Western Civilization

Ideas, Politics & Society

Seventh Edition

Western Civilization

Ideas, Politics & Society

Seventh Edition

Marvin Perry
Baruch College, City University of New York

Myrna Chase
Baruch College, City University of New York

James R. Jacob
John Jay College of Criminal Justice, City University of New York

Margaret C. Jacob
University of California, Los Angeles

Theodore H. Von Laue
Clark University

George W. Bock, *Editorial Associate*

Houghton Mifflin Company Boston New York

Editor-in-Chief: *Jean Woy*
Sponsoring Editor: *Nancy Blaine*
Development Editor: *Julie Dunn*
Senior Project Editor: *Ylang Nguyen*
Editorial Assistant: *Wendy Thayer*
Senior Production Design Coordinator: *Jodi O'Rourke*
Senior Manufacturing Coordinator: *Jane Spelman*
Senior Marketing Manager: *Sandra McGuire*

Printed in the U.S.A.

Library of Congress Card Catalog Number: 2002109657

ISBN: 0-618-271-007

23456789-MV-07 06 05 04 03

Cover Image: *A Lady at the Virginals with a Gentleman* by Johannes Vermeer, 1662–5. Credit: Royal Collection Enterprises Limited.

Text Credits

Page 14: From James B. Pritchard, ed. *The Ancient Near East.* Copyright © 1974 by Princeton University Press. Reprinted by permission of Princeton University Press.
Pages 17, 20: From Adolf Ehrman, ed., *The Ancient Egyptians*, pp. 94, 97, 99, and 76–78. Copyright © 1966. Used by permission of the publishers, Methuen & Co.
Page 21: From John A. Wilson, *The Culture of Ancient Egypt.* Copyright © 1951 by The University of Chicago Press. Reprinted by permission of The University of Chicago Press.
Page 40: From *The TANAKH: The New JPS Translation According to the Traditional Hebrew Text.* Copyright © 1985 by the Jewish Publication Society. Used by permission.
Pages 55–56: Excerpt from *The Iliad* by Homer, translated by E. V. Rieu (Penguin Classics, 1950). Copyright © Estate of E. V. Rieu, 1946. Reprinted with permission of Penguin Press, UK.
Pages 56–57: Excerpt from *The Greeks* by H D F Kitto (Penguin Classics, 1951, Revised edition, 1957). Copyright © H D F Kitto, 1951, 1957. Reprinted with permission of Penguin Press UK.
Page 89: From 'A Girl' by Sappho, *The Oxford Book of Greece Verse in Translation* edited by T.F. Hingham and C.M. Bowra, 1938. Reprinted by permission of Oxford University Press.
Page 93: Reprinted with permission of Pocket Books, an imprint of Simon & Schuster Adult Publishing Group, from *Sophocles: Oedipus the King,* Bernard M.W. Knox, Translator. Copyright © 1959, and renewed © 1987, by Bernard M.W. Knox.
Page 93: From Aeschylus, *The Persians,* translated by Anthony J. Podlecki. Copyright © 1991, published by Bristal Classical Press (Duckworth). Used by permission of the author.
Pages 94–95: From *The Medea,* translated by Rex Warner in *Euripedes, Vol. 3* of Richard Lattimore, *The Complete Greek Tragedies,* p. 101, 96. Copyright © 1959 by The Bodley Head.
Page 132: From Catullus, quoted in E. A. Havelock, *The Lyric Genius of Catullus,* p. 63. Copyright © 1929. Reprinted with permission of Christine M. Havelock.
Page 149: Excerpts from *The Jewish War* by Josephus, translated by G. A. Williamson, revised by E. Mary Smallwood (Penguin Classics, 1959, Revised edition, 1981) Copyright © G. A. Williamson, 1959, 1969. Reprinted with permission of Penguin Press UK.
Page 154: From *The Aeneid of Virgil* by Allen Mandelbaum. Translation copyright © 1971 by Allen Mandelbaum. Used by permission of Bantam Books, a division of Random House, Inc.
Page 262: Excerpts from *The Canterbury Tales* by Geoffrey Chaucer, translated by Nevill Coghill (Penguin Classics, 1951, Fourth revised edition, 1977). Copyright 1951 by Nevill Coghill. Copyright © the Estate of Nevill Coghill, 1958, 1960, 1975, 1977. Reprinted with permission of Penguin Press UK.
Pages 273: From Helen Waddell, *Medieval Latin Lyrics.* Permission to reprint the excerpt from Helen Waddell's translation "Let's away with study..." given by Mary Martin.
Page 273: From David C. Riede and J. Wayne Baker, *The Western Intellectual Tradition, Vol. 1,* 1980. Reprinted with permission of the author.
Page 274: From Anthony Bonner, ed., *Songs of the Troubadours,* pp. 42–43. Copyright © 1972. Reprinted with permission of the author.
Page 320: From Hamlet, Prince of Denmark in *The Complete Plays and Poems of William Shakespeare,* edited by William Allan Neilson and Charles Jarvis Hill, 1942, Houghton Mifflin. Reprinted with permission.
Page 537: From *The Complete Poetical Works of Percy Bysshe Shelley,* edited by Thomas Hutchinson, 1945. Reprinted by permission of Oxford University Press.
Page 589: From Henrik Ibsen, *A Doll's House,* in *Eleven Plays of Henrik Ibsen* (New York: Modern Library, n.d), p. 85–87.
Page 713: From Joseph Conrad, *Heart of Darkness,* 1923, Random House, Inc.
Page 745: From *Collected Poems of Siegfried Sassoon* by Siegfried Sassoon. Copyright © 1918, 1920 by E.P. Dutton. Copyright © 1936, 1946, 1947, 1948 by Siegfried Sassoon. Used by permission of Viking Penguin, a division of Penguin Putnam, Inc.

Brief Contents

Maps xxi
Chronologies xxiii
Preface xxv

Part One

The Ancient World: Foundation of the West to A.D. 500 2

Chapter 1
The Ancient Near East: The First Civilizations 4

Chapter 2
The Hebrews: A New View of God and the Individual 33

Chapter 3
The Greek City-State: Democratic Politics 50

Chapter 4
Greek Thought: From Myth to Reason 74

Chapter 5
The Hellenistic Age: Cultural Diffusion 102

Chapter 6
The Roman Republic: City-State to World Empire 119

Chapter 7
The Roman Empire: A World-State 141

Chapter 8
Early Christianity: A World Religion 171

Part Two

The Middle Ages: The Christian Centuries 500–1400 196

Chapter 9
The Heirs of Rome: Byzantium, Islam, and Latin Christendom 198

Chapter 10
The High Middle Ages: Vitality and Renewal 228

Chapter 11
The Flowering of Medieval Culture: The Christian Synthesis 258

Chapter 12
The Late Middle Ages: Crisis and Dissolution 279

Part Three

Early Modern Europe: from Renaissance to Enlightenment 1350–1789 298

Chapter 13
The Renaissance: Transition to the Modern Age 300

Chapter 14
The Reformation: Shattering of Christendom 323

Chapter 15
European Expansion: Economic and Social Transformations 349

Chapter 16
The Rise of Sovereignty: Transition to the Modern State 377

Chapter 17
The Scientific Revolution: The Mechanical Universe 408

Chapter 18
The Age of Enlightenment: Reason and Reform 426

Part Four

An Age of Revolution: Liberal, National, Industrial 1789–1848 460

Chapter 19
The French Revolution: Affirmation of Liberty and Equality 462

Chapter 20
Napoleon: Subverter and Preserver of the Revolution 488

Chapter 21
The Industrial Revolution: The Transformation of Society 507

Chapter 22
Thought and Culture in the Early Nineteenth Century 529

Chapter 23
Revolution and Counterrevolution: 1815–1848 559

Part Five

An Age of Contradiction: Progress and Breakdown 1848–1914 582

Chapter 24
Thought and Culture in the Mid-Nineteenth Century: Realism and Social Criticism 584

Chapter 25
The Surge of Nationalism: From Liberal to Extreme Nationalism 611

Chapter 26
The Industrial West: Responses to Modernization 637

Chapter 27
Western Imperialism: Global Dominance 667

Chapter 28
Modern Consciousness: New Views of Nature, Human Nature, and the Arts 695

Part Six

World Wars and Totalitarianism: The West in Crisis 1914–1945 726

Chapter 29
World War I: The West in Despair 728

Chapter 30
An Era of Totalitarianism 765

Chapter 31
Thought and Culture in an Era of World Wars and Totalitarianism 808

Chapter 32
World War II: Western Civilization in the Balance 835

Part Seven

The Contemporary World: The Global Age Since 1945 866

Chapter 33
Europe After World War II: Recovery and Realignment, 1945–1989 868

Chapter 34
The Troubled Present 888

Epilogue: Reaffirming the Core Values of the Western Tradition 911

Index I-1

Contents

Maps xxi
Chronologies xxiii
Preface xxv
Acknowledgments xxix
Map Essay before Part One

Part One

The Ancient World: Foundation of the West to A.D. 500 2

Chapter 1
The Ancient Near East: The First Civilizations 4

The Rise to Civilization 5
The Paleolithic Age 5
The Neolithic Revolution 8
The First Civilizations 9

Mesopotamian Civilization 11
Religion: The Basis of Mesopotamian Civilization 12
Government and Law 15
Business and Trade 16
Writing, Mathematics, Astronomy, and Medicine 16

Egyptian Civilization 17
From the Old Kingdom to the Middle Kingdom 17
Religion: The Basis of Egyptian Civilization 18
Divine Kingship 19
Science and Mathematics 20
The New Kingdom and the Decline of Egyptian Civilization 21

Empire Builders 23
Hittites 24
Small Nations 25
Assyria 25
The Neo-Babylonian Empire 26
Persia: Unifier of the Near East 27

The Religious Orientation of the Near East 28
A Mythmaking World-View 29
Near Eastern Achievements 30

Chapter 2
The Hebrews: A New View of God and the Individual 33

Outline of Hebrew History 34
The Israelite Kingdom 35
Conquest, Captivity, and Restoration 36
The Hebrew Scriptures 38

God: One, Sovereign, Transcendent, Good 39

The Individual and Moral Autonomy 40

The Covenant and the Law 41

The Hebrew Idea of History 43

The Prophets 44
Social Justice 45

Universalism 46
Individualism 47
The Legacy of the Ancient Jews 48

Chapter 3
The Greek City-State: Democratic Politics 50
Early Aegean Civilizations 52
The Rise of Hellenic Civilization 54
Homer, Shaper of the Greek Spirit 54
Greek Religion 56
Evolution of the City-State 57
The Break with Theocratic Politics 57
Sparta: A Garrison State 58
Athens: The Rise of Democracy 59
Athenian Greatness 62
The Persian Wars 62
The Delian League 62
The Mature Athenian Democracy 63
Pericles: Symbol of Athenian Democracy 66
The Decline of the City-States 67
The Peloponnesian War 67
The Fourth Century 69
The Dilemma of Greek Politics 69

Chapter 4
Greek Thought: From Myth to Reason 74
Philosophy 75
The Cosmologists: A Rational Inquiry into Nature 76
The Sophists: A Rational Investigation of Human Society 78
Socrates: The Rational Individual 79
Plato: The Rational Society 82
Aristotle: A Synthesis of Greek Thought 86
Art 89
Poetry and Drama 89
Aeschylus 93
Sophocles 93
Euripides 94
Aristophanes 95
History 96
Herodotus 96
Thucydides 97
The Greek Achievement: Reason, Freedom, Humanism 98

Chapter 5
The Hellenistic Age: Cultural Diffusion 102
Alexander the Great 105
Hellenistic Society 106
Competing Dynasties 106
Cosmopolitanism 106
Hellenism and the Jews 109
Hellenistic Culture 110
Literature, History, and Art 110
Science 111
Philosophy 112
The Hellenistic Legacy 117

Chapter 6
The Roman Republic: City-State to World Empire 119
Evolution of the Roman Constitution 120
Roman Expansion to 146 B.C. 124
The Uniting of Italy 124
Conquest of the Mediterranean World 125
Consequences of Expansion 127
Culture in the Republic 130
Collapse of the Republic 132
Crisis in Agriculture 133
The Gracchan Revolution 134
Rival Generals 135
Julius Caesar 136
The Republic's Last Years 138

Chapter 7
The Roman Empire: A World-State 141
Augustus and the Foundations of the Roman Empire 142

The Pax Romana 146
The Successors of Augustus 147
The "Time of Happiness" 150
Roman Culture and Law During the Pax Romana 153

Signs of Trouble 158
Internal Unrest 158
Social and Economic Weaknesses 159
Cultural Stagnation and Transformation 159
The Spread of Mystery Religions 160
The Spiritualization of Philosophy 161

The Decline of Rome 162
Third-Century Crisis 162
Diocletian and Constantine: The Regimented State 164
Tribal Migrations and Invasions 164
Reasons for Rome's Decline 166

The Roman Legacy 169

Chapter 8
Early Christianity: A World Religion 171

Origins of Christianity 172
Judaism in the First Century B.C. 173
Jesus: The Inner Person 175
Saint Paul: From a Jewish Sect to a World Religion 177

The Spread and Triumph of Christianity 179
The Appeal of Christianity 179
Christianity and Rome 181
Christianity and Greek Philosophy 182

The Growth of Christian Organization, Doctrine, and Attitudes 184
The Primacy of the Bishop of Rome 184
The Rise of Monasticism 185
Scriptural Tradition and Doctrinal Disputes 185
Christianity and Society 186
Christianity and the Jews 187

Saint Augustine: The Christian World-View 188

Christianity and Classical Humanism: Alternative World-Views 192

Part Two

The Middle Ages: The Christian Centuries 500–1400 196

Chapter 9
The Heirs of Rome: Byzantium, Islam, and Latin Christendom 198

Byzantine Civilization: The Medieval Christian East 199
Conflict with the Roman Church 200
Imperial Growth and Decline 200
The Bequest of Byzantium 204

Islamic Civilization: Its Development and Dissemination 204
The Prophet: The Founding of a New Religion 204
The Muslim State and Society 206
The Muslim Golden Age 207
Mongol Invasions and Ottoman Dominance 209

Latin Christendom: The Rise of Europe 210
Political and Economic Transformation 210
The Waning of Classical Culture 212

The Church: Shaper of Medieval Civilization 213
The Church as Unifier 213
Monks and the Papacy 214

The Kingdom of the Franks 216
The Era of Charlemagne 217
Carolingian Renaissance 218
The Breakup of Charlemagne's Empire 220

Medieval Society 221
Vassalage 222
Feudal Law 223
Feudal Warriors 223

Noblewomen 224
Agrarian Life 225

Art Essay: The Art of the Ancient World and the Middle Ages after 224

Chapter 10
The High Middle Ages: Vitality and Renewal 228

Economic Expansion 229
- Agricultural Revolution 229
- Revival of Trade 232
- Rebirth of Towns 234

The Rise of States 236
- England 237
- France 238
- Germany 240
- The Emergence of Representative Institutions 241

The Growth of Papal Power 241
- The Sacraments 242
- Gregorian Reform 242
- The Crusades 246
- Dissenters and Reformers 250
- Innocent III: The Apex of Papal Power 253

Christians and Jews 254

Chapter 11
The Flowering of Medieval Culture: The Christian Synthesis 258

Revival of Learning 259

The Medieval World-View 262
- The Universe: Higher and Lower Worlds 263
- The Individual: Sinful but Redeemable 264

Philosophy-Theology 264
- Saint Anselm and Abelard 265
- The Recovery of Aristotle 267
- Saint Thomas Aquinas: Synthesis of Christian Belief and Reason 268
- Strict Aristotelianism: The Challenge to Orthodoxy 270

Science 270

The Recovery of Roman Law 272

Literature 273

Architecture 275

Chapter 12
The Late Middle Ages: Crisis and Dissolution 279

An Age of Adversity 280
- Economic Problems, Black Death, and Social Tension 280
- The Hundred Years' War 284

The Decline of the Papacy 285
- Conflict with France 285
- Critics of Papal Power 287
- The Great Schism and the Conciliar Movement 287
- Fourteenth-Century Heresies 289

Breakup of the Thomistic Synthesis 289

The Middle Ages and the Modern World: Continuity and Discontinuity 290

Part Three

Early Modern Europe: From Renaissance to Enlightenment 1350–1789 298

Chapter 13
The Renaissance: Transition to the Modern Age 300

Italy: Birthplace of the Renaissance 302
- Political Evolution of the City-States 303
- Renaissance Society 306

The Renaissance Outlook: Humanism and Secular Politics 308
- Humanism 308
- A Revolution in Political Thought 310

Renaissance Art 311
- Early Renaissance Art 312
- Late Renaissance Art 314

The Spread of the Renaissance 316

Erasmian Humanism 317
French Humanism 318
Spanish Humanism 318
English Humanism 319

The Renaissance and the Modern Age 320

Art Essay: The Renaissance after 320

Chapter 14

The Reformation: The Shattering of Christendom 323

The Medieval Church in Crisis 325
Wycliffe and Hus 325
Mysticism and Humanism 326
The End of the World 327

The Lutheran Revolt 328
Luther: Humanist, Prophet, and Conservative 328
Luther's Break with Catholicism 328
But Who Is Saved? 331
The Creation and Spread of Lutheranism 331
Religious Reform or Social Revolution? 332

The Spread of the Reformation 335
Calvin and Calvinism 336
France 338
England 340
Southern and Eastern Europe 341
The Radical Reformation 342

The Catholic Response 343

The Reformation and the Modern Age 345

Chapter 15

European Expansion: Economic and Social Transformations 349

European Expansion 351
Forces Behind Expansion 352
The Portuguese Empire 353
The Spanish Empire 355
Black Slavery and the Slave Trade 357

The Price Revolution 359

The Expansion of Agriculture 361
The Old Pattern of Farming 361
Enclosure 361
Convertible Husbandry 362
Agricultural Change in Eastern Europe 363

The Expansion of Trade and Industry 363
The Domestic System 363
Innovations in Business 364
Patterns of Commercial Development 365

The Growth of Capitalism 368
What Is Capitalism? 368
The Fostering of Mercantile Capitalism 368

The Elite and the People 370
Traditional Popular Culture 370
The Reform of Popular Culture 371
Witchcraft and the Witch Craze 372

Economic and Social Transformations 374

Chapter 16

The Rise of Sovereignty: Transition to the Modern State 377

Monarchs and Elites as State Builders 380

The Rise and Fall of Hapsburg Spain 381
Ferdinand and Isabella: Unity and Purity of "Blood" and Religion 381
The Reign of Charles V: Hapsburg, King of Spain, and Holy Roman Emperor 383
Philip II 383
The End of the Spanish Hapsburgs 385

The Growth of French Power 386
Religion and the French State 387
Louis XIV: The Consolidation of French Monarchical Power 388

The Growth of Limited Monarchy and Constitutionalism in England 392
The English Parliament and Constitution 393
The Tudor Achievement 393
The English Revolutions, 1640–1660 and 1688–1689 396

The Netherlands: A Bourgeois Republic 399
The Holy Roman Empire: The Failure to Unify Germany 400
The Emergence of Austria and Prussia 402
Austria 402
Prussia 403
Russia 404
The State and Modern Political Development 405

Chapter 17
The Scientific Revolution: The Mechanical Universe 408
Medieval Cosmology 410
A New View of Nature 411
Renaissance Neo-Platonism 411
Magic and the Search for Nature 412
The Copernican Revolution 412
The Laws of Planetary Motion: Tycho and Kepler 414
Galileo: Experimental Physics 415
The Newtonian Synthesis: Experiment, Mathematics, and Theory 416
Art Essay: Art of the Seventeenth and Eighteenth Centuries after 416
Biology, Medicine, and Chemistry 418
Bacon and Descartes: Prophets of the New Science 420
Bacon 420
Descartes 421
Social Implications of the Scientific Revolution 422
The Meaning of the Scientific Revolution 423

Chapter 18
The Age of Enlightenment: Reason and Reform 426
The Formation of a Public and Secular Culture 429
Salons 430
Freemasons 430
Scientific Academies 432
Alternatives to Orthodoxy 432
Christianity Under Attack 432
Skeptics, Freethinkers, and Deists 432
Voltaire the Philosophe 434
Political Thought 435
Locke 436
Montesquieu 437
Rousseau 437
Social Thought 438
Epistemology and Education 438
Humanitarianism 440
Economic Thought 443
The High Enlightenment 445
European Political and Diplomatic Developments 448
Warfare 448
Enlightened Despotism 449
Effects of Enlightened Despotism 452
The Enlightenment in Eastern Europe 453
The American Revolution 454
The Enlightenment and the Modern World 456

Part Four

An Age of Revolution: Liberal, National, Industrial 1789–1848 460

Chapter 19
The French Revolution: Affirmation of Liberty and Equality 462
The Old Regime 463
The First Estate 464
The Second Estate 465
The Third Estate 465
Inefficient Administration and Financial Disorder 468

The Roles of the Enlightenment and the American Revolution 469
A Bourgeois Revolution? 470

The Moderate Stage, 1789–91 471
The Clash Between the Nobility and the Third Estate 471
Formation of the National Assembly 471
Storming of the Bastille 473
The Great Fear 473
October Days 474
Reforms of the National Assembly 474

The Radical Stage, 1792–94 476
The Sans-Culottes 476
Foreign Invasion 476
The Jacobins 478
Jacobin Achievements 478
The Nation in Arms 479
The Republic of Virtue and the Reign of Terror 479
The Fall of Robespierre 481

The Meaning of the French Revolution 483

Chapter 20
Napoleon: Subverter and Preserver of the Revolution 488

Rise to Power 489
Coup d'État 491
Napoleon's Character 491

Napoleon and France 492
Government: Centralization and Repression 493
Religion: Reconciliation with the Church 493
Law: The Code Napoléon 494
Education: The Imperial University 495
Economy: Strengthening the State 496

Napoleon and Europe 497
Napoleon's Art of War 497
The Grand Empire: Diffusion of Revolutionary Institutions 498

The Fall of Napoleon 500
Failure to Subdue England 500
The Spanish Ulcer 501
The German War of Liberation 501
Disaster in Russia 502
Final Defeat 503

The Legend and the Achievement 504

Chapter 21
The Industrial Revolution: The Transformation of Society 507

Origins of the Industrial Age 509
Europe's Population Explosion 509
Agricultural Revolution 510
Britain First 511
Changes in Technology 513
Changes in Finance 515

Society Transformed 517
Urbanization 518
Changes in Social Structure 520
Working-Class Life 522

Relief and Reform 524

Industrialism in Perspective 526

Chapter 22
Thought and Culture in the Early Nineteenth Century 529

Romanticism: A New Cultural Orientation 530
Exalting Imagination, Intuition, and Feelings 531
Nature, God, History 533
The Impact of the Romantic Movement 535

German Idealism 535
The Challenge Posed by Hume's Empiricism 535
Immanuel Kant 537
G. W. F. Hegel 538

Conservatism: The Value of Tradition 541
Hostility to the French Revolution 541
The Quest for Social Stability 543

Liberalism: The Value of the Individual 543

The Sources of Liberalism 544
Individual Liberty 544
Liberal Economic Theory 545
Liberalism and Democracy 546

Radicalism and Democracy: The Expansion of Liberalism 549
Thomas Paine 549
Jeremy Bentham 550

Early Socialism: New Possibilities for Society 550
Saint-Simon: Technocratic Socialism 551
Fourier: Psychological Socialism 552
Owen: Industrial Socialism 553

Nationalism: The Sacredness of the Nation 553
The Emergence of Modern Nationalism 553
Nationalism and Liberalism 555

Chapter 23
Revolution and Counterrevolution, 1815–1848 559

The Congress of Vienna, 1814–1815 560
Metternich the Archconservative 560
Crisis over Saxony and Poland 563
The Settlement 564

Revolutions, 1820–1829 564

Revolutions, 1830–1832 566

The Rise of Reform in Britain 567

Revolutions of 1848: France 569
The February Revolution 570
The June Days: Revolution of the Oppressed 571

Revolutions of 1848: Germany, Austria, and Italy 572
The German States: Liberalism Defeated 573
Austria: Hapsburg Dominance 575
Italy: Continued Fragmentation 577

Revolutions of 1848: An Assessment 577

Part Five

An Age of Contradiction: Progress and Breakdown 1848–1914 582

Chapter 24
Thought and Culture in the Mid-Nineteenth Century: Realism and Social Criticism 584

Realism and Naturalism 585

Positivism 590

Darwinism 591
Natural Selection 592
Darwinism and Christianity 593
Social Darwinism 593
Religion in a Secular Age 595

Marxism 596
A Science of History 597
Class Conflict 598
Destruction of Capitalism 599
Marxism's Appeal and Influence 600
Critics of Marx 601

Anarchism 602
Pierre Joseph Proudhon 602
Mikhail Bakunin 602

Liberalism in Transition 604
John Stuart Mill 604
Thomas Hill Green 605
Herbert Spencer: Rejection of State Intervention 605

Feminism: Extending the Principle of Equality 606

Chapter 25
The Surge of Nationalism: From Liberal to Extreme Nationalism 611

The Unification of Italy 612
Forces for and Against Unity 612
Failed Revolutions 614
Cavour and Victory over Austria 615
Garibaldi and Victory in the South 616

Italian Unification Completed 617
The Unification of Germany 616
Prussia, Agent of Unification 617
Bismarck and the Road to Unity 619
Nationality Problems in the Hapsburg Empire 622
Magyarization 623
German Versus Czech 623
South Slavs 625
The Rise of Racial Nationalism 625
Volkish Thought 627
Anti-Semitism: The Power and Danger of Mythical Thinking 630

Chapter 26
The Industrial West: Responses to Modernization 637
The Advance of Industry 639

Art Essay: Art of the Late Nineteenth and Twentieth Centuries after 640

Technological Takeoff 641
Accelerated Urbanization 645
Labor's Responses 646
Great Britain: An Industrial Model 648
Labor Unrest 649
The Irish Question 649
The Woman Question 651
Britain on the Eve of War 652
France: Democratic or Authoritarian? 652
Napoleon "le Petit" 652
After the Fall 653
Threats to the Republic 654
France on the Eve of War 655
Germany: Forging an Empire 655
Bismarck's "Struggle for Culture" 656
Germany on the Eve of War 658
Italy: Unfulfilled Expectations 658
Russia: Tsarist Empire 659
The United States: Democratic Giant 662
A Golden Age? 663

Chapter 27
Western Imperialism: Global Dominance 667
Emergence of the New Imperialism 668
Conflicting Interpretations 670
A Global Economy 673
Control and Resistance 674
European Domination of Asia 675
India 675
China 679
Japan 681
The Ottoman Empire 682
Southeast and Central Asia 684
The Scramble for Africa 685
The Berlin Conference 687
Britain in Africa 687
Costs of Colonialism 689
Latin America 690
The Legacy of Imperialism 692

Chapter 28
Modern Consciousness: New Views of Nature, Human Nature, and the Arts 695
Irrationalism 696
Nietzsche 697
Dostoevski 700
Bergson 701
Sorel 702
Freud: A New View of Human Nature 702
Social Thought: Confronting the Irrational and the Complexities of Modern Society 706
Durkheim 706
Pareto 707
Le Bon 708
Weber 708
The Modernist Movement 710
Breaking with Conventional Modes of Esthetics 710
Modern Art 712
Modern Physics 718
The Enlightenment Tradition in Disarray 721

Part Six

World Wars and Totalitarianism: The West in Crisis 1914–1945 726

Chapter 29
World War I: The West in Despair 728

Aggravated Nationalist Tensions in Austria-Hungary 731
The German System of Alliances 732
- The New German Empire 732
- Bismarck's Goals 733

The Triple Entente 734
- Fear of Germany 734
- German Reactions 735

Drifting Toward War 735
- The Bosnian Crisis 735
- Balkan Wars 736
- Assassination of Francis Ferdinand 737
- Germany Abets Austria 738
- The Question of Responsibility 739

War as Celebration 739
Stalemate in the West 742
Other Fronts 746
Collapse of the Central Powers 747
- American Entry 747
- Germany's Last Offensive 748

The Peace Conference 749
- Wilson's Hope for a New World 749
- Problems of Peacemaking 749
- The Settlement 751
- Assessment and Problems 752

The Russian Revolution of 1917 754
- Problems of the Provisional Government 755
- Lenin and the Rise of Bolshevism 755
- Lenin's Opportunity 758
- The Bolsheviks Survive 759

The War and European Consciousness 759

Chapter 30
An Era of Totalitarianism 765

The Nature of Totalitarianism 767
Communist Russia 769
- War Communism and the New Economic Policy 770
- One-Party Dictatorship 770
- The Stalin Revolution 772

The Nature of Fascism 777
The Rise of Fascism in Italy 779
- Postwar Unrest 779
- Mussolini's Seizure of Power 780

The Fascist State in Italy 781
- Consolidation of Power 781
- Control of the Masses 782
- Economic Policies 783
- The Church and the Fascist Regime 783

The New German Republic 783
- Threats from Left and Right 784
- Economic Crisis 785
- Fundamental Weaknesses of the Weimar Republic 786

The Rise of Hitler 787
- The Early Years 787
- The Nazi Party 788
- Hitler's World-View 789
- Hitler Gains Power 791

Nazi Germany 793
- The Leader-State 793
- Economic Life 794
- Nazism and the Churches 795
- Shaping the "New Man" 796
- Anti-Semitic Legislation 797
- Mass Support 798

Liberalism and Authoritarianism in Other Lands 799
- The Spread of Authoritarianism 799
- The Western Democracies 802

Chapter 31
Thought and Culture in an Era of World Wars and Totalitarianism 808

Intellectuals and Artists in Troubled Times 809
Postwar Pessimism 809
Literature and Art: Innovation, Disillusionment, and Social Commentary 812
Communism: "The God That Failed" 817
Reaffirming the Christian World-View 819
Reaffirming the Ideals of Reason and Freedom 821

Existentialism 823
Intellectual Background 823
Basic Principles 824
Nineteenth-Century Forerunners 824
Twentieth-Century Existentialists 825

The Modern Predicament 829

Chapter 32
World War II: Western Civilization in the Balance 835

The Aftermath of World War I 836

The Road to War 838
Hitler's Foreign Policy Aims 838
Breakdown of Peace 839
Czechoslovakia: The Apex of Appeasement 842
Poland: The Final Crisis 843

The Nazi Blitzkrieg 845
The Fall of France 845
The Battle of Britain 848
Invasion of Russia 848

The New Order 850
Exploitation and Terror 850
Extermination 851
Resistance 856

Turn of the Tide 857
The Japanese Offensive 857
Defeat of the Axis Powers 857

The Legacy of World War II 862

Part Seven

The Contemporary World: The Global Age Since 1945 866

Chapter 33
Europe After World War II: Recovery and Realignment, 1945–1989 868

The Cold War 871
Origins 871
Cold War Mobilization 871
Arms Race and Space Race 872
The Vietnam War 874

Building a New Europe 875

The Soviet Bloc 879
Stalin's Last Years 879
After Stalin: Thaw, Détente, Perestroika, and Glasnost 880

Decolonization 884

Chapter 34
The Troubled Present 888

The Demise of Communism 889
1989: Year of Liberation 889
The Collapse of the Soviet Union 893
The Death of an Ideal 894

The Post–Cold War World 896
Post-Communist Russia and the Former Soviet Republics 896

Art Essay: Contemporary Art after 896

Central and Eastern Europe After 1989 899
Western Europe 902

Our Global Age: Tensions and Concerns 905

Epilogue: Reaffirming the Core Values of the Western Tradition 911

Index I–1

Maps

1.1 Mesopotamian and Egyptian Civilizations 11
1.2 Kingdoms and Peoples of the Ancient World 24
1.3 The Assyrian and Persian Empires 26
2.1 Hebrews and Other Peoples of the Ancient Middle East 37
3.1 Greek Colonization of the Mediterranean Basin 55
3.2 The Aegean Basin 63
5.1 Alexander's Conquests 104
5.2 The Division of Alexander's Empire and the Spread of Hellenism 107
6.1 Roman Conquests During the Republic 128
7.1 The Roman Empire Under Augustus and Hadrian 145
7.2 Incursions and Migrations, c. A.D. 300–500 165
8.1 The Journeys of St. Paul 177
8.2 The Spread of Christianity 183
9.1 The Byzantine Empire 201
9.2 The Expansion of Islam, 622–732 209
9.3 The Carolingian World 216
9.4 Ninth-Century Invasions 220
10.1 Medieval Trade Routes 233
10.2 The Kingdom of France, 1180–1314 239
10.3 The Holy Roman Empire, c. 1200 245
10.4 The Routes of the Crusades 248
11.1 Medieval Centers of Learning 260
12.1 Path of the Black Death, 1347–1350 283
13.1 Italian City-States, c. 1494 305
14.1 The Protestant and the Catholic Reformations 339
14.2 Inner Austria and Adjacent Territories 341
15.1 Portuguese and Spanish Empire Building, 1415–1635 356
15.2 Industrial Centers in the Sixteenth Century 367
16.1 Spain from the Ninth to the Sixteenth Century 382
16.2 Europe, 1648 391
16.3 The Growth of Austria and Brandenburg-Prussia, c. 1650–1750 404
18.1 European Expansion, 1715 446
18.2 Europe, 1789 451

18.3 Trade Routes Between the Old and New Worlds 456
19.1 The French Revolution, 1789–1793 467
20.1 Napoleon's Europe, 1810 499
21.1 Industrial Growth in England, Mid-1800s 512
21.2 Industrial Growth on the Continent, Mid-1800s 518
23.1 Peoples of the Hapsburg Monarchy, 1815 563
23.2 Europe, 1815 565
23.3 Europe's Age of Revolutions 578
25.1 Unification of Germany, 1866–1871 618
26.1 European Cities of 100,000 or More, 1800–1900 645
27.1 Asia in 1914 677
27.2 Africa in 1914 687
29.1 The Balkans, 1914 736
29.2 World War I, 1914–1918 740
29.3 Post-World War I: Broken Empires and Changed Boundaries 753
30.1 The Union Republics of the Union of Soviet Socialist Republics (U.S.S.R.) 775
32.1 German and Italian Aggressions, 1935–1939 840
32.2 World War II: The European Theater 846
32.3 World War II: The Pacific Theater 858
33.1 Western Europe After 1945 873
33.2 Southeast Asia and the Vietnam War 875
33.3 Eastern Europe After 1945 882
33.4 Former European Colonies 885
34.1 Post-Cold War Europe and the Former Soviet Union 891

Chronologies

Chronology 1.1 The Near East 6
Chronology 2.1 The Hebrews 35
Chronology 3.1 The Greek City-State 52
Chronology 6.1 The Roman Republic 121
Chronology 7.1 The Roman Empire 143
Chronology 8.1 Early Christianity 173
Chronology 9.1 The Rise of Europe 200
Chronology 10.1 The High Middle Ages 230
Chronology 12.1 The Late Middle Ages 281
Chronology 13.1 The Renaissance 302
Chronology 14.1 The Reformation 326
Chronology 15.1 The Commercial Revolution 351
Chronology 16.1 The Rise of Sovereignty 379
Chronology 18.1 The Enlightenment 428
Chronology 19.1 The French Revolution 464
Chronology 20.1 Napoleon's Career 490
Chronology 23.1 Revolution and Reaction 561
Chronology 25.1 Unification of Italy 613
Chronology 25.2 Unification of Germany 617
Chronology 26.1 Europe in the Age of Industrialization 639
Chronology 27.1 Expansion of Western Dominance 669
Chronology 29.1 World War I 730
Chronology 30.1 Totalitarianism 768
Chronology 32.1 Road to World War II 837
Chronology 32.2 World War II 844
Chronology 33.1 Europe, 1945–1989 870
Chronology 34.1 From the Cold War to Globalism 890

Preface

Western civilization is a grand but tragic drama. The West has forged the instruments of reason that make possible a rational comprehension of physical nature and human culture, conceived the idea of political liberty, and recognized the intrinsic worth of the individual. But the modern West, though it has unraveled nature's mysteries, has been less successful at finding rational solutions to social ills and conflicts between nations. Science, the great achievement of the Western intellect, while improving conditions of life, has also produced weapons of mass destruction. Though the West has pioneered in the protection of human rights, it has also produced totalitarian regimes that have trampled on individual freedom and human dignity. And although the West has demonstrated a commitment to human equality, it has also practiced brutal racism.

Despite the value that westerners have given to reason and freedom, they have shown a frightening capacity for irrational behavior and a fascination for violence and irrational ideologies, and they have willingly sacrificed liberty for security or national grandeur. The world wars and totalitarian movements of the twentieth century have demonstrated that Western civilization, despite its extraordinary achievements, is fragile and perishable.

Western Civilization: Ideas, Politics, and Society examines the Western tradition—those unique patterns of thought and systems of values that constitute the Western heritage. While focusing on key ideas and broad themes, the text also provides a balanced treatment of economic, political, and social history for students in Western civilization courses.

The text is written with the conviction that history is not a meaningless tale. Without a knowledge of history, men and women cannot fully know themselves, for all human beings have been shaped by institutions and values inherited from the past. Without an awareness of the historical evolution of reason and freedom, the dominant ideals of Western civilization, commitment to these ideals will diminish. Without a knowledge of history, the West cannot fully comprehend or adequately cope with the problems that burden its civilization and the world.

In attempting to make sense out of the past, the authors have been careful to avoid superficial generalizations that oversimplify historical events and forces and arrange history into too neat a structure. But we have striven to interpret and to synthesize in order to provide students with a frame of reference with which to comprehend the principal events and eras in Western history.

Changes in the Seventh Edition

For the seventh edition every chapter has been reworked to some extent. The hundreds of carefully selected modifications and additions significantly enhance the text. Some changes deepen the book's conceptual character; others provide useful and illustrative historical details. The concluding essays in several chapters have been enlarged and improved. Chapters treating intellectual history have been expanded and additional quotations from original sources have been inserted. In the last edition, to help students focus on a chapter's key ideas, we reduced the number of review questions and rewrote others. This practice has been continued in this edition. The biographical feature has been retained for this edition: each chapter contains a profile, set off in a box, of a significant historical figure. Among the new personalities featured are Castiglione, Katharina von Bora, Polybius, Josephus, Carl Schurz, Charles Dickens, and Joseph Conrad.

Specific changes in Chapter 1, "The Ancient Near East," include an excerpt from Mesopotamian literature illustrating the sense of insecurity that pervaded the Mesopotamian outlook and an expanded discussion of Hammurabi's Code; as in the past edition, we made a deliberate effort to upgrade the end piece, "The Religious Orientation of the Near East." In Chapter 2, "The Hebrews," the discussions of Hebrew religious-moral thought and the end piece, "The Legacy of the Jews," have been broadened. In Chapter 3, "The Greek City-State," we deepened the analysis of both the strengths and weaknesses of Greek democracy. We added material on early Greek philosophy, the Sophists, Socrates, Plato, and drama in Chapter 4, "Greek Thought." Chapter 5, "The Hellenistic Age," contains expanded discussions of art and Stoicism and a new end piece, "The Hellenistic Legacy." The treatment of Roman politics, expansion, and slavery, has been broadened in Chapter 6, "The Roman Republic." In Chapter 7, "The Roman Empire," we have deepened the discussion of the signs of trouble during the Pax Romana that ultimately contributed to the Empire's decline. In Chapter 8, "Early Christianity," several topics have been given more attention including Jesus' Jewish background and the relationship between Early Christianity and Greek philosophy. In addition, the concluding essay, "Christianity and Classical Humanism: Alternative World-Views," has been enriched. An expanded discussion of Islamic society and culture is the most noteworthy addition to Chapter 9, "The Heirs of Rome." The treatment of medieval Christian perceptions of the Jew in Chapter 10, "The High Middle Ages," has been broadened. Additional excerpts from medieval literature have been inserted in Chapter 11, "The Flowering of Medieval Culture." We have strengthened the conceptual framework of the end piece, "The Middle Ages and the Modern World: Continuity and Discontinuity," in Chapter 12, "The Late Middle Ages." We have broadened the coverage in Chapter 14, "The Reformation," to include more on Eastern Europe. The section on limited monarchy and constitutionalism in England in Chapter 16, "The Rise of Sovereignty," has been enriched.

In recent years, historians have rethought the question: Was the French Revolution a bourgeois revolution? In a previous edition, we incorporated a discussion of this issue in Chapter 19, "The French Revolution." In this edition, more attention is devoted to this question. Other topics given more attention include the reforms of the National Assembly and Robespierre and the Reign of Terror. Here too we have strengthened the concepts in the end piece, "The Meaning of the French Revolution." We have upgraded the treatment of romanticism in Chapter 22, "Thought and Culture in the Early Nineteenth Century." Again consistent with the book's intent, in Chapter 23, "Revolution and Counter Revolution, 1815–1848," we have enriched the end piece, "Revolutions of 1848: An Assessment." In Chapter 24, "Thought and Culture in the Mid-Nineteenth Century, more attention has been given to European realists, particularly Ibsen; additional illustrations of the thought processes of Social Darwinists have been provided; and a new section, "Religion in a Secular Age," has been included.

Chapter 25, "The Surge of Nationalism" contains an expanded treatment of "The Rise of Racial Nationalism." Updates appear throughout Chapter 27, "Western Imperialism," including a revised examination of the legacy of imperialism. In Chapter 28, "Modern Consciousness," we continue to sharpen the treatments of Nietzsche, Freud, Weber, and the ideas incorporated in the end piece, "The Enlightenment Tradition in Disarray."

In Chapter 29, "World War I," the discussion of the causes of the war, the mood at the war's outbreak, the nature of trench warfare, and the Russian Revolution has been enhanced. So too has the end piece, "The War and European Consciousness." In Chapter 30, "An Era of Totalitarianism," we have upgraded the analyses of the nature of totalitarianism, Stalin's dictatorship, and fascism; we also examine in greater depth

Hitler's rise to power and the fascist regimes established in Italy and Germany. Some improvements in the treatment of literature and art have been inserted in Chapter 31, "Thought and Culture in an Era of World Wars and Totalitarianism." Throughout Chapter 32, "World War II," we have upgraded the treatment of the events leading up to the war, the New Order Germany imposed on conquered Europe, the Holocaust, and two major turning points of the war—the battle of Stalingrad and D-Day; the end piece, "The Legacy of World War II," has been significantly expanded. In reworking Chapter 33, "Europe After World War II," we have given more attention to the Soviet invasion of Afghanistan. In light of recent events, including the ethnic cleansing in the Balkans, the problems of the new Russia, and the tragic events of September 11, Chapter 34, "The Troubled Present," has been thoroughly revised.

Many of the illustrations are new for this edition. The four-color art inserts and revised art essays provide a comprehensive treatment of the evolution of Western art styles and are closely linked to the text.

Distinctive Features

The text contains several innovative pedagogical features. Chapter outlines and introductions provide comprehensive overviews of key themes and give a sense of direction and coherence to the flow of history. Many chapters contain concluding essays that treat the larger meaning of the material. Facts have been carefully selected to illustrate key relationships and concepts and to avoid overwhelming students with unrelated and disconnected data. Appropriate quotations, many not commonly found in texts, have been integrated into the discussion. Each chapter contains notes, an annotated bibliography, and review questions that refer students to principal points and elicit thought. The seventh edition has been revised with a new emphasis on the visual aspects of learning. Map captions have been added to all of the maps, helping students to better understand geography and its connection to history. In addition, we have revised and expanded the color insert section, adding a new essay on contemporary art. This essay begins with the post-War period and traces artistic movements up to the present day.

Western Civilization: Ideas, Politics, and Society is available in both one- and two-volume editions, and in a third edition, *From the 1400s. From the 1400s* (22 chapters) has been prepared for those instructors whose courses begin with the Renaissance or the Reformation.

Volume I of the two-volume edition treats the period from the first civilizations in the Near East through the Age of Enlightenment in the eighteenth century (18 chapters). Volume II covers the period from the growth of national-states in the seventeenth century to the contemporary age (19 chapters). Because some instructors start the second half of their course with the period prior to the French Revolution, Volume II incorporates the last three chapters of Volume I: "The Rise of Sovereignty," "The Scientific Revolution," and "The Age of Enlightenment." Volume II also contains a comprehensive introduction that surveys the ancient world, the Middle Ages, and the opening centuries of the modern era; the introduction is designed particularly for students who did not take the first half of the course. *From the 1400s* also contains an introduction that covers the ancient world and the Middle Ages.

Ancillaries

These learning and teaching ancillaries also contribute to the text's usefulness.

Online Study Guide
Instructor's Resource Manual
Test Items
HM ClassPrep with HM Testing
Blackboard™ and WebCT™ course cartridges
GeoQuest:™ and interactive map CD-ROM
Mosaic: Perspectives on Western Civilization web site
Bibliobase: custom coursepacks in Western civilization
Map Transparencies

In lieu of a printed Study Guide, we offer an online Study Guide which features chapter summaries, review questions, web activities, interactive matching exercises, primary source exercises, and web activities as well as a student testing service called ACE (A Cyber Evaluation), which contains self-correcting quizzes.

The *Instructor's Resource Manual* has been revised by Dr. Diane Moczar of Northern Virginia Community College. The *Manual* contains learning objectives, chapter overviews, suggested lecture topics, topics for classroom discussion, ideas for student projects, and a film and multimedia bibliography. Dr. Moczar has added new geography questions throughout the *Manual* and has updated the bibliography. The accompanying *Test Items,* by Professor Matthew Lenoe of Assumption College offers new and revised multiple-choice questions, identification terms, map questions, and essay questions for the seventh edition.

New to this editon is *HM Class Prep with HM Testing,* the latest comprehensive instructor's resource in computerized testing, which includes electronic versions of the Instructor's Resource Manual and Test Items, and PowerPoint maps from the text. Course material is offered in both Blackboard™ and WebCT™ formats for those institutions that use these learning environments. An exciting addition to our map program is a CD-ROM of thirty interactive maps—GeoQuest, available for both instructors and students.

Houghton Mifflin is pleased to announce *Mosiac: Perspectives on Western Civilization.* This web site is a comprehensive, interactive resource that includes primary and secondary documents, interactive maps, examples of fine art, and audio files, providing students with a direct connection to the raw material of Western civilization. Please contact your Houghton Mifflin Company representative for more information about this innovative multimedia program.

We are also proud to call attention to our online primary-source collection, Bibliobase. This resource allows instructors to select from over six hundred documents to create their own customized readers for courses in Western civilization. Visit our web site at **www.bibliobase.com** for more information. Finally, a set of full-color Map Transparencies of all the maps in the text is available on adoption.

The text represents the efforts of several authors. Marvin Perry, general editor of the project, wrote Chapters 1–12, 19–20, 22–25, 28–32, the Epilogue, and the section on the American Revolution in Chapter 18. James R. Jacob is the author of Chapters 13 and 15. Margaret C. Jacob provided Chapters 14 and 16–18. Myrna Chase wrote Chapters 21, 26–27, and contributed to the section on reform in Britain in Chapter 23. Theodore H. Von Laue wrote much of Chapters 33 and 34 and contributed the sections on tsarist Russia to Chapter 26, on the Russian Revolution to Chapter 29, and on Communist Russia to Chapter 30. Since his death, Marvin Perry and Angela Von Laue have revised these chapters. Over the years, Marvin Perry and George Bock have edited the manuscript for continuity and clarity.

Acknowledgments

The authors would like to thank the folowing instructors for their critical reading of sections of the manuscript: Joseph Appiah, J. Sargeant Reynolds Community College; Richard Blanke, University of Maine; Stanislao Rugliese, Hofstra University; Glenn Sanders, Oklahoma Baptist University; Emily J. Teipe, Fullerton College.

Several of their suggestions were incorporated into the final version. We are also grateful to the staff of Houghton Mifflin Company who lent their considerable talents to the project. In particular we would like to thank Julie Dunn, developmental editor, for her conscientiousness and concern; Ylang Nguyen, senior project editor, for her careful attention to detail; Pat Herbst, whose copyediting skills are reflected in the manuscript; and Linda Sykes, for supervising the choice of pictures in the text. This edition rests substantially on the editorial talents of Freda Alexander, who worked closely with us on earlier editions of the text. Both Jean Woy, editor-in-chief, who has been affiliated with the text since the first edition, and Nancy Blaine, senior sponsoring editor, continue to recognize and support what we are trying to do—and for this we remain grateful. The death of Theodore Von Laue, my long time colleague and friend, deeply saddens me. Although his special talents will be missed, his wife Angela Von Laue has added her literary and research skills to the project. I would like to express my personal gratitude to her and to my good friend George Bock, whose creative insights in previous editions continue to contribute to the text's distinguishing character—a concern for crucial concepts and essential relationships. Our often heated, but always fruitful, discussions demonstrate to me the intrinsic value of the Socratic dialogue. And, as always, I am grateful to my wife Phyllis Perry for her encouragement and computer expertise which saved me much time and frustration.

M. P.

Western Civilization

Ideas, Politics & Society

Seventh Edition

Geography of Europe

The map on the following pages shows the continent of Europe and the countries around the Mediterranean Sea, together with the physical features of the land such as major rivers and other bodies of water, mountains and changes of elevation, and the names of countries and their capitals. A knowledge of the geography of this area will help give a sense of the relationship between geography and history, of how the characteristics of the terrain and the availability of rivers and other bodies of water affected the movement of people and the relationship between people and environment throughout history.

Europe is the smallest continent in the world with the exception of Australia. The other continents are Africa, Asia, North America, South America, and Antarctica. The continent of Europe, which can be viewed as the western extension of the Asian landmass, is distinctive in its configuration. Peninsulas make up a significant portion of the continent's land area. This feature gives Europe an unusually long coastline, equal in distance to one and a half times around the equator (37,877 miles). Europe's western boundary is the Atlantic Ocean, while the Ural Mountains, Ural River, and Caspian Sea—in Russia and Kazakhstan—form its eastern boundary. Europe extends southward to the Caucasus Mountains, the Black Sea, and the Mediterranean Sea. The continent extends to the Arctic Ocean in the north. Off the mainland but considered by geographers to be part of Europe are thousands of islands, most notably the British Isles to the northwest.

North Americans are often surprised to discover the small size of the European continent. The geographic area of France, for example, is less than that of Texas; England is similar in size to Alabama. The distance from London to Paris is about the same as from New York to Boston; the distance from Berlin to Moscow is comparable to that of Chicago to Denver. And the entire continent of Europe is about the size of Canada.

Major Peninsulas and Islands There are five major European peninsulas: the Iberian (Portugal and Spain); the Apennine (Italy); the Balkan (Albania, Bulgaria, Greece, and parts of the former Yugoslavian republics and Turkey); the Scandinavian (Norway and Sweden); and Jutland (Denmark). Ireland and the United Kingdom of England, Wales, and Scotland make up the British Isles. Major islands of the Mediterranean Sea include the Balearic Islands, Corsica, Sardinia, Sicily, Crete, and Cyprus.

Seas, Lakes, and Rivers Europe's irregular coastline encloses large areas of the surrounding waters into bays, gulfs, and seas. In the Mediterranean Sea are located, from west to east, the Tyrrhenian Sea (between Italy and Sicily, and Sardinia and Corsica), the Adriatic Sea (between Italy and the former Yugoslavian republics), the Ionian Sea (between Italy and Greece), and the Aegean Sea (between Greece and Turkey).

The Baltic Sea, in the north, is bordered by Finland, Estonia, Latvia, Lithuania, Poland, Germany, and Sweden, and connected by narrow channels to the North Sea, which lies between Great Britain and the countries of the northwestern mainland. The English Channel separates England and France, and the Bay of Biscay borders the west coast of France and the north coast of Spain. The Black Sea, on the southern border of Russia and the Ukraine, is connected by water passages to the Aegean Sea. The Caspian Sea, which lies partly in Russia and Kazakhstan, and

Elevation
Meters
Feet
4,000
13,120
2,000
6,560
500
1,640
200
656
Sea level
Sea level
Below sea level
Below sea level
National capital
Other city
0
100
200
300
400
500 Km.
0
100
200
300
400
500 Mi.
NORWAY
Oslo
SWEI
SCOTLAND
North
Sea
NORTHERN
IRELAND
UNITED
KINGDOM
IRELAND
Dublin
DENMARK
Copenhagen
ENGLAND
WALES
Thames
London
NETHERLANDS
Amsterdam
Elbe
Berlin
English Channel
Brussels
BELGIUM
GERMANY
LUXEMBOURG
Luxembourg
Seine
Paris
Prague
CZEC
REPUB
Loire
Rhine
Bay
of
Biscay
FRANCE
Bern
Vien
SWITZERLAND
AUSTRIA
ATLANTIC
ALPS
SLOVENIA
Ljubljana
Rhône
Po
PYRENEES
Ebro
APENNINES
Adriatic
Se
PORTUGAL
SPAIN
OCEAN
Lisbon
Madrid
Corsica
Rome
ITALY
Balearic Is.
Sardinia
Tyrrhenian
Sea
GIBRALTAR
(Gr. Br.)
Algiers
Rabat
Sicily
Tunis
MALTA
MOROCCO
TUNISIA
Tripoli
ALGERIA
LIBYA

FINLAND
Helsinki
St. Petersburg
Stockholm
Tallinn
ESTONIA
Baltic
Sea
Nizhniy Novgorod
Volga
URAL MTS.
Riga
LATVIA
Moscow
RUSSIA
LITHUANIA
Vilnius
(RUSSIA)
Minsk
BELARUS
KAZAKHSTAN
Ural
Vistula
Warsaw
POLAND
Kiev
Kharkov
CARPATHIAN
MTS.
UKRAINE
Dnieper
SLOVAKIA
slava
Budapest
HUNGARY
MOLDOVA
Kishinev
ROMANIA
Caspian
Sea
CAUCASUS MTS.
Belgrade
AND
OVINA
SERBIA
Bucharest
Danube
Black Sea
GEORGIA
T'bilisi
Baku
AZERBAIJAN
ARMENIA
Yerevan
AZERBAIJAN
(YUGOSLAVIA)
GRO
rica
Sofia
BULGARIA
Skopje
MACEDONIA
Tiranë
ALBANIA
Ankara
TURKEY
IRAN
GREECE
Aegean
Sea
onian
Sea
Athens
Euphrates
Tigris
SYRIA
Baghdad
IRAQ
CYPRUS
LEBANON
Beirut
Damascus
Crete
Mediterranean
Sea
KUWAIT
Kuwait
Jerusalem
Amman
ISRAEL
JORDAN
Cairo
Nile
EGYPT
SAUDI ARABIA

partly in Asia, is the world's largest saltwater lake and is the lowest point in Europe at 92 feet below sea level.

Europe's many rivers have served as transportation routes for thousands of years. Several of the major rivers, including the longest, flow across the Russian plain. The Volga, Europe's longest river (2,194 miles), rises west of Moscow and empties into the Caspian Sea. It is also linked by canals and other river systems to the Arctic Ocean and the Baltic Sea. The Dnieper flows south through the agricultural heartland of the Ukraine into the Black Sea.

Europe's second longest river, the Danube (1,777 miles), is the principal waterway in the southeastern part of the continent. It originates in Germany and flows through Austria, Slovakia, Hungary, the former Yugoslavian republics, Bulgaria, and Romania into the Black Sea. The Rhine winds northward from the Alps through western Germany and the Netherlands into the North Sea, which is also the destination of the Elbe River in eastern Germany. In France, the Rhône flows south into the Mediterranean, and the Seine and Loire flow west to the English Channel and the Bay of Biscay. Other important waterways are the Po in northern Italy, the Vistula in Poland, and the Thames in England.

The proximity of most areas of the European landmass to the coastline or to major river systems is important to understanding the historical development of European civilization. Trading routes and major cities developed along these waterways, and rivers have served as natural boundaries.

Land Regions Europe, despite its small size, presents a wide range of landforms, from rugged mountains to sweeping plains. These landforms can be separated into four major regions: the Northwest Mountains, the Great European Plain, the Central Uplands, and the Alpine Mountain System. The mountains of the Northwest Region cover most of the region, running through northwestern France, Ireland, northern Great Britain, Norway, Sweden, northern Finland, and the northwest corner of Russia.

The Great European Plain covers almost all of the European part of the former Soviet Union, extending from the Arctic Ocean to the Caucasus Mountains. This belt stretches westward across Poland, Germany, Belgium, the western portion of France, and southeastern England.

The Central Uplands is a belt of high plateaus, hills, and low mountains. It reaches from the central plateau of Portugal, across Spain, the central highlands of France, to the hills and mountains of southern Germany, the Czech Republic, and Slovakia.

The Alpine Mountain System is made up of several mountain chains. Included in this system are the Pyrenees between Spain and France, the Alps in southeastern France, northern Italy, Switzerland, and western Austria, and the Apennine range in Italy. Also included are the mountain ranges of the Balkan Peninsula, the Carpathian Mountains in Slovakia and Romania, and the Caucasus Mountains between the Black and Caspian Seas. These mountain ranges have been formidable barriers and boundaries throughout history, affecting the movement of people and the relationship of people to each other and to the land.

When studying the map of Europe, it is important to notice the proximity of western areas of Asia, especially those at the eastern end of the Mediterranean Sea, to areas of North Africa. The cultures of these areas have not only interacted with those of Europe but have also played a significant role in shaping the history of Western civilization.

Western Civilization

Ideas, Politics & Society

Seventh Edition

Part One

The Ancient World: Foundation of the West

to A.D. 500

3000 B.C.

2000 B.C.

1000 B.C.

500 B.C.

100 B.C.

A.D. 200

Politics and Society	Thought and Culture
Rise of civilization in Sumer (c. 3200) Union of Upper and Lower Egypt (c. 2900) Rise of Minoan civilization (c. 2600)	Cuneiform writing in Sumer; hieroglyphics in Egypt
Rise of Mycenaean civilization (c. 2000) Hammurabi of Babylon builds an empire (1792–1750)	*Epic of Gilgamesh* (c. 1900) Code of Hammurabi (c. 1790) Amenhotep IV and a movement toward monotheism in Egypt (c. 1369–1353) Moses and the Exodus (1200s)
The creation of a unified Hebrew monarchy under David (1000–961) Dark Age in Greece (c. 1100–800) Hellenic Age (c. 800–323) Fall of Assyrian empire (612) Persian conquest of Near East (550–525) Formation of Roman Republic (509)	Homer's *Iliad* and *Odyssey* (700s) Age of classical prophecy: flowering of Hebrew ethical thought (750–430)
Persian Wars (499–479) Peloponnesian War (431–404) Conquest of Greek city-states by Philip of Macedon (338) Conquests of Alexander the Great (336–323) Hellenistic Age (323–30) Roman conquest of Carthage and Hellenistic kingdoms (264–146)	Law of the Twelve Tables (c. 450) Rise of Greek philosophy: Ionians, Pythagoreans, Parmenides (500s and 400s) Greek dramatists: Aeschylus, Sophocles, Euripides, Aristophanes (400s) Greek philosophers: Socrates, Plato, Aristotle (400s and 300s) Hellenistic philosophies: Epicureanism, Stoicism, Skepticism, Cynicism
Political violence and civil wars in Rome (88–31) Assassination of Julius Caesar (44) Octavian takes the title Augustus and becomes first Roman emperor (27) Greco-Roman Age (30 B.C.–c. A.D. 500) Pax Romana—the height of Roman Empire (27 B.C.–A.D. 180)	Roman philosophers during the Republic: Lucretius, Cicero (1st cent. B.C.) Rise and spread of Christianity: Jesus (d. A.D. 29); Paul's missionary activity (c. 34–64) Gospel According to Mark (c. 66–70) Roman historians, poets, and philosophers during the Pax Romana: Livy, Tacitus, Virgil, Horace, Ovid, Juvenal, Seneca, Marcus Aurelius
Military anarchy in Rome (235–285) Goths defeat Romans at Adrianople (378) End of Roman Empire in the West (476)	Church fathers: Jerome, Ambrose, Augustine (300s and 400s)

Chapter 1

The Ancient Near East: The First Civilizations

Built as royal tombs, the pyramids at Giza are among the wonders of the ancient world. (Robert Frerck/Woodfin Camp.)

■ **The Rise to Civilization**
The Paleolithic Age
The Neolithic Revolution
The First Civilizations

■ **Mesopotamian Civilization**
Religion: The Basis of Mesopotamian Civilization
Government and Law
Business and Trade
Writing, Mathematics, Astronomy, and Medicine

■ **Egyptian Civilization**
From the Old Kingdom to the Middle Kingdom
Religion: The Basis of Egyptian Civilization
Divine Kingship
Science and Mathematics
The New Kingdom and the Decline of Egyptian Civilization

■ **Empire Builders**
Hittites
Small Nations
Assyria
The Neo-Babylonian Empire
Persia: Unifier of the Near East

■ **The Religious Orientation of the Near East**
A Mythmaking World-View
Near Eastern Achievements

Civilization was not inevitable; it was an act of human creativity. The first civilizations emerged about five thousand years ago, in the Near Eastern river valleys of Sumer and Egypt. Before that time stretched the vast ages of prehistory, when our ancestors did not dwell in cities and knew nothing of writing. Today, when human beings have the capacity to destroy civilization, we might reflect on humanity's long and painful climb to a civilized state.

The Rise to Civilization

The Paleolithic Age

In recent decades, anthropologists and archaeologists have made important discoveries that have shed light on the prehistoric past. Richard E. Leakey speculates about one such find in East Africa:

> *Close to three million years ago on a campsite near the east shore of Kenya's spectacular Lake Turkana, formerly Lake Rudolf, a primitive human picked up a water-smoothed stone, and with a few skillful strikes transformed it into an implement. What was once an accident of nature was now a piece of deliberate technology, to be used to fashion a stick for digging up roots, or to slice the flesh off a dead animal. Soon discarded by its maker, the stone tool still exists, an unbreakable link with our ancestors.*[1]*

The period called the Paleolithic Age, or Old Stone Age, began with the earliest primitive toolmaking human beings who inhabited East Africa nearly three million years ago. It ended ten thousand years ago in parts of the Near East when people discovered how to farm. Our Paleolithic ancestors lived as hunters (no doubt also as scavengers) and food gatherers. Because they had not learned how to farm, they did not establish permanent villages. When their food supplies ran short, they abandoned their caves or tentlike

*Numbered source notes appear at the end of each chapter along with suggested readings and review questions.

Chronology 1.1 ❖ The Near East

3200 B.C.*	Rise of civilization in Sumer
2900	Union of Upper and Lower Egypt
2686–2181	Old Kingdom: essential forms of Egyptian civilization take shape
2180	Downfall of Akkadian empire
1792–1750	Hammurabi of Babylon brings Akkad and Sumer under his control and fashions a code of laws
1570	Egyptians drive out Hyksos and embark on empire building
1369–1353	Reign of Amenhotep IV: a movement toward monotheism
1200	Fall of Hittite empire
612	Fall of Assyrian empire
604–562	Reign of Nebuchadnezzar: height of Chaldean empire
550–525 B.C.	Persian conquests form a world empire

*Most dates are approximations

structures of branches and searched for new dwelling places.

Human social development was shaped by this three-million-year experience of hunting and food gathering. For survival, groups of families formed bands consisting of around thirty people; members learned how to plan, organize, cooperate, trust, and share. The men hunted for meat, and the women cared for the young, tended the fires, and gathered fruits, nuts, berries, and grain. Hunters assisted each other in tracking and killing game, finding cooperative efforts more successful than individual forays. By sharing their kill and bringing some back to their camp for the rest of the group, they reinforced the social bond. So, too, did women who gathered food for the group. Bands that did not cooperate in the hunt, in food gathering, or in food distribution were unlikely to survive.

Although human progress was very slow during the long centuries of the Paleolithic Age, advances occurred that influenced the future enormously. Paleolithic people developed spoken language and learned how to make and use tools. Both accomplishments are evidence of behavior that sets human beings apart from other creatures. To be sure, primates such as apes and chimpanzees utter sounds that express emotions, but they cannot give a name to an object or describe things. And although chimpanzees use a twig as a tool to get at insects, they do not save it for future use or progress in their toolmaking from generation to generation.

Paleolithic people, on the other hand, shaped bone, wood, and stone tools that corresponded to ideas in their minds. They preserved their creations and taught other people how to use them. Succeeding generations improved on what they had learned from their ancestors. With these simple but useful tools, Paleolithic human beings dug up roots, peeled the bark off trees, trapped, killed, and skinned animals, made clothing, and fashioned fishnets. They also discovered how to control fire, which allowed them to cook their meat and provided warmth and protection against predators—lions and leopards, for example—which feared fire. From evidence discovered in caves, it is certain that Paleolithic people had domesticated fire about 500,000 years ago. Some evidence points to fire use as far back as 1.5 million years.

Like toolmaking and the control of fire, language was a great human achievement. Language enabled individuals to acquire and share with one another knowledge, experiences, and feelings. Thus, language was the decisive factor in the development of culture and its transmission from one generation to the next. Language helped par-

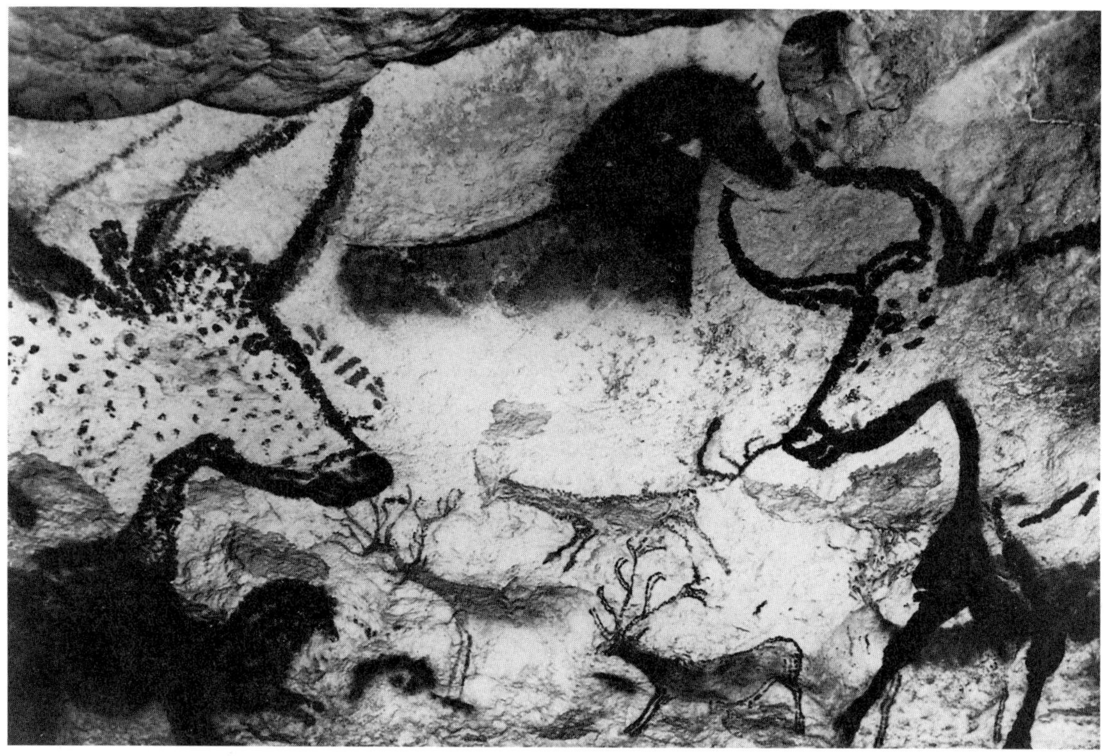

PALEOLITHIC CAVE PAINTING FROM LASCAUX, FRANCE. Produced as part of magical religious rites of hunting, these early paintings display considerable artistic skills. (*French Government Tourist Office.*)

ents teach their children rules of conduct and religious beliefs, as well as how to make tools and light fires.

Most likely, our Paleolithic ancestors developed mythic-religious beliefs to explain the mysteries of nature, birth, sickness, and death. They felt that living powers operated within and beyond the world that they experienced, and they sought to establish friendly relations with these powers. To primitive peoples, the elements—sun, rain, wind, thunder, and lightning—were alive. The natural elements were spirits; they could feel and act with a purpose. To appease these forces of nature, hunters and gatherers made offerings to them. Gradually, there emerged shamans, medicine men, and witch doctors, who, through rituals, trances, and chants, seemed able to communicate with these spirits. Paleolithic people also began the practice of burying their dead, sometimes with offerings, which suggests belief in life after death. Corpses were sometimes dusted with red ocher, which represented blood, a source of life. Another belief is revealed in the many small statues of women, made between forty thousand and twenty-five thousand years ago, that have been found by archaeologists in Europe and Asia. Fashioned from ivory, wood, and clay and often marked by huge breasts and distended stomachs, these fertility figurines represent a mother goddess who gave life, food, and protection.

Between thirty thousand and twelve thousand years ago, Paleolithic people sought out the dark and silent interior of caves, which they probably viewed as sanctuaries, and, with only torches for light, they painted remarkably skillful and perceptive pictures of animals on the cave walls. When these prehistoric artists drew an animal with a spear in its side, they probably believed that this act would make them successful in hunting; when they drew a herd of animals, they probably hoped that this would cause game to be plentiful. This belief that something done to an image of an animal or a person will produce the same effect on the being itself is called *sympathetic magic*. Hunting societies that endured into the modern world still engaged in rituals designed to protect the hunter and to ensure a kill.

Our knowledge of prehistoric art is being expanded by the discovery in December 1994 of a cave in southern France containing more than two hundred paintings made about thirty thousand years ago. Although not yet completely explored, several factors make this discovery so promising: the number of paintings is considerably greater than that found in the famous caves of Lascaux, also in southern France, and Altamira, Spain; included are images of animals—panthers and owls—not found in other caves; and the site seems to have been undisturbed for thousands of years.

The Neolithic Revolution

Some ten thousand years ago, the New Stone Age, or Neolithic Age, began in the Near East. During the Neolithic Age, human beings discovered farming, domesticated animals, established villages, polished stone tools, made pottery, and wove cloth. So important were these achievements that they are referred to as the Neolithic Revolution.

Agriculture—the deliberate planting and cultivation of crops—first developed in the hilly regions of the Near East, where rainfall was plentiful and wheat and barley grew abundantly in the wild. People there also began to domesticate the sheep and wild goats that roamed the hills. In other parts of the world, farming and the domestication of animals developed independently.

Agriculture and the domestication of animals revolutionized life. Whereas Paleolithic hunters and food gatherers had been forced to use whatever nature made available to them, Neolithic farmers altered their environment to satisfy human needs. Instead of spending their time searching for grains, roots, and berries, women and children grew crops near their homes; instead of tracking animals over great distances, men could slaughter domesticated goats or sheep nearby. (Later, horses, camels, and donkeys were tamed, providing people with a means of transportation.) Farming made possible a new kind of community. Because hunters needed to roam over large areas, hunting bands were by necessity small. If the band grew too large, some members formed a new band and moved on. Since farmers had to live near their fields and could store food for the future, farming led to the rise of permanent settlements. Villages containing as many as two hundred or three hundred people had occasionally emerged in late Paleolithic times, before the discovery of agriculture. Hunter-gatherers built such villages in areas that had an abundant, stable food supply—near a river or lake well stocked with fish, or in a valley with plenty of wild wheat and barley and herds of gazelles or goats. The development of farming greatly speeded the shift to villages. It is likely that trade also impelled people to gather in village communities. Herdsmen, hunters, and food gatherers living in regions rich in salt (needed for preserving food), volcanic glass (used for mirrors, blades, and spearheads), or hematite (an iron ore that was a source of red coloring for pottery) formed trading settlements, which exchanged raw materials for food.

Villages changed the patterns of life. A food surplus freed some people to devote part of their time to sharpening their skills as basket weavers or toolmakers. The demand for raw materials and the creations of skilled artisans fostered trade, sometimes across long distances, and the formation of trading settlements. An awareness of private property emerged. Hunters had accumulated few possessions, since belongings presented a burden in moving from place to place. Villagers, however, acquired property and were determined to protect it from one another and from outsiders—nomadic herdsmen who might raid the village. Hunting bands were egalitarian; generally, no one member had more possessions or more power than another. In farming villages, a ruling elite emerged that possessed wealth and wielded power.

No doubt farming also affected our emotional

development. Human beings who had evolved as hunters and foragers, enjoying considerable leisure, personal freedom, independence, and equality, were now forced to adjust to a different tempo of life—unending toil, stifling routine, and the need to obey the commands of the elites. Scholars ponder the psychological dimensions of this shift from the hunter's way of life to sedentary farming.

In recent years, archaeologists have uncovered several Neolithic villages, the oldest of which was established before 8000 B.C. Among the most famous of these sites are Çatal Hüyük in Anatolia (Turkey), Jericho in Palestine, and Jarmö in eastern Iraq. Scholars disagree on whether these communities were just highly developed villages or the first cities. The traditional view is that cities arose about 3000 B.C. in Sumer, the home of the earliest civilization. Some scholars argue that five thousand years before the Sumerian cities Jericho's two thousand inhabitants had created urban life by engaging in trade and embarking on public works. Jericho's walls were six feet six inches thick at the base and in some places twenty feet high. Their construction required cooperation and a division of labor beyond the capacity of an agricultural village. Similar communities, or "primitive cities," spread throughout much of the Near East in late prehistoric times.

Neolithic people made great strides in technology. By shaping and baking clay, they made pottery containers for cooking and for storing food and water. The invention of the potter's wheel enabled them to form bowls and plates more quickly and precisely. Stone tools were sharpened by grinding them on rock. The discoveries of the wheel and the sail improved transportation and promoted trade, and the development of the plow and the ox yoke made tilling the soil easier for farmers.

The Neolithic period also marks the beginning of the use of metals. First used was copper, which was easily fashioned into tools and weapons. Copper implements lasted longer than those made of stone and flint, and they could be recast and reshaped if broken. In time, artisans discovered how to make bronze by combining copper and tin in the proper ratio. Bronze was harder than copper, which made a sharper cutting edge possible.

During the Neolithic Age, the food supply became more reliable, village life expanded, and the population increased. Families that acquired wealth gained a higher social status and became village leaders. Religion grew more formal and structured; nature spirits evolved into deities, each with specific powers over nature or human life. Altars were erected in their honor, and ceremonies were conducted by priests, whose power and wealth increased as people gave offerings to the gods. Neolithic society was growing more organized and complex; it was on the threshold of civilization.

The First Civilizations

What we call *civilization* arose some five thousand years ago in the Near East (in Mesopotamia and Egypt) and then later in the Far East (in India and China). The first civilizations began in cities, which were larger, more populated, and more complex in their political, economic, and social structure than Neolithic villages. Because the cities depended on the inhabitants of adjacent villages for their food, farming techniques must have been developed sufficiently to produce food surpluses. Increased production provided food for urban inhabitants, who engaged in nonagricultural occupations; they became merchants, craftsmen, bureaucrats, and priests.

The invention of writing enabled the first civilizations to preserve, organize, and expand knowledge and to pass it on to future generations; it also allowed government officials and priests to conduct their affairs more efficiently. Moreover, civilized societies possessed organized governments, which issued laws and defined the boundary lines of their states. On a scale much larger than Neolithic communities, the inhabitants erected buildings and monuments, engaged in trade and manufacturing, and used specialized labor for different projects. Religious life grew more organized and complex, and a powerful and wealthy priesthood emerged. These developments—cities, specialization of labor, writing, organized government, monumental architecture, and a complex religious structure—differentiate the first civilizations from prehistoric cultures.

Religion was the central force in these primary civilizations. It provided satisfying explanations for the workings of nature, helped ease the fear of death, and justified traditional rules of morality. Law was considered sacred, a commandment of the gods. Religion united people in the common enterprises needed for survival—for example, the construction and maintenance of irrigation works and the storage of food. Religion also promoted creativity in art, literature, and science. In addition, the power of rulers, regarded as gods or their agents, derived from religion.

The emergence of civilization was a great creative act and not merely the inevitable development of agricultural societies. Many communities had learned how to farm, but only a handful made the leap into civilization. How was it possible for Sumerians and Egyptians, the creators of the earliest civilizations, to make that breakthrough? This question has intrigued and baffled historians, and no single explanation is entirely convincing. Most scholars stress the relationship between civilizations and river valleys. Rivers deposited fertile silt on adjoining fields, provided water for crops, and served as avenues for trade. But environmental factors alone do not adequately explain the emergence of civilization. What cannot be omitted is the human contribution: capacity for thought and cooperative activity.

Both the Tigris and Euphrates Rivers in Mesopotamia and the Nile River in Egypt deposited fertile soil when they overflowed their banks. But before these rivers could be of any value in producing crops, swamps around them had to be drained, jungles had to be cleared, and dikes, reservoirs, and canals had to be built. To construct and maintain irrigation works required the cooperation of large numbers of people, a necessary condition for civilization. As anthropologist Robert J. Braidwood says,

> *Whole villages or groups of people had to turn out to fix dikes or dig ditches. The dikes had to be repaired and the ditches carefully cleared of silt each year, or they would become useless. There also had to be hard and fast rules. The person who lived nearest the ditch or the reservoir must not be allowed to take all the water and leave none for his neighbors. It was not only a business of learning to control the rivers and making their waters do the farmer's work. It also meant controlling men. . . . This learning to work together for the common good was probably the real germ of the Egyptian and the Mesopotamian civilizations.*[2]

In the process of constructing and maintaining irrigation networks, people learned to formulate and obey rules and developed administrative, engineering, and mathematical skills. The need to keep records stimulated the invention of writing. These creative responses to the challenges posed by nature spurred the early inhabitants of Sumer and Egypt to make the breakthrough to civilization, thereby altering the course of human destiny. By the time the Hebrews and the Greeks, the spiritual ancestors of Western civilization, appeared on the stage of history, civilizations had been in existence for some two thousand years.

Civilization also had its dark side. Epidemic disease thrived in urban centers, where people lived close together in unsanitary conditions, drinking contaminated water and surrounded by rotting garbage. The authority wielded by rulers and their officials and the habits of discipline acquired by the community's members made possible the construction of irrigation works, but they were also harnessed for destructive conflicts between states. Such warfare was far more lethal than the sporadic and disorganized acts of violence that occurred in Neolithic times. And warfare fascinated the people who created the first civilizations: scribes recounted battle after battle, warrior-kings boasted of their military conquests, and military heroes were held in the highest esteem. Cultural historian Lewis Mumford observes:

> *War was not a mere residue of more common primitive forms of aggression. . . . In all its typical aspects, its discipline, its drill, its handling of large masses of men as units, in its destructive assaults en masse, in its heroic sacrifices, its final destructions, exterminations, seizures, enslavements, war was rather the special invention of civilization: its ultimate drama.*[3]

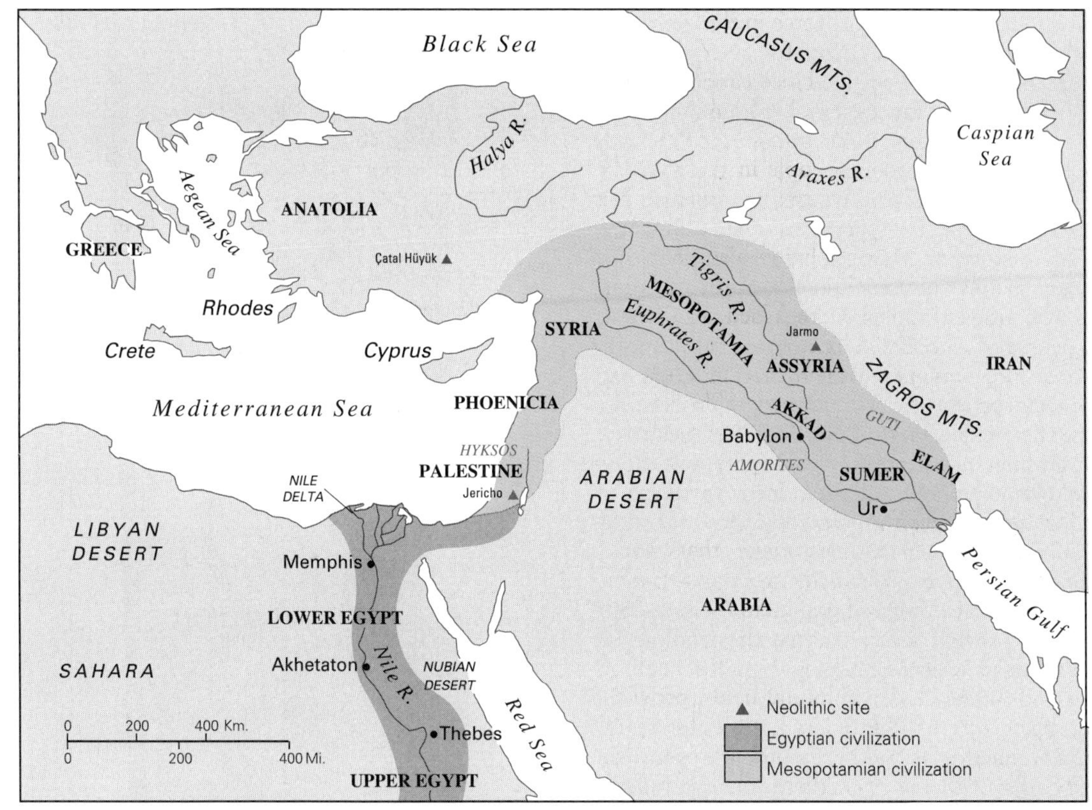

Map 1.1 Mesopotamian and Egyptian Civilizations The first civilizations emerged in river valleys: Mesopotamia in the valleys of the Tigris and Euphrates Rivers, Egypt in the Nile valley.

Mesopotamian Civilization

Mesopotamia is the Greek word for "land between the rivers." It was here, in the valleys of the Tigris and Euphrates Rivers, that the first civilization began. The first to develop an urban civilization in Mesopotamia (modern-day Iraq) were the Sumerians, who colonized the marshlands of the lower Euphrates, which, together with the Tigris, flows into the Persian Gulf. The Sumerians' origin is obscure, although scholars speculate that they migrated from the East, perhaps northern India. They spoke a language unrelated to the tongues of their Semitic neighbors, who had migrated from Arabia into Mesopotamia and adjacent regions.

Through constant toil and imagination, the Sumerians transformed the swamps into fields of barley and groves of date palms. Around 3000 B.C., their hut settlements gradually evolved into twelve independent city-states, each consisting of a city and its surrounding countryside. Among the impressive achievements of the Sumerians were a system of symbol writing (*cuneiform*), in which pictograms and signs for numbers were engraved with a reed stylus on clay tablets to represent ideas; elaborate brick houses, palaces, and temples; bronze tools and weapons; irrigation works; trade with other peoples; an early form of money; religious and political institutions; schools; religious and secular literature; varied art forms; codes of law; medicinal drugs; and a lunar calendar.

Although they spoke a common language and shared the same customs and gods, the Sumerian city-states engaged in frequent warfare with each other, principally over boundaries and water rights (canals built upriver reduced the water available to the cities downriver). Weakened by warfare, the Sumerians lay open to foreign domination.

The history of Mesopotamia is marked by a succession of conquests. To the north of Sumer was a Semitic city called Akkad. About 2350 B.C., the people of Akkad, led by Sargon the Great, the warrior-king, conquered the Sumerian cities. Sargon built the world's first empire, which extended from the Persian Gulf to the Mediterranean Sea. Establishing a pattern that future despotic rulers would emulate, Sargon stationed garrisons in conquered lands and appointed governors and officials to administer the territories, as well as additional bureaucrats to register and parcel out the precious metals, horses, grain, and other commodities exacted from conquered peoples. He also retained a large standing army to quell revolts and to launch new imperialist ventures. The Akkadians adopted Sumerian cultural forms, including cuneiform, and spread them beyond the boundaries of Mesopotamia with their conquests. Mesopotamian religion became a blend of Sumerian and Akkadian elements.

In succeeding centuries, the Sumerian cities were incorporated into various kingdoms and empires. The Sumerian language, replaced by a Semitic tongue, became an obscure language known only to priests, and the Sumerians gradually disappeared as a distinct people. But their cultural achievements endured. Akkadians, Babylonians, Elamites, and others adopted Sumerian religious, legal, literary, and art forms. The Sumerian legacy served as the basis for a Mesopotamian civilization that maintained a distinct style for three thousand years.

Wooden Soundbox of a Sumerian Harp, Ur, c. 2600 B.C. The top panel features a heroic figure embracing two man-faced bulls made from shells inlaid in bitumen. Beneath are three panels with various animals carrying food or drink and musical instruments. The theme may depict a fable of some festive celebration or a ritual myth. (*University Museum, University of Pennsylvania, Negative #S8–22097.*)

Religion: The Basis of Mesopotamian Civilization

Religion lay at the center of Mesopotamian life. Every human activity—political, military, social, legal, literary, artistic—was generally subordinated to an overriding religious purpose. Religion was the Mesopotamians' frame of reference for understanding nature, society, and themselves; it dominated and inspired all other cultural expressions and human activities. Wars between cities, for instance, were interpreted as conflicts between the gods of those cities, and victory ultimately depended on divine favor, not on human effort. Myths—narratives about the activities of the gods—explained the origins of the human species. According to the earliest Sumerian myths, the first human beings issued forth from the earth like plant life, or were shaped from clay by divine craftsmen and granted a heart by the goddess Nammu, or were formed from the blood of two gods sacrificed for that purpose.

The Mesopotamians believed that people were given life so that they could execute on earth the will of the gods in heaven. No important decisions were made by kings or priests without first consulting the gods. To discover the wishes of the gods, priests sacrificed animals and then examined their livers; or the priests might find their answers in the stars or in dreams.

The cities of Mesopotamia were sacred communities dedicated to serving divine masters, and people hoped that appeasing the gods would bring security and prosperity to their cities. The Sumerians erected ziggurats—huge multilevel mounds—on which temples were built. The ziggurat in Ur measured 205 feet by 140 feet at the base and was about 70 feet high; staircases connected its levels and led to the top platform, on which stood a majestic temple.

The ziggurat was surrounded by low walls enclosing offices and houses for the priests and shops where potters, weavers, carpenters, and tanners performed their crafts. The temple was the cultural and economic heart of the city. A particular city belonged to a god, who was the real owner of the land and the real ruler of the city; often a vast complex of temples was built for the god and the god's family. In the temple, the god was offered shelter, food, clothing, and the homage of dutiful servants.

Supervised by priests, the temple was a vital part of the city's life. People congregated there to take part in religious ceremonies. The temple also fulfilled important economic functions. Temple priests collected rents, operated businesses, and received contributions for festivals. Most inhabitants of the city worked for the temple priests as tenant farmers, agricultural laborers, or servants. Anxious to curry favor with the gods and goddesses who watched over the fields, peasants surrendered part of their crops to the temple. Priests coordinated the city's economic activity, supervising the distribution of land, overseeing the irrigation works, and storing food for emergencies. Temple scribes kept records of expenditures and receipts. By serving as stewards of the city's deities and managing their earthly estates, the priests sustained civilized life.

The gods and goddesses, invisible to human eyes but omnipresent, controlled the entire universe and everything in it. The moon, the sun, and the storm, the city, the irrigation works, and the fields—each was directed by a god. Mesopotamians saw gods and demons everywhere in nature. There was a god in the fire and another in the river; evil demons stirred up sandstorms, caused disease, and endangered women in childbirth. To shield themselves from hostile forces, Mesopotamians wore charms and begged their gods for help. Each Mesopotamian offered prayers and sacrifices to a personal god or goddess, who provided protection against evil spirits.

Mesopotamians believed that they were manipulated by divine beings. When misfortune befell them, people attributed it to the gods. Even success was not due to their own efforts but to the intervention of a god who had taken a special interest in them. Compared with the gods, an individual was an insignificant and lowly creature.

Uncertainty and danger filled life in Mesopotamia. Sometimes, the unpredictable waters of the rivers broke through the dikes, flooding fields, ruining crops, and damaging cities. At other times, an insufficient overflow deprived the land of water, causing crops to fail. Great windstorms left the countryside covered with a layer of sand, and heavy thunderstorms turned fields into a sea of mud that made travel impossible. Unlike Egypt, which was protected by vast deserts, Mesopotamia had no natural barriers to invasion. Feeling themselves surrounded by unfathomable and often hostile forces, Mesopotamians lived in an atmosphere of anxiety, which permeated their civilization.

Contributing to this sense of insecurity was the belief that the gods had little love for humanity.

They had created a "savage, 'man' shall be his name . . . [who] shall be charged with the service of the gods that they might be at ease."[4] Toward humans the gods behaved capriciously, maliciously, and vindictively, and it was difficult to please them. The writer of the following verses had done all that he believed the gods wanted of him, yet he continued to suffer physical deterioration and pain:

> *I survived to the next year; the appointed*
> *time passed.*
> *I turned around, but it is bad, very bad;*
> *My* ill luck *increases and I cannot find what*
> *is right.*
> *I called to my god, but he did not show his*
> *face,*
> *I prayed to my goddess, but she did not raise*
> *her head.*[5]

What do the gods demand of me? Is it ever possible to please them? To these questions Mesopotamians had no reassuring answers, for the gods' behavior was a mystery to mere human beings:

> *What is good for oneself may be offense to*
> *one's god,*
> *What in one's own heart seems despicable*
> *may be proper to one's god.*
> *Who can know the will of the gods in heaven?*
> *Who can understand the plans of the*
> *underworld gods?*
> *Where have humans learned the way of a god?*
> *He who was alive yesterday is dead today.*[6]

A Mesopotamian man or woman hoped to experience the good life by being obedient to his or her older brother, father, foreman, priest, and king and to a personal deity, who could influence the decisions of the other gods. The rewards for obedience were long life, health, and worldly success. But the feeling persisted that happiness was either transitory or beyond reach—a pessimism that abounded in Mesopotamian literature.

A mood of uncertainty and anxiety, an awareness of the cosmos as unfathomable and mysterious, a feeling of dread about the fragility of human existence and the impermanence of hu-

King Gudea. Inscriptions written in cuneiform recorded the construction of temples and irrigation works in the Sumerian city-state of Lagash during the reign of King Gudea around 2150 B.C. The inscription on Gudea's image describes a temple dedicated to the goddess Geshtin-anna. (*Louvre © R.M.N.*)

man achievement—these attitudes are as old as the first civilization. The *Epic of Gilgamesh*, the finest work of Mesopotamian literature, masterfully depicts this mood of pessimism and despair. The epic deals with a profound theme: the human protest against death. The death of his close friend causes Gilgamesh to face the reality of his own death. "Despair is in my heart. What my brother is now that shall I be when I am dead. . . . I am afraid of death."[7] Gilgamesh yearns for eternal life, but he learns that when the gods created human beings they allotted to them only death. "Where is the man who can clamber to heaven? Only the gods live forever . . . but as for us men, our days are numbered, our occupations are a breath of wind."[8]

And in contrast to the Egyptians (see "Divine Kingship"), the Mesopotamians had little to look forward to after death. They believed that they would either be confined to a dreary underworld whose rulers would inflict pain on them or be transformed into spirits, flying about and tormenting the living.

Government and Law

The government of early Sumer may have been a "primitive democracy," that is, one in which a council of elders guided everyday affairs and an assembly of citizens appointed a temporary king when war threatened. In time, however, kingship became hereditary and permanent, supplanting rule by the elders. The king's chief duties were to direct the construction and maintenance of temples and irrigation canals and to wage war.

Bestowed on a man by the gods, kingship was the central institution in Mesopotamian society. Unlike Egyptian pharaohs, Mesopotamian kings saw themselves not as gods but rather as great men selected by the gods to represent them on earth. Gods governed through the kings, who reported to the gods about conditions in their land (which was the gods' property) and petitioned the gods for advice.

The Mesopotamians viewed earthly governments as exact replicas of the government of the gods. No one Mesopotamian god was all-powerful; instead, an assembly of gods made decisions as a group. Therefore, a mortal king could not be all-powerful either. For this reason, Mesopotamian kingship usually lacked the sureness, confidence, and absolutism of Egyptian kingship. This view of kingship also contributed to the anxiety in Mesopotamian life, for there was no assurance that a king, mortal and fallible, could correctly ascertain heaven's commands.

The king administered the laws, which came from the gods. Like everyone else in the land, the king had to obey divine laws. These laws provided Mesopotamians with a measure of security. The principal collection of laws in ancient Mesopotamia was the famous code of Hammurabi (c. 1792–c. 1750), the Babylonian ruler. Unearthed by French archaeologists in 1901–1902, the code has provided invaluable insights into Mesopotamian society. The laws were inscribed on a stone slab (stele), near the top of which Hammurabi was depicted, standing reverently before the throne of Shamash, the sun-god and patron of justice. In typical Mesopotamian fashion, Hammurabi claimed that his code rested on the authority of the gods; to violate it was to contravene the divine order.

The code reveals social status and mores in that area and time. Men were the heads of the family, although efforts were made to protect women and children from mistreatment and poverty. Thus, if a man divorced his wife because she did not bear him a son, he had to provide her with money. Punishments were generally severe—"an eye for an eye and a tooth for a tooth." The code prescribed death for housebreaking, kidnapping, aiding the escape of slaves, receiving stolen goods, and bearing false witness; however, it allowed consideration of extenuating circumstances. Being forgiven by the wronged party could also mitigate the penalty. For example, a wife who committed adultery could be spared execution if pardoned by her husband. Class distinctions were expressed in the code. Penalties varied with the status of both the wrongdoer and the victim. For instance, a person received a harsher punishment for harming a noble than for harming a commoner. Government officials engaging in extortion or bribery were punished severely. The code's many provisions relating to business transactions show the importance of trade to Mesopotamian life.

Business and Trade

The economy of Mesopotamian cities depended heavily on foreign and domestic trade. Whereas trade in Egypt was conducted by the state bureaucracy, in Mesopotamia there was greater opportunity for private enterprise. Besides merchants, temple priests engaged in trade because they possessed surplus produce collected as rents from farmers using temple land. Early in Mesopotamian history, merchants were subservient to the king and the temple priests. Over the centuries, however, merchants began to behave as professionals—not just as agents of the palace or temple, but as private entrepreneurs.

Because of trade's importance to the life of the city, governments instituted regulations to prevent fraud. Business transactions had to be recorded in writing, and severe punishments were imposed for dishonesty. A system of weights and measures facilitated trade, and efforts were made to prevent excessive interest rates for loans.

Mesopotamians imported resources not found at home—stone, silver, and timber. In exchange, they exported textiles, fine handicrafts, and (less often because of difficulty in transporting them by donkey) agricultural products. They also imported copper from the Persian Gulf, precious metals from Afghanistan, ivory from Africa and the west coast of India, and cedar and cypress woods, oils, and essences from the Mediterranean coastal areas. Enterprising businessmen set up trading outposts in distant lands, making the Mesopotamians pioneers in international trade.

Writing, Mathematics, Astronomy, and Medicine

The Sumerians established schools, which trained the sons of the upper class in the art of cuneiform writing. Hundreds of tablets on which Sumerian students practiced their lessons have been discovered, testifying to the years of disciplined and demanding work required to master the scribal art. Virtually all scribes were men, but female scribes are at times mentioned in Mesopotamian writings. Noble women in particular were literate.

To assist their pupils, teachers prepared textbooks of word lists and mathematical problems with solutions. In translating Sumerian words into the Akkadian language, they compiled what was probably the world's first dictionary. Students who completed the course of study successfully were employed as archivists, secretaries, or accountants by the temple, the palace, the law courts, or merchants. The Sumerian system of cuneiform writing spread to other parts of the Near East.

The Mesopotamians made some impressive advances in mathematics. They devised multiplication and division tables, including even cubes and cube roots. They determined the area of right-angle triangles and rectangles, divided a circle into 360 degrees, and had some understanding of the principles that centuries later would be developed into the Pythagorean theorem and quadratic equations. But the Babylonians, who made the chief contribution in mathematics, barely advanced to the level of making theories; they did not formulate general principles or furnish proofs for their mathematical operations.

By carefully observing and accurately recording the positions of planets and constellations of stars, Babylonian sky watchers took the first steps in developing the science of astronomy, and they devised a calendar based on the cycles of the moon. As in mathematics, however, they did not form theories to coordinate and illuminate their data. They believed that the position of the stars and planets revealed the will of the gods. Astronomers did not examine the heavens to find what we call cause and effect connections between the phenomena. Rather, they sought to discover what the gods wanted. With this knowledge, people could organize their political, social, and moral lives in accordance with divine commands and escape the terrible consequences that they believed resulted from ignoring the gods' wishes. Thus, despite its impressive achievements, Babylonian astronomy remained essentially a mythical interpretation of the universe.

As was consistent with their religious worldview, the Mesopotamians believed that disease was caused by gods or demons. To cure a patient, priest-physicians resorted to magic; through prayers and sacrifices, they attempted to appease the gods and eject the demons from the sick body. Nevertheless, in identifying illnesses and prescribing appropriate remedies, Mesopotamians demonstrated some accurate knowledge of medicine and pharmacology.

Egyptian Civilization

During the early period of Mesopotamian civilization, the people of another river valley, to the west, put themselves on the path toward civilization. The Egyptians developed their civilization in the fertile valley of the Nile. For good reason, the Greek historian Herodotus called Egypt "the gift of the Nile," for without this mighty river, which flows more than four thousand miles from central Africa northward to the Mediterranean, virtually all Egypt would be a desert. When the Nile overflowed its banks, as it did reliably and predictably, the floodwaters deposited a layer of fertile black earth, which, when cultivated, provided abundant food to support Egyptian civilization. The Egyptians learned how to control the river—a feat that required cooperative effort and ingenuity, as well as engineering and administrative skills.

Nature favored Egypt in a number of ways. Besides water, fish and fowl, and fertile land, the Nile also provided an excellent transportation link between Upper (southern) and Lower (northern) Egypt. Natural barriers—mountains, deserts, cataracts (rapids) in the Nile, and the Mediterranean—protected Egypt from attack, allowing the inhabitants to enjoy long periods of peace and prosperity. Gold, copper, and stone abounded, along with other natural resources. In addition, the climate of Egypt is dry and salutary. To the Egyptians, nature seemed changeless and beneficent. Hence, unlike Mesopotamians, Egyptians derived a sense of security from their environment.

From the Old Kingdom to the Middle Kingdom

About 2900 B.C., a ruler of Upper Egypt, known as Narmer, or Menes, conquered the Nile Delta and Lower Egypt. By 2686 B.C., centralized rule had been firmly established, and great pyramids, which were tombs for the pharaohs, were being constructed. The pyramids required rigorous central planning to coordinate the tens of thousands of laborers drafted to build these immense monuments. During this Pyramid Age, or Old Kingdom (2686–2181 B.C.), the essential forms of Egyptian civilization crystallized.

The Egyptians believed the pharaoh to be both a man and a god, the earthly embodiment of the deity Horus; he was an absolute ruler of the land and held his court at the city of Memphis. The Egyptians regarded the pharaoh as a benevolent protector, who controlled the floodwaters of the Nile, kept the irrigation works in order, maintained justice in the land, and expressed the will of heaven. They expected that when the pharaoh died and joined his fellow gods he would still help his living subjects.

In time, the nobles who served as district governors gained in status and wealth and gradually came to undermine the divine king's authority. The nobles' growing power and the enormous expenditure of Egypt's human and material resources on building pyramids led to the decline of the Old Kingdom. From 2181 to 2040 B.C.—a time called the First Intermediate Period—rival families competed for the throne, thus destroying the unity of the kingdom. The civil wars and the collapse of central authority required to maintain the irrigation system cast a pall over the land, as illustrated in this ancient Egyptian poem:

> *The wrongdoer is everywhere. . . .*
> *Plunderers are everywhere. . . .*
> *Nile is in flood, yet none plougheth for him. . . .*
> *Laughter hath perished and is no longer made.*
> *It is grief that walketh through the land, mingled with lamentations. . . .*
> *The storehouse is bare.*[9]

During what is called the Middle Kingdom (2040–1786 B.C.), strong kings reasserted pharaonic rule and reunited the state. The restoration of political stability reinvigorated cultural life and revived economic activity. Pharaohs extended Egyptian control south over the land of

Nubia, which became a principal source of gold. A profitable trade was carried on with Palestine, Syria, and Crete.

About 1800 B.C., central authority again weakened. In the era known as the Second Intermediate Period (1786–1570 B.C.), the nobles regained some of their power, the Nubians broke away from Egyptian control, and the Hyksos (a mixture of Semites and Indo-Europeans) invaded Egypt. For centuries, desert and sea had effectively guarded Egypt from foreign invasion, but the Hyksos invaders, using horse and chariot and body armor, ended Egyptian complacency. The Hyksos succeeded in dominating Egypt for about a hundred years. Resentful of foreign rule, the Egyptians became more militant and aggressive; they learned to use the Hyksos' weapons and drove out the invaders in 1570 B.C. The period of empire building known as the New Kingdom (1570–1085 B.C.) then began.

The basic features of Egyptian civilization had been forged during the Old and Middle Kingdoms. The Egyptians looked to the past, believing that the ways of their ancestors were best. For almost three thousand years, Egyptian civilization sought to retain a harmony with the order of nature instituted at creation. Believing that the universe was changeless, the Egyptians did not value change or development—what we call progress—but venerated the institutions, traditions, and authority that embodied permanence.

Religion: The Basis of Egyptian Civilization

Religion was omnipresent in Egyptian life and accounted for the outstanding achievements of Egyptian civilization. Religious beliefs were the basis of Egyptian art, medicine, astronomy, literature, and government. The great pyramids, which took decades to finish and required the labor of thousands of people, were tombs for the pharaohs, man-gods. Magical utterances pervaded medical practices, for disease was attributed to the gods. Astronomy evolved to determine the correct time to perform religious rites and sacrifices. The earliest examples of literature dealt wholly with religious themes. The pharaoh was a sacrosanct monarch who served as an intermediary between the gods and human beings. Justice was conceived in religious terms, something bestowed by a creator-god. The Egyptians developed an ethical code, which they believed the gods had approved. In a number of treatises compiled by high officials, now called *Books of Instruction*, Egyptians were urged to tell the truth and to treat others fairly. In one *Book of Instruction* prepared at the end of the second millennium, the author, in a high ethical tone, enjoined Egyptians to express compassion for the poor, widows, and the handicapped.

Egyptian polytheism took many forms, including the worship of animals, for the Egyptians believed that gods manifested themselves in animal shapes. Consequently, crocodiles, cats, bulls, and other animals dwelt in temples and were mummified for burial when they died. Perhaps the Egyptians regarded animals with religious awe because an animal species continues from generation to generation without apparent change. To the Egyptian mind, says Henri Frankfort, a leading scholar in Near Eastern studies, the quality of changelessness made "animal life . . . appear superhuman . . . in that it shared directly, patently, in the static life of the universe."[10]

Certain gods were conceived by the Egyptians as taking various forms. Thoth, for example, was represented as the moon, a baboon, an ibis, and an ibis-headed man. The god Amon was depicted both in human form and as a ram. To the Egyptians, these different representations were not contradictory, for they did not seek logical consistency in religion. The Egyptians also believed great powers in nature—sky, sun, earth, the Nile—to be gods. Thus, the universe was alive with divinities—there were about two thousand gods in the Egyptian pantheon—and human lives were tied to the movements of the sun and the moon and to the rhythm of the seasons. In the heavens the Egyptians found answers to the great problems of human existence.

A crucial feature of Egyptian religion was the afterlife. Through pyramid-tombs, mummification to preserve the dead, and funerary art, the Egyptians showed their yearning for eternity and their desire to overcome death. Mortuary priests recited incantations to ensure the preservation of the dead body and the continuity of existence. Inscribed on the pyramids' interior walls were "pyramid texts," written in *hieroglyphics*—a form of picture writing in which figures, such as crocodiles, sails, eyes, and so forth, represented words or sounds that would be combined to form words. The texts contained fragments from myths, historical annals, and magical lore and provided spells to assist the king in ascending to heaven.

At first, the Egyptians believed that only the pharaoh and the royal family were immortal. In time, the nobility and then the commoners claimed that they, too, could share in the blessings of the "other world." Prayers hitherto reserved for the pharaoh were, for a fee, recited by priests at the burial of commoners. Egyptians believed that their deceased relatives would intercede with the gods in their behalf. They wrote letters to these spirits, petitioning them for help for such problems as infertility, inheritance of property, and family quarrels. To the Egyptians, the other world contained the same pleasures as those enjoyed on earth—friends, servants, fishing, hunting, paddling a canoe, picnicking with family members, entertainment by musicians and dancers, and good food. However, because earthly existence was not fundamentally unhappy, Egyptians did not yearn for death. Unlike early Christians, they did not reject this world or willingly endure martyrdom in order to enter a higher and better world. The following song, inscribed in a pharaoh's tomb, reveals the Egyptians' relish for life.

> *Enjoy yourself while you live,*
> *put on fine linen*
> *anoint yourself with wonderful ointments,*
> *multiply all your fine possessions on earth,*
> *follow your heart's command on earth*
> *be joyful and make merry.*[11]

Pharaoh Mycerinus and His Queen, c. 2525 b.c. Swelling chests and hips idealize the royal couple's humanity, but the cubic feeling of the sculpture and rigid confidence of the pose proclaim their unquestioned divinity. (*Harvard MFA Expedition. Courtesy Museum of Fine Arts, Boston.*)

Divine Kingship

"What is the king of Upper and Lower Egypt? He is a god by whose dealings one lives, the father and mother of men, alone by himself, without an equal."[12] Divine kingship was the basic institution of Egyptian civilization. Perhaps the requirements of the Egyptian environment helped forge the idea of the pharaoh as a living god, because a ruler with supernatural authority, and held in favor by the gods, could hold together the large kingdom and draft the mass labor required to maintain the irrigation system.

Through the pharaoh, the gods made known their wishes for the Egyptian people. As kingship was a divine, not a manmade, institution, it was expected to last for eternity. The Egyptians rejoiced in the rule of an all-powerful, all-knowing god-king, who controlled the Nile, bringing fertility to the land, and could intercede in their behalf with the other deities. To the Egyptians, the pharaoh was "the herdsman of everyone without evil in his heart."[13] They believed that divine kingship was the only acceptable political arrangement, that it was in harmony with the order of the universe, and that it brought stability and authority to the nation.

The power of the pharaoh extended to all sectors of society. Peasants were drafted to serve in labor corps as miners or construction workers. Foreign trade was a state monopoly. The pharaoh authorized commercial ventures—caravan expeditions south to Nubia for ivory, gold, and ebony and sailing expeditions east to Lebanon for timber. Profits from foreign trade enriched the royal treasury. Although private ownership of land was recognized in practice, in theory all land belonged to the pharaoh. As the supreme overlord, the pharaoh oversaw an army of government officials, who collected taxes, managed construction projects, checked the irrigation works, surveyed the land, kept records, and supervised government warehouses, where grain was stored as insurance against a bad harvest. All Egyptians were subservient to the pharaoh, and there was no conception of political liberty.

Egyptian rulers, like their Mesopotamian counterparts, believed that they had an obligation to render justice. Injustice was seen as an offense against the gods. Most pharaohs took their responsibilities seriously and tried to govern as benevolent protectors of the people.

> *Be not evil, it is good to be kindly. . . . Do right so long as thou abidest on the earth. Calm the weeper, oppress no widow, expel no man from the possessions of his father. . . . Take heed lest thou punish wrongfully. . . . Slay not a man whose good qualities thou knowest. . . . Exalt not the son of one of high degree more than him that is of lowly birth, but take to thyself a man because of his actions.*[14]

Egyptians derived a sense of security from the concept of divine kingship. It meant that earthly government and society were in harmony with the cosmos, a divine order that provided justice and security. The Egyptians believed that the institution of kingship dated from the creation of the universe, that as part of the rhythm of the universe kingship was necessary and beneficial to human beings.

The pharaoh was seen as ruling in accordance with Ma'at, which means justice, law, right, and truth. To oppose the pharaoh was to violate the universal and divinely ordained order of Ma'at and to bring disorder to society. Because the Egyptians regarded Ma'at, which was established with the creation of the universe, as the right order of nature, they believed that its preservation must be the object of human activity—the guiding norm of the state and the standard by which individuals conducted their lives. Those who did Ma'at and spoke Ma'at would be justly rewarded. Could anything be more reassuring than this belief that divine truth was represented in the person of the pharaoh, who guaranteed and defended the sacred order of the universe?

Science and Mathematics

Like the Mesopotamians, the Egyptians made practical advances in mathematics and science. They demonstrated superb engineering skills in building pyramids. For example, the pyramid of Khufu, still the largest stone building ever constructed, contains 2.3 million stone blocks, each averaging 2.5 tons. They fashioned an effective system of mathematics, including geometry for measurements, that enabled them to solve relatively simple problems.

Controlling the floodwaters of the Nile required careful planning. Therefore, it was vital to know when the Nile would begin to overflow. Noting that the Nile flooded after the star Sirius appeared in the sky, the Egyptians developed a calendar by which they could predict the time of the flood. Eventually, they fashioned a calendar of twelve months, each having thirty days. To complete the solar year, they added a separate period of five days after the last month. The Egyptian calendar based on the sun was more accurate than the Babylonian lunar calendar.

In the area of medicine, Egyptian doctors were more capable than their Mesopotamian counterparts. They were able to identify illnesses; they recognized that uncleanliness encouraged contagion; they had some knowledge of anatomy and performed operations—circumcision and perhaps the draining of abscessed teeth. Although the progress of medicine was handicapped by the belief that supernatural forces caused illnesses, there is evidence that some Egyptian doctors examined the body in a scientific way. In a scroll, the Edwin Smith Surgical Papyrus (named after the nineteenth-century American Egyptologist who acquired it), the writer omitted all references to divine intervention in his advice for treating wounds and fractures. He described fractures in a matter-of-fact way and recommended healing them with splints and casts. In another papyrus document (papyrus is writing material made from the stalks of the papyrus plant), the writer identified the various snakes, analyzed the effects of their bites, and listed treatments, including the use of specific drugs—and he did so with only minimum references to magical incantations.

The New Kingdom and the Decline of Egyptian Civilization

The New Kingdom began in 1570 B.C. with the war of liberation against the Hyksos. This war gave rise to an intense militancy, which found expression in empire building. Aggressive pharaohs conquered territory that extended as far east as the Euphrates River. From its subject states, Egypt acquired tribute and slaves. Conquests led to the expansion of the bureaucracy, the creation of a professional army to protect the new territorial acquisitions, and the increased power of priests, whose temples shared in the spoils. The formation of the empire ended Egyptian isolation and accelerated commercial and cultural intercourse with other peoples. During this period, Egyptian art, for example, showed the influence of foreign forms.

A growing cosmopolitanism was paralleled by a movement toward monotheism during the reign of Pharaoh Amenhotep IV (c. 1369–1353 B.C.). Amenhotep sought to replace traditional polytheism with the worship of Aton, a single god of all people, a supreme force in nature represented as the sun disk. Amenhotep took the name Akhenaton ("Servant of Aton") and moved the capital from Thebes to a newly constructed holy city called Akhetaten ("Horizon of Aton," which is near modern Tell el-Amarna). The city had palaces, administrative centers, and a temple complex honoring Aton. Akhenaton and his wife, Nefertiti, who played a prominent role in his court, dedicated themselves to Aton—the creator of the world, the maintainer of life, and the god of love, justice, and peace. Akhenaton (or Ikhnaton) also ordered his officials to remove the names and images of other gods from temples and monuments. With awe, Akhenaton celebrated Aton's power and magnificence:

QUEEN NEFERTITI. The painted bust of Queen Nefertiti was discovered in a sculptor's workshop at Amarna, Akhetaten's capital city. She was often depicted with the same tall, blue crown that she is wearing here. (*Aegyptisches Museum, Berlin, SMPK/AKG, London.*)

> *How manifold are thy works!*
> *They are hidden from man's sight.*
> *O sole god, like whom there is no other.*
> *Thou hast made the earth according to thy desire.*[15]

Akhenaton's "monotheism" had little impact on the masses of Egyptians, who remained devoted to their traditional gods and ancient beliefs, and was resisted by priests, who resented his changes. The new religion could not survive the death of its founder. Akhenaton's successor, Tutankhamen (1352–1344 B.C.), abandoned the

Profile

Hatchepsut

Hatchepsut, daughter of Thutmose I (1493–1482 B.C.), was an exceptional figure in Egyptian history—a female pharaoh. As the wife of her half brother, Thutmose II, she did not produce a male heir. When Thutmose II died after a three-year reign, his infant son by a secondary wife inherited the throne. But because of his tender years, Hatchepsut served as regent. By the seventh year of the regency, Hatchepsut had assumed the royal title of king of Egypt. Although females were not officially barred from becoming pharaohs, it was an unchallenged tradition that this revered position was reserved for men. To legitimize her rule, Hatchepsut had a sequence of pictures carved on the porch of her mortuary temple that told the story of her divine birth. She was conceived when the god Amon-Re, disguised as Thutmose I, visited her mother's boudoir. Amon indicated that he intended to father a female, who one

Erich Lessing/Rijksmuseum van Oudheden, Egyptian Collection/Art Resource, NY.

capital at Amarna and returned to Thebes. Tutankhamen was succeeded by an elderly relative, who reigned briefly. In 1340, Horemheb (1340–1315 B.C.), an army commander, seized power and had the monuments to Aton destroyed, along with records and inscriptions bearing Akhenaton's name. And the great visionary was vilified as "The Blashphemer."

Historians are not certain why Akhenaton made such a radical break with tradition by propagating the worship of a single god. Was he trying to strike at the priests, whose wealth and prestige had increased considerably with Egypt's conquests? Did the break stem essentially from the vision of a great prophet? But the most significant historical questions concerning Akhenaton are these: First, was Akhenaton's religion genuine monotheism, which pushed religious thought in a new direction? And second, if this was the case, did it influence Moses, who led the Israelites out of Egypt about a century later?

These two questions have aroused controversy among historians. The principal limitation on the monotheistic character of Atonism is that there were really two gods in Akhenaton's religion—Aton and the pharaoh himself, who was still worshiped as a deity. Egyptologist John A. Wilson sheds light on this notion. Because Egyptians could not break with the central idea of their civilization, divine kingship, "one could say that it was the closest approach to monotheism possible within the thought of the day. That would still fall short of making it a belief in and worship of only one god."[16] Regarding the relationship of Atonism to a later Hebrew monotheism, Wilson says, "The mechanism of transmission from the faith of Akhenaton to the monotheism of Moses is not apparent."[17] Moreover, the Hebrews never identiday would rule Egypt. "Come to me in peace, daughter of my loins, . . . thou art the king who takes possession of the diadem on the Throne of Horus of the Living, eternally."*

Hatchepsut came to be depicted with male attire and a male body. Apparently, by casting off her female appearance, she aimed to be seen as a king, the equal of all other pharaohs, and not as a queen, who was not regarded as divine. Hatchepsut, says Egyptologist Joyce Tyldesley, "needed to make a sharp and immediately obvious distinction between her former position as queen regent and her new role as pharaoh. The change of dress was a clear sign of her altered state."†

During her twenty-year reign, from about 1479 to 1458, Hatchepsut promoted extensive building projects, including her royal tomb, and trading expeditions, particularly to the land of Punt, in modern-day Somaliland. From Punt the Egyptians obtained myrrh and frankincense, precious resins used for making incense that was burned in temple rituals and perfumes and for the mummification of bodies. It was an arduous journey to Punt; the return of the expeditions with these treasures must have greatly increased the prestige of the female pharaoh.

After Hatchepsut's death, her monuments were mutilated and her name and image deleted in a deliberate attempt to obliterate her memory. The campaign was probably initiated by Thutmose III, but his motivation is not clear. Was he demonstrating hatred for his stepmother, who had relegated him to a subordinate role for so many years? Did he try to erase the memory of Hatchepsut in order to prevent the succession in the future of still another female pharaoh in the belief that such a situation was a grave violation of tradition and Ma'at?

---

*Quoted in Joyce Tyldesley, *Hatchepsut: The Female Pharaoh* (New York: Penguin Books, 1998), p. 105.
†Ibid., p. 133.

fied God with the sun or any other object in nature.

Late in the thirteenth century B.C., Libyans, probably seeking to settle in the more fertile land of Egypt, attacked from the west, and the Peoples of the Sea, as unsettled raiders from the Aegean Sea area and Asia Minor were called, launched a series of strikes at Egypt. A weakened Egypt abandoned its empire. In the succeeding centuries, Egypt came under the rule of Libyans, Nubians, Assyrians, Persians, and finally Greeks, to whom Egypt lost its independence in the fourth century B.C. Egyptian civilization had flourished for nearly two thousand years before it experienced an almost one-thousand-year descent into stagnation, decline, and collapse. During its long history, the Egyptians tried to preserve its ancient forms, revealed to them by their ancestors and representing for all time those unchanging values that they believed to be the way of happiness.

Empire Builders

The rise of an Egyptian empire during the New Kingdom was part of a wider development in Near Eastern history after 1500 B.C.—the emergence of international empires. Empire building led to the intermingling of peoples and cultural traditions and to the extension of civilization well beyond the river valleys.

One reason for the growth of empires was the migration of peoples known as Indo-Europeans. Originally from a wide area ranging from southeastern Europe to the region beyond the Caspian Sea, Indo-Europeans embarked, around 2000 B.C.,

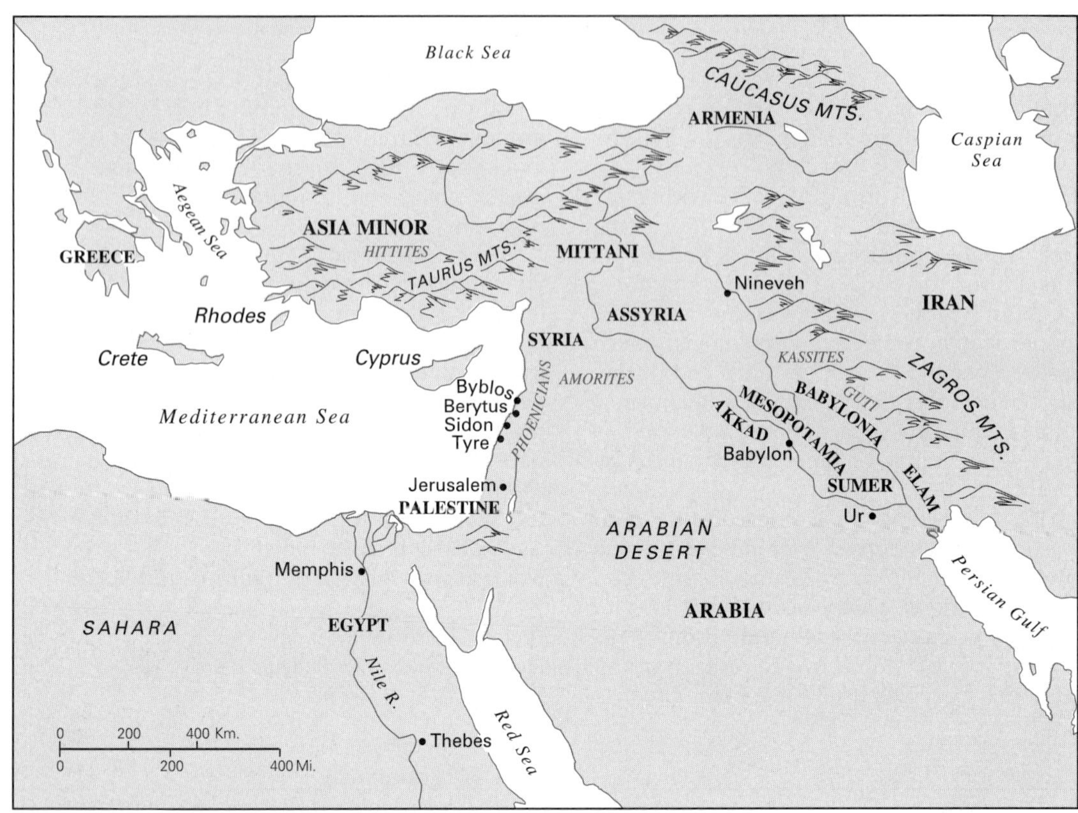

Map 1.2 Kingdoms and Peoples of the Ancient World In addition to the Sumerians and Egyptians, founders of the first civilizations, other peoples contributed to the development of civilization in the Near East. The Hebrews conceived the idea of the one God, the Phoenicians invented the alphabet, and the Hittites developed a substantial iron industry.

on a series of migrations, which eventually brought them into Italy, Greece, Asia Minor, Mesopotamia, Persia, and India. From a core Indo-European tongue emerged the Greek, Latin, Germanic, Slavic, Persian, and Sanskrit languages.

Hittites

Several peoples established strong states in the Near East around 1500 B.C.—the Hurrians in northern Mesopotamia, the Kassites in southern Mesopotamia, and, most importantly, the Hittites in Asia Minor.

Penetrating Asia Minor, Indo-Europeans coalesced with native Hattic-speaking peoples to create the Hittite empire (1450–1200 B.C.). The Hittites ruled Asia Minor and northern Syria, raided Babylon, and challenged Egypt for control of Syria and Palestine.

The Hittites wanted to control the trade routes that ran along the Euphrates River into Syria. Mursilis I, a Hittite king, conquered part of Syria and sacked Babylon in 1595 B.C., ending the Amorite dynasty, which had been established by Hammurabi two centuries earlier. Shortly after the attack, however, the Hittites withdrew from Babylon. In the 1300s, the Hittite empire reached its peak and included much of Asia Minor and northern Syria. The Hittites succeeded because of their well-trained army. Mass attacks by light, horse-drawn chariots demolished enemy lines, while foot soldiers made effective use of the battle-ax and a short curved sword.

The Hittites borrowed several features of Mesopotamian civilization, including cuneiform, legal principles, and literary and art forms. Hittite religion blended the beliefs and practices of Indo-Europeans, native inhabitants of Asia Minor, and Mesopotamians. The Hittites were probably the first people to develop a substantial iron industry. Initially, they apparently used iron just for ceremonial and ritual objects and not for tools and weapons. However, because iron ore was more readily available than copper or tin (needed for bronze), after 1200 B.C. iron weapons and tools spread throughout the Near East, although bronze implements were still used. Around 1200 B.C., the Hittite empire fell, most likely to Indo-European invaders from the north.

Small Nations

During the twelfth century B.C., a temporary lull in empire building permitted a number of small nations in Syria and Palestine to assert their sovereignty. Three of these peoples—the Phoenicians, the Aramaeans, and the Hebrews*—were originally Semitic desert nomads. The Phoenicians were descendants of the Canaanites, a Semitic people who had settled Palestine about 3000 B.C. The Canaanites who had migrated northwest into what is now Lebanon were called Phoenicians.

Settling in the coastal Mediterranean cities of Tyre, Byblos, Berytus (Beirut), and Sidon, the Phoenicians were naturally drawn to the sea. These daring explorers established towns along the coast of North Africa, on the islands of the western Mediterranean, and in Spain, and they became the greatest sea traders of the ancient world. Phoenician merchants exported lumber, glass, copper and bronze utensils, and the purple dye produced from the murex, a mollusk that was plentiful in the coastal waters. The Phoenicians (or their Canaanite forebears) devised the first alphabet—a monumental contribution to writing. Since all words could be represented by combinations of letters, it saved memorizing thousands of diagrams and aided the Phoenicians in transmitting the civilizations of the Near East to the western Mediterranean. Adapted by the Greeks, who added vowels, the phonetic alphabet became a crucial component of European languages.

The Aramaeans, who settled in Syria, Palestine, and northern Mesopotamia, performed a role similar to that of the Phoenicians. As great caravan traders, they carried both goods and cultural patterns to various parts of the Near East. The Hebrews and the Persians, for example, acquired the Phoenician alphabet from the Aramaeans.

*The Hebrews are discussed in Chapter 2.

Assyria

In the ninth century B.C., empire building resumed with the Assyrians, a Semitic people from the region around the upper Tigris River. Because their geographic position made them prey to other peoples in the area, the Assyrians emphasized military prowess to maintain and expand their borders. The Assyrians carefully planned their military campaigns and excelled in siege weapons—battering rams built on massive wheeled frames—which pulverized city walls that had hitherto resisted attackers. Their soldiers wore armor and wielded iron swords, and charging chariots terrorized the foe's infantry, which generally consisted of farmer-soldiers armed with little more than bows and arrows.

Although they had made forays of expansion in 1200 and 1100 B.C., the Assyrians began their march to "world" empire three centuries later. In the eighth and seventh centuries, the Assyrians became a ruthless fighting machine that stormed through Babylonia, Syria, Palestine, and Egypt. Assyrian kings believed that their gods commanded them to conquer and assisted them in their campaigns. At its height, the Assyrian empire extended from the Iranian plateau in the east to the Egyptian city of Thebes.

How did the Assyrians administer such a vast empire? An Assyrian king, who was the representative and high priest of the god Ashur, governed absolutely. Nobles appointed by the king kept order in the provinces and collected tribute, which they probably used for building palaces, temples, and canals. The Assyrians improved roads, established messenger services, and engaged in large-scale irrigation projects to facilitate effective administration

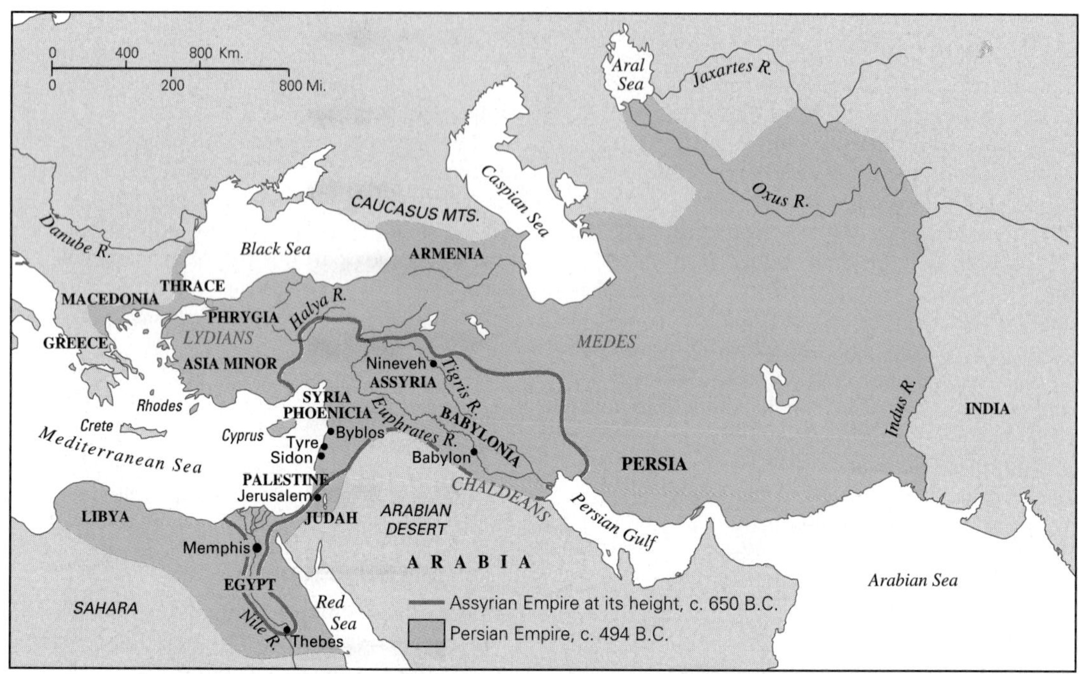

Map 1.3 The Assyrian and Persian Empires In the last part of the sixth century B.C., the Persians established the greatest empire of the ancient Near East, conquering all the lands between the Nile in Egypt and the Indus River in India.

of their conquered lands and promote prosperity. To keep their subjects obedient, the Assyrians resorted to terror and to deportation of troublesome subjects from their home territories. (It is also likely that masses of people were moved around for economic reasons—to replenish a diminishing labor supply.) Assyrian kings boasted of their ruthlessness toward rebellious subjects:

> *13,000 of their warriors I cut down with the sword. Their blood like the water of a stream I caused to run through the squares of their city. The corpses of their soldiers I piled in heaps. . . . [The Babylonian king's] royal bed, his royal couch, the treasure of his palaces, his property, his gods and everything from his palace without number, I carried away. His captive warriors were given to the soldiers of my land like grasshoppers. The city I destroyed, I devastated, I burned with fire.*[18]

Despite an almost all-consuming concern for war, the Assyrians maintained and spread the culture of the past. They copied and edited the literary works of Babylonia, adopted the old Sumerian gods, and used Mesopotamian art forms. The Assyrian king Ashurbanipal (669–626 B.C.) maintained a great library, which contained thousands of clay tablets.

"The king knows that all lands hate us," wrote an official to King Esarhaddon (680–669 B.C.).[19] After a period of wars and revolts weakened Assyria, a coalition of Medes, or Indo-Europeans from Iran, and the Semitic Chaldeans, or Neo-Babylonians, sacked the Assyrian capital of Nineveh in 612 B.C. The conquerors looted and destroyed the city, and the surviving Assyrians fled. Assyrian power was broken.

The Neo-Babylonian Empire

The destruction of the Assyrian empire made possible the rise of a Chaldean empire, which included Babylonia, Assyria, Syria, and Palestine. Under Nebuchadnezzar, who ruled from 604 to

PERSEPOLIS, IRAN, C. 500 B.C. The Persian ruler Darius (522–486 B.C.) constructed a thirty-acre earthen terrace almost fifty feet above the plain and built there a complex of palaces, reception halls, a treasury, and barracks for his royal guards. Persepolis became the ceremonial center of the vast Persian empire until it was destroyed by Alexander the Great's soldiers. (*Photo Researchers © George Holton.*)

562 B.C., the Chaldean, or Neo-Babylonian, empire reached its height. A talented general and statesman, and a brilliant administrator, Nebuchadnezzar had Babylon rebuilt. The new Babylon that arose on the shore of the Euphrates had magnificent procession-ways that led to palaces and temples. On his palace grounds, Nebuchadnezzar created the famous Hanging Gardens for his Median wife, according to legend. The 350-foot building was a series of vaulted terraces and was surrounded by a moat of flowing water. Trees, shrubs, and flowers decorated each terrace. In the interior, vaulted halls were stocked with vessels, fabrics, ornaments, and wines gathered from different regions of the empire. Here guests reclined on divans and were attended by slaves.

Persia: Unifier of the Near East

After Nebuchadnezzar's death, the Chaldean empire was torn by civil war and threatened by a new power—the Persians, an Indo-European people who had settled in southern Iran. Under Cyrus the Great and his son and successor, Cambyses, the Persians conquered all lands between the Nile in Egypt and the Indus River in India. This conquest took twenty-five years, from 550 to 525 B.C. The Near Eastern conception of absolute monarchy justified by religion reached its culminating expression in the person of the Persian king, who, with divine approval, ruled a vast empire, "the four quarters of the earth." Persian kings developed an effective system of administration—based in part on an Assyrian model—which gave stability and a degree of unity to their extensive territories. In so doing, they performed a creative act of statesmanship. The Persian empire was divided into twenty provinces (satrapies), each administered by a governor (satrap) responsible to the emperor. To guard against subversion, the king employed special agents—"the eyes and ears of the emperor"—who supervised the activities of the governors. Persian kings allowed the provincials a large measure of self-rule. They also respected local traditions, particularly in matters of religion, as long as subjects paid their taxes, served in the royal army, and refrained from rebellion; and they deliberately tried to win the goodwill of priests in conquered lands.

The empire was bound together by a uniform language, Aramaic (the language of the Aramaeans of Syria), used by government officials and merchants. Aramaic was written in letters based on the Phoenician alphabet. By making Aramaic a universal language, the Persians facilitated written and oral communication within the empire. The empire was further unified by an elaborate network of roads, an efficient postal system, a common system of weights and measures, and an empirewide coinage, based on an invention of the Lydians from western Asia Minor.

Besides providing impressive political and administrative unity and promoting international trade, the Persians fused and perpetuated the various cultural traditions of the Near East. Persian palaces, for example, boasted the terraces of Babylon, the colonnades of Egypt, the winged bulls that decorated Assyrian palace gates, and the craftsmanship of Median goldsmiths.

The political and cultural universalism of the Persian empire had its counterpart in the emergence of a higher religion, Zoroastrianism. Named for its founder, the Persian prophet Zarathustra (Zoroaster in Greek), who probably lived in the sixth century B.C. (some scholars place him much earlier), this religion taught belief in Ahura Mazda—the Wise Lord—god of light, of justice, wisdom, goodness, and immortality. But, in addition to the Wise Lord, there also existed Ahriman, the spirit of darkness, who was evil and destructive. Ahriman was in conflict with Ahura Mazda. People were free to choose whom they would follow. By choosing Ahura Mazda, they chose good over evil. To serve Ahura Mazda, one had to speak the truth and be good to others; the reward for such behavior was life eternal in paradise, the realm of light and goodness. Followers of the evil spirit could be cast into a realm of darkness and torment. In contrast to the traditional religions of the Near East, Zoroastrianism rejected magic, polytheism, and blood sacrifices and instead stressed ethics.

Persia unified the nations of the Near East into a world-state, headed by a divinely appointed king, and synthesized the region's cultural traditions. Soon it would confront the city-states of Greece, whose political system and cultural orientation differed from that of the Near East.

The Religious Orientation of the Near East

Religion dominated, suffused, and inspired all features of Near Eastern society—law, kingship, art, and science. In the first civilizations, the deepest thoughts of human beings were expressed in the form of religious myths. They were the source of the vitality and creativity of Mesopotamian and Egyptian civilizations. Near Eastern art derived from religion, and science was permeated with it; literature and history dealt with the ways of the gods; and priest-kings or god-kings, their power sanctioned by divine forces, furnished the necessary authority to organize large numbers of people in cooperative ventures. Religion also encouraged and justified wars—including enslavements and massacres—which were seen as conflicts between the gods.

A Mythmaking World-View

A religious or mythopoeic (mythmaking) view of the world gives Near Eastern civilization its distinctive form and allows us to see it as an organic whole. Mesopotamians and Egyptians inherited from their prehistoric ancestors a great variety of communally produced imagery, rituals, and tales accounting for the origin of the world and human life. Giving free play to their imagination, they altered the old myths and elaborated new ones to resolve questions that today we try to answer with science. Mythmaking was humanity's first way of thinking; it was the earliest attempt to explain the beginnings of the universe and human history, to make nature's mysteries and life's uncertainties comprehensible. Appealing primarily to the imagination and emotions, rather than to reason, mythical thinking, as expressed in language, art, poetry, and social organization, has been a fundamental formative element of human culture.

Originating in sacred rites, ritual dances, feasts, and ceremonies, myths narrated the deeds of gods, who, in some remote past, had brought forth the world and human beings. Holding that human destiny was determined by the gods, Near Eastern people interpreted their experiences through myths. Myths also enabled Mesopotamians and Egyptians to make sense out of nature, to explain the world of phenomena. Through myths, the Near Eastern mind sought to give coherence to the universe, to make it intelligible. These myths gave Near Eastern peoples a framework with which to pattern their experiences into a meaningful order, justify their rules of conduct, and try to overcome the uncertainty of existence.

The civilizations of the ancient Near East were based on a way of thinking fundamentally different from the modern scientific outlook. The difference between scientific and mythical thinking is profound. The scientific mind views physical nature as an *it*—inanimate, impersonal, and governed by universal law. The mythmaking mind of the Near East saw every object in nature as a *thou*—personified, alive, with an individual will. It saw gods or demons manipulating things. The world was enchanted, imbued with mysterious spirits. The sun and stars, the rivers and mountains, the wind and lightning were either gods or the dwelling places of gods. Live agents were the forces behind natural events. An Egyptian or a Mesopotamian experienced natural phenomena—a falling rock, a thunderclap, a rampaging river—as life facing life. If a river flooded the region, destroying crops, it was because it wanted to; the river or the gods desired to punish the people.

> *In other words, the ancients told myths instead of presenting an analysis or conclusions. We would explain, for instance, that certain atmospheric changes broke a drought and brought about rain. The Babylonians observed the same facts but experienced them as the intervention of the gigantic bird Imdugud which came to their rescue. It covered the sky with the black storm clouds of its wings and devoured the Bull of Heaven, whose hot breath had scorched the crops.*[20]

The Egyptians believed that Nut, the sky goddess, gave birth to the sun, a deity who sailed west across the celestial sea before descending into his mother's womb to be reborn again in the morning. For the Egyptians, the rising and setting of the sun were not natural occurrences—a celestial body obeying an impersonal law—but a religious drama.

In a Mesopotamian creation myth, Marduk, the chief god of Babylon, slays Tiamat, a primal mother identified with the salt sea.

> *Then the lord paused to view her dead body,*
> *That he might divide the monster and do*
> *artful works.*
> *He split her like a shellfish into two parts;*
> *Half of her he set up and ceiled [covered] it*
> *as sky. . . .*[21]

From the other half of Tiamat's carcass, Marduk proceeded to fashion the earth.

The scientific mind holds that natural objects obey universal rules; hence, the location of planets, the speed of objects, and the onset of a hurricane can be predicted. The mythmaking mind of the ancient Near East was not troubled by contradictions. It did not seek logical consistency and had no awareness of repetitive laws inherent in nature. Rather, it attributed all occurrences to the actions of gods, whose behavior was often erratic and unpredictable. Shamans employed magic to protect people from evil supernatural forces that surrounded them. The scientific mind appeals to reason—it analyzes nature logically and systematically and searches for general principles that govern phenomena. The mythmaking mind appeals to the imagination and feelings and proclaims a truth that is emotionally satisfying, not one that has been arrived at through intellectual analysis and synthesis. Mythical explanations of nature and human experience enrich perception and feeling. Thus, they made life seem less overwhelming and death less frightening.

Of course, Near Eastern people did engage in rational forms of thought and behavior. They certainly employed reason in building irrigation works, preparing a calendar, and performing mathematical operations. Moreover, in their daily life, men and women were often driven by purely pragmatic concerns. Fields had to be planted, goods sold, and household chores attended to. In dealing with these concerns, people did what had to be done in commonsense ways. They planned and prepared, they weighed actions as either beneficial or harmful and behaved accordingly. However, because rational or logical thought remained subordinate to a mythic-religious orientation, they did not arrive at a *consistently* and *self-consciously* rational method of inquiring into physical nature and human culture.

Thus, Near Eastern civilization reached the first level in the development of science—observing nature, recording data, and improving technology in mining, metallurgy, and architecture. But it did not advance to the level of self-conscious philosophical and scientific thought—that is, logically deduced abstractions, hypotheses, and generalizations. Mesopotamians and Egyptians did not fashion a body of philosophical and scientific ideas that were logically structured, discussed, and debated. They had no awareness of general laws that govern particular events. These later developments were the achievement of Greek philosophy. It gave a "rational interpretation to natural occurrences which had previously been explained by ancient mythologies. . . . With the study of nature set free from the control of mythological fancy, the way was opened for the development of science as an intellectual system."[22]

Near Eastern Achievements

Sumerians and Egyptians demonstrated enormous creativity and intelligence. They built irrigation works and cities, organized governments, charted the course of heavenly bodies, performed mathematical operations, constructed large-scale monuments, engaged in international trade, established bureaucracies and schools, and considerably advanced the level of technology. Without the Sumerian invention of writing—one of the great creative acts in history—what we mean by *civilization* could not have emerged.

Many elements of ancient Near Eastern civilization were passed on to the West. The wheeled vehicle, the plow, and the phonetic alphabet—all important to the development of civilization—derive from the Near East. In the realm of medicine, the Egyptians knew the value of certain drugs, such as castor oil; they also knew how to use splints and bandages. The innovative divisions that gave 360 degrees to a circle and 60 minutes to an hour originated in Mesopotamia. Egyptian geometry and Babylonian astronomy were utilized by the Greeks and became a part of Western knowledge. The belief that a king's power came from a heavenly source, a key idea in Western political thought, also derived from the Near East. In Christian art, too, one finds connections to the Mesopotamian art forms—for example, the Assyrians depicted winged angel-like beings.

Both the Hebrews and the Greeks borrowed Mesopotamian literary themes. For example, some biblical stories—the Flood, the quarrel between Cain and Abel, and the Tower of Babel—stem from Mesopotamian antecedents. A similar link exists between the Greek and the earlier Mesopotamian mythologies.

Thus, many achievements of the Egyptians and the Mesopotamians were inherited and assimilated by both the Greeks and the Hebrews, the principal founders of Western civilization. Even more important for an understanding of the essential meaning of Western civilization are the ways in which Greeks and Hebrews rejected or transformed elements of the older Near Eastern traditions to create new points of departure for the human mind.

❖ ❖ ❖

Notes

1. Richard E. Leakey and Roger Lewin, *Origins* (New York: Dutton, 1977), p. 8.
2. Robert J. Braidwood, *Prehistoric Man* (Glenview, Ill.: Scott, Foresman, 1967), p. 141.
3. Lewis Mumford, *Transformation of Man* (New York: Harper Torchbooks, 1972), pp. 46–47.
4. Excerpted in James B. Pritchard, ed., *Ancient Near Eastern Texts Relating to the Old Testament,* 3rd ed., with supplement (Princeton, N.J.: Princeton University Press, 1969), p. 67.
5. Excerpted in James B. Pritchard, ed., *The Ancient Near East: A New Anthology of Texts and Pictures* (Princeton, N.J.: Princeton University Press, 1975), p. 151.
6. Ibid., p. 154.
7. *The Epic of Gilgamesh*, with an introduction by N. K. Sandars (Baltimore: Penguin Books, 1960), p. 94.
8. Ibid., pp. 69, 104.
9. Excerpted in Adolf Ehrman, ed., *The Ancient Egyptians* (New York: Harper Torchbooks, 1966), pp. 94, 97, 99.
10. Henri Frankfort, *Ancient Egyptian Religion* (New York: Harper Torchbooks, 1961), p. 14.
11. Quoted in Eugen Strouhal, *Life of the Ancient Egyptians* (Norman: University of Oklahoma Press, 1992), p. 41.
12. Quoted in Frankfort, *Ancient Egyptian Religion*, p. 43.
13. Quoted in John A. Wilson, "Egypt," in Henri Frankfort et al., *Before Philosophy* (Baltimore: Penguin Books, 1949), p. 88.
14. Excerpted in Erhman, *The Ancient Egyptians*, pp. 76–78.
15. Quoted in John A. Wilson, *The Culture of Ancient Egypt* (Chicago: University of Chicago Press, Phoenix Books, 1951), p. 227.
16. Ibid., p. 225.
17. Ibid., p. 226.
18. Quoted in Joan Oates, *Babylon* (London: Thames & Hudson, 1979), pp. 110–111.
19. Quoted in Georges Roux, *Ancient Iraq* (Harmondsworth, England: Penguin Books, 1966), p. 278.
20. Frankfort et al., *Before Philosophy*, p. 15.
21. James B. Pritchard, ed., *Ancient Near Eastern Texts Relating to the Old Testament,* 2nd ed. (Princeton, N.J.: Princeton University Press, 1955), p. 67.
22. S. Sambursky, *The Physical World of the Greeks* (New York: Collier Books, 1962), pp. 18–19.

Suggested Reading

Campbell, Bernard G., *Humankind Emerging* (1982). The world of prehistory.

Cook, J. M., *The Persian Empire* (1983). An up-to-date history of ancient Persia.

David, Rosalie A., *The Ancient Egyptians* (1982). Focuses on religious beliefs and practices.

Frankfort, Henri, *Ancient Egyptian Religion* (1961). An interpretation of the origins and nature of Egyptian religion.

Frankfort, Henri, et al., *The Intellectual Adventure of Ancient Man* (1946); paperback edition is titled *Before Philosophy.* Brilliant discussions of the role of myth in the ancient Near East by distinguished scholars.

Gowlett, John, *Ascent to Civilization* (1984). An informed study with excellent graphics.

Hallo, W. W., and W. K. Simpson, *The Ancient Near East* (1971). An authoritative survey of the political history of the Near East.

Jacobsen, Thorkild, *The Treasures of Darkness* (1976). Study of Mesopotamian religion by an outstanding scholar.

Kuhrt, Amélie, *The Ancient Near East* (1995). An authoritative two-volume history.

Lewin, Roger, *In the Age of Mankind* (1988). A Smithsonian book on prehistory.

Mertz, Barbara, *Red Land, Black Land* (1966). A social history of the people of Egypt.

Moscati, Sabatino, *The Face of the Ancient Orient* (1962). An illuminating survey of the various peoples of the ancient Near East.

Oates, Joan, *Babylon* (1979). A survey of the history of Babylon from its origin to Hellenistic times; includes a discussion of the legacy of Babylon.

Oppenheim, A. L., *Ancient Mesopotamia* (1964). Stresses social and economic history.

Roux, Georges, *Ancient Iraq* (1964). A balanced survey of Mesopotamian history and society.

Saggs, H. W. F., *The Greatness That Was Babylon* (1962). Strong on social and cultural history.

———, *The Might That Was Assyria* (1984). Survey of Assyrian history and culture.

———, *Civilization Before Greece and Rome* (1989). Focuses on culture and society.

Silverman, David P., ed., *Ancient Egypt* (1997). Clearly written accounts by experts on all phases of ancient Egyptian society.

Strouhal, Eugen, *Life of the Ancient Egyptians* (1992). Daily life of Egyptians; lavishly illustrated.

Tyldesley, Joyce, *Hatchepsut* (1996). A study of the female pharaoh.

von Soden, Wolfram, *The Ancient Orient* (1994). A thematic treatment of ancient Mesopotamian civilization.

Wilson, John A., *The Culture of Ancient Egypt* (1951). An interpretation by a noted Egyptologist.

Review Questions

1. What advances did human beings make during the Paleolithic Age?
2. Why is the development of the Neolithic Age referred to as the Neolithic Revolution?
3. What is meant by *civilization*? Under what conditions did civilization emerge?
4. The Sumerian achievement served as the basis for Mesopotamian civilization. Discuss.
5. How did religion influence Mesopotamian civilization?
6. Define Old Kingdom, Middle Kingdom, and New Kingdom.
7. What role did the pharaoh play in Egyptian life? Do you think that the pharaoh really believed that he was divine? Explain.
8. How did the Egyptians' religious beliefs affect their civilization?
9. What is the historical significance of Akhenaton?
10. The Egyptians would not have comprehended our concept of progress. Explain.
11. What were the achievements of the Phoenicians and the Aramaeans?
12. How did the Persians give unity to the Near East?
13. What advances in science did Near Eastern civilization make? How was science limited by a mythmaking view of nature?
14. What elements of Near Eastern civilization were passed on to Western civilization?

Chapter 2

The Hebrews: A New View of God and the Individual

A sculptured relief from the triumphal Arch of Titus showing Jewish captives bearing the menorah and vessels from the holy temple burned by the Romans at the end of the Jewish revolt, first century A.D. *(Alinari/Art Resource, NY.)*

- **Outline of Hebrew History**
  The Israelite Kingdom
  Conquest, Captivity, and Restoration
  The Hebrew Scriptures
- **God: One, Sovereign, Transcendent, Good**
- **The Individual and Moral Autonomy**
- **The Covenant and the Law**
- **The Hebrew Idea of History**
- **The Prophets**
  Social Justice
  Universalism
  Individualism
- **The Legacy of the Ancient Jews**

Ancient Mesopotamia and Egypt, the birthplace of the first civilizations, are not the spiritual ancestors of the West. For the origins of the Western tradition, we must turn to the Hebrews and the Greeks. Both Greeks and Hebrews, of course, absorbed elements of the civilizations of Mesopotamia and Egypt, but even more significant is how they transformed this inheritance and shaped world-views that differed markedly from the outlooks of these first civilizations. As Egyptologist John A. Wilson writes,

> *The Children of Israel built a nation and a religion on the rejection of things Egyptian. Not only did they see God as one, but they ascribed to him consistency of concern for man and consistency of justice to man. . . . Like the Greeks, the Hebrews took forms from their great neighbors; like the Greeks, they used those forms for very different purposes.*[1]

In this chapter, we examine one source of the Western tradition, the Hebrews, whose conception of God broke with the outlook of the Near East and whose ethical teachings helped fashion the Western idea of the dignity of the individual.

Outline of Hebrew History

The Hebrews originated in Mesopotamia and migrated to Canaan, a portion of which was later called Palestine. The Hebrew patriarchs—Abraham, Isaac, and Jacob, so prominently depicted in the Old Testament—were chieftains of seminomadic clans that roamed Palestine and occasionally journeyed to Mesopotamia and Egypt. The early Hebrews absorbed some features of Mesopotamian civilization. For example, there are parallels between biblical law and the Mesopotamian legal tradition. Several biblical stories—the Creation, the Flood, the Garden of Eden—derive from Mesopotamian sources.

Some Hebrews journeyed from Canaan to Egypt to be herdsmen and farmers, but they eventually became forced laborers for the Egyptians.

Chronology 2.1 ❖ The Hebrews

1250 B.C.*	Hebrew Exodus from Egypt
1024–1000	Reign of Saul, Israel's first king
1000–961	Creation of a united monarchy under David
961–922	Reign of Solomon: construction of the first temple
750–430	Age of classical prophecy
722	Kingdom of Israel falls to Assyrians
586	Kingdom of Judah falls to Chaldeans; the temple is destroyed
586–539	Babylonian exile
538	Cyrus of Persia allows exiles to return to Judah
515 B.C.	Second temple is dedicated

*Most dates are approximations

Fearful of remaining permanent slaves of the pharaoh, the Hebrews yearned for an opportunity to escape. In the early thirteenth century B.C., an extraordinary leader rose among them, called Moses, who came to his people as a messenger of God. Leading the Hebrews in their exodus from Egypt, Moses transformed them during their wanderings in the wilderness of Sinai into a nation, welded together and uplifted by a belief in Yahweh, the one God.

The Israelite Kingdom

The wandering Hebrews returned to Canaan to rejoin other Hebrew tribes that had not migrated to Egypt. The conquest and colonization of Canaan, a gradual process, took many generations. In Canaan, the Israelites did not form a state with a central government but were loosely organized into a tribal confederation bound by a commitment to Yahweh. When enemies threatened, the elders of each of the twelve tribes would decide whether to engage in joint action. During emergencies, judges, who were leaders distinguished by their courage and empowered by "the spirit of Yahweh," rallied the clans against the common enemy. The tribal confederation lasted for about two hundred years, until a threat by the Philistines in the late eleventh century B.C. led the Israelites to draw closer together under a king.

Originally from the islands of the Aegean Sea and the coast of Asia Minor, the Philistines (from whom the name Palestine derives) had invaded Canaan in the early part of the twelfth century B.C. From the coastal regions, they expanded into the interior, extending their dominion over much of the Israelite territory. During this time of crisis, the twelve tribes united under the leadership of Saul, a charismatic hero, whom they acclaimed as their first king. Under Saul's successor, David, a gifted warrior and a poet, the Hebrews (or Israelites) broke the back of Philistine power and subdued neighboring peoples.

The creation of an Israelite kingdom under David and his son Solomon in the tenth century B.C. was made possible by the declining power of other states in the Near East—Babylonia, Assyria, the Hittite kingdom, and Egypt. Solomon's kingdom engaged in active trade with neighboring states, particularly Tyre (located along the Phoenician coast). Solomon's merchant fleet, built and manned by Phoenicians, traded with southerly lands bordering the Red Sea. Another sign of economic progress was extensive construction, especially in Jerusalem, the Hebrew spiritual center, where Solomon erected a royal

HAZOR, NEAR GALILEE. Among the chain of cities fortified by Solomon was this stronghold. The remains of its walls and gate are depicted here. (*Zev Radovan, Jerusalem.*)

palace and beside it a magnificent temple honoring God.

New cities were built, and Jerusalem grew larger. The use of the iron-tipped plow improved agricultural productivity, which, in turn, contributed to a significant population increase. Under Solomon, Israel also experienced a cultural flowering: some magnificent sections of the Old Testament were written, and music flourished.

Old tribal patterns weakened as urban life expanded and some people gained wealth. Tribal society had been distinguished by a large measure of economic equality, but disparity grew between the rich and the poor, between those who considered themselves aristocrats and the common people.

Under Solomon, ancient Israel was at the height of its power and prosperity. However, opposition to Solomon's tax policies and his favored treatment of the region of Judah in the south led to the division of the kingdom after his death in 922 B.C. The tribes loyal to Solomon's son belonged to the kingdom of Judah, whereas the other tribes organized the northern kingdom of Israel. Both second-rate powers, neither Judah nor Israel could hold on to earlier conquests.

Conquest, Captivity, and Restoration

In 722 B.C., Israel fell to the Assyrians, who deported many Hebrews to other parts of the Assyrian empire. These transported Hebrews—the so-called ten lost tribes—merged with neighboring peoples and lost their identity as the people of God. In 586 B.C., the Chaldeans conquered Judah, destroyed Solomon's temple, devastated the land, and deported several thousand Hebrews to Babylon. The prophets Isaiah, Ezekiel, and Jeremiah declared that the destruction of Judah was a punishment that the Hebrews had brought on themselves by violating God's laws. This time was the darkest moment in the history of the Hebrews. Their state was gone; neighboring peoples had overrun their land; and their holy temple was in ruins. Thousands had died in battle, had been executed, or had fled to Egypt and other lands, and thousands more were in exile in Babylon. This exile is known as the Babylonian Captivity.

Still, in what is a marvel of history, the Hebrews survived as a people. Although many of the exiles in Babylon assimilated Babylonian

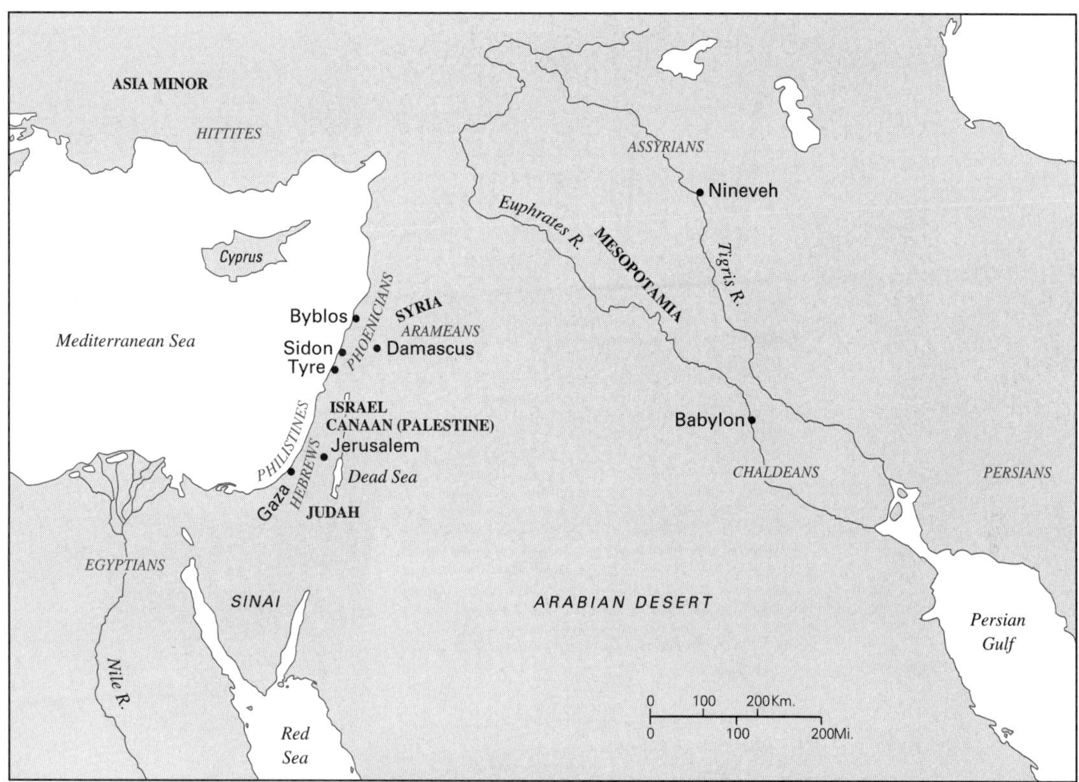

Map 2.1 Hebrews and Other Peoples of the Ancient Middle East
Despite conquest and exile, the Hebrews survived as a people, retained their faith, and remained devoted to their homeland, which, they believed, God had given them.

ways, some remained faithful to their God Yahweh and the Law of Moses and longed to return to their homeland. Priests struggled to understand the misfortunes that had befallen their people and to prevent the erosion of faith in a foreign environment. They codified ancient traditions, records, and practices, particularly laws, in the process creating the Torah (see below). Thus, their faith enabled them to endure conquest and exile. In Babylon, the prophet known as Second Isaiah comforted the uprooted Hebrews. He declared that soon Yahweh, who controlled the course of history, would restore the erring but repentant Hebrews to their land in a second Exodus. When the Persians conquered Babylon, King Cyrus, in 538 B.C., permitted the exiles to return to Judah, now a Persian province, and to rebuild the temple. The majority of Judeans preferred to remain in prosperous and cosmopolitan Babylon. But some of them did return to Judah, and in 515 B.C., the Hebrews, now commonly called Jews, dedicated the second temple at Jerusalem.

During the first half of the fifth century B.C., the restored Jewish community seemed on the verge of disintegration. Exploitation of the poor created internal tensions; intermarriage with non-Jews grew more frequent; and there was spiritual backsliding, including neglect of the Sabbath. Under the leadership of Nehemiah and Ezra in the second half of the fifth century B.C., administrative reforms were introduced and spiritual life was invigorated. Once again, the Jews had overcome threats to their communal existence.

A Dead Sea Scroll, Judea, second century b.c. God's law, as recorded in the Holy Scriptures, still remains a unifying force among Jews. Many ancient Hebrew scrolls were found in caves near the west bank of the Dead Sea beginning in the late 1940s. The scroll depicted here contains the earliest existing copy of a complete Hebrew text of the book of the prophet Isaiah. It barely differs from more modern manuscripts. (© *John C. Trevor, 1970.*)

The Hebrew Scriptures

In the following centuries, the Jews would lose their independence to Rome and become a dispersed people. But they never relinquished their commitment to God and his Law as recorded in the Hebrew Scriptures (Old Testament). Called *Tanak* by Jews, the Old Testament consists of thirty-nine books* by several authors who lived in different centuries. Jews call the first five books of the Old Testament—Genesis, Exodus, Leviticus, Numbers, and Deuteronomy—the Torah (which originally meant "teaching" or "instruction"). Often, the Torah is referred to as the Pentateuch, a Greek word meaning "five books."

The Hebrew Scriptures represent Jewish oral and written tradition dating from about 1250 to 150 b.c. Compiled by religious devotees, not research historians, they understandably contain factual errors, imprecisions, and discrepancies. However, there are also passages that offer reliable history, and historians find the Old Testa-

*In ancient times, the number of books was usually given as twenty-four. Certain books are now divided into two parts, and the twelve works by the minor prophets are now counted as individual books.

ment an indispensable source for studying the ancient Near East. Literary scholars study it for its poetry, legends, and themes, all of which are an integral part of the Western literary tradition. But it is as a work of religious inspiration that the Hebrew Scriptures attain their profoundest importance.

The Old Testament is the record of more than a thousand years of ancient Jewish history. Containing Jewish laws, wisdom, hopes, legends, and literary expressions, it describes an ancient people's efforts to comprehend the ways of God. The Old Testament emphasizes and values the human experience; its heroes are not demigods but human beings. It depicts human strength as well as weakness. Some passages exhibit cruelty and unseemly revenge against the enemies of Israel, while others express the highest ethical values. As set forth in the Hebrew Scriptures, the Hebrew idea of God and his relationship to human beings is one of the foundations of the Western tradition.

God: One, Sovereign, Transcendent, Good

The Hebrew view of God evolved through the history and experiences of the Hebrew people. In the days of the patriarchs, before the sojourn in Egypt, the Hebrews most likely were not monotheists. They probably devoted themselves to the god of their particular clan and expressed no hatred for the idolatrous beliefs of neighboring peoples. The chief of each clan established a special attachment to the god of his fathers, hoping that the deity would protect and assist the clan. Quite likely, the patriarchs' religion contained spiritual elements that later would aid in the transition to monotheism. But this probability cannot be documented with certainty, for much of patriarchal religion still remains a mystery.

Some historians say that Moses' religion was not pure monotheism because it did not rule out the existence of other gods. According to this view, not until the prophets, centuries later, did the Hebrews explicitly deny that other gods existed and proclaim that Yahweh stood alone. Other scholars believe that Moses proclaimed a monotheistic idea, that this idea became the central force in the life of the Hebrews at the time of the Exodus from Egypt, and that it continues to be central today. John Bright, an American biblical scholar, suggests a judicious balance. The religion of Moses "did not deny the existence of other gods," says Bright, but it "effectively denied them status as *gods*."[2] The Hebrews could serve only Yahweh and "accorded all power and authority to Him." Consequently, Israel was

> *forbidden to approach [other deities] as gods. . . . The gods were thus rendered irrelevant, driven from the field. . . . To Israel only the one God was God. . . . The other gods, allowed neither part in creation, nor function in the cosmos, nor power over events . . . were robbed of all that made them gods and rendered non-entities, in short, were "undeified." Though the full implications of monotheism were centuries in being drawn, in the functional sense Israel believed in but one God from the beginning.*[3]

The Hebrew view of the one God marked a profound break with Near Eastern religious thought. The gods of other Near Eastern peoples were not truly free; their power was not without limits. Unlike Yahweh, Near Eastern gods were not eternal but were born or created; they issued from some prior realm. They were also subject to biological conditions, requiring food, drink, sleep, and sexual gratification. Sometimes they became ill or grew old or died. When they behaved wickedly, they had to answer to fate, which demanded punishment as retribution; even the gods were subject to fate's power.

The Hebrews regarded God as *fully sovereign.* He ruled all and was subject to nothing. Yahweh's existence and power did not derive from a preexisting realm, as was the case with the gods of other peoples. The Hebrews believed that no realm of being preceded God in time or surpassed him in power. They saw God as eternal and omnipotent, the source of all in the universe, and having a supreme will. He created and governed the natural world and shaped the moral laws that govern human beings. He was not subservient to fate but determined what happened.

Whereas Near Eastern divinities dwelt within

nature, the Hebrew God was *transcendent,* above nature and not a part of it. Yahweh was not identified with any natural force and did not dwell in a particular place in heaven or on earth. Since God was the creator and ruler of nature, there was no place for a sun-god, a moon-god, a god in the river, or a demon in the storm. Nature was God's creation but was not itself divine. Therefore, when the Hebrews confronted natural phenomena, they experienced God's magnificent handiwork, not objects with wills of their own. All natural phenomena—rivers, mountains, storms, stars—were divested of any supernatural quality. The stars and planets were creations of Yahweh, not divinities or the abodes of divinities. The Hebrews neither regarded them with awe nor worshiped them. This removal of the gods from nature is a necessary prerequisite for scientific thought.

The Hebrews demythicized nature, but concerned as they were with religion and morality, they did not create theoretical science. As testimony to God's greatness, nature inspired people to sing the praises of the Lord; it invoked worship of God, not scientific curiosity. When Hebrews gazed at the heavens, they did not seek to discover mathematical relationships but admired God's handiwork. The Hebrews did not view nature as a system governed by natural law. Rather, they saw the rising sun, spring rain, summer heat, and winter cold as God intervening in an orderly manner in his creation. The Hebrews, unlike the Greeks, were not philosophers. They were concerned with God's will, not with the human intellect; with the feelings of the heart, not the power of the mind; with righteous behavior, not abstract thought. Human wickedness stemmed not from ignorance but from disobedience and stubbornness.

Unlike the Greeks, the Hebrews did not speculate about the origins of all things and the operations of nature; they knew that God had created everything. For the Hebrews, God's existence was based on religious conviction, not on rational inquiry, on revelation, not reason. It was the Greeks, not the Hebrews, who originated systematic rational thought. But Christianity, born of Judaism, retained the Hebrew view of a transcendent God and the orderliness of his creation—concepts that could accommodate Greek science.

The Hebrews also did not speculate about God's nature. They knew only that he was *good* and that he made ethical demands on his people. Unlike Near Eastern gods, Yahweh was not driven by lust or motivated by evil but was "merciful and gracious, long-suffering, and abundant in goodness and truth . . . forgiving iniquity and transgression and sin" (Psalm 145:8).[4*] In contrast to pagan gods, who were indifferent to human beings, Yahweh was attentive to human needs.

By asserting that God was *one, sovereign, transcendent,* and *good,* the Hebrews effected a religious revolution that separated them entirely from the world-view held by the other peoples of the ancient Near East.

The Individual and Moral Autonomy

This new conception of God made possible a new awareness of the individual, who was seen as the culmination and centerpiece of God's creation. Created in the image of God, the human being is unique, qualitatively different from the rest of animate nature. Only the human being has the power of volition, the power to make choices. The Hebrews believed that God, who possessed total freedom himself, had bestowed on his people moral freedom—the capacity to choose between good and evil. Thus, in confronting God, the Hebrews developed an awareness of *self,* or *I*; the individual became conscious of his or her own person, moral autonomy, and personal worth.

Fundamental to Hebrew belief was the insistence that God did not create people to be his slaves. The Hebrews regarded God with awe and humility, with respect and fear, but they did not believe that God wanted people to grovel before him; rather, he wanted them to fulfill their moral potential by freely choosing to follow or not to follow God's Law. Thus, in creating men and women in his own image, God made them autonomous and sovereign. In God's plan for the

*The Bible passages in this chapter are quoted from *The Holy Scriptures* (published by The Jewish Publication Society of America).

universe, human beings were the highest creation, subordinate only to God. Of all his creations, only they had been given the freedom to choose between righteousness and wickedness, between "life and good, and death and evil" (Deuteronomy 30:15). But having the power to choose freely, men and women must bear the responsibility for their choice.

God demanded that the Hebrews have no other gods and that they make no images "nor any manner of likeness, of any thing that is in heaven above, or that is in the earth beneath, . . . thou shalt not bow down unto them nor serve them" (Exodus 20:4–5). The Hebrews believed that the worship of idols deprived people of their freedom and dignity; people cannot be fully human if they surrender themselves to a lifeless idol. Hence, the Hebrews had to destroy images and all other forms of idolatry. A crucial element of Near Eastern religion was the use of images—art forms that depicted divinities—but the Hebrews believed that God, the Supreme Being, could not be represented by pictures or sculpture fashioned by human hands. The Hebrews rejected entirely the belief that an image possessed divine powers that could be manipulated for human advantage. Ethical considerations, not myth or magic, were central to Hebrew religious life.

By making God the center of life, Hebrews could become free moral agents; no person, no human institution, no human tradition could claim their souls. Because God alone was the supreme value in the universe, only he was worthy of worship. Thus, to give *ultimate* loyalty to a king or to a general violated God's stern warning against the worship of false gods. The first concern of the Hebrews was supposed to be righteousness, not power, fame, or riches, which were only idols and would impoverish a person spiritually and morally.

There was, however, a condition to freedom. For the Hebrews, people were not free to create their own moral precepts or their own standards of right and wrong. Freedom meant voluntary obedience to commands that originated with God. Evil and suffering were not caused by blind fate, malevolent demons, or arbitrary gods; they resulted from people's disregard of God's commandments. The dilemma is that in possessing freedom of choice, human beings are also free to disobey God, to commit a sin, which leads to suffering and death. Thus, in the Genesis story, Adam and Eve were punished for disobeying God.

For the Hebrews, to know God was not to comprehend him intellectually, define him, or prove his existence; to know God was to be righteous and loving, merciful and just. When men and women loved God, the Hebrews believed, they were uplifted and improved. Gradually, they learned to overcome the worst elements of human nature and to treat other people with respect and compassion. The Jews came to interpret the belief that man was created in God's image to mean that each human being has a divine spark in him or her, giving every person a unique dignity, which cannot be taken away.

By devotion to God, the Hebrews asserted the dignity and autonomy of human beings. Thus, the Hebrews conceived the idea of moral freedom, that each individual is responsible for his or her own actions. These concepts of human dignity and moral autonomy, which Christianity inherited, are at the core of the Western tradition.

The Covenant and the Law

Central to Hebrew religious thought and decisive in Hebrew history was the covenant, God's special agreement with the Hebrew people:

> *And Moses went up unto God, and the Lord called unto him out of the mountain saying: "Thus shalt thou say to the house of Jacob and tell the children of Israel: Ye have seen what I did unto the Egyptians, and how I bore you on eagles' wings, and brought you unto Myself. Now therefore, if ye will hearken unto My voice indeed, and keep My covenant, then ye shall be Mine own treasure from all peoples; for all the earth is Mine; and ye shall be unto Me a kingdom of priests and a holy nation." (Exodus 19:3–6)*

By this act, the Israelites as a nation accepted God's lordship.

The Hebrews came to see themselves as a unique nation, as a "chosen people," for God had given them a special honor, a profound opportunity, and (as they could never forget) an awesome

Wall Painting from the Synagogue in Dura-Europos. Some time after 1050 B.C., the Israelites engaged the Philistines, formidable warriors who dominated Canaanite cities, in battle near Aphek. The Israelites brought the Ark of the Covenant into their camp, hoping that God's presence would produce victory. However, the Philistines decimated the Israelites and captured the ark. These events are described in 1 Samuel, Chapter 4. This painting from a third-century A.D. synagogue in Roman Syria depicts the ark's capture. (*Yale University Art Gallery, Dura-Europos Collection.*)

responsibility. The Hebrews did not claim that God had selected them because they were better than other peoples or because they had done anything special to deserve God's election. They believed that God, in a remarkable manner, had rescued them from bondage in Egypt and had selected them to receive the Law so that their nation would set an example of righteous behavior—"a light to the nations," said the prophet Isaiah—and ultimately lead other peoples to acknowledge God and his greatness.

This responsibility to be the moral teachers of humanity weighed heavily on the Hebrews. They believed that God had revealed his Law—including the moral code known as the Ten Commandments—to the Hebrew people as a whole, and obedience to the Law became the overriding obligation of each Hebrew. Violating the Law meant breaking the sacred covenant—an act that could lead to national disaster. As the Law originated with the one God, the necessary prerequisite for understanding and obeying it was surrendering belief in other gods forever, since they were barriers to comprehending and carrying out God's universal Law.

Justice was the central theme of Old Testament ethics. The Israelites, liberated from slavery by a righteous and compassionate God, had a moral responsibility to overcome injustice, to care for the poor, the weak, and the oppressed. Ethical concerns resulted in decrees dealing with economic, social, and political relationships—decrees that were designed to give practical expression to God's universal norms of morality. Because the covenant was made with the entire Hebrew nation, society as a whole had a religious obligation to root out evil and make justice prevail. Duty to God demanded also a duty toward one's neighbor: "Thou shalt surely open thy hand unto thy poor and needy brother, in thy land" (Deuteronomy 15:11). Thus, there were laws to protect the poor, widows, orphans, resident aliens, hired laborers, and slaves. For example, in contrast to ancient Near Eastern law, which regarded slaves as property, biblical legislation emphasized the slave's humanity, although it acknowledged the slave's status as chattel. It called for the punishment of masters who used excessive force against slaves, and it required masters to allow slaves to participate in religious observances and to rest on the Sabbath.

Israelite law incorporated many elements from Near Eastern legal codes and oral traditions. But by making people more important than property, by expressing mercy toward the oppressed, and by rejecting the idea that law should treat the poor and the rich differently, Israelite law demonstrated a greater ethical awareness and a more humane spirit than other legal codes of the Near East:

> *And a stranger shalt thou not wrong, neither shalt thou oppress him; for ye were strangers in the land of Egypt. Ye shall not afflict any widow or fatherless child. (Exodus 22:20–21)*
>
> *If thy brother, a Hebrew man, or a Hebrew woman, be sold unto thee, he shall serve thee six years; and in the seventh year thou shalt let him go free from thee. And when thou lettest him go free from thee, thou shalt not let him go empty; thou shalt furnish him liberally. . . . (Deuteronomy 15:12–14)*
>
> *Thou shalt not curse the deaf, nor put a stumbling-block before the blind, but thou shalt fear thy God: I am the Lord. . . . thou shalt love thy neighbor as thyself. (Leviticus 19:14,18)*

Hebrew law regulated all aspects of daily life, including family relationships. The father had supreme authority in the family, and this authority extended to his married sons and their wives if they remained in his household. Although polygamy was permitted, monogamy was the general rule; adultery was punishable by death.

As in other Near Eastern societies, the Jews placed women in a subordinate position. The husband was considered his wife's master, and she often addressed him as a servant or subject would speak to a superior. A husband could divorce his wife, but she could not divorce him. Only when there was no male heir could a wife inherit property from her husband or a daughter inherit from her father. Women were not regarded as competent witnesses in court and played a lesser role than men in organized worship.

On the other hand, the Jews also showed respect for women. Wise women and prophetesses like Judith and Deborah were respected by the community and were consulted by its leaders. Prophets compared God's love for the Hebrews with a husband's love for his wife. The Book of Proverbs describes a woman of valor:

> *Strength and dignity are her clothing;*
> *And she laugheth at the time to come.*
>
> *She openeth her mouth with wisdom;*
> *And the law of kindness is on her tongue.*
> *She looketh well to the ways of her household,*
> *And eateth not the bread of idleness.*
> *Her children rise up and call her blessed;*
> *Her husband also, and he praiseth her. . . .*
> *(Proverbs 31:25–28)*

Jewish law regarded women as persons, not as property. Even female captives taken in war were not to be abused or humiliated. The law required a husband to respect and support his wife and never to strike her. One of the Ten Commandments called for honoring both father and mother.

The Hebrew Idea of History

Their idea of God made the Hebrews aware of the crucial importance of historical time. Holidays commemorating such specific historical events as the Exodus from Egypt, the receiving of the Ten Commandments on Mount Sinai, and the destruction of Solomon's temple kept the past alive and vital. Egyptians and Mesopotamians did not have a similar awareness of the uniqueness of a given event: to them, today's incident merely reproduced events experienced by their ancestors. To the Jews, the Exodus and the covenant at Mount Sinai were singular, nonrepetitive occurrences, decisive in shaping their national history. This historical uniqueness and importance of events derived from the idea of a universal God profoundly involved in human affairs—a God who cares, teaches, and punishes.

The Jews valued the future as well as the past. Regarding human history as a process leading to a goal, they envisioned a great day when God would establish on earth a glorious age of peace, prosperity, happiness, and human brotherhood. This utopian notion has become deeply embedded in Western thought.

The Hebrews saw history as the work of God; it was a divine drama filled with sacred meaning and moral significance. Historical events revealed the clash of human will with God's commands. Through history's specific events, God's presence was disclosed and his purpose made known. When the Hebrews suffered conquest and exile, they interpreted these events as divine retribution for violating the covenant and the Law, sinful acts that brought down the wrath of God upon them. For the Hebrews, history also revealed God's compassion and concern. Thus, the Lord liberated Moses and the Israelites at the Red Sea and appointed prophets to plead for the poor and the oppressed. The ancient Hebrews, says historian Millar Burrows, were convinced that history was "the work of a personal divine will, contending with the foolish, stubborn wills of men, promising and warning, judging and punishing and destroying, yet sifting, saving, and abundantly blessing those found amenable to discipline and instruction."[5] Because historical events revealed God's attitude toward human beings, these events possessed spiritual meaning and were worth recording, evaluating, and remembering.

Wall Painting from the Synagogue in Dura-Europos, Roman Syria, early third century A.D. This painting shows a Hebrew prophet reading from an open scroll. (*Yale University Art Gallery, Dura-Europos Collection.*)

The Prophets

Jewish history was marked by the emergence of spiritually inspired individuals called prophets, who felt compelled to act as God's messengers. The prophets cared nothing for money or possessions, feared no one, and preached without invitation. Often emerging in times of social distress and moral confusion, the prophets pleaded for a return to the covenant and the Law. They exhorted the entire nation and taught that when people forgot God and made themselves the center of all things they would bring disaster to their community. Among the prophets were Amos, a shepherd from Judea in the south; his younger contemporary, Hosea, from Israel in the north; Isaiah of Jerusalem; and Jeremiah, who witnessed the siege of Jerusalem in the early sixth century B.C.

The prophets saw national misfortune as an opportunity for repentance and reform. It is God's wish, they said, to forgive human sins and to renew his relationship with a contrite

Israel. They were remarkably courageous people who did not quake before the powerful. In the late eighth century B.C., an angry Isaiah warned:

> *The Lord will enter into judgment*
> *With the elders of His people, and the princes thereof.*
> *"It is ye that have eaten up the vineyard;*
> *The spoil of the poor is in your houses;*
> *What mean ye that ye crush my people,*
> *And grind the face of the poor?"*
> *(Isaiah 3:14–15)*

Social Justice

The flowering of the prophetic movement—the age of classical, or literary, prophecy—began in the eighth century B.C. In attacking oppression, cruelty, greed, and exploitation, the classical prophets added a new dimension to Israel's religious development. These prophets were responding to problems emanating from Israel's changed social structure. The general lack of class distinctions characterizing a tribal society had been altered by the rise of Hebrew kings, the expansion of commerce, and the growth of cities. By the eighth century, there was a significant disparity between the wealthy and the poor. Small farmers in debt to moneylenders faced the loss of their land or even bondage; the poor were often dispossessed by the greedy wealthy. To the prophets, these social evils were religious sins that would bring ruin to Israel. Amos, a mid-eighth-century prophet, felt a tremendous compulsion to speak out against these injustices. In the name of God, he denounced the pomp of the heartless rich and the hypocrisy of pious Jews who worshiped God in the prescribed manner but neglected their social obligations to their neighbor, and he demanded justice. For Amos, there was no separation between religion and social conduct:

> *I hate, I despise your feasts,*
> *And I will take no delight in your solemn assemblies.*
> *Yea, though ye offer me burnt-offerings and your meal-offerings,*
> *I will not accept them;*
> *Neither will I regard the peace offerings of your fat beasts.*
> *Take thou away from Me the noise of thy songs;*
> *And let Me not hear the melody of the psalteries.*
> *But let justice well up as waters,*
> *And righteousness as a mighty stream.*
> *(Amos 5:21–24)*

God is compassionate, insisted the prophets. He cares for all, especially the poor, the unfortunate, the suffering, and the defenseless. Justice is God's principal concern and his supreme commandment. God's injunctions, declared Isaiah, were to

> *Seek justice, relieve the oppressed,*
> *Judge the fatherless, plead for the widow.*
> *(Isaiah 1:17)*

Prophets stressed the direct spiritual-ethical encounter between the individual and God. Their concern was the inner person rather than the outer forms of religious activity. Holding that the essence of the covenant was universal righteousness, the prophets criticized priests whose commitment to rites and rituals was not supported by a deeper spiritual insight or matched by a zeal for morality in daily life. To the prophets, an ethical sin was far worse than a ritual omission. Above all, said the prophets, God demands righteousness, living justly before God. To live unjustly, to mistreat one's neighbors, to act without compassion—these actions violated God's Law and endangered the entire social order.

The prophets thus helped shape a social conscience that has become part of the Western tradition. This revolutionary social doctrine states that everyone has a God-given right to social justice and fair treatment; that each person has a religious obligation to denounce evil and oppose mistreatment of others; and that the community has a moral responsibility to assist the unfortunate. The prophets held out the hope that life on earth could be improved, that poverty and injustice need not be accepted as part of an unalterable natural order, and that the individual was capable of elevating himself or herself morally and could respect the dignity of others.

Profile

Jeremiah

In 597 B.C., the Babylonians, under King Nebuchadnezzar, captured Jerusalem, looted the temple, removed many leading citizens to Babylon, and placed Zedekiah on the throne of David as a puppet ruler. In 589 B.C., Zedekiah, ignoring the warnings of the prophet Jeremiah (born c. 645 B.C.), rebelled against Babylonian rule.

Jeremiah began prophesying when still in his teens, exhorting the Hebrews to avoid the evils of idol worship and mistreatment of their fellows. If the people did not change their ways, he warned, a "foe from the north"—clearly, he meant the Babylonians—would devastate the land and even destroy the temple. After the Babylonian conquest, Jeremiah warned Zedekiah to accept Babylonian dominion. Nebuchadnezzar, he said, was fulfilling

By permission of the Warden and Fellows, New College, Oxford.

Universalism

Two tendencies were present in Hebrew thought: parochialism and universalism. Parochial-mindedness stressed the special nature, destiny, and needs of the chosen people—a nation set apart from others—for from among all the nations, God had chosen to give it his Law, the Torah. This narrow, tribal outlook was offset by universalism, a concern for all humanity, which found expression in the prophets who envisioned the unity of all people under God. Those prophets told of a great "day" when God, for whom all people were equally precious, would establish everlasting justice and peace among all nations:

> *In that day shall there be a highway out of Egypt to Assyria, and the Assyrian shall come into Egypt, and the Egyptian into Assyria; and the Egyptians shall worship with the Assyrians. In that day shall Israel be the third with Egypt and with Assyria. . . . for that the Lord of hosts hath blessed him saying: "Blessed be Egypt My people and Assyria the work of My hands, and Israel Mine inheritance." (Isaiah 19:23–24)*

Israel was charged with a sacred mission: to lead in the struggle against idolatry and to set an example of righteous behavior for all humanity.

The prophets were not pacifists, particularly if a war was being waged against the enemies of Yahweh. But some prophets denounced war as obscene and looked forward to its elimination. In a world where virtually everyone glorified the warrior, the prophets of universalism envisioned the day when peace would reign over the earth, when nations

> *. . . shall beat their swords into plowshares,*
> *And their spears into pruning-hooks;*
> *Nation shall not lift up sword against nation,*
> *Neither shall they learn war any more.*
> *(Isaiah 2:4)*

God's purpose. God imposed the Babylonian yoke on Judah to provide the people with an opportunity for true contrition and spiritual renewal. To oppose Babylon was to contravene God's plan and bring down his wrath on Judah. Jeremiah told King Zedekiah: "Why should you and your people die by the sword, by famine, and by pestilence, as the Lord has spoken concerning any nation that will not serve the king of Babylon?" (27:12).

Jeremiah's political advice angered royal officials and popular prophets, who urged a war of liberation. When Zedekiah rebelled, Nebuchadnezzar responded with force. The enemies of Jeremiah demanded his execution as a traitor, and he was left to die in a deep cistern. However, Zedekiah allowed the prophet to be rescued but placed him under court arrest. Shortly afterward, the Babylonians poured through Jerusalem's breached walls; they burned the city, destroyed the temple, slaughtered nobles, and forcibly removed many people to Babylon. King Zedekiah met a dreadful end. After being forced to watch the execution of his sons, he was blinded and taken in chains to Babylon.

Nebuchadnezzar ordered Jeremiah's release from prison. Remaining in Jerusalem, the prophet sent out a message of hope to the survivors. God had punished you, he told them, because "your guilt is great, because your sins are so numerous" (30:15). But God, who loved the people of Israel "with an everlasting love" (31:3) and also recognized his abiding commitment to them, will one day "restore the fortunes of my people" (30:3). The exiles will be returned, Jerusalem rebuilt, and the temple restored, he prophesied.

These prophets maintained that when people glorify force they dehumanize their opponents, brutalize themselves, and dishonor God. When violence rules, there can be no love of God and no regard for the individual.

Individualism

The prophets' universalism was accompanied by an equally profound awareness of the individual and his or her worth to God. Before Moses and the later prophets, virtually all religious tradition had been produced communally and anonymously. The prophets, however, spoke as fearless individuals who, by affixing their signatures to their thoughts, fully bore the responsibility of their religious inspiration and conviction.

The notion of individualism is particularly evident in the prophecies of Jeremiah, who in the early sixth century B.C. predicted doom for Judah because of its collective sins in violating God's covenant. In envisioning the day when "everyone shall die for his own iniquity," Jeremiah explicitly emphasized individual responsibility. At that time, God would make a new covenant with the Jews to replace the covenant they had broken. This new covenant would not be written on stone as the Mosaic covenant had been. Rather, it would be a covenant between God and each individual: "I will put My law in their inward parts, and in their heart will I write it" (Jeremiah 31:30–34).

The prophets' emphasis on the individual's responsibility for his or her own actions is a key component of Western thought. In coming to regard God's Law as a *command to conscience, an appeal to the inner person,* the prophets heightened the awareness of the human personality. They indicated that the individual could not know God by merely following edicts and by performing rituals; the individual must experience God. Precisely this *I-Thou* relationship could make the individual fully conscious of self and could deepen and enrich his or her personality. During the Exodus, the Hebrews were a tribal people who obeyed the Law largely out of awe and group compulsion. By the prophets' time, the Jews appeared to be autonomous individuals who heeded the Law because of a deliberate, conscious inner commitment.

The ideals proclaimed by the prophets helped sustain the Jews throughout their long and often painful historical odyssey, and they remain a vital force for Jews today. Incorporated into the teachings of Jesus, these ideals, as part of Christianity, are embedded in the Western tradition.

The Legacy of the Ancient Jews

For the Jews, monotheism had initiated a process of self-discovery and self-realization unmatched by other peoples of the Near East. The great value that westerners give to the individual derives in part from the ancient Hebrews, who held that man and woman were created in God's image and possessed free will and a conscience answerable to God.

Throughout the centuries the Jewish Bible, with its view of God, human nature, divine punishment, and social justice, has played a pivotal and profound role in Jewish life. Moreover, its significance has transcended the Jewish experience; it is also a cornerstone of Western civilization.

Christianity, the essential religion of Western civilization, emerged from ancient Judaism, and the links between the two, including monotheism, moral autonomy, prophetic values, and the Hebrew Scriptures as the Word of God, are numerous and strong. The historical Jesus cannot be understood without examining his Jewish background, and his followers appealed to the Hebrew Scriptures in order to demonstrate the validity of their beliefs. For these reasons, we talk of a Judeo-Christian tradition as an essential component of Western civilization.

The Hebrew vision of a future messianic age, a golden age of peace and social justice, is at the root of the Western idea of progress—that people can build a more just society, that there is reason to be hopeful about the future. This way of perceiving the world has greatly influenced modern reform movements.

In seeking to comprehend their relationship to God, the writers of the Hebrew Scriptures produced a treasury of themes, stories, and models of literary style and craftsmanship that have been a source of inspiration for Western religious thinkers, novelists, poets, and artists to the present day. Historians and archaeologists find the Hebrew Scriptures a valuable resource in their efforts to reconstruct ancient Near Eastern history.

❖ ❖ ❖

Notes

1. John A. Wilson, "Egypt—the Kingdom of the 'Two Lands,'" in *At the Dawn of Civilization,* ed. E. A. Speiser (New Brunswick, N.J.: Rutgers University Press, 1964), pp. 267–268. Vol. 1 in *The World History of the Jewish People.*
2. John Bright, *A History of Israel* (Philadelphia: Westminster Press, 1972), p. 154.
3. Ibid.
4. From *The Holy Scriptures* (Philadelphia: The Jewish Publication Society of America, 1917). The scriptural quotations are used in this chapter with the permission of The Jewish Publication Society of America.
5. Millar Burrows, "Ancient Israel," in *The Idea of History in the Ancient Near East,* ed. Robert C. Denton (New Haven, Conn.: Yale University Press, 1955), p. 128.

Suggested Reading

Albright, W. F., *The Biblical Period from Abraham to Ezra* (1963). Analyzes the culture and history of ancient Israel and explains the growing spiritual nature of the Hebrew conception of God.

Alter, Robert, and Frank Kermode, eds., *The Literary Guide to the Bible* (1987). Specialists discuss the literary qualities and significance of the Old and New Testaments.

Anderson, Bernhard, *Understanding the Old Testament,* 2nd ed. (1966). An excellent survey of the Old Testament in its historical setting.

Armstrong, Karen, *A History of God* (1994). Changing views of God from the ancient Hebrews until today.

Boadt, Lawrence, *Reading the Old Testament* (1984). A study of ancient Israel's religious experience by a sympathetic Catholic scholar.

Bright, John, *A History of Israel* (1972). A thoughtful, clearly written survey; the best of its kind.

de Vaux, Roland, *Ancient Israel,* vol. 1, *Social Institutions* (1965). All phases of Israelite society—family, monarchy, law, war, and so on.

Ehrlich, E. L., *A Concise History of Israel* (1965). An interpretive essay covering the period from the patriarchs to the destruction of the Jerusalem temple in A.D. 70.

Grant, Michael, *The History of Ancient Israel* (1984). A lucid account.

Heschel, Abraham, *The Prophets,* 2 vols. (1962). A penetrating analysis of the nature of prophetic inspiration.

Kaufmann, Yehezkel, *The Religion of Israel* (1960). An abridgment and translation of Kaufmann's classic multivolume work.

Kuntz, Kenneth J., *The People of Ancient Israel* (1974). A useful introduction to Old Testament literature, history, and thought.

Lindblom, J., *Prophecy in Ancient Israel* (1962). By a prominent Swedish scholar.

Metzger, Bruce M., and Michael D. Coogan, eds., *The Oxford Companion to the Bible* (1993). A valuable reference work.

Muilenburg, James, *The Way of Israel* (1961). A discussion of biblical faith and ethics.

Scott, R. B. Y., *The Relevance of the Prophets* (1968). An introduction to the Old Testament prophetic tradition.

Snaith, N. H., *The Distinctive Ideas of the Old Testament* (1964). Discusses those central ideas that distinguish Hebrew religion from other religions of the Near East.

von Rad, Gerhard, *The Message of the Prophet* (1965). An examination of the message of each prophet against the background of his time.

Zeitlin, Irving M., *Ancient Judaism* (1984). A sociologist examines the history and thought of ancient Israel.

Review Questions

1. What role did each of the following play in Jewish history: Moses, Solomon, Babylonian Captivity?
2. In what way did the Hebrew view of God mark a revolutionary break with Near Eastern religious thought?
3. How did Hebrew religious thought promote the idea of moral autonomy?
4. How did the Hebrews interpret the covenant?
5. What was the Hebrew view of women? What, in your opinion, was the significance of this view for Western history?
6. Compare and contrast Hebrew law with law in Mesopotamia and Egypt.
7. Why did the Hebrews consider history to be important?
8. Both parochialism and universalism were evident in ancient Hebrew thought and history. Discuss.
9. What role did the prophets play in Hebrew history? What is the enduring significance of their achievement?
10. Why are the Hebrews regarded as one source of Western civilization?

Chapter 3

The Greek City-State: Democratic Politics

The Acropolis of Athens. (Robert Harding Picture Library.)

■ **Early Aegean Civilizations**

■ **The Rise of Hellenic Civilization**
Homer, Shaper of the Greek Spirit
Greek Religion

■ **Evolution of the City-State**
The Break with Theocratic Politics
Sparta: A Garrison State
Athens: The Rise of Democracy

■ **Athenian Greatness**
The Persian Wars
The Delian League
The Mature Athenian Democracy
Pericles: Symbol of Athenian Democracy

■ **The Decline of the City-States**
The Peloponnesian War
The Fourth Century

■ **The Dilemma of Greek Politics**

The Hebrew conception of ethical monotheism, with its stress on human dignity, is one principal source of the Western tradition. The second major source is ancient Greece. Both Hebrews and Greeks absorbed the achievements of Near Eastern civilizations, but they also developed their own distinctive viewpoints and styles of thought, which set them apart from the Mesopotamians and Egyptians. The great achievements of the Hebrews lay in the sphere of religious-ethical thought; those of the Greeks lay in the development of rational thought. As Greek society evolved, says British historian James Shiel, there

> *was a growing reliance on independent reason, a devotion to logical precision, progressing from myth to logos [reason]. Rationalism permeated the whole social and cultural development. . . . Architecture . . . developed from primitive cultic considerations to sophisticated mathematical norms; sculpture escaped from temple image to a new love of naturalism and proportion; political life proceeded from tyranny to rational experiments in democracy. From practical rules of thumb, geometry moved forward in the direction of the impressive Euclidian synthesis. So too philosophy made its way from "sayings of the wise" to the Aristotelian logic, and made men rely on their own observation and reflection in facing the unexplained vastness of the cosmos.*[1]

The Greeks conceived of nature as following general rules, not acting according to the whims of gods or demons. They saw human beings as having a capacity for rational thought, a need for freedom, and a worth as individuals. Although the Greeks never dispensed with the gods, they increasingly stressed the importance of human reason and human decisions. They came to assert that reason is the avenue to knowledge and that people—not the gods—are responsible for their own behavior. In this shift of attention from the gods to human beings, the Greeks broke with the mythmaking orientation of the Near East and created the rational

Chronology 3.1 ❖ The Greek City-State

1700–1450 B.C.*	Height of Minoan civilization
1400–1230	Height of Mycenaean civilization
1100–800	Dark Age
c. 700	Homer
750–550	Age of Colonization
621	Draco's code of law
594	Solon is elected chief executive
546–527	Under Pisistratus, tyranny replaces oligarchy
507	Cleisthenes broadens democratic institutions
499	Ionians revolt against Persian rule
490	Athenians defeat Persians at battle of Marathon
480	Xerxes of Persia invades Greece; Greek naval victory at Salamis
479	Spartans defeat Persians at Plataea, ending Persian Wars
478–477	Formation of Delian League
431	Start of Peloponnesian War
429	Death of Pericles
413	Athenian defeat at Syracuse
404	Athens surrenders to Sparta, ending Peloponnesian War
399	Execution of Socrates
387	Plato founds a school, the Academy
359	Philip II becomes king of Macedonia
338	Battle of Chaeronea: Greek city-states fall under the dominion of Macedonia
335 B.C.	Aristotle founds a school, the Lyceum

*Some dates are approximations

outlook that is a distinctive feature of Western civilization.

Early Aegean Civilizations

Until the latter part of the nineteenth century, historians placed the beginning of Greek, or Hellenic, history in the eighth century B.C. Now it is known that two related civilizations preceded Hellenic Greece: the Minoan and the Mycenaean. Although the ancient Greek poet Homer had spoken of an earlier Greek civilization in his works, historians believed that Homer's epics dealt with myths and legends, not with a historical past. In 1871, however, a successful German businessman, Heinrich Schliemann, began a search for earliest Greece. Having been enthralled by Homer's epics as a youth, Schliemann was convinced that they referred to an actual civilization.

In excavating several sites mentioned by Homer, Schliemann discovered tombs, pottery, ornaments, and the remains of palaces of what hitherto had been a lost Greek civilization. The ancient civilization was named after Mycenae, the most important city of the time. Mycenaean civilization pervaded the Greek mainland and the islands of the Aegean Sea for much of the second millennium B.C.

In 1900, Arthur Evans, a British archaeologist, made an equally extraordinary discovery. Excavating on the island of Crete, southeast of the Greek mainland, he unearthed a civilization even older than that of the Mycenaean Greeks. The Cretans, or Minoans, were not Greeks and did not speak a Greek language, but their influence on mainland Greece was considerable and enduring. Minoan civilization lasted about 1,350 years (2600 B.C. to 1250 B.C.) and reached its height during the period from 1700 to 1450 B.C.

The centers of Minoan civilization were magnificent palace complexes, whose construction was evidence of the wealth and power of Minoan kings. That the architects of these palaces and the artists who decorated the walls were sensitive to beauty is shown in the ruins uncovered at various Cretan sites. The palaces housed royal families, priests, and government officials and contained workshops that produced decorated silver vessels, daggers, and pottery for local use and for export. Numerous Cretan artifacts have been found in Egypt, Syria, Asia Minor, and Greece, attesting to a substantial export trade.

Judging by the archaeological evidence, the Minoans seemed peaceful. Minoan art did not generally depict military scenes, and Minoan palaces, unlike the Mycenaean ones, had no defensive walls or fortifications. Thus, the Minoans were vulnerable to the warlike Mycenaean Greeks, who invaded and conquered Knossos. The Minoans never recovered from this blow, and within two centuries Minoan civilization faded away.

Who were these Mycenaeans? Around 2000 B.C., Greek-speaking tribes moved southward into the Greek peninsula, where, together with the pre-Greek population, they fashioned the Mycenaean civilization. In the Peloponnesus, the Mycenaeans built palaces that were based in part on Cretan models. In these palaces, Mycenaean kings conducted affairs of state, and priests and priestesses performed religious ceremonies; potters, smiths, tailors, and chariot builders practiced their crafts in the numerous workshops, much like their Minoan counterparts. Mycenaean arts and crafts owed a considerable debt to Crete. A script that permitted record keeping probably also came from Crete. The Mycenaeans were traders, too, exchanging goods with the peoples of Egypt, Phoenicia, Sicily,

SNAKE GODDESS FROM KNOSSOS, CRETE, C. 1600 B.C. With snakes and a dove on her head, this deity is believed to be a household goddess—protector of the household and its inhabitants. Certain features resemble the characteristics of Athena, goddess of Athens in classical times. The exact meaning of the snakes is unknown, except for their link with ancient fertility cults. (*Hirmer Fotoarchiv, München.*)

southern Italy, Macedonia, and the western coast of Asia Minor.

At the apex of Mycenaean society was the king, who headed the armed forces, controlled production and trade, and was the highest judicial authority. Assisting the king were aristocrats, who were officers in the army and held key positions in the administration. The priestesses and priests were also in the upper echelons of the society; they supervised sanctuaries and other properties of the gods. Farmers, stockbreeders, and craftsmen constituted the bulk of the free population. At the bottom of the social pyramid were the slaves—mostly foreign prisoners of war.

Mycenaean civilization, which consisted of several small states, each with its own ruling dynasty, reached its height in the period from 1400 to 1230 B.C. Following that, constant warfare between the Mycenaean kingdoms (and perhaps foreign invasions) led to destruction of the palaces and the abrupt disintegration of the Mycenaean civilization about 1100 B.C. But to the later Greek civilization the Mycenaeans left a legacy of religious forms, pottery making, metallurgy, agriculture, language, a warrior culture and code of honor immortalized in the Homeric epics, and myths and legends, which offered themes for Greek drama.

The Rise of Hellenic Civilization

From 1100 to 800 B.C., the Greek world passed through the Dark Age, an era of transition between a dead Mycenaean civilization and a still unborn Hellenic civilization. The Dark Age saw the migration of Greek tribes from the barren mountainous regions of Greece to more fertile plains, and from the mainland to Aegean islands and the coast of Asia Minor. One group of invaders, the Dorians, penetrated the Peloponnesian peninsula in the south and later founded Sparta. Another group, the Ionians, settled in Attica, where Athens is located, and later crossed to Asia Minor. During this period, the Greeks experienced insecurity, warfare, poverty, and isolation. The bureaucratic system of Mycenaean government had disappeared, extensive trade had ceased, the art of writing had been forgotten, the palace workshops no longer existed, and art had reverted to primitive forms.

After 800 B.C., however, town life revived. Writing again became part of the Greek culture, this time with the more efficient Phoenician script. (Other borrowings from the Near East included artistic imagery and motifs, religious practices, craft skills, and mythological tales that were adapted and transformed by Greek writers.) The population increased dramatically, there was a spectacular rise in the use of metals, and overseas trade expanded. Gradually, Greek cities founded settlements on the islands of the Aegean, along the coast of Asia Minor and the Black Sea, and to the west in Sicily and southern Italy. These colonies, established to relieve overpopulation and land hunger, were independent, self-governing city-states, not possessions of the homeland city-states, although close ties were maintained between the two. During the two hundred years of colonization (750–550 B.C.), trade and industry expanded, the pace of urbanization quickened, and a new class emerged: the merchants, whose wealth derived from goods and money rather than from land. In time, this middle class would challenge the landholding aristocracy.

Homer, Shaper of the Greek Spirit

The poet Homer lived during the eighth century B.C., just after the Dark Age. His great narrative epics, the *Iliad* and the *Odyssey*,* helped shape the Greek spirit and Greek religion. Homer was the earliest molder of the Greek outlook and character. For centuries, Greek youngsters grew up reciting the Homeric epics and admiring the Homeric heroes, who strove for honor and faced suffering and death with courage. Greek thinkers quoted Homer to illustrate moral truths.

In contrast to earlier works of mythology,

*Although scholars agree that Homer composed the *Iliad*, some of them hold that the *Odyssey* was probably the work of an unknown poet, who lived sometime after Homer; some say that Homer composed both epics in their earliest forms and that others altered them.

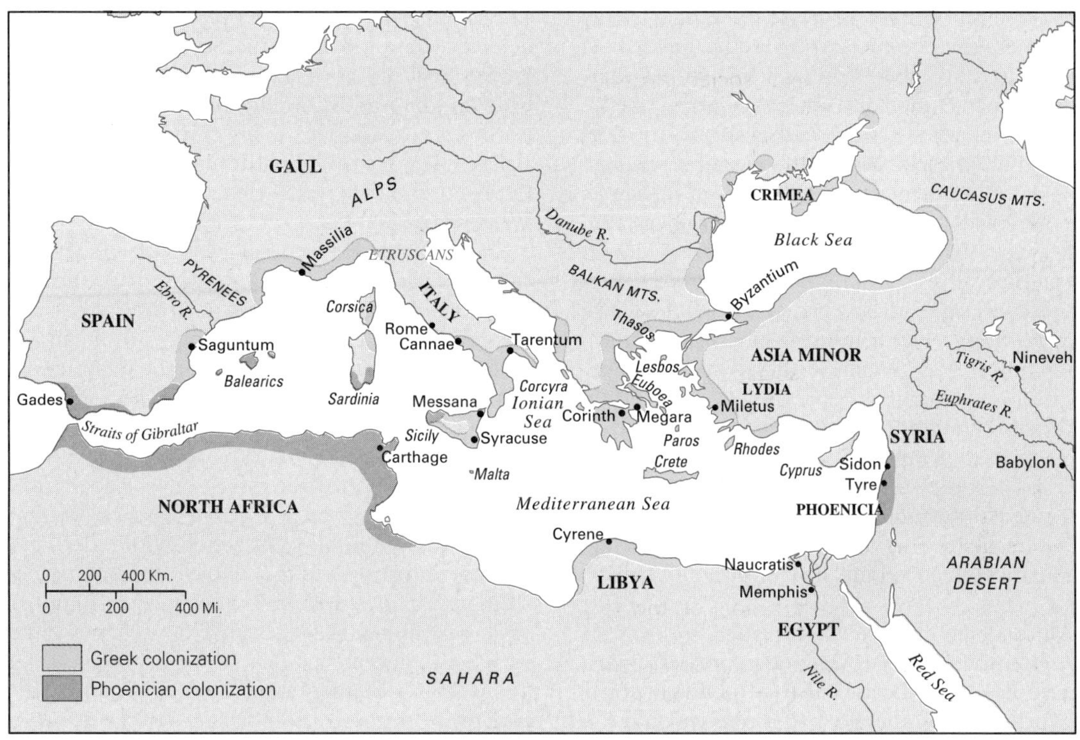

Map 3.1 Greek Colonization of the Mediterranean Basin From 750 to 550 B.C., the Greeks colonized the islands of the Aegean, the coasts of Asia Minor and the Black Sea, and, to the west, Sicily and southern Italy.

Homer dealt not just with a hero's actions, but also with what the hero thought and felt about his behavior. Homer was a poetic genius who could reveal a human being's deepest thoughts, feelings, and conflicts in a few brilliant lines. His characters, complex in their motives and expressing powerful human emotions—wrath, vengeance, guilt, remorse, compassion, and love—would intrigue and inspire Western writers down to the present.

The *Iliad* deals, in poetic form, with a small segment of the tenth and last year of the Trojan War, which had taken place centuries before Homer's time, during the Mycenaean period. At the very beginning, Homer states his theme:

> *The Wrath of Achilles is my theme, that fatal wrath which, in fulfillment of the will of Zeus, brought the Achaeans [Greeks] so much suffering and sent the gallant souls of many noblemen to Hades, leaving their bodies as carrion for the dogs and passing birds. Let us begin, goddess of song, with the angry parting that took place between Agamemnon King of Men and the great Achilles Son of Peleus.*[2]

The story goes on to reveal the cause and tragic consequences of this wrath. In depriving "the swift and excellent" Achilles of his rightful war-prize (the captive young woman Briseis), King Agamemnon has insulted Achilles' honor and has violated the solemn rule that warrior heroes treat each other with respect. His pride wounded, Achilles refuses to rejoin Agamemnon in battle against Troy and plans to affirm his honor by demonstrating that the Achaeans need his valor and military prowess. Not until many brave men have been slain, including his dearest friend Patroclus, does Achilles set aside his quarrel with Agamemnon and enter the battle.

Homer employs a *particular* event, the quarrel between an arrogant Agamemnon and a revengeful Achilles, to demonstrate a *universal* principle: that "wicked arrogance" and "ruinous wrath" will cause much suffering and death. Homer grasps that there is an internal logic to existence. For Homer, says British classicist H. D. F. Kitto, "actions must have their consequences; ill-judged actions must have uncomfortable results."[3] People, and even the gods, operate within a certain unalterable framework; their deeds are subject to the demands of fate, or necessity. With a poet's intuition, Homer sensed what would become a fundamental attitude of the Greek mind: there is a universal order to things. Later Greeks would formulate Homer's poetic insight in philosophical terms.

Although human life is governed by laws of necessity, the Homeric warrior expresses a passionate desire to assert himself, to demonstrate his worth, to gain the glory that poets would immortalize in their songs—that is, to achieve *areté*, excellence. In the *Iliad*, Hector, prince of Troy, does battle with Achilles, even though defeat and death seem certain. He fights not because he is a fool rushing madly into a fray nor because he relishes combat, but because he is a prince bound by a code of honor and conscious of his reputation and of his responsibility to his fellow Trojans. In the code of the warrior-aristocrats, cowardice brought unbearable shame, and honor meant more than life itself. When Hector knows that he is going to be slain by Achilles, he expresses this overriding concern with heroism and glory: "So now I meet my doom. Let me at least sell my life dearly and have a not inglorious end, after some feat of arms that shall come to the ears of generations still unborn."[4]

Heroism, the pursuit of glory, and war's exhilaration are central to the *Iliad*, but Homer is also sensitive to the suffering caused by war. Battlefields littered with dead and maimed warriors fill soldiers with tears. And the grief of widows, orphans, and parents is unremitting.

Homer grasped war's tragic character: it confers honor and dignity on the victorious, but suffering, grief, enslavement, and death on the defeated. And one day, the hero, who had been lauded for his courage and prowess and had brought glory to his family and city, will also perish by the sword. This is his destiny. Homer's insights into life's tragic nature instructed the great Greek dramatists (see Chapter 4) and future Western writers.

In the warrior-aristocrat world of Homer, *excellence* was principally interpreted as bravery and skill in battle. Homer's portrayal also bears the embryo of a larger conception of human excellence, one that combines thought with action. A man of true worth, says the wise Phoenix to the stubborn Achilles, is both "a speaker of words and a doer of deeds." In this passage, we find the earliest statement of the Greek educational ideal: the molding of a man who, says classicist Werner Jaeger, "united nobility of action with nobility of mind," who realized "the whole of human potentialities."[5] Thus, in Homer we find the beginnings of Greek humanism—a concern with man and with his achievements.

To Mesopotamian and Egyptian minds, the gods were primarily responsible for the good or evil that befell human beings. In Homer's work, the gods are still very much involved in human affairs, but Homer also makes the individual a decisive actor in the drama of life. Human actions and human personality are very important. Homer's men demonstrate a considerable independence of will. Human beings pay respect to the gods but do not live in perpetual fear of them; they choose their own way, at times even defying the gods. As British classicist C. M. Bowra notes, "the human actors . . . pursue their own aims and deal their own blows; the gods may help or obstruct them, but success or failure remains their own. The gods have the last word, but in the interval men do their utmost and win glory for it."[6] Homer's view of the eternal order of the world and his conception of the individual striving for excellence form the foundations of the Greek outlook.

Greek Religion

During the Dark Age, Greek religion was a mixture of beliefs and cults of gods and goddesses inherited from the Mycenaean past and from an even older

Indo-European past imported from Asia Minor and from the early civilizations of the Near East. The Greeks had no prophets or works of scripture like the Hebrews, but Homer's epics gave some clarity and structure to Greek religion. They were not intended to have any theological significance, but their treatment of the gods had important religious implications for the Greeks. In time, Homer's epics formed the basis of the Olympian religion accepted throughout Greece. The principal gods were said to reside on Mount Olympus in northern Greece, and on its highest peak was the palace of Zeus, the chief deity. Although all Greeks recognized the Olympian gods, each city retained local gods and rituals that had been transmitted through generations by folk memory.

Many Greeks found an outlet for their religious feelings in the sacred ceremonies of mystic cults. Devotees of the cult of Dionysus, the god of wine and agricultural fertility, engaged in ecstatic dances and frenzied prayers for abundant harvests. Participants in the Eleusinian cult felt purified and reborn through their rituals and believed in a happy life after death. The Orphic cult, which was popular in the sixth century B.C., taught the unimportance of earthly life and the need to prepare for life after the grave. The Orphics believed that the soul, which once enjoyed a happy existence in another world, was imprisoned in the body for an unknown fault, and that if the individual controlled his or her bodily desires the soul would be liberated after death.

In the early stages of Greek history, most people sought to live in accordance with the wishes of the gods. Through prayer, offerings, and ritual purification, they tried to appease the gods and consulted oracles to divine the future. Although religion pervaded daily life, the Greeks had no official body of priests who ruled religious matters and could intervene in politics. Instead, religious ceremonies were conducted by citizens chosen to serve as priests. Nor was there an official creed with established doctrines. Religion was more social than spiritual; that is, it was more a way of expressing attachment to the community than finding inner peace through personal communion with a higher reality. In time, traditional religion would be challenged and undermined by a growing secular and rational spirit.

Evolution of the City-State

The Break with Theocratic Politics

From 750 B.C. to the death of Alexander the Great in 323 B.C., Greek society consisted of independent city-states. The city-state based on tribal allegiances was generally the first political association during the early stages of civilization. Moreover, Greece's many mountains, bays, and islands—natural barriers to political unity—favored this type of political arrangement.

The scale of the city-state, or *polis*, was small; most city-states had fewer than 5,000 male citizens. Athens, which was a large city-state, had some 35,000 to 40,000 adult male citizens; the rest of its population of 350,000 consisted of women, children, resident aliens, and slaves, none of whom could participate in lawmaking. The citizens of the polis, many of whom were related by blood, knew each other well, and together they engaged in athletic contests and religious rituals. The polis gave individuals a sense of belonging, for its citizens were intimately involved in the political and cultural life of the community.

In the fifth century B.C., at its maturity, the Greeks viewed their polis as the only avenue to the good life—"the only framework within which man could realize his spiritual, moral, and intellectual capacities," in the words of Kitto.[7] The mature polis was a self-governing community that expressed the will of free citizens, not the desires of gods, hereditary kings, or priests. In the Near East, religion dominated political activity, and to abide by the mandates of the gods was the ruler's first responsibility. The Greek polis also had begun as a religious institution, in which the citizens sought to maintain an alliance with their deities. But gradually the citizens de-emphasized the gods' role in political life and based government not on the magic powers of divine rulers, but on human intelligence as expressed through the community. Seers, purported to have supernatural skills, might offer advice but could not override the rulings of the Assembly. The great innovation introduced by the Greeks into politics and social theory, says classicist Mason Hammond, was "the view that law did not emanate from gods, or divine rulers, but from the human community."[8] The evolution of the Greek polis from a tribal-religious institution to a secular-rational institution was only a part of the general transition of the Greek mind from myth to reason.

The emergence of rational attitudes did not, of course, spell the end of religion, particularly for the peasants, who remained devoted to their ancient cults, gods, and shrines. Greek commanders and statesmen, at times, were not beyond consulting omens and oracles before making decisions, and a considerable part of Athenian revenue went to the construction of temples and the observance of religious festivals. The Greeks were careful to show respect for the gods, for many believed that these deities could aid or harm a city. Worshiping the god of the city remained a required act of patriotism, to which Greeks unfailingly adhered.

Thus, the religious-mythical tradition never died in Greece but existed side by side with a growing rationalism. As Greek rationalism gained influence, traditional religious beliefs and restrictions either were made to comply more with the demands of reason or grew weaker through neglect and disuse. When Athenian democracy reached its height in the middle of the fifth century B.C., religion was no longer the dominant factor in politics. For many Athenians, religion had become largely ceremonial, a way of expressing loyalty to the city. They had come to rely on human reason, not divine guidance, in their political and intellectual life.

Greek political life was marred by violent party conflicts, demagoguery, intercity warfare, and the exploitation of weak states by stronger ones. Nevertheless, the Greek political achievement was extraordinary. What made Greek political life different from that of earlier Near Eastern civilizations, as well as gave it enduring significance, was the Greeks' gradual realization that community problems are caused by human beings and require human solutions. Thus, the Greeks came to understand law as an achievement of the rational mind rather than as an edict imposed by the gods; law was valued because it expressed the will and needs of the community, not out of fear of the divine. The Greeks also valued free citizenship. An absolute king, a tyrant who ruled arbitrarily and by decree and who was above the law, was abhorrent.

The ideals of political freedom are best exemplified by Athens. Before turning to Athens, however, let us examine another Greek city, which followed a different political course.

Sparta: A Garrison State

Situated on the Peloponnesian peninsula, farther inland than most Greek cities, Sparta had been settled by Dorian Greeks. The Greek city-states dealt with overpopulation and the need for new agricultural land by founding colonies. Sparta, however, established only one colony, Tarentum, in southern Italy. Sparta's chief means of expansion was to conquer, in the eighth century B.C., its neighbors on the Peloponnesian peninsula, including Messenia. Instead of selling the Messenians abroad, the traditional Greek way of treating a defeated foe, the Spartans kept them as state serfs, or *helots*. Helots were owned by the state rather than by individual Spartans. Enraged by their enforced servitude, the Messenians, also a Greek people, desperately tried to regain their freedom. After a bloody struggle, the Spartans suppressed the uprising, but the fear of a helot revolt became indelibly stamped on Spartan consciousness.

To maintain their dominion over the Messenians, who outnumbered them ten to one, the Spartans—with extraordinary single-mindedness, discipline, and loyalty—transformed their own society into an armed camp. Agricultural labor was performed by helots; trade and crafts were left to the *perioikoi*, conquered Greeks who were free but were not citizens and had no political rights. The Spartans learned only one craft, soldiering, and were inculcated with only one conception of excellence: fighting bravely for their city.

The Spartans were trained in the arts of war and indoctrinated to serve the state. Military training for Spartan boys began at age seven; they exercised, drilled, competed, and endured physical hardships. Other Greeks admired the Spartans for their courage, obedience to law, and achievement in molding themselves according to an ideal. Spartan soldiers were better trained and disciplined and were more physically fit than other Greeks. But the Spartans were also criticized for having a limited conception of areté.

Before Sparta converted itself into a military

SPARTAN WOMAN STATUETTE. Spartan women were expected to marry before the age of twenty and to have children. Moreover, it was assumed that while the men and boys underwent military training, the women would keep the household in order. (*National Archaeological Museum, Athens/Archaeological Receipts Fund.*)

state, its cultural development had paralleled that of the other Greek cities. By isolating itself economically and culturally from the rest of Greece, however, Sparta became a closed provincial town and did not share in the cultural enlightenment that pervaded the Greek world. A culturally retarded Sparta paid a heavy price for military strength.

By 500 B.C., Sparta had emerged as the leader of the Peloponnesian League, an alliance of southern Greek city-states whose land forces were superior to those of any other combination of Greek cities. Sparta, though, was concerned with protecting its position, not with expansion. Cautious by temperament and always fearful of a helot uprising, Spartans viewed the Peloponnesian League as an instrument for defense rather than aggression.

Athens: The Rise of Democracy

The contrast between the city-states of Athens and Sparta is striking. Whereas Sparta was a land power and exclusively agricultural, Athens was located on the peninsula of Attica near the coast, possessed a great navy, and was the commercial leader among the Greeks. Reluctant to send soldiers far from home, where they were needed to control the helots, Sparta's leaders pursued an isolationist foreign policy. The daring and ambitious Athenians, on the other hand, endeavored to extend their hegemony over other Greek cities. Finally, Athenians and Spartans differed in their concept of freedom. To the Spartans, freedom meant preserving the independence of their fatherland; this overriding consideration demanded order, discipline, and regimentation. The Athenians also wanted to protect their city from enemies, but, unlike the Spartans, they valued political freedom and sought the full development and enrichment of the human personality. Thus, while authoritarian Sparta became culturally sterile, Athens, with its relatively free and open society, emerged as the cultural leader of Hellenic civilization.

Greek city-states generally moved through four stages: rule by a king (monarchy), rule by landowning aristocrats (oligarchy), rule by one man who seized power (tyranny), and rule by the people (democracy). During the first stage, monarchy, the king, who derived his power from the gods, commanded the army and judged civil cases.

Oligarchy, the second stage, was instituted in Athens during the eighth century B.C. when aristocrats (*aristocracy* is a Greek word meaning "rule of the best") usurped power from hereditary kings. In the next century, aristocratic regimes experienced a social crisis. There was tension between the landholding nobles, who dominated the government, and the newly rich and ambitious merchants, who wanted a share in governing Athens. Furthermore, peasants who borrowed from the aristocracy, pledging their lands as security, lost their property and even became enslaved for nonpayment of their debts. Merchants and peasants also protested that the law, which was based on oral tradition and administered exclusively by aristocrats, was unjust. The embittered and restless middle and lower classes were granted one concession. In 621 B.C., the aristocrats appointed Draco to draw up a code of law. Although Draco's code let the poor know what the law was and reduced the possibilities of aristocratic judges behaving arbitrarily, penalties were extremely severe (hence the word *draconian*), and the code provided no relief for the peasants' economic woes. As the poor began to organize and press for the cancellation of their debts and the redistribution of land, Athens was moving toward civil war.

Solon, the Reformer. In 594 B.C., Solon (c. 640–559 B.C.), a traveler and poet with a reputation for being wise, was elected chief executive. Two years later, the aristocrats, to avert civil war, gave Solon the power to work out a solution to Athens' problems. Solon maintained that a principle of justice, *Diké*, underlies the human community, and that when people violate this standard of justice they bring ruin upon the city. Thus, he held that the wealthy landowners, through their greed, had disrupted community life and brought Athens to the brink of civil war. A distinguishing feature of Greek intellectual life was the belief in the orderliness of the universe. For Solon, universal law also operated in the sphere of social life.

Originally, justice had been conceived in religious terms as the will of Zeus. In regarding justice as a principle operating within society, Solon withdrew justice from the province of religion and gave it a secular foundation. He initiated a rational approach to the problems of society by reducing the gods' role in human affairs. He attributed the city's ills to the specific behavior of individuals; he sought practical remedies for these ills; and he held that written law should be in harmony with the natural order of things. In Solon's career can be detected the embryo of political thought and reform based on reason.

Underlying Solon's reforms were a concern for the interests of the community as a whole, a commitment to moderation, and a desire to avoid radical extremes. Solon aimed at restoring a sick Athenian society to health by restraining the nobles and improving the lot of the poor. To achieve this goal, he canceled debts, freed Athenians enslaved for debt, and brought back to Athens those who had been sold abroad. However, he refused to confiscate and redistribute the nobles' land as the extremists demanded.

Solon recognized that the aristocrats had abused their political power, but he did not believe that the common people were prepared for self-government. His political reforms rested on the assumption that aristocrats would continue to exercise a guiding role in government. At the same time, by broadening political participation, he sought to instill in Athenians of all classes a sense of working for the common good of the city. He permitted all classes of free men, even the poorest, to sit in the Assembly—a body that elected magistrates and accepted or rejected legislation proposed by the Council of Four Hundred, which he had established. Because of property requirements, the new council's membership was limited to the middle and upper classes. Solon also opened the highest offices in the state to wealthy commoners, who had previously been excluded from these positions because they lacked noble birth. Thus, Solon undermined the traditional rights of the hereditary aristocracy and initiated the transformation of Athens from an aristocratic oligarchy into a democracy.

Solon also instituted ingenious economic reforms. Because Attica's soil was too poor for growing grain, he urged the cultivation of grapes for wine and the growing of olives, whose oil could be exported. To encourage industrial expansion, he ordered that all fathers teach their sons a trade and granted citizenship to foreign craftsmen willing to migrate to Athens. These measures and the fine quality of the native reddish-brown clay allowed Athens to become the leading producer and exporter of pottery. Solon's economic policies transformed Athens into a great commercial center.

With imagination and intelligence, Solon reformed Athenian society. He then retired from office. In refusing to use his prestige to become a tyrant, a one-man ruler, Solon demonstrated that his statesmanship rested on the highest moral principles—on a conception of justice. Believing that only the rule of law can hold the community together, Solon refused to act outside the law; wanting to imbue his fellow Athenians with a sense of responsibility, he refused to act irresponsibly. However, Solon's reforms did not eliminate factional disputes among the aristocratic clans or relieve all the discontent of the poor.

Pisistratus, the Tyrant. Pisistratus (c. 605–527 B.C.), another aristocrat, endeavored to take advantage of the general instability to become a one-man ruler. After two abortive efforts, in 561 and 556 B.C., he secured power in 546 B.C. and drove into exile those fellow aristocrats who had opposed him. Tyranny thus had replaced oligarchy.

Tyranny occurred frequently in the Greek city-states. Almost always aristocrats themselves, tyrants generally posed as champions of the poor in their struggle against the aristocracy, another indication that the government had to reckon with the needs of the entire community. To increase their own base of support, some tyrants extended citizenship to the landless and even to foreigners.

Pisistratus sought popular support by having conduits constructed to increase Athens' water supply. Like tyrants in other city-states, he gave to peasants land confiscated from exiled aristocrats and granted state loans to small farmers. By concerning himself with the problems of the common people, Pisistratus continued the trend initiated by Solon. In a deliberate attempt to pacify the population, he exercised personal power without abolishing the existing constitution.

Pisistratus' great achievement was the promotion of cultural life. He initiated grand architectural projects, encouraged sculptors and painters, arranged for public recitals of the Homeric epics, and founded festivals, which included dramatic performances. In all these ways, he made culture, formerly the province of the aristocracy, available to commoners. Pisistratus thus launched a policy that led Athens to emerge as the cultural capital of the Greeks. In further weakening the power of the landed aristocracy, Pisistratus made possible the establishment of democracy under Cleisthenes.

Cleisthenes, the Democrat. After Pisistratus' death in 527 B.C., his power passed to his two sons. One was assassinated, and the other driven from Athens by Spartans, whose intervention had been urged by exiled Athenian aristocrats opposed to one-man rule. In the power vacuum, a faction headed by Cleisthenes, an aristocrat sympathetic to democracy, assumed leadership.

The failure of aristocratic politics to solve pressing socioeconomic problems had led broad sections of the population and emerging political thinkers to move toward an alternative position—involving the population as a whole in Athenian political life. Recognizing this new trend, would-be tyrants, in their struggles with fellow nobles, tried to gain the support of the common people through economic inducements. But, as Cleisthenes recognized, the politically awakened commoners also wanted involvement in decision making. Moreover, he reasoned, only political participation by the broad citizenry could put an end to seizures of political power, arbitrary rule, and factional strife that had marred traditional aristocratic politics.

Cleisthenes reasoned further that the needed transformation of Athenian political life required breaking down the customary divisions of the polis into tribes, clans, and cults. These groupings, inherited from a distant past, consisted of both nobles and commoners. But they were dominated by nobles, who used them to jockey for the chief state positions, a practice that caused much divisiveness, bitterness, and violent conflicts within the city. By an ingenious system of redistricting the city, Cleisthenes replaced this practice, rooted in tradition and authority, with a new approach, devised by reason to ensure that historic allegiance to tribe or clan would be superseded by loyalty to the city as a whole.

Cleisthenes hoped to make democracy the permanent form of government for Athens. To safeguard the city against tyranny, he utilized (or perhaps introduced) the practice of *ostracism.* Once a year, Athenians were given the opportunity to inscribe on a potsherd (*ostracon*) the name of anyone who, they felt, endangered the state. An individual against whom enough votes were cast was ostracized, that is, forced to leave Athens for ten years.

Although some aristocratic features still existed in the government (notably the Council of the Areopagus, consisting of retired high officials), Cleisthenes had firmly secured democratic government in Athens. The Assembly, which Solon had opened to all male citizens, was in the process of becoming the supreme authority in the state. But the period of Athenian greatness lay in the future. The Athenians first had to fight a war of survival against the Persian Empire.

Athenian Greatness

The Persian Wars

In 499 B.C., the Ionian Greeks of Asia Minor rebelled against their Persian overlord. Sympathetic to the Ionian cause, Athens sent twenty ships to aid the revolt, an act that the Greek historian Herodotus said "was the beginning of trouble not only for Greece, but for the rest of the world as well." Bent on revenge, Darius I, king of Persia, sent a small detachment to Attica. In 490 B.C., on the plains of Marathon, the citizen army of Athens defeated the Persians—for the Athenians, one of the finest moments in their history. Ten years later, Xerxes, Darius' son, organized a huge invasion force—some 250,000 men and more than 500 ships—with the aim of reducing Greece to a Persian province. Setting aside their separatist instincts, many of the city-states united to defend their independence and their liberty. Herodotus viewed the conflict as a struggle for freedom.

The Persians crossed the waters of the Hellespont (Dardanelles) and made their way into northern Greece. The historian Herodotus describes their encounter at the mountain pass of Thermopylae with three hundred Spartans, who were true to their training and ideal of areté and "resisted to the last with their swords if they had them, and if not, with their hands and teeth, until the Persians, coming on from the front over the ruins of the wall and closing in from behind, finally overwhelmed them."[9] Northern Greece fell to the Persians, who continued south, burning a deserted Athens.

When it appeared that the Greeks' spirit had been broken, the Athenian statesman and general Themistocles (c. 527–460 B.C.), demonstrating in military affairs the same rationality that Cleisthenes had shown in political life, lured the Persian fleet into the narrows of the Bay of Salamis. Unable to deploy its more numerous ships in this cramped space, the Persian armada was destroyed by Greek ships manned by crews who understood what was at stake. In 479 B.C., a year after the Athenian naval victory at Salamis, the Spartans defeated the Persians in the land battle of Plataea. The inventive intelligence with which the Greeks planned their military operations and a fierce desire to preserve their freedom—which, the war made them realize, was their distinguishing attribute—enabled them to defeat the greatest military power the Mediterranean world had yet seen.

The Persian Wars were decisive in the history of the West. Had the Greeks been defeated, it is very likely that their cultural and political vitality would have been aborted. The confidence and pride that came with victory, however, propelled Athens into a golden age, which became marred by the Athenian urge for dominance in Greece.

The Delian League

The Persian Wars ushered in an era of Athenian imperialism, which had drastic consequences for the future. Immediately after the wars, more than 150 city-states organized a confederation, the Delian League (named after its treasury on the island of Delos), to protect themselves against a renewed confrontation with Persia. Because of its wealth, its powerful fleet, and the restless energy of its citizens, Athens assumed leadership of the Delian League. Largely thanks to the Athenian fleet, the league was able to drive both pirates and Persians from the Aegean Sea. Although it had been conceived as a voluntary association of independent Greek states seeking protection against Persia, the league gradually came under the domination of Athens.

Athenians consciously and rapaciously manipulated the league for their own economic advantage, seeing no conflict between imperialism and democracy. They believed that their freedom and prosperity required subduing, exploiting, and enslaving others, and they adhered to the principle that strong states had a natural right to dominate weaker ones. They relished the empire that gave them wealth, power, and glory. Moreover, the

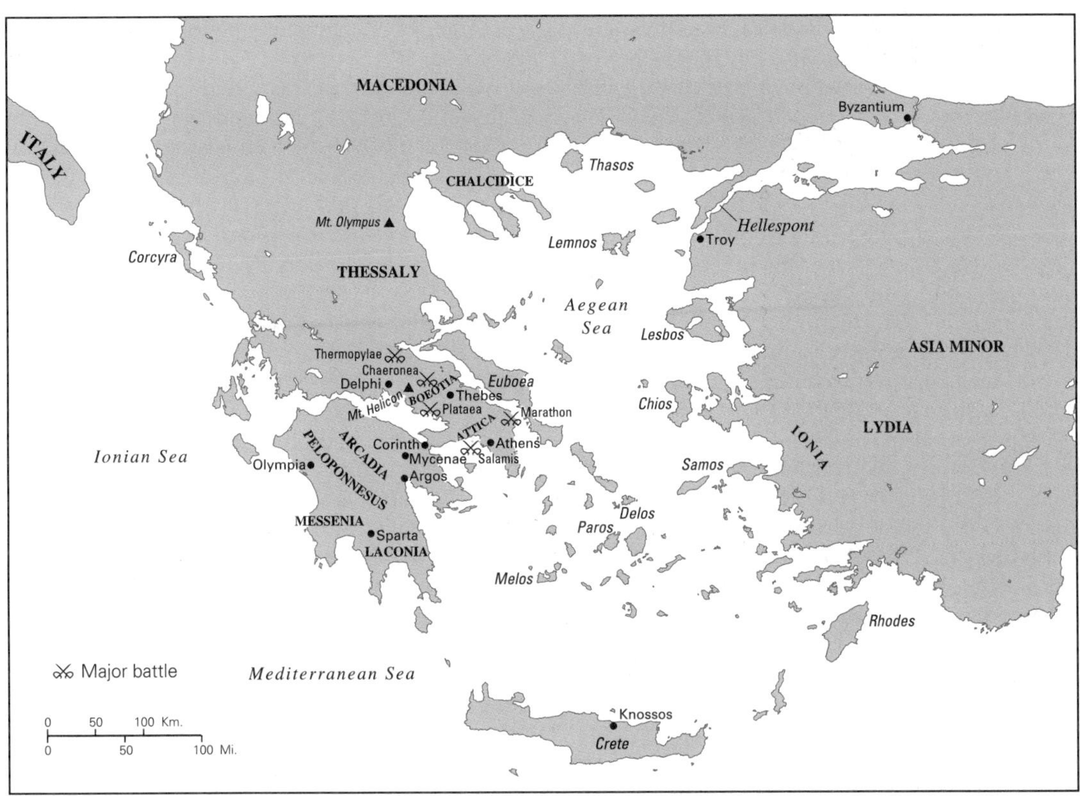

Map 3.2 The Aegean Basin This map shows major battle sites. Note also the Hellespont, where Xerxes' forces crossed into Greece, and Ionia, the coast of Asia Minor, where Greek philosophy was born.

Athenians claimed that the other city-states benefited from Athenian hegemony. Athens forbade member states to withdraw, crushed revolts, and stationed garrisons on the territory of confederate states. It used both tribute from members and the league's treasury to finance public works in Athens.

Although member states did receive protection, were not overtaxed, and enjoyed increased trade, they resented Athenian domination. As the Persian threat subsided, hatred for Athenian imperialism grew. In converting the Delian League into an instrument of Athenian imperialism, Athens may have lost an opportunity to perform a great creative act—forming a broad voluntary confederation that might have forestalled the intercity warfare that gravely weakened Hellenic civilization.

The Mature Athenian Democracy

Athenian imperialism was one consequence of the Persian Wars; another was the flowering of Athenian democracy and culture. Democracy became more firmly entrenched when in 462 B.C. the aristocratic Council of the Areopagus was stripped of its political powers. The Athenian state was a direct democracy, in which the citizens themselves, not elected representatives, made the laws. In the Assembly, which was open to all adult male citizens and which met some forty times a year, Athenians debated and voted on key issues of state; they declared war, signed treaties, and spent public funds. By the middle of the fifth century B.C., the will of the people, as expressed by a majority vote in the Assembly, was supreme. Rejecting the arbitrary rule of tyrants and domination by a small circle of nobles, the Athenians conceived the idea of *isonomy*—equality of political rights for citizens of the polis, that is, the right to vote, to speak before and submit motions to the Assembly, to hold the highest public positions, and to receive equal treatment before the law.

The Council of Five Hundred (which had been established by Cleisthenes to replace Solon's Council of Four Hundred) managed the ports, military installations, and other state properties and prepared the agenda for the Assembly. Because its members were chosen annually by lot and could not serve more than twice in a lifetime, the Council could never supersede the Assembly. Chosen at random, its membership could not become a cabal of the most powerful and ambitious citizens. Some 350 magistrates, also chosen by lot, performed administrative tasks: collecting fines, policing the city, repairing streets, inspecting markets, and so forth. Because of the special competence that their posts required, the ten generals who led the army were not chosen by lot but were elected by the Assembly.

The introduction of pay for government officials marked a great democratic advance. It meant that an average person could afford to leave his job for a year in order to serve on the Council of Five Hundred, on a commission overseeing the administration of the city, or in the law courts.

Athens has been aptly described as a government of amateurs. There were no professional civil servants, no professional soldiers and sailors, no state judges—all legal cases were decided by juries chosen by lot—and no elected lawmakers. The duties of government were performed by ordinary citizens. Such a system rested on the assumption that the average citizen was capable of participating intelligently in the affairs of state and that he would, in a spirit of civic patriotism, carry out his responsibilities to his city. In fifth-century Athens, excellence was equated with good citizenship—a concern for the good of the community that outweighed personal aspirations. Indeed, to a surprisingly large number of Athenians, politics was an overriding concern, and they devoted considerable time and thought to civic affairs. Those who allowed private matters to take precedence over the needs of the community were denounced as useless people living purposeless lives.

Although Athens was a democracy in form, in practice aristocrats continued to dominate political life for most of the fifth century. The generals elected by the people came from noble houses, as did the leading politicians in the Assembly. This situation was not surprising, for aristocrats took for granted a responsibility to exercise leadership and acquired the education, particularly in public speaking and debate, needed to perform this role. Ironically, although it was a struggle against aristocratic power that led to the rise of democracy, aristocratic reformers, like Cleisthenes, not radical commoners, took the lead in this transformation. The economic expansion after the Persian Wars produced a wealthy class of tradesmen, who eventually challenged aristocratic dominance in the Assembly during the last third of the fifth century B.C.

Athenian democracy undoubtedly had its limitations and weaknesses. Modern critics point out that resident aliens were almost totally barred from citizenship and therefore from political participation. Slaves, who constituted about one-fourth of the Athenian population, enjoyed none of the freedoms that Athenians considered so precious. The Greeks regarded slavery as a necessary precondition for civilized life; for some to be free and prosperous, they believed, others had to be enslaved. Whereas people today regard slavery and freedom as contradictory, to the Greeks they were complementary. The large number of slaves available for labor, they believed, permitted free citizens to devote themselves to civic affairs and to fight for the city when needed.

Slaves usually did the same work as Athenian citizens: farming, commerce, manufacturing, domestic chores. Some slaves—the three hundred Scythian archers who made up the police force and those sufficiently educated to serve the state as clerks—enjoyed a privileged position. However, slaves, including preadolescent children, who toiled in the mines suffered a grim fate. In Athens, some slaves were Greeks, but most were foreigners. Slaves were generally prisoners of war and captives of pirates. Sometimes they were foreign children sold by their parents or abandoned infants left to die, a not uncommon practice in ancient Greece and Rome. A person finding the infant might eventually sell the child into slavery.

Athenian women were another group denied legal or political rights. Most Greeks, no doubt, agreed with Aristotle, who said: "[T]he male is by nature superior, and the female inferior; and . . . the one rules and the other is ruled."[10] A girl usually was married at fourteen, to a man twice her age, and the marriage was arranged by a male relative. The wedding day might be the first time that the young bride saw her future husband. Although either spouse could obtain a divorce, the children remained with the father after the marriage was dissolved. Wives did not dine with their husbands and spent much of their time in the women's quarters.

Athenian women were barred from holding public office and generally could not appear in court without a male representative. They could not act in plays, and, when attending the theater, they sat in the rear, away from the men. Greek women received no formal education, although some young women learned to read and write at home. Training in household skills was considered the only education a woman needed. Since it was believed that a woman could not act independently, she was required to have a guardian—normally her father or husband—who controlled her property and supervised her behavior. Convinced that financial dealings were too difficult for women and that they needed to be protected from strangers, men, not women, did the marketing. When a woman left the house, she was usually accompanied by a male. The Athenian wife was treated as a minor; in effect, she was her husband's ward.

Attic Black-Figure Hydria, c. 510 b.c. This hydria, or water jug, shows women drawing water from a fountainhouse. Trips to the fountainhouse provided one of the few opportunities for women to socialize outside the home. (*William Francis Warden Fund. Courtesy Museum of Fine Arts, Boston.*)

Modern critics also point out the failure of Hellenic Greeks to arrive at a conception of what seventeenth- and eighteenth-century liberal thinkers were to call natural or inalienable rights and what are now generally known as human rights. The Greeks limited rights to members of a particular community; they had no awareness of the modern idea that all individuals possess as a birthright basic rights that government must respect.

Ancient critics, too, attacked Athenian democracy. Having no confidence in the ability of the common people to govern, these aristocratic critics equated democracy with mob rule. The Assembly did at times make rash and foolish decisions and was swayed by the oratory of demagogues. For the most part, however, as British historian A. H. M. Jones concludes,

> *the Assembly seems to have kept its head, and very rarely to have broken its rules of procedure. . . . Moreover, the people demanded high standards of its advisors. . . . It was informed advice, and not mere eloquence, that the people expected from rising politicians, and they saw to it that they got it.*[11]

That the Athenians found democracy an indispensable form of government is proved by the paucity of revolts. In the almost two hundred years after Cleisthenes, there were only two attempts to undo the democracy, both made under the stress of the Peloponnesian War and both short-lived.

The flaws in Athenian democracy should not cause us to undervalue its extraordinary achievement. The idea that the state represented a community of free, self-governing citizens remains a crucial principle of Western civilization. Athenian democracy embodied the principle of the legal state—a government based not on force but on laws debated, devised, altered, and obeyed by free citizens.

This idea of the legal state could have arisen only in a society that was aware of and respected the rational mind. In the same way that the Greeks demythicized nature, they also removed myth from the sphere of politics. Holding that government was something that people create to satisfy human needs, the Athenians regarded their leaders neither as gods nor as priests but as men who had demonstrated a capacity for statesmanship. Athens was unique, writes Italian historian Mario Attilio Levi, for Athenians "had the audacity to maintain that human reason is itself the source of legitimacy and therefore of the right to govern and command, in a world in which the only recognized source of legitimacy was the gods."[12]

Both democratic politics and systematic political thought originated in Greece. There people first asked questions about the nature and purpose of the state, rationally analyzed political institutions, speculated about human nature and justice, and discussed the merits of various forms of government. It is to Greece that we ultimately trace the idea of democracy and all that accompanies it: citizenship, constitutions, equality before the law, government by law, reasoned debate, respect for the individual, and confidence in human intelligence.

But there is a fundamental difference between the Greek concept of liberty and our own. We are concerned with protecting the individual from the state, which we often see as a threat to personal freedom and a hindrance to the pursuit of our personal lives. Identifying the good of the individual with the good of the community, the Greeks were not concerned with erecting safeguards against the state; they did not view the state as an alien force, to be feared or to be protected against. Rather, they saw it as a moral association, a second family, which taught proper conduct and enabled them to fulfill their human potential. Given this orientation, they were not much interested in human rights.

Pericles: Symbol of Athenian Democracy

Pericles (c. 495–429 B.C.), a gifted statesman, orator, and military commander, was the central figure in Athenian life during the middle of the fifth century B.C. So impressive was his leadership that this period is called the Age of Pericles. During these years, Athenians achieved greatness in politics, drama, sculpture, architecture, and thought.

In the opening stage of the monumental clash with Sparta, the Peloponnesian War (431–404 B.C.), Pericles delivered an oration in honor of the Athenian war casualties. The oration, as reconstructed by Thucydides, the great Athenian historian of the fifth century B.C., contains a glowing description of the Athenian democratic ideal, which encompassed both civic and personal freedom:

> *We are called a democracy, for the administration is in the hands of the many and not of the few. But while the law secures equal justice to all alike in their private disputes, the claim of excellence is also recognized; and when a citizen is in any way distinguished, he is [selected for] public service . . . as the reward of merit. Neither is poverty a bar, but a man may benefit his country whatever may be the obscurity of his condition. . . . There is no exclusiveness in our public life, and in our private intercourse we are not suspicious of one another, nor angry with our neighbor if he does what he likes; we do not put on sour looks at him which though harmless are unpleasant. . . . a spirit of reverence pervades our public acts; we are prevented from doing wrong by respect for authority and for the laws. . . .*[13]

Throughout the speech, Pericles contrasted the narrow Spartan concept of excellence with the Athenians' humanistic ideal of the full development of the human personality. Unlike Sparta, Athens valued both political freedom and cultural creativity; indeed, as Pericles recognized, freedom released an enormous amount of creative energy, making possible Athens' extraordinary cultural accomplishments. "Our love of what is beautiful does not lead to extravagance, our love of the things of the mind does not make us soft," continued Pericles in praise of Athenian society.[14]

The Decline of the City-States

Although the Greeks shared a common language and culture, they remained divided politically. A determination to preserve city-state sovereignty prevented them from forming a larger political grouping, which might have contained the intercity warfare that ultimately cost the city-state its vitality and independence. But the creation of a Pan-Hellenic union would have required a radical transformation of the Greek character, which for hundreds of years had regarded the city-state as the only suitable political system.

The Peloponnesian War

Athenian control of the Delian League engendered fear in the Spartans and their allies in the Peloponnesian League. Sparta and the Peloponnesian states decided on war because they felt that a dynamic and imperialistic Athens threatened their independence. At stake for Athens was hegemony over the Delian League, which gave Athens political power and contributed to its economic prosperity. Neither Athens nor Sparta anticipated the catastrophic consequences that the war would have for Greek civilization.

The war began in 431 B.C. and ended in 404 B.C., with a temporary and uneasy interlude of peace from 421 to 414 B.C. Possessing superior land forces, the Peloponnesian League invaded Attica and set fire to the countryside. In 430 B.C., a plague, probably coming from Ethiopia by way of Egypt, ravaged Athens, killing about one-third

GRECIAN WARRIORS. The Greek warriors in this vase painting have weapons and armor very much like that used by the Greeks in the Persian Wars. (*Vatican Collection/Scala/Art Resource, NY.*)

of the population, including its leader, Pericles (in 429 B.C.). Because of Athenian sea power and Spartan inability to inflict a crushing defeat on Athenian ground troops, the first stage of the war ended in stalemate. In 421 B.C., the war-weary combatants concluded a peace treaty.

What led to the resumption of the war and the eventual defeat of Athens was the Athenian expedition against Sicily and its largest city, Syracuse. Athenians were intoxicated by an imperialist urge to extend the empire in the west and by prospects of riches. Swayed by speeches that stirred the emotions, the Athenian populace, believing disaster to be impossible and forsaking caution and reason, approved the Sicilian venture. In the words of Thucydides,

> *There was a passion for the enterprise which affected everyone alike. . . . The result of this excessive enthusiasm of the majority was that the few who actually were opposed to the expedition were afraid of being thought unpatriotic if they voted against it, and therefore kept quiet.*[15]

Launched with extravagant expectations, the Sicilian expedition ended in dismal failure. Athens and its allies lost fifty thousand men and two hundred ships in the venture; the expedition also cost Athens all hope of victory in the struggle with Sparta. Fearful that victory in Sicily would increase Athenian manpower and wealth, Sparta had again taken up the sword. Strengthened by financial support from Persia and by the defection of some Athenian allies, Sparta moved to end the war. Finally, its navy decimated and its food supply dwindling, besieged Athens surrendered. Sparta dissolved the Delian League, left Athens with only a handful of ships, and forced the city to pull down its long walls—ramparts designed to protect it against siege weapons. But the Spartans refused to massacre Athenian men and enslave the women and children, as some allies had urged.

The Peloponnesian War shattered the spiritual foundations of Hellenic society. During the course of the long war, men became brutalized, selfish individualism triumphed over civic duty, moderation gave way to extremism, and politics degenerated into civil war.

The deterioration of Greek political life was exemplified by conflicts between oligarchs and democrats. Oligarchs, generally from the wealthier segments of Greek society, wanted to concentrate power in their own hands by depriving the lower classes of political rights. Democrats, generally from the poorer segment of society, sought to preserve the political rights of adult male citizens. Strife between oligarchs and democrats was quite common in the Greek city-states even before the Peloponnesian War. Both sides sought to dominate the Assembly and to manipulate the courts; both resorted to bribery and at times even assassinated opponents. During the Peloponnesian War, these party conflicts erupted into civil war in many cities, including Athens. The moral basis of Hellenic society was wrecked. In the words of Thucydides,

> *Love of power, operating through greed and through personal ambition, was the cause of all these evils. To this must be added the violent fanaticism which came into play once the struggle had broken out. Leaders of parties in professing to serve the public interest . . . were seeking to win the prizes for themselves. In their struggle for ascendancy nothing was barred; terrible indeed were the actions to which they committed themselves, and in taking revenge they went further still. Here they were deterred neither by the claims of justice nor by the interests of the state. . . . Thus neither side had any use for conscientious motives; more interest was shown in those who could produce attractive arguments to justify some disgraceful action. As for the citizens who held moderate views, they were destroyed by both the extreme parties. . . . As the result of these revolutions, there was a general deterioration of character throughout the Greek World.*[16]

Athens shared the political problems of the Greek world during the war. Pericles had provided Athenians with effective leadership in the three decades prior to the war; when the Assembly seemed to support unwise policies, he had won it over with sound arguments. After his death in 429 B.C., the quality of leadership deteriorated. Succeeding statesmen were motivated more by personal ambition than by civic devotion; rather than soberly examine issues, they supported policies that would gain them popularity. Without Pericles' wise statesmanship, the Assembly at times acted rashly, as it did in the case of the Sicilian expedition.

Taking advantage of the decline in morale after the failure of this expedition, oligarchs gained control of Athens in 411 B.C.; a body of citizens, known as the Four Hundred, wielded power. Seeking to deprive the lower classes of political influence, the Four Hundred restricted citizenship to four thousand men. But the crews of

Athenian ships, loyal to democracy, challenged the authority of the Four Hundred, who were forced to flee.

After the defeat of Athens in 404 B.C., oligarchs again gained control, this time with the support of Sparta. A ruling council of thirty men, the so-called Thirty Tyrants, held power. Led by Critias, an extreme antidemocrat, the Thirty trampled on Athenian rights, confiscating property and condemning many people to death. In the winter of 404–403 B.C., returned exiles led an uprising against the Thirty, who were unseated.

The Fourth Century

The Peloponnesian War was the great crisis of Hellenic history. The city-states never recovered from their self-inflicted spiritual wounds. The civic loyalty and confidence that had marked the fifth century B.C. waned, and the fourth century was dominated by a new mentality, which the leaders of the Age of Pericles would have abhorred. A concern for private affairs superseded devotion to the general good of the polis. Increasingly, professionals, rather than ordinary citizens, administered the tasks of government, and mercenaries began to replace citizen soldiers.

The political history of the fourth century can be summed up briefly. Athens, the only state that might have united the Greek world, had lost its chance. A culturally sterile, provincial-minded, and heavy-handed Spartan government lacked the talent to govern the Greeks. In many cities, Sparta replaced democratic governments with pro-Spartan oligarchies under the supervision of a Spartan governor. But Spartan hegemony was short-lived; before long, the Greek city-states had thrown off the Spartan yoke. The quarrelsome city-states formed new systems of alliances and persisted in their ruinous conflicts. Some Greek thinkers, recognizing the futility of constant war, argued that peace should be the goal of Greek politics. But their efforts were in vain.

In addition to wars between city-states, fourth-century Greece experienced a new outbreak of civil wars between rich and poor. Athens largely escaped these ruinous conflicts, but they engulfed many other cities. With good reason, Greek thinkers regarded social discord as the greatest of evils.

While the Greek cities battered one another in fratricidal warfare, a new power was rising in the north—Macedonia. To the Greeks, the Macedonians, a wild mountain people who spoke a Greek dialect and had acquired a sprinkling of Hellenic culture, differed little from other non-Greeks, whom they called barbarians. In 359 B.C., at the age of twenty-three, Philip II (382–336 B.C.) ascended the Macedonian throne. Having spent three years as a hostage in Thebes, Philip had learned the latest military tactics and had witnessed firsthand the weaknesses of the warring Greek states. He converted Macedonia into a first-rate military power and began a drive to become master of the Greeks.

Patient, deceitful, clever, and unscrupulous, Philip gradually extended his power over the Greek city-states. The Greeks did not correctly assess Philip's strength and were slow to organize a coalition against Macedonia, despite the efforts of Demosthenes (c. 384–322 B.C.), the Athenian orator and patriot, who urged the Greeks to unite against this threat to their freedom. In 338 B.C., at Chaeronea, Philip's forces inflicted a decisive defeat on the Greeks, and all of Greece was his. The city-states still existed, but they had lost their independence. The world of the small, independent, self-sufficient polis was drawing to a close, and Greek civilization was taking a different shape.

The Dilemma of Greek Politics

Philip's conquest of the city-states points to fundamental weaknesses of Greek politics. Despite the internal crisis and persistent warfare, the Greeks were unable to fashion any other political framework than the polis. The city-state was fast becoming an anachronism, but the Greeks were unable to see that, in a world moving toward larger states and empires, the small city-state could not compete. An unallied city-state, with its small citizen army, could not withstand the powerful military machine that Philip had created. A challenge confronted the city-states: the need to shape some form of political union, a Pan-Hellenic federation, that would end the suicidal

Profile

Demosthenes

Debates in the Assembly stimulated the development of oratory as an art form in Athens and other city-states. Demosthenes (384–322 B.C.), the greatest of the Greek orators, earned his reputation through disciplined effort, for he was not a naturally gifted speaker. When he first addressed the Assembly, wrote Plutarch, the second-century A.D. biographer, he was "derided for his strange and uncouth style, which was cumbered with long sentences and tortured with formal arguments to a most harsh and disagreeable excess. Besides, he had, it seems, a weakness in his voice, a perplexed and indistinct utterance and a shortness of breath, which by breaking and disjointing his sentences, much obscured the sense and meaning of what he spoke."* But the very determined Demosthenes practiced constantly until he perfected his enunciation and delivery.

Demosthenes' fame rests mainly on his Philippics—speeches delivered over a ten-year period warning Greeks of the threat posed by Philip of Macedon. He urged the city-states of Greece to unite against the common enemy and

Art Resource, NY.

internecine warfare, promote economic well-being, and protect the Greek world from hostile states. Because they could not respond creatively to this challenge, the city-states ultimately lost their independence to foreign conquerors.

The waning of civic responsibility among the citizens was another reason for the decline of the city-states. The vitality of the city-state depended on the willingness of its citizens to put aside private concerns for the good of the community. However, although Athens had recovered commercially from the Peloponnesian War, its citizens had suffered a permanent change in character; the abiding devotion to the polis, which had distinguished the Age of Pericles, greatly diminished during the fourth century. The factional strife, the degeneration of politics into personal ambition, the demagoguery, and the fanaticism that Thucydides had described persisted into the fourth century and were aggravated by the economic discontent of the poor. The Periclean ideal of citizenship dissipated as Athenians neglected the community to concentrate on private affairs or sought to derive personal profit from public office. The decline in civic responsibility could be seen in the hiring of mercenaries to replace citizen soldiers and in the indifference and hesitancy with which Athenians confronted Philip. The Greeks did not respond to the Macedonian threat as they had earlier rallied to fight lamented the deterioration of the Greek character since the heroic struggle against Persia.

> *And we, the Greek community . . . instead of sending embassies to one another about [the danger] and expressing indignation, are in such a miserable state, so intrenched in separate towns, that to this day we can attempt nothing that interest or necessity requires; we cannot combine, or form any association for succour and alliance; we look unconcernedly on the man's growing power, . . . not caring or striving for the salvation of Greece.*†

A passionate patriot, Demosthenes warned his fellow citizens that Philip, an autocratic king, wanted to conquer Athens and put an end to Athenian democracy.

> *there is nothing which [Philip] strives and plots against so much as our constitution, nothing in the world he is so anxious about, as its destruction. . . . first then you must assume that he is an irreconcilable enemy of our constitution and democracy; secondly, you must be convinced that all his operations and contrivances are designed for the injury of our state.*‡

Demosthenes negotiated an alliance between Thebes and Athens, but the two were defeated by Philip at Chaeronea in 338 B.C. Demosthenes, who witnessed the battle, delivered a funeral oration for the Greek dead, but the speech is lost. After the death of Alexander the Great in 323 B.C., Demosthenes helped to organize Greek resistance to Macedonian rule. The Greeks were defeated the following year, and Antipater, the Macedonian governor of Greece, ordered the execution of Demosthenes and other orators who had urged war. The aging orator and passionate patriot took poison.

Demosthenes' speeches served as a model for subsequent orators, including Cicero, Rome's greatest orator. In modern times, patriots and lovers of freedom have evoked Demosthenes' devotion to his city and its free institutions.

---

*Plutarch, *The Lives of Noble Grecians and Romans,* trans. John Dryden, rev. A. H. Clough (New York: Modern Library, n.d.), p. 1025.

†*Demosthenes' Orations,* intro. by John Warrington (London: Dent, Everyman's Library, 1954), Third Philippic, pp. 195–196.

‡Ibid., Fourth Philippic, p. 209.

off the Persian menace because the quality of citizenship had deteriorated.

Greek political life demonstrated the best and worst features of freedom. On the one hand, as Pericles boasted, freedom encouraged active citizenship, reasoned debate, and government by law. On the other, as Thucydides lamented, freedom could degenerate into factionalism, demagoguery, unbridled self-interest, and civil war. Because monarchy deprives people of freedom and self-rule, the Greeks regarded monarchy as a form of government appropriate for uncivilized barbarians. But their political experience showed that free men in a democracy are susceptible to demagogues, will base political decisions on keyed-up emotions rather than on cool reasoning, and are capable of behaving brutally toward political opponents. Moreover, Greek democracy, which valued freedom, was unable to overcome a weakness that has afflicted despotic monarchies: an incautious attitude toward power that causes the state to overreach itself. Such an attitude demonstrated the self-destructive hubris that Greek moralists warned against.

The Athenians, who saw no conflict between imperialism and democracy, considered it natural for stronger states to dominate weaker ones, an attitude that helped to precipitate the destructive Peloponnesian War. A particularly egregious example of this outlook occurred during that war when Athenians decided to invade the island of Melos despite the assurances of the Melians that they represented no threat to Athens. As reported by Thucydides, the Athenian envoys told the Melians that "the strong do what they have the power to do, and the weak accept what they have to accept."[17] When the Melians resisted, the Athenians slaughtered the men, enslaved the women and children, and colonized the territory.

Greek politics also revealed both the capabilities and the limitations of reason. Originally, the polis was conceived as a divine institution in which the citizen had a religious obligation to obey the law. As the rational and secular outlook became more pervasive, the gods lost their authority. When people no longer regarded law as an expression of sacred traditions ordained by the gods but saw it as a merely human contrivance, respect for the law diminished, weakening the foundations of the society. The results were party conflicts, politicians who scrambled for personal power, and moral uncertainty. Recognizing the danger, conservatives insisted that law must again be conceived as issuing from the gods and the city must again treat its ancient traditions with reverence. Although the Greeks originated the lofty ideal that human beings could regulate their political life according to reason, their history, marred by intercity warfare and internal violence, demonstrates the extreme difficulties involved in creating and maintaining a rational society.

Notes

1. James Shiel, ed., *Greek Thought and the Rise of Christianity* (New York: Barnes & Noble, 1968), pp. 5–6.
2. Homer, *The Iliad*, trans. E. V. Rieu (Baltimore: Penguin Books, 1950), p. 23.
3. H. D. F. Kitto, *The Greeks* (Baltimore: Penguin Books, 1957), p. 60.
4. Homer, *The Iliad,* p. 405.
5. Werner Jaeger, *Paideia: The Ideals of Greek Culture,* trans. Gilbert Highet (New York: Oxford University Press, 1945), 1:8.
6. C. M. Bowra, *Homer* (London: Gerald Duckworth, 1972), p. 72.
7. Kitto, *The Greeks*, p. 78.
8. Mason Hammond, *The City in the Ancient World* (Cambridge, Mass.: Harvard University Press, 1972), p. 189.
9. Herodotus, *The Histories*, trans. Aubrey de Sélincourt (Baltimore: Penguin Books, 1954), p. 493.
10. Aristotle, *Politics*, in *Basic Works of Aristotle*, ed., Richard McKeon (New York: Random House, 1941), p. 1132.
11. A. H. M. Jones, *Athenian Democracy* (Oxford: Basil Blackwell, 1969), pp. 132–133.
12. Mario Attilio Levi, *Political Power in the Ancient World* (New York: Mentor Books, 1968), pp. 122–123.
13. Thucydides, *The Peloponnesian War*, trans. B. Jowett (Oxford: Clarendon Press, 1881), bk. 11, chap. 37.
14. Thucydides, *History of the Peloponnesian War*, trans. Rex Warner (Baltimore: Penguin Books, 1954), p. 118.
15. Ibid., p. 382.
16. Ibid., p. 210.
17. Ibid., p. 360.

Suggested Reading

Bowra, C. M., *The Greek Experience* (1957). An excellent introduction to Greek culture and society.

———, *Periclean Athens* (1971). A discussion of Athens at its height.

Claster, J. N., *Athenian Democracy* (1967). A useful collection of readings on the triumphs and failures of Athenian democracy.

Fine, John V. A., *The Ancient Greeks* (1983). An up-to-date, reliable analysis of Greek history.

Finley, M. I., *The Ancient Greeks* (1964). An excellent popular account of Greek civilization.

———, *Early Greece* (1970). A survey of Minoan and Mycenaean civilizations and early Greek history.

Frost, Frank J., *Greek Society* (1987). Social and economic life in ancient Greece.

Grant, Michael, *A Social History of Greece and Rome* (1992). Essays on the rich, the poor, women, slaves, and freedmen and freedwomen.

Hammond, N. G. L., *The Classical Age of Greece* (1975). An interpretation of major developments in Greek history.

History of the Hellenic World (1974–). A multivolume history prepared by leading Greek scholars. It has been translated from the Greek and published by Pennsylvania State University Press. The first volume, *Prehistory and Protohistory*, is excellent for Minoan and Mycenaean civilizations.

Hooper, Finley, *Greek Realities* (1978). A literate and sensitive presentation of Greek society and culture.

Kitto, H. D. F., *The Greeks* (1957). A stimulating survey of Greek life and thought.

———, *Athens: A Portrait of the City in Its Golden Age* (1999). Rich in details and interpretation.

Meier, Christian, *The Greek Discovery of Politics* (1990). Answers the question: How was it that Greek civilization, unlike all others preceding it, gave birth to democracies?

Murray, Oswyn, *Early Greece* (1980). Good on relations with the Near East and lifestyles of the aristocracy.

Nilsson, M. P., *A History of Greek Religion* (1964). A highly regarded work on Greek religion.

Powell, Anton, ed., *The Greek World* (1995). Essays by authorities on all phases of Greek life.

Robinson, C. E., *Hellas* (1948). A useful short survey.

Schein, Seth L., *The Mortal Hero* (1984). An introduction to Homer's *Iliad.*

Starr, Chester G., *The Economic and Social Growth of Early Greece* (1977). Covers the period 800–500 B.C.

Stockton, David, *The Classical Athenian Democracy* (1990). The evolution and nature of Greek democracy.

Taylour, William Lord, *The Mycenaeans* (1983). An account of all phases of Mycenaean life.

Webster, T. B. L., *Athenian Culture and Society* (1973). Discusses Athenian religion, crafts, art, drama, education, and so on.

Willetts, R. F., *The Civilization of Ancient Crete* (1977). An account of all phases of Minoan civilization.

Review Questions

1. What was the legacy of the Mycenaeans to Hellenic civilization?
2. Why is Homer called "the shaper of Greek civilization"?
3. How did the Greek polis break with the theocratic politics of the Near East?
4. Contrast Spartan society with Athenian society.
5. What were the accomplishments of Solon? Pisistratus? Cleisthenes?
6. What was the significance of the Persian Wars?
7. What contradictions do you see between Athenian democratic ideals and Athenian imperialism? Why did no such contradiction exist for the Athenians?
8. Describe the basic features and the limitations of Athenian democracy.
9. Compare and contrast Athenian democracy with American democracy.
10. What were the causes of the Peloponnesian War? What was the significance of the expedition to Sicily? What was the impact of the Peloponnesian War on the Greek world?
11. What problems did the city-states face in the fourth century B.C.?
12. Explain how Greek political life demonstrated both the best and the worst features of freedom and both the capabilities and the limitations of reason.

Chapter 4

Greek Thought: From Myth to Reason

Theater at Epidaurus, Greece, c. 350 B.C. (Hirmer Fotoarchiv, München.)

- **Philosophy**
  The Cosmologists: A Rational Inquiry into Nature
  The Sophists: A Rational Investigation of Human Society
  Socrates: The Rational Individual
  Plato: The Rational Society
  Aristotle: A Synthesis of Greek Thought
- **Art**
- **Poetry and Drama**
  Aeschylus
  Sophocles
  Euripides
  Aristophanes
- **History**
  Herodotus
  Thucydides
- **The Greek Achievement: Reason, Freedom, Humanism**

The Greeks broke with the mythopoeic outlook of the Near East and conceived a new way of viewing nature and human society, which is the basis of the Western scientific and philosophical tradition. After an initial period of mythical thinking, by the fifth century B.C., the Greek mind had gradually applied reason to the physical world and to all human activities. This emphasis on reason marks a turning point for human civilization.

The development of rational thought in Greece was a process, a trend, not a finished achievement. The process began when some thinkers rejected mythical explanations for natural phenomena. The nonphilosophical majority never entirely eliminated the language, attitudes, and beliefs of myth from their lives and thought. For them the world remained controlled by divine forces, which were appeased through cultic practices. Even in the mature philosophy of Plato and Aristotle, mythical modes of thought persisted. What is of immense historical importance, however, is not the degree to which the Greeks successfully integrated the norm of reason, but the fact that they originated this norm, defined it, and consciously applied it to their intellectual and social life.

Philosophy

The first theoretical philosophers in human history emerged in the sixth century B.C., in the Greek cities of Ionia in Asia Minor. Curious about the essential composition of nature and dissatisfied with earlier creation legends, the Ionians sought physical, rather than mythic-religious, explanations for natural occurrences. In the process, they arrived at a new concept of nature and a new method of inquiry. They maintained that nature was not manipulated by arbitrary and willful gods, nor was it governed by blind chance. The Ionians said that there is an intelligible pattern to nature; that nature contains a hidden structure—principles of order or general laws—that governs phenomena; and that these fundamental rules were ascertainable by the human mind. They implied that the origin, composition, and structure of the world can be investigated rationally and systematically. Thus, in seeking to account for rainbows, earthquakes, and eclipses, the Ionians posited entirely naturalistic explanations that excluded the gods. This new outlook marks the beginning of scientific thought.

What conditions enabled the Greeks to make this breakthrough? Perhaps their familiarity with Near Eastern achievements in mathematics and science stimulated their ideas. But this influence should not be exaggerated, says Greek scholar John N. Theodorakopoulos, for Egyptians and Mesopotamians "had only mythological systems of belief and a knowledge of practical matters. They did not possess those pure and crystal-clear products of the intellect which we call science and philosophy. Nor did they have any terminology to describe them."[1] Rooted in mythological thinking, the ancient Near East experienced no eruption of theorizing about nature in pristine philosophical and scientific terms as Greece did beginning in the sixth century B.C. Perhaps the poets' conception of human behavior as subject to universal destiny was extended into the philosophers' belief that nature was governed by law. Perhaps the breakthrough was fostered by the Greeks' freedom from a priesthood and rigid religious doctrines that limit thought. Or perhaps Greek speculative thought was an offspring of the city, because if law governed human affairs, providing balance and order, should not the universe also be regulated by principles of order?

The Cosmologists: A Rational Inquiry into Nature

The first Ionian philosophers are called cosmologists because they sought to discover the underlying principles of the universe: how nature came to be the way it was. They held that some single, eternal, and imperishable substance, which underwent various modifications, gave rise to all phenomena in nature.

Ionian philosophy began with Thales (c. 624–548 B.C.) of Miletus, a city in Ionia. He was a contemporary of Solon of Athens and concerned himself with understanding the order of nature. Thales said that water was the basic element, the underlying substratum of nature, and that through some natural process—similar to the formation of ice or steam—water gave rise to everything else in the world.

Thales revolutionized thought because he omitted the gods from his account of the origins of nature and searched for a natural explanation of how all things came to be. He broke with the commonly held belief that earthquakes were caused by Poseidon, god of the sea, and offered instead a naturalistic explanation for these disturbances: that the earth floated on water and when the water experienced turbulent waves the earth was rocked by earthquakes. Thales was the first person to predict an eclipse of the sun. To do this, he had to dismiss traditional mythical explanations and to grasp a crucial scientific principle—that heavenly objects move in regular patterns, which can be known.

Anaximander (c. 611–547 B.C.), another sixth-century Ionian, rejected Thales' theory that water was the original substance. He rejected any specific substance and suggested that an indefinite, undifferentiated substance, which he called the Boundless, was the source of all things. He believed that from this primary mass, which contained the powers of heat and cold, there gradually emerged a nucleus, the seed of the world. According to Anaximander, the cold and wet condensed to form the earth and its cloud cover, while the hot and dry formed the rings of fire that we see as the moon, the sun, and the stars. The heat from the fire in the sky dried the earth and shrank the seas. From the warm slime on earth arose life, and from the first sea creatures there evolved land animals, including human beings. Anaximander's account of the origins of the universe and nature understandably contained fantastic elements. Nevertheless, by offering a natural explanation for the origin of nature and life and by holding that nature was lawful, it surpassed the creation myths.

Like his fellow Ionians, Anaximenes, who died around 525 B.C., made the transition from myth to reason. He also maintained that a primary substance, air, underlay reality and accounted for nature's orderliness. Air that was rarefied became fire, whereas wind and clouds were formed from condensed air. If the process of condensation continued, it produced water, earth, and eventually stones. Anaximenes also rejected the old belief that a rainbow was the goddess Iris; instead, he saw it as the consequence of the sun's rays falling on dense air.

The Ionians have been called "matter philosophers" because they held that everything issued from a particular material substance. Other sixth-century B.C. thinkers tried a different approach. Pythagoras (c. 580–507 B.C.) and his followers, who lived in the Greek cities in southern Italy, did not find the nature of things in a particular substance but in mathematical relationships. The Pythagoreans discovered that the intervals in the musical scale can be expressed mathematically. Extending this principle of proportion found in sound to the universe at large, they concluded that the cosmos also contained an inherent mathematical order. Thus, the Pythagoreans shifted the emphasis from matter to form, from the world of sense perception to the logic of mathematics. The Pythagoreans were also religious mystics who believed in the immortality and transmigration of souls. Consequently, they refused to eat animal flesh, fearing that it contained former human souls.

Parmenides (c. 515–450 B.C.), a native of the Greek city of Elea in southern Italy, challenged the fundamental view of the Ionians that all things emerged from one original substance. In developing his position, Parmenides applied to philosophical argument the logic used by the Pythagoreans for mathematical thinking. In putting forth the proposition that an argument must be consistent and contain no contradictions, Parmenides became the founder of formal logic.

Despite appearances, asserted Parmenides, reality—the cosmos and all that is within it—is one, eternal, and unchanging. It is made known not through the senses, which are misleading, but through the mind; not through experience, but through reason. Truth could be reached through abstract thought alone. Parmenides' concept of an unchanging reality apprehended by thought alone influenced Plato and is the foundation of metaphysics—the branch of philosophy that attempts to define ultimate reality, or Being.

Parmenides' thought also had religious implications. Although he did not refer to True Being as God, he did ascribe to it the attributes of oneness, transcendence, permanence, and perfection. Such a description of Being abounds with religious meaning. Particularly as developed by Plato, the quest for Being would greatly influence religious thought, including Christian theology, in the ancient world.

Democritus (c. 460–370 B.C.), from the Greek mainland, renewed the Ionians' concern with the world of matter and reaffirmed their confidence in knowledge derived from sense perception—and the senses indicated that change did occur in nature, in contrast to Parmenides' view. But Democritus also retained Parmenides' reverence for reason. His model of the universe consisted of two fundamental realities: empty space and an infinite number of atoms. Eternal, indivisible, and imperceptible, these atoms moved in the void. All things consisted of atoms, and combinations of atoms accounted for all change in nature. In a world of colliding atoms, everything behaved according to mechanical principles. (Of course, Democritus' atomic theory did not derive from any empirical evidence of atoms but was purely speculative.)

Concepts essential to scientific thought thus emerged in embryonic form with Greek philosophers: natural explanations for physical occurrences (Ionians), the mathematical order of nature (Pythagoras), logical proof (Parmenides), and the mechanical structure of the universe (Democritus). By giving to nature a rational, rather than a mythical, foundation and by holding that theories should be grounded in evidence and that one should be able to defend them logically, the early Greek philosophers pushed thought in a new direction. This new approach allowed a critical analysis of theories, whereas myths, accepted unconditionally on faith and authority, did not promote discussion and questioning. For the most part, the early Greek philosophers rejected the old mythical explanations of nature. Nevertheless, when they proclaimed the unity and orderliness of nature and asserted that an ultimate reality underlies the finite world, they were also expressing ideas integral to religious thought.

These early philosophers made possible theoretical thinking and the systematization of knowledge—as distinct from the mere observation and collection of data. The systematization of knowledge extended into several areas. Greek mathematicians, for example, organized the Egyptians' practical experience with land measurements into the logical and coherent science of geometry. They established mathematics as an ordered system based on fundamental premises and necessary connections, and they developed logical procedures for arriving at mathematical proofs.

VASE PAINTING, 520–510 B.C. In this scene painted by the potter Sosias, Achilles is binding up the wounds of his dear friend Patroclus. The artist's careful attention to detail, both physical and psychological, is seen in Patroclus' turned head and open mouth and his propping of the wounded arm. (*Antikenmuseum der Staatlichen Museen/Preussischer Kulturbesitz, Berlin.*)

Both Babylonians and Egyptians had performed fairly complex mathematical operations, but unlike the Greeks, they made no attempt to prove underlying mathematical principles—to demonstrate that certain conclusions must flow from certain hypotheses. In another area, Babylonian priests observed the heavens for religious reasons, believing that the stars revealed the wishes of the gods. The Greeks used the data collected by the Babylonians, but not for a religious purpose; they sought to discover the geometrical laws that govern the motions of heavenly bodies.

A parallel development occurred in medicine. No Near Eastern medical text explicitly attacked magical beliefs and practices. In contrast, Greek doctors, because of the philosophers' work, were able to distinguish between magic and medicine. The school of the Greek physician Hippocrates (c. 460–c. 377 B.C.), located on the island of Cos, off the Asia Minor coast, was influenced by the thought of the early Greek cosmologists. Hippocratic physicians recorded in detail their observations of ill patients, classified symptoms, and predicted the future course of the disease. They also denounced supernatural and magical explanations and cures. The following tract from the school of Hippocrates on epilepsy, which was considered a sacred disease, illustrates the development of a scientific approach to medicine:

> *I am about to discuss the disease called "sacred." It is not, in my opinion, any more divine or sacred than any other disease, but has a natural cause, and its supposed divine origin is due to men's inexperience, and to their wonder at its peculiar character. Now . . . men continue to believe in its divine origin because they are at a loss to understand it. . . . My own view is that those who first attributed a sacred character to this malady were like the magicians, purifiers, charlatans, and quacks of our own day; men who claim great piety and superior knowledge. Being at a loss, and having no treatment which would help, they concealed and sheltered themselves behind superstition, and called this illness sacred, in order that their utter ignorance might not be manifest.*[2]

The Sophists: A Rational Investigation of Human Society

In their effort to understand the external world, the cosmologists had created the tools of reason. These early Greek thinkers were developing a new and profound awareness of the mind's capacity for theoretical thinking. And equally important, they were establishing the mind's autonomy—its ability to inquire into any subject, relying solely on its own power to think. Greek thinkers then turned away from the world of nature and attempted a rational investigation of people and society. The Sophists exemplifed this shift in focus. They were professional teachers who wandered from city to city teaching rhetoric, grammar, poetry, gymnastics, mathematics, and music. The Sophists insisted that it was futile to speculate about the first principles of the universe, for such knowledge was beyond the grasp of the human mind. Instead, they urged that individuals improve themselves and their cities by applying reason to the tasks of citizenship and statesmanship.

The Sophists answered a practical need in

Athens, which had been transformed into a wealthy and dynamic imperial state after the Persian Wars. Because the Sophists claimed that they could teach *political* areté—the skill to formulate the right laws and policies for cities and the art of eloquence and persuasion needed for success in public life—they were sought as tutors by politically ambitious young men, especially in Athens. The Western humanist tradition owes much to the Sophists, who examined political and ethical problems, cultivated the minds of their students, and invented formal secular education.

Traditionally, the Greeks had drawn a sharp distinction between Greeks, the bearers of an enlightened civilization, and uncivilized and immoderate non-Greeks, whom they called barbarians, and held that some people were slaves by nature. The dramatist Euripides expressed these sentiments: "It is natural for Hellenes to rule barbarians and not . . . for barbarians to rule Hellenes. They are a slave race, Hellenes are free."[3] Some Sophists in the fourth century B.C. arrived at a broader conception of humanity. They asserted that slavery was based on force or chance, that people were not slaves or masters by nature, and indeed that all people, Greek and non-Greek, were fundamentally alike.

The Sophists were philosophical relativists—that is, they held that no truth is universally valid. Protagoras, a fifth-century Sophist, said that "man is the measure of all things." By this he meant that good and evil, truth and falsehood, are matters of individual judgment; there are no universal standards that fit all people at all times.

In applying reason critically to human affairs, the Sophists attacked the traditional religious and moral values of Athenian society. Some Sophists taught that speculation about the divine was useless. Others went further, asserting that religion was just a human invention to ensure obedience to traditions and laws. Thus, the Sophist Critias (c. 480–403 B.C.) argued that to deter people from committing "open crimes of violence, . . . a wise and clever man invented fear (of the gods) for mortals, that there might be some means of frightening the wicked, even if they do anything or say or think it in secret. Hence he introduced the Divine (religion), saying that there is a God flourishing with immortal life, . . . who will hear everything said among mortals, and will be able to see all that is done."[4]

The Sophists also applied reason to law, with the same effect: the undermining of traditional authority. The laws of a given city, they asserted, did not derive from the gods; nor were they based on any objective, universal, and timeless standards of justice and good, for such standards did not exist. Each community determined for itself what was good or bad, just or unjust. Beginning with this premise, some Sophists simply urged that laws be changed to meet new circumstances. Some radical Sophists argued that law was merely something made by the most powerful citizens for their own benefit. (Or they said that law was a clever invention of the weak in order to check the strong, who benefited from natural advantages.) This view had dangerous implications: first, law did not need to be obeyed since it rested on no higher principle than might; and second, the strong should do what they have the power to do, and the weak must accept what they cannot resist. Both interpretations were disruptive of community life, for they stressed the selfish interests of the individual over the general welfare of the city.

Some Sophists combined this assault on law with an attack on the ancient Athenian idea of *sophrosyne*—moderation and self-discipline—because it denied human instincts. Instead of moderation, they urged that individuals should maximize pleasure and trample underfoot the traditions that restricted them from fully expressing their desires. As these radical Sophists saw it, the concept of sophrosyne was invented by the weak to enslave nobler natures.

In subjecting traditions to the critique of reason, the radical Sophists triggered an intellectual and spiritual crisis. Their doctrines encouraged loss of respect for authority, disobedience to law, neglect of civic duty, and selfish individualism. These attitudes became widespread during and after the Peloponnesian War, dangerously weakening community bonds.

Socrates: The Rational Individual

In attempting to comprehend nature, the cosmologists had discovered theoretical reason. The Sophists then applied theoretical reason to society. In the process, they created a profound problem for Athens and other city-states: the need to restore the authority of law and a respect for

THE PARTHENON, ATHENS, 447–432 B.C. A masterpiece of the Doric style, the great temple dedicated to Athena Parthenos (the Maiden), the patron goddess of the city, was constructed through the efforts of Pericles. Its cult statue and the sculptural reliefs under its roofline were designed by the outstanding sculptor of the age, Phidias. In post-Hellenistic times, it served as a Christian church and then as a mosque, until it was destroyed in 1687. Between 1801 and 1812, the marble reliefs were removed by the Englishman Lord Elgin and now reside in the British Museum, in London. (*Hirmer Fotoarchiv, München.*)

moral values. Conservatives argued that the only way to do so was by renewing allegiance to the sacred traditions that the Sophists had undermined.

Socrates, one of the most extraordinary figures in the history of Western civilization, took a different position. Born in Athens, probably in 469 B.C., about ten years after the Persian Wars, he was executed in 399 B.C., five years after the end of the Peloponnesian War. His life spanned the glory years of Greece, when Athenian culture and democracy were at their height, as well as the tragic years of the lengthy and shattering war with Sparta.

Both the Sophists and Socrates continued the tradition of reason initiated by the cosmologists, but unlike the cosmologists, both felt that knowledge of the individual and society was more important than knowledge of nature. For both, the old mythological traditions, which had served as a foundation for religion and morality, were no longer valid. Socrates and the Sophists endeavored to improve the individual and thought that this could be accomplished through education. Despite these similarities, Socrates' teaching marks a profound break with the Sophist movement.

Socrates attacked the Sophists' relativism, holding that people should regulate their behavior in accordance with universal values. As he saw it, the Sophists taught skills but had no insights into questions that really mattered: What is the purpose of life? What are the values by which man should live? How does man perfect his character? Here the Sophists failed, said Socrates; they taught the ambitious to succeed in politics, but persuasive oratory and clever reasoning do not instruct a man in the art of living. He felt that the Sophists had attacked the old system of beliefs but had not provided the individual with a satisfactory replacement.

Socrates' central concern was the perfection of individual human character, the achievement of moral excellence. Moral values, for Socrates, did not derive either from a transcendent God, as they did for the Hebrews, or from an inherited mythic-religious tradition. They were attained when the individual regulated his life according to objective standards arrived at through rational reflection: that is, when reason became the formative, guiding, and ruling agency of the soul. For Socrates, true education meant the shaping of character according to values discovered through the active use of reason.

Socrates wanted to subject all human beliefs and behavior to the scrutiny of reason and in this way remove ethics from the realm of authority, tradition, dogma, superstition, and myth. He believed that reason was the only proper guide to the most crucial problem of human existence: the question of good and evil. Socrates taught that rational inquiry—a questioning mind—was a priceless tool, allowing one to test opinions, weigh the merit of ideas, and alter beliefs on the basis of knowledge. To Socrates, when people engaged in critical self-examination and strove tirelessly to perfect their nature, they liberated themselves from prevailing opinions and conventions and based their conduct on convictions that they could rationally defend. Socrates believed that people with questioning minds could not be swayed by sophistic eloquence nor delude themselves into thinking that they knew something when they really did not.

Socrates' fundamental premise was that wrong thinking resulted in wrongdoing and, conversely, that knowledge of what is right gave one the strength of will to do what is right. Critics, including religious thinkers, have castigated this assumption as naive, arguing that Socrates credited others with his own extraordinary inner strength and underestimated the immense power of instinct and passions, which drive people, even those who know better, to do what is wrong.

Dialectics. In urging Athenians to think rationally about the problems of human existence, Socrates offered no systematic ethical theory, no list of ethical precepts. What he did supply was a method of inquiry called *dialectics,* or logical discussion. As Socrates used it, a dialectical exchange between individuals (or with oneself), a *dialogue,* was the essential source of knowledge. It forced people out of their apathy and smugness and made them aware of their ignorance. It compelled them to examine their thoughts critically, confront illogical, inconsistent, dogmatic, and imprecise assertions, and express their ideas in clearly defined terms.

Dialectics affirmed that the acquisition of knowledge was a creative act. The human mind could not be coerced into knowing; it was not a passive vessel into which a teacher poured knowledge. The dialogue compelled the individual to play an active role in acquiring ideas and values by which to live. In a dialogue, individuals became thinking participants in a quest for knowledge. Through relentless cross-examination, Socrates induced his partner in discourse to explain and justify his opinions rationally, for only thus did knowledge become a part of one's being.

Dialogue implied that reason was meant to be used in relations between human beings and that they could learn from each other, help each other, teach each other, and improve each other. It implied further that the human mind could and should make rational choices. To deal rationally with oneself and with others is the distinctive mark of being human. Through the dialectical method, people could make ethical choices, impose rules on themselves, and give form to their existence.

For Socrates, the highest form of excellence was taking control of one's life and shaping it according to ethical values reached through reflection. The good life, the moral life, is attained by the exercise of reason and by the development of intelligence—this precept is the essence of Socratic teaching. Socrates made the individual the center of the universe, reason central to the individual, and moral worth the central aim of human life. In Socrates, Greek humanism found its highest expression.

The Execution of Socrates. Socrates devoted much of his life to what he believed was his mission: pricking the conscience of complacent Athenians and persuading them to think critically about how they lived their lives. "No greater good can happen to a man than to discuss human excellence every day,"[5] he said. Always self-controlled and never raising his voice in anger, Socrates engaged any willing Athenian in conversation about his values. Unlike the Sophists, who were paid professional teachers, Socrates never accepted a fee for his instruction. Through probing questions, he tried to stir people out of their complacency and make them realize how directionless and purposeless their lives were.

For many years, Socrates challenged Athenians without suffering harm, for Athens was generally distinguished by its freedom of speech and thought. In the uncertain times during and immediately after the Peloponnesian War, however, Socrates made enemies. Several of the young men close to him were antidemocrats still mistrusted by some as a threat to the recently restored democracy. When Socrates was seventy, he was accused of corrupting the youth of the city and of not believing in the city's gods but in other, new divinities. Underlying these accusations was the fear that Socrates was a troublemaker, a subversive, a Sophist who threatened the state by subjecting its ancient and sacred values to the critique of thought.

Socrates denied the charges and conducted himself with great dignity at his trial, refusing to grovel and beg forgiveness. Instead, he defined his creed:

> *If you think that a man of any worth at all ought to . . . think of anything but whether he is acting justly or unjustly, and as a good or a bad man would act, you are mistaken. . . . If you were therefore to say to me, "Socrates, . . . We will let you go, but on the condition that you give up this investigation of yours, and philosophy. If you are found following these pursuits again you shall die." I say, if you offered to let me go on these terms, I should reply: . . . As long as I have breath and strength I will not give up philosophy and exhorting you and declaring the truth to every one of you whom I meet, saying, as I am accustomed, "My good friend, you are a citizen of Athens . . . are you not ashamed of caring so much for making of money and for fame and prestige, when you neither think nor care about wisdom and truth and the improvement of your soul?"*[6]

Convicted by an Athenian court, Socrates was ordered to drink poison. Had he attempted to appease the jurors, he probably would have been given a light punishment, but he would not disobey the commands of his conscience and alter his principles even under threat of death.

Socrates did not write down his philosophy and beliefs. We are able to construct a coherent account of his life and ideals largely through the works of his most important disciple, Plato.

Plato: The Rational Society

Plato (c. 429–347 B.C.) used his master's teachings to create a comprehensive system of philosophy, which embraced both the world of nature and the social world. But Plato had a more ambitious goal than Socrates' moral reformation of the individual. He tried to arrange political life according to rational rules and held that Socrates' quest for personal morality could not succeed unless the community was also transformed on the basis of reason. Virtually all the problems discussed by Western philosophers for the past two

ALLEGORY OF THE CAVE. Plato distinguished between a higher world of truth and a lower world of imperfection. He compares people without knowledge of the higher world to prisoners chained to the floor in a dark cave since childhood. Artificial objects, including figures of humans and animals made of wood or stone, are paraded in front of a fire. The prisoners, who cannot turn their heads, can only see the shadows of these objects on the wall in front of them, and they interpret these shadows as reality. When a freed prisoner ascends from the cave into the sunlight (the realm of Truth), he realizes that a totally different reality exists. (*From* The Great Dialogues of Plato, *translated by W. H. D. Rouse. Used by permission of Dutton Signet, a division of Penguin Books USA Inc.*)

millennia were raised by Plato. We focus on two of his principal concerns, the theory of Ideas and the theory of the just state.

Theory of Ideas. Socrates had taught that universal standards of right and justice exist and are arrived at through thought. Building on the insights of his teacher Socrates and of Parmenides, who said that reality is known only through the mind, Plato postulated the existence of a higher world of reality, independent of the world of things that we experience every day. This higher reality, he said, is the realm of Ideas, or Forms—unchanging, eternal, absolute, and universal standards of beauty, goodness, justice, and truth. To live in accordance with these standards constitutes the good life; to know these Forms is to grasp ultimate truth.

Truth resides in this world of Forms and not in the world made known through the senses. For example, a person can never draw a perfect square, but the properties of a perfect square exist in the world of Forms. Also, a sculptor observes many bodies, and they all possess some flaw; in his mind's eye, he tries to penetrate the world of Ideas and to reproduce with art a perfect body. Again, the ordinary person only forms an opinion of what beauty is from observing beautiful things; the philosopher, aspiring to true knowledge, goes beyond what he sees and tries to grasp with his mind the Idea of beauty. Similarly, the ordinary individual has only a superficial understanding of justice or goodness; a true conception of justice or goodness is available only to the philosopher, whose mind can leap from worldly particulars to an ideal world beyond space and time.

Plato saw the world of phenomena as unstable, transitory, and imperfect, whereas his transcendent realm of Ideas was eternal and universally valid. For him, true wisdom was to be obtained through knowledge of the Ideas, not the imperfect reflections of the Ideas perceived with the senses.

A champion of reason, Plato aspired to study human life and arrange it according to universally valid standards. In contrast to Sophist relativism, he maintained that objective and eternal standards do exist. Although Plato advocated the life of reason and wanted to organize society according to rational rules, his writing also reveals a religious-mystical side. At times, Plato seems like a mystic seeking to escape from this world into a higher reality, a realm that is without earth's evil and injustice.

Because Platonism is a two-world philosophy, which believes in a higher world as the source of values and in the soul's immortality, it has had an important effect on religious thought. Christian (as well as Jewish and Muslim) thinkers could harmonize Plato's stress on a higher nonmaterial reality and an immortal soul with their faith. In subsequent chapters, we examine the influence of Platonic otherworldliness on later philosopher-mystics and Christian thinkers.

The Just State. In adapting the rational legacy of Greek philosophy to politics, Plato constructed a comprehensive political theory. What the Greeks had achieved in practice—the movement away from mythic and theocratic politics—Plato accomplished on the level of thought: the fashioning of a rational model of the state.

Like Socrates, Plato attempted to resolve the problem caused by the radical Sophists: the undermining of traditional values. Socrates tried to dispel this spiritual crisis through a moral transformation of the individual, whereas Plato wanted the entire community to conform to rational principles. Plato said that if human beings are to live an ethical life they must do so as citizens of a just and rational state. In an unjust state, people cannot achieve Socratic wisdom, for their souls will mirror the state's wickedness.

Plato had experienced the ruinous Peloponnesian War and the accompanying political turmoil. He saw Athens undergo one political crisis after another; most shocking of all, he had witnessed Socrates' trial and execution. Disillusioned by the corruption of Athenian morality and politics, Plato refused to participate in political life. He came to believe that under the Athenian constitution neither the morality of the individual Athenian nor the good of the state could be enhanced, and that Athens required moral and political reform founded on Socrates' philosophy. Like Socrates, and in contrast to the Sophists' relativism, Plato sought permanent truth and moral certainty.

In his great dialogue *The Republic,* Plato devised an ideal state based on standards that would rescue his native Athens from the evils that had befallen it. *The Republic* attempted to analyze society rationally and to reshape the state so that individuals could fulfill the best within themselves and attain the Socratic goal of moral excellence. For Plato, the just state could not be founded on tradition (for inherited attitudes did not derive from rational standards) or on the doctrine of might being right (a principle taught by radical Sophists and practiced by Athenian statesmen). A just state, for Plato, conformed to universally valid principles and aimed at the moral improvement of its citizens, not at increasing its power and material possessions. Such a state required leaders distinguished by their wisdom and virtue, rather than by sophistic cleverness and eloquence.

Fundamental to Plato's political theory as formulated in *The Republic* was his criticism of Athenian democracy. An aristocrat by birth and temperament, Plato believed that it was foolish to expect the common man to think intelligently about foreign policy, economics, or other vital matters of state. Yet the common man was permitted to speak in the Assembly, to vote, and to be selected, by lot, for executive office. A second weakness of democracy was that leaders were chosen and followed for nonessential reasons, such as persuasive speech, good looks, wealth, and family background.

A third danger of democracy was that it could degenerate into anarchy, said Plato. Intoxicated by liberty, the citizens of a democracy could lose all sense of balance, self-discipline, and respect for law:

> *The citizens become so sensitive that they resent the slightest application of control as intolerable tyranny, and in their resolve to have no master they end up by disregarding even the law, written or unwritten.*[7]

As liberty leads to license, Plato continued, the democratic society will deteriorate morally.

> *The parent falls into the habit of behaving like the child, and the child like the parent: the father is afraid of his sons, and they show no fear or respect for their parents, in order to assert their freedom. . . . To descend to smaller matters, the schoolmaster timidly flatters his pupils, and the pupils make light of their masters. . . . Generally speaking, the young . . . argue with . . . [their elders] and will not do as they are told; while the old, anxious not to be thought disagreeable tyrants, imitate the young and condescend to enter into their jokes and amusements.*[8]

As the democratic city falls into disorder, a fourth weakness of democracy will become evident. A demagogue—often a wealthy, handsome, war hero of noble birth with an ability to stir the multitude with words—will be able to gain power by promising to plunder the rich to benefit the poor. Increasingly the tyrant throws off all constraints and uses his authority to satisfy his desire for power and possessions. To retain his hold over the state, the tyrant

> *begins by stirring up one war after another, in order that the people may feel their need of a leader, and also be so impoverished by taxation that they will be forced to think of nothing but winning their daily bread, instead of plotting against him.*[9]

Because of these inherent weaknesses of democracy, Plato insisted that Athens could not be saved by more doses of liberty. He believed that Athens would be governed properly only when the wisest people, the philosophers, attained power:

> *Unless either philosophers become kings in their countries or those who are now called kings and rulers come to be sufficiently inspired with a genuine desire for wisdom; unless, that is to say, political power and philosophy meet together . . . there can be no rest from troubles . . . for states, nor yet, as I believe, for all mankind.*[10]

Plato rejected the fundamental principle of Athenian democracy: that the average person is capable of participating sensibly in public affairs. People would not entrust the care of a sick person to just anyone, said Plato, nor would they allow a novice to guide a ship during a storm. Yet in a democracy, amateurs were permitted to run the government and to supervise the education of the young. No wonder Athenian society was disintegrating. Plato felt that these duties should be performed only by the best people in the city, philosophers, who would approach human problems with reason and wisdom derived from knowledge of the world of unchanging and perfect Ideas. Only these possessors of truth would be competent to rule, said Plato. Whereas Socrates believed that all people could base their actions on reason and acquire virtue, Plato maintained that only a few were capable of philosophical wisdom and that these few were the state's natural rulers.

The organization of the state, as formulated in *The Republic,* corresponded to Plato's conception of the individual soul, of human nature. Plato held that the soul had three major capacities: reason (the pursuit of knowledge), spiritedness (self-assertion, courage, ambition), and desire (the "savage many-headed monster" that relishes food, sex, and possessions). In the well-governed soul, spiritedness and desire are guided by reason and knowledge—standards derived from the world of Ideas.

Plato divided people into three groups: those who demonstrated philosophical ability should be rulers; those whose natural bent revealed exceptional courage should be soldiers; and those driven by desire, the great masses, should be producers (tradespeople, artisans, or farmers). In what was a radical departure from the general attitudes of the times, Plato held that men and women should receive the same education and have equal access to all occupations and public positions, including philosopher-ruler.

Plato felt that the entire community must recognize the primacy of the intellect and sought to create a harmonious state in which each individual performed what he or she was best qualified to do and preferred to do. This would be a just state, said Plato, for it would recognize human inequalities and diversities and make the best possible use of them for the entire community. Clearly, this conception of justice was Plato's response to the radical Sophists, who taught that justice consisted of the right of the strong to rule in their own interest or that justice was doing whatever one desired.

In *The Republic,* philosophers were selected by

a rigorous system of education open to all children. Those not demonstrating sufficient intelligence or strength of character were to be weeded out to become workers or warriors, depending on their natural aptitudes. After many years of education and practical military and administrative experience, the philosophers were to be entrusted with political power. If they had been properly educated, the philosopher-rulers would not seek personal wealth or personal power; they would be concerned with pursuing justice and serving the community. To prevent the philosopher-rulers from pursuing their own interests rather than the good of the community, they would not be permitted to own property or to have families. Since the children they sired would come from a community of wives, no one would know which child was his.

The philosophers were to be absolute rulers. Although the people would lose their right to participate in political decisions, they would gain a well-governed state, whose leaders, distinguished by their wisdom, integrity, and sense of responsibility, would seek only the common good. Only thus could the individual and the community achieve well-being.

Plato repudiated the fundamental principles of a free community: the right to participate in government, equality before the law, and checks on leaders' power. Even freedom of thought was denied the great mass of people in Plato's state. Philosopher-rulers would search for truth, but the people were to be told clever stories—"noble lies," Plato called them—to keep them obedient. However, the philosopher-rulers, said Plato, would not be seekers of power or wealth. It would not be in their character as wise and virtuous people, the best products of polis education, to behave like ruthless tyrants.

The purpose of *The Republic* was to warn Athenians that without respect for law, wise leadership, and proper education for the young, their city would continue to degenerate. Plato wanted to rescue the city-state from disintegration by recreating the community spirit that had vitalized the polis—and he wanted to recreate it not on the basis of mere tradition but on a higher level, with philosophical knowledge. The social and political institutions of Athens, Plato thought, must be reshaped according to permanent and unalterable ideals of truth and justice, and this could be done only when power and wisdom were joined. He aimed to fashion a just individual and a just state by creating conditions that permitted reason to prevail over the appetites, self-interest, and class and party loyalties.

Aristotle: A Synthesis of Greek Thought

Aristotle (384–322 B.C.) stands at the apex of Greek thought because he achieved a creative synthesis of the knowledge and theories of earlier thinkers. Aristotle studied at Plato's Academy for twenty years. Later, he became tutor to young Alexander the Great, the son of Philip of Macedon. Returning to Athens after Alexander had inherited his father's throne, Aristotle founded a school, the Lyceum.

The range of Aristotle's interests and intellect is extraordinary. He was the leading expert of his time in every field of knowledge, with the possible exception of mathematics. Even a partial listing of his works shows the universal character of his mind and his all-consuming passion to understand the worlds of nature and of humankind: *Logic, Physics, On the Heavens, On the Soul, On the Parts of Animals, Metaphysics, Nicomachean Ethics, Politics, Rhetoric,* and *Poetics.*

Aristotle undertook the monumental task of organizing and systematizing the thought of the Pre-Socratics, Socrates, and Plato. He shared with the natural philosophers a desire to understand the physical universe; he shared with Socrates and Plato the conviction that reason was a person's highest faculty and that the polis was the primary formative institution of Greek life. Out of the myriad of Aristotle's achievements, we discuss only three: his critique of Plato's theory of Ideas, his ethical thought, and his political thought.

Critique of Plato's Theory of Ideas. Like Democritus before him, Aristotle renewed confidence in sense perception, for which Plato had little respect; he wanted to swing the pendulum back from Plato's higher world to the material world. Possessing a scientist's curiosity to understand the facts of nature, Aristotle appreciated the world of phenomena, of concrete things. He respected knowledge obtained through the senses, as the following selection from his observations of a hen's embryo shows:

> *With the common hen after three days and three nights there is the first indication of the embryo. . . . Meanwhile the yolk comes into being . . . and, the heart appears, like a speck of blood, in the white of the egg. This point beats and moves as though endowed with life.*[11]

Aristotle retained Plato's stress on universal principles, but he wanted these principles to derive from human experience with the material world. To the practical and empirically minded Aristotle, the Platonic notion of an independent and separate world of Forms beyond space and time seemed contrary to common sense. To comprehend reality, said Aristotle, one should not escape into another world. For him, Plato's two-world philosophy suffered from too much mystery, mysticism, and poetic fancy; moreover, Plato undervalued the world of facts and objects revealed through sight, hearing, and touch, a world that was important to Aristotle. Like Plato, Aristotle desired to comprehend the essence of things and held that understanding universal principles is the ultimate aim of knowledge. But unlike Plato, he did not turn away from the world of things to obtain such knowledge.

For Aristotle, the Forms were not located in a higher world outside and beyond phenomena but existed in things themselves. He said that through human experience with such things as men, horses, and white objects, the essence of man, horse, and whiteness can be discovered through reason; the Form of Man, the Form of Horse, and the Form of Whiteness can be determined. These universals, which apply to all men, all horses, and all white things, were for both Aristotle and Plato the true objects of knowledge. For Plato, these Forms existed independently of particular objects; the Forms for men or horses or whiteness or triangles or temples existed, whether or not representations of these Ideas in the form of material objects were made known to the senses. For Aristotle, however, universal Ideas could not be determined without examination of particular things. Whereas Plato's use of reason tended to stress otherworldliness, Aristotle tried to bring philosophy back to earth.

By holding that certainty in knowledge comes from reason alone and not from the senses, Plato was predisposed toward mathematics and metaphysics—pure thought, which transcends the world of change and material objects. By stressing the importance of knowledge acquired through the rational examination of sense experience, Aristotle favored the development of empirical sciences—physics, biology, zoology, botany, and other disciplines based on the observation and investigation of nature and the recording of data. Aristotle maintained that theory must not conflict with facts and must make them more intelligible, and that it was the task of science to arrange facts into a system of knowledge.

Ethical Thought. Like Socrates and Plato, Aristotle believed that a knowledge of ethics was possible and that it must be based on reason, for this is what distinguishes human beings from other forms of life. For him, ethical thought derived from a realistic appraisal of human nature and a commonsense attitude toward life. In *Nicomachean Ethics,* he offered this appraisal, as well as a practical guide to proper conduct. The good life, for Aristotle, was the examined life; it meant making intelligent decisions when confronted with specific problems. Individuals could achieve happiness when they exercised the distinctively human trait of reasoning, when they applied their knowledge relevantly to life, and when their behavior was governed by intelligence and not by whim, tradition, or authority.

Aristotle recognized that people are not entirely rational, that the human personality reveals a passionate element, which can never be eradicated or ignored. Aristotle held that surrendering completely to desire meant descending to the level of beasts, but that denying the passions and living as an ascetic was a foolish and unreasonable rejection of human nature. He maintained that by proper training people could learn to regulate their desires. They could achieve moral well-being, or virtue, when they avoided extremes of behavior and rationally chose the way of moderation, which he defined as the mean between two extremes. For example, in one extreme, some people "become angry at the wrong things, more than is right, and longer, and cannot be appeased until they inflict vengeance or punishment." In the other extreme, foolish and slavish people endure every insult without defending themselves. Between these extremes is "the man who is angry at the right thing and with the right people, and, further as he ought, when he ought, and as long as he ought. . . . [T]he good-tempered man tends to be unperturbed and not to be led by passion."[12] "Nothing in excess" is the key to Aristotle's ethics.

Aristotle believed that the contemplative life of the philosopher would yield perfect happiness. The pursuit of philosophical wisdom and beauty, he stated, offered "pleasures marvelous for their purity and their enduringness."[13] But Aristotle did not demand more from an individual than human nature would allow. He did not set impossible standards for behavior, recognizing that all persons cannot pursue the life of contemplation, for some lack sufficient leisure or intelligence. However, by applying reason to human affairs, all individuals could experience a good life.

Political Thought. Aristotle's *Politics* complements his *Ethics*. To live the good life, he said, a person must do so as a member of a political community. Only the polis would provide people with an opportunity to lead a rational and moral existence, that is, to fulfill their human potential. With this assertion, Aristotle demonstrated a typically Greek attitude. At the very moment when his pupil Alexander the Great was constructing a world-state that unified Greece and Persia, Aristotle defended the traditional system of independent city-states. Indeed, his *Politics* summed up the polis-centered orientation of Hellenic civilization.

Also in typically Greek fashion, Aristotle did not want women to participate in the political life of the city. Unlike Plato, who, in *The Republic,* wished to give women an equal opportunity with men, Aristotle, in his *Politics,* put women in an inferior category and maintained that the free male should rule over women. Though Aristotle taught that all human beings share in a rational soul, he felt that women, along with children and slaves, shared in it to a lesser degree:

> *[A]lthough the parts of the soul are present in all of them, they are present in different degrees. For the slave has no deliberative faculty at all; the woman has, but it is without authority, and the child has, but it is immature. . . . Clearly, then, moral virtue belongs to all of them; but the temperance of a man and of a woman, or the courage and justice of a man and of a woman, are not, as Socrates maintained, the same; the courage of a man is shown in commanding, of a woman in obeying. . . . All classes must be deemed to have their special attributes, as the poet says of women, "Silence is a woman's glory," but this is not equally the glory of man.*[14]

Like Plato, Aristotle presumed that political life could be rationally understood and intelligently directed. In *Politics,* as in *Ethics,* he adopted a commonsense, practical attitude. He did not aim at utopia but wanted to find the most effective form of government for most men in normal circumstances. Exemplifying the polis outlook, Aristotle held that enhancing the good of the community is nobler and more virtuous than doing good for oneself, however worthy the act.

Aristotle emphasized the importance of the rule of law. He placed his trust in law rather than in individuals, for they are subject to passions. Aristotle recognized that at times laws should be altered, but he recommended great caution; otherwise, people would lose respect for law and legal procedure:

> *For the law has no power to command obedience except that of habit, which can only be given by time, so that a readiness to change from old to new laws enfeebles the power of the law.*[15]

Tyranny and revolution, Aristotle said, can threaten the rule of law and the well-being of the citizen. To prevent revolution, the state must maintain

> *the spirit of obedience to law, more especially in small matters; for transgression creeps in unperceived and at last ruins the state. [This cannot be done] unless the young are trained by habit and education in the spirit of the constitution. [To live as one pleases] is contradictory to the true interests of the state. . . .*
>
> *Men should not think it slavery to live according to the rule of the constitution, for it is their salvation.*[16]

Aristotle held "that the best political community is formed by citizens of the middle class [those with a moderate amount of property], and that those states are likely to be well-administered in which the middle class is large and stronger if possible than the other classes [the wealthy and the poor].” Both the rich, who excel in “beauty, strength, birth, [and] wealth,” and the poor, who are “very weak or very much disgraced [find it] difficult to follow rational principle. Of these two the one sort grow into violence and great criminals, the other into rogues and petty rascals.” The rich are unwilling “to submit to authority . . . for when they are boys, by reason of the luxury in which they are brought up, they never learn even at school, the habit of obedience.” Consequently, the wealthy “can only rule despotically.” On the other hand, the poor “are too degraded to command and must be ruled like slaves.”[17] Middle-class citizens are less afflicted by envy than the poor and are more likely than the rich to view their fellow citizens as equals.

Art

The classical age of Greek art spans the years from the end of the Persian Wars (479 B.C.) to the death of Alexander the Great (323 B.C.). During this period, standards were established that would dominate Western art until the emergence of modern art in the late nineteenth century.

Greek art coincided with Greek achievement in all other areas. Like Greek philosophy and politics, it too applied reason to human experience and made the transition from a mythopoeic-religious world-view to a world perceived as orderly and rational. It gradually transformed the supernatural religious themes with which it was at first preoccupied into secular human themes. Classical art was representational—that is, it strove to imitate reality, to represent the objective world realistically, as it appeared to the human eye.

Artists carefully observed nature and human beings and sought to achieve an exact knowledge of human anatomy; they tried to portray accurately the body at rest and in motion. They knew when muscles should be taut or relaxed, one hip lower than the other, the torso and neck slightly twisted—in other words, they succeeded in transforming marble or bronze into a human likeness that seemed alive. Yet although it was realistic and naturalistic, Greek art was also idealistic, aspiring to a finer, more perfect representation of what was seen, depicting the essence and form of a thing more truly than it actually appeared. Thus, a Greek statue resembled no specific individual but revealed a flawless human form, without wrinkles, warts, scars, or other imperfections.

In achieving an accurate representation of objects and in holding that there were rules of beauty that the mind could discover, the Greek artist employed an approach consistent with the new scientific outlook. The Greek temple, for example, is an organized unity obeying nature’s laws of equilibrium and harmony; classical sculpture captures the basic laws that govern life in motion. Such art, based on reason, which draws the mind’s attention to the clear outlines of the outer world, also draws attention to the mind itself, making human beings the center of an intelligible world and the masters of their own persons.

Greek artists, just like Greek philosophers, proclaimed the importance and creative capacity of the individual. They exemplified the humanist spirit that characterized all aspects of Greek culture. Classical art placed people in their natural environment, made the human form the focal point of attention, and exalted the nobility, dignity, self-assurance, and beauty of the human being.

Poetry and Drama

Through their awareness of human personality, poets and dramatists, like philosophers and artists, gave expression to the rise of the individual. One of the earliest and best of the Greek poets was Sappho, a woman who lived around 600 B.C. on the island of Lesbos. Sappho established a school to teach music and singing to well-to-do girls and to prepare them for marriage. With great tenderness, Sappho wrote poems of friendship and love: “Some say the fairest thing on earth is a troop of horsemen, others a band of foot-soldiers, others a squadron of ships. But I say the fairest thing is the beloved.”[18] And of her daughter Cleïs, she wrote:

> *I have a child; so fair*
> *As golden flowers is she,*
> *My Cleïs, all my care.*
> *I’d not give her away*
> *For Lydia’s* wide sway*
> *Nor lands men long to see.*[19]

Sappho’s love poetry, addressed also to women,

*Ancient country in Asia Minor.

Profile

Hesiod

The poet Hesiod (c. 700 B.C.) lived on a farm in Boetia, in central Greece, and wrote two major poems. *Theogony* deals with the formation of the universe, and *Works and Days* depicts the life of peasants.

Theogony is replete with mythical imagery, but for several reasons scholars regard it as a precursor of Greek philosophy. First, in explaining the origins of the world through the genealogy of the gods, Hesiod produced an ordered and structured mythology that can be interpreted as nascent rational speculation. Second, the gift of law bestowed by Zeus on humanity can be viewed as an early expression of natural law—the recognition of both a physical and a moral order inherent in the universe. Crucial for philosophic thought, the concept of natural law that Hesiod expressed in mythical-religious terms was explicitly formulated in the rational categories of philosophy by Greek thinkers after Hesiod.

Whereas Homer's epics concentrate on heroes striving to win honor as defined by a chivalric aristocratic ideal, Hesoid's later poem, *Works and Days,* describes the daily ordeal of common folk struggling to feed their families. A man of the soil, Hesiod maintains that honest labor promotes the good life.

Although he was generally pessimistic, Hesiod believed that human beings could improve their lot if they embraced justice, which "is proved the best thing they have." An awareness of justice is what distinguishes human beings from other creatures:

You, Perses, should store away in your mind
all that I tell you,
and listen to justice, and put away
all notions of violence.
Here is the law, as Zeus established it
for human beings;
as for fish, and wild animals, and the flying
birds,
they feed on each other, since there is no idea
of justice among them;

indicates that she was bisexual. This form of sexual behavior was tolerated in ancient Greece, says classicist Lyn Hatherly Wilson, "because it was not procreative, because it did not alter a woman's virginal status, or affect her entry into marriage and male/female relations, except in ways that were considered positive."[20] Sappho was the most prominent female poet in the ancient world. She was depicted on coins and in art, and Plato praised the beauty of her lyric poetry. Sometimes, however, she was treated in an uncomplimentary way by comic playwrights who thought it inappropriate for a woman to write poetry. Her influence endured for centuries: the Roman poets Catullus, Horace, and Ovid alluded to her.

Pindar (c. 518–438 B.C.) was another Greek lyric poet. In his poem of praise for a victorious athlete, Pindar expressed the aristocratic view of excellence. Although life is essentially tragic—triumphs are short-lived, misfortunes are many, and ultimately death overtakes all—man must still demonstrate his worth by striving for excellence:

He who wins of a sudden, some noble prize
In the rich years of youth
Is raised high with hope; his manhood takes
wings;
He has in his heart what is better than wealth
But brief is the season of man's delight.
Soon it falls to the ground;
Some dire decision uproots it.
—Thing of a day! such is man: a shadow in a
dream.
Yet when god-given splendour visits him
A bright radiance plays over him, and how
sweet is life![21]

The high point of Greek poetry is drama, an art

Art Resource, NY.

but to men he gave justice, and she in the end is
proved the best thing
they have. If a man sees what is right and
is willing to argue it,
*Zeus of the wide brows grants him prosperity.**

Human beings are faced with the choice between *Diké* (straight judgment and justice), which safeguards society, and *Hubris* (excessive pride), which destroys it. Honoring justice is what distinguishes a civilized society from a state of savagery.

Throughout *Theogony* and *Works and Days,* Hesiod used the language and imagery of myth to express curiosity about the genesis of the universe, concern for justice, and awareness of a universal moral order. In succeeding centuries, Greek thinkers would discuss these issues using the language and categories of philosophy.

---

*Hesiod, *Works and Days,* in *Hesiod,* trans. Richard Lattimore (Ann Arbor: University of Michigan Press, 1973), p. 51.

form that originated in Greece. The Greek dramatist portrayed the sufferings, weaknesses, and triumphs of individuals. Just as a Greek sculptor shaped a clear visual image of the human form, so a Greek dramatist brought the inner life of human beings, their fears and hopes, into sharp focus and tried to find the deeper meaning of human experience. Thus, both art and drama evidenced the growing self-awareness of the individual.

Drama originated in the religious festivals honoring Dionysus, the god of wine and agricultural fertility. A profound innovation in these sacred performances, which included choral songs and dances, occurred in the last part of the sixth century B.C. when Thespis, the first actor known to history, stepped out of the chorus and engaged it in dialogue. By separating himself from the choral group, Thespis demonstrated a new awareness of the individual.

With only one actor and a chorus, however, the possibilities for dramatic action and human conflicts were limited. Then Aeschylus introduced a second actor in his dramas, and Sophocles a third. Dialogue between individuals thus became possible. The Greek actors wore masks, and by changing them, each actor could play several roles in the same performance. This flexibility allowed the dramatists to depict the clash and interplay of human wills and passions on a greater scale. By the middle of the fifth century B.C., tragedies were performed regularly as civic festivals. The audience sat on wooden bleachers in an open-air, hillside theater (*theatron*). The acoustics of these stone theaters was so superb that a clear voice projected from the front could be heard, without amplification, in the last row. In the staging of these tragedies, the all-male chorus generally danced and sang in a circular area called the *or-*

FLOOR MOSAIC DEPICTING DIONYSUS, THE PATRON GOD OF THE THEATER. The panther's snarl, claws, and craning neck convey a fierceness that vividly contrasts with Dionysus' serene manner. (*Archeological Receipts Fund, Athens.*)

chestra ("dancing place"), which encircled an altar. Their costumes consisted of goat skins (only later did the costumes become elaborate), larger-than-life masks, and elevated shoes.

Because of the grandeur of the dramatists' themes, the eminence of their heroes, and the loftiness of their language, Greek spectators felt intensely involved in the tragedies of the lives portrayed. What they were witnessing went beyond anything in their ordinary lives, and they experienced the full range of human emotions.

A development parallel to Socratic dialectics—dialogue between thinking individuals—occurred in Greek drama. Through the technique of dialogue, early dramatists first pitted human beings against the gods and destiny. Later, by placing characters in conflict with each other, dramatists arrived at the idea of individuals as active subjects responsible for their behavior and decisions, which were based on their own feelings and thoughts. Greek tragedy evolved as a continuous striving toward humanization and individualization.

Like the natural philosophers, Greek dramatists saw an inner logic in the universe and called it Fate or Destiny. When people were stubborn, narrow-minded, arrogant, or immoderate, they were punished. The order in the universe required it, said Sophocles:

The man who goes his way
Overbearing in the word and deed,
Who fears no justice,
Honors no temples of the gods—
May an evil destiny seize him.
And punish his ill-starred pride.[22]

In being free to make decisions, the dramatist says, individuals have the potential for greatness, but in choosing wrongly, unintelligently, they bring disaster on themselves and others. Also like philosophy, Greek tragedy entailed rational reflection. Tragic heroes were not passive victims of fate. They were thinking human beings who felt a need to comprehend their position, explain the reasons for their actions, and analyze their feelings.

The essence of Greek tragedy lies in the tragic hero's struggle against cosmic forces and insurmountable obstacles, which eventually crush him. But what impressed the Greek spectators (and impresses today's readers and viewers of Greek drama) was not the vulnerability or weaknesses of human beings, but their courage and determination in the face of these forces.

Aeschylus

Aeschylus (525–456 B.C.), an Athenian nobleman, had fought in the battle of Marathon. He wrote more than eighty plays, of which only seven survive. They have common themes. As an Athenian patriot, Aeschylus urged adherence to traditional religious beliefs and moral values. Like Solon, the statesman, he believed that the world was governed by divine justice, which could not be violated with impunity; when individuals evinced *hubris* (overweening pride or arrogance), which led them to overstep the bounds of moderation, they must be punished. Another principal theme was that through suffering came knowledge: the terrible consequences of sins against the divine order should remind all to think and act with moderation and caution.

Aeschylus' play *The Persians* dealt with an actual event, the defeat of Xerxes, the Persian emperor, by the Greeks. Xerxes' intemperate ambition to become master of Asia and Greece conflicted with the divine order of the universe. For this hubris, Xerxes must pay:

A single stroke has brought about the ruin of great
Prosperity, the flower of Persia fallen and gone.[23]

The suffering of Xerxes should make people aware of what they can and cannot do:

And heaps of corpses even in generations hence
Will signify in silence to the eyes of men
That mortal man should not think more than mortal thoughts.
For hubris blossomed forth and grew a crop of ruin,
And from it gathered in a harvest full of tears.

In face of this, when Xerxes, who lacks good sense, returns
Counsel him with reasoning and good advice,
To cease from wounding God with overboastful rashness.[24]

Whereas Aeschylean drama dealt principally with the cosmic theme of the individual in conflict with the moral universe, later dramatists, while continuing to use patterns fashioned by Aeschylus, gave greater attention to the psychology of the individual.

Sophocles

Another outstanding Athenian dramatist was Sophocles (c. 496–406 B.C.). His greatness as a playwright lay in both the excellence of his dramatic technique and the skill with which he portrayed character. The people that he created possessed violent passions and tender emotions; they were noble in their nature, though their actions showed human frailty. Sophocles consciously formulated a standard of human excellence: individuals should shape their character in the way a sculptor shapes a form, according to laws of proportion. Sophocles felt that when these principles of harmony were violated by immoderate behavior, a person's character would be thrown off balance and misfortune would strike. The physical world and human activities obey laws, said Sophocles, and human beings cannot violate these laws with impunity.

Whereas Aeschylus concentrated on religious matters and Euripides (see below) dealt with social issues, Sophocles wrote about the perennial problem of well-intentioned human beings struggling valiantly, but unwisely and vainly, against the tide of fate. His characters, bent on some action fraught with danger, resist all appeals to caution and inescapably meet with disaster.

In *Oedipus Rex,* first performed about 429 B.C., Sophocles probes deeply into the human psyche. Oedipus is warned not to pursue the mystery of his birth but insists on searching for the truth about himself: "Nothing will move me. I will find the whole truth." (He had unsuspectingly killed his father and married his mother.*) For this determination, born more of innocence than arrogance, he will suffer. Events do not turn out, as Oedipus discovers, the way a person thinks and desires that they should; the individual is impotent before a relentless fate, which governs human existence. It seems beyond imagining that Oedipus, whom all envied for his intelligence, courage, and good works, would suffer such dreadful misfortune.

But tragedy also gives Oedipus the strength to assert his moral independence. Although struck down by fate, Oedipus remains an impressive figure. The tragedy's catharsis (the purging of the audience's emotions through a work of art) comes from Oedipus' choice of his own punishment, self-inflicted blindness. Oedipus demonstrates that he still possesses the distinctly human qualities of choosing and acting, that he still remains a free man responsible for his actions. Despite his misery, Oedipus is able to confront a brutal fate with courage and to demonstrate nobility of character.

Euripides

The rationalist spirit of Greek philosophy permeated the tragedies of Euripides (c. 485–406 B.C.). Like the Sophists, Euripides subjected the problems of human life to critical analysis and challenged human conventions. It was this critical spirit that prompted the traditionalist Aristophanes (see below) to attack Euripides for introducing the art of reasoning into tragedy. The role of the gods, women's conflicts, the horrors of war, the power of passion, and the prevalence of human suffering and weakness were carefully scrutinized in Euripides' plays. Euripides blends a poet's insight with a psychologist's probing to reveal the tangled world of human passions and souls in torment. Thus, in *Medea,* he presents the deepest feelings of a Greek woman:

> *It was everything to me to think well of one man,*
> *And he, my own husband, has turned out wholly vile.*
> *Of all things which are living and can form a judgement*
> *We women are the most unfortunate creatures.*
> *Firstly, with an excess of wealth it is required*
> *For us to buy a husband and take for our bodies*
> *A master; for not to take one is even worse.*
> *And now the question is serious whether we take*
> *A good or bad one; for there is no easy escape*
> *For a woman, nor can she say no to her marriage.*
> *She arrives among new modes of behaviour and manners,*
> *And needs prophetic power, unless she has learnt at home,*
> *How best to manage him who shares the bed with her.*
> *And if we work out all this well and carefully,*
> *And the husband lives with us and lightly bears his yoke,*
> *Then life is enviable. If not, I'd rather die.*
> *A man, when he's tired of the company in his home,*
> *Goes out of the house and puts an end to his boredom*
> *And turns to a friend or companion of his own age.*
> *But we are forced to keep our eyes on one alone.*

*Sigmund Freud's interpretation of the Oedipus story has had a profound impact on psychoanalytic theory: "[Oedipus'] destiny moves us only because it might have been ours. . . . It is the fate of all of us, perhaps, to direct our first sexual impulse towards our mother and our first hatred and . . . murderous wish against our father. Our dreams convince us that this is so" (*The Interpretation of Dreams*).

What they say of us is that we have a peaceful time
Living at home, while they do the fighting in war.
How wrong they are! I would very much rather stand
Three times in the front of battle than bear one child.[25]

Euripides recognized the power of irrational, demonic forces that seethe within people—what he called "the bloody Fury raised by fiends of Hell."[26] A scorned Medea, seeking revenge against her husband by murdering their children, says:

I know indeed what evil I intend to do,
But stronger than all my afterthoughts is my fury,
Fury that brings upon mortals the greatest evils.[27]

In his plays, Euripides showed that the great tragedy of human existence is that reason can offer only feeble resistance against these compelling, relentless, and consuming passions. The forces that destroy erupt from the volcanic nature of human beings.

A second distinctive feature of Euripidean tragedy is its humanitarianism. No other Greek thinker expressed such concern for a fellow human being, such compassion for human suffering. In *The Trojan Women,* Euripides depicted war as agony and not glory, and the warrior as brutish and not noble. He described the torments of women, for whom war meant the loss of homes, husbands, children, and freedom. In 416 B.C., Athens massacred the men of the small island of Melos, sold its women and children into slavery, and sacked the city. *The Trojan Women,* performed a year later, warned Athenians:

How are ye blind,
Ye treaders down of cities, ye that cast
Temples to desolation, and lay waste
Tombs, the untrodden sanctuaries where lie
The ancient dead; yourselves so soon to die![28]

By exposing war as barbaric, Euripides was expressing his hostility to the Athenian leaders who persisted in continuing the disastrous Peloponnesian War.

Aristophanes

Aristophanes (c. 448–c. 380 B.C.) was the greatest of the Greek comic playwrights. He lampooned Athenian statesmen and intellectuals, censured government policies, and protested against the decay of traditional Athenian values. Behind Aristophanes' sharp wit lay a deadly seriousness, for there was much in Athens during the Peloponnesian War that angered him. As an aristocrat, he was repelled by Cleon, the common tanner who succeeded Pericles. As an admirer of the ancient values of honor, duty, and moderation, he was infuriated by corruption, which he attributed to the Sophists. As a man of common sense, he recognized that the Peloponnesian War must end. In the process of serving as a social critic, Aristophanes wrote some of the most hilarious lines in world literature.

In *Lysistrata,* an antiwar comedy, the women of Greece agree to abstain from having sexual relations with their husbands to compel the men to make peace. Lysistrata reveals the plan:

For if we women will but sit at home,
*Powdered and trimmed, clad in our daintiest lawn,**
Employing all our charms, and all our arts
To win men's love, and when we've won it, then
Repel them firmly, till they end the war,
We'll soon get Peace again, be sure of that.[29]

After the plan has been implemented, many women become "husband-sick" and seek to desert the temple where they have gathered. But the men also suffer:

Oh me! these pangs and paroxysms of love,
Riving my heart, keen as a torturer's wheel![30]

Through these unorthodox methods, the women achieve their goal, peace. Performed during the darkest days of the war, this play reminded its audiences to concentrate their efforts in the real world on securing peace.

In *The Clouds,* Aristophanes ridiculed the Sophist method of education both for turning the

*Fine linen dress

youth away from their parents' values and for engaging the youth in useless, hair-splitting logic. To Aristophanes, the worst of the Sophists was Socrates, who is depicted in *The Clouds* as a fuzzy-minded thinker with both feet planted firmly in the clouds. Socrates is made to look ridiculous, a man who walks on air, contemplates the sun, and teaches such absurd things as "Heaven is one vast fire extinguisher" or "How many feet of its own a flea could jump." The Sophists in the play teach only how "to succeed just enough for my need and to slip through the clutches of the law." A student of these Sophists becomes "a concocter of lies . . . a supple, unprincipled, troublesome cheat."[31] To Aristophanes, Socrates was a subversive who caused Athenians to repudiate civil morality and to speculate about nonsense questions. Clearly, Aristophanes admired the Athens that had bested the Persians at the battle of Marathon and feared the rationalism that Euripides, the Sophists, and Socrates had injected into Athenian intellectual life.

History

The Mesopotamians and the Egyptians kept annals that purported to narrate the deeds of gods and their human agents, the priest-kings or god-kings. These chronicles, filled with religious sayings, royal records, and boastful accounts of military campaigns, are devoid of critical analysis and interpretaton. The Hebrews valued history, but believing that God acted in human affairs, they did not remove historical events from the realm of religious-mythical thought. The Greeks initiated a different approach to the study of history. For the Greeks, history was not the record of God's wrath or benevolence—as it was for the Hebrews—but the actions solely of human beings. As the gods were eliminated from the nature philosophers' explanations for the origins of things in the natural world, mythical elements were also removed from the writing of history.

Greek historians asked themselves questions about the deeds of people, based their answers on available evidence, and wrote in prose, the language of rational thought. They not only narrated events but also examined them, says Italian historian Arnaldo Momigliano, with a "critical attitude . . . enabling [them] to distinguish between facts and fancies. To the best of my knowledge no historiography earlier than the Greek or independent of it developed these critical methods."[32] In the same spirit, British philosopher and historian R. G. Collingwood states:

> *The Greeks quite clearly and consciously recognized both that history is, or can be, a science, and that it has to do with human actions. Greek history is not legend, it is research; it is an attempt to get answers to definite questions about matters of which one recognizes oneself as ignorant. It is not theocratic, it is humanistic; the matters inquired into are not of gods, they are of men. Moreover, it is not mythical. The events inquired into are not events in a dateless past, at the beginning of things; they are events in a dated past, a certain number of years ago. This is not to say that legend, either in the form of theocratic history or in the form of myth, was a thing foreign to the Greek mind. . . . But what is remarkable about the Greeks was not the fact that their historical thought contained a certain residue of elements which we should call non-historical, but the fact that side by side with these, it contained elements of what we call history.*[33]

In several respects, however, the Greeks were unhistorical. To them, history moved in cycles; events and periods repeated themselves. Unlike the Hebrews, they had little awareness of historical uniqueness and progression. Nor was history as vital to the Greeks as it was to the Hebrews. Greek philosophers preferred fixing their minds on eternal and changeless truths rather than on the vicissitudes of history. Aristotle said that poetry (which also included drama) is "more philosophic and of greater import than history, since its statements are of the nature of universals," whereas histories deal only with particular events.[34]

Herodotus

Often called the "father of history," Herodotus (c. 484–c. 424 B.C.) wrote a history of the Persian Wars. Herodotus valued the present and recognized that it is not timeless but has been shaped by earlier happenings. To understand the conflict between Persia and Greece, the most important event during his lifetime, he first inquired into the histories of these societies. Much of his information was derived from posing questions to natives of the lands he visited. Interested in everything, Herodotus frequently interlaced his historical narrative with a marvelous assortment of stories and anecdotes.

The central theme of Herodotus' *Histories* is the contrast between Near Eastern despotism and Greek freedom and the subsequent clash of these two world-views in the Persian Wars. Certain of their superiority, the Greeks considered the non-Hellenic world to be steeped in ignorance and darkness. But Herodotus was generally free of this arrogance. A fair-minded, sympathetic, and tolerant observer, he took joy in examining the wide range of human character and experience.

Though Herodotus found much to praise in the Persian Empire, he was struck by a lack of freedom and by what he considered barbarity. Herodotus emphasized that the mentality of the free citizen was foreign to the East, where men were trained to obey the ruler's commands absolutely. Not the rule of law but the whim of despots prevailed in the East. When a Persian official urged some Greeks to submit to Xerxes, Herodotus wrote that the Greeks said: "You understand well enough what slavery is, but freedom you have never experienced, so you do not know if it tastes sweet or bitter. If you ever did come to experience it, you would advise us to fight for it not with spears only, but with axes too."[35] Of all the Greek city-states, Herodotus admired Athens most. Freedom had enabled Athens to achieve greatness, said Herodotus, and it was this illustrious city that had rescued the Greek world from Persia.

Another theme evident in Herodotus' work was punishment for hubris. In seeking to become king of both Asia and Europe, Xerxes had acted arrogantly; although he behaved as if he were superhuman, "he too was human, and was sure to be disappointed of his great expectations."[36] Like the Greek tragedians, Herodotus drew universal moral principles from human behavior.

In several ways, Herodotus was a historian rather than a teller of tales. First, he recognized that there is value in studying and preserving the past. Second, he asked questions about the past, instead of merely repeating ancient legends; he tried to discover what had happened, analyzed the motivations behind actions, and searched for cause and effect connections. Third, he demonstrated at times a cautious and critical attitude toward his sources, refusing to rely on legends based on little or no objective evidence:

> *The course of my story now leads me to Cyrus: who was this man who destroyed the empire of Croesus, and how did the Persians win their predominant position in Asia? I could, if I wished, give three versions of Cyrus' history, all different from what follows; but I propose to base my account on those Persian authorities who seem to tell the simple truth about him without trying to exaggerate his exploits.*[37]

Fourth, rising above inherited prejudices and a narrow parochialism, he attempted to examine disinterestedly and critically the histories of both Greeks and Persians. Fifth, although the gods appeared in Herodotus' narrative, they played a far less important role than they did in Greek popular mythology. Still, by retaining a belief in the significance of dreams, omens, and oracles and by allowing divine intervention, Herodotus fell short of being a thoroughgoing rationalist. Herodotus' writings contain the embryo of rational history; Thucydides brought it to maturity.

Thucydides

Thucydides (c. 460–c. 400 B.C.) also concentrated on a great political crisis confronting the Hellenic world: the Peloponnesian War. Living in Periclean Athens, whose lifeblood was politics, Thucydides regarded the motives of statesmen and the acts of government as the essence of history. He did not just catalogue facts, but sought those general concepts and principles that the facts illustrated. His history was the work of an intelligent mind trying to make sense of his times.

Thucydides applied to the sphere of political history a rationalist empiricism worthy of the Ionian natural philosophers. He searched for the truth underlying historical events and attempted to present it objectively. From the Sophists, Thucydides learned that the motives and reactions of human beings follow patterns. Therefore, a proper analysis of the events of the Peloponnesian War would reveal general principles that govern human behavior. He intended his history to be a source of enlightenment for future ages, a possession for all time, because the kinds of behavior that caused the conflict between Sparta and Athens would recur regularly through history:

> *Of the events of the war I have not ventured to speak from any chance information, nor according to any notion of my own; I have described nothing but what I either saw myself, or learned from others of whom I made the most careful and particular inquiry. The task was a laborious one, because eyewitnesses of the same occurrences gave different accounts of them, as they remembered or were [partial to] one side or the other. And very likely the strictly historical character of my narrative may be disappointing to the ear. But if he who desires to have before his eyes a true picture of the events which have happened, and of the like events which may be expected to happen hereafter in the order of human things shall pronounce what I have written to be useful, then I shall be satisfied. My history is an everlasting possession, not a prize composition which is heard and forgotten.*[38]

In Thucydides' history, there was no place for myths, for legends, for the fabulous—all hindrances to historical truth. He recognized that a work of history was a creation of the rational mind and not an expression of the poetic imagination. The historian seeks to learn and to enlighten, not to entertain.

Rejecting the notion that the gods interfere in history, Thucydides looked for the social forces and human decisions behind events. Undoubtedly, he was influenced by Hippocratic doctors, who frowned on divine explanations for disease and distinguished between the symptoms of a disease and its causes. Where Herodotus occasionally lapsed into supernatural explanations, Thucydides wrote history in which the gods were absent, and he denied their intervention in human affairs. For Thucydides, history was the work of human beings. And the driving force in history was men's will to power and domination.

In addition to being a historian, Thucydides was also an astute and innovative political thinker with a specific view of government, statesmen, and international relations. He warned against the dangers of extremism unleashed by the strains of war, and he believed that when reason was forsaken, the state's plight would worsen. He had contempt for statesmen who waged war lightly, acting from impulse, reckless daring, and an insatiable appetite for territory. Consequently, he regarded the decision to attack Syracuse in Sicily, which cost so many lives, as a gross political blunder. Although Thucydides admired Athens for its democratic institutions, rule of law, sense of civic duty, and cultural achievements, he recognized an inherent danger in democracy: the emergence of demagogues, who rise to power by stirring up the populace. He extended to international relations the Sophists' insight that people tend to act out of self-interest; national interest, he maintained, was the motivating force in relations between states. And he explicitly formulated the principle of balance of power as a basic formula governing international relations. What caused the Peloponnesian War, he said, was the sudden and spectacular increase of Athenian power and the Spartans' fear that this would upset the balance.

Political scientists, historians, and statesmen still turn to Thucydides for insights into the realities of power politics, the dangers of political fanaticism, the nature of imperialism, the methods of demagogues, and the effects of war on democratic politics.

The Greek Achievement: Reason, Freedom, Humanism

Like other ancient peoples, the Greeks warred, massacred, and enslaved; they could be cruel, arrogant, contentious, and superstitious; and they often violated their ideals. But their achievement was unquestionably of profound historical significance. Western thought essentially begins with the Greeks, who first defined the individual by the capacity to reason. It was the great achievement of the Greek spirit to rise above magic, miracles, mystery, authority, and custom and to discover the procedures and terminology that permit a rational understanding of nature and society. Every aspect of Greek civilization—science, philosophy, art, literature, politics, historical writing—showed a growing reliance on human reason and a diminishing dependence on the gods.

In Mesopotamia and Egypt, people had no clear conception of their individual worth and no understanding of political liberty. They were not citizens but subjects who marched to the command of a ruler whose power originated with the gods. Such royal power was not imposed on an unwilling population but was religiously accepted and obeyed.

In contrast, the Greeks created both civic politics and political freedom. They saw the state as a community of free and equal citizens who made laws in their own interest, and disputes between citizens were decided by a jury of one's peers, not by the whims of a ruler or his officials. The citizens had no other masters but themselves. Denouncing arbitrary rule, they argued that power should be regulated by law and justice. The Greeks held that men are capable of governing themselves, and they valued active citizenship. For the Greeks, the state was a civilizing agent that permitted people to live the good life. Greek political thinkers arrived at a conception of the rational or legal state, in which law was an expression of reason, not of whim or divine commands; of justice, not of might; of the general good of the community, not of self-interest.

The Greeks also gave to Western civilization a conception of inner, or ethical, freedom. People were free to choose between shame and honor, cowardice and duty, moderation and excess. The heroes of Greek tragedy suffered not because they were puppets manipulated by higher powers, but because they possessed the freedom of decision. The idea of ethical freedom reached its highest point with Socrates, who shifted the focus of thought from cosmology to the moral life. To shape oneself according to ideals known to the mind, to develop into an autonomous and self-directed person, became for the Greeks the highest form of freedom.

Underlying everything accomplished by the Greeks was a humanist attitude toward life. The Greeks expressed a belief in the worth, significance, and dignity of the individual. They called for the maximum cultivation of human talent, the full development of human personality, and the deliberate pursuit of excellence. In valuing human personality, the Greek humanists did not approve of living without restraints; they aimed at creating a higher type of man. Such a man would mold himself according to worthy standards; he would make his life as harmonious and flawless as a work of art. This aspiration required effort, discipline, and intelligence. Fundamental to the Greek humanist outlook was the belief that human beings could master themselves. Although people could not alter the course of nature, for there was an order to the universe over which neither human beings nor gods had control, Greek humanists believed that people could control their own lives.

Despite their lauding of the human being's creative capacities, the Greeks were not naive about human nature. Rather, intensely aware of the individual's inherent capacity for evil, Greek thinkers repeatedly warned that without the restraining forces of law, civic institutions, moral norms, and character training, society would be torn apart by the savage elements within human nature.

By discovering theoretical reason, defining political freedom, and affirming the worth and potential of human personality, the Greeks broke with the past and founded the rational and humanist tradition of the West. "Had Greek civilization never existed," wrote poet W. H. Auden, "we would never have become fully conscious, which is to say that we would never have become, for better or worse, fully human."[39]

❖ ❖ ❖

Notes

1. John N. Theodorakopoulos, "The Origins of Science and Philosophy," in *History of the Hellenic World: The Archaic Period* (University Park: Pennsylvania State University Press, 1975), p. 438.
2. Quoted in George Sarton, *A History of Science,* vol. 1 (Cambridge, Mass.: Harvard University Press, 1952), pp. 355–356.

3. Euripides, *Iphigenia at Aulis,* in *Ten Plays by Euripides*, trans. Moses Hadas and John McClean (New York: Bantam Books, 1960), p. 348 (lines 1400–1401).
4. Excerpted in Kathleen Freeman, *Ancilla to the Pre-Socratic Philosophers* (Cambridge, Mass.: Harvard University Press, 1957), pp. 157–158.
5. Plato, *Apology,* trans. F. J. Church, rev. R. D. Cummings (Indianapolis: Bobbs-Merrill, 1956), sec. 28.
6. Ibid., secs. 16–17.
7. Plato, *The Republic,* trans. F. M. Cornford (New York: Oxford University Press, 1945), p. 289.
8. Ibid.
9. Ibid., p. 293.
10. Ibid., pp. 178–179.
11. *Historia Animalium,* in *Works of Aristotle,* vol. 4, trans. D'Arcy Wentworth Thompson (New York: Oxford University Press, 1962), p. 561.
12. *Nicomachean Ethics,* in *Basic Works of Aristotle,* ed. Richard McKeon (New York: Random House, 1941), p. 996.
13. Ibid., p. 1104.
14. *Politics,* in *Basic Works of Aristotle,* ed. McKeon, pp. 1144–45.
15. Ibid., p. 1164.
16. Ibid., pp. 1246, 1251.
17. Ibid., pp. 1220–21.
18. Cited in Werner Jaeger, *Paideia: The Ideals of Greek Culture,* trans. Gilbert Highet (New York: Oxford University Press, 1945), 1:135.
19. Sappho, "A Girl," in *The Oxford Book of Greek Verse in Translation,* ed. T. F. Higham and C. M. Bowra (Oxford: Clarendon Press, 1938), p. 211.
20. Lyn Hatherly Wilson, *Sappho's Sweet Bitter Songs* (London and New York: Routledge, 1966), p. 70.
21. Cited in H. D. F. Kitto, *The Greeks* (Baltimore: Penguin Books, 1957), pp. 174–175.
22. Sophocles, *Oedipus the King,* trans. Bernard M. W. Knox (New York: Washington Square Press, 1959), p. 61.
23. Aeschylus, *The Persians,* trans. Anthony J. Podlecki (Englewood Cliffs, N.J.: Prentice-Hall, 1970), p. 49, lines 250–251.
24. Ibid., pp. 96–97, lines 818–822, 829–831.
25. Euripides, *Medea,* trans. Rex Warner (London: The Bodley Head, 1944), p. 18.
26. *Medea,* trans. Rex Warner, in *Euripides*, vol. 3 of *The Complete Greek Tragedies*, ed. David Grene and Richmond Lattimore (Chicago: University of Chicago Press, 1959–1960), p. 101, line 1260.
27. Ibid., p. 96, lines 1078–80.
28. Euripides, *The Trojan Women,* trans. Gilbert Murray (New York: Oxford University Press, 1915), p. 16, lines 95–97.
29. *Lysistrata*, in *Five Comedies of Aristophanes,* trans. Benjamin Bickley Rogers (Garden City, N.Y.: Doubleday Anchor Books, 1955), p. 292.
30. Ibid., p. 320.
31. *The Clouds,* in *Five Comedies of Aristophanes,* trans. Rogers, pp. 156–157, 169–170.
32. Arnaldo Momigliano, *The Classical Foundations of Modern Historiography* (Berkeley: University of California Press, 1990), p. 30.
33. R. G. Collingwood, *The Idea of History* (New York: Oxford University Press, 1956), pp. 17–18.
34. *Poetics,* in *Basic Works of Aristotle,* ed. McKeon, p. 1464.
35. Herodotus, *The Histories,* trans. Aubrey de Sélincourt (Baltimore: Penguin Books, 1954), p. 458.
36. Ibid., p. 485.
37. Ibid., p. 53.
38. Thucydides, *The Peloponnesian War,* trans. B. Jowett (Oxford: Clarendon Press, 1881), bk. 1, chap. 22.
39. W. H. Auden, ed., *The Portable Greek Reader* (New York: Viking, 1952), p. 38.

Suggested Reading

Boardman, John, et al., *The Oxford History of the Classical World* (1986). Essays on all facets of Greek culture.

Brunschwig, Jacques, and Geoffrey E. R. Lloyd, eds., *Greek Thought* (2000). Essays dealing with many areas of Greek thought.

Copleston, Frederick, *A History of Philosophy*, vol. 1 (1962). An excellent analysis of Greek philosophy.

Cornford, F. M., *Before and After Socrates* (1968). The essential meaning of Greek philosophy clearly presented.

Dodds, E. R., *The Greeks and the Irrational* (1957). Analyzes the role of primitive and irrational forces in Greek culture.

Finley, M. I., ed., *The Legacy of Greece* (1981). Essays on all phases of Greek culture.

Grant, Michael, *The Ancient Historians* (1970). Good material on Herodotus and Thucydides.

Guthrie, W. K. C., *The Greek Philosophers from Thales to Aristotle* (1960). A short, reliable survey of Greek philosophy.

———, *The Sophists* (1971). An assessment of the thought of individual Sophists by a leading student of Greek philosophy.

Jaeger, Werner, *Paideia: The Ideals of Greek Culture* (1939–1944). A three-volume work on Greek culture by a distinguished classicist. The treatment of Homer, the early Greek philosophers, and the Sophists in volume 1 is masterful.

Jones, W. T., *A History of Western Philosophy*, vol. 1 (1962). Clearly written; contains useful passages from original sources.

Kitto, H. D. F., *Greek Tragedy* (1954). A valuable introduction to Greek drama.

Levi, Peter, *The Pelican History of Greek Literature* (1985). Sound insights into Greek writers.

Lloyd, G. E. R., *Early Greek Science* (1970). A survey of Greek science from Thales to Aristotle.

Robinson, J. M., *An Introduction to Early Greek Philosophy* (1968). Combines original sources with lucid discussion.

Snell, Bruno, *The Discovery of the Mind* (1953). A collection of essays focusing on the Greek origins of European thought.

Taylor, A. E., *Socrates* (1951). A discussion of the man and his thought.

Vernant, Jean-Pierre, *The Origins of Greek Thought* (1982). The movement from myth to reason.

Versényi, Laszlo, *Socratic Humanism* (1963). A detailed consideration of Socratic philosophy, especially Socrates' concern for the human individual.

Review Questions

1. What was the achievement of the Ionian natural philosophers?
2. How did Pythagoras, Parmenides, and Democritus contribute to the development of science?
3. How did the Sophists advance the tradition of reason initiated by the natural philosophers? How did they contribute to a spiritual crisis in Athens?
4. What was Socrates' answer to the problems posed by the Sophists?
5. What value does the Socratic dialogue have for education?
6. How did Plato make use of Socrates' thought? What does Plato mean by the realm of Ideas, or Forms?
7. Describe the essential features of Plato's *The Republic* and give the reasons that led him to write it.
8. Discuss whether Plato's political thought has any value for us today.
9. How did Aristotle both criticize and accept Plato's theory of Ideas? What do Aristotle's political thought and ethical thought have in common?
10. Do you agree with Aristotle that "men should not think it slavery to live according to the rule of the constitution, for it is their salvation"? Explain.
11. Greek art was realistic, idealistic, and humanistic. Explain.
12. What did the Greek dramatists have in common with Socrates?
13. Greek dramatists explored the inner life of the individual. Discuss this statement and give examples to support it.
14. Why do the Greek plays have perennial appeal?
15. Why is Herodotus called the "father of history"? In what way did Thucydides surpass Herodotus as a historian? Why is Thucydides still worth reading today?
16. The Greeks broke with the mythopoeic outlook of the ancient Near East and conceived a worldview that is the foundation of Western civilization. Discuss.

Chapter 5

The Hellenistic Age: Cultural Diffusion

Battle of Issus, Roman mosaic. The subject of the mosaic is believed to be Alexander's victory over the Persian king, Darius III, in 333 B.C. at the battle of Issus. On the right side of the mosaic, we see a realistic battle scene filled with both commotion and emotion. (Scala/Art Resource, NY.)

- **Alexander the Great**
- **Hellenistic Society**
  - Competing Dynasties
  - Cosmopolitanism
  - Hellenism and the Jews
- **Hellenistic Culture**
  - Literature, History, and Art
  - Science
  - Philosophy
- **Hellenistic Legacy**

Greek civilization, or Hellenism, passed through three distinct stages: the Hellenic Age, the Hellenistic Age, and the Greco-Roman Age. The Hellenic Age began about 800 B.C. with the early city-states, reached its height in the fifth century B.C., and endured until the death of Alexander the Great in 323 B.C. At that time, the ancient world entered the Hellenistic Age, which ended in 30 B.C., when Egypt, the last major Hellenistic state, fell to Rome. The Greco-Roman Age lasted five hundred years, encompassing the period of the Roman Empire up to the collapse of the Empire's western half in the last part of the fifth century A.D.

Although the Hellenistic Age absorbed the heritage of classical (Hellenic) Greece, its style of civilization changed. During the first phase of Hellenism, the polis was the center of political life. The polis gave Greeks an identity, and only within the polis could Greeks live a good and civilized life. With the coming of the Hellenistic Age, this situation changed. Kingdoms and empires eclipsed the city-state in power and importance. Cities retained a large measure of autonomy in domestic affairs but lost their freedom of action in foreign affairs. Dominated by monarchs, cities were no longer self-sufficient and independent communities as they had been in the Hellenic period. Monarchy—the essential form of government in the Hellenistic world—had not been admired by the Greeks of the Hellenic Age. They agreed with Aristotle that monarchy was suitable only for non-Greeks, who lacked the capacity to govern themselves.

As a result of Alexander the Great's conquests of the lands between Greece and India, tens of thousands of Greek soldiers, merchants, and administrators settled in eastern lands. Their encounters with the different peoples and cultures of the Near East widened the Greeks' horizon and weakened their ties to their native cities. Because of these changes, the individual had to define a relationship not to the narrow, parochial society of the polis, but to the larger world. The Greeks had to examine their place in a world more complex, foreign, and threatening than the polis. They had to fashion a conception of a community that would be more comprehensive than the city-state.

Hellenistic philosophers struggled with these

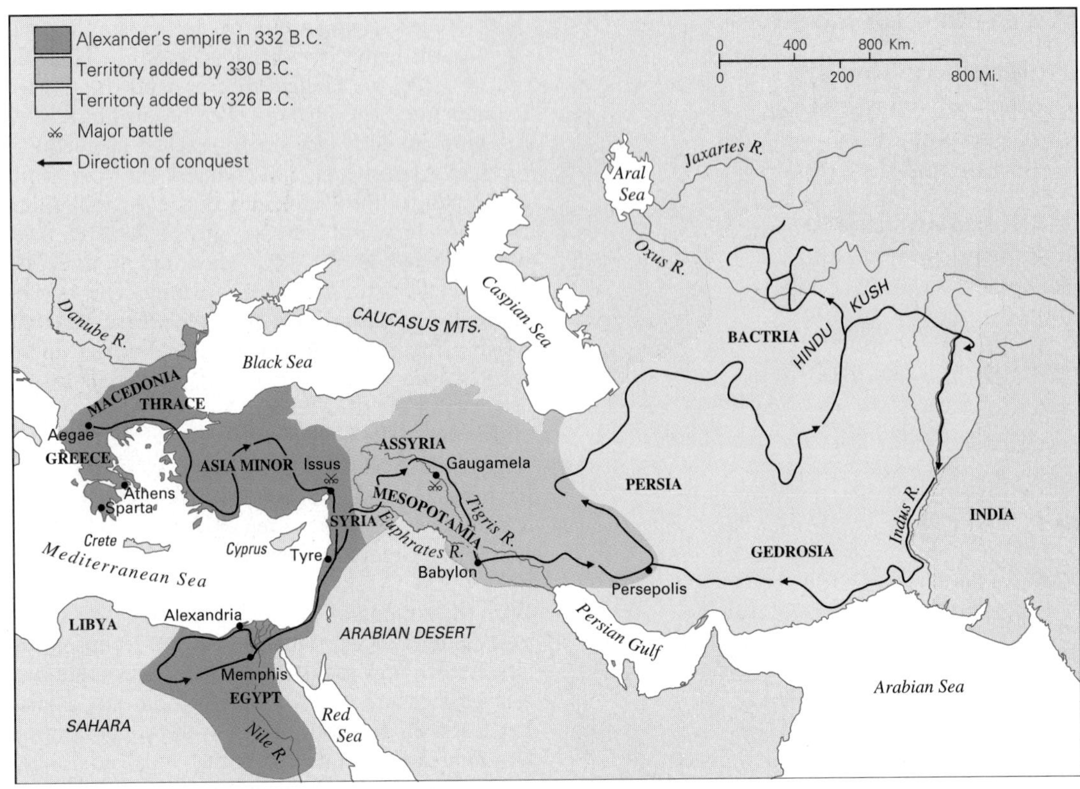

Map 5.1 **Alexander's Conquests** Winning every battle, Alexander the Great carved an empire stretching from Egypt to India.

problems of alienation and community. They sought to give people the inner strength to endure in a world where the polis no longer provided security. In this new situation, philosophers no longer assumed that the good life was tied to the affairs of the city. Freedom from emotional stress—not active citizenship and social responsibility—was the avenue to the good life. This pronounced tendency of people to withdraw into themselves and seek emotional comfort helped shape a cultural environment that contributed to the spread and triumph of Christianity in the Greco-Roman Age.

In the Hellenic Age, Greek philosophers had a limited conception of humanity, dividing the world into Greek and barbarian. In the Hellenistic Age, the intermingling of Greeks and peoples of the Near East caused a shift in focus from the city to the *oikoumene* (the inhabited world); parochialism gave way to cosmopolitanism and universalism as people began to think of themselves as members of a world community. Philosophers came to regard the civilized world as one city, the city of humanity. This new concept was their response to the decline of the city-state and the quest for an alternative form of community.

By uniting the diverse nationalities of the Mediterranean world under one rule, Rome gave political expression to the Hellenistic philosophers' longing for a world community. But the vast and impersonal Roman Empire could not rekindle the sense of belonging, the certainty of identity, that came with being a citizen of a small polis. In time, a resurgence of the religious spirit, particularly in the form of Christianity, helped to overcome the feeling of alienation by offering an image of community that stirred the heart.

Alexander the Great

After the assassination of Philip of Macedon in 336 B.C., his twenty-year-old son, Alexander, succeeded to the throne. Alexander inherited a proud and fiery temperament from his mother. From his tutor Aristotle, Alexander gained an appreciation for Greek culture, particularly the Homeric epics. Undoubtedly, the young Alexander was excited by these stories of legendary heroes, particularly of Achilles, and their striving for personal glory. Alexander acquired military skills and qualities of leadership from his father.

Alexander also inherited from Philip an overriding policy of state: the invasion of Persia. Such an exploit attracted the adventurous spirit of the young Alexander. A war of revenge against the Persians, who were masters of the Greek city-states of Asia Minor, also appealed to his Pan-Hellenic sentiments. Alexander was heir to the teachings of the fourth-century orator Isocrates, who urged a crusade against Persia to unite the Greeks in a common cause. Philip had intended to protect his hold on Greece by driving the Persians from Asia Minor. But Alexander, whose ambition knew no bounds, aspired to conquer the entire Persian Empire. Daring, brave, and intelligent, Alexander possessed the irrepressible energy of a romantic adventurer.

THE "FARNESE PLATE" CAMEO. One of the finest examples of Greek cameos, this one was produced at Alexandria about a century after Alexander's conquest of Egypt. The design was created by carving away portions of the sardonyx stone to set the figures in relief. It depicts Father Nile with the Egyptian goddess Isis and several other Egyptian divinities. (*Museo Nazionale, Naples.*)

With an army of thirty-five thousand men, Alexander crossed into Asia Minor in 334 B.C. After capturing the coast of Asia Minor, he marched into Syria and defeated the Persian army at the battle of Issus. Rather than pursuing the fleeing Persian king, Darius III, Alexander stayed with his master plan, which included the capture of coastal ports in order to crush the Persian navy. He captured Tyre, thought to be an impregnable city, and advanced into Egypt. Grateful to Alexander for having liberated them from Persian rule, the Egyptians made him pharaoh. Alexander appointed officials to administer the country and founded a new city, Alexandria.

Having destroyed or captured the Persian fleet, Alexander, in 331 B.C., moved into Mesopotamia in pursuit of Darius and his army. The Macedonians defeated the numerically superior Persians at Gaugamela, just east of the Tigris River, but Darius escaped. After a stopover at Babylon and at Persepolis, which Alexander burned, perhaps in revenge for Xerxes' destruction of Athens more than 150 years earlier, he resumed the chase. When he finally caught up with Darius, the Persian king was dead, killed by Persian conspirators.

Alexander relentlessly pushed deeper into Asia, crossing from Afghanistan (then called Bactria) into northern India, where he defeated King Porus in a costly battle. When Alexander announced plans to push deeper into India, his troops, exhausted and far from home in a strange land, resisted. Alexander yielded to their wishes and returned to Babylon in 324 B.C. In these campaigns, which covered about ten thousand miles, Alexander proved himself to be a superb strategist and leader of men. Winning every battle, Alexander's army had carved an empire that stretched from Greece to India. Future conquerors, including Caesar and Napoleon, would read of Alexander's career with fascination and longing.

The world after Alexander differed sharply from that existing before he took up the sword. His conquests brought West and East closer together, marking a new epoch. Alexander himself helped implement this transformation. He took a Persian bride, arranged for eighty of his officers and ten thousand of his soldiers to marry oriental women, and planned to incorporate thirty thousand Persian youths into his army. Alexander founded Greek-style cities in Asia, where Greek settlers mixed with the native population.

As Greeks acquired greater knowledge of the Near East, the parochial-mindedness of the polis gave way to a world outlook. As trade and travel between West and East expanded, as Greek merchants and soldiers settled in Asiatic lands, and as Greek culture spread to non-Greeks, the distinctions between barbarian and Greek lessened. Although Alexander never united all the peoples in a world-state, his career pushed the world in a new direction, toward a fusion of disparate peoples and the intermingling of cultural traditions.

Hellenistic Society

Competing Dynasties

In 323 B.C., Alexander, not yet thirty-three years old, died after a sickness that followed a drinking party. He had built an empire that stretched from Greece to the Punjab of India, but he was denied the time needed to organize effective institutions to govern these vast territories. After Alexander's premature death, his generals engaged in a long and bitter struggle to see who would succeed the conqueror. Since none of the generals or their heirs had enough power to hold together Alexander's vast empire, the wars of succession ended in a stalemate. By 275 B.C., the empire was fractured into three dynasties: the Ptolemies in Egypt, the Seleucids in western Asia, and the Antigonids in Macedonia. Macedonia—Alexander's native country—continued to dominate the Greek cities, which periodically tried to break its hold. Later, the kingdom of Pergamum, in western Asia Minor, emerged as the fourth Hellenistic monarchy. These Hellenistic kings were not native rulers enjoying local support (except in Macedonia), but were foreign conquerors. Consequently, they had to depend on mercenary armies and loyal administrators.

In the third century B.C., Ptolemaic Egypt—which ruled Cyprus, islands in the Aegean Sea, cities on the coast of Asia Minor, and southern Syria, including Palestine—was the foremost power in the Hellenistic world. Its great fleet ensured access to its far-flung provinces and protected its trade. Internal revolts, court intrigues, and wars with the kingdom of Seleucia, however, weakened Ptolemaic power in the second century B.C.

The Seleucid Empire, like that of the Ptolemies, was an absolute monarchy in which the king was worshiped as a god. But the Seleucid Empire stretched from the Mediterranean to the frontiers of India and encompassed many different peoples, among them several warlike groups. Thus, this empire was more difficult to control. Attempts by the Seleucids to extend their power in the west were resisted by the Ptolemies. In the third century B.C., these two Hellenistic kingdoms waged five long wars. Finally, the Seleucid ruler Antiochus III (223–187 B.C.) defeated the Ptolemaic forces and established Seleucid control over Phoenicia and Palestine. Taking advantage of Egypt's defeat, Macedonia seized several of Egypt's territories.

In 169–168 B.C., Seleucid Syria invaded Egypt with the intention of annexing it to the Seleucid Empire. This aim would likely have been realized except for the intervention of a new power to the west, Rome. Rome became increasingly drawn into the affairs of the quarrelsome Hellenistic kingdoms; by the middle of the second century B.C., Rome had imposed its will upon them. From that time on, the political fortunes of the western and eastern Mediterranean were inextricably linked.

Cosmopolitanism

Hellenistic society was characterized by a mingling of peoples and an interchange of cultures. Greek traditions spread to the Near East, while Mesopotamian, Egyptian, Hebrew, and Persian traditions—particularly religious beliefs—moved westward. A growing cosmopolitanism replaced the parochialism of the city-state. Although the

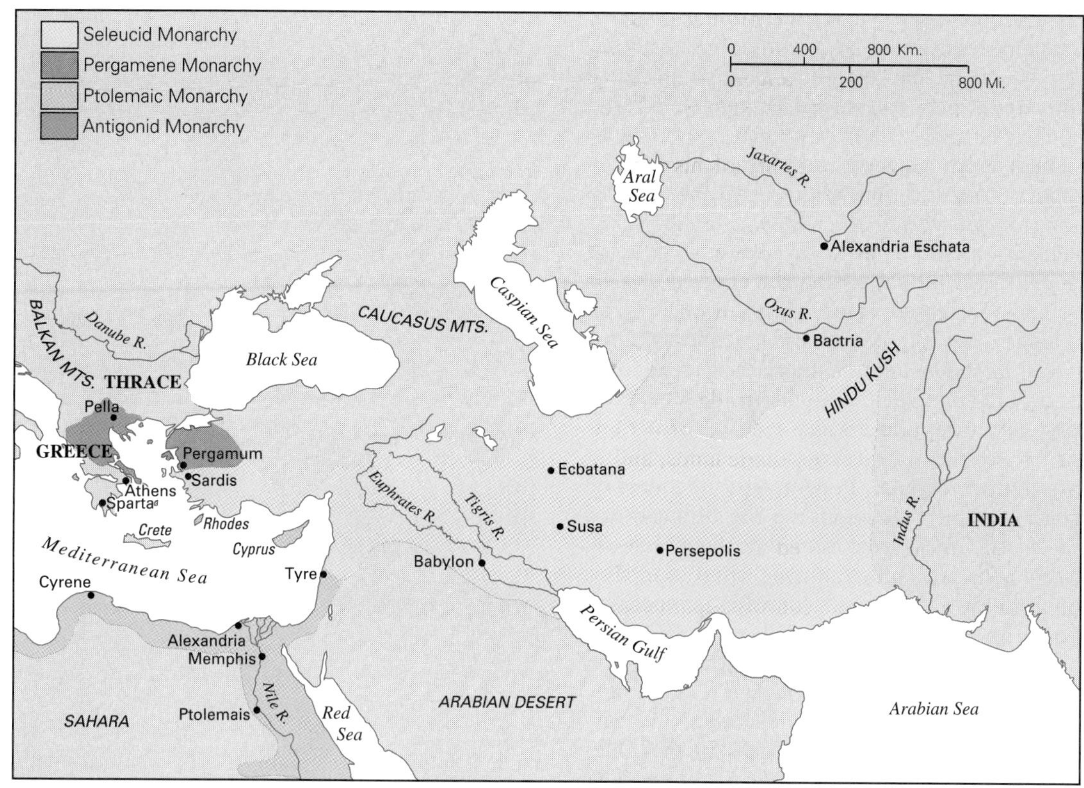

Map 5.2 The Division of Alexander's Empire and the Spread of Hellenism None of Alexander's generals could hold together the vast empire, which fractured into competing dynasties.

rulers of the Hellenistic kingdoms were Macedonians and their high officials and generals were Greeks, the style of government was modeled after that of the ancient oriental kingdoms. In the Hellenic Age, the law had expressed the will of the community, but in this new age of monarchy, the kings laid down the law. The Macedonian rulers encouraged the oriental practice of worshiping the king as a god or as a representative of the gods. In Egypt, for example, the priests conferred on the Macedonian king the same divine powers and titles traditionally held by Egyptian pharaohs. In accordance with ancient tradition, statues of the divine king were installed in Egyptian temples.

Following Alexander's lead, the Seleucids founded cities in the east patterned after the city-states of Greece. The cities, which were often founded to protect trade routes and as fortresses against hostile tribes, adopted the political institutions of Hellenic Greece, including a popular assembly and a council. Hellenistic kings generally did not intervene in the cities' local affairs. Thousands of Greeks settled in these cities, which were Greek in architecture and contained Greek schools, temples, theaters, where performances of classical plays were staged, and gymnasia. Gymnasia were essentially places to exercise, train in sports, and converse, but some had libraries and halls where public lectures and competitions of orators and poets were held. Hellenistic kings brought books, paintings, and statues to their cities from Greece. Hellenistic cities, inhabited by tens of thousands of people from many lands and dominated by a Hellenized upper class, served as centers and agents of Hellenism, which non-

Greeks adopted. The ruling class in each Hellenistic city was united by a common Hellenism, which overcame national, linguistic, and racial distinctions. *Koine* (or shared language), a form of spoken Greek spread by soldiers, administrators, merchants, teachers, and others, became a common tongue throughout much of the Mediterranean world.

Hellenistic cities engaged in economic activity on a much greater scale than the classical Greek city-states. Increased trade integrated the Near East and Greece into a market economy, and business methods became more developed and refined. The middle and upper classes enjoyed homes, furniture, and jewelry more elegant than those of Periclean Athenians, and some people amassed great fortunes. In contrast to the ideal of citizenship, which distinguished the fifth-century polis, many Greeks who settled in Egypt, Syria, and other eastern lands ran roughshod over civil law and moral values and engaged in competitive struggles for wealth and power.

The greatest city of the time and the one most representative of the Hellenistic Age was Alexandria, in Egypt, founded by Alexander. Strategically located at one of the mouths of the Nile, it became a hub of commerce and culture. The most populous city of the Mediterranean world, Alexandria had about 300,000 inhabitants fifty years after its founding. At the beginning of the Christian era, it contained perhaps a million people: Macedonians, Greeks, Romans, Jews, Syrians, Ethiopians, and Arabs.

Alexandria was an unrivaled commercial center; goods from the Mediterranean world, eastern Africa, Arabia, and India circulated in its marketplaces. Two handsome boulevards, squares, fountains, and great temples added to the city's beauty. Its library, created by the first two Ptolemies, had some half a million books. The library was part of a larger complex, the museum, which contained an astronomical observatory and botanical and zoological gardens. Some of the greatest poets, philosophers, physicians, and scientists of the Mediterranean world utilized these facilities.

Aside from the proliferation of Greek urban institutions and ideas, Hellenistic cosmopolitanism expressed itself in an increased movement of peoples, the adoption of common currency standards, and an expansion of trade. International trade was made easier by improvements in navigation techniques, better port facilities, the extension of the monetary economy at the expense of barter, and the rapid development of banking. The makeup of Hellenistic armies also reflected the cosmopolitanism of the age. Serving the Hellenistic kings were men from lands stretching from India to the little-known areas north of the Danube. In Egyptian and Syrian cities, a native elite emerged who spoke Greek, wore Greek-style clothes, and adopted Greek customs.

NIKE, THE GODDESS OF VICTORY, ON A GOLD EARRING, HELLENISTIC PERIOD. The calm, timeless, idealized forms of classical period sculpture gave way to a new style—the Hellenistic, marked by more dynamic, emotion-laden realism. This new aesthetic form reflected the cosmopolitan character of the Greek culture that emerged from Alexander's conquests. (*H. L. Pierce Fund. Courtesy Museum of Fine Arts, Boston.*)

Cultural exchange permeated all phases of cultural life. Sculpture showed the influence of many lands. Historians wrote world histories, not just local ones. Greek astronomers worked with data collected over the centuries by the Babylonians.

Greeks increasingly demonstrated a fascination with Near Eastern religious cults. Philosophers helped to break down the barriers between peoples by asserting that all inhabit a single fatherland. As the philosopher Crates said, "My fatherland has no single tower, no single roof. The whole earth is my citadel, a home ready for us all to live in."[1]

The spread of Greek civilization from the Aegean to the Indus River gave the Hellenistic world a cultural common denominator, but Hellenization did not transform the East and make it one with the West. Hellenization was limited almost entirely to the cities, and in many urban centers it was often only a thin veneer. Many Egyptians in Alexandria learned Greek, generally a necessity for advancement in the state bureaucracy, and some assumed Greek names. But for most, Hellenization did not go much deeper. The countryside lacked even the veneer of Greek culture. Retaining traditional attitudes, the countryside in the East resisted Greek ways. In the villages, local and traditional law, local languages, and family customs remained unchanged; religion, the most important ingredient of the civilizations of the Near East, also kept its traditional character, even if ancestral gods were given Greek names.

Hellenism and the Jews

Like other Near Eastern people, the Jews—both those in Judea and the Diaspora (Jews who lived outside Palestine)—came under the influence of Hellenism. Some Jewish scholars, admiring Greek learning, expressed Jewish religious ideas in philosophical terms; God was identified with reason, and Moses' Law with the rational order of the universe. The Hebrew Scriptures were translated into Greek for use by Greek-speaking Jews living in Alexandria and other areas outside of Judea. Many of these Jews could not understand Hebrew or Aramaic—a Semitic language related to Hebrew that became the common tongue of the Jews after the exile in Babylon. Greek words entered the Hebrew language, and newly constructed synagogues employed Hellenistic architectural styles. Radical Hellenizers, mainly prosperous aristocrats, adopted Greek games, dress, entertainment, and eating habits. These efforts to assimilate pagan ways were resisted by simple folk and the devout, who, clinging tenaciously to Mosaic Law, regarded these alien imports as a great danger to Jewish religious life.

The clash of cultures came to a head when Antiochus IV (174–163 B.C.), the Seleucid king, decided to Hellenize the Jews of Judea. He assumed the title *theos epiphanes* ("god made manifest") because he believed he was Zeus incarnate. In 167 B.C., he desecrated the temple in Jerusalem by erecting an altar to Zeus in the temple court and offering pigs, unclean animals in Jewish law, as a sacrifice. He also forbade ritual circumcision, the sign of the covenant between Jews and their God.

The outrage of loyalist Jews against forced Hellenization was epitomized by Mattathias, a priest who slew the Syrian officer carrying the king's decree to make sacrifices to Zeus. Mattathias' battle cry was "Let everybody who is zealous for the Law and stands by the covenant come out after me." Led by one of Mattathias' sons, Judah Maccabeus (the "hammer"), the Jews successfully fought the Syrians, also venting their anger against the Hellenized Jews who sided with Antiochus. They recaptured Jerusalem in 165 B.C., removed pagan symbols that defiled the temple, and restored Jewish worship. The Jews rededicated the temple and renewed their fidelity to the covenant. (Ever since, this act has been commemorated by Hanukkah—the Festival of Lights.) In 140 B.C., the Jews, under Judah's brother Simon, regained their independence.

Living in the cosmopolitan world of Alexandria dominated by Greek thought and culture, Alexandrian Jews felt compelled to demonstrate that their faith was not incompatible with reason, that there was no insurmountable gulf separating Mosaic religion from Greek philosophy. The leading figure in this effort to explain and justify the Hebrew Scriptures in terms of Greek philosophy—to prove that Mosaic Law, revealed by God, was compatible with truth discovered by natural reason—was Philo of Alexandria (c. 20 B.C.–A.D. 50). Scion of a wealthy, aristocratic Jewish family, Philo was intimately familiar with the Greek cultural tradition and greatly admired Plato. He believed that Plato's view of God, as presented in the *Timaeus,* was compatible with

OLD MARKET WOMAN, C. 2ND CENTURY B.C. Hellenistic genre sculpture depicted people in everyday situations, as individuals, rather than as types. Her stooped shoulders, weighed down by her groceries, also suggest the harsh physical conditions that have worn her down over the years. (*The Metropolitan Museum of Art, New York.*)

the Hebrew Scriptures. In that work, Plato had posited an eternal God, who had existed prior to his creation of the world and continued to exist as an incorporeal and transcendent being.

On several points, Philo disagreed with Greek philosophy. For example, holding that only God was eternal, he could not accept the Platonic view of the eternity of Ideas, or Forms. Nor could he accept the position of Greek philosophy that the laws of nature were inexorable, for this precluded divine miracles. In these and other instances, Philo skillfully used the tools of Greek logic to harmonize differing viewpoints. His blending of Platonism with the Scriptures would be continued by Christian thinkers who admired Philo's achievement.

HELLENISTIC CULTURE

Literature, History, and Art

The Hellenistic Age saw a great outpouring of literary works. Callimachus (c. 305–240 B.C.), an Alexandrian scholar-poet, felt that no one could duplicate the great epics of Homer or the plays of the fifth-century B.C. dramatists. He urged poets to write short, finely crafted poems instead of composing on a grand scale. A student of his, Apollonius of Rhodes, took issue with him and wrote the *Argonautica.* This Homeric-style epic tells the story of Jason's search for the Golden Fleece.

The poet Theocritus (c. 315–250 B.C.), who lived on the island of Sicily, wrote pastorals that showed great sensitivity to natural beauty. He responded with uncommon feeling to the sky and wind, to the hills, trees, and flowers, and to the wildlife of the countryside.

The Athenian playwright Menander (c. 342–291 B.C.) depicted Athenian life at the end of the fourth century. Menander's plays, unlike Aristophanes' lampoons of inept politicians, dealt little with politics. Apparently, Menander reflected the attitude of his fellow Athenians, who, bored with public affairs, had accepted their loss of freedom to Macedonia and were preoccupied with their private lives. Menander dealt sympathetically with human weakness and wrote about stock characters: the clever slave, the young playboy, bragging soldiers, compassionate prostitutes, the elderly seducer, the heroine in trouble. Menander also expressed a warm concern for people, urging them to recognize the humanity of their fellows—whether Greeks, barbarians, or slaves—and to treat each other with kindness and respect.

The leading historian of the Hellenistic Age was Polybius (c. 200–118 B.C.), a Greek, whose history of the rise of Rome is one of the great works of historical literature. Reflecting the universal tendencies of the Hellenistic Age, Polybius endeavored to explain how Rome had progressed from a city-state to a world conqueror.

Hellenistic art, like Hellenistic philosophy, expressed a heightened awareness of the individual. Whereas Hellenic sculpture aimed to depict ideal beauty—the perfect body and face—Hellenistic sculpture, moving from idealism to realism, captured individual character and expression, often of ordinary people—an old fisherman, a crippled man, a drunken lady, a dwarf. Scenes of daily life were realistically portrayed. Wealthy merchants commissioned artists to embellish their private homes. Monarchs, eager to glorify their reigns, sought the services of eminent artists to produce royal portraits, victory monuments, paintings of great battles, temples, and tombs. Continuing a practice initiated during the Hellenic Age, Hellenistic cities commissioned artists. What was new, however, was the proliferation of portrait statues honoring prominent civic leaders, orators, poets, philosophers, and playwrights.

Science

During the Hellenistic Age, Greek scientific achievement reached its height. When Alexander invaded Asia Minor, the former student of Aristotle brought along surveyors, engineers, scientists, and historians, who continued with him into Asia. The vast amount of data in botany, zoology, geography, and astronomy collected by Alexander's staff stimulated an outburst of activity. To integrate so much information, scientists had to specialize in the various disciplines. Hellenistic scientists preserved and expanded the tradition of science developed in the Hellenic Age. They attempted a rational analysis of nature; they engaged in research, organized knowledge in logical fashion, devised procedures for mathematical proof, separated medicine from magic, grasped the theory of experiment, and applied scientific principles to mechanical devices. Hellenistic science, says historian Benjamin Farrington, stood "on the threshold of the modern world. When modern science began in the sixteenth century, it took up where the Greeks left off."[2]

Although Alexandria was the principal center of scientific research, Athens still retained some of its former luster in this area. After Aristotle died in 322 B.C., he was succeeded as head of the Lyceum by Theophrastus and then by Strato. Both wrote treatises on many subjects—logic, ethics, politics, physics, and botany. Theophrastus systematized knowledge of botany in a manner similar to Aristotle's treatment of animals. Strato is most famous for his study of physics. It is likely that Strato, in his investigation of physical problems, did not rely on logic alone but performed a series of experiments to test his investigations.

Because of its library, the finest in the ancient world, and its state-supported museum, Alexandria attracted leading scholars and superseded Athens in scientific investigation. The museum was really a research institute—the first institution in history specifically established for the purpose of scientific research—in which some of the best minds of the day studied and worked.

Alexandrian doctors advanced medical skills. They improved surgical instruments and techniques and, by dissecting bodies, added to anatomical knowledge. Through their research, they discovered organs of the body not known until then, made the distinction between arteries and veins, divided nerves into those comprising the motor and the sensory system, and identified the brain as the source of intelligence. Their investigations advanced knowledge of anatomy and physiology to a level that was not significantly improved until the sixteenth century A.D.

Knowledge in the fields of astronomy and mathematics also increased. Eighteen centuries before Copernicus, Alexandrian astronomer Aristarchus (310–230 B.C.) said that the sun was the center of the universe, that the planets revolved around it, and that the stars were situated at great distances from the earth. But these revolutionary ideas were not accepted, and the belief in an earth-centered universe persisted. In geometry, Euclid, an Alexandrian mathematician who lived around 300 B.C., creatively synthesized earlier developments. Euclid's hundreds of geometric proofs, derived from reasoning alone, are a profound witness to the power of the rational mind.

Alexander's expeditions had opened the eyes of Mediterranean peoples to the breadth of the earth and had stimulated explorations and geographic research. Eratosthenes (c. 275–194 B.C.), an Alexandrian geographer, sought a scientific under-

Profile

Polybius

Rome's expansion from a city-state to a world empire that embraced many different nationalities and the extension of citizenship to non-Romans exemplified the universalism and cosmopolitanism of the Hellenistic Age. So too did Polybius' *Histories,* which sought to account for Rome's unprecedented accomplishment.

In 168 B.C. at the battle of Pynda, the Romans defeated Macedonia, which ruled Greece, ending its independence. After the battle, Polybius, along with a thousand other Greeks who had shown sympathy for Macedonia, was deported to Rome to be questioned. Protected by an influential Roman family, no harm came to him.

In the tradition of Thucydides, Polybius believed that a historian had a duty to teach moral lessons and to enlighten by pointing to general principles governing the course of historical events. Like Thucydides he believed that there

Jose F. Poblete/Corbis.

standing of this enlarged world. He divided the planet into climatic zones, declared that the oceans are joined, and with extraordinary ingenuity and accuracy measured the earth's circumference.

Archimedes of Syracuse (c. 287–212 B.C.), who studied at Alexandria, was a mathematician, a physicist, and an ingenious inventor. His mechanical inventions, including war engines, dazzled his contemporaries. However, Archimedes dismissed his practical inventions, preferring to be remembered as a theoretician. In one treatise, he established the general principles of hydrostatics, a branch of physics that deals with the pressure and equilibrium of liquids at rest.

Philosophy

Hellenistic thinkers preserved the rational tradition of Greek philosophy. Like their Hellenic predecessors, they regarded the cosmos as governed by universal principles intelligible to the rational mind. For the philosophers of both ages, a crucial problem was the achievement of the good life. Also, both Hellenic and Hellenistic thinkers sought rules for human conduct that accorded with rational standards; both believed that individuals attain happiness through their own efforts, unaided by the gods. In the tradition of Socrates, Hellenistic thinkers taught a morality of self-mastery. But although they retained the inheritance of the classical age, they also transformed it, for they had to adapt thought to the requirements of a cosmopolitan society.

In the Hellenic Age, the starting point of philosophy was the citizen's relationship to the city; in the Hellenistic Age, the point of departure was the solitary individual's relationship to humanity and the individual's personal destiny in a larger and more complex world. Philosophy tried to deal with the feeling of alienation resulting from the weakening of the individual's attachment to the polis and to arrive at a conception of community that corresponded to the social realities of a are lessons to be learned from a study of history and that his work would instruct current and future officials regarding the proper course of action under given circumstances. But whereas Thucydides wrote about the Peloponnesian War, which involved the Greek city-states, Polybius, reflecting the spirit of the Hellenistic Age, took the entire Mediterranean world as his subject. His aim was to recount how "the Romans succeeded in less than fifty-three years in bringing under their rule the whole inhabited world, an achievement which is without parallel in human history."* No question was of greater importance, he said, than to understand how Rome acquired this supremacy. Polybius stated explicitly that, unlike his predecessors who wrote specialized narrow studies dealing with aspects of Greek or Persian history, he was attempting a unique project—a systematic world history that "examine[s] the general and comprehensive scheme of events."† Such a study, he held, was an avenue to a wisdom closed to historians who write monographs on parochial, insignificant, and obsure topics.

Among the reasons Polybius gave for Rome's success was its political system, which balanced aristocratic and democratic elements: the Senate, representing the aristocracy, wielded great power, but the Assembly, representing the commoners, also played an important role in political life. Polybius held that such a political balance promoted loyalty and effective government. Polybius was greatly impressed with the Roman army. The discipline and dedication of citizen soldiers, he said, help explain Rome's success in creating a world empire.

*Polybius, *The Rise of the Roman Empire,* trans. Ian Scott-Kilvert (New York: Penguin Classics, 1979), pp. 41.

†Ibid., p. 44.

world grown larger. Unlike Plato and Aristotle, Hellenistic philosophers were moralists, not great speculators and theorists. The Hellenistic schools of philosophy, in contrast to their predecessors, were far less concerned with the scientific understanding of nature. Also in contrast to earlier Greek thinkers, they were less concerned with political organization. Philosophy was now chiefly preoccupied with the life of the individual, and it tried to alleviate spiritual uneasiness and loss of security. It aspired to make people ethically independent so that they could achieve happiness in a hostile and competitive world.

In striving for tranquillity of mind and relief from conflict, Hellenistic thinkers reflected the general anxiety that pervaded their society. They retained respect for reason and aspired to the rational life, but by stressing peace of mind and the effort to overcome anxiety, they were performing a quasi-religious function. Philosophy was trying to provide comfort for the individual suffering from feelings of loneliness and insignificance. This attempt indicated that Greek civilization was undergoing a spiritual transformation. (We examine the full meaning of this transformation in Chapters 7 and 8). The gravitation toward religion in an effort to relieve despair gathered momentum in the centuries that followed. Thus, Hellenistic philosophies helped prepare people to accept Christianity, which promised personal salvation. Ultimately, the Christian answer to the problems of alienation and the need for community would predominate over the Greco-Roman attempt at resolution.

The Hellenistic world gave rise to four principal schools of philosophy: Epicureanism, Stoicism, Skepticism, and Cynicism.

Epicureanism. In the tradition of Plato and Aristotle, Epicurus (342–270 B.C.) founded a school in Athens at the end of the fourth century B.C. He broke with the attitude of the Hellenic Age in significant ways. Unlike classical Greek

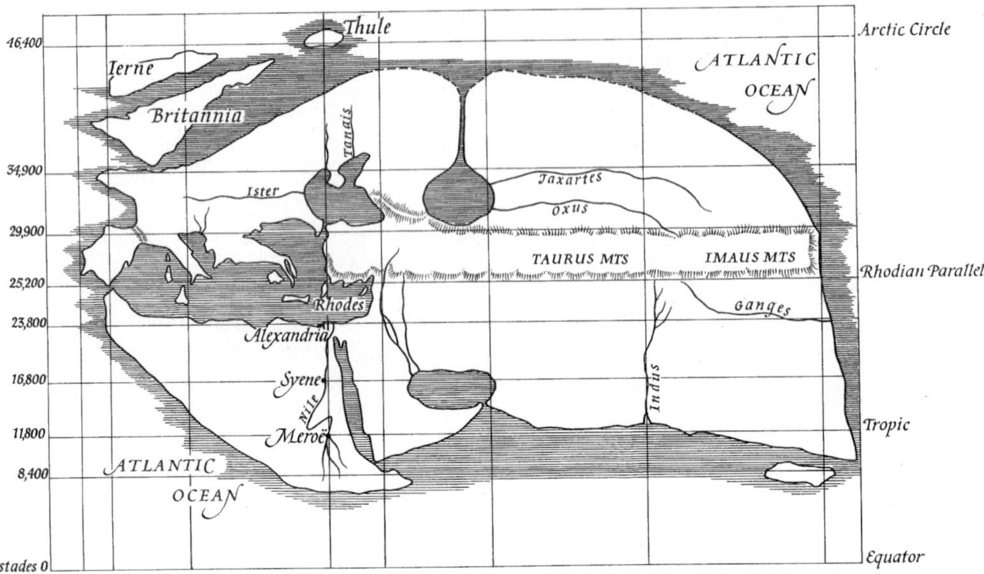

Reconstruction of the Map of the World by Eratosthenes (c. 275–194 b.c.). Geographic knowledge expanded enormously among the Hellenistic Greeks. The first systematic scientific books on geography were credited to Eratosthenes, head of the Alexandrian Library, the greatest scientific and humanistic research center in the Hellenistic world. Eratosthenes estimated the circumference of the earth with remarkable accuracy for his time. His map illustrates the limits of the world known to the Greeks. (*From John Onians,* Art and Thought in the Hellenistic Age [*Thames and Hudson, 1979*]. *Reprinted by permission of Thames and Hudson Ltd.*)

philosophers, Epicurus, reflecting the Greeks' changing relationship to the city, taught the value of passivity and withdrawal from civic life. To him, citizenship was not a prerequisite for individual happiness. Wise persons, said Epicurus, would refrain from engaging in public affairs, for politics could deprive them of their self-sufficiency, their freedom to choose and to act. Nor would wise individuals pursue wealth, power, or fame, as the pursuit would only provoke anxiety. For the same reason, wise persons would not surrender to hate or love, desires that distress the soul. A wise person would also try to live justly, for one who behaves unjustly is burdened with troubles. Nor could there be happiness when one worried about dying or pleasing the gods.

To Epicurus, dread that the gods interfered in human life and could inflict suffering after death was the principal cause of anxiety. To remove this source of human anguish, he favored a theory of nature that had no place for supernatural intervention in nature or in people's lives. Therefore, he adopted the physics of Democritus, which taught that all things consist of atoms in motion. In a universe of colliding atoms, there could be no higher intelligence ordering things; there was no room for divine activity. Epicurus taught that the gods probably did exist, but that they could not influence human affairs; hence it was pointless to worry about them. Individuals should order their lives without considering the gods. Epicurus embraced atomism, not as a disinterested scientist aspiring to truth, but as a moral philosopher seeking to liberate emotional life from fear of the gods.

People could achieve happiness, said Epicurus, when their bodies were "free from pain" and their minds "released from worry and fear." Although Epicurus wanted to increase pleasure for the individual, he rejected unbridled hedonism. Because he believed that happiness must be pur-

MARBLE PORTRAIT OF EPICURUS. The direct gaze and inner calm of the philosopher suggest the essence of his teachings. Epicurus believed that happiness came from a rationally ordered life. He urged his followers to disengage from the uncertainties and stress of politics, business, family, and religion. (*The Metropolitan Museum of Art, Rogers Fund, 1911 [11.90].*)

sued rationally, he thought that the merely sensuous pleasures with unpleasant aftereffects (such as overeating and excessive drinking) should be avoided. In general, Epicurus espoused the traditional Greek view of moderation and prudence. Most important for achieving the good life, said Epicurus, was the company of friends.

By opening his philosophy to men and women, slave and free, Greek and barbarian, and by separating ethics from politics, Epicurus fashioned a philosophy adapted to the post-Alexandrian world of kingdoms and universal culture.

Stoicism. Around the time of the founding of Epicurus' school, Zeno (335–263 B.C.) also opened a school in Athens. Zeno's teachings, called Stoicism, became the most important philosophy in the Hellenistic world. By teaching that the world constituted a single society, Stoicism gave theoretical expression to the world-mindedness of the age. By arriving at the concept of a world-state, the city of humanity, Stoicism offered an answer to the problem of community and alienation posed by the decline of the city-state. By stressing inner strength in dealing with life's misfortunes, Stoicism offered an avenue to individual happiness in a world fraught with uncertainty.

At the core of Stoicism was the belief that the universe contained a principle of order, variously called the Divine Fire, God—more the fundamental force of the universe than a living person—and Divine Reason (*Logos*). This ruling force underlay reality and permeated all things; it ordered the cosmos according to law. The Stoics reasoned that, being part of the universe, people too shared in the Logos that operated throughout the cosmos. The Logos was implanted in every human soul; it enabled people to act virtuously and intelligently and to comprehend the principles of order that governed nature. This natural law provides human beings with an awareness of what is and is not correct behavior, especially when dealing with other human beings. The virtuous person lives in accordance with natural law.

Since reason was common to all, human beings were essentially brothers and fundamentally equal. Reason gave individuals dignity and enabled them to recognize and respect the dignity of others. To the Stoics, all people, Greek and barbarian, free and slave, rich and poor, were fellow human beings, and one law, the law of nature, applied to all of them. What people had in common as fellow human beings far outweighed differences based on culture. All rational human beings were fellow citizens of a world community. Thus, the Stoics, like the Hebrews, arrived at the idea of a common humanity subject to the same moral obligations.

Pericles had spoken of the Athenians' obligation to abide by the laws and traditions of their city; Stoics, viewing people as citizens of the world, emphasized the individual's duty to understand and obey the natural law that governed the cosmos and applied to all. Socrates had taught a morality of self-mastery—reason exercising control over feelings; the Stoics spread Socrates' philosophy beyond Athens, beyond Greece, and enlarged it, offering it as a way of life for all. Like Socrates, the Stoics believed that a person's distinctive quality was the ability to reason and that happiness came from the disciplining of emotions by the rational part of the soul. Also like Socrates, the Stoics maintained that individuals should progress morally, should perfect their character.

In the Stoic view, wise persons ordered their lives according to the natural law—the Logos, or law of reason—that underlay the cosmos. To live in agreement with nature—that is, to follow the dictates of reason—was the aim of moral activity. This harmony with the Logos would give these individuals the inner strength to resist the torments inflicted by others, by fate, and by their own passionate natures. Self-mastery and inner peace, or happiness, would follow. Such individuals would remain undisturbed by life's misfortunes, for their souls would be their own. Even slaves were not denied this inner freedom; although their bodies were subjected to the power of their masters, their minds still remained independent and free.

Stoicism had an enduring influence on the Western mind. To some Roman political and legal thinkers, the Empire fulfilled the Stoic ideal of a world community, in which people of different nationalities held citizenship and were governed by a worldwide law that accorded with the law of reason, or natural law,—a moral order operating throughout the universe. Stoic beliefs—that by nature we are all members of one family, that each person is significant, that distinctions of rank and race are of no account, and that human law should not conflict with natural law—were incorporated into Roman jurisprudence, Christian thought, and modern liberalism. There is continuity between the Stoic idea of natural law and the principle of inalienable rights, rights to which all are entitled by nature, stated in the American Declaration of Independence. In the modern age, the principle of natural law provided theoretical justification for human rights that are the birthright of each individual.

Skepticism. The Epicureans tried to withdraw from the evils of this world and to attain personal happiness by reducing physical pain and mental anguish. The Stoics sought happiness by actively entering into harmony with universal reason. Both philosophies sought peace of mind, but the Stoics did not disengage themselves from political life and often exerted influence over Hellenistic rulers. Skepticism, another school of philosophy, attacked the Epicurean and Stoic belief that there is a definite avenue to happiness. Skeptics held that one could achieve spiritual comfort by recognizing that none of the beliefs by which people lived were true or could bring happiness.

Some Skeptics taught indifference to all theory and urged conformity to accepted views whether or not they were true. This attitude would avoid arguments and explanations. Gods might not exist, said the Skeptics, but to refuse to worship or to deny their existence would only cause trouble; therefore, individuals should follow the crowd. The life of the mind—metaphysical speculation inquiring into the origin of things, and clever reasoning—did not bring truth or happiness; so why should one bother with it? Suspending judgment, recognizing the inability to understand, not committing oneself to a system of belief—by these means one could achieve peace of mind. Instead of embracing doctrines, said the Greek writer Lucian, individuals should go their way "with ever a smile and never a passion."[3] This was the position of those Skeptics who were suspicious of ideas, particularly all-encompassing rational systems, and hostile to intellectuals.

The more sophisticated Skeptics did not run away from ideas but pointed out their limitations; they did not avoid theories but refuted them. In doing so, they did not reject reason. Rather, they focused on a problem of reason: whether indeed it could arrive at truth. Thus, Carneades of Cyrene (213–129 B.C.) insisted that all ideas, even mathematical principles, must be regarded as hypotheses and assumptions, not as absolutes. Just because the universe showed signs of order, Carneades argued, one could not assume that it had been created by God. Since there was never any certainty, only probability, morality should derive from practical experience rather than from dogma.

Cynicism. The Cynics were not theoretical philosophers but supreme individualists who rebelled against established values and conventions—against every barrier of society that restrained individuals from following their own natures. Cynics regarded laws and public opinion, private property and employment, and wives and children as hindrances to the free life. Extreme individualists, the Cynics had no loyalty to family, city, or kingdom and ridiculed religion, philosophy, and literature. They renounced possessions and showed no respect for authority. When Diogenes, a fourth-century B.C. Cynic, met Alexander the Great, he is supposed to have asked only that the great conqueror get out of his light.

Cynics put their philosophy into practice. They cultivated indifference and apathy. To harden themselves against life's misfortunes, they engaged in strenuous exercise, endured cold and hunger, and lived ascetically. Not tied down by property or employment, Cynics wandered shoeless from place to place, wearing dirty and ragged clothes and carrying staffs. To show their disdain for society's customs, Cynics grew long scraggly beards, used foul language, and cultivated bad manners. Diogenes supposedly said: "Look at me, . . . I am without a home, without a city, without property, without a slave; I sleep on the ground; I have neither wife nor children, no miserable governor's mansion, but only earth, and sky, and one rough cloak. Yet what do I lack? Am I not free from pain and fear, am I not free?"[4]

In their attack on inherited conventions, Cynics strove for self-sufficiency and spiritual security. Theirs was the most radical philosophical quest for meaning and peace of soul during the Hellenistic Age.

The Hellenistic Legacy

The Hellenistic Age encompassed the period from the death of Alexander to the formation of the Roman Empire. During these three centuries, Greek civilization spread eastward as far as India and westward to Rome. As Greeks settled in the Near East and intermingled with Egyptians, Syrians, Persians, and others, the parochialism of the Greek polis gave way to a new cosmopolitanism, an interest in the culture of other ethnic groups, and to universalism, an awareness that people were members of a world community that transcended citizenship in one's native city. Both philosophy and the arts reflected these new concerns.

Rome, conqueror of the Mediterranean world and transmitter of Hellenism, inherited the universalist tendencies of the Hellenistic Age and embodied them in its law, institutions, and art. So too did Christianity, which welcomed converts from every ethnic background and held that God loved all people, that Christ died for all humanity. The Stoic idea of natural law that applies to all human beings and its corollary that human beings are fundamentally equal were crucial to the formulation of the modern idea that the individual is endowed with natural rights that no government can violate. A parallel can be drawn between the Hellenistic Age, in which Greek civilization spread to the Near East, and our own age, in which the ideas, institutions, and technology of Western civilization have been exported throughout the globe.

❖ ❖ ❖

Notes

1. Quoted in John Ferguson, *The Heritage of Hellenism* (New York: Science History Publications, 1973), p. 30.
2. Benjamin Farrington, *Greek Science* (Baltimore: Penguin Books, 1961), p. 301.
3. Quoted in J. H. Randall, Jr., *Hellenistic Ways of Deliverance and the Making of the Christian Synthesis* (New York: Columbia University Press, 1970), p. 74.
4. Epictetus, *The Discourses as Reported by Arrian, the Manual and Fragments,* trans. W. A. Oldfather (Cambridge, Mass.: Harvard University Press, 1966), 2:147.

Suggested Reading

Bonnard, André, *Greek Civilization,* vol. 3 (1961). Self-contained chapters on various phases of late classical and Hellenistic periods.

Bury, J. B., et al., *The Hellenistic Age* (1970). First published in 1923; contains valuable essays by leading classicists.

Cary, M., *A History of the Greek World, 323–146 B.C.* (1972). A standard survey of the Hellenistic world.

Ferguson, John, *The Heritage of Hellenism* (1973). A good introduction to Hellenistic culture.

Fox, Robin Lane, *Alexander the Great* (1974). A competent biography.

Grant, Michael, *From Alexander to Cleopatra* (1982). A fine survey of all phases of Hellenistic society and culture.

Green, Peter, *Alexander the Great* (1970). A lavishly illustrated study.

Hadas, Moses, *Hellenistic Culture* (1972). Focuses on the cultural exchanges between East and West.

Koester, Helmut, *Introduction to the New Testament, Volume One: History, Culture and Religion of the Hellenistic Age* (1982). An intelligent guide.

Peters, F. E., *The Harvest of Hellenism* (1970). A comprehensive treatment of Hellenistic history and culture.

Randall, J. H., Jr., *Hellenistic Ways of Deliverance and the Making of the Christian Synthesis* (1970). An astute discussion of Hellenistic and early Christian thought.

Tarn, W. W., *Alexander the Great* (1956). A controversial interpretation.

Wallbank, F. W., *The Hellenistic World* (1982). A survey of the Hellenistic world that makes judicious use of quotations from original sources.

Welles, C. Bradford, *Alexander and the Hellenistic World* (1970). A useful sketch of the political and cultural history of the age.

Review Questions

1. What were the basic differences between the Hellenic Age and the Hellenistic Age?
2. How did Alexander the Great contribute to the shaping of the Hellenistic Age?
3. Provide examples of cosmopolitanism in the Hellenistic period.
4. In what ways is New York City closer to Hellenistic Alexandria than to Hellenic Athens?
5. What was the function of the museum at Alexandria?
6. Hellenistic science stood on the threshold of the modern world. Explain.
7. What problems concerned Hellenistic philosophers?
8. What were the Epicurean, Stoic, Skeptic, and Cynic prescriptions for achieving happiness?
9. What was the enduring significance of Stoicism?
10. Which of the Hellenistic philosophies has the most appeal for you? The least appeal?

Chapter 6

The Roman Republic: City-State to World Empire

The Roman Forum. (Adam Woolfitt/Woodfin Camp.)

■ **Evolution of the Roman Constitution**

■ **Roman Expansion to 146 B.C.**
The Uniting of Italy
Conquest of the Mediterranean World
Consequences of Expansion

■ **Culture in the Republic**

■ **Collapse of the Republic**
Crisis in Agriculture
The Gracchan Revolution
Rival Generals
Julius Caesar
The Republic's Last Years

Rome's great achievement was to transcend the narrow political orientation of the city-state and to create a world-state that unified the different nations of the Mediterranean world. Regarding the polis as the only means to the good life, the Greeks had not desired a larger political unit and had almost totally excluded foreigners from citizenship. Although Hellenistic philosophers had conceived the possibility of a world community, Hellenistic politics could not shape one. Rome overcame the limitations of the city-state mentality and developed an empirewide system of law and citizenship. The Hebrews were distinguished by their prophets and the Greeks by their philosophers. The Romans produced no Amos or Isaiah, and no Plato or Aristotle; their genius found expression in law and government, the practical, not the theoretical.

Historians divide Roman history into two broad periods: the period of the Republic began in 509 B.C., with the overthrow of the Etruscan monarchy; the period of the Empire began in 27 B.C., when Octavian (Augustus) became in effect the first Roman emperor, ending almost five hundred years of republican self-government. By conquering the Mediterranean world and extending Roman law and, in some instances, citizenship to different nationalities, the Roman Republic transcended the parochialism typical of the city-state. The Republic initiated the trend toward political and legal universalism, which reached fruition in the second period of Roman history, the Empire.

Evolution of the Roman Constitution

By the eighth century B.C., peasant communities existed on some of Rome's seven hills near the Tiber River in central Italy. To the north stood Etruscan cities and to the south Greek cities. The more advanced civilizations of both Etruscans and Greeks were gradually absorbed by the Romans.

The origin of the Etruscans remains a mystery, although some scholars believe that they came from Asia Minor and settled in north-central Italy. From them, Romans acquired architectural styles and skills in road construction, sanitation,

Chronology 6.1 ❖ The Roman Republic

509 B.C.	Expulsion of the Etruscan monarch
450	Law of Twelve Tables
287	End of the Struggle of the Orders
264–241	First Punic War: Rome acquires provinces
218–201	Second Punic War: Hannibal is defeated
149–146	Third Punic War: destruction of Carthage
133–122	Land reforms by the Gracchi brothers; they are murdered by the Senate
88–83	Conflict between Sulla and the forces of Marius; Sulla emerges as dictator
79	After restoring rule by Senate, Sulla retires
73–71	Slave revolt is led by Spartacus
58–51	Caesar campaigns in Gaul
49–44	Caesar is dictator of Rome
31 B.C.	Antony and Cleopatra are defeated at Actium by Octavian

hydraulic engineering (including underground conduits), metallurgy, ceramics, and portrait sculpture. Symbols of authority and rule were also borrowed from the Etruscans: purple robes, ivory-veneer chariots, thrones for state officials, and a bundle of rods and an ax held by attendants. Etruscan words and names entered into the Latin language, and Roman religion absorbed Etruscan gods.

The Etruscans had expanded their territory in Italy during the seventh and sixth centuries B.C., and they controlled the monarchy in Rome. But the Etruscan city-states failed to establish a federal union with a centralized government. Defeated by Celts, Greeks, and finally Romans, by the third century B.C., the Etruscans had ceased to exercise any political power in Italy.

Rome became a republic at the end of the sixth century B.C.—the traditional date is 509 B.C.—when the landowning aristocrats, or patricians, overthrew the Etruscan king. As in the Greek cities, the transition from theocratic monarchy to republic offered possibilities for political and legal growth. In the opening phase of republican history, religion governed the people, dictated the law, and legitimized the rule of the patricians—aristocrats by birth who regarded themselves as the preservers of sacred traditions. Gradually, the Romans loosened the ties between religion and politics and hammered out a constitutional system that paralleled the Greek achievement of rationalizing and secularizing politics and law. In time, the Romans, like the Greeks, came to view law as an expression of the public will and not as the creation of god-kings, priest-kings, or a priestly caste.

The impetus for the growth of the Roman constitution came from a conflict—known as the Struggle of the Orders—between the patricians and the commoners, or plebeians. At the beginning of the fifth century B.C., the patrician-dominated government consisted of two elected executives called consuls, the Centuriate Assembly, and the Senate. Patricians owned most of the land and controlled the army. The executive heads of government were the two annually elected consuls, who came from the nobility; they commanded the army, served as judges, and initiated legislation. To prevent either consul from becoming an autocrat, decisions had to be approved by both of them. In times of crisis, the consuls were authorized by the Senate to nominate a dictator; he would possess absolute powers during the emergency, but these powers would expire after six months. The consuls were aided by other annually elected magistrates and administrators.

Etruscan Couple. In Etruscan funerary art the deceased were sometimes represented in full length on the lid of the coffin. Here a husband and wife are shown side by side and smiling. (*Museo Nazionale di Villa Giulia/AKG, London.*)

The Centuriate Assembly was a popular assembly but, because of voting procedures, was controlled by the nobility. The Assembly elected consuls and other magistrates and made the laws, which also needed Senate approval. The Senate advised the Assembly but did not itself enact laws; it controlled public finances and foreign policy. Senators either were appointed for life terms by the consuls or were former magistrates. The Senate was the principal organ of patrician power.

The tension between patricians and commoners stemmed from plebeian grievances, which included enslavement for debt, discrimination in the courts, prevention of intermarriage with patricians, lack of political representation, and the absence of a written code of laws. Resenting their inferior status and eager for economic relief, the plebeians organized and waged a struggle for political, legal, and social equality. They were resisted every step of the way by patricians, who wanted to preserve their own dominance. The plebeians had one decisive weapon: their threat to secede from Rome, that is, not to pay taxes, work, or serve in the army. Realizing that Rome, which was constantly involved in warfare on the Italian peninsula, could not endure without plebeian help, the pragmatic patricians begrudgingly made concessions. Thus, the plebeians slowly gained legal equality.

Early in the fifth century, the plebeians won the right to form their own assembly (the Plebeian Assembly, which was later enlarged and called the Tribal Assembly). This Assembly could elect tribunes, officials who were empowered to protect plebeian rights. As a result of plebeian pressure, in about 450 B.C., the first Roman code of laws was written. Called the Twelve Tables, the code gave plebeians some degree of protection against unfair and oppressive patrician officials, who could interpret customary law in an arbitrary way. Other concessions gained later by the plebeians included the right to intermarry with patricians, access to the highest political, judicial, and religious offices in the state, and the elimination of slavery as payment for debt. In 287 B.C., a date generally recognized as the termination of the plebeian-patrician struggle, laws passed by the Tribal Assembly no longer required Senate approval. Now the plebeians had full civil equality and legal protection and their assembly full power to enact legislation.

Although the plebeians had gained legal equality and the right to sit in the Senate and to hold high offices, Rome was still ruled by an upper class. True, the Tribal Assembly and the tribunes constituted democratic elements and, in theory, seemed to balance the power of the patrician-dominated Senate. Actually, though, power was still concentrated in a ruling oligarchy of wealthy landowners, this time consisting of patricians and influential plebeians who had joined forces with the old nobility. Marriages between patricians and politically powerful plebeians strengthened this alliance. Generally only wealthy plebeians became tribunes, and they tended to side with the old nobility rather than defend the interests of poor plebeians. By using bribes, the ruling oligarchy of patricians and wealthy plebeians maintained control over the Assembly, and the Senate remained a bastion of aristocratic power.

A patron-client relationship extending back to the days of the monarchy reinforced upper-class rule. In early Rome, a plebeian seeking protection for himself and his family in the courts looked to a patrician for assistance. In return, the plebeian gave his patrician patron both military and political support. Enduring over the centuries, the

STATUE PORTRAIT, FIRST CENTURY A.D. The Romans valued family, city, and tradition. Here a noble proudly exhibits the busts of his ancestors. (*Scala/Art Resource, NY.*)

patron-client relationship assured powerful nobles of their commoner clients' support in the Assembly, and it provided clients with food, money, and protection.

Thus, from beginning to end, an upper class—sometimes expanded to allow entry of new talent—governed the Roman Republic. This aristocracy's view of liberty always remained elitist: freedom for Rome's best men to achieve virtue (*virtus*), dignity (*dignitas*), and fame (*fama*) by competing with each other for political power and privilege. Cicero (see below), himself a member of the ruling elite, aptly summed up its outlook: "the safety of the State depends upon the wisdom of its best men, especially since Nature has provided not only that those men who are superior in virtue and in spirit should rule the weaker, but also that the weaker should be willing to obey the stronger."[1] Like others of the upper class, Cicero held that "the perversity and rashness of popular assemblies" precluded them from governing effectively.[2] In the Greek cities, tyrants had succeeded in breaking aristocratic dominance, thereby clearing a pathway for democratic government. But in the Roman Republic, the nobility maintained its tight grip on the reins of power until the civil wars of the first century B.C.

Deeming themselves Rome's finest citizens, the ruling oligarchy led Rome during its period of expansion and demonstrated a sense of responsibility and a talent for statesmanship. In noble families, parents and elders prepared the young for public service. They recounted the glorious deeds of ancestors who had served Rome, and they reminded youngsters of their responsibility to bring additional honors to the family by winning distinction as a commander, orator, or jurist. In this way, a son would prove his worth as a man and as a Roman.

During their two-hundred-year class struggle, the Romans forged a constitutional system based on civic needs rather than on religious mystery. The essential duty of government ceased to be the regular performance of religious rituals and became the maintenance of order at home and the preservation of Roman might and dignity in international relations. Although the Romans retained the ceremonies and practices of their ancestral religion—correct observance was a way of showing respect for tradition—public interest, not religious tradition, determined the content of law and was the standard by which all the important acts of the city were judged. When Romans chose a course of action in public life, they rarely took into consideration the fear of displeasing the gods. By the late Republic, Romans did not seem concerned about divine intervention in their daily lives; the prospect of divine punishment seemed quite remote. In the opening stage of republican history, law was priestly and sacred, spoken only by priests and known only to men of religious families. Gradually, as law was written, debated, and altered, it became disentangled from religion. Another step in this process of secularization and rationalization occurred when the study and interpretation of law passed from the hands of priests to a class of professional jurists, who analyzed, classified, systematized, and sought commonsense solutions to legal problems.

The Roman constitution was not a product of abstract thought, nor was it the gift of a great lawmaker, such as the Athenian Solon. Rather, like the unwritten British constitution, the Roman constitution evolved gradually and empirically in response to specific needs. The Romans, unlike the Greeks, were distinguished by practicality and common sense, not by a love of abstract thought. In their pragmatic and empirical fashion, they gradually developed the procedures of public politics and the legal state.

Undoubtedly, the commoners' struggle for rights and power did arouse hatred on both sides. But in contrast to the domestic strife in Greek cities, Rome's class conflict did not end in civil war. This peaceful solution testifies to the political good sense of the Romans. Fear of foreign powers and the tradition of civic patriotism prevented the patrician-plebeian conflict from turning into a fight to the death. At the time of the class struggle, Rome was also engaged in the extension of its power over the Italian peninsula. Without civic harmony and stability, Rome could not have achieved expansion.

Roman Expansion to 146 B.C.

By 146 B.C., Rome was the dominant state in the Mediterranean world. Roman expansion occurred in three main stages: the uniting of the Italian peninsula, which gave Rome the manpower that transformed it from a city-state into a great power; the collision with Carthage, from which Rome emerged as ruler of the western Mediterranean; and the subjugation of the Hellenistic states, which brought Romans in close contact with Greek civilization. As Rome expanded territorially, its leaders enlarged their vision. Instead of restricting citizenship to people having ethnic kinship, Rome assimilated other peoples into its political community. Just as Roman law had grown to cope with the earlier grievances of the plebeians, so it adjusted to the new situations resulting from the creation of a multinational empire. The city of Rome was evolving into the city of humanity—the cosmopolis envisioned by the Stoics.

The Uniting of Italy

Frequent conflicts with hostile neighbors had forced the Romans to develop militarily and to strengthen their commitment to Rome—circumstances that fostered expansion. During the first stage of this expansion, Rome extended its hegemony over Italy, subduing in the process neighboring Latin kinsmen, semicivilized Italian tribes, the once-dominant Etruscans, and Greek city-states in southern Italy. At the beginning, Roman warfare was principally motivated by the hunger for more farmland. As Rome expanded and its territory and responsibilities increased, it was often drawn into conflict to protect its widened boundaries and its allies. Also fueling Roman expansion was an aristocratic ethos, which placed the highest value on glory and reputation. Demonstrating prowess in war, aristocrats believed, was the finest way to win the esteem of fellow Romans, bring honor to their families, and enhance their own political careers.

Rome's conquest of Italy stemmed in part from superior military organization, training, and iron discipline. From the Greeks they acquired the most advanced methods of siegecraft. Also copying the Greeks, the Romans organized their soldiers into battle formations; in contrast, their opponents often fought as disorganized hordes, which were prone to panic and flight. Fighting as part of a unit strengthened the courage and confidence of the Roman soldier, for he knew that his comrades would stand with him. Roman soldiers who deserted their posts or fled from battle were punished and disgraced, an ordeal more terrible than facing up to the enemy. The promise of glory and rewards also impelled the Roman soldier to distinguish himself in battle.

Ultimately, Rome's success was due to the character of its people and the quality of its statesmanship. The Roman farmer-soldier was dedicated, rugged, persevering, and self-reliant. He could march thirty miles a day laden with arms, armor, and equipment weighing sixty pounds. In the face of danger, he remained resolute and tenacious, obedient to the poet Virgil's maxim: "Yield you not to ill fortune, but go against it with more daring." Romans willingly made sacrifices so that Rome might endure. In conquering Italy, they were united by a moral and religious devotion to their city strong enough to overcome social conflict, factional disputes, and personal ambition.

Despite its army's might, Rome could not have mastered Italy without the cooperation of other Italian peoples. Like other ancient peoples, Rome plundered, enslaved, and brutalized, at times with great ferocity. But it also endeavored, through generous treatment, to gain the loyalty of those it had conquered. Some defeated communities retained a measure of self-government but turned the conduct of foreign affairs over to Rome and contributed contingents to the army when Rome went to war. Other conquered people received partial or full citizenship. In extending its dominion over Italy, Rome displayed a remarkable talent for converting former enemies into allies and eventually into Roman citizens. No Greek city had ever envisaged integrating nonnatives into its political community.

The Italian Confederation formed by Rome was a unique and creative organization that conferred on Italians a measure of security and order previously unknown. Rome prevented internecine wars within the peninsula, suppressed internal revolutions within city-states, and protected the Italians from barbarians (Gallic invaders from the north). In the wars of conquest outside Italy, a share of the glory and plunder fell to all Italians, another benefit of the confederation.

By 264 B.C., Rome had achieved two striking successes. First, it had secured social cohesion by redressing the grievances of the plebeians. Second, it had increased its military might by conquering Italy, thus obtaining the human resources with which it would conquer the Mediterranean world.

Conquest of the Mediterranean World

When Rome finished unifying Italy, there were five great powers in the Mediterranean area: the Seleucid monarchy in the Near East, the Ptolemaic monarchy in Egypt, the kingdom of Macedonia, Carthage in the western Mediterranean, and the Roman-dominated Italian Confederation. One hundred twenty years later, by 146 B.C., Rome had subjected these states to its dominion—"an event for which the past affords no precedent," said the contemporary Greek historian Polybius.

Roman expansion beyond Italy did not proceed according to predetermined design. Indeed, some Roman leaders considered involvement in foreign adventures a threat to both Rome's security and its traditional way of life. But it is difficult for a great power not to get drawn into conflicts as its interests grow, and, without planning it, Rome acquired an overseas empire.

Shortly after asserting supremacy in Italy, Rome engaged Carthage, the other great power in the western Mediterranean, in a prolonged conflict. Founded about 800 B.C. by Phoenicians, the North African city of Carthage had become a prosperous commercial center. Its wealth was derived from a virtual monopoly of trade in the western Mediterranean and along the western coasts of Africa and Europe. The Carthaginians (*Poeni* in Latin) had acquired an empire comprising North Africa and coastal regions of southern Spain, Sardinia, Corsica, and western Sicily.

War between the two great powers began because Rome feared Carthage's designs on the northern Sicilian city of Messana. Rome was apprehensive about the southern Italian city-states that were its allies, fearing that Carthage would use Messana either to attack them or to interfere with their trade. Rome decided that the security of its allies required intervention in Sicily.

The two powers had stumbled into a collision, the First Punic War, 264–241 B.C., that neither had deliberately sought. Although Rome suffered severe losses—including the annihilation of an

Cast Made from Trajan's Column. Emperor Trajan (A.D. 98–117) constructed a column to commemorate his campaigns. One of the reliefs depicts a Roman fleet landing at the port of Acona. During the First Punic War, Rome had become a naval power able to counter Carthage's fleet. (*Alinari/Art Resource, NY.*)

army that had invaded North Africa and the destruction of hundreds of ships in battle and storms—the Romans never considered anything but a victor's peace. Drawing manpower from loyal allies throughout Italy, Rome finally prevailed over Carthage, which had to surrender Sicily to Rome. Three years later, Rome seized the islands of Corsica and Sardinia from a weakened Carthage. With the acquisition of these territories beyond Italy, which were made into provinces, Rome had the beginnings of an empire.

Carthaginian expansion in Spain in order to recoup wealth—Spain was rich in metals—and to obtain manpower for the depleted Carthaginian forces precipitated the Second Punic War (218–201 B.C.). Coming from Spain, the Carthaginian army was commanded by Hannibal (247–183

B.C.), whose military genius astounded the ancients. Hannibal led a seasoned army, complete with war elephants for charging enemy lines, through passes in the Alps so steep and icy that men and animals sometimes lost their footing and fell to their deaths. Some twenty-six thousand men survived the crossing into Italy; fifteen thousand more were recruited from Gallic tribesmen of the Po valley. At the battle of Cannae (216 B.C.), the Carthaginian forces, brilliantly deployed by Hannibal, completely destroyed a Roman army of sixty thousand soldiers, the largest single force Rome had ever put into the field.

Romans were in a state of shock. Mixed with grief for the dead was the fear that Hannibal would crown his victory with an attack on Rome itself. To prevent panic, the Senate ordered women and children indoors, limited mourning to thirty days, and prepared to raise a new army. Adding to Rome's distress was the defection of many southern Italian allies to Hannibal.

These were the Republic's worst days. Nevertheless, says the Roman historian Livy, the Romans did not breathe a word of peace. Hannibal could not follow up his victory at Cannae with a finishing blow, for Rome wisely would not allow its army to be lured into another major engagement. Nor did Hannibal possess the manpower to capture the city itself, with its formidable fortifications. In addition, most of Rome's Italian allies remained loyal. Rome invaded North Africa, threatening Carthage and forcing Hannibal to withdraw his troops from Italy in order to defend his homeland. Hannibal, who had won every battle in Italy, was defeated by Scipio Africanus at the battle of Zama in North Africa in 202 B.C., ending the Second Punic War. Carthage was compelled to surrender Spain and to give up its elephants and its navy.

The Second Punic War left Rome as the sole great power in the western Mediterranean; it also hastened Rome's entry into the politics of the Hellenistic world. In the year after Cannae, during Rome's darkest ordeal, Philip V of Macedonia formed an alliance with Hannibal. Fearing that the Macedonian ruler might have intentions of invading Italy, Rome initiated the First Macedonian War and won it in 205 B.C. To end Macedonian influence in Greece, which Rome increasingly viewed as a Roman protectorate, the Romans fought two other wars with Macedonia. Finally, in 148 B.C., Rome created the province of Macedonia.

Intervention in Greece led to Roman involvement in the Hellenistic kingdoms of the Near East and Asia Minor—Seleucia, Egypt, and Pergamum. The Hellenistic states became client kingdoms of Rome and consequently lost their freedom of action in foreign affairs.

Roman imperialism is a classic example of a great power being snared into overseas adventures. To achieve security, Rome protected its allies, prevented endemic warfare, and thwarted any would-be conquerors of Italy. In the course of these actions came considerable spoils of war, but Rome's principal motives for expansion were strategic and political, not economic.

In 146 B.C., the same year that Rome's hegemony over the Hellenistic world was assured, Rome concluded an unnecessary Third Punic War with Carthage. Although Carthage was by then a second-rate power and no longer a threat to Rome's security, Rome had launched this war of annihilation against Carthage in 149 B.C. The Romans were driven by old hatreds and the traumatic memory of Hannibal's near-conquest. Rome sold Carthaginian survivors into slavery, obliterated the city, and turned the territory into the Roman province of Africa. Rome's savage and irrational behavior toward a helpless Carthage was an early sign of the deterioration of senatorial leadership; there would be others.

Rome had not yet reached the limits of its expansion, but there was no doubt that by 146 B.C. the Mediterranean world had been subjected to its will. No power could stand up to Rome.

Consequences of Expansion

As a result of Rome's eastern conquests, thousands of Greeks came to Rome; many were educated persons who had been enslaved because of the conquests. This influx accelerated the process of Hellenization begun earlier with Rome's contact with the Greek cities of southern Italy.

A crucial consequence of expansion was Roman contact with the legal experience of other peoples, including the Greeks. Roman jurists, demonstrating the Roman virtues of pragmatism and common sense, selectively incorporated into Roman law elements of the legal codes and traditions of these nations. Thus, Roman jurists empirically fash-

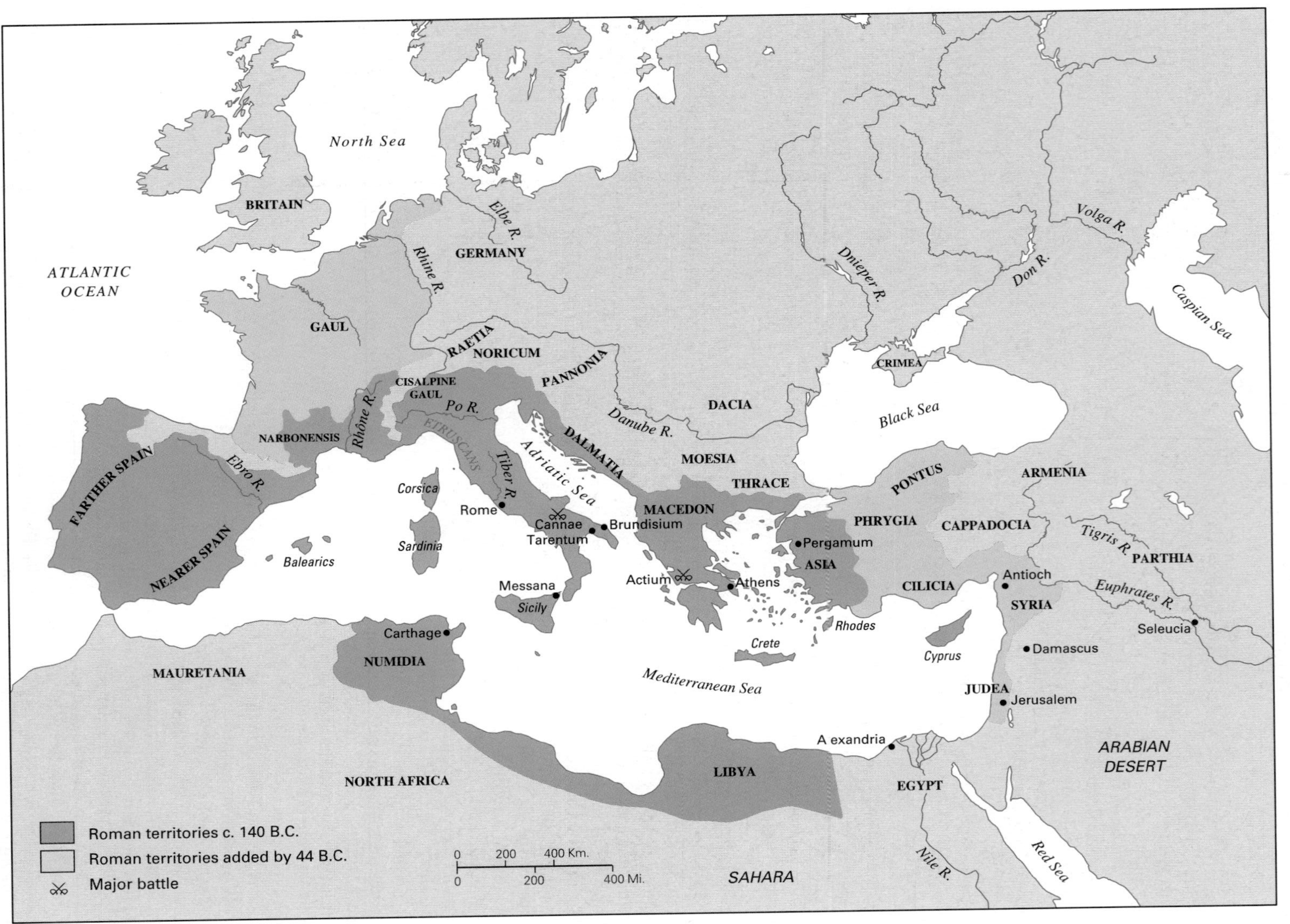
North Sea
ATLANTIC OCEAN
BRITAIN
GAUL
GERMANY
Elbe R.
Rhine R.
RAETIA
NORICUM
PANNONIA
CISALPINE GAUL
Po R.
ETRUSCANS
Rhône R.
NARBONENSIS
Ebro R.
FARTHER SPAIN
NEARER SPAIN
Balearics
Corsica
Sardinia
Tiber R.
Rome
Cannae
Tarentum
Brundisium
Adriatic Sea
DALMATIA
Danube R.
DACIA
MOESIA
THRACE
MACEDON
Actium
Athens
Messana
Sicily
Carthage
NUMIDIA
MAURETANIA
NORTH AFRICA
Mediterranean Sea
Crete
Rhodes
LIBYA
SAHARA
Dnieper R.
Don R.
Volga R.
Caspian Sea
CRIMEA
Black Sea
PONTUS
PHRYGIA
Pergamum
ASIA
CAPPADOCIA
ARMENIA
Tigris R.
PARTHIA
Euphrates R.
Seleucia
CILICIA
Antioch
SYRIA
Damascus
Cyprus
JUDEA
Jerusalem
A exandria
EGYPT
ARABIAN DESERT
Red Sea
Nile R.
Roman territories c. 140 B.C.
Roman territories added by 44 B.C.
Major battle
0 200 400 Km.
0 200 400 Mi.

RUINS IN SPAIN. This Roman aqueduct in Spain stands as an impressive reminder of the ancient Romans' engineering skills. (*Robert Frerck/Woodfin Camp.*)

ioned the *jus gentium,* the law of nations, or peoples, which gradually was applied throughout the Empire (see "Law," in Chapter 7).

Rome's conquests also contributed to the rise of a business class, whose wealth was derived from army supply contracts, construction, and tax collecting in the provinces. Rome had no professional civil service, and the collection of public revenues was open to bidding—the highest bidder receiving a contract to collect customs duties, rents on public lands, and tribute in the provinces. The collector's profit came from milking as much tax money as he could from the provincials. These financiers belonged to a group called the Equites, which also included prosperous landowners. Generally, the interests of the Equites paralleled those of the ruling oligarchy. At times, however, they did support generals—notably Julius Caesar—who challenged senatorial rule.

The immense wealth brought to Rome from the East gave the upper classes a taste for luxury. The rich built elaborate homes, which they decorated with fine furniture and works of art and staffed with servants, cooks, and tutors. They delighted in sumptuous banquets, which contained

◀ *Map 6.1* Roman Conquests During the Republic The conquest of Italy gave Rome the manpower to expand throughout the Mediterranean world. In the Second Punic War, Rome defeated its greatest rival, Carthage.

all types of delicacies. Wealthy matrons wore fancy gowns and elaborate hairstyles. These excesses prompted Roman moralists to castigate the people for violating traditional values.

Roman conquerors had transported to Italy hundreds of thousands of war captives, including Greeks, from all over the Empire. The enslavement and deportations would continue in the first century B.C. (Julius Caesar, for example, enslaved some one million Gauls.) It is estimated that between 80 and 8 B.C. more than two million enslaved aliens were transported to Italy. By the middle of that century, slaves constituted about one-third of Italy's population, compared with about 10 percent before the Second Punic War. The wars of conquest (and piracy) had made the slave trade a vast and lucrative commercial venture. Like the Greeks, Romans considered slavery indispensable for the preservation of civilized life. Roman jurists and intellectuals regarded the division of humanity into masters and slaves as a rule of nature and viewed the slave as an animate tool, an object that produced commodities. The more fortunate or more capable slaves worked as servants, artisans, bookkeepers, scribes, and administrators; the luckless and more numerous toiled on the growing number of plantations or died early laboring in mines under inhuman conditions. Except for the very poor, every free Roman owned at least one slave. Roman masters often treated their slaves brutally, but strong personal bonds between master and slave also existed—for example, there are accounts of slaves enduring torture and death to protect their masters from enemies.

Although slave uprisings were not common, their ferocity terrified the Romans. In 135 B.C., slaves in Sicily revolted and captured some key towns, defeating Roman forces before being subdued. In 73 B.C., gladiators led by Spartacus broke out of their barracks and were joined by tens of thousands of runaways. Spartacus aimed to escape from Italy to Gaul and Thrace, the homelands of many slaves. The slave army, which grew to some 150,000, defeated Roman armies and devastated southern Italy before the superior might of Rome prevailed. Some 6,000 of the defeated slaves were tortured and crucified on the road from Capua to Rome.

Republican Rome treated the people in overseas lands differently from its Italian allies. Italians were drafted into the Roman army, but provincials as a rule served only in emergencies, for Rome was not certain of their loyalty or of their readiness to meet Roman standards of discipline. Whereas Rome had been somewhat generous in extending citizenship to Italians, provincials were granted citizenship only in exceptional cases. All but some favored communities were required to pay taxes to Rome. Roman governors, lesser officials, and businessmen found the provinces a source of quick wealth; they were generally unrestrained by the Senate, which was responsible for administering the overseas territories. Exploitation, corruption, looting, and extortion soon ran rampant. "No administration in history has ever devoted itself so whole-heartedly to fleecing its subjects for the private benefit of its ruling class as Rome of the last age of the Republic," concludes E. Badian.[3] The Roman nobility proved unfit to manage a world empire.

Despite numerous examples of misrule in the provinces, Roman administration had many positive features. Rome generally allowed its subjects a large measure of self-government and did not interfere with religion and local customs. Usually, the Roman taxes worked out to be no higher, and in some instances lower, than those under previous regimes. Most important, Rome reduced the endemic warfare that had plagued these regions.

Essentially, Rome used its power for constructive ends: to establish order; to build roads, aqueducts, and public buildings; and to promote Hellenism. When Rome destroyed, it rebuilt creatively; when it conquered, it spread civilization and maintained peace. But no doubt its hundreds of thousands of prisoners of war, uprooted, enslaved, and degraded, did not view Roman conquest as beneficial; nor did the butchered Spanish tribesmen or the massacred Carthaginians. To these hapless victims, Rome appeared as an evil oppressor, not as the creator of a cosmopolis that brought order and security.

Culture in the Republic

One of the chief consequences of expansion was increased contact with Greek culture. During the third century B.C., Greek civilization started to exercise an increasing and fruitful influence on the

Roman mind. Greek teachers, both slave and free, came to Rome and introduced Romans to Hellenic cultural achievements. As they conquered the eastern Mediterranean, Roman generals began to ship libraries and works of art from Greek cities to Rome. Roman sculpture and painting imitated Greek prototypes. In time, Romans acquired from Greece knowledge of scientific thought, philosophy, medicine, and geography. Roman writers and orators used Greek history, poetry, and oratory as models. Cicero, Rome's greatest orator, tells us that ambitious young men eager to learn the art of oratory but unaware of the existence of any "course of training or any rules of art . . . attain[ed] what skill they could by means of their natural ability. . . . But later, having heard the Greek orators, gained acquaintance with their literature and called in Greek teachers, our people were fired with a really incredible enthusiasm for eloquence."[4]

Adopting the humanist outlook of the Greeks, the Romans came to value human intelligence and eloquent and graceful prose and poetry. Wealthy Romans retained Greek tutors, poets, and philosophers in their households and sent their sons to Athens to study. By the late Republic, educated Romans could speak and read Greek. Thus, Rome creatively assimilated the Greek achievement and transmitted it to others, thereby extending the orbit of Hellenism. To be sure, some conservative Romans were hostile to the Greek influence, which they felt threatened traditional Roman values. Cato the Censor (234–149 B.C.) denounced Socrates for undermining respect for Athenian law and warned that Greek philosophy might lure Roman youth into similar subversive behavior. But the tide of Hellenism could not be stemmed.

Plautus (c. 254–184 B.C.), Rome's greatest playwright, adopted features of fourth- and third-century Greek comedy. His plays had Greek characters and took place in Greek settings; the actors wore the Greek style of dress. His characters resembled those found in Menander's New Comedy: a cunning slave, a lovesick youth, a foolish old man, a braggart soldier. The plots often consisted of a struggle between two antagonists over a woman or money, or both. The plays usually had the ending desired by the audience: the "good guy" won and the "bad guy" received a fitting punishment. The pains of love were a common theme:

> *Not the throes of all mankind*
> *Equal my distracted mind.*
> *I strain and I toss*
> *On a passionate cross;*
> *Love's goad makes me reel,*
> *I whirl on Love's wheel,*
> *In a swoon of despair*
> *Hurried here, hurried there—*
> *Torn asunder, I am blind*
> *With a cloud upon my mind.*[5]

Another playwright, Terence (c. 185–159 B.C.), was originally from North Africa and was brought to Rome as a slave. His owner, a Roman senator, provided the talented youth with an education and freed him. Like Plautus, Terence was influenced by Menander, the fourth-century Athenian comic playwright. Terence's Latin style, graceful and polished, was technically superior to that of Plautus. But Terence's humor, restrained and refined, lacked the boisterousness of Plautus, which appealed to the Roman audience. For this reason, Terence's plays were less popular. Terence demonstrated more humaneness than Plautus, a quality that can be seen in his attitude toward child rearing:

> *I give—I overlook; I do not judge it necessary to exert my authority in everything. . . . I think it better to restrain children through a sense of shame and liberal treatment than through fear. . . . This is the duty of a parent to accustom a son to do what is right rather of his own choice, than through fear of another.*[6]

Catullus (c. 84–c. 54 B.C.) is generally regarded as one of the greatest lyric poets in world literature. He was a native of northern Italy whose father had provided him with a gentleman's education. In his early twenties, Catullus came to Rome and fell in love with Clodia; she was the wife of the governor of Cisalpine Gaul, who was away at the time. For the older Clodia, Catullus was a refreshing diversion from her many other lovers. Tormented by Clodia's numerous affairs, Catullus struggled to break away from passion's grip:

> *I look no more for her to be my lover*
> *As I love her. That thing could never be.*
> *Nor pray I for her purity—that's over.*
> *Only this much I pray, that I be free.*
> *Free from insane desire myself, and guarded*
> *In peace at last. O heaven, grant that yet*
> *The faith by which I've lived may be*
> *rewarded.*
> *Let me forget.*[7]

Lucretius (c. 96–c. 55 B.C.), the leading Roman Epicurean philosopher, was influenced by the civil war fostered by two generals, Marius and Sulla, which is discussed later in this chapter. Distraught by the seemingly endless strife, Lucretius yearned for philosophical tranquillity. Like Epicurus, he believed that religion prompted people to perform evil deeds and caused them to experience terrible anxiety about death and eternal punishment. In his work, *On the Nature of Things,* Lucretius expressed his appreciation of Epicurus. Like his mentor, Lucretius denounced superstition and religion for fostering psychological distress and advanced a materialistic conception of nature, one that left no room for the activity of gods—mechanical laws, not the gods, governed all physical happenings. To dispel the fear of punishment after death, Lucretius marshaled arguments to prove that the soul perishes with the body. He proposed that the simple life, devoid of political involvement and excessive passion, was the highest good and the path that would lead from emotional turmoil to peace of mind. Epicurus' hostility to traditional religion, disparagement of politics and public service, and rejection of the goals of power and glory ran counter to the accepted Roman ideal of virtue. On the other hand, his glorification of the quiet life amid a community of friends and his advice on how to deal with life's misfortunes with serenity had great appeal to first-century Romans like Lucretius, who were disgusted with civil strife.

Rome's finest orator, as well as a leading statesman, Cicero (106–43 B.C.) was an unsurpassed Latin stylist and a student of Greek philosophy. His letters, more than eight hundred of which have survived, provide modern historians with valuable insights into the politics of the late Republic. His Senate speeches have been models of refined rhetoric for all students of the Latin language. Cicero's discussion of such topics as republicanism, citizenship, friendship, virtue, duty, and justice had an enduring influence on Western moral and political thought. Dedicated to republicanism and public-spiritedness, Cicero sought to prevent one-man rule and in his writings exhorted fellow Romans to serve their city.

Cicero was drawn to Stoicism, the most influential philosophy in Rome. Stoicism's stress on virtuous conduct and performance of duty coincided with Roman ideals, and its doctrine of natural law that applies to all nations harmonized with the requirements of a world empire. Cicero admired the Stoic goal of the self-sufficient sage who sought to accord his life with standards of virtue inherent in nature. Natural law commands people to do what is right and deters them from doing what is wrong, and our gift of reason enables us to abide by its commands. Thus, knowledge and virtue are closely linked. Cicero adopted the Stoic belief that the law of the state should conform with the rational and moral norms embodied in natural law, for adherence to such rationally formulated law creates a moral bond among citizens.

He also shared the Stoic view that because natural law applies to all, we are all citizens of a single commonwealth and belong to a society of humanity. As he expressed it,

> *there is no difference in kind between man and man; for Reason, which alone raises us above the level of the beasts and enables us to draw inferences, to prove and disprove, to discuss and solve problems, and to come to conclusions, is certainly common to us all, and though varying in what it learns, at least in the capacity to learn it is invariable. . . . In fact, there is no human being of any race who, if he finds a guide, cannot attain virtue.*[8]

Collapse of the Republic

In 146 B.C., Roman might spanned the Mediterranean world. After that year, the principal concerns of the Republic were no longer foreign invasions but adjusting city-state institutions to the demands of empire and overcoming critical social and political problems at home. The Republic was unequal to either challenge. Instead of developing a professional civil service to administer the conquered lands, Roman leaders attempted to govern an empire with city-state institutions that had evolved for a different purpose. The established Roman administration proved unable to govern the Mediterranean world. In addition, Rome's ruling elites showed little concern for the welfare of its subjects, and provincial rule worsened as governors, tax collectors, and soldiers shamelessly exploited the provincials.

During Rome's march to empire, all its classes had demonstrated a magnificent civic spirit in fighting foreign wars. With Carthage and Macedonia no longer threatening Rome, this cooperation deteriorated, as Cato the Elder (234–149 B.C.) had forewarned: "What was to become of Rome, when she should no longer have any state to fear?"[9] Internal dissension tore Rome apart as the drive for domination formerly directed against foreign enemies turned inward against fellow Romans. Civil war replaced foreign war.

The Romans had prevailed over their opponents partly because of their traditional virtues: resoluteness, simplicity of manners, and willingness to sacrifice personal interests for the good of Rome. But the riches flowing into Rome from the plundered provinces caused these virtues to decay, and rivalry for status and a frenzied pursuit of wealth overrode civic patriotism. This "perverted greed" and "lack of principle," said the poet Horace (65–8 B.C.), has caused "impious slaughter, . . . intestine [domestic] fury, . . . and lawless licence."[10] And the masses, landless and afflicted with poverty and idleness, withdrew their allegiance from the state.

In this time of agony, both great and self-seeking individuals emerged. Some struggled to restore the social harmony and political unity that had prevailed in the period of expansion. Others, political adventurers, attacked the authority of the Senate to gain personal power. The Senate, which had previously exercised leadership creatively and responsibly, degenerated into a self-serving oligarchy that resisted reform and fought to preserve its power and privilege.

Neither the Senate nor its opponents could rejuvenate the Republic. Eventually it collapsed, a victim of class tensions, poor leadership, power-hungry demagogues, and civil war. Underlying all these conditions was the breakdown of social harmony and the deterioration of civic patriotism. The Republic had conquered an empire only to see the character of its citizens decay. In a high moral tone, the historian Sallust (c. 86–34 B.C.) condemned the breakdown of republican values:

> *Growing love of money, and the lust for power which followed it, engendered every kind of evil. Avarice destroyed honor, integrity, and every other virtue, and instead taught men to be proud and cruel, to neglect religion, and to hold nothing too sacred to sell. Ambition tempted many to be false. . . . At first these vices grew slowly and sometimes met with punishments; later on, when the disease had spread like a plague, Rome changed: her government, once so just and admirable, became harsh and unendurable.*[11]

Crisis in Agriculture

The downhill slide of the Republic began with an agricultural crisis. During the long war with Hannibal in Italy, each side had tried to deprive the other of food supplies; in the process, they ruined farmland, destroyed farmhouses and farm equipment, and slaughtered animals. With many Roman soldier-farmers serving in the army for long stretches of time, fields lay neglected. Returning veterans with small holdings lacked the money to restore their land. They were forced to sell their farms to wealthy landowners at low prices.

Another factor that helped to squeeze out the owners of small farms was the importation of hundreds of thousands of slaves to work on large plantations called *latifundia.* This massive use of slaves was unprecedented in Roman history. Farmers who had formerly increased their meager incomes by working for wages on neighboring large estates were no longer needed. Sinking ever deeper into poverty and debt, farmers gave up their lands and went to Rome, seeking work. The dispossessed peasantry found little to do in Rome, where there was not enough industry to provide them with employment and where much of the work was done by slaves. Congregated in rundown, crime-ridden slums, and chronically unemployed, the urban poor faced a daily struggle for survival. The once sturdy and independent Roman farmer, who had done all that his country had asked of him, was becoming part of a vast urban underclass—destitute, embittered, and alienated. The uprooting of a formerly self-reliant peasantry was Hannibal's posthumous revenge on Rome; severing the civic bond, it would prove even more deadly than Cannae.

The Gracchan Revolution

In 133 B.C., Tiberius Gracchus (163–133 B.C.), who came from one of Rome's most honored families, was elected tribune. Distressed by the injustice done to the peasantry and recognizing that the Roman army depended on the loyalty of small landowners, Tiberius made himself the spokesman for land reform. He proposed a simple and moderate solution for the problem of the landless peasants: implementing an old law barring any Roman from using more than 312 acres of the state-owned land obtained in the process of uniting Italy. For many years, the upper class had ignored this law, occupying vast tracts of public land. By reenacting the law, Tiberius hoped to free land for distribution to landless citizens.

Rome's leading families viewed Tiberius as a revolutionary threatening their property and political authority. They thought him a democrat who would undermine the Senate, the seat of aristocratic power, in favor of the Assembly, which represented the commoners. When Tiberius sought reelection as a tribune, a violation of constitutional tradition, the senators were convinced that he was a rabble-rouser who aimed to destroy the republican constitution and become a one-man ruler. To preserve the status quo, with wealth and power concentrated in the hands of a few hundred families, senatorial extremists killed Tiberius and some three hundred of his followers, dumping their bodies into the Tiber.

The cause of land reform was next taken up by Gaius Gracchus (153–121 B.C.), a younger brother of Tiberius. An emotional and gifted speaker, Gaius won the support of the city poor and was elected tribune in 123 B.C. A more astute politician than his brother, Gaius increased his following by favoring the Equites, the new class of plebeian businessmen, and by promising full citizenship to all Italians. He aided the poor by reintroducing his brother's plan for land distribution and by enabling them to buy grain from the state at less than half the market price. But like his brother, Gaius aroused the anger of the senatorial class. A brief civil war raged in Rome, during which Gaius Gracchus (who may have committed suicide) and three thousand of his followers perished.

By killing the Gracchi, the Senate had substituted violence for reason and made murder a means of coping with troublesome opposition. Soon the club and the dagger became common weapons in Roman politics, hurling Rome into an era of political violence that ended with the destruction of the Republic. Though the Senate considered itself the guardian of republican liberty, in reality it was expressing the determination of a few hundred families to retain their control over the state. This is a classic example of a once-creative minority clinging tenaciously to power long after it has ceased to govern effectively or to inspire allegiance. The Senate, which had led Rome to world dominance, became a self-seeking, unimaginative, entrenched oligarchy that was dragging the Republic and the Mediterranean world into disaster.

Rome in the first century B.C. was very different from the Rome that had defeated Hannibal. Entranced by luxuries flowing into Rome from its eastern conquests and determined to retain oligarchic rule, the senatorial families neglected their responsibility to the state. Many upper-class Romans, burning to achieve the dignity that would mark them as great men, tried to climb onto the crowded stage of Roman politics, but the best roles were already reserved for members of the senatorial families. With so few opportunities, aspirants to political power stopped at nothing.

Roman politics in the century after the Gracchi was bedeviled by intrigues, rivalries, personal ambition, and violence. Political adventurers exploited the issue of cheap grain and free land in order to benefit their careers. Whereas the Gracchi were sincere reformers, these later champions of social reform were unscrupulous demagogues who cleverly charmed and manipulated the city poor with bread and circuses: low-cost food and free admission to games. These demagogues aspired to the tribunate of the plebes, an office possessing powers formidable enough to challenge the Senate and not too difficult to obtain, since ten tribunes were elected each year. By riding a wave of popular enthusiasm, these political adventurers hoped to sweep aside the Senate and concentrate power in their own hands. The poor, denied land and employment, demoralized, alienated, and lulled into political ignorance by decades of idleness, food handouts, and free entertainment, were ready to back whoever made the most glittering promises. The Senate behaved like a decadent oligarchy, and the Tribal Assembly, which had become the voice of the urban mob, demonstrated a weakness for demagogues, an openness to bribery, and an abundance of deceit and incompetence. The Roman Republic had passed the peak of its greatness.

Rival Generals

Marius (157–86 B.C.), who became consul in 107 B.C., adopted a military policy that eventually contributed to the wrecking of the Republic. Until about 100 B.C., soldiers served essentially at their own expense, paying for their arms, armor, and food. This meant that only men of some substance could serve. Short of troops for a campaign in Numidia in North Africa, Marius disposed of the traditional property requirement for entrance into the army and filled his legions with volunteers from the urban poor, a dangerous precedent. These new soldiers, disillusioned with Rome, served only because Marius held out the promise of pay, loot, and land grants after discharge. In effect, they were Marius's clients. Their loyalty was not to Rome but to Marius, and they remained loyal to their commander only as long as he fulfilled his promises.

Marius set an example that other ambitious commanders followed. They saw that a general could use his army to advance his political career, that by retaining the confidence of his soldiers he could cow the Senate and dictate Roman policy. The army, no longer an instrument of government, became a private possession of generals. Seeing its authority undermined by generals appointed by the Assembly, the Senate was forced to seek army commanders who would champion the cause of senatorial rule. In time, Rome would be engulfed in civil wars, as rival generals used their troops to strengthen their political affiliations and to further their own ambitions.

Meanwhile, the Senate continued to deal ineffectively with Rome's problems. When Rome's Italian allies pressed for citizenship, the Senate refused to make concessions. The Senate's shortsightedness plunged Italy into a terrible war known as the Social War. As it ravaged the peninsula, the Romans reversed their policy and conferred citizenship on the Italians. The unnecessary and ruinous rebellion petered out.

While Rome was fighting its Italian allies, Mithridates, king of Pontus in northern Asia Minor, invaded the Roman province of Asia. In 88 B.C., he incited the local population to massacre eighty thousand Italian residents of the province. Mithridates and his forces crossed into Greece and occupied Athens and other cities. Faced with this crisis, the Senate entrusted command to Sulla (138–78 B.C.), who had distinguished himself in the Social War. But supporters of Marius, through intrigue and violence, had the order rescinded and the command given to Marius.

Sulla refused to accept his loss of command and, with his loyal troops, proceeded to the capital. This was a fateful moment in Roman history: the first march on Rome, the first prolonged civil war, and the first time a commander and his troops defied the government. Sulla won the first round. But when Sulla left Rome to fight Mithridates in Greece, Marius and his troops retook the city and, in a frenzy, lashed out at Sulla's supporters. The killing lasted for five days and nights.

Marius died shortly afterward. Sulla, on his return, quickly subdued Marius's supporters and became dictator of Rome. He instituted a terror that far surpassed Marius's violence. Without legal sanction and with cold-blooded cruelty, Sulla marked his opponents for death; the state seized their property and declared their children and grandchildren ineligible for public office.

Sulla resolved to use his absolute power to revive the Senate's rule and make it permanent. He

Profile

Cleopatra

Cleopatra (69–30 B.C.), the Greek queen of Egypt, belonged to the Ptolemaic family, the Macedonian Greeks who ruled Egypt during the Hellenistic Age. Cleopatra spoke Greek, received a Greek education, and viewed herself as Greek, but in contrast to her Ptolemaic predecessors, she also learned to speak the Egyptian tongue. Aspiring to revive Ptolemaic power, which had once extended into Palestine and Lebanon, she had the political good sense to realize that this could not be accomplished by antagonizing Rome, which dominated the Mediterranean world.

Cleopatra became Julius Caesar's mistress when the Roman leader stopped at Alexandria. In 47 B.C., she bore a son, declaring that Caesar was the father, and in the next year she followed Caesar to Rome. Three years after Caesar's assassination, she became Mark Antony's lover and bore him twins. She worked closely with Antony, who competed with Octavian for control of the Roman world. After their defeat

Antikenmuseum Berlin, Staatliche Museum, Preussischer Kulturbesitz.

believed that only rule by an aristocratic oligarchy could protect Rome from future military adventurers and assure domestic peace. Therefore, he restored the Senate's right to veto acts of the Assembly, limited the power of the tribunes and the Assembly, and, to prevent any march on Rome, reduced the military authority of provincial governors. To make the Senate less oligarchic, he increased its membership to six hundred. Having put through these reforms, Sulla retired.

Julius Caesar

The Senate failed to wield its restored authority effectively. The Republic was still menaced by military commanders who used their troops for their own political advantage, and underlying problems remained unsolved. In 60 B.C., a triumvirate, a ruling group of three, consisting of Julius Caesar (c. 100–44 B.C.), a politician, Pompey, a general, and Crassus, a wealthy banker, conspired to take over Rome. The ablest of the three was Caesar.

Recognizing the importance of a military command as a prerequisite for political prominence, Caesar gained command of the legions in Gaul in 59 B.C. The following year he began the conquest of the part of Gaul outside of Roman control, bringing the future France into the orbit of Greco-Roman civilization. The campaign was brilliantly described in his *Commentaries*. The successful Gallic campaigns and the invasion of Britain revealed Caesar's exceptional talent for generalship: he acted decisively, moved troops rapidly, and had excellent rapport with his men.

in the naval battle of Actium in 31 B.C., Antony and Cleopatra escaped to Egypt, where Octavian pursued them. When Antony's forces either surrendered to Octavian without a fight or fled, Cleopatra barricaded herself inside her mausoleum. Thinking that she had killed herself, Antony plunged a sword into his body. A messenger told the dying Antony that Cleopatra was still alive and wished to see him. Slaves carried him to her. Since the mausoleum's doors were sealed, he had to be hoisted with great difficulty to an opening in the wall by Cleopatra and her female servants. Plutarch described the scene:

> *Those that were present say that nothing was ever more sad than this spectacle, to see Antony, covered all over with blood and just expiring, thus drawn up, still holding up his hands to her, and lifting up his body with the little force he had left. . . . When she had got him up, she laid him on the bed, tearing all her clothes, which she spread upon him; and beating her breast with her hands, lacerating herself, and disfiguring her own face with the blood from his wounds, she called him her lord, her husband, her emperor.**

Antony died shortly afterward. Captured by the Romans, Cleopatra feared that Octavian would parade her in a victory celebration at Rome. To avoid such a humiliation, the proud Cleopatra poisoned herself, ending the Ptolemaic dynasty in Egypt. In a last letter, she requested to be buried beside Antony.

Cleopatra's life and death have intrigued historians, writers, including Shakespeare, and Hollywood producers. Her true character remains elusive. She had sufficient allure to attract both Caesar and Antony and sufficient ruthlessness to murder her younger brother, and coruler, in order to make her son coruler. No doubt her determination and ambition made her an equal partner with Antony in their political quest.

*Plutarch, *The Lives of Noble Grecians and Romans,* trans. John Dryden, rev. A. H. Clough (New York: The Modern Library, n.d.), p. 1148.

Indeed, Caesar's victories alarmed the Senate, which feared that Caesar would use his devoted troops and soaring reputation to seize control of the state.

Meanwhile, the triumvirate had fallen apart. In 53 B.C., Crassus had perished with his army in a disastrous campaign against the Parthians in the East. The bonds between Pompey and Caesar were weak, consisting essentially of Pompey's marriage to Caesar's daughter Julia. After her death in 54 B.C., Pompey and Caesar grew apart. Pompey, who was jealous of Caesar's success and eager to expand his own power, drew closer to the Senate. Supported by Pompey, the Senate ordered Caesar to relinquish his command. Caesar realized that without his troops he would be defenseless; he decided instead to march on Rome. After Caesar crossed the Rubicon River into Italy in 49 B.C., civil war again ravaged the Republic. Pompey proved no match for so talented a general; the Senate acknowledged Caesar's victory and appointed him to be dictator, a legal office, for ten years.

Caesar realized that republican institutions no longer operated effectively and that only strong and enlightened leadership could permanently end the civil warfare destroying Rome. His reforms were designed to create order out of chaos. Caesar responded to the grievances of the provincial subjects by lowering taxes, making the governors responsible to him, restraining Roman businessmen from ruthlessly draining the provinces' wealth, and generously extending citizenship. To aid the poor in Rome, he began a public works program, which provided employment and beautified the city. He also relocated

BUST OF CAESAR. Julius Caesar tried to rescue a dying Roman world by imposing strong rule. He paved the way for the transition from republican to imperial rule. (*Vatican Museum.*)

more than a hundred thousand veterans and members of Rome's lower class to the provinces, where he gave them land. To improve administration, he reorganized town governments in Italy, reformed the courts, and planned to codify the law. He attempted to conciliate the senatorial class by treating former enemies with moderation and generosity.

In February 44 B.C., Rome's ruling class—jealous of Caesar's success and power and afraid of his ambition—became thoroughly alarmed when his temporary dictatorship was converted into a lifelong office. The aristocracy saw this event as the end of senatorial government and their rule, which they equated with liberty, and as the beginning of a Hellenistic type of monarchy. On March 15 of that year, a group of aristocrats, regarding themselves as defenders of republican traditions more than four and a half centuries old, assassinated Caesar. The group included the general and orator Marcus Junius Brutus. Cicero expressed the feeling that motivated the conspirators:

> *Our tyrant deserves his death, [for his] was the blackest crime of all. [Caesar was] a man who was ambitious to be king of the Roman people and master of the whole world. . . . The man who maintains that such an ambition is morally right is a madman, for he justifies the destruction of law and liberty.*[12]

The Republic's Last Years

The assassination of Julius Caesar did not restore republican liberty but plunged Rome into renewed civil war. Thousands more died in battle or were killed in the proscriptions—lists of Roman citizens declared by their political enemies to be outlaws. Those proscribed had their property confiscated and could be executed. Two of Caesar's trusted lieutenants, Mark Antony and Lepidus, joined with Octavian, Caesar's adopted son, and defeated the armies of Brutus and Cassius, two conspirators in the plot against Caesar. After Lepidus was forced into political obscurity, Antony and Octavian fought each other, with control of Rome as the prize. In 31 B.C., at the naval battle of Actium in western Greece, Octavian crushed the forces of Antony and his wife, Egypt's Queen Cleopatra (who had earlier borne Julius Caesar's son). Octavian emerged as master of Rome and four years later became, in effect, the first Roman emperor. The Roman Republic, whose death throes had lasted for decades and kept the Mediterranean world in turmoil, had finally perished.

The Roman Republic, which had amassed power to a degree hitherto unknown in the ancient world, was wrecked not by foreign invasion but by internal weaknesses: the personal ambitions of power seekers; the degeneration of senatorial leadership and the willingness of politicians to use violence; the formation of private armies, in which soldiers gave their loyalty to their commander rather than to Rome; the transformation of a self-reliant peasantry into an impoverished and demoralized city rabble; and the deterioration of the ancient virtues that had been the source of the state's vitality. Before 146 B.C., the threat posed by foreign enemies, particularly Carthage, had forced Romans to work together for the benefit of the state, and the equilibrium achieved during the patrician-plebeian struggle was maintained. This social cohesion broke down when foreign danger diminished. In the ensuing century of turmoil, the apparatus of city-state government failed to function effectively.

Thus, the high point of Roman rule was not achieved under the Republic. The city-state constitution of the Republic was too limited to govern an immense empire. Rome first had to surpass the narrow framework of city-state government before it could unite the Mediterranean world in peace and law. The genius of Augustus (Octavian), the first emperor, made this development possible.

Notes

1. Cicero, *De Republica*, trans. Clinton Walker Keyes (Cambridge, Mass.: Harvard University Press, Loeb Classical Library, 1994), p. 79.
2. Ibid., p. 81.
3. E. Badian, *Roman Imperialism in the Late Republic* (Ithaca, N.Y.: Cornell University Press, 1971), p. 87.
4. Cicero, *De Oratore*, trans. E. W. Sutton (Cambridge, Mass.: Harvard University Press, Loeb Classical Library, 1967), p. 14.
5. Quoted in J. Wright Duff, *A Literary History of Rome* (New York: Barnes & Noble, 1960), pp. 136–137.
6. Terence, *The Brothers,* trans. H. T. Riley (London: Henry G. Bohn, 1853), pp. 202–203.
7. Catullus, quoted in E. A. Havelock, *The Lyric Genius of Catullus* (New York: Russell and Russell, 1929), p. 63.
8. Cicero, *De Legibus,* trans. C. W. Keyes (Cambridge, Mass.: Harvard University Press, Loeb Classical Library, 1928), pp. 329–330.
9. Quoted in Eli Sagan, *The Honey and the Hemlock* (New York: Basic Books, 1991), p. 25.
10. Horace, *The Odes and Epodes*, trans. C. E. Bennett (Cambridge, Mass.: Harvard University Press, 1988), ode 24, pp. 255–256.
11. Sallust, *The Conspiracy of Catiline,* trans. S. A. Handford (Baltimore: Penguin Books, 1963), pp. 181–182.
12. Cicero, *De Officiis,* trans. Walter Miller (Cambridge, Mass.: Harvard University Press, Loeb Classical Library, 1913), p. 357.

Suggested Reading

Badian, E., *Roman Imperialism in the Late Republic* (1968). An interpretive essay on the interaction between Roman domestic politics and foreign policy.

Boren, H. C., *Roman Society* (1977). A social, economic, and cultural history of the Republic and the Empire, written with the student in mind.

Brunt, P. A., *Social Conflicts in the Roman Republic* (1971). Considers the discontents of the rural and urban poor and the internal struggles within the propertied classes.

Christ, Karl, *The Romans* (1984). A good survey.

Crawford, M., *The Roman Republic* (1982). A reliable survey, with many quotations from original sources.

Dupont, Florence, *Daily Life in Ancient Rome* (1989). Everyday private and public lives of Roman citizens.

Errington, R. M., *The Dawn of Empire: Rome's Rise to World Power* (1972). A study of Rome, the reluctant imperialist.

Gelzer, Matthias, *Caesar: Politician and Statesman* (1968). A revised edition of a classic work first published in 1921.

Grant, Michael, *History of Rome* (1978). A synthesis of Roman history by a leading classical scholar; valuable in regard to both the Republic and the Empire.

———, *Julius Caesar* (1969). The author has a facility for clearly explaining the intricacies of Roman history and politics.

Gruen, E., *The Last Generation of the Roman Republic* (1974). An account of the Roman Republic from Sulla to Caesar; stresses social history.

Harris, William V., *War and Imperialism in Republican Rome, 327–70 B.C.* (1992). The motives behind Roman foreign policy.

Homo, Leon, *Roman Political Institutions* (1962). Reprint of the 1929 classic study of the Roman constitution down to the fall of the Empire in the West.

Lewis, Naphtali, and Meyer Reinhold, eds., *Roman Civilization* (1966). A two-volume collection of source readings. Volume 1 covers the Republic.

Lintott, A. W., *Violence in Republican Rome* (1968). Deals with the corruption of politics through violence.

Mazzolani, L. S., *The Idea of the City in Roman Thought* (1970). How Roman philosophers, poets, and statesmen viewed the polis and the cosmopolis.

Nicolet, C., *The World of the Citizen in Republican Rome* (1980). Daily life of the citizen in the Roman Republic.

Ogilvie, R. M., *Roman Literature and Society* (1980). An introductory survey of Latin literature.

Starr, C. G., *The Emergence of Rome* (1953). A short introduction to the emergence of Roman power in Italy and the Mediterranean.

Review Questions

1. What complaints did the Roman plebeians have at the start of the fifth century B.C.? What was the outcome of the patrician-plebeian conflict?
2. What factors enabled Rome to conquer Italy?
3. Discuss the basic features of Rome's constitutional system around the middle of the third century B.C.
4. What did the first two Punic Wars reveal about the character of the Roman people?
5. What were the consequences of Roman expansion?
6. How did Greek civilization influence Roman cultural life?
7. What were the causes of the agricultural crisis faced by Rome in the second century B.C.?
8. How did the Gracchi brothers try to deal with the agricultural crisis? Why were they opposed by Rome's leading families?
9. What was the significance of the struggle between Marius and Sulla?
10. How did Caesar try to cope with the problems afflicting Rome? Why was he assassinated?
11. Analyze the reasons for the collapse of the Roman Republic.
12. The institutions of the Roman Republic were not suited to governing a world empire. Discuss this statement.

Chapter 7

The Roman Empire: A World-State

Emperor Augustus. The reign of Augustus signified the end of the Roman Republic and the beginning of the Roman Empire. (Cathedral Treasury, Aachen, France/Dagli Orti/The Art Archive.)

- **Augustus and the Foundations of the Roman Empire**
- **The Pax Romana**
  The Successors of Augustus
  The "Time of Happiness"
  Roman Culture and Law During the Pax Romana
- **Signs of Trouble**
  Internal Unrest
  Social and Economic Weaknesses
  Cultural Stagnation and Transformation
  The Spread of Mystery Religions
  The Spiritualization of Philosophy
- **The Decline of Rome**
  Third-Century Crisis
  Diocletian and Constantine: The Regimented State
  Tribal Migrations and Invasions
  Reasons for Rome's Decline
- **The Roman Legacy**

Rome's republican institutions, designed for a city-state, proved incapable of coping with the problems created by the conquest of a world empire. Invincible against foreign enemies, the Republic collapsed from within. But after Octavian's brilliant statesmanship brought order out of chaos, Rome entered its golden age under the rule of emperors. For more than two hundred years, from 27 B.C. to A.D. 180, the Mediterranean world enjoyed unparalleled peace and stability. The Roman world-state, erected on a Hellenic cultural foundation and cemented with empirewide civil service, laws, and citizenship, gave practical expression to Stoic cosmopolitanism and universalism. Yet even this impressive monument had structural defects, and in the third century A.D., the Empire was wracked by crises from which it never fully recovered. In the fifth century, German tribesmen overran the western half of the Empire, which had by then become a shadow of its former self.

During its time of trouble, Rome also experienced an intellectual crisis. Forsaking the rational and secular values of classical humanism, many Romans sought spiritual comfort in Near Eastern religions. One of these religions, Christianity, won out over its competitors and was made the official religion of the Empire. With the triumph of Christianity in the Late Roman Empire, Western civilization took a new direction. Christianity would become the principal shaper of the European civilization that emerged from the ruins of Rome.

Augustus and the Foundations of the Roman Empire

After Octavian's forces defeated those of Antony and Cleopatra at the battle of Actium in 31 B.C., no opponents could stand up to him. The century of civil war, political murder, corruption, and mismanagement had exhausted the Mediterranean world, which longed for order. Like Caesar before him, Octavian recognized that only a strong monarchy could rescue Rome from civil war and anarchy. But learning from Caesar's assassination, he also knew that republican ideals were far from dead. To exercise autocratic power openly, like a Hellenistic monarch, would have

Chronology 7.1 ❖ The Roman Empire

27 B.C.	Senate grants Octavian the title Augustus, and he becomes, in effect, the first Roman emperor; start of the principate and the Pax Romana
A.D. 14	Death of Augustus; Tiberius gains the throne
66–70	Jewish revolt: Romans capture Jerusalem and destroy the second temple
79	Eruption of Mount Vesuvius and destruction of Pompeii and Herculaneum
132–135	Hadrian crushes another Hebrew revolt
180	Marcus Aurelius dies: end of the Pax Romana
212	Roman citizenship is granted to virtually all free inhabitants of Roman provinces
235–285	Military anarchy; Germanic incursions
285–305	Diocletian tries to deal with the crisis by creating a regimented state
378	Battle of Adrianople: Visigoths defeat the Roman legions
406	Imperial borders collapse, and Germanic tribes move into the Empire
410	Rome is plundered by Visigoths
455	Rome is sacked by Vandals
476	End of the Roman Empire in the West

aroused the hostility of the Roman ruling class, whose assistance and good will Octavian desired.

Octavian demonstrated his political genius by reconciling his military monarchy with republican institutions: he held absolute power without abruptly breaking with a republican past. Magistrates were still elected and assemblies still met; the Senate administered certain provinces, retained its treasury, and was invited to advise Octavian. With some truth, Octavian could claim that he ruled in partnership with the Senate. By maintaining the facade of the Republic, Octavian camouflaged his absolute power and contained senatorial opposition, already weakened by the deaths of leading nobles in battle or in the purges that Octavian had instituted against his enemies. Moreover, Octavian's control over the armed forces made resistance futile, and the terrible violence that followed Caesar's assassination made senators amenable to change.

In 27 B.C., Octavian shrewdly offered to surrender his power, knowing that the Senate, purged of opposition, would demand that he continue to lead the state. By this act, Octavian could claim to be a legitimate constitutional ruler leading a government of law, not one of lawless despotism so hateful to the Roman mentality. In keeping with his policy of maintaining the appearance of traditional republican government, Octavian refused to be called king or even, like Caesar, dictator; instead, he cleverly disguised his autocratic rule by taking the inoffensive title *princeps* (first citizen). The Senate also honored Octavian by conferring on him the semireligious and revered name of *Augustus*. (The rule of Augustus and his successors is referred to as the *principate*.)

The reign of Augustus signified the end of the Roman Republic and the beginning of the Roman Empire—the termination of senatorial rule and aristocratic politics and the emergence of one-man rule. The old Roman aristocracy, decimated by war and the proscriptions employed by Antony, Lepidus, and Octavian, had to adjust to a political situation in which they no longer predominated. As the historian Tacitus recognized, Augustus accomplished a profound revolution in Roman political life: "The country had been transformed, and there was nothing left of the

THE PANTHEON, C. A.D. 125. The Pantheon, the most complete surviving building of Roman antiquity, was built by Emperor Hadrian in the second century A.D. In the temple, Greek forms of ornamentation are combined with Roman building techniques. The vast hemispherical dome was constructed by pouring concrete into great wooden forms; then the interior was faced with marble. In contrast to a Greek temple, where the exterior is paramount, the Roman temple emphasizes interior space. (*Anderson/Art Resource.*)

fine old Roman character. Political equality was a thing of the past; all eyes watched for imperial commands."[1] Under Augustus, who ruled from 27 B.C. to A.D. 14, the power of the ruler was disguised; in ensuing generations, however, emperors would wield absolute power openly. As Rome became more autocratic and centralized, it took on the appearance of an oriental monarchy.

Map 7.1 The Roman Empire Under Augustus and Hadrian During the Pax Romana, the Roman Empire expanded beyond the Rhine-Danube Rivers, the imperial boundary during the reign of Augustus.

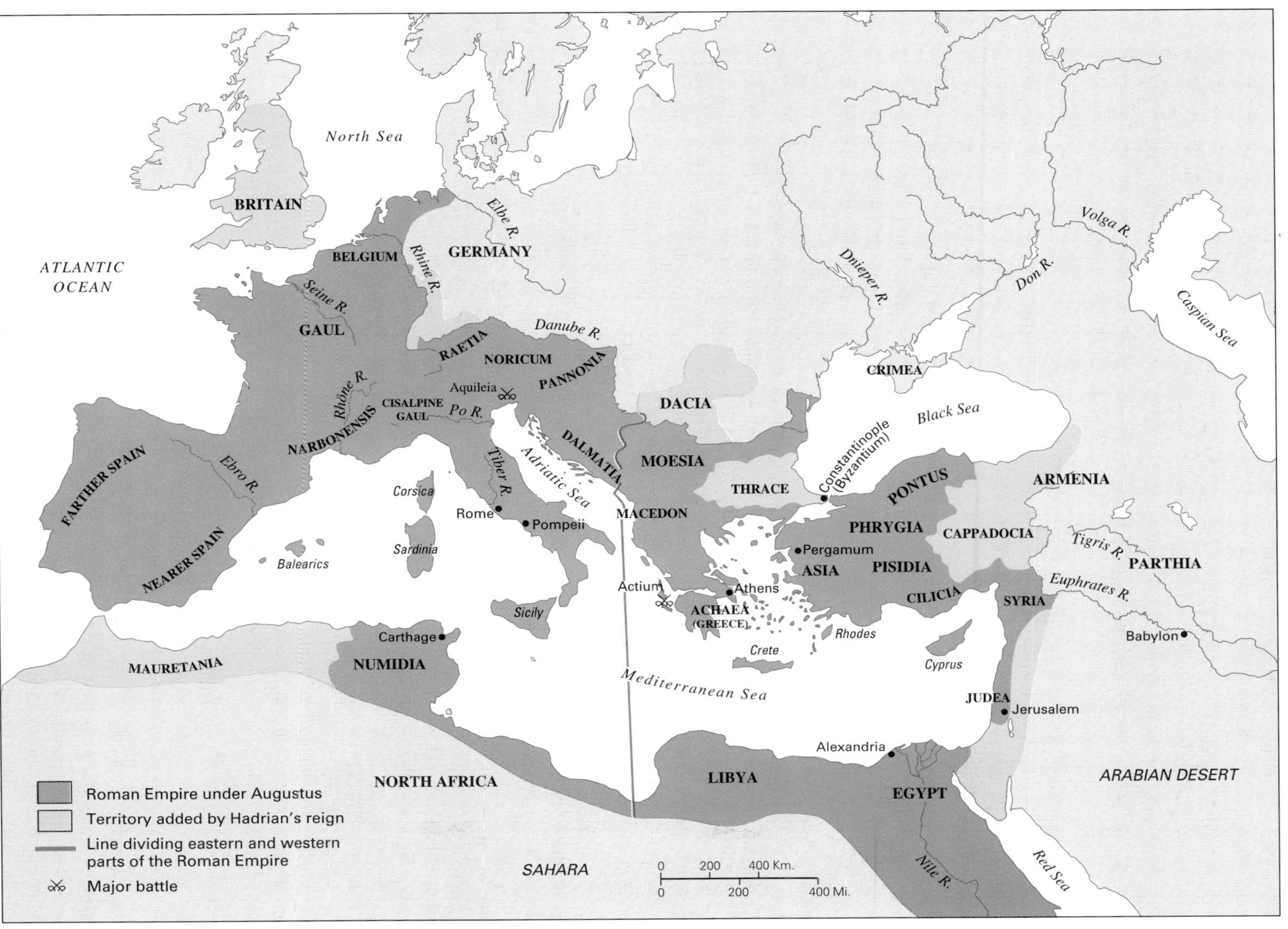

North Sea
BRITAIN
ATLANTIC OCEAN
BELGIUM
Rhine R.
GERMANY
Elbe R.
Seine R.
GAUL
Danube R.
RAETIA
NORICUM
PANNONIA
Aquileia
Rhône R.
CISALPINE GAUL
Po R.
NARBONENSIS
FARTHER SPAIN
Ebro R.
NEARER SPAIN
Balearics
Corsica
Sardinia
Rome
Pompeii
Tiber R.
Adriatic Sea
DALMATIA
Sicily
Carthage
NUMIDIA
MAURETANIA
NORTH AFRICA
SAHARA
DACIA
MOESIA
MACEDON
THRACE
Constantinople (Byzantium)
Actium
Athens
ACHAEA (GREECE)
Crete
Rhodes
Mediterranean Sea
Dnieper R.
Don R.
Volga R.
Caspian Sea
CRIMEA
Black Sea
PONTUS
PHRYGIA
Pergamum
ASIA
PISIDIA
CILICIA
CAPPADOCIA
ARMENIA
Tigris R.
PARTHIA
Euphrates R.
SYRIA
Babylon
Cyprus
JUDEA
Jerusalem
Alexandria
LIBYA
EGYPT
Nile R.
Red Sea
ARABIAN DESERT
Roman Empire under Augustus
Territory added by Hadrian's reign
Line dividing eastern and western parts of the Roman Empire
Major battle
0 200 400 Km.
0 200 400 Mi.

Augustus introduced the practice of emperor worship. In the eastern provinces, where oriental and Hellenistic monarchs had been regarded as divine, the person of Augustus was worshiped as a god. In Italy, where the deification of leaders was alien to the republican spirit, divine honors were granted to Augustus's genius, or spirit of leadership; once deceased, Augustus and his successors were deified. The imperial cult, with its ceremonies, processions, temples, and statues, strengthened the bonds of loyalty that tied subjects to the emperor. By the third century, Italians and other peoples in the western territories viewed the living emperor as a god-king.

Despite his introduction of autocratic rule, Augustus was by no means a self-seeking tyrant, but a creative statesman. Heir to the Roman tradition of civic duty, he regarded his power as a public trust delegated to him by the Roman people. He was faithful to the classical ideal, which required that the state should promote the good life by protecting civilization from barbarism and ignorance; he sought to rescue a dying Roman world by restoring political order and reviving the moral values and civic spirit that had contributed to Rome's greatness.

To prevent a renewal of civil war and to safeguard the borders of the Empire, Augustus reformed the army. As commander in chief, he could guard against the reemergence of ambitious generals like those whose rivalries and private armies had wrecked the Republic. Augustus maintained the loyalty of his soldiers by ensuring that veterans, on discharge, would receive substantial bonuses and land in Italy or in the provinces. By organizing a professional standing army made up mostly of volunteers who generally served for twenty-five years, Augustus was assured a well-trained and loyal force capable of maintaining internal order, extending Roman territory, and securing the frontier.

For the city of Rome, Augustus had aqueducts and water mains built, which brought water to most Roman homes, and he beautified the city by restoring ancient monuments and temples and building new ones. He created a fire brigade, which reduced the danger of great conflagrations in crowded tenement districts, and he organized a police force to contain violence. He improved the distribution of free grain to the impoverished urban masses and financed the popular gladiatorial combats out of his own funds.

In Italy, Augustus had roads repaired, and he fostered public works. He arranged for Italians to play a more important role in the administration of the Empire. For the Italians' security, his army suppressed brigandage, which had proliferated in the countryside during the preceding century of agony, and he guarded the northern borders from barbarian incursions.

By ending the civil wars and their accompanying devastation and by ruling out forced requisition of supplies and extortion of money, Augustus earned the gratitude of the provincials. Also contributing to his empirewide popularity were his efforts to correct tax abuse and to end corruption through improving the quality of governors and enabling aggrieved provincials to bring charges against Roman officials. An imperial bureaucracy, which enabled talented and dedicated men to serve the state, gradually evolved. In addition, Augustus continued the sensible practice of not interfering with the traditional customs and religions of the provinces. During his forty-year reign—the longevity itself was a stabilizing factor—Rome overcame the chaos of the years of revolution. The praise bestowed on him by grateful provincials was not undeserved. One decree from the province of Asia called Augustus

> *the savior of all mankind in common whose provident care has not only fulfilled but even surpassed the hopes of all: for both land and sea are at peace, the cities are teeming with the blessings of concord, plenty, and respect for law, and the culmination and harvest of all good things bring fair hopes for the future and contentment with the present.*[2]

The Pax Romana

The brilliant statesmanship of Augustus inaugurated Rome's greatest age. For the next two hundred years, the Mediterranean world enjoyed the blessings of the Pax Romana, the Roman peace. The ancient world had never experienced such a long period of peace, order, efficient administration, and prosperity. Although both proficient and inept rulers succeeded Augustus, the essential features of the Pax Romana persisted.

The Successors of Augustus

The first four emperors who succeeded Augustus were related either to him or to his third wife, Livia. They constituted the Julio-Claudian dynasty, which ruled from A.D. 14 to 68. Although their reigns were marked by conspiracies, summary executions, and assassinations, the great achievements of Augustus were preserved and strengthened. The Senate did not seek to restore republicanism and continued to assist the princeps; the imperial bureaucracy grew larger and more professional; the army, with some exceptions, remained a loyal and disciplined force.

The Julio-Claudian dynasty came to an end in A.D. 68, when the emperor Nero committed suicide. Nero had grown increasingly tyrannical and had lost the confidence of the people, the senatorial class, and the generals, who rose in revolt. In the year following his death, anarchy reigned as military leaders competed for the throne. After a bloody civil war, the execution of two emperors, and the suicide of another, Vespasian gained the principate. Vespasian's reign (A.D. 69–79) marked the beginning of the Flavian dynasty. By rotating commanding officers and stationing native troops far from their homelands, Vespasian improved discipline and discouraged mutiny. By having the great Colosseum of Rome constructed for gladiatorial contests, he earned the gratitude of the city's inhabitants. Vespasian also had nationalist uprisings put down in Gaul and Judea.

In Judea, Roman rule clashed with Jewish religious-national sentiments. Recognizing the tenaciousness with which Jews clung to their faith, the Roman leaders deliberately refrained from interfering with Hebraic religious beliefs and practices. Numerous privileges, such as exemption from emperor worship because it conflicted with the requirements of strict monotheism, were extended to Jews not only in Judea but throughout the Empire. Sometimes, however, the Romans engaged in activities that outraged the Jews. For example, Pontius Pilate, the Roman procurator in Judea from A.D. 26 to 36, at one point ordered a Roman army unit into Jerusalem with banners bearing the image of the emperor. The entire Jewish nation was aroused. To the Jews, this display of a pagan idol in their holy city was an abomination. Realizing that the Jews would die rather than permit this act of sacrilege, Pilate ordered the banners removed. Another explosive situation emerged when the emperor Caligula (A.D. 37–41) ordered that a golden statue of himself be placed in Jerusalem's temple. Again, the order was rescinded when the Jews demonstrated their readiness to resist.

Relations between the Jews of Judea and the Roman authorities deteriorated progressively in succeeding decades. Militant Jews, who rejected Roman rule as a threat to the purity of Jewish life, urged their people to take up arms. Feeling a religious obligation to reestablish an independent kingdom in their ancient homeland and unable to reconcile themselves to Roman rule, the Jews launched a full-scale war of liberation in A.D. 66. In A.D. 70, after a five-month siege had inflicted terrible punishment on the Jews, Roman armies captured Jerusalem and destroyed the temple, the central site and focus of Jewish religious life. After the conquest of Jerusalem, some fortresses, including Masada on the western side of the Dead Sea, continued to resist. The defenders of Masada withstood a Roman siege until A.D. 73; refusing to become Roman captives, they took their own lives.

Vespasian was succeeded by his sons Titus (A.D. 79–81) and Domitian (A.D. 81–96). The reign of Titus was made memorable by the eruption of Mount Vesuvius, which devastated the towns of Pompeii and Herculaneum. After Titus's brief time as emperor, his younger brother Domitian became ruler. Upon crushing a revolt led by the Roman commander in Upper Germany, a frightened Domitian executed many leading Romans. These actions led to his assassination in A.D. 96, ending the Flavian dynasty. The Flavians, however, had succeeded in preserving internal peace and in consolidating and extending the borders of the Empire.

The Senate selected one of its own, Nerva, to succeed the murdered Domitian. Nerva's reign (A.D. 96–98) was brief and uneventful. But he introduced a wise practice that would endure until A.D. 180: he adopted as his son and designated as

Profile

Josephus

Our knowledge of the Jewish revolt against Rome (A.D. 66–70) derives from *The Jewish Wars,* written by Flavius Josephus (A.D. c. 37–c. 100), who was born Joseph ben Matthias, scion of an eminent priestly Jewish family. Recognizing that a revolt against the overwhelming power of Rome was doomed, he opposed the militants who sought to overthrow Roman rule. Nevertheless, when the revolt broke out, he was given command of the troops in Galilee. When the Romans besieged the town of Jotapata, Josephus, believing that the situation was hopeless, deserted to the Romans, leaving his men behind.

Given favorable treatment by the Romans, Josephus was permitted to observe the terrible siege of Jerusalem. On several occasions he walked around the city's walls, pleading with the defenders to lay down their arms in order to avoid a slaughter. But the vicious struggle went on, and Josephus recalled that "No destruction wrought by god or man approached the wholesale carnage of this war."* Hundreds of thousands perished or were enslaved; those forced to become gladiators died in the arenas for the amusement of the Roman crowd; and the Jews' holy temple was destroyed.

After Jerusalem fell, Josephus proceeded to Rome, where he was granted Roman citizen-

Bettman/Corbis.

his heir a man with proven ability, Trajan, the governor of Upper Germany. This adoptive system assured a succession of competent rulers.

During his rule (A.D. 98–117), Trajan eased the burden of taxation in the provinces, provided for the needs of poor children, and had public works built. With his enlarged army, he conquered Dacia (parts of Romania and Hungary), where he seized vast quantities of gold and silver. He made the territory into a Roman province, adding to the large frontier Rome had to protect. The settlement of the region by many of Trajan's veterans led to its Romanization. Trajan also waged war against Parthia (a kingdom southeast of the Caspian Sea that had once been part of the Hellenistic kingdom of Seleucia), capturing Armenia and advancing to the Persian Gulf. However, overextended lines of communication, revolts by Jews in several eastern provinces, and counterattacks by the Parthians forced his armies to return to Rome.

Trajan's successor, Hadrian (A.D. 117–138), abandoned what remained of Trajan's eastern conquests. He strengthened border defenses in Britain and fought the second Hebrew revolt in Judea (A.D. 132–135). After initial successes, ship and took the name Flavius Josephus. In Rome he wrote *The Jewish Wars.* Historians rely on it for an understanding of the rival Jewish factions prior to the revolt (and at the time of Jesus) and the terrible suffering the revolt brought to the Jews of Judea. Josephus' description of the Roman siege and conquest of Jerusalem is particularly memorable:

> *They poured into the streets sword in hand, cut down without mercy all who came within reach, and burnt the houses of any who took refuge indoors, occupants and all. Many they raided, and as they entered in search of plunder they found whole families dead and the rooms full of the victims of starvation: horrified by the sight, they emerged empty-handed. Pity for those who had died in this way was matched by no such feeling for the living: they ran every man through whom they met and blocked the narrow streets with corpses, deluging the whole City with gore so that many of the fires were quenched by the blood of the slain. At dusk the slaughter ceased, but in the night the fire gained the mastery, and on the 8th September the sun rose over Jerusalem in flames. . . .*
>
> *. . . [T]he aged and infirm were slaughtered; men in their prime who might be useful were herded into the Temple and shut up in the Court of the Women. To guard them Caesar appointed one of his freedmen, and his friend Fronto to decide each man's fate according to his deserts. Those who had taken part in sedition and terrorism informed against each other, and Fronto executed the lot. Of the youngsters he picked out the tallest and handsomest to be kept for the truimphal procession; of the rest, those over seventeen were put in irons and sent to hard labour in Egypt, while great numbers were presented by Titus to the provinces to perish in the theatres by the sword or by wild beasts; those under seventeen were sold. During the days in which Fronto was sorting them out starvation killed 11,000 of the prisoners, some because the guards hated them too bitterly to allow them any food, others because they would not accept it when offered; in any case to fill so many mouths there was not even enough corn. . . .*
>
> *There was no one left for the soldiers to kill or plunder, not a soul on which to vent their fury; for mercy would never have made them keep their hands off anyone if action was possible. So Caesar now ordered them to raze the whole City and Sanctuary to the ground.*[†]

*Josephus, *The Jewish Wars,* trans. G. A. Williamson (Baltimore: Penguin Books, 1967), pp. 337–338.
[†]Ibid., pp. 336–337.

including the capture of Jerusalem, the Jews were again defeated by superior Roman might. The majority of Palestinian Jews were killed, sold as slaves, or forced to seek refuge in other lands. The Romans renamed the province Syria Palestina; they forbade Jews to enter Jerusalem, except once a year, and encouraged non-Jews to settle the land. Although the Jews continued to maintain a presence in Palestine, they had become a dispossessed and dispersed people.

After Hadrian came another ruler who had a long reign, Antoninus Pius (A.D. 138–161). He introduced humane and just reforms. He set limits on the right of masters to torture their slaves to obtain evidence, and he established the principle that an accused person be considered innocent until proven guilty. During the reign of Antoninus, the Empire remained peaceful and prosperous.

Marcus Aurelius (A.D. 161–180), the next emperor, was also a philosopher; his *Meditations* eloquently expressed Stoic thought. Frequent strife marked his reign. Roman forces had to fight Parthians, who had seized Armenia, a traditional bone of contention between Rome and Parthia. The Roman legions were victorious in this campaign but brought back from the East an epi-

Aqueduct at Pont du Gard, Nîmes, France, 19 b.c. The discovery and use of concrete allowed the Romans to carry out a vast program of public works—roads, bridges, aqueducts, harbor facilities, and fortifications. Without such aqueducts to bring clean water from distant sources, the Roman style of urban life would have been impossible. (*Foto Marburg/Art Resource.*)

demic that decimated the population of the Empire. Marcus Aurelius also had to deal with German incursions into Italy and the Balkan peninsula—incursions far more serious than any faced by previous emperors. Roman legions gradually repulsed the Germans, but the wars forced Marcus Aurelius to resort to a desperate financial measure: devaluation of the coinage.

From the accession of Nerva in A.D. 96 to the death of Marcus Aurelius in A.D. 180, the Roman Empire was ruled by the "Five Good Emperors." During this period, the Empire was at the height of its power and prosperity, and nearly all its peoples benefited. The four emperors preceding Marcus Aurelius had no living sons, so they had resorted to the adoptive system in selecting successors, which served Rome effectively. But Marcus Aurelius chose his own son, Commodus, to succeed him. With the accession of Commodus—a misfit and a megalomaniac—in A.D. 180, the Pax Romana came to an end.

The "Time of Happiness"

The Romans called the Pax Romana the "Time of Happiness." They saw it as the fulfillment of Rome's mission: the creation of a world-state that provided peace, security, ordered civilization, and the rule of law. Roman legions defended the Rhine-Danube river frontiers from incursions by German tribesmen, held the Parthians at bay in the east, and subdued the few uprisings that occurred. Nerva's adoptive system of selecting emperors provided Rome with internal stability and a succession of emperors with exceptional ability. These Roman emperors did not use military force needlessly but fought for sensible political goals; generals did not wage war recklessly but tried to limit casualties, avoid risks, and deter conflicts by a show of force.

Constructive Rule. Roman rule was constructive. The Romans built roads—some fifty-three thousand miles of roads, from Scotland to the Euphrates—improved harbors, cleared forests, drained swamps, irrigated deserts, and cultivated undeveloped lands. The aqueducts they constructed brought fresh water for drinking and bathing to large numbers of people, and the effective sewage systems enhanced the quality of life. Goods were transported over roads made safe by Roman soldiers and across a Mediterranean Sea swept clear of pirates.

A wide variety of goods circulated throughout the Empire. From Spain came gold, silver, copper, tin, fruit, and salt; from Gaul, wool, cheese, ham, and glass products; and from Britain, iron, hides, and tin. Greece and Macedonia supplied wine, honey, and marble; and Asia Minor, textiles, olive oil, carpets, and jewels. Syria, Judea, and Arabia offered leather goods, perfume, drugs, and timber; and Egypt, grain. From Parthia, China, and India—lands beyond the eastern borders of the Empire—came silk, spices, pearls and other jewels, cotton, perfumes, and drugs. African lands south of the Sahara yielded gold, ivory, and wild animals. A stable currency, generally not subject to depreciation, contributed to the economic well-being of the Mediterranean world.

Scores of new cities sprang up, and old ones grew larger and wealthier. Although these municipalities had lost their power to wage war and had to bow to the will of the emperors, they retained considerable freedom of action in local matters. Imperial troops guarded against civil wars within the cities and prevented warfare between cities—two traditional weaknesses of city life in the ancient world. The municipalities served as centers of Greco-Roman civilization, which spread to the farthest reaches of the Mediterranean, continuing a process initiated during the Hellenistic Age. Regions of North Africa, Gaul, Britain, and South Germany, hitherto untouched by Hellenism, were brought into the orbit of Greco-Roman civilization. Barriers between Italians and provincials broke down, as Spaniards, Gauls, Africans, and other provincials rose to high positions in the army and in the imperial administration, and even became emperors. Citizenship, generously granted, was finally ex-

BASALT BUST OF LIVIA. Octavian's third wife, Livia (58 B.C.–A.D. 29), was admired for her wisdom and dignity, and the emperor valued her counsel. (*Alinari/Art Resource, NY.*)

tended to virtually all free people by an edict of A.D. 212.

Improved Conditions for Both Slaves and Women. Conditions improved for those at the bottom of society, the slaves. At the time of Augustus, slaves may have accounted for a quarter of the population of Italy. But their numbers declined as Rome engaged in fewer wars of conquest. The freeing of slaves also became more common during the Empire. Urban slaves, who were often skilled artisans, could be induced to work more effectively if there was the hope of manumission. Often, nobles liberated and set up in business skilled and enterprising slaves in return for a share of the profits. Freed slaves became citizens, with most of the rights and privileges of other citizens; their children suffered no legal disabilities. (The poet Terence, the Stoic philosopher Epictetus, and the father of the poet Horace were all freed slaves.)

During the Republic, slaves had been terribly abused; they were often mutilated, thrown to wild beasts, crucified, or burned alive. Several emperors issued decrees protecting slaves from cruel masters. Claudius forbade masters to kill sick slaves; Vespasian forbade masters to sell slaves into prostitution. Domitian prohibited the castration of slaves, and Hadrian barred the execution of slaves without a judicial sentence.

The status of women had been gradually improving during the Republic. In the early days of the Republic, a woman lived under the absolute authority first of her father and then of her husband. By the time of the Empire, a woman could own property and, if divorced, keep her dowry. A father could no longer force his daughter to marry against her will, although upper-class marriages were usually based on political and social considerations. Women could make business arrangements and draw up wills without the consent of their husbands. Roman women, unlike their Greek counterparts, were not secluded in their homes but could come and go as they pleased. Upper-class women of Rome had far greater opportunities for education than did those of Greece, and some formed groups that read and discussed poetry.

Supervising the household remained the principal responsibility of Roman women. The Romans regarded marriage as a sacred civic duty. Seeking to restore traditional values, Augustus issued decrees encouraging Romans to marry. Romans greatly admired the woman who loved only one man and had only one husband, but in reality promiscuity, adultery, divorce, and remarriage were quite common. A wife could obtain a divorce just as easily as her husband, but as a rule children remained with their father. Despite the frequency of divorce, husbands and wives did demonstrate genuine affection for each other. In a eulogy to his recently deceased wife, a grieving Roman noble declared:

> *Why recall your inestimable qualities, your modesty, deference [respectful obedience], affability [courteousness], your amiable disposition, your faithful attention to the household duties, your enlightened religion, your unassuming elegance, the modest simplicity and refinement of your manners? Need I speak of your attachment to your kindred, your affection for your family? . . . These qualities which I claim for you are your own, equalled or excelled by but few; for the experience of men teaches us how rare they are.*[3]

The history of the Empire, indeed Roman history in general, was filled with talented and influential women. Cornelia, the mother of Tiberius and Gaius Gracchus, influenced Roman politics through her sons. The historian Sallust said that Sempronia, the wife of a consul and the mother of Brutus, one of the assassins of Julius Caesar, was "well-educated in Greek and Latin literature. . . . She could write poetry, crack a joke, and converse at will . . . she was in fact a woman of ready wit and considerable charm."[4] Livia, the dynamic wife of Augustus, was often consulted on important government matters, and during the third century there were times when women controlled the throne.

An Orderly World Community. From Britain to the Arabian Desert, from the Danube River to the sands of the Sahara, some fifty to sixty million people with differing native languages, customs, and histories were united by Roman rule into a world community. Unlike officials of the Republic, when corruption and exploitation in

Bas-Relief from Constantine's Arch. Emperor Marcus Aurelius dispenses aid to needy citizens. (*Alinari/Art Resource, NY.*)

the provinces were notorious, officials of the Empire felt a strong sense of responsibility to preserve the Roman peace, institute Roman justice, and spread Roman civilization.

In creating a stable and orderly political community with an expansive conception of citizenship, Rome resolved the problems posed by the limitations of the Greek city-state: civil war, intercity warfare, and a parochial attitude that divided people into Greek and non-Greek. Rome also brought to fruition an ideal of the Greek city-state—the protection and promotion of civilized life. By constructing a world community that broke down barriers between nations, by preserving and spreading Greco-Roman civilization, and by developing a rational system of law that applied to all humanity, Rome completed the trend toward universalism and cosmopolitanism that had emerged in the Hellenistic Age. The Roman world-state was the classical mind's response to the problem of community posed by the decline of the city-state in the era of Alexander the Great. Aelius Aristides, a second-century rhetorician, although Greek, proudly considered himself a Roman and glowingly extolled the Roman achievement:

> *Neither sea nor any intervening distance on land excludes one from citizenship. No distinction is made between Asia and Europe in this respect. Everything lies open to everybody; and no one fit for office or a position of trust is an alien. . . . You have made the word "Roman" apply not to a city but to a universal people. . . . You no longer classify peoples as Greek or barbarian. . . . You have redivided mankind into Romans and non-Romans. . . . Under this classification there are many in each city who are no less fellow citizens of yours than those of their own stock, though some of them have never seen this city.*[5]

Roman Culture and Law During the Pax Romana

During the late Roman Republic, Rome had creatively assimilated the Greek achievement (see Chapter 6) and transmitted it to others who had little or no contact with Hellenism. Rome had acquired Greek scientific thought, philosophy, medicine, and geography. Roman writers used Greek models; sharing in the humanist outlook of the Greeks, they valued human achievement and expressed themselves in a graceful and eloquent style. Roman cultural life reached its high point during the reign of Augustus, when Rome experienced the golden age of Latin literature.

Literature and History. At the request of Augustus, who wanted a literary epic to glorify the Empire and his role in founding it, Virgil (70–19 B.C.) wrote the *Aeneid*, a masterpiece in world literature. The *Aeneid* is a long poem that recounts the tale of Aeneas and the founding of Rome. The first six books, which describe the wanderings of Aeneas, a survivor of Troy, show the influence of Homer's *Odyssey*; the last six, dealing with the wars in Italy, show the *Iliad*'s imprint. Whereas Homer's epics focused on the deeds and misdeeds of heroic warriors, the *Aeneid* is a literary epic of national glory. The profoundest ideas and feelings expressed in the *Aeneid* are Roman virtues—patriotism, devotion to the family, duty to the state, and a strong sense of religion. Intensely patriotic, Virgil ascribed to Rome a divine mission to bring peace and civilized life to the world, and he praised Augustus as a divinely appointed ruler who had fulfilled Rome's mission. The Greeks might be better sculptors, orators, and thinkers, said Virgil, but only the Romans knew how to govern an empire:

> *For other peoples will, I do not doubt,*
> *still cast their bronze to breathe with softer features,*
> *or draw out of the marble living lines, plead causes better,*
> *trace the ways of heaven with wands and tell the rising*
> *constellations; but yours will be the rulership of nations,*
> *remember, Roman, these will be your arts:*
> *to teach the ways of peace to those you conquer, to spare*
> *defeated peoples, to tame the proud.*[6]

In his *History of Rome,* the historian Livy (59 B.C.–A.D. 17) also glorified Roman virtues, customs, and deeds. He praised Augustus for attempting to revive traditional Roman morality, to which Livy felt a strong attachment. Modern historians criticize Livy for failing to utilize important sources of information in this work, for relying on biased authorities, and for allowing fierce patriotism to warp his judgment. Although Livy was a lesser historian than Thucydides or Polybius, his work was still a major achievement, particularly in its depiction of the Roman character, which helped make Rome great.

An outstanding poet, Horace (65–8 B.C.) was the son of a freed slave. He broadened his education by studying literature and philosophy in Athens, and Greek ideals are reflected in his writings. Horace enjoyed the luxury of country estates, banquets, fine clothes, and courtesans, along with the simple pleasures of mountain streams and clear skies. His poetry touched on many themes—the joy of good wine, the value of moderation, and the beauty of friendship. Desiring to blend reason and emotion, Horace urged men to seek pleasurable experiences but to avoid extremes and to keep desire under rational control. He also reminded Romans of the terrible civil wars that had ruined the Republic:

> *What plain is not enriched with Latin blood, to bear witness with its graves to our unholy strife. . . . What pool or stream has failed to taste the dismal war! What sea has Italian slaughter not discolored! What coast knows not our blood!*[7]

Unlike Virgil, Livy, or Horace, Ovid (43 B.C.–A.D. 17) did not experience the civil wars during his adult years. Consequently, he was less inclined to praise the Augustan peace. His poetry showed a preference for romance and humor, and he is best remembered for his advice to lovers contained in his most famous work, *The Art of Love.* Written when Ovid was fifty years old, the work deals with the art of seduction. Book I tells how to attact a woman who is the object of a man's desire; Book II explains how a man can keep a woman's love; Book III advises women about men. To the man who wants to win a woman, Ovid gave this counsel:

> *First of all, be quite sure that there isn't a woman who cannot be won, and make up your mind that you will win her. Only you must prepare the ground.*
>
> *You must play the lover for all you're worth. Tell her how you are pining for her.*
>
> *Never cease to sing the praises of her face, her hair, her taper fingers, and her dainty foot.*
>
> *Tears too are a mighty useful resource in the matter of love. They would melt a diamond.*

> *Make a point, therefore, of letting your mistress see your face all wet with tears.*
>
> *Women are things of many moods. You must adapt your treatment to the special case.*[8]

The writers who lived after the Augustan age were of a lesser quality than their predecessors, although the historian Tacitus (A.D. 55–c. 118) was an exception. Sympathetic to republican institutions, Tacitus denounced Roman emperors and the imperial system in his *Histories* and *Annals*. In *Germania*, he turned his sights on the habits of the Germanic peoples. He described the Germans as undisciplined but heroic, with a strong love of freedom.

The satirist Juvenal (A.D. c. 55–138) attacked the evils of Roman society, such as the misconduct of emperors, the haughtiness of the wealthy, the barbaric tastes of commoners, and the failures of parents. He also described the noise, congestion, and poverty of the capital, as well as its dangers:

> *. . . a piece of pot*
> *Falls down on my head, how often a broken vessel is shot*
> *From the upper windows, with what force it strikes and dints*
> *The cobblestones! . . .*
>
> *But these aren't your only terrors. For you can never restrain*
> *The criminal element. Lock up your house, put bolt and chain*
> *On your shop, but when all's quiet, someone will rob you or he'll*
> *Be a cutthroat perhaps and do you in quickly with cold steel.*[9]

In addition, Juvenal expressed venomous views toward women. He describes the humiliations husbands must face—infidelity, poisonings, public harlotry, and being ignored, intimidated, and dominated. All of this, says Juvenal, is a consequence of a wife's failure to live up to the obligations of the married state—being silent, loyal, obedient, respectful of her husband, and caring for the children.

Philosophy. Stoicism was the principal philosophy of the Pax Romana, and its leading exponents were Seneca, Epictetus (A.D. c. 60–c. 117), and Marcus Aurelius. Perpetuating the rational tradition of Greek philosophy, Roman Stoics saw the universe as governed by reason, and they esteemed the human intellect. Like Socrates, they sought the highest good in this world, not in an afterlife, and envisioned no power above human reason. Moral values were obtained from reason alone. The individual was self-sufficient and depended entirely on rational faculties for knowing and doing good. Stoics valued self-sufficient persons who attained virtue and wisdom by exercising rational control over their lives. Roman thinkers also embraced the Stoic doctrine that all people, because of their capacity to reason, belong to a common humanity.

Lucius Annaeus Seneca (4 B.C.–A.D. 65), a student of rhetoric and philosophy, served the emperor Nero. After Nero accused him of participating in a conspiracy against the throne, Seneca was forced to commit suicide. Seneca's Stoic humanitarianism was expressed in his denunciation of the gladiatorial combats and in his concern for slaves.

> *Were you to consider, that he whom you call your slave, is sprung from the same origin, enjoys the same climate, breathes the same air, and is subject to the same condition of life and death as yourself, you will think it possible to see him as a free-born person, as he is free to see you as a slave. . . .*
>
> *I will not discuss at length the treatment of slaves towards whom we behave cruelly and arrogantly. But this is the essence of what I would prescribe: treat your inferiors as you would have a superior treat you. As often as you think of the power that you have over a slave, reflect on the power that your master has over you. But you say, "I have no master." Be it so. The world goes well with you at present; it may not do so always. You may one day be a slave yourself.*[10]

The emperor Marcus Aurelius, the last of the great Stoics, also had to deal with serious problems confronting the Empire. While commanding troops engaged in fighting plundering tribesmen in the Balkans, he wrote in Greek the *Meditations,* a classic work of Stoic thought. In Stoicism, he sought the strength to overcome the burdens of ruling an empire, the fear of

THE COLOSSEUM, ROME, A.D. 70–80 The joint work of the emperors Vespasian and his sons Titus and Domitian, this huge amphitheater was the largest in the ancient world. It was the site of innumerable spectacles, sham sea battles, gladiatorial games, wild beast hunts, and the deaths of Christian martyrs. (*Photo Researchers/© Louis Renault.*)

death, and the injustices and misdeeds committed by his fellows.

> *Hour by hour resolve firmly, like a Roman and a man, to do what comes to hand with correct and natural dignity, and with humanity, independence, and justice. Allow your mind freedom from all other considerations. This you can do, if you will approach each action as though it were your last, dismissing the wayward thought, the emotional recoil from the commands of reason, the desire to create an impression, the admiration of self, the discontent with your lot. See how little a man needs to master, for his days to flow on in quietness and piety: he has but to observe these few counsels, and the gods will ask nothing more.*[11]

Science. The two most prominent scientists during the Greco-Roman age were Ptolemy, the mathematician, geographer, and astronomer, who worked at Alexandria in the second century A.D., and Galen (A.D. c. 130–c. 201), who investigated medicine and anatomy. Ptolemy's thirteen-volume work, *Mathematical Composition*—more commonly known as the *Almagest,* a Greek-Arabic term meaning "the greatest"—summed up antiquity's knowledge of astronomy and became the authoritative text during the Middle Ages. In the Ptolemaic system, a motionless, round earth stood in the center of the universe, and the moon, sun, and planets moved about the earth in circles, or in combinations of circles. The Ptolemaic system was built on a faulty premise, as modern astronomy eventually showed. However, it did work—that is, it did provide a model of the universe that adequately accounted for most observed phenomena. The Ptolemaic system would not be challenged until the middle of the sixteenth century.

As Ptolemy's system dominated astronomy, so the theories of Galen dominated medicine down to modern times. By dissecting both dead and living animals, Galen attempted a rational investigation of the body's working parts. Although his work contains many errors, he made essential contributions to the knowledge of anatomy. Thanks to Arab physicians who preserved his writings during the Middle Ages, Galen's influence continued in the West into early modern times.

Art, Architecture, and Engineering. Romans borrowed art forms from other peoples, particularly the Greeks, but they borrowed creatively, transforming and enhancing their inheritance. Roman portraiture continued trends initiated during the Hellenistic Age. Imitating Hellenistic models, Roman sculptors realistically carved every detail of a subject's face: unruly hair, prominent nose, lines and wrinkles, a jaw that showed weakness or strength. Sculpture also gave expression to the imperial ideal. Statues of emperors conveyed nobility and authority; reliefs commemorating victories glorified Roman might and grandeur.

The Romans most creatively transformed the Greek inheritance in architecture. The Greek temple was intended to be viewed from the outside; the focus was exclusively on the superbly balanced exterior. By using arches, vaults, and domes, the Romans built structures with large, magnificent interiors. The vast interior, massive walls, and overarching dome of the famous Pantheon, a temple built in the early second century, during the reign of Hadrian, symbolizes the power and majesty of the Roman world-state.

The Romans excelled at engineering. They built amphitheaters, public baths, and aqueducts that carried water to Roman cities—some still survive. Roman engineers with an eye for natural barriers and drainage problems carefully selected routes and designed great embanked roads, the finest in the ancient world.

Law. Expressing the Roman yearning for order and justice, law was Rome's great legacy to Western civilization. Roman law passed through two essential stages: the formation of civil law (*jus civile*) and the formation of the law of nations (*jus gentium*). The basic features of the civil law evolved during the two-hundred-year Struggle of the Orders, at the same time that Rome was extending its dominion over Italy. The Twelve Tables, drawn up in the early days of the patrician-plebeian struggle (described at the beginning of the previous chapter), established for the Roman state written rules of criminal and civil law that applied to all citizens. Over the centuries, the civil law was expanded by statutes enacted by the assemblies, by the legal decisions of jurisdictional magistrates, by the rulings of emperors, and by the commentaries of professional jurists, who, aided by familiarity with Greek logic, engaged in systematic legal analysis.

During the period of the Republic's expansion outside Italy, contact with the Greeks and other peoples led to the development of the second branch of Roman law, jus gentium, which combined Roman civil law with principles selectively drawn from the legal tradition of Greeks and other peoples. Roman jurists identified the jus gentium with the natural law (jus naturale) of the Stoics. The jurists said that a law should accord with rational principles inherent in nature: uniform and universally valid standards that can be discerned by rational people. Serving to bind different peoples together, the law of nations harmonized with the requirements of a world empire and with Stoic ideals, as Cicero pointed out:

> *True law is right reason in agreement with nature; it is of universal application, unchanging and ever lasting. . . . And there will not be different laws at Rome and at Athens or different laws now and in the future, but one eternal and unchangeable law will be valid for all nations and all times.*[12]

The law of nations came to be applied throughout the Empire, although it never entirely supplanted local law. In the eyes of the law, a citizen was not a Syrian or a Briton or a Spaniard but a Roman. In effect, through jus gentium, an international law, Rome transformed what was a theoretical principle for the Stoics into a political reality.

After the fall of the western Roman Empire, Roman law fell into disuse in western Europe. Gradually reintroduced in the twelfth century, it came to form the basis of the common law in all Western lands except Britain and its dependencies. Some provisions of Roman law are readily recognizable in modern legal systems, as the following excerpts illustrate:

> *Justice is a constant, unfailing disposition to give everyone his legal due.*
> *No one is compelled to defend a cause against his will.*
> *No one suffers a penalty for what he thinks.*
> *In the case of major offenses it makes a difference whether something is committed purposefully or accidentally.*
> *The guilt or punishment of a father can impose no stigma upon the son, for every individual is subjected to treatment in accordance with his own action, and no one is made the inheritor of the guilt of another.*
> *In inflicting penalties, the age . . . of the guilty party must be taken into account.*[13]

Entertainment. Despite its many achievements, Roman civilization presents a paradox. On the one hand, Roman culture and law evidence high standards of civilization. On the other, the Romans institutionalized barbaric practices: battles to the death between armed gladiators and the tormenting and slaughtering of wild beasts.

The major forms of entertainment in both the Republic and the Empire were chariot races, wild animal shows, and gladiatorial combat. Chariot races were gala events in which the most skillful riders and the finest and best-trained stallions raced in an atmosphere of incredible excitement. The charioteers, many of them slaves hoping that victory would bring them freedom, became popular heroes. The rich staked fortunes on the races, and the poor bet their last coins.

The Romans craved brutal spectacles. One form of entertainment pitted wild beasts against each other or against men armed with spears. Another consisted of battles, sometimes to the death, between highly trained gladiators. The gladiators, mainly prisoners of war and condemned criminals, learned their craft at schools run by professional trainers. Some gladiators entered the arena armed with a sword, others with a trident and a net. The spectators were transformed into a frenzied mob that lusted for blood. If they were displeased with a losing gladiator's performance, they would call for his immediate execution.

Over the centuries, these spectacles grew more bizarre and brutal. Hundreds of tigers were set against elephants and bulls; wild bulls tore apart men dressed in animal skins; women battled in the arena; dwarfs fought each other. One day in the Colosseum, which could seat fifty thousand people, three thousand men fought each other; on the day the Colosseum opened in A.D. 80, nine thousand beasts were slaughtered. In fact, much of the African trade was devoted to supplying animals for the contests.

Few Romans questioned these barbarities, which became a routine part of daily life. Occasionally, however, thoughtful Romans had strong doubts. After watching a public spectacle, the Stoic philosopher Seneca wrote in disgust: "There is nothing more harmful to one's character than attendance at some spectacle, because vices more easily creep into your soul while you are being entertained. When I return from some spectacle, I am greedier, more aggressive and . . . more cruel and inhuman."[14]

Signs of Trouble

The Pax Romana was one of the finest periods in ancient history. But even during the Time of Happiness, signs of trouble appeared that would grow to crisis proportions in the third century.

Internal Unrest

The Empire's internal stability was always subject to question. Were the economic foundations of the Empire strong and elastic enough to endure hard blows? Could the Roman Empire retain the loyalty of so many diverse nationalities, each with its own religious and cultural traditions? Were the mass of people committed to the values of Greco-Roman civilization, or would they withdraw their allegiance and revert to their native traditions if imperial authority weakened?

During the Pax Romana, dissident elements did surface, particularly in Gaul, Judea, and Egypt. The Jews fought two terrible and futile wars to try to liberate their land from Roman rule. Separatist movements in Gaul were also crushed by Roman forces. To provide free bread for Rome's poor, Roman emperors exploited the Egyptian peasantry. Weighed down by forced labor, heavy taxes, requisitions, and confiscations, Egyptian peasants frequently sought to escape from farmwork.

The unrest in Egypt, Gaul, and Judea demonstrated that not all people at all times welcomed the grand majesty of the Roman peace and that localist and separatist tendencies persisted in a universal empire. In the centuries that followed, as Rome staggered under the weight of economic, political, and military difficulties, these native loyalties reasserted themselves. Increasingly, the masses, and even the Romanized elite of the cities, withdrew their support from the Roman world-state.

Social and Economic Weaknesses

A healthy world-state required empirewide trade to serve as an economic base for political unity, expanding agricultural production to feed the cities, and growing internal mass markets to stimulate industrial production. But the economy of the Empire during the Pax Romana had serious defects. The means of communication and transportation were slow, which hindered long-distance commerce. Roman roads, built for military rather than commercial purposes, were often too narrow for large carts and in places were too steep for any vehicles. Consequently, transporting goods by land, even short distances, necessitated huge price increases that hampered trade. Many nobles, considering it unworthy for a gentleman to engage in business, chose to squander their wealth rather than invest it in commercial or industrial enterprises. Lacking the stimulus of capital investment, the economy could not expand.

Limited employment opportunities resulted from the Greco-Roman civilization's failure to improve its technology substantially and from reliance on slave labor. Also, because manual labor was considered degrading, fit only for a slave, there was little incentive for innovation that might have triggered economic growth and expanded employment opportunities. Because of these factors, millions of people simply did not engage in productive labor. Moreover, scarce employment left the masses with little purchasing power; this too adversely affected business and industry. Many unemployed inhabitants of Italian towns lived on free or cheap grain provided by the state. To feed this unemployed underclass, the government kept the price of grain artificially low. This practice discouraged farmers from planting more crops and expanding grain production and forced many of them to seek other livelihoods. As more farmers left the countryside, the towns became increasingly swollen with an impoverished proletariat. Rural areas eventually faced a serious shortage of laborers due to this population migration.

Ultimately, only a small portion of the urban population—landlords, whose estates were outside the city, merchants, and administrators—reaped the benefits of the Roman peace. They basked in luxury, leisure, and culture. The urban poor, on the other hand, derived few of the economic gains and shared little in the political and cultural life of the city. The privileged classes bought off the urban poor with bread and circuses, but occasionally mass discontent expressed itself in mob violence. Outside the cities, the peasantry—still the great bulk of the population—was exploited to provide cheap food for the city dwellers.

Such a parasitical, exploitative, and elitist social system might function in periods of peace and tranquillity, but could it survive crises? Would the impoverished people of town and country—the overwhelming majority of the population—remain loyal to a state whose benefits barely extended to them and whose sophisticated culture, which they hardly comprehended, virtually excluded them?

Cultural Stagnation and Transformation

Perhaps the most dangerous sign for the future was the spiritual paralysis that crept over the ordered world of Pax Romana. A weary and sterile Hellenism underlay the Roman peace. The ancient world was undergoing a transformation of values that foreshadowed the end of Greco-Roman civilization.

During the second century A.D., Greco-Roman civilization lost its creative energies, and the values of classical humanism were challenged by mythic-religious movements. No longer regarding reason as a satisfying guide to life, the educated elite subordinated the intellect to feelings and an unregulated imagination. No longer finding the affairs of this world to have purpose, people placed their hope in life after death. The Roman world was undergoing a religious revolution and seeking a new vision of the divine.

The application of reason to nature and society, as we have seen, was the great achievement of the Greek mind. Yet despite its many triumphs, Greek rationalism never entirely subdued the mythic-religious mentality, which draws its strength from human emotion. The masses of peasants and slaves remained attracted to religious forms. Ritual, mystery, magic, and ecstasy never lost their hold on the ancient world—nor, indeed, have they on our own scientific and technological society. During the Hellenistic Age, the tide of rationalism gradually receded, and the nonrational, an ever present undercurrent, showed renewed vigor. This resurgence of the mythical mentality could be seen in the popularity of the occult, magic, alchemy, and astrology. Feeling themselves controlled by heavenly powers, burdened by danger and emotional stress, and fearing fate as fixed in the stars, people turned for deliverance to magicians, astrologers, and exorcists.

They also became devotees of the many Near Eastern religious cults that promised personal salvation. More and more people felt that the good life could not be achieved by individuals through their own efforts; they needed outside help. Philosophers eventually sought escape from this world through union with a divine presence greater than human power. Increasingly, the masses, and then even the educated elite, came to believe that the good life could be found not on earth but only in a world beyond the grave. Seeing themselves as isolated souls wandering aimlessly in a social desert, people sought refuge in religion. Reason had been found wanting; the time for faith and salvation was at hand.

The Roman Empire had imposed peace and stability, but it could not alleviate the feelings of loneliness, anxiety, impotence, alienation, and boredom that had been gaining ground in the Mediterranean world since the fourth century B.C. A spiritual malaise descended on the Greco-Roman world. Among the upper classes, the philosophical and scientific spirit withered; rational and secular values were in retreat. Deprived of the excitement of politics and bored by idleness and pleasure, the best minds, says historian Michael Rostovtzeff,

> *lost faith in the power of reason. . . . Creative genius dwindled; science repeated its previous results. The textbook took the place of research; no new artistic discoveries were made, but echoes of the past were heard . . . [writers] amuse[d] the mind but [were] incapable of elevating and inspiring it.*[15]

The Spread of Mystery Religions

The proliferation of Eastern mystery religions was a clear expression of this transformation of classical values. During the Hellenistic era, slaves, merchants, and soldiers brought many religious cults westward from Persia, Babylon, Syria, Egypt, and Asia Minor. The various mystery cults possessed many common features. Converts underwent initiation rites and were bound by oath to secrecy. The initiates, in a state of rapture, attempted to unite with the deity after first purifying themselves through baptism (sometimes with the blood of a bull), fasting, having their heads shaved, or drinking from a sacred vessel. Communion was achieved by donning the god's robe, eating a sacred meal, or visiting the god's sanctuary. This sacramental drama propelled initiates through an intense mystical experience of exaltation and rebirth. Cultists were certain that their particular savior-god would protect them from misfortune and ensure their soul's immortality.

Of special significance was the cult of Mithras, which had certain parallels with early Christianity and was its principal competitor. Originating in Persia, Mithraism spread westward into the Roman Empire. Because it stressed respect for the masculine virtues of bravery and camaraderie, it became particularly popular with the army. The god Mithras, whose birth date was celebrated on December 25, had as his mission the rescuing of humanity from evil. He was said to demand high standards of morality, to judge

STONE RELIEF OF MITHRAS SACRIFICING A BULL. The spread and popularity of Near Eastern mystery cults in the western Roman Empire was a sign of the Hellenistic cosmopolitanism that dominated Roman imperial society. Among the most popular mystery cults, especially among soldiers, was that of Mithras, a Persian warrior-deity also associated with the sun and justice. Mithras promised immortality to those who upheld high ethical standards of conduct and underwent cultic initiation rites. (*Cincinnati Art Museum, Gift of Mr. and Mrs. Fletcher E. Nyce, 1968.*)

souls after death, and to grant eternal life to his faithful followers.

The popularity of magic and mystery demonstrates that many people in Roman society either did not comprehend or had lost faith in the rational and secular values of classical humanism. Religion proved more comforting to the spirit. People felt that the gods could provide what reason, natural law, and civic affairs could not: a sure way of overcoming life's misfortunes and discouragements, a guarantee of immortality, a sense of belonging to a community of brethren who cared, an exciting outlet for bottled-up emotions, and a sedative for anxiety at a time when dissatisfaction with the human condition showed itself in all phases of society and life.

The Spiritualization of Philosophy

The religious orientation also found expression in philosophy, which demonstrated attitudes markedly at odds with classical humanism. These attitudes, commonly associated with religion, included indifference to the world, withdrawal, and pessimism about the earthly state. From trying to understand nature and individuals' relationships to one another, the philosophers more and more aspired to a communion with a higher reality. Like the mystery religions, philosophy reached for something beyond this world in order to comfort the individual. In Neo-Platonism, which replaced Stoicism as the dominant school of philosophy in the Late Roman Empire, religious yearnings were transformed into a religious system that transcended reason.

Plotinus (A.D. c. 205–c. 270), the most influential spokesman of Neo-Platonism, went far beyond Marcus Aurelius's natural religion; in aspiring to the ecstatic union of the soul with God, he subordinated philosophy to mysticism. Plato's philosophy, we have seen, contained both a major and a minor key. The major key stressed a rational interpretation of the human community and called for reforming the polis on the basis of knowledge, whereas the minor key urged the soul to rise to a higher world of reality. Although Plotinus retained elements of Platonic rationalism (he viewed the individual as a reasoning being and used rational argument to explain his religious orientation), he was intrigued by Plato's otherworldliness.

What Plotinus desired was union with the One, or the Good, sometimes called God—the source of all existence. Plotinus felt that the intellect could neither describe nor understand the One, which transcended all knowing, and that joining with the One required a mystical leap, a purification of the soul so that it could return to its true eternal home. For Plotinus, philosophy became a religious experience, a contemplation of the eternal. His successors held that through acts of magic the soul can unite with the One. Compared with this union with the divine One, of what value was knowledge of the sensible world or a concern for human affairs? For Plotinus, this world was a sea of tears and troubles from which the individual yearned to escape. Reality was not in this world but beyond it, and the principal goal of life was not comprehension of the natural world or fulfillment of human potential or betterment of the human community but knowledge of the One. Thus, his philosophy broke with the essential meaning of classical humanism.

Neo-Platonism, concludes historian of philosophy W. T. Stace, "is founded upon . . . the despair of reason." It seeks to reach the Absolute not through reason but through "spiritual intoxication." This marks a radical transformation of philosophical thinking:

> *For philosophy is founded upon reason. It is the effort to comprehend, to understand, to grasp the reality of things intellectually. Therefore it cannot admit anything higher than reason. To exalt intuition, ecstasy, or rapture, above thought—this is the death of philosophy. . . . In Neo-Platonism, therefore, ancient philosophy commits suicide. This is the end. The place of philosophy is taken henceforth by religion.*[16]

By the time of the Late Roman Empire, mystery religions intoxicated the masses, and mystical philosophy beguiled the educated elite. Classical civilization was being transformed. Philosophy had become subordinate to religious belief; secular values seemed inferior to religious experience. The earthly city had raised its eyes toward heaven. The culture of the Roman world was moving in a direction in which the quest for the divine was to predominate over all human enterprises.

The Decline of Rome

Third-Century Crisis

At the death of Marcus Aurelius in A.D. 180, the Empire was politically stable, economically prosperous, and militarily secure. In the third century, the ordered civilization of the Pax Romana ended. Several elements caused this disruption. The Roman Empire was plunged into military anarchy, raided by Germanic tribes, and burdened by economic dislocations. In addition, Eastern religions, which undermined the rational foundations of Greco-Roman civilization, pervaded the Roman world. During these critical times, effective leadership was lacking, for the adoptive system abandoned by Marcus Aurelius was not restored.

The degeneration of the army was a prime reason for the third-century crisis. During the great peace, the army had remained an excellent fighting force, renowned for its discipline, organization, and loyalty. In the third century A.D., however, there was a marked deterioration in the quality of Roman soldiers. Lacking loyalty to Rome and greedy for spoils, soldiers used their weapons to prey on civilians and to make and unmake emperors. Fearful of being killed by their unruly troops who wanted spoils or of being murdered by a suspicious emperor, generals were driven to seize the throne. Once in power, they had to buy the loyalty of their soldiers and guard against assassination by other generals. From A.D. 235 to 285, military mutiny and civil war raged, as legion fought legion. During this period, there were twenty-six soldier-emperors, twenty-five of whom died violently. The once stalwart army neglected its duty of defending the borders and disrupted the internal life of the Empire.

Perhaps this change in attitude can be explained by the liberal granting of citizenship. In A.D. 212, citizenship was extended to virtually all freeborn inhabitants of the Empire. Previously, many army recruits had been drawn from among provincials, who were attracted by the promise of citizenship and its advantages. These recruits generally were men of a high caliber who were interested in bettering themselves and their families' lot. With citizenship no longer an inducement for enlistment, says Edward T. Salmon,

> *recruits were now only too likely to be drawn from the lowest and most primitive elements . . . men of the rough and reckless type, who were joining the army chiefly in order to get weapons in their hands with which they would be able to extort for themselves an even greater share of the Empire's collective wealth . . . men who knew little and cared less about Rome's mission and who, when not preying upon the civilians, had not the slightest compunction about preying upon one another.*[17]

Taking advantage of the military anarchy, Germanic tribesmen crossed the Rhine-Danube frontier to loot and destroy. The Goths raided coastal cities of Asia Minor and Greece and even burned much of Athens. In the West, other Germanic tribes penetrated Gaul, Spain, and Italy and engaged the Romans in a full-scale battle near Milan. At the same time that the European defense lines were being breached, a reborn Persian Empire, led by the Sassanid dynasty, attacked and for a while conquered Roman lands in the East. Some sections of the Empire, notably in Gaul, attempted to break away; these moves reflected an assertion of local patriotism over Roman universalism. The "city of mankind" was crumbling.

These eruptions had severe economic repercussions. Cities were pillaged and destroyed, farmland ruined, and trade disrupted. To obtain funds and supplies for the military, emperors confiscated goods, exacted forced labor, and devalued the currency by reducing the gold and silver content of coins and adding base metals: zinc, tin, and lead. Cheap money caused a ruinous inflation, causing many people to turn to barter as a medium of exchange. These measures led many citizens to withdraw their loyalty from Rome.

Repeated invasions, civil war, pillage by Germans and by Roman soldiers, soaring prices, a debased coinage, declining agricultural production, disrupted transportation, and the excessive demands of the state caused economic havoc and famine in the cities. Compounding the problem was a great plague that spread across North Africa and the Balkans in midcentury. Driven to desperation by famine and plague, by invading barbarians and plundering Roman soldiers, and by the extortions and requisitions of government officials, many people fled the cities. The urban centers of the ancient world, creators and disseminators of high civilization, were caught in a rhythm of breakdown. As cities decayed, the center of life gravitated back to the countryside. Large, fortified estates, or villas, owned by the emperor or wealthy aristocrats, provided refuge for the uprooted and destitute of town and country. In the countryside, people had no deep commitment to classical civilization, which had made little headway against native languages, religions, and manners.

During the third century A.D., the spiritual crisis intensified as the rational foundations of Greco-Roman civilization eroded further. People turned increasingly to the mystery cults, which offered relief from earthly misery, a sense of belonging, and a promise of immortality. In philosophy, creative energies were directed not toward a greater understanding of nature or society but toward a knowledge of the divine, which, taught the philosophers, was the path to happiness. Hellenism was breaking down.

Diocletian and Constantine: The Regimented State

The emperors Diocletian (A.D. 285–305) and Constantine (A.D. 306–337) tried to contain the awesome forces of disintegration. At a time when agricultural production was steadily declining, they had to feed the city poor and an expanded army of more than 500,000, strung out over the Empire. They also had to prevent renewed outbreaks of military anarchy, drive the Germans back across the Danube frontier, and secure the eastern region against renewed aggression from Persia. Their solution was to tighten the reins of government and to extort more taxes and requisitions from the citizens. In the process, they transformed Rome into a bureaucratic, regimented, and militarized state.

Ruling like an oriental despot, Diocletian completed a trend that had been developing for generations. He imitated the pomp of the East, wore magnificent robes and jewels, and demanded that subjects prostrate themselves in his presence. Cities lost their traditional right of local self-government—a loss that also culminated an earlier trend. To increase the size of the army, Diocletian drafted prisoners of war and hired German mercenaries. He also established, on vacant or deserted Roman lands, colonies of Germans from which soldiers could be recruited. To ensure continuous production of food and goods, as well as the collection of taxes, the state forced unskilled workers and artisans to hold their jobs for life and to pass them on to their children. For the same reasons, peasants were turned into virtual serfs, bound to the land that they cultivated. An army of government agents was formed to hunt down peasants who fled the land to escape crushing taxes and poverty.

Also frozen into their positions were city officials, or *curiales*. They often found it necessary to furnish from their own pockets the difference between the state's tax demands and the amount that they could collect from an already overtaxed population. This system of a hereditary class of tax collectors and of crippling taxes to pay for a vastly expanded bureaucracy and military establishment enfeebled urban trade and industry. Such conditions killed the civic spirit of townspeople, who desperately sought escape. By overburdening urban dwellers with taxes and regulations, Diocletian and Constantine helped to shatter the vitality of city life, on which Roman prosperity and civilization depended.

Rome was governed by an oriental despotism, a highly centralized monarchy regimenting the lives of its subjects. Whereas Augustus had upheld the classical ideal that the commonwealth was a means of fostering the good life for the individual, Diocletian adopted the Eastern attitude that the individual lives for the state. The absolutism inherent in the concept of the principate had eclipsed the republican elements that had endured in the Augustan political settlement.

To guard against military insurrection, Diocletian appointed a loyal general as emperor to govern the western provinces of the Empire, while he ruled the eastern regions; although both emperors bore the title Augustus, Diocletian remained superior. (Each emperor then chose an heir-designate, who received his own territory to govern. For a time, the Empire was a tetrarchy—a government by four.) By building an imperial capital, Constantinople, at the Bosporus, a strait where Asia meets Europe, Constantine furthered this trend of dividing the Empire into eastern and western halves.

Tribal Migrations and Invasions

Nearly two centuries after Diocletian's reign, the Roman historian Zosimus described the emperor's accomplishment:

> *By the foresight of Diocletian the frontiers were everywhere studded with cities and forts and towers, and the whole army stationed along them. It was thus impossible for the barbarians to break through, since at every point they encountered an opposing force strong enough to repel them.*[18]

By imposing some order on what had been approaching chaos, Diocletian and Constantine prevented the Empire from collapsing. Rome was given a reprieve. A long period of peace might have brought economic recovery, but misfortune continued to burden Rome, and the process of breakdown and disintegration resumed.

In the last part of the fourth century, the problem of guarding the frontier grew more acute. The Huns, a nomadic people from central Asia, swept across the plains of Russia. With their

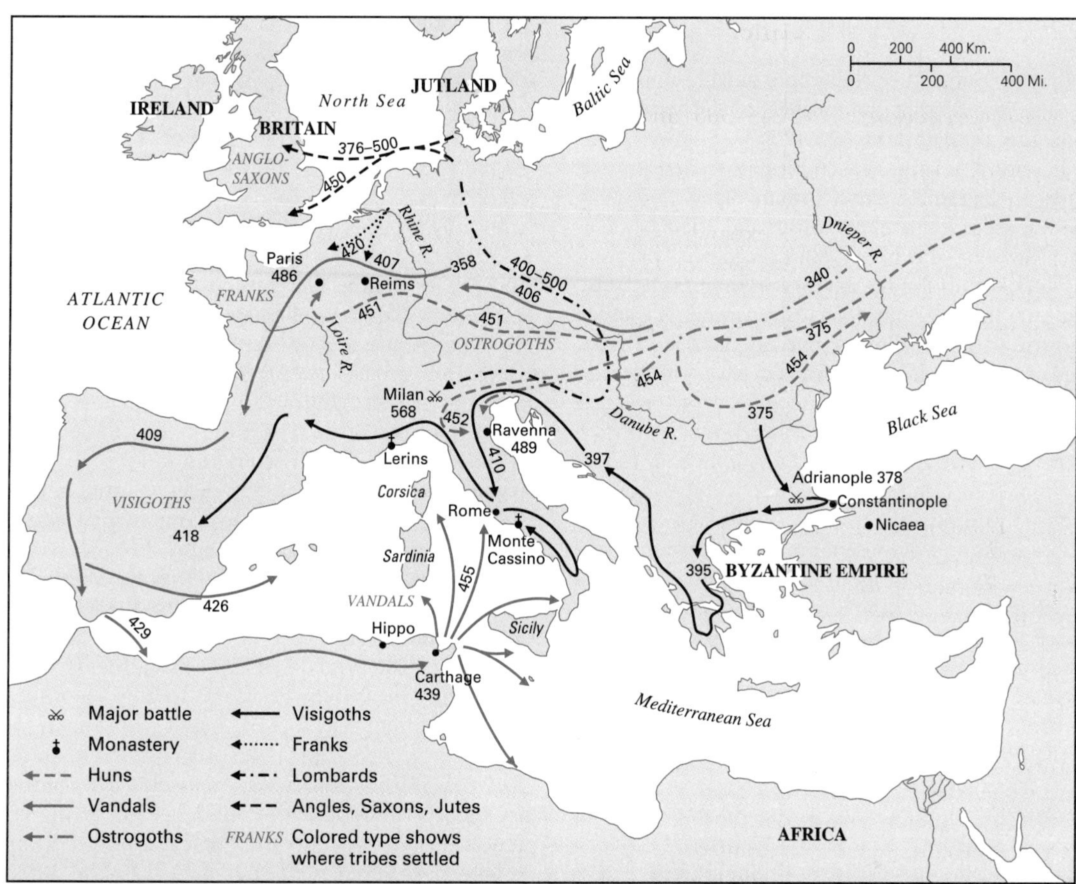

Map 7.2 Incursions and Migrations, c. A.D. 300–500 In the fifth century, German tribes, seeking land and desperate to escape the Huns, overran the weakened Roman borders.

formidible cavalry—the Huns were expert riders and archers—they subdued the Ostrogoths, a Germanic tribe that had established itself in the Ukraine, and forced the Germanic Visigoths, who had migrated along the Danube in what is now Romania, to seek refuge within the eastern Roman Empire. Enraged by their mistreatment at the hands of Roman officials, the Visigoths took up arms. In 378, Goths and Romans fought each other in a historic battle at Adrianople. The Visigoths routed the Roman forces, largely tribal mercenaries, killing and capturing perhaps as many as two-thirds of the Roman army. Emperor Valens perished in what was Rome's worst defeat since Cannae in the war with Hannibal. The Visigoths were on Roman territory to stay. The battle of Adrianople signified that Rome could no longer defend its borders.

Other Germanic tribes increased their pressure on the Empire's borders. Attracted by the warmer climate, riches, and advanced civilization of the Roman Empire, they were also looking for new lands to farm and were frightened by the advent of the Huns. The borders finally collapsed at the very end of 406, as Vandals, Alans, Suebi, and other tribes joined the Goths in devastating and overrunning the Empire's western provinces. In 408–409, the Visigoths, led by Alaric, besieged Rome itself, extorting huge sums in return for permitting food to enter the city. Then in 410, they rampaged through the city, which for eight hundred years had remained free of foreign attack, slaughtering, destroying, and plundering. Saint Jerome lamented: "Who could believe that Rome, built upon the conquest of the whole world, would fall to the ground? that the mother herself would become the tomb of her peoples?"[19]

Economic conditions continued to deteriorate. Cities in Britain, Gaul, Germany, and Spain lay abandoned. Other metropolises saw their populations dwindle and production stagnate. The great network of Roman roads was not maintained, and trade in the West almost disappeared or passed into the hands of Greeks, Syrians, and Jews from the East. Everywhere famine, the extortion of taxes by government officials, and murderous warfare added to the misery of the Roman populace.

In 451, Attila (c. 406–453), who had united Mongol tribes, led his Huns into Gaul, where he suffered his only defeat at the hands of a coalition of Germans and the remnants of the Roman army. He died two years later, having come within a hairsbreadth of turning Europe into a province of a Mongolian empire. But Rome's misfortunes persisted. In 455, Rome was again pillaged, this time by the Vandals. Additional regions fell under the control of Germanic chieftains. Germanic soldiers in the pay of Rome gained control of the government and dictated the choice of emperor. In 476, German officers overthrew the Roman emperor Romulus and placed a fellow German, Odoacer, on the throne. This act is traditionally regarded as the end of the Roman Empire in the West.

Reasons for Rome's Decline

What were the underlying causes of the decline and fall of the Roman Empire in the West? Surely, no other question has intrigued the historical imagination more than this one. Implicit in the answers suggested by historians and philosophers is a concern for their own civilization. Will it suffer the same fate as Rome?

To analyze so monumental a development as the fall of Rome, some preliminary observations are necessary. First, the fall of Rome was a process lasting hundreds of years; it was not a single event that occurred in A.D. 476. Second, only the western half of the Empire fell. The eastern half—wealthier, more populous, less afflicted with civil wars, and less exposed to barbarian invasions—survived as the Byzantine Empire until the middle of the fifteenth century. Third, no single explanation suffices to account for Rome's decline; multiple forces operated concurrently to bring about the fall.

The Role of the Germanic Tribes. Was Rome's fall suicide or murder? Did the Germans walk over a corpse, or did they contribute substantially to Rome's decline and fall? Undoubtedly, an empire enfeebled by internal rot succumbed to the Germanic migrations. Perhaps a stronger Rome might have secured its borders, as it had done during the Pax Romana. But the Germanic attacks occurred mainly in the West, and the western Empire, poorer and less populated than the eastern portion, reeled under these increasingly more numerous and more severe barbarian onslaughts. The pressures exerted by the Germans along an immense frontier also aggravated Rome's internal problems. The barbarian attacks left border regions impoverished and depopulated. The Empire imposed high taxes and labor services on its citizens in order to strengthen the armed forces, causing the overburdened middle and lower classes to hate the imperial government that took so much from them.

Spiritual Considerations. The classical mentality, once brimming with confidence about the potentialities of the individual and the power of the intellect, suffered a failure of nerve. The urban upper class, on whom the responsibility for preserving cosmopolitan Greco-Roman culture traditionally rested, became dissolute and apathetic and no longer took an interest in public life. The aristocrats secluded themselves behind the walls of their fortified country estates; many did not lift a finger to help the Empire. The townspeople demonstrated their disenchantment by avoiding public service and by rarely organizing resistance forces against the barbarian invaders. Hounded by the state and persecuted by the army, many farmers viewed the Germans as liberators. The great bulk of the Roman citizenry, disillusioned and indifferent, simply gave up, despite the fact that they overwhelmingly outnumbered the German invaders.

Political and Military Considerations. The Roman government itself contributed to this spiritual malaise through its increasingly autocratic tendencies, which culminated in the regimented rule of Diocletian and Constantine. The insatiable demands and regulations of the state in the Late Roman Empire sapped the initiative and civic spirit of its citizens. The ruined middle and lower classes withdrew their loyalty. For many, the state had become the enemy, and its administration was hated and feared more than the barbarians. Salvianus of Marseilles (c. A.D. 400–470), a monk from Gaul, described the disaffection toward Rome that led many to welcome the barbarians as liberators:

> *Meanwhile the poor are being robbed, widows groan, orphans are trodden down, so that many, even persons of good birth, who have enjoyed a liberal education, seek refuge with the enemy to escape death under the trials of general persecution. They seek among the barbarians the Roman mercy, since they cannot endure the barbarous mercilessness they find among the Romans. . . . So you find men passing over everywhere, now to the Goths . . . , or whatever other barbarians have established their power anywhere. . . . Hence the name of Roman citizen, once . . . much valued. . . , is now voluntarily repudiated and shunned, and is thought not merely valueless, but even almost abhorrent.*[20]

Related to the political decline was the government's inability to retain the allegiance of its armies and to control ambitious military commanders, who used their troops to seize the throne and its immense power. The internal security and stability of the Empire was thus constantly imperiled by army leaders more concerned with grandiose personal dreams than with defending the Empire's borders. These civil wars imposed terrible financial burdens on the Empire and gravely weakened the frontier defenses—an invitation to the Germans to increase their pressure.

During the Pax Romana, superior training and organization, rigorous discipline, a professional system of command, and a network of walls and forts enabled the Roman legions to protect the frontiers against incursions. The Roman soldier, for whom discipline was a deeply ingrained tradition, knew that his comrades would not desert the field, no matter how hard the fighting—an attitude that usually meant certain victory against untrained barbarian hordes. However, in the Late Roman Empire, the quality of Roman soldiers deteriorated and the legions failed to defend the borders, even though the German invaders were fewer numerically. During the third century, the army consisted predominantly of the provincial peasantry. These nonurban, non-Italian, semicivilized soldiers, often the dregs of society, were not committed to Greco-Roman civilization. They had little comprehension of Rome's mission and at times used their power to attack the cities and towns and to prey on hapless citizens. The emperors also recruited large numbers of Germans into the army to fill depleted ranks. Ultimately, the army consisted predominantly of barbarians, as both legionnaires and officers. Although these Germans made brave soldiers, they too had little loyalty to Greco-Roman civilization and to the Roman state. This deterioration of the Roman army occurred in part because many young citizens evaded conscription. No longer imbued with patriotism, they considered military service a servitude to be shunned.

The deterioration of the Roman army is seen also on the level of tactics. Roman soldiers continued to fight in organized units, but the training and discipline required for fighting in close-order formations had lapsed. Barbarian units serving with the Roman army under their own commanders did not easily submit to traditional discipline. Thus, Rome lost the tactical superiority that it had once enjoyed over the barbarians.

Economic Considerations. Contributing to the decline of the Roman Empire in the West were population decline, the lack of technological advance, the heavy burden of taxation, and economic decentralization, which abetted political decentralization.

During the Late Roman Empire, the population shrank. The epidemic during the reign of Marcus Aurelius, which might have been the bubonic plague, lasted fifteen years. A second plague struck the Empire during the reign of Commodus, Marcus Aurelius's son. Other plagues, in the middle of the third century, and constant warfare further reduced the population. The birthrate did not rise to compensate for these losses. Worsening economic conditions and lack of hope in the future apparently discouraged people from increasing the size of their families.

The decline in population adversely affected the Empire in at least three important ways. First, at the same time that the population was declining, the costs of running the Empire were spiraling, which created a terrible burden for taxpayers. Second, fewer workers were available for agriculture, the most important economic activity of the Empire. Third, population decline reduced the manpower available for the army, forcing emperors to permit the establishment of Germanic colonies within the Empire's borders to serve as feeders for the army. This situation led to the barbarization of the army.

The Roman peace brought stability, but it failed to discover new and better ways of producing goods and agricultural products. To be sure, some advances in technology did take place during the Hellenistic Age and the Pax Romana: rotary mills for grain, screw-presses, and improvements in glass-blowing and field-drainage methods. But the high intellectual culture of Greece and Rome rested on a meager economic and technological foundation. The widespread use of slave labor probably precluded a breakthrough in technology, for slaves had little incentive to invent more efficient ways of producing. The upper classes, identifying manual labor with slavery, would not condescend to engage in the mechanical arts. This failure to improve the level of technology limited employment opportunities for the masses. Because the masses could not increase their purchasing power, business and industry were without a mass internal market that might have acted as a continual stimulus for the accumulation of capital and for economic expansion.

Instead of expanding industry and trade, towns maintained their wealth by exploiting the countryside. The Roman cities, centers of civilized life and opulence, lacked industries. They spent but did not produce. Provided with food and entertainment—"bread and circuses"—the unproductive city dwellers driven out of the labor force by slavery, were a heavy burden for the state. The towns were dominated by landlords whose estates lay beyond the city and whose income derived from grain, oil, and wine. Manufacturing was rudimentary, confined essentially to textiles, pottery, furniture, and glassware. The methods of production were simple; the market was limited; the cost of transportation, particularly by land, was high; and agricultural productivity was low—the labor of perhaps nineteen peasants was required to support one townsman. Such a fundamentally unhealthy economy could not weather the dislocations caused by uninterrupted warfare and the demands of a mushrooming bureaucracy and the military.

With the barbarians pressing on the borders, the increased military expenditures overstrained the Empire's resources. To pay for the food, uniforms, arms, and armor of the soldiers, taxes were raised, growing too heavy for peasants and townspeople, particularly since the large landowners did not pay their fair share. The state also requisitioned wood and grain and demanded that citizens maintain roads and bridges. The government often resorted to force to collect taxes and exact services. Crushed by these demands, many peasants simply abandoned their farms and sought the protection of large landowners or turned to banditry.

Making the situation worse was the administrative separation of the Empire into eastern and western parts, undertaken by Diocletian and Constantine. As a result, western emperors could no longer rely on financial aid from the wealthier East to pay for the defense of the borders. Slow communications and costly transport continued to hamper the empirewide trade, which was required to sustain political unity. Meanwhile, industries gravitated outward, to search for new markets in the frontier army camps and for new sources of slaves in border regions. This dispersion further weakened the bonds of economic unity. Gradually, trade became less international and more local, and provincial regions grew more self-sufficient. The strife of the third century intensified the drift toward economic self-sufficiency in the provinces, a condition that promoted localism and separatism.

Contributing to the economic decentralization was the growth of industries on latifundia, the large, fortified estates owned by wealthy aristocrats. Producing exclusively for the local market, these estates contributed to the impoverishment of urban centers by reducing the number of customers available to buy goods made in the cities. As life grew more desperate, urban craftsmen and small farmers, made destitute by the state, sought the protection of these large landlords, whose estates grew in size and importance. The growth of latifundia was accompanied by the decline of cities and the transformation of independent peasants into virtual serfs.

These great estates were also new centers of political power, which the imperial government could not curb. A new society was taking shape in the Late Roman Empire. The center of gravity shifted from the city to the landed estate, from the imperial bureaucrat to the local aristocrat. These developments epitomized the decay of ancient civilization and presaged a new era, the Middle Ages.

The Roman Legacy

Rome left the West a rich heritage, which endured for centuries. The idea of a world empire united by a common law and effective government never died. In the centuries following the collapse of Rome, people continued to be attracted to the idea of a unified and peaceful world-state. By preserving and adding to the philosophy, literature, science, and the arts of ancient Greece, Rome strengthened the basic foundations of the Western cultural tradition. Latin, the language of Rome, lived on long after Rome perished. The Western church fathers wrote in Latin, and during the Middle Ages, Latin was the language of learning, literature, and law. From Latin came Italian, French, Spanish, Portuguese, and Romanian. Roman law, the quintessential expression of Roman genius, influenced church law and formed the basis of the legal codes of most European states. Finally, Christianity, the core religion of the West, was born within the Roman Empire and was greatly influenced by Roman law and organization.

Notes

1. Tacitus, *The Annals of Imperial Rome,* trans. Michael Grant (Baltimore: Penguin Books, 1959), p. 31.
2. Cited in David Magie, *Roman Rule in Asia Minor* (Princeton, N.J.: Princeton University Press, 1950), p. 490.
3. Excerpted in Dana C. Munro, ed., *A Source Book of Roman History* (Boston: D. C. Heath, 1904), p. 201.
4. Sallust, *The Conspiracy of Cataline,* trans. S. A. Handford (Baltimore: Penguin Books, 1963), p. 193.
5. Excerpted in Naphtali Lewis and Meyer Reinhold, eds., *Roman Civilization, Sourcebook II: The Empire* (New York: Harper & Row, 1966), p. 136.
6. *The Aeneid of Virgil,* trans. Allen Mandelbaum (Berkeley: University of California Press, 1971), pp. 160–161.
7. *The Odes and Epodes of Horace,* trans. C. E. Bennett (Cambridge, Mass.: Harvard University Press, Loeb Classical Library, 1914), p. 109.
8. *The Art of Love and Other Love Books of Ovid* (New York: Grosset & Dunlap, The Universal Library, 1959), pp. 117–118, 130–132, 135.
9. *The Satires of Juvenal,* trans. Hubert Creekmore (New York: Mentor Books, 1963), pp. 58–61, lines 242–248, 269–272, 302–305.
10. Adapted from Seneca, *The Epistles,* trans. Thomas Morell (London: W. Woodfall, 1786), vol. 1, epistle 47.
11. Marcus Aurelius, *Meditations,* trans. Maxwell Staniforth (Baltimore: Penguin Classics, 1964), bk. 2.
12. Cicero, *De Republica,* trans. Clinton Walker Keyes (Cambridge, Mass.: Harvard University Press, Loeb Classical Library, 1994), p. 211.
13. Excerpted in Lewis and Reinhold, eds., *Roman Civilization, Sourcebook II: The Empire,* pp. 535, 539, 540, 547, 548.
14. Seneca, *The Epistles,* vol. 1, epistle 7.
15. Michael Rostovtzeff, *Rome* (New York: Oxford University Press, 1960), p. 322.
16. W. T. Stace, *A Critical History of Greek Philosophy* (London: Macmillan, 1924), p. 377.
17. Excerpted in Mortimer Chambers, ed., *The Fall of Rome* (New York: Holt, Rinehart & Winston, 1963), pp. 45–46.
18. Quoted in Stephen Williams, *Diocletian and the Roman Recovery* (New York: Methuen, 1985), p. 101.
19. Excerpted in James Harvey Robinson, ed., *Readings in European History* (Boston: Ginn, 1904), p. 24.

20. Salvian, *On the Government of God*, trans. Eva M. Sanford (New York: Octagon, 1966), pp. 141–142.

Suggested Reading

Balsdon, J. P. V. D., *Roman Women* (1962). Describes prominent Roman women and treats various topics—marriage, divorce, concubinage—important to an understanding of the position of women.

Boardman, John, et al., eds., *The Oxford History of the Classical World* (1986). Essays on all facets of Roman culture.

Chambers, Mortimer, ed., *The Fall of Rome* (1963). A valuable collection of readings.

Christ, Karl, *The Romans* (1984). Good chapters on social and cultural life in the Empire.

Clarke, M. L., *The Roman Mind* (1968). Studies in the history of thought from Cicero to Marcus Aurelius.

Dupont, Florence, *Daily Life in Ancient Rome* (1989). Social structure, religion, and notions of time and space.

Ferrill, Arther, *The Fall of the Roman Empire* (1986). A military explanation.

Grant, Michael, *The Fall of the Roman Empire* (1990). A clearly written synthesis.

Jenkyns, Richard, ed., *The Legacy of Rome* (1992). Essay on Rome's impact on Western civilization.

Jones, A. H. M., *Augustus* (1970). An authoritative discussion of the Augustan settlement.

Katz, Solomon, *The Decline of Rome* (1955). A helpful introduction.

Lewis, Naphtali, and Meyer Reinhold, eds. *Roman Civilization, Sourcebook II: The Empire* (1966). Primary sources.

MacMullen, Ramsay, *Constantine* (1969). An account of the man and his times.

Mazzarino, Santo, *The End of the Ancient World* (1966). Describes how many thinkers have viewed the idea of the death of Rome and offers a modern interpretation.

Paoli, R. E., *Rome: Its People, Life and Customs* (1963). Surveys all phases of Roman society—women, slavery, clothing, industry, law, medicine, and so on.

Rowell, H. T., *Rome in the Augustan Age* (1962). The city and its people in the era of Augustus.

Southern, Pat, *Augustus* (1998). A recent biography.

Starr, C. G., *Civilization and the Caesars* (1965). A fine interpretive essay on the collapse of classical humanism and the spread of religion in the four centuries from Cicero to Augustine.

Veyne, Paul, ed., *A History of Private Life* (1987). All phases of Roman social life.

Wardman, Alan, *Rome's Debt to Greece* (1976). Roman attitudes toward the Greek world.

Wheeler, Mortimer, *Roman Art and Architecture* (1964). An interpretive study, filled with insight.

White, Lynn, ed., *The Transformation of the Roman World* (1973). A useful collection of essays on the transformation of the ancient world and the emergence of the Middle Ages.

Review Questions

1. In what ways was Augustus a creative statesman?
2. The Roman world-state completed the trend toward cosmopolitanism and universalism that had emerged during the Hellenistic Age. Discuss this statement.
3. Why is the Pax Romana regarded as one of the finest periods in ancient history?
4. Describe the achievements of some Roman writers and scientists during the Pax Romana.
5. How did Roman law incorporate Stoic principles? What does modern law owe to Roman law?
6. What signs of trouble existed during the Pax Romana?
7. Why were people attracted to mystery religions?
8. In what ways was classical humanism in retreat during the second and third centuries A.D.?
9. Describe the crisis that afflicted Rome in the third century.
10. How did Diocletian and Constantine try to deal with the Empire's crisis?
11. What effect did the battle of Adrianople have on the Empire?
12. What role did the barbarians play in the decline of Rome?
13. Analyze the spiritual, military, political, and economic reasons for the decline of the Roman Empire.
14. Could creative statesmanship have saved the Roman Empire? Explain why it might or might not have saved the Empire.

Chapter 8

Early Christianity: A World Religion

Christ Gives the Law to Saints Peter and Paul. 5th century, Santa Costanza, Rome. This mosaic portrays a haloed, beardless Christ bestowing the law in the manner of an emperor delivering an edict. (Scala/Art Resource, NY.)

- **Origins of Christianity**
  Judaism in the First Century B.C.
  Jesus: The Inner Person
  Saint Paul: From a Jewish Sect to a World Religion
- **The Spread and Triumph of Christianity**
  The Appeal of Christianity
  Christianity and Rome
  Christianity and Greek Philosophy
- **The Growth of Christian Organization, Doctrine, and Attitudes**
  The Primacy of the Bishop of Rome
  The Rise of Monasticism
  Scriptural Tradition and Doctrinal Disputes
  Christianity and Society
  Christianity and the Jews
- **Saint Augustine: The Christian World-View**
- **Christianity and Classical Humanism: Alternative World-Views**

As confidence in human reason and hope for happiness in this world waned in the last centuries of the Roman Empire, a new outlook began to take hold. Evident in philosophy and in the popularity of oriental religions, this viewpoint stressed escape from an oppressive world and communion with a higher reality. Christianity evolved and expanded within this setting of declining classicism and heightening otherworldliness. As one response to a declining Hellenism, Christianity offered a spiritually disillusioned Greco-Roman world a reason for living: the hope of personal immortality. The triumph of Christianity marked a break with classical antiquity and a new stage in the evolution of the West, for there was a fundamental difference between the classical and the Christian concepts of God, the individual, and the purpose of life.

Origins of Christianity

A Palestinian Jew named Jesus was executed by the Roman authorities during the reign of Tiberius (A.D. 14–37), who succeeded Augustus. At the time, few people paid much attention to what proved to be one of the most pivotal events in world history. In the quest for the historical Jesus, scholars have stressed the importance of both his Jewishness and the religious ferment that prevailed in Palestine in the first century B.C. Jesus' ethical teachings are rooted in the moral outlook of the Old Testament prophets. Jesus, who prayed as a Jew, taught as a Jew to fellow Jews, and valued Jewish law and prophetic teachings, could only conceive of himself as a Jew. Hans Küng, the prominent German student of religion, elaborates on this point:

> *Jesus was a Jew, a member of a small, poor, politically powerless nation living at the periphery of the Roman Empire. He was active among Jews and for Jews. His mother Mary, his father Joseph, his family, his followers were Jews. His name was Jewish (Hebrew Yeshu'a). . . . His Bible, his worship, his prayers were Jewish. In the situation at that time he could not have thought of any proclamation among the gentiles. His message was for the Jewish people, but for this people in its*

Chronology 8.1 ❖ Early Christianity

c. A.D. 29	Crucifixion of Jesus
c. 34–64	Missionary activity of Saint Paul
c. 66–70	The Gospel According to Mark is written
250–260	A decade of brutal persecution of Christians by the Romans
313	Constantine grants toleration of Christianity
c. 320	First convent is founded
325	Council of Nicaea rules that God and Christ are of the same substance, coequal and coeternal
391–392	Theodosius I prohibits public acts of pagan worship and the public profession of pagan religion; during his reign, Christianity becomes the state religion
430	Death of Saint Augustine
451	Council of Chalcedon rules that Christ is truly God and truly man
529	Saint Benedict founds monastery at Monte Cassino

> *entirety without any exception. From this basic fact it follows irrevocably that without Judaism there would be no Christianity. The Bible of the early Christians was the "Old Testament." The New Testament Scriptures became part of the Bible only by being appended to the Old. The gospel of Jesus Christ everywhere quite consciously presupposes the Torah and the Prophets.*[1]

Judaism in the First Century B.C.

In the first century B.C., four principal social-religious parties, or sects, existed among the Palestinian Jews: Sadducees, Pharisees, Essenes, and Zealots. Composed of the upper stratum of Jewish society—influential landed gentry and hereditary priests, who controlled the temple in Jerusalem—the religiously conservative Sadducees insisted on a strict interpretation of Mosaic Law and the perpetuation of temple ceremonies. Claiming to be the descendants of Sadok, the high priest of Solomon, Sadducees believed that they were maintaining the ancient Hebrew teachings concerning the Torah, which they interpreted literally. Rejecting the concepts of the resurrection of the dead and of an afterlife, they held that God meted out rewards and punishments on earth. Challenging the aristocratic Sadducees, the Pharisees adopted a more liberal attitude toward Mosaic Law (Torah). They allowed discussion on varying interpretations of the Law and granted authority to oral tradition—an "oral Torah," which was communicated from one generation to another—as well as to written Scripture. Unlike the Sadducees, the Pharisees believed in life after death. The concept of personal immortality is barely mentioned in the Hebrew Scriptures. A later addition to Hebrew religious thought, probably acquired from Persia, the idea had gained wide acceptance by the first century A.D. The Pharisees had the support of most of the Jewish people. All later forms of Judaism developed from the Pharisees.

The third religious party, the Essenes, established a semimonastic community near the Dead Sea. Like the Sadducees, they considered themselves to be the true descendants of Sadok, but they rejected the temple priests as corrupt. Only those priests affiliated with their sect were deemed pure. In 1947, leather scrolls in hermetically sealed cylinders were found near the community of Qumran, about fourteen miles from Jerusalem, close to the Dead Sea. Dated from between c. 200 B.C. and A.D. 66–70, the *Wady Qumran Manuscripts,* com-

SARCOPHAGUS OF BAEBIA HERTOFILA, LATE 3RD CENTURY, MUSEO DELLE TERME, ROME. Symbolizing the Christian Eucharist, Jesus distributes the bread and the wine of the Last Supper to his disciples. (*Museo delle Terme, Rome Scala/Art Resource, NY.*)

monly called "The Dead Sea Scrolls," contain the oldest extant Hebrew manuscripts and also documents that are unique to the sect of the Essenes, founded by a man they refer to as the "Teacher of Righteousness." The Essenes believed in the physical resurrection of the body, like the Pharisees, but gave this doctrine a more compelling meaning by tying it to the immediate coming of God's kingdom. Certain that the Messiah was about to come, the Essenes saw themselves as the first generation of God's people.

By adding to our knowledge of Palestinian Judaism in the first century, the scrolls shed light on the period in which Christianity arose and the New Testament was written. Because of the similarity between many of the teachings of Jesus, particularly in the Sermon on the Mount, and the teachings of the Essenes' "Teacher of Righteousness," some modern scholars have suggested that Jesus may have been a member of the Essene community. These scholars argue that the teachings of Jesus concerning the imminent coming of the kingdom of God parallel the messianic expectations of the Essenes.

The fourth sect, the Zealots, demanded that the Jews neither pay taxes to Rome nor acknowledge the authority of the Roman emperor. Devoted patriots, the Zealots engaged in acts of resistance to Rome, which culminated in the great revolt of A.D. 66–70, discussed in Chapter 7.

Besides the afterlife, another widely recognized idea in the first century B.C. was the belief in a Messiah, a redeemer chosen by God to liberate Israel from foreign rule. In the days of the Messiah, it was predicted, Israel would be free, the exiles would return, and the Jews would be blessed with peace, unity, and prosperity. The Messiah, in contrast to wicked Roman rulers, would govern justly and righteously.

Jesus (c. 4 B.C.–c. A.D. 29) practiced his ministry within this context of Jewish religious-national expectations and longings. The hopes of Jesus' early followers encompassed a lower-class dissatisfaction with the aristocratic Sadducees; a Pharisee emphasis on prophetic ideals and the afterlife; an Essene preoccupation with the end-of-days, the nearness of God, and the need for repentance; and a conquered people's yearning for a Messiah who would liberate their land from Roman rule and establish God's reign.

Jesus: The Inner Person

Historians are able to speak with greater certainty about social-religious developments in Judea at the time of Jesus than they can about Jesus himself. In reconstructing what Jesus did and believed, the historian labors under a handicap, for the sources are few. Jesus himself wrote nothing, and nothing was written about him during his lifetime. In the generations following his death, both Roman and Jewish historians paid him scant attention. Consequently, virtually everything known about Jesus derives from the Bible's New Testament, which was written decades after Jesus' death by devotees seeking to convey a religious truth and to propagate a faith.

Modern historians in quest of the historical Jesus have rigorously and critically analyzed the New Testament; their analyses have provided some insights into Jesus and his beliefs. Nevertheless, much about Jesus remains obscure. Very little is known about his childhood. Like other Jewish youths, he was taught Hebrew religious-ethical thought and the many rules that governed daily life. At about the age of thirty, no doubt influenced by John the Baptist, who likely was once part of the Essene community, Jesus began to preach the coming of the reign of God and the need for people to repent—undergo moral transformation—so that they could enter God's kingdom. "Now after John was arrested, Jesus came into Galilee, preaching the gospel of God, and saying, 'The time is fulfilled, and the kingdom of God is at hand; repent, and believe in the gospel' [good news]" (Mark 1:14–15).[2]* This apocalyptic vision that the existing world was coming to an end and would be replaced by God's perfect kingdom had been preached by John the Baptist and other religious thinkers before him.

For Jesus, the coming of the kingdom was imminent; the process leading to the establishment of God's kingdom on earth had already begun. A new order would soon be established in which God would govern his people righteously and mercifully. Hence the present moment became critical for him—a time for spiritual preparedness and repentance—because an individual's thoughts, goals, and actions would determine whether he or she would gain entrance into the kingdom. People had to radically change their lives. They had to eliminate base, lustful, hostile, and selfish feelings; stop pursuing wealth and power; purify their hearts; and show their love for God and their fellow human beings.

Like the Hebrew prophets, Jesus saw ethics as the core of Mosaic Law: "So whatever you wish that men would do to you, do so to them; for this is the law and the prophets" (Matthew 7:12). Like the prophets, he denounced injustice and oppression, urged mercy and compassion, and expressed a special concern for the poor and downtrodden.

Jesus did not intend to lead his fellow Jews, who called him rabbi, away from their ancestral religion: "'Think not that I have come to abolish the law and the prophets; I have come not to abolish them but to fulfil them'" (Matthew 5:17). Although Jesus did not negate the Law, some of his interpretations offended Jewish leaders.

While not seeking to break with his past or to reject Jewish law, Jesus was distressed by the Judaism of his day. Following the prophets, the rabbis taught the Golden Rule, as well as God's love and mercy for his children, but it seemed to Jesus that these ethical considerations were being undermined by an exaggerated rabbinical concern with ritual, restrictions, and the fine points of the Law. Jesus believed that the center of Judaism had shifted from prophetic values to obedience to rules and prohibitions regulating the smallest details of daily life. (To Jewish leaders, of course, these detailed regulations governing eating, washing, Sabbath observance, family relations, and so forth, were God's commands intended to sanctify all human activities.) To Jesus, such a rigid view of the Law distorted the meaning of prophetic teachings. Rules dealt only with an individual's visible behavior; they did not engage the person's inner being and lead to a moral transformation based on love, compassion, and selflessness. Observing the Lord's command to rest on the Sabbath—for example, by not eating an egg laid on Saturday or by not lifting a chair on that day—did not purify a person's heart.

For Jesus, the best way to realize the true meaning of Jewish law was through moral purity, which

*The biblical quotations in this chapter are taken from the Revised Standard Version of the Holy Bible.

finds expression in a love for one's fellows. The inner person concerned Jesus, and it was an inner change that he sought: "'For from within, out of the heart of man, come evil thoughts, fornication, theft, murder, adultery, coveting, wickedness, deceit, licentiousness, envy, slander, pride, foolishness. All these evil things come from within, and they defile a man'" (Mark 7:21–23). Individuals must feel again that God is at hand; they must choose God's way. To Jesus, the spirit of Mosaic Law was more important than the letter of the Law; for him, right living and a pure loving heart were Judaism's true essence. With the fervor of a prophet, he urged a moral transformation of human character through a direct encounter between the individual and God. Jesus also acquired a reputation as a miracle worker who cured the sick and drove demons from the insane.

By preaching active love for others and genuine compassion for sufferers and by stressing a personal and intimate connection between the individual and God, Jesus associated himself more with the Hebrew prophetic tradition than with the Hebrew rituals, rules, and prohibitions that served to perpetuate a national and cultural tradition of a distinct people. Jewish history reveals both universal and parochial components; Jesus' teachings embody the universalism inherent in the concept of the one God and in the prophets' teachings.

It was inevitable that Jewish scribes and priests, guardians of the faith, would regard Jesus, who had become a popular preacher, as a threat to ancient traditions. To Jewish leaders, he was a troublemaker and a subversive. They accused him of associating with social outcasts, sinners, and imperial tax collectors; undermining respect for the Sabbath by violating God's strict command prohibiting any form of labor on this holy day; proclaiming spiritual truth in his own name and on his own authority; and claiming that he, above all other men, had a special and intimate relationship with God and could forgive sins. Stated succinctly, Jewish leaders believed that Jesus was setting the authority of his person over Mosaic Law—an unpardonable blasphemy in their eyes.

The Romans, who ruled Palestine, had little interest in Jewish intrareligious disputes. They feared Jesus as a political agitator, as a charismatic leader who could ignite Jewish messianic expectations into a revolt against Rome. (It is likely that several of Jesus' early followers were Zealots, and the Romans may have viewed Jesus as a Zealot leader; also, Jewish leaders might have wanted Jesus out of the way for fear of repercussions if he ignited a bloody and futile uprising against Rome.) After Jewish leaders turned Jesus over to the Roman authorities, the Roman procurator, Pontius Pilate, sentenced him to death by crucifixion, a customary punishment for someone guilty of high treason. Jesus' execution was consistent with Roman policy in Judea, for the Romans routinely arrested and executed Jews suspected of inciting unrest against Roman rule.

Some Jews, believing that Jesus was an inspired prophet or even the long-awaited Messiah, had become his followers; the chief of these were the Twelve Disciples. At the time of Jesus' death, Christianity was not a separate religion but a small Hebrew sect with dim prospects for survival. What established the Christian movement and gave it strength was the belief of Jesus' followers that he was raised from the dead on the third day after he was buried. The doctrine of the resurrection enabled people to regard Jesus as more than a superb ethical soul, more than a righteous rabbi, more than a prophet, more than the Messiah; it made possible belief in Jesus as a divine savior-god who had come to earth to show people the way to heaven. For early Christians, Jesus' death took on greater importance than his life.

It is the nature of the prophet to propose a new religious-moral vision or to reinterpret an older conception in a profoundly novel way. That is what the charismatic Jesus did. There is no evidence that he intended to establish a new church; this was accomplished by his followers. In the years immediately following the crucifixion, the religion of Jesus was confined almost exclusively to Jews, who could more appropriately be called Jewish-Christians. The word *Christian* came from a name given Jesus: *Christ* (the Lord's Anointed, the Messiah). Missionaries of this dissenting Christian movement within Judaism were called Apostles—those sent out to preach the gospel about Christ. They addressed themselves to Jews and to converts to Judaism who, because they did not adhere fully to Mosaic Law, were not wholly accepted by the Jewish community.

Before this new messianic movement could realize the universal implications of Jesus' teachings and become a world religion, as distinct from a

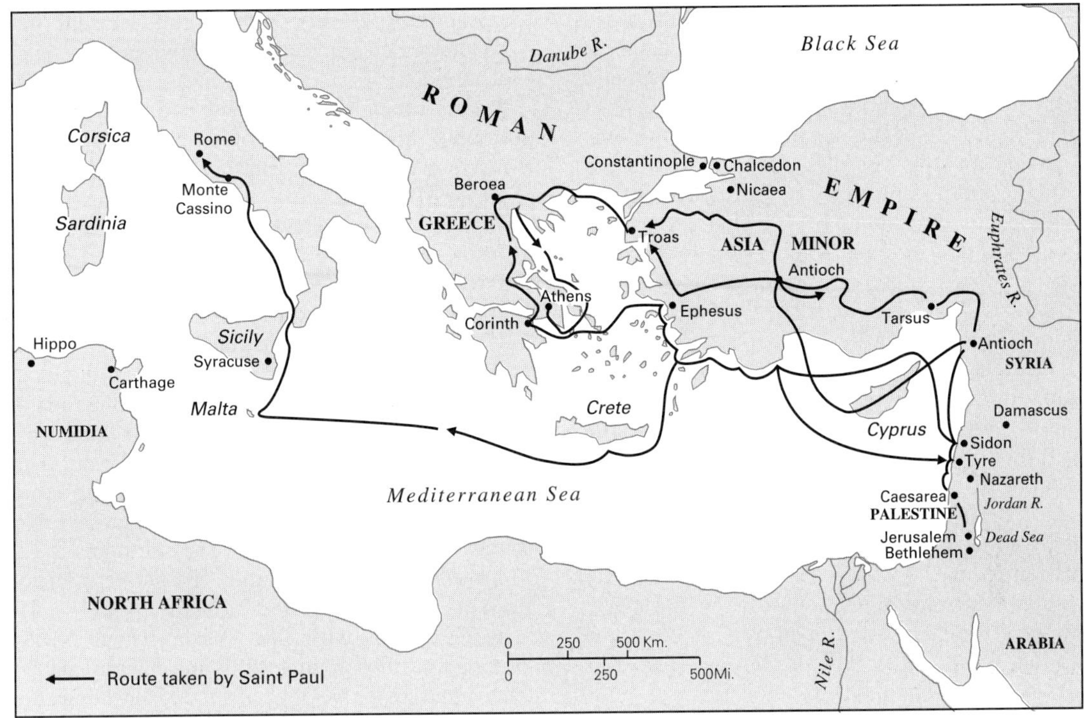

Map 8.1 The Journeys of Saint Paul Paul, a Greek-speaking citizen of Rome and thus free to travel throughtout the Empire, won converts to the new religion.

Jewish sect, it had to extricate itself from Jewish ritual, politics, culture, and history. This achievement was the work of a Hellenized Jew named Saul, known to the world as Saint Paul.

Saint Paul: From a Jewish Sect to a World Religion

Saint Paul (A.D. c. 5–c. 67) came from the Greek city of Tarsus in southeastern Asia Minor. Originally called Saul, he belonged to the Diaspora, or the "Dispersion"—the millions of Jews living outside Palestine. Though the Jews of the Diaspora retained their ancient faith, they were also influenced by Greek culture. An example is the Alexandrian Jew Philo (c. 20 B.C.–c. A.D. 50), who tried to demonstrate that Hebrew Scriptures could be explained and justified in terms of Greek philosophy.

Non-Jews, or *Gentiles* (from Latin *gens,* or "nation"), coming into contact with Jews of the Diaspora were often favorably impressed by Hebrew monotheism, ethics, and family life. Some Gentiles embraced Hebrew monotheism but refused to adhere to provisions of the Law requiring circumcision and dietary regulations. Among these Gentiles and non-Palestinian Jews who were greatly influenced by the Greco-Roman milieu, Jesus' Apostles would find receptive listeners.

Reared in Tarsus, a stronghold of Greek culture, Saul knew Greek well, but it is unlikely, despite a respectable writing style, that he had great knowledge of Greek literature, philosophy, and science. Trained in the outlook of the Pharisees, the young Saul went to Jerusalem to study with Rabban Gamaliel, an outstanding Pharisee teacher. In Jerusalem, Saul persecuted Jesus' followers in the time after his crucifixion, but then Saul underwent a spiritual transformation and became a convert. Serving as a zealous missionary of Jewish Christianity in the Diaspora, Saul, now called by his Roman name, Paul, preached to his fellow Jews in synagogues. Recognizing that the Christian message applied to non-Jews as well, Paul urged spreading it to the Gentiles. His knowledge of Greek was of inestimable value in his missionary work with both Diaspora Jews and Gentiles.

Although he was neither the first nor the only missionary to the Gentiles, Paul was without doubt the most important. In the process of his missionary activity—and he traveled extensively throughout the Roman Empire—he formulated doctrines that represented a fundamental break with Judaism and became the heart of this new religion. Paul taught that all people, both Jews and Gentiles, were sinners as a consequence of Adam's original defiance of God; that Jesus had come to earth to save all people from sin and death; that by suffering and dying on the cross he had atoned for the sins of all and made it possible for people to have eternal life in heaven; and that by believing in Jesus people could gain this salvation. Alone, one was helpless, possessed by sin, unable to overcome one's wicked nature. Jesus was the only hope, said Paul. "Wretched man that I am! Who will deliver me from this body of death? Thanks be to God through Jesus Christ our Lord!" (Romans 7:24–25).

Christ: A Savior-God. To the first members of the Christian movement, Jesus was both a prophet who proclaimed the power and purpose of God and the Messiah whose coming heralded a new age. To Paul, Jesus was a resurrected redeemer who offered salvation to all peoples. Although Paul was not very precise about the divinity of Jesus and his prior existence, he did frequently refer to him as the Son of God and the Divine Wisdom, through whom all things were created and in whom God's purpose is revealed. He taught that the crucified Messiah had suffered and died for the sins of human beings, that through Jesus God had shown his love of humanity and revealed himself to all people, both Jews and Gentiles, and that this revelation supplanted the earlier one to the Jewish people.

Increasingly Jesus' followers came to view the sacrificial Messiah as a savior-god, indeed, as God incarnate. The idea of a slain savior-god was well known in the mystery religions of the eastern Mediterranean. Like these religions, Christianity initiated converts into the mysteries of the faith, featured a sacramental meal, and in time developed a priesthood. But the similarities between Christianity and the mystery cults should not be overstressed, since the differences are more profound.

Unlike the cultic gods, Jesus had actually lived in history. Hence people could identify with him, which enormously increased the appeal of this new religion. Moreover, the deities of the mystery religions were killed against their will by evil powers. In Jesus, it was said, God had become a man and suffered pain and death out of compassion for human beings, to show a floundering humanity the way that would lead from sin to eternal life. This suffering Savior evoked from distressed human beings deep feelings of love and loyalty. Adherents of the mystery cults were not required to undergo a profound moral transformation. Christian converts, however, felt a compelling obligation to make their behavior, in the words of Paul, "worthy of the God who calls you" (Thessalonians 2:12) and to obey Jesus' command: "Be perfect as your heavenly Father is perfect" (Matthew 5:48). Finally, Christians, with their Jewish heritage, would tolerate no other divinity but God. Pagans, on the other hand, often belonged to more than one cult, or at least recognized the divinity of gods in other cults.

The Break with Judaism. In attempting to reach the Gentiles, Paul had to disentangle Christianity from a Jewish sociocultural context. Thus, he held that neither Gentile nor Jewish followers of Jesus were bound by the hundreds of rituals and rules that constitute Mosaic Law. Paul saw no distinctive difference between Jew and Gentile; in his view, the ministry of Jesus was intended for all. As a consequence of Jesus' coming, Paul insisted, Mosaic regulations were obsolete and hindered missionary activity among the Gentiles. For Paul, not the Law of Moses but love of and faith in Christ was the avenue to God and salvation.

To Paul, the new Christian community was the true fulfillment of Judaism; it was granted the promise of a Messiah that God had earlier bestowed on Israel; it was the means to moral transformation and eternal life. The Jews regarded their faith as a national religion, bound inseparably with the history of their people. Paul saw the new Christian community not as a nation but as an oikoumene, a world community. Jesus fulfilled not only the messianic aspirations of the Jews but also the spiritual needs and expectations of all peoples. To this extent, Christianity shared in the universalism of the Hellenistic Age.

In preaching the doctrine of a risen Savior and insisting that Mosaic Law had been superseded, Paul (whatever his intentions) was breaking with his Jewish roots and transforming a Jewish sect into a new religion. Separating Christianity from Judaism enormously increased its appeal for non-Jews, who were attracted to Hebrew ethical monotheism but repelled by practices like circumcision, dietary regulations, and other strict requirements of Mosaic Law. Paul built on the personalism and universalism implicit in the teachings of Jesus (and the Hebrew prophets) to create a religion intended not for a people with its own particular history, culture, and land, but for all humanity.

The Spread and Triumph of Christianity

By establishing Christianity's independence from Judaism and its practices, Paul made the new religion attractive to the Greco-Roman world. Originating in the first century, Christianity took firm root in the second, grew extensively in the third, and became the official religion of the Roman Empire at the end of the fourth century.

The Appeal of Christianity

The triumph of Christianity was related to a corresponding decline in the vitality of Hellenism and a shift in cultural emphasis—a movement from reason to emotion and revelation. Offering comforting solutions to the existential problems of life and death, religion demonstrated a greater capacity than reason to stir human hearts. Hellenism had invented the tools of rational thought, but the power of mythical thought was never entirely subdued. By the Late Roman Empire, science and philosophy were unable to compete with mysticism, myth, and the divine.

This deterioration of the classical outlook was demonstrated by the growing popularity of Eastern religions and the transformation of philosophy. Mystery cults, which promised personal salvation, were spreading and gaining followers. Astrology and magic, which offered supernatural explanations for the operations of nature, were also popular. Stoicism and Epicureanism were performing a religious function by trying to help individuals overcome emotional stress, while Neo-Platonists yearned for a mystical union with the One. This recoil from rational and worldly values helped prepare the way for Christianity. In a culturally stagnating and spiritually troubled Greco-Roman world, Christianity gave new meaning to life and offered new hope to disillusioned men and women.

During the Hellenistic Age, the individual had struggled with the problems of alienation and lack of community. With the decline of the independent city-state, the individual searched for a new frame of reference, a new form of attachment. The Roman Empire represented one possible allegiance. But for many people, it was not a satisfying relationship; the individual found it difficult to be devoted to a political organization so vast, remote, and impersonal. The Christian message of a divine Savior and a concerned Father, as well as of brotherly love, inspired men and women who were dissatisfied with the world of the here and now—who felt no attachment to city or empire, derived no inspiration from philosophy, and suffered from a profound sense of loneliness. Christianity offered the individual what the city and the Roman world-state could not: an intensely personal relationship with God, an intimate connection with a higher world, and membership in a community of the faithful who cared for one another.

Stressing the intellect and self-reliance, Greco-Roman thought did not provide for the emotional needs of many people. Christianity addressed itself to this defect in the Greco-Roman outlook. Particularly those who were poor, oppressed, or enslaved were attracted to the personality, life, death, and resurrection of Jesus, his love for all, and his concern for suffering humanity. They found spiritual sustenance in a religion that offered a hand in love and taught that a person need not be wellborn, rich, educated, or talented to be worthy. To people burdened with misfortune and terrified by death, Christianity held the promise of eternal life, a kingdom of heaven where they would be comforted by God the Father. Thus, Christianity gave to the common person what the aristocratic values of Greco-Roman civilization generally did not: hope, a sense of

Profile

Blandina

Alinari/Art Resource, NY.

During the reign of Marcus Aurelius, a number of Christians in Lyons, Gaul, including Blandina, a frail young slave, were imprisoned, accused of engaging in cannibalism and incest. The Roman authorities tortured Blandina, hoping that she would implicate the Christian community in these abhorrent crimes. Despite the torments inflicted on her, Blandina would not speak falsely against her fellow Christians. The historian Eusebius described her terrible ordeal:

> *Blandina was filled with such power that those who took it in turns to subject her to every kind of torture from morning to night were exhausted by their efforts and confessed themselves beaten—they could think of nothing else to do to her. They were amazed that she was still breathing, for her whole body was mangled and her wounds gaped; they declared that torment of any one kind was enough to part soul and body, let alone a succession of torments of*

dignity, and inner strength. By and large, classical philosophy offered little compassion for the sufferer, but the cardinal principle of Christianity was that Jesus had endured earthly torments because of his love for all human beings and even the lowliest could be redeemed.

Christianity succeeded not only through the appeal of its message but also through the power of its organization. To retain the devotion of the faithful, win new converts, protect itself from opponents, and administer its services, Christianity developed an organized body of followers. This body became the Christian church, which grew into a strong organization uniting the faithful. To city dwellers—lonely, alienated, disillusioned with public affairs, stranded mortals groping for a sense of community—the church that called its members "brother" and "sister" filled an elemental need of human beings to belong. Another attraction for Christian converts was the absence of painful or expensive initiation rites, such as those required for entrance into Mithraism, a leading rival (see "The Spread of Mystery Religions" in Chapter 7). Unlike Mithraism, the church also welcomed women converts, who were often the first to join and who brought their menfolk after them. Among the reasons that the church drew women was its command to husbands to treat their wives kindly, remain faithful, and provide for the children. Moreover, in the eyes of God, women were spirtually equal with men. The church also won new converts and retained the loyalty of its members by furnishing social services for the poor and infirm, welcoming slaves and criminals, sinners, and other outcasts, and offering community and comfort during difficult times.

The ability of an evolving Christianity to assimilate elements from Greek philosophy and even from the mystery religions also contributed in no small measure to its growth. By becoming infused with Greek philosophy, Christianity could present itself in terms intelligible to those *such extreme severity. But the blessed woman, wrestling magnificently, grew in strength as she proclaimed her faith, and found refreshment, rest, and insensibility to her sufferings in uttering the words: "I am a Christian: we do nothing to be ashamed of."*

*For several days Blandina had to watch other Christians being whipped, roasted, and set upon by wild beasts in the amphitheater. Finally, after surviving similar torments, she was "dropped into a basket and thrown to a bull. Time after time the animal tossed her, but she was indifferent now to all that happened to her, because of her hope and sure hold on all that her faith meant, and of her communing with Christ. Then she, too, was sacrificed, while the heathen themselves admitted that never yet had they known a woman suffer so much or so long."**

*Eusebius, *The History of the Church from Christ to Constantine,* trans. G. A. Williamson (New York: New York University Press, 1966), pp. 196, 202.

versed in Greek learning and thus attract educated people. Philosophers who converted to Christianity proved to be able defenders of their newly adopted faith. Because some Christian doctrines (the risen Savior-God, the Virgin and her child, life after death, communion with the divine), practices (purification through baptism), and holy days (December 25 was the birth date of the god Mithras) either paralleled or were adopted from the mystery religions, it became relatively easy to win converts from these rivals.

Christianity and Rome

Generally tolerant of religions, at first the Roman government did not interfere much with the Christian movement. In fact, Christianity benefited in many ways from its association with the Roman Empire. Christian missionaries, among them some of the Twelve Disciples, who were the original followers of Christ, traveled throughout the Empire over roads and across seas made safe by Roman arms. The common Greek dialect, Koine, spoken in most parts of the Empire, facilitated the missionaries' task. Had the Mediterranean world been fractured into separate and competing states, the spread of Christianity might well have faced an insurmountable obstacle. The universalism of the Roman Empire, which made citizenship available to peoples of many nationalities, prepared the way for the universalism of Christianity, which welcomed membership from all nations. Early Christians grafted onto Rome's imperial mission a spiritual evangelical cause: "Go ye therefore and teach all nations" (Matthew 28:19).

As the number of Christians increased, Roman officials began to fear the Christians as subversives, preaching allegiance to God and not to Rome, and as a self-absorbed sect that did not want to fit into the Empire. To many Romans, Christians were enemies of the social order: strange people who would not accept the state gods, would not engage in sacrifices to Roman divinities, scorned gladiatorial contests, stayed away from public baths, glorified nonviolence, refused to honor deceased emperors as gods, and worshiped a crucified criminal as Lord. Romans ultimately found in Christians a scapegoat for the ills burdening the Empire, such as famines, plagues, and military reverses. In an effort to stamp out Christianity, emperors occasionally resorted to persecution. Christians were imprisoned, beaten, starved, burned alive, torn apart by wild beasts in the arena for the amusement of the Romans, and crucified.

However, the early persecutions, beginning with those incited under Emperor Nero in A.D. 64, were local and did not cause much loss of life; they were too sporadic to impede the growth of Christianity. Two centuries later, in A.D. 250, Emperor Decius unleashed against the Christians a brief but brutal terror, which extended throughout much of the Roman Empire. Decius's successors, Gallus (251–253) and Valerian (253–260), also issued anti-Christian edicts and had Christians murdered.

Christians lived in relative peace from 260 to 303, but then Emperor Diocletian (284–305) instituted the most severe persecution they had yet faced, lasting for three years in the West and longer in the East. The persecutions at midcentury and during Diocletian's rule caused the brutal deaths of many Christians. Some, fearful of torture and death, abandoned their faith. However, the persecutions did not last long enough to seriously threaten the new religion. Actually, they strengthened the determination of most of the faithful and won new converts, who were awed by the extraordinary courage of the martyrs willingly dying for their faith.

Unable to crush Christianity by persecution, Roman emperors decided to gain the support of the growing number of Christians within the Empire. In A.D. 313, Constantine, genuinely attracted to Christianity, issued the Edict of Milan, granting toleration to Christians. By allowing the free flow of Christian teachings and instituting legislation favorable to the church, Constantine and his successors accelerated the growth of Christianity and the Christianization of the Empire. By A.D. 392, Theodosius I had made Christianity the state religion of the Empire and declared the worship of pagan gods illegal. Persecution did not end, but its target shifted from Christians to pagans, Jews, and Christians with unorthodox views. The polytheistic religions of the Roman world did not claim to possess an exhaustive truth—did not assert that a particular god or a particular form of worship should prevail over all others and that wrongful religious expressions should be rooted out. People were relatively free to select their own credo and engage in their own acts of worship. Christianity, in contrast, possessing an exclusive attitude toward truth, felt compelled to cleanse society of false gods and beliefs. Such an outlook often led Christians to view nonbelievers as enemies of God deserving of punishment. Thus mobs, often driven by fanatic clergy, hurled non-Christian writings into bonfires, destroyed pagan altars and sacred images, and squelched pagan rites and festivals. Emperors, often pushed by the clergy, passed decrees calling for fining, imprisoning, torturing, and executing adherents of pagan cults.

Christianity and Greek Philosophy

Christianity synthesized both the Hebrew and the Greco-Roman traditions. Having emerged from Judaism, Christianity assimilated Hebrew monotheism and prophetic morality and retained the Old Testament as the Word of God. Without this Hebraic foundation, Christianity cannot be understood. As the new religion evolved, it also assimilated elements of Greek philosophy. The ability to combine a historic Judaic monotheism, which had many admirers in the Gentile world, with Greek rational philosophy was a crucial reason for Christianity's triumph in the Roman Empire. But there was a struggle between conservatives, who wanted no dealings with pagan philosophy, and those believers who recognized the value of Greek thought to Christianity.

To conservative church fathers—early Christian writers whose works are accepted as authoritative by the church—classical philosophy erred completely because it did not derive from divine revelation. They believed that, whereas philosophers merely battled over words, Christianity possessed *the Word,* true wisdom revealed by God in the infallible words of Scripture. As the final statement of God's truth, Christianity superseded both pagan philosophy and pagan religions. According to the church fathers, the simple peasant who accepted Christ possessed more knowledge than the most learned philosopher who did not. These conservatives feared that studying classical authors would contaminate Christian morality (did not Plato propose a community of wives, and did not the dramatists treat violent passions?) and promote heresy (was not classical literature replete with references to pagan gods?). For these church fathers, there could be no compromise between Greek philosophy and Christian revelation. They considered their life's mission to be preaching the Gospel of Jesus, which required no reinforcement from pagan ideas. For them, faith was more reliable than all the demonstrations of human reason. "What indeed has Athens to do with Jerusalem?" asked Tertullian (A.D. 150–225). "With our faith, we desire no further belief. For this is our faith that there is nothing which we ought to believe besides."[3]

Some church fathers, including several who had a Greek education, resisted this anti-intellectualism. Defending the value of studying classical literature, they maintained that such literature, properly taught, could aid in the moral development of children because it presented many examples of virtuous deeds. Some church fathers claimed that Greek philosophy contained a dim glimmer of God's truth, a pre-Christian insight into divine wisdom. Christ had corrected and fulfilled an insight reached by the philosophic mind. Knowledge of Greek philosophy, they

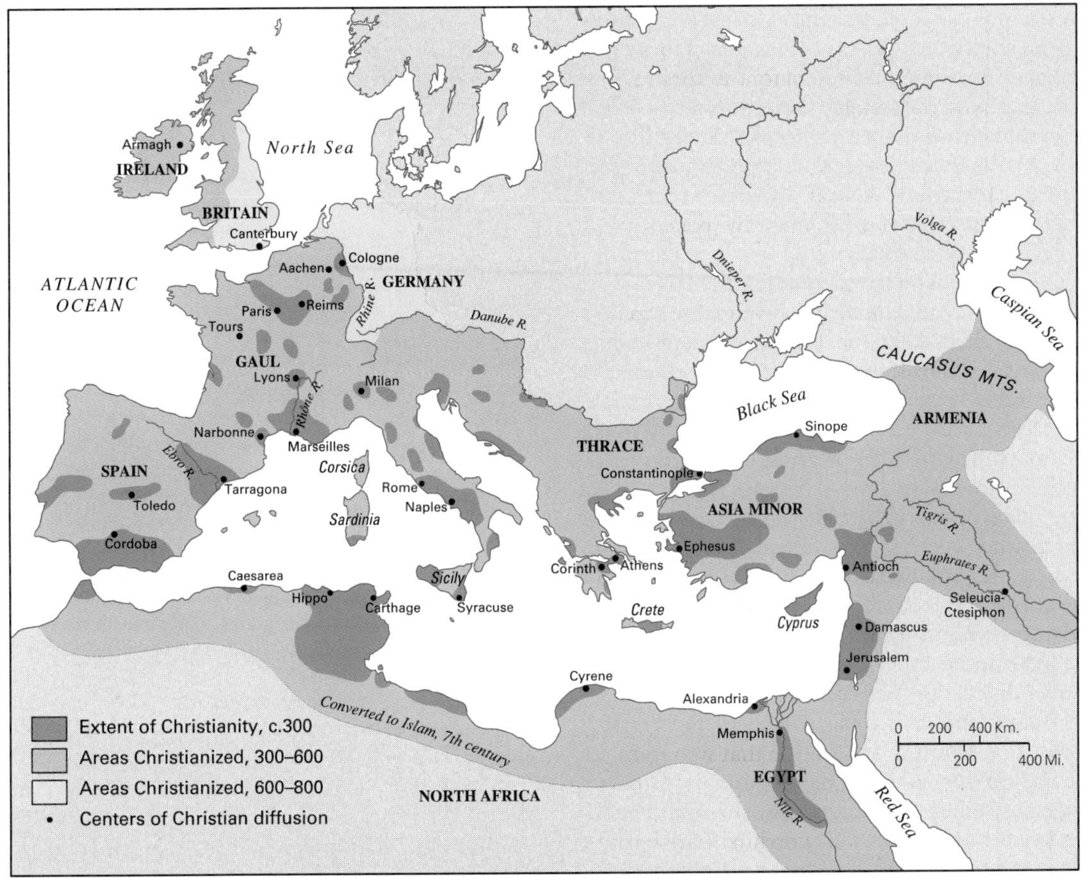

Map 8.2 The Spread of Christianity Aided by dedicated missionaries, Christianity expanded throughout the Mediterranean world and later into Germanic lands.

also contended, helped Christians to explain their beliefs logically and to argue intelligently with pagan critics of Christian teachings. Thus, Clement of Alexandria (c. 150–220) brought reason to the support of faith in his attempt to make Christianity more intellectually respectable in his world:

> *Rather, philosophy is a clear image of truth, a divine gift to the Greeks. Before the advent of the Lord, philosophy helped the Greeks to attain righteousness, and is now conducive to piety, it supplies a preparatory teaching for those who will later embrace the faith. God is the cause of all good things: some given primarily in the form of the Old and the New Testament; others are the consequence of philosophy. Perchance too philosophy was given to the Greeks primarily till the Lord should call the Greeks to serve him. Thus philosophy acted as a schoolmaster to the Greeks, preparing them for Christ, as the laws of the Jews prepared them for Christ.*[4]

Utilizing the language and categories of Greek philosophy, Christian intellectuals transformed Christianity from a simple ethical creed into a theoretical system, a theology. This effort to express Christian beliefs in terms of Greek rationalism is referred to as the Hellenization of Christianity. Greek philosophy enabled Christians to explain rationally God's existence and revelation. Using philosophical concepts, church fathers attempted to show that the Trinity, although a mystery, did not violate the laws of logic: that God the Father, God the Son, and God the Holy Spirit did not conflict with monotheism. They attributed the order and regularity of nature and the natural law (moral principles that apply to all people)—two cardinal principles of Stoic thought—to God, the designer of the universe.

Christ was depicted as the divine or incarnate Logos (reason) in human form. Educated believers could argue that the fundamental principles that Greek philosophers maintained operated in the universe were established by God the Father. The Stoic teaching that all people are fundamentally equal because they share in universal reason could be formulated in Christian terms: all are united in Christ. Christians could interpret the church to be the true fulfillment of the Stoic idea of a polity embracing the entire world. Stoic ethics, which stressed moderation, self-control, and brotherhood, could be assimilated by Christian revelation. Particularly in Platonism, which drew a distinction between a world perceived by the senses and a higher order—a transcendent world that should be the central concern of human existence—Christian thinkers found a congenial vehicle for expressing Christian beliefs. The perfect and universal Forms, or Ideas, which Plato maintained were the true goal of knowledge and the source of ethical standards, were held by Christians to exist in God's mind.

That Greek philosophy had a strong hold on church doctrine was immensely important, for it meant that rational thought, the priceless achievement of the Greek mind, was not lost. However, the Hellenization of Christianity did not mean a triumph of classicism over Christianity but rather the reverse: Christianity triumphed over Hellenism. Greek philosophy had to sacrifice its ability to think freely to the needs of Christian revelation: reason had to serve faith. And in any conflict between reason and faith, faith would prevail. Although Christianity made use of Greek philosophy, Christian truth ultimately rested on faith, not reason. As Tertullian stated, it is precisely because faith in a crucified Lord contradicted all human logic that he would believe: "And the Son of God died; it is by all means to be believed, because it is absurd. And He was buried, and rose again; the fact is certain because it is impossible."[5]

The Growth of Christian Organization, Doctrine, and Attitudes

Early in its history, the church gradually developed along hierarchical lines. Those members of the Christian community who had the authority to preside over the celebration of the Mass—breaking bread and offering wine as Christ had done in the Last Supper—were called either priests or bishops. Gradually, the designation *bishop* was reserved for the one clergyman in the community with the authority to resolve disputes over doctrines and practices. Regarded as the successors to Jesus' Twelve Disciples, bishops supervised religious activities within their regions. The most influential bishops ministered to the leading cities of the Empire: Rome, Alexandria, Antioch, and Milan. In creating a diocese that was supervised by a bishop and had its center in a leading city, the church adapted Roman administrative techniques.

The Primacy of the Bishop of Rome

The bishop of Rome, later called the pope ("father"), claimed primacy over the other bishops, maintaining that the Apostle Peter founded the Roman see (official seat of authority) and that both Peter and Paul were martyred in Rome. Moreover, as the traditional capital of the Empire, Rome seemed the logical choice to serve as the center of the church.

In developing the case for their supremacy over the church organization, bishops of Rome increasingly referred to the famous New Testament passage in which Jesus says to his disciple Simon (also called Peter): "'And I tell you, you are Peter, and on this rock I will build my church'" (Matthew 16:18). Because *Peter* in Greek means "rock" (petra), it was argued that Christ had chosen Peter to succeed him as ruler of the universal church. It was commonly accepted that Saint Peter had established a church in Rome and was martyred there, so it was argued further that the Roman bishop inherited the power that Christ had passed on to Peter. Thus, the argument continued, the bishop of Rome held a unique office: of all the bishops, only he had inherited the powers originally granted by Christ to Peter. Because the Apostles had been subordinate to Peter, so too must the bishops defer to Peter's successor. In the fourth and fifth centuries, popes took a leading part in doctrinal disputes, which threatened to divide the church. More and more Christians came to esteem Rome as the champion of true Christianity.

The Rise of Monasticism

Not all Christians welcomed the growing wealth and power of the church. Some devout Christians committed to living a perfect Christian life were distressed by the wickedness of the world about them, including the moral laxity of those clergy who chased after wealth and pomp. Seeking to escape from the agonies and corruptions of this world, some ardent Christians withdrew to deserts and mountains in search of solitude and spiritual renewal; they were inspired by Jesus' words: "If any man would come after me, let him deny himself and take up his cross and follow me" (Mark 8:34). In their zeal to emulate Jesus' self-denial, they sometimes practiced extreme forms of asceticism: self-flogging, wearing spiked corsets, eating only herbs, or living for years atop a column high above the ground.

Gradually, colonies of these hermits sprang up, particularly in Egypt and Syria; in time, the leaders of these monastic communities drew up written rules for prayer and work. In the first half of the fourth century, Saint Pachomius set up several regulated monasteries in Egypt, and the first convent was founded about 320, in the Egyptian desert, by Mary, Pachomius's sister. Saint Basil (c. 329–c. 379), a Greek who was bishop of Caesarea in Cappadocia (eastern Asia Minor), established the rules that became the standard for monasteries in the East. Basil required monks to refrain from bodily abuses and to engage in manual labor. Through farming, weaving, and construction, monks could make a monastery self-supporting and have the means to assist the needy. Aware of the lure of materialism and selfishness, Basil forbade his monks to own personal property other than clothing and insisted that they spend much of their time in silence.

The monastic ideal spread from east to west. Saint Martin of Tours established a monastery in Gaul, whose monks diligently strove to convert the pagan peasants. But the principal figure in the shaping of monasticism in the West was Saint Benedict (c. 480–c. 543), who founded a monastery at Monte Cassino, Italy, in 529. The Rule of Saint Benedict required the monks to live in poverty and to study, labor, and obey the abbot, the head of the monastery. They had to pray often, work hard, talk little, and surrender private property. In imposing discipline and regulations, Benedict eliminated the excessive and eccentric individualism of the early monks; he socialized and institutionalized the spiritual impulse that had led monks to withdraw from the world. Benedict demonstrated the same genius for administration that the Romans had shown in organizing and governing their Empire. Benedict's rule, which became the standard for monasteries throughout western Europe, also articulated the Christian view of the virtuous life.

Scriptural Tradition and Doctrinal Disputes

The earliest surviving Christian writings are Paul's Epistles, written some twenty-five to thirty years after the death of Jesus. Jesus' sayings were preserved by word of mouth. Sometime around A.D. 66–70, about forty years after the crucifixion, Saint Mark formulated the Christian message from this oral tradition and perhaps from some material that had been put in writing earlier. Later, Saint Matthew and Saint Luke, relying heavily on Mark's account, wrote somewhat longer Gospels. The Gospels of Mark, Matthew, and Luke are called *synoptic* because their approach to Jesus is very similar. The remaining Gospel, written by Saint John around A.D. 110, varies significantly from the synoptic Gospels. The Gospel of John uses the Stoic concept of Logos to present Jesus as the divine being. John identifies Jesus with the eternal word, or Logos, which became the incarnate Son of God: "In the beginning was the Word and the Word was with God, and the Word was God. . . . And the Word became Flesh and dwelt among us" (John 1:1, 14). The synoptic Gospels, the Gospel According to Saint John, Acts of the Apostles, the twenty-one Epistles, including those written by Saint Paul, and Revelation constitute the twenty-seven books of the Christian New Testament. Christians also accepted the Old Testament of the He-

THE ANTIOCH CHALICE: ROMAN SYRIA, SIXTH CENTURY. This richly ornamented silver chalice may have been used to hold the wine that Christians believed became the blood of Christ during the Eucharistic liturgy. (*Metropolitan Museum of Art, The Cloisters Collection, 1950.*)

brews as God's Word. The New Testament was written not by historians with the critical spirit of a Thucydides or a Polybius but by men moved by the fervor of faith. Under these circumstances, it is understandable that it contains discrepancies, some nonhistorical legends, and polemics.

The early Christians had a Bible and a clergy to teach it. But the Holy Writ could be interpreted differently by equally sincere believers, and controversies over doctrine threatened the loose unity of the early church. The most important controversy concerned how people viewed the relationship between God and Christ. Arius (A.D. 250–336), a Greek priest in Alexandria, led one faction; he denied the complete divinity of Christ, one of the basic tenets of the church. To Arius, Christ was more than man but less than God; the Father and the Son did not possess the same nature, or essence. Arius said that there was no permanent union between God and Christ; the Father alone is eternal and truly God.

The Council of Nicaea (A.D. 325), the first assembly, or ecumenical council, of bishops from all parts of the Roman world, was called to settle the controversy. The council condemned Arius and ruled that God and Christ were of the same substance, coequal and coeternal. The position adopted at Nicaea became the basis of the Nicene Creed, which remains the official doctrine of the church. Although Arianism, the name given the heresy of Arius, won converts for a time, it eventually died out, helped along by persecution. The death toll of Arians killed by fellow Christians was far greater than the number of Christan victims of Roman persecution.

Another controversy arose over the relationship between Christ's divine and human natures. Some theologians, viewing Christ as a great ethical soul, tended to emphasize his human nature at the expense of his divine nature. Other theologians argued that Christ's human nature had been absorbed by his divine nature—in effect, that Christ possessed a single divine nature. The Council of Chalcedon in A.D. 451 formulated the orthodox position that Christ is truly God and truly man and that two distinct natures, one divine and the other human, are joined and preserved in his person. The other views were declared heretical but continued to persist in the eastern part of the Empire.

The controversies over Christ's nature and his relationship to God were by no means theological hairsplitting. What was at stake was the central message of Christianity: Christ, the Son of God, had become man and had suffered and died to atone for the sins of all people that they might be saved and have eternal life.

Christianity and Society

Although salvation was their ultimate aim, Christians still had to dwell within the world and deal with its imperfections. In the process, Christian thinkers challenged some of the mores of Greco-Roman society and formulated attitudes that would endure for centuries.

Influenced by passages in the New Testament that condemned acts of revenge and the shedding of blood, and concerned only with the heavenly kingdom, some early Christians refused military service. Others, however, held that in a sinful world, defense of the state was necessary, and without concealment or apology, they served in the army.

After Roman emperors professed Christianity, Christians began to serve the government more often. With the barbarians menacing the borders, these Christian officials could not advocate nonviolence. Christian theorists began to argue that under certain circumstances—to punish injustice or to restore peace—war was just. But even such wars must not entail unnecessary violence.

Christians denounced the gladiatorial combats and contests between men and beasts as blood lust and murder. Nevertheless, these spectacles persisted even after the majority of the population had converted to Christianity. When the games finally ended, it was probably due more to the growing poverty of the western Empire than to the Christian conscience.

The early Christian view of women was rooted in the patriarchal tradition of Jewish society. Paul subjected the wife to her husband's authority. "Wives, be subject to your husbands, as to the Lord. For the husband is the head of the wife as Christ is the head of the church" (Ephesians 5:22–23). Paul wanted women to remain quiet at church meetings. "If there is anything they desire to know, let them ask their husbands at home. For it is shameful for a woman to speak in church" (I Corinthians 14:35). But Paul also held that all are baptized in Christ: "There is neither Jew nor Greek, there is neither slave nor free, there is neither male nor female; for you are all one in Christ Jesus" (Galatians 3:28). Consequently, both sexes were subject to divine law, and both possessed moral autonomy. The early church held to strict standards on sexual matters. It condemned adultery and esteemed virginity pledged for spiritual reasons.

Christians waged no war against slavery, which was widely practiced and universally accepted in the ancient world. Paul commanded slaves to obey their masters, and many Christians were slave owners. While Christians did not try to alter the legal status of slaves, they did teach that slaves, too, were children of God, they sought their conversion, and they urged owners not to treat slaves harshly. In the modern world, the Christian teaching that all persons are spiritually equal before God would arouse some Christians to fight for the abolition of slavery.

Christianity and the Jews

The central theme of the New Testament Gospels is love of both God and fellow human beings. But the Gospels also devote considerable attention to the fallen angel, Satan, and the evil demons that inhabit his kingdom. Increasingly, Christians identified opponents—Jews, pagans, and heretics—with Satan and viewed conflicts in a moral context: a struggle between God's faithful and Satan's servants. Over the centuries, the view that they were participants in a cosmic struggle between good and evil led Christians to demonize adversaries, a practice that exacerbated hatred and justified mistreatment, even massacre. Christian attitudes and behavior toward Jews poignantly illustrate this point.

Numerous links connect early Christianity and Judaism. Jesus himself and his earliest followers, including the Twelve Disciples, were Jews who were faithful to Jewish law. Jesus' message was first spread in synagogues throughout the Roman Empire. Early Christianity's affirmation of the preciousness of the human being, created in God's image, its belief that God rules history, its awareness of human sinfulness, its call for repentance, and its appeal to God for forgiveness are rooted in Judaism. The Christian reference to God as a "merciful Father" derives from Jewish prayer. Also rooted in Judaism are the moral norms proclaimed by Jesus in the Sermon on the Mount and on other occasions. For example, "Thou shalt love thy neighbor as thyself" was the motto of the Jewish sage Hillel, a contemporary of Jesus, who founded a school. The great value that the Torah gives to charity was inherited by Christianity. Jesus' use of parables to convey his teachings, the concept of the Messiah, respect for the Sabbath, and congregational worship also stem from Judaism. And, of course, Christians viewed the Hebrew Scriptures as God's word.

However, over the years, particularly after more and more non-Jews became followers of Christ, Christians forgot or devalued this relationship to Judaism, and some thinkers began to show hostility toward Judaism and Jews that had tragic consequences in later centuries. Several factors fueled this anti-Judaism: resentment against Jews for their refusal to embrace Jesus; the polemics of the Jewish establishment against followers of Jesus; the role in Jesus' death ascribed to Jews by the New Testament; resentment against those Christians who Judaized, that is, continued to observe Jewish festivals and the Jewish Sabbath, regard the synagogue as holy, and practice circumcision; and anger that Judaism remained a vital religion, for this undermined the conviction that Christianity was the fulfillment of Judaism and the one true faith.

What made Christian anti-Judaism particularly ominous was the effort of some theologians to demonize the Jewish people. The myth emerged that the Jews, murderers of the incarnate God who embodied all that was good, were a cursed people, children of the Devil, whose suffering was intended by God. Thus Origen (c. 185–c. 251) maintained that "the blood of Jesus [falls] not only upon those who lived then but also upon all generations of the Jewish people following afterwards until the end of the world."[6] In the late fourth century, John Chrysostom described Jews as "inveterate murderers, destroyers, men possessed by the Devil." "[T]hey murder their offspring and immolate them to the devil." The synagogue, he said, was "the domicile of the devil as is also the soul of the Jews." Their rites are "criminal and impure," their religion is "a disease." For the "odious assassination of Christ," there is "no expiation possible, . . . no pardon." Jews will live "under the yoke of servitude without end."[7] Since the Devil was very real to early and medieval Christians, the Jew became identified with evil. Christians developed a mindset, concludes the Rev. Robert A. Everett, that was "unable to see anything positive in Judaism. . . . Judaism and the Jewish people came to have no real value for Christians except as a negative contrast to Christianity."[8] Because of this "teaching of contempt" and the "diabolization of the Jew," the Christian ethic of love did not extend to Jews:

> *[O]nce it is established that God has cursed the Jews, how can one argue that Christians should love them? If Jews have been fated by God to have . . . a long history of suffering, who are Christians to alter their history by doing anything to relieve Jewish suffering? The theology of victimization thus precludes Christian love as a basis of relating to Jews.*[9]

The diabolization of the Jew, which bore no relationship to the actual behavior of Jews or to their highly ethical religion, and the "theology of victimization," which held that the Jews were collectively and eternally cursed for denying Christ, became powerful myths, which, over the centuries, poisoned Christians' hearts and minds against Jews, spurring innumerable humiliations, persecutions, and massacres by Christians who believed that their actions were pleasing to God. Alongside this hatred of Jews and antipathy to their suffering, there also evolved the belief that the Jews, faithless and perfidious though they were, should be permitted to survive, for one day they would see the light and convert to the true faith.

Saint Augustine: The Christian World-View

During the early history of Christianity, learned fathers of the church explained and defended church teachings. Most of the leading early fathers wrote in Greek, but in the middle of the fourth century, three great Latin writers—Saint Jerome, Saint Ambrose, and Saint Augustine—profoundly influenced the course of Christianity in the West.

As a youth, Saint Jerome (A.D. c. 340–420) studied Latin literature in Rome. Throughout his life, he remained an admirer of Cicero, Virgil, Lucretius, and other great Latin writers, and he defended the study of classical literature by Christians. Baptized in his mid-twenties, Jerome lived for a while as a hermit in the desert of Chalcis, near Antioch. After becoming a priest, he became secretary to Pope Damascus. Criticized for attacking the luxurious living and laxness of the clergy, he left Rome and established a monastery near Bethlehem, where he devoted himself to prayer and study.

Saint Jerome wrote about the lives of the saints and promoted the spread of monasticism. But his greatest achievement was the translation of the Old and New Testaments from Hebrew and Greek into Latin. Jerome's text, the common, or Vulgate, version of the Bible, became the official edition of the Bible for the Western church.

Saint Ambrose (A.D. 340–397), bishop of Milan,

CHRIST ENTHRONED. Detail from the funerary sarcophagus of Junius Bassus, A.D. 359. (*Hirmer Fotoarchiv, München.*)

Italy, composed religious hymns and wrote books on Scripture, dogma, and morality. In his work on the duties of the clergy, Ambrose provided humane rules for dealing with the poor, the old, the sick, and the orphaned. He urged clerics not to pursue wealth but to practice humility and avoid favoring the rich over the poor. Ambrose sought to defend the autonomy of the church against the power of the state. Emperors are not the judges of bishops, he wrote. His dictum that "the Emperor is within the church, not above it" became a cardinal principle of the medieval church.

The most important Christian theoretician in the Late Roman Empire was Saint Augustine (A.D. 354–430), bishop of Hippo, in North Africa. Born in the North African province of Numidia, Augustine attended school at Carthage, where he studied the Latin classics. Struggling to find meaning in a world that abounded with evil, Augustine turned to Manichaeism, an Eastern religious philosophy whose central doctrine was the struggle of the universal forces of light and good against those of darkness and evil. But Augustine still felt spiritually restless. In Milan, inspired by the sermons of Ambrose, he abandoned Manichaeism and devoted his life to following Christ's teachings. After serving as a priest, he was appointed bishop of Hippo in 395.

In his autobiography, the *Confessions,* Augustine described his spiritual quest and appealed to devotees of Manichaeism and to adherents of pagan philosophy to embrace Christianity. At the turn of the fifth century, when the Greco-Roman world-view was disintegrating and the Roman world-state was collapsing, Augustine wrote his greatest and most influential work, *The City of God.* He became the chief architect of the Christian outlook that succeeded a dying classicism.

In 410, when Augustine was in his fifties, Visigoths sacked Rome—a disaster for which the classical consciousness was unprepared. Throughout the Empire, people panicked. Non-Christians blamed the tragedy on Christianity, saying that the Christians had predicted the end of the world and by refusing to offer sacrifices to ancient gods had turned those deities against Rome. They also accused Christians of undermining the Empire by refusing to serve in the army. Even Christians expressed anxiety. Why were the righteous also suffering? Where was the kingdom of God on earth that had been prophesied in the Scriptures?

Augustine's *City of God* was a response to the crisis of the Roman Empire, just as Plato's *The Republic* had been a reaction to the crisis of the Athenian polis. Whereas Plato expressed hope that a state founded on rational principles could remedy the abuses of Athenian society, Augustine maintained that the worldly city could never be the central concern of a Christian. The ideal state, he wrote, could not be realized on earth; it existed only in heaven. The misfortunes of Rome, therefore, should not distress a Christian unduly, for Christianity belonged to the realm of the spirit and could not be identified with any state.

The meaning of history, Augustine believed, was to be found not in Rome's mission to bring peace and order to the world, but in God's intention for human beings. The collapse of Rome did not diminish the greatness of Christianity because the true Christian was a citizen of a heavenly city that could not be pillaged by ungodly barbarians but would endure forever. Compared with God's heavenly city, Rome and its decline were unimportant. What really mattered in history, Augustine said, was not the coming to be or the passing away of cities and empires, but the individual's spiritual destiny, his or her entrance into heaven or hell.

Yet Augustine remained a man of this world. Although the earthly city was the very opposite of the heavenly city, he insisted that people must still deal with this earthly abode. Christians could not reject their city entirely but must bend it to fit a Christian pattern. The city that someday would rise from the ruins of Rome must be based on Christian principles. Warfare, economic activity, education, and the rearing of children should all be conducted in a Christian spirit. The church could not neglect the state but must guide it to protect human beings from their own sinful natures. The state must employ repression and punishment to restrain people, who were inherently sinful, from destroying each other and the few good men and women whom God had elected to save from hell. But the earthly city would never know tranquillity, said Augustine, for it would always be inhabited predominantly by wretched sinners. People should be under no illusion that it could be transformed into the City of God. Because human beings are infected with sin, everywhere in human society we see

> *love for all those things that prove so vain and . . . breed so many heartaches, troubles, griefs, and fears; such insane joys in discord, strife, and war; such wrath and plots of enemies . . . such fraud and theft and robbery; such perfidy . . . homicide and murder, cruelty and savagery, lawlessness and lust; all the shameless passions of the impure—fornication and adultery . . . and countless other uncleannesses too nasty to be mentioned; the sins against religion—sacrilege and heresy . . . the iniquities against our neighbors—calumnies and cheating, lies and false witness, violence to persons and property . . . and the innumerable other miseries and maladies that fill the world, yet escape attention.*[10]

Augustine did not hold that Christ, by his sacrificial death, had opened the door to heaven for all. Most of humanity remained condemned to eternal punishment, said Augustine; only a handful had the gift of faith and the promise of heaven. People could not overcome a sinful nature by their own efforts; moral and spiritual regeneration stemmed not from human will power but from God's grace. And God determined who would be saved and who would be damned.

Whereas the vast majority of people, said Augustine, were citizens of a doomed earthly city, the small number endowed with God's grace constituted the City of God. These people lived on earth as visitors only, for they awaited deliverance to the Kingdom of Christ, where together with the good angels and God they would know perfect happiness. But the permanent inhabitants of the earthly city were destined for eternal punishment in hell. A perpetual conflict existed between the two cities and between their inhabitants; one city stood for sin and corruption, the other for God's truth and perfection. For Augustine, the highest good was not of this world but consisted of eternal life with God.

Augustine's distinction between this higher world of perfection and a lower world of corruption remained influential throughout the Middle Ages. But the church, rejecting Augustine's doctrine that only a limited number of people are predestined for heaven, emphasized that Christ had made possible the salvation of all who would embrace the precepts and injunctions of the church. The Protestant reformers of the sixteenth century, however, accepted Augustine's position.

Augustine repudiated the distinguishing feature of classical humanism: the autonomy of reason. For him, ultimate wisdom could not be achieved through rational thought alone. Reason had to be guided by faith. Without faith, there could be no true knowledge, no understanding. Philosophy had no validity if it did not first accept as absolutely true the existence of God and the authority of his revelation. Valid ethical standards could not be formulated by reason alone but were revealed to people by the living God. Christian truth did not rest on theoretical excellence or logical consistency; it was true because its source was God.

Augustine's belief contrasts with that of Socrates, who insisted that through rational reflection each individual could arrive at standards of good and evil. For the humanist Socrates, ultimate values were something that the individual could grasp through thought alone and could defend rationally. For Augustine, reason alone could not serve as a proper guide to life. He maintained that individuals, without divine guidance, lacked the capacity to comprehend ultimate truth or to regenerate themselves morally. Without God, they could not attain wisdom or liberate themselves from a wicked and sinful human nature: "the happiness of man can come not from himself but only from God, and . . . to live according to oneself is sin."[11]

Thus, against the classical view that asserted the primacy of reason, Augustine opposed the primacy of faith. But he did not necessarily regard reason as an enemy of faith, and he did not call for an end to rational speculation. What he denied of the classical view was that reason *alone* could attain wisdom, could instruct people how to live. The wisdom that Augustine sought was

Saint Augustine in His Studio. Saint Augustine was the most influential Christian theoretician in the Late Roman Empire. This painting of him in his studio depicts him as a serious thinker. (*Corbis-Bettmann.*)

Christian wisdom, God's revelation to humanity. The starting point for this wisdom, he said, was belief in God and the Scriptures. For Augustine, secular knowledge for its own sake had little value; the true significance of knowledge lay in its role as a tool for comprehending God's will. Let us utilize truths useful to the faith that pagan philosophers might have chanced upon, he said. Augustine adapted the classical intellectual tradition to the requirements of Christian revelation.

With Augustine, the human-centered outlook of classical humanism, which for centuries had been undergoing transformation, gave way to a God-centered world-view. The fulfillment of God's will, not the full development of human talent, became the chief concern of life.

Augustinian Christianity is a living philosophy because it still has something vital to say about the human condition. To those who believe that people have the intelligence and goodwill to transform their earthly city into a rational and just community that promotes human betterment, Augustine offers a reminder of human sinfulness, weakness, and failure. Nor will new and ingenious political and social arrangements alter a defective human nature. He cautions the optimist that progress is not certain, that people, weak and ever prone to wickedness, are their own worst enemies, that success is illusory, and that misery is the essential human reality.

Christianity and Classical Humanism: Alternative World-Views

Christianity and classical humanism are the two principal components of the Western tradition. The value that modern Western civilization places on the individual derives ultimately from classical humanism and the Judeo-Christian tradition. Classical humanists believed that human worth came from the capacity of individuals to reason, and to shape their character and life according to rational standards. Christianity also places great stress on the individual. In the Christian view, God cares for each person; he wants people to behave righteously and to enter heaven; Christ died for all because he loves humanity. Christianity espouses active love and genuine concern for fellow human beings. Without God, people are as Augustine described them: "foul, crooked, sordid, . . . vicious." With God, the human personality can undergo a moral transformation and become loving, good, and free. The idea of a Christian conscience, prompted by God and transcending all other loyalties, reinforces respect for all human beings regardless of cultural and national differences. Also promoting respect for each person is the presupposition of natural equality stemming from the Christian belief that each individual, regardless of birth, wealth, or talent, is precious to God.

But Christianity and classical humanism also represent two essentially different world-views. The triumph of the Christian outlook signified a break with the essential meaning of classical humanism; it pointed to the end of the world of antiquity and the beginning of an age of faith, the Middle Ages. With the victory of Christianity, the ultimate goal of life shifted. Life's purpose was no longer to achieve excellence in this world through the full and creative development of human capacities, but to attain salvation in a heavenly city. A person's worldly accomplishments amounted to very little if he or she did not accept God and his revelation. The Christian ideal of the isolated and contemplative monk, who rejected the world in order to serve God, was alien to the spirit of classical humanism, which valued active citizenship and active participation in worldly activities. Equally foreign to the Greco-Roman mind was another idea introduced by Christianity: the need to escape from a sinful human nature, a consequence of Adam and Eve's defiance of God. This view of a corrupt human nature and an unclean human body, particularly in Augustine's formulation, became deeply embedded in the European mind during the Christian centuries—the Middle Ages.

In the classical view, history had no ultimate end, no ultimate meaning; periods of happiness and misery repeated themselves endlessly. In the Christian view, history is filled with spiritual meaning. It is the profound drama of individuals struggling to overcome their original sin in order to gain eternal happiness in heaven. History began with Adam and Eve's fall and would end when Christ returns to earth, evil is eradicated, and God's will prevails. For the Christian the coming of Christ was both the central event and a turning point in world history.

Classicism held that there was no authority higher than reason, that individuals had within themselves, through unaided reason, the ability to understand the world and life. Christianity teaches that, without God as the starting point, knowledge is formless, purposeless, and prone to error. Classicism, unlike Judaism or Christianity, possessed no truths or moral precepts revealed by a divine power. Rather, classicism held that ethical standards were expressions of universal reason, laws of nature, which reason could discover. Through reason, individuals could discern the norms by which they should regulate their lives. Reason would enable them to govern desires and will; it would show where their behavior was wrong and teach them how to correct it. Because individuals sought what was best for themselves, they would obey the voice of reason. Christianity, on the other hand, maintains that ethical standards emanate from the personal will of God. Without submission to God's commands, people remain wicked forever; the human will, essentially sinful, cannot be transformed by the promptings of reason. Only when individuals turn to God for forgiveness and guidance can they find the inner strength to overcome their sinful nature. People cannot perfect themselves through scientific knowledge; it is spiritual insight and belief in God that they require and that must serve as the first principle of their lives. For classicism, the ultimate good was sought through independent thought and action; for Christianity, the ultimate good comes through knowing, obeying, and loving God.

Christian thinkers respected Greek philosophy, however, and did not seek to eradicate the intellectual heritage of Greece. Rather, they sought to fit it into a Christian framework—that is, rational inquiry must be guided by and never conflict with Christian teachings. By preserving the Greek philosophical tradition—even if it remained subordinate to the Christian outlook—Christian thinkers performed a task of immense historical significance.

Christianity inherited the Hebrew view of the overriding importance of God for humanity: God, who is both Lawgiver and Judge, makes life intelligible and purposeful. For the Christian, God is a living being, loving and compassionate, in whose company one seeks to spend eternity; one knows God essentially through faith and feeling. Although the Greek philosophers had a conception of God, it was not comparable to the God of Hebrews and Christians. For the Greeks, God was a logical abstraction, a principle of order, the prime mover, the first cause, the mind of the universe, pure thought, the supreme good, the highest truth; God was a concept, impersonal, unfeeling, and uninvolved with human concerns. The Greeks approached God through the intellect, not the heart; they neither loved nor worshiped God. In addition, because religion was at the periphery, not the center, of classical humanism, the idea of God did not carry the same significance as it did for Christianity.

The Ascension of Jesus into Heaven: A Miniature Painting c. A.D. 586. In this illustration contained in a manuscript produced by a monk at Saint John's Abbey, Zagba, Mesopotamia, the upper zone of the painting reflects a vision of the prophet Ezekiel (1:3–28). The lower zone shows Jesus' Disciples and his mother Mary with two angels as witnesses to Jesus' ascension into heaven. (Acts 1:7–14). (*Courtesy Biblioteca Medicea Laurenziana, Florence. Photo by Donato Pineides.*)

In the classical world, the political community was the avenue to justice, happiness, and self-realization. In Christianity, the good life was identified not with worldly achievement but with life eternal, and the ideal commonwealth could only be one that was founded and ruled by Christ. It was entrance into God's kingdom that each person must make the central aim of life. For the next thousand years, this distinction between heaven and earth, this otherworldly, theocentric outlook, would define the Western mentality.

In the Late Roman Empire, when classical values were in decay, Christianity was a dynamic and creative movement. Possessing both institutional and spiritual strength, Christianity survived the fall of Rome. Because it retained elements of Greco-Roman civilization and taught a high morality, Christianity served as a civilizing agent in the centuries that followed Rome's collapse. Indeed, Christianity was the essential shaper of the European civilization that emerged in the Middle Ages.

❖ ❖ ❖

Notes

1. Hans Küng, "Christianity and Judaism," in *Jesus' Jewishness,* ed. James H. Charlesworth (New York: Crossroad, 1991), p. 259.
2. The biblical quotations, used with permission, are from the Holy Bible, Revised Standard Version (New York: Thomas Nelson & Sons, 1952). The Revised Standard Version is the text used for biblical quotations throughout, except where noted otherwise.
3. Tertullian, "On Prescription Against Heretics," chap. 7, in Alexander Roberts and James Donaldson, eds., *The Ante-Nicene Fathers* (New York: Charles Scribner's Sons, 1918), 3:246.
4. Clement of Alexandria, *Stromata (Miscellanies),* trans. William Wilson, in Alexander Roberts and James Donaldson, *Ante-Nicene Christian Library* (Edinburgh: T & T Clark, 1867–1872), vol. 4, *The Writings of Clement of Alexandria,* pp. 303–304.
5. Tertullian, "On the Flesh of Christ," in Roberts and Donaldson, *The Ante-Nicene Fathers,* p. 525.
6. *Origenis, Commentariorum in Evangelium Secundum Matthaeum* in *Patrologiae Cursus Completus,* Series Graeca Prior, ed. J. P. Migne (Paris: Parisiorum, 1862), vol. 13, cols. 1494–1495, pars. 775–776; trans. J. Castora for this volume.
7. Quoted in Edward H. Flannery, *The Anguish of the Jews* (London: Macmillan, 1965), p. 48.
8. Randolph Braham, ed., *The Origins of the Holocaust: Christian Anti-Semitism* (Boulder, Colo: Social Science Monographs and Institute for Holocaust Studies of the City University of New York, 1986), p. 36.
9. Ibid., p. 37.
10. Saint Augustine, *The City of God,* trans. Gerald G. Walsh et al., abridged (Garden City, N.Y.: Doubleday Image Books, 1958), p. 519.
11. Ibid., p. 300.

Suggested Reading

Armstrong, A. H., and R. A. Markus, *Christian Faith and Greek Philosophy* (1960). A presentation of the dialogue between Christianity and Greek philosophy.

Armstrong, Karen, *A History of God* (1994). Good material on early Christianity.

Benko, Stephen, *Pagan Rome and the Early Christians* (1984). How Romans and Greeks viewed early Christianity.

Chadwick, Henry, *The Early Church* (1967). A survey of early Christianity in its social and ideological context.

Charlesworth, James, ed., *Jesus' Jewishness* (1991). Essays by prominent scholars exploring the Jewish context of early Christianity.

Davies, J. G., *The Early Christian Church* (1967). A splendid introduction to the first five centuries of Christianity.

Ferguson, Everett, ed., *Encyclopedia of Early Christianity* (1990). Entries on all aspects of early Christianity.

———, *Backgrounds of Early Christianity* (1993). A clear and thorough examination of the milieu in which Christianity was born.

Fredricksen, Paula, *From Jesus to Christ* (1998). Christian origins and the images of Jesus in the New Testament.

Frend, W. H. C., *The Rise of Christianity* (1984). A valuable reference work for early church history.

Gager, John G., *The Origins of Anti-Semitism* (1983). Anti-Semitism as essentially a Christian phenomenon.

Grant, Michael, *Jesus* (1977). An examination of the Gospels.

Latourette, K. S., *A History of Christianity* (1953). Clearly written and eminently readable.

Mattingly, Harold, *Christianity in the Roman Empire* (1967). A brief, well-informed survey.

Meeks, Wayne A., *The Moral World of the First Christians* (1986). Continuity and discontinuity between the moral outlook of early Christianity and that of Jewish and Greco-Roman thought.

Nicholls, William, *Christian Antisemitism* (1993). A Christian scholar analyzes the Christian roots of anti-Judaism.

Nock, A. D., *St. Paul* (1963). A highly respected account of the principal Christian Apostle to the Greco-Roman world.

———, *Early Christianity and Its Hellenistic Background* (1964). A superb scholarly treatment of the relationship of Christianity to the wider cultural setting.

Pelikan, Jaroslav, *The Christian Tradition* (1971), vol. 1, *The Emergence of the Catholic Tradition.* The first of a five-volume series on the history of Christian doctrine.

Perkins, Pheme, *Reading the New Testament* (1978). Introduces the beginning student to the New Testament.

Perry, Marvin, and Frederick M. Schweitzer, eds., *Jewish-Christian Encounters over the Centuries* (1994). Useful essays on Jesus, Paul, the Dead Sea Scrolls, and early Christian anti-Judaism.

Segal, Allan F., *Rebecca's Children* (1986). Judaism and Christianity in the Roman world.

Wilkin, Robert L., *The Christians as the Romans Saw Them* (1984). Pagan reaction to the rise of Christianity.

Review Questions

1. Why does the life of Jesus present a problem to the historian?
2. What were Jesus' basic teachings?
3. What is the relationship of early Christianity to Judaism?
4. What was the historical significance of the belief in Jesus' resurrection?
5. How did Saint Paul transform a Jewish sect into a world religion?
6. What factors contributed to the triumph of Christianity in the Roman Empire?
7. Why did some early Christian thinkers object to the study of classical literature? What arguments were advanced by the defenders of classical learning? What was the outcome of this debate? Why was it significant?
8. What is the historical significance of Saint Basil, Saint Martin of Tours, and Saint Benedict?
9. What factors contributed to the rise of anti-Judaism among early Christians? Define and explain the historical significance of "diabolization of the Jew," "teaching of contempt," and "theology of victimization."
10. How did Saint Augustine view the fall of Rome, the worldly city, humanity, and Greek philosophy?
11. Compare and contrast the world-views of early Christianity and classical humanism.

Part Two

The Middle Ages: The Christian Centuries

500–1400

500

600

700

800

900

1000

1100

1200

1300

Politics and Society	Thought and Culture
Germanic kingdoms established on former Roman lands (5th and 6th cent.) Saint Benedict founds monastery at Monte Cassino (529) Pope Gregory I sends missionaries to convert Anglo-Saxons (596)	Boethius, *Consolation of Philosophy* (523) Law code of Justinian (529) Byzantine church Hagia Sophia (532–537) Cassiodorus establishes a monastic library at Vivarium (540)
Spread of Islam (622–732)	The Koran
Charles Martel defeats Muslims at Tours (732)	Bede, *Ecclesiastical History of the English People* (c. 700) Muslim Golden Age (700s and 800s)
Charlemagne crowned emperor of Romans Alfred the Great, ruler of Saxon kingdom of Wessex (871–899) Muslim, Magyar, and Viking invasions of Latin Christendom (9th and early 10th cent.) Growth of feudalism (800–1100)	Carolingian Renaissance (768–814) Alfred the Great promotes learning in England (871–899)
German king Otto I becomes first Holy Roman Emperor (962)	
Split between the Byzantine and Roman churches (1054) Norman conquest of England (1066) Start of First Crusade (1096)	Romanesque style in architecture (1000s and 1100s)
Philip Augustus expands central authority in France (1180–1223) Development of common law and jury system in England (1100s) Pontificate of Innocent III: height of papal power (1198–1216)	Flowering of medieval culture (12th and 13th cent.): universities, Gothic architecture, scholastic philosophy, revival of Roman law
Magna Carta (1215) Destruction of Baghdad by Mongols (1258)	Aquinas, *Summa Theologica* (1267–1273)
Hundred Years' War (1337–1453) Black Death (1347–1351) Great Schism of papacy (1378–1417)	Dante, *Divine Comedy* (c. 1307–1321) Chaucer, *Canterbury Tales* (c. 1388–1400)

Chapter 9

The Heirs of Rome: Byzantium, Islam, and Latin Christendom

Coronation of Charlemagne. (Scala/Art Resource, NY.)

- **Byzantine Civilization: The Medieval Christian East**
  Conflict with the Roman Church
  Imperial Growth and Decline
  The Bequest of Byzantium
- **Islamic Civilization: Its Development and Dissemination**
  The Prophet: The Founding of a New Religion
  The Muslim State and Society
  The Muslim Golden Age
  Mongol Invasions and Ottoman Dominance
- **Latin Christendom: The Rise of Europe**
  Political and Economic Transformation
  The Waning of Classical Culture
- **The Church: Shaper of Medieval Civilization**
  The Church as Unifier
  Monks and the Papacy
- **The Kingdom of the Franks**
  The Era of Charlemagne
  Carolingian Renaissance
  The Breakup of Charlemagne's Empire
- **Medieval Society**
  Vassalage
  Feudal Law
  Feudal Warriors
  Noblewomen
  Agrarian Life

The triumph of Christianity, the decay of the Roman Empire, and the establishment of Germanic kingdoms on once Roman lands constituted a new phase in Western history: the end of the ancient world and the beginning of the Middle Ages, a period that spanned a thousand years. In the ancient world, the locus of Greco-Roman civilization had been the Mediterranean Sea; the heartland of Western medieval civilization gradually shifted to the north, to regions of Europe that Greco-Roman civilization had barely penetrated. Latin Christendom (western and central Europe) was only one of three new civilizations based on religion that emerged after the decline of the Roman Empire; Byzantium and Islam were the other two. Both of these Eastern civilizations influenced the emerging Europe in important ways.

Byzantine Civilization: The Medieval Christian East

Although the Roman Empire in the West fell to the German tribes, the eastern provinces of the Empire survived. They did so because they were richer, more urbanized, and more populous and because the main thrust of the Germanic and Hunnish invaders had been directed at the western regions. In the eastern parts, Byzantine civilization took shape. Its religion was Christianity, its culture Greek, and its machinery of administration Roman. The capital, Constantinople, was built on the site of the ancient Greek city of Byzantium, on a peninsula in the Straits of Bosporus—the dividing line between Asia and Europe. Constantinople was a fortress city perfectly situated to resist attacks from land and sea.

During the Early Middle Ages (500–1050), Byzantine civilization was economically and culturally far more advanced than the Latin West. At a time when few westerners (Latin Christians) could read or write, Byzantine scholars studied the literature, philosophy, science, and law of ancient Greece and Rome. Whereas trade and urban life had greatly declined in the West, Constantinople was a magnificent Byzantine city of

Chronology 9.1 ❖ The Rise of Europe

496	Clovis adopts Roman Christianity
523	Boethius writes *Consolation of Philosophy*
540	Cassiodorus establishes a monastic library at Vivarium
596	Pope Gregory I sends missionaries to convert the Anglo-Saxons
717	Charles Martel becomes mayor of the palace under a weak Merovingian king
732	Charles Martel defeats the Muslims at Tours
751	Pepin the Short, with papal support, deposes the Merovingian ruler and becomes king of the Franks
755	Pepin donates to the papacy lands taken from the Lombards
768	Charlemagne becomes king of the Franks
774	Charlemagne defeats the Lombards
782	Alcuin of York heads Charlemagne's palace school
c. 799	Charlemagne subdues the Saxons
800	Charlemagne is crowned emperor of the Romans by Pope Leo III
814	Charlemagne dies and is succeeded by his son, Louis the Pious
840	Death of Louis the Pious: the empire is divided among his sons
c. 840s	Height of Viking attacks
c. 890	Magyars invade central Europe

schools, libraries, open squares, and bustling markets.

Conflict with the Roman Church

Over the centuries, many differences developed between the Eastern church and the Roman church. The pope in Rome resisted domination by the Byzantine emperor, and the Byzantines denied the pope's claim to authority over all Christians. The two churches quarreled over ceremonies, holy days, the display of images, and the rights of the clergy. The final break came in 1054. The Christian church split into the Roman Catholic in the West and the Eastern (Greek) Orthodox in the East, a division that still persists.

Political and cultural differences widened the rift between Latin Christendom and Byzantium. Latin Christians refused to recognize that the Byzantine emperors were, as they claimed, successors to the Roman emperors. In the Byzantine Empire, Greek was the language of religion and intellectual life; in the West, it was Latin.

Imperial Growth and Decline

Byzantine emperors were absolute rulers who held that God had chosen them to rule and to institute divine will on earth. As successors to the Roman emperors, they claimed to rule all the lands once part of the Roman Empire. The first great Byzantine ruler was Justinian, who reigned nearly forty years, from 527 to 565. Justinian often relied on the advice of his wife, Theodora. Theodora's background was unusual for an empress; she was not from the nobility but was the daughter of a bear trainer in the circus and had been an actress, a profession most people considered degrading. In a number of crises, the strong-

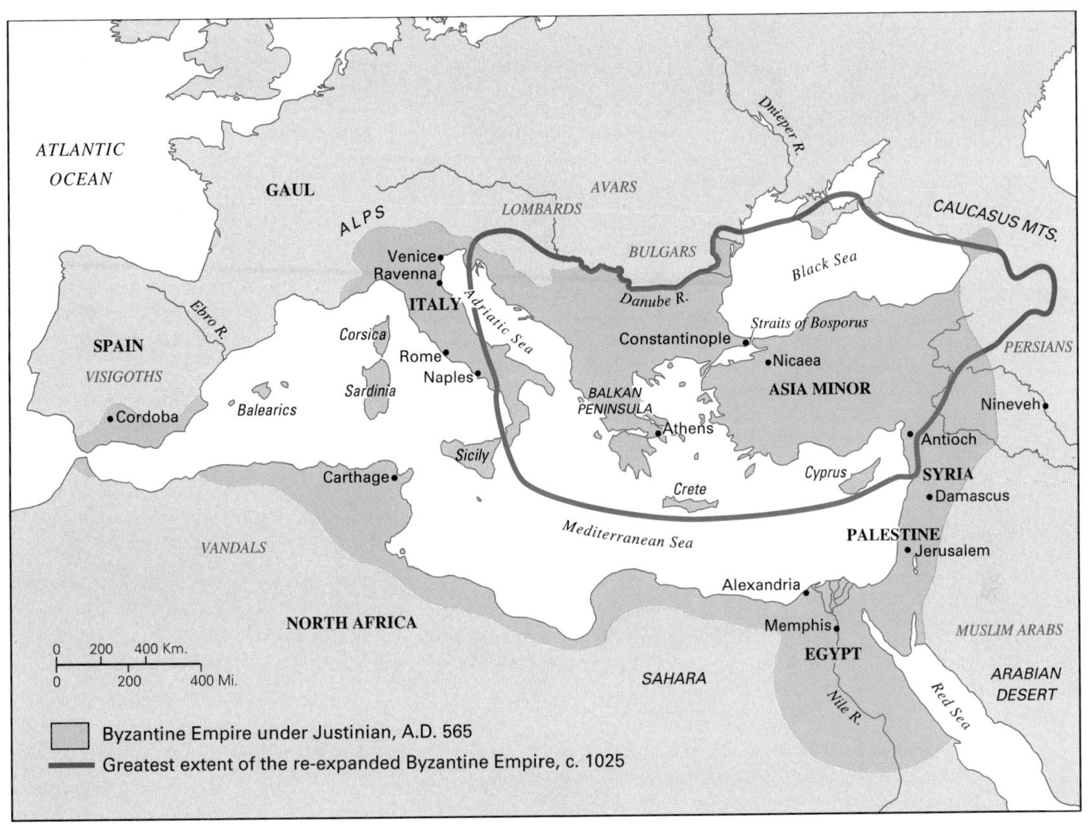

Map 9.1 The Byzantine Empire In the centuries after Justinian regained lands in the western Mediterranean that had been lost to Germanic invaders, the Byzantines faced attacks from Avars, Bulgars, Lombards, Persians, Arabs, Latin Christians, Seljuk Turks, and the Ottoman Turks, who captured Constantinople in 1453.

willed and astute Theodora gave Justinian the courage to act decisively.

Justinian's most lasting achievement was the appointment of a commission of scholars to collect and codify Rome's ancient laws and the commentaries of learned jurists. The result was the *Corpus Juris Civilis,* which became the official body of law of the Byzantine Empire. In the twelfth century, it was gradually reintroduced into western Europe, where it became the basis of common law in many European lands.

Justinian sought to regain the lands in the western Mediterranean that had been conquered by Germanic invaders. During his reign, Byzantine forces retook North Africa from the Vandals, part of southern Spain from the Visigoths, and Italy from the Ostrogoths, establishing a western capital at Ravenna.

Besides draining the treasury, the long and costly wars led to the neglect of defenses in the Balkan Peninsula and the Near East. The Balkans were invaded by Slavic tribes from the Black Sea region and by Avars and Bulgars, originally from central Asia; Syria was ravaged by the Persians. Nor were the conquered territories in the west secure. The Germanic Lombards, who had moved into northern Italy in the late sixth century, conquered much Byzantine territory that had been recently recovered from the Ostrogoths. By 629, the Visigoths had driven the Byzantines from Spain.

In the early seventh century, the Byzantines faced a renewed threat from the Persians, who

Ravenna Mosaics. Theodora, emperor Justinian's wife, was a strong-willed woman who exercised considerable authority and often advised her husband on matters of state. (*AKG London.*)

seized the Byzantine provinces of Syria, Palestine, and Egypt. In an all-out effort, however, Emperor Heraclius (610–641) regained the provinces and in 627 crushed the Persians near the ruins of the ancient city of Nineveh. But the exhausted Byzantine Empire had become vulnerable to the Muslim Arabs, who had moved swiftly out of the Arabian Desert seeking to propagate Islam, their new faith (discussed later in this chapter).

By 642, the Arabs had stripped the Byzantine Empire of Syria, Palestine, and Egypt, and by the beginning of the eighth century, they had taken North Africa. Near the end of the seventh century and again in 717, the Muslims besieged Constantinople. But the Byzantine fleet was armed with a new weapon, "Greek fire"—a fiery explosive liquid shot from tubes—which set enemy ships aflame and made blazing pools on the water's surface. Thus, the light Byzantine ships were able to repulse the better-built Arabian ships.

The Arabs' failure to take Constantinople was crucial not only for the Byzantine Empire but also for the history of Christianity. Had this Christian fortress fallen in the eighth century, the Arabs would have been able to overrun the Balkan Peninsula and sail up the Danube River into the European heartland. After this defeat, however, Islamic armies largely concentrated their conquests outside Europe.

From the late ninth to the early eleventh century, the Byzantine forces grew stronger and even took the offensive against the Muslims. But soon

Church of the Holy Wisdom (Hagia Sophia), Constantinople, A.D. 532–537. The largest church ever built in the Byzantine world, Hagia Sophia was constructed by Emperor Justinian. The interior of its immense dome was decorated with golden mosaics simulating the light of heaven. After the Turkish conquest of Constantinople in A.D. 1453, the mosaics were painted white, the church was converted into a mosque, and minarets (towers from which the faithful were summoned for prayer five times a day) were constructed. (*Gary Yeowell/Tony Stone.*)

new enemies threatened. By 1071, the Normans from France had driven the Byzantines from Italy. In the same year, the Seljuk Turks, a people from central Asia who had adopted Islam, defeated the Byzantines in Asia Minor and subjugated most of the peninsula, the heart of the Byzantine Empire. Internal dissension, however, led to the breakup of the Seljuk Empire.

Seeking to exploit Seljuk weakness and to regain lost territories, the Byzantines appealed to Latin Christians for help. Although European Christians had little love for the Byzantines, they did want to free Christian holy places from the Muslims. For this purpose, they undertook a series of Crusades, beginning in the late eleventh century (see Chapter 10). In 1204, during the Fourth Crusade, Latin Christian knights (greedy for riches) and Venetian merchants (eager to gain control of the rich Byzantine trade) decided to take Constantinople rather than fight the Muslims.

The Latin Christians looted the city, destroying sacred books, vandalizing churches, and carrying huge amounts of gold, jewels, Christian relics, and works of art back to western Europe. They also seized islands along Constantinople's major trade routes, set up kingdoms on Byzantine lands, and tried to force Latin forms of Christianity on the Byzantine Greeks. The Orthodox Greeks resisted, and for nearly sixty years Latin and Greek Christians fought one another. Not until 1261 were the westerners driven from Constantinople. The Byzantine Empire regained its independence, but its power was disastrously weakened. Crushing taxes, decreasing agricultural production, declining trade, and civil war continued to sap the tottering empire.

The deathblow to the empire was dealt by another group of Turks from central Asia. The Ottoman Turks had accepted Islam and had begun to build an empire. They drove the Byzantines from Asia Minor and conquered much of the Balkans. By the beginning of the fifteenth century, the Byzantine Empire consisted of only two small territories in Greece and the city of Constantinople. In 1453, the Ottoman Turks broke through Constantinople's great walls and plundered the city. After more than ten centuries, the Byzantine Empire came to an end.

The Bequest of Byzantium

During its thousand years, Byzantium made a significant impact on world history. First, it prevented the Muslim Arabs from advancing into eastern Europe. Had the Arabs broken through Byzantine defenses, much of Europe might have been converted to the new faith of Islam. A far-reaching accomplishment was the codification of the laws of ancient Rome under Justinian. This monumental achievement preserved Roman law's principles of reason and justice. Today's legal codes in much of Europe and Latin America trace their roots to the Roman law recorded by Justinian's lawyers. The Byzantines also preserved the philosophy, science, mathematics, and literature of ancient Greece.

Contacts with Byzantine civilization stimulated learning in both the Islamic world to the east and Latin Christendom to the west. Speros Vryonis, a student of Byzantine civilization, states: "The Byzantines carried the torch of civilization unextinguished at a time when the barbarous Germanic and Slav tribes had reduced much of Europe to near chaos: and they maintained this high degree of civilization until Western Europe gradually emerged and began to take form."[1] Byzantium exerted an important religious, cultural, and linguistic influence on Latin Romanians, eastern Slavs (Russians and Ukrainians), and southern Slavs (Serbs and Bulgars). From Byzantium, the Slavs acquired legal principles, art forms, and an alphabet (the Cyrillic, based on the Greek) for writing their languages. (On the other hand, the western Slavs—Poles, Czechs, and Slovaks—came under the influence of Latin Christianity and Latin culture.)

Islamic Civilization: Its Development and Dissemination

The Prophet: The Founding of a New Religion

The second eastern civilization to arise after Rome's fall was based on the vital new religion of Islam, which emerged in the seventh century among the Arabs of Arabia. Its founder was Muhammad (c. 570–632), a prosperous merchant in Mecca, a trading city near the Red Sea. When Muhammad was about forty, he believed that he was visited in his sleep by the angel Gabriel, who ordered him to "recite in the name of the Lord!" Transformed by this experience, Muhammad came to believe that he had been chosen as a prophet.

Although most desert Arabs worshiped tribal gods, in the towns and trading centers many Arabs were familiar with Judaism and Christianity, and some had accepted the idea of one God. Rejecting the many deities of the tribal religions, Muhammad offered the Arabs a new monotheistic faith, Islam, which means "surrender to Allah" (God).

Islamic standards of morality and rules governing daily life are set by the Koran, the book that Muslims believe contains the words of Allah as revealed to Muhammad. Muslims see their religion as the completion and perfection of Judaism and Christianity; they believe both of those monotheistic predecessors were superseded by Allah's revelation to Muhammad. Muslims regard the ancient Hebrew prophets as sent from God and value their messages about compassion and the oneness of humanity. They also regard Jesus as a great prophet but do not consider him divine. They see Muhammad as the last and greatest of the prophets and be-

MOSQUE OF MOHAMMED ALI, CAIRO, TWELFTH CENTURY A.D. This mosque was a gathering place for prayer, preaching, and study of the Koran. Mosques were usually rectangular buildings, with arcaded porticos surrounding an open court. Inside, the focal point was an apse facing Mecca from which the local *Imam* (holy man) led the congregation in prayer. Nearby was a pulpit for preaching and a copy of the Koran on a lectern. In the outer court were pools or fountains for ritual purification. At the Cairo mosque, the fountains were covered by a domed building. Attached to the mosque were minarets for calling the faithful to daily prayers. (*Courtesy Trans World Airlines.*)

lieve that he was entirely human, not divine. Muslims worship only Allah, the creator and ruler of heaven and earth, a single, all-powerful God who is merciful, compassionate, and just. According to the Koran, on the Day of Judgment, unbelievers and the wicked "shall dwell amidst scorching winds and seething water: in the shade of pitch-black smoke . . . sinners that deny the truth . . . shall eat . . . [bitter] fruit . . . [and] drink boiling water."[2] Faithful Muslims who have lived virtuously are promised paradise, which they believe to be a garden where they will experience bodily pleasures and spiritual delights.

An essential feature of Islam is the obligation of the faithful to obey the Five Pillars of the faith: (1) A Muslim must accept and repeat the statement of faith: "There is no God but Allah, and Muhammad is his Prophet." (2) At least five

Shi'a Manuscript, c. 1307. The Shi'ites give their loyalty to the house of Ali, cousin and son-in-law of Muhammad. In this picture, Muhammad, on the left, declares Ali his successor. (*Special Collections, Edinburgh University Library.*)

times a day, a believer must face the holy city of Mecca and pray. (3) Muslims have a religious duty to be generous to the poor. (4) During the holy month of Ramadan, believers should not eat or drink between sunrise and sunset. (5) Muslims are expected to make at least one pilgrimage to the holy city of Mecca.

Muhammad's religion began to win followers, but the ruling elite of Mecca would not accept this new faith. To escape persecution, Muhammad and his small band of followers left Mecca in 622 for Medina, a town about two hundred miles away. Their flight, known as the *Hegira,* or "emigration," is one of the most important events in Muslim history and is commemorated by yearly pilgrimages. The date of the Hegira became year one of the Muslim calendar.

In Medina, Muhammad gained converts and won respect as a judge, rendering decisions on such matters as family relations, property inheritance, and criminal behavior. Preaching a holy war against unbelievers, Muhammad urged followers to raid the trading caravans from Mecca and to subdue unfriendly Bedouin tribes. He tried to convert the Jews of Medina, but they would not accept him as a prophet and mocked his unfamiliarity with the Hebrew Scriptures and the learned writings of the rabbis. To a large extent, political considerations determined Muhammad's attitude toward Jews, who sided with his Meccan enemies. He expelled several thousand Jews from Medina, seized Jewish property, beheaded some six hundred Jewish men, and enslaved women and children. Later, he permitted the Arabian Jews the free exercise of their religion and guaranteed the security of their property. In 630, Mecca surrendered to a Muslim army without a fight. Soon Bedouin tribes all over Arabia embraced Islam and recognized the authority of the Prophet Muhammad.

In a little more than two decades, Muhammad united the often feuding Arabian tribes into a powerful force dedicated to Allah and the spreading of the Islamic faith. After Muhammad's death in 632, his friend and father-in-law, Abu Bakr, became his successor, or caliph. Regarded as the defender of the faith, whose power derived from Allah, the caliph governed in accordance with Muslim law as defined in the Koran.

Islam gave the many Arab tribes the unity, discipline, and organization to succeed in their wars of conquest. Under the first four caliphs, who ruled from 632 to 661, the Arabs, with breathtaking speed, overran the Persian Empire, seized some of Byzantium's provinces, and invaded Europe. Muslim warriors believed that they were engaged in a holy war, *jihad*—literally, striving in the path of God—to spread Islam to nonbelievers and that those who died in the jihad were assured a place in paradise. A desire to escape from the barren Arabian Desert and to exploit the rich Byzantine and Persian lands was another compelling reason for expansion. In the east, Islam's territory eventually extended into India and to the borders of China; in the west, it encompassed North Africa and most of Spain. The Muslims' northward push lost momentum and was halted in 717 by the Byzantines at Constantinople and in 732 by the Franks at the battle of Tours, in central France.

The Muslim State and Society

After the death of Muhammad, Muslims sought authoritative guidance on religious, social, and moral questions that the Koran did not specifically address. The most important source for such guidance was *Hadith*—a collection of sayings, stories, and actions of the Prophet on a wide range of topics. The early Hadith were transmitted by his trusted companions and constitute the literary record of his *sunna,* or customary practice. Aisha, Muhammad's youngest wife, was the source of several thousand Hadith, but within two centuries about 600,000 Hadith existed. The Koran coupled with the Hadith provided directions for a complete way of life for Muslims.

The Islamic state was a theocracy: government and religion were inseparable; there could be no distinction between secular and spiritual authority. Muslims viewed God as the source of all law and political authority and the caliph as his earthly deputy. Divine law regulated all aspects of human relations. The ruler who did not enforce Koranic law failed in his duties. Thus, Islam was more than a religion; it was also a system of government, society, law, and thought that bound its adherents into an all-encompassing community. The idea of a single society governed by the Koran remained in the Muslim mind over the centuries and is a principal aim of Muslim fundamentalists today. The separation of church and state, which became firmly rooted in the West in modern times, still remains an alien concept in much of the Muslim world.

Christians and Jews who lived in Islamic lands had fewer rights than Muslims—they could not bear arms, were assessed a special tax, and, at times, were barred from testifying in court against a Muslim. Nevertheless, as "people of the book," Jews and Christians were protected communities, and despite instances of loss of property or life, or both, the two groups generally went about their business and practiced their religions free of persecution. In fact, Jews were physically safer in Muslim than in Christian lands, and unlike medieval Christians, Muslims did not demonize Jews as a hateful and cursed people deserving divine punishment.

Muslims perceived themselves as members of a single community of the faithful, but the emergence of sects ruptured the unity of Islam. In the Muslim world, dissent from the established social and political order was expressed through religious movements that challenged orthodoxy. The principal division—one that still incites bitter animosity—was between the Sunnis and the Shi'ites. The Sunnis, who were in the majority, followed traditional teachings and established practices as defined by the consensus of the Muslim community. The Shi'ites (*Shi'a* means "Party") maintained that not the existing caliphs but the descendants of Muhammad, starting with Ali, cousin and son-in-law of Muhammad and the fourth caliph, were the rightful rulers of the Islamic community.

Ali had been murdered in 661, his older son in 669. The massacre in 680 of Ali's younger son, Husayn, and some of Husayn's followers and relatives gave rise to passionate devotion to the house of Ali, which is still expressed in processions, poetry, and self-mortification. To Shi'ites, the anniversary of Husayn's death remains the most important religious holiday in the Muslim calendar. Because suffering and martyrdom are central to Shi'a, it has had great appeal to the oppressed masses of Muslim society.

Shi'ites viewed Ali and his descendants as *Imams,* holy men, innocent of all sin, the most excellent of beings, selected by God to inherit Muhammad's spiritual and political powers. The Imams linked the new generation with Muhammad's original inspiration. Shi'ites believed that without the Imams' guidance, the true meaning of Islam could not be grasped. Counting from Ali, the leading branch of Shi'a, known as the Twelvers, held that there were twelve Imams. Twelver Shi'ites continue to believe that the twelfth Imam is still alive but remains in hiding and that one day he will return as a messianic leader, the Mahdi, and, guided by God, will set the world right. This form of Shi'a has been the official religion of Iran since the sixteenth century.

The Muslim Golden Age

In the eighth and ninth centuries, under the Abbasid caliphs, based in Baghdad, Muslim civilization entered its golden age. Islamic civilization creatively integrated Arabic, Byzantine, Persian, and Indian cultural traditions. During the Early Middle Ages, when learning was at a low point in western Europe, the Muslims forged a high civilization.

Muslim science, philosophy, and mathematics, based largely on the achievements of the ancient Greeks, made brilliant contributions to the sum

ANCIENT MEDICINE. For much of the Middle Ages, Muslim physicians were more skilled than their counterparts in the West. Here an Arab doctor performs a type of cataract operation. (*World Health Organization.*)

of knowledge at a time when Latin Christendom had lost much of Greco-Roman thought and culture. The Muslims had acquired Greek learning from the older Persian and Byzantine civilizations, which had kept alive the Greek inheritance. By translating Greek works into Arabic and commenting on them, Muslim scholars performed the great historical task of preserving the philosophical and scientific heritage of ancient Greece. Along with this heritage, the original contributions of Muslim scholars and scientists were also passed on to Christian Europe, a transmission of immense historical significance, as the historian W. Montgomery Watt explains:

> *When one becomes aware of the full extent of Arab experimenting, Arab thinking and Arab writing, one sees that without the Arabs European science and philosophy would not have developed when they did. The Arabs were no mere transmitters of Greek thought, but genuine bearers, who both kept alive the disciplines they had been taught and extended their range. When about 1100 Europeans became seriously interested in . . . science and philosophy . . . [they] had to learn all they could from the Arabs before they themselves could make further advances.*[3]

There are numerous examples of Muslim brilliance in mathematics, medicine, science, and philosophy. From India the Muslims acquired the concept of the zero and "Arabic" numerals, passing these ideas on to the West. Muslim mathematicians did original work in algebra and trigonometry; Muslim astronomers corrected the observations made by ancient astronomers, particularly Ptolemy. In physics, the Muslim Arabs' most significant contribution was in the field of optics. Rejecting Euclid's and Ptolemy's explanation that the eye emits visual rays, they recognized that vision is a consequence of rays of light. Building on the medical knowledge of the Greeks, Muslim physicians became the best-trained and most skillful doctors of the time. Surgeons performed amputations, removed cancerous tissue, devised new medicines, and used anesthetics when performing operations. The best Muslim hospitals had separate wards for fevers, surgical cases, eye diseases, and dysentery. Well ahead of their time were those Muslim doctors who recommended humane treatment for the mentally ill. The Persian al-Razi, or Rhazes, who headed the hospital in Baghdad in the ninth century, wrote a medical encyclopedia, in which he discussed measles, kidney stones, poisons, skin diseases, and ways of maintaining one's health. The works of Rhazes, translated into Latin, were widely consulted in Latin Christendom.

Muslim thinkers employed the categories of Greek philosophy to explain Islamic doctrine. Al-Farabi (c. 870–950), who wrote commentaries on Aristotle, offered proofs for God's existence based on Aristotelian logic that were later studied by medieval Christian philosophers. The most eminent Muslim thinker, Ibn-Sina, known to the West as Avicenna (980–1037), was a poet, doctor, scientist, and philosopher who wrote on every field of knowledge. His philosophical works, which relied heavily on Aristotle, had an important influence on medieval Christian thinkers. Another giant of Muslim learning was Ibn-Rushd, whom westerners call Averroës (1126–1198). Averroës insisted that the Koran did not oppose the study of philosophy and held

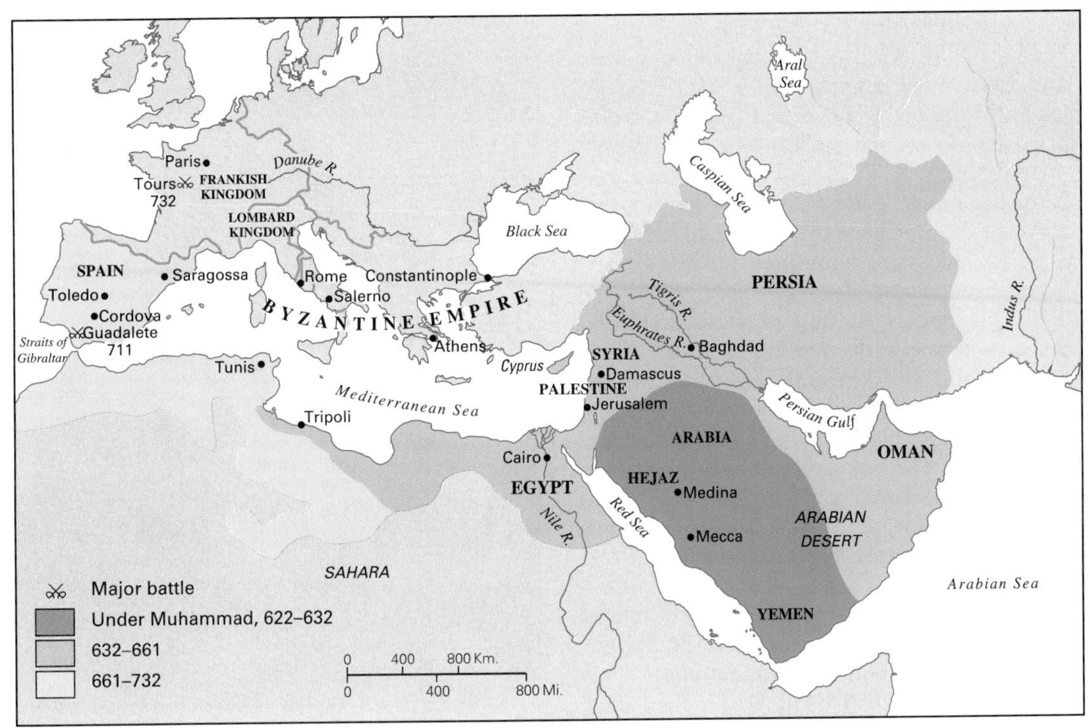

Map 9.2 The Expansion of Islam, 622–732 From 632 to 661, the Arabs, with breathtaking speed, overran the Persian Empire, seized some of Byzantium's provinces, and invaded southern Europe. Their northward momentum was halted in 717 by the Byzantines at Constantinople and in 732 by the Franks at the battle of Tours in central France.

that the ancient Greeks—even though they were not Muslims—had discovered truth. His commentaries on Aristotle were studied in western universities, where they sparked an important controversy (see page 270).

Mongol Invasions and Ottoman Dominance

The Arab empire, stretching from Spain to India, was unified by a common language (Arabic), a common faith, and a common culture. By the eleventh century, however, the Arabs began losing their dominance in the Islamic world. The Seljuk Turks, who had taken Asia Minor from the Byzantines, also conquered the Arabic lands of Syria, Palestine, and much of Persia. Although the Abbasid caliphs remained the religious and cultural leaders of Islam, political power was exercised by Seljuk sultans. In the eleventh and twelfth centuries, the Muslims lost Sicily and most of Spain to Christian knights, and European Crusaders carved out kingdoms in the Near East.

In the thirteenth century came a new wave of invaders, the Mongols from central Asia. Led by Genghis Khan, Mongolian archers, mounted on fast-moving ponies, poured across Asia into Muslim lands. By 1227, when Genghis Khan died, the eastern part of the Muslim world had fallen to the Mongols. After the death of Genghis Khan, some Mongol forces swept across Russia and threatened central Europe; others continued to advance on Muslim lands in the Near East. Storming Baghdad in 1258, the Mongols burned, plundered, and killed with savage fury; among the fifty thousand people slaughtered was the last Abbasid caliph. The Mongols devastated the palaces, libraries, and schools that had made Baghdad the cultural capital of the Islamic world. A year later, they marched into Syria, again killing and looting. Their brutal advance westward was finally stopped in 1260 in Palestine by Egyptian forces.

By the beginning of the fourteenth century, the Muslim world seemed less threatened. In the Near East, the Muslims had recaptured the last Christian state founded by the Crusaders, while the Mongols, who had by this time converted to Islam, remained in Persia and were unable to advance westward. In the late fourteenth century, however, the Mongols, under Tamerlane, again menaced the Near East. Another bloody conqueror, Tamerlane cowed opposition with huge pyramids built from the skulls of thousands of slaughtered victims. After Tamerlane's death in 1404, his empire disintegrated, and its collapse left the way open for the Ottoman Turks.

The Ottoman Empire reached its height in the sixteenth century with the conquest of Egypt, North Africa, Syria, and the Arabian coast. The Turkish conquest of much of Hungary in the 1520s and the siege of Vienna (1529) spread panic in Europe. The Ottomans developed an effective system of administration but could not restore the cultural brilliance, the thriving trade, or the prosperity that the Muslim world had known under the Abbasid caliphs of Baghdad. The vitality that had kept the Muslim world more advanced than western Europe for most of the Middle Ages dissipated.

Clovis. The conversion of Clovis to Roman Catholicism ultimately made possible an alliance between the papacy and Frankish rulers. (*Private collection/Bridgeman Art Library.*)

Latin Christendom: The Rise of Europe

The centuries of cultural greatness of the Islamic and the Byzantine civilizations enriched the Western world. They did not, however, produce the major breakthroughs in science, technology, philosophy, economics, and political thought that gave rise to the modern world. That process was the singular achievement of Europe. During the Middle Ages, a common European civilization—Latin Christendom—evolved. It integrated Christian, Greco-Roman, and German elements. Christianity was at the center of medieval civilization, Rome was the spiritual capital and Latin the language of intellectual life, and Germanic customs pervaded social and legal relationships.

During the Early Middle Ages (500–1050), Latin Christendom was culturally far behind the two Eastern civilizations and did not catch up until the twelfth century. In succeeding centuries, however, it produced the movements that ushered in the modern age: the Renaissance, the Reformation, the Scientific Revolution, the Age of Enlightenment, the French Revolution, and the Industrial Revolution.

Political and Economic Transformation

From the sixth to the eighth century, Europeans struggled to overcome the disorder created by the breakup of the Roman Empire and the deterioration of Greco-Roman civilization. In the process, a new civilization, with its own distinctive style, took root. Christianity had already intermingled with the Greco-Roman tradition in the final centuries of the Empire. Another element, the Germanic tradition, came during the fifth century and after with the invading tribes of Visigoths, Vandals, Franks, Angles, Saxons, Ostrogoths, and others, who founded kingdoms in North Africa, Italy, Spain, Gaul, and Britain—lands formerly belonging to Rome.

Even before the invasions, these Germanic tribes had acquired some knowledge of Roman culture and were attracted to it. Therefore, the new rulers sought not to destroy Roman civilization but to share in its advantages. For example, Theodoric the Great (474–526), the Ostrogoth ruler of Italy, retained the Roman Senate, civil service, and schools; and rich aristocratic Roman families continued to hold high government offices. The Burgundians in Gaul and the Visigoths in Spain maintained Roman law for their conquered subjects; and the Frankish ruler Clovis (c. 466–511) wore Roman imperial colors and took Roman titles. All the Germanic kingdoms tried to maintain Roman systems of taxation; furthermore, Latin remained the official language of administration.

However, torn by warfare, internal rebellion, and assassination, the Germanic kingdoms provided a poor political base on which to revive a decadent and dying classical civilization. Most of the kingdoms survived for only a short time and had no enduring impact. In 533–534, Byzantium destroyed the Vandal kingdom in North Africa, and the Vandals disappeared as a people; a similar fate befell the Ostrogoth kingdom in Italy two decades later. In the early eighth century, Muslim Arabs destroyed the Visigoth kingdom in Spain. An exception to this trend occurred in Gaul and south-central Germany, where the most successful of the Germanic kingdoms was established by the Franks—the founders of the new Europe.

The Roman world was probably too far gone to be rescued, but even if it had not been, the Germans were culturally unprepared to play the role of restorer. By the end of the seventh century, the old Roman lands in western Europe showed a marked decline in central government, town life, commerce, and learning. Though vigorous and brave, the German invaders were essentially a rural and warrior people, tribal in organization and outlook. Their native culture, without cities or written literature, was primitive compared with the literary, philosophical, scientific, and artistic achievements of the Greco-Roman world. The Germans were not equipped to reform the decaying Roman system of administration and taxation or cope with the economic problems that had burdened the Empire. Nor could they maintain roads and irrigation systems, preserve skills in the arts of stoneworking and glassmaking, or breathe new life into the dying humanist culture.

Roman ideas of citizenship and the legal state were totally alien to Germanic tradition. The Germans gave loyalty to their kin and to a tribal chief, not to an impersonal state that governed citizens of many nationalities. The king viewed the land he controlled as a private possession that could be divided among his sons after his death—a custom that produced numerous and devastating civil wars and partitions. Unlike the Romans, the Germanic invaders had no trained civil servants to administer the state and no organized system of taxation to provide a secure financial base for government. Barbarian kings subdivided their kingdoms into districts and chose members of the great noble families to administer each district. These noble counts dispensed justice, maintained order, and collected rents and dues owed the king in their districts. The danger always existed that the counts would usurp the monarch's authority.

The Germans also found Roman law strange. Roman law incorporated elements of Greek philosophy and was written, whereas German law at the time of the invasions consisted of unwritten tribal customs. Roman law applied to all people throughout the Empire, regardless of nationality; a German could be judged only by the law of his own tribe. Roman judges investigated evidence and demanded proof; German courts, in the absence of clear evidence, relied on trial by ordeal. In a typical ordeal, a bound defendant was thrown into a river. Sinking meant innocence; floating was interpreted as divine proof of guilt, because the pure water had "rejected" the evildoer. Although primitive by Roman standards, Germanic law did help to lessen blood feuds between families. Before long, the Germanic kingdoms began to put customary tribal law, which had absorbed and continued to absorb elements from Roman law, into writing. Replacing Roman law and spreading throughout Europe, Germanic law became an essential element of medieval society.

The distinguishing feature of classical civilization, its vital urban institutions, had deteriorated in the Late Roman Empire. The shift from an urban to a rural economy accelerated under the kingdoms created by Germanic chieftains. Although the German kings retained Roman cities as capitals, they did not halt the process of decay that had overtaken urban centers. These rulers settled their people in the countryside, not in towns; they did not significantly utilize cities as instruments of local government; and they failed to maintain Roman roads. Although towns did not vanish altogether, they continued to lose control over the surrounding countryside and to decline in wealth and importance. They were the episcopal seats (sees) of bishops, rather than centers of commerce and intellectual life. Italy remained an exception to this general trend. There, Roman urban institutions persisted, even during the crudest period of the Early Middle Ages. Italian cities kept some metal currency in circulation and traded with one another and with Byzantium.

Shrinking commerce during the Early Middle Ages was part of the process of decline begun in the Late Roman Empire. Although commerce never wholly disappeared—and, indeed, experienced temporary periods of renewed activity—it was predominantly localized. Furthermore, it was controlled by colonies of Jews, Syrians, and Greeks—a sign of the economic inertia of Latin Christians. From the last decade of the fifth century to the middle of the seventh century, Byzantine merchants established themselves in the western lands and exchanged papyrus, spices, and textiles for European slaves. Then, in the second half of the seventh century, this trade dropped off greatly; as Muslim power expanded to control the Mediterranean, Byzantine merchants had to turn eastward for markets. Thus, the bonds between East and West weakened, and Europe shifted its axis northward, away from the Mediterranean. Few goods exchanged hands and few coins circulated; people produced for themselves what they needed.

The Waning of Classical Culture

Greco-Roman humanism, in retreat since the Late Roman Empire, continued its decline in the centuries immediately following Rome's demise. The old Roman upper classes abandoned their heritage and absorbed the ways of their Germanic conquerors, the Roman schools closed, and Roman law faded into disuse. Aside from clerics, few people could read and write Latin, and even learned clerics were rare. Europeans' knowledge of the Greek language was almost totally lost, and the Latin rhetorical style deteriorated. Many literary works of classical antiquity were either lost or unread. Raids by Germanic tribes and later by Muslims, Magyars, and Vikings (see below) devastated libraries. Many works by great authors were lost forever. For example, only seven of the one hundred dramas written by Sophocles have survived. European culture was much poorer than the high civilizations of Byzantium, Islam, and ancient Rome.

During this period of cultural poverty, the few persons who were learned generally did not engage in original thought but salvaged and transmitted remnants of classical civilization. Given the context of the times, this was a considerable achievement. These individuals retained respect for the inheritance of Greece and Rome while remaining devoted to Christianity. In a rudimentary way, they were struggling to create a Christian culture that combined the intellectual tradition of Greece and Rome with the religious teachings of the Christian church.

An important figure in the intellectual life of this transitional period was Boethius (480–c. 525), a descendant of a noble family. Boethius had received a classical education at the Platonic Academy at Athens before Emperor Justinian closed it in 529. He was the last Latin-speaking scholar of the Roman world to have mastered the Greek language and to have intimate knowledge of Greek philosophy. Later, Boethius served the Ostrogoth Theodoric I, who ruled Italy. Recognizing that Greco-Roman civilization was dying, Boethius tried to rescue the intellectual heritage of antiquity. He translated into Latin some of Aristotle's treatises on logic and wrote commentaries on Aristotle, Cicero, and Porphyry (a Neo-Platonist philosopher). He also wrote treatises on theology and textbooks on arithmetic, astronomy, and music. A sudden turn of fortune deprived him of power, prestige, and possessions and confronted him with imminent death when Theodoric ordered him executed in 524 or 525 for allegedly participating in a plot against the throne.

While in prison awaiting execution, Boethius wrote *The Consolation of Philosophy,* which is regarded as one of the masterpieces of world literature. In it, Boethius pondered life's meaning: "Think you that there is any certainty in the affairs of mankind when you know that often one swift hour can utterly destroy a man?"[4] Alone in his dungeon, he turned for guidance and consolation not to Christ but to the philosophical training of his youth. He derived comfort from Lady Philosophy, who reassured him, in the tradition of Socrates and the Stoics, that "if then you are master of yourself, you will be in possession of that which you will never wish to lose, and which Fortune will never be able to take from you."[5] No tyrant can "ever disturb the peculiar restfulness which is the property of a mind that hangs together upon the firm basis of its reason."[6] In the life and thought of Boethius, the classical tradition lived on. He was a bridge between a classical civilization too weakened to be revived and a Christian civilization still in embryo.

Until the twelfth century, virtually all that Latin Christendom knew of Aristotle came from Boethius's translations and commentaries. Similarly, his work in mathematics, which contains fragments from Euclid, was the principal source for the study of that discipline in the Early Middle Ages. Boethius also bequeathed to future generations basic philosophical definitions and terms. In his theological writings, he strove to demonstrate that reason did not conflict with orthodoxy—an early attempt to attain a rational comprehension of belief, or, as he expressed it, to join faith to reason. Boethius's effort to examine Christian doctrines rationally, a principal feature of medieval philosophy, would grow to maturity in the twelfth and thirteenth centuries. Writing in the sixth century, Boethius was a forerunner of this movement.

Cassiodorus (c. 490–575), a contemporary of Boethius, was born in southern Italy of a good family; he served three Ostrogoth kings. Although Cassiodorus wrote the twelve-volume *History of the Goths* and some theological treatises, his prime legacies were the establishment of a monastic library containing Greek and Latin manuscripts and his advocacy of higher education to improve the quality of the clergy. In his educational writings, he justified the importance of studying secular literature as an aid to understanding sacred writings. Even though his works were not original, they did rescue some ideas of the ancients from oblivion; these ideas would bear fruit again in later centuries. Cassiodorus's plans for founding a university in Rome modeled after the one in Alexandria did not materialize; in fact, six hundred years would elapse before universities would arise in Latin Christendom. Leaving political office, Cassiodorus retired to a monastery, where he initiated the monastic practice of copying ancient texts. Without this tradition, many key Christian and Greco-Roman works would undoubtedly have perished.

In Spain, Isidore of Seville (c. 576–636) compiled an encyclopedia, *Etymologiae,* covering a diversity of topics from arithmetic and God to furniture. Isidore derived his information from many secular and religious sources. Quite understandably, his work contained many errors, particularly in its references to nature. For centuries, though, the *Etymologiae* served as a standard reference work and was found in every monastic library of note.

The translations and compilations made by Boethius, Cassiodorus, and Isidore, the books collected and copied by monks and nuns, and schools established in monasteries (particularly those in Ireland, England, and Italy) kept intellectual life from dying out completely in the Early Middle Ages. Amid the deterioration of political authority, the stagnation of economic life, and the decline in learning, a new civilization was emerging. German and Roman peoples intermarried, and Roman, German, and Christian traditions intermingled. But it was the church more than anything else that gave form and direction to the emerging civilization.

The Church: Shaper of Medieval Civilization

The Church as Unifier

Christianity was the integrating principle and the church was the dominant institution of the Middle Ages. During the Late Roman Empire, as the Roman state and its institutions decayed, the church gained power and importance; its organization grew stronger and its membership increased. Unlike the Roman state, the church was a healthy and vital institution. The elite of the Roman Empire had severed their commitment to the values of classical civilization, whereas church leaders were intensely devoted to their faith.

During the invasions of the fifth and sixth centuries, the church assumed many political functions formerly performed by the Roman state and continued to convert the Germanic tribes. By teaching a higher morality, the church tamed the warrior habits of the German peoples. By preserving some of the high culture of Greece and Rome, it opened German minds to new ideas. When the Empire collapsed, the church retained its administrative system and preserved elements of its civilization. A unifying and civilizing agent, the church provided people with an intelligible and purposeful conception of life and death. In a dying world, the church was the only institution capable of reconstructing civilized life.

Thus, the Christian outlook, rather than the traditions of the German tribes, was the foundation of medieval civilization. During the course of the Middle Ages, people came to see themselves as participants in a great drama of salvation. There was only one truth: God's revelation to humanity. There was only one avenue to heaven, and it passed through the church. God had established the church to administer the rites through which his love was bestowed on people. The church had the awesome responsibility of caring for human souls. Without the church, it was believed, people would remain doomed sinners. To the medieval mind, society without the church was inconceivable. Membership in a universal church replaced citizenship in a universal empire. Across Europe, from Italy to Ireland, a new society centered on Christianity was forming.

Painting of Saint Matthew from the Gospel Book of Charlemagne, c. 800–810. Handwritten and very costly, sacred books were often lavishly illustrated with miniature paintings. In this painting, Saint Matthew, wearing a Roman toga, is depicted with his pen poised, writing his Gospel. Because of the painting's clear Hellenistic style, scholars believe the artist was trained in an Italian or Byzantine school. (*Kunsthistorisches Museum, Vienna.*)

Monks and the Papacy

Monks helped construct the foundations of medieval civilization. During the seventh century, intellectual life on the European continent continued its steady decline. In the monasteries of Ireland and England, however, a tradition of learning persisted. Early in the fifth century, Saint Patrick began the conversion of the Irish to Christianity. In Ireland, Latin became firmly entrenched as the language of both the church and scholars at a time when it was in danger of disappearing in many parts of Europe. Irish monks preserved and cultivated Latin and even kept some knowledge of Greek alive; during their missionary activities, they revived the use of Latin. Irish scholars engaged in biblical analysis, and, besides copying manuscripts, they decorated them, with an exquisite eye for detail. In England, the Anglo-Saxons, both women and men, who converted to Christianity mainly in the seventh century, also established monasteries that kept learning alive. Double monasteries existed, in which monks and nuns obeyed a common rule and one superior, sometimes an abbess. The Venerable Bede (673–735) wrote commentaries on Scripture and translated the fourth Gospel (Saint John's) into Anglo-Saxon. Bede is best known for his *Ecclesiastical History of the English People,* one of the finest medieval historical works.

In the sixth and seventh centuries, Irish monks and nuns built monasteries in continental Europe and converted people in the surrounding areas. Many converted Anglo-Saxons embraced Benedictine monasticism and, continuing the efforts of Irish monks, became the chief agents in Christianizing people in northern Europe. Thus, monks and nuns made possible a unitary European civilization based on a Christian foundation. By copying and preserving ancient texts, they also kept alive elements of ancient civilization.

During the Early Middle Ages, when cities were in decay, monasteries, whose libraries contained theological works and ancient Latin classics, were the main cultural centers; they would remain so until the rebirth of towns in the High Middle Ages. By instructing peasants in superior methods of farming, monks were partly responsible for the reclamation of lands that had been neglected or devastated during the great invasions. Monasteries also offered succor to the sick and the destitute and served as places of refuge for travelers. To the medieval mind, the monks' and nuns' selfless devotion to God, adoption of apostolic poverty, and dedication to prayer and contemplation represented the highest expression of the Christian way of life; it was the finest and most certain path to salvation. It was not uncommon for both men and women, with old age or even death approaching, to take the vows so they might die as monks or nuns. Regarding the monks as soldiers in the war against paganism, unorthodoxy, and heresy, the popes protected monasteries and encouraged their spread.

The Early Middle Ages was a formative period for the papacy, as well as for society in general. The status of the papacy was closely tied to events in Italy. In the sixth century, the Byzantine emperor Justinian, viewing the breakup of the Roman Empire as only temporary, sought to regain western lands lost to the Germanic invaders. In 533–34, a force led by his able general Belisarius destroyed the Vandal kingdom in North Africa. The Byzantines then invaded Italy, breaking the power of the Ostrogoths. The destruction of the Ostrogoth kingdom opened the way for the Lombards, the last Germanic people to settle in once Roman lands. During the second half of the sixth century, the Lombards invaded Italy and seized much of the territory that the Byzantines had regained from the Ostrogoths.

The Lombard invasion gave the papacy an opportunity to free itself from Byzantine domination. Increasingly, popes assumed control over the city of Rome and the surrounding territory, while seeking to protect these lands from the Lombards. At this critical stage, Gregory I, the Great (590–604), became pope. A descendant of a prominent Roman family and a monk, Gregory turned out to be one of the ablest medieval popes. He used Roman methods of administration effectively to organize and administer papal property in Italy, Sicily, Sardinia, Gaul, and other regions. The papacy owned huge estates worked by serfs. It also owned timberlands and mines, which provided the income for maintaining the clergy, churches, monasteries, hospitals, and orphanages in Rome and other places. Because of Gregory's efforts, the papacy became the leading financial institution of the day.

Gregory tried to strengthen the pope's authority within the church, insisting that all bishops and the Byzantine church in Constantinople were subject to papal authority. Establishing monasteries, he tightened the bonds between the monks and the papacy, and it was he who dispatched Benedictine monks to England to win over the Anglo-Saxons. The newly established Anglo-Saxon church looked to Rome for leadership. Gregory realized that to lead Christendom effectively the papacy must exercise authority over churches outside Italy—a policy adopted by popes who succeeded him.

Besides providing the papacy with a sound financial base and strengthening its ties with monasteries and non-Italian churches, Gregory engaged in other activities. He wrote commentaries on the books of the Bible and authored many works dealing with Christian themes: the duties of bishops, the lives of saints and monks, miracles, and purgatory. Because of his many

Map 9.3 The Carolingian World Resting more on the personal qualities of Charlemagne than on any firm economic or political foundation, the Carolingian empire did not survive the emperor's death in 814.

writings, Gregory is regarded as a father of the Latin church. An astute diplomat, he knew that the papacy required the political and military support of a powerful kingdom to protect it from its enemies, especially the Lombards. Accordingly, he set his sights on an alliance with the Franks. Finally materializing 150 years later, this alliance between the papacy and Frankish kings helped shape medieval history.

The Kingdom of the Franks

From their homeland in the Rhine River valley, the Frankish tribes had expanded into Roman territory during the fourth and fifth centuries. The ruler Clovis united the various Frankish tribes and conquered most of Gaul. In 496, he converted to Roman Christianity through the efforts of his wife, Chlotilde. Clovis's conversion to

Catholicism was an event of great significance. A number of other German kings had adopted the Arian form of Christianity, which the church had declared heretical (see page 186). By embracing Roman Christianity, the Franks became a potential ally of the papacy.

After Clovis's death in 511, the Frankish lands suffered hard times. His kingdom was divided, and the Merovingian rulers (so named after Merovech, a semilegendary ancestor of Clovis) engaged in fratricidal warfare and brutal murder. In the seventh century, the various Merovingian rulers had become ineffective and lost much of their power to great landowners. The real ruler of each Frankish realm was the king's chief officer, the mayor of the palace. One of these, Pepin II of Heristal (687–714), triumphed over his rival mayors and became ruler of Frankland. Pepin was the founder of the Carolingian dynasty (so named after Charlemagne, the greatest of the Carolingians). Pepin's son, Charles Martel, who served as mayor of the palace from 717 to 741, succeeded Pepin.

Charles Martel subdued entrenched nobles and hostile tribes, thus strengthening Carolingian rule. Muslim Arabs and Berbers from North Africa, who had conquered Visigoth Spain in the early eighth century, crossed the Pyrenees into Frankish Gaul and advanced northward along the old Roman road. At the battle of Tours in 732, the Franks defeated the Muslims. Although the Muslims continued to occupy the Iberian Peninsula, they would advance no farther north into Europe. Charles Martel was succeeded by his son, Pepin the Short, who in 751 deposed the last Merovingian king. With the approval of the papacy and his nobles, Pepin was crowned king by Boniface, a prominent bishop. Originally an English Benedictine, Saint Boniface had been instrumental in converting Germans to Christianity, firmly linking the Franks to Rome.

In approving Pepin's royal accession, the papacy was continuing Gregory's earlier efforts to gain an ally in its struggle against the Lombards, who still had designs on papal territory. In 753, Pope Stephen II journeyed across the Alps to confer with Pepin, who welcomed the pontiff with respect. The pope anointed Pepin again as king of the Franks and appealed to him to protect the papacy from the Lombards. Pepin invaded Italy, defeated the Lombards, and turned over captured lands to the papacy. Pepin's donation made the pope ruler of the territory between Rome and Ravenna, which became known as the Papal States.

The Era of Charlemagne

The alliance between the Franks and the papacy was continued by Pepin's successor, Charlemagne (Charles the Great), who ruled from 768 to 814. Charlemagne continued the Carolingian policy of expanding the Frankish kingdom. He destroyed the Lombard kingdom and declared himself king of the Lombards. He added Bavaria to his kingdom, and after long, terrible wars, he compelled the Saxons to submit to his rule and convert to Christianity—thousands were beheaded when they were slow to choose between baptism or execution. He also conquered a region in northern Spain, the Spanish March, which served as a buffer between the Christian Franks and the Muslims in Spain.

Immense difficulties arose in governing the expanded territories. Size seemed an insuperable obstacle to effective government, particularly since Charlemagne's administrative structure, lacking trained personnel, was primitive by Islamic, Byzantine, or Roman standards. The empire was divided into about 250 counties administered by counts—nobles personally loyal to the ruler. Men from powerful families, the counts served as generals, judges, and administrators, implementing the king's decisions. To supervise the counts, Charlemagne created *missi dominici* (royal messengers)—generally two laymen and a bishop or abbot—who made annual journeys to the different counties. The purpose of the missi dominici was to prevent counts and their subordinates from abusing their power and undermining Charlemagne's authority.

On Christmas Day in Rome in the year 800, Pope Leo III crowned Charlemagne emperor of the Romans. The initiative for the coronation probably came from the papacy, not from Charlemagne. The meaning of this event has aroused conflicting opinions among historians, but certain conclusions seem justified. The title signified that the tradition of a world empire

Profile

Saint Boniface

Of the many English monks and nuns who converted inhabitants of the Netherlands and Germany, none was more important than Saint Boniface (c. 680–754). In 716, Boniface, then a monk called Wynfrid who had earned a reputation as a Latin scholar, left England for Frisia in order to restore the churches that had been destroyed when the Frisians revolted against Frankish rule and Christian proselytizing. Consecrated bishop in 722, he extended his missionary activity into Bavaria and Thuringia. Working closely with the papacy, he founded monasteries, including the famous Abbey of Fulda, converted pagans, and imposed Christian standards of behavior on both clergy and laypeople. For example, he prohibited idol worship and the selling of slaves to heathens for sacrifices. In a letter to Pope Zacharias, he expressed his displeasure with deacons who "have four or five concubines in their beds, still read

Alinari/Art Resource, NY.

still survived, despite the demise of the western Roman Empire three hundred years earlier. But because it was the pope who crowned Charlemagne, this meant that the emperor had a spiritual responsibility to spread and defend the faith. Thus, Roman universalism was fused with Christian universalism.

The Frankish empire, of course, was only a dim shadow of the Roman Empire. The Franks had no Roman law or Roman legions; there were no cities that were centers of economic and cultural activity; and officials were not trained civil servants with a world outlook, but uneducated war chieftains with a tribal viewpoint. Yet Charlemagne's empire did embody the concept of a universal Christian empire, an ideal that would endure throughout the Middle Ages.

The crowning of a German ruler as emperor of the Romans by the head of the church represented the merging of German, Christian, and Roman traditions, which is the essential characteristic of medieval civilization. This blending of traditions was also evident on a cultural plane, for Charlemagne, a German warrior-king, showed respect for classical learning and Christianity, both non-Germanic traditions.

Carolingian Renaissance

Charlemagne felt that it was his religious duty to raise the educational level of the clergy so that they understood and could properly teach the faith. To do so required overcoming the illiteracy or semiliteracy of clergymen and preparing sacred Scriptures that were uniform, complete, and free of errors. Charlemagne also fostered education to train administrators who would be capable of overseeing his empire and the royal estates; such men had to be literate.

To achieve his purpose, Charlemagne gathered some of the finest scholars in Europe. Alcuin of York, England (735–804), was given charge of the palace school attended by Charlemagne and the Gospel and are not ashamed or afraid to call themselves deacons—nay rather, entering upon the priesthood, they continue in the same vices, add sin to sin, declare that they also have a right . . to celebrate mass."* He also denounced "any layman, be he emperor, king, official, or count [who] may capture a monastery from the power of a bishop, an abbot, or an abbess and begin to hold property bought by the blood of Christ—the ancient fathers called such a man a robber, sacrilegious, a murderer of the poor, a devil's wolf entering the sheepfold of Christ, to be condemned with the ultimate anathema before the judgment of Christ."†

Boniface maintained a correspondence with his cousin Lioba, an English-born nun, who became abbess of the convent Boniface founded at Tauberbischofsheim, near the Main River. Shortly before his death, Boniface visited with Lioba at her convent. He urged her not to "forsake the land of your pilgrimage. . . . Hold bravely to your course, carry on the good work day by day, and heed not the body's weakness. Time is not long, suffering is not hard, if your eyes are set upon eternity."‡

When Boniface died, Archbishop Cuthbert of Canterbury praised him for bringing "savage peoples from their long and devious wanderings in the wide abyss of eternal perdition into the glorious pathways of the heavenly fatherland by the inspiration of his holy words and by the example of his pious and gentle life."§ When Lioba died in 780, she was buried at Fulda to be joined with Boniface.

**The Letters of Saint Boniface,* trans. Ephraim Emerton (New York: Columbia University Press, 1940), p. 80.

†Ibid., p. 140.

‡Quoted in Eleanor Duckett, *The Wandering Saints of the Early Middle Ages* (New York: Norton, 1959), p. 227.

§*The Letters of Saint Boniface,* p. 184.

his sons and daughters, high lords, and youths training to serve the emperor. Throughout France, Alcuin expanded schools and libraries, promoted the copying of ancient manuscripts, and imposed basic literary standards on the clergy.

The focus of the Carolingian Renaissance was predominantly Christian: an effort to train clergymen and improve their understanding of the Bible and the writings of the church fathers. This process raised the level of literacy and improved the Latin style. Most important, monastic copyists continued to preserve ancient texts, which otherwise might never have survived; the oldest surviving manuscripts of many ancient works are Carolingian copies. Carolingian scholars thus helped to fertilize the cultural flowering known as the Twelfth-Century Awakening—the high point of medieval civilization.

Compared with the Greco-Roman past, with the cultural explosion of the twelfth and thirteenth centuries, or with the great Italian Renaissance of the fifteenth century, the Carolingian Renaissance seems slight indeed. Although it did rediscover and revive ancient works, it did not recapture the spirit of Greece and Rome. Carolingian scholars did not engage in independent philosophical speculation or search for new knowledge, nor did they achieve that synthesis of faith and reason that would be constructed by the great theologians of the twelfth and thirteenth centuries. The Carolingian Renaissance did, however, reverse the process of cultural decay, which had characterized much of the Early Middle Ages. Learning would never again fall to the low level it had reached during the centuries following the decline of Rome.

During the era of Charlemagne, a distinct European civilization took root. It blended the Roman heritage of a world empire, the intellectual achievement of the Greco-Roman mind, Christian otherworldliness, and the customs of the Germanic peoples. This nascent western European civilization differed from Byzantine and

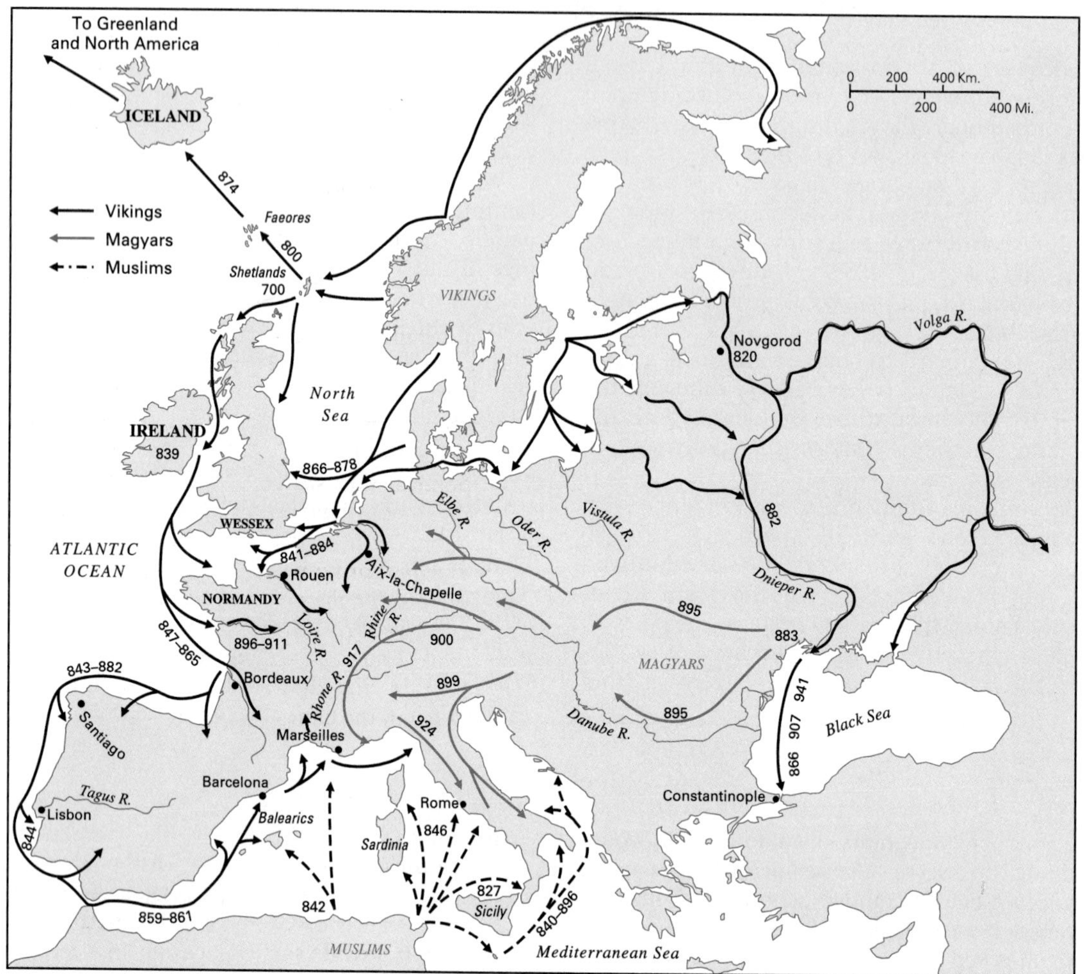

Map 9.4 Ninth-Century Invasions Invasions by Vikings, Magyars, and Muslims in the ninth century heightened political insecurity and accelerated the process of decentralization characterized by feudalism.

Islamic civilizations, and Europeans were growing conscious of the difference. But the new medieval civilization was still centuries away from its high point, which would be reached in the twelfth and thirteenth centuries.

Charlemagne's empire also engendered the ideal of a unified Latin Christendom: a single Christian community under one government; this new collectivity would supersede the seperate German tribal units. Over the centuries, the pursuit of this ideal of a Christian world-state, Christendom, would inspire many people, both clergy and laity.

The Breakup of Charlemagne's Empire

After Charlemagne's death in 814, his son, Louis the Pious, inherited the throne. Louis aimed to preserve the empire, but the task was virtually impossible. The empire's strength rested more on the personal qualities of Charlemagne than on any firm economic or political foundation. Moreover, the empire was simply too large and consisted of too many diverse peoples to be governed effectively. Besides Frankish nobles, who sought to increase their own power at the emperor's expense, Louis had to deal with his own rebellious sons. After Louis died in 840, the empire was divided among the three surviving sons.

The Treaty of Verdun in 843 gave Louis the German the eastern part of the empire, which marked the beginning of Germany; to Charles the Bald went the western part, which was the start of France; and Lothair received the Middle Kingdom, which extended from Rome to the North Sea. This Middle Kingdom would become a source of conflict between France and Germany into the twentieth century. As central authority waned, large landowners increasingly exercised authority in their own regions. Simultaneous invasions from all directions furthered this movement toward localism and decentralization.

In the ninth and tenth centuries, Latin Christendom was attacked on all sides. From bases in North Africa, Spain, and Sicily, Muslims ravaged regions of southern Europe, even as far as the suburbs of Rome. The Magyars, originally from western Asia and linguistically related to Finns and Turks, crossed the Carpathian Mountains in the ninth century and established themselves on the plains of the Danube; their horsemen launched lightning raids into northern Italy, western Germany, and parts of France. Defeated in Germany in 933 and again in 955, the Magyars withdrew to what is now Hungary; they ceased their raids and adopted Christianity.

Still another group of invaders, the Northmen, or Vikings, sailed from Scandinavia in their long, open, wooden ships to raid the coasts and river valleys of western Europe. Superb seamen, the Vikings crossed the North Atlantic and settled in Iceland and Greenland; from there, they almost certainly traveled to and landed on the coast of North America. They also produced rich poetry, excelled at crafts, and contributed greatly to the revival of trade in the High Middle Ages.

In pursuit of slaves, jewels, and precious metals hoarded in monasteries, the Viking invaders plundered, destroyed, raped, and murdered. Villages were devastated, ports were ruined, and the population was decimated. Trade was at a standstill, coins no longer circulated, and farms were turned into wastelands. The European economy, already gravely weak, collapsed, the political authority of kings disappeared, and cultural life and learning withered.

These terrible attacks heightened political insecurity and accelerated anew the process of decentralization that had begun with the decline of Rome. During these chaotic times, counts came to regard as their own the land that they administered and defended for their king. Similarly, the inhabitants of a district looked on the count or local lord as their ruler, for his men and fortresses protected them. In their regions, nobles exercised public power formerly held by kings, an arrangement later designated as feudalism.

In instances where great lords failed to protect their territories from neighboring counts or from invaders, political power was further fragmented. In other areas, local nobles chipped away at a count's authority in his county. In many regions, the political unit shrank from the county to the *castellany*, the land close to a lord's castle. In such areas, the local lord exercised virtually supreme authority; people turned to him for protection and for the administration of justice. Europe had entered an age of feudalism, in which the essential unit of government was not a kingdom but a county or castellany and political power lay in the hands of local lords.

Medieval Society

Arising during a period of collapsing central authority, invasion, scanty public revenues, and declining commerce and town life, feudalism attempted to provide some order and security. Feudalism was not a planned system devised logically from general principles, but an improvised response to the challenge posed by ineffectual central authority. Feudal practices differed from locality to locality and in some regions barely took root. Although it was only a stopgap means of government, feudalism did bring some order, justice, and law during an era of breakdown, localism, and transition. It would remain the predominant political arrangement until kings reasserted their authority in the High and Late Middle Ages.

Feudalism made an enduring impact on Western civilization. It contributed to Western notions about honor, gentlemen, and romantic love (see Chapter 11). Most important, feudal traditions laid the groundwork for the principle of limiting a king's power and for the practice of parliamentary government (see Chapters 10 and 12).

Feudalism was built on an economic foundation known as *manorialism.* Although pockets of free peasantry remained, a village community, or manor, consisting of serfs bound to the land became the essential agricultural arrangement for much of the Middle Ages. The manorial village was the means of organizing an agricultural society with limited markets and money. Neither lords nor priests performed economically productive work. Their ways of life were made possible by the toil of serfs.

Manorialism and feudalism presupposed a stable social order: clergy who prayed, lords who warred, and serfs who toiled. People believed that society functioned smoothly when individuals accepted their status and performed their proper role. In the words of an eleventh-century cleric,

> *Mankind, since the beginning of time has been divided in three, those who pray, those who cultivate, those who fight, and each of the three is comforted on either side by the two others. He who, forsaking the world, gives himself to a life of prayer owes it to the warriors that he is able to carry out his holy task in safety, while he owes his bodily nourishment to the farmers. Similarly, the farmers ascend to God through the prayers of the ecclesiastics and are defended by the weapons of the warriors. So also, the warriors are fed by the produce of the fields and benefit from the income therefrom, while the holy prayers of the pious whom they protect will expiate the crimes which they commit in battle.*[7]

A person's rights, duties, and relationship to law depended on his or her ranking in the social order. To change position was to upset the organic unity of society. And no one, serfs included, should be deprived of the traditional rights associated with his or her rank. This arrangement was justified by the clergy:

> *God himself has willed that among men, some must be lords and some serfs, in such a fashion that the lords venerate and love God, and that the serfs love and venerate their lord following the word of the Apostle; serfs obey your temporal lords with fear and trembling; lords treat your serfs according to justice and equity . . .* [8]

Vassalage

Feudal relationships enabled lords to increase their military strength. The need for military support was the principal reason for the condition of vassalage. A vassal was a knight who in a solemn ceremony pledged loyalty to a lord. This feature of feudalism derived from an ancient German ceremony during which warriors swore personal allegiance to the head of the war-band. Among other things, the vassal gave military service to his lord and received in return a *fief,* which was usually land sufficient to support his needs. This fief was inhabited by peasants, and the crops that they raised provided the vassal with his means of support.

Besides rendering military assistance and supplying knights, the vassal owed several other obligations to his lord in return for the fief and the lord's protection. These duties included sitting in the lord's court and judging cases, such as the breach of feudal agreements between the lord and his other vassals; providing lodgings when the lord traveled through the vassal's territory; offering a gift when the lord's son was knighted or when his eldest daughter married; and raising a ransom should the lord be captured by an enemy.

Both lord and vassal felt honor-bound to abide by the oath of loyalty. It became an accepted custom for a vassal to renounce his loyalty to his lord if the latter failed to protect him from enemies, mistreated him, or increased the vassal's obligations as fixed by the feudal contract. Similarly, if a vassal did not live up to his obligations, the lord would summon him to his court, where he would be tried for treachery. If found guilty, the vassal could lose his fief and perhaps his life. Sometimes disputes between vassals and lords erupted into warfare. Because a vassal often held land from more than one lord and sometimes was himself a lord to vassals, situations frequently became awkward, complex, and confusing. On occasion, a vassal had to decide to which lord he owed *liege homage* (prime loyalty).

As feudalism evolved, the king came to be regarded as the chief lord, who had granted fiefs to the great lords, who in turn had divided them into smaller units and regranted them to vassals. Thus, all members of the ruling class, from the lowliest knights to the king, occupied a place in the feudal hierarchy. In theory, the king was the highest political authority and the source of land tenure, but in actual fact he was often less powerful than other nobles of the realm.

Feudalism would decline when kings converted their theoretical powers into actual powers. The decline of feudalism was a gradual process; conflict between the crown and the aristocracy would persist, with varying degrees of intensity, for several centuries, but the future belonged to the centralized state being shaped by kings, not to feudal fragmentation.

Feudal Law

Feudal law, which incorporated many features of traditional German law, differed markedly from Roman law. Roman law was universal, having been enacted by a central government for a world empire. It was also rational, for it sought to be in accord with natural law that applied to all; and it was systematic, for it offered a framework of standards that applied to individual cases. Feudal law, in contrast, was local, covering only a small region. Moreover, it was personal. In the Roman view, the individual as a citizen owed obligations to the state, whereas under feudalism, a vassal owed loyalty and service to a lord according to the terms of a personal agreement made between them.

In the feudal view, lords and kings did not make law; rather, they were guided by tradition and precedent. They discovered and confirmed law by examining ancient customs. Therefore, feudal patterns of landownership, military service, and wardship came to be regarded an expression of ancient, unchanging, and inviolable custom. Consequently, if the vassal believed that his lord had violated the feudal agreement, that is, had broken faith with him and had transgressed tradition, the vassal would demand restoration of customary rights before an audience of his fellow vassals. Often lords battled each other, believing that they were defending their rights. Similarly, lords claimed the right to resist kings who did not honor their feudal agreements.

Feudal Warriors

Feudal lords viewed manual labor and commerce as degrading for men of their rank. They considered only one vocation worthy: that of warrior. Through combat, the lord demonstrated his valor, earned his reputation, measured his individual worth, derived excitement, added to his wealth, and defended his rights. Warfare was his whole purpose in life. During the twelfth century, to relieve the boredom of peacetime, nobles staged gala tournaments in which knights, fighting singly or in teams, engaged each other in battle to prove their skill and courage. The victors in these pageants gained prestige in the eyes of fellow nobles and admiring ladies and received prizes—falcons, crowns, and substantial amounts of money. The feudal glorification of combat became deeply ingrained in Western society and endured into the twentieth century. Over the centuries, a code of behavior, called *chivalry,* evolved for the feudal nobility. A true knight was expected to fight bravely, demonstrate loyalty to his lord, and treat other knights with respect and courtesy.

In time, the church interjected a religious element into the warrior culture of the feudal knight. It sought to use the fighting spirit of the feudal class for Christian ends: knights could assist the clergy in enforcing God's will. Thus, to the Germanic tradition of loyalty and courage was added a Christian component. As a Christian gentleman, a knight was expected to honor the laws of the church and to wield his sword in the service of God. He was supposed to protect women, children, and the weak and to defend the church against heretics and infidels. The very ceremony of knighthood was placed within a Christian framework. A priest blessed the future knight's arms and prayed that the knight would always "defend the Just and Right."

Regarding the private warfare of lords as lawless violence that menaced social life, the church, in the eleventh century, imposed strictures called the Peace of God and the Truce of God. These restrictions limited feudal warfare to certain days of the week and certain times of the year. Thus, the church tried to regulate warfare according to moral principles. Although only partially effective, the Peace of God did offer Christian society some respite from plundering and incessant warfare.

Noblewomen

Feudal society was very much a man's world. In theory, women were deemed to be physically, morally, and intellectually inferior to men; in practice, they were subjected to male authority. Fathers arranged the marriages of their daughters. Girls from aristocratic families were generally married at age sixteen or younger to a man often twice as old. The wife of a lord was at the mercy of her husband; if she angered him, she might expect a beating. A French law code of the thirteenth century stated: "In a number of cases men may be excused for the injuries they inflict on their wives, nor should the law intervene. Provided he neither kills nor maims her, it is legal for a man to beat his wife when she wrongs him."[9] Although the church taught that both men and women were precious to God and spiritual equals, church tradition also regarded women as agents of the devil—evil temptresses who, like the biblical Eve, used their sexuality to lure men into sin—and church law also permitted wife beating.

In Mary, the mother of Jesus, however, Christians had an alternative image of women to the image suggested by Eve, one that placed women in a position of honor. Devotion to the Virgin Mary reached its high point in the twelfth and thirteenth centuries with the growing belief in the Immaculate Conception (the idea, which later became a doctrine, that Mary was conceived free of original sin and remained free of sin throughout her life*). Moreover, medieval Christians believed that Mary, by dedicating her entire life to Jesus in his work of redemption, cooperated with him in his ministry and could intercede with him in behalf of individual Christians. The numerous artistic depictions of Mary as the Mother of God and the Queen of Heaven, as well as the multitude of churches named after the Virgin, are evidence of the popular piety the cult of Mary generated throughout the Middle Ages.

Noblewomen. At times, medieval ladies joined their husband's hunting party. (*Universitat Bibliothek, Heidelberg, cod. Pal. Germ.048 fol, 64r/AKG London.*)

Aristocratic girls who did not marry often entered a convent. (Peasant daughters, because they were needed on the farm—they probably worked as hard and as well as men—rarely became nuns. Moreover, their parents could not afford the dowry, payable in land, cash, or goods, required by the convent for admission.) The nunneries provided an outlet for the talents of unmarried noblewomen. Abbesses demonstrated organizational skills in supervising the convent's affairs. Some nuns acquired an education and, like their male counterparts, copied manuscripts and thus

*The Immaculate Conception did not become Roman Catholic dogma until 1854, when Pope Pius IX promulgated the bull *Ineffabilis Deus*.

The Art of the Ancient World and the Middle Ages

The art of the classical period (c. fifth century B.C.) was important not only to the ancient Greeks but also to the Romans and to later generations, from the Renaissance to the postmodern period of the late twentieth century. Through the ages, classical art has been kept alive—adopted, adapted, altered, and appreciated—by artists and craftspeople. Why has the classical style remained at the forefront of artistic endeavor?

The classical period has given us the first works of the Western world to represent the human form with accuracy. The body itself was the sculptors' subject. Their aim was to shape their marble so as to make a general and schematic figure lifelike. Classical sculpture has been a powerful learning device for aspiring artisans from Michelangelo to nineteenth-century artists such as Auguste Rodin. Ancient sculptures—and plaster casts made from them—have been used as teaching tools by educators since the Renaissance. Learning to draw from casts of ancient works was the traditional first step in an artist's education; even many abstract artists of the twentieth century had a

1. Praxiteles. *Hermes with Young Dionysus*, c. 350 B.C. *(Olympia Museum/Bridgeman Art Library.)*

10. Hubert or Jan Van Eyck. *The Last Judgement,* c. 1420–1425. *(Metropolitan Museum of Art, NY.)*

11. Giotto di Bondone. *Kiss of Judas,* c. 1305. Scrovengi Chapel, Padua, Italy. *(Alinari/Art Resource.)*

The Art of the Ancient World and the Middle Ages

1. Praxiteles. *Hermes with Young Dionysus*, c. 350 B.C. *(Olympia Museum/Bridgeman Art Library.)*

The art of the classical period (c. fifth century B.C.) was important not only to the ancient Greeks but also to the Romans and to later generations, from the Renaissance to the postmodern period of the late twentieth century. Through the ages, classical art has been kept alive—adopted, adapted, altered, and appreciated—by artists and craftspeople. Why has the classical style remained at the forefront of artistic endeavor?

The classical period has given us the first works of the Western world to represent the human form with accuracy. The body itself was the sculptors' subject. Their aim was to shape their marble so as to make a general and schematic figure lifelike. Classical sculpture has been a powerful learning device for aspiring artisans from Michelangelo to nineteenth-century artists such as Auguste Rodin. Ancient sculptures—and plaster casts made from them—have been used as teaching tools by educators since the Renaissance. Learning to draw from casts of ancient works was the traditional first step in an artist's education; even many abstract artists of the twentieth century had a

2. Venus de Milo. Greek statue from the first century B.C., probably an imitation of a fourth-century work. *(Louvre/Giraudon/Art Resource.)*

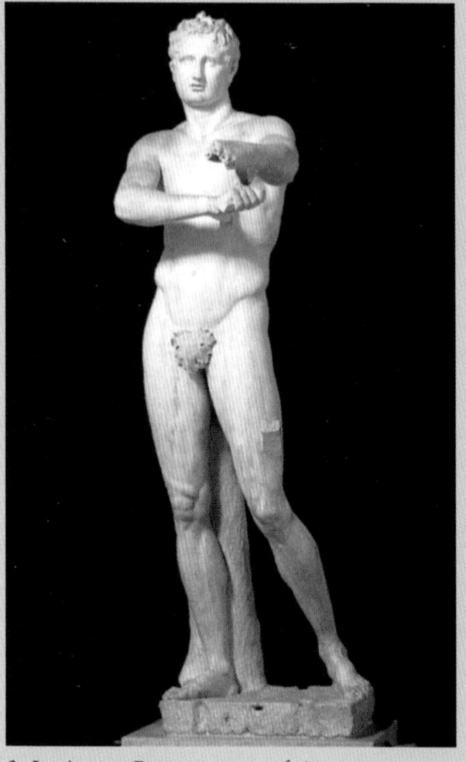

3. Lysippos. Roman copy of *Apoxyomenos*, original c. 325–300 B.C. *(Museo Pio Clementino, Vatican Museums, Vatican State/Scala/Art Resource.)*

solid grounding in works of the classical period.

The balanced, rhythmical composition of classical sculpture and architecture is another element that has influenced later artists. Earlier works—from the Greek Archaic period (sixth century B.C.) as well as works from ancient Egypt and Mesopotamia—are solid, blocklike, and devoid of any sense of movement. Classical sculptors, by contrast, were able to bring the stone alive with innovative poses, luxuriant drapery, and a careful balancing between relaxation and tension.

The works of Praxiteles embody the ideal of classical sculpture and offer visual proof that the Greeks' search for beauty and truth extended beyond their literature and philosophy.

Praxiteles (fl. 375–330 B.C.) is renowned for the quality of his marble sculpture, such as the *Hermes with Young Dionysus* (Figure 1), considered one of his finest works. Little is known of Praxiteles himself, but much has been written about his art.

The Hermes statue has many of the attributes that distinguish the best classical sculpture. The stance is relaxed: an S-curve takes the weight off one leg and shifts it to the opposite hip. This *contrapposto*, or counterbalanced, pose draws attention to every part of the god's body. The turned and slightly tilted head is a departure from the fully frontal works of earlier periods. The drapery is a careful, three-dimensional rendering of drapery in vase painting from the same period. It is realistic and so fluid that viewers might forget they are looking at marble.

A roughly contemporary work, the *Venus de Milo* (Figure 2), by an unidentified artist, embodies many of the same principles as the Hermes figure. Venus puts her weight on one leg, tensing some muscles and relaxing others. Drapery loosely covers her waist and has the look of soft cotton.

A contemporary of Praxiteles, Lysippos (fl. fourth century B.C.), is credited with changing the "Canon of Proportions" established by his predecessor Polyclitus. The "Canon of Proportions," rules that earlier sculptors followed in carving their masterpieces, assured a certain uniformity in the rendering of the human form. Heads were always a certain proportion of the whole; eyes were placed at a certain level within the face; and so on. But the work of Lysippos is notably different.

One of Lysippos's best-known works, the *Apoxyomenos* (*Scraper*) (Figure 3), shows a youthful athlete cleaning himself with a *strigyl* (scraper) after exercising. What distinguishes this work from the works of other artists are the proportions. Lysippos's youth has a smaller head and a more slender body. Although he stands with his weight on one foot, his hips are not as sharply angled as the hips of other classical figures, in whom the S-curve is more clearly pronounced. Even the face of the athlete foretells a new era in art. Unlike the serene, perfect faces of other classical figures, the Apoxyomenos' expression seems thoughtful and dreamy, not remote and dispassionate.

Distinguished by its portrayal of emotion and drama, *The Laocoön Group* (Figure 4) is one of the most famous works of Western art. Dated to the second century B.C., the work depicts the death of Laocoön, a priest of the god Apollo, and his twin sons, killed by sea serpents because they tried to prevent the entry into Troy of the huge wooden horse in which Greek warriors were concealed. The sculptors, Agesander, Atheodorou, and Polydoros of Rhodes, convey the violence and intensity of events through the exaggeration of facial features, musculature, and pose.

This work from the Hellenistic period differs from its classical predecessors in its emotionality and exaggeration of the human form. Laocoön's face shows anguish over the loss of his sons, and his muscles bulge as he strains to wrest himself from the serpent's grasp. Laocoön's children are depicted as smaller than their father yet as fully mature men.

4. Hellenistic sculpture. *The Laocoön Group*, second century B.C. *(Museo Pio Clementino, Vatican Museums, Vatican State/Scala/Art Resource.)*

Many historians have described the art of Rome as unoriginal and deriving from classical Greek works. The Romans did make multiple copies of many Greek prototypes, but they also excelled in areas of the decorative arts in which we have no evidence of Greek virtuosity. The Romans developed distinctive styles in wall painting (fresco), mosaic, and minor metal arts; their contributions to architecture are also noteworthy.

Frescoes are made by painting directly on wet or damp plaster. Some fresco painters limit their work to small scenes; others cover entire walls with landscapes, people, and architectural elements. Roman fresco painters were adept at reproducing the look of marble and

5. Detail of a Pompeian wall fresco. *Lady Playing the Cithera,* first century B.C. *(Metropolitan Museum of Art, NY.)*

other materials. The *trompe l'oeil* (literally "fool the eye") style of Roman fresco painters demonstrates their skill at reproducing the world around them.

As can be seen in Figure 5, Roman painters were able to convincingly present three-dimensional objects on a two-dimensional surface. This first-century B.C. fresco, *Lady Playing the Cithera* (a harplike musical instrument), from a villa at Boscoreale, near Pompeii, is an excellent example of the fresco painter's art. Though painted on a flat surface, the chair is set at an angle and projects outward toward the viewer. The chair's three-dimensionality is further emphasized by the placement of the young attendant, who stands behind it, holding on to its back.

Roman sculptors tended to follow closely the classical Greek and Hellenistic traditions. Some art historians assert that originality in Roman sculpture is evident only in lifelike portrait busts of the emperors, often planted firmly on the necks of copies of Greek or Hellenistic gods and heroes. To an extent, this is the case with the life-size *Augustus of the Prima Porta* (Figure 6), a work probably completed during the reign of Augustus (27 B.C.–A.D. 14) or shortly after his death and deification. Many elements of this work are direct borrowing from classical and Hellenistic prototypes. It is the head, however, that sets this work apart from its forebears. The face of Augustus is a lifelike representation of the emperor, if we assume that the great number of coins bearing Augustus's image offer an accurate likeness. Unlike Greek sculpture, which idealized the human form, this Roman work presents an image that would be recognized by all who viewed it.

Roman works such as the Augustus statue also served as illustrations of contemporary events. Carvings on the breastplate in *Augustus of the Prima Porta* portray the Romans' victory over the Parthians. Pictorial narratives of other Roman achievements were sculpted on free-standing columns and triumphal arches, as well as on the walls of buildings. In this way, Roman rulers were able to transmit news and information throughout their vast empire to people who could not read or who did not speak Latin.

The art and architecture of the Byzantine era and the Middle Ages show a transformation in subject matter. Christianity, with its theme of resurrection and salvation, dominated the period. Both Latin and Greek churches used art to spread Christian teachings and to buttress their authority. Because few people could read or write, both churches relied on sculpture, painting, and drawing to convey the essence of Christianity.

Figure 7, the mosaic *The Court of Justinian,* from the Church of San Vitale in the Italian city of Ravenna, shows the emperor Justinian and his attendants and dates to c. A.D. 547. The emperor stands in the center of the scene and is flanked by officials and local clergy. The contrast between this work and the Boscoreale fresco (Figure 5) is noteworthy. Here, the emphasis is on two-dimensionality and the vertical. All of the figures face front; there is little attempt to show depth or three-dimensionality, except for the somewhat unsuccessful overlapping of figures. These Byzantine figures, with small heads, tiny feet, and disproportionate arms, are elongated and slender, unlike the figures of the Roman painting or the Greek sculptures shown earlier.

As political and spiritual ruler of the Byzantine Empire, Justinian is flanked by twelve companions, drawing a parallel between him and Jesus Christ. His golden halo brings to mind the one usually shown around Christ's head; the attributes of Christianity, including a cross, a censer (incense burner), and a shield bearing a symbolic version of Jesus' name, remind viewers of Justinian's dual roles.

Easily recognized symbols such as the halo became common devices for transmitting the message of Christ and the church. To understand the extent to which symbols and images became the common language, consider two representations of the Madonna and Child: *Enthroned Madonna and Child,* from the Byzantine school (Figure 8), and *Madonna Enthroned Between Saints Peter and Leonard,* by the Magdalen Master of the Tuscan school (Figure 9). Both date from the thirteenth century. The similarities between them are noteworthy. The Madonna is shown in what now seems to be a conventional pose—seated on an elaborate chair or throne, facing front, holding the child on her left knee, and supporting him with her left hand. The Madonna is heavily robed, although in neither work was the artist able to depict the clothes with the fluidity of the painter responsible for the Boscoreale fresco (Figure 5).

The *Enthroned Madonna and Child*'s origins are Eastern—the Byzantine school having developed in Byzantium, the capital of the eastern Roman Empire. Byzantium (renamed Constantinople in A.D. 330) had a certain sphere of influence in the West, attested to by the Ravenna mosaic (Figure 7), and as a result, a fusion of Eastern and Western styles is evident in works such as the *Enthroned Madonna.* What is typically Byzantine about this work is the richness of color and the use of gold—in the background and in the Madonna's robes. The faces of the figures owe more to Western art, however. Soft modeling and careful shading make them look almost as if they were superimposed by another artist at another time.

6. *Augustus of the Prima Porta. (Vatican Museums, Vatican State/Scala/Art Resource.)*

The *Madonna Enthroned Between Saints Peter and Leonard* is from Italy. The artist, a conservative painter, used many elements familiar to us from the Byzantine work. Such characteristics as the smaller narrative elements that surround the central figures, the poses, the facial expressions, and the stylized painting of the drapery are all standard for the Middle Ages.

At this point, Western art begins to undergo another transformation. Styles and subject matter change, paralleling developments in

7. Mosaic. *The Court of Justinian,* c. A.D. 547. *(Church of San Vitale, Ravenna/Scala/Art Resource.)*

politics and society. Artists working at the end of the Middle Ages and on the verge of the Renaissance include the brothers Jan and Hubert Van Eyck. Figure 10 shows *The Last Judgement* (c. 1420–1425), one panel of a diptych (a two-paneled work) painted by one or both of them (the other panel portrays the Crucifixion). *The Last Judgement* illustrates some of the stylistic elements that distinguish these artists. The image is divided in two horizontally. In the upper half, which represents heaven, the mood is one of calm and order; below, on earth and in hell, pandemonium reigns. This suggestion of the promise of heaven and the threat of hell was intended to motivate people to heed Christian teachings and clerical authority.

The Van Eycks portrayed this idea with a clarity and realistic feeling unseen in other works. Their virtuosity is paralleled by the work of a slightly earlier Italian artist, Giotto di Bondone (1267–1337), whose style also marked a definite break with his peers, and whose work stands on the cusp between the Renaissance and what preceded it.

Giotto's *Kiss of Judas*, in the Scrovengi Chapel in Padua, dates from 1305 (Figure 11). A work of the Late Middle Ages, or Gothic period, it represents a major shift in artistic direction; its lifelike depiction of the human figures seen in the lower foreground anticipates later perspectival painting. To understand this change in representational art in the fourteenth century, it is necessary to remember what was happening in Italy at the time. Although the art was meant to reflect the kingdom of heaven,

8. Byzantine school. *Enthroned Madonna and Child,* thirteenth century. *(National Gallery of Art, Washington, D.C. Gift of Mrs. Otto H. Kahn, 1940.)*

9. Magdalen Master, Tuscan school. *Madonna Enthroned Between Saints Peter and Leonard,* c. 1270. *(Yale University Art Gallery, New Haven, Connecticut. University purchase from James Jackson Jarves.)*

actual events in the kingdom on earth played a great role.

As noted earlier, Byzantium and Byzantine art influenced Italian art and society in the medieval period. Images, symbols, and techniques that flourished in Eastern workshops took root in Italy, culminating in what art historians call a "neo-Byzantine style" in the early thirteenth century, soon after the Crusaders conquered Constantinople in 1204. Italian artists adopted the Byzantine style, which had its roots in classical Greek prototypes. The combination of Byzantine, Greek, and native Italian styles produced the new way of seeing epitomized by Giotto.

10. Hubert or Jan Van Eyck. *The Last Judgement*, c. 1420–1425. *(Metropolitan Museum of Art, NY.)*

11. Giotto di Bondone. *Kiss of Judas*, c. 1305. Scrovengi Chapel, Padua, Italy. *(Alinari/Art Resource.)*

preserved knowledge and ideas of the past. The nun Hroswitha (c. 935–c. 1001) of Gandersheim, in Saxony, Germany, produced poetry, history, and plays. Inspired by the Roman poet Terence, she wrote six dramas—the first since Roman times—along with a history of German rulers and one of her own convent.

As the lady of the castle, the lord's wife performed important duties. She assigned tasks to the servants, made medicines, preserved food, taught young girls how to sew, spin, and weave—she was responsible for providing the lord and his companions with most of the clothes they required—and, despite her subordinate position, took charge of the castle when her husband was away. If the lord was taken prisoner in war, she raised the ransom to pay for his release. Sometimes she put on armor and went to war. For amusement, noblewomen enjoyed chess and other board games, played musical instruments, or embroidered tapestries to cover castle walls. A lady might also join her husband on the hunt, a favorite recreation of the medieval nobility.

Agrarian Life

The origins of manorialism can be traced in part to the Late Roman Empire, when peasants depended on the owners of large estates for protection and security. This dependence increased during the Early Middle Ages, especially during the invasions of Northmen, Magyars, and Muslims in the ninth and tenth centuries. Peasants continued to sacrifice their freedom in exchange for protection, or, in some cases, they were too weak to resist the encroachments of local magnates. Like feudalism, manorialism was not an orderly system but consisted of improvised relationships and practices that varied from region to region.

A lord controlled at least one manorial village; great lords might control hundreds. A small manor included a dozen families; a large one, as many as fifty or sixty. The manorial village was never completely self-sufficient because salt, millstones, and metalware were generally obtained from outside sources; it did, however, constitute a balanced economic setting. Peasants grew grain and raised cattle, sheep, goats, and hogs; blacksmiths, carpenters, and stonemasons built and repaired dwellings and implements; the village priest cared for the souls of the inhabitants; and the lord defended the manor and administered the customary law.

The serf and his family lived in a dismal, one-room cottage that they shared with chickens and pigs. In the center burned a small fire, the smoke escaping through a hole in the roof. In cold weather when the fire was strong, the room filled with smoke. When it rained, water came through the thatched roof and turned the earth floor into mud. The odor from animal excrement was ever present.

Poor roads, few bridges, and dense forests made travel difficult; thieves and warring knights made it unsafe. Peasants generally lived, worked, and died on the lord's estate and were buried in the village churchyard. Few had any contact with the world beyond the village of their birth. When a manor was attacked by another lord, the peasants found protection inside the walls of their lord's house. In many places, by the twelfth century, this building had become a well-fortified stone castle.

In return for protection and the right to cultivate fields and to pass these holdings on to their children, serfs owed obligations to their lord, and their personal freedom was restricted in a variety of ways. Bound to the land, they could not leave the manor without the lord's consent. Before a serf could marry, he had to obtain the lord's permission and pay a fee. The lord could select a wife for his serf and force him to marry her. Sometimes a serf, objecting to the lord's choice, preferred to pay a fine: "Thomas of Oldbury came on summons and was commanded to take Agatha of Halesowen to wife; he said he would rather be fined."[10] These rules also applied to serfs' children, who inherited their parents' obligations. In addition to working their allotted land, the serfs had to tend the fields reserved for the lord. Other services exacted by the lord included digging ditches, gathering firewood, building fences, repairing roads and bridges, and sewing clothes. Probably somewhat more than half of a serf's workweek was devoted to these labor obligations.

Serfs also paid a variety of dues to the lord. These included the annual *capitation,* a tax considered a sign of servitude; the *taille,* a tax on the serf's property; and the *heriot,* an inheritance tax imposed when a deceased serf's sons acquired the right to their father's lands. In addition, serfs paid *banalities* for using the lord's mill, bake-oven, and winepress.

Serfs did derive some benefits from manorial relationships. They received protection during a chaotic era, and they possessed customary rights, which the lord often respected, to cottages and farmland. But in a world periodically threatened with famine and epidemics, serfs faced an unrelenting struggle to survive, a struggle made all the more difficult by the contempt lords had for them. If a lord demanded more services or dues than were customary, or if he interfered with their right to cottages or strips of farmland, the peasants might demonstrate their discontent by refusing to work for the lord. Up to the fourteenth century, however, open rebellion was rare because lords possessed considerable military and legal power. The manorial system promoted attitudes of dependency and servility among the serfs; their hopes for a better life were directed toward heaven.

Medieval agriculture suffered from several deficiencies. Among them was the short supply of fertilizer; farmers depended solely on animal manure. Inadequate wooden plows and primitive methods of harnessing draft animals resulted in low yields. Yet as the Middle Ages progressed, important improvements in agriculture (discussed in Chapter 10) took place and had wide ramifications for medieval economic and social life. In the High Middle Ages, the revival of an urban economy and the reemergence of central authority would undermine manorial (and feudal) relationships.

Notes

1. Speros Vryonis, Jr., *Byzantium and Europe* (New York: Harcourt, Brace & World, 1967), p. 193.
2. The Koran, tr. N. J. Dawood (Baltimore: Penguin Books, 1961), pp. 108–109.
3. W. Montgomery Watt, *The Influence of Islam on Medieval Europe* (Edinburgh: Edinburgh University Press, 1972), p. 43.
4. Boethius, *The Consolation of Philosophy,* trans. W. V. Cooper (New York: Modern Library, 1943), p. 26.
5. Ibid., p. 29.
6. Ibid., p. 34.
7. Quoted in Jean-Pierre Poly and Eric Bournazel, *The Feudal Transformation 900–1200,* trans. Caroline Higgitt (New York: Holmes & Meier, 1991), p. 149.
8. Quoted in V. H. H. Green, *Medieval Civilization in Western Europe* (New York: St. Martin's Press, 1971), p. 35.
9. Cited in Frances Gies and Joseph Gies, *Women in the Middle Ages* (New York: Thomas Y. Crowell, 1978), p. 46.
10. Quoted in G. G. Coulton, *Medieval Village, Manor, and Monastery* (New York: Harper Torchbooks, 1960), p. 82.

Suggested Reading

Barber, Richard, *The Knight and Chivalry* (1982). The world of the feudal warrior.

Bark, W. C., *Origins of the Medieval World* (1960). The Early Middle Ages as a fresh beginning.

Burns, Thomas, *A History of the Ostrogoths* (1984). A study of Roman-Ostrogothic relations.

Dawson, Christopher, *The Making of Europe* (1957). Stresses the role of Christianity in shaping European civilization.

Duby, Georges, *The Early Growth of the European Economy* (1974). By a leading French medievalist.

Focillon, Henri, *The Year 1000* (1971). Conditions of life toward the end of the Early Middle Ages.

Ganshof, F. L., *Feudalism* (1964). A concise treatment of feudal institutions.

Gies, Frances, and Joseph Gies, *Women in the Middle Ages* (1978). The narrative weaves in valuable quotations from medieval sources.

———, *Life in a Medieval Castle* (1974). The castle as the center of medieval life; passages from journals, songs, and account books.

Herrin, Judith, *The Formation of Christendom* (1987). The transition from antiquity to the Middle Ages.

Hodgson, Marshall G. S., *The Venture of Islam,* 2 vols. (1974). A magisterial survey of Islamic culture.

Holmes, George, ed., *The Oxford History of Medieval Europe* (1988). Essays by several scholars; good opening essay on transformation of the Roman world.

Keen, Maurice, *The Pelican History of Medieval Europe* (1969). A brief survey.

Kitzinger, Ernst, *Early Medieval Art* (1983). Originally published in 1940, it provides valuable insights into the transition of art from classical naturalism to Christian religious fervor.

Kritzeck, James, ed., *Anthology of Islamic Literature.* A rich sampling.

Laistner, M. L. W., *Thought and Letters in Western Europe A.D. 500 to 900* (1957). A comprehensive survey of European thought in the Early Middle Ages.

Latouche, Robert, *The Birth of Western Economy* (1966). Economic decline during the Early Middle Ages.

LeGoff, Jacques, *Medieval Civilization* (1990). Selected topics on medieval civilization by a leading French historian.

Lewis, A. R., *Emerging Medieval Europe* (1967). Good discussions of both economic and social changes.

Lewis, Bernard, *The Arabs in History* (1966). A valuable survey.

Lucas, Angela M., *Women in the Middle Ages* (1983). Women and religion, marriage, and letters.

Nasr, Seyyed Hossein, *Science and Civilization in Islam* (1968). An analysis of Islamic science with many illuminating extracts from medieval works.

Rowling, Marjorie, *Life in Medieval Times* (1973). All phases of medieval daily life.

Shahar, Shulamith, *The Fourth Estate* (1983). Women in the Middle Ages.

Thompson, J. W., and E. N. Johnson, *An Introduction to Medieval Europe* (1937). Still a valuable text.

Tierney, Brian, *Western Europe in the Middle Ages* (1970). An outstanding text.

Zacour, Norman, *An Introduction to Medieval Institutions* (1969). Comprehensive essays on all phases of medieval society.

Review Questions

1. What factors led to a rift between Byzantium and the Latin West?
2. Discuss Byzantium's long-term influence on world history.
3. What does Islam have in common with Christianity? How do they differ?
4. What is the importance of each of the following to the history of Islam: Hegira, Koran, jihad, and Shi'a?
5. Characterize and discuss the significance of the Muslim intellectual achievement.
6. Why did the Muslim empire decline?
7. In what ways were Greco-Roman ideas and institutions alien to Germanic traditions?
8. How was the Roman world in the West transformed by the seventh century?
9. How did Latin Christendom blend Christian, Greco-Roman, and Germanic traditions?
10. What was the significance of monks and nuns to medieval civilization?
11. Explain the significance of the following Frankish rulers: Clovis, Charles Martel, and Pepin the Short.
12. What crucial developments occurred during the reign of Charlemagne? Why were they important?
13. Discuss the causes and effects of the breakup of Charlemagne's empire.
14. What conditions led to the rise of feudalism? How did feudal law differ from Roman law?
15. What conditions led to the rise of manorialism? What obligations did a serf have to the lord? What did the serf get in return?

Chapter 10

The High Middle Ages: Vitality and Renewal

Miniature Painting of Flemish Citizens Receiving a City Charter, Chronique de Hainout, Fifteenth Century. (Koninklijke Bibliotheek Albert 1st, Brussels.)

- **Economic Expansion**
  - Agricultural Revolution
  - Revival of Trade
  - Rebirth of Towns
- **The Rise of States**
  - England
  - France
  - Germany
  - The Emergence of Representative Institutions
- **The Growth of Papal Power**
  - The Sacraments
  - Gregorian Reform
  - The Crusades
  - Dissenters and Reformers
  - Innocent III: The Apex of Papal Power
- **Christians and Jews**

By the end of the eleventh century, Europe showed many signs of recovery and vitality. The invasions of Magyars and Vikings had ended, and powerful lords and kings imposed greater order on their territories. Improvements in technology and the clearing of new lands increased agricultural production. More food, the fortunate absence of plagues, and the limited nature of feudal warfare contributed to a population increase. The revival of long-distance trade and the emergence of towns were other visible signs of economic expansion. Offensives against the Muslims—in Spain, in Sicily, and (at the end of the century) in the Holy Land—demonstrated Europe's growing might and self-confidence. So too did the German conquest and colonization of lands on the northeastern frontier of Latin Christendom.

Reform movements strengthened the bonds between the church and the people and increased the power of the papacy. During the High Middle Ages (1050–1300), the pope, as Christ's deputy, sought to direct, if not rule, all Christendom. European economic and religious vitality was paralleled by a cultural flowering in philosophy, literature, and the visual arts. The civilization of Latin Christendom had entered its golden age.

Economic Expansion

A period of economic expansion, the High Middle Ages witnessed an agricultural revolution, a commercial revolution, the rebirth of towns, and the rise of an enterprising and dynamic middle class.

Agricultural Revolution

During the Middle Ages, important advances were made in agriculture. Many of these innovations occurred in the Early Middle Ages but were adopted only gradually and were not used everywhere. In time, however, they markedly increased production. By the end of the thirteenth century, medieval agriculture had reached a technical level far superior to that of the ancient world.

One innovation was a heavy plow that cut deeply into the soil. This new plow enabled farm-

Chronology 10.1 ❖ The High Middle Ages

910	Founding of the Abbey of Cluny
962	Otto I crowned emperor of the Romans, beginning the Holy Roman Empire
987	Hugh Capet becomes king of France
1054	Split between the Byzantine and the Roman churches
1061–1091	Norman conquest of Sicily
1066	Norman conquest of England
1075	Start of the Investiture Controversy
1096	First Crusade begins
c. 1100	Revival of the study of Roman law at Bologna
1163	Start of the construction of the Cathedral of Notre Dame
1198–1216	Pontificate of Innocent III: height of the church's power
1267–1273	Saint Thomas Aquinas writes *Summa Theologica*
c. 1321	Dante completes *Divine Comedy*

ers to work more quickly and effectively. As a result, they could cultivate more land, including the heavy, moist soils of northern Europe, which had offered too much resistance to the light plow. Another important advance in agricultural technology was the invention of the collar harness. The old yoke harness worked well with oxen but tended to choke horses, which, because they move faster and have greater stamina than oxen, are more valuable for agricultural work. The introduction of the horseshoe to protect the soft hoofs of horses added to their ability to work on difficult terrain.

Two other developments were the widening use of the water mill by the tenth century and the introduction of windmills, which came into use in the twelfth century. Replacing ancient hand-worked mills, both inventions saved labor in grinding grain.

The gradual emergence of the three-field system of managing agricultural land, particularly in northern Europe, increased production. In the old, widely used two-field system, half the land was planted in autumn with winter wheat, while the other half was left fallow to restore its fertility. In the new three-field system, one-third of the land was planted in autumn with winter wheat, a second third was planted the following spring with oats and vegetables, and the last third remained fallow. The advantages of the three-field system were that two-thirds of the land were farmed and only one-third was left unused and that the diversification of crops made more vegetable protein available.

Higher agricultural production reduced the number of deaths caused by starvation and dietary disease and thus contributed to a population increase. Grain surpluses also meant that draft animals and livestock could survive the winter. The growing numbers of animals provided a steady source of fresh meat and milk and increased the quantity of manure for fertilizer.

Soon the farmland of a manorial village could not support the growing village population. Consequently, peasants had to look beyond their immediate surroundings and colonize trackless wasteland. Lords vigorously promoted this conversion of uncultivated soil into agricultural land because it increased their incomes. Monastic communities also actively engaged in this enterprise. Almost everywhere peasants were draining swamps, clearing forests, and establishing new villages. Their endeavors during the eleventh and

Agricultural Improvements. The invention of the heavy plow and the horse collar and the switch to a three-field system greatly expanded agricultural production. The increase in the food supply was a principal reason for the growth of towns. (*Bibliothèque Nationale de France, Paris*)

twelfth centuries brought vast areas of Europe under cultivation for the first time. New agricultural land was also acquired through expansion, the most notable example being the organized settlement of lands toward the east by German colonists.

The colonizing and cultivation of virgin lands contributed to the decline of serfdom. Lords owned vast tracts of forests and swamps that would substantially increase their incomes if cleared, drained, and farmed. But serfs were often unwilling to move from their customary homes and fields to do the hard labor needed to cultivate these new lands. To lure serfs away from their villages, lords promised them freedom from most or all personal services. In many cases, the settlers fulfilled their obligations to the lord by paying rent rather than by performing services or providing foodstuffs, thus making the transition from serfs to freemen. In time, they came to regard the land as their own. As a result of these changing economic conditions, the percentage of French peasants who were serfs fell from 90 percent in 1050 to about 10 percent in 1350.

The improvement in agricultural technology and the colonization of new lands altered the conditions of life in Europe. Surplus food and the increase in population freed people to work at nonfarming occupations, making possible the expansion of trade and the revival of town life.

Revival of Trade

Expanding agricultural production, the end of Viking attacks, greater political stability, and an increasing population produced a revival of commerce. During the Early Middle Ages, Italians and Jews kept alive a small amount of long-distance trade between Catholic Europe and the Byzantine and Islamic worlds. In the eleventh century, sea forces of Italian trading cities cleared the Mediterranean of Muslim fleets, which had blocked trade. As in Roman times, goods could circulate once again from one end of the sea to the other. The cities of Venice, Amalfi, Genoa, and Pisa grew prosperous from the lucrative Mediterranean trade. The expanding population of northern Europe provided a market for Eastern silks, sugar, spices, and dyes, and Italian merchants were quick to exploit this demand.

By the start of the eleventh century, the European economy showed unmistakable signs of recovery from the disorders of the previous century. During the next two centuries, local, regional, and long-distance trade gained such momentum that some historians describe the period as a commercial revolution that surpassed the commercial activity of the Roman Empire during the Pax Romana. A class of traders emerged who had business contacts in other lands, know-how, and ambition.

Crucial to the growth of trade were international fairs, where merchants and craftspeople set up stalls and booths to display their wares: swords, leather saddles, tools, rugs, shoes, silks, spices, furs, fine furniture, and other goods. Because of ever-present robbers, lords provided protection for merchants carrying their wares to and from fairs. Each fair lasted about three to six weeks; then the merchants would move on to another site. The Champagne region in northeastern France was the great center for fairs.

The principal arteries of trade flowed between the eastern Mediterranean and the Italian cities, between Scandinavia and the Atlantic coast, between northern France, Flanders, and England, and from the Baltic Sea in the north to the Black Sea and Constantinople via Russian rivers. The fine woolen cloth manufactured in Flanders provided the main stimulus for commerce along the Atlantic coast, and Flemish merchants prospered. In exchange for Flemish cloth, Scandinavians traded hunting hawks and fur; the English traded raw wools; and the Germans traded iron and timber. A wine trade also flourished between French vineyards and English wine merchants.

Because of their strategic position, Italian towns acted as intermediaries between the trade centers of the eastern Mediterranean and those of Latin Christendom. Luxury goods from as far away as India and China were transported to Italy by Italian ships, and then taken overland to parts of Germany and France. In addition, the Italians extended their trade and increased their profits by sailing westward into the Atlantic Ocean and then north to the markets of Spain, the Netherlands, and England. On return voyages, they brought back wool and unfinished cloth, which in turn stimulated the Italian textile industry. Since individual merchants often lacked sufficient capital for these large-scale enterprises, groups of merchants formed partnerships. By enabling merchants to pool their capital, reduce their risks, and expand their knowledge of profit-making opportunities, these arrangements furthered commerce.

Increased economic activity led to other advances in business techniques. Underwriters insured cargoes; the development of banking and credit instruments made it unnecessary for merchants to carry large amounts of cash. The international fairs not only were centers of international trade but also served as capital markets for international credit transactions. The arrangements made by fair-going merchants to settle their debts were the origin of the bill of exchange, which allowed one currency to be converted into another. The invention of double-entry bookkeeping gave merchants an overview of their financial situation: the value of their goods and their ready cash. Without such knowledge, no large-scale commercial activity could be conducted on a continuous basis. Another improvement in business techniques was the formation of commercial law, which defined the rules of conduct for debts and contracts.

Map 10.1 Medieval Trade Routes ▶
Expanding agricultural production, the end of Viking raids, greater political stability, and an increasing population produced a revival of commerce in the eleventh century.

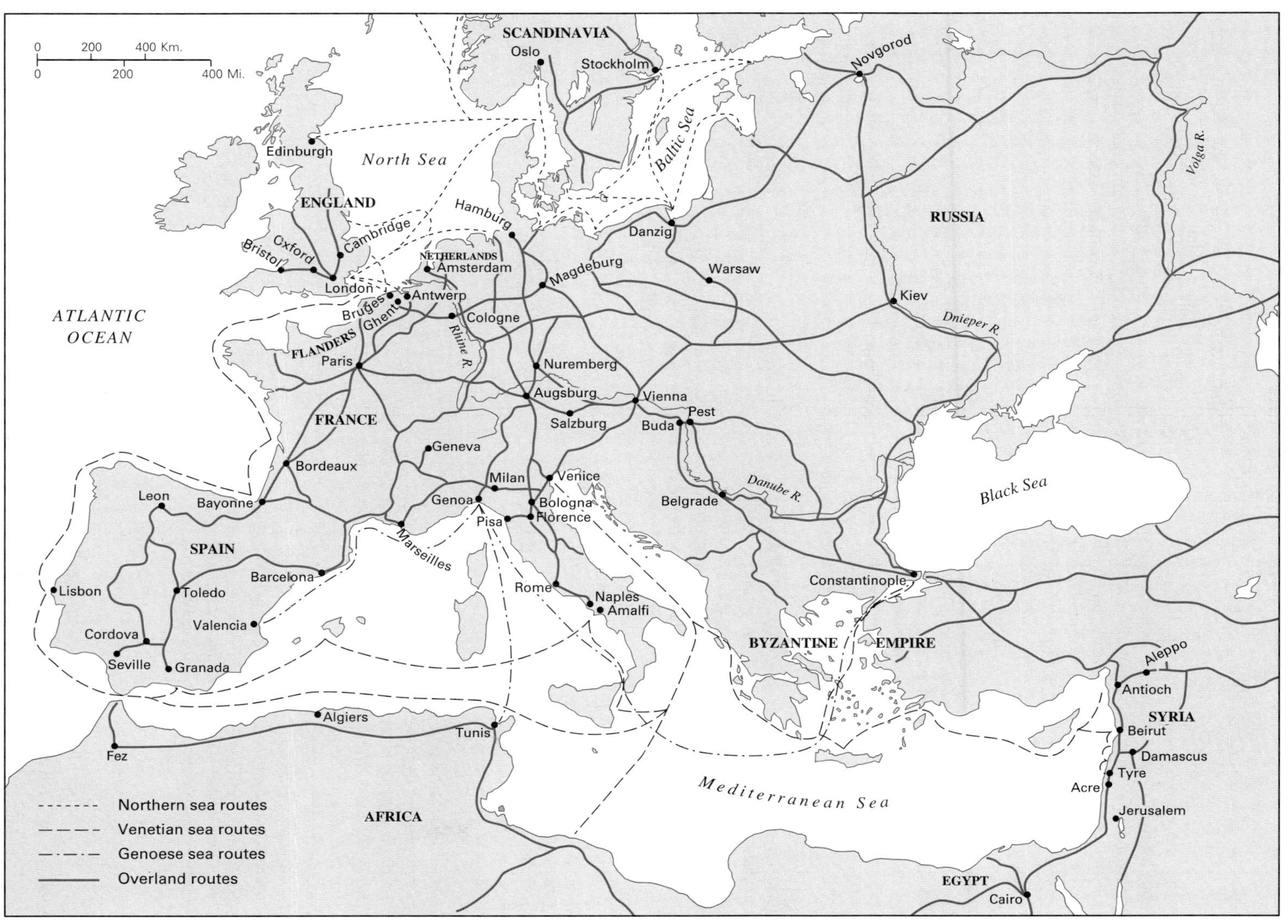

0 200 400 Km.
0 200 400 Mi.
SCANDINAVIA
Oslo
Stockholm
Novgorod
Edinburgh
North Sea
Baltic Sea
Volga R.
ENGLAND
Hamburg
Danzig
RUSSIA
Cambridge
Oxford
Bristol
London
NETHERLANDS
Amsterdam
Magdeburg
Warsaw
Kiev
Antwerp
Bruges
Ghent
Cologne
Dnieper R.
ATLANTIC OCEAN
FLANDERS
Rhine R.
Paris
Nuremberg
Augsburg
Vienna
Pest
Buda
Salzburg
FRANCE
Geneva
Bordeaux
Milan
Venice
Danube R.
Black Sea
Leon
Bayonne
Genoa
Bologna
Belgrade
Pisa
Florence
SPAIN
Marseilles
Barcelona
Lisbon
Toledo
Rome
Constantinople
Naples
Amalfi
Valencia
Cordova
BYZANTINE EMPIRE
Aleppo
Seville
Granada
Antioch
SYRIA
Algiers
Tunis
Beirut
Fez
Damascus
Tyre
Acre
Mediterranean Sea
Jerusalem
AFRICA
EGYPT
Cairo
Northern sea routes
Venetian sea routes
Genoese sea routes
Overland routes

Rebirth of Towns

In the eleventh century, towns emerged anew throughout Europe, and in the next century, they became active centers of commercial and intellectual life. Towns were a revolutionary force—socially, economically, and culturally. Because they provided new opportunities, other than food production, for commoners, towns contributed to the decline of manorialism. A new class of merchants and craftspeople came into being. This new class—the middle class—comprised those who, unlike the lords and serfs, were not affiliated with the land. The townsman was a new man, with a value system different from that of the lord, the serf, or the cleric.

What spurred town growth was the increased food supply resulting from advances in agricultural technology. Surplus farm production meant that the countryside could support an urban population of artisans and professionals. Expanding trade, too, fostered urbanization. Towns emerged in places that were natural for trade: seacoasts, riverbanks, crossroads, and market sites. They also sprang up outside fortified castles and monasteries and on surviving Roman sites. The colonies of merchants who gathered at these locations were joined by peasants skilled in crafts or willing to work as laborers. From a medieval record comes this description of a town taking shape:

> *After this castle was built, certain traders began to flock to the place in front of the gate to the bridge of the castle, that is merchants, tavernkeepers, then other outsiders drifted in for the sake of food and shelter of those who might have business transactions with the count, who often came there. Houses and inns were erected for their accommodation, since there was not room for them within the chateau. These habitations increased so rapidly that soon a large ville came into being.*[1]

Medieval towns were protected from outside attack by thick, high walls, towers, and drawbridges. Most towns had a small population. The largest ones—Florence, Ghent, and Paris—had between fifty thousand and a hundred thousand inhabitants by the start of the fourteenth century; Venice and Milan had somewhat more than a hundred thousand. Covering only small areas, these walled towns were crowded with people. Booths and wares of merchants and artisans lined the narrow and crooked streets, which were strewn with refuse—animal blood and bones dumped by butchers, rotten fish discarded by fishmongers, and human waste thrown from windows. Such unsanitary conditions were a breeding ground for contagious disease.

During the day, the streets were jammed with merchants hawking their goods, women carrying baskets, men carting produce and merchandise, beggars pleading, and children playing. A festive occasion, such as a procession honoring a patron saint, sometimes brought traffic to a standstill. A hanging, a beheading, or the burning of a heretic was looked upon as another festive occasion and always attracted a huge crowd. At night, the streets were deserted; few people ventured forth because the few elderly watchmen were no match for the numerous thieves. Even greater danger came from fires, which raged through overcrowded streets lined with wooden houses.

Merchants and craftspeople organized guilds to protect themselves from outside competition. The merchant guild in a town prevented outsiders from doing much business. A craftsman new to a town had to be admitted to the guild of his trade before he could open a shop. Competition between members of the same guild was discouraged. To prevent any one member from making significantly more money than another, a guild required its members to work the same number of hours, pay employees the same wages, produce goods of equal quality, and charge customers a just price. These rules were strictly enforced. Guilds also performed social and religious functions. Guild members attended meetings in the guildhall, celebrated holidays together, and marched in processions. The guilds cared for members who were ill or poor and extended help to widows and children of deceased members.

Women took an active part in the economic life of towns, working with men, usually their husbands, in the various crafts—as cobblers, tailors, hatters, bakers, goldsmiths, and so forth. Women brewed beer, made and sold charcoal, sold vegetables, fish, and poultry, and ran inns. In many towns, the wives and widows of master craftsmen were admitted to guilds. These guildswomen had many of the privileges of a master, including the right to train apprentices.

Because many towns were situated on land belonging to lords or on the sites of old Roman towns ruled by bishops, these communities at first came under feudal authority. In some instances, lords encouraged the founding of towns, for urban industry and commerce brought wealth to the region. However, tensions soon developed between merchants, who sought freedom from feudal restrictions that interfered with their pursuit of financial gain, and lords and bishops, who wanted to preserve their authority over the towns. Townspeople, or burghers (a *burg* is a fortified town), refused to be treated as serfs bound to a lord and liable for personal services and customary dues. The burghers wanted to travel, trade, marry, and dispose of their property as they pleased; they wanted to make their own laws and levy their own taxes. Sometimes by fighting, but more often by payments of money, townspeople obtained charters from the lords giving them the right to set up their own councils. These assemblies passed laws, collected taxes, and formed courts, which enforced the laws. Towns became more or less self-governing city-states, the first since Greco-Roman days.

The leading citizens of the towns, the patricians, were members of the merchant guilds who engaged in commerce, industry, and banking. Some patricians in the prosperous Italian towns enjoyed great wealth, owned considerable real estate, and conducted business transactions involving large sums. These people generally dominated town politics; often they obtained country estates and intermarried with the feudal aristocracy. Successful doctors and lawyers also belonged to the urban elite. Below them on the social scale were master craftsmen in the more lucrative crafts (goldsmiths, for example) and large retailers. Then came small retailers, masters in the less profitable crafts, and journeymen training to be masters. At the bottom were the laboring poor—the bulk of the population—who had no special skills and were subject to unemployment.

In virtually every medieval city, the church was the largest property owner. Because the church frowned on the pursuit of wealth, many businessmen had guilt pangs, particularly in old age, about the way they had earned their livelihood. Compounding their guilt and fear of hellfire was an awareness of having violated the church's strict prohibitions against practicing usury. To allay these concerns about the destiny of their souls, business people often bequeathed money and property to the church. These bequests helped to finance hospitals and schools, which were the church's responsibility.

In a number of ways, towns loosened the hold of lords on serfs. "City air makes a man free," went a medieval proverb. Seeking freedom and fortune, serfs fled to the new towns, where, according to custom, lords could no longer reclaim them after a year and a day. Enterprising serfs earned money by selling food to townspeople. When the serfs acquired a sufficient sum of money, they bought their freedom from lords, who needed cash to pay for goods bought from merchants. Lords increasingly began to accept fixed cash payments from serfs in place of labor services or foodstuffs. As serfs met their obligations to lords with money, they gradually became rent-paying tenants and, in time, were no longer bound to the lord's land. The manorial system of personal relations and mutual obligations was disintegrating.

The activities of townspeople made them a new breed; they engaged in business and had money and freedom. Their world was the market rather than the church, the castle, or the manor. Townspeople were freeing themselves from the prejudices both of feudal aristocrats, who considered trade and manual work degrading, and of the clergy, who cursed the pursuit of riches as an obstacle to salvation. They revived the Greco-Roman ideal of active citizens devoted to their city. Processions, celebrations, and feasts commemorating holy days or memorable events in the town's history strengthened civic bonds. An emerging secular civic life, combined with the new value given to business, produced a spiritual counterforce to Christian otherworldliness that would gain momentum in succeeding centuries. The townspeople were critical, dynamic, and progressive—a force for change. Medieval towns nurtured the origins of the *bourgeoisie* (literally, "citizens of the burg," the walled town), the urban middle class, which would play a crucial role in modern European history.

The Battle of Hastings, a.d. 1066: Scene from the Bayeux Tapestry, France, eleventh century. This battle sealed the conquest of England by William, duke of Normandy. The French-speaking Normans now governed the native Anglo-Saxons; eventually, both Normans and Anglo-Saxons fused into a single people, the English. The Bayeux Tapestry depicts seventy scenes of the conquest and is significant as both a work of art and a historical source. (*Art Resource.*)

The Rise of States

The revival of trade and the burgeoning of towns signaled a growing vitality in Latin Christendom. Another sign of strength was the greater order and security provided by the emergence of states. While feudalism fostered a Europe that was split into many local regions, each ruled by a lord, the church envisioned a vast Christian commonwealth, *Respublica Christiana,* governed by an emperor who was guided by the pope. During the High Middle Ages, the ideal of a universal Christian community seemed close to fruition. Never again would Europe possess such spiritual unity.

But other forces were propelling Europe in a different direction. Aided by educated and trained officials who enforced royal law, tried people in royal courts, and collected royal taxes, kings expanded their territory and slowly fashioned strong central governments. Gradually, subjects began to transfer their prime loyalty from the church and the lords to the person of the king. These developments laid the foundations of European states. Not all regions followed the same pattern. Whereas England and France achieved a large measure of unity during the Middle Ages, the areas that later became Germany and Italy remained divided, with numerous independent territories.

England

After the Roman legions abandoned England in the fifth century, the Germanic Angles and Saxons invaded the island and established several small kingdoms. In the ninth century, the Danes—one group of the Northmen who raided western Europe—conquered most of Anglo-Saxon England. But the Saxon kingdom of Wessex, ruled by Alfred the Great (871–899), survived. To resist the Danes, Alfred strengthened his army and built a fleet. To stem the decline of learning that accompanied the Danish invasions, Alfred, like Charlemagne, founded a palace school, bringing to it scholars from other areas. Alfred himself studied Latin and translated a work of Pope Gregory I into Anglo-Saxon. He also had other works translated into Anglo-Saxon, including Boethius's *Consolation of Philosophy.* Alfred's descendants gradually regained land from the Danes and reestablished Anglo-Saxon control over the island.

In 1066, the Normans—those Northmen who had first raided and then settled in France—defeated the Anglo-Saxons in the battle of Hastings and became masters of England. Determined to establish effective control over his new kingdom, William the Conqueror (1027–1087), duke of Normandy (in western France), kept one-sixth of conquered England for himself. In accordance with feudal practice, he distributed the rest among his Norman nobles, who swore an oath of loyalty to him and provided him with military assistance. But William made certain that no feudal baron had enough land or soldiers to threaten his power. The Norman conquest led to the replacement of an Anglo-Saxon aristocracy with a Norman one, and it strengthened the king's position as never before.

To tighten royal control, William retained some Anglo-Saxon administrative practices. The land remained divided into *shires* (counties) administered by *sheriffs* (royal agents). This structure gave the king control over local government. To determine how much money he could demand, William ordered a vast census taken of people and property in every village. Census data, compiled in the *Domesday Book,* indicated the number of tenants, cattle, sheep, and pigs and the quantities of farm equipment throughout the realm. Thus, better than any other monarch of his day, William knew what the assets of his kingdom were. Because William conquered England in one stroke, his successors did not have to travel the long, painful road to national unity that French monarchs had to take.

Crucial to shaping national unity was the development of common law. When Henry I became king in 1100, England had conflicting baronial claims and legal traditions, which were a barrier to unity. These legal traditions included Anglo-Saxon law, feudal law introduced by the Normans from France, church law, and the commercial law emerging among the town businesspeople. During the reigns of Henry I (1100–1135) and Henry II (1154–1189), royal judges traveled to different parts of the kingdom. Throughout England, important cases began to be tried in the king's court rather than in local courts, thereby increasing royal power. The decisions of royal judges were recorded and used as guides for future cases. In this way, a law common to the whole land gradually came to prevail over the customary law of a specific locality. Because common law applied to all England, it served as a force for unity. It also provided a fairer system of justice. Common law remains the foundation of the English legal system and the legal systems of lands settled by English people, including the United States.

Henry II made an early form of trial by jury a regular procedure for many cases heard in the king's court, laying the foundations of the modern judicial system. Twelve men familiar with the facts of the case appeared before the king's justices and were asked under oath if the plaintiff's statement was true. The justices based their decisions on the answers. Henry II also ordered representatives of a given locality to report under oath to visiting royal judges any local persons who were suspected of murder or robbery. This indictment jury was the ancestor of the modern grand jury.

The growth of an efficient financial administration paralleled the development of a strong judicial system. The Exchequer, the royal accounting office, was formed during the early years of Henry I's reign. Its officials saw to the collection of all revenues owed the king. Like the judges, these officials formed a class of professional administrators who were personally loyal to the king.

King John (1199–1216) inadvertently precipitated a situation that led to another step in the political development of England. Fighting a costly and losing war with the king of France, John had coerced his vassals into giving him more and more revenue; he had also punished some vassals without a proper trial. In 1215, the angry barons rebelled and compelled John to fix his seal to a document called Magna Carta, or Great Charter. Magna Carta is celebrated as the root of the uniquely English respect for basic rights and liberties. Although essentially a feudal document directed against a king who had violated rights of feudal barons, Magna Carta stated certain principles that eventually could be interpreted more widely.

Over the centuries, these principles were expanded to protect the liberties of the English against governmental oppression. Magna Carta stated that no unusual feudal dues "shall be imposed in our kingdom except by the common consent of our kingdom." In time, this right came to mean that the king could not levy taxes without the consent of Parliament, the governmental body that represents the English people. Magna Carta also provided that "no freeman shall be taken or imprisoned . . . save by the lawful judgment of his peers or by the law of the land." The barons who drew up the document had intended it to mean that they must be tried by fellow barons. As time passed, these words were regarded as a guarantee of trial by jury for all men, a prohibition against arbitrary arrest, and a command to dispense justice fully, freely, and equally. Implied in Magna Carta is the idea that the king cannot rule as he pleases but must govern according to the law: not even the king can violate the law of the nation. Centuries afterward, when the English sought to limit the king's power, they would interpret Magna Carta in this way.

Anglo-Saxon England retained the Germanic tradition that the king should consider the advice of the leading men in the land. William the Conqueror continued this practice by seeking the opinions of leading nobles and bishops. In the thirteenth century, it became accepted custom that the king should not decide major issues without consulting these advisers, who assembled together as the Great Council. Lesser nobility and townspeople also began to be summoned to meet with the king. These two groups were eventually called the House of Lords (bishops and nobles) and the House of Commons (knights and burghers). Thus did the English Parliament evolve, and by the mid-fourteenth century, it was a permanent institution of government.

WOMEN WORKERS. At times noble ladies fought side by side with men when their castle was attacked. Here women hurl rocks and shoot arrows at the attackers. (*Bibliothèque royale Albert 1er, Brussels.*)

Frequently in need of money but unable to levy new taxes without the approval of Parliament, the king had to turn to that body for help. Parliament used this control over money matters to enhance its power. The tradition grew that the power to govern rested not with the king alone but with the king and Parliament together.

During the Middle Ages, England became a centralized and unified state. But the king did not have unlimited power; he was not above the law. The rights of the people were protected by certain principles implicit in the common law and in Magna Carta and by the power of Parliament.

France

In the 150 years after Charlemagne's death, the western part of his empire, which was destined to become France, faced terrible ordeals. Charlemagne's heirs fought one another for the crown;

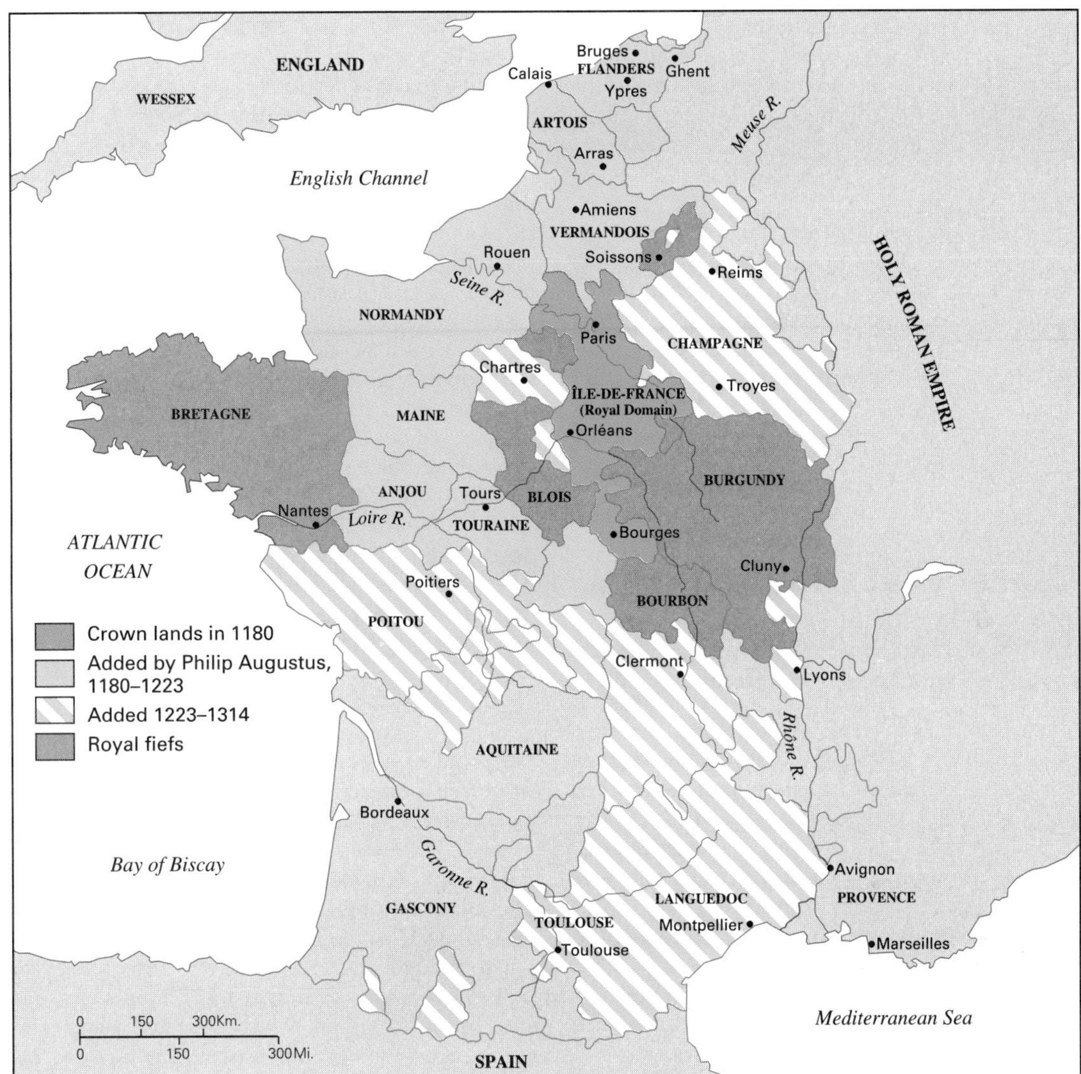

Map 10.2 The Kingdom of France, 1180–1314 Through wars, alliances, and marriages, French kings expanded their territory.

the Vikings raided everywhere their ships would carry them; Muslims from Spain plundered the southern coast; and strong lords usurped power for themselves. With the Carolingian family unable to maintain the throne, the great lords bestowed the title of king on one of their own. In 987, they chose Hugh Capet (987–996), the count of Paris. Because many great lords held territories far larger than those of Hugh, the French king did not seem a threat to noble power. But Hugh strengthened the French monarchy by having the lords also elect his son as his coruler. This practice continued, until it became understood that the crown would remain with the Capetian family.

With the accession of Louis VI (1108–1137), a two-hundred-year period of steadily increasing royal power began. Louis started this trend by successfully subduing the barons in his own duchy. A decisive figure in the expansion of French royal sway was Philip Augustus (1180–

1223). Philip struck successfully at King John of England (of Magna Carta fame), who held more territory as feudal lord in France than Philip did. By stripping John of most of his French lands (Normandy, Anjou, and much of Aquitaine), Philip tripled the size of his kingdom and became stronger than any French lord.

How the king of England came to hold so much of France is a convoluted tale. It began when William, duke of Normandy, conquered England in 1066, becoming ruler of both territories. Later, William's great-grandson, Henry, acquired much of southern France through his marriage to Eleanor of Aquitaine (c. 1122–1204), perhaps the most powerful queen of the medieval era. First married to Louis VII, she had reigned as queen of France for fifteen years and had even gone with Louis on the Second Crusade. This marriage was annulled in 1152, and shortly afterward Eleanor married Henry Plantagenet, who became King Henry II of England in 1154. She bore Henry eight children, among them Richard the Lion-Hearted and John (whom Philip Augustus defeated), both of whom became kings of England. Thus, as a result of the Norman Conquest and intermarriage, the destinies of France and England were closely intertwined until the end of the Middle Ages.

Louis IX (1226–1270)—pious, compassionate, and conscientious and a genuine lover of peace—was perhaps the best-loved French monarch of the Middle Ages. Departing from feudal precedent, Louis issued ordinances for the entire realm without seeking the consent of his vassals. One ordinance prohibited private warfare among the nobility. Another promoted the nationwide circulation of coins produced by royal mints. These ordinances furthered royal power and promoted order.

Under Louis IX and his successors, the power of the French monarch continued to grow. Kings added to their lands by warfare and marriage; they devised new ways of raising money, including taxing the clergy. A particularly effective way of increasing the monarch's power was by extending royal justice. In the thirteenth century, the king's court, the *parlement,* became the highest court in France. Quarrels between the king and his vassals were resolved in the parlement, and many cases previously tried in lords' courts were transferred to the king's court. Moreover, because the decision of feudal courts could be appealed to the parlement, lords no longer had the last say on legal questions.

At the beginning of the fourteenth century, Philip IV (the Fair) engaged in a struggle with the papacy (see page 285). Seeking to demonstrate that he had the support of his subjects, Philip summoned representatives of the church (First Estate), the nobility (Second Estate), and the townspeople (Third Estate) to meet in a national assembly known as the Estates General. This assembly would be called again to vote funds for the crown. Unlike the English Parliament, the Estates General never became an important body in French political life, and it never succeeded in controlling the monarch. Whereas the basis for limited monarchy had been established in England, no comparable checks on the king's power developed in France. By the end of the Middle Ages, French kings had succeeded in creating a unified state. But regional and local loyalties remained strong and persisted for centuries.

Germany

After the destruction of Charlemagne's empire, its German territories were broken into large duchies. Following traditional Germanic practice, the ruling dukes elected one of their own as king. The German king, however, had little authority outside his own duchy. Some German kings tried not to antagonize the dukes, but Otto the Great (936–973) was determined to control them. He entered into an alliance with German bishops and archbishops, who could provide him with fighting men and trained administrators—a policy continued by his successors.

In 951, Otto marched into northern Italy in an attempt to assert his influence. Ten years later, he returned to protect the pope from his Italian enemies. In 962, emulating the coronation of Charlemagne, the pope crowned Otto "Emperor of the Romans" (later the title would be changed to "Holy Roman Emperor").

The revival of the empire meant that the history of medieval Germany was closely tied to that of Italy and the papacy. Otto and his successors wanted to dominate both Italy, which had been part of Charlemagne's empire, and the pope—an ambition that embroiled the Holy Roman Emperor in a life-and-death struggle with the papacy. The papacy allied itself with the German dukes and the Italian cities, enemies of the emperor. German intervention in papal and Italian politics was the principal reason why German territories did not achieve unity in the Middle Ages.

The Emergence of Representative Institutions

One great contribution of the Middle Ages to the modern world was the representative institution. Representative assemblies, or parliaments, had their beginnings at the end of the twelfth century in the Spanish kingdom of León. In the thirteenth century, they developed in other Spanish kingdoms—Castile, Aragon, Catalonia, and Valencia—as well as in Portugal, England, and the Holy Roman Empire. In the fourteenth century, parliaments formed in France and the Netherlands.

Kings generally came to accept the principles that parliamentary consent was required for levying taxes and that the king should consult parliament about important laws and obtain its approval. By and large, the parliaments had grown out of royal dependence on the nobility for military support. Because of this dependence, monarchs considered it wise to listen to the opinions of the lords. Consequently, it became customary for the king to summon councils to discuss matters of war and peace and other vital questions. Since the high clergy constituted an important group in the realm, they too were consulted. As towns gained in wealth and significance, townspeople were also asked to royal councils. Leading nobles came to represent the nobility as an order of society; members of the upper clergy—archbishops, bishops, and abbots—represented the entire clergy; and deputies from the towns represented the townspeople. An important tradition had been established: the duty of the monarch to seek advice and consent on issues of concern to his subjects. Perhaps the practice of representative government was influenced by those church lawyers who held that the pope should seek the guidance of the Christian community as expressed in church councils—meetings of representatives of the clergy.

Thirteenth-Century Politics. The representative assembly, antecedent of the modern parliament, was an original achievement of the Middle Ages. Here the king of Aragon presides over the *cortes*, an assembly representing clergy, nobles, and townspeople. (*MAS Barcelona.*)

To be sure, in succeeding centuries, parliaments would be either ignored or dominated by kings. Nevertheless, the principle of constitutional government—government by consent—was woven into the fabric of Western society. The representative parliament is unique to Western civilization; it has no parallel in the political systems of the non-European world. Originating in the Middle Ages, the representative assembly is a distinct achievement and contribution of Western civilization.

The Growth of Papal Power

In the High Middle Ages, a growing spiritual vitality accompanied economic recovery and increasing political stability. It was marked by several developments. The common people were showing greater devotion to the church. Within the church, reform movements were attacking clerical abuses, and the papacy was becoming more powerful. A holy war against the Muslims was drawing the Christian community closer together. During this period, the church tried with great determination to make society follow divine standards: it tried to shape institutions and cultural expressions according to a comprehensive Christian outlook.

The Sacraments

As the sole interpreters of God's revelation and the sole ministers of his sacraments—sacred rites—the clergy imposed and supervised the moral outlook of Christendom. Divine grace was channeled through seven sacraments, which could be administered only by the clergy, the indispensable intermediary between individuals and God. On persons who resisted its authority, the church could impose the penalty of excommunication (expulsion from the church and denial of the sacraments, without which there could be no salvation).

The seven sacraments involved the church in the lives of individuals from birth to death. Baptism cleansed individuals—usually infants—of the stain of original sin. Confirmation granted additional grace to previously baptized young adults. Matrimony made marriage a holy union. Extreme unction, administered to the dying, was intended to remove the remains of sin. The sacrament of the Eucharist, derived from Gospel accounts of Christ's Last Supper, took place within a liturgical service, the Mass. In a solemn ceremony, bread and wine were miraculously transformed into the substance of the body and blood of Christ, which the priest administered, allowing believers to partake of Christ's saving grace. The sacrament of penance required sinners to show sorrow for their sins, to confess them to a priest, and to perform an act of contrition: prayer, fasting, almsgiving, or a pilgrimage to a holy shrine. Through the priest, the sinner could receive absolution and be rescued from spending eternity in hell. This sacrament enabled the church to enforce its moral standards throughout Latin Christendom. The final sacrament, ordination, consecrated men to serve as clergy.

Gregorian Reform

By the tenth century, the church was western Europe's leading landowner, possessing perhaps a third of the land in Italy and vast properties in other lands. However, the papacy was in no position to exercise commanding leadership over Latin Christendom. The office of pope had fallen under the domination of aristocratic families, who conspired and on occasion murdered in order to place one of their own on the wealthy and powerful throne of Saint Peter. As the papacy became a prize for Rome's leading families, it was not at all unusual for popes themselves to be involved in conspiracies and assassinations. Also weakening the authority of the papacy were local lords, who dominated churches and monasteries by appointing bishops and abbots and by collecting the income from church taxes. The bishops and abbots appointed by lords for political reasons lacked the spiritual devotion to maintain high standards of discipline among the priests and monks.

What raised the power of the papacy to unprecedented heights was the emergence of a reform movement, especially in Burgundian and German monasteries. High-minded monks called for a reawakening of spiritual fervor and the elimination of moral laxity among the clergy. They attacked particularly a concern for worldly goods, the taking of mistresses, and a diminishing commitment to the Benedictine rule. Of the many monasteries that took part in this reform movement, the Benedictine monks of Cluny in Burgundy, France, were the most influential.

Founded in 910, Cluny soon established daughter houses in France, Germany, England, and Italy, which were supervised by the mother monastery. Cluniac monks strove to impose Christian ideals on society. They demanded that clergymen not take wives or mistresses and not purchase their offices in the church. The monks tried to liberate their monasteries from the control of lords and commanded them to use their arms not for personal advantage but for Christian goals—the protection of the church and the unfortunate.

In the middle of the eleventh century, popes came under the influence of the monastic reformers. In 1059, a special synod convened by the reform-minded Pope Nicholas II moved to end the interference of Roman nobles and German Holy Roman Emperors in the selection of the pope. Henceforth, a select group of clergymen in Rome, called *cardinals,* would be responsible for choosing the pontiff.

The reform movement found its most zealous exponent in the person of Hildebrand, who became Pope Gregory VII in 1073. Gregory insisted that human society was part of a divinely ordered universe, governed by God's universal law, and that the pope, as the supreme spiritual leader of Christendom, was charged with the mission of establishing a Christian society on earth. As successor to Saint Peter, the pope had the final word on matters of faith and doctrine. All bishops came under his authority; so did kings, whose powers should be used for Christian ends. Gregory and other medieval popes often argued that just as the soul is superior to the body and commands it, and just as heavenly dignity excels the earthly, so too does priestly authority predominate over royal power. Thus, disobeying the pope—God's viceroy on earth—constituted disobedience to God himself. The pope was responsible for instructing rulers in the proper use of their God-given power, and kings had the solemn duty to obey these instructions. If a king failed in his Christian duty, the pope could deny him his right to rule. Responsible for implementing God's law, the pope could never take a subordinate position to kings or lords.

THE STRUGGLE BETWEEN THE PAPACY AND THE EMPIRE: A PAINTING OF POPE GREGORY VII, EMPEROR HENRY IV, AND COUNTESS MATILDA OF TUSCANY, TWELFTH CENTURY. Matilda, a strong ally of the Gregorian reform movement, tried unsuccessfully to mediate the dispute between the German king and the pope over the issue of lay investiture. Both Germany and Italy were plunged into civil war by partisans of each faction. Some fifty years later, in 1122, a compromise was reached but enmity and suspicion between popes and emperors continued for centuries. (*Coll. Biblioteca Vaticana, Madeline Grimaldi Archives.*)

Like no other pope before him, Gregory VII made a determined effort to assert the preeminence of the papacy over the church hierarchy and secular rulers. This determination led to a bitter struggle between the papacy and the German monarch and future Holy Roman Emperor Henry IV. The dispute was a dramatic confrontation between two competing versions of the relationship between secular and spiritual authority.

Through his reforms, Gregory VII intended to improve the moral quality of the clergy and to liberate the church from all control by secular authorities. He forbade priests who had wives or concubines to celebrate Mass; he deposed clergy who had bought their offices; he excommunicated bishops and abbots who had received their estates from a lay lord; and he expelled from the church lay lords who invested bishops with their office. The appointment of bishops, Pope Gregory insisted, should be controlled entirely by the church.

This last point touched off a conflict, called the Investiture Controversy, between King Henry IV and Pope Gregory VII. Bishops served a dual function. On the one hand, they belonged to the spiritual community of the church; on the other, as holders of estates and members of the nobility, they were also integrated into the feudal order.

Traditionally, emperors had both granted bishops their feudal authority and invested them with their spiritual authority. In maintaining that no lay rulers could confer ecclesiastical offices on their appointees, Pope Gregory threatened Henry's authority.

In earlier times, German kings seeking allies in conflicts with feudal nobility had made vassals of members of the upper clergy. In return for a fief, bishops would agree to provide troops for a monarch in his struggle against the lords. German monarchs viewed bishops as officers of the state who served the throne. If kings had no control over the appointment of bishops—as Pope Gregory maintained—they would lose the allegiance, military support, and financial assistance of their most important allies. Moreover, by agreeing to Gregory's demands, German kings would lose their freedom of action and be dominated by the Roman pontiff.

Henry IV regarded Gregory VII as a fanatic who trampled on custom, meddled in German state affairs, and challenged legitimate rulers established by God, thereby threatening to subordinate kingship to the papacy. With the approval of the German bishops, Henry called for Pope Gregory to descend from the throne of Saint Peter. Gregory in turn excommunicated Henry and deposed him as king. Soon German lands were embroiled in a civil war, as German lords used the quarrel to strike at Henry's power. The princes declared that they would not recognize Henry as king until the ban of excommunication was lifted, and they invited Gregory to meet with them in Germany.

Henry, who did not want Gregory to come to Germany and stir up his rebellious subjects, shrewdly planned to journey to Italy and appeal to Gregory to remove the stigma of excommunication. As Christ's vicar, Gregory was obligated to forgive a humble penitent. In midwinter, the German monarch crossed the Alps into northern Italy and headed for Canossa, a castle of Mathilda of Tuscany, where Gregory was staying on his way to Germany to preside at a meeting called by German lords to elect a new king. After three days, the pope forgave Henry. Henry's act of humility produced, in a sense, a victory for the king because once the ban of excommunication was removed he could deal more effectively with his rebellious lords. But the image of the German emperor pleading for forgiveness also enhanced the prestige of the papacy.

Still, the civil war persisted. The lords declared Henry deposed and elected Rudolf as his successor. Gregory, again disillusioned with Henry, recognized Rudolf as the new king. Not to be outdone, Henry, with the support of his warrior bishops, declared Pope Gregory deposed. Finally, Henry's troops crossed the Alps, successfully attacked Rome, and installed a new pope, who, in turn, crowned Henry emperor of the Romans. Gregory died in exile.

The papacy was resilient, however. Gregory's successors were energetic men who skillfully promoted papal interests. Finally in 1122, the papacy and Emperor Henry V reached a compromise, the Concordat of Worms. Bishops were to be elected exclusively by the church and invested with the staff and the ring—symbols of spiritual power—by the archbishop, not the king. This change signified that a bishop owed his role as spiritual leader to the church only. The king would grant the bishop the scepter to indicate that the bishop was also the recipient of a fief and the king's vassal, owing feudal obligations to the crown. This compromise recognized the dual function of the bishop as a spiritual leader in the church and a feudal landowner. The church had reached similar settlements with the kings of France and England about five years earlier.

The Investiture Controversy had important consequences both for German territories and for the papacy. As a result of the civil war, the great German lords strengthened their control over their lands, thereby thwarting the unifying and centralizing efforts of the monarchy. Unlike England and France, Germany, because of its conflict with the papacy, did not emerge from the Middle Ages as a unified state. Despite the exile of Gregory VII and the appointment of a new pope by Henry IV, the Investiture Controversy was no defeat for the papacy. The Concordat of Worms recognized that the church was an independent

Map 10.3 The Holy Roman Empire, c. 1200 ▶
Unable to overcome the German princes, Holy Roman Emperors, unlike French and English rulers, could not build a unified state during the Middle Ages. Germany did not achieve unity until the late nineteenth century.

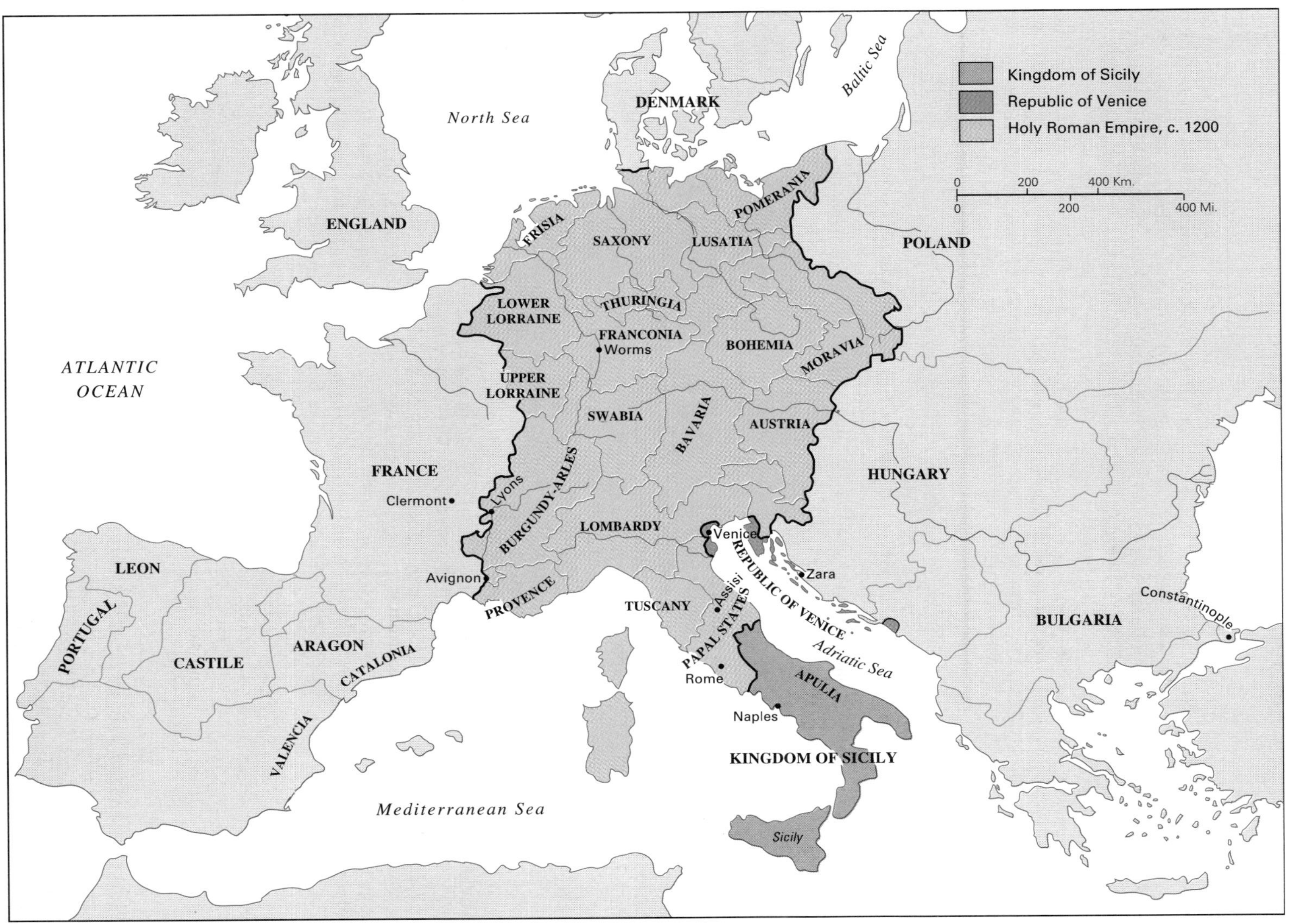

Kingdom of Sicily
Republic of Venice
Holy Roman Empire, c. 1200
0
200
400 Km.
0
200
400 Mi.
North Sea
DENMARK
Baltic Sea
ENGLAND
POLAND
FRISIA
SAXONY
LUSATIA
POMERANIA
LOWER LORRAINE
THURINGIA
FRANCONIA
Worms
BOHEMIA
MORAVIA
ATLANTIC OCEAN
UPPER LORRAINE
SWABIA
BAVARIA
AUSTRIA
FRANCE
HUNGARY
Clermont
Lyons
BURGUNDY-ARLES
LOMBARDY
Venice
REPUBLIC OF VENICE
Zara
LEON
Avignon
PROVENCE
TUSCANY
Assisi
PAPAL STATES
Constantinople
BULGARIA
PORTUGAL
CASTILE
ARAGON
CATALONIA
Adriatic Sea
Rome
APULIA
Naples
VALENCIA
KINGDOM OF SICILY
Mediterranean Sea
Sicily

body headed by the pope, over whom rulers had no authority; it was free of state control. Moreover, Gregory's vision of a Christendom guided by the pontiff, and of the state subordinate to and in the service of the papacy, persisted. Sharing his vision, future popes would raise the papacy to new heights of power.

The conflict between the papacy and the German rulers continued after the Concordat of Worms—a contest for supremacy between the heir of Saint Peter and the heir of Charlemagne. German monarchs wanted to control the papacy and the prosperous northern Italian cities. However, when Frederick I (1152–1190), known as Frederick Barbarossa (Red Beard), tried to reassert authority over these cities, they resisted. In 1176, the armies of an alliance of Italian cities, supported by the pope, trounced Frederick's forces at the battle of Legnano. The Italian infantry showed that it could defeat knights on horseback, and Frederick was compelled to recognize the independence of the Italian cities. His numerous expeditions to Italy weakened his authority. German princes strengthened themselves at the expense of the monarchy, thereby continuing to preclude German unity.

Frederick, however, did achieve a diplomatic triumph. He arranged for his son, Henry VI, to marry the heiress to the kingdom of Sicily. Consisting of the island of Sicily and most of the Italian mainland south of Rome, the kingdom was well run and economically advanced. The papacy, which feared the extension of the emperor's power so close to its own territory, waged a relentless struggle to separate Sicily from the Holy Roman Empire. In attempting to join Sicily to Germany, Henry and his successors severely strained German resources. Taking advantage of the emperor's difficulties in Sicily, German princes continued to consolidate their power at home.

The Crusades

Like the movement for spiritual renewal associated with the Cluniac reformers, the Crusades—wars to regain the Holy Land from the Muslims—were an outpouring of Christian zeal and an attempt by the papacy to assert its preeminence. Along with the renewal of commerce and the growth of towns, the Crusades were a sign of vitality and self-confidence in western Europe. The victims of earlier Muslim attacks, Latin Christians now took the offensive. Furthermore, the Crusades were part of a general movement of European expansion during the High Middle Ages. Latin Christians were venturing forth as pioneers to open new lands to cultivation and as conquerors to expand the borders of Christendom.

By the middle of the eleventh century, forces from the cities of Genoa and Pisa had driven the Muslims from Sardinia. In 1087, these northern Italians successfully attacked the North African port of Tunis, a leading base for Muslim pirates, and forced the emir of Tunis to free Christian captives and to favor Genoese and Pisan merchants. By 1091, Normans had taken Sicily from the Muslims and southern Italy from Byzantium. With the support of the papacy, Christian knights engaged in the long struggle to drive the Muslims from Spain; by 1248, after more than two centuries of conflict, only the small southern kingdom of Granada remained in Muslim hands. Germans conquered and colonized lands south of the Baltic coast inhabited by non-Christian Slavs, Balts, and Prussians. German settlers brought with them Christianity and German language and culture. They cleared vast tracts of virgin land for farming and established towns, bishoprics, and monasteries in a region where urban life had been virtually unknown.

In the eleventh century, the Seljuk Turks, who had earlier embraced Islam, conquered vast regions of the Near East, including Anatolia, a province of the Byzantine Empire. With the death of the Turkish sultan in 1092, the Seljuk Empire broke up, which reduced the pressure on Byzantium. Seeking to strengthen his army in preparation for the reconquest of Anatolia, Byzantine emperor Alexius appealed to Western rulers for mercenaries.

Pope Urban II, at the Council of Clermont (in France) in 1095, exaggerated the danger confronting Eastern Christianity. He called for a holy crusade against the heathen Turks, whom he accused of defiling and destroying Christian churches. Several months later, he expanded his objectives to include the conquest of Jerusalem. A Christian army, mobilized by the papacy to defend the faith and to regain the Holy Land from nonbelievers, accorded with the papal concept of a just war; it would channel the endemic violence

THE CRUSADES. Among the many fortresses built by the Crusaders in the Near East was this one located in northern Syria. Note the massive walls. (*Michael Nicholson/Corbis.*)

of Europe's warrior class in a Christian direction. A crusade against the Muslims also held the promise of bringing the Eastern church, which had formally broken with Rome in 1054, under papal leadership. In organizing a crusade for Christian ends, Urban II, like Gregory VII in his struggle with Henry IV, sought to demonstrate the supremacy of the pope.

What motivated the knights and others who responded to Urban's appeal? To some younger sons with no hope of inheriting land at home, a crusade offered an opportunity to gain land by conquest. No doubt the Crusaders regarded themselves as armed pilgrims dedicated to rescuing holy places from the hated Muslims. Through the years, Christian pilgrims had made the journey to Jerusalem to do penance for crimes against the church and to demonstrate their piety. These pilgrims and other devout Christians found it deplorable that Christian holy places were controlled by heathen Muslims. Moreover, Urban declared that participation in a crusade was itself an act of penance, an acceptable way of demonstrating sorrow for sin. In their eagerness to recruit warriors, popular preachers went even further: they promised cancellation of penalties for sin. To a knight, a crusade was no doubt a great adventure that promised land, glory, and plunder, but it was also an opportunity to remit sins by engaging in a holy war. The enthusiasm with which knights became Christian warriors demonstrated the extent to which the warrior mentality of the nobles had become permeated by Christian principles.

Stirred by popular preachers, the common people also became gripped by the crusading spirit. The most remarkable of the evangelists was Peter the Hermit. Small and thin, with a long gray beard caked with mud, Peter rode his donkey through the French countryside arousing the religious zeal of plain folk. Swayed by the old man's eloquence, thousands of poor people abandoned their villages and joined Peter's march to Jerusalem. As this army of the poor crossed Germany, the credulous peasants expected to find Jerusalem just beyond the horizon; some thought that Peter was leading them straight to heaven. While Peter's army made its way to Constantinople, another army of commoners recruited in Germany began their crusade by massacring the Jews of the Rhineland, despite the efforts of bishops to protect them. Unlike Peter's army, these commoners never reached Constantinople; after plundering Hungary, they were slaughtered by Hungarians (Magyars). Camped in the suburbs of Constantinople, Peter's restless recruits crossed from Byzantine-controlled land into Turkish territory, where they too were massacred. Faith alone could not win Jerusalem.

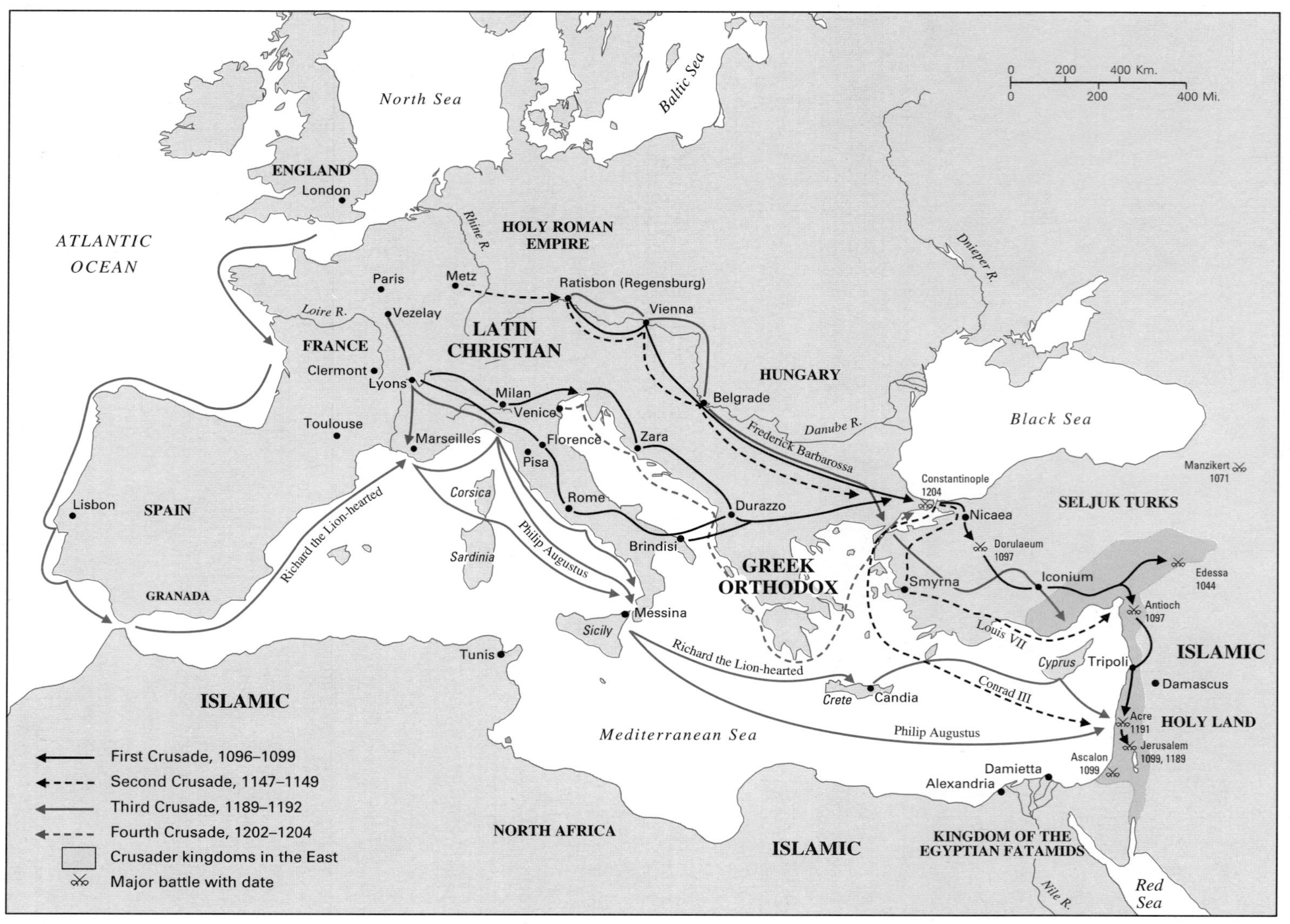

North Sea
Baltic Sea
0 200 400 Km.
0 200 400 Mi.
ENGLAND
London
ATLANTIC OCEAN
HOLY ROMAN EMPIRE
Rhine R.
Dnieper R.
Paris
Metz
Ratisbon (Regensburg)
Vienna
Loire R.
Vezelay
LATIN CHRISTIAN
FRANCE
Clermont
Lyons
HUNGARY
Milan
Venice
Belgrade
Toulouse
Marseilles
Florence
Pisa
Zara
Danube R.
Black Sea
Frederick Barbarossa
Constantinople 1204
Manzikert 1071
Nicaea
SELJUK TURKS
Lisbon
SPAIN
Corsica
Rome
Durazzo
Brindisi
Dorulaeum 1097
Sardinia
Philip Augustus
Richard the Lion-hearted
GREEK ORTHODOX
Smyrna
Iconium
Edessa 1044
GRANADA
Messina
Sicily
Antioch 1097
Louis VII
Tunis
Richard the Lion-hearted
Cyprus
Tripoli
ISLAMIC
Damascus
ISLAMIC
Crete
Candia
Conrad III
Mediterranean Sea
Philip Augustus
Acre 1191
HOLY LAND
Jerusalem 1099, 1189
Ascalon 1099
Damietta
Alexandria
First Crusade, 1096–1099
Second Crusade, 1147–1149
Third Crusade, 1189–1192
Fourth Crusade, 1202–1204
Crusader kingdoms in the East
Major battle with date
NORTH AFRICA
ISLAMIC
KINGDOM OF THE EGYPTIAN FATAMIDS
Nile R.
Red Sea

Departing later than the commoners, an army of knights assembled at Constantinople in the spring of 1097. After enduring the long march through Anatolia, the Christian army arrived at Antioch in Syria, which it captured after a long siege. In June 1099, three years after Urban's appeal, the soldiers of the First Crusade (1096–1099) stood outside the walls of Jerusalem. Using siege weapons, they broke into the city and slaughtered Muslims and Jews.

Weakened by local rivalries and religious quarrels, the Muslim world failed to unite against the Christian invaders, who, besides capturing Jerusalem, carved out four small states in Syria and Palestine. How long could these Christian states, islands in a Muslim sea, endure against a Muslim counteroffensive?

Never resigned to the establishment of Christian states in their midst, Muslim leaders called for a jihad, or holy war. In 1144, one of the Crusader states, the County of Edessa, in Syria, fell to the resurgent forces of Islam. Alarmed by the loss of Edessa, Pope Eugenius II called for the Second Crusade (1147–1149). In 1147, King Louis VII of France and Emperor Conrad III of Germany led their forces across the Balkans into Asia Minor. Both armies, traveling independently, were decimated by Seljuk Turks, and only a fraction of the Christians reached their goal. The Second Crusade was a complete failure.

After 1174, Saladin, a brilliant commander, became the most powerful leader in the Muslim Near East. In 1187, he invaded Palestine, annihilated a Christian army near Nazareth, and recaptured Jerusalem. In contrast to Christian knights of the First Crusade, who filled Jerusalem with blood and corpses, Saladin permitted no slaughter. The capture of Jerusalem led to the Third Crusade (1189–1192), in which some of Europe's most prominent rulers participated—Richard I, the Lion-Hearted, of England, Philip Augustus of France, and Frederick Barbarossa of Germany. The Crusaders captured Acre and Jaffa, but Jerusalem remained in Muslim hands.

◀ *Map 10.4* The Routes of the Crusades
In 1291, almost two hundred years after Pope Urban II's appeal for a crusade, the last Christian stronghold in the Near East had fallen.

Pope Innocent III called the Fourth Crusade (1202–1204), to demonstrate anew that the papacy was the shepherd of Christendom. In 1202, ten thousand Crusaders gathered in Venice, preparing to depart for the East. But the Venetians, who had agreed to provide transport and food, would not set sail because the Crusaders produced less money than the agreement had called for. The wily Venetians then proposed a new deal. They would allow the Crusaders to postpone payment in exchange for their cooperation in capturing the trading port of Zara, a rival of Venice controlled by the king of Hungary. Infuriated by this attack against a Christian city, Innocent excommunicated the Crusaders and the Venetians, but anxious to save the Crusade, he quickly lifted the sentence on the soldiers.

Again the Crusade was diverted. Alexius IV, pretender to the throne of Byzantium, offered the Venetians and the Christian army a huge sum in exchange for their aid in restoring his throne. While some Crusaders rejected the bribe and sailed to Syria to fight the Muslims, the bulk of the crusading army attacked Constantinople in 1204. In a display of barbarism, they looted and defiled churches and massacred citizens. This shameful behavior, along with the belief that the papacy was exploiting the crusading ideal to extend its own power, weakened both the crusading zeal of Christendom and the moral authority of the pope.

Other Crusades followed, including even the Children's Crusade in 1212. Stirred by Stephen of Cloyes, a young shepherd boy who claimed that Christ had communicated with him, thousands of French peasant children, accompanied by priests, marched to Marseilles, where they expected the Mediterranean Sea to part, permitting them to continue their march to the Holy Land. When the miracle did not occur, the children boarded seven ships offered to them by William the Pig and Hugo the Iron, two seemingly pious townsmen. Two of the ships were lost in a terrible storm, and the other five were captured by Muslim pirates, with whom William and Hugo had worked out a deal. The children were sold into slavery in North Africa, and as far as is known none ever returned (one priest eventually did). At about the same time, another Children's Crusade, this one originating in Germany, also ended in the deaths of thousands of children.

Profile

Saladin

Salah al-Din Yusuf (1137–1193), known to the Western world as Saladin, recaptured Jerusalem from the Franks in 1187. Born into a prominent Kurdish family, Saladin served the emir of Syria, whose troops invaded Egypt in 1167. Rising quickly, Saladin was appointed vizier of Egypt and then confirmed as sultan of Egypt and Syria. After extending his authority over Muslim-controlled territories of Egypt, Syria, and Palestine, Saladin, deeply committed to the jihad, turned against the Franks. In particular, he vowed to liberate Islamic holy places in Jerusalem from Christian control.

In 1187, Saladin lured the Franks into an engagement at Hittin, near Tiberias, in northern Palestine. Marching all day, the exhausted and thirst-crazed Franks suffered terrible losses

British Library.

Meanwhile, the position of the Christian states in the Near East continued to deteriorate. In 1291, almost two centuries after Pope Urban's appeal, the last Christian strongholds in the Near East fell.

The Crusades had some immediate effects on Latin Christendom. They may have contributed to the decline of feudalism and the strengthening of monarchy because many lords were killed in battle or squandered their wealth financing expeditions to the Holy Land. The Crusades did foster trade between Latin Christendom and the East, but the revival of trade had already begun and would have proceeded without the Crusades. Although the Crusades sparked an interest in geography and travel and became a theme in literature, they did not significantly influence European cultural progress. The Crusaders had no contact with Muslim centers of learning in the Near East; it was through Spain and Sicily that Muslim learning penetrated Latin Christendom and helped stimulate the cultural awakening of the twelfth and thirteenth centuries. Over the centuries, some have praised the Crusades for inspiring idealism and heroism. Others, however, have castigated the movement for corrupting the Christian spirit and unleashing religious intolerance and fanaticism—including the massacre of Jews in the Rhineland and of Muslims and Jews in Jerusalem—which would lead to strife in future centuries.

Dissenters and Reformers

Freedom of religion is a modern concept; it was totally alien to the medieval outlook. Regarding itself as the possessor and guardian of divine, and therefore ultimate, truth, the church felt a profound obligation to purge Christendom of heresy—beliefs that challenged Christian orthodoxy. To the church, heretics had committed when, in desperation, they threw themselves at the prepared Muslim lines, which blocked the Franks from reaching Lake Tiberias and its life-giving water. After the victory at Hittin, Saladin's forces took several Christian strongholds, most of them surrendering without a fight. Then Saladin turned on Jerusalem.

Living up to his reputation as a man of honor and magnanimity, Saladin made the Christian inhabitants of Jerusalem a generous proposal. If the Franks surrendered, Christians would be free to leave the city with their property, and Christian pilgrims would not be harmed. But the Frankish lords would not surrender without a fight the city where Jesus was crucified. On September 20, 1187, Saladin's soldiers besieged Jerusalem and began battering its walls. A Muslim historian noted: "Then began the fiercest struggle imaginable; each side looked on the fight as an absolute religious obligation. There was no need for a superior authority to drive them on."* On October 2, the Muslims rushed through the breached walls and captured the city. In stark contrast to the Christian conquest of Jerusalem in 1099, Saladin permitted no massacre and no plundering. The Franks could escape enslavement by paying a moderate ransom, and in an extraordinary display of tolerance, Saladin guarded Christian holy places from Muslims seeking revenge for earlier Frankish brutalities.

*Excerpted in Francesco Gabriel, ed., *Arab Historians of the Crusades* (Berkeley: University of California Press, 1969), p. 130.

treason against God and were carriers of a deadly infection. Heresy was the work of Satan; lured by false ideas, people might abandon the true faith and deny themselves salvation. The church could never create a Christian world community if heretics rebelled against clerical authority and created divisions among the faithful. In the eyes of the church, heretics not only obstructed individual salvation but also undermined the foundations of society. The church believed that it had a sacred duty to eradicate this moral defect.

To compel obedience, the church used its power of excommunication. An excommunicated person could not receive the sacraments or attend church services—fearful punishments in an age of faith. In dealing with a recalcitrant ruler, the church could declare an interdict on his territory, which in effect denied the ruler's subjects the sacraments (although exceptions could be made). The church hoped that the pressure exerted by an aroused populace would compel the offending ruler to mend his ways.

The church also conducted heresy trials. Before the thirteenth century, local bishops were responsible for locating heretics and putting them on trial. Gregory IX (1227–1241) started to use Franciscans and Dominicans (see page 252) as official investigators, in effect creating a permanent tribunal, the Inquisition, directly under the pope's authority. An inquisitor and his staff established themselves in a region suspected of heresy. After taking testimony, often in secret, the inquisitors summoned suspects to answer accusations made against them. The accused were not told the names of their accusers, nor could they have legal defense or examine evidence of witnesses. They were tortured (torture had been sanctioned by Roman law), and those who persisted in their beliefs might be turned over to the civil authorities to be burned at the stake.

Dissent in the Middle Ages was often reformist in character. Inspired by the Gospels, reformers criticized the church for its wealth and involvement in worldly affairs. They called for a return to the simpler, purer life of Jesus and the Apostles. Reform movements drew support from the new class of town dwellers; the church often rebuked the way of life in towns and only slowly adjusted to the townsmen's spiritual needs.

The Waldensians. In their zeal to emulate the moral purity and material poverty of the first followers of Jesus, reform-minded dissenters attacked ecclesiastical authority. The Waldensians, followers of Peter Waldo, a rich merchant of Lyons, were a case in point. Peter was greatly moved by a passage in Matthew: "If thou wilt be perfect go sell what thou hast and give to the poor and thou shalt have treasure in heaven" (19:22). In the 1170s, Peter distributed his property to the poor and attracted both male and female supporters. Like their leader, they committed themselves to poverty and to preaching the Gospel in the vernacular, or native tongue, rather than in the church's Latin, which many Christians did not understand. The Waldensians considered themselves true Christians, faithful to the spirit of the apostolic church. Repelled by Waldensian attacks against the immorality of the clergy and by the fact that these laymen were preaching the Gospel without the permission of ecclesiastical authorities, the church condemned the movement as heretical. Despite persecution, however, the Waldensians continued to survive as a group in northern Italy.

The Cathari. Catharism was the most radical heresy to confront the medieval church. This belief represented a curious mixture of Gnosticism and Manichaeism—Eastern religious movements that had competed with Christianity in the days of the Roman Empire—and of doctrines condemned as heretical by the early church. Carried to Italy and southern France by Bulgarian missionaries, Catharism gained followers in regions where opposition to the worldliness and wealth of the clergy was already strong.

Cathari tenets differed considerably from those of the church. The Cathari believed in an eternal conflict between the forces of the god of good and those of the god of evil. Because the evil god, whom they identified with the God of the Old Testament, created the world, this earthly home was evil. The soul, spiritual in nature, was good but was trapped in wicked flesh. Because sexual activity was responsible for imprisoning the spirit in the flesh, the Cathari urged abstinence to avoid the birth of still another wicked human being. They also abstained from eggs, cheese, milk, and meat because these foods were the products of sexual activity. (This rigorous asceticism was demanded only of a select few, the *perfecti* [perfect ones]; simple believers could marry and their diets were not restricted.) The Cathari taught that, since the flesh is evil, Christ would not have taken a human form; hence he could not have suffered on the cross or have been resurrected. Nor could God have issued forth from the evil flesh of the Virgin. According to Catharism, Jesus was not God but an angel. In order to enslave people, the evil god created the church, which demonstrated its wickedness by pursuing power and wealth. Repudiating the church, the Cathari organized their own ecclesiastical hierarchy.

The center for the Catharist heresy was southern France, where a strong tradition of protest existed against the moral laxity and materialism of the clergy. When the Cathari did not submit to peaceful persuasion, Innocent III called on kings and lords to exterminate Catharism with the sword. Lasting from 1208 to 1229, the war against the Cathari was marked by brutality and fanaticism. An army of crusading knights led by a papal legate assembled in northern France; it headed south, massacring heretics. Soon command of the crusading army passed to Simon de Montfort, a minor baron with great ambition. De Montfort slaughtered suspected heretics throughout the county of Toulouse, and for a short time he held the title of count of Toulouse. The crusading knights had effectively broken the power of the nobles who had protected the heretics. Innocent III sent legates to the region to arrest and try the Cathari. Under his successor, Dominican and Franciscan inquisitors completed the task of exterminating them.

The Franciscans and the Dominicans. Driven by a zeal for reform, devout laypeople condemned the clergy for moral abuses. Sometimes their piety and resentment exploded into heresy; at other times it was channeled into movements that served the church. Such was the case with the two great orders of friars, the Franciscans and the Dominicans.

Like Peter Waldo, Saint Francis of Assisi (c. 1181–1226) came from a wealthy merchant family. After undergoing an intense religious experience, Francis abandoned his possessions and devoted his life to imitating Christ. Dressed as a beggar, he wandered into villages and towns preaching, healing, and befriending. Unlike the monks who withdrew into walled fortresses, Francis proclaimed Christ's message to the poor of the towns. Like Peter Waldo, he preached a religion of personal feeling; like Jesus, he stretched out a hand of love to the poor, to the helpless, to the sick, and even to lepers, whom everyone feared to approach. The saintly Francis soon attracted disciples, called Little Brothers, who followed in the footsteps of their leader.

To suspicious churchmen, the Little Brothers seemed to be another heretical movement protesting against a wealthy and worldly church. However, Francis respected the authority of the priesthood and the validity of the sacraments. Recognizing that such a popular movement could be useful to the church, Innocent III allowed Francis to continue his mission. Innocent hoped that the Franciscans would help keep within the church those members of the laity who had deep religious feelings but were dissatisfied with the leadership of the traditional hierarchy.

As the Franciscans grew in popularity, the papacy exercised greater control over their activities; in time, the order was transformed from a spontaneous movement of inspired laymen into an organized agent of papal policy. The Franciscans served the church as teachers and missionaries in eastern Europe, North Africa, the Near East, and China. The papacy set aside Francis's prohibition against the Brothers owning churches, houses, and lands corporately. His desire to keep the movement a lay order was abandoned when the papacy granted the Brothers the right to hear confession. Francis's opposition to formal learning as irrelevant to preaching Gospel love was rejected when the movement began to urge university education for its members. Those who protested against these changes as a repudiation of Francis's spirit were persecuted, and a few were even burned at the stake as heretics.

The Dominican order was founded by Saint Dominic (c. 1170–1221), a Spanish nobleman who had preached against the Cathari in southern France. Believing that those well versed in Christian teaching could best combat heresy, Dominic, unlike Francis, insisted that his followers engage in study. In time, the Dominicans became some of the leading theologians in the universities. Like the Franciscans, they went out into the world to preach the Gospel and to proselytize. Dominican friars became the chief operators of the Inquisition. For their zeal in fighting heresy, they were known as "hounds of the Lord."

Innocent III: The Apex of Papal Power

During the pontificate of Innocent III (1198–1216), papal theocracy reached its zenith. More than any earlier pope, Innocent made the papacy the center of European political life. In the tradition of Gregory VII, he forcefully asserted the theory of papal monarchy. As head of the church, Vicar of Christ, and successor of Saint Peter, Innocent claimed the authority to intervene in the internal affairs of secular rulers when they threatened the good order of Christendom. According to Innocent, the pope, "lower than God but higher than man . . . judges all and is judged by no one."[2] And again, "Princes have power on earth, priests over the soul. As much as the soul is worthier than the body, so much worthier is the priesthood than the monarchy. . . . No king can reign rightly unless he devoutly serve Christ's vicar."[3]

Innocent applied these principles of papal supremacy in his dealings with the princes of Europe. When King Philip Augustus of France repudiated Ingeborg of Denmark the day after their wedding and later divorced her to marry someone else, Innocent placed an interdict on France to compel Philip to take Ingeborg back. For two decades, Innocent III championed Ingeborg's cause until she finally became the French queen. When King John of England rejected the papal candidate for archbishop of Canterbury, Stephen Langton, Innocent first laid an interdict on the country. Then he excommunicated John, who expressed his defiance by confiscating church property and by forcing many bishops into exile. However, when Innocent urged Philip Augustus of France to invade England, John backed down. He accepted Innocent's nominee for archbishop, returned the property to the church, welcomed the exiles back, and, as a sign of complete capitulation, turned his kingdom over to Innocent to receive it back as a fief. Thus, as vassals of the papacy, John and his successors were obligated to do homage to the pope and to pay him a feudal tribute. Innocent also laid interdicts on the Spanish kingdoms of Castile and León and on Norway.

In addition, Pope Innocent sought to separate Sicily from the Holy Roman Empire. When the candidacy for Holy Roman Emperor was disputed, Innocent backed young Frederick II, king of Sicily and grandson of Frederick Barbarossa. In return for Innocent's backing, Frederick agreed never to unite Sicily and the Holy Roman Empire. When Frederick (1215–1250) emerged victorious over his rival, Otto of Brunswick, Innocent thought that the Holy Roman Emperor would finally be subservient to the papacy. But Frederick, breaking his promise, refused to renounce Sicily. Subsequently, Frederick II (as well as his heirs) and the successors of Innocent III waged a furious struggle for power. The outcome was a disaster for the Holy Roman Emperor, who lost Sicily and saw his authority over the German princes evaporate. Once again, because of the Italian adventures of the emperors, Germany stayed fragmented; it would remain broken into separate and independent territories until the last part of the nineteenth century.

Innocent called the Fourth Crusade against the Muslims and a crusade against the heretical Cathari. The culminating expression of Innocent's supremacy was the Fourth Lateran Council, summoned in 1215. Comprising some twelve hundred clergy and representatives of secular rulers, the council issued several far-reaching decrees. It maintained that the Eastern Orthodox church was subordinate to the Roman Catholic church, prohibited the state from taxing the clergy, and declared laws detrimental to the church null and void. The council made bishops responsible for ferreting out heretics in their dioceses and ordered secular authorities to punish convicted heretics. Insisting on high standards of behavior for the clergy, it also required each Catholic to confess his or her sins to a priest at least once a year and to perform the prescribed penance. Through this directive, the church tightened its control over the conscience of Europe. The council also decreed that in the sacrament of the Eucharist the body and blood of Christ are actually present in the bread and wine used in the sacrament. This meant that the priest at the altar was God's agent in the performance of a wondrous miracle.

Christians and Jews

In their relations with heretics, pagans, and Muslims, medieval Christians demonstrated a narrow and hostile attitude that ran counter to the Gospel message that all human beings were children of God and that Christ had suffered for all humanity. Muslims were seen, in the words of Pope Urban II, as a "vile breed," "infidels," and "enemies of God." While the clergy denounced war among Christians, they considered it a duty to wage holy war against non-Christians, and knights regarded fighting the Muslims in Spain or the Holy Land as the highest expression of the chivalric ideal.

Medieval Christians also showed hatred for Jews—a visibly alien group in a society dominated by the Christian world-view. In 1096, bands of Crusaders massacred Jews in French and German towns. In the city of Mainz, more than a thousand Jews lost their lives. Some, in an act of martyrdom, chose to kill themselves and their children rather than submit to forced baptism or face a crueler death at the hands of the Crusaders. One contemporary wrote:

> *I know not whether by a judgment of the Lord, or by some error of mind, they rose in a spirit of cruelty against the Jewish people scattered throughout these cities and slaughtered them without mercy, . . . asserting it to be their duty against the enemies of the Christian faith. . . . The Jews of [Mainz], knowing of the slaughter of their brethren, . . . fled in hope of safety to Bishop Rothard. . . . He placed the Jews in the very spacious hall of his own house, [but the crusaders] attacked the Jews in the hall with arrows and lances. Breaking the bolts and doors, they killed the Jews, about seven hundred in number, who in vain resisted the force and attack of so many thousands. They killed the women, also, and with their swords pierced tender children of whatever age and sex.*[4]

Viewing the Jews as possessions to be exploited, kings and lords taxed and fined them re-

ANTI-SEMITISM. Holding the Jews responsible for the Black Death, Christians committed mass murder. In Basel several hundred Jews were herded into a wooden house and burned to death. Some six thousand Jews were burned alive in Mainz. Flames consumed another two thousand in a huge pyre outside Strasbourg, and their property was distributed to the local townspeople. In this picture depicting the slaughter of the Jews of Strasbourg, the townspeople evidently enjoy the spectacle. (*Koninklijke Bibliotheek Albert 1st, Brussels.*)

lentlessly and periodically expelled Jews from their territories in order to confiscate their property. In 1290, Jews were expelled from England, and in 1306, from France. Between 1290 and 1293, expulsions, massacres, and forced conversions led to the virtual disappearance of a centuries-old Jewish community life in southern Italy. In Germany, savage riots periodically led to the torture and murder of Jews. In 1348–49, when the Black Death (see page 281) raged across Europe, Jews were accused of spreading the plague by poisoning well water; thousands of them were burned alive in Basel, Freiburg, Strasbourg, Mainz, and other towns.

Several factors contributed to anti-Jewish feelings during the Middle Ages. To medieval Christians, the refusal of the Jews to embrace Christianity was an act of wickedness, particularly since the church taught that the coming of Christ had been prophesied by the Old Testament. Related to this prejudice was the portrayal of the Crucifixion in the Gospels. In the minds of medieval Christians, the crime of deicide—the killing of God—eternally stained the Jews as a people, and, as Christian theologians taught, they were to remain forever in subjection to Christians. It was just such a view that led town magistrates and princes periodically to confiscate Jewish property, at times after burning the helpless Jews alive in a public spectacle. The flames of hatred were fanned by the absurd allegation that Jews, made bloodthirsty by the spilling of Christ's blood, tortured and murdered Christians, particularly children, to obtain blood for ritual purposes. This blood libel was widely believed by the credulous masses and incited numerous riots, which led to the torture, burning alive, pillaging of property, and expulsion of countless Jews, despite the fact that some popes condemned the charge as groundless.

The role of Jews as moneylenders also provoked animosity toward them. Jews were increasingly excluded from international trade and most professions and were barred from the guilds and in some areas from landholding as well. Hence virtually the only means of livelihood open to them was moneylending. This activity, which was in theory forbidden to Christians, aroused the hatred of the individual peasants, clergy, lords, and kings who did the borrowing.

The policy of the church toward the Jews was that they should not be harmed but should live in humiliation, a fitting punishment for their act of deicide and continued refusal to embrace Christianity. Thus, the Fourth Lateran Council barred Jews from public office, ordered them to remain off the streets during Christian festivals, and required them to wear a distinguishing badge on their clothing, a symbol of their degradation. Christian art, literature, and religious instruction depicted the Jews in a derogatory manner, often identifying them with the Devil, who was very real and very terrifying to medieval Christians. Such people deserved no mercy, reasoned medieval Christians. Indeed, nothing was too bad for them. Because Jews were seen as evil allies of Satan engaged in a diabolical plot against God and Christendom, Jew-hatred was regarded as an expression of Christian virtue. Deeply etched into the minds and hearts of Christians, the distorted image of the Jew as a contemptible creature persisted in the European mentality into the twentieth century.

Despite their precarious position, medieval Jews maintained their faith, expanded their tradition of biblical and legal scholarship, and developed a flourishing Hebrew literature. The work of Jewish translators, doctors, and philosophers contributed substantially to the flowering of medieval culture in the High Middle Ages. The foremost Jewish scholar of the Middle Ages was Moses ben Maimon (1135–1204), also called by the Greek name Maimonides. He was born in Córdoba, Spain, then under Muslim rule. After his family emigrated from Spain, Maimonides went to Egypt, where he became physician to the sultan. During his lifetime, Maimonides achieved fame as a philosopher, theologian, mathematician, and physician. He was recognized as the leading Jewish sage of his day, and his writings were respected by Christian and Muslim thinkers as well. Like Christian and Muslim philosophers, Maimonides tried to harmonize faith with reason, to reconcile the Hebrew Scriptures and the Talmud (Jewish biblical commentary) with Greek philosophy. In his writings on ethical themes, Maimonides demonstrated piety, wisdom, and humanity.

❖ ❖ ❖

Notes

1. Quoted in J. W. Thompson, *Social and Economic History of the Middle Ages* (New York: Frederick Ungar, 1959), 2:772.
2. Excerpted in Brian Tierney, ed., *The Crisis of Church and State, 1050–1300* (Englewood Cliffs, N.J.: Prentice-Hall, 1964), p. 132.
3. Quoted in James Westfall Thompson and Edgar Nathaniel Johnson, *An Introduction to Medieval Europe* (New York: Norton, 1937), p. 645.
4. Excerpted in A. C. Krey, ed., *The First Crusade: The Accounts of Eye-Witnesses and Participants* (Princeton, N.J.: Princeton University Press, 1921), pp. 54–55.

Suggested Reading

Brooke, Christopher, and Rosalind Brooke, *Popular Religion in the Middle Ages* (1984). How the common people viewed the clergy, the Bible, the saints, judgment, heaven, and hell.

Cantor, Norman F., ed., *The Medieval Reader* (1994). Well-chosen firsthand accounts.

Chazan, Robert, *Medieval Stereotypes and Modern Antisemitism* (1997). The deterioration of the image of the Jew in the High Middle Ages.

Cohen, Jeremy, *The Friars and the Jews* (1982). The evolution of medieval anti-Judaism among the Dominicans and Franciscans.

Duby, Georges, ed., *A History of Private Life, vol. 2, Revelations of the Medieval World* (1988).

Among the topics covered are sex, child-rearing, old age, and aristocratic households.

Gimpel, Jean, *The Medieval Machine* (1977). Technological advances in the Middle Ages.

Gregg, Joan Young, *Devils, Women, and Jews* (1997). The demonization of women and Jews in medieval sermon stories.

Lawrence, C. H., *Medieval Monasticism* (1989). Discusses various monastic movements and the mendicant friars.

LeGoff, Jacques, ed., *The Medieval World* (1990). Profiles of medieval people, including the monk, the warrior, the peasant, the merchant, and the intellectual, written by leading medievalists.

Lopez, R. S., *The Commercial Revolution of the Middle Ages, 950–1350* (1976). How an undeveloped society succeeded in developing itself.

Mayer, H. E., *The Crusades* (1972). A short, scholarly treatment.

Mundy, J. H., *Europe in the High Middle Ages, 1150–1309* (1973). All phases of society in the High Middle Ages.

Pernoud, Regine, ed., *The Crusades* (1964). A compilation of original sources.

Peters, Edward, *Inquisition* (1988). A recent account by a leading scholar.

Phillips, J. R. S., *The Medieval Expansion of Europe* (1990). Contacts between Europe and other parts of the world from the tenth through the fifteenth century.

Pounds, N. J. G., *An Economic History of Medieval Europe* (1974). A lucid survey.

Rorig, Fritz, *The Medieval Town* (1971). A study of medieval urban life.

Schafer, William, ed., *The Gregorian Epoch* (1964). Readings on the Cluniac movement, Gregory VII, and the Investiture Controversy.

Strayer, J. R., *On the Medieval Origins of the Modern State* (1970). Characteristics of medieval state building.

Synan, Edward A., *The Popes and the Jews in the Middle Ages* (1965). An exploration of Jewish-Christian relations in the Middle Ages.

Tierney, Brian, ed., *The Crisis of Church and State, 1050–1300* (1964). Contains many documents illustrating this crucial medieval development.

Trachtenberg, Joshua, *The Devil and the Jews* (1961). The medieval conception of the Jew and its relationship to modern anti-Semitism.

White, Lynn, Jr., *Medieval Technology and Social Change* (1964). A study of medieval advances in technology.

Review Questions

1. What advances in agriculture occurred during the Middle Ages and what effect did they have?
2. What factors contributed to the rise of towns? What was the significance of the medieval town?
3. Identify and explain the importance of the following: William the Conqueror, common law, Magna Carta, and Parliament.
4. Identify and explain the significance of the following: Hugh Capet, Philip Augustus, Louis IX, and Estates General.
5. Why did Germany not achieve unity during the Middle Ages?
6. What is the historical significance of the medieval representative institution?
7. What were the goals of Cluniac reformers?
8. How did Gregory VII view the papacy? How was the Investiture Controversy resolved? What was the significance of this controversy?
9. Why did Urban II call a crusade against the Turks? What prompted lords and commoners to go on a crusade? What was the final importance and outcome of the Crusades?
10. Why did the church regard Waldensians and Cathari as heretics?
11. What were the achievements of Saint Francis and Saint Dominic?
12. Papal power reached its height under Innocent III. Discuss this statement.
13. What factors contributed to the rise of anti-Semitism during the Middle Ages? How does anti-Semitism demonstrate the power of mythical thinking?
14. The High Middle Ages showed many signs of recovery and vitality. Discuss this statement.

Chapter 11

The Flowering of Medieval Culture: The Christian Synthesis

Notre-Dame de la Belle Verrière, c. 1170, Notre-Dame de Chartes, France. (© Clive Hicks.)

■ **Revival of Learning**

■ **The Medieval World-View**
The Universe: Higher and Lower Worlds
The Individual: Sinful but Redeemable

■ **Philosophy-Theology**
Saint Anselm and Abelard
The Recovery of Aristotle
Saint Thomas Aquinas: Synthesis of Christian Belief and Reason
Strict Aristotelianism: The Challenge to Orthodoxy

■ **Science**

■ **The Recovery of Roman Law**

■ **Literature**

■ **Architecture**

Europe in the High Middle Ages showed considerable vitality. The population grew, long-distance trade revived, new towns emerged, states started to take shape, and papal power increased. The culminating expression of this recovery and resurgence was the cultural flowering in philosophy, the visual arts, and literature. Creative intellects achieved on a cultural level what the papacy accomplished on an institutional level: the integration of life around a Christian viewpoint. The High Middle Ages saw the restoration of some of the learning of the ancient world, the rise of universities, the emergence of an original form of architecture (the Gothic), and the erection of an imposing system of thought, called *scholasticism*. Medieval theologian-philosophers fashioned Christian teachings into an all-embracing philosophy, which represented the spiritual character of medieval civilization. They perfected what Christian thinkers in the Roman Empire had initiated and what the learned men of the Early Middle Ages were groping for: a synthesis of Greek philosophy and Christian revelation.

Revival of Learning

In the late eleventh century, Latin Christendom began to experience a cultural revival; all areas of life showed vitality and creativeness. In the twelfth and thirteenth centuries, a rich civilization with a distinctive style united the educated elite in the lands from England to Sicily. Gothic cathedrals, an enduring testament to the creativeness of the religious impulse, were erected throughout Europe. Universities sprang up in several cities. Roman authors were again read, and their style was imitated. The quality of written Latin—the language of the church, learning, and education—improved, and secular and religious poetry, both in Latin and in the vernacular, abounded. Roman law emerged anew in Italy, spread to northern Europe, and regained its importance (lost since Roman times) as worthy of study. Some key works of ancient Greece were translated into Latin and studied in universities. Employing the rational tradition of Greece, men of genius harmonized Christian doctrines and Greek philoso-

Map 11.1 Medieval Centers of Learning Medieval universities established in the West a tradition of learning that never died. There is direct continuity between the universities of our own day and the medieval centers of learning.

SCHOOL OF BOLOGNA MANUSCRIPT ILLUMINATION. After a text had been transcribed, it could then be illuminated. This was accomplished by applying decoration in the spaces left blank by the scribe. One illuminator was charged with the pen decoration, executed with colored inks. Another was the overseer of all the painted ornamentation, including borders, frames, and decorated letters. The amount of time required to illuminate a manuscript was dependent on the size of the undertaking and how many layers of color were used, because each fresh layer required its own drying time. (*Staatliche Museen zu Berlin/Bildarchiv Preussischer Kulturbesitz.*)

phy. During this period, the status and influence of learned men grew considerably.

Several conditions contributed to this cultural explosion, known as the Twelfth-Century Awakening. As attacks of Vikings, Muslims, and Magyars ended and kings and great lords imposed more order and stability, people found greater opportunities for travel and communication. The revival of trade and the growth of towns created a need for literacy and provided the wealth required to support learning. Increasing contact with Islamic and Byzantine cultures in Spain and Sicily led to the translation into Latin of ancient Greek works preserved by these Eastern civilizations. By preserving Greek philosophy and science—and by commentating creatively on these classical works—Islamic civilization acted as a bridge between antiquity and the cultural revival of the High Middle Ages. The Twelfth-Century Awakening was also kindled by the legacy of the Carolingian Renaissance, whose cultural lights had dimmed but never wholly vanished in the period of disorder after the dissolution of Charlemagne's empire.

In the Early Middle Ages, the principal educational centers were the monastic schools. During the twelfth century, cathedral schools in towns gained importance. Paid a stipend by a local church, their teachers taught grammar, rhetoric, and logic. But the chief expression of expanding intellectual life was the university, a distinct creation of the Middle Ages.

The origins of the medieval university are obscure and varied. The first universities were not planned but grew spontaneously. They developed as students eager for knowledge and skills needed for high positions in government gathered around prominent teachers. The renewed importance of Roman law for business and politics, for example, drew students to Bologna to study with acknowledged masters.

The university was really a guild or corporation of masters or students who joined together to defend their interests against church or town authorities or the townspeople. A university might emerge when students united because of common needs, such as protection against townspeople who overcharged them for rooms and necessities. Organized into a body, students could also make demands on their instructors. At Bologna, professors faced fines for being absent or for giving lectures that drew fewer than five students; they were required to leave behind a deposit as security to ensure their return if they took a journey. A corporation of students formed the University at Bologna. The University of Paris, which evolved from the Cathedral School of Notre Dame, was the creation of a corporation of masters.

University students attended lectures, prepared for examinations, and earned degrees. They studied grammar, rhetoric, logic, arithmetic, geometry, astronomy, music, medicine, and, when ready, church law and theology, which was considered queen of the sciences. The curriculum relied heavily on Latin translations of ancient texts, chiefly the works of Aristotle. In mathematics and astronomy, students read Latin translations of Euclid and Ptolemy, while students of medicine studied the works of two great medical men of the ancient world, Hippocrates and Galen.

But sometimes students followed other pursuits. Instead of studying, they turned to drinking, gambling, and fighting. At Oxford University, it was reported that students "went through the streets with swords and bows and arrows and assaulted all who passed by."[1] Fathers complained that their sons preferred "play to work and strumming a guitar while the others are at their studies."[2] Students often faced financial problems, and they knew whom to ask for help: "Well-beloved father, to ease my debts . . . at the tavern, at the baker's, with the doctor . . . and to pay . . . the laundress and the barber, I send you word of greetings and of money."[3]

In *The Canterbury Tales,* Geoffrey Chaucer (c. 1340–1400), the leading English writer of the Middle Ages, provided a memorable description of the serious, dedicated medieval student:

> *An* Oxford Cleric, *still a student though,*
> *One who had taken logic long ago,*
> *Was there; his horse was thinner than a rake,*
> *And he was not too fat, I undertake,*
> *But had a hollow look, a sober stare;*
> *The thread upon his overcoat was bare.*
> *He had found no preferment in the church*
> *And he was too unworldly to make search*
> *For secular employment. By his bed*
> *He preferred having twenty books in red*
> *And black, of Aristotle's philosophy,*
> *To having fine clothes, fiddle or psaltery.*
> . . . .
> *The thought of moral virtue filled his speech*
> *And he would gladly learn, and gladly teach.*[4]

Universities performed a crucial function in the Middle Ages. Students learned the habit of reasoned argument. Universities trained professional secretaries and lawyers, who administered the affairs of church and state and of the growing cities; these institutions of learning also produced theologians and philosophers, who shaped the climate of public opinion. Since the curriculum and the texts studied were essentially the same in all lands, the learning disseminated by universities tightened the cultural bonds that united Christian Europe. Medieval universities established in the West a tradition of learning that has never died; there is direct continuity between the universities of our own day and the medieval ones.

The Medieval World-View

A distinctive world-view, based essentially on Christianity, evolved during the Middle Ages. This outlook differed from both the Greco-Roman and the modern scientific and secular views of the world. In the Christian view, not the individual but the Creator determined what constituted the good life. Thus, reason that was not illuminated by revelation was either wrong or inadequate, for God had revealed the proper rules for the regulation of individual and social life. Ultimately, the good life was not of this world but came from a union with God in a higher world. This Christian belief as formulated by the church made life and death purposeful and intelligible; it dominated the thought of the Middle Ages.

The Universe: Higher and Lower Worlds

Medieval thinkers sharply differentiated between spirit and matter, between a realm of grace and an earthly realm, between a higher world of perfection and a lower world of imperfection. Moral values derived from the higher world, which was also the final destination for the faithful. Two sets of laws operated in the medieval universe, one for the heavens and one for the earth. The cosmos was a giant ladder, with God at the summit; earth, composed of base matter, stood at the bottom, just above hell, where, farthest from God, dwelled Satan, his evil spirits, and the souls of the damned.

From Aristotle and Ptolemy, medieval thinkers inherited the theory of an earth-centered universe—the *geocentric theory*—which they imbued with Christian symbolism. The geocentric theory held that revolving around the motionless earth at uniform speeds were seven transparent spheres, in which were embedded each of the seven "planets"—the moon, Mercury, Venus, the sun, Mars, Jupiter, and Saturn. A sphere of fixed stars (that is, the stars, like chandeliers in a ceiling, stayed in a constant relationship to each other) enclosed this planetary system. Above the firmament of the stars were the three heavenly spheres. The outermost, the Empyrean Heaven, was the abode of God and the Elect. Through the sphere below—the Prime Mover—God transmitted motion to the planetary spheres. Underneath this was the lowermost sphere, the Crystalline Heaven, composed of a clear transparent substance.

An earth-centered universe accorded with the Christian idea that God created the universe for men and women and that salvation was the primary aim of life. Because God had created people in his image, they deserved this central position. Though they might be at the bottom of the cosmic ladder, only they, of all living things, had the capacity to ascend to heaven, the realm of perfection.

God as Architect of the Universe, French Old Testament Miniature Painting, thirteenth century. To the medieval Christian, God was the creator of the world. The universe had a known hierarchical order, a "great chain of being" extending from God downward to the lowest form of being. (*Osterreichische Nationalbibliothek, Vienna.*)

Also acceptable to the Christian mentality was the sharp distinction drawn by Aristotle between the world above the moon and the one below it. Aristotle held that terrestrial bodies were made of four elements: earth, water, air, fire. Celestial bodies, which occupied the region encompassing the moon and the area above, were composed of a fifth element, the ether—too clear, too pure, and too perfect to be found on earth. The planets and stars existed in a world apart; they were made of the divine ether and followed celestial laws, which did not apply to earthly objects. Whereas earthly bodies underwent change—ice converting to water, a burning log converting to ashes—heavenly objects were incorruptible, immune to all change. Unlike earthly objects, they were indestructible.

Heavenly bodies also followed different laws of motion than earthly objects. Aristotle said that it was natural for celestial bodies to move eternally in uniform circles, such motion being considered a sign of perfection. According to Aristotle, it was also natural for heavy bodies (stone) to fall downward and for light objects (fire, smoke) to move upward toward the celestial world; the falling stone and the rising smoke were finding their natural place in the universe. This view of the universe would be shattered by the Scientific Revolution of the sixteenth and seventeenth centuries.

The Individual: Sinful but Redeemable

At the center of medieval belief was the idea of a perfect God, who had conceived and created the universe, and wretched and sinful human beings. God had given Adam and Eve freedom to choose; rebellious and presumptuous, they had used their freedom to disobey God. In doing so, they made evil an intrinsic part of the human personality. But God, who had not stopped loving human beings, showed them the way out of sin. God became man and died so that human beings might be saved. Men and women were weak, egocentric, and sinful. With God's grace, they could overcome their sinful nature and gain salvation; without grace, they were utterly helpless.

The medieval individual's understanding of self stemmed from a comprehension of the universe as a hierarchy instituted by and culminating in God. On earth, the basest objects were lifeless stones devoid of souls; higher than stones were plants, endowed with a primitive type of soul, which allowed for reproduction and growth. Still higher were animals, which had the capacity for motion and sensation. The highest of the animals were human beings; unlike other animals, they could grasp some part of universal truth. Far superior to them were the angels, for they apprehended God's truth without difficulty. At the summit of this graduated universe was God, who was pure Being, without limitation, and the source of all existence. God's revelation reached down to humanity through the hierarchical order. From God, revelation passed to the angels, who were also arranged hierarchically. From the angels, the truth reached men and women, grasped first by prophets and apostles and then by the multitudes. Thus, all things in the universe, from angels, men, and women to the lowest earthly objects, occupied a place peculiar to their nature and were linked by God in a great, unbroken chain.

Medieval individuals derived a sense of security from this hierarchical universe, in which the human position was clearly defined. Although they were sinners who dwelt on a corruptible earth, at the bottom of the cosmic hierarchy, they *could* ascend to the higher world of perfection above the moon. As children of God, they enjoyed the unique distinction that each human soul was precious; all individuals commanded respect, unless they were heretics. (A heretic forfeited dignity and could be justly executed.)

Medieval thinkers also arranged knowledge in a hierarchical order: knowledge of the spiritual surpassed all worldly knowledge, all the sciences. Therefore, the true Christian understood that the pursuit of worldly knowledge could not proceed properly unless guided by divine revelation. To know what God wanted of the individual was the summit of self-knowledge and permitted entry into heaven. Thus, God was both the source and the end of knowledge. The human capacity to think and to act freely constituted the image of God within each individual; it ennobled man and woman and offered them the promise of associating with God in heaven.

True, human nobility derived from intelligence and free will. But if individuals disobeyed God, they brought misery on themselves. To challenge the divine will with human will constituted the sin of pride, contempt for God, and a violation of the divine order. Such sinful behavior invited self-destruction.

In the medieval view, neither nature nor the human being could be understood apart from God and his revelation. All reality emanated from God and was purposefully arranged in a spiritual hierarchy. Three great expressions of this view of life were scholastic philosophy, *The Divine Comedy* of Dante, and the Gothic cathedral.

Philosophy-Theology

Medieval philosophy, or scholasticism, applied reason to revelation. It explained and clarified Christian teachings by means of concepts and principles of logic derived from Greek philosophy. Scholastics tried to show that the teachings of faith, though not derived from reason, were not contrary to reason, that logic could confirm church dogma. They tried to prove through reason what they already held to be true through faith. For example, the existence of God and the immortality of the soul, which every Christian accepted as articles of faith, could also, they thought, be demonstrated by reason. In struggling to harmonize faith with reason, medieval thinkers constructed an extraordinary synthesis of Christian revelation and Greek thought.

The scholastic masters used reason not to challenge but to serve faith: to elucidate, clarify, and buttress it. They did not break with the central concern of Christianity, that of earning God's grace and achieving salvation. Although this goal could be realized solely through faith, scholastic thinkers insisted that a science of nature did not obstruct the pursuit of grace and that philosophy could assist the devout in the contemplation of God. They did not reject those Christian beliefs that were beyond the grasp of human reason and therefore could not be deduced by rational argument. Instead, they held that such truths rested entirely on revelation and were to be accepted on faith. To medieval thinkers, reason did not have an independent existence but ultimately had to acknowledge a suprarational, superhuman standard of truth. They wanted rational thought to be directed by faith for Christian ends and guided by scriptural and ecclesiastical authority. Ultimately, faith had the final word.

Not all Christian thinkers welcomed the use of reason. Regarding Greek philosophy as an enemy of faith (would not reason lead people to question belief in miracles?), a fabricator of heresies (would not reason encourage disbelief in essential church teachings?), and an obstacle to achieving communion of the soul with God (would not a deviation from church teachings, under the influence of pagan philosophy, deprive people of salvation?), conservative theologians opposed the use of reason to elucidate Christian revelation. For if reason could demonstrate the proof of Christian teachings, as its advocates insisted, it could also be used, warned conservatives, to challenge and reject those teachings. In a sense, the conservatives were right. By revitalizing Greek thought, medieval philosophy nurtured a powerful force that eventually would shatter the medieval concepts of nature and society and weaken Christianity. Modern Western thought was created by thinkers who refused to subordinate reason to religious authority. Reason proved to be a double-edged sword: it both ennobled and undermined the medieval world-view.

Saint Anselm and Abelard

An early scholastic, Saint Anselm (1033–1109) was abbot of the Benedictine monastery of Bec in Normandy. He used rational argument to serve the interests of faith. Like Augustine before him and other thinkers who followed him, Anselm said that faith was a precondition for understanding. Without belief there could be no proper knowledge. He developed philosophical proof for the existence of God. Anselm argued as follows: We can conceive of no being greater than God. But if God were to exist only in thought and not in actuality, his greatness would be limited; he would be less than perfect. Hence he exists. Anselm's motive and method reveal something about the essence of medieval philosophy. He does not begin as a modern might: "If it can be proven that God exists, I will adopt the creed of Christianity; if not, I will either deny God's existence (atheism) or reserve judgment (agnosticism)." Rather, Anselm accepts God's existence as an established fact because he believes what Holy Scripture says and what the church teaches. He then proceeds to employ logical argument to demonstrate that God can be known not only through faith but also through reason. He would never use reason to subvert what he knows to be true by faith. In general, this attitude would characterize later medieval thinkers, who also applied reason to faith.

As a young teacher of theology at the Cathedral School of Notre Dame, Peter Abelard (1079–1142) acquired a reputation for brilliance and combativeness. His tragic affair with Héloise, whom he tutored and seduced, has become one of the great romances in Western literature. Héloise had a child and entered a nunnery; Abelard was castrated on orders of Canon Fulbert, Héloise's guardian, and sought temporary refuge in a monastery. After resuming his career as a teacher in Paris, Abelard again had to seek refuge, this time for writing an essay on the Trinity that church officials found offensive. After further difficulties and flights, he again returned to Paris to teach dialectics. Not long

Profile

Abelard and Héloise

Scala/Art Resource, NY.

Our knowledge of the love affair of Abelard and Héloise derives essentially from the candid autobiography Abelard wrote—something highly unusual for medieval scholars—and the exchange of letters between the two lovers. Abelard was nearly forty when Fulbert, the canon of Notre Dame, asked the famous scholar to tutor his bright and attractive seventeen-year-old niece. In *The Story of My Misfortunes,* Abelard described the tutorial:

> *Under a pretence of study, we gave ourselves up wholly to love. The lessons furnished us with the means to those mysterious communings dictated by vows of love. The books were open, but our words were more of love than of philosophy, and there were more kisses than explanations. My hands wandered more often to her breast than to our books and our eyes turned lovingly on one another more often than on the texts before us.**

When Héloise gave birth to a son, Abelard proposed marriage. Sharing the widely accepted view that married life was a barrier to scholarly pursuits, Héloise at first resisted but then relented. The couple tried to hide their marriage by living apart, but the news of their betrothal spread quickly. Canon Fulbert was

afterward, his most determined opponent, Bernard of Clairvaux, accused Abelard of using the method of dialectical argument to attack faith. To Bernard, a monk and mystic, subjecting revealed truth to critical analysis was fraught with danger:

> *[T]he deepest matters become the subject of undignified wrangling. . . . Virtues and vices are discussed with no trace of moral feelings, the sacraments of the Church with no evidence of faith, the mystery of the Holy Trinity with no spirit of humility or sobriety: all is presented in a distorted form, introduced in a way different from the one we learned and are used to.*[5]

Hearkening to Bernard's powerful voice, the church condemned Abelard and confined him to a monastery for the rest of his days.

Abelard believed that it was important to apply reason to faith and that careful and constant questioning led to wisdom. Since all knowledge derives from God, said Abelard, it is good to pursue learning. In *Sic et Non* (Yes and No), he took 150 theological issues and, by presenting passages from the Bible and the church fathers, showed that there pleased with the marriage, which salvaged his niece's honor. However, when Héloise, always concerned with the best interests of her beloved, swore that no marriage had taken place, Fulbert placed her in a convent and subjected Abelard "to the most barbarous and shameful revenge."

The castrated Abelard retreated to the Abbey of Saint Denis, but soon resumed his teaching at a school near the monastery. His talents undiminished, Abelard continued to attract many students. But his misfortunes persisted. In 1121, a church council ruled that his *Treatise on the Unity and Trinity of God* be burned and that its author retire to Saint Denis.

More than a decade after their romance, Abelard was the reform-minded abbot of Saint Gildas and Héloise the abbess of the Paraclete, a newly established convent. Still in love, Héloise wrote to Abelard:

> *Those lovers' delights we enjoyed together were so sweet to me that I cannot find it in my heart to condemn them, or even wipe out the memory of them without pain. Whichever way I turn, they are always in my sight, they and their desires. Even while I sleep, their illusions pursue me. Always, even in the most solemn moments of the mass, when prayer should be most pure, the obscene images of these pleasures still enthrall my poor soul so that I give myself up to this depravity rather than to prayer. I, who should bemoan what I have done, sigh instead after that which I have lost. And not only those things we have done, but the very times and places in which we did them together are so graven in my heart that I see them all again with you and am not free from them even in my sleep. Sometimes even the movements of my body reveal the thoughts that are in my soul, and they betray themselves by involuntary words. I am so unhappy and with what justice I repeat the lament of a soul in torment: "Wretched that I am, who will deliver me from this living death?"*

In a gentle rebuke, Abelard replied that their sexual encounter, in which he "slaked my miserable desires [did] not deserve the name of love," and beseeched her to direct all her love to Christ. Abelard died in 1142 at the age of sixty-three. When Héloise died twenty-two years later, also at the age of sixty-three, she was buried at his side. Their remains are still together, though not in the original gravesite.

---

*The passages from Abelard's *The Story of My Misfortunes* and from his correspondence with Héloise are taken from the admirable translations of selected passages from these works found in Philippe Wolf, *The Cultural Awakening,* trans. Anne Carter (New York: Pantheon, 1968), pt. 1, chap. 3.

were conflicting opinions. He suggested that the divergent opinions of authorities could be reconciled through proper use of dialectics. But like Anselm before him, Abelard did not intend to refute traditional church doctrines. Reason would buttress, not weaken, the authority of faith. Abelard wrote after his condemnation in 1141:

> *I will never be a philosopher, if this is to speak against St. Paul, I would not be an Aristotle if this were to separate me from Christ. . . . I have set my building on the cornerstone on which Christ has built his Church. . . . I rest upon the rock that cannot be moved.*[6]

The Recovery of Aristotle

During the Early Middle Ages, scholars in the Muslim world translated the works of Aristotle into Arabic and wrote commentaries on them. The preservation of ancient Greek thought was a major contribution of Islamic civilization. During the High Middle Ages, these works were translated into Latin by learned Europeans.

The introduction into Latin Christendom of the major works of Aristotle created a dilemma for religious authorities. Aristotle's comprehensive philosophy of nature and man, a product of human reason alone, conflicted in many instances with essential Christian doctrine. For Aristotle, God was an impersonal principle that accounted for order and motion in the universe, the unmoved mover. For Christianity, not only was God responsible for order in the physical universe, but he was also a personal being—a loving Father concerned about the deeds of his children. Whereas Christianity taught that God created the universe at a specific point in time, Aristotle held that the universe was eternal. Nor did Aristotle believe in the personal immortality of the soul, another cardinal principle of Christianity. For Aristotle, it was impossible for the soul to exist independently of the body.

Some church officials feared that the dissemination of Aristotle's natural philosophy would endanger faith. Would the teachings of Christ and the church fathers have to answer to pagan philosophy? Would Athens prevail over Jerusalem? At various times in the first half of the thirteenth century, the teaching of Aristole's scientific works was forbidden at the University of Paris. However, because the ban did not apply throughout Christendom and was not consistently enforced in Paris, Aristotle's philosophy continued to be studied.

The Triumph of Saint Thomas Aquinas: Wall Painting, the Spanish Chapel, Church of Santa Maria Novella, Florence, fourteenth century. In a church built by his fellow Dominican friars, the saint, theologian, and philosopher Thomas Aquinas sits enthroned, expounding Christian theology illuminated by the principles of Aristotle. This painting is by Taddeo Gaddi, a pupil of the master painter Giotto. (*Photo Alinari-Giraudon.*)

Saint Thomas Aquinas: Synthesis of Christian Belief and Reason

Rejecting the position of conservatives, who insisted that philosophy would contaminate faith, Saint Thomas Aquinas (c. 1225–1274) upheld the value of human reason and natural knowledge. He set about reconciling Aristotelianism with Christianity. Aquinas taught at Paris and at various institutions in Italy. His greatest work, *Summa Theologica,* is a systematic exposition of Christian thought. As a devout Catholic and member of the Dominican order, he of course accepted the truth of revelation. He never used reason to undermine faith.

Aquinas divided revealed truth into two categories: beliefs whose truth can be demonstrated by reason and beliefs that reason cannot prove to be either true or false. For example, he believed that philosophical speculation could prove the existence of God and the immortality of the human soul but could not prove or disprove the doctrines of the Trinity, the Incarnation, and the Redemption, because those articles of faith wholly surpassed the capacity of human reason. This fact, however, did not detract from their certainty. Doctrines of faith did not require rational proof to be valid. They were true because they originated with God, whose authority is unshakable.

Can the teachings of faith conflict with the evidence of reason? For Aquinas, the answer was emphatically no. He said that revelation could not be the enemy of reason because revelation did not contradict reason and reason did not corrupt the purity of faith. Revelation supplemented and perfected reason. If there appeared to be a conflict between philosophy and faith, it was certain that reason had erred somewhere, for the doctrines of faith were infallible. Since *both* faith and reason came from God, they were not in competition with each other but, properly understood, supported each other and formed an organic unity. Consequently, reason should not be feared, for it was another avenue to God. Because there was an inherent agreement between true faith and correct reason—they both ultimately stemmed from God—contradictions between the two were only a misleading appearance. Although philosophy had not yet been able to resolve the dilemma, for God no such contradictions existed. In heaven, human beings would attain complete knowledge, as well as complete happiness. While on earth, however, they must allow faith to guide reason; they must not permit reason to oppose or undermine faith.

Because reason was no enemy of faith, applying it to revelation need not be feared. As human reasoning became more proficient, said Aquinas, it also became more Christian, and apparent incompatibilities between faith and reason disappeared. Recognizing that both faith and reason point to the same truth, the wise person accepts the guidance of religion in all questions that relate directly to knowledge needed for salvation. There also existed a wide range of knowledge that God had not revealed and that was not required for salvation. Into this category fell much knowledge about the natural world of things and creatures, which human beings had perfect liberty to explore.

Thus, in exalting God, Aquinas also paid homage to human intelligence, proclaimed the value of rational activity, and asserted the importance of physical reality revealed through human senses. Consequently, he valued the natural philosophy of Aristotle. Correctly used, Aristotelian thought would assist faith. Aquinas's great effort was to synthesize Aristotelianism with the divine revelation of Christianity. That the two could be harmonized he had no doubt. He made use of Aristotelian categories in his five proofs of God's existence. In his first proof, for example, Aquinas argued that a thing cannot move itself. Whatever is moved must be moved by something else, and that by something else again. "Therefore, it is necessary to arrive at a first mover, moved by no other; and this everyone understands to be God."[7]

Aquinas also found a place for Aristotle's conception of man. Aristotle, said Aquinas, was correct to regard man as a natural being and to devise for man a natural system of ethics and politics. Aristotle, however, did not go far enough. Aquinas said that, in addition, human beings are also special children of God. Consequently, they must define their lives according to the standards God has set. Aquinas insisted that much of what Aristotle had to say about man was accurate and valuable, for he was a gifted philosopher, but he possessed no knowledge of God. The higher insight provided by revelation did not disqualify what natural reason had to say about human beings but improved on it.

Aquinas upheld the value of reason. To love the intellect was to honor God and not to diminish the truth of faith. He had confidence in the power of the rational mind to comprehend most of the truths of revelation, and he insisted that in nontheological questions about specific things in nature—those questions not affecting salvation—people should trust only to reason and experience.

Aquinas gave new importance to the empirical world and to scientific speculation and human knowledge. The traditional medieval view, based largely on Saint Augustine, drew a sharp distinction between the higher world of grace and the lower world of nature, between the world of spirit and the world of sense experience. Knowledge derived from the natural world was often seen as an obstacle to true knowledge. Aquinas altered this tradition by affirming the importance of knowledge of the social order and the physical world. He gave human reason and worldly knowledge a new dignity. Thus, the City of Man was not merely a sinful place from which people tried to escape in order to enter God's city; it was worthy of investigation and understanding. But Aquinas remained a medieval thinker, for he always maintained that secular knowledge should be supervised and corrected by revealed truth, and he never questioned the truth of the medieval Christian view of the world and the individual. As historian Steven Ozment explains,

> *Aquinas brought reason and revelation together, but strictly as unequals. . . . In this union, reason, philosophy, nature, secular*

> *man and the state ultimately had value only in subservience to the higher goals of revelation, theology, grace, religious man, and the church. . . . Thomist theology was the most sophisticated statement of the medieval belief in the secondary significance of the lay and secular world, a congenial ideology for a church besieged by independent and aggressive secular political powers.*[8]

Strict Aristotelianism: The Challenge to Orthodoxy

Some teachers in the Faculty of Arts at Paris, relying heavily on the commentaries of Averroës, the great Muslim thinker (see page 208), found Aquinas's approach of Christianizing or explaining away Aristotle unacceptable. Unlike Aquinas, they did not seek to reconcile Aristotle's philosophy with Christian dogma. They held that certain Aristotelian propositions contradicting faith were philosophically true, or at least could not be proven false. These teachers maintained that it was impossible to refute these propositions by natural reason alone—that is, without recourse to faith. For example, by reason alone Aristotle had demonstrated that the world was eternal and that the processes of nature were unalterable. The first doctrine conflicted with the Christian belief that God created the universe at a point in time; the second conflicted with the belief that God could work miracles.

But these teachers did not take the next step and argue that Aristotle was correct and faith wrong. They maintained only that Aristotle's arguments could not be refuted by natural reason, and that philosophers—as philosophers, not as Christians—should base their judgments on rational arguments only, not on miracles and revelation. These strict Aristotelians did not deny the truths of faith, but they did assert that natural reason could construct conclusive proofs for propositions that the church had explicitly stated to be false.

In 1277, the bishop of Paris condemned 219 propositions, many of them taught by these expositors of Aristotle at the University of Paris. Included in the condemnation were some propositions held by the great Aquinas. This move attempted to prevent Aristotle's philosophical naturalism from undermining Christian beliefs. Consequently, the condemnation was a triumph for conservative theologians, who had grown increasingly worried about the inroads made by Aristotelianism. To them, even the Christian Aristotelianism of Aquinas was suspect.

Condemnations generally hinder the pursuit of knowledge, but, ironically, the condemnation of 1277 may have had the opposite effect. It led some thinkers to examine critically and reject elements of Aristotle's natural philosophy. This development may have served as a prelude to modern science, which, born in the sixteenth and seventeenth centuries, grew out of a rejection of Aristotelian physics.

Science

During the Early Middle Ages, few scientific works from the ancient world were available to western Europeans. Scientific thought was at its lowest ebb since its origination more than a thousand years earlier in Greece. By contrast, both Islamic and Byzantine civilizations preserved and, in some instances, added to the legacy of Greek science. In the High Middle Ages, however, many ancient texts were translated from Greek and Arabic into Latin and entered Latin Christendom for the first time. The principal centers of translation were Spain, where Christian and Muslim civilizations met, and Sicily, which had been controlled by Byzantium up to the last part of the ninth century and then by Islam until Christian Normans completed the conquest of the island by 1091. Often learned Jews, who knew both Arabic and Latin, served as translators. These translations of ancient Greek scientific works and of Arabic commentaries stimulated interest in nature.

In the thirteenth and fourteenth centuries, a genuine scientific movement did occur. Impressed with the naturalistic and empirical approach of Aristotle, some medieval schoolmen spent time examining physical nature. Among them was the Dominican Albert the Great (Albertus Magnus). Born in Germany, Albert (c. 1206–1280) studied at Padua and taught at the University of Paris, where Thomas Aquinas was his student. To Albert, philosophy meant more than employing Greek reason to contemplate divine wisdom: it also meant making sense of nature. Albert devoted himself to mastering, editing, and commenting on the vast body of Aristotle's works.

While retaining the Christian stress on God, revelation, the supernatural, and the afterlife, Albert (unlike many earlier Christian thinkers) considered nature a valid field for investigation. In his writings on geology, chemistry, botany, and zoology, Albert, like Aristotle, displayed respect for the concrete details of nature, utilizing them as empirical evidence:

> *I have examined the anatomy of different species of bees. In the rear, i.e. behind the waist, I discovered a transparent, shining bladder. If you test this with your tongue, you find that it has a slight taste of honey. In the body there is only an insignificant spiral-shaped intestine and nerve fibers which are connected with the sting. All this is surrounded with a sticky fluid.*[9]

Showing a modern-day approach, Albert approved of inquiry into the material world, stressed the value of knowledge derived from experience with nature, sought rational explanations for natural occurrences, and held that theological debates should not stop scientific investigations. He pointed to a new direction in medieval thought.

Robert Grosseteste (c. 1175–1253), chancellor of Oxford University, was also a scholar of the scientific movement. He declared that the roundness of the earth could be demonstrated by reason. In addition, he insisted that mathematics was necessary in order to understand the physical world, and he carried out experiments on the refraction of light.

Another Englishman, the monk and philosopher Roger Bacon (c. 1214–1294), foreshadowed the modern attitude of using science to gain mastery over nature. He recognized the practical advantages that might come and predicted these great changes:

> *Machines for navigation can be made without rowers so that the largest ships on rivers or seas will be moved by a single man in charge with greater velocity than if they were full of men. Also oars can be made so that without animals they will move with unbelievable rapidity.... Also flying machines can be constructed so that a man sits in the midst of the machine revolving some engine by which artificial wings are made to beat the air like a flying bird. Also a machine small in size can be made for walking in the sea and rivers, even to the bottom without danger.*[10]

Bacon valued the study of mathematics and read Arabic works on the reflection and refraction of light. Among his achievements were experiments in optics and the observation that light travels much faster than sound. His description of the anatomy of the vertebrate eye and optic nerves was the finest of that era, and he recommended dissecting the eyes of pigs and cows to obtain greater knowledge of the subject.

The study of the ancient texts of Hippocrates and Galen and their Islamic commentators, particularly Avicenna's *Canon of Medicine,* which synthesized Greek and Arabic medicine, elevated medicine to a formal discipline. Although these texts contained numerous errors and contradictions, they had to be mastered, if only to be challenged, before modern medicine could emerge. In addition, medieval doctors dissected animals and, in the late fourteenth century, human bodies. From practical experience, medieval doctors, monks, and laypersons added to the list of plants and herbs that would ease pain and heal.

Medieval scholars did not make the breakthrough to modern science. They kept the belief that the earth was at the center of the universe and that different sets of laws operated on earth and in the heavens. They did not invent analytic geometry or calculus or arrive at the modern concept of inertia. Although some medieval thinkers explicitly urged seeking natural explanations to account for physical occurrences, medieval science was never wholly removed from a theological setting. Modern science self-consciously seeks the advancement of specifically scientific knowledge, but in the Middle Ages, many questions involving nature were raised merely to clarify a religious problem.

Medieval scholars and philosophers, however, did advance knowledge about optics, the tides, and mechanics. They saw the importance of mathematics for interpreting nature, and they performed some experiments. By translating and commenting on ancient Greek and Arabic works, medieval scholars provided future ages with ideas to reflect on and to reject and surpass, a necessary precondition for the emergence of modern science.

Medieval thinkers also developed an anti-Aristotelian physics, which some historians of science believe influenced Galileo, the creator of modern mechanics, more than two centuries later. To explain why heavy objects do not always fall downward—why an arrow released by a bow moves in a straight line before it falls—Aristotle said that when the arrow leaves the bow, it separates the air, which then moves behind the arrow and pushes it along. Aristotle, of course, had no comprehension of the law of inertia, which, as formulated by Isaac Newton in the seventeenth century, states that a body in motion will continue in a straight line unless interfered with. Unable to imagine that being in motion is as natural a condition as being at rest, Aristotle concluded that an outside force must maintain continual contact with the moving object. Hence, the flying arrow requires the "air-engine" to keep it in motion.

In the fourteenth century, Jean Buridan, a professor at the University of Paris, rejected Aristotle's theory. Buridan argued that the bowstring transmits to the arrow a force called impetus, which keeps the arrow in motion. Whereas Aristotle attributed the arrow's motion to the air, which was external to the arrow, Buridan found the motive force to be an agent imparted to the arrow by the bowstring. Though still far from the modern theory of inertia, Buridan's impetus theory was an advance over Aristotle's air-engine. In the impetus theory, a moving body requires a cause to keep it in motion. In the theory of inertia, as noted above, once a body is in motion, no force is required to keep it moving in a straight line.

Late medieval physics went beyond Aristotle in other ways as well, particularly in the importance given to expressing motion mathematically. The extent to which late medieval thinkers influenced the thinkers of the Scientific Revolution is a matter of debate. Some historians view modern science as a child of the Middle Ages. Other historians believe that the achievements of medieval science were slim and that modern science owes very little to the Middle Ages.

The Recovery of Roman Law

During the Early Middle Ages, western European law essentially consisted of Germanic customs, some of which had been written down. Although some elements of Roman law endured as custom, the formal study of Roman law disappeared. The late eleventh and the twelfth centuries saw the revival of Roman law, particularly in Bologna, Italy. Irnerius lectured on the *Corpus Juris Civilis,* Roman laws and judicial commentaries codified by Byzantine jurists in the sixth century by order of the emperor Justinian. He made Bologna the leading center for the study of Roman law. Irnerius and his students applied to the study of law the methods of organization and logical analysis that scholastic theologians used in studying philosophical texts.

Unlike traditional Germanic law, which was essentially tribal law, Roman law assumed the existence of universal principles, which could be grasped by the human intellect and expressed in the law of the state. Roman jurists had systematically and rationally structured the legal experience of the Roman people. The example of Roman law stimulated medieval jurists to organize their own legal tradition. Intellectuals increasingly came to insist on both a rational analysis of evidence and judicial decisions based on rational procedures. Law codes compiled in parts of France and Germany and in the kingdom of Castile were influenced by the recovery of Roman law.

The Roman legal experience contained political principles that differed markedly from feudal practices. According to feudal tradition, lords, by virtue of their large estates, were empowered to exercise political authority. Roman jurists, in contrast, had attributed governmental powers to the state and had granted wide powers to the emperor. The *Corpus Juris Civilis* stated that the power to make laws had originally resided with the Roman people but they had surrendered this power to the emperor. Medieval lawyers in the service of kings used this concept to justify royal absolutism, holding that the monarch possessed the absolute powers that the Roman legal tradition had granted to the Roman emperor. This strong defense of the monarch's power helped kings maintain their independence from the papacy.

Roman law also influenced church law, which was derived from the Bible, the church fathers, church councils, and the decisions of popes. In the last part of the eleventh century, church scholars began to codify church (or canon) law and were helped by the Roman legal tradition.

Literature

Medieval literature was written both in Latin and in the vernacular—the normal spoken language, as distinct from the language of learning. Much of medieval Latin literature consisted of religious hymns and dramas depicting the life of Christ and saints. The following hymn by Saint Thomas Aquinas is typical:

Sing, my tongue, the Savior's glory
Of his Flesh the mystery sing;
Of the Blood, all price exceeding,
Shed by our immortal King,
Destined for the world's redemption,
From a noble womb to spring.[11]

Medieval university students, like their modern counterparts, lampooned their elders and social conventions, engaged in drinking bouts, and rebelled against the rigors of study. They put their feelings into poetry written in Latin:

We in our wandering,
Blithesome and squandering;
Tara, tantara, teino!
Eat to satiety,
Drink with propriety;
Tara, tantara, teino!

Laugh till our sides we split,
Rags on our hides we fit;
Tara, tantara, teino!
Jesting eternally,
Quaffing infernally;
Tara, tantara, teino![12]

For them, youth and study did not mix:

Let's away with study,
Folly's sweet.
Treasure all the pleasure of our youth:
Time enough for age
To think of Truth.

So short a day,
And life so quickly hasting
And is study wasting
Youth that would be gay![13]

And, of course, their thoughts turned to romance:

All I care for is to play,
Gaze upon my treasure,
Now and then to touch her hand,
Kiss is modest measure;
But the fifth act of love's game,
Dream not of that pleasure![14]

Vernacular literature emerged in the High Middle Ages. The French *chansons de geste*—epic poems of heroic deeds that had first been told orally—were written in the vernacular of northern France. The poems dealt with Charlemagne's battles against the Muslims, with rebellious nobles, and with feudal warfare. The finest of these epic poems, *The Song of Roland,* expressed the feudal ethic—loyalty to one's lord and devotion to Christianity were the highest virtues and treachery an impardonable crime. Roland, Charlemagne's nephew, who was killed in a battle with the Muslims, is idealized as the brave Christian knight who battles God's enemies, a warrior of heroic proportions with great physical prowess, who is loyal to God, king, and his knightly entourage.

The *Nibelungenlied,* the best expression of the heroic epic in Germany, is often called "the *Iliad* of the Germans." Like its French counterpart, it dealt with heroic feats:

In stories of our fathers, high marvels we are told
Of champions well-approved in perils manifold.
Of feasts and merry meetings, of weeping and of wail,
And deeds of gallant daring I'll tell you in my tale.[15]

The *roman*—a blending of old legends, chivalric ideals, and Christian concepts—combined love with adventure, war, and the miraculous. Among the romans were the tales of King Arthur and his Round Table. Circulating by word of mouth for centuries, these tales spread from the British Isles to France and Germany. In the twelfth century, they were put into French verse.

Another form of medieval poetry, which flourished particularly in Provence, in southern France, dealt with the romantic glorification of women. Sung by *troubadours,* many of them nobles, the courtly love poetry expressed a changing attitude

TROUBADOURS. Troubadours composed and sang love songs that praised noble ladies for their beauty and charm and expressed both the joys and pains of love. In this thirteenth-century manuscript illumination, a troubadour entertains a royal couple. (*Biblioteca Real, El Escorial, Madrid, Spain/Giraudon/Art Resource, NY.*)

toward women. Although medieval men generally regarded women as inferior and subordinate, courtly love poetry ascribed to noble ladies superior qualities of virtue. To the nobleman, the lady became a goddess worthy of devotion, loyalty, and worship. He would honor her and serve her as he did his lord; for her love, he would undergo any sacrifice. Troubadours sang love songs that praised ladies for their beauty and charm and expressed both the joys and the pains of love:

I sing of her, yet her beauty
is greater than I can tell,
with her fresh color, lively eyes,
and white skin, untanned
and untainted by rouge.
She is so pure and noble
that no one can speak ill of her.
But above all, one must praise,
it seems to me, her truthfulness,
her manners and her gracious speech
for she never would betray a friend. . . .[16]

Noblewomen actively influenced the rituals and literature of courtly love. They often invited poets to their courts and wrote poetry themselves. Sometimes a lady troubadour expressed disdain for her husband and desire for the knight whom she truly loved:

I should like to hold my knight
Naked in my arms at eve,
That he might be in ecstasy
As I cushioned his head against my breast,
For I am happier far with him
Than Floris with Blancheflor;
I grant him my heart, my love,
My mind, my eyes, my life.

Fair friend, charming and good,
When shall I hold you in my power?
And lie beside you for an hour
And amorous kisses give to you;
Know that I would give almost anything
To have you in my husband's place,
But only if you swear
To do everything I desire.[17]

Ladies demanded that knights treat them with gentleness and consideration and that knights dress neatly, bathe often, play instruments, and compose (or at least recite) poetry. To prove worthy of his lady's love, a knight had to demonstrate patience, charm, bravery, and loyalty. It was believed that a knight would ennoble his character by devoting himself to a lady.

Courtly love involved not a husband-wife relationship but a noble's admiration and yearning for another woman of his class. Among nobles, marriages were arranged for political and economic reasons. The rituals of courtly love, it has been suggested, provided an outlet for erotic feelings condemned by the church. They also enhanced the skills and refined the tastes of the noble. The rough warrior acquired wit, manners, charm, and a facility with words. He was becoming a courtier and a gentleman.

The greatest literary figure of the Middle Ages was Dante Alighieri (1265–1321) of Florence.

Dante appreciated the Roman classics and wrote not just in Latin, the traditional language of intellectual life, but also in Italian, his native tongue. In this respect, he anticipated the Renaissance. In the tradition of the troubadours, Dante wrote poems to his beloved Beatrice:

> *My lady carries love within her eyes:*
> *All that she looks on is made pleasanter;*
> *Upon her path men turn to gaze at her;*
> *He whom she greeteth feels his heart to rise,*
> *And droops his troubled visage, full of sighs,*
> *And of his evil heart is then aware:*
> *Hate loves, and Pride becomes a worshipper.*
> *O women, help to praise her in somewise.*
> *Humbleness, and the hope that hopeth well,*
> *By speech of hers into the mind are brought,*
> *And who beholds is blessed often-whiles.*
> *The look she hath when she smiles*
> *Cannot be said, nor holden in the thought;*
> *'Tis such a new and gracious miracle.*[18]

In *The Divine Comedy,* Dante synthesized the various elements of the medieval outlook and summed up, with immense feeling, the medieval understanding of the purpose of life. Written while Dante was in exile, *The Divine Comedy* describes the poet's journey through hell, purgatory, and paradise. Dante arranges hell into nine concentric circles; in each region, sinners are punished in proportion to their earthly sins. The poet experiences all of hell's torments—burning sand, violent storms, darkness, and fearful monsters that whip, claw, bite, and tear sinners apart. The ninth circle, the lowest, is reserved for Lucifer and traitors. Lucifer has three faces, each a different color, and two batlike wings. In each mouth he gnaws on the greatest traitors in history: Judas Iscariot, who betrayed Jesus, and Brutus and Cassius, who assassinated Caesar. Those condemned to hell are told: "All hope abandon, ye who enter in."

In purgatory, Dante meets sinners who, although they undergo punishment, will eventually enter paradise. He and Beatrice ascend to the highest heaven, a realm of light that radiates truth, goodness, and gentleness. In paradise, the poet meets the great saints and the Virgin Mary. He glimpses the Vision of God. In this mystical experience, the aim of life is realized.

VIRGIL AND DANTE WATCH LUCIFER: A MINIATURE PAINTING IN AN EARLY MANUSCRIPT OF *THE DIVINE COMEDY*. Dante reserved the lowest depth of hell for those guilty of treason. Lucifer, the angel who betrayed God, is depicted as a monster with three mouths. With these he perpetually chews on Judas Iscariot, Brutus, and Cassius. (*Trivulzian Library, Milan.*)

ARCHITECTURE

Two styles of architecture evolved during the Middle Ages: Romanesque and Gothic. The Romanesque style dominated the eleventh century and the greater part of the twelfth. In imitation of ancient Roman structures, Romanesque buildings used massive walls to support stone barrel and groin vaults with rounded arches. Thick walls were needed to hold up the great weight of the roofs. Because the walls had few spaces for windows, little light entered the interior of Romanesque buildings.

The development of the pointed arch permitted supports that lessened the bearing pressure of the roof on the walls. This new style, called Gothic, allowed buildings to have lofty, vaulted ceilings and huge windows. Whereas Romanesque buildings produced an impression of massive solidity, Gothic buildings created an illusion of soaring energy. The

The Romanesque Nave of the Cathedral of Saint Sernin, Toulouse. The nave is covered by a stone barrel vault, replacing earlier wooden roofs, which were susceptible to fire. The columns, thick walls, and small windows were required structurally to bear the great weight of the roof vaulting. Little light penetrated the interior. (*Caisse Nationale des Monuments Historiques, Paris.*)

The Gothic Nave and Choir of Notre Dame Cathedral, Paris, twelfth century. The Gothic nave is wider than the Romanesque nave because pointed arches can bridge a wider space and carry a roof with less heavy vaulting. The walls are raised higher and are thinner and punctured with larger open spaces for windows than were possible in Romanesque buildings. The weight of the roof and walls is borne by flying buttresses, stone arched supports external to the walls. (*Jean Roubier.*)

Gothic cathedral gave visual expression to the medieval conception of a hierarchical universe. As the historian Joan Gadol puts it, "Inside and out, the Gothic cathedral is one great movement upward through a mounting series of grades, one ascent through horizontal levels marked by arches, galleries, niches, and towers . . . the material ascends to the spiritual, the natural is assumed into the supernatural—all in a graduated rise."[19] This illusion is created by the tall and narrow proportions of the interior spaces, the springing pointed arches, and the marching patterns of closely spaced columns and colonnettes.

The magnificently designed stained-glass windows and complex sculptural decoration of Gothic cathedrals depicted scenes from the Bible and the lives of saints, as well as scenes from daily life, for the worshipers, many of whom were illiterate. The reduction of wall space, which allowed these massive glass illustrations, was made possible by the flying buttresses on the buildings' exteriors. These great arcs of masonry carry the weight and thrust of the stone vaults out to the exterior walls. The light cage of buttresses surrounding the cathedral makes the exterior silhouette appear as airy and diffuse as the interior spaces.

Gothic cathedrals took many decades to complete. Only in an age of intense religious faith could such energy have been spent to glorify God. These vast building projects, many of them in northern France, were made possible by economic prosperity. Funds were raised from a variety of sources. Cathedrals owned income-producing properties, such as farmland, mills, and forests, and received donations from pilgrims visiting the relics of famous saints. Clerics also collected tolls and taxes on goods shipped to fairs through their region.

The Gothic style was to remain vigorous until the fifteenth century, spreading from France to England, Germany, Spain, and beyond. Revived from time to time thereafter, it has proved to be one of the most enduring styles in Western art and architecture.

Not too long ago, some intellectuals viewed the Middle Ages as a period of ignorance and superstition, an era of cultural sterility that stood between the high civilizations of ancient Greece and Rome and the modern West. This view of the Middle Ages as a dark age has been abandoned, and quite properly so, for the High Middle Ages saw the crystallizing of a rich and creative civilization. To be sure, its religious orientation sets it apart both from classical civilization and from our own modern secular and scientific civilization. But the *Summa Theologica* of Aquinas, *The Divine Comedy* of Dante, and the Gothic cathedral all attest to the creativeness and genius of the medieval religious spirit.

❖ ❖ ❖

Notes

1. Quoted in G. G. Coulton, *Life in the Middle Ages* (New York: Macmillan, 1928), 1:74.
2. Quoted in Charles Homer Haskins, *The Rise of Universities* (Ithaca, N.Y.: Cornell University Press, 1957), p. 79.
3. Quoted in Coulton, *Life in the Middle Ages*, 3:113.
4. Geoffrey Chaucer, *The Canterbury Tales*, trans. Neville Coghill (Baltimore: Penguin Books, 1958), p. 27.
5. Quoted in Anders Piltz, *The World of Medieval Learning* (Oxford: Blackwell, 1981), p. 83.
6. Quoted in David Knowles, *The Evolution of Medieval Thought* (New York: Vintage Books, 1964), p. 123.
7. *Summa Theologica*, excerpted in Anton C. Pegis, ed., *Introduction to Saint Thomas Aquinas* (New York: Modern Library, 1948), p. 25.
8. Steven Ozment, *The Age of Reform* (New Haven, Conn.: Yale University Press, 1980), p. 20.
9. Quoted in Piltz, *The World of Medieval Learning*, p. 176.
10. Quoted in A. C. Crombie, *Medieval and Early Modern Science* (Garden City, N.Y.: Doubleday Anchor Books, 1959), 1:55–56.
11. Excerpted in Charles W. Jones, ed., *Medieval*

Literature in Translation (New York: Longmans, Green, 1950), p. 903.

12. Quoted in Haskins, *The Rise of Universities,* pp. 86–87.
13. Quoted in Marcia L. Colish, *Medieval Foundations of the Western Intellectual Tradition, 400–1400* (New Haven, Conn.: Yale University Press, 1997), p. 202.
14. Excerpted in David C. Riede and J. Wayne Baker, eds., *The Western Intellectual Tradition,* vol. 1 (Dubuque, Ia.: Kendall/Hunt, 1980), p. 62.
15. *The Fall of the Nibelungers,* trans. William Nanson Lettsom (London: Williams & Norgate, 1890), p. 1.
16. Excerpted in Anthony Bonner, ed., *Songs of the Troubadours* (New York: Schocken Books, 1972), pp. 42–43.
17. Quoted in Frances Gies and Joseph Gies, *Women in the Middle Ages* (New York: T. Y. Crowell, 1978), p. 45.
18. Dante Alighieri, *The New Life,* trans. Dante Gabriel Rossetti (London: Elis & Elvey, 1899), pp. 82–83.
19. Joan Gadol, *Leon Battista Alberti, Universal Man of the Early Renaissance* (Chicago: The University of Chicago Press, 1969), pp. 149–150.

Suggested Reading

Baldwin, John W., *The Scholastic Culture of the Middle Ages* (1971). A useful introductory survey.

Bonner, Anthony, ed., *Songs of the Troubadours* (1972). Collection of troubadour poetry.

Brooke, Christopher, *The Twelfth-Century Renaissance* (1969). Surveys schools, learning, theology, literature, and leading figures.

Copleston, F. C., *Aquinas* (1955). A study of Aquinas's thought.

———, *A History of Medieval Philosophy* (1974). A lucid, comprehensive survey of medieval philosophy.

Crombie, A. C., *Medieval and Early Modern Science,* 2 vols. (1959). All phases of medieval science.

Flanagan, Sabina, *Hildegard of Bingen* (1989). A biography of a remarkable medieval woman who distinguished herself as a mystic, poet, and naturalist.

Gilson, Etienne, *Reason and Revelation in the Middle Ages* (1966). A superb brief exposition of the medieval philosophical tradition.

Gimpel, Jean, *The Cathedral Builders* (1984). The financial, political, and spiritual forces behind the building of cathedrals.

Haskins, C. H., *The Renaissance of the Twelfth Century* (1957). Reprint of a still useful work.

Knowles, David, *The Evolution of Medieval Thought* (1964). One of the best of its kind.

Mâle, Emile, *The Gothic Image* (1958). A valuable study of medieval art.

Pieper, Josef, *Scholasticism* (1964). Written with intelligence and grace.

Piltz, Anders, *The World of Medieval Learning* (1981). A clearly written, informative survey of medieval education and learning.

Wagner, David L., ed., *The Seven Liberal Arts in the Middle Ages* (1983). Essays on the place of liberal arts in medieval culture.

Wieruszowski, Helene, *The Medieval University* (1966). A good survey, followed by documents.

Review Questions

1. What factors contributed to the revival of learning in the late eleventh and twelfth centuries?
2. What was the significance of medieval universities?
3. Compare and contrast medieval universities with universities today.
4. Describe the essential features of the medieval view of the universe. How does it differ from the modern view?
5. What were scholastic philosophers trying to accomplish?
6. Does the scholastic goal have any relevance for us today?
7. Aquinas did not consider reason to be an enemy of faith. Explain this statement.
8. What was the significance of Aquinas's thought?
9. What would Socrates have thought of Aquinas?
10. Discuss the contribution of the Middle Ages to the growth of science.
11. What was the significance of the revival of Roman law?
12. Describe what each of the following tells about the attitudes and interests of medieval people: troubadour poetry, *The Canterbury Tales, The Divine Comedy,* and Gothic cathedrals.

Chapter 12

The Late Middle Ages: Crisis and Dissolution

The Jacquerie: Enraged French Peasants Attack the Castle of a Lord. (Bibliothèque Nationale, Paris.)

- **An Age of Adversity**
  Economic Problems, Black Death, and Social Tension
  The Hundred Years' War
- **The Decline of the Papacy**
  Conflict with France
  Critics of Papal Power
  The Great Schism and the Conciliar Movement
  Fourteenth-Century Heresies
- **Breakup of the Thomistic Synthesis**
- **The Middle Ages and the Modern World: Continuity and Discontinuity**

By the start of the fourteenth century, Latin Christendom had experienced more than 250 years of growth. On an economic level, agricultural production had expanded, commerce and town life had revived, and the population had increased. On a political level, kings had become more powerful, bringing greater order and security to large areas. On a religious level, the papacy had demonstrated its strength as the spiritual leader of Christendom, and the clergy had been reformed. On a cultural level, a unified world-view, blending faith and reason, had been forged.

During the Late Middle Ages, roughly the fourteenth and early fifteenth centuries, medieval civilization was in decline. The fourteenth century, an age of adversity, was marked by crop failures, famine, population decline, plagues, stagnating production, unemployment, inflation, devastating warfare, and abandoned villages. Violent rebellions by the poor of the towns and countryside were ruthlessly suppressed by the upper classes. The century witnessed flights into mysticism, outbreaks of mass hysteria, and massacres of Jews; it was an age of pessimism and general insecurity. The papacy declined in power, heresy proliferated, and the synthesis of faith and reason, erected by Christian thinkers during the High Middle Ages, began to disintegrate. These developments were signs that the stable and coherent civilization of the thirteenth century was drawing to a close.

But all was not decline and gloom. On the positive side, representative institutions developed, and thinkers showed a greater interest in the world of nature. And in Italy, the dynamic forces of urbanism and secularism were producing a period of cultural and humanistic flowering known as the Renaissance.

An Age of Adversity

Economic Problems, Black Death, and Social Tension

In the Late Middle Ages, Latin Christendom was afflicted with severe economic problems. The earlier increases in agricultural production did not continue. Limited use of fertilizers and limited

Chronology 12.1 ❖ The Late Middle Ages

1303	The French attack papal summer palace at Anagni
1309–1377	Babylonian Captivity: the popes, all French, reside at Avignon and are influenced by the French monarchy
1323–1328	Peasants revolt in Flanders
1328	End of France's Capetian dynasty; Edward III of England tries to gain the French throne
1337–1453	Hundred Years' War between England and France
1346	Battle of Crécy: the English defeat the French
1347–1351	Black Death reaches Italian ports and ravages Europe
1356	Battle of Poitiers: the English defeat the French
1358	Jacquerie, the French peasants' revolt
1377	Pope Gregory XI returns papacy to Rome
1378	Florentine laborers revolt
1378–1417	Great Schism: Christendom has two and then three popes
1381	English peasants revolt
1382	Weavers revolt in Ghent
1415	Battle of Agincourt: Henry V of England defeats the French; Jan Hus, a Bohemian religious reformer, is burned at the stake
1429	Joan of Arc liberates Orléans
1431	Joan of Arc is condemned as a witch
1453	The English are driven from France, except Calais: end of the Hundred Years' War
1460	Pope Pius II condemns the Conciliar Movement as heretical

knowledge of conservation exhausted the topsoil. As more grazing land was converted to the cultivation of cereals, animal husbandry decreased, causing a serious shortage of manure needed for arable land. Intermittent bouts of prolonged heavy rains and frost also hampered agriculture. From 1301 to 1314, there was a general shortage of food, and from 1315 to 1317, famine struck Europe. Throughout the century, starvation and malnutrition were widespread. In Bruges, for example, two thousand of the town's thirty-five thousand inhabitants died of starvation.

Other economic problems abounded. A shortage of silver, caused by technical problems in sinking deeper shafts in mines, led to the debasement of coins and spiraling inflation, which hurt the feudal nobility in particular. Prices for manufactured luxury goods, which the nobility craved, rose rapidly. At the same time, the dues that the nobility collected from peasants diminished. To replace their revenues, lords and knights turned to plunder and warfare.

Compounding the economic crisis was the Black Death, or bubonic plague. This disease was carried by fleas on black rats and probably first struck Mongolia in 1331–32. From there, it crossed into Russia. Carried back from Black Sea ports, the plague reached Sicily in 1347. Spreading

THE BLACK DEATH. The bubonic plague, or Black Death, ravaged Europe in the middle of the fourteenth century, killing one-quarter to one-third of the population. This picture depicts victims of the worst natural disaster in recorded history. (*Bettmann/Corbis.*)

swiftly throughout much of Europe through human contact, the plague attacked an already declining and undernourished population. The first crisis lasted until 1351, and other serious outbreaks occurred in later decades. The crowded cities and towns had the highest mortalities. Perhaps twenty million people—about one-quarter to one-third of the European population—perished in the worst disaster in recorded history caused by natural forces. Contemporaries viewed the disaster as divine punishment for humanity's sins.

Panic-stricken people drifted into debauchery, lawlessness, and frenzied forms of religious life. Organized bands of flagellants marched from region to region beating themselves and each other with sticks and whips in a desperate effort to appease God, who, they believed, had cursed them with the plague. Art concentrated on morbid scenes of decaying flesh, open graves laden with worm-eaten corpses, dances of death, and the torments of hell. Sometimes this hysteria was directed against Jews, who were accused of causing the plague by poisoning wells. Terrible massacres of Jews, often by mass burnings, occurred despite the pleas of the papacy.

The millions of deaths caused production of food and goods to plummet and some prices to soar. Nobles tried to make peasants bear the brunt of the crisis, as the value of land decreased and agricultural income lessened. A law decreed in England in 1349 required peasants to work for lords at fixed wages. Similar regulations of wages in German, Spanish, and Portuguese principalities aggravated tensions between peasants and nobles.

Economic and social tensions, some of them antedating the Black Death, escalated into rebel-

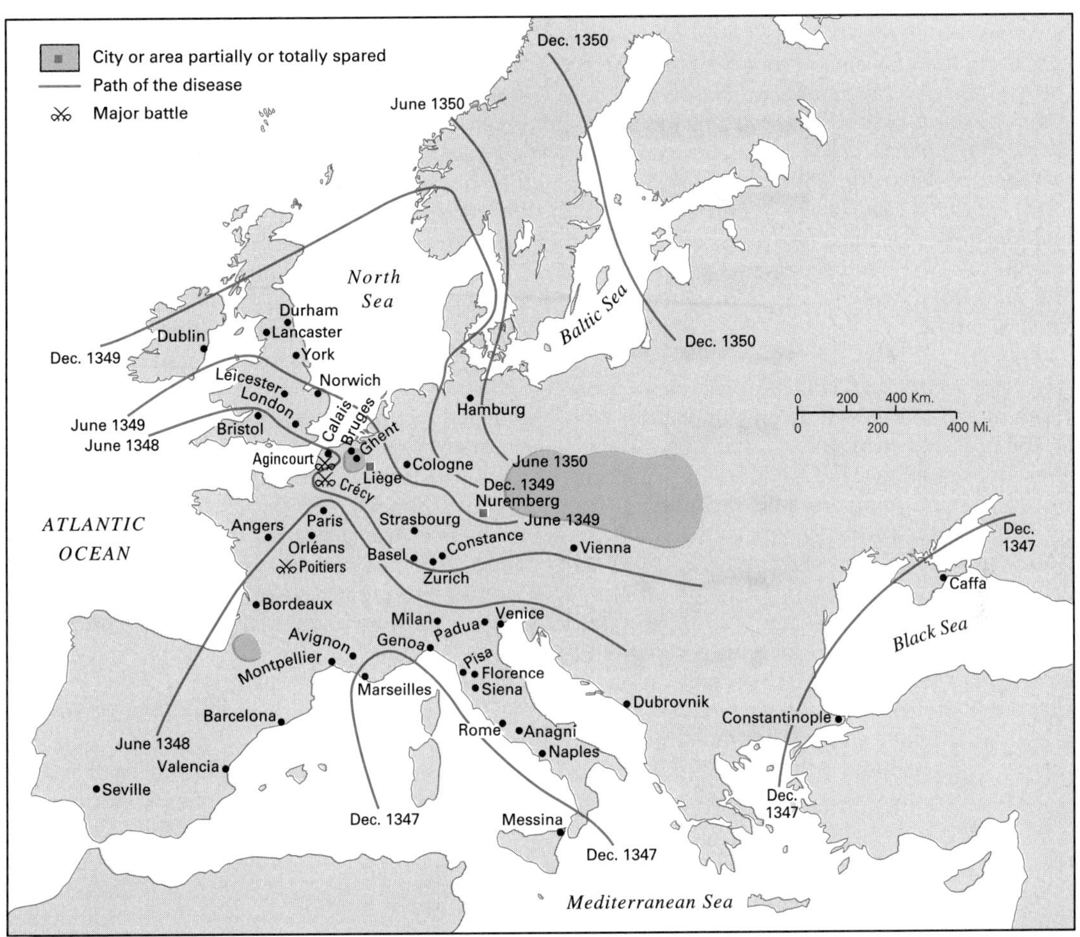

Map 12.1 Path of the Black Death, 1347–1350 The Black Death took the lives of some twenty million people. The crowded cities and towns had the highest mortality rate.

lions. Each rebellion had its own specific causes, but a general pattern characterized the uprisings in the countryside. When kings and lords, breaking with customary social relationships, imposed new and onerous regulations, the peasants rose in defense of their traditional rights. No doubt their revolt was also fueled by an instinctive hatred for the haughty lords, who, for centuries, had treated peasants with contempt. In 1323, the lords' attempt to reimpose old manorial obligations infuriated the free peasants of Flanders, whose condition had improved in earlier decades. The Peasants' Revolt lasted five bloody years. In 1358, French peasants took up arms in protest against the plundering of the countryside by soldiers. Perhaps twenty thousand peasants died in the uprising known as the Jacquerie. In 1381, English peasants revolted, angered over legislation that tied them to the land and imposed new taxes. John Ball, who claimed to be a priest, expressed egalitarian sentiments:

> *My good friends, things cannot go on well in England, nor ever will until everything shall be in common; when there shall neither be vassal nor lord, and all distinctions leveled; when the lords shall be no more masters than ourselves. But ill have they used us! and for*

> *what reason do they thus hold us in bondage? Are we not all descended from the same parents, Adam and Eve? and what can they show, or what reasons give, why they should be more the masters than ourselves? except, perhaps, in making us labor and work, for them to spend. . . . They have handsome manors, when we must brave the wind and rain in our labors in the field; but it is from our labor they have wherewith to support their pomp.*[1]

Like the revolts in Flanders and France, the uprising in England failed. To the landed aristocracy, the peasants were sinners attacking a social system ordained by God. Possessing superior might, the nobility suppressed the peasants, sometimes with savage cruelty.

Social unrest afflicted the towns, as well as the countryside. The wage earners of Florence (1378), the weavers of Ghent (1382), and the poor of Paris (1382) rose up against the ruling oligarchy. These revolts were generally initiated not by the poorest and most downtrodden but by those who had made some gains and were eager for more. The rebellions of the urban poor were crushed just like the peasant uprisings.

Fourteenth-century Europeans suffered because of the numerous long wars, which devastated towns and farmland and seriously hampered economic life. To deprive an invading army of food, fields were laid waste. Invaders, too, decimated farms to destroy the enemy's morale, and discharged soldiers plundered the countryside.

The Hundred Years' War

In earlier centuries, wars had generally been short and small in scale, sparing noncombatants the worst effects. In the fourteenth century, this trend changed. The most destructive war was the series of conflicts between France and England known as the Hundred Years' War (1337–1453). Because English kings had ruled parts of France, conflicts between the two monarchies had been common. By 1214, the French monarchy had succeeded in acquiring most English territories in France. In 1328, the Capetian dynasty came to an end with the death of Charles IV, the son of Philip IV, the Fair. An assembly of French barons gave the crown to Philip VI of Valois, nephew of Philip the Fair. Edward III, king of England, insisted that he had a superior claim to the throne because his mother was Philip the Fair's daughter. Edward's attempt to gain the French throne was one reason for a new conflict. Another was the effort of the French monarch to squeeze taxes from Flemish towns, such as Bruges, which had grown rich as trade and cloth-making centers. Dependent on English wool and resentful of the French monarchy's demands, the Flemish towns threw their support behind Edward III.

In the opening phase of the war, the English inflicted terrible defeats on French knights at the battles of Crécy (1346) and Poitiers (1356). Using longbows, which allowed them to shoot arrows rapidly, English archers cut down wave after wave of charging French cavalry. The war continued on and off throughout the fourteenth century. During periods of truce, gangs of unemployed soldiers roamed the French countryside killing and stealing, actions that precipitated the Jacquerie, the peasant uprising.

After the battle of Agincourt (1415), won by the English under Henry V, the English controlled most of northern France. It appeared that England would shortly conquer France and join the two lands under one crown. At this crucial moment in French history, a young and illiterate peasant girl, Joan of Arc (1412–1431), helped rescue France. Believing that God commanded her to drive the English out of France, Joan rallied the demoralized French troops, leading them in battle. In 1429, she liberated the besieged city of Orléans. Imprisoned by the English, Joan was condemned as a heretic and a witch in 1431 by a handpicked church court and was burned at the stake. The English intended to undermine the French cause by demonstrating that Joan was not divinely chosen. But Joan's life and death inspired the French people with a sense of devotion to their country. The reorganized and aroused French army recaptured Paris. By 1453, the English were driven from all French territory except the port of Calais.

During the Hundred Years' War, French kings introduced new taxes, which added substantially to their incomes. These monies furnished them with the means to organize a professional army of well-paid and loyal troops. By evoking a sense

PORTRAIT OF JOAN OF ARC: WITCH OR SAINT? Claiming that heavenly voices had called upon her to lead the armies of France to victory over the English, a young peasant girl, Joan of Arc, persuaded the French crown prince to give her command of his army. Victorious in battle, she fulfilled all that was required of her, including the crowning of the new king at Rheims. Captured soon after, she was tried as a witch by an English-dominated court and executed in Rouen in 1431. She has been a heroine and inspiration to many modern artists, poets, and dramatists. (*Archives Nationales, Paris.*)

of pride and oneness in the French people, the war also contributed to a growing, but still incomplete, national unity. The English, too, emerged from the war with a greater sense of solidarity, and Parliament, because it had to finance the war, gained in stature.

However, the war had terrible consequences for the French peasants. Thousands of farmers were killed and valuable farmland was destroyed by English armies and marauding bands of mercenaries. In another portentous development, the later stages of the Hundred Years' War saw the use of gunpowder and heavy artillery.

THE DECLINE OF THE PAPACY

The principal sign of breakdown in the Late Middle Ages was the waning authority and prestige of the papacy. In the High Middle Ages, the papacy had been the dominant institution in Christendom, but in the Late Middle Ages, its power disintegrated. The medieval ideal of a unified Christian commonwealth guided by the papacy was shattered. Papal authority declined in the face of the growing power of kings, who championed the parochial interests of states. The papacy's prestige and its capacity to lead diminished as it became more embroiled in European politics. Many pious Christians felt that the pope behaved more like a secular ruler than like an Apostle of Christ. Political theorists and church reformers further undermined papal authority.

Conflict with France

Pope Boniface VIII (1294–1303) vigorously upheld papal claims to supremacy over secular rulers. In the famous bull *Unam Sanctam* (1302), he declared:

> *... if the earthly power errs, it shall be judged by the spiritual power ... but [the pope] can be judged only by God not by man. ... Whoever therefore resists this power so ordained by God resists the ordinance of God. ... Therefore, we declare, state, define, and pronounce that it is altogether necessary to salvation for every human creature to be subject to the Roman Pontiff.*[2]

But in trying to enforce this idea of papal supremacy on proud and increasingly more powerful kings, Boniface suffered defeat and humiliation.

Philip IV of France (1285–1314) and Edward I of England (1272–1307) taxed the churches in their lands to raise revenue for the war they planned to wage. By doing so, they disregarded

The Battle of Crécy, 1346. English claims to the French throne led to the Hundred Years' War between the French and the English monarchies. The English victory at Crécy was catastrophic for the French mounted knights, who fell in droves under the withering fire of English longbowmen. In the end, however, the English effort was unsuccessful; although France was devastated by invading armies and internal revolts, the English kings lost almost all their French possessions. (*Photo Hachette.*)

the church's prohibition against the taxing of its property by the state without papal permission. In the bull *Clericis Laicos* (1296), Boniface decreed that kings and lords who imposed taxes on the clergy and the clergy who paid them would be excommunicated. However, Boniface badly misjudged the situation. Far from bowing to the pope's threat, both Edward and Philip acted forcefully to assert their authority over the churches in their kingdoms. Boniface backed down from his position, declaring that the French king could tax the clergy in times of national emergency. Thus, the matter was resolved to the advantage of the state.

A second dispute had more disastrous consequences for Boniface. Philip tried and imprisoned a French bishop despite Boniface's warning that this was an illegal act and a violation of church law and tradition, which held that the church, not the state, must judge the clergy. Philip summoned the first meeting of the Estates General to gain the backing of the nation. Shortly afterward, Boniface issued the bull *Unam Sanctam,* quoted earlier, and he threatened to excommunicate Philip. The outraged monarch decided to seize Boniface and to replace him with a new pope. Aided by Italian mercenaries and enemies of Boniface, French conspirators raided the papal summer palace at Anagni in September 1303 and captured the pope. Although Boniface was released, this terrible event proved too much for him, and a month later he died.

Boniface's successors, Benedict XI (1303–1304) and Clement V (1305–1314), tried to conciliate Philip. In particular, Clement agreed to suppress the Templars, a wealthy religious-military order to which the French crown was in debt. Another victory for Philip was Clement's decision to remain at Avignon, a town on the southeastern French frontier, where he had set up a temporary residence.

From 1309 to 1377, a period known as the Babylonian Captivity, the popes were all French and resided in Avignon, not Rome. Factional violence in Rome and the Papal States had driven them from Italy. During this time, the papacy, removed from Rome and deprived of revenues from the Papal States, was often forced to pursue policies favorable to France. Also detrimental to the papal image was the antipapalism growing among members of the laity repelled by the luxurious style of living at Avignon and by the appointment of high churchmen to areas where they did not know the local language and where they demonstrated little concern for the local population. Under these circumstances, more and more people questioned the value of the papacy and the need for it.

Critics of Papal Power

The conflict between Boniface and Philip provoked a battle of words between proponents of papal supremacy and defenders of royal rights. In his treatise *On Ecclesiastical Power,* Giles of Rome (c. 1245–1316) vigorously supported the doctrine of papal power. Because the spiritual is inherently superior to the temporal, he argued, the pope has the authority to judge temporal rulers. All temporal lords ought to be governed by spiritual and ecclesiastical authority, and especially by the pope, who heads the church.

Defenders of royal prerogatives challenged the pope's claim to primacy over both secular rulers and the clergy. In taking this position, they weakened the medieval church. *On Kingly and Papal Power* (1302) by John of Paris (c. 1241–1306) attacked the theory of papal monarchy championed by Giles of Rome and asserted the independence of the French monarchy. For John, the church was primarily a spiritual body charged with administering the sacraments; as such, its authority did not extend to temporal affairs. Indeed, clerical interference in secular affairs threatened the state's stability. While granting that "the priest is superior to the ruler in dignity," John maintained that "it is not necessary to be superior to him in all things." Since both rulers and priests derive their power from God, said John, they are each superior in their own spheres. "The priest is, therefore, superior in spiritual matters and conversely, the ruler is superior in temporal matters."[3]

The most important critique of clerical intrusion into worldly affairs was *The Defender of the Peace* (1324) by Marsiglio of Padua (c. 1290–c. 1343). Marsiglio held that the state ran according to principles that had nothing to do with religious commands originating in a higher realm. Religion dealt with a supernatural world and with principles of faith that could not be proved by reason, wrote Marsiglio. Politics, in contrast, dealt with a natural world and with the affairs of the human community. Political thinkers should not try to make the earthly realm conform to articles of faith. According to Marsiglio, the state was self-sufficient; it needed no instruction from a higher authority. Thus, Marsiglio denied the essential premises of medieval papal political theory: that kings received their power from God; that the pope, as God's vicar, was empowered to guide kings; that the state, as part of a divinely ordered world, must conform to and fulfill supranatural ends; and that the clergy were above the laws of the state. Marsiglio viewed the church as a spiritual institution with no temporal power. This outlook anticipates modern political thought.

The Great Schism and the Conciliar Movement

The Avignon popes were often competent men who, despite the hard times that had overtaken the papacy, tried to bolster papal power. They tightened their hold over church administration by reserving for themselves certain appointments and collections of fees formerly handled by local bishops. Through a deliberate effort at financial centralization, including the imposition of new

A Dead Man Before His Judge: A Miniature Painting from the *Rohan Book of Hours*, France, c. 1420. God the Father, bearing the orb and sword of universal sovereignty, hears the final prayer of a dying man and sends an angel to liberate the man's soul from the clutches of a demon. A preoccupation with death and demons was characteristic of late medieval Christian art. (*Bibliothèque Nationale, Paris.*)

taxes and the more efficient collection of old ones, the Avignon popes substantially increased papal income.

Although Pope Gregory XI returned the papacy to Rome in 1377, the papacy was to suffer another humiliation: the Great Schism. Elected pope in 1378, Urban VI immediately displayed tactlessness, if not mental imbalance, by abusing and even imprisoning cardinals. Fleeing from Rome, the cardinals declared that the election of Urban had been invalid and elected Clement VII as the new pope. Refusing to step down, Urban excommunicated Clement, who responded in kind. To the utter confusion and anguish of Christians throughout Europe, there were now two popes: Urban ruling from Rome and Clement from Avignon.

Prominent churchmen urged the convening of a general council, the Council of Pisa, to end the disgraceful schism, which obstructed the papacy from performing its sacred duties. Held in 1409 and attended by hundreds of churchmen, the Council of Pisa deposed both Urban and Clement and elected a new pope. Since neither deposed pope recognized the council's decision, Christendom then had three popes. A new council was called at Constance in 1414. In the struggle that ensued, each of the three popes either abdicated or was deposed in favor of an appointment by the council. In 1417, the Great Schism ended.

During the first half of the fifteenth century, church councils met at Pisa (1409), Constance (1414–1418), and Basel (1431–1449) in order to end the schism, combat heresy, and reform the church. The Conciliar Movement attempted to transform the papal monarchy into a constitutional system in which the pope's power would be regulated by a general council. Supporters of the movement held that the papacy could not reform the church as effectively as a general council representing the clergy. But the Conciliar Movement ended in failure. As the Holy Roman Emperor and then the French monarch withdrew their support from the councils, the papacy regained its authority over the higher clergy. In 1460, Pope Pius II condemned the Conciliar Movement as heretical.

Deeply embroiled in European power politics and the worldly life of Renaissance Italy, the papacy often neglected its spiritual and moral responsibilities. Many devout Christians longed for religious renewal, a return to simple piety; the papacy did not hear this cry for reform. The papacy's failure to provide creative leadership for reform made possible the Protestant Reformation of the sixteenth century. By splitting Christendom into Catholic and Protestant, the Reformation destroyed forever the vision of a Christian world commonwealth guided by God's vicar, the pope.

Fourteenth-Century Heresies

Another threat to papal power and to the medieval ideal of a universal Christian community guided by the church came from radical reformers who questioned the function and authority of the entire church hierarchy. These heretics in the Late Middle Ages were forerunners of the Protestant Reformation. The two principal dissenters were the Englishman John Wycliffe (c. 1320–1384) and the Czech Jan Hus (c. 1369–1415).

By stressing a personal relationship between the individual and God and by claiming that the Bible itself, rather than church teachings, is the ultimate Christian authority, Wycliffe, a respected English theologian teaching at the University of Oxford, challenged the fundamental position of the medieval church: that the avenue to salvation passed through the church alone. He argued that Scripture, which was the final authority, needed no further development by church authorities and that the sacraments are not necessary for salvation. He denounced the wealth of the higher clergy and sought a return to the spiritual purity and material poverty of the early church. To Wycliffe, the wealthy, elaborately organized hierarchy of the church was unnecessary and wrong. The splendidly dressed and propertied bishops bore no resemblance to the simple people who first followed Christ. Indeed, these worldly bishops, headed by a princely and tyrannical pope, were really anti-Christians, the "fiends of Hell." Wycliffe wanted the state to confiscate church property and the clergy to embrace poverty. By denying that priests changed the bread and wine of communion into the substance of the body and blood of Christ, Wycliffe rejected the special powers of the clergy.

In Bohemia, Wycliffe's ideas were enthusiastically received by Czech reformers led by Jan Hus. Like Wycliffe, Hus advocated vernacular translations of the Bible, which would be accessible to common people, and he upbraided the upper clergy for their luxury and immorality.

Both movements were declared heretical. The church deprived the Lollards—an order of poor priests that spread Wycliffe's teachings—of their priestly functions. In the early fifteenth century, some of Wycliffe's followers were burned at the stake, and Hus was burned at the stake. Nevertheless, the church could not crush the dissenters' followers or eradicate their teachings. To some extent, the doctrines of the Reformation would parallel the teachings of Wycliffe.

Breakup of the Thomistic Synthesis

In the Late Middle Ages, the papacy lost power, as kings, political theorists, and religious dissenters challenged papal claims to supreme leadership. The great theological synthesis constructed by the scholastic theologians of the twelfth and thirteenth centuries was also breaking down. The process of fragmentation evident in the history of the church took place in philosophy as well.

Saint Thomas Aquinas's system culminated the scholastic attempt to show the basic agreement of philosophy and religion. In the fourteenth century, a number of thinkers cast doubt on the possibility of synthesizing Aristotelianism and Christianity, that is, reason and faith. Consequently, philosophy grew more analytical and critical. Denying that reason could demonstrate the truth of Christian doctrines with certainty, philosophers tried to separate reason from faith. Whereas Aquinas had said that reason proved or clarified much of revelation, fourteenth-century thinkers asserted that the basic propositions of Christianity were not open to rational proof. Whereas Aquinas had held that faith supplemented and perfected reason, some philosophers were now proclaiming that reason often contradicted faith.

Duns Scotus (1265–1308), a Scottish Franciscan, held that human reason cannot prove that God is omnipotent, that he forgives sins, that he rewards the righteous and punishes the wicked, or that the soul is immortal. These Christian doctrines, which scholastic philosophers believed could be proven by reason, were for Scotus the province of revelation and faith, not reason.

To be sure, this new outlook did not urge abandoning faith in favor of reason. Faith had to prevail in any conflict with reason because faith rested on God, the highest authority in the universe. But the relationship between reason and revelation was altered. Articles of faith, it was now held, had nothing to do with reason; they were to be believed, not proved. Reason was not an aid to theology but a separate sphere of activity. This new attitude snapped the link between reason and faith that Aquinas had so skillfully forged. The scholastic synthesis was disintegrating.

The chief proponent of the new outlook was William of Ockham (c. 1285–1349). In contrast to Aquinas, Ockham insisted that natural reason could not prove God's existence, the soul's immortality, or any other essential Christian doctrine. Reason could say only that God probably exists and that he probably endowed humankind with an immortal soul. But it could not prove these propositions with certainty. The tenets of faith were beyond the reach of reason, said Ockham; there was no rational foundation to Christianity. For Ockham, reason and faith did not necessarily complement each other as they did for Aquinas; it was neither possible nor helpful to join reason to faith. Ockham, however, sought not to undermine faith—only to disengage it from reason.

In the process of proclaiming the authority of theology, Ockham furthered the use of reason to comprehend nature. His approach, separating natural knowledge from religious dogma, made it easier to explore the natural world empirically without fitting it into a religious framework. Ockham, thus, is a forerunner of the modern mentality, which is characterized by a separation of reason from religion and an interest in the empirical investigation of nature.

The Middle Ages and the Modern World: Continuity and Discontinuity

Medieval civilization began to decline in the fourteenth century, but no dark age comparable to the three centuries following Rome's fall descended on Europe; its economic and political institutions and technological skills had grown too strong. Instead, the waning of the Middle Ages opened up possibilities for another stage in Western civilization: the modern age.

The modern world is linked to the Middle Ages in innumerable ways. European cities, the middle class, the state system, English common law, universities—all had their origins in the Middle Ages. During medieval times, important advances were made in business practices, including partnerships, systematic bookkeeping, and the bill of exchange. By translating and commenting on the writings of Greek and Arabic thinkers, medieval scholars preserved a priceless intellectual heritage without which the modern mind could never have evolved. In addition, numerous strands connect the thought of the scholastics and that of early modern philosophers.

Feudal traditions lasted long after the Middle Ages. Up to the French Revolution, for instance, French aristocrats enjoyed special privileges and exercised power over local government. In England, the aristocracy controlled local government until the Industrial Revolution transformed English society in the nineteenth century. Retaining the medieval ideal of the noble warrior, aristocrats continued to dominate the officer corps of European armies through the nineteenth century and even into the twentieth. Aristocratic notions of duty, honor, loyalty, and courtly love have endured into our own day.

During the Middle Ages, Europeans began to take the lead over the Muslims, the Byzantines, the Chinese, and all the other peoples in the use of technology. Medieval technology and inventiveness stemmed in part from Christianity, which taught that God had created the world specifically for human beings to subdue and exploit. Consequently, medieval people tried to employ animal power and laborsaving machinery to relieve human drudgery. Moreover, Christianity taught that God was above nature, not within it, so the Christians faced no spiritual obstacle to exploiting nature—unlike, for instance, the Hindus. In contrast to classical humanism, the Christian outlook did not consider manual work degrading; even monks combined it with study.

The Christian stress on the sacred worth of the individual (each person had an immortal soul that was God's concern), on human equality (differences in rank and birth were of no account to God on Judgment Day), and on the higher law of God (divine precepts had a greater pull on conscience than did the state's laws) has never ceased to influence Western civilization. Even though in modern times the various Christian churches have not often taken the lead in political and social reform, the ideals identified with the Judeo-Christian tradition have become part of the Western heritage. As such, they have inspired social reformers who may no longer identify with their ancestral religion.

Believing that God's law was superior to state or national decrees, medieval philosophers provided a theoretical basis for opposing tyrannical kings who violated Christian principles. The idea that both the ruler and the ruled are bound by a higher law would, in a secularized form, become a principal element of modern liberal thought.

Feudalism also contributed to the history of liberty. According to feudal custom, the king, as a member of the feudal community, was duty-bound to honor agreements made with his vassals. Lords possessed personal rights, which the king was obliged to respect. Resentful of a king who ran roughshod over customary feudal rights, lords also negotiated contracts with the crown, such as Magna Carta (1215), to define and guard their customary liberties. To protect themselves from the arbitrary behavior of a king, feudal lords initiated what came to be called *government by consent* and the *rule of law*.

During the Middle Ages, then, there gradually emerged the idea that law was not imposed on inferiors by an absolute monarch but required the collaboration of the king and his subjects; that the king, too, was bound by the law; and that lords had the right to resist a monarch who violated agreements. A related phenomenon was the rise of representative institutions, with which the king was expected to consult on the realm's affairs. The most notable of such institutions was the British Parliament; though subordinate to the king, it became a permanent part of the state. Later, in the seventeenth century, Parliament would successfully challenge royal authority. Thus, continuity exists between the feudal tradition of a king bound by law and the modern practice of limiting the authority of the head of state.

Although the elements of continuity are clear, the characteristic outlook of the Middle Ages is as different from that of the modern age as it was from the outlook of the ancient world. Religion was the integrating feature of the Middle Ages, whereas science and secularism—a preoccupation with worldly life—determine the modern outlook. The period from the Italian Renaissance of the fifteenth century through the eighteenth-century Age of Enlightenment saw a gradual breaking away from the medieval world-view—a rejection of the medieval conception of nature, the individual, and the purpose of life. The transition from medieval to modern was neither sudden nor complete, for there are no sharp demarcation lines separating historical periods. While many distinctively medieval ways endured in the sixteenth, seventeenth, and even eighteenth centuries, these centuries saw as well the rise of new intellectual, political, and economic forms, which marked the emergence of modernity.

Medieval thought began with the existence of God and the truth of his revelation as interpreted by the church, which set the standards and defined the purposes for human endeavor. The medieval mind rejected the fundamental principle of Greek philosophy: the autonomy of reason. Without the guidance of revealed truth, reason was seen as feeble.

Scholastics engaged in genuine philosophical speculation, but they did not allow philosophy to challenge the basic premises of their faith. Unlike either ancient or modern thinkers, medieval schoolmen ultimately believed that reason alone could not provide a unified view of nature or society. A rational soul had to be guided by a divine light. For all medieval philosophers, the natural order depended on a supernatural order for its origin and purpose. To understand the natural world properly, it was necessary to know its relationship to the higher world. The discoveries of reason had to accord with Scripture as interpreted by the church. In medieval thought, says the historian-philosopher Ernst Cassirer,

> *neither science nor morality, neither law nor state, can be erected on its own foundations. Supernatural assistance is always needed to bring them to true perfection. . . . Reason is and remains the servant of revelation; within the sphere of natural intellectual and psychological forces, reason leads toward, and prepares the ground for, revelation.*[4]

In the modern view, both nature and the human intellect are self-sufficient. Nature is a

Profile

Christine de Pisan

British Library/AKG London.

At the end of the Middle Ages, a remarkable woman took up the task of defending women from their many male detractors. Christine de Pisan (c. 1364–c. 1430) was born in Venice but moved with her parents to Paris, where her father was court physician and astrologer. She married a court notary when she was fifteen, had three children, and was left a widow and penniless ten years later. Although she had only an elementary education, she decided to use her literary interests to become a professional writer, an unheard-of occupation for a woman at that time. She won the friendship and patronage of noble ladies at the French royal court and produced courtly love poetry as well as poems about the French court, and books, including several polemical attacks on the poets who slandered womankind. She addressed such weighty issues as the ability of women to govern, their aptitude for learning, and the criminality of rape. In *The City of Ladies,* written in 1405, she argued that women possess the same moral and intellectual qualities as men. In one dialogue with Lady Reason, Christine asks whether God has honored women with the capacity of "high understanding and great learning. I wish very much to know this because men maintain that the mind of

mathematical system that operates without miracles or any other form of divine intervention. To comprehend nature and society, the mind needs no divine assistance; it accepts no authority above reason. The modern mentality finds it unacceptable to reject the conclusions of science on the basis of clerical authority and revelation or to ground politics, law, or economics on religious dogma. It refuses to settle public issues by appeals to religious belief, which is now seen as a strictly private conern.

The medieval philosopher understood both nature and society to be a hierarchical order. God was the source of moral values, and the church was responsible for teaching and upholding these ethical norms. Kings acquired their right to rule from God. The entire social structure constituted a hierarchy: the clergy guided society according to Christian standards; lords defended Christian society from its enemies; and serfs, lowest in the social order, toiled for the good of all. In the hierarchy of knowledge, a lower form of knowledge derived from the senses, and the highest type of knowledge, theology, dealt with God's revelation. To the medieval mind, this hierarchical ordering of nature, society, and knowledge had a divine sanction.

Rejecting the medieval division of the universe into higher and lower realms and superior and inferior substances, the modern view postulated the women can learn very little." Lady Reason responds like a contemporary feminist:

"My daughter, since I told you before, you know quite well that the opposite of their opinion is true, and to show you this even more clearly, I will give you proof through examples. I tell you again—and don't doubt the contrary—if it were customary to send daughters to school like sons, and if they were then taught the natural sciences, they would learn as thoroughly and understand the subleties of all the arts and sciences as well as sons. And by chance there happen to be such women, for, as I touched on before, just as women have more delicate bodies than men, weaker and less able to perform many tasks, so do they have minds that are freer and sharper whenever they apply themselves."

"My lady, what are you saying? With all due respect, could you dwell longer on this point, please. Certainly men would never admit this answer is true, unless it is explained more plainly, for they believe that one normally sees that men know more than women do."

She answered, "Do you know why women know less?"

"Not unless you tell me, my lady."

"Without the slightest doubt, it is because they are not involved in many different things, but stay at home, where it is enough for them to run the household, and there is nothing which so instructs a reasonable creature as the exercise and experience of many different things."

"My lady, since they have minds skilled in conceptualizing and learning, just like men, why don't women learn more?"

*She replied, "Because, my daughter, the public does not require them to get involved in the affairs which men are commissioned to execute, just as I told you before. It is enough for women to perform the usual duties to which they are ordained. As for judging from experience, since one sees that women usually know less than men, that therefore their capacity for understanding is less, look at men who farm the flatlands or who live in the mountains. You will find that in many countries they seem completely savage because they are so simple-minded. All the same, there is no doubt that Nature provided them with the qualities of body and mind found in the wisest and most learned men. . . ."**

*Christine de Pisan, *The Book of the City of Ladies*, translated by Earl Jeffrey Richards.

uniformity of nature and of nature's laws: the cosmos knows no privilege of rank; heavenly bodies follow the same laws of nature as earthly objects. Space is geometric and homogeneous, not hierarchical, heterogeneous, and qualitative. The universe was no longer conceived as finite and closed but as infinite, and the operations of nature were explained mathematically. The modern thinker studies mathematical law and chemical composition, not grades of perfection. Spiritual meaning is not sought in an examination of the material world. Roger Bacon, for example, described seven coverings of the eye and then concluded that God had fashioned the eye in this manner in order to express the seven gifts of the Spirit. This way of thinking is alien to the modern outlook. So, too, is the medieval belief that natural disasters, such as plagues and famines, are God's punishments for people's sins.

The outlook of the modern West also broke with the rigid division of medieval society into three orders: clergy, nobles, and commoners. The intellectual justification for this arrangement, as expressed by the English prelate John of Salisbury (c. 1115–1180), has been rejected by modern westerners: "For inferiors owe it to their superiors to provide them with service, just as the superiors in their turn owe it to their inferiors to provide them with all things needful for their protection and succor."[5] Opposing the feudal principle that an indi-

Wisdom Urges Medieval Scholars Forward. During the Middle Ages, Europeans made considerable advances in technology. The astrolabe, quadrant, sundials, and mechanical clocks shown here exemplify medieval technical skills. (*Bibliothèque royale Albert 1er, Brussels.*)

vidual's obligations and rights are a function of his or her rank in society, the modern view stressed equality of opportunity and equal treatment under the law. It rejected the idea that society should be guided by clergy who were deemed to possess a special wisdom; by nobles who were entitled to special privileges; and by monarchs who were thought to receive their power from God.

The modern West also rejected the personal and customary character of feudal law. As the modern state developed, law assumed an impersonal and objective character. For example, if the lord demanded more than the customary forty days of military service, the vassal might refuse to comply because he would see the lord's request as an unpardonable violation of custom and agreement, as well as an infringement on his liberties. In the modern state, with a constitution and a representative assembly, if a new law increasing the length of military service is passed, it merely replaces the old law. People do not refuse to obey it because the government has broken faith or violated custom.

In the modern world, the individual's relationship to the universe has been radically transformed. Medieval people lived in a geocentric universe that was finite in space and time. The universe was small, enclosed by a sphere of stars, beyond which were the heavens. The universe, it was believed, was some four thousand years old, and, in the not-too-distant future, Christ would return and human history would end. People in the Middle Ages knew why they were on earth and what was expected of them; they never doubted that heaven would be their reward for living a Christian life. Preparation for heaven was the ultimate aim of life. J. H. Randall, Jr., a historian of ideas, eloquently sums up the medieval view of a purposeful universe in which the human being's position was clearly defined:

> *The world was governed throughout by the omnipotent will and omniscient mind of God, whose sole interests were centered in man, his trial, his fall, his suffering and his glory. Worm of the dust as he was, man was yet the central object in the whole universe. . . . And when his destiny was completed, the heavens would be rolled up as a scroll and he would dwell with the Lord forever. Only those who rejected God's freely offered grace and with hardened hearts refused repentance would be cut off from this eternal life.*[6]

This comforting medieval vision is alien to the modern outlook. Today, in a universe some twelve to fifteen billion years old, in which the earth is a tiny speck floating in an endless cosmic ocean, where life evolved over tens of millions of years, many westerners no longer believe that human beings are special children of God; that heaven is their ultimate goal; that under their feet is hell, where grotesque demons torment sinners; and that God is an active agent in human history. To many intellectuals, the universe seems unresponsive to the religious supplications of people, and life's purpose is sought within the limits of earthly existence. Science and secularism have driven Christianity and faith from their central position to the periphery of human concerns.

In the nineteenth and twentieth centuries, Christian thinkers lamented the waning of faith. Distressed by all-consuming secularism, crude materialism, and vicious class and national antagonisms, these thinkers attributed the ills of the modern West to a diminishing commitment to Christianity and called for spiritual renewal. Some of them, looking back nostalgically to the Middle Ages when life had an overriding religious purpose and few doubted the truth of Christian teachings, contended that the modern West would benefit from a reaffirmation of those Christian concerns and values that had energized medieval society.

The modern outlook developed gradually in the period from the Renaissance to the eighteenth-century Age of Enlightenment. Mathematics rendered the universe comprehensible. Economic and political thought broke free of the religious frame of reference. Science became the great hope of the future. The thinkers of the Enlightenment wanted to liberate humanity from superstition, ignorance, and traditions that could not pass the test of reason. They saw themselves as emancipating culture from theological dogma and clerical authority. Rejecting the Christian idea of a person's inherent sinfulness, they held that the individual was basically good and that evil resulted from faulty institutions, poor education, and bad leadership. Thus, the concept of a rational and free society in which individuals could realize their potential slowly emerged.

❖ ❖ ❖

Notes

1. Jean Froissart, *Chronicles of England, France, Spain* (London: Henry G. Bohn, 1849), p. 653.
2. Excerpted in Brian Tierney, ed., *The Crisis of Church and State, 1050–1300* (Englewood Cliffs, N.J.: Prentice-Hall, 1964), p. 189.
3. Excerpted in Ralph Lerner and Muhsin Mahdi, eds., *Medieval Political Philosophy* (New York: Free Press, 1963), pp. 413–414.
4. Ernst Cassirer, *The Philosophy of the Enlightenment* (Boston: Beacon Press, 1955), p. 40.
5. John of Salisbury, *Policraticus,* trans. John

Dickinson (New York: Russell & Russell, 1963), pp. 243–244.

6. J. H. Randall, Jr., *The Making of the Modern Mind* (Boston: Houghton Mifflin, 1940), p. 34.

Suggested Reading

Bowsky, W. M., ed., *The Black Death* (1971). Readings on the impact of the plague.

Hay, Denys, *Europe in the Fourteenth and Fifteenth Centuries* (1966). A good survey of the Late Middle Ages.

Hilton, Rodney, *Bond Men Made Free* (1977). An analysis of medieval peasant movements.

Holmes, George, *Europe: Hierarchy and Revolt, 1320–1450* (1975). A good survey of the period.

Huizinga, Johan, *The Waning of the Middle Ages* (1924). An old but still valuable discussion of late medieval culture.

Lerner, Robert E., *The Age of Adversity* (1968). A short, readable survey of the fourteenth century.

McFarlane, K. B., *John Wycliffe and the Beginnings of English Nonconformity* (1952). The man and his influence.

Mollat, Guillaume, *The Popes at Avignon* (1963). The papacy in the fourteenth century.

Ozment, Steven E., *The Age of Reform, 1250–1550* (1980). An intellectual and religious history of late medieval and Reformation Europe.

Perroy, Edouard, *The Hundred Years' War* (1965). The best treatment of the conflict.

Russell, Burton Jeffrey, *Witchcraft in the Middle Ages* (1972). Describes the development of a phenomenon that is deeply rooted in the nonrational.

Spinka, M., *John Hus and the Czech Reform* (1941). A reliable work on Hus and the Hussite wars.

Ziegler, Philip, *The Black Death* (1969). The spread and impact of the great plague.

Review Questions

1. What economic problems made the fourteenth century an age of adversity?
2. What were the principal reasons for peasant uprisings in the fourteenth century?
3. What was the fundamental issue at stake in the conflict between Boniface VIII and Philip IV?
4. How did John of Paris and Marsiglio of Padua challenge the pope's claim to primacy over secular authority?
5. Identify and explain the historical significance of the Babylonian Captivity, the Great Schism, and the Conciliar Movement.
6. Why did the church regard Wycliffe and Hus as heretics?
7. What was the significance of Ockham's philosophy?
8. What is the legacy of the Middle Ages to the modern world?
9. How does the characteristic outlook of the Middle Ages differ from that of the modern age?

Part Three

Early Modern Europe: From Renaissance to Enlightenment

1350–1789

1300

1400

1500

1600

1700

Politics and Society	*Thought and Culture*
Hundred Years' War (1337–1453)	Italian Renaissance begins (c. 1350)
War of Roses in England (1455–1485) Rule of Ferdinand and Isabella in Spain (1469–1516) Charles VIII of France (1483–1498) Henry VII; beginning of Tudor dynasty in England (1485–1509) French invasion of Italy (1494) Columbus reaches America (1492)	Early Renaissance artists: Brunelleschi, Masaccio, van Eyck Printing with movable type (c. 1445) Humanists: Valla, Pico della Mirandola Late Renaissance artists: Botticelli, Leonardo da Vinci, Michelangelo, Raphael, Bellini, Giorgione, Titian Renaissance spreads to northern Europe (late 15th–early 16th cent.)
Henry VIII of England (1509–1547) Francis I of France (1515–1547) Charles V, Holy Roman Emperor (1519–1556) Henry VIII of England breaks with Rome (1529–1536) Council of Trent (1545–1563) Treaty of Augsburg in Germany (1555) Philip II of Spain (1556–1598) Elizabeth I of England (1558–1603) Religious wars in France (1562–1598) Revolt of the Netherlands from Spain (1566–1609) Defeat of Spanish Armada (1588)	Humanists: Castiglione, Erasmus, Montaigne, Rabelais, More, Machiavelli, Cervantes, Shakespeare Luther writes Ninety-five Theses (1517) Calvin, *The Institutes of the Christian Religion* (1536) Copernicus, *On the Revolution of the Heavenly Spheres* (1543)
Thirty Years' War (1618–1648) English Revolutions (1640–1660, 1688–1689) Louis XIV of France (1643–1715) Peter the Great of Russia (1682–1725)	Scientists: Kepler, Galileo, Newton Philosophers: Bacon, Descartes, Spinoza, Hobbes, Bayle, Locke
War of Spanish Succession (1702–1714) War of Austrian Succession (1740–1748) Frederick the Great of Prussia (1740–1786) Maria Theresa of Austria (1740–1780) Seven Years' War (1756–1763) Catherine the Great of Russia (1762–1796) American Declaration of Independence (1776) American Revolution (1776–1783) Beginning of French Revolution (1789)	Enlightenment thinkers: Voltaire, Montesquieu, Rousseau, Diderot, Hume, Adam Smith, Thomas Jefferson, Kant

Chapter 13

The Renaissance: Transition to the Modern Age

The School of Athens by Raphael (1483–1520). The ancient Greek philosophers, with Plato and Aristotle at the center, are depicted here, assembled in classical grandeur. Painted to decorate the Vatican, the papal palace in Rome, the picture exudes the Renaissance reverence for classical antiquity and reflects the widely held view that ancient philosophy represented a foreshadowing of Christianity and was essentially in harmony with it. (Stanza della segnaturna, Vatican Palace, Vatican State/Art Resource, NY.)

- **Italy: Birthplace of the Renaissance**
  Political Evolution of the City-States
  Renaissance Society
- **The Renaissance Outlook: Humanism and Secular Politics**
  Humanism
  A Revolution in Political Thought
- **Renaissance Art**
  Early Renaissance Art
  Late Renaissance Art
- **The Spread of the Renaissance**
  Erasmian Humanism
  French Humanism
  Spanish Humanism
  English Humanism
- **The Renaissance and the Modern Age**

From the Italian Renaissance of the fifteenth century through the Age of Enlightenment of the eighteenth century, the outlook and institutions of the Middle Ages disintegrated and distinctly modern forms emerged. The radical change in European civilization could be seen on every level of society. On the economic level, commerce and industry expanded greatly, and capitalism in some countries largely replaced medieval forms of economic organization. On the political level, central government grew stronger at the expense of feudalism. On the religious level, the rise of Protestantism fragmented the unity of Christendom. On the social level, middle-class townspeople, increasing in number and wealth, were playing a more important role in economic and cultural life. On the cultural level, the clergy lost its monopoly over learning, and the otherworldly orientation of the Middle Ages gave way to a secular outlook in literature and the arts. Theology, the queen of knowledge in the Middle Ages, surrendered her crown to science. Reason, which in the Middle Ages had been subordinate to revelation, asserted its independence.

Many of these tendencies manifested themselves dramatically during the Renaissance. The word *renaissance* means "rebirth," and it is used to refer to the attempt by artists and thinkers to recover and apply the ancient learning and standards of Greece and Rome. In historical terms, the Renaissance is both a cultural movement and a period. As a movement, it was born in the city-states of northern Italy and spread to the rest of Europe. As a period, it runs from 1350 to 1600. Until the late fifteenth century, the Renaissance was restricted to Italy. What happened there in the fourteenth and fifteenth centuries sharply contrasts with civilization in the rest of Europe, which, until the end of the fifteenth century, still belonged to the Late Middle Ages.

The nineteenth-century historian Jacob Burckhardt in his classic study, *The Civilization of the Renaissance in Italy* (1860), held that the Renaissance is the point of departure for the modern world. During the Renaissance, said Burckhardt, individuals showed increasing concern with worldly life and self-consciously aspired to shape their destinies—attitudes that are the key to modernity.

Chronology 13.1 ❖ The Renaissance

1200–1300	Bologna, Padua, and Ravenna become centers of legal studies
1300–1450	Republicanism reigns in northern Italian city-states
1304–1374	Petrarch, "father of humanism"
1378	Ciompi revolt in Florence
c. 1407–1457	Lorenzo Valla, author of *Declamation Concerning the False Decretals of Constantine*
c. 1445	Johann Gutenberg invents movable metal type
1454	Peace of Lodi is signed
1494	Charles VIII of France invades northern Italy; Pope Julius II commissions frescoes by Michelangelo for the Vatican's Sistine Chapel
1513	Machiavelli writes *The Prince*
1528	*The Book of the Courtier,* by Baldesar Castiglione, is published
1535	Sir Thomas More, English humanist and author of *Utopia,* is executed for treason

Burckhardt's thesis has been challenged, particularly by medievalists, who view the Renaissance as an extension of the Middle Ages, not as a sudden break with the past. These critics argue that Burckhardt neglected important links between medieval and Renaissance culture. One distinguishing feature of the Renaissance, the revival of classical learning, had already emerged in the High Middle Ages to such an extent that historians speak of "the renaissance of the twelfth century" and the "Twelfth-Century Awakening." The Renaissance owes much to the legal and scholastic studies that flourished in the Italian universities of Padua and Bologna before 1300. Town life and trade, hallmarks of Renaissance society, were also a heritage from the Middle Ages.

To be sure, the Renaissance was not a complete and sudden break with the Middle Ages. Many medieval ways and attitudes persisted. Nevertheless, Burckhardt's thesis that the Renaissance represents the birth of modernity has much to recommend it. Renaissance writers and artists themselves were aware of their age's novelty. They looked back on the medieval centuries as the "Dark Ages" that followed the grandeur of ancient Greece and Rome, and they believed that they were experiencing a rebirth of cultural greatness. Renaissance artists and writers were fascinated by the cultural forms of Greece and Rome; they sought to imitate classical style and to capture the secular spirit of antiquity. In the process, they broke with medieval artistic and literary forms. They valued the full development of human talent and expressed fresh excitement about the possibilities of life in this world. This outlook represents a new trend in European civilization.

The Renaissance, then, was an age of transition that saw the rejection of certain elements of the medieval outlook, the revival of classical cultural forms, and the emergence of distinctly modern attitudes. As mentioned earlier, this rebirth began in Italy during the fourteenth century. It gradually spread north and west to Germany, France, England, and Spain during the late fifteenth and sixteenth centuries.

Italy: Birthplace of the Renaissance

The city-states of northern Italy that spawned the Renaissance were developed urban centers where the elite had the wealth, freedom, and inclination to cultivate the arts and to enjoy the fruits of worldly life. In Italy, moreover, reminders of ancient Rome's grandeur were visible everywhere. Roman roads, monuments, and manuscripts intensified Italians' links to their Roman past.

Political Evolution of the City-States

During the Middle Ages, the feudal states of northern Italy had been absorbed into the Holy Roman Empire. They continued to owe nominal allegiance to the German emperor during the early Renaissance. But protracted wars with the papacy had sapped the empire's vitality. Its consequent weakness allowed the states of northern Italy to develop as autonomous political entities. The weakening of the papacy in the fourteenth century also promoted this development.

In their size and their varied types of governments, the city-states in northern Italy resembled those of ancient Greece. Among the more important were Rome, Milan, Florence, Venice, Mantua, Ferrara, Padua, Bologna, and Genoa. They differed markedly from most of Europe in two fundamental respects.

First, by the late eleventh and twelfth centuries, these city-states were flourishing commercial and banking centers and monopolized trade in Mediterranean areas, including trade between the Orient and the West. Merchant fleets, especially those of Venice and Genoa, carried goods from ports in the eastern Mediterranean westward into the Atlantic and from there north to the Baltic Sea. In contrast to the rest of Europe, the wealth of these cities lay not in land but in commerce and industry. When popes, monarchs, and feudal magnates of Europe needed money, they borrowed it from Italian, especially Florentine, merchant-bankers.

Second, the predominance of business and commerce within these city-states meant that the feudal nobility, which held the land beyond the city walls, played a much lesser role in government than they did elsewhere in Europe. By the end of the twelfth century the city-states no longer were dominated by the feudal nobility, or landed aristocracy. The aristocracy and the rich merchants had to share power, and when their alliances broke down, as they often did, the two groups struggled for power based on their opposing interests and outlooks. The interests of the smaller merchants and the artisans in the towns also had to be catered to. When they were not, those groups rioted and rebelled, as they did, for instance, in 1378, during the revolt of the *Ciompi* (wool-workers) in Florence.

Politically, the city-states in Northern Italy were inherently unstable. The instability had two sources: internal conflicts between merchants and nobles and external rivalries among the city-states themselves. The city-states managed to keep both the papacy and the Holy Roman Empire at bay, sometimes by playing one giant against the other, as Third World nations do today. But the price of this continued independence was that the city-states, without any externally imposed power structure, had to seek their own solutions to their instability. Out of this situation came experiments in the form and technique of government. The origins of modern political thought and practice can be discerned in this experimentation, which is an important link between the Renaissance and the modern age.

The political experimentation in the northern Italian city-states can usefully, if only roughly, be divided into two periods: the first (1300–1450) marked by the defense of republicanism; the second (1450–1550), by the triumph of despotism. By the end of the twelfth century, the city-states had adopted a fairly uniform pattern of republican self-government built around the office of a chief magistrate. Elected by the citizens on the basis of a broad franchise, he ruled with the advice of two councils—a large public one and a small secret one. His powers were tightly circumscribed by the constitution; with his term of office restricted ordinarily to six months, he could be removed from government or punished at the end of his tenure.

The city-states not only developed republican institutions; they also devised important theories to defend and justify their liberty and self-government in the face of their external enemies, the papacy and the empire. With the emperor, they argued that their customary feudal subjection to imperial authority must be radically adjusted to fit the changed reality that they were in fact self-governing. With the papacy, they contended that Christ had denied all political jurisdiction to the clergy, including the pope, and that this fact un-

LUDOVICO GONZAGA, HIS FAMILY AND COURT: A FRESCO PAINTED BY ANDREA MANTEGNA, 1465–1474. The Gonzaga family came to power as princes of Mantua, selling their services as condottieri to the Venetians, Milanese, and others as their interests dictated. Ludovico (1414–1478) presided over Mantua at a time of great prosperity. He commissioned the famous painter Andrea Mantegna to decorate his palace, and the architect Leon Battista Alberti to build several churches. His patronage of humanistic scholars, poets, and philosophers enhanced the prestige of both the city and its princely ruler. (*Scala/Art Resource, NY.*)

dercut the papal claim to political control in Italy and elsewhere.

However, given the city-states' internal instability and rivalry, their republicanism proved precarious. During the fourteenth and early fifteenth centuries, the republican institutions in one city after another toppled in favor of despotic rule. Three conditions were responsible for this development. First, class war between rich merchants and nobles caused one group or the other, or both, to seek a resolution of the crisis by turning to one-man rule. Second, the economic disasters, famine, and disease of the period from 1350 to 1450 encouraged the drift toward despotism. Northern Italy was particularly hard hit by the bubonic plague. The citizenry lost faith in the ability of short-term republican governments to cope with such emergencies and put its trust in long-term, one-man rule. Third, and perhaps most important, the city-states, in wars with their rivals, had come to rely on mercenary troops. The

Map 13.1 Italian City-States, c. 1494 ▶
During the Renaissance, Italy was divided between large kingdoms in the south, dominated by the Spanish monarchy, and smaller city-states in the north, each with its own government and army and often hostile to one another. The French king Charles VIII took advantage of these divisions by invading and occupying much of northern Italy beginning in 1494.

0
50
100 Km.
0
50
100Mi.
OTTOMAN EMPIRE
DUCHY OF SAVOY
DUCHY OF MILAN
Milan
Turin
Pavia
Lodi
Padua
M. OF MANTUA
Mantua
Venice
REPUBLIC OF VENICE
SALUZZO
Po R.
REP. OF GENOA
Genoa
Ferrara
D. OF FERRERA
D. OF MODENA
Bologna
Ravenna
REP. OF LUCCA
Arno R.
Pisa
REP. OF FLORENCE
Florence
Urbino
DALMATIA
Siena
Tiber R.
Assisi
REP. OF SIENA
CORSICA
PAPAL STATES
Adriatic Sea
Rome
KINGDOM OF NAPLES
Bari
SARDINIA
Naples
Salerno
Palermo
Mediterranean Sea
KINGDOM OF SICILY

leaders of those troops, the notorious *condottieri*—unschooled in and owing no loyalty to the republican tradition—simply seized power during emergencies.

Some city-states held out for a long time against the trend toward despotism. Among those that did, Florence was by far the most successful. In the process, the Florentines developed new arguments and theories for the maintenance of republicanism and liberty (see below). But by the middle of the fifteenth century, even Florentine republicanism was giving way before the intrigues of a rich banking family, the Medicis. They had installed themselves in power in the 1430s, with the return of Cosimo de Medicis from exile. Cosimo's grandson, Lorenzo the Magnificent, completed the destruction of the republican constitution in 1480, when he managed to set up a government staffed by his own supporters.

The one city-state where republicanism survived until the advent of Napoleon was Venice. Protected from the rest of Italy by lagoons, Venice, during the Middle Ages, controlled a far-flung and exceptionally lucrative seagoing trade and a maritime empire stretching along the Adriatic and the eastern Mediterranean Seas. Venetian maritime commercial successes were matched by political ones at home. For centuries, Venice managed to govern itself without a major upheaval; its republican constitution made this stability possible. Its chief executive offices, the Council of Ten, were elective, but after 1297, both these offices and the electorate were narrowly restricted by law to old patrician families. Venice was an aristocratic republic. The government proved remarkably effective because the ruling elite was able to instill in its young a sense of public duty that was passed on from one generation, and one century, to the next. Because Venetian government was at once stable and republican, it served as a model to republican theorists in seventeenth- and eighteenth-century Europe.

Aside from Venice, the city-states in Northern Italy were not only internally unstable but also constantly warring with each other. By the middle of the fifteenth century, however, five major powers had emerged from the fighting: the kingdom of Naples and Sicily in the south; the Papal States, a papacy-controlled territory running across the center of the Italian peninsula; and the city-states of Florence, Venice, and Milan in the north. In 1454, these five powers, largely through the efforts of Cosimo de Medicis, concluded the Peace of Lodi. For the next forty years, they were relatively peaceful, until the French king Charles VIII invaded northern Italy in 1494.

The Peace of Lodi endured so long thanks to diplomacy. The essential techniques of modern diplomacy were worked out and applied in the second half of the fifteenth century in Italy. The practices of establishing embassies with ambassadors, sending and analyzing intelligence reports, consulting and negotiating during emergencies, and forming alliances all developed during this period. Some historians also see this time in Italian history as the seedbed for the notion of balance of power, which eventually became fundamental to the diplomacy of all Europe. Later, in the early modern period, European governments formed alliances so that no single state or group of allied states could dominate the Continent. Some elements of this balance of power were anticipated in the struggles among the Italian city-states.

Renaissance Society

The new way of life in the city-states paralleled developments in relations among them. Prosperous merchants played a leading role in the political and cultural life of the city. With the growth of commerce and industry, the feudal values of birth, military prowess, and a fixed hierarchy of lords and vassals decayed in favor of ambition and individual achievement, whether at court, in the countinghouse, or inside the artist's studio. The old feudal chivalric code was not destroyed but transformed to serve different purposes.

The new urban, commercial oligarchies could not justify their power in the old way, through heredity. Moreover, they had to function within the inherently unstable political climate of the city-states. Faced with this dual problem, the oligarchs fell back on the feudal idea of honor and developed elaborate codes. These codes differed in significant ways from their medieval antecedents. First came a depreciation (though never a complete elimination) of birth as a basis of merit, and a corresponding emphasis on effort, talent, and (in the case of the artist) creative genius. Second, honor was no longer defined in narrow, largely military terms; it was expanded to include both the civic and courtly virtues of the worthy citizen and courtier and the artistic achievement of the painter, sculptor, architect, and poet.

The new code, however, did remain elitist and even aristocratic. Indeed, the new oligarchs of the Renaissance, because of their newness and insecurity, were all the more anxious to adopt the aristocratic outlook of the old nobility. The *nouveaux riches* (newly rich) aped the feudal aristocracy in dress and manners, even as they accommodated the code of knightly chivalry to the demands of a new urban and commercial culture. Renaissance society was a highly unstable compound of old and new.

Marriage and Family Life. City life profoundly altered family structure, marriage patterns, and relations between the sexes. Elsewhere in Europe, most people still lived on the land and tended to marry early in order to produce large families to work the fields. But in cities, early marriage could be a liability for a man who was attempting to make his fortune. The results were that older men married young brides and that wives usually outlived their husbands. Because a widow inherited her husband's property, she was not pressed to remarry and was likely to bring up her children in a single-parent household. According to the historian David Herlihy, the fact that so many women were responsible for nurturing their children may have encouraged the development of the Renaissance ideal of a gentleman, which emphasized civility, courtliness, and an appreciation of art, literature, and the feminine graces.

The large number of single, relatively prosperous, and leisured adults probably explains why Renaissance cities were notorious for sodomy, prostitution, and triangles involving an older husband, a young wife, and a young lover. Such sexual behavior was encouraged by the relative anonymity of the large cities and by the constant influx of young men of talent from the country districts.

Whatever the effect on their sons, upper-class women enjoyed greater freedom in greater numbers than they had since the fall of Rome. If they were married, they had the income to pursue pleasure in the form of clothes, conversation, and romance. If a well-to-do husband died while his wife was still young, she had no financial reasons to remarry and was free, to a degree previously unknown, to go her own way.

Patronage of the Arts. Members of the urban upper class became patrons of the arts, providing funds to support promising artists and writers. Urban patricians, whose wealth was based on commerce and banking, not land, had become dominant in both republican Florence and despotic Milan. Unable to claim power by birth or to rely on traditional loyalties, they looked to culture to provide the trappings and justification of power.

For the newly rich, art could serve a political function. In its sheer magnificence, art could manifest power. Art, like literature, could also serve as a focus of civic pride and patriotism. Just as insecure rulers contended on the battlefield, they competed for art and artists to bolster their egos. Art became a desirable political investment, especially when, in the fifteenth century, economic investments were not offering as much return as they had a century or two before. The popes invested in art as well. Having lost the battle for temporal dominion in Europe, the papacy concentrated on increasing its direct dominion in Italy by consolidating and expanding the Papal States. As an adjunct to this policy, the popes heaped wealth on artists to enhance papal prestige. Indeed, the popes became the most lavish patrons of all, as the works of Michelangelo, Botticelli, and Raphael testify.

The result of this new patronage by popes and patricians was an explosion of creativity. The amount, and especially the nature, of this patronage also helped to shape both art and the artist. For the first time since antiquity, portraiture became a separate genre and was developed much further than ever before. Patrician rivalry and insecurity of status, fed by the Renaissance ethic of achievement and reward, produced a scramble for honor and reputation. This fostered the desire to be memorialized in a painting, if not in a sculpture. A painter like Titian was in great demand.

Secularism. Renaissance society was marked by a growing secular outlook. Intrigued by the active life of the city and eager to enjoy the worldly pleasures that their money could obtain, wealthy merchants and bankers moved away from the medieval preoccupation with salvation. Although they were neither nonbelievers nor atheists, for them religion increasingly had to compete with worldly concerns. Consequently, members of the urban upper class paid religion less heed or at least did not allow it to interfere with their quest for a full life. The challenge and pleasure of living well in this world seemed more exciting than the promise of heaven. This outlook found expression in Renaissance art and literature.

Individualism. Individualism was another hallmark of Renaissance society. Urban life released people of wealth and talent from the old constraints of manor and church. The urban elite sought to assert their own personalities, discover and express their individual feelings, and demonstrate their unique talents. They strove to win fame and glory and to fulfill their ambitions. This Renaissance ideal was explicitly elitist. It applied only to the few, entirely disregarding the masses, and it valued what was distinctive and superior in an individual, not what was common to all. Concerned with the distinctions of the few, it did not consider the needs or rights of the many. Individualism became deeply embedded in the Western soul and was expressed by artists who sought to capture individual character, by explorers who ventured into uncharted seas, by conquerors who carved out empires in the New World, and by merchant-capitalists who amassed fortunes.

The Renaissance Outlook: Humanism and Secular Politics

Humanism

The most characteristic intellectual movement of the Renaissance was *humanism,* an educational and cultural program based on the study of ancient Greek and Roman literature. The humanist attitude toward antiquity differed from the attitude of medieval scholars, who had taken pains to fit classical learning into a Christian worldview. Renaissance humanists did not subordinate the classics to the requirements of Christian doctrines; rather, they valued ancient literature for its own sake—for its clear and graceful style and its insights into human nature. From the ancient classics, humanists expected to learn much that could not be provided by medieval writing: for instance, how to live well in this world and how to perform one's civic duties. For the humanists the classics were a guide to the good life, the active life. To achieve self-cultivation, to write well, to speak well, and to live well, it was necessary to know the classics. In contrast to scholastic philosophers, who used Greek philosophy to prove the truth of Christian doctrines, Italian humanists used classical learning to nourish their new interest in a worldly life.

Whereas medieval scholars were familiar with only some ancient Latin writers, Renaissance humanists restored to circulation every Roman work that could be found. Similarly, knowledge of Greek was very rare in Latin Christendom during the Middle Ages, but Renaissance humanists increasingly cultivated the study of Greek in order to read Homer, Demosthenes, Plato, and other ancients in the original.

Although predominantly a secular movement, Italian humanism was not un-Christian. True, humanists often treated moral problems in a purely secular manner. Yet in dealing with religious and theological questions, they did not challenge Christian belief or question the validity of the Bible. They did, however, attack scholasticism for its hairsplitting arguments and preoccupation with trivial questions. They stressed instead a purer form of Christianity, based on direct study of the Bible and writings by the church fathers.

The early humanists, sometimes called the fathers of humanism, were Petrarch (1304–1374) and Boccaccio (1313–1375). Petrarch, Boccaccio, and their followers carried the recovery of the classics further by making a systematic attempt to discover the classical roots of medieval Italian rhetoric. Petrarch's own efforts to learn Greek were largely unsuccessful, but by encouraging his students to master the ancient tongue, he advanced humanist learning. Petrarch was particularly drawn to Cicero, the ancient Roman orator. Following the example of Cicero, Petrarch insisted that education should consist not only of learning and knowing things but also of learning how to communicate one's knowledge and how to use it for the public good. Therefore, the emphasis in education should be on rhetoric and moral philosophy, wisdom combined with eloquence. As Bartolommeo della Fonte (1446–1513), professor of rhetoric at Florence, said, such a program of instruction would fit a man for effective rule: that is, "to punish the wicked, to care for the good, to embellish his native land and to benefit all mankind."[1] Thus, Petrarch helped make Ciceronian values dominant among the humanists. His followers set up schools to inculcate the new Ciceronian educational ideal.

Implicit in the humanist educational ideal was a radical transformation of the medieval (Augustinian) view of men and women. According to this view, since human beings were completely subject to divine will, not only were they incapable of attaining excellence through their own efforts and talents, but it was wrong and sinful for them even to try. In contrast, the humanists, recalling the classical Greek concept of areté, made the achievement of excellence through individual striving the end not only of education but of life itself. Moreover, because individuals were capable of this goal, it was their duty to pursue it as the end of life, although the pursuit was not effortless and indeed demanded extraordinary energy and skill.

People were deemed capable of excellence in every sphere and duty-bound to make the effort. This emphasis on human creative powers was one of the most characteristic and influential doctrines of the Renaissance. A classic expression of it is found in the *Oration on the Dignity of Man* (1486) by Giovanni Pico della Mirandola (1463–1494). Man, said Pico, has the freedom to shape his own life. Pico has God say to man: "We have made you a creature" such that "you may, as the free and proud shaper of your own being, fashion yourself in the form you may prefer."[2]

Pico also spelled out another implication of man's duty to realize his potential: through his own exertions, man can come to understand and control nature. One of the new and powerful Renaissance images of man was as the *magus,* the magician. The vision of the mastery of nature would continue to inspire experimentalists, like Francis Bacon, and natural philosophers, like Robert Boyle and Isaac Newton, until at least the early eighteenth century. A major psychological driving force of the Scientific Revolution, this vision stemmed in large part from the philosophy of Italian humanists like Pico.

The attack on the medieval scholastics was implicit in the humanist educational ideal. From the humanist perspective, scholasticism failed not only because its terms and Latin usage were barbarous but also because it did not provide useful knowledge. This humanist emphasis on the uses of knowledge offered an additional stimulus to science and art.

So hostile were the humanists to all things scholastic and medieval that they reversed the prevailing view of history. The Christian view saw history as a simple unfolding of God's will and providence. The humanists stressed the importance of human actions and human will in history—of people as active participants in the shaping of events. The humanists rejected the providentialist scheme in favor of a cyclical view deriving from the ancients, particularly Aristotle, Polybius, and Cicero. History alternated between times of darkness and times of light, of ignorance and illumination, of decline and rebirth.

This cyclical view allowed the humanists to characterize the preceding epoch as a period of decline from classical heights. It also let them see their own time as a period of rebirth, the recovery of classical wisdom and ideals. On the basis of this cyclical view, the humanists invented the notion of the Middle Ages as a gulf of darkness separating the ancient world from their own. To the humanists, then, we owe the current periodization of history into ancient, medieval, and modern. The humanists' view also contained an element of today's idea of progress: they dared to think that they, "the moderns," might even surpass the ancient glories of Greece and Rome.

The humanist emphasis on historical scholarship yielded a method of critical inquiry that, in the right hands, could help undermine traditional loyalties and institutions. The work of Lorenzo Valla (c. 1407–1457) provides the clearest example of this trend. Educated as a classicist, Valla trained the guns of critical scholarship on the papacy in his most famous work, *Declamation Concerning the False Decretals of Constantine.* The papal claim to temporal authority rested on a document that purported to verify the so-called Donation of Constantine, whereby the emperor Constantine, when moving the capital of the Roman Empire to Constantinople in the fourth century, bestowed on the pope dominion over all of the western Empire. Valla proved that the document was based on an eighth-century forgery, because some of the language it contained was unknown in Constantine's time and did not come into use until much later.

Also embedded in the humanist reevaluation of individual potential was new appreciation of the moral significance of work. For the humanist, the honor, fame, and even glory bestowed by one's city or patron for meritorious deeds were the ultimate rewards for effort. The humanist pursuit of praise and reputation became something of a Renaissance cult.

In fourteenth- and fifteenth-century republican Florence, at least until the Medicis took control, Petrarchan humanism was not meant for a court elite. Humanism was a civic idea: to educate and inform citizens so that they could contribute to the common good to the greatest possible extent. In this sense, humanism was put in the service of republican values and the republican cause, and the mixture of the two is what has come to be called *civic humanism* by recent historians. This civic ideal developed furthest in the Florentine republic.

By the second half of the fifteenth century, as the Medicis gained increasing control, the civic ideal was being replaced by an ideal more fitting to the times, the ideal of princely rule. This ideal borrowed much from civic humanism even though it was directed toward princes and courtiers and not toward citizens. The emphasis on the pursuit of virtue and honor continued. Like the ideal gentleman, the ideal prince would evolve through humanistic education, which would so prepare him for the struggle between virtue and fortune that virtue would prove victorious.

The similarities between the civic and princely ideals, however, were not as important as the differences. The aim of princely rule was not liberty but peace and security, and the best means to this end was not a republic but hereditary monarchy. This new princely ideal was reflected in a new spate of advice books, the most influential of which was *The Book of the Courtier,* written between 1513 and 1518 by Baldesar Castiglione (1478–1529). These books promoted the notion that the ideal ruler should be universally talented and skillful, equally commanding on the battlefield, at court, and in the state, and virtuous throughout. These advice books, especially Castiglione's, were to serve as indispensable handbooks for courtiers and would-be gentlemen not only in Renaissance Italy but throughout Europe for centuries.

A Revolution in Political Thought

One advice book transcended all the others: *The Prince,* written in 1513 by the Florentine Niccolò Machiavelli (1469–1527). It offered a critique of the humanist ideal of princely rule and in so doing made some fundamental contributions to political theory. Indeed, Machiavelli may be called the first major modern political thinker. To Machiavelli, the humanist ideal was naive in its insistence on the prince's virtues and eloquence to the exclusion of all other considerations. He attacked the medieval and humanist tradition of theoretical politics:

> *Since my intention is to say something that will prove of practical use to the inquirer, I have thought it proper to represent things as they are in real truth, rather than as they are imagined. Many have dreamed up republics and principalities which have never in truth been known to exist; the gulf between how one should live and how one does live is so wide that a man who neglects what is actually done for what should be done learns the way to self-destruction.*[3]

Politics, Machiavelli argued, requires the rational deployment of force, as well as, and even prior to, the exercise of virtue.

On this point, Machiavelli's advice is quite specific. He wrote *The Prince* in part as a plea. Since 1494, Italy had fallen prey to France and Spain. Their great royal armies overpowered the mercenary armies of the city-states and proceeded to lay waste to Italy in their struggle for domination of the peninsula. To prevent this, Machiavelli said, the Italians should unite behind a leader—the prince—whose first act would be to

Niccolò Machiavelli (1469–1527). Machiavelli looked back to the ancient Roman republic for his ideals and spent his life serving the city-state of Florence, but as the author of *The Prince,* his name became a byword for atheism and deceit. "Machiavellian" is still used to describe an unscrupulous politician. (*Palazzo Vecchio, Florence, Italy/Erich Lessing/Art Resource, NY.*)

disband the mercenaries and forge a new citizen army worthy of the glorious Roman past and capable of repelling the "barbarian" invasion. "Mercenaries," Machiavelli claimed, "are useless and dangerous." They are useless because "there is no . . . inducement to keep them on the field apart from the little they are paid, and this is not enough to make them want to die for you." And they are dangerous because their leaders, the infamous *condottieri,* "are anxious to advance their own greatness" at the expense of the city-state. Reliance on mercenaries was the sole cause of "the present ruin of Italy," and the cure lay in the creation of a national militia, led by a prince.[4]

This prince had to be both wily and virtuous, not just virtuous (as humanists had said): "The fact is that a man who wants to act virtuously in every way necessarily comes to grief among so many who are not virtuous." So Machiavelli scandalized Christian Europe by asserting that "if a prince wants to maintain his rule he must learn how not to be virtuous, and to make use of this or not according to his need."[5] Even more shocking, the prince must know how to dissemble, that is, to make all his actions appear virtuous, whether they are so or not. In ironic parody of conventional advice-book wisdom, Machiavelli argued that a ruler must cultivate a *reputation* for virtue rather than virtue itself. In this connection, Machiavelli arrived at a fundamental political truth: politics (and especially the relationship between the ruler and the ruled) being what it is, the road to success for the prince lies in dissimulation. As he put it, "Everyone sees what you appear to be, few experience what you really are. And those few dare not [contradict] the many who are backed by the majesty of the state."[6] Here again the Renaissance arrived at modernity.

Machiavelli broke with both the medieval and the humanist traditions of political thought. He was a secularist who tried to understand and explain the state without recourse to Christian teachings. Influenced by classical thought, especially the works of Livy, he rejected the prevailing view that the state is God's creation and the ruler should base his policies on Christian moral principles. For Machiavelli, religion was not the foundation for politics but merely a useful tool in the prince's struggle for success. The prince might even dissemble, if he thought he had to, in matters of the faith, by appearing pious, whether he was or not, and by playing on and exploiting the piety of his subjects.

Renaissance Art

The most vivid image of the Renaissance is conveyed through its architecture, sculpture, and painting. Renaissance examples of all three art forms display a style that stressed proportion, balance, and harmony. These artistic values were achieved through a new, revolutionary conceptualization of space and spatial relations. To a considerable extent, Renaissance art also reflects the values of Renaissance humanism, in the use of classical models in architecture, in the rendering of the nude human figure, and in the heroic vision of human beings.

Profile

A Renaissance Man

Baldesar Castiglione (1478–1529), poet and diplomat, spent his life in the service of princes. Out of that experience he wrote *The Book of the Courtier* (1528), one of the most famous and important examples of the Renaissance genre known as the advice book. He meant his work to offer instruction in manners and morals—to teach individual men how to live up to Renaissance ideals and become what was known as a "universal man."

Castiglione argued that the focus of government and society should be the court of the ruler, or prince. The prince, Castiglione said, possesses and exercises the real power, but his retinue of courtiers and court ladies—men and women of high rank living in the prince's palace or nearby—plays no small role in his success. It is their duty to advise and instruct the prince, to teach him to be virtuous and rational and to lead a civilized life free of the ignorance and barbarism of the Dark Ages. This is no mean feat, Castiglione warns, because the court is a dangerous place inhabited by many who will try to flatter, deceive, and corrupt an unwary prince, sap his power, and destroy his government. The perfect courtier "strives to

Louvre, Paris/Erich Lessing/Art Resource, NY.

Medieval art sought to represent spiritual aspiration; the world was a veil merely hinting at the other perfect eternal world. Renaissance art expresses spiritual aspiration, but its setting and character differ altogether. This world is no longer a veil but the *place* where people live, act, and worship. The reference is less to the other world and more to this world, and people are treated as creatures who find their spiritual destiny as they fulfill their human one.

The Middle Ages had produced a distinctive art known as the Gothic. By the fourteenth and fifteenth centuries, Gothic art had evolved into the International Style, characterized by careful drawing, flowing and delicate lines, harmonious composition, and delightful naturalistic detail. Italian Renaissance art at its most distinctive represents a conscious revolt against this late Gothic trend. The revolt produced revolutionary discoveries, which served as the foundation of Western art up to this century. In art, as in philosophy, the Florentines played a leading role in this esthetic transformation. They, more than anyone else, were responsible for the way artists saw and drew for centuries and for the way most Western people still see or want to see.

Early Renaissance Art

The first major contributor to Renaissance painting was the Florentine painter Giotto (c. 1276–1337). Borrowing from Byzantine painting, he ensure that his prince is not deceived, does not listen to flatterers, and distinguishes between good and evil, loving the one and detesting the other."* If such courtiers are successful, the prince can become the best possible ruler, and his court will set an example of order and harmony for the whole society, "since subjects always imitate the behavior of their rulers."†

To do his job properly, a courtier must have a multitude of skills, including the ability to fight in battle and lead an army. For this he needs strength and agility, which must be developed through athletic training. Castiglione recommended a regimen of wrestling, tennis, horseback riding, and swimming. The mind, too, must be developed: a courtier must learn the arts of peace, including languages and literature, music and painting, oratory and philosophy. Finally, the social graces must be acquired: a courtier must know how to dress, dance, converse, and amuse the ladies. A man well skilled in these areas has the qualifications necessary to be considered a "universal man."

Castiglione's message was frankly aristocratic and elitist. *The Book of the Courtier* provided a powerful model of the way government and society should be constituted and operate, and it remained influential through the nineteenth century.

But Castiglione did not stop there. Unlike many of his contemporaries, he refused to believe that women were naturally inferior to men. While others said, for example, "women bring no benefit to the world, save the bearing of children,"‡ Castiglione thought that women could be as universally talented as the perfect courtier in the rarefied world of the court, if not further down the social scale. Remarkably he said, "Don't you think that we might find many women just as capable of governing cities and armies as men?"§ Castiglione was Machiavelli's contemporary, and Castiglione's arguments often ran counter to those marshalled by Machiavelli in *The Prince* (see pp. 310–311). And although Machiavelli's ideas are often said to look forward to modern politics and modern times, on the fundemental issue of gender equality Castiglione was the clear harbinger of modernity.

---

*Castiglione, *The Book of the Courtier,* trans. George Bull (New York: Viking Penguin, 1987), p. 285.
†Ibid., pp. 88–89.
‡Ibid., p. 242.
§Ibid., p. 216

created figures modeled by chiaroscuro, alternations of light and shade. He also developed several techniques of perspective, representing three-dimensional figures and objects on two-dimensional surfaces so that they appear to stand in space. Giotto's figures look remarkably alive. They are drawn and arranged in space to tell a story, and the expressions they wear and the illusion of movement they convey heighten the dramatic effect. Giotto's best works were *frescoes,* wall paintings painted while the plaster was still wet, or fresh. Lionized in his day, Giotto had no immediate successors, and his ideas were not taken up and developed further until almost a century later.

By the early fifteenth century, the revival of classical learning had begun in earnest. In Florence, it had its artistic counterpart among a circle of architects, painters, and sculptors who sought to revive classical art. The leader of this group was an architect, Filippo Brunelleschi (1377–1446). He abandoned Gothic prescriptions altogether and designed churches, such as the Church of San Lorenzo in Florence, reflecting classical models. To him, we also owe the discovery of the rules of perspective. Giotto had revived the ancient technique of foreshortening; Brunelleschi's renderings of spatial relationships were mathematically precise. Brunelleschi's devotion to ancient models and his new tool of mathematical perspective set the stage for the further development of Renaissance painting.

Early Renaissance artists were dedicated to representing things as they are, or at least as they are seen to be. Part of the inspiration for this goal was also classical. The ancient ideal of beauty was the beautiful nude. Renaissance admiration for ancient art meant that for the first time since the fall of Rome artists studied anatomy; they learned to draw the human form by having models pose for them, a practice fundamental to artistic training to this day. Another member of Brunelleschi's circle, the Florentine sculptor Donatello (1386–1466), also showed renewed interest in the human form and conscious rejection of Gothic taste.

Another approach to the observation of nature, besides imitation of the ancients, developed in northern Europe, principally in the Netherlands. Its original exponent was Jan van Eyck (c. 1390–1441), who worked mostly in what is now Belgium. Van Eyck's art developed out of the International Style. Within that style, there was an interest in the faithful depiction of objects and creatures in the natural world. Van Eyck carried this tendency so far that it became the principal aim of his art: his pictures are like photographs in their infinitely scrupulous attention to the way things look. Unlike his contemporaries in Florence, van Eyck subordinated accuracy and perspective to appearance—the way things look—and showed no interest in classical models. In his concern to paint what he saw, he developed oil painting. At that time, most paints were egg-based. Oil-based paints allowed van Eyck to obtain more lifelike and virtuoso effects. The technique spread quickly to Italy, with astonishing results.

GIOVANNI ARNOLFINI AND HIS BRIDE, BY JAN VAN EYCK (C. 1390–1441). The painting uses the new technique of perspective and draws a careful, and idealized, portrait of a prosperous married couple in their bedroom. It depicts a world that values privacy, sober prosperity, and intimacy of a certain kind: he stares out at us, while she looks deferentially at him. (*Reproduced by courtesy of the Trustees, The National Gallery, London.*)

Late Renaissance Art

The use of perspective posed a fundamental problem for Renaissance painters: how to reconcile perspective with composition—dramatic arrangement—and the search for harmony. The chief interest of later fifteenth-century Italian painting lay in how artists tackled this problem.

Among the Florentine artists from the second half of the fifteenth century who strove for a solution of this question was the painter Sandro Botticelli (c. 1444–1510). *The Birth of Venus,* one of his most famous pictures, depicts not a Christian legend but a classical myth. Representing, as it does, the way that beauty came into the world, this painting is another expression of the Renaissance desire to recover the lost wisdom of the ancients. Botticelli succeeded in rendering a perfectly harmonious pattern, but at the cost of sacrificing solidity and anatomical correctness. In *The Birth of Venus,* what the viewer notices are the graceful, flowing lines that unify and vivify the painting. Even the liberties that Botticelli took with nature—for example, the unnatural proportions of Venus's neck and shoulders—enhance the esthetic outcome.

New approaches to this problem of perspective and composition were developed by the three greatest artists of the Renaissance: Leonardo da Vinci (1452–1519), Michelangelo Buonarroti (1475–1564), and Raphael Santi (1483–1520).

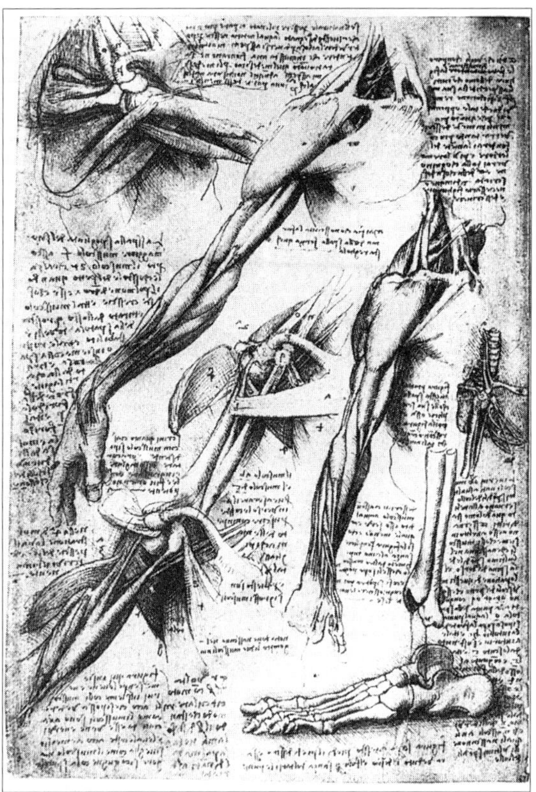

ANATOMICAL DRAWING BY LEONARDO DA VINCI (1452–1519). These drawings show the close connection between art and scientific anatomy and provide evidence of da Vinci's universal genius. (*Corbis-Bettmann.*)

All of them were closely associated with Florence, and all three were contemporaries.

Leonardo was a scientist and engineer, as well as a great artist. He was an expert at fortifications and gunnery, an inventor, an anatomist, and a naturalist. He brought this close observation of nature to his paintings and combined it with powerful psychological insight to produce works that, although few in number, are of unsurpassed genius. Among the most important of these are *The Last Supper, St. John,* and *La Gioconda,* or the Mona Lisa. The Mona Lisa is an example of an artistic invention of Leonardo's—what the Italians call *sfumato.* Leonardo left the outlines of the face a little vague and shadowy, thus freeing it of any wooden quality that more exact drawing would have imparted and making it more lifelike and mysterious. Here was a major breakthrough in solving the problem of perspective. The artist must not be too exact and rigid in adhering to the rules; he must introduce a correcting softness and atmosphere to achieve a reconciliation between perspective and the demands of design.

Michelangelo's creation of artistic harmony derived from his mastery of anatomy and drawing. His model in painting came from sculpture; his paintings are sculpted drawings. He was, of course, a sculptor of the highest genius, whose approach to his art was poetic and visionary. Instead of trying to impose form on marble, he thought of sculpting as releasing the form from the rock. Among his greatest sculptures are *David, Moses,* and *The Dying Slave.* Michelangelo was also an architect. Patronized by the pope, he designed the dome of the new Saint Peter's Basilica in Rome. But perhaps his most stupendous work is the frescoes he painted on the ceiling of the Sistine Chapel in the Vatican, commissioned by Pope Julius II. In four years, working with little assistance, Michelangelo covered the empty space with the most monumental pictures ever painted, pictures that summarize the Old Testament story. *The Creation of Adam* is the most famous of these superlative frescoes.

Raphael, the last of these three artistic giants, was the complete master of design in painting. His balanced compositions sacrifice nothing to perspective. Rather, perspective becomes just another tool, along with sfumato and mathematical proportion, for achieving harmony. Raphael is especially famous for the sweetness of his Madonnas. But he was also capable of painting other subjects and conveying other moods, as his portrait *Pope Leo X with Two Cardinals* reveals (Pope Leo was his patron).

Renaissance painting came late to Venice, but when it arrived in the late fifteenth and early sixteenth centuries, it produced a tradition of sustained inventiveness whose keynote was the handling of color. Giovanni Bellini (c. 1431–1516) may be said to have discovered color as a tool of composition. He borrowed perspective from Florentine painting, but he also used color to achieve unity and harmony.

This use of color was extended in a revolutionary direction by another Venetian, Giorgione (c. 1478–1510), to whom only five paintings can be ascribed with absolute certainty. Until Giorgione, landscape had functioned primarily as a decorative, and sometimes imaginative, background, as in the Mona Lisa. Giorgione made landscape part of the subject of his paintings and, through his handling of light and color, used it to unify and integrate his canvases. According to the art historian E. H. Gombrich, "This was almost as big a step forward . . . as the invention of perspective had been."[7] Perhaps Giorgione's greatest experiment in this respect was *The Tempest.*

The Spread of the Renaissance

The Renaissance spread to Germany, France, England, and Spain in the late fifteenth and the sixteenth centuries. In its migration northward, Renaissance culture adapted itself to conditions unknown in Italy, such as the growth of the monarchical state and the strength of lay piety. In England, France, and Spain, Renaissance culture tended to be court centered and hence antirepublican, as it was, for instance, under Francis I in France and Elizabeth I in England. In Germany and the Rhineland, no monarchical state existed, but a vital tradition of lay piety was present in the Low Countries. For example, the Brethren of the Common Life was a lay movement emphasizing education and practical piety. Intensely Christian and at the same time anticlerical, the people in such lay movements found in Renaissance culture tools for sharpening their wits against the clergy—not to undermine the faith but rather to restore it to its apostolic purity.

Thus, northern humanists were profoundly devoted to ancient learning, just as the humanists in Italy had been. But nothing in northern humanism compares to the paganizing trend associated with the Italian Renaissance. The northerners were chiefly interested in the problem of the ancient church and, in particular, the question of what constituted original Christianity. They sought a model in the light of which they might reform the corrupted church of their own time.

Everywhere, two factors operated to accelerate the spread of Renaissance culture after 1450: growing prosperity and the printing press. Prosperity, brought on by peace and the decline of famine and plague, led to the founding of schools and colleges. The sons (women were excluded) of gentlemen and merchants were sent to school to receive a humanistic education imported from Italy. The purpose of such education was to prepare men for a career in the church or the civil service of the expanding state and for acceptance into higher social spheres.

Printing with movable type, which was invented in the middle of the fifteenth century, quickened the spread of Renaissance ideas. Back in the Late Middle Ages, the West had learned, through the Muslims from the Chinese, of printing, paper, and ink. However, in this block printing process, a new block had to be carved from wood for each new impression, and the block was discarded as unusable as soon as a slightly different impression was needed. About 1445, Johann Gutenberg (c. 1398–1468) and other printers in Mainz in the Rhineland invented movable metal type to replace the cumbersome blocks. It was possible to use and reuse the separate pieces of type—as long as the metal in which they were cast did not wear down—simply by arranging them in the desired order.

With the advent of the printing press, the book-publishing industry began to develop. The first printed books were religious: Bibles, sermons, and prayer books. But other kinds soon followed because there was a ready market for books on a great variety of secular subjects. The market was enormous and continued to expand during the sixteenth century. Printed books were much cheaper than the earlier hand-copied ones, and many more people could now afford to buy them. Publishers catered to every taste in reading—learned and popular, technical and imaginative, serious and light. Books became big business, driven by both consumer demand and the profit motive. Fifteen or twenty million books had already been published by 1500, and another 150 million more a century later.

Not only were books cheaper and more numerous, but printing made it easier to learn to read. Literacy rates were still very low, especially among women and the poor, but the clerical and gentry monopoly on reading had been broken. More and more books were also published in the vernacular (rather than Latin), which helped standardize written language and stimulated the development of national literatures all across Europe. Printing, moreover, provided a surer basis for scholarship and prevented the further corruption of texts through hand copying. By giving all scholars the same text to work from, it made progress in critical scholarship and science faster and more reliable.

But in early modern Europe printing was not an unmixed blessing. Elite opinion was often divided, or at least ambivalent, on the issue. Printing was an obvious boon; the authorities, however, saw the need for censorship, for imposing controls on what was published. Today, ours is a pluralistic society that values new ideas and a variety of opinions, even differences of opinion, at least up to a point. Early modern Europeans were not so tolerant; in fact, they were suspicious of intellectual novelty and variety and sometimes downright hostile to heterodox thinking. For centuries, leaders in church and state had tried to build unity by enforcing Christian orthodoxy and punishing heresy. The motto of the French monarchy aptly sums up the point: "One king, one law, one faith." The Catholic church established an *Index of Prohibited Books* in the mid-sixteenth century, and books like Machiavelli's *The Prince* were put on the list. Protestant authorities also set up machinery for regulating the book trade. Printers of "dangerous" books were punished, sometimes executed, and their book stocks confiscated. All intellectual life would be affected by this atmosphere: the tension between the power of print and the desire to control opinion.

Erasmian Humanism

To Desiderius Erasmus (c. 1466–1536) belongs the credit for making Renaissance humanism an international movement. He was educated in the Netherlands by the Brethren of the Common Life, which was one of the most advanced religious movements of the age, combining mystical piety with rigorous humanist pedagogy. Erasmus traveled throughout Europe as a humanist educator and biblical scholar. Like other Christian humanists, he trusted the power of words and used his pen to attack scholastic theology and clerical abuses and to promote his philosophy of Christ. His weapon was satire, and his *Praise of Folly* and *Colloquies* won him a reputation for acid wit vented at the expense of conventional religion.

ERASMUS, BY QUENTIN MASSYS, 1517. Erasmus (c. 1466–1536) was a great biblical scholar and Christian humanist who hoped to purify the Catholic church by calling for moral reform and criticizing clerical wealth and corruption. (*The Royal Collection © Her Majesty Queen Elizabeth II.*)

True religion, Erasmus argued, does not depend on dogma, ritual, or clerical power. Rather, it is revealed clearly and simply in the Bible and therefore is directly accessible to all people, from the wise and great to the poor and humble. Nor is true religion opposed to nature. Rather, people are naturally capable of both apprehending what is good as set forth in the Scriptures and living in accordance with it. Perfect harmony between human nature and true religion allows humanity to attain, if not perfection, at least the next best thing, peace and happiness in this life.

This clear but quiet voice was drowned out by the storms of the Reformation (see Chapter 14), and the weight Erasmus gave to the individual's natural capacities could not hold its own before the renewed emphasis on human sinfulness and dogmatic theology. Erasmus was caught in the middle and condemned by both sides; for him, the Reformation was both a personal and a historical tragedy. He had worked for peace and unity and was treated to a spectacle of war and fragmentation. Erasmian humanism, however, survived these horrors as an ideal, and during the next two centuries, whenever thinkers sought toleration and rational religion (Rabelais and Montaigne, for instance), they looked back to Erasmus for inspiration.

French Humanism

German and French humanists pursued Christian humanist aims. They used humanist scholarship and language to satirize and vilify medieval scholastic Christianity and to build a purer, more scriptural Christianity. These northern humanists had great faith in the power of words. The discovery of accurate biblical texts, it was hoped, would lead to a great religious awakening. Protestant reformers, including Martin Luther, relied on humanist scholarship.

French thinkers of the next generation exploited and carried the humanist legacy in more radical directions. Among them, two were outstanding: Michel de Montaigne (1533–1592) and François Rabelais (c. 1494–1553). Both thought and wrote in reaction to the religious wars resulting from the Reformation. In the face of competing religious dogmatisms—Catholic, Protestant, and sectarian—Montaigne advanced a skepticism in which he maintained that one can know little or nothing with certainty. He therefore advocated political quietism and acceptance of Christianity on faith. This skepticism also entailed tolerance. An individual was not fully responsible for his or her beliefs, since they were the product of frail reason and force of circumstance. Thus, Montaigne argued, people should not be punished for their beliefs, and the only ones who deserved to be severely dealt with were the dogmatists in religion. These people deserved to be punished because their certainty and self-righteousness flew in the face of a fundamental epistemological fact: that reason cannot be relied on, especially in matters of religion.

Montaigne was not a systematic philosopher but devoted himself to what he could learn by Socratic self-examination, the results of which he set down in his *Essays.* In their urbane and caustic wit and their intense self-absorption, the *Essays* betray a crucial shift in humanist thought, which became more pronounced in the next century. Gone is the optimism and emphasis on civic virtue of the High Renaissance. In their place come skepticism and introspection, the attempt to base morality on the self rather than on public values. As Montaigne says, "Let us learn to be no more avid of glory than we are capable of it."[8] This shift, produced by the increasing scale and violence of religious war, represented a retreat from the idealism of Renaissance humanism.

Rabelais took a different route from Montaigne's. In response to religious dogmatism, he asserted the essential goodness of the individual and the right to be free to enjoy the world rather than being bound down, as John Calvin later would have it, by fear of a vengeful God. Rabelais's folk-epic, *Gargantua and Pantagruel,* in which he celebrates earthly and earthy life, is the greatest French work of its kind and perhaps the greatest in any literature. Rabelais said that, once freed from dogmatic religion, people could, by virtue of their native goodness, build a paradise on earth and disregard the one dreamed up by theologians. In *Gargantua and Pantagruel,* he imagined a monastery where men and women spend their lives "not in laws, statutes, or rules, but according to their own free will and pleasure." They sleep and eat when they desire and learn to "read, write, sing, play upon several musical instruments, and speak five or six . . . languages and compose in them all very quaintly." They observed one rule: "DO WHAT THOU WILT."[9]

Spanish Humanism

Spanish humanism represents a special case. The church hierarchy gained such a tight grip in Spain during the late fifteenth and early sixteenth centuries that it monopolized humanist learning and exploited it for its own repressive purposes. In contrast to Germany, France, or England, there was little or no room for a dissenting humanist voice. The mastermind behind this authoritarian Spanish humanism was Cardinal Francisco Jiménez de Cisneros (1436–1517). Jiménez founded the University of Alcalá, not far from Madrid, for the instruction of the clergy. He also sponsored and published the Complutensian Polyglot Bible, with Hebrew, Latin, and Greek texts in parallel columns. Jiménez, like Christian humanists elsewhere, sought to enlighten the clergy through a return to the pure sources of religion, and he saw his Polyglot Bible as one of the chief means of realizing that goal.

A century after Jiménez, Miguel de Cervantes Saavedra (1547–1616) produced his great novel, *Don Quixote,* in which he satirized the ideals of knighthood and chivalry. Don Quixote, the victim of his own illusions, roams the countryside looking for romance and an opportunity to prove his knightly worth. To Quixote's servant Sancho Panza, Cervantes assigned the role of pointing up the inanity of his master's quest by always acting prudently and judging according to common sense. Despite his earthy realism, however, Panza must share his master's misfortunes—so much for realism in a world run by men full of illusions. Cervantes's satire is very gentle. That knightly valor was still a valid subject for satire indicates how wedded Spain was even in the early seventeenth century to the conservative values of its crusading past.

English Humanism

Christian humanism in England sharply contrasted with that in Spain. It was developed by secular men in government as much as by clerics, and its objectives were often opposed to authority and tradition. Various Italian humanists came to England during the fifteenth century as bishops, merchants, court physicians, or artists. Englishmen also studied in Italy, especially in Florence, and introduced the serious humanistic study of the classics at Oxford University toward the end of the century.

The most influential humanist of the early English Renaissance was Sir Thomas More (1478–1535), who studied at Oxford. His impact arose from both his writing and his career. Trained as a lawyer, he became a successful civil servant and member of Parliament. His most famous book is *Utopia,* the major utopian treatise to be written in the West since Plato's *Republic* and one of the most original works of the entire Renaissance.

Many humanists had attacked private wealth as the source of pride, greed, and human cruelty. But in *Utopia,* More went further. He argued that an acquisitive society is by nature both unjust and unprosperous. "For, when everyone is entitled to get as much for himself as he can, all available property . . . is bound to fall into the hands of a small minority, which means that everyone else is poor." The unscrupulous few win out over the many who remain honest and decent. For More, the conclusion was inescapable: "I am quite convinced that you will never get a fair distribution of goods . . . until you abolish private property altogether."[10] But to balance things out, he stated the economic case against communism as well. In the absence of a profit motive, "there would always tend to be shortages because nobody would work hard enough. . . . Then when things really got short, the . . . result would be a series of murders and riots."[11] But More accused those who took this view of lacking the imagination to conceive of a truly just society. In *Utopia,* he set out to make up for this deficiency by inventing an ideal society in which private ownership was abolished and poverty eliminated because everyone had to work in order to eat. Such a system even produced surpluses, which allowed people the leisure for instruction and recreation.

More succeeded Cardinal Wolsey as lord chancellor under Henry VIII. But when the king broke with the Roman Catholic church, More resigned, unable to reconcile his conscience with the king's rejection of papal supremacy. Three years later, in July 1535, More was executed for treason for refusing to swear an oath acknowledging the king's ecclesiastical supremacy.

William Shakespeare (1564–1616), widely considered the greatest playwright the world has ever produced, gave expression to conventional Renaissance values: honor, heroism, and the struggle against fate and fortune. But there is nothing conventional about Shakespeare's treatment of characters possessing these virtues. His greatest plays, the tragedies (*King Lear, Julius Caesar,* and others), explore a common theme: men, even heroic men, despite virtue, are able only with the greatest difficulty, if at all, to overcome their human weaknesses. What fascinated Shakespeare was the contradiction between the Renaissance image of nobility, which is often the self-image of Shakespeare's heroes, and man's capacity for evil and self-destruction. Thus, Ophelia says of Hamlet, her lover, in the play of the same name:

O, what a noble mind is here o'erthrown!
The courtier's, soldier's, scholar's, eye, tongue, sword;
The expectancy and rose of the fair state,
The glass of fashion and the mould of form,
The observ'd of all observers, quite, quite down!
[And] I, of ladies most deject and wretched,
That suck'd the honey of his music vows,
Now see that noble and most sovereign reason,
Like sweet bells jangled, out of tune and harsh;
That unmatch'd form and feature of blown youth
Blasted with ecstasy. O, woe is me,
T' have seen what I have seen, see what I see![12]

The plays are intensely human—so much so that humanism fades into the background. Thus, art transcends doctrine to represent life itself.

The Renaissance and the Modern Age

The Renaissance, then, marks the birth of modernity—in art, in the idea of the individual's role in history and nature, and in society, politics, war, and diplomacy. Central to this birth is a bold new view of human nature: individuals in all endeavors are free of a given destiny imposed by God from the outside—free to make their own destiny, guided only by the example of the past, the force of present circumstances, and the drives of their own inner nature. Individuals, set free from theology, are seen to be the products, and in turn the shapers, of history. Their future is not wholly determined by Providence but is partly the work of their own free will.

Within the Italian city-states, where the Renaissance was born, rich merchants were at least as important as the church hierarchy and the old nobility. The city-states were almost completely independent because of the weakness of church and empire. So the northern Italians were left free to invent new forms of government, in which merchant-oligarchs, humanists, and condottieri played a more important part than priests and nobles, who dominated politics in the rest of Europe. Along with the inventiveness, however, this newness and lack of tradition produced disorder and violence. Condottieri grabbed power from hapless citizens, and republics gave way to despotism.

But the problems created by novelty and instability demanded solutions, and the wealth of the cities called forth the talent to find them. Commercial wealth and the new politics produced a new culture: Renaissance art and humanism. Talented individuals—scholars, poets, artists, and government officials—returned to classical antiquity, which in any case lay near at hand in Italy and Greece. Ancient models in art, architecture, literature, and philosophy provided answers to their questions. This return to antiquity also entailed a rejection of the Middle Ages as dark, barbarous, and rude. The humanists clearly preferred the secular learning of ancient Greece and Rome to the clerical learning of the more recent past. The reason for this was obvious: the ancients had the same worldly concerns as the humanists; the scholastics did not.

The revival of antiquity by the humanists did not mean, however, that they identified completely with it. The revival itself was done too self-consciously for that. In the very act of looking back, the humanists differentiated themselves from the past and recognized that they were different. They were in this sense the first modern historians, because they could study and appreciate the past for its own sake and, to some degree, on its own terms.

In the works of Renaissance artists and thinkers, the world was, to a large extent, depicted and explained without reference to a higher supernatural realm of meaning and authority. This is clearly seen in Machiavelli's analysis of politics. Closely associated with this secular element in Renaissance culture was a new realism that beckoned toward the modern outlook. What else is Machiavelli's new politics but a politics of realism, dealing with the world as he found it rather than as it ought to be? This realism also manifests itself in the realm of art, where mathematical perspective renders the world in its spatial dimension and gives it the solidity and

The Renaissance

1. Filippo Brunelleschi. Church of San Lorenzo. Interior, looking toward the apse. Florence, Italy. *(Erich Lessing/Art Resource.)*

The Renaissance period in the visual arts is characterized by the same humanist vision that prevailed in literature, drama, music, and the minor arts during the fifteenth and sixteenth centuries. Although the term *Renaissance*, literally "rebirth," was coined by Italian writers of that period, it is important to remember that change in artistic style and temperament did not take place overnight.

By the late fifteenth and sixteenth centuries the styles of the Renaissance spread from Italy to the Low Countries (the Netherlands, Belgium, and Luxembourg), Germany, France, England, and Spain. These styles were not exported wholesale; rather, elements of the Renaissance fused with local traditions to produce new styles and variants of the Italian themes. What is consistent from one country to the next, however, is the extent to which Renaissance art really was a rebirth—a departure from the style of the medieval period.

As we have seen, the dramatic work of Giotto marked the end of the stiff, otherworldly style of the Middle Ages. The artists who followed Giotto diverged from his style and subject matter. Although Christianity was still an important theme, Renaissance artists also depicted subjects from Greek and Roman mythology, as well as scenes from everyday life.

Painting, sculpture, architecture, and the

2. Donatello. *David*, c. 1425–1430. *(Museo Nazionale del Bargello, Florence/Scala/Art Resource.)*

minor arts evolved at a different pace throughout this period. It was not as if all artists declared themselves to be Renaissance figures simultaneously. Instead, styles changed with new artistic sensibilities, technological advances, and the requests of new patrons.

Rarely can one ascribe the development of an entire period of art to a single individual. Such is the case of Renaissance architecture, however. Filippo Brunelleschi (c. 1377–1446) began his career as a sculptor in Florence. He turned to architecture sometime after 1402 and traveled to Rome, where he studied the remains of imperial Roman buildings and monuments. Brunelleschi learned the theory of scientific perspective, perhaps while trying to draw on paper three-dimensional images of the monuments. He also developed a method of building double domes linked to reinforce each other. This lightened the weight of the dome, allowing the structure beneath to be built with fewer supporting elements.

One of the earliest expressions of his architectural skill can be seen in the Church of San Lorenzo in Florence (1421–1469) (Figure 1). Thanks to the benevolence of the Medici family, Brunelleschi was granted license to design an entire building himself. The Church of San Lorenzo was a new structure, not an adaptation of or an addition to an older, medieval building. Although some of its elements may have derived from earlier prototypes, the new building was distinct in its symmetry and regularity. Its floor plan shows a markedly regular repetition of equal-size squares to establish the nave, transept, and aisles. The centrally planned chapel, with its strict adherence to mathematical proportion, distinguishes the Church of San Lorenzo from the medieval Gothic cathedral. Brunelleschi's ability to grasp the concept of perspective in two dimensions is translated into three dimensions by the strong use of line and rhythmical arches that draw the eye to the altar.

Brunelleschi effected the same fusion of antique and Christian as his contemporaries did in other fields. Poets and writers experimented with classical and Christian styles; so, too,

3. Sassetta. *Saint Anthony Tempted by the Devil in the Form of a Woman*, c. 1430. *(Yale University Art Gallery, New Haven, Connecticut. University Purchase from James Jackson Jarves.)*

did Brunelleschi. Note, for example, the Corinthian capitals topping the San Lorenzo columns, whereas the floor plan is in the shape of a cross.

Architecture was not the only medium that combined experimentation and echoes of the past; sculpture did as well. Whereas Brunelleschi can be viewed as the father of Renaissance architecture, a host of sculptors advanced the Renaissance style in their medium. Prominent among them in the early Renaissance was Donatello (1386–1466), whose works distinguished him as a master even in his own time. The bronze *David* (c. 1425–1430) is perhaps the most controversial of his best-known sculptures (Figure 2). The first life-size, free-standing nude sculpture since antiquity, this work is still something of an enigma.

Art historians assume that the statue was to have been exhibited outdoors, or at least in a central location, because it was meant to be viewed from all sides. The young David is wear-

4. Pietro Perugino. *The Delivery of the Keys,* 1481. *(Sistine Chapel, Vatican Palace, Vatican State/Scala/Art Resource.)*

ing only a hat and high boots. Unlike the well-muscled athletes of the classical period, however, he is slender and slight, an adolescent instead of a developed adult. Donatello does pay homage to classical prototypes in the stance of his David—a *contrapposto*, or counterbalanced, pose, in which the weight on the legs is uneven (compare David's stance with Hermes' stance in Figure 1 of the first art essay).

Symbolic devices provide the key to the significance of the sculpture. David represents the city of Florence itself, and the helmet of Goliath under his feet represents the duchy of Milan, which at the time was at war with Florence. David's nudity may allude to the city's classical past, and the wreathed hat may suggest victory.

In painting, experiments in depth and linear perspective stand out as the major developments. Artists were seeking ways of making two-dimensional surfaces seem three-dimensional. Brunelleschi was the first to develop a system in which all parallel lines of a scene converge in one central point on the horizon; other artists adopted his scheme and carried it further.

An early Renaissance work from Siena, *Saint Anthony Tempted by the Devil in the Form of a Woman* (c. 1430) (Figure 3), foreshadows developments that distinguish later paintings. The artist is on the brink of discovering the mechanics of perspective. The path taken by Saint Anthony leads back into the hills, which are shown on a curved horizon. The work, which is more than five hundred years old, is strangely modern in its abstraction, stripped of many of the decorative elements that mark both earlier and later works.

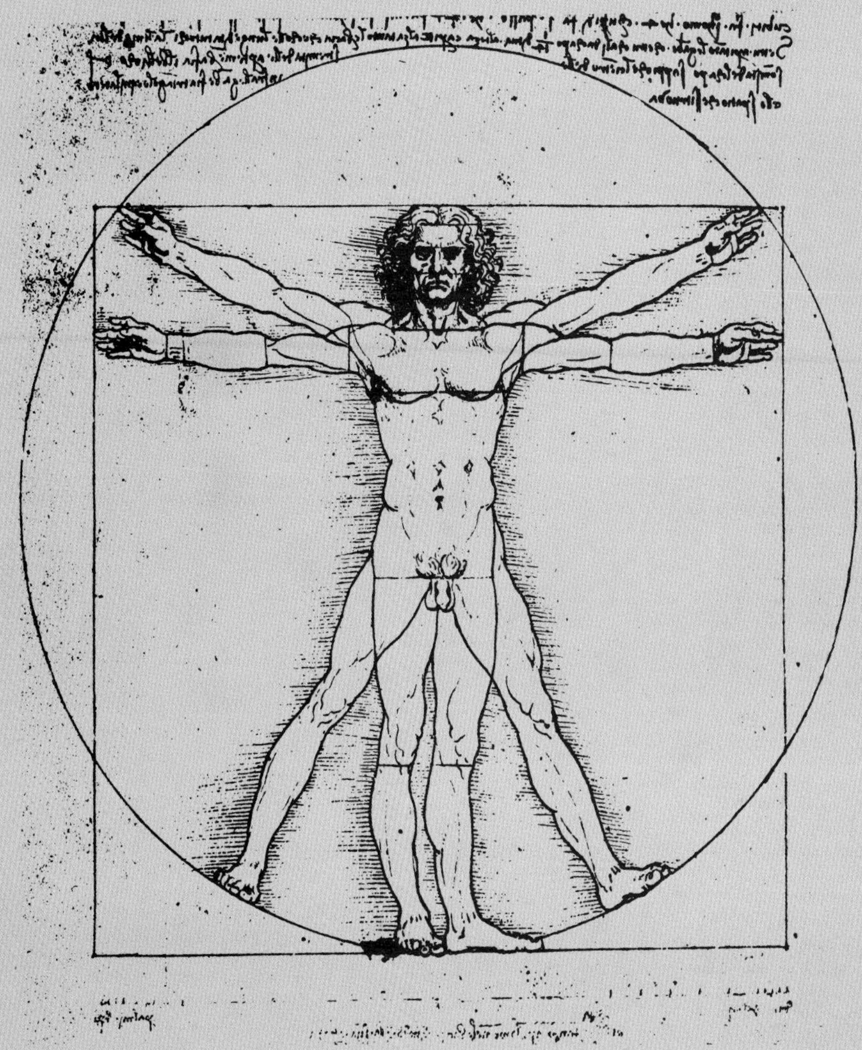

5. Leonardo da Vinci, *The Proportions of Man,* from his notebooks. *(Hulton Archive/ Getty Images.)*

Pietro Perugino's *The Delivery of the Keys*, a fresco from the Sistine Chapel in the Vatican (1481) (Figure 4), illustrates the enthusiasm with which other artists achieved perspective. Note that all the parallel lines in the foreground converge at the church in the center of the background. The viewer's eye is drawn into the painting, and figures seem real, not flat. Compare this portrayal with the flat and linear rendering of Justinian and his retinue in the mosaic from Ravenna. There, the effect is two-dimensional, and the viewer does not expect to see beyond the layer of figures. In the Perugino, by contrast, the figures are full and exist in a three-dimensional space.

The works of Leonardo da Vinci (1452–1519)—his drawings, paintings, sculpture, innumerable inventions, and copious writings—exemplify the Renaissance spirit. He expands the idea of three-dimensional, perspectival space to include the living form of things, their mathematical proportions. He announced a new way

6. Michelangelo Buonarroti. *Creation of Adam*, 1510. *(Vatican Museum and Galleries, Rome/Bridgeman Art Library.)*

of looking at nature and the individual. For Leonardo, visual art offered a means of arriving at nature's truths. Truth was attained when the artist brought both human reason and creative capacity to bear on the direct experience of the senses. Leonardo examined objects in all their diversity and represented them realistically. He visually delineated the natural world with unprecedented scientific precision, and he asserted his spiritual and intellectual freedom to do so. Through his art, Leonardo helped lay the foundations for modern science.

In his notebooks, Leonardo sketched an infinite variety of objects—inorganic, organic, human—and recorded fragmentary thoughts about them. Everywhere, he demonstrated concern for the concrete specificity of things, which he depicted in minute detail. He was perpetually engaged in a quest for the essential living form of a thing, the relationship of its parts to the whole, the numerical ratios subsisting among the parts, and the laws operative in the ratios. He found such ratios and laws everywhere, in both animate and inanimate objects. He was particularly fascinated by the human body, and in his notebook his written observations are accompanied by a marvelous sketch of the body, *The Proportions of Man* (Figure 5), conceived and framed with realism and mathematical proportion.

By the end of the fifteenth century, Renaissance art in Italy had reached its height. The so-called High Renaissance flowered in the visual arts as well as in other areas of culture. Michelangelo, Titian, and Giorgione are among the best-known artists of this era.

7. Titian. *Bacchus and Ariadne*, 1523. *(Erich Lessing/Art Resource.)*

The works of Michelangelo Buonarroti (1475–1564)—paintings, sculpture, literature, and architecture—epitomize the Renaissance. Looking at his paintings—for instance, *Creation of Adam* on the ceiling of the Vatican's Sistine Chapel (1510) (Figure 6)—a viewer is struck by the extent to which he learned from the art of the ancient world. Nevertheless, Michelangelo's reliance on the classical is subordinate to his Renaissance vantage point. Here, the figures float freely through a celestial landscape and depict the biblical story of creation.

But the artists of the Renaissance looked to the classical past not only for technique; they also borrowed and adapted subject matter. Unlike the art of the Middle Ages, which concentrated on Christian themes, Renaissance paintings also illustrated the myths of ancient Greece and Rome.

The Venetian artist Titian (1488/90–1576) was well known for his use of both mythology and biblical themes. His *Bacchus and Ariadne* (1523) (Figure 7) illustrates his independence from the stylistic conventions of other High Renaissance schools. Titian offers a sensual rendering of the classical tale, in which the young Ariadne marries Bacchus (Dionysus), the god of wine, after being abandoned by the Greek king Theseus. Titian's use of *chiaroscuro* (alternating areas of light and dark) is pronounced. The general feeling of the work is much looser and freer than the feelings of the carefully constructed canvases produced by his contemporaries. The painting also has a roughness, as though it were

8. Pieter Brueghel the Elder. *Leading the Blind*, 1568. *(Museo Nazionale di Capodimonte, Naples/Erich Lessing/Art Resource.)*

unfinished—a quality that marks a departure from the meticulously realistic works of other High Renaissance artists.

As the artistic styles of the Italian Renaissance spread northward, they were adapted and superimposed on a different set of political and religious circumstances, resulting in a fusion of Renaissance method and local themes. Pieter Brueghel the Elder's (1525/30–1569) *Leading the Blind* (1568) (Figure 8) exemplifies this trend. The artist uses line and motion as Titian did. But the image he presents, though derived from a biblical quotation, offers a contemporary view of humankind, reflecting the upheavals felt as the Reformation moved through Europe.

drama that constitute a modern visual and esthetic realism. The sources for both the esthetic and the political realism were the cultural forms of ancient Greece and Rome.

Renaissance humanism exuded deep confidence in the capacities of able people, instructed in the wisdom of the ancients, to understand and change the world. Renaissance realism, then, was mixed with idealism, and this potent combination departed sharply from the medieval outlook. In place of Christian resignation there grew a willingness to confront life directly and a belief that able human beings can succeed even against great odds.

This new confidence is closely related to another distinctive feature of the Renaissance: the cult of the individual. Both prince and painter were motivated in part by the desire to display their talents and to satisfy their ambitions. Such individual striving was rewarded and encouraged by the larger society of rich patrons and calculating princes, who valued ability. Gone was the medieval Christian emphasis on the virtue of self-denial and the sin of pride. Instead, the Renaissance placed the highest value on self-expression and self-fulfillment, on the realization of individual potential, especially of the gifted few. The Renaissance fostered an atmosphere in which talent, even genius, was allowed to flourish. The ideal, at least, was meritocracy.

To be sure, the Renaissance image of the individual and the world, bold and novel, was the exclusive prerogative of a small, well-educated urban elite and did not reach down to include the masses. Nevertheless, the Renaissance set an example of what people might achieve in art and architecture, taste and refinement, education, and urban culture. In many fields, the Renaissance set the cultural standards of the modern age.

❖ ❖ ❖

Notes

1. Quoted in Quentin Skinner, *The Foundations of Modern Political Thought,* 2 vols. (Cambridge: Cambridge University Press, 1978), 1:89.
2. Giovanni Pico della Mirandola, *Oration on the Dignity of Man,* trans. A. Robert Caponigri (Chicago: Henry Regnery, 1956), p. 7.
3. Niccolò Machiavelli, *The Prince,* trans. George Bull (Harmondsworth, England: Penguin Books, 1961), pp. 90–91.
4. Ibid., pp. 77–78.
5. Ibid., p. 91.
6. Ibid., p. 101.
7. E. H. Gombrich, *The Story of Art,* 12th ed. (London: Phaidon, 1972), p. 250.
8. Quoted in Eugen Weber, ed., *The Western Tradition,* 2 vols., 4th ed. (Lexington, Mass., and Toronto: D. C. Heath, 1990), 1:395.
9. François Rabelais, *Gargantua and Pantagruel,* trans. Sir Thomas Urquhart (1883), bk. 1, chap. 57.
10. Thomas More, *Utopia,* trans. Paul Turner (Harmondsworth, England: Penguin Books, 1965), p. 66.
11. Ibid., p. 67.
12. From *Hamlet, Prince of Denmark,* in *The Complete Plays and Poems of William Shakespeare,* ed. William Allan Neilson and Charles Jarvis Hill (Boston: Houghton Mifflin, 1942), p. 1067.

Suggested Reading

Baron, Hans, *The Crisis of the Early Italian Renaissance* (1966). An influential interpretation of the origins of civic humanism.

Bouwsma, William J., *Venice and the Defense of Republican Liberty* (1968). The Venetian origins of Western republicanism.

Brucker, Gene A., *Renaissance Florence,* rev. ed. (1983). An excellent analysis of the city's physical character, its economic and social structure, its political and religious life, and its cultural achievements.

Burckhardt, Jacob, *The Civilization of the Renaissance in Italy* (1860), 2 vols. (1958). The first major interpretative synthesis of the Renaissance; still an essential resource.

Burke, Peter, *Popular Culture in Early Modern Europe* (1978). A fascinating account of the social underside from the Renaissance to the French Revolution.

Copenhaver, Brian P., and Charles B. Schmitt, *Renaissance Philosophy* (1992). A useful, readable survey.

Eisenstein, Elizabeth, *The Printing Press as an Agent of Change,* 2 vols. (1978). The definitive treatment—informative, argumentative, and suggestive.

Ginzburg, Carlo, *The Cheese and the Worms* (1982). A lively, penetrating account of the cosmos as seen from the point of view of a sixteenth-century Italian miller.

Hale, John, *The Civilization of Europe in the Renaissance* (1994). An informed and entertaining survey, full of interesting illustrations.

Huizinga, Johan, *Erasmus and the Age of Reformation* (1957). A brief study of the greatest northern European humanist.

Kelley, Donald R., *Renaissance Humanism* (1991). A concise treatment of a complicated subject.

King, Margaret L., *Women of the Renaissance* (1991). A useful survey of a burgeoning field of scholarship.

Pocock, J. G. A., *The Machiavellian Moment* (1975). A heady adventure in the history of ideas, tracing republicanism from its Italian Renaissance origins through the English and American Revolutions.

Pullan, Brian S., *A History of Early Renaissance Italy* (1973). A solid, brief account.

Skinner, Quentin, *The Foundations of Modern Political Thought,* 2 vols. (1978). The first volume covers the Renaissance; highly informed.

Wittkower, R., *Architectural Principles in the Age of Humanism* (1952). Architecture as the expression of Renaissance values and ideas.

Review Questions

1. What does the word *renaissance* mean, and where and when did the Renaissance first occur?
2. What is the connection between the Renaissance and the Middle Ages? What special conditions gave rise to the Italian Renaissance?
3. Which forms of government predominated among the Italian city-states? In the end, which was the most successful? Why?
4. In what ways did the social patterns of Renaissance Italy depart from those of the rest of Europe?
5. What are some connections between Renaissance society and Renaissance art and culture?
6. What is humanism and how did it begin? What did the humanists contribute to education and history?
7. What is the difference between civic humanism and the princely ideal of government, and from what does this difference come?
8. How can it be said that Machiavelli invented a new politics by standing the ideal of princely rule on its head?
9. What is perspective? To whom do we owe the discovery of its rules?
10. What is the basic difference between Early and Late Renaissance painting?
11. What factors encouraged the spread of the Renaissance into the western European monarchies and the Rhineland?
12. To what key invention do we owe the rise of the printing press? What were the effects of the printing press on European civilization?
13. Why is the Renaissance considered the departure from the Middle Ages and the beginning of modernity?

Chapter 14

The Reformation: The Shattering of Christendom

Martin Luther was both a dour and thoughtful man with great determination. (Uffizi, Florence/Erich Lessing/Art Resource, NY.)

■ **The Medieval Church in Crisis**
Wycliffe and Hus
Mysticism and Humanism
The End of the World

■ **The Lutheran Revolt**
Luther: Humanist, Prophet, and Conservative
Luther's Break with Catholicism
But Who Is Saved?
The Creation and Spread of Lutheranism
Religious Reform or Social Revolution?

■ **The Spread of the Reformation**
Calvin and Calvinism
France
England
Southern and Eastern Europe
The Radical Reformation

■ **The Catholic Response**

■ **The Reformation and the Modern Age**

By the early sixteenth century, the only European institution that transcended geographic, ethnic, linguistic, and national boundaries was under severe attack from reformers. For centuries, the Catholic church, with its center in Rome, had been extending its influence into every aspect of European society, culture, and politics. To some observers, the church's desire to amass wealth and extend its power appeared to outweigh its commitment to the search for holiness in this world and salvation in the next. Preoccupied by wealth, addicted to international power, and protective of their own interests, the clergy, from the pope down, became the center of a storm of criticism. Humanists, made self-confident by the new learning of the Renaissance, called for the reform and renewal of the church, setting the stage for the Protestant Reformation. Eventually, though, that movement deviated significantly from what the Renaissance humanists had in mind. The Reformation brought into being a new form of Christianity, Protestantism, and not reform of the Cathlic church from within.

Schooled in techniques of criticism developed during the Renaissance, humanists first used those techniques on documents that supposedly justified papal authority. Lorenzo Valla, for instance, refuted the so-called Donation of Constantine (see "Humanism" in Chapter 13). But the fraud that especially vexed the humanists lay not on parchments but in the very practices by which the church governed the faithful.

The Protestant Reformation, however, did not originate in elite circles of humanistic scholars. It began in the mind of Martin Luther, an obscure German monk and a brilliant theologian. Luther rejected the church's claim that it was the only vehicle for human salvation, and he defied the pope's right to silence, reprimand, and excommunicate any Christian who rejected papal authority or denied the truth of certain church teachings. In public defiance, but only after much soul-searching, Luther started a rebellion against the church's authority that in less than one decade shattered irrevocably the religious unity of Christendom. This rebellion also worked a quiet revolution in the lives of men and women. Marriage rather than celibacy became an ideal, as did preaching and education. People became less intimidated by authority but probably more self-questioning and self-chastising. For all these reasons, the Reformation dominated European history throughout much of the sixteenth century.

The Medieval Church in Crisis

By the Late Middle Ages, the church had entered a time of crisis. Between 1350 and 1480, theologians and political theorists rejected the pope's claim to supremacy over kings and to spiritual sovereignty over all of Western Christendom. They argued that the church had become inefficient and corrupt and that the papacy in Rome was to blame. Some reformers sought to wrest power from the pope and give it to a general council of the church's hierarchy. This was one of the aims—in addition to ending the Great Schism and combating heresy—of the conciliar movement before 1480. However, the Councils of Constance and of Basel failed to leave a meaningful inheritance to the church, largely because the special interests of kings and the papacy undercut the councils' authority. The failure of the conciliar movement prevented the church from reforming itself from within and made possible a broader reformation. The invention of printing gave literate people access to what the reformers were demanding.

Wycliffe and Hus

The two most significant attempts to reform the church, prior to Luther, occurred in the late fourteenth century in England and Bohemia. The leaders of these movements, John Wycliffe in England and Jan Hus in Bohemia, were learned theologians who attacked some church doctrines and practices. By expressing their ideas in precise language, Wycliffe and Hus made heresy intellectually respectable. The influence of Wycliffe's and later Hus's movement also contributed to the long-term success of Protestantism in England and to its short-term success in portions of eastern Europe. Hus laid the ground for the conversion of the Hungarian nobility. Even without access to printing presses, both Wycliffe and Hus appealed for mass support, prefiguring the populist quality of the Reformation.

John Wycliffe (c. 1320–1384), a master at Oxford University, attacked the church's authority by arguing simply that the church did not control the individual's eternal destiny. He said that salvation came only to those who possess faith, a gift freely given by God and not contingent on participation in the church's rituals or sacraments. This position made the clergy far less important. Wycliffe attacked the church's wealth and argued that all true believers in Christ were equal and, in effect, Christ's priests. To make faith accessible to them, Wycliffe and his followers translated portions of the Bible into English. Much that Wycliffe preached foreshadowed the teachings of Luther.

Wycliffe received staunch support from some members of the English nobility. However, when his ideas were taken up by articulate peasants during an abortive peasants' revolt in 1381, Wycliffe lost many powerful backers. In the end, his attempt to reform the church by bringing it under secular control failed. Partly because he retained strong supporters and was more interested in scholarship than leadership, Wycliffe survived the failure of his movement and died a natural death. His ideas remained alive in popular religious beliefs, and his followers, called Lollards, helped foster Protestantism during the sixteenth-century English Reformation.

A harsher fate awaited the Bohemian (Czech) reformer Jan Hus (c. 1369–1415): he was burned at the stake in 1415. Partly under the influence of Wycliffe's writings, Hus, in his native Prague, attacked the sacramental system of the church, as well as its wealth and power. He also preached for Bohemian independence at a time when the Holy Roman Emperor sought to continue his control over that territory. After Hus's execution, his followers broke with the Roman Catholic church. For a brief time, they nationalized the Bohemian church. Like the Lollards in England, the Hussites prepared the ground for the success of the Protestant Reformation. Until well into the seventeenth century, Bohemia remained a battleground of popular Protestantism against the official church and also a site over which the Ottoman Turks exercised influence.

Chronology 14.1 ❖ The Reformation

1381	English peasants revolt and support John Wycliffe, an early reformer
1414–1418	Council of Constance
1431–1449	Council of Basel
1517	Martin Luther writes the Ninety-five Theses and the Reformation begins; thousands of printed copies circulate
1520	Pope Leo X excommunicates Luther
1524–1526	German peasants revolt
1526	Hungary falls to the Ottoman Turks, and its Diet is dissolved; it is powerless to stop the spread of Lutheranism
1529	English Parliament accepts Henry VIII's Reformation
1534	Henry VIII is declared head of the Church of England; Francis I of France declares Protestants heretics; Ignatius Loyola founds the Society of Jesus; Anabaptists, radical reformers, capture Münster in Westphalia
1536	John Calvin publishes *Institutes of the Christian Religion*
1536–1564	Calvin leads the Reformation in Geneva with William Farel
1545–1563	Council of Trent
1553–1558	Mary, Catholic queen of England, persecutes Protestants; many flee to Geneva
1555	Peace of Augsburg
1561	Scotland turns Presbyterian under John Knox
1562–1598	French wars of religion between Catholics and Protestants are settled by the Edict of Nantes in 1598
1640–1660	English Revolution; rise and defeat of the Puritans

Mysticism and Humanism

Wycliffe's and Hus's reform attempts coincided with a powerful new religiosity. Late medieval mystics sought to have immediate and personal communication with God and to renew the church's spirituality. Many late medieval mystics were women, who, by virtue of their sex, were deprived of an active role in governing the church. First mysticism and then Protestantism offered women a way of expressing their independence in religious matters.

The church hierarchy inevitably regarded mysticism with suspicion. If individuals could experience God directly, they would have little need for the church and its rituals. In the fourteenth century, mystical movements seldom became heretical. But in the sixteenth and seventeenth centuries, radical reformers, some of them women preachers, often found in Christian mysticism a powerful alternative to institutional control and even to the consolation offered by priests and the sacraments.

In the Low Countries, the Brethren of the Common Life propounded a religious movement known as the *devotio moderna,* which was inspired by mysticism. A semimonastic order of laity and clergy, the Brethren expressed their

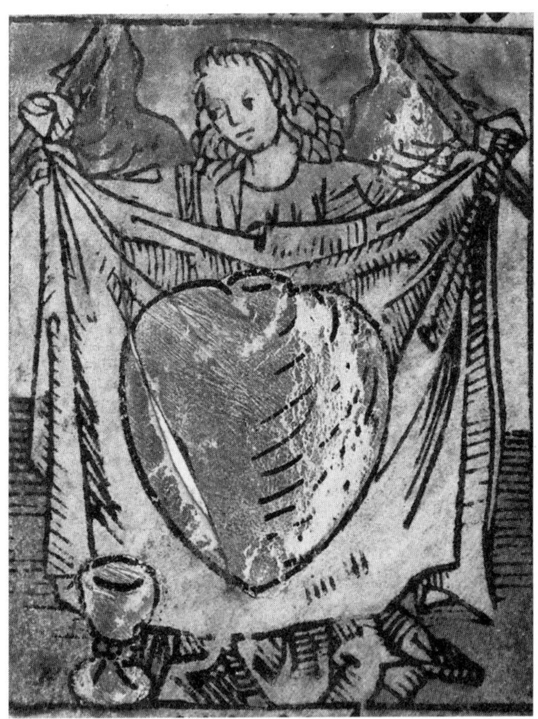

THE SACRED HEART OF JESUS, A HAND-COLORED WOODCUT SOLD AS AN INDULGENCE, NUREMBERG, 1480s. The sale of indulgences to erase purgatory time disgusted Martin Luther. The veneration of relics—objects associated with the life of Christ or his saints, even bones and hair—was also condemned. Rival churches often claimed to have the "only authentic" head of a certain saint. (*Metropolitan Museum of Art, Bequest of James Clark McGuire, 1931. 31.54.142.*)

practical piety by dedicating their lives to the service of the entire community. With their teaching, they trained a new generation of urban-based scholars and humanists, who became some of the church's severest critics.

The humanist Erasmus of Rotterdam thought that critical words would suffice to show the clergy the folly of their ways, which he ridiculed in *The Praise of Folly* (1509). Yet neither mysticism, with its emphasis on inner spirituality, nor humanism, with its stress on classical learning, could capture the attention of thousands of ordinary Europeans. A successful reform movement required leaders of an active and aggressive temperament who could do battle with political realities and win lay support against the local and international power of the church.

Millenarianism, the belief that after the Last Judgment Christ would institute a thousand-year rule of saints on earth, gave its believers a radical and religious justification for attacking established institutions and institutional corruption. That Christ would rule in a future paradise meant that the society of their own day was ruled by the Antichrist. The end of the world would be ushered in by the righteous.

The End of the World

In the movements inspired by Wycliffe and Hus, as well as in the peasant revolts often spurred by economic grievances, a sense of urgency became apparent during the fourteenth and fifteenth centuries. These movements and the millenarian beliefs of their adherents—who believed that they were living in the "final days" before the end of the world—foreshadowed the popular unrest characteristic of the Reformation. Millenarians took inspiration from biblical prophecy and looked forward to the moment of divine intervention when the world would be destroyed, sinfulness overwhelmed, and a paradise on earth created, where God's chosen would rule. Millenarian reformists took a doctrine accepted but not promoted by the church and reinterpreted it to express their vision of a society where religion ensures justice for the poor and oppressed. According to the church, someday the world would end, Christ would come again to judge everyone, and those whom Christ chose to be with him would be called "saints" and would reign with him in heaven. Reformers reinterpreted Catholic millenarian doctrine. According to them, Christ would condemn the rich and propertied and establish a new society, not in heaven but on earth, which the poor would inherit, and for a thousand years—a millennium—the poor would rule in Christ's kingdom.

By 1500, the biblical concept of the Antichrist and the image of the "whore of Babylon" became a shorthand for the corruption of the church. When in the early sixteenth century Luther and other reformers called the pope himself the Antichrist or the whore of Babylon, they were appealing to a millenarian tradition of reform and protest that had existed in the West for centuries.

The Lutheran Revolt

Only an attack on papal and clerical authority could strike at the church's power. To succeed, the attack had to address the multitudes while appealing to princes. Heresy had to be made respectable. This feat demanded someone whose inner struggle mirrored the widespread discontent with the church's care for souls, someone who could translate the agony of the search for salvation into language accessible to all Christians. Martin Luther (1483–1546) had experienced a personal crisis of faith, and he possessed the will, the talent, and the intellectual vigor to offer it as an example for other Christians. Luther wrote voluminously and talked freely to his friends and students. Using this mass of recorded material, historians have been able to reconstruct the life and personality of this Augustinian friar and theologian who began the Reformation.

Luther: Humanist, Prophet, and Conservative

Martin Luther was born in eastern Germany to relatively uneducated parents of humble origins. His father, Hans Luther, was exceptionally ambitious. Born a peasant, he left the land and became a miner and finally a manager of several mines, in an industry that was booming in late-fifteenth-century Germany. Like many newly successful individuals, Hans Luther had ambitious plans for his son; he wanted Martin to study law at the university in order to attain the status of an educated man. Luther's mother displayed an intense and humble piety, thus putting Luther in closer touch with German popular religion than was common among contemporary scholars.

At the university, Luther embarked on an intellectual career that was to make him one of the foremost theologians and biblical scholars of his day. As a young student, he fulfilled his father's wish and studied law. His earlier education gave him a fine grounding in classical and humanistic learning; he knew the writings of Erasmus and others.

At the age of twenty-one, in 1504, Luther suddenly abandoned his legal studies to enter the Augustinian monastery at Erfurt. The actual decision was made swiftly. In later life, Luther recounted that the decision had been made in fear, as a vow to Sainte Anne in the midst of a fierce lightning storm, by a young man convinced that his death at that moment would bring him eternal damnation. Why Luther thought he was damned is not known, but his guilt conspired with his vivid imagination to kindle what must have been a growing resentment against his father's domination.

Luther was also a millenarian, and he believed that the time available to all Christians was limited by the prospect of Christ's return; he thought that he was living in the last days of the world. Eventually, as he became the leader of an international religious movement, Luther grew convinced that he was the long-foretold, divinely ordained prophet chosen to announce the coming Final Judgment. As the leader of the German Reformation, he also had to take clear political stands and pick his allegiances. Without hesitation and with deep conviction, Luther chose to preserve the social order, to support the power of princes and magistrates, and to maintain social hierarchy.

Luther's Break with Catholicism

As he studied and prayed, Luther grew increasingly terrified by the possibility of his damnation. As a monk, he sought union with God, and he understood the church's teaching that salvation depended on faith, works (meaning acts of charity, prayer, fasting, and so on), and grace. He participated in the sacraments of the church, which according to its teaching were intended to give God's grace. Indeed, after his ordination, Luther administered the sacraments. Yet he still felt the weight of his sins, and nothing the church offered seemed to relieve that burden.

Even the mystery of the Mass and the conversion of bread and wine into the body and blood of Christ brought Luther little inner peace. Seeking solace and salvation, he increasingly turned to reading the Bible. Two passages spoke directly to him: "For therein is the righteousness of God revealed from faith to faith: as it is written, 'He who through faith is righteous shall live'" (Romans 1:17); and "They are justified by his grace as a gift, through the redemption which is in Christ Jesus" (Romans 3:24). In these two passages, Luther found, for the first time in his adult life, some hope for his own salvation. They said to him that faith, freely given by God through Christ, enables the recipient to obtain salvation, and that human beings, powerless because of their fallen and sinful nature, are rescued by divine mercy.

The concept of salvation by faith alone provided an answer to Luther's spiritual quest. Practicing good works such as prayer, fasting, pilgrimages, and participation in the Mass and the other sacraments would not in themselves lead to grace. No amount of good works, however necessary for maintaining the Christian community, would bring salvation. Through reading the Bible and through faith alone, the Christian could find the meaning of earthly existence. For Luther, the true Christian was a courageous figure who faced the terrifying quest for salvation armed only with the hope that God had granted the gift of faith. The new Christian served others, not to trade good works for salvation but solely to fulfill the demands of Christian love. Nuns left their convents and married in the belief that their faith and service to the comunity would save them. So too did priests leave the church to become, like Luther, leaders of their own churches. Luther's odyssey provided the foundation for a new, Protestant piety.

Pursuing his theological and biblical studies, Luther became a professor at the nearby university at Wittenberg and a preacher in that city's church. He shared his personal and intellectual struggle with his students and his congregations. At the University of Wittenberg and in the province of Saxony in general, Luther found an audience receptive to his views, and his popularity and reputation grew as a result. Before 1517, he was considered a dynamic and controversial preacher, whose passionate interest lay in turning Christians away from their worldly interests and from reliance on good works, while focusing their attention on Christ and the truth contained within Scripture. After 1517, he became a figure of international reputation and eventually a publicly condemned heretic in the eyes of the church.

The starting point for the Reformation was Luther's attack in 1517 on the church's practice of selling indulgences. The church taught that some individuals go directly to heaven, some go directly to hell, others go to heaven after spending time in purgatory. Punishment in purgatory is necessary for those who sinned excessively but had the good fortune to repent before death. Dying in a state of mortal sin (that is, without repenting) meant suffering in hell eternally. Naturally, people worried about how long they might have to suffer in purgatory. Indulgences were intended to remit portions of that time and punishment and were granted to individuals by the church in exchange for their prayers, attendance at Mass, and almost any acts of charity—including monetary offerings to the church itself. This last was the most controversial; it could easily appear that the church was selling and people were buying admittance to heaven.

In the autumn of 1517, a friar named Tetzel was selling indulgences near Wittenberg. Some of the money he obtained was for rebuilding Saint Peter's Basilica in Rome, and the rest was for paying off debts incurred by a local archbishop in purchasing his office from the pope. Although Luther did not know about this second purpose, he was incensed both by Tetzel's crude manner and by his flagrant exploitation of the people's ignorance and misuse of their money. Luther launched his attack on Tetzel and the selling of indulgences by tacking on the door of the Wittenberg castle church his Ninety-five Theses.* Luther's theses (propositions) challenged the entire notion of selling indulgences not only as a corrupt practice but also as resting on a

*Some scholars debate whether this public display ever occurred, but the document itself was soon printed and widely circulated.

Selling Letters of Indulgence Before the Reformation. This engraving shows activities in the pope's audience-viewing room. Peasants and religious men are giving money to the church and receiving blessings after making their payments. (*Corbis/Bettmann.*)

theologically unsound assumption—namely, that salvation could be earned by good works.

The outline of Luther's later theology and his reliance on faith as the only means to salvation are implicit in the Ninety-five Theses. In that document he wrote:

> *6. The Pope has no power to remit any guilt, except by declaring and warranting it to have been remitted by God. . . . 33. We must especially beware of those who say that these pardons from the Pope are an inestimable gift of God. . . . 37. Every Christian . . . has a share of all the benefits of Christ and of the Church, given by God, even without letters of pardon.*[1]

Luther was blunt about his dispute with the church's hierarchy and, in particular, with the papacy: he challenged its sole authority to save souls and to guard the entrance into heaven.

Luther's argument in the Ninety-five Theses and in his later writings rested on the belief that Christian salvation through personal piety requires contrition for sins and trust in God's mercy. Luther also believed that church attendance, fasting, pilgrimages, and charity alone did not earn salvation. The church, in contrast, held that *both* faith and good works were necessary for salvation. Luther further insisted that every individual could discover the meaning of the Bible unaided by the clergy. The church maintained that only the clergy could read and interpret the Bible properly. Luther argued that in matters of faith there was no difference between the clergy and the laity; indeed, each person could receive faith directly and freely from God. The church held that the clergy were intermediaries between individuals and God: Christians reached eternal salvation through the church and its clergy. For Luther, no priest, no ceremony, no sacrament, and certainly no confinement in convents or monasteries could bridge the gulf between the Creator and his creatures, and the possibility of personal damnation remained a distinct reality. Hope lay only in a personal relationship between the individual and God, as expressed through faith in God's mercy and grace. In Luther's view, no church could mediate that faith for the individual, and to that extent Luther's theology destroyed the foundations of the church's spiritual power. By declaring that clergy and church rituals do not hold the key to salvation, Luther rejected the church's claim that it alone offered the way to eternal life.

But Who Is Saved?

If faith alone, freely given by God, brings salvation to the believer, how can a man or woman know whether he or she has faith? Luther seemed content to assert that the search itself by a pious and penitent supplicant was a sign of God's favor. In Luther's doctrine of faith, the notion of *predestination* is barely beneath the surface. Luther never chose to bring forth the implications of his doctrine. His contemporary, the great French theologian John Calvin, however, made predestination central to his version of reformed Christianity. This belief made salvation an intensely personal matter—some might say an intensely terrifying or liberating matter.

The discussion about predestination continues today; it is one of the most difficult theological issues. Predestination rests on the assumption that God is all-knowing and eternal and his will is absolute: he gives faith to whomever he chooses and does so for his own inscrutable reasons. Because God's existence and will are timeless, God knows the fate of every person even as individuals are searching for salvation. Given God's foreknowledge, it may be said that every person is predestined for either heaven or hell. But for believers the problem remains, how can individuals know whether God has chosen them for salvation?

Luther said simply that men and women could hope and trust in salvation but would know whether they had been granted it only after death. Subsequent reformers would make much of the doctrine of predestination in their struggle to systematize Protestant doctrine and to create an identifying experience for all true Christians. Calvin and his followers, who became numerically the largest group of European and American Protestants, believed firmly that some are chosen and others damned.

The Creation and Spread of Lutheranism

Although Luther did not realize it in 1517, the Reformation was under way. Quickly translating his theses from Latin into German, his students printed and distributed them, first in Saxony and eventually throughout Germany. Local church authorities recognized in Luther a serious threat and prepared to silence him. But Luther was tenacious; he began to write and preach his theology with increasing vigor. With the aid of the printing press, by 1525 there were probably three million Protestant pamphlets circulating in Germany. Students flocked to Wittenberg from eastern Europe as well as Germany.

At this point, politics intervened. Recognizing that his life might be in danger if he continued to preach without a protector, Luther appealed for support to the prince of his district, Frederick, the elector of Saxony. The elector was a powerful man in international politics—one of the seven lay and ecclesiastical princes who chose the Holy Roman Emperor. Frederick's support for his most famous university professor convinced church officials, including the pope, that this friar would have to be dealt with cautiously.

The years 1518 and 1519 were momentous ones for the Holy Roman Empire. Before his death in 1519, the Holy Roman Emperor Maximilian I wanted to see his grandson, Charles, king of Spain, elected to succeed him. The papacy at first opposed Charles's candidacy, even looking to Frederick of Saxony as a possible alternative. Frederick wisely declined. However, because he was one of the seven electors, the contenders—Charles, Francis I of France, and Henry VIII of England—counted on him for his vote. Charles bribed the electors, and the title became his. Therefore, during this crucial period and for years afterward, he had to proceed cautiously on issues that might offend powerful German princes.

These political considerations explain the delay in Luther's official condemnation and excommunication by the pope. When in late 1520 the pope finally acted against him, it was too late; Luther had been given the time needed to promote his views. He proclaimed that the pope was the Antichrist and that the church was the "most lawless den of robbers, the most shameless of all brothels, the very kingdom of sin, death and Hell."[2] When the papal bull excommunicating him was delivered, Luther burned it.

Luther and his followers established congregations for Christian worship throughout Germany. To find protectors, in 1520 Luther published the *Address to the Christian Nobility of the German Nation.* In it, he appealed to the German princes to reform the church and cast off their allegiance to the pope, who, he argued, had used taxes and political power to exploit them for centuries. His appeal produced some success; the Reformation flourished on the resentment against foreign papal intervention that had long festered in Germany. Luther also wrote to the German people and conveyed the meaning of his personal experience as a Christian. In *The Freedom of the Christian Man* (1520), he called on Germans to strive for true spiritual freedom through faith in Christ, to discipline themselves, to obey legitimate political authority, and to perform good works according to the dictates of Christian love. In these treatises, Luther made his conservatism clear: he wanted to present no threat to legitimate political authority, that is, to the power of German princes.

In 1521, Charles V, the Holy Roman Emperor and a devout Catholic, summoned Luther to Worms, giving him a pass of safe conduct. There Luther was to answer to the charge of heresy, both an ecclesiastical and a civil offense. On his journey, Luther received a warm public response from great crowds of people, but the emperor and his officials coldly demanded that he recant. Luther's reply, delivered after some deliberation, is undoubtedly his most famous statement: "Unless I am convinced of error by the testimony of Scripture or by clear reason . . . I cannot and will not recant anything, for it is neither safe nor honest to act against one's conscience. God help me. Amen."

Shortly after this confrontation with the emperor, Luther went into hiding to escape arrest. During that one-year period, he translated the New Testament into German. With this work, he offered his compatriots the opportunity to take the same arduous spiritual odyssey that he had undergone and to join him as a new type of Christian. These followers, or Lutherans, were eventually called *Protestants,* those who protested against the established church, and the term became generic for all supporters of the Reformation.

Religious Reform or Social Revolution?

Luther looked to every level of German society for support. In a country of many small towns with printing presses, the literate urban population responded dramatically to his call. Led by city fathers and preachers, individuals converted to the new Protestant churches or turned their own Catholic church into a Protestant one. The new faith made men and women bold. When a teenage boy married of his own will without consulting his family in Nuremberg, he defended his actions by saying that God "ordained that it happen this way by his divine will."[3] Priests were now expected to marry. Even though Protestants insisted that women marry and be silent and obedient, a Swiss Protestant woman who refused marriage justified her wanting to remain "masterless" by saying: "Those who have Christ for a master are not masterless."

Luther was a brillant preacher, and clearly his message could inspire people to be defiant as well as devout. Protestantism came to be seen not only as a source of personal revitalization and salvation, but also as a force that could renew society and government.

The same issues that moved Germans appealed to people in towns and cities in Austria, Hungary, Poland, the Netherlands, and Switzerland. Even in Paris and London, as well as in northern Italy by the late 1520s, followers or readers of Luther could easily be found, and lives changed profoundly. Katharina von Bora, who married Martin Luther, left her convent and then spent the rest of her life raising their six children and presiding over a large house, with visitors from every part of Europe. Luther valued her strength and zeal for his

Profile

Katharina von Bora

The Granger Collection.

Katharina von Bora (1499–1552) and Martin Luther had a marriage that, though imperfect, well represents the Protestant model. Although Katharina came from a noble background, her family was not well off. After a few years of religious education, she entered a nunnery—a common choice for women without dowries for marriage. Katharina and other women in the convent soon became disillusioned with the cloistered life. Somehow, Martin Luther learned of their plight and decided to help. In April 1523 he aided eleven nuns—among them Katharina—in their escape from the cloister. Legend has it that they hid in empty smoked herring barrels.

Two years later, Katharina and Martin were married. Their marriage became a love match that lasted all of their lives. Katharina and Martin became role models for other Protestant clergy. Protestant doctrine taught women that marriage and child-rearing, combined with obedience to one's husband, led to holiness. Katie, as Martin called her, ran a household with over forty rooms in addition to buying and running a farm. She raised six children and was a devoted Protestant wife. Her last recorded words are, "I will stick to Christ as a burr to a topcoat." Beginning with Katharina and Martin, Protestant ministers married and raised families while serving their congregations.

cause so much that he called her his "Moses." There were thousands of devout and defiant Katharinas throughout Europe.

Despite repression by the Catholic church, in 1550 Protestants were probably in the majority in some German towns, in much of Hungary and Bohemia, in Sweden, and in various Swiss cantons. In France, more than a million people converted to Calvin's version of Protestantism. How could this have happened in one generation?

In the sixteenth century, any new religious or political movement needed the support of the nobility. Early on, Luther appealed to them and they responded. Their motives were as diverse as piety and political ambition. The Reformation provided the nobility with the unprecedented opportunity to confiscate church lands, eliminate church taxes, and gain the support of their subjects by serving as leaders of a popular and dynamic religious movement. The Reformation also gave the nobles a way

ICONOCLAST JURY. In the sixteenth century reformers tore out the statues and stained glass in Protestant churches, arguing that decoration distracts from the Bible and the word of God. (*The Granger Collection.*)

to resist the Catholic Holy Roman Emperor Charles V, who wanted to extend his authority over the German princes. Resenting Italian domination of the church, many other Germans who supported Martin Luther believed that they were freeing German Christians from foreign control. The same spirit motivated the nobility in France, the Low Countries, Poland, and Lithuania.

First and foremost, however, Lutheranism was a popular evangelical movement. Its battle cry became "The Word of God"; faith and the Bible were its hallmarks. Luther turned his wrath on the clergy: on the "detestable tyranny of the clergy over the laity; [the clergy] almost look upon them as dogs, unworthy to be numbered in the Church along with themselves . . . they dare to command, exact, threaten, drive, and oppress, at their will."[4]

Nevertheless, as a political conservative, Luther hesitated to challenge secular authority. To him, the good Christian was an obedient citizen. The freedom of the Christian was an inward, spiritual freedom. Yet he could not stop his ideas from spreading to the poor and the peasantry, often by word of mouth. The population of Germany was about 16 million, of which probably no more than 400,000 could read. For the illiterate and largely rural people, Lutheranism came to mean not only religious reform but also an evangelical social movement that would address their poverty. In addition, the peasants believed that the end of the world was near and that God would soon impose justice. Millenarianism and poverty inspired social revolution.

Although Luther had spoken forcefully about the discontent of Christians with their church, he never understood that, in the minds of the poor and socially oppressed, the church's abuses were visible signs of the exploitation they encountered in their daily lives. The wealthy and powerful feudal lords who dominated every aspect of their existence, and the prosperous townspeople who bought their labor for the lowest possible wages, seemed no different from the venal clergy; indeed, in some cases the lord was also a local bishop.

In the early sixteenth century, a rapid population explosion throughout Europe had produced severe inflation, high unemployment, and low wages. These conditions seriously affected the poor. The peasantry in Germany was probably worse off than the peasantry in England and the Low Countries; in the German states, the feudal power of lords over peasant life remained unbroken. In 1524, long-suffering peasants openly rebelled against their lords. The peasants' revolt spread to over one-third of Germany; some 300,000 people took up arms against their masters. Luther's successful confrontation with the church authorities had inspired them. Had he not chastised the nobles for failing to care for the poor as commanded in the Gospel?

Luther, however, had no intention of associating his movement with a peasant uprising at the risk of alienating the nobility from the Reformation. Luther virulently attacked the rebellious peasants, urging the nobility to become "both judge and executioner" and to "knock down, strangle, and stab . . . and think nothing so venomous, pernicious, Satanic as an insurgent. . . . Such wonderful times are these that a prince can merit heaven better with bloodshed than another with prayer."[5] By 1525, the peasants had been put down by the sword. Thousands died or were left homeless, and many were permanently alienated from Lutheranism. Because of the failure of the revolt, the German peasantry remained relatively backward and oppressed well into the nineteenth century. In Germany, the Reformation meant religious reform but not social revolution or even social reform.

The Spread of the Reformation

Lutheranism spread in waves and in every direction, if we take Wittenberg, the training ground for Protestant clergy, as its center. In northern Europe, where the Alps and the Pyrenees formed natural borders, the Reformation spread rapidly. In southern Europe, where the church and the Inquisition were strongest, the Reformation made fewer inroads. Thus, the spread of Protestantism had a pattern. It grew strong in northern Germany, Scandinavia, the Netherlands, Scotland, and England but failed in the Romance countries, though not without a struggle in France.

Protestantism also appeared simultaneously in different places—a sure indication of its popular roots. For example, in the Swiss city of Zurich, the priest and reformer Ulrich Zwingli (1484–1531) preached a form of Christianity very close to that of Luther and claimed that he developed his ideas independently of Luther. Zwingli and Luther both sought an alternative to the doctrine of *transubstantiation*—the priest's transformation of communion bread and wine into the substance of Christ's body and blood—which gave enormous power to the priesthood. But the two reformers differed bitterly over the form and meaning of the ceremony. Luther retained the traditional Catholic form and meaning. Zwingli radically altered the communion service, and for his followers it became solely a commemoration of the Last Supper. Their quarrel anticipates the fate that awaited many reformers. Once free to read and interpret the Bible for themselves, they could not agree on its meaning or on the ritual expressions they would give their new versions of Christianity.

Zwingli died on the battlefield in a war to defend the Reformation. His teachings laid the foundation for a thorough reformation in Switzerland, and the major reform movement of the next generation, Calvinism, benefited from Zwingli's reforms. Both forms of the Reformation spread into eastern Europe.

In Germany, the strife created by the Reformation was settled, though not to everyone's satisfaction, by the Peace of Augsburg (1555). It decreed, by the famous dictum *cuius regio, eius religio* ("whoever rules, his religion"), that each territorial prince should determine the religion of his subjects. Broadly speaking, northern Germany became largely Protestant, and Bavaria and other southern territories remained in the Roman Catholic church. The victors were the local princes. Toward the end of his life, Charles V expressed bitter regret for not intervening more

INTERIOR OF ST. ODULPHUS, ASSENDELFT, THE NETHERLANDS. Early Calvinism was an austere faith that is manifest in the exact and simple construction of Protestant churches in the Dutch Republic, as shown in this painting by Pieter Saenredam. Many of these churches are still standing. (*Rijksmuseum-Stichting, Amsterdam.*)

forcefully in those early years. The decentralization of the empire and its division into Catholic and Protestant areas blocked German unity until the last part of the nineteenth century. In eastern Europe, both forms of Christianity showed hostility to Islam, and it was returned in kind.

Calvin and Calvinism

The success of the Reformation outside Germany and Scandinavia derived largely from the work of John Calvin (1509–1564), a French scholar and theologian. By the 1530s, Lutheran treatises circulated widely in Paris. Some university students, including the young John Calvin, were impressed by Luther's ideas.

Calvin was born into a French family of recent and substantial bourgeois status; his father, somewhat like Luther's, was self-made and ambitious. A lawyer and administrator, the elder Calvin served ecclesiastical authorities until a dispute over finances led to his excommunication. He desired prosperous careers for his sons. John first studied to be a priest and then, at his father's insistence, took up the study of law at the University of Orléans. Unlike the rebellious Luther, Calvin waited until his father's death to return to Paris and resume his theological studies. Even more so than Luther, Calvin was trained as a humanist. He knew the ancient languages, as well as philosophy and theology, and he knew the Bible. From all those sources, Calvin fashioned the most compelling version of Protestantism to come out of the Reformation.

Sometime in 1533 or 1534, Calvin met French

followers of Luther and became convinced of the truth of the new theology. He began to spread its beliefs immediately after his conversion, and within a year he and his friends were in trouble with the civil and ecclesiastical authorities. Calvin was arrested but was released because of insufficient evidence.

King Francis I, a bitter rival of the Holy Roman Emperor, could countenance Protestantism in Germany but would never permit disruptive religious divisions in France. Riots had already broken out in Paris between Catholics and supporters of the Reformation. In 1534, the French church, backed by a royal decree, declared the Protestants heretics and subjected them to arrest and execution.

Within a year, young Calvin abandoned his literary studies to become a preacher of the Reformation. Calvin explained his conversion as an act of God: "He subdued and reduced my heart to docility, which, for my age, was over-much hardened in such matters."[6] Calvin emphasized the power of God over sinful and corrupt humanity; his God thundered and demanded obedience, and the terrible distance between God and the individual was mediated only by Christ.

In his search for spiritual order and salvation, Calvin spoke to his age. His anxiety was widely shared. He feared disorder and ignorance, sinfulness, and simply the unpredictable quality of human existence. As he put it, "We are perturbed and tremble at the least change . . . We must struggle not only with the affliction of present evils, but also with the fear and anxiety with which impending dangers may harass us."[7]

The only solution to anxiety lay in unshakable faith in God, knowledge of his laws, and absolute adherence to righteous conduct. We must see God's order everywhere, especially in nature, in "the symmetry and regulation" of the universe.[8] Faith in God is so obviously our salvation that, according to Calvin, only the damned, the reprobate, would turn their back on him and live in disorder. Calvin assured his congregations that God "will give a good result to everything we do . . . God will cause our enterprises to prosper when our purpose is right and we attempt nothing except what he wills."[9] With Calvin, the doctrine of predestination became the centerpiece of Protestant theology: some people are saved, others damned at birth; inward belief and outward righteousness and integrity may signal a person's fate, but God alone knows what the future holds.

The social and political implications of predestination were immediate: Calvinists became militant Protestants capable of ruling their towns or cities with the same iron will they used to control their unruly passions. Like Luther, Calvin always stressed that Christians should obey legitimate political authority. But Calvinists were individuals who assumed that unfailing dedication to God's law could signal salvation; their obedience to human laws would always be contingent on their inner sense of righteousness. Thus, Calvinism made for stern men and women, active in their churches and willing to suppress vice in themselves and others. Calvinism also could produce revolutionaries willing to defy any temporal authorities seen to violate God's laws. Obedience to Christian law became the dominating principle of Calvin's life. Rigorous enforcement of the law ensured obedience to God's law; it also served as an alternative to the decrees and obligations formerly imposed by the Catholic church.

The political situation in France forced Calvin to leave. After his flight from Paris, he finally sought safety in Geneva, a small, prosperous Swiss city near the French border. There Calvin eventually established a militant Protestant church that dominated the lives of many others less committed to the Reformation.

French-speaking Switzerland was a logical choice. Before Calvin's arrival, Geneva's citizens were in revolt against their Catholic bishops. The French-born reformer William Farel led a small Protestant congregation there and implored Calvin to stay to continue the work of the Reformation. Together, they became leaders of the Protestant movement in Geneva. After many setbacks, Calvin emerged as the most dynamic agent of reform in the city. Until his death in 1564, his beliefs and actions ruled Geneva's religious and social life.

Calvin established an unofficial Calvinist *theocracy*—a society where Calvinist elders regulated citizens' personal and social lives and did so through church courts that were independent of state institutions. Older, pious male members of the community governed the city. These elders of the Calvinist church imposed strict discipline in dress, sexual mores, church attendance, and business affairs; they severely punished irreligious and sinful behavior. This rigid discipline contributed to Geneva's prosperity; indeed, Calvin instituted the kind of social discipline that some of the merchants had always wanted. Prosperous merchants, as well as small shopkeepers, saw in Calvinism a series of doctrines that justified the self-discipline they already exercised in their own lives and wished to impose on the unruly masses. They particularly approved of Calvin's economic views, for Calvin, unlike the Catholic church, saw nothing sinful in commercial activities and even gave his assent to the practice of charging interest.

Geneva became the center of international Protestantism. Calvin trained a new generation of Protestant reformers of many nationalities who carried his message back to their homelands. Calvin's *Institutes of the Christian Religion* (1536), in its many editions, became (after the Bible) the leading textbook of the new theology. In the second half of the sixteenth century, Calvin's theology of predestination spread into France, England, Scotland, the Netherlands, and parts of the Holy Roman Empire.

Calvin always opposed any recourse to violence and supported the authority of magistrates. Yet when monarchy became a persecutor, his followers felt compelled to respond. Calvinist theologians became the first political theoreticians of modern times to publish cogent arguments for opposition to monarchy and eventually for political revolution. In France and later in the Netherlands, Calvinism became a revolutionary ideology, complete with an underground organization of dedicated followers who challenged monarchical authority. (In the seventeenth century, the English version of Calvinism—Puritanism—performed the same function.) In certain circumstances, Calvinism possessed the moral force to undermine the claims of the monarchical state on the individual.

France

Although Protestantism was illegal in France after 1534, its persecution was halfhearted and never systematic. The Calvinist minority in France, the Huguenots, grew and become a well-organized underground movement that attracted nobles, urban dwellers, some peasants, and especially women. Huguenot churches, often under the protection of powerful nobles, assumed an increasingly political character in response to the monarchy-sponsored persecution. By 1559, French Protestants were sufficiently organized and militant to challenge their persecutors, King Henry II and the Guise—one of the foremost Catholic families in Europe, tied by marriage and conviction to the Spanish monarchy and its rigorous form of Catholicism. Guise power in the French court meant that all Protestant appeals for lenient treatment went unheeded, and in 1562, civil war erupted between Catholics and Protestants. What followed was one of the most brutal religious wars in the history of Europe. In 1572, an effort at conciliation through the marriage of a Protestant leader into the royal family failed when Catholics, urged on by the queen-mother, Catherine de Medicis, murdered the assembled Protestant wedding guests. Over the next week, a popular uprising left thousands of Protestants dead; the streets, according to eyewitness accounts, were stained red with blood. These murders and the ensuing slaughter, known as the Saint Bartholomew's Day Massacre, inspired the pope to have a Mass said in thanksgiving for a Catholic "victory." Such was the extent of religious hatred in late-sixteenth-century Europe.

After nearly thirty years of brutal fighting throughout France, victory went to the Catholic side—but just barely. Henry of Navarre, the Protestant bridegroom who in 1572 had managed to escape the fate of his supporters, became King Henry IV, but only after reconverting to Catholicism. He established a tentative peace by granting Protestants limited toleration. In 1598, he issued the Edict of Nantes, the first document in any nation-state that attempted to institutionalize a degree of religious toleration. In the seventeenth century, the successors of Henry IV (he was assassinated by a priest in 1610) gradually weakened and then in 1685 revoked the edict. The foundations of toleration, in theory and practice, remained tenuous in early modern France. Every

Map 14.1 The Protestant and Catholic ▶ Reformations Europe fractured into competing camps, and religious warfare became a way of life.

0 200 400 Km.
0 200 400 Mi.
Lutheran
Calvinist (Reformed)
Church of England
Roman Catholic
Huguenot centers
Spread of Calvinism
ATLANTIC OCEAN
North Sea
Baltic Sea
Bay of Biscay
Mediterranean Sea
Adriatic Sea
Black Sea
SCOTLAND
Edinburgh
IRELAND
Dublin
ENGLAND
Oxford
London
NORWAY
SWEDEN
DENMARK
LITHUANIA
PRUSSIA
POLAND
Warsaw
Hamburg
BRANDENBURG
Berlin
Wittenberg
Amsterdam
NETHERLANDS
Münster
HOLY
ROMAN
EMPIRE
WESTPHALIA
Leipzig
Brussels
Noyon
Paris
SAXONY
Prague
BOHEMIA
Worms
Nuremberg
MORAVIA
Orléans
Nantes
Strasbourg
Augsburg
Munich
BAVARIA
Vienna
AUSTRIA
Pest
Buda
TRANSYLVANIA
Basel
Zurich
FRANCE
SWITZERLAND
HUNGARY
Geneva
Trent
Milan
Venice
Bordeaux
Loyola
Toulouse
Avignon
ITALY
Rome
Naples
Corsica
Sardinia
SPAIN
Madrid
PORTUGAL
Lisbon
OTTOMAN EMPIRE

French king of the seventeenth century tried to decrease the number of Protestants in the kingdom.

England

The Reformation in England could not have differed more from the continental Reformations. The king, Henry VIII (1509–1547), and not clergymen in revolt, made it happen. The pope refused to grant Henry an annulment of his marriage to his first wife, which had failed to produce a male heir. So this self-confident Renaissance king, bent on having a new wife and new sources of revenue, removed the English church from papal jurisdiction.

Unlike the French and Spanish kings, the English Tudors never frightened the papacy. Henry VII (1485–1509), the first Tudor monarch, and his son, Henry VIII, enjoyed a good measure of control over the English church but never played a major role in European and papal politics. When Henry VIII decided that he wanted a divorce (he called it an annulment) from the Spanish princess Catherine of Aragon, in 1527–28, the pope in effect ignored his request. Henry had a shaky case from a theological point of view and not enough international political power to force his will on the papacy. As the pope stalled, Henry grew more desperate; he needed a male heir and presumed that the failure to produce one lay with his wife. At the same time, he desired the shrewd and tempting Anne Boleyn. But Spain's power over the papacy, symbolized by Charles V's army, which had sacked Rome in 1525, ensured that Henry's pleas for an annulment would go unheeded.

Anticlericalism and resentment toward the papacy were rife throughout Europe in the early sixteenth century. The English tradition of opposing the church, however, stretched back to Wycliffe in the fourteenth century. Aware of that long tradition, Henry VIII arranged to grant himself a divorce by severing England from the Roman Catholic church. To do so, he summoned Parliament, which in turn passed a series of statutes drawn up at his initiative and guided through Parliament by his political adviser, Thomas Cromwell. Beginning in 1529, Henry convinced both houses of Parliament to accept his Reformation and so began an administrative and religious revolution. In 1534, Henry had himself declared supreme head of the Church of England (also known as the Anglican church). In 1536, he dissolved English monasteries and seized their property, which was distributed or sold to his loyal supporters. In most cases, it went to the lesser nobility and landed gentry. By involving Parliament and the gentry, Henry VIII turned the Reformation into a national movement.

In the eleven years after Henry's death in 1547, three more Tudor monarchs ascended the throne of England. Henry was succeeded by his son, Edward VI, a Protestant, who reigned from 1547 to 1553. On his death, Edward was succeeded by his Catholic half sister, Mary (1553–1558), the daughter of Henry VIII and Catherine of Aragon, the divorced first wife, who had been sent into exile. With the remaining Catholic minority in England, Mary persecuted Protestants severely. On her death, she was succeeded by her Protestant half sister, Elizabeth I (1558–1603), Henry's daughter by Anne Boleyn, and England became a Protestant country again.

The Anglican church as it developed in the sixteenth century differed only to a limited degree in its customs and ceremonies from the Roman Catholicism it replaced. Large sections of the English population, including aristocratic families, remained Catholic and even used their homes as centers for Catholic rituals performed by clandestine priests. Thus, the exact nature of England's Protestantism became a subject of growing dispute. Was the Anglican church to be truly Protestant? Was its hierarchy to be responsive to, and possibly even appointed by, the laity? Were its services and churches to be simple, lacking in "popish" rites and rituals and centered only on Scripture and sermon? Was Anglicanism to conform to Protestantism as practiced in Switzerland, either in Calvinist Geneva or in Zwinglian Zurich? The clergy, especially the English bishops, would accept no form of Protestantism that might limit their ancient privileges, ceremonial functions, and power. Mary's persecutions, however, had forced leading English Protestants into exile in Geneva and into the waiting arms of the Calvinist church.

Despite these religious issues, raised by the growing number of English Calvinists, or Puritans, as they were called, Elizabeth's reign was

Map 14.2 Inner Austria and Adjacent Territories The Protestant Reformation sought converts throughout Hapsburg Europe and also confronted Islam in the Ottoman Empire. In both places the Reformation was only minimally successful, although Hungary is a major exception and by the end of the century the Hapsburgs got a large portion of it.

characterized by a heightened sense of national identity and by the persecution of Catholics, who were seen as threats to national security. At this same time, Calvinism flourished in Scotland. In Ireland, elites and peasants spurned the Reformation and remained staunch Catholics.

Southern and Eastern Europe

In Spain and Italy, where the Inquisition was powerful, the Reformation struggled but failed to take hold. In Venice, as late as the 1560s, it was possible to find Protestants of all sorts—Lutherans, Calvinists, radical millenarians. We know about them from the interrogation reports filled out by their Catholic inquisitors. The Italian Inquisition had the backing of the papacy and the population. Humanism, which might have given support to Protestantism, had never possessed a popular base in Italy, and the universities and printing presses, so vital to the Reformation north of the Alps, remained in Italy firmly under clerical control.

Luther's writings circulated in Spain for a time, but there, too, the authorities, both lay and clerical, quickly and thoroughly stamped out Protestantism. In the Middle Ages, the Spanish church and state had successfully joined in a religious and nationalist crusade to drive out the Muslims, and this effort forged strong links between the Spanish monarchy and the church. About a quarter of the Spanish population held a church office of one kind or another, and the church owned half of Spain's land. Allied with the state, the Inquisition enforced public and private morality. In southern Europe, the Reformation simply could not evade clerical authorities.

In eastern Europe, the pattern was quite different and more complex than in Italy and Spain. In Hungary, warfare between Christians and Turks led to the collapse of the nobility, three-quarters of whom were killed in one battle in 1526. The weakness of Austrian Hapsburg authority in the country, coupled with the demise of the local elite, created a power vacuum into which the Reformation rushed. Many Hungarian intellectuals had studied humanism in Italy and were predisposed to listen favorably to the European reformers. Franciscan priests like Mathias Devái Biró led the exodus from the Catholic church.

Hungarian reformers like Biró (1523–1545) and Stephen Kis (1505–1572) studied with Luther in Wittenberg and returned to Budapest to preach the Lutheran gospel. But as the number of their converts grew, Catholic and Turkish authorities became alarmed. They imprisoned Kis and Biró, confiscated their libraries, and fought the Reformation at every turn. Yet the Protestants did make converts among the Hungarian nobility, as well as among the townspeople. Not until the seventeenth century and the Hapsburg-led Counter Reformation did Hungary return to the church. Even in the eighteenth century, during the Enlightenment, Hungarian Protestants were influential in the intellectual life of the country.

The influence of the papacy in Bohemia (the Czech homeland), Poland, and Lithuania had always been problematical. In the Late Middle Ages, heresy could be found in all three places:

among the followers of Peter Waldo, the twelfth-century heretic, in Poland, and Lithuania; and among the followers of Wycliffe and then Hus in Bohemia and Poland. In Poland, the progress of the Reformation was most dramatic.

Lutheranism came first to Gdańsk, led by a local monk who was protected by the local aristocracy. In a pattern similar to the German Reformation, Poland embraced Lutheranism under the leadership of its nobility and its cities. Even the private confessor of the queen of Poland became a Lutheran. The Catholic church and the Inquisition, however, fought back. Priests as well as artisans who took up the Reformation were imprisoned. In 1539, an eighty-year-old Kraków woman, Catherine Zalaszowska, the wife of a city councilor, was burned at the stake. She had refused to adore the Eucharist held by a priest and thus implied that she did not accept either his authority or the doctrine of transubstantiation. In 1544, the death penalty was introduced for selling heretical books. Yet in 1569, when the Polish Diet of noblemen met, 58 out of the 133 delegates were Protestants; one-sixth of all Polish parishes had joined the Reformation. In 1573, religious toleration had to be granted in Poland; it had become the center of Protestantism in eastern Europe.

The pattern of the Reformation in the East followed that in the rest of Europe. It began in the cities, succeeded where it was supported by the nobility or where traditional authority was weak, and lasted when it took root among the general population. In Poland that had occurred; in neighboring Lithuania, only the nobility, already immensely powerful, took up Protestantism. When the church, led by the Jesuits, fought back, it easily triumphed in those areas where the Reformation lacked popular support. Very slowly, Poland was brought back into the church; in Lithuania, by the late sixteenth century, Protestantism had all but disappeared. Throughout the region Christians, Muslims, and Jews lived side by side, but with tensions always present.

The Radical Reformation

The mainstream of the Protestant Reformation can be described as *magisterial* because the leading reformers generally supported established political authorities, whether they were territorial princes or urban magistrates. For the reformers, human freedom was a spiritual, not a social, concept. Yet the Reformation did help trigger revolts among the artisan and peasant classes of central and then western Europe. Indications are that church doctrine had not made great inroads into the folk beliefs of large segments of the European masses. Late medieval records of church interrogations, usually in towns and villages where heresy or witchcraft was suspected, show that people deviated to an extraordinary degree from official doctrines and beliefs. For example, some peasants held the very un-Christian belief that Nature was God or that witches had as much spiritual power as priests did. By the 1520s, several radical reformers arose, often from the lower classes of European society, and attempted to channel popular religion and folk beliefs into a new version of reformed Christianity that spoke directly to the temporal and spiritual needs of the oppressed.

The proliferation of radical groups throughout Europe makes them difficult to classify. Nevertheless, some beliefs constituted what may be called the *Radical Reformation.* Appealing to the poor and oppressed, the radicals argued that ordinary men and women, even if illiterate, have certain knowledge of their salvation through an *inner light*—a direct communication from God to his chosen "saints"—men and women predestined for salvation. That knowledge makes the saint free. For the radicals, such spiritual freedom justified their demands for social and economic freedom and equality. Protestantism, radically interpreted, proclaimed the righteousness and the priesthood of all believers. It said that all people can have faith if God wills it and that God would not abandon the wretched and humble of the earth.

The radicals said, as did the Bible, that the poor shall inherit the earth, which is ruled at present by the Antichrist, and that the end of the world had been proclaimed by Scripture. The saint's task was to purge this earth of evil to make it ready for Christ's Second Coming. For the radicals, the faith-alone doctrine meant certain salvation for the poor and lowly, and the Scriptures became an inspiration for social revolution. The doctrine could also inspire quietism, retreat from this world in anticipation of a better world to come. Luther, Calvin, and the other reformers vigorously condemned the social doctrines that were preached by the radical reformers, whether activist or quietist.

The largest group in the Radical Reformation prior to 1550 has the general name of Anabaptists. On receiving the inner light—the message of salvation—the Anabaptist felt born anew and yearned to be rebaptized. This notion had a revolutionary implication: the first baptism—one's first Christian allegiance to an established church (Protestant or Catholic)—did not count. The Anabaptist was a new Christian, a new person led by the light of conscience to seek reform and renewal of all institutions in preparation for the Second Coming of Christ. Millenarian doctrines about the end of the world provided a sense of time and of the urgency of the moment.

In 1534, Anabaptists captured the city of Münster in Westphalia, near the western border of Germany. They seized the property of nonbelievers, burned all books except the Bible, and in a mood of jubilation and sexual excess openly practiced a repressive (as far as women were concerned) polygamy. All the while, the Anabaptists proclaimed that the Day of Judgment was close at hand. The radical leaders at Münster were men totally unprepared for power, and their actions led to universal condemnation. They were defeated by the army led by a Lutheran prince, Philip of Hesse, and the local Catholic bishops brutally suppressed them. In early modern Europe, *Münster* became a byword for dangerous revolution. In Münster today, the cages still hang from the church steeple where the Anabaptist leaders were tortured and left to die as a warning to all would-be imitators.

By the late sixteenth century, many radical movements had either gone underground or grown quiet. But a century later, during the English Revolution of 1640 to 1660, the beliefs and political goals of the Radical Reformation resurfaced, threatening to push the political revolution in a direction that its gentry leaders desperately feared. Although the radicals failed in England, they left a tradition of democratic and antihierarchical thought. The radical assertion that saints, who have received the inner light, *are the equal of anyone,* regardless of social status, helped shape modern democratic thought.

The Catholic Response

The Catholic church did not foresee that the Protestant Reformation would gain such strength or that it would attract so many powerful noble families. The papacy was slow to respond. Initially, the energy for reform came from ordinary clergy, as well as laypeople such as Ignatius Loyola (1491–1556), rather than from the hierarchy or the established religious orders. Trained as a soldier, this pious Spanish reformer sought to create a new religious order fusing the intellectual excellence of humanism with a reformed Catholicism that would appeal to powerful economic and political groups. Founded in 1534, the Society of Jesus, commonly known as the Jesuits, became the backbone of the Catholic Reformation (also called the Counter Reformation) in southern and western Europe.

The Jesuits strove to bypass local corruption and appealed to the papacy to lead a truly international movement to revive Christian universalism. The Jesuits saw most clearly the bitter fragmentation produced by the Reformation. Moreover, they perceived one of the central flaws in Protestant theology. Predestination offered salvation to the literate and prosperous laity and, at least in theory, to the poor as well. However, it also included the possibility of despair for the individual and a life tormented by fear of inescapable damnation. In response, the Jesuits offered hope: a religious revival based on ceremony, tradition, and the power of the priest to offer forgiveness.

The Jesuits pursued positions as confessors to princes and urged them to press their efforts to strengthen the church in their territories. They even sought to develop a theology that permitted "small sins" in the service of an ultimately just cause. In this way, the Jesuits, by the seventeenth century, became the greatest teachers in Europe and also the most controversial religious group within the church. Were they the true voice of a reformed church, or did they use religion simply as a disguise to seek political power of their own, to make themselves the Machiavellian servants of princes? It was a controversy that neither their contemporaries nor historians have resolved.

The forces of the Catholic revival built schools and universities throughout Europe, designed

BAROQUE CATHOLIC ALTAR FROM KODEN, POLAND. (*Art Resource, NY.*)

churches, and even fostered a distinct style of art and architecture: cherubic angels grace the ornate decor of Counter Reformation churches; heaven-bound saints beckon the penitent. This baroque style, so lavish and emotive, was intended to move the heart, just as the skilled preacher sought to move the intellect. It was, in part, a response to the Protestant message that religion is ultimately a private, psychological matter, not always satisfied by scholastic argumentation.

By the 1540s, the Counter Reformation was well under way. The attempt to reform the church from within combined several elements that had always stood for renewal within traditional Catholicism. For example, the Jesuits were imitating such preaching orders of the Middle Ages as the Dominicans and the Franciscans, and some Catholic reformers looked to Renaissance humanism, like that of Erasmus, as the key to the church's total reformation. The leaders of this Catholic movement attacked many of the same abuses that had impelled Luther to speak out, but they avoided a break with the doctrinal and spiritual authority of the pope and the clergy.

The Counter Reformation also turned aggressive and hostile toward Protestants. The church tried to counter the popular appeal of Protestantism by offering dramatic, emotional, and even sentimental piety to the faithful. In regard to individuals who were unmoved by this appeal to sentiment or by the church's more traditional spirituality and who allied themselves with Protestant heresy, the church resorted to sterner measures. The Inquisition expanded its activities, and wherever Catholic jurisdiction prevailed, unrepentant heretics—Protestants, Jews, and even Muslims—were subject to death or imprisonment. Catholics did not hold a monopoly on persecution: wherever Protestantism obtained official status—in England, Scotland, Ireland, and Geneva, for instance—Catholics or religious radicals also sometimes faced persecution. Calvin, for example, approved the execution in 1563 of the naturalist and skeptic Michael Servetus, who opposed the doctrine of the Trinity. (In 1600, the Catholic church burned Giordano Bruno for similar reasons.)

Aside from torture and imprisonment, one of the Catholic church's main tools was censorship. By the 1520s, the impulse to censor and burn dangerous books intensified as the church tried to prevent the rapid spread of Protestant ideas. In the rush to eliminate heretical literature, the church condemned the works of reforming Catholic humanists as well as those of Protestants. The *Index of Prohibited Books* became an institutional part of the church's life. Over the centuries, the works of many leading European thinkers were placed on the *Index,* which was not abolished until 1966.

These Counter Reformation policies of education, vigorous preaching, church building, persecution, and censorship succeeded in bringing thousands of people, Germans and Bohemians in particular, back into the church. Furthermore, the church implemented some concrete changes in policy and doctrine. In 1545, the Council of Trent met to reform the church and strengthen it for confronting the Protestant challenge. Over the many years that it was convened (until 1563), the council modified and unified church doctrine; abolished many corrupt practices, such as the selling of indulgences; and vested final authority in the papacy, thereby reasserting its power. The Council of Trent purged the church and gave it doctrinal clarity on such matters as the roles of faith and good works in attaining salvation. It passed a decree that the church shall be the final arbiter of the Bible and demanded that texts be taken literally wherever possible. Galileo Galilei, the Italian physicist and astronomer, was to experience great difficulties in the next century because that decree implied that the motion of the earth contradicted Scripture. But the intention of the decree was to offer the church as a clear voice amid the babble of Protestant tongues. Priests were accorded considerable latitude in their daily lives. All compromise with Protestantism was rejected (not that Protestants were anxious for it). The Reformation had split Western Christendom irrevocably.

The Reformation and the Modern Age

At first glance, the Reformation would seem to have renewed the medieval stress on otherworldliness and reversed the direction toward a secularized humanism taken by the Renaissance. Yet a careful analysis shows decisively modern elements in Reformation thought, as well as antiauthoritarian tendencies in its political history. The Reformation shattered the religious unity of Europe, the chief characteristic of the Middle Ages, and further weakened the principal institution of medieval society, the church, whose moral authority and political power waned considerably. To this day, western Europe remains an area of Catholic and Protestant traditions. Although doctrinal rigidity (and in some places church attendance) has largely disappeared, the split between the southern Catholic countries and the mostly Protestant north is still visible in various customs and rituals. In eastern European countries, where the churches, both Catholic and Protestant, emerged from the early modern period as powerful political forces, governments had to be cautious in dealing with them. During the 1980s, Lutheran and Catholic churches became focal points for anti-Soviet activities. In the same period, Northern Ireland stood as a reminder of the religious tensions that had once plagued the whole of Europe. Also in the same period, the centuries of tensions between Christians and Muslims in eastern Europe led to new nationalistic passions.

By strengthening the power of monarchs and magistrates at the expense of religious bodies, the Reformation furthered the growth of the modern state. Protestant rulers completely repudiated the pope's claim to temporal power and extended their authority over Protestant churches in their lands. In predominantly Catholic lands, the church reacted to the onslaught of Protestantism by supporting the monarchies, but at the same time it preserved a significant degree of political independence. Protestantism did not create the modern secular state; it did, however, help to free the state from subordination to religious authority. Such autonomy is an essential feature of modern political life.

Indirectly, Protestantism contributed to the growth of political liberty: another ideal, though not always a reality, in the modern West. To be sure, neither Luther nor Calvin championed political freedom. Luther said that subjects should obey the commands of their rulers, and Calvinists created in Geneva a theocracy that closely regulated its citizens. Nevertheless, tendencies in the Reformation provided a basis for challenging monarchical authority. During the religious wars, both Protestant and Catholic theorists supported resistance to monarchs whose edicts, they believed, defied God's Law. Moreover, the Protestant view that all believers—laity, clergy, lords, and kings—were masters of their own spiritual destiny eroded hierarchical authority and accorded with emerging constitutional government.

The Reformation also contributed to the creation of an individualistic ethic. Protestants sought a direct and personal relationship with God and interpreted the Bible for themselves. Facing the prospect of salvation or damnation entirely on their own, without the church to provide aid and security, and believing that God had chosen them to be saved, Protestants developed inner confidence and assertiveness. This religious individualism was the counterpart of the intellectual individualism of the Renaissance humanists.

The Protestant ethic of the Reformation developed concurrently with a new economic system. Theorists have argued ever since about whether the new individualism of the Protestants brought on the growth of capitalism or whether the capitalistic values of the middle class gave rise to the Protestant ethic. In the middle of the nineteenth century, Karl Marx theorized that Protestantism gave expression to the new capitalistic values of the bourgeois: thrift, hard work, self-reliance, and rationality. Hence, Marx argued, the success of Protestantism can be explained by reference to the emergence of Western capitalism.

In 1904, the German sociologist Max Weber argued that Marx had got it backward—that Protestantism encouraged the growth of capitalism, not vice versa.[10] Weber began with the assumption that religious beliefs do in fact have relevance to the way individuals act in the world. He perceived in the Protestant ethic of the Reformation, as it evolved through the life experiences of its followers, the spirit of a nascent capitalism. Weber saw the spirit of capitalism embodied in the entrepreneur, the parvenu, the self-made person. Such people strive for business success and bring to their enterprises self-discipline and self-restraint. They make profit not for pleasure but for the sake of more profit. They bring to their enterprises moral virtues of frugality and honesty. They also plan work and business and strive to render them efficient, with profits carefully accumulated over time. For Weber, Protestants made the best capitalists because predestination made them *worldly ascetics:* Christians forced to find salvation without assistance and through activity in this world. The reformers had condemned the monastery as an unnatural life; their concomitant emphasis on human sinfulness established a psychology of striving that could be channeled only into worldly activity. So Protestant men and women fulfilled their vocation, or calling, by service to the community or state and by dedication to this daily work. If Weber is right, commerce or family life could become sanctified. But this ethic did little to alleviate the condition of the poor, which had worsened by the end of the sixteenth century.

By the late seventeenth century, the center of economic growth in Europe was shifting from Mediterranean and Catholic countries toward northern Atlantic areas: England, the Netherlands, and parts of northern France. Protestant cities, with their freer printing presses, were also developing into centers of intellectual creativity. The characteristics of the modern world—individual expression, economic development, and scientific learning—were to become most visibly present in western European Protestant cities, such as London, Amsterdam, and Geneva. By 1700, both the Protestant entrepreneur and the Protestant intellectual began to symbolize the most advanced forms of economic and creative life. Sixteenth-century Protestantism had created a new spirituality. Survival in this world, as well as salvation in the next, came to depend on inner faith and self-discipline. For the prosperous, both eventually became useful in a highly competitive world where individuals rule their own lives and the labor of others and represent themselves and others in government. The tension between the Roman church and Protestantism set the former in the direction of opposing modernity. By 1800, the church in Rome—but by no means all Catholics—viewed change with deep suspicion.

❖ ❖ ❖

Notes

1. Eugen Weber, ed., *The Western Tradition,* 2 vols., 4th ed. (Lexington, Mass., and Toronto: D. C. Heath, 1990), 1:334–335.
2. John Dillenberger, ed., *Martin Luther: Selections from His Writings* (New York: Doubleday, 1961), p. 46, taken from *The Freedom of a Christian Man* (1520).
3. Steven Ozment, ed., *Three Behaim Boys: Growing Up in Early Modern Germany* (New Haven, Conn.: Yale University Press, 1990), p. 79.
4. Martin Luther, *On the Babylonish Captivity of*

the Church, quoted in Weber, *Western Tradition,* p. 338.

5. Martin Luther, *Luther's Works,* ed. Robert Schultz (Philadelphia: Fortress Press, 1967), 46:50–52.
6. François Wendel, *Calvin* (Paris: Presses Universitaires de France, 1950), p. 20.
7. Quoted in William J. Bouwsma, *John Calvin, A Sixteenth-Century Portrait* (New York: Oxford University Press, 1988), p. 39.
8. Ibid., p. 104.
9. Ibid., p. 96.
10. See Max Weber, *Protestant Ethic and the Spirit of Capitalism,* trans. Talcott Parsons (New York: Charles Scribner's Sons, 1958).

Suggested Reading

Blickle, P., H. C. Rublack, and W. Schulze, *Religion, Politics and Social Protest: Three Studies on Early Modern Germany* (1984). A short, readable account of the volatile mixture of religion and politics in the German Reformation.

Cottret, Bernard, *Calvin: A Biography* (2000). A superb French historian shows Calvin as a remote, even shy man. The case of Servetus is well handled.

Davidson, N. S., *The Counter-Reformation* (1987). A short, readable account.

Delumeau, J., *Catholicism Between Luther and Voltaire* (1977). An intelligent general account.

Holt, Mack P., *The French Wars of Religion 1562–1629* (1995). Discusses the dark side of religious intolerance and hatred.

Koenigsberger, H. G., and George L. Mosse, *Europe in the Sixteenth Century* (1987). A good general survey, with bibliography.

Major, J. Russell, *From Renaissance Monarchs to Absolute Monarchy* (1994). An important account of political developments in the period when religion and politics were inseparable.

McClendon, Muriel, ed., *Protestant Identities: Religion, Society, and Self-Fashioning in Post-Reformation England* (1999). Good portraits of individuals by a new generation of historians.

McGrath, Alister E., *Reformation Thought: An Introduction* (1999). A solid account of difficult ideas made understandable.

Pettegrew, A., ed., *The Early Reformation in Europe* (1992). Essays by experts on different countries, from Spain to Hungary.

Wiesner-Hanks, Merry, ed., *Converts Confront the Reformation: Catholic and Protestant Nuns in Germany* (1996). A lively introduction to different sides in the Protestant-Catholic divide of the 1520s.

For sources on the Internet, see

http://www.ic/net.org/pub/resources/text/wittenberg/wittenberg-home.html
This site gives a cross section of texts written by Lutherans, many of them in English.

http://www.luc.edu/libraries/science/jesuits/index.html
Documents the Jesuits' interest in science and contains articles and biographical information for the period 1540 to 1773.

Review Questions

1. Why did the Reformation begin in the early sixteenth century rather than in the fourteenth century, at the time of Hus and Wycliffe? Describe the conditions and personalities responsible for starting the Reformation.
2. How did Martin Luther's personality traits relate to his role and actions in the Reformation? In what ways did Luther's theology mark a break with the church? Why did many Germans become followers of Luther?
3. What role did the printing press play in the Reformation?
4. Did the Reformation make the lives of clergymen easier by allowing them to marry?
5. What were Calvin's major achievements?
6. Explain predestination.
7. In what ways did the radical reformers differ from other Protestants? Did Luther betray the peasants?
8. Were women better off as nuns or as married Protestants?
9. What did *Münster* symbolize in early modern Europe? Was the symbolism fair?
10. How did the Reformation in England differ

from that in Germany? How did it differ in Hungary from what it was in Poland?

11. Why did France not become a Protestant country? Give the reasons and describe the circumstances.
12. What role did the Jesuits and the Inquisition play in the Counter Reformation? What did the Counter Reformation accomplish in western and in eastern Europe? Were Protestants more tolerant than Catholics?
13. Which features of Protestantism point toward the modern world?

Chapter 15

European Expansion: Economic and Social Transformations

A Street in Haarlem, c. 1680, by G. A. Berckheyde (1638–1698). There was a ready market for such pictures in the seventeenth-century Dutch Republic, or United Provinces. Haarlem was one of several major Dutch cities where growing trade and industry created wealth and fostered civic pride. (Gemaldegalerie, Alte Meister, Dresden/AKG London.)

- **European Expansion**
  Forces Behind Expansion
  The Portuguese Empire
  The Spanish Empire
  Black Slavery and the Slave Trade
- **The Price Revolution**
- **The Expansion of Agriculture**
  The Old Pattern of Farming
  Enclosure
  Convertible Husbandry
  Agricultural Change in Eastern Europe
- **The Expansion of Trade and Industry**
  The Domestic System
  Innovations in Business
  Patterns of Commercial Development
- **The Growth of Capitalism**
  What Is Capitalism?
  The Fostering of Mercantile Capitalism
- **The Elite and the People**
  Traditional Popular Culture
  The Reform of Popular Culture
  Witchcraft and the Witch Craze
- **Economic and Social Transformations**

During the period from 1450 to 1750, western Europe entered an era of overseas exploration and economic expansion that transformed society. By 1450, Europe had recovered from the severe contraction of the fourteenth century, produced by plague and marginal agriculture, and was resuming the economic growth that had been the pattern in the twelfth and early thirteenth centuries. This new period of growth, however, was no mere extension of the earlier one but a radical departure from medieval economic forms.

Overseas exploration changed the patterns of economic growth and society. European adventurers discovered a new way to reach the rich trading centers of India by sailing around Africa. They also conquered, colonized, and exploited a new world across the Atlantic. These discoveries and conquests brought about an extraordinary increase in business activity and the supply of money, which stimulated the growth of capitalism. People's values changed in ways that were alien and hostile to the medieval outlook. By 1750, the model Christian in northwestern Europe was no longer the selfless saint but the enterprising businessman. The era of secluded manors and walled towns was drawing to a close. A world economy was emerging in which European economic life depended on the market in Eastern spices, African slaves, and American silver. During this age of exploration and commercial expansion, Europe generated a peculiar dynamism unmatched by any other civilization. A process was initiated that, by 1900, would give Europe mastery over most of the globe and wide-ranging influence over other civilizations.

The economic expansion from 1450 to 1650 or 1700 did not, however, raise the living standards of the masses. The vast majority of the people, 80 to 90 percent, lived on the land, and their main business was the production of primary goods: food, especially cereals, and wool. For most of these people, life hovered around the subsistence level, sometimes falling below subsistence during times of famine and disease. Whenever the standard of living improved, any surplus resources were soon taken up by the survival of more children and hence more mouths to feed. The beneficiaries of the commercial expansion, those whose income rose, were the rich, especially the *nouveaux riches* (new rich).

Chronology 15.1 ❖ The Commercial Revolution

1394–1460	Henry the Navigator, prince of Portugal, encourages expansion into Africa for gold and his anti-Muslim crusade
1430	The Portuguese expand into the Canaries and the Azores
1488	Bartholomeu Dias reaches the tip of Africa
1492	Christopher Columbus reaches the Caribbean island of Española on his first voyage; the Jews are expelled from Spain; Granada, the last Muslim kingdom in Spain, is conquered, completing the Reconquest
1497	Vasco da Gama sails around Cape of Good Hope (Africa) to India
1509	The Portuguese defeat Muslim fleet at Diu in the Indian Ocean
1513	Balboa discovers the Pacific Ocean at the Isthmus of Panama
1519–1521	Hernando Cortés conquers the Aztecs in Mexico
1520–1521	Magellan's soldiers circumnavigate the globe
1531–1533	Francisco Pizarro conquers the Incas in Peru
1545	Silver is discovered by the Spaniards at Potosí, Peru
1552	Silver from the New World flows into Europe via Spain, contributing to a price revolution
1590s	The Dutch develop shipping carriers for grain
1602–1609	Dutch East India Company is founded; Bank of Amsterdam is founded, expanding credit
1651	Navigation Act is passed in England to accomplish the goals of mercantilism
1694	Bank of England is founded

In these respects, then, early modern Europe was comparable to an underdeveloped country today whose society consists of two main economic groups: a small, wealthy elite and a large and growing population that exists on the margin of subsistence and is racked by recurrent hunger and disease. Developments during overseas exploration and economic expansion should be viewed in the context of these social conditions.

European Expansion

During the Middle Ages, the frontiers of Europe had expanded, even if only temporarily in some instances. The Crusaders carved out feudal kingdoms in the Near East. Christian knights pushed back the Muslims on the Iberian Peninsula and drove them from Mediterranean islands. Germans expanded in the Baltic region at the expense of non-Christian Balts, Prussians, and Slavs. Genoa and Venice established commercial ports in the Adriatic Sea, the Black Sea, and the eastern Mediterranean. In the fifteenth and sixteenth centuries, western Europeans embarked on a second and more lasting movement of expansion, which led them onto the uncharted waters of the Atlantic, Indian, and Pacific Oceans. Combined forces propelled Europeans outward and enabled them to dominate Asians, Africans, and American Indians.

Forces Behind Expansion

The population of western Europe increased rapidly between 1450 and 1600, at all levels of society. Among the gentry (hereditary landlords), population growth was translated into land hunger. As the numbers of those in the landed classes exceeded the supply of available land, the sons of the aristocracy looked beyond Europe for the lands and fortunes denied them at home. Nor was it unnatural for them to do so by plunder and conquest; their ancestors had done the same thing for centuries. Exploits undertaken and accomplished in the name of family, church, and king were deemed legitimate, perhaps the most legitimate, ways of earning merit and fame, as well as fortune. So the gentry provided the leadership—Hernando Cortés is an example—for the expeditions to the New World.

Merchants and shippers, as well as the sons of the aristocracy, had reason to look abroad. Trade between Europe, Africa, and the Orient had gone on for centuries, but always through intermediaries, who increased the costs and decreased the profits on the European end. Gold had been transported by Arab nomads across the Sahara from the riverbeds of West Africa. Spices had been shipped from India and the East Indies by way of Muslim and Venetian merchants. Western European merchants now sought to break those monopolies by going directly to the source: to West Africa for gold, slaves, and pepper, and to India for pepper, spices, and silks. Moreover, the incentive for such commercial enterprise grew because between 1450 and 1600 the wealth of prosperous Europeans increased dramatically. This wealth was translated into new purchasing power and the capacity to invest in foreign ventures that would meet the rising demand for luxury goods among the prosperous.

The centralizing monarchical state also played its part in expansion. Monarchs who like Ferdinand and Isabella of Spain had successfully established royal hegemony at home sought opportunities to extend their control overseas. The Spanish rulers looked over their shoulders at their neighbors, the Portuguese, and this competition spurred the efforts of both countries in their drive to the East. Later, the Dutch, the English, and the French engaged in a century-long rivalry. From overseas empires came gold, silver, and commerce that paid for ever more expensive royal government at home and for war against rival dynasties abroad.

Finally, religion helped the expansion. The crusading tradition was well established, especially on the Iberian Peninsula, where a five-hundred-year struggle known as the Reconquest had taken place to drive out the Muslims. Cortés, for example, saw himself as following in the footsteps of Paladin Roland, a medieval military hero who had fought to drive back Muslims and pagans. The Portuguese, too, were imbued with the crusading mission. Prince Henry the Navigator hoped that the Portuguese expansion into Africa would serve two purposes: the discovery of gold and the extension of Christianity at the expense of Islam. In this second aim, his imagination was fired by the legend of Prester John, which told of an ancient Christian kingdom of fabled wealth in the heart of Africa. If the Portuguese could reach that land, Prince Henry reckoned, the two kingdoms would join in a crusade against Islam.

Thus, expansion involved a mixture of economic, political, and religious forces and motives. The West had a crusading faith; divided into a handful of competing, warlike states, it expanded by virtue of forces built into its structure and culture. But besides the will to expand, the West also possessed the technology needed for successful expansion. This factor distinguished the West from China and the lands of Islam and helps explain why the West, rather than the Eastern civilizations, launched an age of conquest resulting in global mastery.

Not since the Early Middle Ages had there been such a rapid technological revolution as that which began in the fifteenth century. Europeans had already learned about gunpowder from the Chinese in the late thirteenth century, and by the fifteenth century, its military application had become widespread. The earliest guns were big cannon meant to knock holes in the walled defenses characteristic of the Middle Ages. In the sixteenth and seventeenth centuries, handheld firearms (particularly the musket) and smaller, more mobile field artillery were perfected. Dynastic and religious wars and overseas expansion kept demand for armaments high, and as a result, the armament industry was important to the growth of trade and manufacturing.

Another technological development during the period from 1400 to 1650 was the sailing ship. The vessels of the ancient world had been driven primarily by oars and human energy. Called galleys, they were suitable for the shorter distances, calmer waters, and less variable conditions of the Mediterranean and the Black and Red Seas—but not for the Atlantic and other great oceans, which Europeans began to ply in the early sixteenth century. Moreover, by the fifteenth century in western Europe, labor was in short supply, making it difficult to recruit or condemn men to the galleys. For these reasons, the Portuguese, the Dutch, and the English abandoned the galley in favor of the sailing ship.

The sail and the gun were crucially important in allowing Europeans to overcome non-Europeans and penetrate and exploit their worlds. Western Europeans combined these devices in the form of the gunned ship. Not only was the sailing vessel more maneuverable and faster in the open seas than the galley, but the addition of guns gave it another tactical advantage over its rivals. The galleys of the Arabs in the Indian Ocean and the junks of the Chinese were not armed with guns below deck for firing at a distance to cripple or sink the enemy. In battle, they relied instead on the ancient tactic of coming up alongside the enemy vessel, shearing off its oars, and boarding to fight on deck.

The gunned ship gave the West naval superiority from the beginning. The Portuguese, for example, made short work of the Muslim fleet sent to drive them out of the Indian Ocean in 1509. That victory at Diu, off the western coast of India, indicated that the West not only had found an all-water route to the Orient but was there to stay. Material and religious motives led Europeans to explore and conquer; superior technology ensured the success of their enterprises.

The Portuguese Empire

Several reasons account for Portugal's overseas success. Portugal's long Atlantic coastline ensured that its people would look to the sea—initially for fishing and trade and then for exploration. A sunny climate also spurred seafaring and commercial expansion. Portugal was northern Europe's closest supplier of subtropical products: olive oil, cork, wine, and fruit. The feudal nobility, typically antagonistic to trade and industry, was not as powerful in Portugal as elsewhere in Europe. Although feudal warriors had carved Portugal out of Moorish Iberia in the twelfth century, their descendants were blocked from further interior expansion by the presence of the strong Christian kingdom of Castile in the east. The only other outlet for expansion was the sea.

Royal policy also favored expansion. The central government promoted trading interests, especially after 1385, when the merchants of Lisbon and the lesser ports helped establish a new dynasty in opposition to the feudal aristocracy. In the first half of the fifteenth century, a younger son of the king, named Prince Henry the Navigator (1394–1460) by English writers, sponsored voyages of exploration and the nautical studies needed to undertake them. In these endeavors, he spent his own fortune and the wealth of the church's crusading order that he headed. Prince Henry sought to revive the anti-Muslim crusade, to which Portugal owed its existence as a Christian state. This connection between the medieval Crusades and the early modern expansion of Europe ran through Portuguese and Spanish history.

As early as the fifteenth century, the Portuguese expanded into islands in the Atlantic Ocean. In 1420, they began to settle Madeira and raise food there, and in the 1430s, they pushed into the Canaries and the Azores in search of new farmland and slaves for their colonies. In the middle decades of the century, they moved down the West African coast to the mouth of the Congo River and beyond, establishing trading posts as they went.

By the last quarter of the century, they had developed a viable imperial economy among the ports of West Africa, their Atlantic islands, and western Europe—an economy based on sugar, black slaves, and gold. Africans panned the gold in the riverbeds of central and western Africa, and the Portuguese purchased it at its source. They paid in cloth and slaves at a profit of at least 500 percent. Then the Portuguese trans-

PORTUGUESE IN INDIA. A charming watercolor by a Portuguese traveler in India, this painting mixes what to Western eyes was strange and foreign with the more familiar. The elephant, the clothes, and the elaborate parasols held high by turbaned servants may have seemed exotic, but the hunt, the horse, and the hunting dogs had their counterparts in western European landed society. (*Biblioteca Casanatense, Rome. Photo: Humberto Nicoletti Serra.*)

ported the gold to Europe, where they sold it for even more profit. Slaves figured not only in the purchase of gold but also in the production of sugar. On their Atlantic islands, the Portuguese grew sugar cane, and little else by the end of the century, as a cash crop for European consumption, and slaves were imported from West Africa to do the work. There was also a lively trade in slaves to Portugal itself and elsewhere in southern Europe.

The Portuguese did not stop in western Africa. By 1488, Bartholomeu Dias had reached the southern tip of the African continent; a decade later, Vasco da Gama sailed around the Cape of Good Hope and across the Indian Ocean to India. By discovering an all-water route to the Orient, Portugal broke the commercial monopoly on Eastern goods that Genoa and Venice had enjoyed.

In search of spices, the Portuguese went directly to the source, to India and the East Indies. As they had done along the African coast, they established fortified trading posts—most notably at Goa, on the western coast of India (Malabar) and at Malacca (now Singapore), on the Malay Peninsula.

Demand for spices was insatiable. Pepper and other spices are relatively unimportant items in the modern diet, but in the era before refrigeration, fresh meat was available only at slaughtering time, customarily twice a year. The rest of the year the only meat available, for those who could afford it at all, was dried, stringy, and tough; spices made meat and other foods palatable.

The infusion of Italian, particularly Genoese, investment and talent contributed to Portuguese expansion. As Genoese trade with the Near East, especially the Black Sea, shrank due to the expansion of the Ottoman Empire, Genoese merchants shifted more and more of their capital and mercantile activities from the eastern to the western Mediterranean and the Atlantic—that is, to Spain and Portugal and their possessions overseas. This shift is evident in the life of Christopher Columbus (1451–1506), a Genoese sailor, who worked in Portugal before finally winning acceptance at the court of Castile in Spain for his scheme to find a westward route to the spices of the East. Initially, much of the Genoese investment was in the sugar plantations in Portuguese colonies in the Atlantic. The Portuguese gained not only Genoese capital but also the expertise to put it to use. The Genoese had established their own sugar colonies in Cyprus and Crete two centuries before, and they knew from long experience what would work. The plantation system based on slave labor was an Italian import; only now the slaves were black Africans instead of Slavs, as they had often been in the eastern Mediterranean.

The Spanish Empire

Spain stumbled onto its overseas empire, which nonetheless proved to be the biggest and richest of any until the eighteenth century. Columbus won the support of Isabella, queen of Castile. But on his first voyage (1492), he landed on a large Caribbean island, which he named Española (Little Spain). To the end of his life, even after subsequent voyages, Columbus believed that the West Indies were part of the East. Two forthcoming events would reveal that Columbus had discovered not a new route to the East but new continents: Vasco Nuñez de Balboa's discovery of the Pacific Ocean at the Isthmus of Panama in 1513 and Ferdinand Magellan's circumnavigation of the globe (1520–21) through the strait at the tip of South America that now bears his name.

The Spanish found no spices in the New World, but they were more than compensated by the abundant land and the large quantities of precious metals. Stories of the existence of larger quantities of gold and silver to the west lured the Spaniards from their initial settlements in the Caribbean to Mexico. In 1519, Hernando Cortés landed on the Mexican coast with a small army. During two years of campaigning, he managed to defeat the native rulers, the Aztecs, and to conquer Mexico for the Spanish crown. A decade later, Francisco Pizarro achieved a similar victory over the mountain empire of the Incas in Peru. Both Cortés and Pizarro exploited the hostility that the subject tribes of Mexico and Peru felt toward their Aztec and Incan overlords, a strategy that accounts to some extent for the Spaniards' success. But the most important reason was probably the spread of infectious diseases among the native population, including the armies—diseases carried by the Europeans to which the Indians apparently had little or no resistance and which so weakened them that the Spanish forces could win despite being vastly outnumbered. This is one of the signal examples in world history where a nonhuman biological agency brought about the decisive turning point in the flow of events.

For good reasons, the Mexican and Peruvian conquests became the centers of the Spanish overseas empire. First, there were the gold hoards accumulated over the centuries by the rulers of these lands for religious and ceremonial purposes. Once these supplies were exhausted, the Spanish discovered silver at Potosí in Upper Peru in 1545 and at Zacatecas in Mexico a few years later. From the middle of the century, the annual treasure fleets sailing to Spain became the financial bedrock of Philip II's war against the Muslim Turks and the Protestant Dutch and English.

Not only gold and silver lured Spaniards to the New World. The crusading tradition also acted as a spur. Cortés, Pizarro, and many of their followers were *hidalgos*—lesser gentry whose status depended on the possession of landed estates and whose training and experience taught that holy war was a legitimate avenue to wealth and

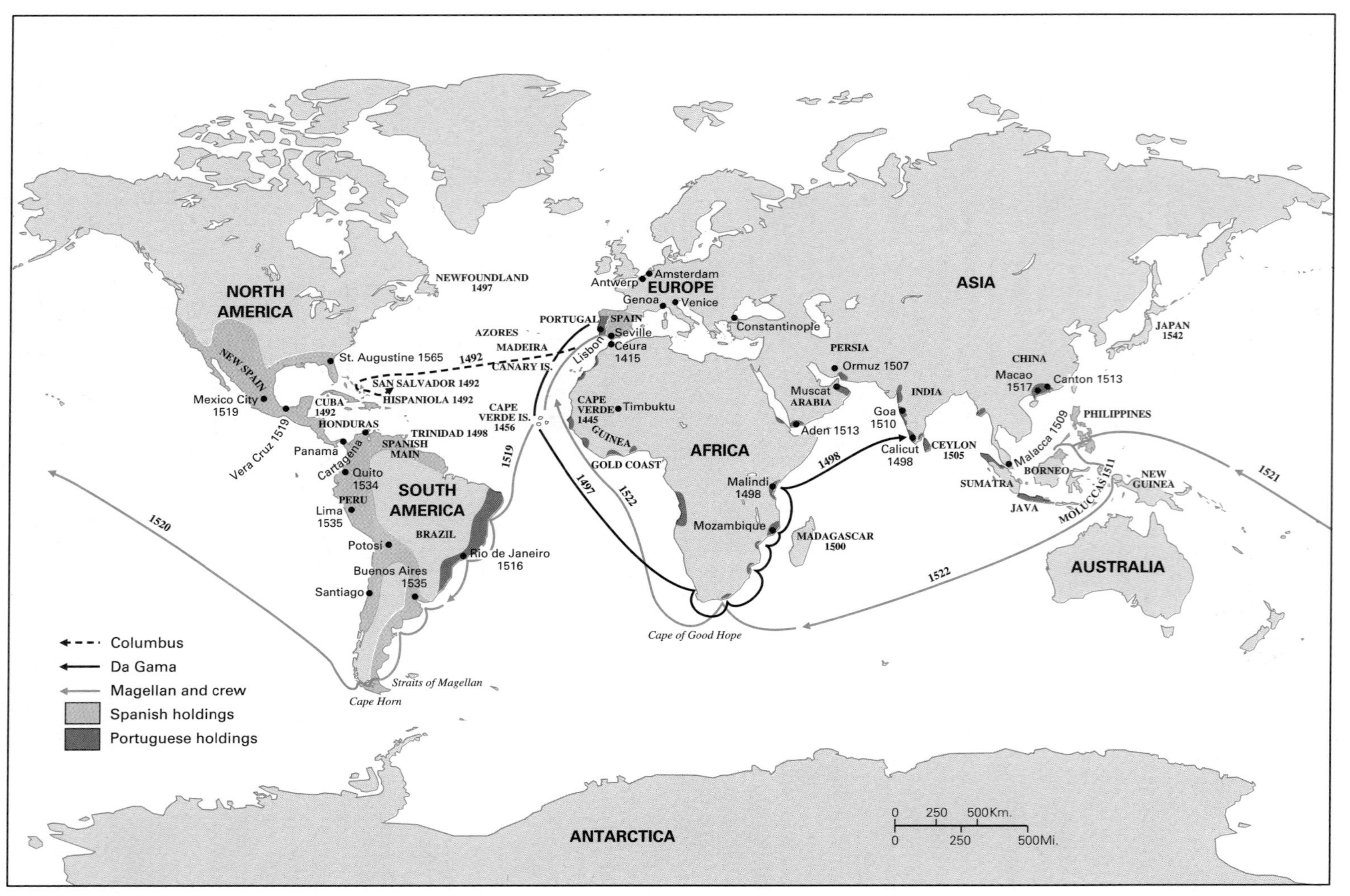

NORTH AMERICA
NEWFOUNDLAND 1497
NEW SPAIN
St. Augustine 1565
Mexico City 1519
Vera Cruz 1519
CUBA 1492
HONDURAS
SAN SALVADOR 1492
HISPANIOLA 1492
1492
TRINIDAD 1498
SPANISH MAIN
Panama
Cartagena
Quito 1534
PERU
Lima 1535
SOUTH AMERICA
BRAZIL
Potosí
Buenos Aires 1535
Santiago
Rio de Janeiro 1516
Straits of Magellan
Cape Horn
AZORES
MADEIRA
CANARY IS.
CAPE VERDE IS. 1456
PORTUGAL
SPAIN
Lisbon
Seville
Ceura 1415
Antwerp
Amsterdam
EUROPE
Genoa
Venice
Constantinople
CAPE VERDE 1445
Timbuktu
GUINEA
GOLD COAST
AFRICA
Malindi 1498
Mozambique
MADAGASCAR 1500
Cape of Good Hope
PERSIA
Ormuz 1507
Muscat
ARABIA
Aden 1513
INDIA
Goa 1510
Calicut 1498
CEYLON 1505
ASIA
CHINA
Macao 1517
Canton 1513
JAPAN 1542
PHILIPPINES
Malacca 1509
BORNEO
SUMATRA
JAVA
MOLUCCAS 1511
NEW GUINEA
AUSTRALIA
ANTARCTICA
1497
1498
1519
1520
1521
1522
1522
Columbus
Da Gama
Magellan and crew
Spanish holdings
Portuguese holdings
0 250 500Km.
0 250 500Mi.

power. Their fathers had conquered Granada, the last Muslim kingdom in Spain, in 1492; they had expelled the Jews the same year and had carried the Christian crusade across to North Africa. The conquest and conversion of the peoples of the New World was an extension of the crusading spirit that marked the five previous centuries of Spanish history. The rewards were the propagation of the true faith, service to the crown, land grants, and control over the inhabitants, who would work the fields. The land was especially attractive in the sixteenth century because the number of hidalgos was increasing with the general rise in population, and as a result, the amount of land available to them at home was shrinking.

The conquerors initially obtained two kinds of grants from the crown: *encomiendas* and *estancias*. The latter were land grants, either of land formerly belonging to the native priestly and noble castes or of land in remoter and less fertile regions. Encomiendas were royal grants of authority over the natives. Those who received such authority, the *encomenderos,* promised to give protection and instruction in the Christian religion to their charges. In return, they gained the power to extract labor and tribute from the peasant masses, who were worked beyond their capacity.

The royal grants of encomiendas during the first generation of Spanish settlement were partially responsible for the decimation of the native peoples in the New World within a century of European occupation. Between 1500 and 1600, the number of natives shrank from about twenty million to perhaps no more than two million. The major cause of this catastrophe, however, was not forced labor but the diseases introduced from Europe—dysentery, malaria, hookworm, and smallpox—against which the natives had little or no natural resistance. Beginning in the 1540s, the position of the natives gradually improved as the crown withdrew grants that gave authority over the natives and took increasing responsibility for controlling the Indians.

◀ *Map 15.1* Portuguese and Spanish Empire Building, 1415–1635 Not only did Spain and Portugal carve out empires in different parts of the world, but, as the map shows, they built two different kinds of empires. Portugal established small colonies along the seacoast. Spain went in for conquering and governing large territories and large populations in the New World.

Power and wealth became concentrated in fewer and fewer hands. As the Spanish landholders lost authority over the native population to royal officials and their associates, the latter gained substantially in power and privilege. As recurrent depressions ruined smaller landowners, they were forced to sell out to their bigger neighbors. On their conversion to Christianity, the Indians were persuaded to give more and more land to the church. Thus, Spanish America became permanently divided between the privileged elite and the impoverished masses.

Black Slavery and the Slave Trade

One group suffered even more than the Indians: the black slaves originally brought over from West Africa. During the long period of their dominance in North Africa and the Middle East (from the seventh to the nineteenth century), the Muslim states relied on slave labor and slave soldiers from black Africa south of the Sahara. Blacks were captured and transported across the Sahara to be sold in the slave markets of North Africa. It was common for such slaves, especially soldiers, to be eventually freed by their Muslim masters, a practice sanctioned by the Koran. So it was necessary to replenish the stock of slaves from south of the Sahara in every generation. At its height in the eighteenth century, this trans-Saharan trade may have risen to some ten thousand slaves a year.

But this annual traffic was eventually dwarfed by the slave trade between West Africa and the European colonies in the New World, which began in earnest in the early sixteenth century. The Portuguese dominated the Atlantic slave trade for a century and a half after 1450; during that time, it never rose beyond some five thousand black slaves a year. The Dutch edged out the Portuguese in the seventeenth century and com-

Profile

Bartolomé de las Casas

Library of Congress.

Bartolomé de las Casas (1474–1566), a Dominican friar, excited in his youth by Columbus's discoveries, set out for the New World in 1502 and spent the rest of his life as a missionary to the Amerindians. Not only did he preach to them and convert them to Christianity, but, appalled by the cruelty of the Spanish conquest, he joined others in his order in defending the Indians against their oppressors.

Some argued that the brutal treatment of the Indians, the confiscation of their lands, and even their enslavement were justified because the Indians fit Aristotle's definition of "natural slaves": people whose behavior and customs, such as human sacrifice, betrayed them as being less than rational and therefore subhuman. In book after book, de las Casas attacked such views. He pointed out that the Indians often lived up to a higher standard of civilized life than so-called civilized European Chris-

peted with the French and the British for dominance. In the eighteenth century, the British gained control of at least 50 percent of the trade. As Roland Oliver notes in *The African Experience,* "By the end of the seventeenth century, stimulated by the growth of plantation agriculture in Brazil and the West Indies, Atlantic shipments had increased to about thirty thousand a year, and by the end of the eighteenth century they were nearly eighty thousand."[1]

Captured in raids by African slavers, the victims were herded into specially built prisons on the West African coast. Those accepted for sale were "marked on the breast with a red-hot iron, imprinting the mark of the French, English or Dutch companies so that each nation may distinguish their own property."[2] Across the centuries, some 11 or 12 million blacks in all were exported to the New World. Of these, some 600,000 ended up in the thirteen colonies of British North America, forming the basis of the slave population of the new United States at the end of the American Revolution.

The conditions of the voyage from Africa, the so-called middle passage, were brutal. Crammed into the holds of ships, some 13 to 30 percent of blacks died on board. On arrival in the New World, slaves were greased with palm oil to improve their appearance and paraded naked into the auction hall for the benefit of prospective buyers who paid top prices for "the strongest, youthfullest, and most beautiful."[3] The standard workload for slaves everywhere was ten or eleven hours a day six days a week. But some distinction must be made between slavery in the American South and elsewhere in the New World. In Brazil and the West Indies, slaves were worked to exhaustion and death and then replaced. Slaves formed a large matians—for example, in sexual conduct, choice of rulers, military discipline, child-rearing, and (something especially important to a monk) giving relief to the poor. In addition, de las Casas was impressed by the Incas' feats of engineering, especially the highways they had built through the Andes, which excelled anything he had seen that the Romans had done.

This radical champion of Indian rights also dreamed of building a New Jerusalem in the New World. He called for the creation of a new kind of empire, in which Philip II would still be emperor but most of the Spanish colonists would be forced to leave. The missionaries would stay on, protected by a small Spanish army, to guide the Indians toward realizing this millennial vision. For his contemporaries, the most extreme aspect of the view de las Casas propounded was that the Indians should regain possession of all the land the Spanish had taken, including rights to all the gold and silver that lay beneath.

jority there and were concentrated on very large plantations. Revolts were frequent but always crushed and savagely punished. In the American South, by contrast, slaves were a minority dispersed over relatively small holdings; large plantations were few. As a result, revolts and deadly epidemics were rare. After 1808, when the United States abolished the external slave trade, slaveholders could not ruthlessly exploit their slaves if they were to meet the growing need for workers caused by the increasing industrial demand for raw cotton. By 1830, the slave population of the southern states rose through natural increase to more than two million, which represented over one-third of all slaves in the New World.

Why had the Atlantic slave trade grown to such a large volume by the eighteenth century? On the American side, economics provide the answer. In the New World, fields and mines had to be worked, but since the native population had been decimated, an enormous labor shortage existed. Black slaves were imported to satisfy the demand. Not only were they plentiful and cheap to maintain, but they were also skilled in farming and mining and could withstand tropical heat, insects, and disease, including the infections brought over from Europe to which the Indians had succumbed.

On the African side, how did suppliers continue to meet this large and growing New World demand? First, the demand was greater for males than for females, and males constituted two-thirds of those transported. Since all African peoples were polygynous (men might take more than one wife), the women and girls left behind in Africa continued to breed, so that the population did not shrink and there was always a supply of blacks to be captured and enslaved. Second, by 1700, a new factor was introduced, which proved decisive: guns, imported from Europe, were now commonly traded for slaves. With the guns, the West African rulers built armies for capturing other peoples to sell to the Europeans, while protecting themselves from being enslaved by rival forces. The desire for profit led to the need for more captives to sell for still more firearms to take still more slaves. All the ingredients were now in place for a deadly arms race, and the result was "a spiral of mounting violence," which could not be broken.[4] But from the point of view of the Atlantic trade, this grisly scenario guaranteed a steady supply of human cargo to satisfy a steeply rising New World demand.

The Price Revolution

Linked to overseas expansion was another phenomenon: unprecedented inflation during the sixteenth century, known as the price revolution. Evidence is insufficient on the general rise in prices. Cereal prices, however, multiplied by eight times or more in certain regions during the sixteenth century and continued to rise, though more slowly, during the first half of the next century. After 1650, prices leveled off or fell in most places. This pattern continued throughout the eighteenth century in England and off and on in France up to the Revolution. Economic historians have generally assumed that the prices of goods other than cereals increased by half as much as

A New World Sugar Refinery, Brazil. Sugar was the main and most profitable crop of plantation agriculture until the late eighteenth century, when cotton took the lead, at least in some places. On the plantation, the cane was not only grown but also processed into a variety of products—sugars, molasses, and rum—that were exported to Europe to meet a rising demand. Black slaves did the work under efficient but brutal conditions and often at great profit to the plantation owners. (*Mansell Collection.*)

grain prices. Since people at that time did not understand why prices rose so rapidly, inflation was not subject to control. On the contrary, the remedies governments applied, such as currency debasement, often worsened the problem.

Like colonization, the price revolution played an enormous role in the commercial revolution and may have resulted partially from the silver mining conducted in New Spain. The main cause of the price revolution, however, was population growth during the late fifteenth and sixteenth centuries.

The population of Europe almost doubled between 1460 and 1620; then it leveled off and decreased in some places. The patterns of population growth and of cereal prices thus match in the sixteenth and seventeenth centuries. Before the middle of the seventeenth century, the number of mouths to feed outran the capacity of agriculture to supply basic foodstuffs, causing the vast majority of people to live close to subsistence. Until food production could catch up with the increasing population, prices, especially those of the staple food, bread, would continue to rise.

Why population grew so rapidly in the fifteenth and sixteenth centuries is not known, but we do know the reasons for the population decline in the seventeenth century. By then, the population had so outgrown the food supply that scarcity began to take its toll. Malnourishment, starvation, and disease pushed the death rate higher than the birthrate. With time, of course, prices decreased as population and hence demand declined in the 1600s.

The other principal cause of the price revolution was probably the flow of silver into Europe from the New World by way of Spain beginning in 1552. But as a cause, the influx of silver lies on shakier ground than the inflationary effects of an expanding population. Increases in production and consumption following the growth in population would, to some degree, have necessitated an increase in the money supply to accommodate the greater number of commercial transactions. At some point, it is assumed, the influx of silver exceeded the necessary expansion of the money supply and itself began contributing to the inflation. The most that can be said now is that the price revolution was caused by *too many people with too much money chasing too few goods.* The effects of the price revolution were momentous.

The Expansion of Agriculture

The price revolution had its greatest effect on the land. Rising roughly twice as much as the prices of other goods, food prices spurred ambitious farmers to take advantage of the situation and produce for the expanding market. The opportunity for profit drove some farmers to work harder and manage their land better, and the impact of the price revolution came from that incentive. The most important changes occurred in England and the Netherlands.

The Old Pattern of Farming

All over Europe, landlords held their properties in the form of manors. A particular type of rural society and economy evolved on these manors in the Late Middle Ages. By the fifteenth century, much manor land was held by peasant-tenants according to the terms of a tenure known in England as *copyhold.* The tenants had certain hereditary rights to the land in return for the performance of certain services and the payment of certain fees to the landlord. Principal among these rights was the use of the commons—a tract of land consisting of pasture, woods, and a pond—by all tenants of a manor. For the copyholder, access to the commons often made the difference between subsistence and real want because the land tilled on the manor might not produce enough to feed a family.

Arable land was worked according to ancient custom. The land was divided into strips, and each peasant of the manor was assigned a certain number of strips. This whole pattern of peasant tillage and rights in the commons was known as the *open-field system.* After changing little for centuries, it was met head-on by incentives generated by the price revolution.

Enclosure

The open-field system, geared to providing subsistence for local villages, prevented large-scale farming for distant markets. The commons could not be diverted to the production of crops for sale, and the division of arable land into strips made it difficult to engage in profitable commercial agriculture. In the sixteenth century, English landlords aggressively pursued the possibilities for profit resulting from the inflation of farm prices and launched a two-pronged attack against the open-field system in an effort to transform their holdings into market-oriented, commercial ventures. First, they resorted to *enclosure,* fencing off the commons and thereby depriving their tenant peasantry of the use of the common land. Restriction of rights to the commons deprived tenants of critically needed produce. Then landlords changed the conditions of tenure from copyhold to leasehold. Copyhold was heritable and fixed; leasehold was not. When a lease came up for renewal, the landlord could raise the rent beyond the tenant's capacity to pay. Both acts of the landlord forced peasants off the manor or into the landlord's employ as farm laborers.

MEDIEVAL AGRICULTURE. A manuscript page from a book copied about 1500 in what is now Belgium. Agriculture was the foundation of economic life, and because the population was growing rapidly, every effort was being made to increase food production. (*Corbis-Bettmann.*)

Rural poverty and violence increased because of the mass evictions of tenant farmers.

With tenants gone, fields could be incorporated into larger, more productive units. Subsistence farming gave way to commercial agriculture: the growing of a surplus for the marketplace. Landlords would either hire laborers to work recently enclosed fields or rent these fields to prosperous farmers in the neighborhood. Either way, landlords stood to gain. They could hire labor at bargain prices because of the swelling population and the large supply of peasants forced off the land by enclosure. If landlords chose to rent out their fields, they also profited. Prosperous farmers, who themselves grew for the market, could afford to pay higher rents than the previous tenants, the subsistence farmers, and they were willing to pay more because farm prices tended to rise even faster than rents.

The existence of prosperous farmers, known collectively as the *yeomanry,* was crucial to the commercialization of farming in England. Yeomen were men who might not own much land but rented enough to produce a marketable surplus, sometimes a substantial one. They emerged as a discernible rural group in the High Middle Ages and were a product of the unique English inheritance custom of *primogeniture,* observed by peasantry and gentry alike.

Because of the rights of primogeniture, the eldest son inherited his parents' entire estate, and younger sons had to fend for themselves. Thus, land remained undivided and heirs often had enough land to produce a surplus for sale. Many a gentleman landowner enclosed his fields not to work them himself but to rent them to neighboring yeomen at rates allowing him to keep abreast of spiraling prices. Yeomen were better suited to work the land than the landlord, depending on it as they did for their livelihood.

One other process growing out of the price revolution promoted enclosure and the commercialization of farming. Rising prices forced less businesslike landlords, who did not take advantage of the profits to be made from farming, to sell property in order to meet current expenses. The conditions of the price revolution thus tended to put an increasing amount of land into more productive hands.

Convertible Husbandry

In the Netherlands, the effect of the price revolution on agriculture was as dramatic and important as in England. By the seventeenth century, the Dutch population had soared, and the majority of people had moved to the cities. As a result, a situation unique in all Europe—the problem of land use—became vitally important, especially as there was so little land to start with. The Dutch continued their efforts to reclaim land from the sea, as they had begun to do in the Middle Ages. More significant, however, was their development, in the fifteenth and sixteenth centuries, of a new kind of farming known as *convertible husbandry*. This farming system employed a series of innovations that replaced the old three-field system of crop rotation, which had left one-third of the land unplanted at any given time. The new techniques allowed farmers to cultivate all their land every year and diversified agriculture.

Convertible husbandry alternated the planting of soil-depleting cereals with the planting of soil-restoring legumes and grazing. For a couple of years, a field would be planted in cereals; in the third year, peas or beans would be sown to return essential nitrogen to the soil; then for the next four or five years, the field would become pasture for grazing animals, whose manure would further restore the soil for replanting cereals and restarting the cycle. Land thus returned to grain produced much more than land used in the three-field system. This method of increasing productivity, when exported from the Netherlands and applied in England and France between 1650 and 1750, played an essential role in the complicated process by which these countries eventually became industrialized. For industrialization requires agriculture productive enough to feed large, nonfarming urban populations.

Agricultural Change in Eastern Europe

In the portion of Europe that stretches from the Elbe River across the Baltic plain to Russia, the effects of the price revolution were as dramatic as they were in England. The Baltic plain played an essential role in the European economy in the fifteenth, sixteenth, and early seventeenth centuries. Because western Europeans continued to outrun their food supply (in some places until the middle of the seventeenth century), they turned to the Baltic lands for regular shipments of grain.

Thus, the landlords in the Baltic plain became commercial farmers producing for an international market. This trade led to a reorganization in the region south and east of the Baltic. There, as in England, enclosure to produce an agricultural surplus took place on a vast scale. But in contrast to the English experience, the peasant-tenants who had engaged in subsistence farming on these lands for generations were not evicted; nor did they become farm laborers working for low wages. Instead, they remained on the land, and the terms of their tenure gradually shifted toward serfdom. A two-caste society emerged in eastern Europe: a world of noble landlords and serfs.

The Expansion of Trade and Industry

The conditions of the price revolution also caused trade and industry to expand. Population growth, which exceeded the capacity of local food supplies, stimulated commerce in basic foodstuffs—for example, the Baltic trade with western Europe. Equally important as a stimulus to trade and industry was the growing income of landlords, merchants, and, in some instances, peasants. This income created a rising demand for consumer goods, which helps explain several activities already mentioned. For example, the Portuguese spice trade with the East and the sugar industry in the Portuguese islands developed because prosperous people wanted such products. Higher income also created a demand for farm products other than cereals—meat, cheese, fruit, wine, and vegetables—and for fine cloth. The resulting land use reduced the area available for grain production and contributed to the rise in bread prices, which meant even larger profits.

Another factor propelling commercial and industrial expansion was the growth of the state. With increasing amounts of tax revenue to spend, the expanding monarchies of the sixteenth and seventeenth centuries bought more and more supplies—ships, weapons, uniforms, paper—and so spurred economic development.

The Domestic System

Along with commercial and industrial expansion came a change in the nature of the productive enterprise. Just as the price revolution produced, in the enclosure movement, a reorganization of agriculture and agrarian society, it similarly affected trade and manufacturing. The reorganization there took place especially in the faster-growing industries—woolen and linen textiles—where an increasingly large mass market outpaced supply and thus made prices rise. This basic condition of the price revolution operated, just as it did in food production, to produce expansion. In the textile industries, increasing demand promoted specialization. For example, eastern and southwestern England made woolens, and northwestern France and the Netherlands produced linen.

Markets tended to shift from local to regional or even to international, a condition that gave rise to the merchant-capitalist. Merchant-capitalists' operations, unlike those of local producers, extended across local and national boundaries. Such mobility allowed these capitalists to buy or produce goods where costs were lowest and to sell where prices and volume were highest. Because of the size and range of a business, an individual capitalist could control the traditional local producers, who increasingly depended on him for the widespread marketing of their expanded output.

This procedure, which was well developed by the seventeenth century, gave rise to what is known as the domestic system of cottage industry. The manufacture of woolen textiles is a good example of how the system worked. A merchant-capitalist would buy raw wool from English landlords, who had enclosed the common grazing land on their manors to take advantage of the rising price of wool. The merchant's agents collected the wool and took it (put it out) to nearby villages for spinning, dyeing, and weaving. The work was done in the cottages of peasants, many of whom had been evicted from the surrounding manors as a result of enclosure and therefore had to take whatever work they could get at whatever wages they were offered. When the wool was processed into cloth, it was picked up and shipped to market.

The domestic system represents an important step in the evolution of capitalism. It was not industrial capitalism, because there were no factories and the work was done by hand rather than by power machinery; nevertheless, the domestic system significantly broke with the medieval guild system. The new merchant-capitalists saw to it that the work was performed in the countryside, rather than in the cities and towns, to avoid guild restrictions on output, quality, pay, and working conditions. The medieval distinction between a master and an apprentice who would someday replace the master in the guild framework gave way to the distinction between the merchant-owner (the person who provided the capital) and the worker (the person who provided the labor in return for wages and would probably never be an owner).

Enclosure also served to capitalize industry. Mass evictions lowered the wages of cottage workers because labor was so plentiful. This condition provided an additional incentive for merchant-capitalists to invest in cottage industry. The changes in farming, however, were much more important to the economic development of Europe than the changes in industry, because agriculture represented a much larger share of total wealth.

Innovations in Business

A cluster of other innovations in business life, some of them having roots in the Middle Ages, accompanied the emergence of the merchant-capitalist and the domestic system. Banking operations grew more sophisticated. It became possible for depositors to pay their debts by issuing written orders to their banks to make transfers to their creditors' accounts—the origins of the modern check. Accounting methods also improved. The widespread use of double-entry bookkeeping made errors immediately evident and gave a clear picture of the financial position of a commercial enterprise. Although known in the ancient world, double-entry bookkeeping was not widely practiced in the West until the fourteenth century. In this and other business practices, the lands of southern Europe, especially Italy, were the forerunners; their accounting techniques spread to the rest of Europe in the sixteenth century.

Business practices related to shipping also developed in the fourteenth century. A system of maritime insurance, without which investors would have been highly reluctant to risk their money on expensive vessels, evolved in Florence. By 1400, maritime insurance had become a regular

View of a Sixteenth-Century Marketplace. Market towns were growing all over western Europe after 1500. The increasing population made for brisk business in the marketplace. Note the ships in the harbor, the churches, and the variety of products available to those who could afford them. (*Private Collection/ Bridgeman Art Library.*)

item of the shipping business, and it was destined to play a major role in the opening of Atlantic trade. At least equally important to overseas expansion were business enterprises known as joint-stock companies, which allowed small investors to buy shares in a large venture. These companies made possible the accumulation of the huge amounts of capital needed for large-scale operations such as the building and deployment of merchant fleets—amounts quite beyond the resources of one person.

Patterns of Commercial Development

Responses to the price revolution in trade and industry hinged on social and political conditions and thus differed in various parts of Europe. In the United Provinces (the Netherlands) and England, there were far fewer strictures on trade and industry than in France and Spain. So in the sixteenth and seventeenth centuries, England and the United Provinces were better placed than France and Spain to take advantage of conditions favorable for business expansion. In the United Provinces, favorable conditions resulted from the weakness of Dutch feudal culture and values in comparsion with commercial ones, the small land area, and a far larger percentage of urban population than elsewhere in western Europe.

England's advantage derived from another source: not the weakness of the landed gentry but its habits. Primogeniture operated among the owners of large estates just as it did among the yeomanry, with much the same effect. Younger sons were forced to make their fortunes elsewhere. Those who did so by going into business would often benefit from an infusion of venture capital that came from their elder brothers' landed estates. And, of course, capital was forthcoming from such quarters because of the profitable nature of English farming. In a reverse process, those who made fortunes in trade would typically invest money in land and rise gradually into landed society. The skills that had brought wealth in commerce would then be applied to new estates, usually with equal success.

England and the Netherlands. In both England and the United Provinces the favorable conditions led to large-scale commercial expansion. In the 1590s, the Dutch devised a new ship, the *fluit,* or flyboat, to handle bulky grain shipments at the lowest possible cost. This innovation permitted them to capture the Baltic trade, which became the main source of their phenomenal commercial expansion between 1560 and 1660. Equally dramatic was their commercial penetration of the Orient. Profits from the European carrying trade built ships that allowed the Dutch first to challenge and then to displace the Portuguese in the spice trade with the East Indies during the early seventeenth century. The Dutch chartered the United East India Company in 1602 and established trading posts in the islands—the beginnings of the Dutch empire, which lasted until World War II.

The English traded throughout Europe in the sixteenth and seventeenth centuries, especially with Spain and the Netherlands. The staples of this trade were raw wool and woolens, but increasingly the trade included such items as ships and guns. The seventeenth century saw the foundation of a British colonial empire along the Atlantic seaboard in North America, from Maine to the Carolinas, and in the West Indies, where the English managed to dislodge the Spanish in some places.

In seventeenth-century England, the central government increasingly took the side of the capitalist producer. At the beginning of the century, the king had imposed feudal fees on landed property, acted against enclosures, and granted monopolies in trade and manufacture to court favorites, which restricted opportunities for investment. The king also spent revenues on maintaining an unproductive aristocracy. But by the end of the century, because of the revolutionary transfer of power from the king to Parliament, economic policy more closely reflected the interests of big business, whether agricultural or commercial. Landowners no longer paid feudal dues to the king. Enclosure went on unimpeded, in fact abetted, by parliamentary enactment.

The Navigation Act, first passed in 1651, allowed all English shippers to carry goods anywhere, replacing the old system that had restricted trade with certain areas to specific traders. The act also required that all goods be carried in English ships, enabling merchants, as Christopher Hill writes, "to buy English and colonial exports cheap and sell them dear abroad, to buy foreign goods cheap and sell them dear in England."[5] English shippers also gained the profits of the carrying trade, one factor leading to the displacement of the Dutch by the English as the leading power in international commerce after 1660.

France and Spain. France benefited from commercial and industrial expansion, but not to the same degree as England. The principal reason for the difference was the aristocratic structure of French society. Family ties and social intercourse between aristocracy and merchants, such as existed in England, were largely absent in France. Consequently, the French aristocracy remained contemptuous of commerce. Also inhibiting economic expansion were the guilds—remnants of the Middle Ages that restricted competition and production. In France, there was relatively less opportunity than in England for merchant-capitalists operating outside the guild structures.

Spain presents an even clearer example of the failure to grasp the opportunities afforded by the price revolution. By the third quarter of the six-

Map 15.2 Industrial Centers in the Sixteenth Century ▶ This map of Europe (c. 1500) indicates the population of the most important cities (Naples is the largest). It also shows the centers of three kinds of industry: textiles, metals, and finance. Cloth making (textile production) was the most important industry in Europe in the early modern period.

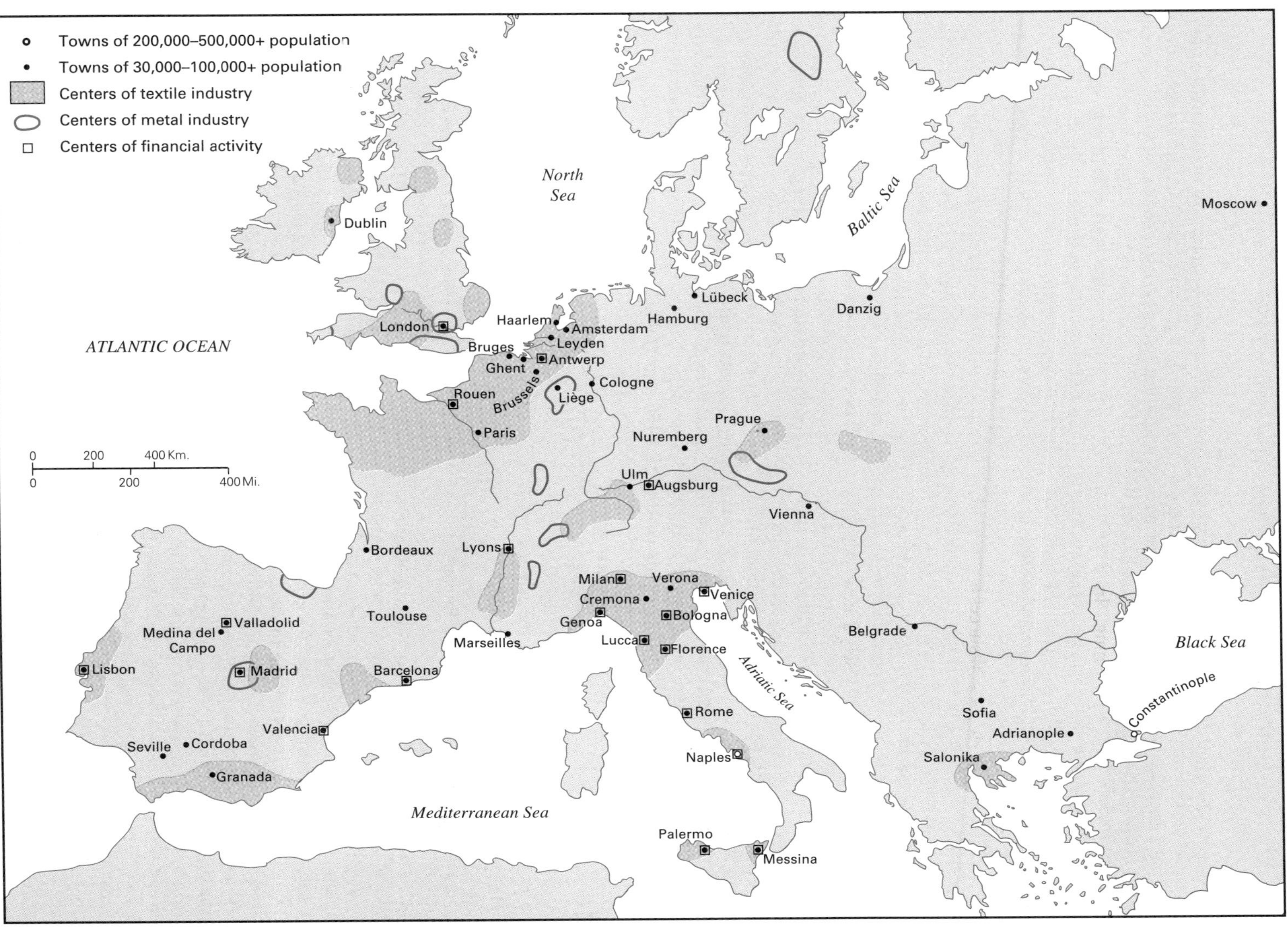
Towns of 200,000–500,000+ population
Towns of 30,000–100,000+ population
Centers of textile industry
Centers of metal industry
Centers of financial activity
0 200 400 Km.
0 200 400 Mi.
ATLANTIC OCEAN
North Sea
Baltic Sea
Mediterranean Sea
Adriatic Sea
Black Sea
Moscow
Dublin
London
Haarlem
Amsterdam
Leyden
Bruges
Ghent
Antwerp
Brussels
Cologne
Liège
Rouen
Paris
Hamburg
Lübeck
Danzig
Prague
Nuremberg
Ulm
Augsburg
Vienna
Bordeaux
Lyons
Toulouse
Marseilles
Milan
Verona
Venice
Cremona
Genoa
Bologna
Lucca
Florence
Rome
Naples
Palermo
Messina
Belgrade
Sofia
Adrianople
Constantinople
Salonika
Valladolid
Medina del Campo
Lisbon
Madrid
Barcelona
Valencia
Seville
Cordoba
Granada

teenth century, Spain possessed the makings of economic expansion: unrivaled amounts of capital in the form of silver, a large and growing population, rising consumer demand, and a vast overseas empire. These factors did not bear fruit because the Spanish value system regarded business as a form of social heresy. The Spanish held in high esteem gentlemen who possessed land gained through military service and crusading ardor, which enabled them to live on rents and privileges. Commerce and industry remained contemptible pursuits.

Numerous wars in the sixteenth century (with France, the Lutheran princes, the Ottoman Turks, the Dutch, and the English) increasingly strained the Spanish treasury, despite the annual shipments of silver from the New World. Spain spent its resources on maintaining and extending its imperial power and Catholicism, rather than on investing in economic expansion. In the end, the wars cost even more than Spain could handle. The Dutch for a time, and the English and the French more permanently, displaced Spain as the great power. The English and the Dutch had taken advantage of the opportunities presented by the price revolution; the Spanish had not.

The Growth of Capitalism

What Is Capitalism?

The changes described—especially in England and the Netherlands—represent a crucial stage in the development of the modern economic system known as *capitalism.* This is a system of *private enterprise:* the main economic decisions (what, how much, where, and at what price to produce, buy, and sell) are made by private individuals in their capacity as owners, workers, or consumers. Capitalism is also said to be a system of *free enterprise:* the basic decisions are not left only to individuals; these decisions are also made in response to market forces. People are free, in other words, to obey the law of supply and demand. When goods and labor are scarce, prices and wages rise; when they are plentiful, prices and wages fall.

In the Middle Ages, capitalistic enterprise was not widespread because the market was severely restricted, and, consequently, so was the operation of market forces. The vast majority of people lived as self-sufficient subsistence farmers (peasants or serfs) on the land. There was some trade and a few small cities, especially in Italy, where capitalistic enterprise was conducted, but this commerce accounted for only a tiny fraction of total economic activity. Even in the cities, capitalistic forms of enterprise were hampered by guild restrictions, which set limits on production, wages, and prices without regard to market forces. In addition, the economic decay of the fourteenth and early fifteenth centuries did not predispose those who had surplus money to gamble on the future.

But conditions changed in certain quarters beginning in the fifteenth and sixteenth centuries, generating the incentive to invest—to take risks for future profit rather than to consume. This process was due, more than anything else, to the economic situation prevailing in Europe between 1450 and 1600.

The Fostering of Mercantile Capitalism

Several conditions sustained the incentive to invest and reinvest—a basic factor in the emergence of modern capitalism. One was the price revolution stemming from a supply of basic commodities that could not keep pace with rising demand. Prices continued to climb, creating the most powerful incentive of all to invest rather than to consume. Why spend now, those with surplus wealth must have asked, when investment in commercial farming, mining, shipping, and publishing (to name a few important outlets) is almost certain to yield greater wealth in the future? The price revolution reduced the risk involved in investment, thus helping overcome the reluctance of the wealthy to engage in capitalistic enterprise.

Another condition that encouraged investment was the distribution of wealth in a way promoting investment. Three distinct patterns of distribution worked to this effect. First, inflation widened the gap between the rich and the poor during the sixteenth century; the rich who chose to invest garnered increasing amounts of wealth, which probably added to their incentive to continue investing. Because of the growing population and the resulting shortage of jobs, employers could pay lower and lower wages; thus, again, their profits increased, encouraging reinvestment. Merchant-capitalists were an important group of investors who gained from these conditions. As they grew, they were able to exercise a controlling influence in the marketplace because they operated on a large scale, from regional to international; thus, they were able to dictate terms of production and employment, displacing the local guilds. This displacement was also favorable to investment and growth. Mercantile capitalism did not benefit everyone equally; in fact, it produced increasing inequities between rich and poor, owners and workers, and independent merchant-capitalists and members of local guilds.

The second pattern of wealth distribution that encouraged investment, especially in England, grew out of the practice of primogeniture. The concentration of inherited property in the hands of the eldest child (usually the oldest son) meant that he had sufficient wealth to be persuaded to invest at least part of it. Any younger sons were left to make their own way in the world and often turned their drive and ambition into profits.

Finally, a pattern of international distribution of wealth promoted investment in some lands. The classic example is that of Spain in relation, say, to England. Spain in the sixteenth century devoted its wealth and energies to religious war and empire and relied on producers elsewhere for many of its supplies. So Spanish treasure was exported to England to pay for imports, stimulating investment there rather than in Spain. Capitalism did not develop everywhere at the same pace, and as the Spanish case shows, the very conditions that discouraged it in one place encouraged it somewhere else.

Two additional stimuli for investment came from governments. First, governments acted as giant consumers, whose appetites throughout the early modern period were expanding. Merchants, who supplied governments with everything from guns to frescoes, not only prospered but reinvested as well because of the constancy and growth of government demand. Governments also sponsored new forms of investment, whether to satisfy the taste for new luxuries at the king's court or to meet the requirements of the military. Moreover, private investors reaped incalculable advantages from overseas empires. Colonies supplied cheap raw materials and cheap (slave) labor and served as markets for exports. They greatly stimulated the construction of ships and harbor facilities and the sale of insurance.

The second government stimulus comprised state policies meant to increase investment, which they no doubt sometimes did, though not always. Collectively, these policies constitute what is known as *mercantilism:* the conscious pursuit by governments of courses of action supposed to augment national wealth and power. One characteristic expression of mercantilism was the pursuit of a favorable balance of international payments. According to conventional wisdom, wealth from trade was measured in gold and silver, of which there was believed to be a more-or-less fixed quantity. The state's goal in international trade became to sell more abroad than it bought, that is, to establish a favorable balance of payments. When the amount received for sales abroad was greater than the amount spent for purchases, the difference would be an influx of precious metal into the state. By this logic, mercantilists were led to argue for the goal of national sufficiency: a country should try to supply most of its own needs to keep imports to a minimum. This argument, of course, ignored the fact that, in international trade, the more a country buys, the more it can sell because its purchases abroad create purchasing power for its goods overseas.

Mercantilism did have a positive side. Governments increased economic activity by employing the poor, subsidizing new industries, and chartering companies to engage in overseas trade. Particularly valuable were the steps taken by states to break down local trade barriers, such as guild regulations and internal tariffs, in an attempt to create national markets and internal economic unity.

The English, moreover, saw that mercantilistic calculations of national wealth should be made over the long run. For example, Thomas Mun (1571–1641) argued that a country might import more than it exported in the short run and still come out ahead in the end because raw materials that are imported and then reprocessed for export would eventually yield a handsome profit.

In addition, Mun was one of the first to discern the virtues of *consumerism,* a phenomenon that is still extremely important for achieving sustained economic growth. Speaking of foreign trade, he maintained that the more English merchants did to advertise English goods to potential customers, the greater the overseas market for those goods would be. In other words, demand can be *created.* Just as there is an urge to invest and make profits, so there is an appetite to consume and enjoy the products of industry, and both inclinations have played their part in the growth of capitalism. Nor was the message restricted to the foreign market. Between 1660 and 1750, England became the world's first consumer society: more and more people had more and more money to spend, and they acquired a taste for conspicuous consumption (which had always before been confined to the aristocracy). Discretionary goods were available—lace, tobacco, housewares, flowers—and consumers wanted them. Concomitantly, just as today, the stronger the stimulus to buy, the harder the consumer worked, which induced further growth.

The price revolution, the concentration of wealth in private hands, and government activity combined to provide the foundation for sustained investment and for the emergence of mercantile capitalism. This new force in the world should not be confused with industrial capitalism. The latter evolved with the first Industrial Revolution in eighteenth-century England, but mercantile capitalism paved the way for it.

The Elite and the People

Traditional Popular Culture

Europe's economic expansion was accompanied by equally important social and cultural changes in the relations between ordinary people and their rulers, whether kings, nobles, landlords, or clergy. Throughout the Middle Ages, there had always been two cultures: the elite culture of the royal court, the feudal lords, and the educated clergy, and the popular culture of largely illiterate peasants and artisans.

Over the centuries, the common people had evolved a distinctive culture, which their rulers patronized and, to some degree, participated in. This popular culture consisted of a mosaic of the customs of various groups of people—shepherds, peasants, cobblers, weavers, miners—each group with its own traditions. Even a youth culture of apprentices was to be found in the towns. Furthermore, besides the settled culture of the villages and towns, there was a vagabond culture of sailors, soldiers, beggars, thieves, and other "masterless men."[6]

The prosperous and the powerful called on the services of learned professionals—clergy, physicians, and lawyers. Ordinary people had their own humbler and cheaper equivalents—lay preachers, folk healers, and witches (that is, sorcerers and fortunetellers). The royal courts, manor houses, monasteries, and universities were centers of elite culture. Ordinary people worked, played, and worshiped in meaner settings: the village church, the tavern, the street, and especially the marketplace or village square. In the church and churchyard, they danced, feasted, and performed religious pageants; in the tavern and street, they gossiped, played games, watched puppet shows, staged cockfights, listened to folk preachers, and consulted healers, astrologers, and magicians.

Certain special occasions granted people the freedom to express themselves. Beginning in the thirteenth century, the most important of these occasions was the carnival, the three- to six-day festival preceding the onset of Lent. The carnival was a time of revelry and ritual processions through church and streets, excessive eating and drinking, and a sharp increase in sexual activity. It was also a time during which ordinary people, at least in their parades and public displays, engaged in what was called "turning the world upside down." So, for instance, in a procession a horse would be made to walk backward with its rider facing its tail. Popular illustrations of the era show a son beating his father, a pupil beating his teacher, servants giving orders to their masters, the laity preaching to the clergy, the husband minding the baby, and the wife smoking and holding a gun. What does all this mean? Was it a safety valve, allowing the people to blow off the steam generated by an otherwise oppressive and monotonous existence? Perhaps, but it sometimes led to real violence, and the elite, by the sixteenth century at any rate, looked on such behavior as subversive and fraught with danger. As a noble said on the occasion of the carnival at Palermo in 1648, "On the pretext of these assemblies of the people for these ridiculous spectacles, factious spirits would be able . . . to encourage some new riot."[7]

Nor was the carnival the only occasion for this ritual mockery of authority. The calendar year was punctuated by the observance of religious feast days on which similar behavior took place. So, for instance, in France, on the Feast of Fools (the Innocents) on December 28, an abbot or bishop of fools was elected, and a mock Mass took place in which the clergy dressed in women's clothes, played cards, ate sausages, sang ribald songs, and cursed their congregations instead of blessing them.

Among the most prevalent popular traditions was the ritual mockery of marriage known as the *charivari*. Only unconventional marriages qualified for such rude treatment at the hands of one's neighbors: an old man and a young wife, a second marriage, a husband beaten or cuckolded by his wife. The charivari consisted of a ritual procession in which the victim or his effigy would be mounted backward on an ass and drawn through the streets accompanied by "rough music" (the beating of pots and pans). Charivaris were sometimes conducted at the expense of tax collectors, preachers, and landlords. Here then was a kind of popular justice, another version of the world turned upside down.

The Reform of Popular Culture

Throughout the Middle Ages and until the early sixteenth century, elite culture and popular culture existed in more-or-less stable balance. Indeed, the two worlds, high and low, occupied considerable common ground. Landlords and clergy took part in village games and feasts and shared with their inferiors an outlook that stressed communal values: pulling together in a subsistence world, making sure that everyone had enough for survival, and extending relief to those in need. The emphasis was on communalism, not individualism, especially in the countryside.

In the sixteenth century, however, a drastic change took place in the attitude of the elite toward ordinary people. No longer willing to patronize and foster popular culture, the elite became increasingly suspicious of and hostile to it. This shift occurred for two reasons. The first was the elite's fear of the growing numbers of the poor and fear of the growing numbers of people, some poor and some not, who, inspired by the new religious movements and the new printed literature, were beginning to question the old authorities and sometimes even joined in rebellion against them. Encouraged by the greater accessibility of printed books and by the Protestant emphasis on Bible reading, more and more people became literate, and a popular literature of religious instruction, astrological almanacs, and chivalric romances poured from the presses to meet the growing demand. On this score, too, the authorities had their misgivings; books of the right sort were acceptable, even useful, but a little learning was thought to be a dangerous thing.

The second reason for the shift in elite attitudes toward ordinary people was not fear but hope. Not only were the elite alarmed by the growing poverty and unrest among the people; they also thought that they knew how to control the unrest and even perhaps in some measure overcome it. Just as religion inspired the people, so the Reformation, the Counter Reformation, and the Christian humanism of the Renaissance inspired leaders to reform society and in particular to attack popular culture for being both too pagan and too disorderly. The customs of the people, it was thought, needed to be purified, made more decent and sober, and the people themselves needed to be disciplined so that they might become obedient subjects of king and church. Society came to be seen as divided between the godly (among whom the elite included themselves) and the ungodly multitude, who needed to be controlled and, if possible, educated for service in the Christian commonwealth.

What followed was a wide-ranging onslaught

against all forms of traditional popular culture—what one historian has called "the triumph of Lent" over "the world of Carnival."[8] This reform movement included attacks on popular festivals, lay preaching, and "the world turned upside down." The Florentine ruler Girolamo Savonarola, a few days before the carnival of 1496, preached a sermon recommending that "boys should collect alms for the respectable poor, instead of mad pranks, throwing stones and making floats."[9] A century later, in England, Phillip Stubbe drew up a comprehensive indictment of May games, Lords of Misrule, Christmas feasting, church ales, wakes, bearbaiting, cockfighting, and dancing. Popular religious dramas disappeared in northern Italy during the third quarter of the sixteenth century and in England by the end of that century.

The new bureaucratic state joined the clergy in the reforming enterprise. In the sixteenth and seventeenth centuries, many forms of behavior that had been thought of as spiritual sins became secular crimes as well, subject to prosecution and punishment by the state. These newly criminalized activities included adultery, blasphemy, sodomy, infanticide, and witchcraft. In this period, too, public brothels, which had existed for centuries, were gradually shut down, a process beginning in Lutheran Germany between 1530 and 1560. The state enforced what the new moral puritanism decreed.

Hans Baldung Grien (1485–1545). Witches' Sabbat (1510) depicts both learned and popular beliefs concerning witches. For example, the night ride through the air, the naked feasting, and orgiastic concourse with the Devil all reflect the view that witchcraft was an extremely dangerous heresy that sought to overthrow Christianity and put Devil worship in its place. (*Germanisches Nationalmuseum Nürnberg.*)

Witchcraft and the Witch Craze

The prosecution of witches constitutes a particularly important chapter in this attack on popular culture. Although it had always been suspect, witchcraft had been a part of traditional village culture for centuries. There were two kinds of witchcraft, known at the time as black and white. The white variety involved healing and fortunetelling. Black witchcraft conjured evil powers by a curse or by the manipulation of objects, such as the entrails of animals.

The medieval church developed a more theological and sinister interpretation of the phenomenon: that witches conspired with the Devil to work against God and human society, held secret meetings, and had carnal relations with the Devil. In the late twelfth century, Christian thinkers began to emphasize the idea of a Devil who roamed the world at the head of an army of demons, attempting to undermine the saving mission of Christ and tempting people to sin. Witches were regarded as those who had succumbed to temptation and entered into a pact to worship Satan in place of God. This worship was thought to take place at secret, nocturnal meetings (the legendary witches' Sabbats), during which witches and demons were supposed to engage in sexual orgies, sacrifice infants, and desecrate the Eucharist.

As early as the thirteenth century, bishops and popes prosecuted witches for heresy. Confessions were usually extracted by means of torture. Those found guilty were burned at the stake (on the Continent) or hanged (in England), and their property was confiscated by the authorities. The church held that a witch's "only hope of salvation was to be arrested and to recant before her execution. By such reasoning the torment and killing of witches was for their own good as well as that of God and society."[10]

The growth of printed literature on the subject of witchcraft was especially influential in the spread of the church's view that witchcraft involved a diabolical plot. In 1486, there appeared a handbook called *Malleus Maleficarum, The Hammer of Witches,* by two German Dominicans who claimed to show what witches did at the Devil's behest. These Dominicans had tried almost fifty people for witchcraft, all but two of them women.

By the sixteenth century, the linkage of women to witchcraft had been firmly established. Men could also be accused of the crime, but almost everywhere that witches were tried in the sixteenth and seventeenth centuries more than 75 percent were women, often elderly widows and spinsters. The so-called witch craze is a phenomenon of these two centuries, when perhaps as many as 110,000 people were prosecuted and 60,000 executed all over Europe.

Why were most of the accused women? No doubt this pattern reflected an ancient prejudice that women were less rational and more lustful than men and so more susceptible to the Devil's wiles. As the authors of *The Hammer of Witches* declared, "Witchcraft comes from carnal lust, which is in woman insatiable."[11]

One view of English witch-hunts during the period may help explain the predominance of women among the accused. In traditional society, widows and the elderly were objects of local charity. An old woman, so the theory goes, would beg for alms and be rebuffed by a more prosperous neighbor; later, some misfortune would befall the neighbor, and he would blame it on the old woman, accusing her of witchcraft as a way of assuaging his guilt for having refused her request for help. According to this interpretation, such behavior characterizes a period of rapid transition from communal subsistence to an ethic of economic individualism that demanded that each person look out for himself or herself. Just such a period in England coincided with the large number of witchcraft prosecutions brought against poor old women.

By 1700, the witch craze had ended in western Europe—first in Holland, the most tolerant country, and in Spain, the most intolerant because the Spanish Inquisition provided another focus for persecutions. Two factors probably helped to put an end to the witch-hunts.

First, the religious turmoil unleashed by the Reformation, on which the witch craze fed, also triggered an intellectual backlash that led some to wonder whether fanaticism had not got the better of reason and to call for a tempering of inflamed passions and the exercise of a greater degree of skepticism in matters of faith. "It is rating our conjectures too high to roast people alive for them," the skeptic Michel de Montaigne exclaimed.[12] Thus, judges in seventeenth-century France imposed stricter tests and demanded that more conclusive evidence be presented before convicting people tried for witchcraft. In 1682, Louis XIV himself declared the phenomenon to be a kind of fraud.

Second, during the last half of the seventeenth century, another shift was taking place in relations between the elite and the common people. The elite began to associate belief in astrology, magic, and witches with the people. Both cultures had once shared these beliefs, but now the elite spurned them as representing so many vulgar superstitions. This shift owed something to the growth of skepticism and the impact of science. It also indicated a hardening of the lines drawn between the two cultures and a greater willingness by the elite to accept, if not foster, the resulting divisions. By the early eighteenth century, although almost nobody would admit to having given up the belief in the existence of witches, serious discussion, let alone prosecution, of witchcraft cases had been read out of polite society. The reason was not that the belief had been proved wrong, but that to talk about it, except by way of ridicule, was deemed unseemly. The belief in witchcraft declined in part by being rendered taboo in the upper reaches of society. It lost its appeal as much through social snobbery as through science and skepticism.

Economic and Social Transformations

The transformations considered in this chapter were among the most momentous in the world's history. In an unprecedented development that may never be repeated, one small part of the world, western Europe, became lord of the sea-lanes, master of many lands throughout the globe, and banker and profit taker in an emerging world economy. Western Europe's global hegemony was to last well into the twentieth century. By conquering and settling new lands, Europeans exported Western culture around the globe, a process that accelerated in the twentieth century.

The overseas expansion had profound effects. The native populations of the New World were decimated. To ease the labor shortage, millions of blacks were imported from Africa to work as slaves on plantations and in mines. Black slavery would produce large-scale effects on culture, politics, and society, which have lasted to the present day.

The widespread circulation of plant and animal life also had great consequences. Horses and cattle were introduced into the New World. (The Aztecs were so amazed to see a man on horseback that they thought horse and rider were one demonic creature.) In return, the Old World sampled such novelties as corn, the tomato, and most important, the potato, which was to become a staple of the northern European diet. Manioc, from which tapioca is made, was transplanted from the New World to Africa, where it helped sustain the population.

Western Europe was wrenched out of the subsistence economy of the Middle Ages and launched on a course of sustained economic growth. This transformation resulted from the grafting of traditional forms, such as primogeniture and holy war, onto new forces, such as global exploration, price revolution, and convertible husbandry. Out of this change emerged the beginnings of a new economic system, mercantile capitalism, which in large measure provided the economic thrust for European world predominance and paved the way for the Industrial Revolution of the eighteenth and nineteenth centuries.

Finally, these economic changes were accompanied by a major shift in relations between the rulers and the ruled. For centuries, the elite had tolerated and even patronized the culture of the common people. But under the impact of the commercial revolution and the Reformation, the authorities became increasingly suspicious of the people and undertook to purify and reform popular culture. The degree to which they succeeded remains an open question. But the gap between the elite and the people widened, as the elite found less and less in popular culture to identify with and more and more to condemn or try to undo. The elite distanced themselves from ordinary people even as they attempted to impose their will. The result was the emergence of two separate cultures, divorced from and hostile to each other. Only in moments of mass hysteria, such as during the witch craze, could the people and their rulers join forces against a common and defenseless victim.

❖ ❖ ❖

Notes

1. Roland Oliver, *The African Experience* (New York: HarperCollins, 1991), p. 123.
2. Quoted in Basil Davidson, *Africa in History* (New York: Collier Books, 1991), p. 215.
3. Quoted in Richard S. Dunn, *Sugar and Slaves*

(Chapel Hill: University of North Carolina Press, 1972), p. 248.

4. Quoted in Davidson, *Africa in History,* p. 223.
5. Christopher Hill, *Reformation to Industrial Revolution* (Baltimore: Penguin Books, 1969), pp. 159–160.
6. Christopher Hill, *The World Turned Upside Down* (New York: Viking, 1972), ch. 3.
7. Quoted in Peter Burke, *Popular Culture in Early Modern Europe* (New York: Harper & Row, 1978), p. 203.
8. Ibid., chs. 7–8.
9. Ibid., p. 217.
10. Jeffrey B. Russell, *A History of Witchcraft* (London: Thames & Hudson, 1980), p. 78.
11. Quoted in Margaret L. King, *Women of the Renaissance* (Chicago: University of Chicago Press, 1993), p. 155.
12. Quoted in Russell, *A History of Witchcraft,* p. 73.

Suggested Reading

Bernard, Carmen, *The Incas: People of the Sun* (1994). Richly illustrated.

Boxer, C. R., *The Portuguese Seaborne Empire, 1415–1825* (1969). A comprehensive treatment.

Cipolla, Carlo M., *Guns, Sails and Empires* (1965). Connections between technological innovation and overseas expansion, 1400 to 1700.

Davis, David Brion, *The Problem of Slavery in Western Culture* (1966). Authoritative and full of insight.

Davis, Ralph, *The Rise of the Atlantic Economies* (1973). A reliable survey of early modern economic history.

Haley, K. H. D., *The Dutch in the Seventeenth Century* (1972). A little classic.

Kamen, Henry, *The Iron Century* (1971). Insight into the social and class basis of economic change.

Kolchin, Peter, *American Slavery: 1619–1877* (1993). An informed synthesis.

Pagden, Anthony, *Spanish Imperialism and the Political Imagination: Studies in European and Spanish-American Social and Political Theory, 1513–1830* (1990). A rich treatment of ideas behind overseas expansion.

Parker, Geoffrey, *The Military Revolution: Military Innovation and the Rise of the West, 1500–1800* (1988). Sweeping coverage of a crucial topic.

Parry, J. H., *The Age of Reconnaissance* (1963). A short survey of overseas exploration.

Sharpe, J. A., *Early Modern England,* 2nd ed. (1997). A standard account, offering a readable overview.

Review Questions

1. What links the Middle Ages and early modern overseas expansion? What were the new forces for expansion operating in early modern Europe?
2. Compare Spanish and Portuguese overseas expansion in terms of the motives, the areas of expansion, and the character of the two empires.
3. What is the connection between the price revolution and overseas expansion? What was the principal cause of the price revolution? Why?
4. Compare the conditions of slavery under the Muslims in Africa with those in the New World. Where did the slaves originate and what caused the slave trade to continue in each case?
5. What was enclosure? How did the price revolution encourage it?
6. Compare open-field farming and enclosure in terms of who worked the land, how the land was worked, and the results of each method.
7. What was convertible husbandry, where did it originate, and why was it such an important innovation?
8. What was the domestic system? What were its advantages over the guilds and what long-term effect did it have?
9. Define mercantile capitalism. What three patterns of the distribution of wealth fostered its development?
10. What was the traditional relationship between the people and their rulers? How and why did

this relationship begin to change in the sixteenth century, and with what result?

11. What accounts for the witch craze and its decline? Why were most of its victims women?

Chapter 16

The Rise of Sovereignty: Transition to the Modern State

Louis XIV sought by every gesture and pose to display grandeur and to embody monarchy. His dress and affect were meant to awe and intimidate. (Giraudon/Art Resource.)

- **Monarchs and Elites as State Builders**
- **The Rise and Fall of Hapsburg Spain**
  - Ferdinand and Isabella: Unity and Purity of "Blood" and Religion
  - The Reign of Charles V: Hapsburg, King of Spain, and Holy Roman Emperor
  - Philip II: Religious Zealot
  - The End of the Spanish Hapsburgs
- **The Growth of French Power**
  - Religion and the French State
  - Louis XIV: The Consolidation of French Monarchical Power
- **The Growth of Limited Monarchy and Constitutionalism in England**
  - The English Parliament and Constitution
  - The Tudor Achievement
  - The English Revolutions, 1640–1660 and 1688–1689
- **The Netherlands: A Bourgeois Republic**
- **The Holy Roman Empire: The Failure to Unify Germany**
- **The Emergence of Austria and Prussia**
  - Austria
  - Prussia
- **Russia: Great Nobles and Starving Peasants**
- **The State and Modern Political Development**

From the thirteenth to the seventeenth century, a new and unique form of political organization emerged in the West: the dynastic, or national, state, which, through taxes and war, harnessed the power of its nobility and the material resources of its territory. Neither capitalism nor technology could have enabled the West to dominate other lands and peoples had it not been for the power of the European states. They directed the energies of the landed elite into national service and international competition. A degree of domestic stability ensued, and the states encouraged commerce and industry, which could in turn be taxed. Although they nurtured the aristocracy, many states also required that both lord and peasant serve in national armies for the purpose of foreign conquest, as well as for defense.

In most emerging states, monarchs and their court bureaucracies were the key players in the process of state formation. Generally, they developed forms of government that historians describe by the term *absolutism.* For centuries, kings seemed invincible. Nevertheless, one other form of government emerged in early modern Europe: *republican,* or *constitutional,* states. By 1800, the future lay with this other, more participatory system, which gave greater power to landed or mercantile elites than to kings and their courts.

Although kings in some medieval lands had begun to forge national states, medieval political forms differed considerably from those that developed in the early modern period. During the Middle Ages, feudal lords gave homage to their kings but continued to rule over their local territories, resisting the centralizing efforts of monarchs. Local and even national representative assemblies, which met occasionally to give advice to kings, at times acted as a brake on the king's power. City-states enjoyed considerable autonomy. The clergy supported the monarch but governed as separate spiritual realms. The papacy challenged the authority of those monarchs who, it believed, did not fulfill their duty to rule in accordance with Christian teachings as interpreted by the church. In early modern times, powerful monarchs subdued these competing systems of political authority and established strong central governments at the expense of all who opposed them.

Chronology 16.1 ❖ The Rise of Sovereignty

1469	Ferdinand and Isabella begin their rule of Castile and Aragon
1485	Henry VII begins the reign of the Tudor dynasty in England
1517	The Protestant Reformation starts in Germany
1519	Charles V of Spain becomes Hapsburg emperor of the Holy Roman Empire
1556–1598	Philip II of Spain persecutes Jews and Muslims
1559	Treaty of peace between France and Spain
1560s–1609	Netherlands revolts against Spanish rule
1562–1589	Religious wars in France
1572	Saint Bartholomew's Day Massacre: Queen Catherine of France thought to have ordered thousands of Protestants executed
1579	*Vindiciae contra Tyrannos,* published by Huguenots, justifies regicide
1588	English fleet defeats the Spanish Armada
1590s	A reaction in Russia against Ivan IV, the Terrible
1593	Henry IV of France renounces his Protestantism to restore peace in France
1598	French Protestants granted limited religious toleration by the Edict of Nantes
1640–1660	Revolution in England
1648	Treaty of Westphalia ends Thirty Years' War
1649	Charles I, Stuart king of England, is executed by an act of Parliament
1649–1660	England is coruled by Parliament and the army under Oliver Cromwell
1660	Charles II returns from exile and becomes king of England
1683	Turks attack Vienna and are defeated
1685	Louis XIV of France revokes the Edict of Nantes
1688–1689	Revolution in England: end of absolutism; religious toleration for all Protestants
1699	Treaty of Karlowitz marks Austrians' victory over Turks and affirms Austria's right to rule Hungary, Transylvania, and parts of Croatia
1701	Louis XIV tries to bring Spain under French control
1702–1714	War of the Spanish Succession establishes a balance of power between England and France

Monarchs and Elites as State Builders

At first, the pivotal figures in the development of states were the kings. European elites, whether landed or urban, grudgingly gave allegiance to these ambitious, and at times ruthless, authority figures. In general, a single monarch seemed the only alternative to the even more brutal pattern of war and disorder so basic to the governing habits of the feudal aristocracy. In the process of increasing their own power, the kings of Europe subordinated the aristocracy to their needs and interests and gained firm control over the Christian churches in their territories. Gradually, religious zeal was made compatible with and largely supportive of the state's goals, rather than papal dictates or even universal Christian aspirations. The demise of medieval representative assemblies—with the notable exception of the English Parliament—is a dramatic illustration of how monarchs subjected to their will all other political authorities, whether local, regional, or national.

Monarchs needed and employed a variety of tools for extending their power. All encouraged the use of vernacular languages—English, French, Spanish, and so on—to foster a common identity, as well as counteract the church's monopoly over the international language of the time, Latin. But more important than words were arms. The foundations of monarchical power were the standing army and a system of tax collection that permitted war to be waged. The two were inseparable. The goal of the monarch was to have independent wealth and power. In general, only war justified taxes. "Was [absolute monarchy] in reality ever anything but a constant search for new funds to pay for an over-ambitious foreign policy?" asks the British historian William Doyle.[1] The rise and fall of the great European powers of the early modern period, first Spain, then France and England, can be traced directly in the fortunes of their armies on the battlefield and the fullness of the king's treasury. Only the rise of the Dutch Republic broke with the pattern of king-army-taxes as the key to the creation of a centralized state. The Dutch case was the very antithesis of absolutism because the rich, urban, Protestant elite lent the state money at interest and in the process created the first system of national bonds and a citizen-financed national debt. As a result, a nation was created, but one without a strong central (as opposed to local) government. Local elites held most of the power, just as they held the state bonds.

In most monarchical states, however, anything that stood in the way of royal power had to be subdued, remolded, or destroyed. Where early modern monarchs succeeded in subduing, reconstituting, or destroying local aristocratic and ecclesiastical power systems, strong dynastic states emerged. Where the monarchs failed, as they did in the Holy Roman Empire and Italy, no viable states evolved until well into the nineteenth century. Those failures derived from the independent authority of local princes or city-states, and in the case of Italy, from the decentralizing influence of papal authority. In the Holy Roman Empire, feudal princes found allies in the newly formed Protestant communities, and in such a situation, religion worked as a decentralizing force. Once given the power to protect the local religion, German princes also maintained their peasants as virtual serfs.

Successful early modern kings subordinated religion to the needs of the state. They did so not by separating church and state (as was later done in the United States), but rather by linking their subjects' religious identity with national identity. For example, in England, by the late seventeenth century, to be a true Protestant was to be a true English subject, while in Spain the same equation operated for the Catholic (as opposed to the Muslim or the Jew, who came to be regarded as non-Spanish).

In the thirteenth century, most Europeans still identified themselves with their localities: their villages, manors, or towns. They gave political allegiance to their local lord or bishop. They knew little, and probably cared less, about the activities of the king and his court, except when the monarch called on them for taxes or military service. By the late seventeenth century, in contrast, aristocrats in many European countries defined their political power in terms of their relationship to king and court. By then, the lives of very ordinary people were being affected by national systems of tax collection, by the doctrines and practices of national churches, and by conscription.

Increasingly, prosperous town dwellers, the bourgeoisie, also realized that their prosperity hinged, in part, on court-supported foreign and domestic policies. If the king assisted their commercial ventures, the town dwellers gave their support to the growth of a strong central state. In only two states, England and the Netherlands, did landed and mercantile elites manage to redistribute political power so that by the late seventeenth century it could be shared by monarchy and Parliament in England or, in the Netherlands, monopolized by a social oligarchy.

The effects of European state building were visible by the late seventeenth century. Commercial rivalry between states and colonial expansion, two major activities of the period, were directly related to the ability of elites to protect their interests under the mantle of the state, and to the state's willingness to encourage world trade in order to enrich its own treasury. Monarchs and the states they helped to create ushered in the modern world just as surely as did commercial expansion, capitalism, and science. They also enshrined political power as a masculine preserve, with consequences for women that persist to this day.

The Rise and Fall of Hapsburg Spain

The Spanish political experience of the sixteenth century stands as a model of the interconnectedness of king, army, and taxation. It was also one of the most spectacular examples in Western history of the rise and equally dramatic fall of a great power. In the course of their rise, the Spanish kings built a dynastic state that burst through its frontiers and encompassed Portugal, part of Italy, the Netherlands, and enormous areas of the New World. Spain became an intercontinental empire—the first in the West since Roman times.

Hispania as a concept and geographical area existed in Roman times, and citizens of Portugal, Castile, Aragon, Catalonia, and Andalusia, to name only the larger and more important areas of the Iberian Peninsula, recognized a certain common identity—no more, no less. Until 1469, however, Spain did not exist as a political entity. In that year, Ferdinand, heir to the throne of Aragon, married his more powerful and prosperous cousin, Isabella, heiress of Castile. Yet even after the unification of Castile and the crown of Aragon (Catalonia, Aragon, and Valencia), relations among the fiercely independent provinces of Spain were often tense. Only through dynastic marriage of their offspring to a German-speaking family of central Europe, the Hapsburgs, did the Spanish monarchs emerge on the international scene. Marriage became a key piece in the puzzle of state development.

Ferdinand and Isabella: Unity and Purity of "Blood" and Religion

During their rule (1479–1516), which took many years to establish firmly, Ferdinand and Isabella laid the foundation for the Spanish empire and Spanish domination of European affairs throughout the sixteenth century. Together, they sought to build the army and the state by waging a campaign to reconquer Spanish territory still held by the Muslims. At the same time, they strove to bring the church into alliance with the state and forge a Spanish identity based on "blood" ancestry as well as religion. It became necessary to prove that no Jews or non-Spaniards could be found in a family's lineage.

In order to develop a strong monarchy, the Spanish rulers had to bring the church's interests in line with their own. Ferdinand and Isabella's alliance with the church and their war against the Muslims in the southern portion of the peninsula were interrelated. A crusade against the Muslims presupposed an energetic church and a deep and militant Catholicism, with the rulers committed to the aims of the church, and the church to the aims of the rulers. While other Europeans, partly under the impact of the Renaissance, questioned the church's leadership and attacked its corruption, the Catholic Kings (as Ferdinand and Isabella were called) reformed the church, making it responsive to their needs and also invulnerable to criticism. Popular piety and royal policy led in 1492 to a victory over Granada, the last Muslim-ruled territory of Spain.

The five-hundred-year struggle for Christian hegemony in the Iberian Peninsula left the Spanish fiercely religious and strongly suspicious of foreigners. Despite centuries of intermarriage with non-Christians, by the early sixteenth century, purity of blood and orthodoxy of faith became neces-

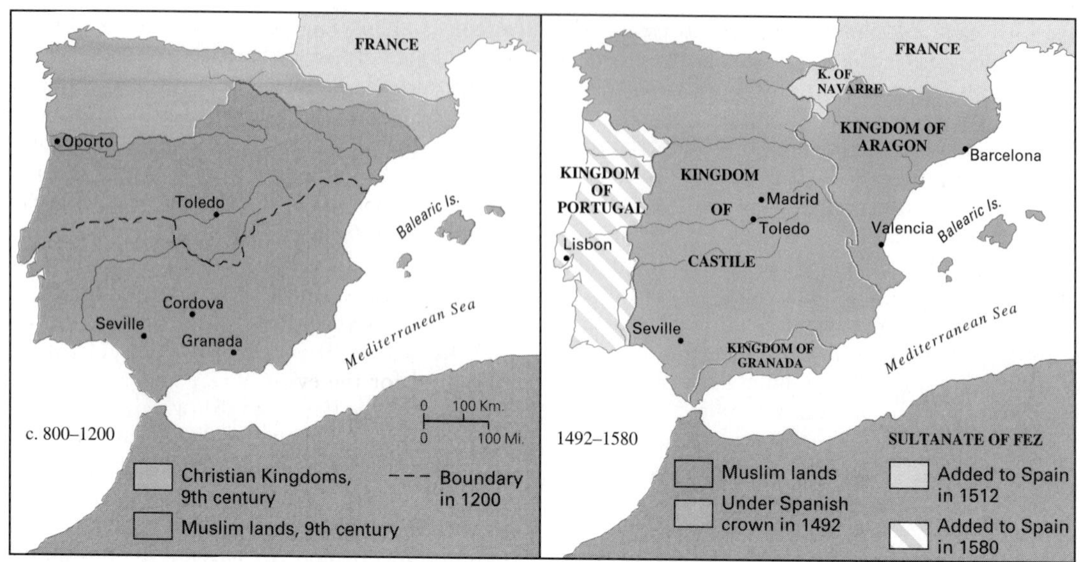

Map 16.1 Spain from the Ninth to the Sixteenth Century Spain became a nation gradually, and eventually Portugal split away to become a separate state.

sary for, and synonymous with, Spanish identity. The Spanish state and church were actively engaged in persecuting Muslims and Jews, who for centuries had contributed substantially to Spanish cultural and economic life.

In 1492, in a move to enforce religious uniformity, the crown expelled from Spain Jews unwilling to accept baptism. Some 150,000 (some estimates are considerably higher) were driven out. The thousands of Jews who underwent conversion were watched by a church tribunal, the Inquisition, for signs of backsliding. The clerical inquisitors employed sophisticated means of interrogation and torture to ferret out newly converted Christians and their descendants suspected of practicing Judaism. Death by fire, sometimes in elaborate public ceremonies, was the ultimate penalty. Muslims also bore the pain of persecution: forced conversions; investigations, torture, and executions conducted by the Inquisition; and finally, mass expulsion in 1609–1614. The Inquisition represented the dark side of the Spanish genius for conquest and administration, and its shadow stretched down through the centuries well into the twentieth and the repressive regime of Francisco Franco.

The wars against the Muslims gave the Spanish invaluable military experience and rendered their army one of the finest in Europe. The wars also created a pattern in the growth of the Spanish empire: its victories always lay in the south—in Italy, in Latin America, and against the Turks—while its defeats and setbacks occurred in the north—in the Netherlands, in opposition to the Lutheran Reformation in the Holy Roman Empire, and in war against England.

With a superior army, with the great magnates pacified, and with the church and the Inquisition under monarchical control, the Catholic Kings expanded their interests and embarked on an imperialist foreign policy in Europe and abroad, which had extraordinary consequences. Ultimately, it made Spain dominant in the New World.

Ferdinand and Isabella gambled on Columbus's voyage, and they won. Then, beginning in 1519 in Mexico, the conquistador Hernando Cortés defeated the Aztec nation with six hundred foot soldiers and sixteen horses. This feat was partly due to the superiority of Spanish technology, but it was also made possible by the condition of the Aztec nation, which was struggling to maintain a hold over its own people and over scores of other Mexican tribes that it had, in some cases, brutally subdued. The Spanish forces were led by members of the minor aristocracy, *hidalgos*. Their role was distinctive yet typical of the role played by the minor aristocracy in the building of other European nation-states. For them, as younger sons of impoverished aristocrats, war was a means to riches and land. Unlike the great and wealthy aristocrats, they would serve the crown at home and abroad as soldiers and often as bureaucrats. Their loyalty to the king was matched only by their fierce ambition. The bureaucracy and army of the early modern states were very important avenues for obtaining or retaining elite status.

The Reign of Charles V: Hapsburg, King of Spain, and Holy Roman Emperor

Through a series of shrewd marriage agreements for their children, Ferdinand and Isabella strengthened their international alliances. As a result, their grandson, Charles, who ruled from 1516 to 1556, inherited Spain, the Netherlands, Austria, Sardinia, Sicily, the kingdom of Naples, and Franche-Comté. In 1519, the same year as the conquest of Mexico, he was also elected Holy Roman Emperor (partly through bribery). Thus, he became the most powerful monarch in Europe. But in the course of his reign, he saw problems emerge that would eventually lead to Spain's decline and weaken the Hapsburg dynasty to which, through marriage, he had been heir.

Charles's inheritance was simply too vast to be governed effectively. However, that was only dimly perceived at the time. The Lutheran Reformation proved to be the first successful challenge to Hapsburg power. It was the first phase of a religious and political struggle between Catholic Spain and Protestant Europe: a struggle that would dominate the last half of the sixteenth century and ultimately reduce Spanish influence.

The achievements of Charles V's reign rested on the twin instruments of army and bureaucracy. The Hapsburg Empire in the New World was vast, and, on the whole, effectively administered and policed. The Catholic clergy were key players in this process. Out of a sprawling empire, with its exploited native populations, came the greatest flow of gold and silver ever witnessed by Europeans. Constant warfare in Europe, in Italy and against the Turks in the Mediterranean, coupled with the immensity of the Spanish administrative network, required a steady intake of capital. But this easy access to income appears to have been detrimental in the long run to the Spanish economy. There was no incentive for the development of domestic industry, entrepreneurship, or international commerce. Moreover, constant war engendered and perpetuated a social order geared to the aggrandizement of a military class rather than to the development of a commercial class. Although war expanded Spain's power in the sixteenth century, it also sowed the seeds for the financial crises of the 1590s and beyond, and for the eventual decline of Spain as a world power.

Philip II

In the reign of Philip II (1556–1598), the strengths and weaknesses of the Spanish state became fully evident. That period is pivotal in early modern Spanish history. Philip II inherited the throne from his father, Charles V, who abdicated in 1556 and left his son with a large empire in both the Old World and the New. Although this empire had been administered effectively enough, it was facing the specters of bankruptcy and heresy. Heresy, more than any other problem, compelled the attention of this obsessively devout monarch, whose zeal for Catholicism ruled his private conduct and infused his foreign policy. Philip bided his time with foreign infidels and heretics and waited for the moment when the crown would possess the revenue needed to launch an offensive against the Turks and international Protestantism.

To Philip II, being truly Spanish meant being Christian in faith and blood; the racist tendencies already evident in the later fifteenth century gained full expression during his reign. Increasingly, the country came to be ruled by an exclusive class of old Christians, who claimed to be untainted because for centuries they had refused to marry Muslims or Jews. Traditional in their thinking, the old Christians controlled the church, religious orders, and the Inquisition—all to preserve an imperial system in need of reform.

Melancholic and standoffish by temperament, Philip II worked arduously and declined most of life's enjoyments. He pored over his ministers' reports, editing and commenting, yet in the end he was strangely indecisive. Some problems re-

Allegory of the Abdication of Charles V, by Frans Francken II, 1556. Emperor Charles V, who ruled half of Europe and most of the Americas, abdicated in 1556, giving his German imperial crown to his brother Ferdinand, archduke of Austria, and the kingdoms of Spain and the Netherlands to his son Philip II. The Hapsburg dynasty ruled Spain until the eighteenth century and Austria and Hungary until the early twentieth century. (*Rijksmuseum, Amsterdam.*)

mained unsolved for years, as frustrated advisers begged in vain for the king to take action.

In the 1560s, Philip sent the largest land army ever assembled in Europe into the Netherlands with the intention of crushing Protestant-inspired opposition to Spanish authority. The ensuing revolt of the Netherlands lasted until 1609, and in losing the Netherlands, Spain lost its industrial heartland. In 1576, the Spanish army, in a desperate attempt to defeat the rebels, flooded and sacked Antwerp, the leading commercial and banking city in northern Europe. Antwerp's trade and many of its educated elite gradually moved to Amsterdam, a Protestant stronghold, which replaced its southern rival as an international capital and the center of the new Dutch national state.

By the 1580s, Philip's foreign policy was overextended in every direction, and his religious zeal shaped all his decisions. He intervened in the French religious wars on the Catholic side, although his intervention gave little to Spain in the way of power or influence. Philip's disastrous attempt to invade England was also born of religious zeal.

Philip regarded an assault on England, the main Protestant power, as a holy crusade against the "heretic and bastard" Queen Elizabeth; he particularly resented English assistance to Protestant Dutch rebels. Sailing from Lisbon in May

1588, the Spanish Armada, twenty-two-thousand men strong, met with humiliating defeat. Its ships were too cumbersome to negotiate the treacherous English Channel, where the English ships easily outmaneuvered them and broke their formation by sending fire ships crashing into them. Moreover, strong winds, typical for this time of year, drove the Armada out of striking position.

The defeat had a psychological effect on the Spanish. They openly pondered what they had done to incur divine displeasure. Protestant Europe, however, hailed the victory as a sign of its election, and the "Protestant wind" stirred by divine intervention entered the mythology of English nationalism. In the rise and fall of nations, self-assurance has played a crucial, if inexplicable, role. The cultural renaissance associated with the England of Shakespeare owed its vigor and confidence in part to its pride at being Protestant and independent of Spanish influence.

The End of the Spanish Hapsburgs

After the defeat of the Armada, Spain gradually and reluctantly abandoned its imperial ambitions in northern Europe. The administrative structure built by Charles V and Philip II did remain strong throughout the seventeenth century; nevertheless, by the first quarter of the century, enormous weaknesses had surfaced in Spanish economic and social life. In 1596, Philip II was bankrupt, his vast wealth overextended by the cost of foreign wars. Bankruptcy reappeared at various times in the seventeenth century, while the agricultural economy, at the heart of any early modern nation, stagnated. The Spanish in their golden age had never devoted enough attention to increasing domestic production.

Despite these setbacks, Spain was still capable of taking a very aggressive posture during the Thirty Years' War (1618–1648). The Austrian branch of the Hapsburg family joined forces with their Spanish cousins, and neither the Swedes and Germans nor the Dutch could stop them. Only French participation in the Thirty Years' War on the Protestant side tipped the balance decisively against the Hapsburgs. Spanish aggression brought no victories, and with the Peace of Westphalia (1648), Spain officially recognized the independence of the Netherlands and cut its ties with the Austrian branch of the family.

By 1660, the imperial age of the Spanish Hapsburgs had come to an end. The rule of the Protestant princes had been secured in the Holy Roman Empire; the largely Protestant Dutch Republic flourished; Portugal and its colony of Brazil were independent of Spain; and dominance over European affairs had passed to France. The quality of material life in Spain deteriorated rapidly, and the ever-present gap between the rich and the poor widened even more drastically. The traditional aristocracy and the church retained their land and power but failed conspicuously to produce effective leadership. With decline came rigidity of institutions and values. Spain remained authoritarian far longer than other European countries. Democratic revolutions did not occur in a country dominated exclusively by the landed elite and the church. The commercial elite that became increasingly important in England, the Netherlands, and France failed to develop in monarchical and agricultural Spain.

The Spanish experience illustrates two aspects of the history of the European state. First, the state as empire could survive and prosper only if the domestic economic base continued to expand. Living off the colonies ultimately meant economic stagnation and the absence of technological innovation at home. Second, the states where a vital and aggressive mercantile class developed generally prospered in the early modern period. In such states, the elite no longer consisted exclusively of those with landed wealth; rather, it comprised those who invested, or even participated, in the market and manufacturing. However, in Spain, the old aristocracy and the church continued to dominate and control society and its mores. They not only despised manual labor and profit taking through trade, but also showed little interest in science and technology.

Although the major states had been created by kings and shrewd dynastic marriages, after 1700 they were increasingly nurtured by an expansion of the elite to include merchants. Eventually, some of the merchants began to look and act like aristocrats. France became such an early modern absolutist state.

As the educated and commercial elites in the early modern states widened, courts and kings began to seem less and less necessary. The English constitutional model of government, complete with a representative assembly, started to look more attractive to reformers. Meanwhile, absolutist monarchies like France continued to function, but only with a vast and expensive bureaucracy that tried to stimulate commerce and industry.

The Growth of French Power

Two states in the early modern period succeeded most effectively in consolidating the power of their central governments: France and England. Each became a model of a very different form of statehood. The English model evolved into a constitutional monarchy in which the king's power was limited by Parliament and the rights of the English people were protected by law and tradition. The French model emphasized at every turn the glory of the king and, by implication, the sovereignty of the state and its right to stand above the interests of its subjects. France's monarchy became absolute, although the evolution of the French state was a very gradual process, not completed until the late seventeenth century.

When Hugh Capet became king of France in 987, he was, in relation to France's other great feudal lords, merely first among equals. From this small power base, more symbolic than real, Hugh Capet's successors extended their territory and dominion at the expense of the feudal lords' power. To administer their territories, the Capetians established an efficient bureaucracy composed of townsmen and trustworthy lesser nobles who, unlike the great feudal lords, owed their wealth and status directly to the king. These royal officials, an essential element of monarchical power, collected the king's feudal dues and administered justice. At the same time, French kings emphasized that they had been selected by God to rule, a theory known as the *divine right of kings.* This theory gave monarchy a sanctity that various French kings relied on to enforce their commands to rebellious feudal lords and defend themselves against papal claims of dominance over the French church.

Yet medieval French kings never sought absolute power. Not until the seventeenth century was the power base of the French monarchy consolidated to the extent that kings and their courts could attempt to rule without formal consultations with their subjects. In the Middle Ages, the French monarchs recognized the rights of, and consulted with, local representative assemblies, which represented the three estates, or orders, in society. These assemblies (whether regional or national) consisted of deputies drawn from the various elites: the clergy, the nobility, and significantly, the leadership of cities and towns in a given region. The Estates met as circumstances—such as wars, taxes, or local disputes—warranted, and the nationally representative assembly, the Estates General, was always summoned by the king. Medieval French kings consulted these assemblies mainly to give legitimacy to their demands and credibility to their administration. They also recognized that the courts—especially the highest court, the Parlement of Paris—had the right to administer the king's justice with a minimum of royal interference. Medieval kings did not see themselves as originators of law; they were its guarantors and administrators.

War came to serve the interests of a monarchy bent on consolidating its power and authority. As a result of the Hundred Years' War (1337–1453), the English were eventually driven from France, their claims to the French throne dashed. In the process of war, the French monarchy grew richer. War enabled the French kings to levy new taxes, often enacted without the consent of the Estates General, and to maintain a large standing army under royal command. The Hundred Years' War also inspired allegiance to the king as the visible symbol of France. The war heightened the French sense of national identity; the English were a common enemy, discernibly different in manners, language, dress, and appearance.

With revenue and an army at their disposal, the French kings subsequently embarked on territorial aggrandizement. Charles VIII (1483–1498) invaded Italy in 1494. Always a shrewd assessor of the implications of power, Machiavelli observed that Italy's weakness resulted from its lack of unity, whereas the power of this new cohesive state of France derived in large measure from the strength of its prince and his huge and mostly native-born army. Although the French gained little territory from the Italian campaign, they did effectively challenge Spanish power in Italy and intimidate an already weakened papacy.

Religion and the French State

In every emergent state, tension existed between the monarch and the papacy. At issue was control over the church within that territory—over its personnel, its wealth, and, of course, its pulpits, from which an illiterate majority learned what their leaders wanted them to know, not only in matters of religious belief but also about questions of obedience to civil authority. The monarch's power to make church appointments could ensure a complacent church. A church that was willing to preach about the king's divine right and was compliant on matters of taxes was especially important in France because, legally, the church had to pay no taxes and had only to give donations to the crown. Centuries of tough bargaining with the papacy paid off when, in 1516, Francis I (1515–1547) concluded the Concordat of Bologna, by which Pope Leo X permitted the French king to nominate, and therefore effectively to appoint, men of his choice as bishops in the French church.

The Concordat of Bologna laid the foundation for what became known as the *Gallican church*—a term signifying the immense power and authority of the Catholic church in France as sanctioned and overseen by the French kings. By the early sixteenth century, religious homogeneity had strengthened the central government at the expense of papal authority and the traditional privileges enjoyed by local aristocracy. This ecclesiastical and religious settlement lay at the heart of monarchical authority. Consequently, the Protestant Reformation threatened the very survival of France as a unified state. Throughout the early modern period, the French kings had assumed that their realms must be governed by one king, one faith, and one set of laws. Any alternative to that unity offered local power elites, whether aristocratic or clerical, the opportunity to channel religious dissent into their service at the expense of royal authority. Once linked, religious and political opposition to any central government could be extremely dangerous.

During the decades that followed, partly through the efforts of the Huguenot (Protestant) underground and partly because the French king and his ministers vacillated in their attempts at persecution, the Protestant minority grew in strength and dedication. By challenging the authority of the Catholic church, Protestants were also inadvertently challenging royal authority, for the French church and the French monarchy supported each other. Protestantism became the basis for a political movement of an increasingly revolutionary nature.

From 1562 to 1598, France experienced waves of religious wars, which cost the king control over vast areas of the kingdom. In 1579, extreme Huguenot theorists published the *Vindiciae contra Tyrannos*. This anonymous attack on the rights of kings, combined with a call to action, was the first of its kind in early modern times. It justified rebellion against, and even the execution of, an unjust king. European monarchs might claim power and divinely sanctioned authority, but by the late sixteenth century, their subjects had available the moral justification to oppose their monarch's will, by force if necessary, and this justification rested on Scripture and religious conviction. Significantly, this same treatise was translated into English in 1648, a year before Parliament publicly executed Charles I, king of England.

The French monarchy struggled when faced with a combined religious and political opposition. The era of royal supremacy ushered in by Francis I came to an abrupt end during the reign of his successor, Henry II (1547–1559). Wed to Catherine de Medicis, a member of the powerful Italian banking family, Henry occupied himself not with the concerns of government but with the pleasures of the hunt. The sons who succeeded Henry—Francis II (1559–1560), Charles IX (1560–1574), and Henry III (1574–1589)—were uniformly weak. In this power vacuum, their mother, Catherine, emerged as virtual ruler—a queen despised as an Italian and a nonaristocrat, as a woman, and as a backstairs intriguer. One of the most hated figures of her day, Catherine de Medicis defies dispassionate assessment. She probably ordered the execution of Protestants by royal troops in Paris—the beginning of the infamous Saint Bartholomew's Day Massacre (1572). The massacre, with the bloodbath that followed, became both a symbol and a legend in subsequent European history: a symbol of the excesses of religious zeal and a legend of Protestant martyrdom, which gave renewed energy to the cause of international Protestantism.

The civil wars begun in 1562 were renewed in the massacre's aftermath. They dragged on until the death of the last Valois king in 1589. The Valois failure to produce a male heir to the throne placed Henry, duke of Bourbon and a Protestant, in line to succeed to the French throne. Realizing that the overwhelmingly Catholic population would not accept a Protestant king, Henry (apparently without much regret) renounced his adopted religion and embraced the church. His private religious beliefs may never be known, but outward conformity to the religion of the Catholic majority was the only means to effect peace and reestablish political stability. Under the reign of Henry IV (1589–1610), the French throne acquired its central position in national politics. Henry granted to his Protestant subjects and former followers a degree of religious toleration through the Edict of Nantes (1598), but they were never welcomed in significant numbers into the royal bureaucracy. Throughout the seventeenth century, every French king attempted to undermine the Protestants' regional power bases and ultimately to destroy their religious liberties.

Louis XIV: The Consolidation of French Monarchical Power

The defeat of Protestantism as a national force set the stage for the final consolidation of the French state under the great Bourbon kings, Louis XIII and Louis XIV. Louis XIII (1610–1643) realized that his rule depended on an efficient and trustworthy bureaucracy, a renewable treasury, and constant vigilance against the localized claims to power by the great aristocracy and Protestant cities and towns. Cardinal Richelieu, who served as the young Louis XIII's chief minister from 1624 to 1642, became the great architect of French absolutism.

Richelieu's morality rested on one sacred principle, embodied in a phrase he invented: *raison d'état,* reason of state. Richelieu applied the principle when he brought under the king's control the disruptive and antimonarchical elements within French society. He increased the power of the central bureaucracy, attacked the power of independent, and often Protestant, towns and cities, and harassed their Huguenot inhabitants. Above all, he humbled the great nobles by limiting their effectiveness as councilors to the king and prohibiting their traditional privileges, such as using a duel rather than court action to settle grievances. Reason of state also guided Richelieu's foreign policy. It required that France turn against Catholic Spain and join the Protestant, and hence anti-Spanish, side in the war that was raging at the time in the Holy Roman Empire. France's entry into the Thirty Years' War (1618–1648) resulted in a decisive victory for French power on the Continent.

Richelieu died in 1642, and Louis XIII the following year. Mazarin, a cardinal who had never been ordained a priest and an Italian by birth, took charge during the minority of Louis XIV (he was five years old when Louis XIII died) and continued Richelieu's policies. Mazarin's heavy-handed actions produced a rebellious reaction, the *Fronde:* a series of street riots that eventually cost the government control over Paris and lasted from 1648 to 1653. Centered in Paris and supported by the great aristocracy, the courts, and the city's poorer classes, the Fronde threatened to develop into a full-scale uprising. It might have done so but for one crucial factor: its leadership was divided. Court judges (lesser nobles who had often just risen from the ranks of the bourgeoisie) deeply distrusted the great aristocrats and refused in the end to make common cause with them. And both groups feared disorders among the urban masses.

When Louis XIV finally assumed responsibility for governing in 1661, he vowed that the events he had witnessed as a child in Paris, when the Fronde had brought street rioters to the palace windows, would never be repeated. In his reign, Louis XIV crafted the absolutist state and became the source of all power, which was in turn administered by his bureaucracy. The local elites or officials were expected to look to the central government for everything, from taxes to noble titles and exclusive privileges for perfume manufacturing or coal extraction. Provincial bureaucrats reported to ministers based in Paris. Indeed, even road engineers were sent out from Paris. The army was made larger and more professional, gaining, in addition, an architecture and engineering corps. The state also established a military school and sponsored academies for science, literature, and language. Intellectuals re-

THE HALL OF MIRRORS IN THE ROYAL PALACE AT VERSAILLES. Immense and grand, Versailles was the wonder of the age. Like the person of the king, it said to his subjects: I am grandeur incarnate. Even by today's standards, it is an impressive building, both inside and out. (*C. L. Chrysun/The Image Bank/Getty Images.*)

ceived court patronage and pensions but were expected to say what officials liked to hear.

Under Louis XIV, the state became the major player in everything, from dredging the rivers to awarding manufacturing monopolies. No absolute monarch in western Europe had ever before held so much personal authority or commanded such a vast and effective military and administrative machine. Louis XIV's reign represents the culmination of the process of increasing monarchical authority that had been under way for centuries. Intelligent, cunning, and possessing a unique understanding of the requirements of his office, Louis XIV became the envy of his age.

Perhaps the most brilliant of Louis XIV's many policies was his treatment of the aristocracy. He simply dispensed with their services as influential advisers. He treated the aristocrats to elaborate rituals, feasts, processions, displays, and banquets, but amid all these celebrations their political power dwindled. The wiser members of the aristocracy stayed home and managed their estates; others made their way at court as minor functionaries and basked in the glory of the Sun King. A lengthy visit to Versailles—a necessity for any aristocrat who wanted his views and needs attended to—could bankrupt the less well-to-do.

Louis XIV's domestic policies centered on his incessant search for new revenues. His palace at Versailles cost a fortune. So too did his wars, which Louis XIV waged to excess. To raise capital, he used the services of Jean Baptiste Colbert, a brilliant administrator, who improved methods of tax collecting, promoted new industries, and encouraged international trade. Such ambitious national policies were possible because Louis XIV inherited the efficient system of administration introduced by Richelieu. Instead of relying on the local aristocracy to collect royal taxes and to administer royal policies, Richelieu had appointed the king's own men as *intendants,* or functionaries dispatched with wide powers into the provinces. At first, their mission had been temporary and their success minimal, but gradually they became a permanent feature of royal administration. During the reign of Louis XIV, the country was divided into thirty-two districts, controlled by intendants. Operating with a total bureaucracy of about a thousand officials and no longer bothering even to consult the parlements or the Estates, Louis XIV ruled absolutely.

Why did such a system of absolute authority work? Did the peasants not revolt? Why did the old aristocracy not rise in rebellion? For the aristocrats, the loss of political authority was not accompanied by a comparable loss in wealth and social position; indeed, quite the contrary was true. During the seventeenth century, the French nobility—2 percent of the population—controlled approximately 20 to 30 percent of the total national income. The church, too, fared well under Louis, receiving good tax arrangements, provided it preached about the king's divinely given rights. Although there were peasant upheavals throughout the century, the sheer size of the royal army and police—more than 300,000 by the end of Louis's reign—made successful revolt nearly impossible. When in the early 1700s a popular religious rebellion led by Protestant visionaries broke out in the south, royal troops crushed it. Thus, absolutism rested on the complicity of the old aristocracy, the self-aggrandizement of government officials, the church's doctrines, the revenues squeezed out of the peasantry, and the power of a huge military machine.

Yet Louis XIV's system was fatally flawed. Without any effective check on his power and on his dreams of international conquest, no limit was imposed on the state's capacity to make war or on the ensuing national debt. Louis XIV coveted the section of the Holy Roman Empire that led to the Rhine; he also sought to curb Dutch commercial prosperity and had designs on the Spanish Netherlands (the Franco-Dutch War, 1672–1678). By the 1680s, his domestic and foreign policies turned violently aggressive. In 1685, he revoked the Edict of Nantes, forcing many of the country's remaining Protestants to flee. In 1689, he embarked on a military campaign to gain territory from the Holy Roman Empire. And in 1701, he tried to bring Spain under the control of the Bourbon dynasty. Louis XIV, however, underestimated the strength of his northern rivals, England and the Netherlands. Their combined power, in alliance with the Holy Roman Empire and the Austrians, defeated Louis XIV's ambitions.

The War of the Spanish Succession was essentially a land war fought on the battlefields of northern Europe. Out of it, the Austrians acquired the southern Netherlands (Belgium) and thus a buffer against the possibility of a French overrun of the Low Countries. Most dramatically, however, the war created a balance of power in Europe. Britain emerged as a major force in European affairs, the counterweight against the French colossus. The relative peace of the eighteenth century has often been attributed to the creation of this real, but fragile, balance among the major European powers.

Louis XIV's participation in these long wars emptied the royal treasury. By the late seventeenth century, taxes had risen intolerably and were levied mostly on those least able to pay: the peasants. In the 1690s, the combination of taxes, bad harvests, and plague led to widespread poverty, misery, and starvation in large areas of France. Thus, for the great majority of French people, absolutism meant a decline in living standards and a significant increase in mortality rates. Absolutism also meant increased surveillance of the population. Royal authorities censored books, spied on heretics, Protestants, and freethinkers, and even tortured and executed opponents of state policy.

By 1715, France was a tightly governed society whose treasury was bankrupt. Protestants had been driven into exile or forced to convert. Strict censorship laws closely governed publishing, causing a brisk trade in clandestine books and manuscripts. Direct taxes burdened the poor and

Map 16.2 Europe, 1648 ▶
Europe in 1648, exhausted by war.

0 200 400 Km.
0 200 400 Mi.
Austrian Hapsburg lands
Spanish Hapsburg lands
Prussian lands
German states
Swedish lands
Boundary of Holy Roman Empire
ATLANTIC OCEAN
North Sea
English Channel
Baltic Sea
Black Sea
Mediterranean Sea
SCOTLAND
Edinburgh
IRELAND
Dublin
Durham
ENGLAND
London
NORWAY
SWEDEN
FINLAND
ESTONIA
LIVONIA
RUSSIA
JUTLAND
DENMARK
Copenhagen
SCHLESWIG
Danzig
PRUSSIA
Vilna
MECKLEN-BURG
Hamburg
POMERANIA
BRANDENBURG
Berlin
Warsaw
POLAND
UNITED NETHERLANDS
Amsterdam
Antwerp
SPANISH NETHERLANDS
Cologne
WEST-PHALIA
HESSE
Mainz
Worms
SAXONY
SILESIA
BOHEMIA
Prague
MORAVIA
BAVARIA
Augsburg
Vienna
AUSTRIA
TRANSYLVANIA
MOLDAVIA
WALLACHIA
Belgrade
OTTOMAN EMPIRE
Paris
Nantes
FRANCE
FRANCHE-COMTÉ
SWITZERLAND
Geneva
SAVOY
PIEDMONT
MILAN
GENOA
FLORENCE
PAPAL STATES
REPUBLIC OF VENICE
Rome
Naples
NAPLES
Corsica (to Genoa)
Sardinia
Palermo
Sicily
Lepanto
Athens
Crete (To Rep. of Venice)
PORTUGAL
Lisbon
CASTILE
Madrid
SPAIN
CATALONIA
ARAGON
VALENCIA
ANDALUSIA
Granada

POOR WOMAN WITH CHILDREN, BY J. DUMONT (1701–1781). Louis XIV may have been grand, but he was also callous. He impoverished the poor even further, and by the end of his reign famine had returned to parts of France. (*Pushkin Museum, Moscow/Bridgeman Art Library.*)

were legally evaded by the aristocracy. Critics of state policy within the church had been effectively marginalized. And over the long run, foreign wars had brought no significant gains.

In the France of Louis XIV, the dynastic state reached maturity and began to display some of its classic characteristics: centralized bureaucracy; royal patronage to enforce allegiance; a system of taxation universally but inequitably applied; and suppression of political opposition, either through the use of patronage or, if necessary, through force. Another important feature was the state's cultivation of the arts and sciences as a means of increasing national power and prestige. Together, these policies enabled France and its monarchs to achieve political stability, enforce a uniform system of law, and channel the country's wealth and resources into the service of the state as a whole.

Yet at his death in 1715, Louis XIV left his successors a bureaucracy and onerous taxation that were vastly in need of overhaul. Because this system endorsed the traditional social privileges of the church and nobility, reforming it was virtually impossible. Although the pattern of war, excessive taxation of the lower classes, and spending beyond revenues had damaged French finances, the bureaucracy of the absolutist state continued to function, extending its influence over every area of trade and manufacturing, transportation, and agriculture. To this day, perfectly preserved pieces of silk and cotton cloth made in every French province sit in the Parisian archives of the government. In the eighteenth century, they had been sent there for inspection. Only when the king's ministers had approved the samples could the cloth from which they had been cut be sold in the open market, with the king's seal. By the 1780s, manufacturers clamored for freer markets, fewer, or at least faster, inspections, and more freedom to experiment. They smuggled and cheated the inspectors while looking across the Channel at England with envy at the power, wealth, and freedom of its industry and its merchants. The discontent of French manufacturers contributed to the causes of the 1789 French Revolution.

THE GROWTH OF LIMITED MONARCHY AND CONSTITUTIONALISM IN ENGLAND

England achieved national unity earlier than any other major European state. Its island geography freed it from the border disputes that plagued emerging states in continental Europe. By an accident of fate, its administrative structure also developed in such a way as to encourage centralization. In 1066, William, duke of Normandy and vassal to the French king, had invaded and conquered England, acquiring at a stroke the entire kingdom. In contrast, the French kings took centuries to make the territory of France their domain.

As conquerors, the Norman kings pursued a policy of intermarriage and consultation. They consulted with their powerful subjects—archbishops, bishops, earls, and barons. By the middle of the thirteenth century, these consultations, or *parlays,* came to be called *parliaments.* Increasingly, the practice grew of inviting to these parliaments representatives from the counties—knights and burgesses. Gradually, these lesser-than-noble but often wealthy and prominent representatives came to regard Parliament as a means of self-expression for redressing their grievances. In turn, the later medieval kings saw Parliament as a means of exercising control and raising taxes. By 1297, the Lords (the upper house) and Commons (as the lower house was called) had obtained the king's agreement that no direct taxes could be levied without their consent. By the fourteenth century, Parliament had become a permanent institution of government. Its power was entirely subservient to the crown, but its right to question royal decisions had been established.

The English Parliament and Constitution

The medieval English Parliament possessed two characteristics that distinguished it from its many Continental counterparts, such as the various French Estates. The English Parliament was national, not provincial; more important, its representatives were elected across caste lines, with voting rights dependent on property, not on noble birth or status. These representatives voted as individuals, rather than collectively as clergy, nobles, or commoners, that is, as Estates. In the Middle Ages, Parliament and the monarchy were interdependent; they were seen not as rivals but as complementary forms of centralized government. That very interdependence, however, would ultimately lead to conflict.

The constitution, too, emerged during the Middle Ages in England. It comprised unwritten and written precedents, laws, and royal acts that came to embody the basic principles of government. (In contrast to the French model, England developed into a *constitutional* monarchy.) The most famous document, Magna Carta (1215), guaranteed certain aristocratic privileges and was read at the opening meeting of almost every Parliament the king called. This theoretical foundation—until now not written as a single document—grew out of legal practices and customs described under the generic title *common law.* Whereas feudal law applied only to a local region, common law extended throughout the realm and served as a unifying force.

The Tudor Achievement

Emphasis on the medieval evolution of Parliament and the constitution should not obscure the fact that England in the fifteenth century could be a lawless place where local nobility ran their estates and made war on their neighbors largely unchecked by central government. One such war, the War of the Roses (1455–1485) pitted two noble families against each other in a struggle for domination. Out of it, the Tudors emerged triumphant, in the person of Henry VII (1485–1509), who spent much of his reign consolidating and extending his authority. In the process, he revitalized and remade the institutions of central government. Henry VII's goal was to check the unruly nobility. Toward this end, he brought commoners into the government. These commoners, unlike the great magnates, could be channeled into royal service because they craved what the king offered: financial rewards and elevated social status. Although they did not fully displace the aristocracy, commoners were brought into Henry VII's inner circle, into the Privy Council, into the courts, and eventually into all the highest offices of the government. The strength and efficiency of Tudor government were shown during the Reformation, when Henry VIII (1509–1547) made himself head of the English church. He was able to take this giant step (known as the Henrican Revolution) toward increasing royal power because his father had restored order and stability.

The Protestant Reformation in England was a revolution in royal, as well as ecclesiastical, government. It attacked and defeated a main obstacle to monarchical authority: the power of the papacy. At the same time, the Reformation greatly enhanced the power of Parliament. Henry used Parliament to make the Reformation because he knew that he needed the support of the lords, the country gentry, and the merchants. No change in religious practice could be instituted by the monarchy alone. Parliament's participation in the Reformation gave it a greater role and sense of importance than it had ever possessed in the past.

Profile

Elizabeth I, Queen of England (1558–1603)

By kind permission of the Marquess of Tavistock, and the Trustees of the Bedford Estates.

Born in 1533, Elizabeth, the daughter of Henry VIII and his second wife, Anne Boleyn, was raised as a Protestant by her father. Fidelity to the Anglican church may have been basic to Henry's interests, but fidelity to his marriage vows was not. He put Anne Boleyn to death on charges of treason. His marriage to her had led to England's break with the Roman Catholic church, which would not grant him a divorce from his first wife, Catherine of Aragon, with whom he had failed to produce a male heir. When Henry's second mariage also did not produce the male heir he so deeply desired, he tired of Elizabeth's mother. Hence her tragic end.

The church of Rome regarded Elizabeth as a bastard and never accepted Henry's self-decreed divorce from his first wife. Not surprisingly, in her youth Elizabeth came to fear

Nonetheless, the final outcome of this administrative revolution enhanced monarchical power. By the end of his reign, Henry VIII easily possessed as much power as his French rival, Francis I. Indeed, until the early seventeenth century, the history of monarchical power in England, with its absolutist tendencies, was remarkably similar to the Continental pattern.

At Henry's death, the Tudor bureaucracy and centralized government were strained to the utmost, yet survived. The government weathered the reign of Henry's sickly son, Edward VI (1547–1553), and the extreme Protestantism of some of his advisers, and it survived the brief and deeply troubled reign of Henry's first daughter, Mary (1553–1558), who brutally tried to return England to Catholicism. At Mary's death, England came dangerously close to the religious instability and sectarian tension that undermined the French kings during the final decades of the sixteenth century.

Henry's second daughter, Elizabeth I, became queen in 1558 and reigned until her death in 1603. The Elizabethan period was characterized by a heightened sense of national identity. The English Reformation enhanced that sense, as did the increasing fear of foreign invasion by Spain. The fear was real enough and lessened only with the defeat of the Spanish Armada in 1588. For the English the victory was like that of David over Goliath, and its value was both symbolic and real. For the Spanish the defeat was also deeply affecting: they asked how had they gone wrong. In the seventeenth century, the English would look back on Elizabeth's reign as a golden age. It was the calm before the storm, a time when a new commercial class was formed, which, in the seventeenth century, would demand a greater say in government operations.

The social and economic changes of the Elizabethan age can be seen, in microcosm, by looking at the Durham region in northern England. From marriage and to regard her claim to the English throne as precarious. She became queen in 1558—after the deaths of her half sister, Mary, and half brother, Edward, each of whom had short, tumultuous reigns. With Elizabeth's accession to the throne, England and Wales returned to the fold of the Henrican Reformation, repudiating the efforts of Queen Mary to force them to revert to Roman Catholicism. Because Mary executed Protestant leaders, she went down in history as "Bloody Mary."

At Elizabeth's accession, male contemporaries worried in print whether she would be up to the task of ruling and urged her court and Privy Council to keep her in line. They were in for a shock as Elizabeth proved to be one of the most able monarchs; she did not hesitate to set policy as she saw fit, much to the annoyance of her advisers. Even the earl of Leicester, widely regarded as one of her suitors, said in 1578 that "our conference with her Majesty about affairs is both seldom and slender."

Elizabeth faced the possibility of rebellion led by her Catholic cousin, Mary Queen of Scotland, and in the end Elizabeth saw her executed. Elizabeth's greatest test came in 1588 when the Spanish king, Philip II, sent his Armada to invade England for the purpose of restoring it to Catholicism. Consulting her astrologers but armed for battle, Elizabeth rallied the country, and the English fleet got very lucky. A gale-force wind blew the Spanish ships out of striking distance of the mouth of the Thames River, and, pursued by the faster English ships, the Armada was virtually destroyed. The wind that blew that day became known as "the Protestant wind," and Elizabeth went down in history as "good Queen Bess."

More even than her father, Elizabeth secured England, though not Ireland, for the Protestant cause. She also gave her name to the age, and Elizabethan England flourished culturally. During her reign, William Shakespeare wrote many of his greatest plays and had them performed.

1580 to 1640, a new coal-mining industry developed there through the efforts of entrepreneurs—gentlemen with minor lands who exploited their mineral resources. The wool trade also prospered in Durham. By 1600, social and political tensions had developed. The wool merchants and the entrepreneurial gentry were demanding a greater say in governing the region. They were opposed by the traditional leaders of Durham society: the bishops and the dozen or so aristocratic families with major landholdings and access to the court in London.

This split can be described as one between "court" and "country." In this context, *court* refers to the traditional aristocratic magnates, the church hierarchy, and royal officialdom, and *country* denotes a loose coalition of merchants and rising agricultural and industrial entrepreneurs from the prosperous gentry class, whose economic worth far exceeded their political power. The pattern found in Durham was repeated in other parts of England, generally where industry and commerce grew and prospered. The gentry gained social status and wealth. In the seventeenth century, these social and economic tensions between court and country would help foment revolution.

By the early seventeenth century in England, the descendants of the old feudal aristocracy differed markedly from their Continental counterparts. Isolation from the great wars of the Reformation had produced an aristocracy less militaristic and more ceremonial and commercial in orientation. Furthermore, the lesser ranks of the landowning aristocracy, gentlemen without titles (the gentry), had prospered significantly in Tudor times. In commercial matters, they were often no shrewder than the great landed magnates, but they had in Parliament, as well as in their counties, an effective and institutionalized means of expressing their political interests. The great nobles, in contrast, had largely abandoned

HENRY VIII. Although the ruler of a second-rate power, Henry VIII sought to impress upon his subjects that he was a new and powerful monarch. He sought to compete in style, if not power, with the French and the Spanish kings. (*Walker Art Gallery, Liverpool.*)

the sword as the primary expression of their political authority without putting anything comparable in its place. Gradually, political initiative was slipping away from the great lords and into the hands of a gentry that was commercially and agriculturally innovative as well as fiercely protective of its local base of political power.

Religion played a vital role in this realignment of political interests and forces. Many of the old aristocracy clung to the Anglicanism of the Henrican Reformation, with bishops and liturgy intact, and some even clung to Catholicism. The newly risen gentry found in the Protestant Reformation a form of religious worship more suited to their independent spirit. They felt that it was their right to appoint their own preachers and that the church should reflect local tastes and beliefs rather than doctrines and ceremonies inherited from a discredited Catholicism. In late Tudor times, gentry and merchant interests fused with Puritanism—the English variety of Calvinism—to produce a political-religious vision with ominous potential.

The English Revolutions, 1640–1660 and 1688–1689

The religious and political forces threatening the monarchy were dealt with ineffectively by the first two Stuart kings: James I (1603–1625) and Charles I (1625–1649). Like their Continental counterparts, both believed in royal absolutism. Essentially, what these Stuart kings tried to do in England was what Louis XIV later tried to do in France: establish crown and court administrators as the sole governing bodies within the state. The Stuarts, however, lacked an adequate social and institutional base for absolutism, not least of all a standing army. They did not possess the vast independent wealth of the French kings.

Through the established church, the Stuarts preached the doctrine of the divine right of kings. James I, an effective and shrewd administrator, conducted foreign policy without consulting Parliament. In a speech before Parliament, he stated that "it is sedition in subjects to dispute what a king may do in the height of his power . . . I will not be content that my power be disputed upon."[2]

James I made the standard moves toward creating an absolute monarchy: he centralized and consolidated the power of the government and tried to win over the aristocracy by giving them new offices and titles. He gave royal monopolies to merchants of everything from soap to coal. James I did not have a sufficient economic base to pay for his largesse. His son and successor, Charles I, had the same problem. But he suspended Parliament in 1629 and attempted to rule through his advisers. He had two major goals: to rid the nation of Puritans and to root out the "country" opposition. Charles also tried to collect taxes without the Parliament's consent. These policies ended in disaster; by 1640, the Puritans and the gentry opposition had grown closer together.

The first English Revolution began in 1640 because Charles I needed money to defend the realm against a recent Scottish invasion. Being staunch Calvinists, the Scots had rebelled against Charles's religious policies. Moreover, their clan leaders saw rebellion as a way to get back at the Stuart kings, who long had been a thorn in their side, first when they had been in Edinburgh and now from their base in London. Charles had no alternative but to call Parliament, which could then dictate the terms: no concessions from Charles, then no taxes to fight the Scots, who were also demanding money for every day they occupied the northern territory. Parliament countered the king's requests with demands for rights: consultations with Parliament in matters of taxation, trial by jury, habeas corpus, and a truly Protestant church responsive to the beliefs and interests of its laity. Charles refused these demands, viewing them as an assault on royal authority. He even tried to arrest the leaders of Parliament. In 1642, civil war began. Directed by Parliament and financed by taxes and the merchants, the war was fought by the New Model Army led by Oliver Cromwell (1599–1658), a Puritan squire with a gift for military leadership.

The two English Revolutions need to be seen as part of a constitutional crisis that lasted two generations. The crisis began in 1640, degenerated into civil war in 1642, and culminated in regicide in 1649. After the restoration of monarchy in 1660, the crisis flared up again in 1679–81 and was finally resolved by the Revolution of 1688–89—sometimes called the Glorious Revolution. The crisis affected England, Scotland, Ireland, and Wales differently, but in all cases led to the consolidation of English power over these territories. Perhaps the native Irish fared worst of all as Cromwell drove thousands to the western, barren part of the island.

The civil war of the 1640s generated a new type of military organization. The New Model Army was financed by Parliament's rich supporters and led by gentlemen farmers. Its ranks were filled by religious zealots, along with the usual cross section of poor artisans and day laborers. This citizen army defeated the king, his aristocratic followers, and the Anglican church's hierarchy.

In January 1649, Charles I was publicly executed by order of Parliament. During the interregnum (time between kings) of the next eleven years, Parliament joined with the army to govern the country as a republic. In the distribution of power between the army and the Parliament, Cromwell proved to be a key element. He had the support of the army's officers and some of its rank and file, and he had been a member of Parliament for many years. However, he gained control over the army only after it was purged of radical groups. Some of these radicals wanted to level society, that is, to redistribute property by ending monopolies and to give the vote to all male citizens. In the context of the 1650s, Cromwell was a moderate republican who also believed in limited religious toleration for Protestants, yet history has painted him, somewhat unjustly, as a military dictator.

Both English Revolutions were led by a loose coalition of urban merchants and landed gentry imbued with the strict Protestantism of the Continental Reformation. In the 1650s, their success was jeopardized by growing discontent from the poor, who made up the rank and file of the army and demanded that their economic and social grievances be rectified. The radicals of the first English Revolution—men like Gerrard Winstanley, the first theoretician of social democracy in modern times, and John Lilburne, the Leveller—demanded redistribution of property, even communal property; voting rights for the majority of the male population; and abolition of religious and intellectual elites, whose power and ideology supported the interests of the ruling classes. The radicals rejected Anglicanism, moderate Puritanism, and even, in a few cases, the lifestyle of the middle class; they opted instead for radical politics and free lifestyles. They spurned marriage, and the Quakers even allowed women to preach. The radicals terrified devoted Puritans such as Cromwell. By 1660, two years after Cromwell's death, the country was adrift, without effective leadership.

Parliament, having secured the economic interests of its constituency (gentry, merchants, and some small landowners), chose to restore court and crown and invited the exiled son of the executed king to return to the kingship. Having learned the lesson his father had spurned, Charles II (1660–1685) never instituted royal absolutism, although he did try to minimize Parliament's role in the government. His court was a far more open institution than his father's had been, for Charles II feared a similar death.

Charles's brother James II (1685–1688), however, was a foolishly fearless Catholic and admirer of French absolutism. Having gathered at his court a coterie of Catholic advisers (among them Jesuits) and supporters of royal prerogative, James attempted to bend Parliament and local government to the royal will. James's Catholicism was the crucial element in his failure. The Anglican church would not back him, and political forces similar to those that had gathered against his father, Charles I, in 1640 descended on him. The ruling elites, however, had learned their lesson back in the 1650s: civil war would produce social discontent among the masses. The upper classes wanted to avoid open warfare and preserve the monarchy as a constitutional authority but not as an absolute one. Puritanism, with its sectarian fervor and its dangerous association with republicanism, was allowed to play no part in the second English Revolution.

In early 1688, Anglicans, some aristocrats, and opponents of royal prerogative (members of the Whig party, along with a few Tories) formed a conspiracy against James II. Their purpose was to invite his son-in-law, William of Orange, stadholder (head) of the Netherlands and husband of James's Protestant daughter Mary, to invade England and rescue its government from James's control. The final outcome of this invasion was determined by William and his conspirators, in conjunction with a freely elected Parliament. This dangerous plan succeeded for three main reasons: William and the Dutch desperately needed English support against the threat of a French invasion; James had lost the loyalty of key men in the army, powerful gentlemen in the counties, and the Anglican church; and the political elite was committed and united in its intentions. William and Mary were declared king and queen by act of Parliament, and William defeated James II's army in Ireland. The last revolution in English history defeated royal absolutism forever. Ironically, while political freedom increased in England, Scotland soon lost its parliament, and Catholics in Ireland were systematically repressed.

This bloodless revolution—the Glorious Revolution—created a new political and constitutional reality. Parliament gained the rights to assemble regularly and to vote on all matters of taxation; the rights of habeas corpus and trial by jury (for men of property and social status) were also secured. These rights were in turn legitimated in a constitutionally binding document, the Bill of Rights (1689). All Protestants, regardless of their sectarian bias, were granted toleration.

The Revolution Settlement of 1688–89 resolved the profound constitutional and social tensions of the seventeenth century and laid the foundations of the English government that exists today. The year 1688 saw the creation of a new public and political order that would become the envy of enlightened reformers. The Glorious Revolution, says the historian J. H. Plumb, established "the authority of certain men of property, particularly those of high social standing, either aristocrats or linked with aristocracy, whose tap root was in land but whose side roots reached out to commerce, industry and finance."[3] Throughout the eighteenth century, England was ruled by kings and Parliaments that represented the interests of an oligarchy, whose cohesiveness and prosperity ensured social and political stability.

The English Revolutions in the end established English parliamentary government and the rule of law; they also provided a degree of freedom for the propertied. In retrospect, we can see that absolutism according to the French model probably never had a chance in England. It had too many gentlemen who possessed enough land to be independent of the crown, yet not so much that they could control whole sections of the kingdom. In addition, monarchs had no effective standing army. But to contemporaries, the issues seemed different: English opponents of absolutism spoke of their rights as granted by their ancient constitution and the feudal law, of the need to make the English church truly Protestant, and, among the radicals, of the right of lesser men to establish their property. These opponents possessed an institution—Parliament—through which they could express their grievances. Eventually, they also acquired an army, which waged war to protect property and commercial rights. In 1689, the propertied classes invented limited monarchy and a constitutional system based on laws made by

Parliament and sanctioned by the king. Very gradually, the monarchical element in that system would yield to the power and authority of parliamentary ministers and state officials.

In the nineteenth and twentieth centuries, parliamentary institutions would be gradually and peacefully reformed to express a more democratic social reality. The events of 1688–89 have rightly been described as "the year one," for they fashioned a system of government that operated effectively in Britain and could also be adopted elsewhere with modification. The British system became a model for other forms of representative government, adopted in France and in the former British colonies, beginning with the United States. It was the model that offered a viable alternative to absolutism.

Oliver Cromwell. Cromwell wore the simple black of the Puritan gentry and sought to portray himself as a pious warrior. Yet in this portrait he does have a somewhat regal bearing, and his task demanded that he act like a king without ever becoming one. (*AKG, London.*)

The Netherlands: A Bourgeois Republic

One other area in Europe developed a system of representative government that also survived for centuries. The Netherlands (the Low Countries, that is, the seven Dutch provinces and Belgium) had been part of Hapsburg territory since the fifteenth century. When Charles V ascended the Spanish throne in 1516, the Netherlands became an economic linchpin of the Spanish empire. Spain exported wool and bullion to the Low Countries in return for manufactured textiles, hardware, grain, and naval stores. Flanders, with Antwerp as its capital, was the manufacturing and banking center of the Spanish empire.

To the north, cities like Rotterdam and Amsterdam built and outfitted the Spanish fleet. In The Hague, printers published the Bible in Spanish and in Dutch or Flemish (actually the same language). But in the north, too, Protestantism made significant inroads.

During the reign of Charles V's successor, Philip II, a tightly organized Calvinist minority, with its popular base in the cities and its military strategy founded on sea raids, at first harassed and then aggressively challenged Spanish power. In the 1560s, the Spanish responded by trying to export the Inquisition into the Netherlands and sending an enormous standing army there under the duke of Alva. It was a classic example of overkill; thousands of once-loyal Flemish and Dutch subjects turned against the Spanish crown. The people either converted secretly to Calvinism or aided the revolutionaries. Led by William the Silent (1533–1584), head of the Orange dynasty, the seven northern provinces (Holland, Zeeland, Utrecht, Gelderland, Overijssel, Friesland, and Groningen) joined in the Union of Utrecht (1579) to protect themselves against Spanish aggression. Their determined resistance, coupled with the serious economic weaknesses of the overextended Spanish empire, eventually produced unexpected success for the northern colonies.

By 1609, the seven northern provinces were effectively free of Spanish control and loosely tied together under a republican form of government.

Seventeenth-century Netherlands (that is, the Dutch Republic) became a prosperous bourgeois state. Rich from the fruits of manufacture and trade in everything from tulip bulbs to ships—and, not least, slaves—Dutch merchants ruled their cities and provinces with a fierce pride. By the early seventeenth century, this new nation of only 1.2 million people was practicing the most innovative commercial and financial techniques in Europe.

In this fascinating instance, capitalism and Protestantism fused to do the work of princes; the Dutch state emerged without absolute monarchy, and indeed in opposition to it. From that experience, the ruling Dutch oligarchy retained a deep distrust of hereditary monarchy and of central government. The exact position of the House of Orange remained a vexing constitutional question until well into the eighteenth century. The oligarchs and their party, the Patriots, favored a republic without a single head, ruled by them locally and in the Estates General meeting in The Hague. The Calvinist clergy, old aristocrats, and a vast section of the populace—all for very different reasons—wanted the head of the House of Orange to govern as stadholder of the provinces—in effect, as a limited monarch in a republican state. These unresolved political tensions between the center and the localities prevented the Netherlands from developing a form of republican government to rival the stability of the British system of limited monarchy. The Dutch achievement came in other areas.

Calvinism had provided the ideology of revolution and national identity. Capital, in turn, created a unique cultural milieu in the Dutch urban centers of Amsterdam, Rotterdam, Utrecht, and The Hague. Wide toleration without a centralized system of censorship made the Dutch book trade, which often disseminated works by refugees from the Spanish Inquisition and later by French Protestants, the most vital in Europe right up to the French Revolution. And the sights and sounds of an active and prosperous population, coupled with a politically engaged and rich bourgeoisie, fed the imagination, as well as the purses, of various artistic schools. Rembrandt van Rijn, Jan Steen, Frans Hals, Jan Vermeer, and Jan van del Velde are at the top of a long list of great Dutch artists—many of them also refugees. They left timeless images portraying the people of the only republican national state to endure throughout the seventeenth century.

The Holy Roman Empire: The Failure to Unify Germany

In contrast to the English, French, Spanish, and Dutch experiences in the early modern period, the Germans failed to achieve national unity. The German failure to unify is tied to the history of the Holy Roman Empire. That union of various central European territories was created in the tenth century, when Otto I, in a deliberate attempt to revive Charlemagne's empire, was crowned "Emperor of the Romans" by the pope. Later, the title was changed to "Holy Roman Emperor." The empire consisted of mostly German-speaking principalities.

Otto and his medieval successors busied themselves not with administering their territories but with attempting to gain control over the rich Italian peninsula and dealing with the challenges presented by powerful popes. Meanwhile, the German nobility extended and consolidated their rule over their peasants and over various towns and cities within the empire. Their aristocratic power remained a constant obstacle to German unity. Only by incorporating the nobility into the fabric of the state's power, court, and army and by sanctioning their oppressive control of the peasants would Holy Roman Emperors manage to create a unified German state.

In the medieval and early modern periods, the Holy Roman Emperors depended on powerful noble lords—including archbishops and bishops—for support, because the office of emperor was elective, not hereditary. German noble princes—including the archbishops of Cologne and Mainz, the Hohenzollern ruler of Brandenburg, and the duke of Saxony, who were electors responsible for choosing the Holy Roman Emperor—were fiercely independent. All belonged to the empire yet regarded themselves as autonomous powers. These decentralizing tendencies were highly developed by the thirteenth century, and the emperors gradually realized that they were losing control of the outer frontiers of the empire. The French had conducted a successful military incursion into northern Italy and on the western frontier of the empire. Hungary had fallen to the Turks, and the Swiss were hard to govern (besides, given their terrain, they were impossible to beat into submission). At the same time, Hapsburg princes maneuvered themselves into a position from which they could monopolize the imperial elections.

The Holy Roman Empire in the reigns of the Hapsburg emperors Maximilian I (1493–1519) and Charles V (1519–1556) might have achieved a degree of cohesion comparable with that in France and Spain. Certainly, the impetus of war—against France and against the Turks—required the creation of a large standing army and the taxation to maintain it. Both could have worked to the benefit of a centralized, imperial power. But the Protestant Reformation, which began in 1517, meshed with already well-developed tendencies toward local independence and destroyed the last hope of Hapsburg domination and German unity. The German nobility were all too ready to use the Reformation as a vindication of their local power, and indeed Martin Luther made just such an appeal to their interests.

At precisely the moment in the 1520s when Charles V had to act with great determination to stop the spread of Lutheranism, he was at war with France over its claims to Italian territory. Charles had no sooner won his Italian territories, in particular the rich city-state of Milan, when he had to make war against the Turks, who in 1529 besieged Vienna. Not until the 1540s was Charles V in a position to attack the Lutheran princes. By then, they had had considerable time to solidify their position and had united for mutual protection in the Schmalkaldic League.

War raged in Germany between the Protestant princes and the imperial army led by Charles V. In 1551, Catholic France entered the war on the Protestant side, and Charles had to flee for his life. Defeated, Charles abdicated and retired to a Spanish monastery. The Treaty of Augsburg (1555) gave every German prince the right to determine the religion of his subjects. The princes had won their local territories, and a unified German state was never constructed by the Hapsburgs.

When Emperor Charles V abdicated in 1556, he divided his kingdom between his son Philip and his brother Ferdinand. Philip inherited Spain and its colonies, as well as the Netherlands. Ferdinand acquired the Austrian territories. The Spanish and Austrian branches of the Hapsburg family were thus created, and well into the late seventeenth century they defined their interests in common and often waged war accordingly. The enormous international power of the Hapsburgs was checked only by their uncertain authority over the German states within the Holy Roman Empire. Throughout the sixteenth century, the Austrian Hapsburgs barely managed to control these sprawling and deeply divided German territories. Protestantism, as protected by the Treaty of Augsburg, and the particularism and provinciality of the German nobility continued to prevent the creation of a German state.

The Austrian Hapsburg emperors, however, never missed an opportunity to further the cause of the Counter Reformation and to court the favor of local interests opposed to the nobility. No Hapsburg was ever more fervid in that regard than the Jesuit-trained Archduke Ferdinand II, who ascended the throne of the Holy Roman Empire in Vienna in 1619. He immediately embarked on a policy of Catholic revival and used Spanish officials as his administrators. His policies provoked within the empire a war that engulfed the whole of Europe.

The Thirty Years' War (1618–1648) began when the Bohemians, whose anti-Catholic tendencies can be traced back to the Hussite reformers of the early fifteenth century, attempted to put a Protestant king on their throne. The Austrian and Spanish Hapsburgs reacted by sending an army into the kingdom of Bohemia, and suddenly the whole empire was forced to take sides along religious lines. The Bohemian nobility, after centuries of enforcing serfdom, failed to rally the rural masses behind them, and victory went to the emperor. Bohemia and the German states suffered almost unimaginable devastation; ravaging Hapsburg armies sacked and burned three-fourths of each kingdom's towns and practically exterminated its aristocracy.

Until the 1630s, it looked as if the Hapsburgs would be able to use the war to enhance their power and promote centralization. But the intervention of Lutheran Sweden, led by Gustavus Adolphus and encouraged by France, wrecked Hapsburg ambitions. The ensuing military conflict devastated vast areas of northern and central Europe. The civilian population suffered untold hardships: soldiers raped women and pillaged the land, and thousands of refugees took to the roads and forests. Partly because the French finally intervened directly, the Spanish Hapsburgs emerged from the Thirty Years' War with no benefits. At the Treaty of Westphalia (1648), their Austrian cousins reaffirmed their right to govern the eastern states of the kingdom, with Vienna as their capital. Austria took shape as a dynastic state, and the German territories in the empire remained fragmented by the independent interests of their largely recalcitrant feudal nobility. In consequence, the Thirty Years' War shaped the course of German history into the nineteenth century.

The Emergence of Austria and Prussia

Austria

As a result of the settlement at Westphalia, the Austrian Hapsburgs gained firm control over most of Hungary and Bohemia, where they installed a virtually new and foreign nobility. At the same time, they strengthened their grip on Vienna. In one of the few spectacular successes achieved by the Counter Reformation, the ruling elites in all three territories were forcibly, or in many cases willingly, converted back to Catholicism. At long last, religious predominance could be used as a force—long delayed in eastern Europe because of the Protestant Reformation—for the creation of the Austrian dynastic state.

One severe obstacle to territorial hegemony remained: the military threat posed by the Turks, who sought to control much of Hungary. During the reign of the Austrian emperor Leopold I (1658–1705), warfare against the Ottoman Empire—a recurrent theme in Hapsburg history beginning with Charles V—once again erupted, and in 1683 the Turks again besieged Vienna. However, the Ottoman Empire lacked its former strength and cohesiveness. A Catholic and unified Austrian army, composed of a variety of peoples and assisted by the Poles, managed to defeat the Turks and recapture the whole of Hungary and Transylvania and part of Croatia. Austria's right to govern these lands was firmly accepted by the Turks at the Treaty of Karlowitz (1699).

The Austrian Hapsburgs and their victorious army had entered the larger arena of European power politics. In 1700, at the death of the last Spanish Hapsburg, Leopold I sought to place his second son, Archduke Charles, on the Spanish throne. But this attempt brought Leopold into a violent clash with Louis XIV. Once again, Bourbon and Hapsburg rivalry, a dominant theme in early modern history, provoked a major European war.

In the War of the Spanish Succession (1702–1714), the Austrians, with their army led by the brilliant Prince Eugene of Savoy, joined forces with the English and the Dutch. This war brought rewards in western Europe to the Austrian Hapsburgs: they acquired the Spanish Netherlands (Belgium today), as well as Milan and small holdings in Italy. But the Hapsburgs did not succeed in capturing the Spanish throne.

Up to the early eighteenth century, the Austrian Hapsburgs had struggled to achieve territorial hegemony and to subdue the dissident religious groups (Protestants and Turkish Muslims) that in very different ways threatened to undermine their authority. Warfare and the maintenance of a standing army had taken precedence over administrative reform and commercial growth. Military victory created the conditions within which centralization could occur.

The Austrian achievement of the eighteenth century, which made Austria a major force in European affairs, stemmed from the administrative reforms and cultural revival initiated by Charles VI (assisted militarily by Eugene of Savoy) and continued by his successors, Maria Theresa and Joseph II. These eighteenth-century monarchs embraced a style of government sometimes described as *enlightened*. Through education and liberal policies, they sought to catch up with the more established and older dynastic states of Europe, and in the process they created what has come to be known as *enlightened despotism*.

Prussia

By the late seventeenth century in northern Europe, a cohesive state governed by an absolute monarch emerged first in Prussia. Serfdom had largely disappeared in western Europe by the late sixteenth century, although it remained in parts of central and eastern Europe. No longer free to play at war or to control the lives of their peasants, progressive German aristocrats improved their agricultural systems or sought offices and military commands in the service of the absolutist state.

Prussia was different. It was a state within the Holy Roman Empire, and its territorial ambitions could be checked by the other princely states or the empire. Although Prussia developed an absolute monarchy like France, its powerful aristocracy acquiesced to monarchical power only in exchange for guarantees of their feudal power over the peasantry. In 1653, the Prussian nobility granted the Hohenzollern ruler of Prussia power to collect taxes for the maintenance of a strong army, but only after he issued decrees rendering serfdom permanent.

The Hohenzollerns, the ruling dynasty of Prussia, had had a most inauspicious beginning in the later Middle Ages. These rulers were little more than dukes in the Holy Roman Empire until 1415, when Holy Roman Emperor Sigismund made one of them an imperial elector with the right to choose imperial successors. For centuries, the Hohenzollerns had made weak claims to territory in northern Germany. They finally achieved control over Prussia and certain other smaller principalities by claiming the inheritance of one wife (1608) and by single-minded, ruthless aggression.

The most aggressive of these Hohenzollerns was the elector Frederick William (1640–1688), who played a key role in forging the new Prussian state. Frederick William inherited the territories of the beleaguered Hohenzollern dynasty, whose main holding, Brandenburg in Prussia, was very poor in natural resources. Indeed, Prussia barely survived the devastation wreaked by the Thirty Years' War, especially the Swedish army's occupation of the electorate.

Distaste for foreign intervention in Prussia, and for the accompanying humiliation and excessive taxes, prompted the Junker class (the landed Prussian nobility) to support national unity and strong central government. But they would brook no threat to their economic control of their lands and peasants. By 1672, the Prussian army, led by Junker officers, was strong enough to enter the Franco-Dutch War on the Dutch side. The war brought no territorial gains but allowed the elector to raise taxes. Once again, the pattern of foreign war, taxes, and military conscription led to an increase in the power of the central government. But in Prussia, in contrast to lands to the west, the bureaucracy was entirely military. No clerics or rich bourgeois shared power with the Junkers. The pattern initiated by the Great Elector (Frederick William) would be continued in the reigns of his successors: Frederick I (d. 1713), Frederick William I, and Frederick the Great.

The alliance between the aristocracy and the monarchy was especially strengthened in the reign of Frederick William I (1713–1740). In the older dynastic states, absolute monarchs tried to dispense with representative institutions once the monarchy had grown strong enough. So, too,

MARIA THERESA AND JOSEPH. By the middle of the eighteenth century the nuclear family was being valorized even among the monarchs of Europe. Here Maria Theresa and Joseph pose with their family. (*Château de Versailles, Versailles, France/Reunion des Musees Nationaux/Art Resource, NY.*)

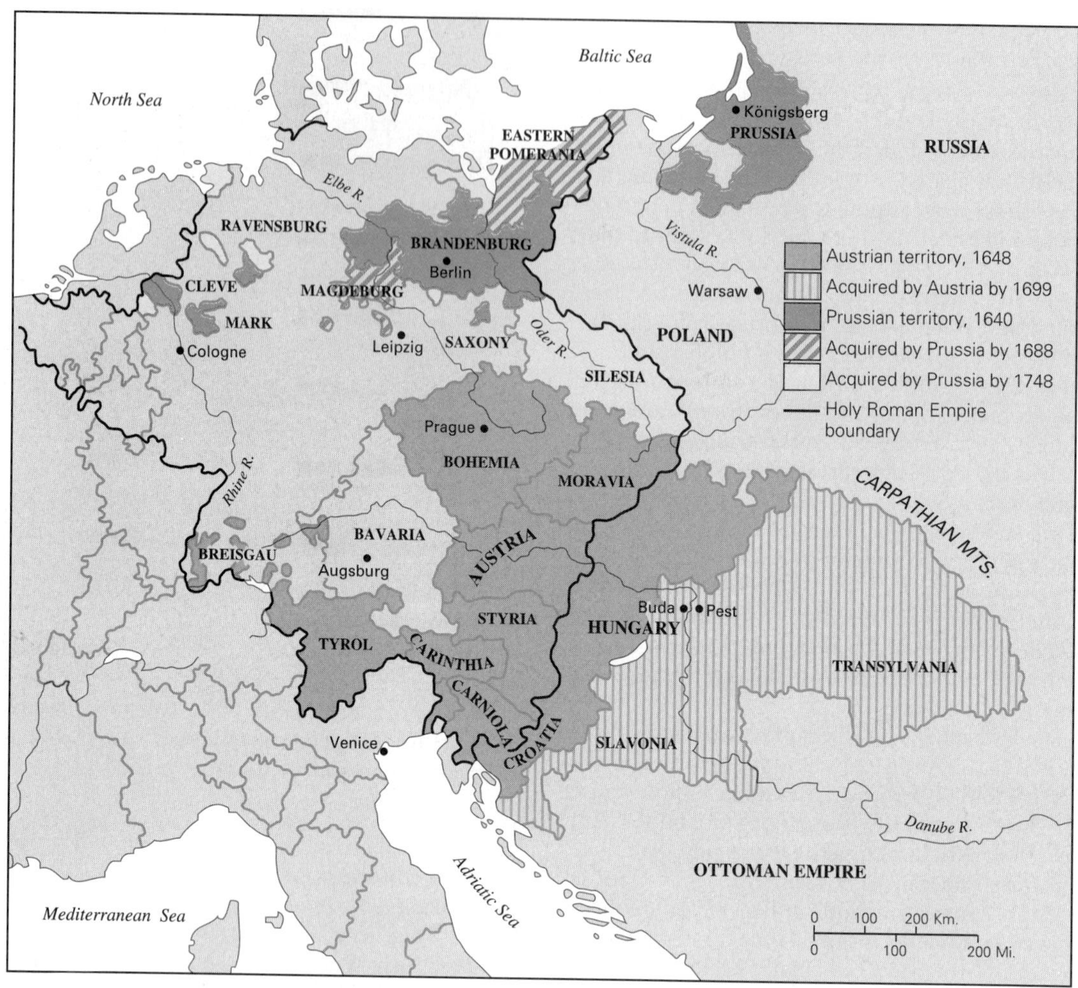

Map 16.3 **The Growth of Austria and Brandenburg-Prussia, c. 1650–1750** The process laid the foundation for modern Germany and also for tension between Christianity and Islam.

did Frederick William finally undercut the Prussian provincial assemblies, the *Landtage,* which still had some power over taxation and army recruitment. He was able to do so only by bringing the landowning Junker class into the government—especially into the army—and by keeping the tax-paying peasants in the status of serfs.

Since representative institutions in twentieth-century Germany struggled, often unsuccessfully, for survival, it is interesting to note that in early-eighteenth-century Prussia such institutions did exercise considerable influence. Like the Austrian monarchy the Prussians embarked on a program of reforms, consolidation, and improvements, sometimes described as enlightened. But always at the heart of the Prussian state stood a military elite with little interest in reform.

Russia

Although remote from developments in western Europe, Russia in the early modern period took on some characteristics remarkably similar to those of western European states. It relied on absolute monarchy reinforced by a feudal aristocracy. As in Europe, the power of the aristocracy to wreak havoc had to be checked and its energies channeled into the state's service. But the Russian pattern of absolutism broke with the Western model and resembled that adopted in Prussia, where serfdom increased as the power of centralized monarchy grew. The award of peasants was the bribe by which the monarchy secured aristocrats' cooperation in the state's growth.

Russian absolutism experienced a false start under Ivan IV, the Terrible (1547–1584). Late in the sixteenth century, Ivan sought to impose a tsarist autocracy. He waged a futile war against Sweden and created an internal police force, which he entrusted with the administration of central Russia. His failure in war and an irrational policy of repression (fueled in part by his mental instability) doomed his attempt to impose absolutism. Much of Ivan's state building was undone with his death, which launched the Time of Troubles: a period of foreign invasion and civil warfare that endured for years.

Order was restored in 1613, when the Romanovs gained the support of the aristocracy. The accession of Michael Romanov as tsar marks the beginning of the Romanov dynasty and the emergence of a unified Russian state. Of that dynasty, by far the most important ruler was Peter the Great (1682–1725). He ruthlessly suppressed the independent aristocrats while inventing new titles and ranks for his supporters. The army was reformed in accordance with military standards in western Europe. The peasants were made the personal property of their lords. From 1700 to 1707, taxes on the peasants multiplied five times over. Predictably, the money went toward the creation of a professional army along European lines and toward making war. The preparation led this time to victory over the Swedes. Finally, Peter brought the Russian Orthodox church under the control of the state by establishing a new office, called the Holy Synod; its head was a government official.

Peter managed to wed the aristocracy to the absolutist state, and the union was so successful that strong Russian monarchs in the eighteenth century, like Catherine the Great, could embrace enlightened reforms without jeopardizing the stability of their regimes. Once again, repression and violence in the form of taxation, serfdom, and war led to the creation of a dynastic state—one that proved least susceptible to reform and was eventually dismantled in 1917 by the Russian Revolution.

PETER THE GREAT. Peter the Great looked westward and outward and sought to modernize Russia. (*Rijksmuseum-Stichting, Amsterdam.*)

THE STATE AND MODERN POLITICAL DEVELOPMENT

By the early seventeenth century, Europeans had developed the concept of the *state:* an active political entity to which its subjects owed duties and obligations. That concept became the foundation of the modern science of politics. The one essential ingredient of the Western concept of the state, as it emerged in the early modern period, was the notion of *sovereignty:* the view that the state was supreme within its borders and other institutions and organizations—by implication even the church—were allowed to exist only if they recognized the state's authority. The art of government thus entailed molding the ambitions and strength of the powerful into service to the state. The state, its power growing through war and taxation, became the basic unit of political authority in the West.

Interestingly, the concept of human liberty,

now so basic to Western thought, was not articulated first in the sovereign states of Europe. Rather, the idea was largely an Italian creation, discussed with great vehemence by Italian theorists of the later Middle Ages and the Renaissance. These humanists lived and wrote in the independent city-states, and they often aimed their treatises against the encroachments of the Holy Roman Emperor—in short, against princes and their search for absolute power. In the sixteenth and seventeenth centuries, the idea of liberty was rarely discussed and was generally found only in the writings of Calvinist opponents of absolutism. Not until the mid-seventeenth century in England did a body of political thought emerge that argued that human liberty can be ensured within the confines of a powerful national state: one governed by mere mortals and not by divinely sanctioned and absolute kings. In general, despite the English and Dutch developments, absolutism in its varied forms (Spanish, French, Prussian) dominated the political development of early modern Europe.

Although first articulated in the Italian republics and then enacted briefly in England and more durably in the Netherlands, the republican ideal did not gain acceptance as a viable alternative to absolutism until the European Enlightenment of the eighteenth century. At the heart of that ideal lay the notion that the state serves the interests of those who support and create it. In the democratic and republican revolutions of the late eighteenth century, western Europeans and Americans repudiated monarchical systems of government in response to the republican ideal. By then, princes and the aristocratic and military elites had outlived their usefulness in many parts of Europe. The states they had created, mostly to further their own interests, had become larger than their creators. Eventually, the national states of western Europe, as well as of the Americas, proved able to survive and prosper without kings or aristocrats, though they retained the administrative and military mechanisms so skillfully and relentlessly developed by early modern kings and their court officials.

By the eighteenth century, the state, not the locality, had become the focal point of Western political life. Peace depended on the art of balancing the powers of the various European states so that no single state could expect to win domination, or *hegemony,* over all the others. Whenever a European state believed that it could dominate, war resulted. In early modern times, first the Spanish under Charles V and Philip II and then the French under Louis XIV sought, and for a brief time achieved, hegemony over European politics. Ultimately, however, these great states faltered because of the internal pressures that war making created. Nonetheless, the belief persisted, until 1945, that one state could dominate Western affairs. In the twentieth century, that belief produced not simply war but world war. By then, the power of Western states had overtaken vast areas of the world, and the ability to impose a balance of power became a matter of world survival.

❖ ❖ ❖

Notes

1. William Doyle, *The Ancien Régime* (Atlantic Highlands, N.J.: Humanities Press, 1988), p. 19.
2. Quoted from *True Law of Free Monarchies,* excerpted in Marvin Perry et al., *Sources of the Western Tradition* (Boston: Houghton Mifflin, 1999), pp. 358–359.
3. J. H. Plumb, *The Growth of Political Stability in England: 1675–1725* (London: Macmillan, 1967), p. 69.

Suggested Reading

Braudel, F., *The Mediterranean and the Mediterranean World in the Age of Philip II* (1973). One of the most important and beautifully written books ever done on early modern social and political development.

Brenner, Robert, *Merchants and Revolution. Commercial Change, Political Conflict, and London's Overseas Traders, 1550–1653* (1993). Lays to rest the notion that the English civil wars were just a contest between a stubborn king and his subjects who were religious fanatics.

Burke, Peter, *The Fabrication of Louis XIV* (1992). A good antidote for those who think that Madison Avenue invented advertising and image building.

Doyle, William, *The Ancien Régime* (1988). An excellent, short survey that also reviews how historians have understood absolutism.

Elliott, J. H., *Imperial Spain, 1469–1716* (1963). Now a classic and the best account available of early modern Spain.

Hill, Christopher, *The English Bible and the Seventeenth-Century Revolution* (1993). Gives insight into the values and beliefs of a people who could execute their king.

Jacob, Margaret C., and W. W. Mijnhardt, eds., *The Dutch Republic in the Eighteenth Century: Decline, Enlightenment, and Revolution* (1992). Essays survey Dutch history but also look at the republic in decline.

Kennedy, Paul, *The Rise and Fall of the Great Powers: Economic Change and Military Conflict, 1550 to 2000* (1987). A courageous book that seeks to assess early modern militarism in relation to recent American history.

Koenigsberger, H. G., *Monarchies, States, Generals and Parliaments* (2001). An excellent survey of the Dutch scene by a master historian.

Smith, Lacey Baldwin, *This Realm of England, 1399–1688,* rev. ed. (1983). A good, readable survey.

Sturdy, John, *Fractured Europe, 1600–1721* (2002). A very readable survey.

For sources on the Internet, see
http://library.byu.edu/~rdh/eurodocs/
An excellent collection of primary source materials for European political history.

http://www.idbus.edu/courses/hy101/english/01
Articles on the English civil war.

Review Questions

1. What role did the aristocracy play in the formation of the European states?
2. In what ways did early modern kings increase their power, and what relationship did they have to the commercial bourgeoisie in their countries?
3. What is meant by *raison d'état* and by *divine right of kings*?
4. What role did religion and national churches play in creating or dismembering the state?
5. Discuss the strengths and weaknesses of the Spanish state.
6. Why did England move in the direction of parliamentary government while most countries on the Continent embraced absolutism? Indicate the main factors.
7. What made the Dutch state so different from its neighbors? Describe the differences. Are we justified in calling it "bourgeois"?
8. What made the Prussian, Russian, and Austrian experiences of statehood roughly comparable?
9. Discuss the differences between the treatment of the peasants in eastern and western Europe.
10. Government has sometimes been described as being, in the final analysis, organized violence. Is that an appropriate description of early modern European governments?

Chapter 17

The Scientific Revolution: The Mechanical Universe

When Galileo looked through his telescope he saw shadows. But shadows meant depth and contour and that meant real, solid matter. The notion that the planets were ethereal globes of light gave way to their being just matter like the earth. (The Granger Collection.)

- **Medieval Cosmology**
- **A New View of Nature**
  Renaissance Neo-Platonism
  Magic and the Search for Nature
  The Copernican Revolution
  The Laws of Planetary Motion: Tycho and Kepler
  Galileo: Experimental Physics
- **The Newtonian Synthesis: Experiment, Mathematics, and Theory**
- **Biology, Medicine, and Chemistry**
- **Bacon and Descartes: Prophets of the New Science**
  Bacon
  Descartes
- **Social Implications of the Scientific Revolution**
- **The Meaning of the Scientific Revolution**

In the fifteenth century, the cohesive medieval view of the world began to disintegrate. By the late seventeenth century, educated Europeans no longer believed in it. Thus, the collapse of medieval institutions such as feudalism and serfdom had an intellectual parallel. The Renaissance and the Reformation aided the collapse, but no movement was as important in shaping the modern world-view as the Scientific Revolution of the seventeenth century. It made physical nature a valid object for experimental inquiry and mathematical calculation. For the new science to arise, a philosophical break with the medieval conception of nature had to occur. The medieval approach to nature sought to explain nature's appearances. To the naked eye, the earth seems to be in the center of our universe. Medieval philosophy explained how and why the earth was in the center; how and why heavy bodies fell toward it and light ones rose away from it. The philosophical revolution of the seventeenth century demolished such explanations. At the heart of the Scientific Revolution was the assumption that appearances could lie, that truth lay in conceptualizing the universe as an abstract entity: as matter in motion, as geometrical shapes, and as weight and number.

The Scientific Revolution brought a new, mechanical conception of nature that enabled westerners to discover and explain the laws of nature mathematically. They came to see nature as composed solely of matter, whose motion, occurring in space and measurable by time, is governed by the push and pull of bodies and by laws of force. This philosophically elegant construction rendered the physical world knowable and even possibly manageable. It also contributed decisively to the formulation of applied mechanics.

The Scientific Revolution rested on a new, replicable methodology. Because of successful experiments performed by scientists and natural philosophers such as Galileo Galilei, William Harvey, Robert Boyle, and Isaac Newton, Western science acquired its still-characteristic methods of observation, experimentation, and replication. By the late seventeenth century, no one could entertain a serious interest in the physical order without actually doing—and recording—experiments or without observing, in a rigorous and systematic way, the behavior of physical phenomena. The scientific method was now seen as an avenue to truth.

The mechanical concept of nature, coupled with a rigorous methodology, gave modern scientists the means to unlock and explain nature's secrets.

Mathematics increasingly became the language of the new science. For centuries, Europeans had used first geometry and then algebra to explain certain physical phenomena. With the Scientific Revolution came a new mathematics, the infinitesimal calculus. Even more important, philosophers became increasingly convinced that all nature—physical objects, as well as invisible forces—could be expressed mathematically. By the late seventeenth century, even geometry had become so complex that a gifted philosopher like John Locke (1632–1704), a friend and contemporary of Isaac Newton, could not understand the sophisticated mathematics used by Newton in the *Principia*. A new scientific culture had been born. During the eighteenth-century Enlightenment (Chapter 18), it provided the model for progress in the natural sciences and in the human sciences that were to imitate them.

Medieval Cosmology

The unique character of the modern scientific outlook is most easily grasped through contrast with the medieval understanding of the natural world and its physical properties. That understanding rested on a blend of Christian thought with theories derived from ancient Greek writers, such as Aristotle and Ptolemy.

Aristotle (384–322 B.C.) had argued simply that it was in the nature of things to move in certain ways. A stone falls because it is absolutely heavy; fire rises because it is absolutely light. Weight is an absolute property of a physical thing; therefore, motion results from the properties of bodies, and not from the forces that impinge on them. It follows (logically but incorrectly) that if the medium through which a body falls is taken as a constant, then the speed of its fall could be doubled if its weight were doubled. Only rigorous experimentation could refute this erroneous concept of motion; it was many centuries before such experimentation was undertaken.

Aristotle's physics fitted neatly into his *cosmology*, or world picture. The earth, being the heaviest object, lay stationary and suspended at the center of the universe. The sun, planets, and moon revolved in circles around the earth. Aristotle presumed that since the planets were round themselves, always in motion, and seemingly never altered, the most "natural" movement for them should be circular, for it is perfect motion.

Aristotle's physics and cosmology were unified. He could put the earth at the center of the universe and make it stationary because he presumed its absolute heaviness; all other heavy bodies that he had observed fall toward it. He presumed that the planets were made of a fine, luminous ether and held in their circular orbits by luminous spheres, or "tracks." These spheres possessed a certain reality, though invisible to human beings, and hence they came to be known as the crystalline spheres.

Aristotle believed that everything in motion had been moved by another object that was itself in motion—a continuing chain of movers and moved. By inference, this belief led back to some object or being that began the motion. Christian philosophers of the Middle Ages argued that Aristotle's Unmoved Mover must be the God of Christianity. For Aristotle, who had no conception of a personal God or an afterlife of rewards or punishments and who believed that the universe was eternal rather than created at a specific point in time, such an identification would have been meaningless.

Although Aristotle's cosmology never gained the status of orthodoxy among the ancient Greeks, by the second century A.D. in Alexandria, Greek astronomy became codified and then rigid. Ptolemy of Alexandria produced the *Almagest* (A.D. 150), a handbook of Greek astronomy based on the theories of Aristotle. The crucial assumption in the *Almagest* was that a motionless earth stood at the center of the universe (although some Greeks had disputed the notion) and that the planets moved about it in a series of circular orbits, interrupted by smaller circular orbits, called epicycles. The epicycles explained why at certain times a planet was visibly closer to the earth. As Ptolemy put it, if the earth moved, "living things and individual heavy objects would be left behind . . . the earth itself would very soon have fallen completely out of the heavens."[1] By the Late Middle Ages, Ptolemy's handbook had come to represent standard astronomical wisdom. As late as the 1650s, more than a hundred years after the Polish astronomer Nicolaus Copernicus had argued mathematically that the sun was the center of the universe, educated Europeans in most universities still believed that the earth held the central position.

In the thirteenth century, mainly through the philosophical efforts of Thomas Aquinas (1225–1274), Aristotle's thought was adapted to Christian beliefs, often in ingenious ways. Aquinas emphasized that order pervaded nature and that every physical effect had a physical cause. The tendency in Aquinas's thought and that of his followers, who were called scholastics by their seventeenth-century critics, was to search for these causes—again, to ask *why* things move, rather than *how* they move. But Aquinas denied that these causes stretched back to infinity. Instead, he insisted that nature proves God's existence; God is the First Cause of all physical phenomena. The world picture taught by the scholastics affirmed the earth and humankind as the center of the Christian drama of birth, death, and salvation.

Medieval thinkers integrated the cosmology of Aristotle and Ptolemy into a Christian framework that drew a sharp distinction between the world beyond the moon and the earthly realm. Celestial bodies were composed of the divine ether, a substance too pure and too spiritual to be found on earth; heavenly bodies, unlike earthly bodies, were immune to all change and obeyed different laws of motion. The universe was not homogeneous but divided into a higher world of the heavens and a lower world of earth. Earth could not compare with the heavens in spiritual dignity, but God had nevertheless situated it in the center of the universe. Earth deserved this position of importance, for only here did Christ live and die for humankind. This vision of the universe was to be shattered by the Scientific Revolution.

Also shattered by the philosophy of nature articulated in the seventeenth century was the belief that all reality, natural as well as human, could be described as consisting of *matter* and *form*. Following Aristotle, the scholastics argued that matter was inchoate, lifeless, and indistinguishable, and that form gave it shape and identity. A table, for instance, possessed a recognizable shape and could be identified as a table because it possessed the form of tableness. A human being existed only because the matter of the body was given life by the soul, by its form. This doctrine was central to both medieval philosophy and theology. Important beliefs were justified by it. For example, the church taught that the priest, when performing the sacrament of the Eucharist, had the power to transform bread and wine into the body and blood of Christ. This was possible because, theologians argued, the matter of the bread and wine remained the same (and hence looked the same), but its form was changed by the power of the priest. Consequently, the Mass could be explained without recourse to magic, which was highly suspect. Similarly, medieval people believed that the king's power resided within him; kingness was part of his essence. So, too, nobility was a quality said to adhere to the person of the nobleman or noblewoman. The mechanical philosophy of Galileo, Boyle, and Newton, which was central to the Scientific Revolution, denied the existence of form. Matter was simply composed of tiny corpuscles, or atoms, which were hard and impenetrable and were governed by the laws of impact or force. Such a conception of nature threatened whole aspects of medieval and even Christian doctrine; ultimately, for society its implications proved to be democratic.

A New View of Nature

Renaissance Neo-Platonism

Italian Renaissance thinkers rediscovered the importance of the ancient Greek philosopher Plato (c. 429–347 B.C.). Plato taught that the philosopher must look beyond the appearances of things to an invisible reality, which is abstract, simple, rational, and best expressed mathematically. For Plato, the greatest achievements of the human mind were mathematics and music; both revealed the inherent harmony and order within nature.

Renaissance Platonists interpreted Plato from a Christian perspective, and they believed that the Platonic search for truth about nature, about God's work, was but another aspect of the search for knowledge about God. The Italian universities and academies became centers where the revival of Plato flourished among teachers and translators, who came to be known as *Neo-Platonists.* Central to their humanist curriculum was the study of philosophy, mathematics, music, Greek and Latin, and in some cases Arabic. Those languages made available the world of pagan, pre-Christian learning and its many different philosophies of nature. The leading thinkers of the Scientific Revolution were all inspired by Renaissance Neo-Platonism. They revered Plato's search for a truth that was abstract and mathematically elegant, and they explored the ancient writers and their theories about nature. Some of the ancients had been atomists; a few had even argued that the sun might be at the center of the universe. They had also invented geometry.

With the impulse to mathematize nature came the desire to measure and experience it. The rediscovery of nature as mappable and quantifiable found expression in the study of human anatomy, as well as in the study of objects in motion. Renaissance art shows the fruits of this inquiry, for artists tried to depict the human body as exactly as possible yet to give it ideal form. The revival of artistic creativity associated with the Renaissance is linked to an interest in the natural world and to Neo-Platonism.

Magic and the Search for Nature

The thinkers of the Scientific Revolution also drew on a body of magical and mystical thought drawn from the first and second centuries A.D. Many of these anonymous students of magic believed that there had once been an ancient Egyptian priest, Hermes Trismegistus, who had possessed secret knowledge about nature's processes and the ultimate forces at work in the universe. In the second century A.D., this magical tradition was written down in a series of mystical dialogues about the universe. When Renaissance Europeans rediscovered these second-century writings, they erroneously assumed the author to be Hermes. Hence the writings seemed to be even older than the Bible.

Hermetic literature stated that true knowledge comes from a contemplation of the One, or the Whole—a spiritual reality higher than, yet embedded in, nature. Some of these ancient writings argued that the sun was the natural symbol of this Oneness, and such an argument seemed to give weight to a heliocentric picture of the universe. The Hermetic approach to nature also incorporated elements of the Pythagorean and Neo-Platonic traditions, which emphasized the inner mathematical harmony pervading nature. A follower of Hermeticism might approach nature mathematically, as well as magically. For example, Johannes Kepler (see below) was both a fine mathematician and a believer in the magical power of nature. Though not directly influenced by Hermeticism as a system of belief, for much of his life Isaac Newton saw no contradiction in searching for the mathematical laws of nature while practicing alchemy—the illusive search for a way to transform ordinary metals into gold.

In early modern Europe, the practitioners of alchemy and astrology could also be mathematicians and astronomers, and the sharp distinction drawn today between magic and science—between the irrational and the rational—would not have been made by many of the leading natural philosophers who lived in the sixteenth and seventeenth centuries.

The Renaissance revival of ancient learning contributed a new approach to nature, one that was simultaneously mathematical, experimental, and magical. Although the achievements of modern science depend on experimentation and mathematics, the impulse to search for nature's secrets presumes a degree of self-confidence best exemplified and symbolized by the magician. One of the important byproducts of the Scientific Revolution was that eventually the main practitioners of the new science repudiated magic, largely because of its secretiveness and its associations with pagan religion. But this repudiation should not obscure the initial role of magic, among many other factors, as a stimulus to scientific inquiry and enthusiasm.

The Copernican Revolution

Nicolaus Copernicus was born in Poland in 1473. As a young man, he enrolled at the University of Kraków, where he may have come under the influence of Renaissance Platonism, which was spreading outward from the Italian city-states.

COPERNICAN SYSTEM. In his *On the Revolutions of the Heavenly Spheres* Copernicus proposed a heliocentric model in which the planets orbit around the sun. (*The Granger Collection.*)

Copernicus also journeyed to Italy, and in Bologna and Padua he may have become aware of ancient Greek texts containing arguments for the sun being the center of the universe. We know very little about his early education.

Copernicus's interest in mathematics and astronomy was stimulated by contemporary discussions of the need for calendar reform, which required a thorough understanding of Ptolemaic astronomy. The mathematical complexity of the Ptolemaic system troubled Copernicus, who believed that truth was the product of elegance and simplicity. In addition, Copernicus knew that Ptolemy had predecessors among the ancients who philosophized about a heliocentric universe or who held Aristotle's cosmology and physics in little regard. Thus, his Renaissance education gave Copernicus not a body of new scientific truth, but rather the courage to break with traditional truth taught in the universities.

Toward the end of his stay in Italy, Copernicus became convinced that the sun was at the center of the universe. So he began a lifelong task to work out mathematical explanations of how a heliocentric universe operated. Unwilling to engage in controversy with the followers of Aristotle, Copernicus did not publish his findings until 1543, the year of his death, in a work titled *On the Revolutions of the Heavenly Spheres*. Legend says that his book, which in effect began the Scientific Revolution, was brought to him on his deathbed. Copernicus died a Catholic priest, hoping only that his book would be read sympathetically.

The treatise retained some elements of the Aristotelian-Ptolemaic system. Copernicus never doubted Aristotle's basic idea of the perfect circular motion of the planets or the existence of crystalline spheres within which the stars revolved, and he retained many of Ptolemy's epicycles—orbits within the circular orbits of the sun and planets. But Copernicus proposed a heliocentric model of the universe that was mathematically simpler than Ptolemy's earth-centered universe. Thus, he eliminated some of Ptolemy's epicycles and cleared up various problems that had troubled astronomers who had based their work on an earth-centered universe.

Copernicus's genius was expressed in his ability to pursue an idea—the concept of a sun-centered universe—and to bring to that pursuit lifelong dedication and brilliance in mathematics. By removing the earth from its central position and by giving it motion—that is, by making the earth just another planet—Copernicus undermined the system of medieval cosmology and made possible the birth of modern astronomy.

But because they were committed to the Aristotelian-Ptolemaic system and to biblical statements that they thought supported it, most thinkers of the time rejected Copernicus's conclusions. They also raised specific objections. The earth, they said, is too heavy to move. How, some of Copernicus's colleagues asked, can an object falling from a high tower land directly below the point from which it was dropped if the earth is moving so rapidly?

The Laws of Planetary Motion: Tycho and Kepler

Copernicus laid the foundation for the intellectual revolution that overturned the medieval conception of the universe and ushered in modern cosmology. But it fell to other observers to fill in the important details. Tycho Brahe (1546–1601) never accepted the Copernican system, but he saw that it presented a challenge to astronomers. Aided by the king of Denmark, Tycho built the finest observatory in Europe. In 1572, he observed a new star in the heavens. Its existence offered a direct and serious challenge to the Aristotelian and scholastic assumption of unalterable, fixed, and hence perfect heavens. To this discovery of what eventually proved to be an exploding star, Tycho added his observations on the comet of 1577. He demonstrated that it moved unimpeded through the areas between the planets and passed right through the crystalline spheres. This finding raised the question of whether such spheres existed, but Tycho himself remained an Aristotelian. Although his devotion to a literal reading of the Bible led Tycho to reject the Copernican sun-centered universe, he did propose an alternative system, in which the planets revolved around the sun but the sun moved about a motionless earth.

Ultimately, Tycho's fame rests on his skill as a practicing astronomer. He bequeathed to future generations precise calculations about the movements of heavenly bodies. These calculations proved invaluable. They were put to greatest use by Johannes Kepler (1571–1630), a German who collaborated with Tycho during the latter's final years. Tycho bequeathed his astronomical papers to Kepler, who brought to these data a scientific vision that was both experimental and mystical.

Kepler searched persistently for harmonious laws of planetary motion. He did so because he believed profoundly in the Platonic ideal. According to this ideal, a spiritual force infuses the physical order, beneath appearances are harmony and unity, and the human mind can begin to comprehend that unity only through *gnosis*—a direct and mystical realization of unity—and through mathematics. Kepler believed that both approaches were compatible, and he managed to combine them. He believed in and practiced astrology (as did Tycho) and throughout his lifetime tried to contact an ancient but lost and secret wisdom.

In the course of his observations of the heavens, Kepler discovered the three basic laws of planetary motion. First, the orbits of the planets are elliptical, not circular as Aristotle and Ptolemy had assumed, and the sun is one focus of the ellipse. Unlike Tycho, Kepler accepted Copernicus's theory and provided proof for it. Kepler's second law demonstrated that the velocity of a planet is not uniform, as had been believed, but increases as its distance from the sun decreases. Kepler's third law—that the squares of the times taken by any two planets in their revolutions around the sun are in the same ratio as the cubes of their average distances from the sun—brought the planets into a unified mathematical system.

The significance of Kepler's work was immense. He gave sound mathematical proof to Copernicus's theory, eliminated forever the use of epicycles, which had saved the appearance of circular motion, and demonstrated that mathematical relationships can describe the planetary system. But Kepler left a significant question unresolved: what kept the planets in their orbits? Why did they not fly out into space or crash into the sun? The answer would be supplied by Isaac Newton, who synthesized the astronomy of Copernicus and Kepler with the new physics developed by Galileo.

Galileo: Experimental Physics

At the same time that Kepler was developing a new astronomy, his contemporary, Galileo Galilei (1564–1642), was breaking with the older physics of Aristotle. A citizen of Pisa by birth, Galileo lived for many years in Padua, where he conducted some of his first experiments on the motion of bodies. Guided by the dominant philosophy of the Italian Renaissance—the revived doctrines of Plato—Galileo believed that beyond the visible world lay certain universal truths, subject to mathematical verification. Galileo insisted that the study of motion entails not only the use of logic (as Aristotle had believed) but also the application of mathematics. For this Late Renaissance natural philosopher, mathematics became the language of nature. Galileo also believed that only after experimenting with the operations of nature can the philosopher formulate harmonious laws and give them mathematical expression. Galileo was also trained in the practices of Renaissance art, in using shades to show depth and perspective. When he first looked at the moon through his telescope, that training became very important.

In his mechanical experiments, Galileo discovered that, all other things being equal, bodies of unequal weight will experience a uniform acceleration (due to gravity). He demonstrated that bodies fall with arithmetic regularity. Motion could, therefore, be treated mathematically.

Galileo established a fundamental principle of modern science: the order and uniformity of nature. There are no distinctions in rank or quality between the heavens and earth; heavenly bodies are not perfect and changeless as Aristotle had believed. In 1609, Galileo built a telescope through which he viewed the surface of the moon. The next year, in a treatise called *The Starry Messenger,* he proclaimed to the world

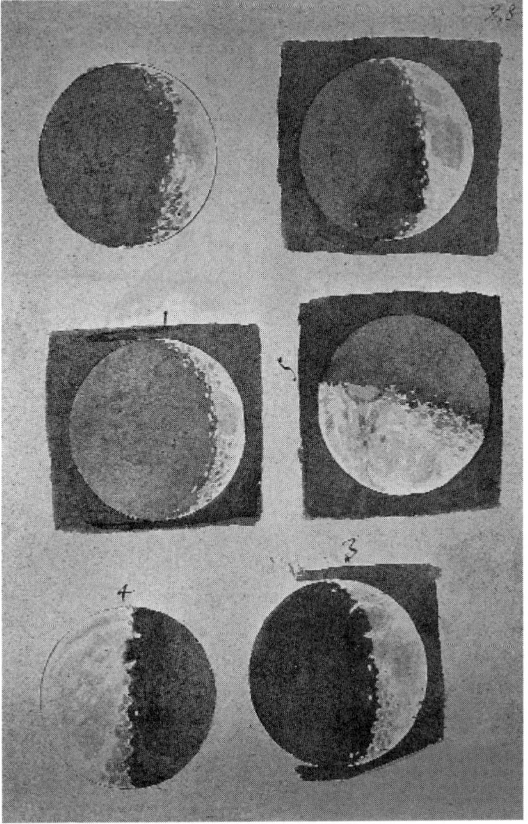

Notebook Sketches of the Phases of the Moon by Galileo Galilei, 1609–1610. Galileo saw only shadows when he looked into his telescope. But because he was trained as an artist in the principles of light and dark coloring to emphasize or shorten distance, he knew that what he saw represented real objects, in this case mountains and valleys. Somewhat satirically, he compared the moon to Bohemia. (*Biblioteca Nazionale Centrale, Florence.*)

that the moon "is not smooth, uniform, and precisely spherical as a great number of philosophers believe it and the other heavenly bodies to be, but is uneven, rough, and full of cavities . . . being not unlike the face of the earth, relieved by chains of mountains and deep valleys."[2] In addition, Galileo noticed spots on the sun, providing further evidence that heavenly objects, like earthly objects, undergo change. There are no higher and lower worlds; nature is the same throughout.

When he saw shadows through his telescope, he assumed that actual bodies were casting them, just as they do on an earthly landscape. The art and science of his age were of a piece.

Through his telescope, Galileo also observed moons around Jupiter—a discovery that helped support the Copernican hypothesis. If Jupiter had moons, then all heavenly bodies did not orbit the earth. The moons of Jupiter removed a fundamental criticism of Copernicus and opened up the possibility that the earth, with its own moon, might be just like Jupiter and that both might in turn revolve around a central point—the sun.

With Galileo, the science of Copernicus and the assault on Aristotle entered a new phase. Scholastic priests began to attack Galileo from their pulpits in Florence, backed by teachers within the academic community who routinely taught the old astronomy. These teachers saw a threat to their own power in Galileo's public notoriety and in his following among the laity. A secret group of priests and academics, named the Liga, formed with the express purpose of silencing Galileo; they used Aristotle and the Bible to attack him. But Galileo was also a courtier with friends in high places, so he dared to challenge the clergy and to offer his science directly to the laity. He argued publicly with the theologians. In the early seventeenth century, the Catholic church saw danger on every front: Protestants in Germany, Jews and Muslims in the East, and a laity demanding new schools that would provide practical education for their children. Now Galileo offered a view of the universe that conflicted with certain scriptural texts.

Historians used to believe that the church attacked Galileo solely because he was a Copernican, that is, because he believed the sun to be at the center of the universe. New evidence from the recently opened Vatican archives suggests that the church may also have worried about his theory of matter and his abandonment of the scholastics' view of the relationship between matter and form. That view went to the heart of the doctrine of the Eucharist, and the church saw, rightly, that the new science threatened the philosophical foundations of certain key doctrines.

In 1632, Galileo's teachings were condemned, and he was placed under house arrest. These actions cut short the open pursuit of science in many Catholic countries of the seventeenth century. Where the Inquisition was strong, the new science would be viewed as subversive. Censorship worked to stifle public intellectual inquiry. By the midcentury, science had become an increasingly Protestant and northern European phenomenon.

The Newtonian Synthesis: Experiment, Mathematics, and Theory

By 1650, the works of Copernicus and especially of Galileo had dethroned the physics and astronomy of Aristotle and Ptolemy. A new philosophy of nature tied to observation and Neo-Platonism had come into existence; its essence lay in the mathematical expression of physical laws that describe matter in motion. Yet no single overriding law had been articulated that would bring together the experimental successes of the new science, its mathematical sophistication, and its philosophical revolution. This law was supplied by Isaac Newton.

Newton was born in 1642, in Lincolnshire, England, the son of a modest yeoman. Because of his intellectual promise, he obtained a place at Trinity College, Cambridge, and there he devoted himself to natural philosophy and mathematics. Newton's student notebooks survive and show him mastering philosophical texts while also trying to understand the fundamental truths of Protestant Christianity as taught at Cambridge. Combining Christian Neo-Platonism with a genius for mathematics, Newton produced a coherent synthesis of the science of Kepler and Galileo, which eventually captured the imagination of European intellectuals.

In 1666, Newton formulated the mathematics for the universal law of gravitation, and in the same year, after rigorous experimentation, he determined the nature of light. The sciences of physics and optics were transformed. However, for many years, Newton did not publish his discoveries, partly because even he did not grasp the immense significance of his work. Finally, another mathematician and friend, Edmund Halley, persuaded him to publish under the sponsorship of the Royal Society. The result was the *Principia*

Art of the Seventeenth and Eighteenth Centuries

1. Peter Paul Rubens. *The Betrothal of Saint Catherine,* sketch for a large altar painting, c. 1628. *(Staatliche Gemalde-Galerie, Berlin/Bridgeman Art Library.)*

The influence of political, economic, and social change permeates the visual arts of the seventeenth and eighteenth centuries. Perhaps most significant to the artists who made their living by providing paintings with religious themes for churches, as well as for private patrons, were the religious conflicts that split apart European society. Catholics and Protestants quarreled and openly fought over doctrine and dogma; as a result of the struggles, artists had to decide how best to please patrons whose religious sympathies may have changed or developed in new directions. Politically, the seventeenth and eighteenth centuries are also marked by the emergence of new sovereign states and by a change in the nature of artistic patronage.

Although a number of terms are used to describe the seventeenth and eighteenth centuries, the one most commonly applied by art historians is *baroque*. The word literally means irregularly shaped, whimsical, grotesque, or odd. Its origin is French, but it is generally agreed that the baroque style of art originated in Rome.

Baroque art is hard to explain within the context of the social and political changes that were sweeping over Europe. Some historians see it as illustrative of the Counter Reformation; others point out that the style was equally appealing to Catholics and Protestants. Nor

2. Giovanne Benedetto Castiglione. *Melancholia*, mid-seventeenth century. *(Philadelphia Museum of Art. Pennsylvania Academy Fine Arts Collection.)*

was baroque favored only by the absolute rulers of France or other monarchs; it was also a style of the bourgeois.

One of the most famous baroque painters was Peter Paul Rubens (1577–1640) of Flanders, which, prospering from its commercial connections, was home to many successful artists and patrons in this period. To study painting, Rubens traveled to Rome in 1600 and spent many years visiting other artistic centers in Italy. There he learned to paint on large-scale canvases and play with the size and weight of his subjects. Despite the influence of his southern contemporaries, however, his style remained essentially Flemish.

In his painting *The Betrothal of Saint Catherine* (Figure 1), we immediately sense the energy and fullness of the figures typical among Italian artists. But we also notice that Rubens's palette is much lighter than theirs, and consequently, the figures of Saint Catherine and the saints who surround her seem to move lightly as well.

Noteworthy, too, in this canvas is the depiction of the figures, whose hairstyles and mode of dress is contemporary rather than suggestive of biblical times. This juxtaposition of scenes from the Bible with the flavor of everyday life in the seventeenth century reveals much about the connection between the artist and his own surroundings.

The baroque style of highly finished, realistic works is very familiar to us. But we must also recall that baroque artists were skilled draftsmen. As an example, there is Giovanne Benedetto Castiglione's *Melancholia* (mid-seventeenth century) (Figure 2), a brush drawing in oil with added red chalk. Works on paper do not always survive as well as those on board or canvas. The drawings we do have attest to the artistic skill of seventeenth-century artists, who used line and shadow as well as did their Renaissance predecessors.

Melancholia is an allegory about the human dilemma of choosing among the worlds of art, religion, science, and learning. Symbols from each of these worlds—scientific tools, musical instruments, a globe, and the like—surround the figure of Genius, who sits in a contemplative pose.

Although by and large the artists of the baroque period were not well-rounded humanists like those of the Renaissance, some of them could work in two- and three-dimensional art forms. For example, Gian Lorenzo Bernini (1598–1680) distinguished himself as a sculptor as well as an architect.

Bernini was responsible for the sculptural program of Saint Peter's Basilica in the Vatican. He also completed sculptures in other Roman churches, including the Cornaro Chapel in the Church of Santa Maria della Vittoria. His *The Ecstasy of Saint Teresa* (1644–1647) (Figure 3) is a remarkable work that tells a dramatic story. The heart of Saint Teresa of Avila was said to have been pierced by an angel's golden arrow; the pain was exquisite, for not only was it the pain of death but also the pleasure of everlasting life in the arms of God. Bernini skillfully portrays the exact moment of Saint Teresa's ecstasy, in a theatrical setting using not only sculpture but also the architectural elements of the chapel.

3. Gian Lorenzo Bernini. *The Ecstasy of Saint Teresa,* 1644–1647. *(Church of Santa Maria della Vittoria, Rome/Scala/Art Resource.)*

The saint and the angel are carved of white marble and seem to be floating on a cloud. The sculpted golden rays, which descend from a point above the figures, are bathed in light by a window hidden behind the frame that surrounds the two figures. Bernini decorated the entire chapel to follow the theme of Saint Teresa; ceiling frescoes show clouds of angels celebrating the event.

While Bernini was gaining fame in Italy, a French painter—one who spent almost his entire career in Rome—was winning an international reputation. Nicolas Poussin (1593/4–1665) relied strongly on the art of the classical and especially the Hellenistic periods for his inspiration. His *The Rape of the Sabine Women* (c. 1636–37) (Figure 4), a lavish and richly painted canvas, captures action like a carefully posed photograph. Indeed, if Bernini was theatrical in his portrayal of Saint Teresa, one could say that Poussin is cinematographic.

The story depicted in *The Rape of the Sabine Women* is derived from classical mythology; the poses of the figures hark back to the Hellenistic period. Compare the positioning of the arms of the women on the left of the canvas with the tortured stance of Laocoön, in the sculpture shown in Figure 4 of the first art

4. Nicolas Poussin. *The Rape of the Sabine Women,* c. 1636–37. *(Metropolitan Museum of Art, NY.)*

essay. Other groups in the Poussin canvas are also reminiscent of that sculpture. As another bow to the ancient past, Poussin paints in the background buildings that are faithful to Roman prototypes. Such reliance on archaeology and mythology are typical of his work.

While paintings depicting mythological, historical, or religious themes dominated the major art markets during the baroque era, patrons in Holland sought paintings that related more to their own experience. For that reason, the genre of the still life—paintings of flowers, fruit, dishes, food, and other familiar objects—reached its zenith in that country.

Willem Kalf (1622–1693), among the most skilled of Dutch still-life masters, was able to take a collection of objects and turn it into an object of art. His *Still Life* (Figure 5) showcases his meticulous, almost photo-realistic style. In particular, it focuses on the way in which glass reflects light and on the juxtaposition of different textures. Although modern art historians view some still lifes as merely ornamental displays of technical skill, there was a reason for them. The popularity of still lifes, and of landscapes, probably has to do with the human desire for reassurance that "things are as they should be," that the status quo is being maintained, regardless of the religious or political turmoil affecting other aspects of life. No matter what was going on politically, no matter what religious dispute was being negotiated, people could find a degree of comfort in being surrounded by familiar objects or scenes.

While Kalf distinguished himself as a still-life painter, another Dutch master, Rembrandt van Rijn (1606–1669) gained fame for his historical and religious canvases. Rembrandt was influenced in his early years by Italian painters, especially by their use of light. But that was not his only strength. His reputation as a portrait painter brought him renown and fortune in Amsterdam.

Even more impressive were his self-portraits, which he painted not for the commissions of patrons but entirely for himself in the pursuit of truth. For an artist to paint as many self-portaits as Rembrandt did in the seventeenth century was very unusual. Self-portraits are anlogous to autobiographics: in both, the artist examines himself because he believes his own self is worthy of self-examination.

Rembrandt's quest for the meaning of the inner life is compatible with the growing introspectiveness of the seventeenth century, an age that also produced Descartes's dictum that to think is to be, the soliloquies of Shakespeare's Hamlet, and the hallucinations of Cervantes' Don Quixote.

5. Willem Kalf. *Still Life*, c. 1660. *(Hermitage, St. Petersburg/Scala/Art Resource.)*

Rembrandt produced a series of sixty-two self-portraits during the course of his lifetime, an exhaustive autobiography in pictures in which he seemed to engage in a dialogue with himself in a variety of atttitudes and poses: vigorous, youthful, heroic, flamboyant, melodramatic, enigmatic, aging, distraught, struggling with despair, grimly resolved, disdainful, strong, weak. Rembrandt completed *Self-Portrait at Old Age*, 1669 (Figure 6), the fifty-fifth in a corpus of sixty-two self-portraits, in the last year of his life. It is among a cluster of self-portraits in which he appears to have "pulled himself together" and defined his identity. In it, we find Rembrandt staring back at us with the calm assurance of a man who has mastered his art and life, and surpassed his time and place.

The later part of the eighteenth century marks the beginning of the rococo and neoclassical periods in art history. Especially popular in France, the rococo and neoclassical movements owed much to political and social forces. The term *rococo* describes a style that is frothy and frivolous and compatible with the peripheral concerns of royalty. In 1698, King Louis XIV ordered the redecoration of his palace at Versailles with works that were lighthearted and youthful instead of stodgy and serious. His dabbling with artistic matters led to quarrels and esthetic disagreements in the artistic community.

An example of the rococo is François Boucher's (1703–1770) *The Toilet of Venus* (1751) (Figure 7). Although some art historians describe his work as slick and artificial, Boucher became the darling of the French court. In his *The Toilet of Venus*, the goddess is full figured and lush, surrounded by all the sensual accouterments that the goddess of love and erotic pleasure should have. Given her appearance and her surroundings, Boucher's Venus looks as though she would have been comfortable in period dress, supervising the decor of her boudoir at the palace at Versailles. Clearly, Boucher understood his audience well.

While Boucher exemplified the light and airy sentiment of the rococo, Jacques Louis David (1748–1825) typified the neoclassical.

6. Rembrandt van Rijn. *Self Portrait at Old Age*, 1669. *(Erich Lessing/National Gallery, London/Årt Resource, NY.)*

The neoclassical style represents a return to the rationality and harmony of the classical past; many of the works from this period also reflect contemporary political events.

Justice, honor for one's country, and the need to portray inspirational themes were the guideposts of the neoclassical artists. Their training ground was Italy, primarily because it was the source of the classical prototypes from which they could learn. Jacques Louis David's *The Death of Marat* (1793) (Figure 8) captures the essence of that event in a manner that combines the best of Poussin and Rubens.

The subject matter is important because it illuminates the neoclassical concept of virtue, represented by the martyrdom of Marat, a revolutionary. The style borrows from Poussin's ability to capture a scene with photographic stillness, rendering the figures in an almost sculptural way. But David has also appropriated Rembrandt's technique of skillfully juxtaposing light and shadow. While the neoclassicists sometimes paid homage to their distant past in subject matter, they also showed their reverence for the revolutionary ideals of their own time.

7. François Boucher. *The Toilet of Venus,* 1751. *(Metropolitan Museum of Art, NY.)*

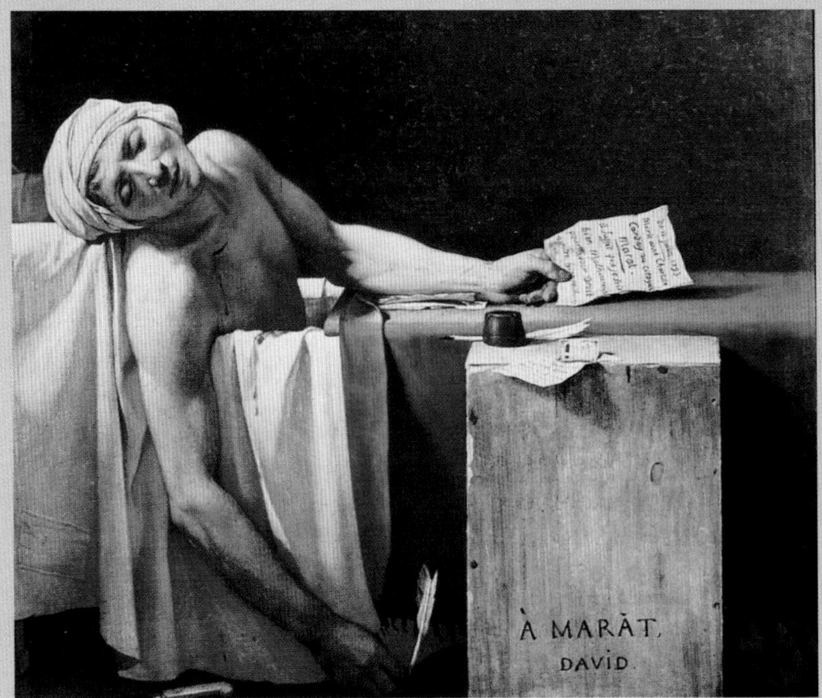

8. Jacques Louis David. *The Death of Marat*, 1793. *(Royal Museum of Fine Arts, Brussels/Giraudon/Art Resource.)*

SIR ISAAC NEWTON (1642–1727). In 1666, Newton's mathematical formulation of the law of universal gravitation and his experiments in the nature of light opened a new stage in human understanding of the physical universe. The poet Alexander Pope expressed Newton's contemporaries' view of his achievements: "Nature, and Nature's Laws lay hid in Night. God said, 'Let Newton be!' and All was Light." (*The Granger Collection.*)

Mathematica of 1687. In 1704, Newton published his *Opticks* and revealed his theory that light was corpuscular in nature and that it emanated from luminous bodies in a way that scientists later described as waves.

Of the two books, both monumental achievements in the history of science, the *Principia* made the greater impact on contemporaries. Newton offered universal mathematical laws, as well as a philosophy of nature that sought to explain the essential structure of the universe: matter is always the same; it is atomic in structure, and in its essential nature it is dead or lifeless; and it is acted upon by immaterial forces that are placed in the universe by God. Newton said that the motion of matter could be explained by three laws: inertia, that a body remains in a state of rest or continues its motion in a straight line unless impelled to change by forces impressed on it; acceleration, that the change in the motion of a body is proportional to the force acting on it; and that for every action there is an equal and opposite reaction.

Newton argued that these laws apply not only to observable matter on earth but also to the motion of planets in their orbits. He showed that planets did not remain in their orbits because circular motion was "natural" or because crystalline spheres kept them in place. Rather, said Newton, planets keep to their orbits because every body in the universe exercises a force on every other body, a force that he called *universal gravitation.* Gravity is proportional to the product of the masses of two bodies and inversely proportional to the square of the distance between them. It is operative throughout the universe, whether on earth or in the heavens, and it is capable of mathematical expression. Newton built his theory on the work of other scientific giants, notably Kepler and Galileo. No one before him, however, had possessed the breadth of vision, mathematical skill, and dedication to rigorous observation to combine this knowledge into one grand synthesis.

The universe could now be described as matter in motion; it was governed by invisible forces that operated everywhere, both on earth and in the heavens, and these forces could be expressed mathematically. The medieval picture of the universe as closed, earthbound, and earth centered was replaced by a universe seen to be infinite and governed by universal laws. The earth was now regarded as simply another moving planet. Newtonian principles were taught by generations of Newton's followers as, in effect, applied mechanics. A revolution in thought had changed Western ideas about nature forever.

But what was God's role in this new universe? Newton and his circle labored to create a mechanical world-view dependent on the will of God. At one time, Newton believed that gravity was simply the will of God operating on the universe. As he wrote in the *Opticks,* the physical order "can be the effect of nothing else than the wisdom and skill of a powerful ever-living agent."[3] Because of his strong religious convictions, Newton allowed his science to be used in the service of the established Anglican church, and his followers argued for social stability anchored in an ordered universe and an established church. Newton, a scientific genius, was also a deeply religious thinker committed to the maintenance of Protestantism in England. Among his contemporaries, however, were free-thinkers who like John Toland (see "Skeptics, Free-thinkers, and Deists" in Chapter 18) used his ideas to argue that nature can operate on its own, without the assistance of a providential God.

Biology, Medicine, and Chemistry

The spectacular advances in physics and astronomy in the sixteenth and seventeenth centuries were not matched in the biological sciences.

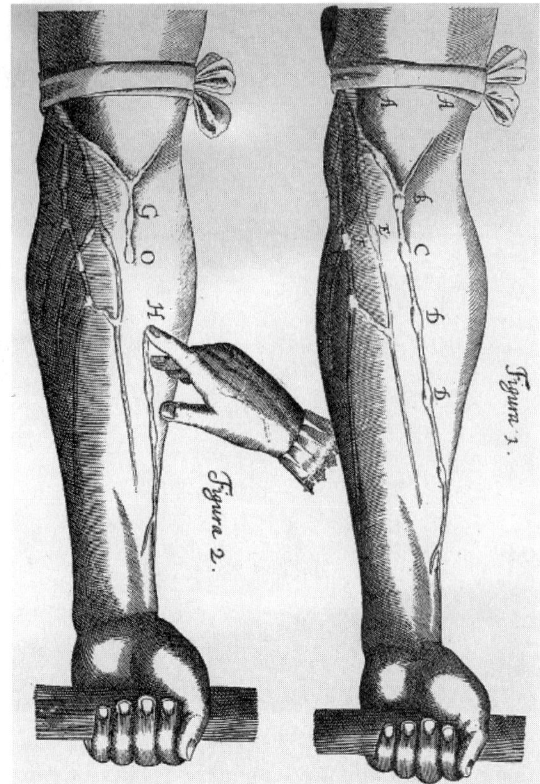

Science and Blood. For centuries it was believed that blood carried character traits as well as nobility. The English experimenter William Harvey viewed blood as simply a liquid that circulated in the body in a uniform way. Illustrations such as this one made the point graphically. (*Corbis.*)

Indeed, the day-to-day practice of medicine throughout western Europe changed little in the period from 1600 to 1700, for much of medical practice relied, as it had since the Middle Ages, on astrology.

Doctors clung to the teachings of the ancient practitioners Galen and Hippocrates. In general, Galenic medicine paid little attention to the discovery of specific cures for particular diseases. As a follower of Aristotle, Galen emphasized the elements that make up the body; he called their manifestations *humors.* A person with an excess of blood was sanguine; a person with too much bile was choleric. Health consisted of a restoration of balances among these various elements, so Galenic doctors often prescribed purges of one sort or another. The most famous of these was bloodletting, but sweating was also a favorite remedy. Taught devotedly in the medical schools of Europe, these methods were often as dangerous as the diseases they sought to cure.

Despite the tenacity of Galenic medicine, sixteenth- and seventeenth-century innovators and reformers did try to challenge and overturn medical orthodoxy. With an almost missionary zeal, Paracelsus (1493–1541), a Swiss-German physician and Hermeticist, introduced the concept of diagnostic medicine. He argued that particular diseases can be differentiated and are related to chemical imbalances. His treatments relied on chemicals and not on bloodletting or the positions of the stars (although he did not discount such influences), and he proclaimed an almost ecstatic vision of human vitality and longevity. In most universities, the faculties of medicine bitterly opposed his views, but by 1650 in England and later in that century in France, Paracelsian ideas had many advocates. Support for Paracelsian medicine invariably accompanied an attack on the traditional medical establishment and its professional monopoly, and it often indicated support for the new science in general. The struggle between Galenists and Paracelsians quickly took on a social dimension; the innovators saw themselves pitted against a medical elite, which, in their opinion, had lost its commitment to medical research and existed solely to perpetuate itself. In the eighteenth century, Paracelsian ideas, stripped of their magical associations, became commonplace.

The medical reforms of the eighteenth century did not rest solely on the Paracelsian approach; they also relied heavily on the experimental breakthroughs made in the science of anatomy. A pioneer in this field was the Belgian surgeon Andreas Vesalius (1515–1564), who published *The Structure of the Human Body* in 1543. Opposing Galenic practice, Vesalius argued for observation and anatomical dissection as the keys to knowing how the human body works. By the late seventeenth century, doctors had learned a great deal about the human body, its structure, and its chemistry.

The study of anatomy yielded dramatic results. In 1628, William Harvey (1578–1657) announced that he had discovered the circulation of blood. Harvey compared the functioning of the heart to that of a mechanical pump, and once again the tendency to mechanize nature, so basic to the Scientific Revolution in physics, led to a significant discovery. Yet the acceptance of Harvey's work was very slow, and the practical uses of his discovery were not readily perceived.

The experimental method in medicine produced other innovations, among them systematic examination not only of corpses but also of patients. In the late 1600s, the finest doctor of the age, Herman Boerhaave, taught his students in Leiden, in the Netherlands, by taking them on house calls, arguing that nothing in medicine can be known without a careful and rigorous examination of the body. He proclaimed that he was trying to bring the methods and philosophy of the new science to medicine, and he pioneered hands-on medical techniques.

Just as Newton applied the theory and method of science to the heavens, his contemporaries on both sides of the English Channel sought to utilize science to illuminate every object we experience. Protestantism inspired them to be aggressive in their assault on scholasticism. Indeed, the most original experimenter of the age, who codified the experimental method as we know it, was a devout English Protestant. Robert Boyle (1627–1691) believed that Aristotle's physics and the philosophy that supported it promoted Catholic teachings and thus amounted to little more than magic. At a time when English Protestants feared a revival of Catholic and absolutist monarchy, Boyle wanted to abolish the invisible forces on which Catholic theology rested. He also wished to defeat the magic of what he called "the vulgar," that is, the beliefs of the populace, whose disorder and tendencies to rebellion he feared.

To accomplish these aims, Boyle urged scientists to adopt the zeal of the magicians, but without their secretive practices and their conjuring with spirits. As an alternative to spirits, Boyle advocated the atomic explanation of matter: that matter consists of small, hard, indestructible particles that behave with regularity. According to Boyle, the existence of these particles explained the changes in gases, fluids, and solids.

Boyle pioneered the experimental method with such exciting and accurate results that by the

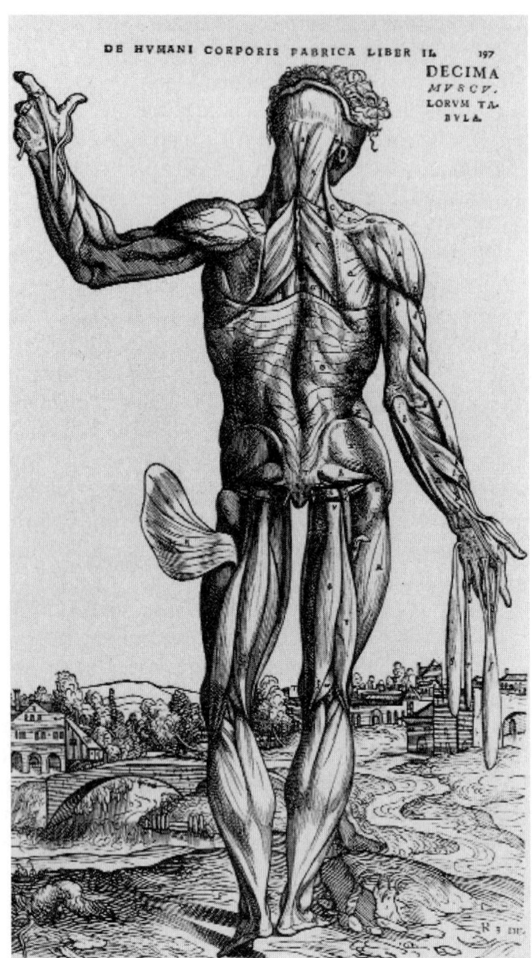

Woodcut from "On the Structure of the Human Body" by Andreas Vesalius, 1543. Vesalius was a professor at Padua. Originally a follower of Galen's teachings, he carried out many exacting dissections of corpses, which he documented with his vividly realistic drawings. (*Royal College of Physicians.*)

time of his death no serious scientist could attempt chemical experiments without following his guidelines. Thus, the science of chemistry acquired its characteristic experimentalism; it was also based on an atomic theory of matter. But not until late in the eighteenth century was this new discipline applied to medical research.

Bacon and Descartes: Prophets of the New Science

The new science needed prophets and social theorists to give it direction and to assess its implications. During the early modern period, two major reformers tried, in disparate ways, to channel science into the service of specific social programs: Francis Bacon (1561–1626) and René Descartes (1596–1650).

Bacon

The decidedly practical and empirical Francis Bacon stands as the most important English proponent of the new science, though not its most important practitioner. Bacon became profoundly suspicious of magic and the magical arts, not because they might not work but because he saw secrecy and arrogance as characteristic of their practitioners. Bacon was lord chancellor of England under James I, and he wrote about the usefulness of science partly in an effort to convince the crown of its advantages. He wanted science to serve the interests of strong monarchy.

Yet no philosopher of modern science has surpassed Bacon in elevating the study of nature to a humanistic discipline. In the *Advancement of Learning* (1605), Bacon argued that science must be open and all ideas must be allowed a hearing. Science must have human goals: the improvement of humanity's material condition and the advancement of trade and industry, but not the making of war or the taking of lives. Bacon also preached the need for science to possess an inductive methodology grounded in experience; the scientist should first of all be a collector of facts.

Although Bacon was rather vague about how the scientist as a theorist actually works, he knew that preconceived ideas imposed on nature seldom yield positive results. An opponent of Aristotle, Bacon argued that university education should move away from the ancient texts and toward the new learning. A powerful civil servant, he was not afraid to attack the guardians of tradition. The Baconian vision of progress in science leading to an improvement of the human condition and the security of the state inspired much scientific activity in the seventeenth century, particularly in England.

Descartes

René Descartes, a French philosopher of the first half of the seventeenth century, went to the best French schools and was trained by the Jesuits in mathematics and scholastic philosophy. Yet in his early twenties, he experienced a crisis of confidence. He felt that everything he had been taught was irrelevant and meaningless.

Descartes began to search within himself for what he could be sure was clear and distinct knowledge. All he could know with certainty was the fact of his existence, and even that he knew only because he experienced not his body but his mind: "I think, therefore I am." From this point of certitude, Descartes deduced God's existence. God exists because Descartes had in his mind an idea of a supreme, perfect being, and, Descartes reasoned, this idea could have been put there only by such a being, not by any ordinary mortal. Therefore, God's existence means that the physical world must be real, for no Creator would play such a cruel trick and invent a vast hoax.

For Descartes, the new science meant confidence: in his own mind, in the knowability of the physical world, and in mathematics and reason. Scientific thought meant an alternative to everything he associated with the medieval: confusion, disorder, conflict between church and state, fear of the unknown, and magic. Turning his back on the centuries immediately preceding his own, Descartes, possibly as a result of knowing Bacon's ideas for practical science, proclaimed that "it is possible to attain knowledge which is very useful in life, and that, instead of that speculative philosophy which is taught in the schools [that is, scholasticism], we may find a practical philosophy by means of which . . . we can . . . render ourselves the masters and possessors of nature."[4] Descartes was the first person to dream about the capacity of science to control and dominate nature, though he could not imagine its potential to destroy nature.

In order to affirm the existence of anything other than the abstractions of mathematics,

René Descartes (1596–1650). This is a fanciful engraved portrait of Descartes done long after his death by C. Hellemans. Descartes looks ready to meditate and very resolved. (*Bibliothèque Nationale, Paris.*)

Descartes had to proclaim the existence of God and the Universe, largely because both were ideas in his mind. He radically separated matter from spirit, mind from nature, and in the process he widened a gap in Western thought that would haunt philosophers for centuries. What if a thinker who understood the implications of Descartes's separation of matter from spirit was to argue that only matter existed? The thinker who did so was Benedict de Spinoza (1632– 1677). Born in Amsterdam of recently immigrated Jewish parents, he was trained in classical languages and Hebrew thought. His genius drew him to the new science, and he became an early explicator of Descartes's philosophy, in which he spied a central weakness: its inability to explain the linkage between matter and spirit or to connect God to nature in any meaningful way. Spinoza's solution was radical, logical, and thoroughly heretical to Christian thinkers: he argued that God is Nature, that matter and spirit in effect are one.

To this day, philosophers dispute Spinoza's purpose. Was he an atheist who wanted to do away with the Judeo-Christian conception of God, or was he a mystic who wished to infuse God into Nature? His contemporaries of every religious persuasion (he was expelled from his Amsterdam synagogue) deemed him an atheist and thought that he had become one by reading too much science. Their condemnation made "spinozism" a byword for atheism and freethinking. In the Enlightenment, freethinkers and materialists would claim to have been inspired by Spinoza.

The thoughts and visions of Bacon and Descartes revealed the power and importance of scientific knowledge. Science could promote human well-being, as Bacon insisted; it could make human beings and nature the foundation of all meaningful knowledge, as Descartes assumed; it could express pantheism, as Spinoza showed; or it could justify a belief in Nature as God, as it did for Spinoza. Whichever position educated westerners embraced by the late 1600s, science would be used to challenge the traditional authority of the clergy, whether Catholic or fundamentalist Protestant. Why believe in dogmas and texts when nature offered another kind of truth—universal and, just as important, applicable to human problems? For good or ill, the Scientific Revolution gave its followers a sense of power and self-confidence unimagined even by Renaissance proponents of individualism or by the theorists of absolute state power.

Social Implications of the Scientific Revolution

Perhaps the critical factor in causing the historical phenomenon called the Scientific Revolution was the acceptance and use of the new science by educated elites. Without such acceptance, the science of Galileo, Kepler, Descartes, Boyle, and Newton would have remained the specialized knowledge of the few—or, worse still, a suspect, even heretical, approach to nature. Galileo could not have succeeded as much as he did in disseminating his theories (despite the hostility of the church) without his large European following and his many aristocratic patrons, particularly in Florence.

Access to the printing press in Europe was also critical to the acceptance of the new mechanical understanding of nature. Descartes understood that fact when he left France, after the condemnation of Galileo, and published and lived in the Netherlands. Persecution and censorship meant that the new science made far less of an impact in Catholic than in Protestant Europe.

Equally important, the new science offered the dream of power to both governments and early promoters of industry. In the seventeenth century, this dream enticed monarchs and statesmen to give their patronage to scientific academies and projects. The achievements of the new science were quickly institutionalized in academies dominated either by the state, as in France, or by the landed and commercial elite, as in England. Founded in the 1660s, scientific academies such as the Royal Society in England became centers for the dissemination of science at a time when many universities, still controlled by the clergy, were hostile to its attack on scholasticism.

The new mechanical learning—not widely communicated by Newton's *Principia,* which was far too technical for most people, but rather passed on as mechanical information in handbooks and lectures—began to be applied in Britain and Scotland during the second half of the eighteenth century. The applied mechanics that improved the steam engine and utilized it in coal mining and water engineering stemmed from Newtonian lectures and books, which proliferated in Britain during the 1700s. The road from the Scientific Revolution leads more directly to the Industrial Revolution than is often realized. James Watt, who perfected the steam engine, had been tutored in Newtonian mechanics. His engine revolutionized the manufacturing of cotton.

In the same period, the scientific gentleman and woman, like the French chemist Lavoisier and his wife, Marie Anne, became fashionable icons. Elite and mildly prosperous families brought microscopes and globes into their homes. Owning these objects caused the family's status to rise, even if no one in the family became an engineer or doctor. Science had captured the Western imagination.

The Meaning of the Scientific Revolution

The Scientific Revolution was decisive in shaping the modern mentality; it shattered the medieval view of the universe and replaced it with a wholly different world-view. Gone was the belief that a motionless earth lay at the center of a universe that was finite and enclosed by a ring of stars. Gone, too, was the belief that the universe was divided into higher and lower worlds and that different laws of motion operated in the heavens and on earth. The universe was now viewed as a giant machine functioning according to universal laws, which could be expressed mathematically. Nature could be mastered conceptually.

The methodology that produced this view of nature—the new science—played a crucial historical role in reorienting Western thought from medieval theology and metaphysics to the study of physical and human problems. In the Late Middle Ages, most men of learning were Aristotelians and theologians. By the mid-eighteenth century, knowledge of Newtonian science and the dissemination of useful learning had become the goal of the educated classes. All knowledge, it was believed, could emulate scientific knowledge: it could be based on observation, experimentation, or rational deduction; and it could be systematic, verifiable, progressive, and useful. This new approach to learning used the scientists of the sixteenth and seventeenth centuries as proof that no institution or dogma had a monopoly on truth; the scientific approach would yield knowledge that might, if properly applied for the good of all people, produce a new and better age. Such an outlook gave thinkers new confidence in the power of the human mind to master nature and led them to examine European institutions and traditions with an inquiring, critical, and skeptical spirit. Scientific societies and academies sprang up all over Europe. In the Dutch Republic in 1785, a society was also founded by women interested in receiving a scientific education. Most scientific academies, however, excluded women into the twentieth century.

The Scientific Revolution ultimately weakened traditional Christianity. God's role in a mechanical universe was not clear. Newton had argued that God not only set the universe in motion but

James Watt (1736–1819). An engraved portrait of James Watt rendered in his successful years. His somewhat grim affect is consonant with the depression he often described in his letters. (*The Granger Collection.*)

still intervened in its operations, thus leaving room for miracles. Others retained a place for God as Creator but regarded miracles as limitations on nature's mechanical perfection. Applied to religious doctrines, Descartes's reliance on methodical doubt and clarity of thought and Bacon's insistence on careful observation led thinkers to question the validity of Christian teachings. Theology became a separate and somewhat irrelevant area of intellectual inquiry, not fit for the interests of practical, well-informed people. Not only Christian doctrines but also various popular beliefs grew suspect. Magic, witchcraft, and astrology, still widespread among the European masses, were regarded with disdain by elite culture. The masses of people remained devoted to some form of traditional Christianity, and the uncertainty of a universe governed by devils, witches, or the stars continued to make sense to peasants and laborers, who remained powerless

Profile

Madame du Châtelet

Giraudon/Art Resource, NY.

In the eighteenth century, women entered the world of science for the first time. The most accomplished and famous among these scientists was Madame du Châtelet (1706–1749). One of the foremost mathematicians of her era, she helped to bring Newtonian science to France. Her translation of Newton's *Principia* remains the only French translation. Her mathematical skill was formidable, as was her ability to convey complex scientific ideas in a readable form. She realized earlier than many French professors that Newton's calculus was superior to the Cartesian system.

Madame du Châtelet and Voltaire were lovers, and both were at the center of the French Enlightenment. In matters scientific, however, he was her pupil. When the first scientific society for women in the world was founded in 1785 in the Dutch Republic, her name was invoked in its founding documents. Like so many women of her time, she died in childbirth.

in the face of nature or the domination of the rich and landed.

In Catholic countries, where the Scientific Revolution began, hostility toward scientific ideas gathered strength in the early 1600s. The mentality of the Counter Reformation enabled lesser minds to exercise their fears and arrogance against any idea they regarded as suspicious. Galileo was caught in this hostile environment, and the Copernican system was condemned by the church in 1616. In Spain and Poland, it was not officially taught until the 1770s.

Gradually, the science of Newton became the science of western Europe: nature mechanized, analyzed, regulated, and mathematized. As a result of the Scientific Revolution, learned westerners came to believe more strongly than ever that nature could be mastered. Mechanical science—applied to canals, engines, pumps, and levers—became the science of industry. Thus, the Scientific Revolution, operating on both intellectual and commercial levels, laid the groundwork for two major developments of the modern West: the Age of Enlightenment and the Industrial Revolution.

Notes

1. Quoted in Jean D. Moss, *Novelties in the Heavens* (Chicago: University of Chicago Press, 1993), p. 33.
2. Excerpted in *Discoveries and Opinions of Galileo,* ed. Stillman Drake (Garden City, N.Y.: Doubleday, 1957), p. 28.
3. Excerpted in *Newton's Philosophy of Nature,* ed. H. S. Thayer (New York: Hafner, 1953), p. 177.

4. Excerpted in *Descartes' Philosophical Writings,* ed. Norman Kemp Smith (New York: Modern Library, 1958), pp. 130–131.

Suggested Reading

Appleby, J., L. Hunt, and M. Jacob, *Telling the Truth About History* (1994). Discusses the issues raised by the heroic model of science that came out of the Scientific Revolution and relates the issues to today's attitudes toward science.

Brooke, John H., *Science and Religion. Some Historical Perspectives* (1991). A lively, intelligent discussion of the tensions between science and religion since the sixteenth century.

Jacob, James R., *The Scientific Revolution* (1998). The best, most readable account of events from Copernicus to Newton.

Jacob, Margaret, *Scientific Culture and the Making of the Industiral West* (1997). Combines intellectual, social, and economic history.

Laudan, Larry, *Science and Relativism. Some Key Controversies in the Philosophy of Science* (1990). Debates some of the implications of being for or against science; intended for students.

Moss, Jean Dietz, *Novelties in the Heavens. Rhetoric and Science in the Copernican Controversy* (1993). The way scientists from Copernicus to Galileo described their discoveries tells us about their beliefs and values.

Oster, Malcolm, ed., *Science in Europe, 1500–1800: A Primary Sources Reader, A Secondary Sources Reader* (2002). A wonderful resource for students.

Schiebinger, Londa, *Nature's Body. Gender in the Making of Modern Science* (1993). Discusses how scientists project their own values on the things they study, from plants to apes and people.

Watson, Richard, *Cogito Ergo Sum. The Life of René Descartes* (2002). This is a very readable book by a scholar who can write to a wide audience.

Review Questions

1. What was the difference between the new scientific understanding of the universe and the medieval understanding of it?
2. Describe the major achievements of Copernicus, Kepler, Galileo, and Newton.
3. How did the practice of medicine change during the Scientific Revolution? Describe the changes.
4. Does modern science conform to Francis Bacon's ideals? List these ideals and discuss why it does or does not conform.
5. Was the Scientific Revolution essentially the achievement of a few men of genius, or was the process more complex than that? What were its implications?
6. What are the important contributions made by Newton?
7. What was the relationship between science and magic in this period?
8. What role did the Scientific Revolution play in shaping a modern mentality? Why have some people in the early twenty-first century become antiscience?

Chapter 18

The Age of Enlightenment: Reason and Reform

Madame Geoffrin's Salon. (Giraudon/Art Resource, NY.)

- **The Formation of a Public and Secular Culture**
  - Salons
  - Freemasons
  - Scientific Academies
- **Alternatives to Orthodoxy**
  - Christianity Under Attack
  - Skeptics, Freethinkers, and Deists
  - Voltaire the Philosophe
- **Political Thought**
  - Locke
  - Montesquieu
  - Rousseau
- **Social Thought**
  - Epistemology and Education
  - Humanitarianism
- **Economic Thought**
- **The High Enlightenment**
- **European Political and Diplomatic Developments**
  - Warfare
  - Enlightened Despotism
  - Effects of Enlightened Despotism
- **The Enlightenment in Eastern Europe**
- **The American Revolution**
- **The Enlightenment and the Modern World**

The eighteenth century's most exciting intellectual movement is called the Enlightenment. So powerful was its dedication to toleration and rational thought that until quite recently the era was sometimes characterized as the Age of Reason. The turn toward what became known by 1750 as the Enlightenment began in the late seventeenth century. Three factors were critically important in this new intellectual ferment: revulsion against monarchical and clerical absolutism, especially as practiced by Louis XIV in France; a new freedom of publishing and, with it, the rise of a new public and a secular culture, especially in England and the Dutch Republic; and, not least, the impact of the Scientific Revolution, particularly the excitement generated by Newton's *Principia* (1687).

When Newton's great work appeared, censorship or imprisonment for ideas disliked by church or state was still commonplace. Protestants languished in French prisons. Opponents of the Calvinist clergy in the Netherlands could be detained indefinitely; one man died after three years in jail without a trial, probably a suicide. In England, Oxford University routinely expelled students whose ideas were seen to be heretical or unorthodox. In the papal territories, Jewish children were still forcibly baptized and removed from their homes. By 1750, such extreme measures were rare anywhere north of the Alps or in the American colonies.

The promoters of science and religious tolerance had secured new freedoms, many of them given by sleight of hand. Rationality and order—imitative of the order found in Newton's universe—seemed to be gaining momentum. The leaders of the Enlightenment sought to impose an ordered freedom on social and political institutions. They were prepared to attack in print, though sometimes anonymously, the attitudes and beliefs that stood in the way of tolerance, freedom, and rationality. As combative intellectuals and pundits, they earned the name *philosophes*—simply the French word for "philosophers"—now used in many languages to describe the bold and witty satirists of clergymen, courtiers, and the pious in general. Thinkers as diverse as Voltaire in France, Benjamin Franklin in America, and Immanuel Kant (1724–1804), an abstract philosopher in Germany, may be labeled *philosophes*.

Chronology 18.1 ❖ The Enlightenment

1685	Revocation of the Edict of Nantes; persecution of Protestants in France
1687	Publication of Newton's *Principia*
1688–1689	Revolution in England: the clergy's power is weakened and censorship loosened
1690	Publication of Locke's *Two Treatises of Government*
1695	Publication of Locke's *Reasonableness of Christianity*
1696	Toland's *Christianity Not Mysterious* makes the case for deism
1717	Founding of the Grand Lodge, London; the beginning of organized Freemasonry
1733	Voltaire publishes *Letters Concerning the English Nation*
1740	Frederick the Great invades Silesia; the War of the Austrian Succession ensues
1748	Hume publishes *An Enquiry Concerning Human Understanding;* Montesquieu publishes *The Spirit of the Laws*
1751	Publication of Diderot's *Encyclopedia* in Paris
1756–1763	Seven Years' War
1762	Rousseau publishes *Émile* and *The Social Contract*
1775	American Revolution begins
1776	Adam Smith publishes *The Wealth of Nations*
1785	Russian Charter of Nobility; the servitude of the peasants is guaranteed
1787	Dutch Revolution begins
1789	French Revolution begins

Late in the eighteenth century, Kant gave a succinct definition of *enlightenment:* bringing "light into the dark corners of mind," dispelling ignorance, prejudice, and superstition. Kant went to the heart of one aspect of the Enlightenment: its insistence that each individual should reason independently, without recourse to the authority of schools, churches, or clergymen.[1]

Being a political moderate and living in Prussia, Kant hoped that the call for self-education and critical thought would mean no disruption of the political order, at least at home. In his moderation he was similar to most philosophes. Distrusting the uneducated people, these intellectual leaders sought a gradual transformation of the human condition. But there were radical thinkers during the late eighteenth century, such as the American revolutionary Thomas Jefferson (1743–1826) and the feminist Mary Wollstonecraft (1759–1797), who were prepared to endorse an immediate political disruption of the traditional authority of monarchy, aristocracy, fathers, and churchmen. Whether radical or moderate, the philosophes were united by certain key ideas. They believed in the new science, were critical of clergy and all rigid dogma but tolerant of people's right to worship freely, and believed deeply in freedom of the press. They were also willing to entertain, though not necessarily accept, new heresies—such as pantheism, or the belief that the earth had gradually evolved or the view that the Bible was a series of wise stories but not the literal word of God.

Philosophes were found most commonly in the major European cities, where they clubbed and socialized in literary and philosophical societies. By the 1770s, Paris was the center of the Enlightenment, but circles of philosophes could be found in Berlin, Moscow, Budapest, London, The Hague, and, across the Atlantic, in Philadelphia. Their writings spread far and wide because they adopted a new style for philosophical discussion: clear, direct, witty, satirical, even naughty and audacious. At times, they were more like journalists, propagandists, writers of fiction, even pornographers, who sought to live by their pens. Their success owed much to the growing literacy of urban men and women, a new prosperity that made books affordable, and the existence of an audience that liked what they had to say. The philosophes' readers, too, were fed up with all vestiges of medieval culture. They resented priestly privileges, protected social classes, monarchical decrees in place of deliberation in representative assemblies, and restrictions on who could manufacture what and where.

Appealing to the professional classes, literate merchants, and women with leisure to read, the philosophes opposed the old scholastic learning of the universities, mocked the clergy, and denied the Christian mysteries. They expressed confidence in science and reason, called for humanitarian treatment of slaves and criminals, and played a cat-and-mouse game with censors. Dedicated to freedom of thought and person, they combined these liberal values with a secular orientation and a belief in future progress. The philosophes helped shape, if not define, modern beliefs in tolerance, human rights, and free speech.

The Formation of a Public and Secular Culture

In England and the Dutch Republic, by 1700, freedom of the press was a practical or a legal reality. During the same period, in 1685, Louis XIV outlawed Protestants from France. Faced with forced conversion or imprisonment, thousands of highly educated Protestants (as well as menial workers) fled to England or the Netherlands. They set up journals and newspapers, formed new clubs, and began a vast international discussion—conducted in French, the language of all well-educated Europeans—aiming it against the injustices of monarchical absolutism and the evils of religious persecution. In journals and newspapers, the reformers endorsed the need for political change.

At the same time, relative freedom of assembly in the cities of western Europe (even in Paris, which was too big to police) gave rise to a new public and secular sphere: a zone for social life outside the family but not attached to churches or courts. The new public sphere, found in *salons* (gatherings in private homes), coffee houses, and Masonic lodges, as well as in academies for scientific learning like the Royal Society of London, laid the ground for the emergence of the Enlightenment.

All these autonomous and voluntary groups helped create a new secular and public culture. In this new and free mental space, what we now call civil society, people mingled with strangers, politeness and conviviality became norms of behavior, and informal learning flourished. Lecturers gave scientific demonstrations, ordinary men learned to vote for their leaders or to debate publicly, and women met outside the home to discuss novels or politics. Indeed, in some of the Parisian salons, women were often the key organizers. By the 1780s, throughout western Europe no town of any size was without a private association, club, and newspaper. In the Dutch Republic, in 1785, the first scientific society founded by and for women met in the town of Middleburg (located in the province of Zeeland and no larger than about 17,000 souls).[2] The women chose a Freemason and follower of Voltaire to give scientific demonstrations, and they set about learning Newtonian mechanics with such dedication that their society lasted for over a hundred years.

Men and women met at these sociable gatherings not because they were relatives, belonged to the same religion, or practiced the same trade or profession, but because they had a common interest in politics, science, the new novels, or self-improvement. Members of these new clubs shared certain characteristics: they were highly literate; they possessed some surplus wealth and leisure time; and, if titled aristocrats, they were not opposed to mixing with bourgeois lawyers, doctors, civil servants, and merchants. Such cosmopolitan men and women made the theories of the philosophes come alive. The new societies thus became schools where the literate expanded their universe, learning about peoples of the Orient and the Americas and about the Newtonian heavens. In the words of Kant, they dared to think for themselves.

This training in self-governance, self-education, and social criticism helped prepare the way for the liberal revolutions that swept across Europe at the end of the eighteenth and during the first half of the nineteenth century. In the first years of the French Revolution, one of the earliest activities of the revolutionaries was to set up clubs based on equality and fraternity and modeled after the clubs and lodges of the Enlightenment. As the revolutions spread, these societies spread the principles of the French Revolution, among them nationalist fervor. In the nineteenth century every nation had its patriotic clubs, but with them came the demise of the cosmopolitan ideals of the enlightened fraternities and salons. The Enlightnment could be smug and self-righteous, but it looked across national borders and its leaders were seldom dull.

Salons

Perhaps the most famous of the many new forms of secular culture were the salons, often run by women and mostly found in Paris. Intellectually ambitious women, such as Madame Necker and Madame Geoffrin, organized regular evening receptions in their drawing rooms. There philosophes gathered to discuss ideas in an atmosphere that was civilized, independent of the crown and the nobility, and open. Originally, the salon was an institution found only in noble homes, where the room designated for leisure activities gave the gathering its name. The Parisian women and their philosophe friends transformed the custom into gatherings where men and women could educate themselves and where some of the most outrageous ideas of the age could be openly discussed. The habits of luxurious feasting and gaming disappeared and in their place came serious, if somewhat formal, egalitarian conversation. Salons also developed an international correspondence; letters from all over Europe were read to the assembled guests. The notion of a republic of letters and the goal of cosmopolitanism were actually experienced in the salons. Some salons, however, excluded women, who were attacked as frivolous and gossipy. The free mixing of women and men always generated controversy in the eighteenth century.

Freemasons

As the search for a new religiosity during the Enlightenment came to mean a search for an alternative to traditional beliefs and practices, societies with a ritual and ethical component began to flourish. Among them were the Freemasons, a fraternity that evolved in the late seventeenth century in England and Scotland out of the guilds of stonemasons. In 1717, a group of London gentlemen, many of them very interested in the new science, founded the Grand Lodge, a collection of various Masonic lodges that met in pubs around the city. From that date onward, Freemasonry spread throughout Britain and then to continental Europe. It was often exported by British ambassadors, who brought it in the 1730s to Paris and The Hague and who used membership in the lodges to foster interest in British customs and institutions.

In the lodges, men, and eventually some women, were meant to meet "upon the level," that is, as fraternal equals, to hold elections, and to live under a constitution patterned on the rules that the old lodges had evolved during the seventeenth century. On the Continent, however, such practices as annual elections, representative government within the framework of a constitution, and habits of self-governance were new and experimental. The lodges sought to make their members virtuous, disciplined, and civilized. For some men, this experience came to rival that found in the churches. Philosophes, such as Benjamin Franklin and, late in his life, Voltaire, joined lodges; in some cities, lodges became cultural centers. In Vienna, Mozart was a Freemason and wrote music for his lodge; in Berlin, Frederick the Great cultivated the lodges, which in turn became centers for the cult of enlightened monarchy.

By the middle of the eighteenth century, perhaps

FREEMASONS' CEREMONY, VIENNA. To the right, in avid conversation, we can see one of the most famous Freemasons of the 1780s, the composer Wolfgang Amadeus Mozart. The play of light in the masonic "temple," the blindfolding, and the elegance were all intended to give importance to this new form of social life. (*Erich Lessing/Art Resource, NY.*)

as many as fifty thousand men belonged to lodges in just about every major European city. British constitutionalism, as well as the old fraternal ideals of equality and liberty, took on new meaning in these private gatherings. In France, in the 1780s, the national Grand Lodge instituted a national assembly of elected representatives, as well as a monthly payment of charity for impoverished brothers. The lodges for women became places where women and men actually talked about the meaning of liberty and equality for their own lives. Many lodges were dominated by the most elite elements in Old Regime society, who found themselves giving allegiance, and often considerable financial support, to a new system of belief and governance—a system that was ultimately incompatible with the principles of birth and inheritance on which their power rested. In 1738 the pope condemned membership in the lodges. At the time of the French Revolution, its opponents claimed that the lodges were responsible for the uprising. There was no truth to the claim, which opponents of all reforms and revolutions have often repeated. The subversive quality of the lodges lay not in any conspiracy but rather in the freedom they allowed for thought, self-governance, and discussion.

Scientific Academies

By midcentury, there were provincial scientific academies all over the Continent. The first scientific societies had formed in the 1660s in London and Paris. They continued to flourish and were imitated in Turin, Budapest, Berlin, and small cities of the Dutch Republic, such as Haarlem and Middelburg. Members of all these societies performed experiments of greater or lesser sophistication, listened to learned papers, and collected samples. Each society kept a cabinet of "rarities" containing everything from rocks to deformed animal bones. Any man who possessed what the age called curiosity could join one of these groups and try to become a man of science. Gradually, women were admitted—not as members but as spectators. By the 1770s, these scientific societies served as models for groups specifically interested in the application of scientific knowledge, or in useful learning. The new groups became centers for the reformers and critics of the age, who sought to turn the Enlightenment into a movement for changing society and government.

In Germany and France, where the scientific academies tended to be dominated by aristocratic leadership, new societies with a utilitarian purpose were founded and had to compete with the older societies. As a result, the turn toward the applied and the utilitarian was not as visible as in England and Scotland. In France, the academies became centers for abstract and advanced science and mathematics—for important and original contributions with little practical application. During the French Revolution, however, the academies were purged, and emphasis was then placed on applications of mechanics and chemistry.

Alternatives to Orthodoxy

Christianity Under Attack

No single thread had united Western culture more powerfully than Christianity. Until the eighteenth century, educated people, especially rulers and servants of the state, had to give allegiance to one or another of the Christian churches—however un-Christian their actions. The Enlightenment produced the first widely read and systematic assault on Christianity launched from within the ranks of the educated. The philosophes argued that many Christian dogmas defied logic—for example, the conversion of the substance of bread and wine into the body and the blood of Christ during the Eucharist. They also ridiculed theologians for arguing about obscure issues that seemed irrelevant to the human condition and a hindrance to clear thinking. "Theology amuses me," wrote Voltaire. "That's where we find the madness of the human spirit in all its plenitude." In the same vein, the philosophes denounced the churches for inciting the fanaticism and intolerance that led to the horrors of the Crusades, the Inquisition, and the wars of the Reformation. They viewed Christianity's preoccupation with salvation and its belief in the depravity of human nature, a consequence of Adam and Eve's defiance of God, as barriers to social improvement and earthly happiness.

Skeptics, Freethinkers, and Deists

An early attack on Christian dogma was made by the skeptic Pierre Bayle (1647–1706), who came to distrust Christian dogma and to see superstition as a social evil far more dangerous than atheism. Bayle was a French Protestant forced to flee to the Netherlands as a result of Louis XIV's campaign against Protestants. Although a Calvinist in background, Bayle also ran into opposition from the strict Calvinist clergy, who regarded him as lax on doctrinal matters. He attacked his critics and persecutors in a new and brilliant form of journalism, his *Historical and Critical Dictionary* (1697), which was more an encyclopedia than a dictionary. Under alphabetically arranged subjects and in copious footnotes, Bayle discussed the most recent learning of the day on various matters and never missed an opportunity to ridicule the dogmatic, the superstitious, or the just plain arrogant. In Bayle's hands, the ancient philosophy of skepticism—the doubting of all dogma—was revived and turned into a tool; rigorous questioning of accepted ideas became a method for arriving at new truths. As Bayle noted in his *Dictionary,* "It is therefore only religion that has anything to fear from Pyrrhonism [that is, skepticism]."[3] In this same critical spirit, Bayle, in his dictionary article entitled "David," compared Louis XIV to Goliath. The message was clear enough: great tyrants and the clergy who prop them up should beware of self-confident, independently minded citizens who are skeptical of the claims of authority made by kings and churches and are eager to use their own intellects to search for truth.

Bayle's *Dictionary,* which was in effect the first encyclopedia, had an enormous impact throughout Europe. Its very format captured the imagination of the philosophes. Here was a way of simply, even scientifically, classifying and ordering knowledge. Partly through Bayle's writings, skepticism became an integral part of the Enlightenment approach to religion. It taught its readers to question the clerical claim that God's design governs human events—that "God ordains" certain human actions. Skepticism dealt a serious blow to revealed religion and seemed to point in the direction of "natural" religion, that is, toward a system of beliefs and ethics designed by rational people on the basis of their own needs.

The religious outlook of the philosophes was also colored by late-seventeenth- and early-eighteenth-century English freethinkers. These early representatives of the Enlightenment used the term *freethinking* to signal their hostility to established church dogmas and their ability to think for themselves. They looked back to the English Revolution of 1640–1660 for their ideas about government; many English freethinkers were republicans in the tradition established by important figures of the interregnum. Indeed, the English freethinkers of the 1690s and beyond helped popularize English republican ideas at home and in the American colonies, where in 1776 these views would figure prominently in the thinking of American revolutionaries.

The freethinkers had little use for organized religion or even for Christianity itself. In 1696, the freethinker John Toland (1670–1722) published *Christianity Not Mysterious.* In it he argued that most religious doctrines seemed to contradict reason or common sense and ought to be discarded along with such beliefs as the resurrection of Jesus and the miracles of the Bible. Toland also attacked the clergy's power; in his opinion, the Revolution of 1688–89 had not gone far enough in undermining the power of the established church and the king. Toland and his freethinking associates wanted England to be a republic governed by "reasonable" people who worshiped, as Toland proposed, not a mysterious God but intelligible nature. For Toland, Newton's science made nature intelligible, and he used it as a stick with which to beat at the doctrines of revealed religion.

Combining science with skepticism, freethinking, and anticlericalism, thoughtful critics found ample reason for abandoning all traditional authority. By 1700, a general crisis of confidence in established authority had been provoked by the works of Bayle, the freethinkers, and philosophers such as Descartes. Once started in England and the Netherlands and broadcast via Dutch and French refugee printers, the Enlightenment quickly became international.

Some of the early proponents of the Enlightenment were atheists. They often published clandestinely. A particularly early and outrageous example of their thinking appeared under the title *The Treatise on the Three Imposters* (1719), which identified Jesus, Moses, and Muhammad as the impostors. However, most of the philosophes were simply deists, who believed only those Christian doctrines that could meet the test of reason. For example, they considered it reasonable to believe in God, for only with a creator, they said, could such a superbly organized universe have come into being. But, in their view, after God set the universe in motion, he took no further part in its operations. Thus, although deists retained a belief in God the Creator, they rejected clerical authority, revelation, original sin, and miracles. They held that biblical accounts of the resurrection and of Jesus walking on water or raising the dead could not be reconciled with natural law. Deists viewed Jesus as a great moral teacher, not as the Son of God, and they regarded ethics, not faith, as the essence of religion. Rational people, they said, served God best by treating their fellow human beings justly.

David Hume (1711–1776), a Scottish skeptic, attacked both revealed religion and the deists' natural religion. He maintained that all religious ideas, including Christian teachings and even the idea of God, stemmed ultimately from human fears and superstitions. Hume rejected the deist argument that this seemingly orderly universe required a designing mind to create it. The universe, said Hume, might very well be eternal and the seemingly universal order simply be more in our heads than in reality. Hume laid great emphasis on social conventions, with which he associated religion. Reason should best be expressed through skepticism.

Voltaire the Philosophe

The French possessed a vital tradition of intellectual skepticism going back to the late sixteenth century, as well as a tradition of scientific rationalism exemplified by Descartes. In the early eighteenth century, however, the French found it difficult to gain access to the new literature of the Enlightenment because the French printing presses were among the most tightly controlled and censored in Europe. As a result, a brisk but risky traffic developed in clandestine books and manuscripts subversive of authority, and French-language journals poured from Dutch presses.

As a poet and writer struggling for recognition in Paris, the young François Marie Arouet, known to the world as Voltaire (1694–1778), encountered some of the new ideas that were being discussed in salons in Paris. In the French capital, those educated people who wanted to read books and discuss ideas hostile to the church or to the Sorbonne, the clerically controlled university, had to proceed with caution. Individuals had been imprisoned for writing, publishing, or owning books hostile to Catholic doctrine. Although Voltaire learned something of the new enlightened culture in Paris, it was in 1726, when he journeyed to London, that Voltaire the poet became Voltaire the philosophe. Voltaire fled Paris after he was arbitrarily arrested when defending himself in a fight with a local aristocrat.

In England, Voltaire became acquainted with the ideas of John Locke and Isaac Newton. From Newton, Voltaire learned the mathematical laws that govern the universe; he witnessed the power of human reason to establish general rules that seemed to explain the behavior of physical objects. From Locke, Voltaire learned that people should believe only the ideas received from the senses. Locke's theory of learning, his *epistemology*, impressed many of the proponents of the Enlightenment. Again, the implications for religion were most serious: if people believed only what they experienced, they would not accept mysteries and doctrines simply because they were taught by churches and clergy. Voltaire enjoyed considerable freedom of thought in England and saw a social and religious toleration that contrasted sharply with French absolutism and the power of the French clergy. He also witnessed a freer mix-

VOLTAIRE AND KING FREDERICK. The roundtable was beloved by the aristocracy because it claimed everyone as an equal. Here Voltaire visits with Frederick the Great and perhaps imagined himself as an equal. (*Bildarchiv Preussischer Kulturbesitz.*)

ing of bourgeois and aristocratic social groups than was permitted in France at this time.

Throughout his life, Voltaire fiercely supported toleration and free inquiry. He criticized churches and the Roman Catholic Inquisition. His books were banned in France, but he probably did more there than any other philosophe to popularize the Enlightenment. In *Letters Concerning the English Nation* (1733), Voltaire offered constitutional monarchy, new science, and religious toleration as models to be followed by all of Europe. In the *Letters,* he praised English society for its encouragement of these ideals. As he put it, "This is the country of sects. An Englishman, as a free man, goes to Heaven by whatever road he pleases."[4] Voltaire never ceased to ridicule the purveyors of superstition and blind obedience to religious authority. In such works as *Candide* (1759) and *Micromegas* (1752), he castigated the clergy, as well as other philosophical supporters of the status quo who would have people believe that this was the best of all possible worlds.

Voltaire was also a practical reformer who campaigned for the rule of law, a freer press, religious toleration, humane treatment of criminals, and a more effective system of government administration. His writings constituted a radical attack on several aspects of eighteenth-century French society. Yet, like so many philosophes, Voltaire feared the power of the people, especially if goaded by the clergy. He was happiest in the company of the rich and powerful, provided they tolerated his ideas and supported reform. Not surprisingly, Voltaire was frequently disappointed by eighteenth-century monarchs, like Frederick the Great in Prussia, who promised enlightenment but sought mainly to increase their own power and that of their armies.

Perhaps the happiest decision of Voltaire's life was to team up with the scientist and philosophe Madame du Châtelet (1706–1749). Together they read Newton, although she became the more proficient mathematician. Before her death during the birth of their child, Madame du Châtelet made the only French translation of the *Principia,* explicated it, and trained scientists who took up Newtonian ideas and spread them throughout western Europe.

Political Thought

With the exception of Machiavelli in the Renaissance and Thomas Hobbes and the republicans during the English Revolution of 1640–1660, the Enlightenment produced the greatest originality in modern political thought witnessed in the West up to that time. Three major European thinkers and a host of minor ones wrote treatises on politics that remain relevant to this day: John Locke, *Two Treatises of Government* (1690); Baron de la Brède et de Montesquieu, *The Spirit of the Laws* (1748); and Jean Jacques Rousseau, *The Social Contract* (1762). All repudiated the divine right of kings and strove to check the power of monarchy; each offered different formulas for achieving that goal. These major political theorists of the Enlightenment were also aware of the writings of Machiavelli and Hobbes and, though often disagreeing with them, borrowed some of their ideas.

During the Renaissance, Machiavelli (d. 1527) analyzed politics in terms of power, fortune, and the ability of the individual ruler; he did not call in God to justify the power of princes or to explain their demise. Machiavelli also preferred a republican form of government to monarchy, and his republican vision did not lose its appeal during the Enlightenment. Very late in the eighteenth century, most liberal theorists recognized that the republican form of government, or at least the virtues practiced by citizens in a republic, offered the only alternative to the corruption and repression associated with absolute monarchy.

Political thinkers of the Enlightenment were ambivalent toward much of the writing of Thomas Hobbes (1588–1679). All, however, liked his belief that self-interest is a valid reason for engaging in political activity and his refusal to bring God into his system to justify the power of kings. Hobbes said that power did not rest on divine right but arose out of a contract made among men who agreed to elevate the state, and hence the monarch, to a position of power over them. That contract, once made, could not be broken. As a consequence, the power of the government, whether embodied in a king or a parliament, was absolute.

Hobbes published his major work, *Leviathan,* in 1651, soon after England had been torn by civil war; thus, he was obsessed with the issue of political stability. He feared that, left to their own devices, men would kill one another; the "war of all against all"[5] would prevail without the firm hand of a sovereign to stop it. Hobbes's vision of human nature was dark and forbidding. In the state of nature, the original men had lived lives that could only have been "nasty, brutish, and short." Their sole recourse was to set up a power over themselves that would restrain them. For Hobbes, the state was, as he put it, a "mortal god," the only guarantee of peace and stability. He was the first political thinker to realize the extraordinary power that had come into existence with the creation of strong centralized governments. Most Enlightenment theorists, however, beginning with John Locke, denied that governments possessed absolute power over their subjects, and to that extent they repudiated Hobbes. Many European thinkers of the eighteenth century, including Rousseau, also rejected Hobbes's gloomy view that human nature is greedy and warlike. Yet Hobbes lurks in the background of the Enlightenment. He is the first wholly secular political theorist, and he sounded the death knell for theories of the divine right of kings. The Enlightenment theorists started where he left off.

LOCKE ON THE CONTINENT. John Locke enjoyed an international reputation. This highly stylized portrait of him is adorned with French text. Locke had lived in the Dutch Republic and his writings were taken and promoted by French Huguenot refugees who hated the monarchy they left behind. (*Corbis.*)

Locke

Probably the most widely read political philosopher during the first half of the eighteenth century was John Locke (1632–1704). Locke came to maturity in the late 1650s, and like so many of his contemporaries, he was drawn to science. Although he became a medical doctor, his major interest lay in politics and political theory. His *Two Treatises of Government* was seen as a justification for the English Revolution of 1688–89 and the notion of government by consent of the people. (Although the treatises were published in 1690, Locke wrote them before the Glorious Revolution; that fact, however, was not known during the Enlightenment.)

Locke's theory, in its broad outlines, stated that the right to govern derived from the consent of the governed and was a form of contract. When people gave their consent to a government, they expected it to govern justly, protect their property, and ensure certain liberties for the propertied. If a government attempted to rule absolutely and arbitrarily—if it violated the natural rights of the individual—it reneged on its contract and forfeited the loyalty of its subjects. Such a government could legitimately be overthrown. Locke believed that a constitutional government that limited the power of rulers offered the best defense of property and individual rights. He also advocated religious toleration for religious groups whose beliefs did not threaten the state. Locke denied toleration to Catholics because of their association with the Stuarts and to atheists because their oaths to God could not be trusted. He also promoted the necessity for education, particularly for those who saw themselves as the natural leaders of society. And not least, he advocated commerce and trade as one of the foundations of England's national strength.

Late in the eighteenth century, Locke's ideas were used to justify liberal revolutions in both Europe and America. His *Treatises of Government* had been translated into French early in the century by Huguenot refugees. These Protestant victims of French absolutism, persecuted for their religion, saw that the importance of Locke's political philosophy was not simply in his use of contract theory to justify constitutional government; he also asserted that the community could take up arms against its sovereign in the name of the natural rights of liberty and property. Locke's ideas about the foundation of government had greater impact on the European continent and in America during the eighteenth century than in England.

Montesquieu

Baron de la Brède et de Montesquieu (1689–1755) was a French aristocrat who, like Voltaire, visited England late in the 1720s and knew the writings of Locke. Montesquieu had little sympathy for revolutions, but he did approve of constitutional monarchy. His primary concern was to check the unbridled authority of the French kings. In opposition to the Old Regime, Montesquieu proposed a balanced system of government, with an executive branch offset by a legislature whose members were drawn from the landed and educated elements in society. From his writings we derive our notion of government divided into branches. Montesquieu genuinely believed that the aristocracy possessed a natural and sacred obligation to rule and that their honor called them to serve the community. He also sought to fashion a government that channeled the interests and energies of its people, a government that was not bogged down in corruption and inefficiency.

In stressing the rule of law and the importance of nonmonarchical authority, Montesquieu became a source for legitimating the authority of representative institutions. Hardly an advocate of democracy, Montesquieu was nonetheless seen as a powerful critic of royal absolutism. His writings, particularly *The Spirit of the Laws,* established him both as a major philosophe who possessed republican tendencies and as a critic of the Old Regime in France. Once again, innovative political thinking highlighted the failures of absolutist government and pointed to the need for some kind of representative assembly in every European country. In addition, Montesquieu's ideas on a balanced system of government found favor in the new American republic.

Rousseau

Not until the 1760s did democracy find its champion: Jean Jacques Rousseau (1712–1778). Rousseau based his politics on contract theory and his reading of Hobbes. For Rousseau, the people choose their government and, in so doing, effectively give birth to civil society. But he further demanded (in contrast to Hobbes) that the contract be constantly renewed and that government be made immediately and directly responsible to the will of the people. *The Social Contract* opened with this stirring cry for reform, "Man is born free; and everywhere he is in chains," and went on to ask how that restriction could be changed. Freedom is in the very nature of man: "to renounce liberty is to renounce being a man, to surrender the rights of humanity and even its duties."[6]

Rousseau's political ideal was the city-state of ancient Greece, where men (but not women) participated actively and directly in politics and were willing to sacrifice self-interest to the community's needs. To the ancient Greek, said Rousseau, the state was a moral association that made him a better person, and good citizenship was the highest form of excellence. In contrast, modern society was prey to many conflicting interests; the rich and powerful used the state to preserve their advantages and power, and the poor and powerless viewed it as an oppressor. Consequently, the obedience to law, the devotion to the state, and the freedom that had characterized the Greek city-state had been lost.

In *The Social Contract,* Rousseau tried to resolve the conflict between individual freedom and the demands of the state. His solution was a small state, modeled after his native city of Geneva as well as after the Greek city-state. Such a state, said Rousseau, should be based on the

Jean Jacques Rousseau Alone, a Self-Exile from the City. Rousseau viewed nature and solitude as curative. He also advocated reading for introspection and enlightenment. (*Photographie Bulloz.*)

general will: that which is best for the community, which expresses its common interests. Rousseau wanted laws of the state to coincide with the general will. He felt that people have the wisdom to arrive at laws that serve the common good, but to do so, they must set aside selfish interests for the good of the community. For Rousseau, freedom consisted of obeying laws prescribed by citizens inspired by the general will. The citizens themselves must constitute the lawmaking body; lawmaking cannot be entrusted to a single person or a small group.

In Rousseau's view, those who disobey laws—who act according to their private will rather than in accordance with the general will as expressed in law—degrade themselves and undermine the community. Therefore, government has the right to force citizens to be obedient, to compel them to exercise their individual wills in the proper way. He left the problem of minority rights unresolved.

No philosopher of the Enlightenment was more dangerous to the Old Regime than Rousseau. His ideas were perceived as truly revolutionary: a direct challenge to the power of kings, the power of the church, and the power of aristocrats. Although Rousseau thought that many leaders of the Enlightenment had been corrupted by easy living and the life of the salons, with their attendant aristocrats and dandies, he nevertheless earned an uneasy place in the ranks of the philosophes. In the French Revolution, his name would be invoked to justify democracy, and of all the philosophes, Rousseau would probably have been the least horrified by the early phase of that revolutionary upheaval.

Social Thought

Rousseau looked on society as the corrupter of human beings, who, left to their own devices, were inherently virtuous and freedom loving. A wide spectrum of thinkers in the Enlightenment also viewed society, if not as corrupting, at least as needing constant reform. Some enlightened critics were prepared to work with those in power to bring about social reforms. Other philosophes believed that the key to reform lay not in social and political institutions but in changing the general mentality through education and knowledge. All developed new ideas about humankind as travelers told of new peoples and places where commonplace concepts, such as the Judeo-Christian God, had never existed. The societies of Native Americans fascinated Europeans, who vacillated between feeling superior and believing themselves mired in baroquely rigid customs.

Epistemology and Education

Just as Locke's *Two Treatises of Government* helped shape the political thought of the Enlightenment, his *Essay Concerning Human Understanding* (1689) provided the theoretical foundations for an unprecedented interest in education. Locke's view that at birth the mind is blank—a clean slate, or *tabula rasa*—had two important implications. First, if human beings did

Profile

Mary Wollstonecraft

The Board of Trustees of the National Museums and Galleries on Merseyside, Walker Art Gallery.

One of the founders of modern feminism and a deeply committed defender of liberty, human rights, and the French Revolution, Mary Wollstonecraft (1759–1797) came to maturity in a circle of English radicals. Her friends included the Unitarian ministers Richard Price and Joseph Priestley, and she knew the British-born American radical Thomas Paine. Although she received little formal education, she taught herself languages, made a living as a translator, read Rousseau critically, and began an intellectual odyssey that took her from liberal Protestantism to freethinking and possibly atheism. She went to France during its Revolution and wanted to raise her daughter there because she believed that in France she would be freer. By far her most famous book is ***The Vindication of the Rights of Women*** (1792), a classic statement of women's rights and the causes of prejudice and inequality. Since the two hundredth anniversary of Wollstonecraft's famous book, her writings have been revived, and she has been placed at the center of the European Enlightenment as an embodiment of its belief in science and the possibility of human emancipation.

not come into this world with innate ideas, then they were not, as Christianity taught, inherently sinful. Second, a person's environment was the decisive force in shaping his or her character and intelligence. Nine of every ten men, wrote Locke, "are good or evil, useful or not, [because of] their education." Such a theory was eagerly received by the reform-minded philosophes, who preferred attributing wickedness to faulty institutions, improper rearing, and poor education rather than to a defective human nature.

In the Enlightenment view, the proper study of humanity addressed the process by which people can and do know. Locke had said that individuals take the information produced by their senses and reflect on it; in that way, they arrive at complex ideas. Aside from an environment promoting learning, education obviously requires the active participation of students. Merely receiving knowledge not tested by their own sense experience is inadequate.

More treatises were written on education during the eighteenth century than in all previous centuries combined. On the Continent, where the clergy controlled many schools and all the universities, the educated laity began to demand state regulation and inspection of educational facilities. This insistence revealed a growing discontent with the clergy and their independent authority. By the second half of the century, new schools and universities in Prussia, Belgium, Austria, Hungary, and Russia attempted to teach practical subjects suited to the interests of the laity. Predictably, science was given a special place in these new institutions. In France, for all the interest in education on the part of the philosophes, by 1789 probably only 50 percent of the men and about 20 percent of the women were literate.

The standards of education for girls and women were appalling. Only a few philosophes, mostly women, and the occasional clergyman who had seen firsthand the poor quality of female education in reading and writing called for reform. But reform did not come till after 1800, when industrialization put more women in the workforce and required some literacy. As for higher education, women were excluded, with a few exceptions. Madame du Châtelet in France had studied mathematics with a private tutor; and in Italy, Laura Bassi became the first woman to teach in a European university, at Bologna. In the Netherlands, women founded a scientific academy in 1785. However, these were isolated waves in a sea of largely clerical indifference.

Generally, Protestant countries were better at ensuring basic literacy and numeracy for boys and probably also for girls. Lutheran Prussia and Presbyterian Scotland excelled in the field of education, but for very different reasons. In Prussia, Frederick the Great decreed universal public education for boys as part of his effort to surpass the level of technical expertise found in other countries. His educational policy was another example of his using the Enlightenment to increase the power of the central government. In Scotland, improvements in education were sponsored mainly by the established Presbyterian (Calvinist) church. The Protestant universities were by and large more progressive intellectually than their Catholic counterparts. The Jesuits, for instance, resisted teaching the new science. By contrast, medicine at the universities of Edinburgh—along with medicine at the University of Leiden in the Netherlands—became the most advanced of the century. But ironically, the universities were never at the forefront of the Enlightenment. For the latest ideas, one went to the salons rather than consulted the professors.

That fact fitted in very well with Locke's doctrine that knowledge comes primarily through experience. Rousseau took it up and brought it to its logical conclusion. In *Émile* (1762), he argued that individuals learn from nature, from people, or from things. Indeed, Rousseau wanted the early years of a child's education to be centered on developing the senses and not spent with the child chained to a schoolroom desk. Later, attention would be paid to intellectual pursuits, and then finally to morality. Rousseau grasped a fundamental principle of modern psychology: the child is not a small adult, and childhood is not merely preparation for adulthood but a particular stage in human development with its own distinguishing characteristics.

Rousseau appealed especially to women to be virtuous and to protect their children from social convention, that is, to teach their children about honesty and sentiment. There were problems with Rousseau's educational system. He would make the family the major educational force, and he wanted the products of such education to be cosmopolitan and enlightened individuals, singularly free from superstition and prejudice. However, women (whom Rousseau would confine to the home) were to bear the burden of instilling enlightenment, although they had little experience of the world beyond the family and in France their education was entirely in the hands of nuns.

Rousseau's contradictions, particularly about women, sprang in large measure from his desperate search for an alternative to aristocratic mores and clerical authority. He also shared in the gender bias of his age, although what may seem bias to us may also have reflected his belief that women sought the home as a solace and refuge. Certainly, many women read him critically, but essentially as an ally and defender.

Humanitarianism

Crime and Punishment. No society founded on the principles of the Enlightenment could condone the torture of prisoners and the inhumanity of a corrupt legal system. On those points, all the philosophes were clear, and they had plenty of evidence from their own societies on which to base their condemnation of torture and the inhumanity of the criminal justice system.

Whether an individual was imprisoned for unpaid debts or for banditry or murder, prison conditions differed little. Prisoners were often starved

Tortures of the Inquisition. Torture was part of everyday criminal justice in every European country. Only around the middle of the eighteenth century did the practice come under withering attack by enlightened thinkers. (*The Granger Collection.*)

or exposed to disease, or both. In many continental European countries, where torture was still legal, prisoners could be subjected to brutal interrogation or to random punishment. In 1777, English reformer John Howard published a report in England and Wales that documented how prisoners went without food or medical assistance.

To imagine that the enlightened reformers invented the techniques of discipline and punishment—as some philosophers in the twentieth century have thought—denies the historical record. It was the reformers of the Enlightenment who began to agitate against the prison conditions of the day. Even if torture was illegal, as was the case only in England, prison conditions were often as harmful as torture to the physical and mental health of inmates. Conditions still present in some prisons today would have been intolerable to the philosophe-reformers.

Although there is something particularly reprehensible about the torturer, his skills were consciously applauded in many countries during the eighteenth century. Fittingly, the most powerful critique of the European system of punishment came from Italy, where the Inquisition and its torture chambers had reigned with little opposition for centuries. In Milan, during the early 1760s, the Enlightenment had made very gradual inroads, and in a small circle of reformers the practices of the Inquisition and the relationship between church and state in the matter of criminal justice were avidly discussed.

Out of that intellectual ferment came one of the most important books of the Enlightenment: *Of Crime and Punishment* (1764), by the Milanese reformer Cesare Beccaria (1738–1794). For centuries, sin and crime had been wedded in the eyes of the church; the function of the state was to punish crime because it was a manifestation of sin. Beccaria cut through that thicket of moralizing. He argued that the church should concern itself with sin and should abandon its prisons and courts. Instead, the state should concern itself with crimes against society, and the purpose of punishment should be to reintegrate the individual into society. Punishment should be swift but intended to rehabilitate.

Beccaria also inquired into the causes of crime. Abandoning the concept of sin, Beccaria, rather like Rousseau, who perceived injustice and corruption in the very fabric of society, regarded private property as the root of social injustice and hence the root of crime. Pointedly, he asked, "What are these laws I must respect, that they leave such a huge gap between me and the rich? Who made these laws? Rich and powerful men. . . . Let us break these fatal connections. . . . let us attack injustice at its source."[7]

Beccaria's attackers labeled him a *socialist*—the first time (1765) that term was used—by which they meant that Beccaria paid attention only to people as social creatures and that he wanted a society of free and equal citizens. In contrast, the defenders of the use of torture and capital punishment, and of the necessity of social inequality, argued that Beccaria's teachings would lead to chaos and to the loss of all property rights and legitimate authority. These critics sensed the utopian aspect of Beccaria's thought. His humanitarianism was not directed toward the reform of the criminal justice system alone; he sought to restructure society in such a way as to render crime far less prevalent and, whenever possible, to reeducate its perpetrators.

When Beccaria's book and then the author himself turned up in Paris, the philosophes greeted them with universal acclaim. All the leaders of the period—Voltaire, Rousseau, Denis Diderot, and the atheist d'Holbach—embraced one or another of Beccaria's views. But if the criminal justice system and the schools were subject to scrutiny by enlightened critics, what did the philosophes have to say about slavery, the most pernicious of all Western institutions?

Slavery. On both sides of the Atlantic during the eighteenth century, criticism of slavery was growing. At first, it came from religious thinkers like the Quakers, whose own religious version of enlightenment predated the European-wide phenomenon by several decades. The Quakers were born out of the turmoil of the English Revolution, and their strong adherence to democratic ideas grew out of their conviction that the light of God's truth works in every man and woman. Many philosophes on both sides of the Atlantic knew Quaker thought, and Voltaire, who had mixed feelings about slavery, and Benjamin Franklin, who condemned it, admired the Quakers and their principles.

On the problem of slavery, some philosophes were strangely ambivalent. In an ideal world—just about all agreed—slavery would not exist. But the world was not ideal, and given human wickedness, greed, and lust for power, Voltaire thought that both slavery and exploitation might be inevitable. "The human race," Voltaire wrote in his *Philosophical Dictionary* (1764), "constituted as it is, cannot subsist unless there be an infinite number of useful individuals possessed of no property at all."[8] Diderot thought that slavery was probably immoral but concluded that, given the importance of slavery in the colonies and the fact that the French monarchy provided no leadership in changing the situation, there was no point in trying to abolish slavery at the time. Indeed, not until 1794, and only after agonized debate, did the French government, no longer a monarchy, finally abolish slavery in its colonies.

It must be remembered that political thinkers of the Enlightenment, among them Locke (who condoned slavery) and Montesquieu (whose ideas were used to condone it), rejected God-given political authority and argued for the rights of property holders and for social utility as the foundations of good government. Those criteria, property and utility, played right into the hands of the proslavery apologists. Montesquieu condemned slavery, but that did not stop its apologists from using his ideas about the relationship between hot climates and sloth to justify making Africans slaves. Even radicals inspired by the French Revolution, like the British manufacturer Thomas Cooper, could emigrate and become slave owners and apologists for the system.

Yet if the principle held, as so many philosophes argued, that human happiness was the greatest good, how could slavery be justified? In his short novel *Candide,* Voltaire has his title character confront the spectacle of a young African who has had his leg and arm cut off merely because it is the custom of a country. Candide's philosophical optimism is shattered as he reflects on the human price paid by this slave, who harvested the sugar that Europeans enjoyed so abundantly. Throughout the eighteenth century, the emphasis placed by the Enlightenment on moral sensibility produced a literature that used shock to emphasize over and over again, and with genuine revulsion, the inhumanity of slavery.

By the second half of the century, a new generation of philosophes launched strongly worded attacks on slavery. With Rousseau in the vanguard, they condemned slavery as a violation of the natural rights of man. The philosophes invented the concept of *human rights*. In a volume issued in 1755, the great *Encyclopedia* of the Enlightenment, edited by Diderot, condemned slavery in no uncertain terms: "There is not a single one of these hapless souls . . . who does not have the right to be declared free . . . since neither his ruler nor his father nor anyone else had the right to dispose of his freedom."[9] That statement appeared in thousands of copies and various editions of an encyclopedia that was probably the most influential publication resulting from the French Enlightenment. Indeed, French writers led the enlightened attacks on slavery. The Dutch novelist Betje Wolff had to translate French writers when, in 1790, she launched her attack on the Dutch slave trade.

These writers tipped the scales to put the followers of the Enlightenment in the antislavery camp. But that victory was clouded by ambiguous language coming straight from the pens of some of Europe's supposedly most enlightened thinkers and by their prejudice against blacks as non-Europeans.

Social Equality. The humanitarian impulse inevitably entailed taking a cold, hard look at social inequalities, which were very obvious in a century when dress, speech, body gestures, and even smell told all. The poor were visibly underfed; workers wore the costumes of their trade; aristocrats, both men and women, dressed in elaborate wigs, shoes, silks, jewels, and lace. Devout Calvinist women often wore black, and only their rings or headpieces betrayed their social status. How could the ideal of human equality be conceptualized in such a society?

Voltaire despised the lower classes. Kant said that women should feel and not reason: "her philosophy is not to reason, but to sense."[10] Women had few property rights, and the poor had even fewer; the Lockean contract seemed irrelevant to their circumstances. Yet in the American and French Revolutions, the leaders proclaimed human equality as an ideal. But though France freed the slaves in the colonies, the Jacobins closed down women's political clubs. In the new American republic, women began to take a more active role in civil society; slavery, however, remained (yet in every northern state, it was abolished by 1804). Modern critics condemn the Enlightenment for being inconsistent, but historical reality can be understood only in relation to the backward alternatives offered by absolute monarchs and established churches.

More than any other previous historical movement, the Enlightenment put human equality on the mental agenda of Western societies. Men and women could meet as equals at social gatherings, the new novels could depict the suffering of women at the hands of brutal men or describe the wretched life of the poor, women could travel abroad as never before, and traveling scientific lecturers frequently sought their tuition. Leisure, literacy, public and secular culture, fiery journalism, local newspapers, travelers' reports, even the new and naughty pornography, all attacked the superstitions and contradictions that centuries of custom had enshrined. The new science pointed to a universe where matter was everywhere the same—the atoms are all equal—and it universally obeyed impersonal and impartial laws. The struggle to achieve democratic equality—the dilemma of modern life—first came to the surface in countless acts of reading and conversing in the new enlightened and urban culture. It continues to this day.

Economic Thought

The Enlightenment's emphasis on property as the foundation for individual rights and its search for uniform laws inspired by Newton's scientific achievement led to the development of the science of economics. Appropriately, that intellectual achievement occurred in the most advanced capitalistic nation in Europe, Great Britain. Not only were the British in the vanguard of capitalist expansion, but by the third quarter of the eighteenth century, that expansion had started the Industrial Revolution. Britain's new factories and markets for the manufacture and distribution of goods provided a natural laboratory where theorists schooled in the Enlightenment's insistence on observation and experimentation could watch the ebb and flow of capitalist production and distribution. In contrast to its harsh criticisms of existing institutions and old elites, the Enlightenment on the whole approved of the independent businessman—the entrepreneur. And there was no one more approving than Adam Smith (1732–1790), whose *Wealth of Nations* (1776) became a kind of bible for those who regarded capitalist activity as uniformly worthwhile and never to be inhibited by outside regulation.

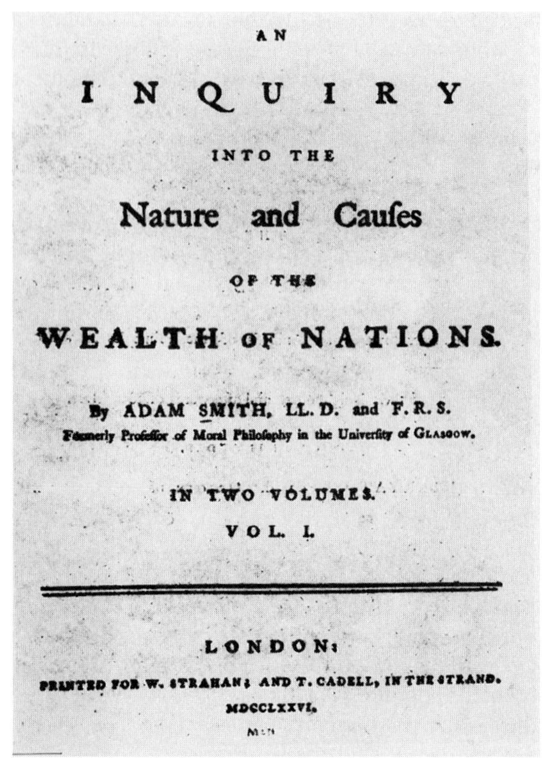

AN

INQUIRY

INTO THE

Nature and Cauſes

OF THE

WEALTH OF NATIONS.

By ADAM SMITH, LL. D. and F. R. S.

Formerly Profeſſor of Moral Philoſophy in the Univerſity of Glasgow.

IN TWO VOLUMES.

VOL. I.

LONDON:

PRINTED FOR W. STRAHAN; AND T. CADELL, IN THE STRAND.

MDCCLXXVI.

Plain Adam Smith. Smith's classic—the most often cited defense of capitalism—appeared in a plain binding, with no fancy artwork. The genius lay in the text of 1776. (*Corbis.*)

Throughout the seventeenth century in England, there had been a long tradition of economic thought. The resulting ideology stressed independent initiative and the freedom of market forces to determine the value of money and the goods it can buy. By 1700, English economic thought was already well ahead of what could be found on the Continent, with the exception of some Dutch writings. That sophistication undoubtedly reflected the complexity of market life in cities like London and Amsterdam.

One important element in seventeenth-century economic thought, as well as in the most advanced thinking on ethics, was the role of self-interest. Far from being considered crude or socially dangerous, it was seen as a good thing, to be cautiously accepted. In the mid-seventeenth century, Hobbes took the view that self-interest lay at the root of political action. By the end of the century, Locke argued that government, rather than primarily restraining the extremes of human greed and the search for power, should promote the interests of its citizens. By the middle of the eighteenth century, enlightened theorists all over Europe—especially in England, Scotland, and France—had decided that self-interest was the foundation of all human actions and that at every turn government should aid people in expressing their interests and thus in finding true happiness.

Of course, in the area of economic life, government had for centuries regulated most aspects of the market. The classic economic theory behind such regulation was mercantilism. Mercantilists believed that a constant shortage of riches—bullion, goods, whatever—existed and that governments must so direct economic activity in their states as to compete successfully with other nations for a share of the world's scarce resources. There was also another assumption implicit in mercantilist theory: that money has a "real" value, which governments must protect. The value is not to be determined solely by market forces.

It required faith in the inherent usefulness of self-interest to assert that government should cease regulating economic activity and that the market should be allowed to be free. The doctrine of *laissez faire*—leaving the market to its own devices—was the centerpiece of Adam Smith's massive economic study on the origins of the wealth of nations.

As a professor in Glasgow, Scotland, Smith actually went to factories to observe the work. He was one of the first theorists to see the importance of the division of labor in making possible the manufacture of more and cheaper consumer goods. Smith viewed labor as the critical factor in a capitalist economy: the value of money, or of an individual for that matter, rested on the ability to buy labor or the byproducts of labor, namely goods and services. According to *The Wealth of Nations,* "labor is the real measure of the exchangeable value of all commodities."[11] The value of labor is in turn determined by market forces, by supply and demand. Before the invention of money or capital, labor belonged to the laborer, but in the money and market society, which had evolved since the Middle Ages, labor belonged to the highest bidder.

Smith was not bothered by the apparent randomness of market forces, although he was distressed by signs of greed and exploitation. Beneath the superficial chaos of commerce, he saw order—the same order that he saw in physical nature through his understanding of the new science. He used the metaphor of "the invisible hand" to explain the source of this order; by that he probably meant Newton's regulatory God, made very distant by Smith, who was a deist. That hand would invisibly reconcile self-interest to the common or public interest. With the image of the invisible hand, Smith expressed his faith in the rationality of commercial society and laid the first principle for the modern science of capitalist economics. He did not mean to license the oppression of the poor and the laborer. Statements in *The Wealth of Nations* such as "Landlords, like all other men, love to reap where they never sowed" or "Whenever there is great property, there is great inequality"[12] reveal Smith to be a moralist. Yet he knew of no means to stop the exploitation of labor. He believed that its purchase at market value ensured the working of commercial society, and he assumed that the supply of cheap labor was inexhaustible.

British theorists like Smith looked at commerce and industry as the keys to national wealth. But on the Continent most theorists saw agriculture, not industry, as the engine of wealth and progress. This physiocratic philosophy, as it was called, was particularly commonplace in France, where the richness and diversity of the climate produced fine crops and luxury items such as wine and perfume from flowers and herbs. Despite this relative abundance, physiocratic doctrine reluctantly permitted state intervention to ensure that food would be evenly distributed. Right up to the 1780s, the poor needed and expected such intervention. But because of their dedication to agriculture and the commerce that came with it, few physiocrats foresaw the immense importance that manufacturing and steam power would assume by 1800.

For all their differences, Smith and the French physiocrats shared certain characteristics common to enlightened economic theorists. They wanted to find the laws that regulated economic life; in that search they imitated the successes of the new science. In addition, they believed that progress was possible and that wealth and well-being could be increased for all. Knowledge is progressive; hence, by implication, the human condition also yields to constant improvement. This vision sometimes made the theorists myopic when it came to poverty and the injustice of the market. What they bequeathed to the modern age was a belief in the inevitability of progress wedded to capitalism and free trade—a belief that remains powerful to this day.

The High Enlightenment

More than any other political system in western Europe, the Old Regime in France was directly threatened by the doctrines and reforming impulse of the Enlightenment. The Roman Catholic church was deeply entrenched in every aspect of life: landownership, control over the universities and the presses, and access to both the court and, through the pulpit, the people. For decades the church had brought its influence to bear against the philosophes, yet by 1750, the Enlightenment had penetrated learned circles and academies in Paris and the provinces. After 1750, censorship of

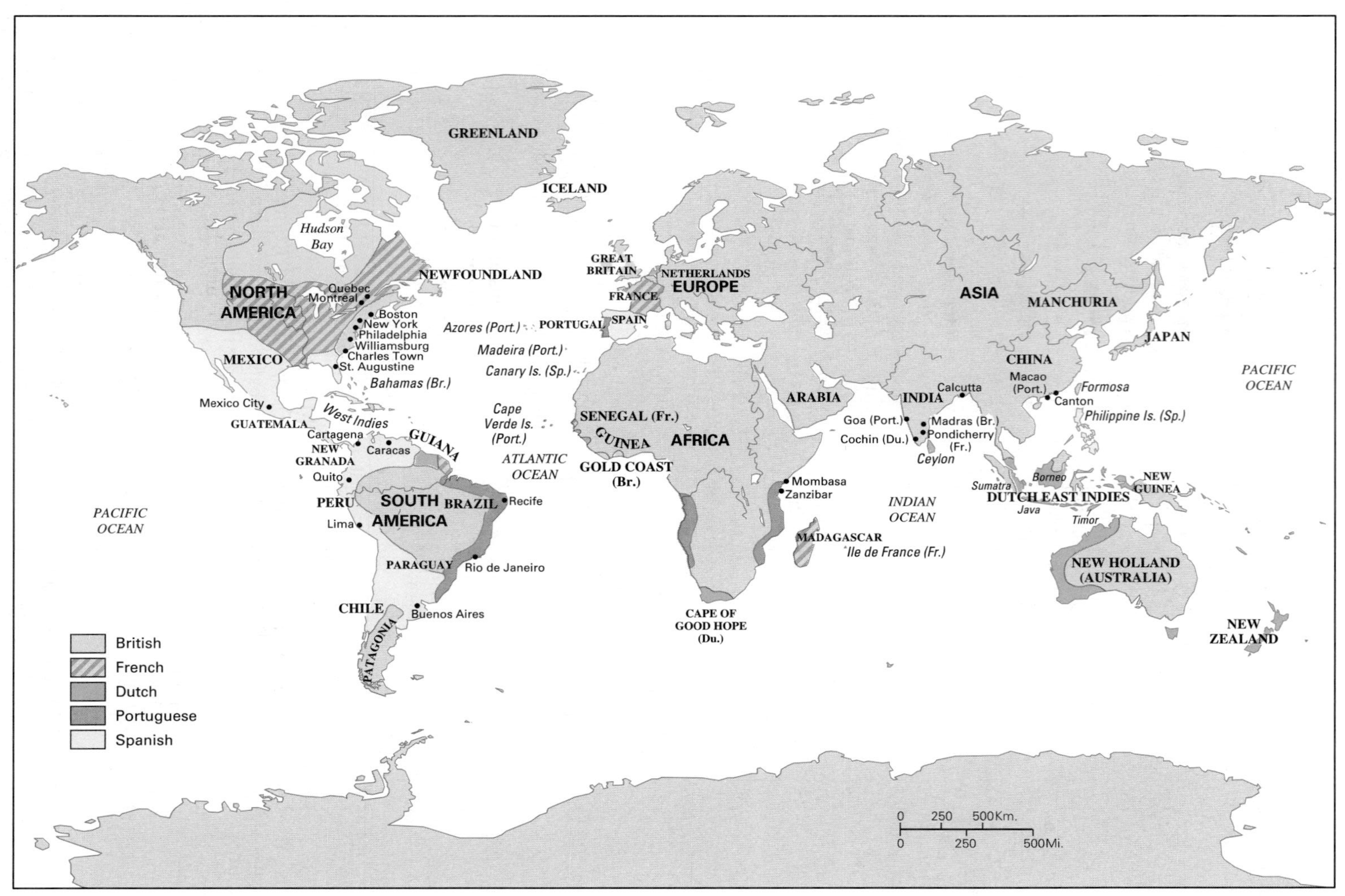
GREENLAND
ICELAND
Hudson Bay
NEWFOUNDLAND
NORTH AMERICA
Quebec
Montreal
Boston
New York
Philadelphia
Williamsburg
Charles Town
St. Augustine
MEXICO
Bahamas (Br.)
Mexico City
GUATEMALA
West Indies
Cartagena
NEW GRANADA
Caracas
GUIANA
Quito
PERU
SOUTH AMERICA
BRAZIL
Recife
Lima
PARAGUAY
Rio de Janeiro
CHILE
Buenos Aires
PATAGONIA
PACIFIC OCEAN
Azores (Port.)
Madeira (Port.)
Canary Is. (Sp.)
Cape Verde Is. (Port.)
ATLANTIC OCEAN
GREAT BRITAIN
NETHERLANDS
EUROPE
FRANCE
PORTUGAL
SPAIN
SENEGAL (Fr.)
GUINEA
AFRICA
GOLD COAST (Br.)
CAPE OF GOOD HOPE (Du.)
ARABIA
Mombasa
Zanzibar
MADAGASCAR
Ile de France (Fr.)
INDIAN OCEAN
ASIA
MANCHURIA
JAPAN
CHINA
Macao (Port.)
Canton
Formosa
Philippine Is. (Sp.)
INDIA
Calcutta
Goa (Port.)
Madras (Br.)
Pondicherry (Fr.)
Cochin (Du.)
Ceylon
Sumatra
Borneo
DUTCH EAST INDIES
Java
Timor
NEW GUINEA
NEW HOLLAND (AUSTRALIA)
NEW ZEALAND
PACIFIC OCEAN
British
French
Dutch
Portuguese
Spanish
0 250 500Km.
0 250 500Mi.

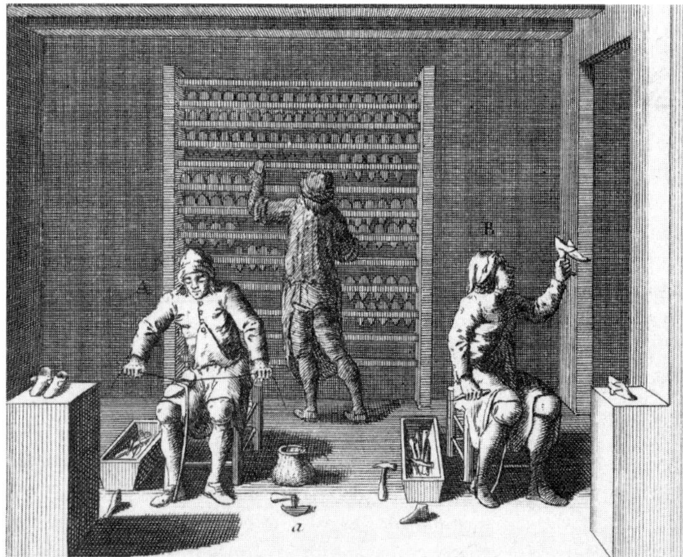

Diderot and Artisans. There are many extraordinary aspects of Diderot's great *Encyclopedia.* Among the most noted are the quality and precision of the engravings that depict workers at their crafts. To this day the volumes remain important sources for knowledge about every craft of the age. (*Corbis.*)

the press was relaxed by a new censor deeply influenced by Enlightenment ideals. In fact, censorship had produced the opposite of the desired effect: the more irreligious and atheistic the book or manuscript, the more attractive and sought after it became.

By the 1740s, the fashion among proponents of the Enlightenment was to seek an encyclopedic format for presenting their ideas. After Bayle's *Dictionary,* the first successful encyclopedia was published in England by Ephraim Chambers in 1728, and before too long, a plan was under way for its translation into French. A leading Freemason in France, the chevalier Ramsay, advocated that all the Masonic lodges in Europe should make a financial contribution to this effort, but few, if any, responded to the call.

◀ *Map 18.1* European Expansion, 1715
Globalization as a process began in the eighteenth century with European trade, exploration, and colonization.

Four aggressive Parisian publishers took up the task of producing the encyclopedia. One of them had had some shady dealings in clandestine literature, which had acquainted him with the more irreligious and daring philosophes in Paris. Hence he knew the young Denis Diderot (1713–1784), who had spent six months in jail for his philosophical and pornographic writings. Out of that consortium of publishers and philosophes came the most important book of the Enlightenment, Diderot's *Encyclopedia.* Published in 1751 and in succeeding years and editions, the *Encyclopedia* initiated a new stage in the history of Enlightenment publishing. In the process, it brought to the forefront materialistic ideas, which, until that time, only the most radical freethinkers in England and the Netherlands had openly written about. The new era thus ushered in, called the High Enlightenment, was characterized by a violent attack on the church's privileges and the very foundations of Christian belief. From the 1750s to the 1780s, Paris shone as the capital of the Enlightenment. The philosophes were no longer a persecuted minority. Instead, they became cultural heroes. The *Encyclopedia* had to be read by anyone claiming to be educated.

In his preface to the *Encyclopedia,* Diderot's collaborator, Jean D'Alembert (c. 1717–1783), summed up the principles on which it had been compiled. In effect, he wrote a powerful summation of the Enlightenment's highest ideals. He also extolled Newton's science and gave a short description of its universal laws. The progress of geometry and mechanics in combination, d'Alembert wrote in his preface, "may be considered the most incontestable monument of the success to which the human mind can rise by its efforts."[13] In turn, he urged that revealed religion be reduced to a few precepts to be practiced; religion should, he implied, be made scientific and rational. The *Encyclopedia* itself explicitly followed Francis Bacon's admonition that the scientist should first of all be a collector of facts; in addition, it gave dozens of examples of useful new mechanical devices.

D'Alembert in the preface also praised the epistemology of Locke: all that is known, is known through the senses. He declared that all learning should be catalogued and readily available, that the printing press should enlighten, and that literary societies should encourage men of talent. These societies, he added, "should banish all inequalities that might exclude or discourage men who are endowed with talents that will enlighten others."[14]

During the High Enlightenment, reformers dwelled increasingly on the Old Regime's inequalities, which seemed to stifle men of talent. The aristocracy and the clergy were not always talented, and seldom were they agitators for enlightenment and reform. Their privileges seemed increasingly less rational. By the 1780s, Paris had produced a new generation of philosophes, for whom Voltaire, Diderot, and Rousseau were aged or dead heroes. But these young authors found the life of the propagandist to be poor and solitary, and they looked at society's ills as victims rather than as reformers. They gained firsthand knowledge of the injustices catalogued so brilliantly by Rousseau in *The Social Contract.*

The High Enlightenment's systematic, sustained, and occasionally violent attacks on the clergy and the irrationality of privilege link that movement with the French Revolution. The link did not lie in the comfortable heresies of the great philosophes, ensconced as they were in the fashionable Parisian salons. Rather, it was to be found in the way those heresies were interpreted by a new generation of reformers—Marat and Robespierre among them—who in the early days of the Revolution used the Enlightenment as a mirror on which they reflected the evils of the Old Order.

European Political and Diplomatic Developments

Warfare

The dreams of the philosophes seemed unable to forestall imperial developments in power politics, war, and diplomacy. The century was dominated by two areas of extreme conflict: Anglo-French rivalry over control of territory in the New World and hegemony in northern Europe; and intense rivalry between Austria and Prussia over control of central Europe. These major powers, with their imperialistic ambitions, were led by cadres of aristocratic ministers or generals. The Enlightenment did little to displace the war-making role that had belonged to the aristocracy since the Middle Ages. In Berlin some philosophes enjoyed the brilliance of court life and turned a blind eye to Prussian militarism.

France and England were the great rivals in the New World, although colonization had been well under way since the early sixteenth century. Spain had been the first sovereign state to establish an empire in America; located principally in South America and Central America, this empire was based on mining gold and silver, trade, and slaves. The English and the Dutch had followed, first as settlers and then also as slave traders, but their colonies lay to the north—in Virginia, New Amsterdam (later to become New York), and New England. Farther north, the French explored and exploited Canada and the region now known as the midwestern United States. Early in the eighteenth century, the Dutch and the Spanish had largely dropped out of the race for colonies in North America, leaving the field to the French and the English.

By the middle of the eighteenth century, the rivalry of these two powers for territory in the

New World increased tension in the Old World. Earlier, the British had sought to contain the French colossus and ensure their historic trading interests in the Low Countries and the Rhineland by allying themselves with the Dutch Republic and the Austrians, who controlled what is today called Belgium. The alliance of the Maritime Powers (Britain and the Netherlands) with Austria tilted the balance of power against France for the entire first half of the eighteenth century.

Meanwhile, Prussia under Frederick the Great was entering the ranks of the major powers. In 1740, Frederick launched an aggressive foreign policy against neighboring states and ruthlessly seized the Austrian province of Silesia. The forces of the new Austrian queen, Maria Theresa, were powerless to resist this kind of military onslaught. In two years, Prussia acquired what was probably the largest territory captured by any continental European state in that era. Silesia augmented the Prussian population by 50 percent, and Frederick also gained a relatively advanced textile manufacturing area. The Austrians never forgave his transgression.

In 1756, Maria Theresa formed an alliance with France against Prussia; the ensuing Seven Years' War (1756–1763) involved every major European power. Austria's alliance with France in 1756, which ended the historic rivalry between France and the House of Hapsburg, is known as the "diplomatic revolution." The Austrians had grown to fear Prussia in the north more than they feared the French. From the Austrian point of view, Prussia had stolen Silesia in 1740, and regaining it was more important than preserving historic rivalries with France. On the French side, King Louis XV longed for an alliance with a Roman Catholic power and for peace in Europe so that France would be better able to wage war against Britain in the New World.

For their part, the British sought an ally in the newer, stronger Prussia, and reneged on their traditional ally, Austria. Frederick the Great stood at the head of a new state that was highly belligerent yet insecure, for all the European powers had reasons to want to keep Prussia weak and small. The Seven Years' War—which seesawed between the opponents, with French, Austrian, and Russian forces ranged against Frederick's Prussians—changed things little in Europe but did reveal the extraordinary power of the Prussian war machine. Prussia joined the ranks of the Great Powers.

Hostilities in North America tipped the balance of power there in favor of the English. From 1754 to 1763, the French and the English fought over their claims in the New World. England's victory in this conflict—which was also part of the Seven Years' War—led ultimately to the American Revolution. England secured its claim to control the colonies of the eastern seaboard, a market that would enrich its industrialists of the next generation enormously—though, from the colonists' point of view, unjustly.

While the major western European powers were growing stronger, some eastern European countries were falling further under the domination of the Ottoman (Turkish) Empire as the result of warfare. Only Hungary decidedly benefited from the wars led by Austria against the Turks. With its new independence finally secured from the Turks in 1718, Hungary entered an era of peace and enlightenment.

Empires and nation-states were the beneficiaries of eighteenth-century war and diplomacy. Only in the Dutch Republic did a little-noticed revolution in 1747–48 provide any indication that the Great Powers or the merchant capitalists had anything to fear from their home populations. The Dutch Revolution was led by men who identified with the Enlightenment and who wanted to reform the institutions of government. Inspired by the restoration of the House of Orange, Amsterdam rose in a democratic rebellion headed by a coalition of small merchants and minor philosophes. In 1748 they failed to effect any meaningful changes, but the calls they made for reform and renewal would be heard again in Amsterdam in 1787 and in Paris in 1789. On the latter occasion, the world would listen. For most of the eighteenth century, however, warfare seemed only to confirm the internal security and stability of the ruling monarchs and elites controlling most European states.

Enlightened Despotism

Enlightened despotism, an apparent contradiction in terms, was used as a phrase by the French philosophe Diderot as early as the 1760s. Wherever the philosophes used this phrase, it referred to an ideal shared by many of them: the strong monarch who would implement rational reforms, removing obstacles to freedom, ending book censorship, and allowing the laws of nature to work, particularly in trade and commerce. When historians use the term *enlightened despotism,* they generally are describing the reigns of specific European monarchs and their ministers: Frederick the Great in Prussia; Catherine the Great in Russia; Charles III in Spain; Maria Theresa and, to a greater extent, her son Joseph II in Austria; and Louis XV in France.

These eighteenth-century monarchs instituted specific reforms in education, trade, and commerce and against the clergy. This type of enlightened government must be understood in context: these countries developed late relative to the older states of Europe. Prussia, Austria, and Russia had to move very quickly if they were to catch up to the degree of centralization achieved in England and France. And when monarchies in France and Spain also occasionally adopted techniques associated with enlightened despotism, they generally did so to compete against a more advanced rival—for example, France against England and Spain against France.

Austria. In the course of the eighteenth century, Austria became a major centralized state as a result of the administrative reforms of Charles VI and his successors. Though Catholic and devout at home, Charles allied himself abroad with Protestant Europe against France. In the newly acquired Austrian Netherlands, he supported the progressive and reforming elements in the nobility, which opposed the old aristocracy and clergy. His daughter Maria Theresa (1740–1780) continued this pattern, and the Austrian administration became one of the most innovative and progressive on the Continent. Many of its leading ministers, like the Comte du Cobenzl in the Netherlands or Gerard van Swieten, Joseph II's great reforming minister, were Freemasons. This movement often attracted progressive Catholics (as well as Protestants and freethinkers), who despised what they regarded as the medieval outlook of the traditional clergy.

Dynastic consolidation and warfare did contribute decisively to the creation of the Austrian state. But in the eighteenth century, the intellectual and cultural forces of the Enlightenment enabled the state to establish an efficient system of government and a European breadth of vision. With these attributes, Austria came to rival (and, in regard to Spain, surpass) older, more established states in Europe. Frustrated in their German territories, the Austrian Hapsburgs concentrated their attention increasingly on their eastern states. Vienna gave them a natural power base, and Catholic religiosity gradually united the ruling elites in Bohemia and Hungary with their Hapsburg kings. Hapsburg power created a dynastic state in Austria, yet all efforts to consolidate the German part of the empire and to establish effective imperial rule met with failure. Also problematic were Joseph II's interventions in the southern Netherlands. He offended the clergy without winning liberal support. Revolution erupted in Brussels in 1787.

Prussia. German unification proceeded very slowly, and even enlightened despotism could not achieve it. Under the most famous and enlightened Hohenzollerns of the eighteenth century, Prussian absolutism acquired some unique and resilient features. Frederick II, the Great (1740–1786), pursued a policy of religious toleration and, in so doing, attracted French Protestant refugees, who had manufacturing and commercial skills. Intellectual dissidents, such as Voltaire, were also attracted to Prussia. Voltaire eventually went home disillusioned with this new Prussian "enlightened despotism," but not before Frederick had used him and in the process acquired a reputation for learning. By inviting various refugees from French clerical oppression, Frederick gave Berlin a minor reputation as a center for Enlightenment culture. But alongside Frederick's courtship of the French philosophes, with their enlightened ideals, there remained the reality of Prussia's militarism and the serfdom of its peasants.

Yet the Hohenzollern dynasty succeeded in cre-

Map 18.2 Europe, 1789 ▶

The Hapsburgs had vast holdings and this did not make the other German states feel secure. This entire map would change after 1800 as Napoleon swept through Europe.

0
200
400 Km.
0
200
400 Mi.
Austrian Hapsburg territories
Prussian territories
Boundary of Holy Roman Empire
ATLANTIC OCEAN
North Sea
Baltic Sea
Black Sea
Mediterranean Sea
SCOTLAND
Edinburgh
IRELAND
GREAT BRITAIN
ENGLAND
London
NORWAY
KINGDOM OF NORWAY AND DENMARK
DENMARK
KINGDOM OF SWEDEN
St. Petersburg
Moscow
RUSSIA
LITHUANIA
POLAND
Warsaw
PRUSSIA
Berlin
HANOVER
SAXONY
UNITED NETHERLANDS
Amsterdam
AUSTRIAN NETHERLANDS
GERMAN STATES
Prague
AUSTRIA
BAVARIA
Vienna
Buda
Pest
HUNGARY
ROMANIA
Paris
FRANCE
SWITZERLAND
SAVOY
MILAN
Venice
REPUBLIC OF VENICE
Avignon
GENOA
TUSCANY
PAPAL STATES
Rome
Naples
KINGDOM OF THE TWO SICILIES
Sicily
Corsica (To France)
KINGDOM OF SARDINIA
Sardinia
PORTUGAL
Lisbon
SPAIN
Madrid
ALBANIA
(Ven. Rep.)
OTTOMAN EMPIRE
Constantinople

ating a viable state, built by the labor of its serfs and the power of its Junker-controlled army. This state managed to survive as a monarchy until World War I. By the middle of the eighteenth century, this small nation, of no more than 2.5 million inhabitants, exercised inordinate influence in European affairs because of its military prowess.

Prussian absolutism rested on the nationally conscripted army and the Junker class, and its economy was state directed and financed. Its court expenses were held to a minimum; most state expenditures went into maintaining an army of 200,000 troops, the largest in relation to population in all Europe.

Russia. Russia during the eighteenth century made significant strides, under various monarchs, toward joining the European state system. During the reign of Peter the Great (1682–1725), the Russians established strong diplomatic ties in almost every European capital. In addition, the Russian metal industry became vital to European development. The English, who lacked the forestland and wood necessary to fire smelting furnaces, grew dependent on Russian-produced iron.

Catherine the Great (1762–1796) consciously pursued policies intended to reflect her understanding of the Enlightenment. These presented contradictions. She entered into respectful correspondence with philosophes but at the same time extended serfdom to the entire Ukraine. She promulgated a new, more secular educational system and sought at every turn to improve Russian industry, but her policies rested on the aggrandizement of the agriculturally based aristocracy. The Charter of Nobility in 1785 forever guaranteed the aristocracy's right to hold the peasants in servitude. As interpreted by this shrewd monarch, the Enlightenment completed the tendency to monarchical absolutism that had been well under way since the sixteenth century.

CATHERINE THE GREAT. Catherine the Great adorned herself to show her aristocracy that she was its superior. (*The Luton Hoo Foundation.*)

Effects of Enlightened Despotism

Enlightened despotism was, in reality, the use of Enlightenment principles by monarchs to enhance the central government's power and thereby their own. These eighteenth-century monarchs knew, in ways their predecessors had not, that knowledge is power; they saw that application of learned theories to policy can produce useful results.

But did these enlightened despots try to create more humanitarian societies in which individual freedom would flourish on all levels? In this area, enlightened despotism must be pronounced a shallow deployment of Enlightenment ideals. For example, Frederick the Great decreed the abolition of serfdom in Prussia, but he had no means to force the aristocracy to conform because he desperately needed their support. In the 1780s, Joseph II instituted liberalized publishing laws in Austria; but when artisans began reading pamphlets about the French Revolution, the state quickly retreated and reimposed censorship. In the 1750s, Frederick the Great too had loosened the censorship laws, and writers were free to attack traditional religion; however, they were never allowed to criticize the army, the key to Frederick's aggressive foreign policy. Although Catherine the Great gave Diderot a pension, she would hear of nothing that compromised her political power, and her ministers were expected to give her unquestioning service.

Finally, if the Enlightenment means the endorsement of reason over force, and peace and cosmopolitan unity over ruthless competition, then the foreign policies of these enlightened despots were uniformly despotic. The evidence lies in a long series of aggressions, including Frederick's invasion of Silesia in 1740, Austria's secret betrayal of its alliance with the English and Dutch and the ensuing Seven Years' War, and Austria's attempt in the 1770s to claim Bavaria. In short, the Enlightenment provided a theory around which central and eastern European states that were only recently unified could organize their policies. The theory also justified centralization over the power of local elites grown comfortable during centuries of unopposed authority. There were no major philosophes who did not grow disillusioned with enlightened monarchs on the rare occasions when their actions could be observed at close range. The Enlightenment did provide new principles for the organization of centralized monarchical power, but centralization with economic rationalization and management did not make their practitioners or beneficiaries any more enlightened. Enlightened despotism was extinguished largely by the democratic revolutions of the late eighteenth century.

The Enlightenment in Eastern Europe

The impact of the Enlightenment in the countries of eastern Europe varied enormously. Where it made greatest inroads, we see the subsequent emergence of discernibly modern social and political ideas and aspirations. In Hungary, for example, independence from the Ottoman Empire in 1718 left a country that was still essentially feudal yet eager for reform and renewal. In the 1720s, peace brought regeneration. The population doubled in the course of the eighteenth century; agricultural techniques markedly improved; and by midcentury, schools and universities had begun to teach the new science. Hungarian Protestants who had traveled and studied abroad came home with the ideas of the philosophes. A lay intelligentsia was created and with it came new literature and drama, as well as Western-style civil society: lodges, salons, clubs, and societies. By 1790, the Enlightenment and the French Revolution had inspired a movement for Hungarian nationalism and against the control of the Austrians and Hapsburgs. Then in 1795, its leaders were executed. However, their nationalistic ideals survived well into the nineteenth and twentieth centuries.

In Poland and Lithuania, the influence of the Jesuits remained strong even after they were expelled from other eastern European countries, such as Hungary. In Poland, the Catholic clergy continued to control education, and the Enlightenment remained a deeply censored, almost underground movement. Yet it did exist and influence educational reform, especially after the expulsion of the Jesuits in 1773. Those who advocated the Enlightenment allied themselves with the monarchy, which they saw as the only force that might be strong enough to oppose the entrenched clergy and aristocracy. The power of the Polish nobility had dire historical consequences for the country. No central authority emerged in eighteenth-century Poland comparable in its unifying ability to the monarchs of Prussia, Austria, and Russia. Not once but three times, in 1772, 1793, and 1795, Poland was partitioned by these three potent neighbors, who took portions of it. Some Poles resisted; a Polish nobleman even appealed to Rousseau in 1771 to help draft a constitution for his beleaguered country. The document in which Rousseau expressed his thoughts on Polish government was cautious and judicious, giving power to all the various elements within Polish elite society.

The failure of the Enlightenment to take hold in parts of eastern Europe had far-reaching consequences, with which the people of those countries continue to grapple. In the 1990s, those countries—such as Hungary and the Czech Republic—that experienced the Enlightenment seemed to show the greatest cohesiveness in the struggle to create a unified, secular, tolerant, and independent state.

The American Revolution

England's victory over France in the Seven Years' War set in motion a train of events that culminated in the American Revolution. The war drained the British treasury, and now Britain faced the additional expense of paying for troops to guard the new North American territories that it had gained in the war. Strapped British taxpayers could not shoulder the whole burden, so the members of Parliament thought it quite appropriate that American colonists should help to pay the bill; they reasoned that Britain had protected the colonists from the French and was still protecting them in their conflicts with Indians. Thus, new colonial taxes and import duties were imposed. Particularly galling to the colonists were the Stamp Act (which placed a tax on newspapers, playing cards, liquor licenses, and legal documents) and the Quartering Act (which required colonists to provide living quarters and supplies to English troops stationed in America).

Vigorous colonial protest compelled the British Parliament to repeal the Stamp Act, but new taxes were imposed, raising the price of many everyday articles, including tea. The stationing of British troops in Boston, the center of rebelliousness, worsened tensions. In March 1770, a crisis ensued after a squad of British soldiers fired into a crowd of Bostonians who had been taunting them and pelting them with rocks and snowballs. Five Bostonians died, and six were wounded. A greater crisis occurred in 1773, when Parliament granted the East India Company exclusive rights to sell tea in America. The colonists regarded this as yet another example of British tyranny. When a crowd of Bostonians dressed as Indians climbed aboard East Indian ships and dumped about ninety thousand pounds of tea overboard, the British responded with a series of repressive measures, which included suppressing self-government in Massachusetts and closing the port of Boston.

The quarrel turned to bloodshed in April and June 1775. On July 4, 1776, delegates from the thirteen colonies adopted the Declaration of Independence, written mainly by the philosophe Thomas Jefferson. Applying Locke's theory of natural rights, this document declared that government derives its power from the consent of the governed, that it is the duty of a government to protect the rights of its citizens, and that people have the right to "alter or abolish" a government that deprives them of their "unalienable rights."

Why were the American colonists so ready to revolt? For one thing, they had brought to North America a highly idealized understanding of English liberties. Long before 1776, they had extended representative institutions to include small property owners who probably could not have voted in England. The colonists had come to expect representative government, trial by jury, and protection from unlawful imprisonment. Each of the thirteen colonies had an elected assembly that acted like a miniature parliament; in these assemblies, Americans gained political experience and quickly learned self-government.

Familiarity with the thought of the Enlightenment and the republican writers of the English Revolution also contributed to the Americans' awareness of liberty. The ideas of the philosophes traversed the Atlantic and influenced educated Americans, particularly Jefferson and Benjamin Franklin. Like other philosophes, American thinkers expressed growing confidence in reason, valued freedom of religion and of thought, and championed the principle of natural rights.

Another source of hostility toward established authority among the American colonists was their religious traditions, particularly Puritanism, which viewed the Bible as infallible and its teachings as a higher law than the law of the state. Like their counterparts in England, American Puritans challenged political and religious authorities who, in their view, contravened God's law. Thus, Puritans acquired two habits that were crucial to the development of political liberty: dissent and resistance. When transferred to the realm of politics, these Puritan tendencies led Americans to resist authority that they considered unjust.

American victory came in 1783 as a result of several factors. George Washington proved to be a superior leader, able to organize and retain the loyalty of his troops. France, seeking to avenge its defeat in the Seven Years' War, helped the Americans with money and provisions and then in 1778 entered the conflict. Britain had difficulty shipping supplies across three thousand miles of

THE BOSTON TEA PARTY. The engraver chose to depict free blacks as well as whites applauding one of the early acts that led to the American Revolution. (*AKG, London.*)

ocean, was fighting the French in the West Indies and elsewhere at the same time, and ultimately lacked commitment to the struggle.

Reformers in other lands quickly interpreted the American victory as a successful struggle of liberty against tyranny. During the Revolution, the various former colonies drew up constitutions based on the principle of popular sovereignty and included bills of rights that protected individual liberty. They also managed, somewhat reluctantly, to forge a nation. Rejecting both monarchy and hereditary aristocracy, the Constitution of the

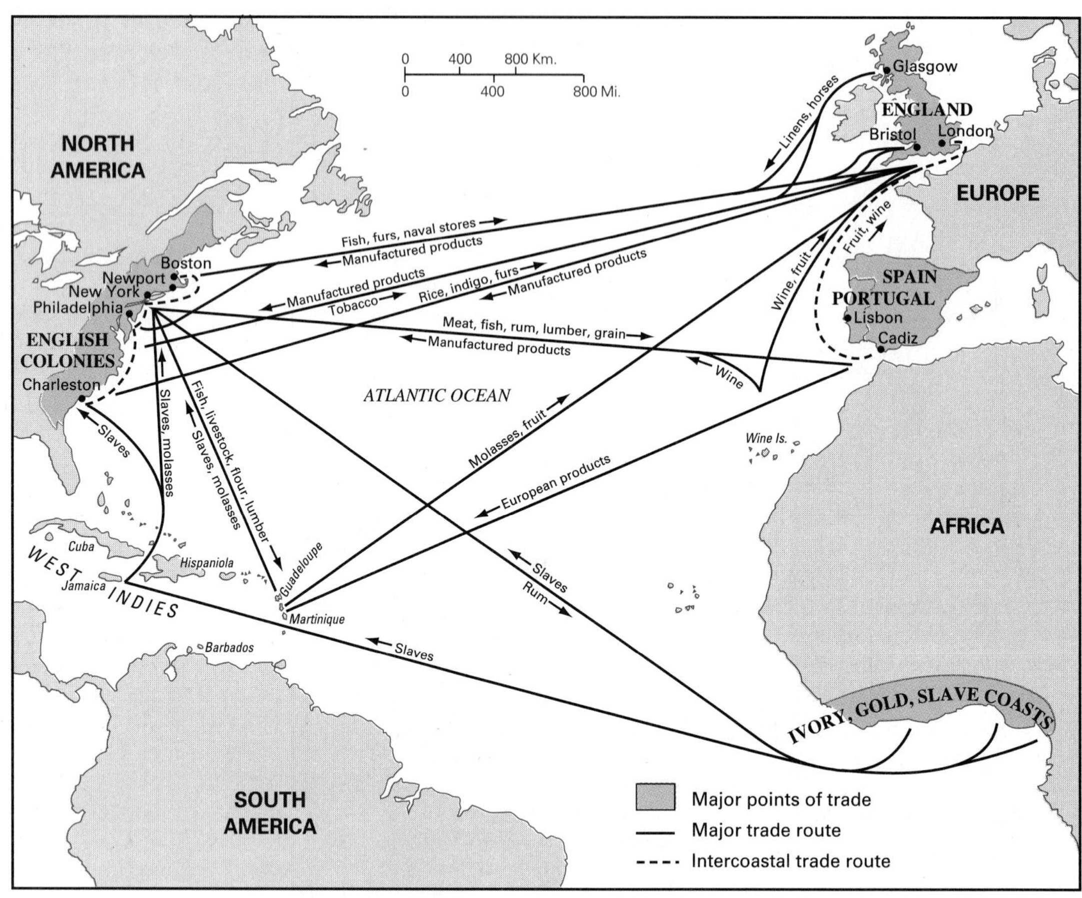

Map 18.3 Trade Routes Between the Old and New Worlds The trade routes of the eighteenth century foreshadow the globalization of trade with which we are familar.

United States created a republic in which power derived from the people. A system of separation of powers and checks and balances set safeguards against the abuse of power, and the Bill of Rights provided for protection of individual rights. To be sure, the ideals of liberty and equality were not extended to all people. Slaves knew nothing of the freedom that white Americans cherished, and women were denied the vote and equal opportunity; human equality remained an issue throughout the nineteenth and twentieth centuries. To reform-minded Europeans, however, it seemed that Americans were fulfilling the promise of the Enlightenment. They were creating a freer and better society.

The Enlightenment and the Modern World

Enlightened thought culminated a trend begun by Renaissance humanists, who attacked medieval otherworldliness and gave value to individual achievement and the worldly life. It was a direct outgrowth of the Scientific Revolution, which provided a new method of inquiry and verification and demonstrated the power and self-sufficiency of the human intellect. If nature were autonomous—that is, if it operated according to natural laws that did not require divine intervention—then the human intellect could also be autonomous. Through its own powers, it could uncover the general principles that operate in the social world, as well as in nature.

The philosophes sought to analyze nature, government, religion, law, economics, and education through reason alone, with little reference to Christian teachings, and they rejected completely the claims of clerics to a special wisdom. The philosophes broke decisively with the medieval view that the individual is naturally depraved, that heaven is the true end of life, and that human values and norms derive from a higher reality and are made known through revelation. Instead, they upheld the potential goodness of the individual, regarded the good life on earth as the true purpose of existence, and insisted that individuals could improve themselves and their society by the light of reason.

In addition, the political philosophies of Locke, Montesquieu, and Rousseau were based on an entirely new (and modern) concept of the relationship between the state and the individual: states should exist not simply to accumulate power but also to enhance human happiness. From that perspective, monarchy, and even oligarchy not based on merit, began to seem increasingly less useful. And if happiness is a goal, then it must be assumed that some sort of progress is possible in history.

When we observe societies that have never experienced their own version of enlightenment, we see oftentimes the oppression of women and authoritarian governments sometimes run by clergymen. Religion can turn to intolerance or fanaticism if unchecked by questioning, or even by doubting.

The philosophes wanted a freer, more humane, and more rational society, but they feared the people and their potential for revolutionary action. As an alternative to revolution, most philosophes offered science as the universal improver of the human condition. Faith in reform without the necessity of revolution proved to be a doctrine for the elite of the salons. In that sense, the French Revolution can be said to have repudiated the essential moderation of philosophes like Voltaire, d'Alembert, and Kant.

However, the Enlightenment established a vision of humanity so independent of Christianity and so focused on the needs and abuses of the society of the time that no established institution, once grown corrupt and ineffectual, could long withstand its penetrating critique. To that extent, the writings of the philosophes point toward the democratic revolutions of the late eighteenth century. To a lesser extent, the writers of the Enlightenment also point toward ideals that remain strong in most democratic Western societies: religious toleration, a disdain for prejudice and superstition, a fear of unchecked political authority, and, of course, a belief in the power of the human mind to recognize the irrational and attempt to correct it.

Notes

1. "An Answer to the Question: 'What Is Enlightenment?'" in *Kant's Political Writings,* ed. Hans Reiss (Cambridge: Cambridge University Press, 1970), pp. 54–60.
2. *Wetten van het Natuurkundig Genootschap, door eenige Dames opgericht, binnen Middelburg den 6 August. 1785.* (Rules for the Scientific Society established by women within Middelburg on 6 August 1785), Middelburg, [1785], p. 29. The only known copy is to be found in the Provincial Library in Zeeland, the Netherlands.
3. Pierre Bayle, *Historical and Critical Dictionary,* ed. Richard H. Popkin (New York: Bobbs-Merrill, 1965), p. 195.
4. Voltaire, *Philosophical Letters* (New York: Bobbs-Merrill, 1961), p. 22.
5. Thomas Hobbes, *Leviathan,* ed. C. B. Macpherson (Harmondsworth, England: Penguin, 1977), p. 189.
6. Jean Jacques Rousseau, *The Social Contract and Discourses* (New York: Dutton, 1950), pp. 3, 9.
7. Quoted in Franco Venturi, *Utopia and Reform in the Enlightenment* (Cambridge: Cambridge University Press, 1971), p. 101.
8. Voltaire, *Philosophical Dictionary,* ed. Theo-

dore Besterman (Harmondsworth, England: Penguin, 1974), p. 183.

9. Quoted in David B. Davis, *The Problem of Slavery in Western Culture* (Harmondsworth, England: Penguin, 1970), p. 449.
10. Immanuel Kant, *Beobachtungen* (1900–1919), in *Kants Werke,* ed. Dilthey, 2:230.
11. Adam Smith, *The Wealth of Nations,* ed. George Stigler (New York: Appleton, 1957), p. 3.
12. Ibid., p. 98.
13. Jean Le Rond d'Alembert, *Preliminary Discourse to the Encyclopedia of Diderot,* trans. Richard N. Schwab (New York: Bobbs-Merrill, 1963), p. 22.
14. Ibid., pp. 101–102.

Suggested Reading

Applewhite, Harriet B., and Darline G. Levy, eds., *Women and Politics in the Age of the Democratic Revolution* (1990). Lively essays about real women in Europe and America.

Chartier, Roger, *The Cultural Origins of the French Revolution* (1991). A good map through the French Enlightenment; weak on women.

Cranston, Maurice, *Philosophers and Pamphleteers: Political Theorists of the Enlightenment* (1986). A clear, readable account of the major French thinkers.

Darnton, Robert, *The Literacy Underground of the Old Regime* (1982). A collection of essays by a master storyteller.

Gay, Peter, *The Enlightenment, An Interpretation,* 2 vols. (1966–1969). Probably the best synthesis of the period ever written.

Hunt, Lynn, ed., *The Invention of Pornography: Obscenity and the Origins of Modernity* (1993). Pornography arose in the late seventeenth century and was tied to social criticism and eventually to the Enlightenment. It was very different then from what it has subsequently become.

———, ed., *Human Rights and the French Revolution* (1997). Shows how people in the eighteenth century arrived at principles that remain revolutionary in many societies today.

Jacob, Margaret, *The Enlightenment: A Brief History with Documents* (2001). A long introduction precedes selections from Locke, Diderot, and others.

Lukes, Steven, *The Curious Enlightenment of Professor Caritat: A Comedy of Ideas* (1995). A delightful story that makes eighteenth-century ideas accessible and relevant to today's world.

Maza, Sarah, *Private Lives and Public Affairs: The Causes Célèbres of Prerevolutionary France* (1993). Shows what the press can do to deflate the authority of kings and aristocrats; fine reading.

Skinner, Quentin, *Reason and Rhetoric in the Philosophy of Hobbes* (1996). A very readable examination of Hobbes's philosophy that emphasizes his debt to the Renaissance.

Starobinski, Jean, *Jean-Jacques Rousseau: Transparency and Obstruction* (1971). One of the greatest biographies ever written of the most important philosophe.

Williams, David, ed., *The Enlightenment* (1999). Contains political writings by Voltaire, Hume, Condorcet, and others.

Review Questions

1. What is meant by the term *enlightenment?* Where did the Enlightenment begin, and what contributed to its spread?
2. Describe the new public sphere, and name some of the societies that sprang up within it.
3. Why did Christianity come under attack by deists, skeptics, and freethinkers? What sorts of things did they say about it?
4. In what ways did Voltaire and Madame du Châtelet exemplify the philosophes?
5. What were the essential characteristics of the political thought of Hobbes, Locke, Montesquieu, and Rousseau? Make relevant comparisons and contrasts.
6. Describe Locke's theory of learning. What was its significance for the Enlightenment?
7. How did the philosophes come to terms with the status of slaves and criminals?
8. What were the views of the philosophes on the position of women in society? Did women have an Enlightenment?
9. Did the philosophes approve of capitalism? Explain why or why not.
10. What made the High Enlightenment different

from what preceded it? Describe how it differed. How did the *Encyclopedia* exemplify the High Enlightenment?

11. List the major military conflicts of the eighteenth century. Discuss the significance of each.
12. Enlightened despotism was in reality the use of Enlightenment principles by monarchs to enhance the central government's power and thereby their own. Discuss this statement.
13. In what ways was the American Revolution based on Enlightenment principles?
14. The Enlightenment was a pivotal period in the shaping of the modern mentality. Discuss this statement.

Part Four

An Age of Revolution: Liberal, National, Industrial

1789–1848

1780

1790

1800

1810

1820

1830

1840

Politics and Society	Thought and Culture
French Revolution begins (1789) Declaration of the Rights of Man and of the Citizen (1789)	Kant, *Critique of Pure Reason* (1781) Bentham, *Principles of Morals and Legislation* (1789)
France declares war on Austria (1792) Execution of Louis XVI (1793) Reign of Terror (1793–94) Napoleon seizes power (1799)	Burke, *Reflections on the Revolution in France* (1790) Wollstonecraft, *Vindication of the Rights of Woman* (1792) De Maistre, *Reflections on the State of France* (1796) Wordsworth, *Lyrical Ballads* (1798) Malthus, *Essay on the Principle of Population* (1798)
Battle of Trafalgar—French and Spanish fleets defeated by the British (1805) Napoleon defeats Prussians at Jena (1806) Napoleon defeats Russians at Friedland (1807)	Beethoven, Fifth Symphony (1807–08) Goethe, *Faust* (1808, 1832)
Napoleon invades Russia (1812) Napoleon defeated at Waterloo (1815) Congress of Vienna (1814–15)	Byron, *Childe Harold* (1812)
Revolutions in Spain, Italy, Russia, and Greece (1820–1829)	Shelley, *Prometheus Unbound* (1820) Ricardo, *Principles of Political Economy* (1817) Hegel, *The Philosophy of History* (1822–1831)
Revolutions in France, Belgium, Poland, and Italy (1830–32) Reform in Britain: Reform Act of 1832; slavery abolished within British Empire (1833); Factory Act (1833)	Fourier, *Treatise on Agrarian Domestic Fellowship* (1822) Comte, *Course in Positive Philosophy* (1830–1842)
Irish famine (1845–1849) Revolutions in France, Germany, Austria, and Italy (1848)	Proudhon, *What Is Property?* (1840) De Tocqueville, *Democracy in America* (1835–1840) Gaskell, *Mary Barton* (1848) Marx, *Communist Manifesto* (1848)

Chapter 19

The French Revolution: Affirmation of Liberty and Equality

The Storming of the Bastille, July 14, 1789. (AKG, London.)

- **The Old Regime**
  - The First Estate
  - The Second Estate
  - The Third Estate
  - Inefficient Administration and Financial Disorder
  - The Roles of the Enlightenment and the American Revolution
  - A Bourgeois Revolution?
- **The Moderate Stage, 1789–91**
  - The Clash Between the Nobility and the Third Estate
  - Formation of the National Assembly
  - Storming of the Bastille
  - The Great Fear
  - October Days
  - Reforms of the National Assembly
- **The Radical Stage, 1792–94**
  - The Sans-Culottes
  - Foreign Invasion
  - The Jacobins
  - Jacobin Achievements
  - The Nation in Arms
  - The Republic of Virtue and the Reign of Terror
  - The Fall of Robespierre
- **The Meaning of the French Revolution**

The outbreak of the French Revolution in 1789 stirred the imagination of Europeans. Both participants and observers sensed that they were living in a pivotal age. On the ruins of the Old Order, founded on privilege and despotism, a new era was forming, and it promised to realize the ideals of the Enlightenment. These ideals included the emancipation of the human personality from superstition and tradition, the triumph of liberty over tyranny, the refashioning of institutions in accordance with reason and justice, and the tearing down of barriers to equality. It seemed that the natural rights of the individual, hitherto a distant ideal, would now become reality, and centuries of oppression and misery would end. Never before had people shown such confidence in the power of human intelligence to shape the conditions of existence. Never before had the future seemed so full of hope.

This lofty vision kindled emotions akin to religious enthusiasm and attracted converts throughout the Western world. "If we succeed," wrote the French poet André Chénier, "the destiny of Europe will be changed. Men will regain their rights and the people their sovereignty."[1] The editor of the Viennese publication *Wiener Zeitung* wrote to a friend: "In France a light is beginning to shine which will benefit the whole of humanity."[2] British reformer John Cartwright expressed the hopes of reformers everywhere: "Degenerate must be that heart which expands not with sentiments of delight at what is now transacting in . . . France. The French . . . are not only asserting their own rights, but they are asserting and advancing the general liberties of mankind."[3]

The Old Regime

Eighteenth-century French society was divided into three orders, or Estates, which were legally defined groupings. The clergy constituted the First Estate, the nobility the Second Estate, and everyone else (about 96 percent of the population) the Third Estate. The clergy and nobility, totaling about 500,000 out of a population of 26 million, enjoyed special privileges, receiving pensions and profitable positions from the king. The social structure of the Old Regime, based on priv-

Chronology 19.1 ❖ The French Revolution

July 1788	Calling of the Estates General
May 5, 1789	Convening of the Estates General
June 17, 1789	Third Estate declares itself the National Assembly
July 14, 1789	Storming of the Bastille
Late July 1789	The Great Fear
August 4, 1789	Nobles surrender their special privileges
June 1791	Flight of Louis XVI
October 1791	Legislative Assembly succeeds the National Assembly
April 20, 1792	Legislative Assembly declares war on Austria
August 10, 1792	Parisians attack the king's palace
September 1792	September Massacres
September 20, 1792	Battle of Valmy
September 21–22, 1792	Abolition of the monarchy
January 21, 1793	Execution of Louis XVI
June 1793	Jacobins replace Girondins as the dominant group in the National Convention
July 28, 1794	Robespierre is guillotined
1795 and 1796	Failed insurrections by the poor of Paris
September 1797	Royalist coup d'état against the Directory is crushed
November 1799	Napoleon seizes power

ileges and inequalities sanctioned by law, produced tensions that contributed to the Revolution.

The First Estate

The powers and privileges of the French Catholic church made it a state within a state. As it had done for centuries, the church registered births, marriages, and deaths; collected tithes (a tax on products from the soil); censored books considered dangerous to religion and morals; operated schools; and distributed relief to the poor. Since it was illegal for Protestants to assemble publicly for prayer, the Catholic church enjoyed a monopoly on public worship. Although it owned an estimated 10 percent of the land, which brought in an immense revenue, the church paid no taxes. Instead, it made a "free gift" to the state (the church determined the amount), which was always smaller than direct taxes would have been. Critics denounced the church for promoting superstition and obscurantism, impeding reforms, and being more concerned with wealth and power than with the spiritual message of Jesus.

The clergy reflected the social divisions in France. The upper clergy shared the attitudes and way of life of the nobility from which they sprang. The parish priests, commoners by birth, resented the haughtiness and luxurious living of the upper clergy. In 1789, when the Revolution began, many priests sympathized with the reform-minded people of the Third Estate.

The Second Estate

Like the clergy, the nobility was a privileged order. Nobles held the highest positions in the church, army, and government. They were exempt from most taxes (or used their influence to evade taxes), collected manorial dues from peasants, and owned between one-quarter and one-third of the land. In addition to the income they drew from their estates, nobles were becoming increasingly involved in such nonaristocratic enterprises as banking, finance, commerce, and industry. Many key philosophes—Montesquieu, Condorcet, d'Holbach—were nobles, and nobles were the leading patrons of the arts. Most nobles, however, were suspicious and intolerant of the liberal ideas advanced by the philosophes.

All nobles were not equal; there were gradations of dignity among the 350,000 members of the nobility. Enjoying the most prestige were *nobles of the sword:* families that could trace their aristocratic status back several centuries. Many of these noblemen were officers in the king's army. The highest of the ancient nobles were engaged in the social whirl at Versailles and Paris, receiving pensions and sinecures from the king but performing few useful services for the state. Most nobles of the sword, unable to afford the gilded life at court, remained on their provincial estates, the poorest of them barely distinguishable from prosperous peasants.

Alongside this ancient nobility, a new nobility had arisen, created by the monarchy. To obtain money, reward favorites, and weaken the old nobility, French kings had sold titles of nobility to members of the bourgeoisie and had conferred noble status on certain government offices bought by wealthy bourgeois. Particularly significant were *nobles of the robe,* who had purchased judicial offices in the parlements—the high law courts—and whose ranks included many former bourgeois.

Opinion among the aristocrats was divided. Influenced by the liberal ideals of the philosophes, some nobles sought to reform France; they wanted to end royal despotism and establish a constitutional government. To this extent, the liberal nobility had a great deal in common with the bourgeoisie. These liberal nobles saw the king's difficulties in 1788 as an opportunity to regenerate the nation under enlightened leadership. When they resisted the king, they claimed that they were attacking despotic rule. But many nobles, concerned with preserving their privileges and honorific status, were hostile to liberal ideals and opposed reform.

The Third Estate

The Third Estate comprised the bourgeoisie, peasants, and urban laborers. Although the bourgeoisie provided the leadership for the Revolution, its success depended on the support given by the rest of the Third Estate.

The Bourgeoisie. The bourgeoisie consisted of merchant-manufacturers, wholesale merchants, bankers, master craftsmen, doctors, lawyers, intellectuals, and government officials below the top ranks. Although the bourgeoisie had wealth, it lacked social prestige. A merchant, despite his worldly success, felt that his occupation denied him the esteem enjoyed by the nobility. "There are few rich people who at times do not feel humiliated at being nothing but wealthy," observed an eighteenth-century Frenchman.[4]

Influenced by the aristocratic values of the day and envious of the nobility's lifestyle, the bourgeosie sought to erase the stigma of common birth and to rise socially by becoming landowners. By 1789, the bourgeoisie owned about 20 percent of the land. Traditionally, some members of the bourgeoisie had risen socially either by purchasing a judicial or political office that carried with it a title of nobility or by gaining admission to the upper clergy and the officer ranks of the army. Access to the nobility remained open throughout the eighteenth century. Nevertheless, since the highest and most desired positions in the land were reserved for the nobility, able bourgeois were often excluded, for a variety of reasons: the high cost of purchasing an office, the limited number of new offices created, the resistance of nobles to their advancement, or the hostility of the older nobility toward those recently ennobled. No doubt these men felt frustrated and came to resent a social system that valued birth more than talent. For most of the century, however, the bourgeoisie did not challenge the existing social structure, including the special privileges of the nobility.

By 1789, the bourgeois had many grievances. They wanted all positions in church, army, and state to be open to men of talent regardless of birth. They sought a parliament that would make laws for the nation; a constitution that would limit the king's power and guarantee freedom of thought, a fair trial, and religious toleration; and administrative reforms that would eliminate waste, inefficiency, and interference with business.

The Peasantry. The condition of the more than twenty-one million French peasants was a paradox. On the one hand, they were better off than peasants in Austria, Prussia, Poland, and Russia, where serfdom still predominated. In France, serfdom had largely disappeared; many peasants owned land, and some were even prosperous. But most French peasants lived in poverty, which worsened in the closing years of the Old Regime.

Peasants owned between 30 and 40 percent of the land, but the typical holding was barely large enough to eke out a living. The rising birthrate (between 1715 and 1789, the population may have increased from eighteen million to twenty-six million) led to the continual subdivision of farms among heirs. Moreover, many peasants did not own land but rented it from a nobleman or a prosperous neighbor. Others worked as sharecroppers, turning over to their creditors a considerable portion of the harvest.

"Let's Hope That the Game Finishes Well." This political cartoon shows a laboring-class woman carrying smug representatives of the privileged orders on her back. (*Musée de la Ville de Paris.*)

Owning too little land to support themselves, many peasants tried to supplement their incomes. They hired themselves out for whatever employment was available in their region: as agricultural day laborers, charcoal burners, transporters of wine, or textile workers in their own homes. Landless peasants tried to earn a living in such ways. The increasing birthrate resulted in an overabundance of rural wage earners. This worsened the plight of small landowners and reduced the landless to beggary. "The number of our children reduces us to desperation,"[5] was a common complaint of the peasants by 1789.

An unjust and corrupt system of taxation weighed heavily on the peasantry. Louis XIV had maintained his grandeur and financed his wars by milking ever more taxes from the peasants, a practice that continued throughout the eighteenth century. An army of tax collectors victimized the peasantry. In addition to royal taxes, peasants paid the tithe to the church and manorial dues to lords.

Although serfdom had ended in most parts of France, lords continued to demand obligations from peasants as they had done in the Middle Ages. Besides performing labor services on the lord's estate, peasants still had to grind their corn in the lord's mill, bake their bread in his oven, press their grapes in his winepress, and give him part of their produce in payment. (Their fees were called *banalities.*) In addition, the lord collected a land rent from peasant proprietors, levied dues on goods at markets and fairs, and exercised exclusive hunting rights on lands tilled by peasants. The last was a particularly onerous right, for the

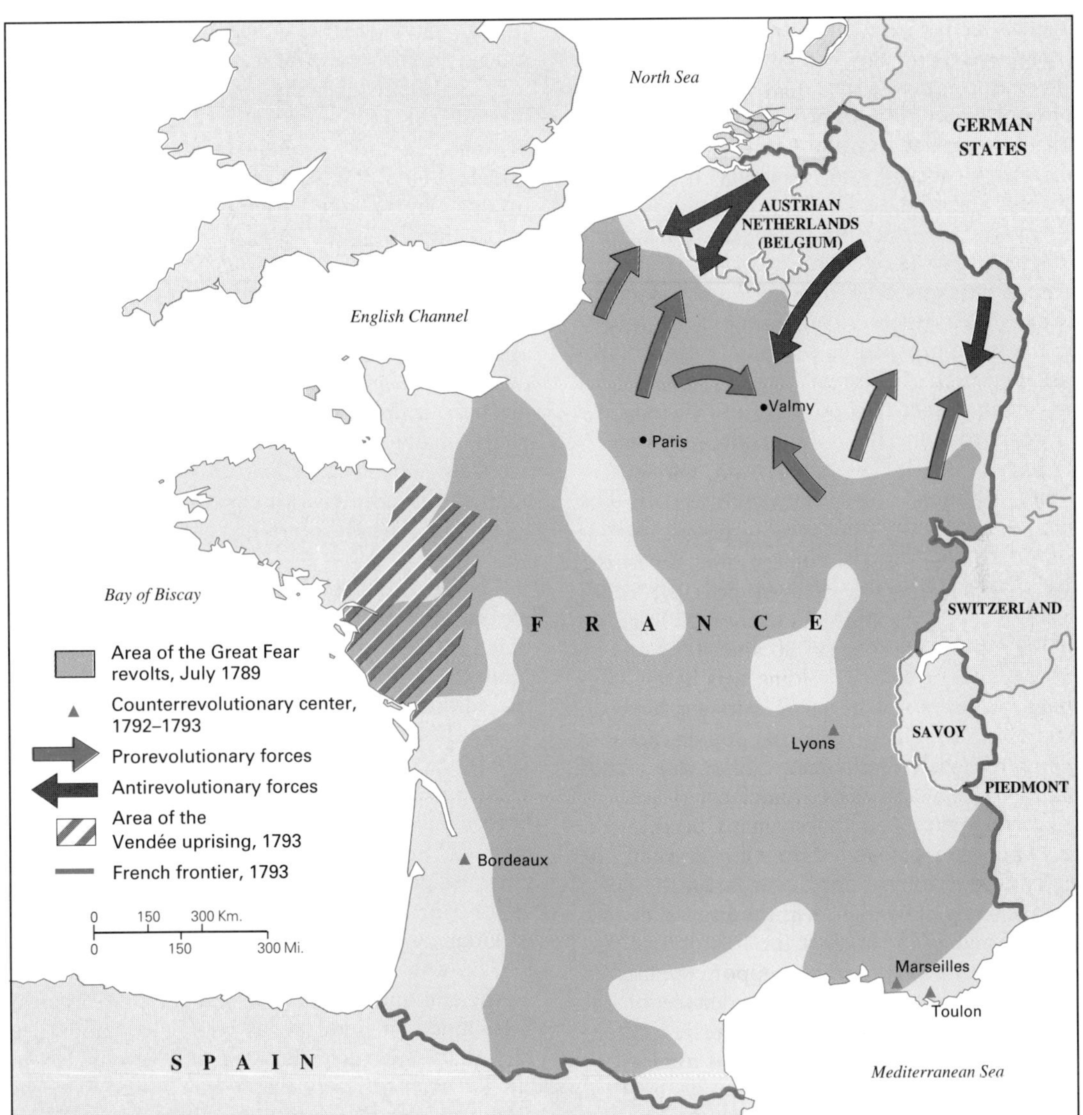

Map 19.1 The French Revolution, 1789–1793 French revolutionaries had to deal with both internal enemies and foreign invasion.

lord's hunting parties damaged crops. Lords were determined to hold on to these privileges, not only because of the income they brought but because they were symbols of authority and social esteem. The peasants, however, regarded these obligations as hateful legacies of the past from which they derived no benefit.

In the last part of the eighteenth century, lords sought to exact more income from their lands by reviving manorial dues that had not been collected for generations, increasing the rates on existing dues, and contracting businessmen to collect payments from the peasants. These capitalists naturally tried to squeeze as much income as possible from the peasants, making them hate the whole system of manorial obligations even more.

Inefficient farming methods also contributed to the poverty of the French peasants. In the eighteenth century, France did not experience a series of agricultural improvements comparable to those in England. Failure to invest capital in modernizing agricultural methods meant low yields per acre and a shortage of farm animals.

A rise in the price of necessities during the closing years of the Old Regime worked hardship on those peasants who depended on wages for survival. With prices rising faster than wages, only the more prosperous peasants with produce to sell benefited. The great majority of peasants were driven deeper into poverty, and the number of beggars roaming the countryside increased. A poor harvest in 1788–89 aggravated peasant misery and produced an atmosphere of crisis. The granaries were empty; the price of bread, the staple food of the French, soared; and starvation threatened. Hatred of the manorial order and worsening poverty sparked a spontaneous and autonomous peasant revolution in 1789.

Urban Laborers. The urban laboring class in this preindustrial age consisted of journeymen working for master craftsmen, factory workers in small-scale industries, and wage earners such as day laborers, gardeners, handymen, and deliverymen, who were paid by those they served. The poverty of the urban poor, like that of the peasant wage earners, worsened in the late eighteenth century. From 1785 to 1789, the cost of living increased by 62 percent, while wages rose only 22 percent. For virtually the entire decade of the Revolution, urban workers struggled to keep body and soul together in the face of food shortages and rising prices, particularly the price of their staple food, bread. Material want drove the urban poor to acts of violence that affected the course of the Revolution.

Inefficient Administration and Financial Disorder

Eighteenth-century France was in theory an absolute monarchy. The king claimed that his power derived from God, and, unlike Britain, France had no parliament that represented the people and met as a continuous body. The administration of the country was complex, confusing, and ineffective. The practice of buying state offices from the king, introduced as a means of raising money, brought in many incompetent officeholders. "When his Majesty created an office," stated one administrator, "Providence called into being an imbecile to buy it."[6] Tariffs on goods shipped from one French province to another and differing systems of weights and measures hampered trade. No single law code applied to all the provinces; instead, there were overlapping and conflicting law systems based on old Roman law or customary feudal law, which made the administration of justice slow, arbitrary, and unfair. To admirers of the philosophes, the administrative system was an insult to reason. The Revolution would sweep the system away.

Financial disorders also contributed to the weakness of the Old Regime. In the regime's last years, the government could not raise sufficient funds to cover expenses. Servicing the debt incurred during the War of the Austrian Succession (1740–1748) and the Seven Years' War (1756–1763) placed an immense burden on the treasury. This burden reached crisis proportions when France incurred additional expenses by aiding the colonists in the American Revolution. The king's gifts and pensions to court nobles and the extravagant court life further drained the treasury.

Finances were in a shambles, not because France was impoverished but because it had an inefficient and unjust tax system. Few wealthy Frenchmen, including the bourgeois, paid their fair share of taxes. Because tax revenue came chiefly from the peasants, it was bound to be inadequate. Excise duties and indirect taxes on consumer goods yielded much-needed revenue in the last decades of the Old Regime. However, instead of replenishing the royal treasury, these additional funds were pocketed by rich tax collectors, who, for a fixed payment to the state, had obtained the right to collect these indirect taxes. Although serious, the financial crisis could have been solved if the clergy, nobility, and bourgeoisie paid their fair share of taxes. Some progressive ministers recognized the need for comprehensive reforms, but nobles and clergy resisted them, clinging tenaciously to their ancient privileges. The irresolution of the king and the intrigues, rivalries, and incompetence of his ministers also impeded reform.

The nobles were able to thwart royal will mainly through the parlements. Many parlementaires were originally wealthy bourgeois who had purchased their offices from the state (nobles of the robe). Both the office and status of nobility remained within the family. The Paris parlement and twelve provincial parlements reviewed the judgments of lower courts and registered royal edicts. The parlements had the right to *remonstrate,* that is, to pass judgment on the legality of royal edicts before registering them. If the courts considered the king's new laws at variance with previous legislation or ancient traditions, they would refuse to register them. (Generally, it was the Paris parlement that set the example.) The king could revise the edicts in accordance with the parlements' instructions or force their registration by means of a *lit de justice:* a solemn ceremony in which the monarch appeared before the court. If the parlementaires stood firm in their resistance, the king might order the arrest of their leaders. Although the king could force his will on the parlements, their bold opposition damaged royal prestige.

With France on the brink of bankruptcy, the king's ministers proposed that the nobility and the church surrender some of their tax privileges. The parlements protested and remonstrated. Some nobles resisted because they were steadfast defenders of noble prerogatives; the more liberal nobles resisted because they saw an opportunity to check absolutism and introduce fundamental reforms that would regenerate the nation.

The resistance of the nobility forced the government, in July 1788, to call for a meeting of the Estates General—a medieval representative assembly, which had last met in 1614—to deal with the financial crisis. The body was to convene in May 1789. Certain that they would dominate the Estates General, the nobles intended to weaken the power of the throne. Once in control of the government, they would introduce financial reforms. But the revolt of the nobility against the crown had unexpected consequences. It opened the way for revolutions by the Third Estate, which destroyed the Old Regime and with it the aristocracy and its privileges.

The Roles of the Enlightenment and the American Revolution

Revolutions are born in the realm of the spirit. Revolutionary movements, says George Rudé, a historian of the French Revolution, require "some unifying body of ideas, a common vocabulary of hope and protest, something, in short, like a common 'revolutionary psychology.'"[7] For this reason, many historians see a relationship between the Enlightenment and the French Revolution. Although the philosophes themselves were not revolutionaries, their attacks on the pillars of the established order helped create a revolutionary psychology. As Henri Peyre observes,

> *Eighteenth-century philosophy taught the Frenchman to find his condition wretched, or in any case, unjust and illogical and made him disinclined to the patient resignation to his troubles that had long characterized his ancestors. . . . The propaganda of the "Philosophes" perhaps more than any other factor accounted for the fulfillment of the preliminary condition of the French Revolution, namely discontent with the existing state of things.*[8]

As the Revolution progressed, its leaders utilized the philosophes' ideas and language to justify their own reform program.

The American Revolution, which gave practical expression to the liberal philosophy of the philosophes, also helped pave the way for the French Revolution. The Declaration of Independence, which proclaimed the natural rights of man and sanctioned resistance against a government that deprived men of these rights, influenced the framers of the Declaration of the Rights of Man and of the Citizen. The United States showed that a nation could be established on the principle that sovereign power derived from the people. The Americans set an example of social equality unparalleled in Europe. In the United States, there was no hereditary aristocracy, no serfdom, and no state church. Liberal French aristocrats, such as the marquis de Lafayette, who had fought in the American Revolution, returned to France more optimistic about the possibilities of reforming French society.

A Bourgeois Revolution?

Because the bourgeois were the principal leaders and chief beneficiaries of the French Revolution, many historians have viewed it, along with the English Revolutions of the seventeenth century and the growth of capitalism, as "an episode in the general rise of the bourgeoisie."[9] Those who regard the Revolution as a "bourgeois revolution" argue that in the last part of the eighteenth century it became increasingly difficult for the bourgeoisie to gain the most honored offices in the land. According to this view, in the eighteenth century, a decadent and reactionary aristocracy sought to regain the powers that it had lost under Louis XIV. Through parlements, aristocrats blocked reforms proposed by the king that threatened their privileges, and they united to prevent commoners from entering their ranks. The nobility's determination to safeguard its power and social exclusiveness clashed head-on with the aspirations of a wealthy, talented, and progressive bourgeoisie. Finding the path to upward mobility and social dignity barred, the bourgeoisie, imbued with the rational outlook of the Enlightenment, came to perceive nobles as an obstacle to its advancement and the nation's progress. "The essential cause of the Revolution," concludes the French historian Albert Soboul, "was the power of a bourgeoisie arrived at its maturity and confronted by a decadent aristocracy holding tenaciously to its privileges."[10] Thus, when the bourgeois found the opportunity during the Revolution, they ended the legal division of France into separate orders.

In recent decades, some historians have challenged this interpretation. These revisionists argue that before 1789 France did not have a self-conscious bourgeois class aspiring to take control of the state in order to promote a capitalist economy, that the nobles and the bourgeoisie did not represent antagonistic classes divided by sharp differences. On the contrary, they were not clearly distinguishable from each other. The bourgeois aspired to noble status, and many nobles were involved in business enterprises—mining, metallurgy, textiles, and overseas trading companies—traditionally considered the province of the bourgeoisie. Abandoning a traditional aristocratic disdain for business, many nobles had acquired the capitalist mentality associated with the middle class. Some nobles also shared with the bourgeois the liberal values of the philosophes and a desire to do away with monarchical despotism and reform France according to rational standards. Thus, French nobles, particularly those who lived in urban centers or had traveled to Britain and the American colonies, were receptive both to new means of livelihood and to progressive ideas. Moreover, the French nobility was constantly infused with new blood from below. During the eighteenth century, thousands of bourgeois, through marriage, the purchase of an office that carried with it a title of nobility, or service as local officials—mayors, for example—had some entitlement of nobility. As the British historian William Doyle puts it, "the nobility was an open elite, not a hereditary class apart. Nor is it now possible to maintain that this elite grew less open as the eighteenth century went on thanks to some exclusive 'aristocratic reaction.'"[11]

Just prior to 1789, revisionists contend, nobles and prosperous bourgeois were no longer clearly differentiated; the traditional distinctions that had set them apart were now obsolete. France's social elite actually consisted not of a hereditary nobility but of *notables*—both nobles and bourgeois—distinguished more by wealth than by birth. Bourgeois notables were essentially moderate; they did not seek the destruction of the aristocracy that was accomplished in the opening stage of the Revolution. The elimination of aristocratic privileges was not part of a preconceived bourgeois program, revisionists maintain, but an improvised response to the violent upheavals in the countryside in July and August 1789. Moreover, not until early 1789, when a struggle erupted over the composition of the Estates General (see the next section), did the bourgeoisie start to become conscious of itself as a class with interests that clashed with those of the aristocracy. Until then, both the bourgeoisie and many aristocrats were united around a common and moderate reform program.

Finally, revisionists argue that the nobility was not as decadent or reactionary as traditional accounts would have it. The nobles resisted the king's reforming ministers because they doubted the ability of a despotic and incompetent state to solve the financial crisis. To be sure, there were aristocrats who selfishly wanted to cling to their privileges, but many also aspired to serve the public good by instituting structural changes that would liberate the nation from despotic and inefficient rule and reform its financial and administrative system. It was this desire to institute crucial changes in French political life, say revisionists, that led nobles to press for the convening of the Estates General.

The Moderate Stage, 1789–91

The Clash Between the Nobility and the Third Estate

Frenchmen in great numbers met in electoral assemblies to elect deputies to the Estates General. Churchmen and nobles voted directly for their representatives. Most deputies of the clergy were parish priests, many of them sympathetic to reform. Although the majority of deputies of the Second Estate were conservative country nobles, there was a sizable liberal minority (including some who had fought in the American Revolution), that favored reform; political liberalism was not a monopoly of the bourgeoisie. The representatives from the Third Estate were elected indirectly, with virtually all taxpaying males over the age of twenty-five being eligible to vote. The delegates of the Third Estate consisted predominantly of bourgeois drawn from government service and the professions, including many articulate lawyers.

Each Estate drew up lists of grievances and suggestions *(cahiers de doléances)*. The cahiers from all three orders expressed loyalty to monarchy and church. Many cahiers of the nobility insisted on the preservation of manorial rights and honorific privileges, whereas cahiers prepared by the urban bourgeoisie often demanded the abolition of serfdom, the fees paid by peasants to lords, the lords' courts, and the lords' exclusive hunting rights. On the other hand, cahiers drawn up by liberal nobles agreed with bourgeois demands on many crucial issues. Both groups called for the establishment of a national assembly that would meet periodically and consent to taxation. Both also wanted a written constitution, financial reforms, including the surrender of tax exemptions, a guarantee of personal liberty, and freedom of the press. There was general agreement that a constitutional government that met regularly to pass laws was preferable to absolute monarchy, which ruled by decree. Both reform-minded nobles and bourgeois held great hopes for the regeneration of France and the advancement of liberty.

At this stage, then, with a significant number of nobles sympathetic to reform, there was no inseparable gulf between the Second and the Third Estates. However, it soon became clear that the hopes of reformers clashed with the intentions of many aristocrats. What had started as a struggle between the crown and the aristocracy was turning into something far more significant: a conflict between the two privileged orders on one side and the Third Estate on the other. As one keen observer noted in early 1789, "The public debate has changed. Now the King, despotism, the constitution are merely secondary: it is a war between the Third Estate and the other two orders."[12] One pamphleteer, Abbé Sieyès (1748–1836), expressed the hatred that the bourgeoisie had for the aristocracy. "The privileged order has said to the Third Estate: 'Whatever be your services, whatever be your talents, you shall go thus far and no farther. It is not fitting that you be honored.'" The higher positions in the land, said Sieyès, should be the "reward for talents," not the prerogative of birth. Without the Third Estate, "nothing can progress"; without the nobility, "everything would proceed infinitely better."[13] What triggered the conflict between them was the issue of representation in the Estates General—a medieval assembly divided into the traditional orders of clergy, aristocracy, and commoners.

Formation of the National Assembly

The Estates General convened at Versailles on May 5, 1789, but was stalemated by the question of procedure. Seeking to control the assembly, the nobil-

Formation of the National Assembly, by Jacques Louis David (detail). By forming the National Assembly in June 1789, the Third Estate successfully challenged the nobility and defied the king. In this painting glorifying the event, aristocrat, clergyman, and commoner embrace before a cheering National Assembly. (*Versailles © Réunion des Musées Nationaux.*)

ity insisted that the three Estates follow the traditional practice of meeting separately and voting as individual bodies. Because the two privileged orders were likely to stand together, the Third Estate would always be outvoted, two to one. The delegates from the Third Estate, unwilling to allow the nobility and the higher clergy to dominate the Estates General, proposed instead that the three Estates meet as one body and vote by head. There were some 610 delegates from the Third Estate; the nobility and clergy together had an equivalent number. Since the Third Estate could rely on the support of sympathetic parish priests and liberal nobles, it would be assured a majority if all orders met together. As aristocrats and bourgeois became more polarized, antinoble rhetoric gained a growing audience among all segments of the Third Estate. Many commoners now saw the aristocracy as the chief obstacle to reform.

On June 10, the Third Estate broke the stalemate. It invited the clergy and nobility to join with it in a common assembly; if they refused, the Third Estate would go ahead without them. A handful of priests answered the roll call, but not one noble. On June 17, the Third Estate made a revolutionary move. It declared itself the National Assembly. On June 20, locked out of their customary meeting hall (apparently by accident), the Third Estate delegates moved to a nearby tennis court and took a solemn oath not to disband until a constitution had been drawn up for France. By these acts, the bourgeois delegates demonstrated their desire and determination to reform the state.

Louis XVI commanded the National Assembly to separate into orders, but the Third Estate held firm. The steadfastness of the delegates and the menacing actions of Parisians who supported the National Assembly forced Louis XVI to yield. On June 27, he ordered the nobility (some had already done so) and the clergy (a majority had already done so) to join with the Third Estate in the National Assembly. The Third Estate had successfully challenged the nobility and defied the king. It would use the National Assembly to institute reforms, including the drawing-up of a constitution that limited the king's power.

But the victory of the bourgeoisie was not yet secure, for most nobles had not resigned themselves to a bourgeois-dominated National Assembly. Recognizing that France was on the threshold of a social revolution that jeopardized their power and status, many nobles now reversed their position of previous years and joined with the king in an effort to crush the National Assembly. Louis XVI, influenced by his wife, Queen Marie Antoinette, as well as his brother the comte d'Artois and court aristocrats, ordered special foreign regiments to the outskirts of Paris and Versailles. He also replaced Jacques Necker, a reform-minded minister, with a nominee of the queen. It appeared that Louis XVI, overcoming his usual hesitancy and vacillation, had resolved to use force against the National Assembly and to stop the incipient revolution. At this point, uprisings by the common people of Paris and peasants in the countryside saved the National Assembly, exacerbated hostilities between the Third Estate and the nobility, and ensured the victory of the forces of reform.

Storming of the Bastille

In July 1789, the level of tension in Paris was high for three reasons. First, the calling of the Estates General had aroused hopes for reform. Second, the price of bread was soaring: in August 1788, a Parisian laborer had spent 50 percent of his income on bread; by July 1789, he was spending 80 percent. The third element in the tension was the fear of an aristocratic plot to crush the National Assembly. Frightened that royal troops would bombard and pillage the city, Parisians searched for weapons.

On July 14, eight hundred to nine hundred Parisians gathered in front of the Bastille, a fortress used as a prison and a despised symbol of royal despotism. They gathered primarily to obtain gunpowder and to remove the cannon that threatened a heavily populated working-class district. Fearing an attack, the governor of the Bastille, Bernard Jordan de Launay, ordered his men to fire into the crowd; they killed ninety-eight and wounded seventy-three people. When the tables were turned and five cannon were aimed on the main gate of the Bastille, de Launay surrendered. Despite the promise that he would not be harmed, de Launay and five of his men were killed, and their heads were paraded on pikes through the city.

Historians hostile to the French Revolution have long depicted the besiegers of the Bastille as a destructive mob made up of the dregs of society—smugglers, beggars, bandits, degenerates. However, more recent scholarship reveals that the Bastille crowd was not drawn from the criminal elements but consisted almost entirely of small tradesmen, artisans, and wage earners—concerned citizens driven by hunger, fear of an aristocratic conspiracy, and hopes for reform.[14]

The fall of the Bastille had far-reaching consequences: a symbol of the Old Regime had fallen; some court nobles hostile to the Revolution decided to flee the country; the frightened king told the National Assembly that he would withdraw all the troops ringing Paris. The revolutionary act of the Parisians had indirectly saved the National Assembly and with it the bourgeois revolution.

The Great Fear

The uprising of the Parisians strengthened the hand of the National Assembly. Revolution in the countryside also served the interests of the reformers. The economic crisis of 1788–89 had worsened conditions for the peasantry; the price of bread soared, and the number of hungry beggars wandering the roads and spreading terror multiplied. Peasants feared that the beggars would seize their crops, which would soon be ready for harvest. Also contributing to the revolutionary mentality were the great expectations unleashed by the summoning of the Estates General, for like the urban poor, the peasants hoped that their grievances would be remedied. In the spring of 1789, peasants were attacking food convoys and refusing to pay royal taxes, tithes, and manorial dues. These revolutionary outbreaks intensified in the last weeks of July. Inflamed by economic misery and stirred by the uprisings of the Parisians, peasants began to burn manor houses and destroy the registers on which their obligations to the lords were inscribed.

The flames of the peasants' insurrection were fanned by rumors that aristocrats were organizing bands of brigands to attack the peasants. The large number of vagrants roaming the countryside helped trigger irrational fears among the peasantry. The mythical army of brigands never materialized, but the Great Fear, as this episode is called, led more peasants to take up arms against the lords. Convinced that aristocrats were plotting to block reforms, the peasants attacked the lords' chateaux with greater fury.

The peasant upheavals in late July and early August, like the insurrection in Paris, worked to the advantage of the reformers. The attacks provided the National Assembly with an opportunity to strike at noble privileges by putting into law what the peasants had accomplished with the torch—the destruction of feudal remnants. On the night of August 4, 1789, aristocrats, seeking to restore calm in the countryside, surrendered their special privileges: exclusive hunting rights, tax exemptions, monopoly on highest offices, manorial courts, and the right to demand labor services from peasants. The Assembly maintained that "the feudal regime had been utterly destroyed."*

In the decrees of August 5 and 11, the National Assembly implemented the resolutions of August 4. The Assembly also declared that the planned constitution should be prefaced by a declaration of rights. On August 26, it adopted the Declaration of the Rights of Man and of the Citizen.

*This was not entirely true. Some peasant obligations were abolished outright. However, for being released from other specified obligations, peasants were required to compensate their former lords. The peasants simply refused to pay, and in 1793 the Jacobins, recognizing reality, declared the remaining debt null and void.

October Days

Louis XVI, cool to these reforms, postponed his approval of the August Decrees and the Declaration of Rights. It would require a second uprising by the Parisians to force the king to agree to the reforms and to nail down the victory of the reformers.

On October 5, 1789, Parisian housewives (and men) marched twelve miles to Versailles to protest the lack of bread to the National Assembly and the king. A few hours later, twenty thousand Paris Guards, a citizen militia sympathetic to the Revolution, also set out for Versailles in support of the protesters. The king had no choice but to promise bread and to return with the demonstrators to Paris. Two weeks later, the National Assembly abandoned Versailles for Paris.

Once again, the "little people" had aided the bourgeoisie. Louis XVI, aware that he had no control over the Parisians and fearful of further violence, approved the August Decrees and the Declaration of the Rights of Man and of the Citizen. Nobles who had urged the king to use force against the Assembly and had tried to block reforms fled the country in large numbers.

Reforms of the National Assembly

With resistance weakened, the National Assembly continued the work of reform begun in the summer of 1789. By abolishing both the special privileges of the nobility and the clergy and the absolutism based on the divine right of kings, the National Assembly completed the destruction of the Old Regime.

1. *Abolition of special privileges.* By ending the special privileges of the nobility and the clergy in the August Decrees, the National Assembly legalized the equality that the bourgeoisie had demanded. The aristocratic structure of the Old Regime, a remnant of the Middle Ages that had hindered the progressive bourgeoisie, was eliminated.

2. *Statement of human rights.* The Declaration of the Rights of Man and of the Citizen expressed liberal and universal goals of the philosophes and the particular interests of the bourgeoisie. To contemporaries, it was a refuta-

tion of the Old Regime, a statement of ideals that, if realized, would end long-standing abuses and usher in a new society. In proclaiming the inalienable right to liberty of person and freedom of religion and thought and to equal treatment under the law, the declaration affirmed the dignity of the individual. It asserted that government belonged not to any ruler but to the people as a whole, and that its aim was the preservation of the natural rights of the individual. Because the declaration contrasted sharply with the principles espoused by an intolerant clergy, a privileged aristocracy, and a despotic monarch, it has been called the death warrant of the Old Regime.

The declaration expressed the view of the philosophes that people need not resign themselves to the abuses and misfortunes of human existence: through reason, they can improve society. But in 1789, the declaration was only a statement of intent. It remained to be seen whether its principles would be achieved. A significant example of the new leadership's commitment to equality and religious toleration was the law passed in 1791 granting civil rights to Jews. In theory, Jews were now free to leave the ghetto, to which they had been forcibly confined for centuries in order to keep them apart from gentiles, and to participate in French society as equal citizens.

3. *Subordination of church to state.* The National Assembly also struck at the privileges of the Roman Catholic church. The August Decrees declared the end of tithes. To obtain badly needed funds, the Assembly in November 1789 confiscated church lands and put them up for sale. In 1790, the Assembly passed the Civil Constitution of the Clergy, which altered the boundaries of the dioceses, reducing the number of bishops and priests, and transformed the clergy into government officials elected by the people and paid by the state.

Almost all bishops and many priests opposed the Civil Constitution. One reason was that the reorganization deprived a sizable number of clergymen of their positions. Moreover, in theory, Protestants and nonbelievers could participate in the election of Catholic clergy. In addition, the Assembly had issued the decree without consulting the pope or the French clergy as a body. When the Assembly required the clergy to take an oath that they would uphold the Civil Constitution, only about one-half would do so, and many believing Catholics supported the dissenting clergy. The Civil Constitution divided the French and gave opponents of the Revolution an emotional issue around which to rally supporters.

4. *A constitution for France.* In September 1791, the National Assembly achieved the goal at which it had been aiming since June 1789: a constitution limiting the power of the king and guaranteeing all French citizens equal treatment under the law. Citizens paying less than a specified amount in taxes could not vote. Probably about 30 percent of the males over the age of twenty-five were excluded by this stipulation, and only the more well-to-do citizens qualified to sit in the Legislative Assembly, a unicameral parliament created to succeed the National Assembly. The drafters of the contitution did not trust illiterate and propertyless men to vote and enact legislation. Nevertheless, the suffrage requirements under the constitution of 1791 were far more generous than in Britain.

5. *Administrative and judicial reforms.* The National Assembly sought to reform the chaotic administrative system of France. It replaced the patchwork of provincial units with eighty-three new administrative units, or departments, approximately equal in size. The departments and their subdivisions were allowed a large measure of self-government.

Judicial reforms complemented the administrative changes. A standardized system of courts replaced the innumerable jurisdictions of the Old Regime, and the sale of judicial offices was ended. All judges were selected from graduate lawyers, and citizen juries were introduced in criminal cases. In the penal code completed by the National Assembly, torture and barbarous punishments were abolished.

6. *Aid for business.* The National Assembly put an end to all tolls and duties on goods transported within the country, maintained a tariff to protect French manufacturers, and insisted that French colonies trade only with the mother country. The Assembly also established a uniform system of weights and measures, eliminated the guilds (medieval survivals that blocked business expansion), and forbade workers to form unions or to strike.

By ending absolutism, striking at the privileges

of the nobility, and preventing the mass of people from gaining control over the government, the National Assembly consolidated the rule of the bourgeoisie. With one arm, it broke the power of the aristocracy and throne; with the other, it held back the common people. Although the reforms benefited the bourgeoisie, it would be a mistake to view them merely as a selfish expression of bourgeois interests. The Declaration of the Rights of Man and of the Citizen was addressed to all; it proclaimed liberty and equality as the right of all and called upon citizens to treat one another with respect. Both French and foreign intellectuals believed that the Revolution would lead ultimately to the emancipation of humanity. "The men of 1789," says the French historian Georges Lefebvre, "thought of liberty and equality as the common birthright of mankind."[15] These ideals became the core of the liberal-democratic credo that spread throughout much of the West in the nineteenth century.

The Radical Stage, 1792–94

The Sans-Culottes

Pleased with their accomplishments—equality before the law, careers open to talent, a written constitution, parliamentary government—the men of 1789 wished the Revolution to go no further. But revolutionary times are unpredictable. Soon the Revolution moved in a direction neither anticipated nor desired by the reformers. A counterrevolution, led by irreconcilable nobles and alienated churchmen, gained the support of strongly Catholic peasants. It began to threaten the changes made by the Revolution, forcing the revolutionary leadership to resort to extreme measures.

The discontent of the *sans-culottes**—small shopkeepers, artisans, and wage earners—also propelled the Revolution toward radicalism. Although they had played a significant role in the Revolution, particularly in the storming of the Bastille and the October Days, they had gained little. The sans-culottes, says the French historian Albert Soboul, "began to realize that a privilege of wealth was taking the place of a privilege of birth. They foresaw that the bourgeoisie would succeed the fallen aristocracy as the ruling class."[16] Inflamed by poverty and their hatred of the rich, the sans-culottes insisted that it was the government's duty to guarantee them the "right of existence"—a policy that ran counter to the economic individualism of the bourgeoisie. They demanded that the government increase wages, set price controls on food supplies, end food shortages, punish food speculators and profiteers, and deal severely with counterrevolutionaries.

Although most sans-culottes upheld the principle of private property, they wanted laws to prevent extremes of wealth and poverty. Socially, their ideal was a nation of small shopkeepers and small farmers. "No one should own more than one workshop or one store," read a sans-culotte petition.[17] Whereas the men of 1789 sought equality of rights, liberties, and opportunities, the sans-culottes expanded the principle of equality to include narrowing the gap between the rich and poor. To reduce economic inequality, the sans-culottes called for higher taxes for the wealthy and the redistribution of land. Politically, they favored a democratic republic in which the common man had a voice.

In 1789, the bourgeoisie had demanded equality with the aristocrats: the right to hold the most honored positions in the nation and an end to the special privileges of the nobility. By the close of 1792, the sans-culottes were demanding equality with the bourgeois. They wanted political reforms that would give the poor a voice in the government and social reforms that would improve their lot.

Foreign Invasion

Despite the pressures exerted by reactionary nobles and clergy on the one hand and discontented sans-culottes on the other, the Revolution might not have taken a radical turn had France remained at peace. The war that broke out with Austria and Prussia in April 1792 exacerbated internal dissensions, worsened economic conditions, and threatened to undo the reforms of the Revolution. It was in these circumstances that the Revolution moved from its moderate stage into a radical one, which historians refer to as the Second French Revolution.

In June 1791, Louis XVI and the royal family,

*Literally, *sans-culottes* means "without culottes" and refers to the people who wore the simple trousers of a laborer and not the knee breeches that aristocrats wore before the Revolution.

traveling in disguise, fled Paris for the northeast of France to join with *émigrés* (nobles who had left revolutionary France and were organizing a counterrevolutionary army) and to rally foreign support against the Revolution. Discovered at Varennes by a village postmaster, they were brought back to Paris as virtual prisoners. The flight of the king turned many French people against the monarchy, strengthening the position of the radicals who wanted to do away with kingship altogether and establish a republic. But it was foreign invasion that ultimately led to the destruction of the monarchy.

In the Legislative Assembly, the lawmaking body that had succeeded the National Assembly in October 1791, one group, called the Girondins, urged an immediate war against Austria, which was harboring and supporting the émigrés. The Girondins believed that a successful war would unite France under their leadership, and they were convinced that Austria was already preparing to invade France and destroy the Revolution. Moreover, regarding themselves as crusaders in the struggle of liberty against tyranny, the Girondins hoped to spread revolutionary reforms to other lands to provoke a war of the people against kings.

On April 20, 1792, the Legislative Assembly declared war on Austria. Commanded by the duke of Brunswick, a combined Austrian and Prussian army crossed into France. French forces, short of arms and poorly led (about six thousand of some nine thousand officers had abandoned their command), could not halt the enemy's advance. Food shortages and a counterrevolution in the West increased the unrest. In an atmosphere already charged with tension, the duke of Brunswick issued a manifesto declaring that if the royal family were harmed he would exact a terrible vengeance on the Parisians. On August 10, 1792, enraged Parisians and militia from other cities attacked the king's palace, killing several hundred Swiss guards.

In early September, as foreign troops advanced deeper into France, there occurred an event analogous to the Great Fear of 1789. As rumors spread that jailed priests and aristocrats were planning to break out of their cells to support the duke of Brunswick, Parisians panicked. Driven by fear, patriotism, and murderous impulses, they raided the prisons and massacred eleven to twelve hundred prisoners. Most of the victims were not political prisoners but ordinary criminals.

THE EXECUTION OF LOUIS XVI. The king died with dignity. His last words were, "I forgive my enemies; I trust that my death will be for the happiness of my people, but I grieve for France, and I fear that she may suffer the anger of the Lord." (*Giraudon/Art Resource, NY.*)

On September 21 and 22, 1792, the National Convention (the successor to the Legislative Assembly) abolished the monarchy and established a republic. In December 1792, Louis XVI was placed on trial, and in January 1793, he was executed for conspiring against the liberty of the French people. The execution of Louis XVI intensified tensions between the revolutionaries and the crowned heads of Europe. The uprising of August 10, the September Massacres, the creation of a republic, and the execution of Louis XVI all confirmed that the Revolution was taking a radical turn.

Meanwhile, the war continued. Short of supplies, hampered by bad weather, and possessing insufficient manpower, the duke of Brunswick never did reach Paris. Defeated by superior artillery at Valmy on September 20, 1792, the foreign forces retreated to the frontier, and the armies of the republic took the offensive. By the beginning of 1793, French forces had overrun Belgium (then a part of the Austrian Empire), the German Rhineland, and the Sardinian provinces of Nice and Savoy. To the peoples of Europe, the National Convention solemnly announced that it was waging a popular crusade against privilege and tyranny, against aristocrats and princes.

These revolutionary political and social ideas, the execution of Louis XVI, and, most important, French expansion that threatened the balance of power frightened the rulers of Europe. Urged on by Britain, by the spring of 1793, they formed an anti-French alliance. The allies' forces pressed toward the French borders, endangering the republic.

Counterrevolutionary insurrections further undermined the fledgling republic. In the Vendée, in western France, peasants who were protesting against taxation and conscription and were still loyal to their priests and Catholic tradition, which the Revolution had attacked, took up arms against the republic. Led by local nobles, the peasants of the Vendée waged a guerrilla war for religion, royalism, and their traditional way of life. In some provinces, federalists objecting to the power wielded by the centralized government in Paris also revolted. The republic was unable to exercise control over much of the country.

The Jacobins

As the republic tottered under the weight of foreign invasion, internal insurrection, and economic crisis, the revolutionary leadership grew still more radical. In June 1793, the Jacobins replaced the Girondins as the dominant group in the National Convention. The Girondins favored a government in which the departments would exercise control over their own affairs. The Jacobins wanted a strong central government, with Paris as the center of power. The Girondins also opposed government interference in business, whereas the Jacobins supported temporary governmental controls to deal with the needs of war and economic crisis. This last point was crucial; it won the Jacobins the support of the sans-culottes.

Both the Girondins and the Jacobins came from the bourgeoisie, but some Jacobin leaders were more willing to listen to the economic and political demands of the hard-pressed sans-culottes. Besides, the Jacobins wanted an alliance with the sans-culottes in order to defend the Revolution against foreign and domestic enemies. The Jacobins had a further advantage in the power struggle: they were tightly organized, well disciplined, and convinced that only they could save the republic. On June 2, 1793, some eighty thousand armed sans-culottes surrounded the Convention and demanded the arrest of Girondin delegates—an act that enabled the Jacobins to gain control of the government.

The problems confronting the Jacobins were staggering. They had to cope with civil war, particularly in the Vendée, economic distress, blockaded ports, and foreign invasion. They lived with the terrible dread that if they failed, the Revolution for liberty and equality would perish. Only strong leadership could save the republic. It was provided by the Committee of Public Safety. Serving as a cabinet for the Convention, the Committee of Public Safety organized the nation's defenses, formulated foreign policy, supervised ministers, ordered arrests, and imposed the central government's authority throughout the nation. The twelve members of the committee, all ardent patriots and veterans of revolutionary politics, constituted "a government of perhaps the ablest and most determined men who have ever held power in France."[18]

Jacobin Achievements

The Jacobins continued the work of reform. A new constitution, in 1793, expressed Jacobin enthusiasm for political democracy. It contained a new Declaration of Rights, which affirmed and amplified the principles of 1789. By giving all adult males the right to vote, it overcame sans-culotte objections to the constitution of 1791. However, the threat of invasion and the revolts caused the implementation of the new constitution to be postponed, and it was never put into effect. Furthermore, by abolishing both slavery in the French colonies and imprisonment for debt and by making plans for free public education, the Jacobins revealed their humanitarianism and their debt to the philosophes.

Jacobin economic policies derived from the exigencies of war. To halt inflation and gain the support of the poor—both necessary for the war effort—the Jacobins decreed the *law of the maximum,* which fixed prices on bread and other essential goods. To win over the peasants, the Jacobins made it easier for them to buy the property of émigré nobles. To equip the Army of the Republic, the Committee of Public Safety requisitioned grain, wool, arms, shoes, and other items from individual citizens, required factories and mines to produce at full capacity, and established state-operated armament and munitions plants.

The Nation in Arms

For the war against foreign invaders, the Jacobins, in an act that anticipated modern conscription, drafted unmarried men between eighteen and twenty-five years of age. They mobilized all the resources of the nation, infused the army with a love for *la patrie* (the nation), and in a remarkable demonstration of administrative skill, equipped an army of more than 800,000 men. In creating the nation in arms, the Jacobins heralded the emergence of modern warfare. Inspired by the ideals of liberty, equality, and fraternity and commanded by officers who had proved their skill on the battlefield, the citizen-soldiers of the republic won decisive victories. In May and June 1794, the French routed the allied forces on the vital northern frontier, and by the end of July, France had become the triumphant master of Belgium.

By demanding complete devotion to the nation, the Jacobin phase of the Revolution also heralded the rise of modern nationalism. In the schools, in newspapers, speeches, and poems, on the stage, and at rallies and meetings of patriotic societies, the French people were told of the glory won by republican soldiers on the battlefield and were reminded of their duties to la patrie. "The citizen is born, lives and dies for the fatherland."[19] These words were written in public places for all citizens to read and ponder. The soldiers of the Revolution fought not for money or for a king but for the nation. "When *la patrie* calls us for her defense," wrote a young soldier to his mother, "we should rush to her. . . . Our life, our goods, and our talents do not belong to us. It is to the nation, to *la patrie,* to which everything belongs."[20] Could this heightened sense of nationality, which concentrated on the special interests of the French people, be reconciled with the Declaration of the Rights of Man, whose principles were addressed to all humanity? The revolutionaries themselves did not understand the implications of the new force that they had unleashed.

The Republic of Virtue and the Reign of Terror

Robespierre. At the same time that the Committee of Public Safety was forging a revolutionary army to deal with external enemies, it was also waging war against internal opposition. The pivotal personality in this struggle was Maximilien Robespierre (1758–1794). Robespierre, who had served in the National Assembly and was an active Jacobin, was distinguished by a fervent faith in the rightness of his beliefs, a total commitment to republican democracy, and an integrity that earned him the appellation "the Incorruptible." In the early stage of the Revolution, Robespierre had strongly supported liberal reforms. He attacked, at times with great fervor, slavery, capital punishment, and censorship; he favored civil rights for Jews; and, in what was considered a radical measure, he supported giving all men the vote regardless of how much property they owned.

Robespierre wanted to create a better society founded on reason, good citizenship, and patriotism. In his Republic of Virtue, there would be no kings or nobles; men would be free, equal, and educated; and reason would be glorified and superstition ridiculed. There would be no extremes of wealth or poverty; a person's natural goodness would prevail over vice and greed; and laws would preserve, not violate, inalienable rights. In this utopian vision, an individual's duties would be "to detest bad faith and despotism, to punish tyrants and traitors, to assist the unfortunate, to respect the weak, to defend the oppressed, to do all the good one can to one's neighbor, and to be-

The Reign of Terror. During the Terror thousands of men and women were condemned to death by the guillotine, often in front of cheering crowds. In this painting a court official reads the names of those sentenced for execution. (*Hulton/Getty Images.*)

have with justice towards all men."[21] Motivated by a sense of integrity, people would actively put the public good ahead of private interests.

A disciple of Rousseau, Robespierre considered the national general will to be ultimate and infallible. Its realization meant the establishment of a Republic of Virtue; its denial meant the death of an ideal and a return to despotism. Robespierre believed that he and his colleagues in the Committee of Public Safety had correctly ascertained the needs of the French people. He was certain that the committee members were the genuine interpreters of the general will, and he felt duty-bound to ensure its realization. He pursued his ideal society with religious zeal. Knowing that the Republic of Virtue could not be established while France was threatened by foreign and civil war, Robespierre urged that enemies of the republic "be prosecuted by all not as ordinary enemies, but as rebels, brigands, and assassins."[22]

To preserve republican liberty, the Jacobins made terror a deliberate government policy. Robespierre declared:

> *Does not liberty, that inestimable blessing . . . have the . . . right to sacrifice lives, fortunes, and even, for a time, individual liberties? . . . Is not the French Revolution . . . a war to the death between those who want to be free and those content to be slaves? . . . There is no middle ground; France must be entirely free or perish in the attempt, and any means are justifiable in fighting for so fine a cause.*[23]

With Robespierre playing a key role, the Jacobin leadership attacked those they considered enemies of the republic: Girondins who challenged Jacobin authority; federalists who opposed a strong central government emanating from Paris; counterrevolutionary priests and nobles and their peasant supporters; and profiteers who hoarded food. The Robespierrists also executed Jacques Danton, a hero of the Revolution, who wished to end the terror and negotiate peace with the enemy. The Jacobins even sought to discipline the ardor of the sans-culottes, who had given them power. Fearful that sans-culotte spontaneity would undermine central authority and promote anarchy, Robespierrists brought about the dissolution of sans-culotte societies. In addition, they executed radical revolutionaries known as the *enragés* (literally, madmen), who had considerable influence on the Paris sans-culottes. The leaders of the enragés threatened insurrection against Jacobin rule and pushed for more social reforms than the Jacobins would allow, including setting limits on incomes and on the size of farms and businesses.

Robespierre and his fellow Jacobins did not resort to the guillotine because they were bloodthirsty or power mad. Instead, they sought to establish a temporary dictatorship in a desperate attempt to save the republic and the Revolution. Deeply devoted to republican democracy, the Jacobins viewed themselves as bearers of a higher faith. Like all visionaries, Robespierre was convinced that he knew the right way and that the new society he envisaged would benefit all humanity. He saw those who impeded its implementation not just as opponents but as sinners who had to be liquidated for the general good.

Special courts were established in Paris and other cities to try suspects. The proceedings were carried on in haste, and most judgments called either for acquittal or execution. In the Vendée, where civil war raged, many of the arrested were executed by firing squads, without trial; some five thousand were loaded onto barges, which were then sunk in the middle of the Loire River.

Ironically, most of the executions took place after the frontiers had been secured and the civil war crushed. In many ways, the Terror was less a means of saving the beleaguered republic and more a way of shaping the new republican society and the new individual in accordance with the radical Jacobin ideology. Of the 500,000 people imprisoned for crimes against the republic, some 16,000 were sentenced to death by guillotine and another 20,000 perished in prison before they could be tried. More than 200,000 died in the civil war in the provinces, some 40,000 summarily executed by firing squad, guillotine, and mass drownings ordered by military courts authorized by the Convention.

The Jacobins did save the republic. Their regime expelled foreign armies, crushed the federalist uprisings, contained the counterrevolutionaries in the Vendée, and prevented anarchy. Without the discipline, order, and unity imposed on France by the Jacobins, it is likely that the republic would have collapsed under the twin blows of foreign invasion and domestic anarchy.

Significance of the Terror. The Reign of Terror poses fundamental questions about the meaning of the French Revolution and the validity of the Enlightenment conception of the individual. To what extent was the Terror a reversal of the ideals of the Revolution as formulated in the Declaration of the Rights of Man? To what extent did the feverish passions and the fascination with violence demonstrated in the mass executions in the provinces and in the public spectacles in Paris indicate a darker side of human nature, beyond control of reason? Did Robespierre's religion of humanity revive the fanaticism and cruelty of the wars of religion, which had so disgusted the philosophes? Did the Robespierrists, who considered themselves the staunchest defenders of the Revolution's ideals, soil and subvert these ideals by their zeal? The Jacobins mobilized the might of the nation, created the mystique of la patrie, and imposed dictatorial rule in defense of liberty and equality; they also legalized and justified terror committed in the people's name, that is, in the cause of democracy. In so doing, were they unwittingly unleashing new forces that, in later years, would be harnessed by totalitarian ideologies consciously resolved to stamp out the liberal heritage of the Revolution? Did 1793 mark a change in the direction of Western civilization: a movement away from the ideals of the philosophes and the opening of an age of political coercion and ideological fanaticism, which would culminate in the cataclysms of the twentieth century?

The Fall of Robespierre

The Terror had been instituted during a time of crisis and keyed-up emotions. By the summer of 1794, with the victory of the republic seemingly assured, fear of an aristocratic conspiracy had subsided, the will to punish "traitors" had slackened, and popular fervor for the Terror had diminished. As the need and enthusiasm for the Terror abated, Robespierre's political position weakened.

Opponents of Robespierre in the Convention, feeling the chill of the guillotine blade on their

Profile

Gracchus Babeuf

In 1796, militant supporters of the poor conspired to overthrow the Directory, which was dominated by moderate bourgeois. Among the plotters was Gracchus Babeuf (1760–1797), whose newspaper, *Tribune of the People,* founded in 1794 shortly after the fall of Robespierre, regularly attacked the government. Made aware of the plot—known as the Conspiracy of the Equals—by informers, the Directory ordered the conspirators rounded up. Most of those indicted were freed, seven were deported, and two, including Babeuf, were executed.

The historical significance of Babeuf and his associates derives not from their inconsequential conspiracy but from their call to abolish private property and end the division of society into exploiter and exploited. Historians view the conspirators as pre-Marxist socialists who, like their Marxist successors, aspired to seize power in order to radically transform society.

Giraudon/Art Resource, NY.

own necks, ordered the arrest of Robespierre and some of his supporters. On July 28, 1794, the tenth of Thermidor according to the new republican calendar, Robespierre was guillotined. Parisian sans-culottes might have saved him but made no attempt to do so. With their political clubs dissolved, they lacked the organization needed for an armed uprising. Moreover, the sans-culottes' ardor for Jacobinism had waned. They resented Robespierre for having executed their leaders, and apparently the social legislation instituted by the Robespierrist leadership had not been sufficient to soothe sans-culotte discontent.

After the fall of Robespierre, the machinery of the Jacobin republic was dismantled. Leadership passed to the property-owning bourgeois who had endorsed the constitutional ideas of 1789–91, the moderate stage of the Revolution. The new leadership, known as Thermidoreans until the end of 1795, wanted no more of the Jacobins or of Robespierre's society. They had considered Robespierre a threat to their political power because he would have allowed the common people a considerable voice in the government. They had also viewed him as a threat to their property because he would have introduced some state regulation of the economy to aid the poor.

The Thermidorean reaction was a counterrevolution. The new government purged the army of officers who were suspected of Jacobin leanings, abolished the law of the maximum, and declared void the constitution of 1793. A new constitution, approved in 1795, reestablished property requirements for voting. The counterrevolution also produced a counterterror, as royalists and Catholics massacred Jacobins in the provinces.

At the end of 1795, the new republican government, the Directory, was burdened by war, a sagging economy, and internal unrest. The Directory crushed insurrections by Parisian sans-culottes, maddened by hunger and hatred of the rich (1795, 1796), and by royalists seeking to re-

In the spirited defense he gave at his trial, Babeuf often quoted passages from *Tribune of the People,* such as the following, which reveals the socialist character of his thought.

> *The masses can no longer find a way to go on living; they see that they possess nothing and that they suffer under the harsh and flinty oppression of a greedy ruling class. The hour strikes for great and memorable revolutionary events, already foreseen in the writings of the times, when a general overthrow of the system of private property is inevitable, when the revolt of the poor against the rich becomes a necessity that can no longer be postponed. . . .*
>
> *Nature has placed everyone under an obligation to work. None may exempt himself from work without committing an antisocial action. Work and its fruits should be common to all. Oppression exists when one man is ground down by toil and lacks the barest necessaries of life, while another revels in luxury and idleness. It is impossible for anyone, without committing a crime, to appropriate for his own exclusive use the fruits of the earth or of manufacture.*
>
> *In a truly just social order there are neither rich nor poor. The rich, who refuse to give up their superfluous wealth for the benefit of the poor, are enemies of the people.*
>
> *None may be permitted to monopolize the cultural resources of society and hence to deprive others of the education essential for their wellbeing. Education is a universal human right.*
>
> *The purpose of the Revolution is to abolish inequality and to restore the common welfare. The Revolution is not yet at an end, since the wealthy have diverted its fruits, including political power, to their own exclusive use, while the poor in their toil and misery lead a life of actual slavery and count for nothing in the State.**

**The Defense of Gracchus Babeuf,* ed. and trans. John Anthony Scott (New York: Schocken Books, 1972), pp. 45–46.

store the monarchy (1797). As military and domestic pressures increased, power began to pass into the hands of generals. One of them, Napoleon Bonaparte, seized control of the government in November 1799, pushing the Revolution into yet another stage.

The Meaning of the French Revolution

The French Revolution was a decisive period in the shaping of the modern West. It implemented the thought of the philosophes, destroyed the hierarchical and corporate society of the Old Regime, which was a legacy of the Middle Ages, promoted the interests of the bourgeoisie, and quickened the growth of the modern state.

The Revolution also weakened the aristocracy. With their ancient feudal rights and privileges eliminated, the nobles became simply ordinary citizens. Throughout the nineteenth century, France would be governed by both aristocrats and bourgeois. Property, not noble birth, determined the composition of the new ruling elite—a trend already in evidence before the Revolution.

The principle of careers open to talent gave the bourgeoisie access to the highest positions in the state. Having wealth, talent, ambition, and now opportunity, the bourgeoisie would play an ever more important role in French political life. Throughout continental Europe, the reforms of the French Revolution served as a model for progressive bourgeois who, sooner or later, would challenge the Old Regime in their own lands.

The French Revolution transformed the dynastic state, on which the Old Regime was based, into the modern state: national, liberal, secular, and rational. When the Declaration of the Rights of Man and of the Citizen asserted that "the source of all sovereignty resides essentially in the nation," the concept of the state took on a new meaning. The state was no longer merely a territory or a federation of provinces; it was not the private possession of the king claiming to be God's lieutenant on earth. In the new conception, the state belonged to the people as a whole, and the individual, formerly a subject, was now a citizen with both rights and duties and was governed by laws that drew no distinction on the basis of birth.

The liberal thought of the Enlightenment found practical expression in the reforms of the Revolution. Absolutism and divine right of monarchy, repudiated in theory by the philosophes, were invalidated by constitutions affirming that sovereignty resides with the people, not with a monarch, and setting limits on the powers of government and by elected parliaments representing the governed. By providing for equality before the law and the protection of human rights—habeas corpus, trial by jury, and freedom of religion, speech, and the press—the Revolution struck at the abuses of the Old Regime. Because of violations and interruptions, these gains seemed at times more theoretical than actual. Nevertheless, these liberal ideals reverberated throughout the Continent. In the early nineteenth century, reformers in France and other lands, aspiring for political and social change, took the French Revolution as their inspiration, and the pace of reform quickened.

During the nineteenth century, the French Revolution served as a frame of reference for the various political constellations: liberalism, socialism, conservatism. Bourgeois liberals took as their model the moderate stage of the Revolution, which advanced the cause of liberty and equality and reformed a decaying Old Regime. At the same time, the Revolution presented a dilemma for bourgeois liberals, who valued reforms promoting liberty and equality but also feared the entrance into politics of the uneducated and unpropertied sans-culottes, with their demand for state intervention in the economy to improve living standards. And bourgeois moderates were haunted by memories of Jacobin radicalism. The Terror was a frightening demonstration of how liberty could degenerate into a new kind of despotism. With the demands of the sans-culottes for political democracy and for social reform, the voice of the urban poor began to be heard in politics, a phenomenon that would intensify with growing industrialization. Emerging socialists who embraced the cause of the laboring poor employed the rhetoric of the sans-culottes leaders in order to launch a social revolution that would improve the status of the downtrodden.

LIBERTY ARMED WITH THE SCEPTER OF REASON STRIKES DOWN IGNORANCE AND FANATICISM, AN ENGRAVING BY JEAN-BAPTISTE CHAPUY, C. 1793. Using a scepter given to her by Reason standing at the left, Liberty strikes down ignorance and fanaticism, usually identified with religion. Many of these prints were produced in 1793 and 1794, when there was a concerted effort to replace traditional Christianity with a civic religion, the Cult of Reason. (*Bibliothèque Nationale, Paris.*)

If European liberals embraced the philosophy of the moderate reformers of 1789–91 while rejecting the extremism of the radical Jacobins, conservatives throughout the nineteenth century regarded the Revolution in all its stages as an unmitigated disaster and wanted to undo reforms introduced by the Revolution. Hostility to the Revolution and to the Enlightenment defined extreme conservatism during the nineteenth century and found its ultimate expression in the fascist movements of the twentieth century, which explicitly attacked the universal ideals expressed in the Declaratrion of the Rights of Man and of the Citizen.

By disavowing any divine justification for the monarch's power and by depriving the church of its special position, the Revolution accelerated the secularization of European political life. Sweeping aside the administrative chaos of the Old Regime, the Revolution attempted to impose rational norms on the state. The sale of public offices, which had produced ineffective and corrupt administrators, was eliminated, and the highest positions in the land were opened to men of talent regardless of birth. The Revolution abolished the peasantry's manorial obligations, which had hampered agriculture, and it swept away barriers to economic expansion. It based taxes on income and streamlined their collection. By destroying feudal remnants and eliminating internal tolls and guilds, it speeded up the expansion of a competitive market economy. In the nineteenth century, reformers in the rest of Europe would follow the lead set by France.

By showing that a decadent old order could be toppled and supplanted by a new one, the French Revolution inspired generations of revolutionaries aspiring to end long-standing abuses and remodel society. In the process, it unleashed three potentially destructive forces identified with the modern state: total war, nationalism, and a fanatic utopian mentality. All of these forces contradicted the rational and universal aims of the Declaration of the Rights of Man.

Whereas eighteenth-century wars were fought by professional soldiers for limited aims, the French Revolution, says the British historian Herbert Butterfield,

> *brings conscription, the nation in arms, the mobilization of all the resources of the state for unrelenting conflict. It heralds the age when peoples, woefully ignorant of one another, bitterly uncomprehending, lie in uneasy juxtaposition watching one another's sins with hysteria and indignation. It heralds Armageddon, the giant conflict for justice and right between angered populations each of which thinks it is the righteous one. So a new kind of warfare is born—the modern counterpart to the old conflicts of religions.*[24]

The world wars of the twentieth century are the terrible fulfillment of this new development in warfare.

The French Revolution also gave birth to modern nationalism. During the Revolution, loyalty was directed to the entire nation, not to a village or province or to the person of the king. The whole of France became the fatherland. Under the Jacobins, the French became converts to a secular faith preaching total reverence for the nation. "In 1794 we believed in no supernatural religion; our serious interior sentiments were all summed up in the one idea, how to be useful to the fatherland. Everything else . . . was, in our eyes, only trivial. . . . It was our only religion."[25] Few suspected that the new religion of nationalism was fraught with danger. Louis-Antoine de Saint-Just, a young, ardent Robespierrist, was gazing into the future when he declared: "There is something terrible in the sacred love of the fatherland. This love is so exclusive that it sacrifices everything to the public interest, without pity, without fear, with no respect for the human individual."[26] The philosophes would have deemed nationalism, which demanded total dedication of body and soul to the nation and eclipsed thought, to be a repudiation of their universalism and hopes for rational solutions to political conflicts. It was a new dogma capable of evoking wild and dangerous passions and a setback for the progress of reason.

The French Revolution gave rise to still another potentially destructive force: a revolutionary mentality that sought to demolish an unjust traditional society and create a new social order that would restore individuals to their natural goodness. The negative side of this lofty vision was its power to whip up extremism that justified mass murder in the name of a higher good. Such was the case with Robespierre and other Jacobins. In the twentieth century, Nazis in Germany and radical socialists in Russia, China, and Cambodia, seeing themselves as idealists striving for a social regeneration of humanity, oppressed, terrorized, and murdered with intense dedication—and a clear conscience.

The Revolution attempted to reconstruct society on the basis of Enlightenment thought. The Declaration of the Rights of Man and of the Citizen, whose spirit permeated the reforms of the Revolution, upheld the dignity of the individual, demanded respect for the individual, attributed to each person natural rights, and barred the state from denying these rights. It insisted that society and the state have no higher duty than to promote the freedom and autonomy of the individual. "It is not enough to have overturned the throne," said Robespierre; "our concern is to erect upon its remains holy Equality and the sacred Rights of Man."[27] The tragedy of the Western experience is that this humanist vision, brilliantly expressed by the Enlightenment and given recognition in the reforms of the French Revolution, would be undermined in later generations. And, ironically, by its fanatical commitment to a seductive ideology that promised worldly salvation—the creation of a republic of virtue and truth—the French Revolution itself contributed to the shattering of this vision. It had spawned total war, nationalism, terror as government policy, and a revolutionary mentality that sought to change the world through coercion and violence. In the twentieth century, these dangerous forces almost succeeded in crushing the liberty and equality so valued by the French reformers.

Notes

1. Quoted in G. P. Gooch, *Germany and the French Revolution* (New York: Russell & Russell, 1966), p. 39.
2. Quoted in Ernst Wangermann, *From Joseph II to the Jacobin Trials* (New York: Oxford University Press, 1959), p. 24.
3. Excerpted in Alfred Cobban, ed., *The Debate on the French Revolution* (London: Adam & Charles Black, 1960), p. 41.
4. Quoted in Elinor G. Barber, *The Bourgeoisie in Eighteenth-Century France* (Princeton, N.J.: Princeton University Press, 1967), p. 57.
5. Quoted in C. B. A. Behrens, *The Ancien Régime* (New York: Harcourt, Brace & World, 1967), p. 43.
6. Quoted in Leo Gershoy, *The French Revolution and Napoleon* (New York: Appleton-Century-Crofts, 1933), p. 18.
7. George Rudé, *Revolutionary Europe, 1783–1815* (New York: Harper Torchbooks, 1966), p. 74.
8. Henri Peyre, "The Influence of Eighteenth-Century Ideas on the French Revolution," *Journal of the History of Ideas,* 10 (1949):73.
9. Georges Lefebvre, *The French Revolution from 1793 to 1799,* trans. John Hall Stewart and James Friguglietti (New York: Columbia University Press, 1964), 2:360.
10. Quoted in T. C. W. Blanning, *The French Revolution: Aristocrats Versus Bourgeois?* (Atlantic Highlands, N.J.: Humanities Press, 1987), p. 9.
11. William Doyle, *Origins of the French Revolution* (New York: Oxford University Press, 1980), p. 21.
12. Quoted in Blanning, *French Revolution,* p. 38.
13. Excerpted in John Hall Stewart, ed., *A Documentary Survey of the French Revolution* (New York: Macmillan, 1951), pp. 43–44.
14. See George Rudé, *The Crowd in the French Revolution* (New York: Oxford University Press, 1959).
15. Georges Lefebvre, *The Coming of the French Revolution* (Princeton, N.J.: Princeton University Press, 1967), p. 210.
16. Albert Soboul, *The Parisian Sans-Culottes and the French Revolution, 1793–94,* trans. Gwynne Lewis (London: Oxford University Press, 1964), pp. 28–29.
17. Quoted in Soboul, *Parisian Sans-Culottes,* p. 64.
18. Alfred Cobban, *A History of Modern France* (Baltimore: Penguin, 1961), 1:213.
19. Quoted in Hans Kohn, *Nationalism: Its Meaning and History* (Princeton, N.J.: D. Van Nostrand, 1965), p. 25.
20. Quoted in Carlton J. H. Hayes, *The Historical Evolution of Modern Nationalism* (New York: Richard R. Smith, 1931), p. 55.
21. Excerpted in George Rudé, ed., *Robespierre* (Englewood Cliffs, N.J.: Prentice-Hall, 1976), p. 72.
22. Ibid., p. 57.
23. Excerpted in E. L. Higgins, ed., *The French Revolution* (Boston: Houghton Mifflin, 1938), pp. 306–307.
24. Herbert Butterfield, *Napoleon* (New York: Collier Books, 1962), p. 18.
25. Quoted in Hayes, *Evolution of Modern Nationalism,* p. 55.
26. Quoted in Hans Kohn, *Making of the Modern*

French Mind (New York: D. Van Nostrand, 1955), p. 17.

27. Quoted in Christopher Dawson, *The Gods of Revolution* (New York: New York University Press, 1972), p. 83.

Suggested Reading

Blanning, T. C. W., *The French Revolution: Aristocrats Versus Bourgeois?* (1987). Summarizes recent scholarship on the question; a volume in Studies of European History series.

———, ed., *The Rise and Fall of the French Revolution* (1996). A collection of recent articles, some by prominent students of the Revolution.

Campbell, Peter Robert, *The Ancien Régime in France* (1988). An incisive essay on French society prior to the Revolution.

Carr, John L., *Robespierre* (1972). A biography of the revolutionary leader.

Doyle, William, *The Oxford History of the French Revolution* (1990). A narrative history that incorporates new thinking on the causes and nature of the Revolution.

Forrest, Alan, *The French Revolution* (1995). Social, political, and ideological changes brought about by the Revolution.

Furet, François, and Mona Ozouf, eds., *A Critical Dictionary of the French Revolution* (1989). Articles on many topics pertaining to the Revolution.

Gershoy, Leo, *The Era of the French Revolution* (1957). A brief survey with useful documents.

Gourbet, Pierre, *The Ancien Régime* (1973). A survey of French society from 1600 to 1750.

Higgins, E. L., ed., *The French Revolution* (1938). Excerpts from contemporaries.

Kafker, F. A., and J. M. Laux, *The French Revolution: Conflicting Interpretations* (1976). Excerpts from leading historians.

Lefebvre, Georges, *The French Revolution,* 2 vols. (1962, 1964). A detailed analysis by a master historian.

———, *The Coming of the French Revolution* (1967). A brilliant analysis of the social structure of the Old Regime and the opening phase of the Revolution.

Palmer, R. R., *The Age of the Democratic Revolution,* 2 vols. (1959, 1964). The French Revolution as part of a revolutionary movement that spread on both sides of the Atlantic.

———, *Twelve Who Ruled* (1965). An admirable treatment of the Terror.

Rudé, George, *The Crowd in the French Revolution* (1959). An analysis of the composition of the crowds that stormed the Bastille, marched to Versailles, and attacked the king's palace.

———, *Robespierre: Portrait of a Revolutionary Democrat* (1976). An admirable biography.

Soboul, Albert, *The Sans-Culottes* (1972). An abridgment of the classic study of the popular movement of 1793–94.

Stewart, J. H., *A Documentary Survey of the French Revolution* (1951). A valuable collection.

Sutherland, D. M. G., *France 1789–1815* (1986). Like Doyle, Sutherland departs from the classic theory of the bourgeois revolution.

Review Questions

1. What privileges did clergy and nobility enjoy in the Old Regime?
2. What were the grievances of the bourgeoisie, the peasantry, and the urban laborers?
3. Why was France in financial difficulty?
4. Why do some historians regard the French Revolution as a bourgeois revolution? Why do revisionists dispute this view?
5. Identify and explain the significance of the following: the formation of the National Assembly, the storming of the Bastille, the Great Fear, and the October Days.
6. Analyze the nature and significance of the reforms of the National Assembly.
7. What were the grievances of the sans-culottes?
8. Identify and explain the significance of the following: flight of the king, the Brunswick manifesto, and the September Massacres.
9. What were the principal differences between the Jacobins and the Girondins?
10. What were the accomplishments of the Jacobins?
11. How did Robespierre justify the Terror? What meaning do you ascribe to the Terror?
12. Why was the French Revolution a decisive period in the shaping of the West?

Chapter 20

Napoleon: Subverter and Preserver of the Revolution

In this painting by Jacques Louis David, Napoleon is depicted as a heroic commander. (© Réunion des Musées Nationaux/Art Resources, NY.)

■ **Rise to Power**
Coup d'État
Napoleon's Character

■ **Napoleon and France**
Government: Centralization and Repression
Religion: Reconciliation with the Church
Law: The Code Napoléon
Education: The Imperial University
Economy: Strengthening the State

■ **Napoleon and Europe**
Napoleon's Art of War
The Grand Empire: Diffusion of Revolutionary Institutions

■ **The Fall of Napoleon**
Failure to Subdue England
The Spanish Ulcer
The German War of Liberation
Disaster in Russia
Final Defeat

■ **The Legend and the Achievement**

The upheavals of the French Revolution made possible the extraordinary career of Napoleon Bonaparte. This popular general, who gained control over France in 1799, combined a passion for power with a genius for leadership. Under Napoleon's military dictatorship, the constitutional government for which the people of 1789 had fought and the republican democracy for which the Jacobins had rallied the nation seemed lost. Nevertheless, during the Napoleonic era, many achievements of the Revolution were preserved, strengthened, and carried to other lands.

Rise to Power

Napoleon was born on August 15, 1769, on the French-ruled island of Corsica, the son of a petty noble. After finishing military school in France, he became an artillery officer; the wars of the French Revolution gave him an opportunity to advance his career. In December 1793, Napoleon's brilliant handling of artillery forced the British to lift their siege of the city of Toulon. Two years later, he saved the Thermidorean Convention from a royalist insurrection by ordering his troops to fire into the riotous mob—the famous "whiff of grapeshot." In 1796, he was given command of the French Army of Italy. His star was rising.

In Italy, against the Austrians, Napoleon demonstrated a dazzling talent for military planning and leadership, which earned him an instant reputation. Having tasted glory, he could never do without it. Since he had experienced only success, nothing seemed impossible. He sensed that he was headed for greatness. Years later, he recalled: "[In Italy] I realized I was a superior being and conceived the ambition of performing great things, which hitherto had filled my thoughts only as a fantastic dream."[1]

In November 1797, Napoleon was ordered to plan an invasion of England. Aware that the French navy was weak, he recommended postponing the invasion. He urged instead that an expedition be sent to the Near East to strike at British power in the Mediterranean and British commerce with India, and perhaps to carve out a French empire in the Near East. With more than

Chronology 20.1 ❖ Napoleon's Career

1796	Napoleon gets command of the French Army of Italy
1798	Battle of the Nile: the British annihilate Napoleon's fleet
November 10, 1799	Napoleon helps to overthrow Directory's rule, establishing a strong executive in France
1802	He becomes first consul for life; peace is made with Austria and Britain
March 21, 1804	Civil Code (called Code Napoléon in 1807)
December 2, 1804	Napoleon crowns himself emperor of the French
October 1805	French forces occupy Vienna
October 21, 1805	Battle of Trafalgar: French and Spanish fleets are defeated by the British
December 1805	Battle of Austerlitz: Napoleon defeats Russo-Austrian forces
1806	War against Prussia and Russia
October 1806	Napoleon defeats Prussians at Jena, and French forces occupy Berlin
June 1807	French victory over Russians at Friedland
1808–1813	Peninsular War: Spaniards, aided by the British, fight against French occupation
September 14, 1812	Grand Army reaches Moscow
October–December 1812	Grand Army retreats from Russia
October 1813	Allied forces defeat Napoleon at Leipzig
1814	Paris is captured, and Napoleon is exiled to Elba
March 20, 1815	Escaping, Napoleon enters Paris and begins "hundred days" rule
June 1815	Defeated at Waterloo, Napoleon is exiled to Saint Helena

thirty-five thousand troops, Napoleon set out for Egypt, then a part of the Turkish empire. Although he captured Cairo, the Egyptian campaign was far from a success. At the battle of the Nile (1798), the British, commanded by Admiral Horatio Nelson, annihilated Napoleon's fleet. Deprived of reinforcements and supplies, with his manpower reduced by battle and plague, Napoleon was compelled to abandon whatever dreams he might have had of threatening India. Although the Egyptian expedition was a failure, Napoleon, always seeking to improve his image, sent home glowing bulletins about French victories. To people in France, he was the conqueror of Egypt, as well as of Italy.

Meanwhile, political unrest, financial disorder, and military reversals produced an atmosphere of crisis in France. Napoleon knew that in such times people seek out a savior. A man of destiny must act. Without informing his men, he slipped out of Egypt, avoided British cruisers, and landed in France in October 1799.

Coup d'État

When Napoleon arrived in France, a conspiracy was already under way against the government of the Directory. Convinced that only firm leadership could solve France's problems, some politicians plotted to seize power and establish a strong executive. Needing the assistance of a popular general, they turned to Napoleon, whom they thought they could control. Although the hastily prepared coup d'état was almost bungled, the government of the Directory was overthrown. The French Revolution entered a new stage, that of military dictatorship.

Demoralized by a decade of political instability, economic distress, domestic violence, and war, most of the French welcomed the leadership of a strong man. The bourgeois, in particular, expected Napoleon to protect their wealth and the influence they had gained during the Revolution.

The new constitution (1799) created a strong executive. Although three consuls shared the executive office, the first consul, Napoleon, monopolized power. Whereas Napoleon's fellow conspirators, who were political moderates, sought only to strengthen the executive, Napoleon aspired to personal rule. He captured the reins of power after the coup, and his authority continued to expand. In 1802, he was made first consul for life, with the right to name his successor. And on December 2, 1804, in a magnificent ceremony at the Cathedral of Notre Dame in Paris, Napoleon crowned himself emperor of the French. General, first consul, and then emperor—it was a breathless climb to the heights of power. Napoleon, who once said that he loved "power as a musician loves his violin,"[2] was determined never to lose it.

Napoleon's Character

What sort of man was this on whom the fate of France and Europe depended? Napoleon's complex and mysterious personality continues to baffle biographers. However, certain distinctive characteristics are evident. Napoleon's intellectual ability was impressive. His mind swiftly absorbed and classified details, which his photographic memory stored. With surgical precision, he could probe his way to the heart of a problem while still retaining a grasp of peripheral considerations. Ideas always danced in his head, and his imagination was illuminated by sudden flashes of insight. He could work for eighteen or twenty hours at a stretch, deep in concentration, ruling out boredom or fatigue by an act of will. Napoleon, man of action, warrior par excellence, was in many ways, says Georges Lefebvre, "a typical man of the eighteenth century, a rationalist, a *philosophe* [who] placed his trust in reason, in knowledge, and in methodical effort."[3]

Rationalism was only one part of his personality. There was also that elemental, irresistible urge for action, "the romantic Napoleon, a force seeking to expand and for which the world was no more than an occasion for acting dangerously."[4] This love of action fused with his boundless ambition. Lefebvre continues:

> *His greatest ambition was glory. "I live only for posterity," he exclaimed, "death is nothing, but to live defeated and without glory is to die every day." His eyes were fixed on the world's great leaders: Alexander who conquered the East and dreamed of conquering the world; Caesar, Augustus, Charlemagne. . . . They were for him examples, which stimulated his imagination and lent an unalterable charm to action. He was an artist, a poet of action, for whom France and mankind were but instruments.*[5]

He also exuded an indefinable quality of personality, a charismatic force that made people feel that they were in the presence of a superior man. Contemporaries remarked that his large gray eyes, penetrating, knowing, yet strangely expressionless, seemed to possess a hypnotic power. He was capable of moving men to obedience, to loyalty, and to heroism.

The rationalist's clarity of mind and the romantic's impassioned soul, the adventurer's love of glory and the hero's personal magnetism and iron will—these were the components of Napoleon's personality. There was also an aloofness—some would say callousness—that led him to regard peo-

Coronation of Napoleon and Josephine, by David. Napoleon crowned himself emperor in a magnificent ceremony. To French émigrés and nobles throughout Europe, he was the "crowned Jacobin" who threatened aristocratic privileges and European stability. (*Louvre © Réunion des Musées Nationaux.*)

ple as pawns to be manipulated in the pursuit of his destiny. "A man like me," he once said, "troubles himself little about the lives of a million men."[6]

Napoleon's genius might have gone unheralded and his destiny unfulfilled had it not been for the opportunities created by the French Revolution. By opening careers to talent, the Revolution enabled a young Corsican of undistinguished birth to achieve fame and popularity. By creating a national army and embroiling France in war, it provided a military commander with enormous sources of power. By plunging France into one crisis after another, it opened up extraordinary possibilities for a man with a gift of leadership and an ambition "so intimately linked with my very being that it is like the blood that circulates in my veins."[7] It was the Revolution that made Napoleon conscious of his genius and certain of his destiny.

Napoleon and France

Living in a revolutionary age, Napoleon had observed firsthand the precariousness of power and the fleetingness of popularity. A superb realist, he knew that his past reputation would not sustain him. If he could not solve the problems caused by a decade of revolution and war and bind together the different classes of French people, his prestige would diminish and his power collapse. The general must become a statesman and, when necessary, a tyrant. His domestic policies, showing the influence of both eighteenth-century enlightened despotism and the Revolution, affected every aspect of society and had an enduring impact on French history. They continued the work of the Revolution in destroying the institutions of the Old Regime.

Government: Centralization and Repression

In providing France with a strong central government, Napoleon continued a policy initiated centuries earlier by Bourbon monarchs. The Bourbons, however, had not been able to overcome completely the barriers presented by provinces, local traditions, feudal remnants, and corporate institutions. Napoleon, in contrast, succeeded in giving France administrative uniformity. An army of officials, subject to the emperor's will, reached into every village, linking together the entire nation. This centralized state suited Napoleon's desire for orderly government and rational administration, enabled him to concentrate power in his own hands, and provided him with the taxes and soldiers needed to fight his wars. To suppress irreconcilable opponents, primarily die-hard royalists and republicans, Napoleon used the instruments of the police state: secret agents, arbitrary arrest, summary trials, and executions.

Napoleon also shaped public opinion to prevent hostile criticism of his rule and to promote popular support for his policies and person. In these actions, he was a precursor of twentieth-century dictators. Liberty of the press came to an end. Printers swore an oath of obedience to the emperor, and newspapers were converted into government mouthpieces. Printers were forbidden to print and booksellers to sell or circulate "anything which may involve injury to the duties of subjects toward the sovereign or the interests of the state."[8] When Napoleon's secretary read him the morning newspapers, Napoleon would interrupt, "Skip it, skip it. I know what is in them. They only say what I tell them to."[9] These efforts at indoctrination even reached schoolchildren, who were required to memorize a catechism glorifying the ruler, which ran, in part, as follows:

> *Q. What are the duties of Christians with respect to the princes who govern them, and what in particular are our duties toward Napoleon I, our Emperor?*
>
> *A. Christians owe to the princes who govern them, and we owe in particular to Napoleon I, our Emperor, love, respect, obedience, fidelity, military service; . . . we also owe him . . . prayers for his safety. . . .*
>
> *Q. Why are we bound to all these duties towards our Emperor?*
>
> *A. First of all, because God, who creates emperors and distributes them according to his will, in loading our Emperor with gifts, both in peace and war, has established him as our sovereign. . . . To honor and to serve our Emperor is then to honor and to serve God himself.*
>
> *Q. What . . . of those who may be lacking in their duty towards our Emperor?*
>
> *A. . . . they would be resisting the order established by God himself and would make themselves worthy of eternal damnation.*[10]

By repressing liberty, subverting republicanism, and restoring absolutism, Emperor Napoleon reversed some of the liberal gains of the Revolution. Although favoring equality before the law and equality of opportunity as necessary for a well-run state, Napoleon believed that political liberty impeded efficiency and threatened the state with anarchy. He would govern in the interest of the people as an enlightened but absolute ruler.

Religion: Reconciliation with the Church

For Napoleon, who was a deist, if not an atheist, the value of religion was not salvation but social and political cohesion. It promoted national unity and prevented class war. He stated:

> *Society cannot exist without inequality of fortunes, and inequality of fortunes cannot exist without religion. When a man is dying of hunger alongside another who stuffs himself, it is impossible to make him accede to the difference unless there is an authority which says to him God wishes it thus; there must be some poor and some rich in the world, but hereafter*

Profile

François Dominique Toussaint L'Ouverture

In 1791, in the midst of the French Revolution, black slaves on San Domingo, the rich French sugar colony in the West Indies, revolted, murdering their masters, burning down plantations, and crying "Vengeance! Vengeance!" Their hatred of servitude, which had ignited slave revolts in previous decades, was intensified by the ideals of liberty and equality reverberating across the Atlantic.

François Dominique Toussaint L'Ouverture (c. 1743–1803) joined the rebellion and quickly rose to a position of command. Toussaint was the son of a petty African chief from Dahomey who, like millions of other Africans, had been captured in war, sold to westerners, and brought in chains to toil on plantations in the New World. Toussaint, the eldest of eight children, was born in captivity. A remarkable old black taught him French and some Latin and geometry, and his master, recognizing Toussaint's ability, made him first a coachman and

Roger-Viollet.

> *and for all eternity the division will be made differently.*[11]

This is what Napoleon probably had in mind when he said: "Men who do not believe in God—one does not govern them, one shoots them."[12]

Napoleon tried to close the breach between the state and the Catholic church, which had appeared during the Revolution. Such a reconciliation would gain the approval of the mass of the French people, who still remained devoted to their faith, and would reassure the peasants and bourgeoisie who had bought confiscated church lands. For these reasons, Napoleon negotiated an agreement with the pope. The Concordat of 1801 recognized Catholicism as the religion of the great majority of the French, rather than as the official state religion (the proposal that the pope desired). The clergy were to be paid and nominated by the state but consecrated by the pope.

In effect, the Concordat guaranteed the reforms of the Revolution. The church did not regain its confiscated lands or its right to collect the tithe. The French clergy remained largely subject to state control. And by not establishing Catholicism as the state religion, the Concordat did not jeopardize the newly won toleration of Jews and Protestants. Napoleon had achieved his aim. The Concordat made his regime acceptable to Catholics and to owners of former church lands.

Law: The Code Napoléon

Under the Old Regime, France was plagued with numerous and conflicting law codes. Reflecting local interests and feudal traditions, these codes obstructed national unity and administrative efficiency. Efforts by the revolutionaries to draw up then steward of the plantation's livestock, a position almost never held by a nonwhite.

At the time of the rebellion, 42,000 whites, employing brutal means of repression—whipping, chaining, roasting, and mutilation—dominated 500,000 black slaves, often working them like beasts. Complicating the social structure were mulattos, people of mixed race who were granted French citizenship in 1793 out of fear that they would side with the rebellious black slaves.

Aspiring to eliminate slavery entirely, Toussaint organized an army consisting mainly of illiterate slaves into a fighting force capable of defeating European-trained soldiers. In 1794, the Jacobins abolished slavery over the opposition of the white planters, and Toussaint, who had distinguished himself as a military commander, was appointed assistant governor. Toussaint was also a man of vision, deeply committed to the revolutionary ideals of liberty and equality and to introducing economic, administrative, and educational reforms in San Domingo. Contrary to the wishes of the more radical black officers, he permitted whites and mulattos to hold important positions in the bureaucracy. Toussaint's reluctance to declare independence from France also angered the radicals.

In 1801, two years after seizing power in France, Napoleon sent twenty thousand troops to San Domingo to restore slavery and to subdue Toussaint, whose power had increased considerably. The old warrior, having lost none of his skills in guerrilla warfare, was at the point of defeating the French when he proposed peace. The French commander tricked Toussaint into believing that if he retired, France would negotiate a favorable settlement with San Domingo. Shortly after he retired to his farm, Toussaint was arrested and sent to prison in France, where he suffered abuse and humiliation until his death in 1803. On January 1, 1804, revolutionaries on the island established the independent state of Haiti, whose foundation Toussaint L'Ouverture had laid.

a unified code of laws bogged down. Recognizing the value of such a code in promoting effective administration throughout France, Napoleon pressed for the completion of the project. The Code Napoléon incorporated many principles of the Revolution: equality before the law, the right to choose one's profession, freedom of religion, protection of property rights, the abolition of serfdom, and the secular character of the state.

The code also had its less liberal side, denying equal treatment to workers in their dealings with employers, to women in their relations with their husbands, and to children in their relations with their fathers. By making wives inferior to their husbands in matters of property, adultery, and divorce, the code reflected both Napoleon's personal attitude and the general view of the times toward women and family stability. Of women, he once said that "the husband must possess the absolute power and right to say to his wife: 'Madam, you shall not go out, you shall not go to the theater, you shall not receive such and such a person: for the children you shall bear shall be mine!'"[13]

Adopted in lands conquered by France, the Code Napoléon helped to weaken feudal privileges and institutions and clerical interference in the secular state. With justice, Napoleon could say: "My true glory is not to have won forty battles. . . . Waterloo will erase the memory of so many victories. . . . But what nothing will destroy, what will live forever, is my Civil Code."[14]

Education: The Imperial University

Napoleon's educational policy was an elaboration of the school reforms initiated during the Revolution. Like the revolutionaries, Napoleon favored a system of public education, with a sec-

Admiring Napoleon. The emperor's charisma and conquests earned him the adoration of the French people. In this print the peasant pointing to Napoleon tells the priest: "For me he will always be Our Father." (*Bibliothèque Nationale, Paris.*)

ular curriculum and minimum church involvement. For Napoleon, education served a dual purpose: it would provide him with capable officials to administer his laws and trained officers to lead his armies; and it would indoctrinate the young in obedience and loyalty. He established the University of France, a giant board of education that placed education under state control. To this day, the French school system, unlike that in the United States, is strictly centralized, with curriculum and standards set for the entire country.

The emperor did not consider education for girls important, holding that "marriage is their whole destination."[15] In his view, whatever education girls did receive should stress religion. "What we ask of education is not that girls should think but that they should believe. The weakness of women's brains, the instability of their ideas, the place they fill in society, their need for perpetual resignation . . . all this can only be met by religion."[16]

Economy: Strengthening the State

Napoleon's financial and economic policies were designed to strengthen France and enhance his popularity. To stimulate the economy and to retain the favor of the bourgeois, who supported his seizure of power, Napoleon aided industry through tariffs and loans. He fostered commerce (while also speeding up troop movements) by building or repairing roads, bridges, and canals. To protect the currency from inflation, he established the Bank of France, which was controlled by the nation's leading financiers. By keeping careers open to talent, he endorsed one of the key demands of the bourgeoisie during the Revolution. Fearing a revolution based on lack of bread, he provided food at low prices and stimulated employment for the laboring poor. He endeared himself to the peasants by not restoring feudal privileges and by allowing them to keep the land they had obtained during the Revolution.

Napoleon did not identify with the republicanism and democracy of the Jacobins, which he equated with mob rule. Rather, by preserving many social gains of the Revolution while suppressing political liberty, he showed himself to be an heir of enlightened despotism. Like the reforming despots, Napoleon admired administrative uniformity and efficiency, hated feudalism, religious persecution, and civil inequality, and favored government regulation of trade and industry.

Napoleon Crossing the Great Saint Bernard Pass. Integral to Napoleon's art of war was his ability to move his troops quickly across difficult terrain and surprise his opponents with confounding tactics. (*Bulloz, Paris.*)

Napoleon and Europe

Although Napoleon's domestic policies gained him wide support, it was his victories on the battlefield that mesmerized the French people and gratified their national vanity. Ultimately, his popularity and his power rested on the sword. In 1802, he declared,

> *My power proceeds from my reputation, and my reputation from the victories I have won. My power would fail if I were not to support it with more glory and more victories. Conquest has made me what I am; only conquest can maintain me.*[17]

Napoleon, the Corsican adventurer, realized Louis XIV's dream of French mastery of Europe. Between 1805 and 1807, Napoleon decisively defeated Austria, Prussia, and Russia, becoming the virtual ruler of Europe. In these campaigns, as in his earlier successes in Italy, Napoleon demonstrated his greatness as a military commander.

Napoleon's Art of War

Although forgoing a set battle plan in favor of flexibility, Napoleon was guided by certain general principles, which constituted his art of war. He stressed the advantage of "a rapid and audacious attack" in preference to waging defensive war from a fixed position. "Make war offensively; it is the sole means to become a great captain and to fathom the secrets of the art."[18] Warfare could not be left to chance but required mastering every detail and anticipating every contingency. "I am accustomed to thinking out what I shall do three or four months in advance, and I base my calculations on the worst of conceivable circumstances."[19] Every master plan contained numerous alternatives to cover all contingencies.

Surprise and speed were essential ingredients of Napoleonic warfare. Relying heavily on surprise, Napoleon employed various stratagems to confuse and deceive his opponents: providing newspapers with misleading information and launching secondary offensives. Determined to strike unexpectedly and consequently demoralize the enemy by arriving at a battlefield ahead of schedule, he carefully selected the best routes to the chosen destination, eliminated slow-moving supply convoys by living off the countryside, and inspired his men to incredible feats of marching as they drew closer to the opposing army. In the first Italian campaign, his men covered 50 miles in thirty-six hours; in 1805, against Austria, they marched 275 miles in twenty-three days.

His campaigns anticipated the blitzkrieg, or lightning warfare, of the twentieth century. By rapid marches, Napoleon would concentrate a superior force against a segment of the enemy's strung-out forces. Here the hammer blow would fall. Employing some troops to pin down the opposing force, he would move his main army to the enemy's rear or flank, cutting off the enemy supply line. Conducted with speed and deception, these moves broke the spirit of the opposing troops. Heavy barrages by concentrated artillery opened a hole in the enemy lines, which was penetrated first by infantry and then by shock waves of cavalry. Unlike the typical eighteenth-century commander, who maneuvered for position and was satisfied with his opponent's retreat, Napoleon sought to annihilate the enemy's army, thereby destroying its source of power.

The emperor thoroughly understood the importance of morale in warfare. "Moral force rather than numbers decides victory," he once said.[20] He deliberately sought to shatter his opponent's confidence by surprise moves and lightning thrusts. He also recognized that he must maintain a high level of morale among his own troops. By sharing danger with his men, he gained their affection and admiration. He inspired his men by appealing to their honor, vanity, credulity, and love of France. "A man does not have himself killed for a few halfpence a day or for a petty distinction," he declared. "You must speak to the soul in order to electrify the man."[21] This Napoleon could do. It was Napoleon's charisma that led the duke of Wellington to remark: "I used to say of him that his presence on the field made a difference of 40,000 men."[22]

Eighteenth-century military planners had stressed the importance of massed artillery, rapid movement, deception, living off the countryside, and the annihilation of the enemy army. Napoleon alone had the will and ingenuity to convert these theories into battlefield victories. Napoleon also harnessed the military energies generated during a decade of revolutionary war. The Revolution had created a mass army, had instilled in the republican soldier a love for la patrie, and had enabled promising young soldiers to gain promotions on the basis of talent rather than birth. Napoleon took this inheritance and perfected it.

The Grand Empire: Diffusion of Revolutionary Institutions

By 1810, Napoleon dominated continental Europe, except for the Balkan Peninsula. The Grand Empire comprised lands annexed to France, vassal states, and cowed allies. The French republic had already annexed Belgium and the German Left Bank of the Rhine. Napoleon incorporated several other areas into France: German coastal regions as far as the western Baltic and large areas of Italy, including Rome, Geneva and its environs, Trieste, and the Dalmatian coast. Vassal states in the Grand Empire included five kingdoms ruled by Napoleon's relatives: two kingdoms in Italy and the kingdoms of Holland, Westphalia, and Spain.

Besides the five satellite kingdoms, there were several other vassal states within the Grand Empire. Napoleon formed the Confederation of the Rhine in 1806. Its members, a loose association of sixteen (later eighteen) German states, were subservient to the emperor, as were the nineteen cantons of the Swiss confederation. The Grand Duchy of Warsaw, formed in 1807 from Prussia's Polish lands, was placed under the rule of the German king of Saxony, one of Napoleon's vassals. Finally, the Grand Empire included states compelled to be French allies—Austria, Prussia, and Russia, as well as Sweden and Denmark.

Map 20.1 Napoleon's Europe, 1810 ▶
By 1810, Napoleon dominated much of the Continent. His Grand Empire comprised lands annexed to France, vassal states, and cowed allies.

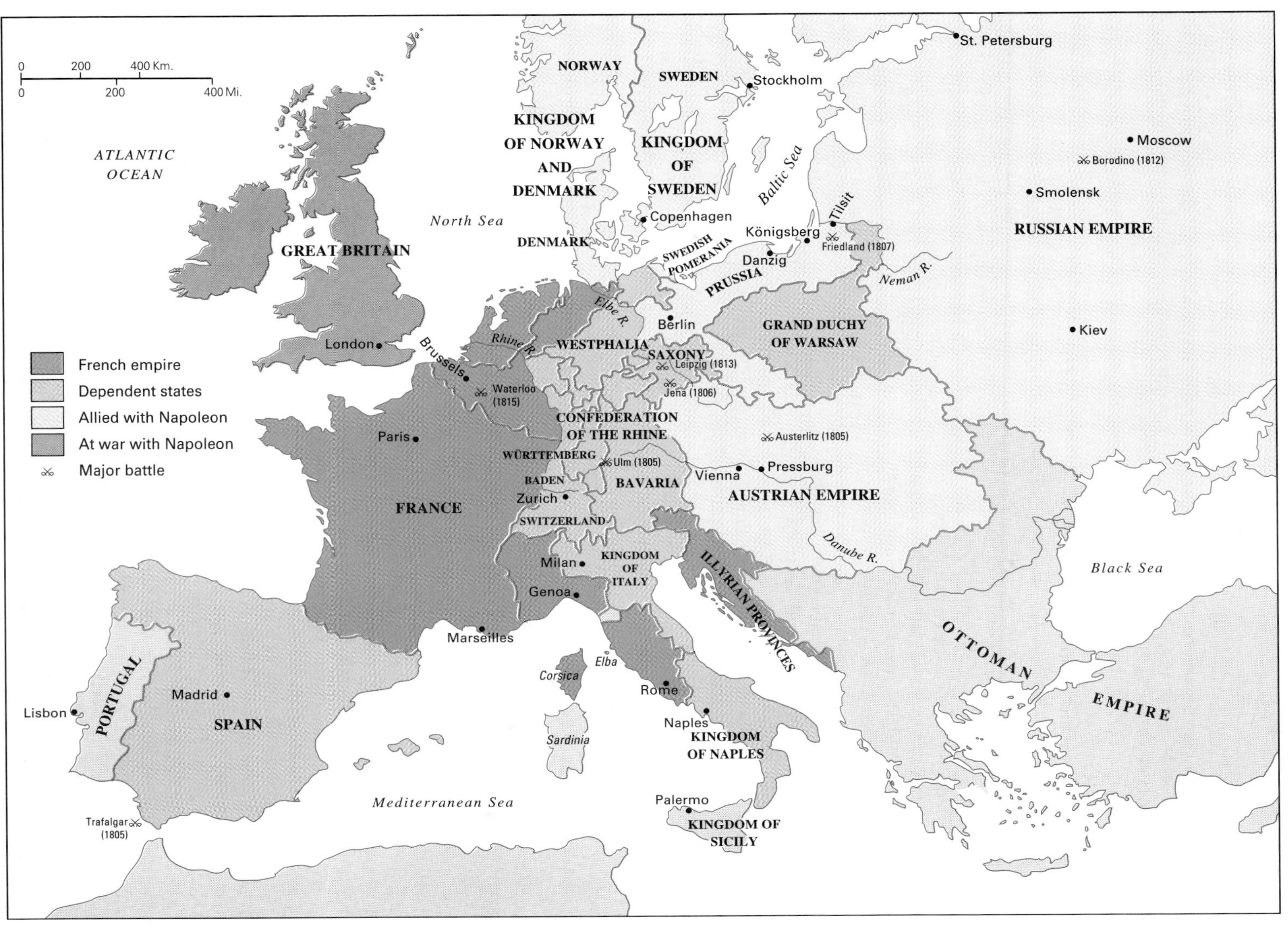
0
200
400 Km.
0
200
400 Mi.
ATLANTIC OCEAN
North Sea
Baltic Sea
Black Sea
Mediterranean Sea
French empire
Dependent states
Allied with Napoleon
At war with Napoleon
Major battle
GREAT BRITAIN
London
NORWAY
KINGDOM OF NORWAY AND DENMARK
DENMARK
SWEDEN
KINGDOM OF SWEDEN
Stockholm
Copenhagen
St. Petersburg
Moscow
Borodino (1812)
Smolensk
RUSSIAN EMPIRE
Kiev
Tilsit
Königsberg
Friedland (1807)
Danzig
SWEDISH POMERANIA
PRUSSIA
Neman R.
Elbe R.
Berlin
GRAND DUCHY OF WARSAW
Rhine R.
Brussels
Waterloo (1815)
WESTPHALIA
SAXONY
Leipzig (1813)
Jena (1806)
CONFEDERATION OF THE RHINE
Austerlitz (1805)
Paris
FRANCE
WÜRTTEMBERG
Ulm (1805)
Vienna
Pressburg
BADEN
BAVARIA
AUSTRIAN EMPIRE
Zurich
SWITZERLAND
Danube R.
Milan
KINGDOM OF ITALY
ILLYRIAN PROVINCES
Genoa
Marseilles
Corsica
Elba
Rome
OTTOMAN EMPIRE
Lisbon
PORTUGAL
Madrid
SPAIN
Sardinia
Naples
KINGDOM OF NAPLES
Palermo
KINGDOM OF SICILY
Trafalgar (1805)

With varying degrees of determination and success, Napoleon extended the reforms of the Revolution to other lands. His officials instituted the Code Napoléon, organized an effective civil service, opened careers to talent, and equalized the tax burden. Besides abolishing serfdom, manorial payments, and the courts of the nobility, they did away with clerical courts, promoted freedom of religion, permitted civil marriage, pressed for civil rights for Jews, and fought clerical interference in secular matters. They also abolished guilds, introduced a uniform system of weights and measures, eliminated internal tolls, and built roads, bridges, and canals. They promoted secular education and improved public health. Napoleon had launched a Europe-wide social revolution that attacked the privileges of the aristocracy and the clergy and hastened the modernization of nineteenth-century Europe.

Napoleon had a twofold purpose in implementing these reforms: promoting administrative efficiency and winning the support of conquered peoples. Pleased by the overhaul of feudal practices and the reduction of clerical power, many Europeans, particularly the progressive bourgeoisie, welcomed Napoleon as a liberator.

But there was another side to Napoleon's rule. The tyrant of Europe turned conquered lands into satellite kingdoms and exploited them for the benefit of France. In a letter to Prince Eugène, viceroy of Italy, Napoleon revealed his policy:

> *All the raw silk from the Kingdom of Italy goes to England. I wish to divert it from this route to the advantage of my French manufacturers: otherwise my silk factories, one of the chief supports of French commerce, will suffer substantial losses. My principle is France first. You must never lose sight of the fact that . . . France should claim commercial supremacy on the continent.*[23]

The satellite states and annexed territories were compelled to provide recruits for Napoleon's army and taxes for his war treasury. Opponents of Napoleon faced confiscation of property, the galleys, and execution.

These methods of exploitation and repression increased hatred for Napoleon and French rule. Subject peoples, including bourgeois liberals who felt that he had betrayed the ideals of the Revolution, came to view Napoleon as a tyrant ready for his downfall.

The Fall of Napoleon

Aside from the hostility of subject nationals, Napoleon had to cope with the determined opposition of Great Britain. Its subsidies and encouragement kept resistance to the emperor alive. But perhaps Napoleon's greatest obstacle was his own boundless ambition, which warped his judgment. From its peak, the emperor's career soon slid downhill to defeat, dethronement, and deportation.

Failure to Subdue England

Britain was Napoleon's most resolute opponent. It could not be otherwise, for any power that dominated the Continent could organize sufficient naval might to threaten British commerce, challenge its sea power, and invade the island kingdom. Britain would not make peace with any state that sought European hegemony, and Napoleon's ambition would settle for nothing less.

Since he could not make peace with Britain, Napoleon resolved to crush it. Between 1803 and 1805, he assembled an invasion flotilla in the English Channel. But there could be no invasion of Britain while British warships commanded the channel. In 1805, the battle of Trafalgar demonstrated British naval power when Admiral Nelson devastated a combined French and Spanish fleet. Napoleon was forced to postpone his invasion scheme indefinitely.

Unable to conquer Britain by arms, Napoleon decided to bring what he called "the nation of shopkeepers" to its knees by damaging the British economy. His plan, called the Continental System, was to bar all countries under France's control from buying British goods. Although hurt, Britain escaped economic ruin by smuggling goods onto the Continent and increasing trade with the New World. But the Continental System also punished European lands dependent on British imports; hundreds of ships lay idle in European ports, and industries closed down. Though generally supportive of Napoleon's social and administrative reforms, the bourgeoisie turned against him because of the economic distress caused by the Continental System. Furthermore, Napoleon's efforts to enforce the system enmeshed him in two catastrophic blunders: the occupation of Spain and the invasion of Russia.

The Spanish Ulcer

An ally of France since 1796, Spain proved a disappointment to Napoleon. It failed to prevent the Portuguese from trading with Britain and contributed little military or financial aid to France's war effort. Napoleon decided to incorporate Spain into his empire; in 1808, he deposed the Spanish ruler and designated his brother Joseph as king of Spain.

Napoleon believed that the Spanish would rally round the gentle Joseph and welcome his liberal reforms. This confidence was a fatal illusion. Spanish nobles and clergy feared French liberalism; the overwhelmingly peasant population, fanatically religious and easily stirred up by the clergy, viewed Napoleon as the Devil's agent. Loyal to the Spanish monarchy and faithful to the church, the Spanish fought a "War to the Knife" against the invaders.

Both sides in the Peninsular War displayed extreme cruelty. Guerrilla bands, aided and encouraged by priests preaching holy war, congregated in mountain hideouts. Striking from ambush, they raided French convoys and outposts. The war waged by Spanish partisans foreshadowed a twentieth-century phenomenon: the inability of a great power, using trained soldiers and modern weapons, to subdue peasant guerrillas.

The intervention of British troops, commanded by Sir Arthur Wellesley, the future duke of Wellington, led to the ultimate defeat of Joseph in 1813. The "Spanish ulcer" drained Napoleon's treasury, tied down French troops, enabled Britain to gain a foothold on the Continent from which to invade southern France, and

AND THERE IS NO REMEDY, ETCHING BY FRANCISCO GOYA (1746–1828). Spaniards resisted the installation of Joseph, Napoleon's brother, as king of Spain. Both sides engaged in terrible atrocities in the ensuing Peninsular War. The Spanish painter Francisco Goya captured the war's brutality. (*Philadelphia Museum of Art: SmithKline Beecham Corporation Fund.*)

inspired patriots in other lands to resist the French emperor.

The German War of Liberation

Anti-French feeling also broke out in the German states. Hatred of the French invaders evoked a feeling of national outrage among some Germans, who up to this time had thought only in terms of their own particular state and prince. Some German intellectuals, using the emotional language of nationalism, called for a war of liberation against Napoleon and, in some instances, for the creation of a unified Germany.

Besides arousing a desire for national independence and unity, the defeat of the Prussians at Jena (1806) and French domination of Germany stimulated a movement for reform among members of the Prussian high bureaucracy and officer corps. To survive in a world altered by the French Revolution, Prussia would have to learn the principal lessons of the Revolution: that aroused citizens fighting for a cause make better soldiers than mercenaries and oppressed serfs and that officers selected for daring and intelligence command better than nobles possessing only a gilded birthright. The reformers believed that the elimination of social abuses would overcome defeatism and apathy and encourage Prussians to serve the state willingly and to fight bravely for national honor. A revitalized Prussia could then deal with the French.

Among the important reforms introduced in Prussia between 1807 and 1813 were the abolition of serfdom, the granting to towns of a large measure of self-administration, the awarding of army commissions on the basis of merit instead of birth, the elimination of cruel punishment in the ranks, and the establishment of national conscription. In 1813, the reform party forced King Frederick William III to declare war on France. The military reforms did improve the quality of the Prussian army. In the War of Liberation (1813), Prussian soldiers demonstrated far more enthusiasm and patriotism than they had at Jena in 1806, and the French were driven from Germany. The German War of Liberation came on the heels of Napoleon's disastrous Russian campaign.

Disaster in Russia

The unsuccessful invasion of Russia in 1812 diminished Napoleon's glory and hastened the collapse of his empire. Deteriorating relations between Russia and France led Napoleon to his fatal decision to attack the eastern giant. Unwilling to permit Russia to become a Mediterranean power, the emperor resisted the tsar's attempts to acquire Constantinople. Napoleon's creation of the Grand Duchy of Warsaw irritated the tsar, who feared a revival of Polish power and resented French influence on Russia's border. Another source of friction between the tsar and Napoleon was Russia's illicit trade with Britain in violation of the Continental System. Napoleon reasoned that if he permitted the tsar to violate the trade regulations, other lands would soon follow and England would never be subdued. No doubt Napoleon's inexhaustible craving for power also compelled him to strike at Russia.

Napoleon assembled one of the largest armies in history: some 614,000 men, 200,000 animals, and 20,000 vehicles. Frenchmen constituted about half of the *Grande Armée de la Russie;* the other soldiers, many serving under compulsion, were drawn from a score of nationalities. The emperor intended to deal the Russians a crushing blow, forcing Tsar Alexander I to sue for peace. But the Russians had other plans: to avoid pitched battles, retreat eastward, and refuse to make peace with the invader. Napoleon would be drawn ever deeper into Russia in pursuit of the enemy.

In June 1812, the Grand Army crossed the Neman River into Russia. Fighting only rear-guard battles and retreating according to plan, the tsar's forces lured the invaders into the vastness of Russia, far from their lines of supply. In September, the Russians made a stand at Borodino, some seventy miles west of Moscow. Although the French won, opening the road to Moscow, they lost forty thousand men and failed to destroy the Russian army, which withdrew in order. Napoleon still did not have the decisive victory with which he hoped to compel the tsar to make peace. At midnight on September 14, the Grand Army, its numbers greatly reduced by disease, hunger, exhaustion, desertion, and battle, entered Moscow. Expecting to be greeted by a deputation of nobles, Napoleon found instead that the Muscovites had virtually evacuated their holy city. To show their contempt for the French conquerors and to deny the French shelter, the Russians set fire to the city, which burned for five days.

Taking up headquarters in Moscow, Napoleon waited for Alexander I to admit defeat and come to terms. But the tsar remained intransigent. Napoleon was in a dilemma: to penetrate deeper into Russia was certain death; to stay in Moscow with winter approaching meant possible starvation. Faced with these alternatives, Napoleon was forced to retreat westward to his sources of supply. On October 19, 1812, ninety-five thousand troops and thousands of wagons loaded with loot left Moscow for the long trek back.

In early November came the first snow and

Disaster in Russia. Lacking winter provisions, Napoleon's Grand Army abandoned Moscow in October 1812. The retreating French were decimated by hunger, winter, and Russian attacks. (*Musée de l'Armée.*)

frost. Army stragglers were slaughtered by Russian Cossacks and peasant partisans. Hungry soldiers pounced on fallen horses, carving them up alive. The wounded were left to lie where they dropped. Some poor wretches, wrote a French officer, "dragged themselves along, shivering . . . until the snow packed under the soles of their boots, a bit of debris, a branch, or the body of a fallen comrade tripped them and threw them down. Then their moans for help went unheeded. The snow soon covered them up and only low white mounds showed where they lay. Our road was strewn with these hummocks, like a cemetery."[24]

In the middle of December, with the Russians in pursuit, the remnants of the Grand Army staggered across the Neman River into East Prussia. Napoleon had left his men earlier in the month and, traveling in disguise, reached Paris on December 18. Napoleon had lost his army; he would soon lose his throne.

Final Defeat

After the destruction of the Grand Army, the empire crumbled. Although Napoleon raised a new army, he could not replace the equipment, cavalry horses, and experienced soldiers squandered in Russia. Now he had to rely on schoolboys and overage veterans.

Most of Europe joined in a final coalition against France. In October 1813, allied forces from Austria, Prussia, Russia, and Sweden defeated Napoleon at Leipzig; in November, Anglo-Spanish forces crossed the Pyrenees into France. Finally, in the spring of 1814, the allies captured Paris. Napoleon abdicated and was exiled to the tiny island of Elba, off the coast of Italy. The Bourbon dynasty was restored to the throne of France in the person of Louis XVIII, younger brother of the executed Louis XVI and the acknowledged leader of the émigrés.

Only forty-four years of age, Napoleon did not believe that it was his destiny to die on Elba. On March 1, 1815, he landed on the French coast with a thousand soldiers. Louis XVIII ordered his troops to stop Napoleon's advance. When Napoleon's small force approached the king's troops, Napoleon walked up to the soldiers who blocked the road. "If there is one soldier among you who wishes to kill his Emperor, here I am." It was a brilliant move by a man who thoroughly understood the French soldier. The king's troops shouted, "Long live the Emperor!" and joined Napoleon. On March 20, 1815, Napoleon entered Paris to a hero's welcome. He had not lost his charisma.

Raising a new army, Napoleon moved against the allied forces in Belgium. There the British, led by the duke of Wellington, and the Prussians, led by Field Marshal Gebhard von Blücher, defeated Napoleon at Waterloo in June 1815. Napoleon's desperate gamble to regain power—the famous "hundred days"—had failed. This time the allies sent Napoleon to Saint Helena, a lonely island in the South Atlantic, a thousand miles off the coast of southern Africa. On this gloomy and rugged rock, Napoleon Bonaparte, emperor of France and would-be conqueror of Europe, spent the last six years of his life.

The Legend and the Achievement

"Is there anyone whose decisions have had a greater consequence for the whole of Europe?" asks the Dutch historian Pieter Geyl about Napoleon.[25] It might also be asked: Is there anyone about whom there has been such a wide range of conflicting interpretations? Both Napoleon's contemporaries and later analysts have seen Napoleon in many different lights.

Napoleon himself contributed to the historical debate. Concerned as ever with his reputation, he reconstructed his career while on Saint Helena. His recorded reminiscences are the chief source of the Napoleonic legend. According to this account, Napoleon's principal aim was to defend the Revolution and consolidate its gains. He emerges as a champion of equality and supporter of popular sovereignty who destroyed aristocratic privileges, restored order, and opposed religious intolerance. He appears as a lover of peace forced to take up the sword because of the implacable hatred of Europe's reactionary rulers. According to this reconstruction, Napoleon meant to spread the blessings of the Revolution to the Germans, Dutch, Spaniards, Poles, and Italians; he wished to create a United States of Europe, a federation of free and enlightened nations living in peace.

Undoubtedly, Napoleon did disseminate many gains of the Revolution. Nevertheless, say his critics, this account overlooks much. It ignores the repression of liberty, the subverting of republicanism, the oppression of conquered peoples, and the terrible suffering resulting from his pursuit of glory. The critics see the reminiscences as another example of Napoleonic propaganda.

Although the debate over Napoleon continues, historians agree on two points. First, his was no ordinary life. A self-made man who harnessed the revolutionary forces of the age and imposed his will on history, Napoleon was right to call his life a romance. His drive, military genius, and charisma propelled him to the peak of power; his inability to moderate his ambition bled Europe, distorted his judgment, and caused his downfall. His overweening pride, the hubris of the Greek tragedians, would have awed Sophocles; the dimensions of his mind and the intricacies of his personality would have intrigued Shakespeare; his cynicism and utter unscrupulousness would have impressed Machiavelli. Second, historians agree that by spreading revolutionary ideals and institutions, Napoleon made it impossible for the traditional rulers to restore the Old Regime intact after the emperor's downfall. He had assured not only the destruction of feudal remnants and the secularization of society, but also the transformation of the dynastic state into the modern national state and the prominence of the bourgeoisie.

The new concept of warfare and the new spirit of nationalism also became an indelible part of the European scene. In the course of succeeding generations, the methods of total warfare in the service of a belligerent nationalism would shatter Napoleon's grandiose vision of a united Europe. They would also subvert the liberal humanism that was the essential heritage of the Enlightenment and the French Revolution.

❖ ❖ ❖

Notes

1. Quoted in Felix Markham, *Napoleon and the Awakening of Europe* (New York: Collier Books, 1965), p. 27.
2. Excerpted in J. Christopher Herold, ed., *The Mind of Napoleon* (New York: Columbia University Press, 1955), p. 260.
3. Georges Lefebvre, *Napoleon,* trans. J. E. Anderson (New York: Columbia University Press, 1969), 2:65.
4. Ibid., p. 67.
5. Ibid., p. 66.
6. Quoted in David Chandler, *The Campaigns of Napoleon* (New York: Macmillan, 1966), p. 157.
7. Excerpted in Maurice Hutt, ed., *Napoleon* (Englewood Cliffs, N.J.: Prentice-Hall, 1972), p. 3.
8. Excerpted in David L. Dowd, ed., *Napoleon: Was He the Heir of the Revolution?* (New York: Holt, Rinehart, & Winston, 1966), p. 42.
9. Quoted in Felix Markham, *Napoleon* (New York: Mentor Books, 1963), p. 100.
10. Excerpted in Frank Malloy Anderson, ed., *The Constitution and Other Select Documents Illustrative of the History of France* (Minneapolis: H. W. Wilson, 1908), pp. 312–313.
11. Quoted in Robert B. Holtman, *The Napoleonic Revolution* (Philadelphia: Lippincott, 1967), pp. 123–124.
12. Quoted in Holtman, *Napoleonic Revolution,* p. 121.
13. Quoted in Markham, *Napoleon,* p. 97.
14. Excerpted in Dowd, *Napoleon,* p. 27.
15. Quoted in Holtman, *Napoleonic Revolution,* p. 143.
16. Excerpted in Hutt, *Napoleon,* pp. 49–50.
17. R. M. Johnston, ed., *The Corsican: A Diary of Napoleon's Life in His Own Words* (Boston: Houghton Mifflin, 1910), p. 166.
18. Quoted in Chandler, *Campaigns of Napoleon,* p. 145.
19. Ibid.
20. Ibid., p. 155.
21. Ibid.
22. Ibid., p. 157.
23. Excerpted in Dowd, *Napoleon,* p. 57.
24. Quoted in J. Christopher Herold, *The Age of Napoleon* (New York: Dell, 1963), p. 320.
25. Pieter Geyl, *Napoleon: For and Against* (New Haven, Conn.: Yale University Press, 1964), p. 16.

Suggested Reading

Chandler, David, *The Campaigns of Napoleon* (1966). An analysis of Napoleon's art of war.

Cronin, Vincent, *Napoleon Bonaparte* (1972). A highly acclaimed biography.

Geyl, Pieter, *Napoleon: For and Against* (1964). A critical evaluation of French writers' views of Napoleon.

Herold, J. Christopher, ed., *The Mind of Napoleon* (1955). Valuable selections from the written and spoken words of Napoleon.

———, *The Horizon Book of the Age of Napoleon* (1965). Napoleon and his times.

Holtman, Robert B., *The Napoleonic Revolution* (1967). Particularly good on Napoleon the propagandist.

Hutt, Maurice, ed., *Napoleon* (1972). Excerpts from Napoleon's words and the views of contemporaries and later historians.

Lefebvre, Georges, *Napoleon,* 2 vols. (1969). An authoritative biography.

Markham, Felix, *Napoleon* (1963). A first-rate short biography.

———, *Napoleon and the Awakening of Europe* (1965). An exploration of Napoleon's influence on other lands.

Review Questions

1. How was Napoleon able to gain power?
2. What personality traits did Napoleon exhibit?

3. What principles underlay Napoleon's domestic reforms?
4. What was Napoleon's "art of war"?
5. How did Napoleon both preserve and destroy the ideals of the French Revolution?
6. Why did England feel compelled to resist Napoleon?
7. Describe the purpose and significance of Prussia's reforms.
8. Account for Napoleon's downfall.
9. Identify and explain the historical significance of the battle of Leipzig and the "hundred days."
10. What were Napoleon's greatest achievements? What were his greatest failures?

Chapter 21

The Industrial Revolution: The Transformation of Society

European machine-produced textile printing copied traditional Indian textile designs. Indian weavers, spinners, printers—an entire cast of craftsmen—were driven to despair and destitution trying to compete with the European women and children who toiled long hours to manufacture the cheap calicos. (Lewis Hine/Hulton Archive/Getty Images.)

- **Origins of the Industrial Age**
  Europe's Population Explosion
  Agricultural Revolution
  Britain First
  Changes in Technology
  Changes in Finance
- **Society Transformed**
  Urbanization
  Changes in Social Structure
  Working-Class Life
- **Relief and Reform**
- **Industrialism in Perspective**

In the second half of the eighteenth century, such significant changes took place in the ways western Europeans labored and traded that historians call the total process the Industrial Revolution. Although this revolution had no start, no single set pattern, and little planning, its effects dominated the following two centuries, changing the lives and society of Europeans and spreading throughout the world.

The term *Industrial Revolution* refers to the shift from an agrarian, handicraft, labor-intensive economy to an economy dominated by machine manufacture, specialization of tasks or division of labor, factories and cities, and a worldwide market for goods, services, and capital. These changes began in England, amazing contemporaries with inventions that, though actually simple on-the-job changes made by laborers, nonetheless "revolutionized" human tasks. Today the aspects of the Industrial Revolution that stand out for us are the increase in agricultural productivity; the population growth and the rapid development of cities; the new and more efficient ways of organizing tasks to use plentiful labor and stretch limited natural resources; and the innovative ways of expanding capital.

Industrial progress that spanned a century in Britain and as much as two centuries in the rest of the developed world hardly seems revolutionary. But the transformation of human existence between the eighteenth century and the present is so great that no terms other than *revolution* seem appropriate. In fact, historians see multiple industrial revolutions: one from 1750 to 1850 in western Europe, one from the mid-nineteenth century including the United States, another in the first half of the twentieth century, and yet another within the last fifty years.

Industrial development did not proceed at the same pace everywhere. The changes begun in England in the mid 1700s were delayed in France by political and social conflict until after the French Revolution. In the German and Italian states, the lack of political unity slowed the growth of industry. The German states began industrializing in the 1840s, nearly a century after England. Even after German unification in 1870, when industry grew phenomenally, much of the traditional economy persisted alongside the new. In Italy, too, industrialization began slowly. It was hampered by the sharp economic divisions between north and south, the comparative lack of natural resources, and the slow political unification of the peninsula. Eastern Europe did not start industrializing until the 1890s, and in some cases not until the twentieth century.

Britain, thus, had stepped out ahead. European states copied its techniques, borrowed and stole its plans, imported its engineers as advisers, borrowed its capital, and carefully studied its politics, ideas, and society to imitate whatever seemed essential to industrialization. By the second half of the nineteenth century, Germany, France, and the United States moved into genuine competition with Britain; and Italy, Russia, and Austria-Hungary raced to catch up. Almost inevitably, Europeans and Americans, and eventually other peoples around the globe, were driven to adopt the changes in agriculture and industry that had originated in England. Everywhere, as the economy changed, the conditions of labor and life were profoundly altered.

Origins of the Industrial Age

Why did industrialization begin in western Europe rather than elsewhere in the world? Why had not the wealth and skills of the Chinese or the Moguls in India made these radical changes in economy and society? After all, the desire for Asia's superior products had launched Europeans on their aggressive commercial expansion in the sixteenth century. These counter-factual questions—that is, questions asking *why not* rather than *why*—furnish us with complex answers that illustrate the characteristics of the actual revolution.

From the fifteenth to the eighteenth century, western Europe accumulated substantial wealth, and this wealth was spread across more classes of people. In the late Middle Ages improved agriculture increased population. The widespread practice of diverse rural handicrafts provided the foundations for the relatively rapid expansion of trade, both overseas and on the Continent, in the next two centuries. This expansion resulted from an aggressive search for new markets rather than from new methods of production; it built on the capitalist practices of medieval and Renaissance bankers and merchants, and it tapped the wealth of a much larger world than the Mediterranean lands accessible to earlier generations. Thus, the resources of the New World and of Africa, both human and material, fueled Europe's accumulation of wealth.

In the early modern period, the states that had centralized power in the hands of a strong monarch—England, Spain, Portugal, and France, as well as the much less centralized Netherlands—competed for markets, territory, and prestige in ways that contributed to economic expansion. Engaged in fierce military and commercial rivalries with one another, these states, with varying degrees of success, actively promoted industries to manufacture weaponry, uniforms, and ships; they also encouraged commerce for the sake of tax revenues. This growth in commerce nurtured a greatly expanded economy, in which many levels of society took part: owners of large estates, merchant princes, innovative entrepreneurs, the sugar plantation colonials, slave traders, sailors, and even peasants.

Europe's Population Explosion

Several factors, each linked to the increase in the labor supply, led to the ultimate industrialization of much of Europe. In the eighteenth century, there was an enormous growth in the rural population. This increase coincided with the breaking up of traditional patterns of farming in western Europe and their replacement by capitalist farming for the market: an agricultural revolution. The conjunction of the population explosion and the rise in agricultural productivity did not bring famine, disease, and misery to Europe as it had so many times before, and as it has continued to do in so many other regions, particularly Asia and Africa, until recently. The effects of the conjunction actually freed much of Europe's labor to take part in industrialization. In labor-scarce areas such as Russia, the United States, and much of Latin America, however, labor remained bound to the land in serfdom, slavery, and peonage deep into the nineteenth century. Even the strong monarchs of western Europe were not powerful enough to keep labor tied to the land. The rapidly growing population provided both the laborers

THE AGRICULTURAL REVOLUTION: THE MCCORMICK REAPER. Harvesting grain with a horse-drawn machine released great numbers of laborers from farms to work in factories and cities. The great demand for labor may explain, in part, the constant search for and investment in mechanical devices for farm and factory in the United States, a major food exporter even today. (*State Historical Society of Wisconsin.*)

and the consumers of the products of economic development.

Most of Europe's explosive population growth took place after the middle of the eighteenth century and continued into the nineteenth. In 1800, Europe had about 190 million people; by 1850, 260 million. By 1914, it had 460 million, and some 200 million other Europeans had settled throughout the world. Virtually simultaneous with this population boom were two major changes in agriculture: a "green revolution" of new crops, and new and different ways of utilizing land and labor. With these changes, productivity rose sufficiently to feed the increasing population and at the same time to improve the diet of Europeans. Better nutrition meant better health, more births, and fewer deaths of both young and old. Surviving children grew stronger and taller (the average European man was five foot six in 1900; a mere five feet in 1800). They worked harder and longer and were abler intellectually. Girls began to menstruate earlier; women married at a younger age (on average, three years earlier), which meant more births. Greater demand meant higher prices for food and profits for land entrepreneurs. At the same time, this relative agricultural prosperity contributed to the poverty of the rural poor.

Agricultural Revolution

By the eighteenth century, traditional patterns of farming were breaking up in western Europe. Capitalist agriculture, which had developed in England and the Netherlands, spread to other areas; production was for the market, not for family or village consumption. Many people, aristocrats as well as peasants, persisted in traditional patterns and obligations: the social economy of reciprocity and redistribution. But powerful forces gradually drew most farmers to the marketplace, first in western, then in central, and finally in eastern Europe. Land that was freed from traditional obligations became just another commodity to be bought, sold, traded, and managed for profit.

Peasants freed from manorial obligations joined the ranks of entrepreneurs, tenants, or wage laborers—all farming for the market. Undeveloped land was brought under cultivation; common land once used for grazing animals was claimed as private property, generally by great landowners, whose political power gave them an advantage. This process, known as *enclosure,* took place over much of Europe. In England, most enclosure occurred two centuries earlier when powerful landlords increased and consolidated their holdings. The much smaller number of enclosures in the 1700s were, nonetheless, responsible for much rural poverty. At least two generations tried to eke out a living as day laborers for the commercial farming landowners, who were glad to have the cheap labor when there was work to do but resented the poor in the off-season. The pressure to make a living drove the poor to work as weavers or spinners in their own cottages. Entrepreneurs "farmed out" some manufacturing processes to displaced rural labor. In the long run, the new trends forced farmers to emigrate either to cities or to the Americas or Australia.

The agricultural revolution of the 1700s meant changes in landholding, soil usage, and animal husbandry. Land use grew more efficient. Convertible husbandry cycled land from grain production through soil-restoring crops of legumes, then pasturage, and back to grain production. Land no longer needed to lie fallow. These methods were first developed by landlords seeking to improve production but gradually extended to the peasantry. In some areas, however—within every country, and particularly in southern and eastern Europe—the old practices continued well into the 1800s.

By the middle of the nineteenth century—after two centuries of increasing agricultural productivity with little change in technology—the application of technical ingenuity to farming brought steel plows, improved reapers, horse-drawn rakes, and threshers. (The Americans were very inventive in this area; agricultural machinery formed a substantial part of their manufacturing exports.) These changes greatly increased efficiency and production; fewer men and women could produce more food and raw materials.

Britain First

Why did Britain industrialize first? At the beginning of the eighteenth century, Britain's advantages were not so apparent. The Netherlands and France were as wealthy, if not more so. They possessed an empire equal to England's in trading importance, and their populations were equally skilled and industrious. The scientific and intellectual life of both rivaled that of England. The French government, if anything, was more responsive than Britain's to the need for transportation and communication; it supported engineering and innovation with subsidies and prizes. It had also established schools for technicians and trained civil engineers for public works such as waterworks, canals, roads, and bridges.

The French, however, seemed less willing than the British to change the traditional ways of agriculture or craft production. The size of the landholdings, smaller than in England, may have discouraged experimentation. By and large, the French populace lived less well than the English but had enough wealth to make an effective demand for products at home. Well into the nineteenth century, the French produced fine goods by hand for the few, rather than cheap goods by machine for the many. As a result of these commercial and cultural differences, French industrialization was slow. Furthermore, a number of serious obstacles—particularly, internal tariffs, government monopolies and charters, and strong craft guilds—hampered industrialization in France, as well as in the countries of central Europe. In England, these hindrances to the free flow of goods either were less powerful or did not exist.

In some ways, the French Revolution, which gave so much political freedom and economic opportunity, perpetuated traditional agricultural and commercial practices. Peasants who acquired land in the Revolution often gained plots so small that the new farming methods were difficult to apply. Because French peasants tried to restrict

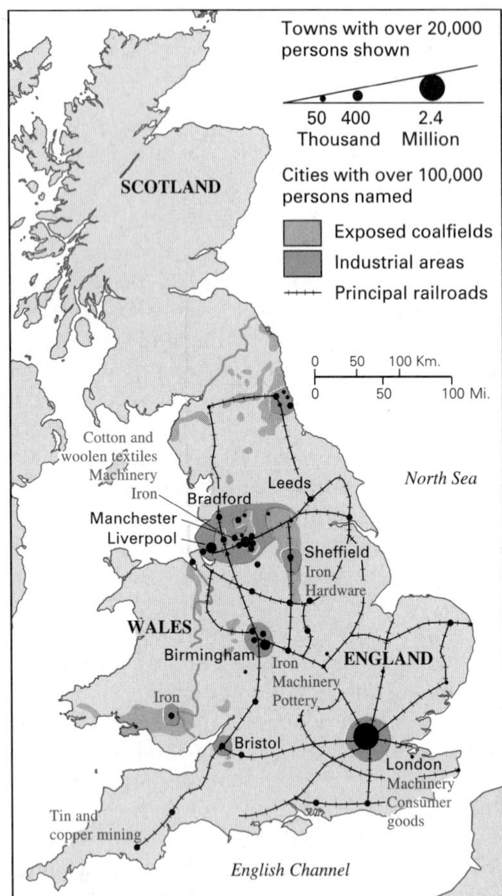

Map 21.1 Industrial Growth in England, Mid 1800s Textiles, metallurgy, and mining made England the model of industrial growth.

their family size in order to feed themselves, France lacked a large supply of cheap labor. Inefficient small farms did not produce a surplus for the market. The impact of industrial change in France was more violent, more dependent on agriculture, and subject to greater fluctuations than in Britain. Political instability made it hard for the French to develop or maintain the optimism and the willingness to take risks that contribute to economic development. Small wonder the French approached industrial change with caution.

The Netherlands, too, had sufficient wealth to support industrialization. During the seventeenth century, the Dutch had developed techniques of finance and commerce that every nation tried to imitate. They had a good transportation system, a fine navy, and technical know-how. They were also skilled farmers. However, they lacked natural resources.

Britain, thus, possessed several advantages enabling it to become the workshop of the world. First, it had a labor pool of hardworking, skilled farmers who could no longer earn a living for their families on the land. Britain also possessed large and easily developed supplies of coal and iron and a long tradition of metallurgy and mining. In the early stages of industrialization, Britain's river transportation system was supplemented by canals and toll roads (turnpikes), which private entrepreneurs financed and built for profit. Private enterprise played a vital role in Britain's economic development; no other country relied as completely on private capital resources and individual entrepreneurs for its industrial development. Small wonder, then, that free trade and economic individualism had so many champions there.

The state did contribute to Britain's industrial revolution, however. British business thrived in a climate favorable to economic expansion—a stable environment of law, order, and protection of private property. Laws allowed the enclosure of common lands, pushing small farmers off the land and permitting the consolidation of large holdings. Parliament chartered businesses, such as toll bridge and canal builders and the East Indies Company, that expanded trade routes and enriched the British economy. By the eighteenth century, a British entrepreneur had remarkable freedom of entry into the economy because he was not as restricted by monopolies, charters, and guilds as were other Europeans.

Even Britain's culture spurred industrialization, because it encouraged consumption and permitted social mobility. The British aspired to the lifestyles of their social superiors, creating a broad-based consuming public. Consumption was a great incentive to production and trade. Debt carried no social stigma, as it did in other cultures; rather, it was a sign of class. Moreover, although the upper class had a social prejudice against trade, there were no rigid barriers. A fortune accumulated by hard work or by marriage could overcome almost any social handicap within a generation or two.

Changes in Technology

When most people think of the Industrial Revolution, they think of the inventions that changed handicrafts to machine-made goods and substituted other sources of energy for human and animal power. Innovations also led to the development of new products. In the long run, inventions would have revolutionary implications for politics and society, as well as for the economy, but the early stages of technological development grew from the simple changes workers made as they plied their crafts. Eager artisans quickly picked up on small improvements to lessen their burdens and increase their productivity and profits. Examination of some key industries indicates how the process took off.

Cotton Textiles. Britain jumped ahead in cotton production because it was already the home of an important wool trade. Cotton production was actually the first indstry to grow at unprecedented rates, expanding tenfold between 1760 and 1785 and another tenfold between 1785 and 1825. In 1733, long before expansion started, a simple invention—John Kay's flying shuttle—allowed weavers to double their output. This shuttle, which could be used in the home, was a device that had been used in the wool trade for generations. It enabled weavers to produce faster than spinners—until James Hargreaves's spinning jenny, perfected by 1768, allowed an operator to work several spindles at once, powered only by human energy. Within five years, Richard Arkwright applied a water-frame spinning machine, which could be powered by water or animals. Samuel Crompton's spinning mule (1779) powered many spindles, first by human and later by animal and water energy. These changes improved spinning productivity so much that there were bottlenecks in weaving until Edmund Cartwright developed a power loom in 1787. To the end of the century, there was a race first speeding up the spinning and then the weaving by applying water power to looms or new, larger devices to the jenny.

These inventions drastically altered the social conditions of the workplace. At first, people worked in their cottages; women and children spun while men wove. Then, when more than human strength was needed to power the looms, and the water frame was used, it became more efficient to bring workers together than to send work out to workers' homes. The family moved to factories, usually located by streams for the water power. Steam meant factories could be built anywhere. If coal was nearby costs were cut considerably. Then, the work separated into specialized factories for weaving or spinning. Power-driven weaving was done primarily by men, spinning by women. Odd jobs were handled by children. Within two or three generations, the factory system revolutionized labor. It also urbanized labor.

These were not the only social changes. The invention of Eli Whitney's cotton gin (1793), which removed seeds from raw cotton quickly and cheaply, brought about a social revolution because farmers and plantation owners devoted more land to production. The higher demand for field labor brought far-reaching changes in the system of slavery, just as other inventions caused the shift from the domestic production system to a factory one.

Weavers and spinners—not technicians, engineers, or scientists—invented simple devices modeled after machines already in use. These inventions did not cause the cotton industry's expansion; that was the result of social and economic demand. Once begun, the expansion was so great, the demand so urgent, and the potential profits so great that more and more complicated technology was developed. A role emerged for the engineer who was an expert in building or adapting machines and in utilizing different sources of power.

Steam Power. Roughly the same process took place in steam. James Watt's steam engine dates from the 1760s, but it was too expensive to be widely adapted to production. Women, children, and even men laborers were cheaper than steam-

WOMAN AT HARGREAVES'S SPINNING JENNY. The cotton textile trade was one of the first to be mechanized. In cottage industries, the whole family contributed to the making of thread and cloth. Hargreaves's spinning jenny, one of the early inventions made by the workers themselves, was an adaptation of his wife's thread-spinning tool. (*Mary Evans Picture Library.*)

powered machinery. Within two generations, by the 1830s in England, engines and fuel became cheaper, entrepreneurs began to use them, and expansion became rapid. Steam engines ran on coal or wood, not water power, which meant flexibility in locating factories. (Any factory already located by water would continue to use that much cheaper source of power, of course.) Steam also powered transportation—trains and carts—but again cost might lead a businessman to use canal transportation. By the midcentury, steam was widely applied, causing the incredible rate of change generally identified with the Industrial Revolution. In the two previous centuries, increasing productivity, the accumulation of capital, and the provisioning of a growing population had been powered by people, animals, and water—an extraordinary feat. With steam, work was revolutionized because weaker, younger, and less-skilled workers could perform the few simple necessary tasks. Moreover, as steam took hold, human participation in the process of manufacture diminished; engines replaced people, and workers became "hands" that drove machines.

The New Iron Age. Steam power enabled employers to hire the weak to operate the machinery, but it required strong machines to withstand its force. As with textiles and power, the history of the search for better iron illustrates how developments in one industry prompted change in related industries and in society.

Until the eighteenth century, making iron had not changed much since the Middle Ages. By trial-and-error methods, entrepreneurs such as the Darbys, in England, replaced the burning of scarce and valuable wood with coal or coke in the manufacture of cast iron and later wrought iron. Coal made brittle metal though, until Henry Cort copied the French practice of using a furnace with two separate compartments, one for the coke and one for the iron ore. By the 1780s, trial and error, copying, and adapting had perfected wrought iron so that it became the most widely used metal in construction and machinery. In the 1860s steel began to be produced cheaply. Henry Bessemer converted pig iron into steel by removing impurities in the iron. William Siemens and Pierre and Émile Martin developed the open-hearth process, which could handle much greater amounts of metal than Bessemer's converter. Steel became so cheap to produce that it quickly replaced iron in building and in industry. The age of steel was born.

Producing iron or steam power required coal. Britain's production of coal kept pace with the demand and with the industrial growth that it fueled. Sixteen million tons were mined at the end of the Napoleonic wars; thirty million in 1836; and sixty-five million in 1856. All this coal was mined by human beings—entire families, whole villages—because steam engines were too expensive to replace human labor. Steam engines were used to pump water and to haul the carts or the miners up from the main shaft to the surface. Once steam engines were applied to mining itself, rich veins in existing mines became accessible, stoking this early industrialization.

Transportation and Communication. Revolutionized transportation provided a network to support expansion. Major road building took place in the eighteenth century in England and in France, and later in the rest of Europe. Both Britain and the United States experienced a boom in canal construction between 1760 and 1820. But canals were quickly outmoded by railroads, which, though more expensive, were more flexible. They caught the public imagination much as automobiles and airplanes would in the twentieth century. Steam-powered engines began to replace horse-powered railroads in the 1820s. Deeming railroads essential to their strength and unity, Continental governments expended major efforts to develop rail networks, particularly where canals or roads were inadequate. Railroads were so successful that by the middle of the nineteenth century, English roads were just paths leading to the station. Stations all over Europe looked like palaces. Not until the twentieth century and the advent of the automobile was a complete network of roads deemed crucial to public transport in Britain.

Communication changed as spectacularly as transportation. Britain inaugurated the penny post in 1840, making it possible to send a letter to any part of the kingdom for about half an American penny. But the cost of postage was so high elsewhere that letters were rarely written; many letters of the time fill every space on a single sheet of paper because the postage rate was cheapest for one sheet. When the telegraph was invented, it developed rapidly because business demanded cheap and fast communications. The first telegraphic message was sent from Baltimore to Washington, D.C., in 1844. Within seven years, the first undersea cable was laid under the English Channel, and by 1866, transatlantic cable was operating. Although certainly not cheap, the telegraph was quickly employed by ever-expanding business.

Unprecedented amounts of private British capital built Britain's system of roads, canals, railways, and steamships. Continental states were slower to adopt steam transport just because they lacked capital and skilled civil engineering. Only France invested a great percentage of private capital in building a Europe-wide transportation system. Various failures of management and inadequate financing led the French government to take control of its railroads, but in most of Europe, state construction and control was the rule. In the United States, Congress gave enormous grants of land to railroad companies to encourage the laying of tracks, usually by cheap immigrant labor. Everywhere during the nineteenth-century railroad-building boom, financiers invested heavily in railroads. The flow of capital from western Europe, particularly Britain and France, to other lands in Europe and America was an awe-inspiring achievement. The flow of finance across borders and oceans was matched only by the flow of labor, as Europeans and Asians built railroad networks to support the expanding agriculture and industry of the Americas.

Changes in Finance

The first stages of industrialization—the use of new crop mixes and tools in agriculture and the first changes in spinning and weaving—did not require much capital. Neither did the early adap-

Profile

The Darby Family

By trial and error, three generations of an English family of iron manufacturers developed new ways of producing the precious metal of industrialization. As in so many enterprises of the Industrial Revolution, the innovative methods and capital investments came from a single family from the seventeenth to the nineteenth century.

Abraham Darby (1677–1717), a workman in Coalbrookdale, England, built a blast furnace for casting iron. He is believed to be the first to have used coke in iron smelting while trying to replace expensive charcoal. Coke made less brittle iron than raw coal because it contained less sulphur. With larger furnaces Darby was able to make superior iron, which was used for casting quality cannon for the Royal Navy, a good contract but not a subsidy.

By the time of Abraham II (1711–1763) coke smelting was the dominant technique for making cast iron, but the Darbys had no exclusive rights to the process. The industry (still consisting of small, competing firms) was concen-

Spectrum Color Library.

tations in the iron industry. Subsequent growth, however—from the spread of factories and the extensive application of machinery in agriculture to the expansion of mining and construction in the cities—required the investment of enormous capital. Railroads and steamship lines were often so expensive that only governments could finance them; even in Belgium, where they were privately financed at first, the king was the major investor. Large capital infusions were also needed to fund the steel industry.

In the beginning, the owning family was the source of a company's financing, its management, and even its technical innovation. Family firms dominated industry. But outside investment grew steadily from 1860 to World War I (1914). In Britain, wealthy merchants and landlords invested, and low interest rates encouraged borrowing. On the Continent, where the supply of capital was limited, the British became international investors of the first rank, furnishing much of the capital for the industrialization of other nations. French investors, who were sometimes reluctant to invest at home for fear of political instability, financed railroads in central Europe. They were also the major investors in the Suez Canal and in the first canal project in Panama, which failed. Among banking families—including the Barings of London and the Rothschilds of France, England, and Germany—kinship ties joined together large amounts of investment capital. People of the same religion or region would often band together to gather capital for development, as the Protestant and Jewish bankers of trated in coal-rich regions such as Coalbrookdale to reduce transportation costs.

Abraham III (1750–1791) was the pride of the family and of England when in 1779 he built the first cast-iron bridge: a semicircular arch across the Severn River. The Severn bridge was a major technological feat. Darby rebuilt his grandfather's furnaces to cast large enough pieces for a bridge that is one hundred feet long with forty-five-foot-high castings. It has 378 tons of interlocking iron pieces held together by bolts or rivets. Engineers and travelers from all over Europe came to see this marvel.

The story of the Darbys and the Severn bridge symbolizes English industrialization. When John Wilkinson, another small ironmonger, failed to get together the capital for the bridge, Darby designed, cast, and built it in his small enterprise. Darby also financed the bridge. He laid out half of the total funds and got the other half from private funds—none came from government. A technological marvel, the bridge was a financial one as well, capitalized by a workman-entrepreneur who wasn't even incorporated.

France did. These investor groups fueled European industrialization.

Banking, however, was risky business in the nineteenth century; dozens of banks failed in every financial crisis. Lacking insurance for deposits and possessing only limited resources, banks tended to be cautious about risks. They diversified their investments so as not to lose everything in the failure of a single industry. Thus, in any given country, the number of industries able to borrow substantial amounts of capital was limited. In many countries, bankers preferred safe investments in government debt, a preference that slowed the development of industry.

Financing industry was difficult until there was some organization to enable a number of people to pool their capital safely. In the existing joint-stock companies, individuals could be held responsible for all the debts of the enterprise. Despite this risk, more and more individuals joined together, retaining the right to transfer their shares without the consent of other stockholders. England was innovative in finance, repealing the laws against joint-stock companies in 1825 and permitting incorporation in 1844. Investors were liable for a corporation's debts only in proportion to the number of shares they owned. This legal change meant that investors endangered only the amount that they had paid for their stock, and not all the funds that they or their family possessed. In 1844, after nearly a century of industrial progress, England had almost 1,000 such companies—with a stock value of £345 million—compared with only 260 in France. In the 1850s, limited liability was applied to the stock of most English businesses, and a little later it was extended to banking and insurance companies. By the 1860s, France, Germany, and the United States permitted limited liability, which released a flow of savings into industry.

Like so much of the Industrial Revolution, solving the problems of organizing, structuring, and managing firms and of acquiring funds for the development of industry was a matter of trial and error, experiment, and innovation. These inventions of the mind and culture were as important to the expanding revolution as the invention of machines.

Society Transformed

European society remained overwhelmingly rural, and much of the old life continued while the foundations of the new society were being laid. Landed property was still the principal form of wealth and the source of social and political power. Large landowners, as leaders of families and kinship groups, continued to exert political and social influence, usually on the local or regional level. From England to Russia, families of landed wealth (often the old noble families) still constituted the social elite.

Industrialization brought a new world, with many forms of property and power. Individuals became increasingly important—before the law, in trade, in political thought, and in politics. Ultimately, the nation became more important than the province, region, or local area, but even in

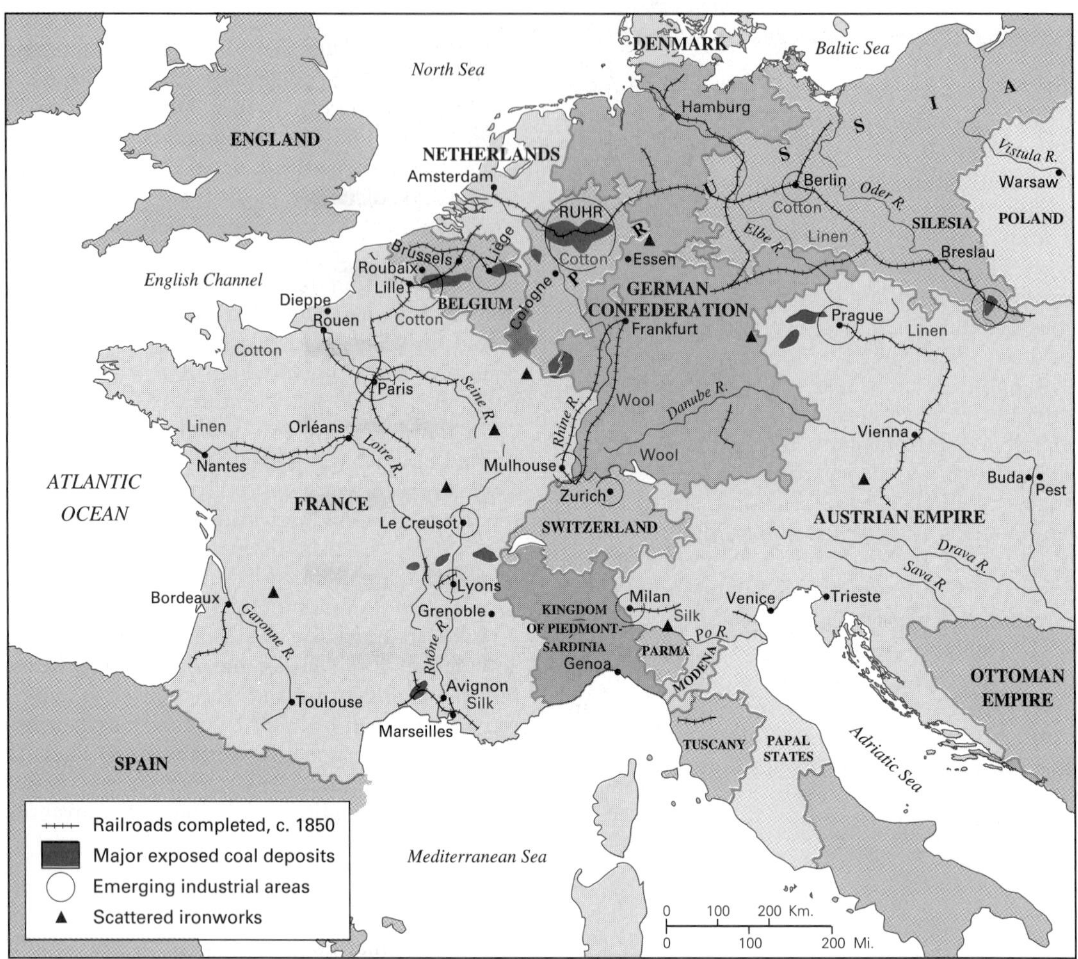

Map 21.2 Industrial Growth on the Continent, Mid 1800s Industry created a market and production unit in northwestern Europe even before central Europe (Germany and Italy) were national units.

western Europe, this did not happen for most people until the last quarter of the nineteenth century. Contemporaries viewed the growth of cities and industrial towns as they did so many aspects of industrialization—as a sudden and complete break with the past. For them it was the shattering of traditional moral and social patterns. Some people remembered the past clearly, but others idealized it as a golden age in which the relations between master and worker had been based on values other than the cash nexus—other than wages, hours, and production.

Urbanization

The urbanization of Western society greatly accelerated during the Industrial Revolution. Classical civilization had been urban, and medieval cities had been the centers of commerce and government. But in the nineteenth century, cities became places of manufacture and industry, growing in number, size, and population. Before 1800, about 10 percent of the European population lived in cities (20 percent in Great Britain and the Netherlands, the leading areas of urban

London Row Houses. This painting by the French artist Gustave Doré depicts overcrowded and unsanitary conditions in industrial London. Workers and their families lived side by side in row houses, each only one room wide with a tiny yard in back. (*Prints Division, New York Public Library, Astor, Lenox, and Tilden Foundations.*)

living). Only forty-five cities in the *world* had more than 100,000 people. Halfway through the nineteenth century, when 52 percent of the English lived in cities, just 25 percent of the French, 36 percent of the Germans, 7 percent of the Russians, and 10 percent of U.S. inhabitants were urban dwellers.

Most of the shift from rural to urban living in the West occurred in the twentieth century, as industrialization spread. But the increase in Europe's urban population during the 1800s was acute, occurring overnight in some regions: the Midlands in England, the Lowlands in Scotland, the northern plains in France, the German Rhineland, the northeastern United States, and parts of northern Italy. Unlike capital cities, industrial ones, particularly in England, grew rapidly, without planning or much regulation by local or national governments. Government and business were reluctant to finance remedies for poor working and living conditions, which they saw as the workers' problem or perhaps the responsibility of a particular industry or group of businessmen but not of taxpayers as a whole. Private funds were too weak and unwilling to combat the effects of unregulated private enterprise. In the rest of Europe, where industrialization came later, states were more willing to regulate industrial and urban development. They also had a bureaucracy for planning and regulation, although such efforts were still woefully inadequate.

So much growth with so little planning or control led to cities with minimal sanitation, no street lighting, wretched housing, poor transportation, and scant security. Cities had grown without planning before, but they had not been home and workplace for such large numbers of people, many of them new arrivals. Rich and poor alike suffered in this environment of disease, crime, and ugliness, although the poor obviously bore the brunt of these evils.

Major industrial cities developed similar housing patterns, mainly because of the wide disparity in economic and social power between the classes. By the middle of the nineteenth century, the wealthiest inhabitants circled the city's edge and were close to the country, living in "suburbs," which were roomier and cleaner than the city proper. As a general rule, the farther one lived from the central city, the wealthier one was. Suburban houses were not row houses; they stood alone and usually had gardens. The outermost ring of the city itself was preferred by the middle class; it had many of the characteristics of the wealthier suburbs. In an inner ring were artisans' dwellings, ranging from small detached middle-class residences to one- and two-story row houses, perhaps with small yards. In the center of industrial towns were workers' row houses, several stories high, jammed together as close to the factories as possible, separated from each other by a strip of mud or cobblestones with a pump in the middle that served all the residents in the surrounding buildings. When public transportation developed in the second half of the century, workers' districts dispersed, sometimes to encircle great governmental cities, such as London and Paris. The wealthy monopolized the central city. In industrial cities, the earlier pattern remained, although new workers' housing might be scattered.

Almost universally, those who wrote about industrial cities—England's Manchester, Leeds, and Liverpool, and France's Lyons—described the stench, the filth, the inhumane crowding, the poverty, and the immorality. The novelists Charles Dickens, George Sand, and Émile Zola captured the horrors of urban industrial life and the plight of the poor. In *Bleak House,* Dickens, referring to one of the characters in the novel, warned about the effects of such wretchedness: "There is not an atom of Tom's slime . . . not a wickedness, not a brutality of his committing, but shall work its retribution, through every order of society, up to the proudest of the proud and the highest of the high."[1] Factual parliamentary reports read like the novels when describing a London row. An 1842 government report from Leeds described the conditions there:

> *Walls unwhitewashed for years, black with the smoke of foul chimneys, without water . . . with floors unwashed from year to year, without out-offices [lavatories]. Outside there are streets, raised a foot, sometimes two above the level of the causeway, by the accumulation of years . . . stagnant puddles here and there . . . and excrementitious deposits on all sides as a consequence, undrained, unpaved, unventilated, uncared-for by any authority but the landlord, who weekly collects his miserable rents from his miserable tenants.*

This report indicated landlords' responsibility; others blamed tenants and workers, who were often new arrivals from rural areas or from Scotland and Ireland. The parliamentary reports and the press helped mold English public opinion until it forced some regulation of urban building, transportation, sanitation, and public health. On the Continent, where the state was less committed to laissez-faire ideology, it took a much more active role in controlling urban conditions.

Changes in Social Structure

The Industrial Revolution destroyed forever the old division of society into clergy, nobility, and commoners. The development of industry and commerce caused a corresponding development of a bourgeoisie—a middle class comprising people of common birth who engaged in trade and other capitalist ventures. Usually referred to as the middle classes because of the several economic layers, the wealthiest bourgeois were bankers, factory and mine owners, and merchants, but shopkeepers, managers, lawyers, and doctors were included. The middle classes stressed the virtues of work, thrift, ambition, and caution. Their critics believed that the bourgeois perverted these virtues into materialism, selfishness, and callousness. Generally, critics saw the bourgeoisie as culturally smug and bound by convention.

The Industrial Revolution began in an agrarian society dominated by landowning and labor-controlling aristocracy. From the eighteenth century on, as industry and commerce developed, the middle class grew in size, first in England and then throughout western Europe. Its larger size did not automatically bring greater power. The middle class struggled to end the political, economic, and social discrimination against it. Wherever industrial wealth became more important, the middle class gained political power and social respectability. The bourgeoisie was indeed able to force important changes, but its members still functioned in a political and social world that had existed long before they gained power and influence.

By the end of the century, bourgeois politicians held the highest offices in much of western Europe, sharing power with aristocrats, but in central and eastern Europe, aristocrats remained dominant into the twentieth century. Wealthy bourgeois emulated the aristocracy—buying great estates, marrying their daughters to sons of aristocrats—but they were the elite of the new industrial age, not of the Old Regime.

Although industrialization may have reduced some barriers between the landed elites and the middle class, it sharpened distinctions between the middle and laboring classes. Equally as diverse as the middle class, laborers encompassed different economic levels—rural laborers, miners, and city workers. Rural laborers included farmers and "cottage workers." In the 1700s and 1800s, an important segment of production was done in the villages, usually in the home, hence the name *domestic system.* A middleman would supply materials to a worker, who wove or spun them at piecework rates. This system, which preceded factory production, undercut workers' livelihoods and ultimately forced their children or grandchildren into urban labor. In the first years of the Industrial Revolution, rural workers responded to the harsh conditions and low wages by destroying machinery and engaging in other acts of violence. In England, they called themselves "king Ludd's men" (Ludd was the name they gave to their Robin Hood) and raided farms in the night, breaking the machines or burning effigies of the farmers who they thought caused their misery. In all of Europe, peasants and artisans responded in that way to the introduction of machinery. In France, they dropped wooden shoes (*sabots*) into the works to slow the machinery, giving us the word *sabotage.*

Three broad distinctions existed among city workers; there were artisans, factory workers, and servants. Factory workers were the newest and most rapidly growing social group. At mid-century, however, they did not constitute a majority of laboring people in any large city. For example, as late as 1890, they made up only one-sixth of London's population.

The artisans were the largest group of city workers until the 1850s, and in some places for much longer. Some of them worked in construction, printing, small tailoring or dressmaking establishments, food preparation, and food processing. Others were craftspeople who produced such luxury items as furniture, jewelry, lace, and velvet. As a group, artisans were distinct from factory workers; their technical skills were difficult to learn, and traditionally their crafts were regulated by guilds, which still served both social and economic functions. Artisans were usually educated (they could read and write), lived in a city or village for generations, and maintained stable families, often securing places for their children in their crafts.

As the Industrial Revolution progressed, artisans faced competition from cheap, factory-produced goods. They began to downgrade their skills by dropping apprenticeship training, forcing journeymen to work longer hours with shoddy materials, and loosening the rules of the guilds. In 1848, artisans, rather than factory workers, were at the forefront of the revolutionary movement as they tried to save themselves from the effects of the Industrial Revolution.

Servants, the third group of urban workers, were especially numerous in the capitals. During the first half of the nineteenth century, in cities such as Paris and London, servants outnumbered factory workers. The great increase in domestic labor—a middle-class family employed at least one servant—changed the daily life of middle-class women.

Working in a middle- or upper-class household, urban servants lived in a world apart from factory workers and artisans. They were often women who had come to the city from the country, where they might also have been servants. They were completely at the mercy of their employers. They might be treated decently or exploited, but they had little recourse when they were abused. Some worked their entire lives as servants; some women left service to marry working-class men. (Domestic help could not keep their jobs when they married.) Servants usually had some education. If they married and had a family, they taught their children to read and write and sometimes to observe the manners and values of the household in which the parent had worked. Often these servants taught their children their own deference to authority and their aspirations to bourgeois status, which may have limited social discontent and radical political activity.

Working-Class Life

Life was difficult for the early factory workers. Usually recent arrivals from agricultural areas, where they had been driven off the land, they had no special skills or traditions of working with others in a craft. Frequently, male factory workers moved to the city without their families, leaving wives and children behind until they could afford to support them in town. Other workers were single men or women who could find no jobs as servants or farm laborers in their villages. These people entered rapidly growing industries, where long hours—sometimes fifteen a day—were common. Farming had meant long hours, too, as had the various forms of home-based labor for piecework rates, but the pace of the machine and the routine made factory work oppressive. Machines required highly regulated human labor: generally menial, often dangerous, and usually boring.

In the mines, steam engines did not chop coal from the veins; they did not even haul the coal wagons to the main shaft. Men, women, and small children hacked out the coal and sorted it, while horses and mules—and sometimes humans—pulled coal wagons on rails to the main shaft, where steam-powered engines lifted the coal to the surface. The miners labored to keep pace with the machines. They faced cave-ins, explosions, and deadly fumes. Deep under the earth's surface, life was dark, cold, wet, and uncertain. The work could be literally backbreaking. Their bodies stunted and twisted, their lungs wrecked, miners labored their lives away in "the pits." Technological advances, such as special lamps that would not ignite underground gases, saved their lives, but almost a century passed before working conditions improved, sometimes as a result of unions or government regulation and sometimes because labor-saving machinery became affordable.

Factory workers fared a little better than miners. Sometimes workers' standards of living rose when they moved from farms to cities, particularly if all family members found work together. The pay earned by a family might exceed what they could have earned for farm labor, though in a rural area they might have been able to supplement earnings with food. Working conditions, however, were terrible, as were living conditions. Factories were dirty, hot, unventilated, and frequently dangerous. Housing was overcrowded, dirty, and badly built. Workers who were unmarried or had left their families in the country often lived in barracks with other members of their sex. If they lost their jobs, they also lost their shelter.

The lives of factory workers were depressing. They had few links to their surroundings, and like immigrants to a new country, they lived with hardship and deprivation. In the villages they left behind, they were poor but socially connected to family, to church, and even to local landlords. In the cities, they labored in plants with twenty to a hundred workers and had little contact with their employers; instead, foremen pushed them to work hard and efficiently for long hours to keep up with the machines. They had little time to socialize with other workers; they were fined for talking to one another, as well as for lateness and for many petty infringements. To keep their jobs, they often had to compete with each other. Lacking organization, comradeship, education, and experience of city life, they found little comfort when times were bad.

Yet factory workers did make lives for them-

ENGRAVING FROM THE *ILLUSTRATED TIMES,* 1859. As unemployed workers flooded into the great cities of Europe, homelessness became a pressing social problem. To keep dry and warm, homeless men sometimes slept in coffins made for the living and lined up in a factory or prisonlike building. These facilities were charitable institutions—not poor-law workhouses—but they reflected the common belief that poverty was the fault of the poor, who should learn to help themselves. (*Mansell Collection.*)

selves. They married or entered into some relationship at a younger age than artisans and, on the average, had more children than other classes. A wife and children were an economic asset because they worked to help the family. When workers grew old or were disabled, their children were their only "pension." As mechanization progressed, women and children were generally driven out of the factory labor force, but in the early years they were the mainstay of the industrial process.

Many workers developed a life around the pub, the café, or some similar gathering place, where there were drinks and games and the gossip and news of the day. On Sundays, their one day off, workers drank and danced; absenteeism was so great on Monday that the day was called "holy Monday." Gin drinking was denounced on all sides; workers, their wives, and reformers alike urged temperance. Most workers did not attend church, but when they did, they frequented those churches that tried to reach them—usually not the established churches, which seemed to care only about the wealthy. In England, workers attended revivals; Methodists and other Dissenters welcomed them. The Catholic church had a particularly strong following among Irish workers. Many workers played sports, and some social organizations grew up around their sporting games. In these and other ways, workers developed a culture of their own—a culture misunderstood and often deplored by middle-class reformers.

Industrial workers rarely protested their conditions violently; in some countries they did so more than in others. For the most part, workers endured their lack of political and economic rights. They toiled long hours, were fined for mistakes and even for accidents, were fired at the whim of the employer or foreman, and suffered from job insecurity. Yet they rarely broke machines—unlike country laborers. Factory workers had few organizations and no political rights. Although they lacked the traditions and organizations of craftspeople, they did join with artisans in movements for political rights: the Chartists in England and the republicans in France. When workers protested, they were repressed. Even a peaceful demonstration, during which they sang hymns and prayed, might be disrupted by soldiers and gunfire. Workers who protested lost their jobs and were "blacklisted" (employers circulated their names so that other employers would not hire them). The law might say that they were equal, but workers were neither wealthy enough nor sufficiently organized to take offending employers to court for violating the law.

Workers' political agitation did not achieve much in the first half of the nineteenth century, but they made some progress in attaining a minimum of economic security. They formed "friendly" or "mutual aid" societies and cooperatives to help themselves when they were out of work or sick. They paid some dues or took up special collections when one of their members died or was killed on the job. They also created clubs, where they could learn to read and write or someone could read to them or write a letter for them. Self-help organizations often developed into unions; sometimes they were unions in disguise to circumvent the law.

Many workers and radicals believed that the only hope for their class lay in unified action through trade unions, mutual aid societies, cooperatives, or political organizations. Workers developed a culture of solidarity, a sense of what was fair and unfair in relations with one another and with employers. In England and western Europe, trade unions grew, even when they were illegal. Unions made some headway in protecting their members from unemployment and dangerous working conditions, but strikes were rarely successful. Often suppressed by force, strikes were usually misunderstood by the general public, which was imbued with individualist and laissez-faire principles and saw strikes as an attack on the businessman's right to carry on trade. Not until the 1870s and 1880s was widespread discontent expressed by militant trade unions.

In England, unions were legalized in 1825 but were forbidden to strike. The law made no special provision for them as it did for corporations; for example, if a union's officer ran away with its treasury, English law did not protect the workers' dues. Small unions were powerless. An 1834 attempt to gain strength by joining all unions together in a Grand National Consolidated Trades Union failed because measures that would help one trade would not necessarily help another. In the 1850s, highly skilled workers joined together in a single craft union, which was a more successful tactic because employers found it difficult to replace a skilled worker. Still, the vast majority of workers were not organized during much of the nineteenth century.

Relief and Reform

Moralists said that there had always been poor people, but with industrialization, the economic and psychological hardships borne by the work force seemed worse. Many people believed that the condition of the poor had actually deteriorated in the midst of increased wealth. If machines could produce so much wealth and so many products, why were there so many poor people living in such misery?

Britain was the first nation to face the worsening condition of the poor. In the eighteenth century, English agricultural laborers had a higher standard of living than their counterparts on the Continent. As Britain rapidly industrialized, the changing conditions convinced observers that both rural and urban workers' lives had worsened. Parliamentary investigations by civic-minded citizens documented the suffering for all to read. Many leaders believed that only increasing economic capacity would end distress. But would the economy expand fast enough to benefit the lowliest workers through laissez faire, or did it need direction from the state? Socialists, utilitarians, and practical reformers believed that better organization of industry and government was necessary to relieve the situation.

The English Factory Acts were a series of measures, beginning in 1802, that limited the hours of those (especially women and children) who labored in mines and factories. By 1833, children under thirteen could work no more than nine hours a day and no one aged thirteen to eighteen could work more than twelve hours or at night. The acts also required children to go to school for two hours a day, but the law did not furnish funds for schools. England was much slower than France or Germany to provide state schools; whatever initiative was taken in this regard came from private enterprise and charities, rather than government. Controversy erupted among the religious sects about which of them should educate the children, who remained uneducated or self-educated amid the conflict. Sometimes there were schools for boys but not for girls. It was argued that for moral reasons the sexes should not mix in the classroom, even though they worked side by side in the factories and mines.

In 1847, women and children were no longer permitted to work more than ten hours a day. Many employers switched to a single system of ten-hour shifts, but a loophole in the Ten Hours Act allowed some to develop a "relay system," in which children worked intermittently during the day for a total of ten hours. Men could still work as much as sixteen hours but did not in actual practice because it was difficult to organize many different shifts in a large factory. At first, workers resented the regulations because family income declined if children could not work. Gradually, they realized that the humanitarian protection of women and children might make their own lives easier and safer and their wages higher. However, a ten-hour day for adult male workers was not enacted until 1874, despite two generations of agitation.

In 1834, a reform of the Poor Law, which dated from the reign of Queen Elizabeth I, tried to differentiate between the "deserving" poor and the "undeserving" poor. The New Poor Law required anyone receiving assistance to live in a prisonlike workhouse. Legislators thought only those who were truly needy would submit to such conditions just to receive a meal and shelter. They were proved right. The poor and the unemployed working class hated and feared the workhouse, where families were separated by age and sex, miserably fed, and hired out to manufacturers and farmers for less than the going wage. The poor feared "pauperization." Humanitarians protested. In the "hungry forties," when want was widespread, because there were not enough workhouses for the homeless and the jobless, forced relegation to the workhouses failed.

In contrast to Britain, people on the Continent more readily accepted the idea that the state could interfere with the market to protect labor. Most states in Europe had large bureaucracies to enforce regulations and to carry out relief measures. There was concern, however, that too much interference with employers would handicap businesses competing with the English. Governments in Germany, France, and Belgium did not always follow a policy of unrestricted industry, but sometimes they did. Such policies deepened class bitterness and disaffection.

Historians still debate how bad workers' conditions were in the early stages of industrialization. Workers' testimony of acute distress, particularly in the 1780–1830 period and again in the 1840s, has left a powerful impression of their misery. Their champions—humanitarians, novelists, radicals, and socialists—defended them from inhumane treatment and dreadful lives. However, from the limited statistics that are available and governmental and humanitarian reports, historians generally conclude that standards of living actually improved during the eighteenth and early nineteenth centuries. They stress the higher wages, greater opportunities, and more choices for men and women. Still, few would deny that the rapidity of change caused great hardship for the workers of all countries, who endured cruel conditions in factories and slums. Machines destroyed crafts and displaced the craftsmen. A million Irish farm laborers starved during the great famine. Those who emigrated to England, British colonies, or the United States may have escaped starvation but still lived desperately hard lives. As for the workers who did not emigrate, statistical evidence showing an increase in their living standard does not reveal much about the radically reduced quality of life that men, women, and children experienced as they moved from rural communities to urban factories and slums—and to daily insecurity. Their grim experiences were relived by workers in the rest of Europe and the United States later in the century and in much of the world in the twentieth century.

The Great Exhibition of 1851, by Dickinson. The Crystal Palace exhibition drew enormous crowds from all over Europe to see the products and processes of machine and craft industries. The building itself was a glass structure supported by a cast-iron frame, a construction imitated in many grand railroad terminals, department stores, and auditoriums throughout Europe and the United States. (*By permission of the Houghton Library, Harvard University.*)

Industrialism in Perspective

Like the French Revolution, the Industrial Revolution modernized Europe. Eventually, it transformed every facet of society and even the natural world. In preindustrial society—Europe in the mid-eighteenth century—agriculture was the dominant economic activity and peasants were the most numerous class. Peasant life centered on the family and the village, which country folk rarely left. The new rational and critical spirit associated with the Enlightenment hardly penetrated rural Europe; there, religious faith, clerical authority, and ancient superstition remained firmly entrenched. The richest and most powerful class was the aristocracy, whose wealth stemmed from land and whose privileges were protected by custom and law. The French Revolution undermined the traditional power structure of king, aristocracy, and clergy.

The Industrial Revolution accelerated the pace of modernization. In time, agricultural villages and handicraft manufacturing were eclipsed in importance by cities and factories. The very geography of the world changed with the construction of dams, canals, roads, railroads, cities, and factories. In the society fashioned by industrialization and urbanization, aristocratic power and values declined. At the same time, the bourgeoisie increased in number, wealth, importance, and power. More and more, a person was judged by talent or income rather than by birth, and opportunities for upward social mobility expanded. In time, the Industrial Revolution became a great force for democratization; during the nineteenth century, first the middle class and then the working class gained the vote.

The Industrial Revolution also hastened the secularization of European life. In the cities, former villagers, separated from traditional communal ties, drifted away from their ancestral religion. Along with urban living, the increase in governments' power over individuals through public education and required military service contributed greatly to the molding of a secular, as well as a nationalistic, society. Modernization did not proceed everywhere at the same pace and with the same thoroughness. Generally, premodern social and institutional forms remained deeply entrenched in eastern and southern Europe and persisted there well into the twentieth century.

As noted earlier, historians see several phases of industrial revolution: one from 1750 to 1850 in western Europe, one from the mid-nineteenth century including the United States, another in the early twentieth century, and another within the last fifty years. Despite the many problems it created, some of which still remain, the Industrial Revolution was a great triumph. Ultimately, it made possible the highest standard of living in human history and created new opportunities for social advancement, political participation, and educational and cultural development. In the second half of the nineteenth century, industrialization widened the science and technology gap between the West and the rest of the world. Western states were able to extend their power so that by the twentieth century virtually the entire globe came under Western dominance. In the twenty-first century, the world is still engaged in the process of industrialization, and the process is, indeed, worldwide, encompassing most of the peoples and places of the globe.

Note

1. Charles Dickens, *Bleak House* (Harmondsworth, England: Penguin, 1971), p. 683.

Suggested Reading

The Cambridge Economic History of Europe, vol. 6 (1965). Includes several fine essays on industrialization by specialists in central and eastern Europe.

Crafts, N. F. R., *British Economic Growth During the Industrial Revolution* (1985). Argues that industrialization was much slower and less transforming in the nineteenth century than the phrase Industrial Revolution connotes.

Crouzet, F., *The First Industrialists: The Problem of Origins* (1985). Addresses the question of the class origins of the pioneers of industry. Were they middle class, workers, craftsmen in social background?

Deane, Phyllis, *The First Industrial Revolution, 1750–1850* (1965). An early and excellent introduction.

Fisher, Douglas, *Industrial Revolution* (1992). Incorporates the latest scholarship on British industrialization.

Himmelfarb, Gertrude, *The Idea of Poverty: England in the Early Industrial Age* (1983). A brilliant history of English social thought focused on the condition of the poor.

Hobsbawm, Eric, *The Age of Capital* (1988). *The Age of Revolution: 1789–1848* (1964). A Marxist survey of this tumultuous period, stressing the connections between economic, social, and political revolution.

Jones, E. L., *Growth Recurring* (1988). Addresses the important question of why industrialization took place in Europe.

Landes, David, *The Unbound Prometheus: Technological Change and Industrial Development in Western Europe from 1750 to the Present* (1969). Beautifully written, this book, and Landes's subsequent studies, have influenced a generation arguing for European industrial advancement.

Langer, William L., *Political and Social Upheaval: 1832–1852* (1969). The complexities and interrelationships of economic and social change and politics are underlined in this classic. There are many monographs but this is a good overview.

McPherson, Natalie, *Machines and Economic Growth* (1994). A return to the question of inventions and economic growth from recent scholarship.

Milward, A. S., *Economic Development of Continental Europe, 1780–1870* (1973).

Mokyr, Joel, *The British Industrial Revolution: An Economic Perspective* (1993). Economic emphasis rather than social or political by a scholar with wide interests.

———, *A Lever of Riches* (1990). The role of laborers and small entrepreneurs in the Industrial Revolution.

Pomerantz, Ken, *The Great Divergence: Europe, China and Making of World Economy* (2000). A "big question" study that tries to answer why northwestern Europe, which, as late as the 1700s, was comparable to China in that it was not much more advanced, industrialized first and more intensively.

Sewell, William H., Jr., *Work and Revolution in France: The Language of Labor from the Old Regime to 1848* (1980). A review of labor's involvement in this turbulent period.

Stearns, Peter, *The Industrial Revolution in World History* (1993). A readable book with a broad perspective.

Thompson, E. P., *The Making of the English Working Class* (1966). A dramatic and enormously influential book.

Novels of Special Note

Balzac, Honoré de, *Eugénie Grandet; Père Goriot; César Birotteau.* A great novelist's studies of the decay of human character under social and economic pressures.

Dickens, Charles, *Hard Times; Our Mutual Friend; Oliver Twist; Bleak House.* The great humanitarian's social protest novels.

Disraeli, Benjamin, *Sybil.* A politician's program in novel form.

Eliot, George, *Adam Bede; Middlemarch.* These two great novels show a wealth of nineteenth-century life, including social attitudes and moral dilemmas.

Gaskell, Elizabeth, *North and South; Mary Barton.* A woman's vision of industrial and social change.

Zola, Émile, *Germinal.* Describes the condition of miners in the 1850s and 1860s. Very interesting to compare with Richard Llewellyn's novel of Welsh miners, *How Green Was My Valley.*

Review Questions

1. Why did England experience industrialization before the rest of Europe? How did political and social factors influence industrialization in England?
2. How did political and social factors promote or delay industrialization in France, in the German states, and in the Netherlands?
3. How did changes in European agriculture in the early 1800s reflect the impact of capitalism and industrialization?
4. What factors promoted the growth of cities between 1800 and 1860?
5. What arguments could be made that industrialization was a slow process? What arguments could be made that industrialization in the period 1750–1850 was revolutionizing?
6. Which groups were designated the "middle classes" and which were considered the "working classes," or "lower orders," in nineteenth-century Europe? Why did contemporaries and some historians make the terms plural?
7. Why did organized religion play a decreasing role or a role different from its traditional spiritual one in the lives of working-class people in the mid 1800s?
8. What aspects of working-class life and culture did the middle class try to change in the nineteenth century?
9. How did the law discriminate against and punish the working class during the early stages of industrialization? How did it try to protect this class?

Chapter 22

Thought and Culture in the Early Nineteenth Century

Traveller Looking Over a Sea of Fog, by Caspar David Friedrich. (Hamburger Kunsthalle.)

- **Romanticism: A New Cultural Orientation**
  Exalting Imagination, Intuition, and Feelings
  Nature, God, History
  The Impact of the Romantic Movement
- **German Idealism**
  The Challenge Posed by Hume's Empiricism
  Immanuel Kant
  G. W. F. Hegel
- **Conservatism: The Value of Tradition**
  Hostility to the French Revolution
  The Quest for Social Stability
- **Liberalism: The Value of the Individual**
  The Sources of Liberalism
  Individual Liberty
  Liberal Economic Theory
  Liberalism and Democracy
- **Radicalism and Democracy: The Expansion of Liberalism**
  Thomas Paine
  Jeremy Bentham
- **Early Socialism: New Possibilities for Society**
  Saint-Simon: Technocratic Socialism
  Fourier: Psychological Socialism
  Owen: Industrial Socialism
- **Nationalism: The Sacredness of the Nation**
  The Emergence of Modern Nationalism
  Nationalism and Liberalism

In 1815, the armies of France no longer marched across Europe, and Napoleon was imprisoned on an island a thousand miles off the coast of Africa. The traditional rulers of the Continent, some of them recently restored to power, were determined to protect themselves and society from future Robespierres who organized reigns of terror and Napoleons who obliterated traditional states. As defenders of the status quo, they attacked the reformist spirit of the philosophes, which had produced the French Revolution. In *conservatism,* which championed tradition over reason, hierarchy over equality, and the community over the individual, they found a philosophy to justify their assault on the Enlightenment and the Revolution.

But the forces unleashed by the French Revolution had penetrated European consciousness too deeply to be eradicated. One of them was *liberalism,* which aimed to secure the liberty and equality proclaimed by the Revolution. Another was *nationalism,* which sought to liberate subject peoples and unify broken nations.

The early 1800s also saw the flowering of a new cultural orientation. *Romanticism,* with its plea for the liberation of human emotions and the free expression of personality, challenged the Enlightenment stress on rationalism. Although primarily a literary and artistic movement, romanticism also permeated philosophy and political thought, particularly conservatism.

Still another force emerging in the post-Napoleonic period was socialism. Reacting to the problems spawned by the Industrial Revolution, socialists called for creating a new society, based on cooperation rather than on capitalist competition. A minor movement in the era from 1815 to 1848, socialism in its Marxist version became a major intellectual and social force in the last part of the century.

Romanticism: A New Cultural Orientation

The Romantic Movement, which began in the closing decades of the eighteenth century, dominated European cultural life in the first half of the nineteenth. Historians recognize the prominence of romanticism in nineteenth-century cultural life, but the movement was so complex and the differences among the various romantic writers, artists, and musicians so numerous that historians cannot agree on a definition of romanticism. Romantics were both liberals and conservatives, revolutionaries and reactionaries; some were preoccupied with religion and God, while others paid little attention to faith.

Most of Europe's leading cultural figures came under the influence of the Romantic Movement. Among the exponents of romanticism were the poets Shelley, Wordsworth, Keats, and Byron in England; the novelist Victor Hugo and the Catholic novelist and essayist Chateaubriand in France; and the writers A. W. and Friedrich Schlegel, the dramatist and poet Schiller, and the philosopher Schelling in Germany. Caspar David Friedrich in Germany and John Constable in England expressed the romantic mood in art, and Beethoven, Schubert, Chopin, and Wagner expressed it in music.

Exalting Imagination, Intuition, and Feelings

Perhaps the central message of the romantics was that the imagination of the individual should determine the form and content of an artistic creation. This outlook ran counter to the rationalism of the Enlightenment, which itself had been a reaction against the otherworldly Christian orientation of the Middle Ages. The philosophes had attacked faith because it thwarted and distorted reason; romantic poets, philosophers, and artists now denounced the scientific rationalism of the philosophes because it crushed the emotions and impeded creativity.

According to the romantics, the philosophes had turned flesh-and-blood human beings into soulless thinking machines. The philosophes' geometric spirit, which sought to fit all life into a mechanical framework, had diminished and demeaned the individual. Such shallow thinking had stifled imagination and spontaneity, preventing people from realizing their human potential. To be restored to their true nature and made whole again, human beings must be emancipated from the tyranny of excessive intellectualizing; their feelings must be nourished and expressed. Taking up one of Rousseau's ideas, romantics yearned to rediscover in the human soul the pristine freedom and creativity that had been squashed by habits, values, rules, and standards imposed by civilization.

Abstract reason and scientific knowledge, said the romantics, are insufficient guides to knowledge. They provide only general principles about nature and people; they cannot penetrate to what really matters—the uniqueness of each person, of each robin, of each tree, cloud, and lake. The philosophes had concentrated on people in general, focusing on the elements of human nature shared by all people. The romantics, in contrast, emphasized human uniqueness and diversity: the traits that set one person apart from others. Discover and express your true self, romantics commanded: cultivate your own imagination; play your own music; write your own poetry; paint your own personal vision of nature; live, love, and suffer in your own way. The philosophes had asserted the mind's autonomy—its capacity to think for itself and not depend on authority. Romantics gave primary importance to the autonomy of the personality—the individual's need and right to find and fulfill an inner self. This intense introspection, the individual's preoccupation with human feelings, is the distinguishing feature of romanticism. In the opening lines of his autobiography, *The Confessions,* Jean Jacques Rousseau, a romantic in an age of reason, expressed the passionate subjectivism that was to characterize the Romantic Movement:

> *I am commencing an undertaking, hitherto without precedent and which will never find an imitator. I desire to set before my fellows the likeness of a man in all the truth of nature, and that man myself. Myself alone! I know the feelings of my heart, and I know men. I am not made like any of those I have seen. I venture to believe that I am not made like any of those who are in existence. If I am not better, at least I am different.*[1]

Whereas the philosophes had regarded feelings as an obstacle to clear thinking, to the romantics they were the human essence. People could not live by reason alone, said the romantics. They agreed

Dante's Inferno: The Whirlwind of Lovers, by William Blake (1757–1827). A radical romantic painter and poet, Blake totally rejected the artistic conventions of the past. His religious and political beliefs were as unique as his art; he spent his life trying to convey tormented inward visions. He was a prolific illustrator, and his imaginative genius was stimulated by great literature, such as Dante's *Divine Comedy*. (*National Gallery of Art, Washington, D.C. Gift of W. G. Allen.*)

with Rousseau's words that "For us, to exist is to feel and our sensibility is incontestably prior to our reason."[2] For the romantics, reason was cold and dreary, its understanding of people and life meager and inadequate. Reason could not comprehend or express the complexities of human nature or the richness of human experience. By always dissecting and analyzing, by imposing deadening structure and form, and by demanding adherence to strict rules, reason crushed inspiration and creativity and barred true understanding. "The Reasoning Power in Man," wrote William Blake, the British poet, artist, and mystic, is "an Incrustation [scab] over my Immortal Spirit."[3]

The avenue to truth for the romantics was spontaneous human emotion rather than the intellect. By cultivating emotions, intuition, and the imagination, individuals could experience reality and discover their authentic selves. The romantics wanted people to feel and to experience—"To bathe in the Waters of Life," said Blake.[4] Or as Johann Goethe, Germany's great poet, wrote in *Faust,* "My worthy friend, gray are all theories,/ And green alone Life's golden tree."[5]

Consequently, the romantics insisted that imaginative poets had a deeper insight into life than analytical philosophers. Poetry is a true philosophy, the romantics said; it can do what rational analysis and geometric calculations cannot do—speak directly to the heart, clarify life's deepest mysteries, participate in the eternal, and penetrate to the depths of human nature. To think profoundly, one has to feel deeply, said the romantics. For reason to function best, it must be nourished by the poetic imagination; that alone extricates and ennobles feelings hidden in the soul. "I am certain of nothing but of the holiness of the Heart's affections and the truth of Imagination," wrote John Keats. "O for a Life of Sensations rather than of Thoughts."[6] In his preface to *The Lyrical Ballads* (1798), often called the manifesto of romanticism, William Wordsworth (1770–1850) held that poetry—that is, imagination and feeling—not mathematics and logic, yielded the highest truth.

The Enlightenment mind had been clear, critical, and controlled. It had adhered to standards of esthetics, thought to be universal, that had dominated European cultural life since the Renaissance. That mind stressed technique, form, and changeless patterns and tended to reduce the imagination to mechanical relationships. "Analysis and calculation make the poet, as they make the mathematician," wrote Étienne Condillac, a prominent French philosophe. "Once the material of a play is given, the invention of the plot, the characters, the verse, is only a series of algebraic problems to be worked out."[7] Following in this tradition, Népomucène Lemercier determined that there were twenty-six rules for tragedy, twenty-three for comedy, and twenty-four for the epic; he proceeded to manufacture plays and epics according to this formula.

Romantic poets, artists, and musicians broke with the traditional styles and uniform standards, essentially those inherited from the classical traditions, and created new cultural forms and techniques. "We do not want either Greek or Roman Models," Blake declared, "but [should be] just & true to our own Imaginations."[8] Victor Hugo (1802–1885), the dominant figure among French romantics, urged: "Freedom in art! . . . Let us take the hammer to the theories, the poetics [the analysis of poetry] and the systems."[9] Yearning for unhindered self-expression, the romantics believed that one did not learn how to write poetry or paint pictures by following textbook rules, nor could one grasp the poet's or artist's intent by judging works according to fixed standards. Only by trusting their own feelings could individuals attain their creative potential and achieve self-realization. Hence, the most beautiful works of art were not photographic imitations of nature but authentic and spontaneous expressions of the artist's feelings, fantasies, intuition, and dreams. It was the artist's inner voice that gave a work of art its supreme value. Caspar David Friedrich declared: "The artist should not only paint what he sees in front of him, but also what he sees inside himself."[10] Similarly, the romantics were less impressed by Beethoven's structure than by the intensity and power of his music. Thus, a contemporary of Beethoven's said that his "music moves the levers that open the floodgates of fear, terror, of horror, of pain and arouses the longing for the eternal which is the essence of Romanticism."[11]

The romantics explored the inner life of the mind, which Freud would later call *the unconscious*. "It is the beginning of poetry," wrote Friedrich Schlegel, "to abolish the law and the method of the rationally proceeding reason and to plunge us once more into the ravishing confusion of fantasy, the original chaos of human nature."[12] It was this dimension of the mind—mysterious, primitive, more elemental and more powerful than reason, the wellspring of creativity—that the romantics longed to revitalize and release. Some romantics had an intuitive awareness of the dark side of the unconscious. Buried there, they sensed, were our worst fears and most hideous desires. When we dig deeply into our "most cherished reveries," Hugo warned, we discover a spiral that

> *. . . is deep, and when one descends into it*
> *It continues ceaselessly and broadens out,*
> *And because one has touched some fatal*
> *enigma,*
> *One often returns pale from this dark*
> *journey.*[13]

Nature, God, History

The philosophes had viewed nature as a lifeless machine, a giant clock, all of whose parts worked together in perfect precision and harmony. Nature's laws, operating with mathematical certainty, were uncovered by the methodology of science. The romantics rejected this impersonal, mechanical model. Inspired and awed by nature's beauty and majesty, they responded emotionally to nature and sought a mystical union with it. To the romantics, nature was alive and suffused with God's presence. Nature stimulated the creative energies of the imagination; it taught human beings a higher form of knowledge. As William Wordsworth wrote,

> *One impulse from a vernal [springtime]*
> *wood*
> *May teach you more of man,*
> *Of moral evil and of good,*
> *Than all the sages can.*[14]

Wordsworth felt that the poet had a unique capacity to know nature. Interaction with nature fostered self-discovery. Thus, Wordsworth saw in nature

> *The anchor of my purest thoughts, the nurse,*
> *The guide, the guardian of my heart, and soul*
> *Of all my moral being.*[15]

For the romantics, the poet's imagination unlocked nature's most important secrets. In perhaps the most impassioned application of this principle, English romantics decried their country's drab factories—the "dark satanic mills," which deprived life of its joy and separated people from nature.

Regarding God as a great watchmaker—a detached observer of a self-operating mechanical universe—the philosophes tried to reduce religion to a series of scientific propositions. Many romantics, on the contrary, viewed God as a spiritual force that inspired people and enriched life, and they deplored the decline of Christianity. The cathedrals and ceremonies, poetic and mysterious, satisfied the esthetic impulse; Christian moral commands, compassionate and just, elevated human behavior to a higher level. Consequently, the romantics condemned the philosophes for weakening Christianity by submitting its dogmas to the test of reason, and they recoiled with anger at the philosophes' relegation of God to the status of a watchmaker. As Samuel Taylor Coleridge (1772–1834), poet and conservative political thinker, wrote: "What indeed but the wages of death can be expected from a doctrine which degrades the Deity into a bland hypothesis, and that the hypothesis of a clockwork-maker . . . a godless nature, and a natureless, abstract God . . . the Sunday name of gravitation."[16] The romantics' call to acknowledge the individual as a spiritual being and to cultivate the religious side of human nature accorded with their aim of restoring the whole personality, which had been fragmented by the philosophes' excessive emphasis on the intellect.

The Middle Ages, too, appeared as a very different era to the philosophes and the romantics. To the former, that period was a time of darkness, when superstition and fanaticism reigned; surviving medieval institutions and traditions served only to bar progress. The romantics, in contrast, revered the Middle Ages. The wars of the French Revolution, Napoleon, and the breakdown of political equilibrium had produced a sense of foreboding about the future. Some sought spiritual security by looking back to the Middle Ages, when Europe was united by a single faith and the fabric of society seemed intact and strong. To the romantic imagination, the Middle Ages, steeped in religious faith, had nurtured social harmony and abounded with heroic and chivalrous deeds as well as colorful pageantry.

The romantics and the philosophes also diverged in their conception of history. For the philosophes, history served a didactic purpose by providing examples of human folly. Such knowledge helped people prepare for a better future, and for that reason alone history should be studied. To the romantics, a historical period, like an individual, was a unique entity with its own soul. They wanted the historian to portray and analyze the variety of nations, traditions, and institutions that constituted the historical experience, always recognizing what is particular and unique to a given time, place, and people. The romantics' feeling for the uniqueness of phenomena and their appreciation of cultural differences laid the foundation of modern historical scholarship. For they sought to study the specific details of history and culture and to comprehend them in their own terms within the context of their own times.

Searching for universal principles, the philosophes dismissed folk traditions as peasant superstitions and impediments to progress. Rebelling against the standardization of culture, the romantics saw native languages, songs, and legends as the unique creations of a people and the deepest expression of national feeling. The romantics regarded the legends, myths, and folk traditions of a people as the wellspring of poetry and art and as the spiritual source of that people's cultural vitality, creativity, and identity. Hence they examined these earliest cultural expressions with awe and reverence. They discovered the nation's past for their kinsmen. In this way, romanticism helped shape modern nationalism.

The Impact of the Romantic Movement

The romantic revolt against the Enlightenment had an important and enduring impact on European history. By focusing on the creative capacities inherent in the emotions—intuition, spontaneity, instinct, passion, will, empathy—the romantics shed light on a side of human nature that the philosophes often overlooked or undervalued. By encouraging personal freedom and diversity in art, music, and literature, they greatly enriched European cultural life. Future artists, writers, and musicians would proceed along the path cleared by the romantics. Modern art, for example, owes much to the Romantic Movement's emphasis on the legitimacy of human feeling and to its exploration of the hidden world of dreams and fantasies. The romantic emphasis on feeling sometimes found expression in humanitarian movements that fought slavery, child labor, and poverty. Romantics were among the first to attack the emerging industrial capitalism for subordinating individuals to the requirements of the industrial process and treating them as mere things. By recognizing the distinctive qualities of historical periods, peoples, and cultures, the romantics helped create the modern historical outlook. By valuing a nation's past, romanticism contributed to modern nationalism and conservatism.

However, the Romantic Movement had a potentially dangerous side: it served as background to the extreme nationalism of the twentieth century. As Ernst Cassirer points out, the romantics "never meant to politicize but to 'poeticize' the world," and their deep respect for human individuality and national diversity was not compatible with Hitler's racial nationalism. Yet by waging their attack on reason with excessive zeal, the romantics undermined respect for the rational tradition of the Enlightenment and thus set up a precondition for the rise and triumph of fascist movements. Although their intention was cultural and not political, by idealizing the past and glorifying ancient folkways, legends, native soil, and native language, the romantics introduced a highly charged nonrational component into political life. In later generations, romanticism, particularly in Germany, fused with political nationalism to produce "a general climate of inexact thinking, an intellectual . . . dreamworld and an emotional approach to problems of political action to which sober reasoning should have been applied."[17]

The philosophes would have regarded the romantics' veneration of a people's history and traditions as a barbarous regression to superstition and a triumph of myth over philosophy. Indeed, when transferred to the realm of politics, the romantics' idealization of the past and fascination with inherited national myths as the source of wisdom did reawaken a way of thinking about the world that rested more on feeling than on reason. In the process, people became committed to nationalist and political ideas that were fraught with danger. The glorification of myth and the folk community constitutes a link, however unintended, between romanticism and extreme nationalism, which culminated in the world wars of the twentieth century.

German Idealism

The romantics' stress on the inner person also found expression in the school of German philosophy called *idealism.* Idealists did not see the world as something objective, that is, existing independently of individual consciousness. Rather, they held that human consciousness, the knowing subject, builds the world and determines its form. German idealism arose in part as a response to the challenge posed by David Hume, the Scottish empiricist and skeptic.

The Challenge Posed by Hume's Empiricism

Enlightenment thinkers believed that physics and astronomy, epitomized by Newton, provided the kind of certainty that other forms of inquiry, no-

Profile

Percy Bysshe Shelley

Percy Bysshe Shelley (1792–1822) was destined to follow his father into a parliamentary career and received a traditional classical education. Flamboyantly imaginative, he had little in common with his peers and was tormented and bullied at school. This treatment resulted in a lifelong hatred of authority, joined by recklessness, intellectual brilliance, great personal charm, and a vivid emotional temperament.

Expelled from Oxford for writing a pamphlet advocating atheism, Shelley eloped with a sixteen-year-old bride and began a life of exile, shifting from place to place in England and Europe with an ever-changing number of family members and friends. His brief, stormy life—the suicide of his first wife, his marriage to Mary Godwin (the daughter of Mary Wollstonecraft and author of *Frankenstein*), personal misfortunes, passionate friendships, financial problems, and bouts of depression—culminated in death by drowning in Italy. Throughout it all

Corbis.

tably theology, could not. But in his *Treatise of Human Nature* (1739–40) and *Enquiry Concerning Human Understanding* (1748), Hume cast doubt on the view that scientific certainty was possible. He demolished the religious argument for miracles and the deist argument for a Creator; he also called into question the very notion of scientific law.

Science rests on the conviction that regularities observed in the past and the present will be repeated in the future: that there does exist an objective reality, which rational creatures can comprehend. Hume, however, argued that science cannot demonstrate a *necessary connection* between cause and effect. Because we repeatedly experience a burning sensation when our fingers have contact with a flame, we assume a cause and effect relationship. This assumption is unwarranted, says Hume. All we can acknowledge is that there is a constant conjunction between the flame and the burning sensation.

According to Hume, a thoroughgoing empiricist, sense perception is the only legitimate source of knowledge, and our sense experiences can never prove a necessary connection between what we customarily perceive as cause and effect. We can see things happening, but we cannot see why they happen. Experience tells us only what happens at a particular moment; it cannot tell us with certainty that the same combination of events will be repeated in the future. Based on past experience, the mind expects the flame to burn, but we cannot prove that there is a law at work in nature guaranteeing that a specific cause will produce a specific effect. What we mean by cause and effect is simply something that the mind, through habit, imposes on our sense per-he poured out an incessant stream of poetry, prose, and translations from five languages. Like his contemporaries in the Romantic Movement he responded emotionally to politics, the natural world, love, and poetry. "A poem," he wrote, "is the very image of life expressed in its eternal truth."

A radical in politics, Shelley was inspired by the ideals of the French Revolution, abhorred the oppressive conservatism of English politics, and was frustrated by his inability to influence events. His sonnet "England in 1819" described his disgust with a country ruled by "An old, mad, blind, despised and dying king." His lyrical poetry was composed in a spontaneous rush of feeling. He celebrated the natural world from the grandeur of crashing waves and mountains to quietly radiant landscapes, and he identified himself in relation to the natural world. In "Ode to the West Wind" he compared himself with the driving wind: "A heavy weight of hours has chained and bowed/One too like thee: tameless, and swift, and proud."

Shelley was notorious for his irregular lifestyle and had little literary success in his lifetime; his life contained more pain than pleasure. In "Adonais," which he wrote on the death of fellow poet John Keats, who died in 1821 at the age of twenty-six, Shelley seemed to be prefiguring his own early death:

He has outsoared the shadow of our night;
Envy and calumny and hate and pain,
And that unrest which men miscall delight,
Can touch him not and torture not again;
From the contagion of the world's slow stain
He is secure, and now can never mourn
A heart grown cold, a head grown gray in vain;
*Nor, when the spirit's self has ceased to burn,**
With sparkless ashes load an unlamented urn.

*From "Adonais," in *The Complete Works of Percy Bysshe Shelley,* ed. by T. Hutchinson (London: Oxford University Press, 1945), p. 440.

ceptions. For practical purposes, we can say that two events are in association with each other, but we cannot conclude with certainty that the second was caused by the first—that natural law is operating within the physical universe. Such a radical empiricism undermines the very foundations of science, so revered by progressive thinkers.

Immanuel Kant

In the *Critique of Pure Reason* (1781), Immanuel Kant, the German philosopher and proponent of Newtonianism and the scientific method, undertook the challenge of rescuing reason and science from Hume's empiricism. Kant rejected Hume's (and Locke's) underlying premise that all knowledge derives from sense experience, which imprints impressions on the mind. The mind, said Kant, is not a *tabula rasa,* a blank slate, passively receiving sense impressions, but an active instrument that structures, organizes, and interprets the multiplicity of sensations coming to it. The mind can coordinate a chaotic stream of sensations because it contains its own inherent logic; it is equipped with several categories of understanding, including cause and effect. These categories are a priori and universal: that is, they are necessary constituents of all human minds and exist independently of and prior to experience.

For Kant, cause and effect has an objective existence; it exists as an a priori component of human consciousness. Because of the way the human mind is constituted, we presuppose a relationship of cause and effect in all our experiences with the objects of this world. The mind does not treat the physical world in an arbitrary or random way; it imposes structure and order on our sense experience. Cause and effect, space and time, and other categories of the mind permit us to attribute certainty to scientific knowledge. The physical world must possess certain definite characteristics because these characteristics conform to the categories of the mind. The object, said Kant, must "accommodate itself to the subject."

Kant rescued science from Hume's assault: the laws of science are universally valid. But in the process, Kant made scientific law dependent on the mind and its a priori categories. We see nature in a certain way because of the mental apparatus that we bring to it. The mind does not derive the laws of nature from the physical world. Indeed, the reverse is true. The mind imposes its own laws on nature—on the raw impressions received by the senses—giving the physical world form, structure, and order. By holding that objects must conform to the rules of the human mind, that it is the knowing subject that creates order within nature, Kant gave primacy to the knower rather than to the objects of knowledge. He saw the mind as an active agent, not a passive receptacle for sensations. This "turn in philosophy," which Kant considered as revolutionary as the Copernican theory had been for astronomy, gave unprecedented importance to the individual mind and its inherent capacity for knowing.

It is a fundamental principle of Kant's thought that we cannot know ultimate reality. Our knowledge is limited to the phenomenal world, the realm of natural occurrences. We can know only the things that we experience, that is, things we grasp through the active intervention of the mind's categories. We can have no knowledge of a thing-in-itself, that is, of an object's ultimate or real nature—its nature as it is independently of the way we experience it, apart from the way our senses receive it. The human mind can acquire knowledge only of that part of reality revealed through sense experience. We can say nothing about the sun's true nature but only describe the way the sun appears to us: that is, our impression of the sun formed by the mind's ordering of our sense experiences of it. Thus, at the same time that Kant reaffirmed the validity of scientific law, he also limited the range of science and reason.

G. W. F. Hegel

Kant had insisted that knowledge of what lies beyond the phenomena—knowledge of ultimate or absolute reality itself—is forever denied us. Georg Wilhelm Friedrich Hegel (1770–1831), another German philosopher, could not accept this. He constructed an all-embracing metaphysical system that attempted to explain all reality and uncover the fundamental nature and meaning of the universe and human history—to grasp the wholeness of life. In the process, he synthesized the leading currents of thought of his day: the rationalism of the Enlightenment, romanticism, and Kantian philosophy.

Hegel inherited from the philosophes a respect for reason and the conviction that the human intellect can make sense out of nature and human experience—that the universe is intelligible. The romantics taught him to appreciate the wide diversity of human experience and to search for truth in the varieties of cultural life and history rather than in an unchanging natural order. Like the romantics, Hegel held that the scientific method provided only a partial and limited view of reality. He also acquired from the romantics the idea that we should aspire to see things wholly, as an organic unity of interdependent parts, rather than as separate atoms in isolation.

Adopting Kant's notion that the mind imposes its categories on the world, Hegel emphasized the importance of the thinking subject in the quest for truth. However, Kant held that we can have knowledge only of how a thing appears to us, not of the thing-in-itself. Hegel, in contrast, maintained that ultimate reality, total truth, is knowable to the human mind: the mind can comprehend the principles underlying all existence and can grasp the essential meaning of human experience.

Kant had asserted the essential idealist position that it is the knowing subject that organizes our experiences of the phenomenal world. Hegel went a giant step beyond that by positing the existence of a universal Mind—Absolute Spirit—that differentiates itself in the minds of thinking individuals. He saw Mind, the thing-in-itself, as a universal agent, whose nature can be apprehended through thought.

Hegel in His Study. Georg Wilhelm Friedrich Hegel (1770–1831) constructed a comprehensive philosophical system that sought to explain all reality. His philosophy of history, particularly the theories of dialectical conflict and of progression toward an ultimate end, greatly influenced Karl Marx. (*Bildarchiv Preussischer Kulturbesitz, Berlin.*)

Absolute Spirit is truth in its totality and wholeness. Plato believed that true reality, the Idea, was static, timeless, and unchanging and existed in a higher, superterrestrial world, apart from the transitory world of phenomena that we observe every day. But Hegel held that ultimate reality was characterized by change and development and was to be found in the concrete world of human experience; in cultural life and political conflicts, the Idea or Spirit becomes actualized. To discover ultimate truth, the mind does not flee from the objects of this world to a higher reality; rather, it aspires to a deeper understanding of existing things.

Because Hegel viewed Absolute Spirit not as fixed and static but as evolving and developing, history plays a central role in his philosophical system. History is the development of Spirit in time. In the arena of world history, truth unfolds and makes itself known to the human mind. Like the romantics, Hegel said that each historical period has a distinctive character that separates it from every preceding age and enables us to see it as an organic whole. The art, science, philosophy, religion, politics, and leading events are sufficiently interconnected that the period may be said to possess an organic unity, a historical coherence.

Does history contain an overarching meaning? Are past, present, and future linked together by something more profound, more unifying than random chance? Hegel believed that world history reveals a rational process progressing toward a final destination. An internal principle of order underlies historical change. There is a purpose and an end to history: the unfolding of Absolute Spirit. In the course of history, an immanent Spirit manifests itself; gradually, progressively, and nonrepetitively, it actualizes itself, becoming itself fully. Nations and exceptional human beings, "World-Historical" individuals—Alexander the Great, Caesar, Napoleon—are the vehicles through which Spirit realizes its potentiality and achieves self-consciousness. Hegel's philosophy of history gives meaning, purpose, and direction to historical events. Where is history taking us? What is its ultimate meaning? For Hegel, history is humanity's progress from lesser to greater freedom: "The History of the World is none other than the progress of the consciousness of Freedom . . . [It is] the absolute goal of history."[18]

According to Hegel, Spirit manifests itself in history through a dialectical conflict between opposing forces; the struggle between one force (thesis) and its adversary (antithesis) is evident in all spheres of human activity. This clash of opposites gains in intensity, ending eventually in a resolution that unifies both opposing views. Thought and history then enter a new and higher stage, that of synthesis, which, by absorbing the truths within both the thesis and the antithesis, achieves a higher level of truth and a higher stage of history. Soon this synthesis itself becomes a thesis that enters into another conflict with another opposing force. This conflict too is resolved by a still higher synthesis. Thus, the dynamic struggle between thesis and antithesis—sometimes expressed in revolutions and war, and sometimes in art, religion, and philosophy—and its resolution into a synthesis accounts for movement in history. Or, in Hegelian language, Spirit is closer to realization: its rational structure is progressing from potentiality to actuality. The dialectic is the march of Spirit through human affairs. Historical change is often instituted by world-historical individuals who, unknown to themselves, are agents of Spirit in its march through history. Since Hegel held that freedom is the essence of Spirit, it is through history that human beings progress toward consciousness of their own freedom. They become self-consciously aware of their own self-determination—their ability to regulate their lives rationally according to their own consciousness. For Hegel, two developments stand out in the evolution of individual freedom: Socrates, who taught people to examine inherited values with a critical spirit, and the Protestant Reformation, which held that salvation is a matter of personal conscience.

But for individual freedom to be realized, said Hegel, social and political institutions must be rationally determined and organized; that is, the will of the individual must be harmonized with the needs of the community. For Hegel, freedom is not a matter of securing abstract natural rights for the individual, which was the goal of the French Revolution. Rather, true freedom is attained only within the social group. Thus, in Hegel's view, human beings discover their essential character—their moral and spiritual potential—only as citizens of a cohesive political community. This view goes back to the city-states of ancient Greece, which Hegel admired.

Like Rousseau, Hegel sought to bring the individual's free choice into harmony with the needs of society as a whole. Hegel linked freedom to obedience to the state's commands. In the state's laws and institutions, which are manifestations of reason, the objectivization of Spirit, individuals find a basis for rationally determining their own lives. In this way, the private interests of citizens become one with common interests of the community. For Hegel, Absolute Spirit, which is also Ultimate Reason, realizes itself in the state, the highest form of human association. The state joins fragmented individuals together into a community and substitutes a rule of justice for the rule of instincts. It permits individuals to live the ethical life and to develop their human potential. An individual cannot achieve these goals in isolation.

The rationally organized community favored by Hegel was a constitutional monarchy. Yet he also reached the perplexing conclusion that the pinnacle of the consciousness of freedom was to be found in the Germany of his day. Germans recognized the value of monarchical leadership, he said, but also assimilated the Christian principle of the individual's infinite worth.

In deeming the Prussian state, which had an autocratic king, no constitution, no popularly elected parliament, and government-imposed censorship, to be the pinnacle of freedom and the goal for which history had been striving, Hegel's thought reveals a powerful undercurrent of statism—that is, the exaltation of the state and the subordination of the individual to it. For Hegel, the national state was the embodiment of Universal Reason and the supreme achievement of Absolute Spirit:

> *It must . . . be understood that all the worth which the human being possesses—all spiritual reality, he possesses only through the State. . . . Thus only is he fully conscious; thus only is he a partaker of morality—of a just and moral social and political life. For Truth is the unity of the universal . . . and the Universal is to be found in the State, in its laws, its universal and rational arrangements. The state is the Divine Idea as it exists on Earth.*[19]

German conservatives used Hegel's idea that existing institutions have a rational legitimacy to support their opposition to rapid change. Existing reality, even if it appears cruel and hateful, is the actualization of Absolute Spirit. Therefore, it is inherently necessary and rational and should not be altered.

Some of Hegel's followers, known as Young Hegelians, interpreted Hegel in a radical sense. They rejected his view that the Prussian state, or any German state, was the goal of world history, the realization of freedom. The Germany of their day, held the Young Hegelians, had not attained a harmony between the individual and society: it was not rationally organized and did not foster freedom. These Young Hegelians saw Hegel's philosophy as a means for radically altering the world to make existing society truly rational. The most important of the radical Young Hegelians was Karl Marx. Marx retained Hegel's overarching principles that history contains an inner logic, that it is an intelligible process, and that a dialectical struggle propels history from a lower stage to a higher stage.

Conservatism: The Value of Tradition

To the traditional rulers of Europe—kings, aristocrats, and clergy—the French Revolution was a great evil that had inflicted a near-fatal wound on civilization. As far as they were concerned, the revolutionaries heralded chaos when they executed Louis XVI, confiscated the land of the church, destroyed the special privileges of the aristocracy, and instituted the Reign of Terror. Then the Revolution gave rise to Napoleon, who deposed kings, continued the assault on the traditional aristocracy, and sought to dominate Europe. Disgusted and frightened by the revolutionary violence, terror, and warfare, the traditional rulers sought to refute the philosophes' world-view, which had spawned the Revolution. To them, natural rights, equality, the goodness of man, and perpetual progress were perverse doctrines that had produced the Jacobin "assassins." In conservatism, they found a political philosophy to counter the Enlightenment ideology.

Edmund Burke's *Reflections on the Revolution in France* (1790) was instrumental in shaping conservative thought. Burke (1729–1797), an Anglo-Irish philosopher and statesman, wanted to warn his countrymen of the dangers inherent in the ideology of the revolutionaries. Although writing in 1790, Burke astutely predicted that the Revolution would lead to terror and military dictatorship. In Burke's view, fanatics armed with abstract ideas divorced from historical experience had dragged France through the mire of revolution. Burke developed a coherent political philosophy, which served as a counterweight to the ideology of the Enlightenment and the Revolution.

The leading conservative theorists on the Continent—more aptly called reactionaries—were Joseph de Maistre (1753–1821) and Vicomte Louis de Bonald (1754–1840). De Maistre, who fled his native Piedmont (northern Italy) in 1792 and again in 1793, after the invasion by the armies of the new French republic, vociferously denounced the philosophes for undermining belief and authority. He called their activity an "insurrection against God." In *Reflections on the State of France* (1796) and other works, he attacked the philosophes and the French Revolution, which he blamed them for inciting. Committed to authority and order, de Maistre fought any kind of political or religious liberalism. To him, the Revolution was a satanic evil; all its pronouncements must be totally condemned and its roots expunged from the soil of Christian Europe.

Like de Maistre, de Bonald, a French émigré, detested the French Revolution, staunchly defended monarchy, and attacked the rational spirit of the Enlightenment as an enemy of faith. His Catholicism and monarchism are summarized in his famous remark: "When God wished to punish France, he took away the Bourbon from her governance."

Hostility to the French Revolution

Entranced by the great discoveries in science, the philosophes and French reformers had believed that the human mind could also transform social institutions and ancient traditions according to rational models. Progress through reason became their faith. Intent on creating a new future, the revolutionaries abruptly dispensed with old habits, traditional authority, and familiar ways of thought.

To conservatives, who like the romantics venerated the past, this was supreme arrogance and wickedness. They regarded the revolutionaries as presumptuous men who recklessly severed society's links with ancient institutions and traditions and condemned venerable religious and moral beliefs as ignorance. De Maistre called Voltaire the man "into whose hands hell has given all its power."[20] Moreover, the revolutionaries forgot—

or never knew—that the traditions and institutions that they wanted to destroy did not belong solely to them. Past generations and, indeed, future generations had a claim on these creations of French genius. By attacking time-honored ways, the revolutionaries had deprived French society of moral leadership and opened the door to anarchy and terror. "You began ill," wrote Burke of the revolutionaries, "because you began by despising everything that belonged to you. . . . When ancient opinions and rules of life are taken away, the loss cannot possibly be estimated. From that moment we have no compass to govern us; nor can we know distinctly to what port we steer."[21]

The philosophes and French reformers had expressed unlimited confidence in the power of human reason to understand and to change society. Although conservatives also appreciated human rational capacities, they recognized the limitations of reason. "We are afraid to put men to live and trade each on his own private stock of reason," said Burke, "because we suspect that this stock in each man is small, and that the individuals would do better to avail themselves of the general bank and capital of nations and of ages."[22] Conservatives saw the Revolution as a natural outgrowth of an arrogant Enlightenment philosophy that overvalued reason and sought to reshape society in accordance with abstract principles.

Conservatives did not regard human beings as good by nature. Human wickedness was not due to a faulty environment, as the philosophes had proclaimed, but was at the core of human nature, as Christianity taught. Evil was held in check not by reason but by tried and tested institutions, traditions, and beliefs. Without these habits inherited from ancestors, said conservatives, the social order was threatened by sinful human nature.

Because monarchy, aristocracy, and the church had endured for centuries, argued the conservatives, they had worth. The clergy taught proper moral values; monarchs preserved order and property; aristocrats guarded against despotic kings and the tyranny of the common people. All protected and spread civilized ways. By despising and uprooting these ancient institutions, the revolutionaries had hardened the people's hearts, perverted their morals, and caused them to commit terrible outrages on each other and on society.

Conservatives detested attempts to transform society according to a theoretical model. They considered human nature too intricate and social relations too complex for such social engineering. In the conservatives' view, the revolutionaries had reduced people and society to abstractions divorced from their historical settings. Consequently, they had destroyed ancient patterns that seemed inconvenient and had drawn up constitutions based on the unacceptable principle that government derives its power from the consent of the governed.

The art of politics, argued Burke, entails practical reason: pursuing limited and realizable goals for a particular community at a particular time. The wise statesman, said traditionalists, abhors abstract principles and spurns ideal models. Rather, he values the historical experiences of his nation and is concerned with real people in specific historical situations. He recognizes that institutions and beliefs do not require theoretical excellence; they do not have to meet the test of reason or of nature in order to benefit society. Statesmen who ignore these truisms and strive to reform a commonwealth according to a priori models—political formulas that do not fit the realities of history and the social order—plunge the nation into anarchy. To Burke, the revolutionaries were zealots who, like the religious radicals during the Reformation, resorted to force and terror in order to create a new man and a new society. In politics, experience is the best teacher and prudence the best method of procedure. Burke warned:

> *[I]t is with infinite caution that any man ought to venture upon pulling down an edifice which has answered in any tolerable degree for ages the common purposes of society, or on building it up again, without having models and patterns of approved utility before his eyes.*[23]

For conservatives, God and history were the only legitimate sources of political authority. States were not made; rather, they were an expression of the nation's moral, religious, and historical experience. No legitimate or sound constitution could be drawn up by a group assembled for that purpose. Scraps of paper with legal terminology and philosophic visions could not produce an effective government. Instead, a sound political system evolved gradually and inexplicably in response to circumstances. For this reason, conservatives admired the English constitution. It was not a product of abstract thought; no assembly had convened to fashion it. Because it grew imperceptibly out of the historical experience and needs of the English people, it was durable and effective.

Conservatives viewed society not as a machine with replaceable parts but as a complex and delicate organism. Tamper with its vital organs, as the revolutionaries had done, and it would die.

The Quest for Social Stability

The liberal philosophy of the Enlightenment and the French Revolution started with the individual. The philosophes and the revolutionaries envisioned a society in which the individual was free and autonomous. Conservatives, in contrast, began with the community; they believed that the individual could function well only as part of a social group: family, church, or state. Alone, a person would be selfish, unreliable, and frail. Through membership in a social group, however, individuals learned cooperation and manners. From the conservative perspective, by exalting the individual, the revolutionaries had threatened to dissolve society into disconnected parts. Individualism would imperil social stability, destroy obedience to law, and fragment society into self-seeking isolated atoms.

Holding that the community was more important than the individual, conservatives rejected the philosophy of natural rights. Rights were not abstractions that preceded an individual's entrance into society and pertained to all people everywhere. Rather, the state, always remembering the needs of the entire community and its links to past generations, determined what rights and privileges its citizens might have. There were no "rights of man," only rights of the French, the English, and so forth, as determined and allocated by the particular state.

Conservatives viewed equality as another pernicious abstraction that contradicted all historical experience. Since for conservatives, society was naturally hierarchical, they believed that some men, by virtue of their intelligence, education, wealth, and birth, were best qualified to rule and instruct the less able. They blamed the revolutionaries for uprooting a long-established ruling elite and thus depriving society of effective leaders, causing internal disorder, and paving the way for a military dictatorship.

Whereas the philosophes had attacked Christianity for promoting superstition and fanaticism, conservatives saw religion as the basis of civil society. They were convinced that excess liberty and the weakening of religion had brutalized people and shattered the foundations of society. Conservatives denounced the Enlightenment for unshackling dangerous instincts that religion had held in check. Catholic conservatives, in particular, held that God had constituted the church and monarchy to rein in sinful human nature. "Christian monarchs are the final creation of the development of political society and of religious society," said Louis de Bonald. "The proof of this lies in the fact that when monarchy and Christianity are both abolished society returns to savagery."[24]

Conservatism exposed a limitation of the Enlightenment by pointing out that human beings and social relationships are far more complex than the philosophes had imagined. People do not always accept the rigorous logic of the philosopher and are not eager to break with ancient ways, however illogical they appear to the intellect. They often find familiar customs and ancestral religions more satisfying guides to life than the blueprints of philosophers. The granite might of tradition remains an obstacle to the visions of reformers. Conservative theorists warned that revolutionary violence in the pursuit of utopian dreams transforms politics into an ideological crusade that ends in terror and despotism. These warnings bore bitter fruit in the twentieth century.

Liberalism: The Value of the Individual

The decades after 1815 saw a spectacular rise of the bourgeoisie. Talented and ambitious bankers, merchants, manufacturers, professionals, and officeholders wanted to break the stranglehold of the landed nobility, the traditional elite, on political power and social prestige. They also wanted to eliminate restrictions on the free pursuit of profits.

The political philosophy of the bourgeoisie

was most commonly liberalism. While conservatives sought to strengthen the foundations of traditional society, which had been severely shaken in the period of the French Revolution and Napoleon, liberals strove to alter the status quo. Believing in the goodness of human nature and the capacity of individuals to control their own lives, they hoped to realize the promise of the Enlightenment and the French Revolution.

The Sources of Liberalism

In the long view of Western civilization, liberalism is an extension and development of the democratic practices and rational outlook that originated in ancient Greece. Also flowing into the liberal tradition was the Judeo-Christian affirmation of the worth and dignity of the individual endowed by God with freedom to make moral choices. Moreover, certain developments in the Middle Ages were instrumental in the development of freedom: the emergence of representative institutions, the tradition that rulers had to respect the customary rights of feudal lords, and the rise of an enterprising and self-governing middle class. But the immediate historical roots of nineteenth-century liberalism extended back to seventeenth-century England. At that time, the struggle for religious toleration by English Protestant dissenters advanced the principle of freedom of conscience, which is easily transferred into freedom of opinion and expression in all matters. The Glorious Revolution of 1688 set limits on the power of the English monarchy. In that same century, John Locke's natural-rights philosophy proclaimed that the individual was by nature entitled to freedom, and it justified revolutions against rulers who deprived citizens of their lives, liberty, or property. The expansion of a market economy, particularly in Britain, the American colonies, and Holland, showed the virtues of individual initiative and voluntary human actions, uncoerced by the authority of government.

The French philosophes also helped shape liberalism. From Montesquieu, liberals derived the theory of the separation of powers and of checks and balances: principles intended to guard against autocratic government. The philosophes had supported religious toleration and freedom of thought, expressed confidence in the capacity of the human mind to reform society, maintained that human beings are essentially good, and believed in the future progress of humanity—all fundamental tenets of liberalism.

The American and French Revolutions were crucial phases in the history of liberalism. The Declaration of Independence gave expression to Locke's theory of natural rights; the Constitution of the United States incorporated Montesquieu's principles and demonstrated that people could create an effective government; and the Bill of Rights protected the person and rights of the individual. In destroying the special privileges of the aristocracy and opening careers to talent, the French National Assembly of 1789 implemented the liberal ideal of equality under the law. It also drew up the Declaration of the Rights of Man and of the Citizen, which affirmed the dignity and rights of the individual, and a constitution that limited the king's power. Both Revolutions explicitly called for the protection of property rights, another basic premise of liberalism.

Individual Liberty

The liberals' primary concern was the enhancement of individual liberty. They agreed with Kant that every person exists as an end in himself or herself and not as an object to be used arbitrarily by others. If uncoerced by government and churches and properly educated, a person could develop into a good, productive, and self-directed human being. People could make their own decisions, base actions on universal moral principles, and respect each other's rights.

Liberals rejected a legacy of the Middle Ages, the classification of the individual as commoner or aristocrat on the basis of birth. They held that a man was not born into a certain station in life but made his way through his own efforts. Taking their cue from the French Revolution, liberals called for an end to all privileges of the aristocracy.

In the tradition of the philosophes, liberals stressed the preeminence of reason as the basis of political life. Unfettered by ignorance and tyranny, the mind could eradicate evils that had burdened people for centuries and begin an age of free institutions and responsible citizens. For this reason, liberals supported the advancement of education. They believed that educated people apply reason to their political and social life, and thus they act in ways beneficial to themselves and society and are less likely to submit to tyrants.

Liberals attacked the state and other authorities that prevented the individual from exercising the right of free choice, interfered with the right of free expression, and impeded the individual's self-determination and self-development. They agreed with John Stuart Mill, the British philosopher, that "over his own body and mind, the individual is sovereign . . . that the only purpose for which power can be rightly exercised over any member of a civilized community, against his will, is to prevent harm to others."[25]

The great question confronting nineteenth-century liberals was the relationship between state authority and individual liberty. To guard against the absolute and arbitrary authority of kings, liberals demanded written constitutions that granted freedom of speech, of the press, and of religion; freedom from arbitrary arrest; and the protection of property rights. To prevent the abuse of political authority, liberals called for a freely elected parliament and the distribution of power among the various branches of government. Liberals held that a government that derived its authority from the consent of the governed, as given in free elections, was least likely to violate individual freedom. A corollary of this principle was that the best government is the one that governs least—that is, one that interferes as little as possible with the economic activities of its citizens and does not involve itself in their private lives or their beliefs.

Liberal Economic Theory

Bourgeois liberals thought that the economy, like the state, should proceed according to natural laws rather than the arbitrary fiat of rulers. Adopting the laissez-faire theory of Adam Smith, they argued that a free economy, in which private enterprise was unimpeded by government regulations, was as important as political freedom to the well-being of the individual and the community. When people acted from self-interest, the liberals said, they worked harder and achieved more. Self-interest and natural competitive impulses spurred economic activity and ensured the production of more and better goods at the lowest possible price, thereby benefiting the entire nation. For this reason, the government must neither block free competition nor deprive individuals of their property, which gave them the incentive to work hard and efficiently. The state contributed to the nation's prosperity when it maintained domestic order; it endangered economic development when it tampered with the free pursuit of profits.

Believing that individuals were responsible for their own misfortunes, liberals were often unmoved by the suffering of the poor. Indeed, they used the principle of laissez faire—that government should not interfere with the market—to justify their opposition to humanitarian legislation intended to alleviate the misery of the factory workers. Liberals regarded such social reforms as unwarranted and dangerous meddling with the natural law of supply and demand.

One theorist upholding this view was Thomas R. Malthus (1766–1834), an Anglican cleric and professor of history and political economy. In his *Essay on the Principle of Population* (published in 1798 and then in a second, much enlarged, edition in 1803), Malthus asserted that population grows at a much faster rate than the food supply, resulting in food shortages, irregular employment, lower wages, and high mortality. The poor's distress, said Malthus, was not due to faulty political institutions or existing social and property relations. Its true cause was the number of children they had:

> *When the wages of labour are hardly sufficient to maintain two children, a man marries and has five or six. He of course finds himself miserably distressed. . . . He accuses his parish. . . . He accuses the avarice of the rich. He accuses the partial and unjust institutions of society. . . . In searching for objects of accusation, he never alludes to the quarter from which all his misfortunes originate. The last person that he would think of accusing is himself.*[26]

The state cannot ameliorate the poor's misery, said Malthus; "the means of redress are in their own hands, and in the hands of no other persons whatever."[27] This "means of redress" would be a lowering of the birthrate through late marriages and chastity, but Malthus believed that the poor lacked the self-discipline to refrain from sexual activity. When they receive higher wages, they have more children, thereby upsetting the population-resource balance and bringing misery to themselves and others.* The view of poverty as an iron law of nature, which could not be undone by the good intentions of the state through philanthropy, buttressed supporters of strict laissez faire and eased the consciences of the propertied classes. Compassion for the poor was simply a misplaced emotion; government reforms were doomed to fail and higher wages provided no relief. Malthus's theory also flew in the face of adherents of human perfectibility and inevitable progress. Poverty, like disease, was simply a natural phenomenon—a law of nature that could not be eliminated. No wonder his contemporaries called economics "the dismal science."

In *Principles of Political Economy* (1817), David Ricardo (1772–1823) gave support to Malthus's gloomy outlook. Higher wages, said Ricardo, lead workers to have more children, causing an increase in the labor supply. Competition for jobs by an expanding labor force brings down wages. This "iron law of wages" offered bleak prospects for the working poor:

> *When, however, by the encouragement which high wages give to the increase of population, the number of labourers is increased, wages again fall to their natural price [to a subsistence level] and indeed from a reaction sometimes fall below it. . . . It is a truth which admits not a doubt, that the comforts and well-being of the poor cannot be permanently secured without some regard on their part, or some effort on the part of the legislature, to regulate the increase of their numbers, and to render less frequent among them early and improvident marriages.*[28]

Liberals of the early nineteenth century saw poverty and suffering as part of the natural order and beyond the scope of government. They feared that state intervention in the economy to redress social ills would disrupt the free market, threatening personal liberty and hindering social well-being. Thus, on May 13, 1848, an editorial in the *Economist* protesting against a bill before Parliament that sought to improve housing and sanitation declared: "suffering and evil are nature's admonitions; they cannot be got rid of; and the impatient attempts of benevolence to banish them from the world by legislation . . . have always been productive of more evil than good." Government interference, liberals also argued, discouraged the poor from finding work and so promoted idleness. According to liberal political economy, unemployment and poverty stemmed from individual failings.

A particularly glaring example of the coldness and harshness of liberals toward suffering was their response to the Irish famine of 1845–1849. While the Irish were dying of starvation, the liberal leadership in Britain, fearing that government intervention would promote dependence, did little to lessen the suffering. "The more I see of government interference," wrote Sir Charles Wood, chancellor of the Exchequer, "the less I am disposed to trust it, and I have no faith in anything but private capital employed under the individual charge."[29] To some hardhearted liberals, the famine, which killed about 1.5 million people, was simply nature's way of dealing with Ireland's excess population. A dogmatic commitment to laissez faire discouraged British officials from coping humanely and creatively with this disaster.

In the last part of the century, liberals modified their adherence to strict laissez faire, accepting the principle that the state had a responsibility to protect the poor against the worst abuses of rapid industrialization.

Liberalism and Democracy

The French Revolution presented a dilemma for liberals. They supported the reforms of the moderate stage: the destruction of the special privileges of the aristocracy, the drawing up of a declaration of rights and a constitution, the establishment of a parliament, and the opening of ca-

*In later editions of his work, Malthus was more hopeful that checks on fertility through later marriage and "moral restraint" would lead to moderate improvements in the standard of living.

ALEXIS DE TOCQUEVILLE. Alexis de Tocqueville, French statesman and political analyst, grasped the growing importance of common people in politics. Although an aristocrat by birth, he recognized that the destruction of aristocracy, a system based on rank and privilege, and the march toward democracy could not be curbed. (*The Granger Collection.*)

reers to talent. But they repudiated Jacobin radicalism. Liberals were frightened by the excesses of the Jacobin regime: its tampering with the economy, which, to liberals, violated the rights of private property; its appeal to the "little people," which liberals saw as inviting mob rule; its subjection of the individual to the state, which they regarded as the denial of individual rights; and its use of terror, which awakened the basest human feelings.

Although many liberals still adhered to the philosophy of natural rights, some who were disturbed by the Jacobin experience discarded the theory underlying the reforms of the Revolution. Fearing social disorder as much as conservatives did, these liberals did not want to ignite revolutions by the masses. In the hands of the lower classes, the natural-rights philosophy was too easily translated into the democratic creed that all people should share political power, a prospect that the bourgeois regarded with horror. To them, the participation of commoners in politics meant a vulgar form of despotism and the end of individual liberty. They saw the masses—uneducated, unpropertied, inexperienced, and impatient—as lacking both the ability and the temperament to maintain liberty and protect property.

Few thinkers in the first half of the nineteenth century grasped the growing significance of the masses in politics as did Alexis de Tocqueville (1805–1859), the French political theorist and statesman. In the wake of the French Revolution, de Tocqueville, an aristocrat by birth but a liberal by temperament, recognized that the destruction of aristocracy—a system based on rank—and the march toward democracy could not be curbed. In *Democracy in America* (1835–1840), based on his travels in the United States, de Tocqueville analyzed, with cool detachment and brilliance, the nature, merits, and weaknesses of American democratic society. In contrast to the France of the Old Regime, wrote de Tocqueville, American society had no hereditary aristocracy with special privileges; the avenues to social advancement and political participation were open to all. Arguing that democracy was more just than aristocratic government, de Tocqueville saw it as the political system of the future. But he also recognized the dangers inherent in democracy.

In a democratic society, he noted, people's passion to be equal outweighs their commitment to liberty. Spurred by the ideal of equality, people in a democracy desire the honors and possessions that they deem to be their due. They demand that the avenues to social, economic, and political advancement be opened to all; and they no longer accept the disparity in wealth and position as part of the natural order. However, since people are not naturally equal in ability, many are frustrated and turn to the state to secure for them the advantages that they cannot obtain for themselves. To improve their material well-being, they are willing to sacrifice political liberty. Consequently, democracies face an ever present danger that people, craving equality, will surrender their liberty to a central government if it promises to provide them with property and other advantages.

Granted ever more power by the people, the state would regulate its citizens' lives and crush local institutions that impede centralized control. Liberty would be lost, not to the despotism of kings but to the tyranny of the majority. To prevent democracy from degenerating into state despotism, de Tocqueville urged strengthening institutions of local government, forming numerous private associations over which the state would have no control, protecting the independence of the judiciary, and preserving a free press—all of which promote active and responsible citizenship.

Another danger in a democratic society, said de Tocqueville, is the tendency of the majority to demand conformity of belief. Since the majority's power can be absolute and irresistible, the minority fears to stray from the prescribed track.

According to de Tocqueville, democracy also spawns a selfish individualism, which could degenerate into vulgar hedonism. Driven by an overriding concern for possessions and profits, people can lose their taste for political participation and their concern for the public good. If narrow self-interest prevails over a sense of public duty, liberty cannot long endure.

Although recognizing the limitations of democracy, de Tocqueville did not seek to reverse its growth. In this new age that is dawning, he wrote,

> *all who shall attempt . . . to base freedom upon aristocratic privilege will fail . . . all who shall attempt to draw and to retain authority within a single class, will fail. . . . All . . . who would establish or secure the independence and the dignity of their fellow-men, must show themselves the friends of equality. . . . Thus the question is not how to reconstruct aristocratic society, but how to make liberty proceed out of that democratic state of society in which God has placed us.*[30]

The problems of democracy, declared de Tocqueville, must be resolved without jeopardizing freedom. The task of a democratic society is to temper extreme individualism and unrestrained acquisitiveness by fostering public spirit. Without direct participation by cooperating citizens—that is, without a concern for the common good—democracy faces a bleak future. Freedom depends less on laws than it does on cultivating the sentiments and habits of civic virtue.

Because bourgeois liberals feared that democracy could quash personal freedom as ruthlessly as any absolute monarch, they called for property requirements for voting and officeholding. They wanted political power to be concentrated in the hands of a safe and reliable—that is, a propertied and educated—middle class. Such a government would prevent revolution from below, a prospect that caused anxiety among bourgeois liberals.

When liberals of the early nineteenth century engaged in revolutions, their aims were always limited. Once they had destroyed absolute monarchy and gained a constitution and a parliament or a change of government, they quickly tried to terminate the revolution. When the fever of revolution spread to the masses, liberals either withdrew or turned counterrevolutionary, for they feared the stirrings of the multitude.

Although liberalism was the political philosophy of a middle class generally hostile to democracy, the essential ideals of democracy flowed logically from liberalism. Eventually, democracy became a later stage in the evolution of liberalism because the masses, their political power enhanced by the Industrial Revolution, would press for greater social, political, and economic equality. Thus, by the early twentieth century, many European states had introduced universal manhood suffrage, abandoned property requirements for officeholding, and improved conditions for workers.

But the fears of nineteenth-century liberals were not unfounded. In the twentieth century, the participation of common people in politics indeed threatened freedom. Impatient with parliamentary procedures, the masses, particularly when troubled by economic problems, in some instances gave their support to demagogues who promised swift and decisive action. The granting of political participation to the masses has not always made people freer. The confidence of democrats was shaken in the twentieth century by the seeming willingness of common people to trade freedom for state authority, order, economic security, and national power. Liberalism is based on the assumption that human beings can and do respond to rational argument and that reason will prevail over base human feelings. The history of the twentieth century shows that this may be an overly optimistic assessment of human nature.

Radicalism and Democracy: The Expansion of Liberalism

In the early 1800s, democratic ideals were advanced by thinkers and activists called radicals. Inspired by the democratic principles expressed in Rousseau's *Social Contract* and by the republican stage of the French Revolution, French radicals championed popular sovereignty—rule by the people. In contrast to liberals, who feared the masses, French radicals trusted the common person. Advocating universal manhood suffrage and a republic, radicalism gained the support of French workers in the 1830s and 1840s.

British radicals, like their liberal cousins, inherited the Enlightenment's confidence in reason and its belief in the essential goodness of the individual. In the 1790s, British radicals expressed sympathy for the French Revolution, approving its concern for natural rights and its attack on feudal privileges. In the first half of the nineteenth century, English radicals sought parliamentary reforms because some heavily populated districts were barely represented in Parliament, while lightly populated districts were overrepresented. They demanded payment for members of Parliament to permit the nonwealthy to hold office; they sought universal manhood suffrage to give the masses representation in Parliament; and they insisted on the secret ballot to prevent intimidation of and reprisals against voters. Radicals attacked the hereditary aristocracy and fought corruption. Some, like William Cobbett, a crusading journalist, supported the struggle of the working class to improve its condition. He described the workers' penury:

> *A labouring man in England with a wife and only three children, though he never lose a day's work, though he and his family be economical, frugal and industrious in the most extensive sense of these words, is not now able to procure himself by his labour a single meal of meat from one end of the year into the other. Is this a state in which the labouring man ought to be?*[31]

English radicalism embodied the desires of parliamentary reformers for broader political representation and the hopes of the laboring poor for a better life. Two important theorists of the movement were Thomas Paine and Jeremy Bentham.

Thomas Paine

Thomas Paine (1737–1809), responding to Burke's *Reflections on the Revolution in France* with *The Rights of Man* (published in two parts in 1791 and 1792), denounced reverence for tradition, defended the principle of natural rights, and praised as progress the destruction of the Old Regime. Paine shared the conviction of other Enlightenment thinkers that superstition, intolerance, and despotism had interfered with human progress in the past, and he staunchly supported the American and French Revolutions. To initiate a true age of enlightenment, he said, it is necessary to recognize that "all the great laws of society are laws of nature,"[32] and to reconstitute the social and political order in accordance with these principles inherent in nature. Paine denounced all hereditary monarchy and aristocracy as wretched systems of slavery, which deprived people of their inherent right to govern themselves and exploited them financially in order to raise money for war. The only legitimate government, he claimed, was representative democracy, in which the right of all men to participate was assured. Paine believed that republican governments would be less inclined than hereditary ones to wage war and more concerned with the welfare of the common person.

From Paine, the English radical tradition acquired a faith in reason and human goodness, a skeptical attitude toward established institutions, an admiration for the open and democratic society being shaped in the United States, and a dislike of organized religion. It also gained the belief that the goal of government was the greater happiness of ordinary people and that excluding common people from political participation was unjust.

Jeremy Bentham

In contrast to Paine, Jeremy Bentham (1748–1832) rejected the doctrine of natural rights as an abstraction with no basis in reality, and he regarded the French Revolution as an absurd attempt to reconstruct society according to principles as misguided as those that had supported the Old Regime. Bentham's importance to the English radical tradition derives from the principle of *utility*, which he offered as a guide to reformers. The central fact of human existence, said Bentham, is that human beings seek to gratify their desires, that they prefer pleasure to pain, and that pleasure is intrinsically good and pain bad. In Bentham's view, human beings are motivated solely by self-interest, which they define in terms of pleasure and pain: "Nature has placed mankind under the governance of two sovereign masters, *pain* and *pleasure*. It is for them alone to point out what we ought to do, as well as to determine what we shall do."[33] Consequently, every political, economic, judicial, or social institution and all legislation should be judged according to a simple standard: does it bring about the greatest happiness for the greatest number? If it does not, it should be swept away.

Bentham believed that he had found an objective and scientific approach to the study and reform of society. By focusing on the necessity for change and improvement on every level of society and by encouraging a careful and objective analysis of social issues, Bentham and his followers, called philosophical radicals, contributed substantially to the shaping of the English reform tradition.

According to Bentham, those in power had always used what they considered the highest principles—God's teachings, universal standards, and honored traditions—to justify their political and social systems, their moral codes, and their laws. On the basis of these principles, they persecuted and abused people, instituted practices rooted in ignorance and superstition, and imposed values that made people miserable because they conflicted with human nature and the essential needs of men and women. Bentham contended that the principle of utility—that one should act always to derive the greatest happiness for the greatest number of people—permits the reforming of society in accordance with people's true nature and needs. It does not impose unrealistic standards on men and women but accepts people as they are. Utilitarianism, he declared, bases institutions and laws on an objective study of human behavior rather than on unsubstantiated religious beliefs, unreliable traditions, and mistaken philosophical abstractions. Its goal is to propose measures that augment rather than diminish the community's happiness. In his desire to make people happier, Bentham was representative of the humanitarianism of the Enlightenment.

Bentham's utilitarianism led him to press for social and political reforms. The aristocratic ruling elite, he said, were interested not in producing the "greatest happiness of the greatest number" but in furthering their own narrow interests. Only if the rulers came from the broad masses of people would government be amenable to reforms based on the principle of greatest happiness. Thus, he supported extension of the suffrage and a secret ballot and attacked political corruption and clerical control over education. Bentham wanted to do away with the monarchy and the House of Lords and to disestablish the Anglican church. In contrast to laissez-faire liberals, Benthamites argued for legislation to protect women and children in the factories. They also sought to improve sanitation in the cities and to reform the archaic British prison system.

Early Socialism: New Possibilities for Society

A new group, called socialists, went further than either the liberals or the radicals. Socialists argued that the liberals' concern for individual freedom and the radicals' demand for extension of the suffrage had little impact on the poverty, oppression, and gross inequality of wealth that plagued modern society. Asserting that the liberals' doctrine of individualism degenerated into selfish egoism, which harmed community life, socialists demanded the creation of a new society based on cooperation rather than on competition. Reflecting the spirit of the Enlightenment and the French Revolution, socialists, like liberals, denounced the status quo for perpetuating injustice and held that people could create a better world. Like liberals, too, they placed the highest value on a rational analysis of society and on transforming society in line with scientifically valid premises, whose truth rational people could grasp. Socialists believed that they had discerned a pattern in human society, which, if properly understood and acted upon, would lead men and women to an earthly salvation. Thus, early socialists were also romantics, for they dreamed of a new social order, a future utopia, where each individual could find happiness and self-fulfillment.

The most important early socialist thinkers—Saint-Simon, Fourier, and Owen—espoused a new social and economic system in which production and distribution of goods would be planned for the general benefit of society. The current organization of society was unjust, for it kept great masses of people in poverty, oppression, and despair. Society was also mismanaged, for people were prevented from working for the common good. The thought of the early socialists influenced Karl Marx and Friedrich Engels, who, in the second half of the nineteenth century, became the most influential formulators and propagators of socialism. There were also Christian communitarians, who protested the treatment of the poor and the unsettling conditions caused by industrialization. These Christian "socialists" urged believers to share their property and labor and live together in model communities.

Socialists questioned the assumption that society was made up of isolated and self-seeking individuals, and they challenged the laws of economics as formulated by the laissez-faire economists. Denying that human beings fared best as competing individuals, they argued that people achieved more happiness for themselves and for others as members of a cooperative community that lived, worked, and planned together. Some socialists urged voluntary divorce from the larger society. They proposed communes or model factory towns as places to apply the principles of socialism or communitarianism. Some were very perceptive about the nature of industrialization and the future of industrial society. Others romantically longed for the past and created schemes that would preserve the values and ethics of village life as it existed before the Industrial Revolution. All socialists denounced as hollow and hypocritical the liberals' preoccupation with liberty and equality, arguing that to the lower classes devastated by poverty these ideals were merely formal principles. They protected the person and property of the wealthy while the majority were mired in poverty and helplessness. Although they sought to replace the existing social order with a more just arrangement, these early socialists, unlike Marx, did not advocate class warfare. They aspired to create a new harmonious social order that would reconcile different classes; for Marx, by necessity a new social order entailed the destruction of the bourgeoisie.

Saint-Simon: Technocratic Socialism

Descended from a distinguished French aristocratic family, Henri Comte de Saint-Simon (1760–1825) renounced his title during the French Revolution and enthusiastically preached the opportunity for a new society. He regarded his own society as defective and in need of reorganization: the critical philosophy of the Enlightenment had shattered the Old Order but had not provided a guide for reconstructing society. Saint-Simon believed that he had a mission to set society right by providing an understanding of the new age being shaped by science and industry. Many of the brightest young people in France believed in his mission.

Saint-Simon argued, however, that just as Christianity had provided social unity and stability during the Middle Ages, so scientific knowledge would bind the society of his time. Scientists, industrialists, bankers, artists, and writers would replace the clergy and the aristocracy as the social elite. Saint-Simon had a romantic love of genius and talent. In the new industrial age, he thought, the control of society must pass to the *industriels*—those who produce or who make it possible to produce. These manufacturers, bankers, engineers, intellectuals, and scientists would harness technology for the betterment of humanity. Saint-Simon's disciples championed efforts to build great railway and canal systems, including the Suez and Panama Canals. His vision of a scientifically organized society led by trained experts was a powerful force among intellectuals in the nineteenth century and is very much alive today among those who believe in a technocratic society.

Like the philosophes, Saint-Simon valued science, had confidence in the power of reason to improve society, and believed in the certainty of progress according to laws of social development. Also like the philosophes, he attacked the clergy for clinging to superstition and dogma at the expense of society. The essence of Christianity was the golden rule: the sublime command that people should treat each other like brothers and sisters. According to Saint-Simon, the traditional clergy, having placed dogma above moral law, had forfeited its right to lead Europe, just as the aristocracy had, before the French Revolution, forfeited its right to rule. He called for "a new Christianity" (the title of one of his books) to serve as an antidote to selfish interests and to abjure the narrow nationalism that divided the peoples of Europe.

Saint-Simon's thought reveals several socialist elements: that industrial society constitutes a new stage in history, that unchecked individualism is detrimental to society, and that creative and collective planning is necessary to cope with social ills. He argued, as Marx would later, that liberalism failed to deal with the deprivation of the workers, the real producers of wealth. But a crucial socialist conception was absent from his thought: he did not view society as divided into classes with competing interests that necessitated violent conflict.

Fourier: Psychological Socialism

Another early French socialist was Charles Fourier (1772–1837), who believed, as the romantics did, that society conflicted with the natural needs of human beings and that this tension was responsible for human misery. Only the reorganization of society so that it would satisfy people's desire for pleasure and contentment would end that misery. Whereas Saint-Simon and his followers had elaborate plans to reorganize society on the grand scale of large industries and giant railway and canal systems, Fourier sought to create small communities that would allow men and women to enjoy life's simple pleasures. These communities of about sixteen hundred people, called *phalansteries,* would be organized according to the unchanging needs of human nature.

Fourier was not greatly concerned about the realities of industrialization, and his ideas reflect the artisan society that existed in France when he was growing up. In the phalansteries, no force would coerce or thwart innocent human drives. All the people would work at tasks that interested them and produce things that brought them and others pleasure. Like Adam Smith, Fourier understood that specialization bred boredom and alienation from work and life. Unlike Smith, he did not believe that vastly increased productivity compensated for the evils of specialization. In the phalansteries, money and goods would not be equally distributed; those with special skills and responsibilities would be rewarded accordingly. This system conformed to nature because people have a natural desire to be rewarded for their achievements.

Both Fourier and the Saint-Simonians supported female equality, placing them among the first social thinkers to do so. Fourier did not define female equality merely in political terms. He thought that marriage distorted the natures of both men and women because monogamy restricted their sexual needs and narrowed the scope of their lives to the family alone. Instead, people should think of themselves as part of the family of all humanity. Because married women had to devote all their strength and time to household and children, they had no time or energy left to enjoy life's pleasures. Fourier did not call for the abolition of the family, but he expressed the hope that it would disappear on its own as society adjusted to his theories. Men and women would find new ways of fulfilling themselves sexually, and the community would be organized so that it could care for the children. Fourier's ideas found some acceptance in the United States, where in the 1840s at least twenty-nine communities were founded on Fourierist principles. None, however, lasted more than five or six years.

Owen: Industrial Socialism

In 1799, Robert Owen (1771–1858) became part owner and manager of the New Lanark cotton mills in Scotland. Distressed by widespread mistreatment of workers, Owen resolved to improve the lives of his employees without destroying profits. He raised wages, upgraded working conditions, refused to hire children under ten, and provided workers with neat homes, food, and clothing, all at reasonable prices. He set up schools for children and for adults. In every way, he demonstrated his belief that healthier, happier workers produced more than less fortunate ones. Like Saint-Simon, Owen believed that industry and technology could enrich humankind if organized according to the proper principles. Heads of state, members of parliaments, and business leaders came from all over Europe to see Owen's factories.

Just like many philosophes, Owen was convinced that the environment was the principal shaper of character: that the ignorance, alcoholism, and crime of the poor derived from bad living conditions. Public education and factory reform, said Owen, would make better citizens of the poor. When Parliament balked at reforms, Owen even urged the creation of a grand national trade union of all the workers in England. In the earliest days of industrialization, with very few workers organized in unions, this dream seemed an impossible one. Owen came to believe that the entire social and economic order must be replaced by a new system based on harmonious group living rather than on competition. He established a model community at New Harmony, Indiana, but it was short-lived. Even in his factory in Scotland, Owen had some difficulty holding on to workers, many of whom were devout Christians and resented his secular ideas and the dancing taught to their children in his schools.

Nationalism: The Sacredness of the Nation

Nationalism is a conscious bond shared by a group of people who feel strongly attached to a particular land and who possess a common language, culture, and history, marked by shared glories and sufferings. Nationalists contend that one's highest loyalty and devotion should be given to the nation. They exhibit great pride in their people's history and traditions and often feel that their nation has been specially chosen by God or history. They assert that the nation—its culture and history—gives meaning to an individual's life and actions. Like a religion, nationalism provides the individual with a sense of community and with a cause worthy of self-sacrifice. Identifying with the nation's collective achievements can enhance the feeling of self-worth.

In an age when Christianity was in retreat, nationalism became the dominant spiritual force in nineteenth-century European life. Nationalism provided new beliefs, martyrs, and "holy" days that stimulated feelings of reverence; it offered membership in a community, which satisfied an overwhelming psychological need of human beings for fellowship and identity. And nationalism supplied a mission—the advancement of the nation—to which people could dedicate themselves.

The Emergence of Modern Nationalism

The essential components of nationalism emerged during the French Revolution. The Revolution asserted the principle that sovereignty derived from the nation, from the people as a whole: the state was not the private possession of the ruler but the embodiment of the people's will. The nation-state was above king, church, estate, guild, or province, superseding all other loyalties. The French people must view themselves not as subjects of the king, not as Bretons or Normans, nobles or bourgeois, but as citizens of a united fatherland, la patrie. These two ideas—that the people possess unlimited sovereignty and that they are united in a nation—were crucial in fashioning a nationalist outlook.

As the Revolution moved from the moderate to the radical stage, French nationalism intensified. In 1793–94, when the republic was threatened by foreign invasion, the Jacobins created a national army, demanded ever greater allegiance to and sacrifice for the nation, and called for the expansion of France's borders to the Alps and the Rhine. With unprecedented success, the Jacobins used every means—press, schoolroom, and rostrum—to instill a love of country.

The Romantic Movement also awakened nationalist feelings. By examining the language, literature, and folkways of their people, romantic thinkers instilled a sense of national pride in their compatriots. Johann Gottfried Herder (1744–1803), a prominent German writer, conceived the idea of the *Volksgeist*—the spirit of the people. For Herder, each people was unique and creative; each expressed its peculiar genius in language, literature, monuments, and folk traditions. Herder did not make the theoretical jump from a spiritual or cultural nationalism to political nationalism; he did not call for the formation of states based on nationality. But his emphasis on the unique culture of a people and his assertion that an individual is defined as a member of a specific culture or nation stimulated a national consciousness among Germans and the various Slavic peoples who lived under foreign rule. Fascination with the Volksgeist prompted intellectuals to investigate the past of their own people, to rediscover their ancient traditions, and to extol their historic languages and cultures. From this cultural nationalism, it was only a short step to a political nationalism that called for national liberation, unification, and statehood.

The romantics were the earliest apostles of German nationalism. Resisting the French philosophes, who sought to impose universal norms on all peoples, German romantics stressed the uniqueness of the German nation and its history. They restored to consciousness memories of the German past, and they emphasized the distinct qualities of the German folk and the special destiny of the German nation. The romantics glorified medieval Germany and valued hereditary monarchy and aristocracy as vital links to the nation's past. They saw the existence of each individual as inextricably bound up with folk and fatherland, and they found the self-realization for which they yearned in the uniting of their own egos with the national soul. To these romantics, the national community was the source of artistic and spiritual creativity and the vital force that gave the individual both an identity and a purpose in life. The nation stood above the individual; the national spirit linked isolated souls into a community of brethren. In unmistakably romantic tones, poet Ernst Moritz Arndt (1769–1860) urged Germans to unite against Napoleon:

> *German man, feel again God, hear and fear the eternal, and you hear and fear also your Volk [people], you feel again in God the honor and dignity of your fathers, their glorious history rejuvenates itself in you, their firm and gallant virtue reblossoms in you, the whole German Fatherland stands again before you in the august halo of past centuries. No longer Catholics and Protestants, no longer Prussians and Austrians, Saxons and Bavarians, Silesians and Hanoverians, no longer of different faith, different mentality, and different will—be Germans, be one, will to be one by love and loyalty, and no devil will vanquish you.*[34]

Most German romantics expressed hostility to the liberal ideals of the French Revolution. They condemned the reforms of the Revolution for trying to reconstruct society by separating individuals from their national past, for treating them as isolated abstractions. They held that the German folk spirit should not be polluted by foreign French ideas.

To the philosophes, the state was a human institution, a rational arrangement between individuals that safeguarded their rights and permitted them to realize their individual goals. To German romantics such a state was an artificial and lifeless construction. The true German state was something holy, the expression of the divine spirit of the German people; it could not be manufactured to order by the intellect. The state's purpose was neither the protection of natural rights nor the promotion of economic well-being; rather, the state was a living organism that linked each person to a sacred past and reconciled and united heterogeneous wills, imbuing them with a profound sense of community, with which one entered into mystical communion. "This 'Romantic' image of a state founded not on any rational idea of the functions and purposes of a state but on love and perfect communion, is of course a formula for totalitarianism," observes R. J. Hollingdale, "and it was towards a state modeled on this formula that German nationalism continually moved."[35] Building on the romantics' views, radical German nationalists came to propound the dangerous racist idea that national identity was an inherited characteristic—that being and feeling German depended on birth rather than acculturation. Holding this belief, some German national-

MASSACRE AT CHIOS. In the Greek War of Independence, 1821–1830, the Turks took the island of Chios and either massacred or sold into slavery most of the Greek inhabitants. French artist Eugene Delacroix depicted the atrocity in this famous painting. (*Louvre, Paris Reunion des Musées Nationaux/Art Resource, NY.*)

ists maintained that Jews, no matter how many generations they had resided in Germany, could never be truly German.

Nationalism and Liberalism

In the early 1800s, liberals were the principal leaders and supporters of nationalist movements. They viewed the struggle for national rights—the freedom of a people from foreign rule—as an extension of the struggle for the rights of the individual. There could be no liberty, said nationalists, if people were not free to rule themselves in their own land.

Liberals called for the unification of Germany and Italy, the rebirth of Poland, the liberation of Greece from Turkish rule, and the granting of autonomy to the Hungarians of the Austrian Empire. Liberal nationalists envisioned a Europe of independent states based on nationality and popular sovereignty. Free of foreign domination and tyrant princes, these newly risen states would protect the rights of the individual and strive to create a brotherhood of nationalities in Europe.

In the first half of the nineteenth century, few intellectuals recognized the dangers inherent in nationalism or understood the fundamental conflict between liberalism and nationalism. For the liberal, the idea of universal natural rights transcended all national boundaries. Inheriting the cosmopolitanism of the Enlightenment, liberalism emphasized what all people had in common, called for all individuals to be treated equally under the law, and preached toleration. Nationalists, manifesting the particularist attitude of the in-group and the tribe, regarded the nation as the essential fact of existence. Consequently, they often willingly subverted individual liberty for the sake of national grandeur. The liberal sought to protect the rights of all within the state, whereas the nationalist often ignored or trampled on the rights of individuals and national minorities. Liberalism grew out of the rational tradition of the West; nationalism derived from the emotions. Because it fulfilled an elemental yearning for community and kinship, nationalism exerted a powerful hold over human hearts, often driving people to political extremism. Liberalism demanded objectivity in analyzing tradition, society, and history, but nationalism evoked a mythic and romantic past that often distorted history.

"Nationalism requires . . . much belief in what is patently not so," wryly observes the British historian E. J. Hobsbawm.[36] Thus nationalists inflated their people's past achievements and attributed to the nation a peculiar inner spirit that set it apart from others and accounted for its superiority. While constantly declaiming the wrongs that others had inflicted on them, they turned a blind eye to their own mistreatment of others. Nationalists interpreted history to serve political ends: the unity of their people and the creation of an independent nation-state.

In the last part of the nineteenth century, the irrational and mythic quality of nationalism intensified. By stressing the unique qualities and history of a particular people, nationalism promoted hatred between nationalities. By kindling deep love for the past, for community, and for kinship, it often raised emotions to fever pitch. It shattered rational thinking, dragged the mind into a world of fantasy and myth, and introduced extremism into politics. Love of nation became an overriding passion, threatening to extinguish the liberal ideals of reason, freedom, and equality.

Notes

1. Jean Jacques Rousseau, *The Confessions* (New York: Modern Library, 1950), p. 2.
2. Quoted in H. G. Schenk, *The Mind of the European Romantics* (Garden City, N.Y.: Doubleday, 1969), p. 4.
3. William Blake, Milton, in *The Poetry and Prose of William Blake,* ed. David V. Erdman (Garden City, N.Y.: Doubleday, 1965), bk. 2, plate 40, lines 34–36.
4. Ibid., plate 41, line 1.
5. Johann Goethe, *Faust,* trans. Bayard Taylor (New York: Modern Library, 1950), pt. 1, sc. 4.
6. Letter of John Keats, November 22, 1817, in *The Letters of John Keats,* ed. Hyder E. Rollins (Cambridge, Mass.: Harvard University Press, 1958), 1:184–185.
7. Quoted in John Herman Randall, Jr., *The Career of Philosophy* (New York: Columbia University Press, 1965), 2:80.
8. Blake, *Milton,* Preface.
9. Quoted in Robert T. Denommé, *Nineteenth-Century French Romantic Poets* (Carbondale: Southern Illinois University Press, 1969), p. 28.
10. Quoted in T. C. W. Blanning, ed., *The Oxford Illustrated History of Modern Europe* (New York: Oxford University Press, 1996), p. 124.
11. Quoted in Frederic Ewen, *Heroic Imagination* (Secaucus, N.J.: Citadel Press, 1984), p. 276.
12. Quoted in Ernst Cassirer, *An Essay on Man* (New York: Bantam Books, 1970), p. 178.
13. Victor Hugo, "La Pente de la Rêverie," *Les Feuilles D'Automne* (Paris: J. Hetzel, 1831), p. 157.
14. From "The Tables Turned," in *The Complete Poetical Works of Wordsworth,* ed. Andrew J. George (Boston: Houghton Mifflin, 1904, rev. ed. 1982), p. 83.
15. From "Lines Composed a Few Miles Above Tintern Abbey," *The Complete Poetical Works of William Wordsworth* (Philadelphia: Porter & Coates, 1851), p. 194.
16. Quoted in R. W. Harris, *Romanticism and the*

Social Order, 1780–1830 (New York: Barnes & Noble, 1969), pp. 223–224.

17. Horst von Maltitz, *The Evolution of Hitler's Germany* (New York: McGraw-Hill, 1973), p. 217.
18. G. W. F. Hegel, *The Philosophy of History,* trans. J. Sibree (New York: Dover, 1956), pp. 19, 23.
19. Ibid., p. 39.
20. Quoted in George Brandes, *Revolution and Reaction in Nineteenth Century French Literature* (New York: Russell & Russell, reprint ed., n.d.), pp. 106–107.
21. Edmund Burke, *Reflections on the Revolution in France* (New York: Liberal Arts Press, 1955), pp. 40, 89.
22. Ibid., p. 99.
23. Ibid., p. 70.
24. Quoted in Frederick B. Artz, *Reaction and Revolution, 1814–1832* (New York: Harper Torchbooks, 1963), p. 73.
25. John Stuart Mill, *On Liberty,* ed. Currin V. Shields (Indianapolis: Bobbs-Merrill, 1956), chap. 1.
26. Thomas Robert Malthus, *First Essay on Population,* reprinted for the Royal Economic Society (London: Macmillan, 1926), p. 16.
27. Ibid., p. 17.
28. Excerpted in Allan Bullock and Maurice Shock, eds., *The Liberal Tradition from Fox to Keynes* (London: Adam & Charles Black, 1956), pp. 31–32.
29. Quoted in Anthony Arblaster, *The Rise and Decline of Western Liberalism* (Oxford: Basil Blackwell, 1984), p. 258.
30. Alexis de Tocqueville, *Democracy in America,* trans. Henry Reeve (New York: Oxford University Press, 1924), pp. 493–494.
31. Quoted in Raymond Williams, *Culture and Society, 1780–1945* (New York: Columbia University Press, 1983), p. 14.
32. Quoted in Francis Canavan, "Thomas Paine," in *History of Political Philosophy,* ed. Leo Strauss and Joseph Cropsey (Chicago: Rand McNally, 1963), p. 594.
33. Jeremy Bentham, *An Introduction to the Principles of Morals and Legislation,* together with *A Fragment on Government* (London: Basil Blackwell, 1948), chap. 1, sec. 1, p. 125.
34. Quoted in Hans Kohn, *Prelude to Nation-States* (Princeton, N.J.: D. Van Nostrand, 1967), p. 262.
35. R. J. Hollingdale, *Nietzsche* (London: Routledge & Kegan Paul, 1973), p. 25.
36. E. J. Hobsbawm, *Nations and Nationalism Since 1870* (Cambridge, England: Cambridge University Press, 1992), p. 12.

Suggested Reading

Arblaster, Anthony, *The Rise and Decline of Western Liberalism* (1984). A critical analysis of liberalism, its evolution and characteristics.

Bullock, Alan, and Maurice Shock, eds., *The Liberal Tradition from Fox to Keynes* (1956). Selections from the works of British liberals.

Denommé, Robert T., *Nineteenth-Century French Romantic Poets* (1969). The genesis of romanticism in France.

de Ruggiero, Guido, *The History of European Liberalism* (1927). A classic study.

Epstein, Klaus, *The Genesis of German Conservatism* (1966). An analysis of German conservative thought as a response to the Enlightenment and the French Revolution.

Fried, Albert, and Ronald Sanders, eds., *Socialist Thought* (1964). Selections from the writings of socialist theorists.

Harris, R. W., *Romanticism and the Social Order, 1780–1830* (1969). Involvement of English romantics in social and political questions.

Honour, Hugh, *Romanticism* (1979). A study of the influence of romanticism on the visual arts.

Kohn, Hans, *The Idea of Nationalism* (1961). A comprehensive study of nationalism by a leading student of the subject.

———, *Prelude to Nation-States* (1967). The emergence of nationalism in France and Germany.

Manuel, Frank, *The Prophets of Paris* (1962). Good discussions of Saint-Simon and Fourier.

Markham, F. M. H., ed., *Henri Comte de Saint-Simon* (1952). Selected writings.

Schapiro, J. S., *Liberalism: Its Meaning and History* (1958). A useful survey with readings.

Schenk, H. G., *The Mind of the European Romantics*

(1969). A comprehensive analysis of the Romantic Movement.

Shafer, B. C., *Faces of Nationalism* (1972). The evolution of modern nationalism in Europe and the non-European world; contains a good bibliography.

Simon, W. M., *French Liberalism 1789–1848* (1972). Selections from the writings of French liberals.

Weiss, John, *Conservatism in Europe, 1770–1945* (1977). Conservatism as a reaction to social modernization.

Review Questions

1. The Romantic Movement was a reaction against the dominant ideas of the Enlightenment. Discuss this statement.
2. What was the significance of the Romantic Movement?
3. How did Kant try to resolve the problem posed by Hume's empiricism?
4. What was Hegel's view of history? What influence did it have?
5. What were the attitudes of the conservatives toward the philosophes and the French Revolution?
6. Why did conservatives reject the philosophy of natural rights?
7. What were the sources of liberalism?
8. Contrast the views of early-nineteenth-century liberals and conservatives regarding the individual's relationship to society.
9. What fundamental difference existed between French radicals and liberals?
10. What did British radicalism owe to Paine and Bentham?
11. What basic liberal-capitalist doctrines were attacked by early socialists?
12. Why are Saint-Simon, Fourier, and Owen regarded as early socialists?
13. How did the French Revolution and romanticism contribute to the rise of modern nationalism?
14. What is the relationship between nationalism and liberalism?
15. Account for nationalism's great appeal.

Chapter 23

Revolution and Counterrevolution, 1815–1848

Barricades in the streets of Frankfurt, 1848. In 1848 revolutionary fever spread from France to Germany. In several German states, liberals fought for written constitutions that protected basic rights and parliamentary government that represented the people. At first the ruling princes made concessions but quickly regained their nerve and ordered their professional soldiers to crush the revolutionaries. (The Granger Collection, New York.)

- **The Congress of Vienna, 1814–1815**
  Metternich the Archconservative
  Crisis over Saxony and Poland
  The Settlement
- **Revolutions, 1820–1829**
- **Revolutions, 1830–1832**
- **The Rise of Reform in Britain**
- **Revolutions of 1848: France**
  The February Revolution
  The June Days: Revolution of the Oppressed
- **Revolutions of 1848: Germany, Austria, and Italy**
  The German States: Liberalism Defeated
  Austria: Hapsburg Dominance
  Italy: Continued Fragmentation
- **The Revolutions of 1848: An Assessment**

During the years 1815 through 1848, the forces unleashed by the French Revolution clashed with the traditional outlook of the Old Regime. The period opened with the Congress of Vienna, which drew up a peace settlement after the defeat of Napoleon, and closed with the revolutions that swept across most of Europe in 1848.

Much of the Old Regime outside France survived the stormy decades of the French Revolution and Napoleon. Monarchs still held the reins of political power. Aristocrats, particularly in central and eastern Europe, retained their traditional hold on the army and administration, controlled the peasantry and local government, and enjoyed tax exemptions. Determined to enforce respect for traditional authority and to smother liberal ideals, the conservative ruling elites resorted to censorship, secret police, and armed force.

The French Revolution, however, had shown that absolutism could be successfully challenged and feudal privileges abolished. Inspired by the revolutionary principles of liberty, equality, and fraternity, liberals and nationalists continued to engage in revolutionary action.

The Congress of Vienna, 1814–1815

Metternich the Archconservative

After the defeat of Napoleon, representatives of European powers convened in Vienna to draw up a peace settlement. The pivotal figure at the Congress of Vienna was Prince Klemens von Metternich (1773–1859) of Austria, who had organized the coalition that triumphed over Napoleon.

A man of the Old Order, Metternich hated the new forces of nationalism and liberalism. He regarded liberalism as a dangerous disease carried by middle-class malcontents, and he believed that domestic order and international stability depended on rule by monarchy and respect for aristocracy. The misguided liberal belief that society could be reshaped according to the ideals of liberty and equality, said Metternich, had led to twenty-five years of revolution, terror, and war.

Chronology 23.1 ❖ Revolution and Reaction

1820	Revolt in Spain
1821	Austria crushes revolts in Italy
1823	French troops crush revolt in Spain
1825	Uprising in Russia crushed by Nicholas I
1829	Greece gains independence from the Ottoman Empire
1830	July Ordinances in France are followed by a revolution, which forces Charles X to abdicate
August 1830	Belgian revolution
October 1830	Belgians declare their independence from Holland, establishing a liberal government
1831	Polish revolution fails
1831–32	Austrian forces crush a revolution in Italy
1832	Reform Act extends suffrage to the middle class in Britain
1848	Year of revolution
February 1848	Revolution in Paris: Louis Philippe abdicates, and France becomes a republic
March 1848	Uprisings in capital cities of the German states lead to liberal reforms
March 18–22, 1848	"Five Glorious Days" in Milan
March 22, 1848	Citizens of Venice declare their freedom from Austria and establish a republic
June 1848	June Days of Paris: revolutionaries are beaten by professional soldiers
August 1848	Constitutional Assembly meets in Vienna and abolishes serfdom in the Austrian Empire
December 1848	Louis Napoleon is elected president of the Second Republic of France
August 1849	Hungarians' bid for independence is crushed by Hapsburg forces, aided by Russian troops

In order to restore stability and peace, the old Europe must suppress liberal ideas and quash the first signs of revolution. If the European powers did not destroy the revolutionary spirit, they would be devoured by it.

Metternich also feared the new spirit of nationalism. Because Austria was a multinational empire, it was particularly vulnerable to nationalist unrest. If its many ethnic groups—Poles, Czechs, Magyars, Italians, South Slavs, and Romanians—became infected with the nationalist virus, they would shatter the Hapsburg Empire. A highly cultured, multilingual, and cosmopolitan aristocrat, Metternich considered himself the defender of European civilization. He thought that by arousing the masses and setting people against people nationalism could undermine the foundations of European civilization.

Metternich's critics accuse him of shortsightedness. Instead of harnessing and directing the new forces let loose by the French Revolution, he sought to stifle them. Instead of trying to rebuild

Congress of Vienna, 1815, by Jean Baptiste Isabey (1767–1855). The delegates to the Congress of Vienna sought to reestablish many features of Europe that existed before the French Revolution and Napoleon. They can be accused of shortsightedness; nevertheless, the balance of power that they formulated preserved international peace. Metternich is standing in front of a chair at left. (*The New York Public Library.*)

and remodel, he sought to prop up dying institutions. Regarding all reforming as an invitation to radicalism and revolution, Metternich refused to make any concessions to liberalism.

Metternich wanted to return to power the ruling families deposed by more than two decades of revolutionary warfare. He also sought to restore the balance of power so that no one country could be in a position to dominate the European continent as France under Napoleon had done. Metternich was determined to end the chaos of the Napoleonic period and restore stability to Europe. There must be no more Napoleons who obliterate states, topple kings, and dream of European hegemony. Although he served the interests of the Hapsburg monarchy, Metternich also had a sense of responsibility to Europe as a whole. He sought a settlement that would avoid the destructiveness of a general war.

The other nations at the Congress of Vienna included Britain, Russia, France, and Prussia. Representing Britain was Robert Stewart, Viscount Castlereagh (1769–1822), the realistic British foreign secretary. Though an implacable enemy of Napoleon, Castlereagh demonstrated mature statesmanship by not seeking to punish France severely. Tsar Alexander I (1777–1825), steeped in Christian mysticism, wanted to create a European community based on Christian teachings. Alexander regarded himself as the savior of Europe, an attitude that caused other diplomats to view him with distrust. Representing France was Prince

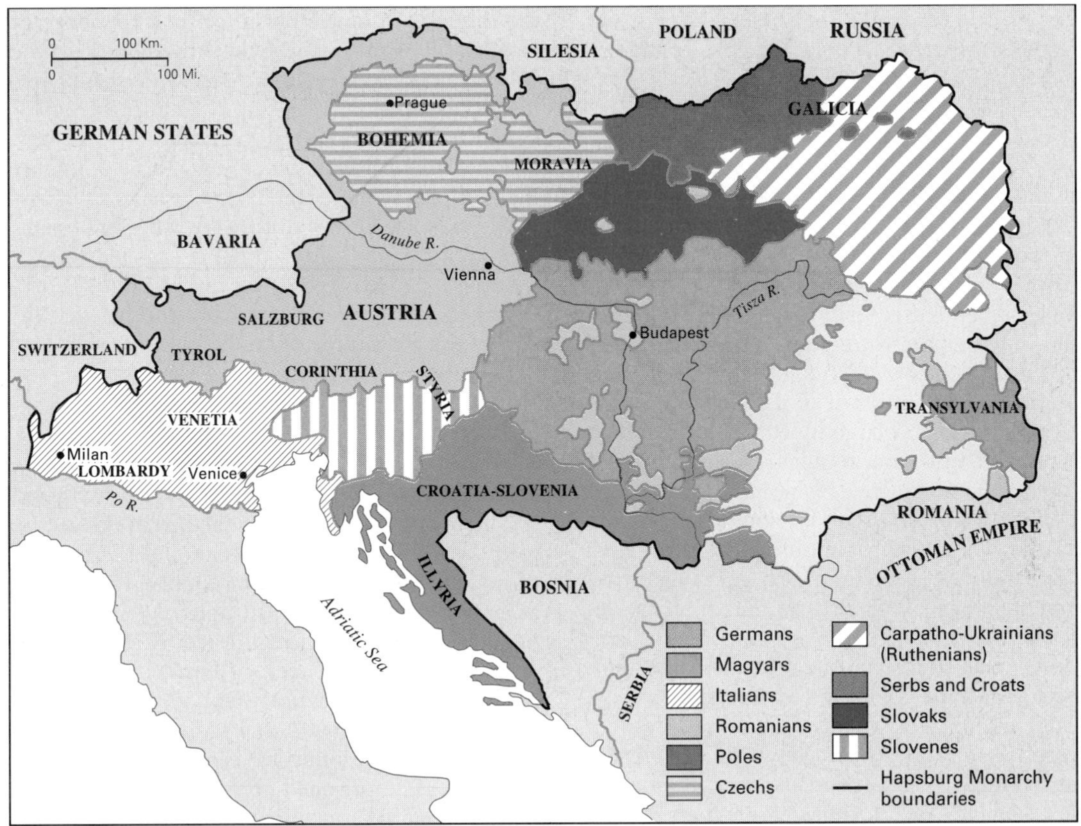

Map 23.1 Peoples of the Hapsburg Monarchy, 1815 In 1815, Austria was a multinational empire dominated by Germans. As nationalism among the various ethnic groups grew stronger, fear of dissolution became the principal concern of Hapsburg leaders.

Charles Maurice de Talleyrand-Périgord (1754–1838). A devoted patriot, Talleyrand sought to remove from France the stigma of the Revolution and Napoleon. The aging Prince Karl von Hardenberg (1750–1822) represented Prussia. Like Metternich, Castlereagh, and Talleyrand, the Prussian statesman believed that the various European states, besides pursuing their own national interests, should concern themselves with the well-being of the European community as a whole.

Crisis over Saxony and Poland

Two interrelated issues threatened to disrupt the conference and enmesh the Great Powers in another war. One was Prussia's intention to annex the German kingdom of Saxony; the other was Russia's demand for Polish territories. The tsar wanted to combine the Polish holdings of Russia, Austria, and Prussia into a new Polish kingdom under Russian control. Britain and Austria saw such an extension of Russia's power into central Europe as a threat to the balance of power. Metternich declared that he had not fought Napoleon to prepare the way for the tsar. Britain agreed that Russia's westward expansion must be checked.

Prince Talleyrand of France suggested that Britain, Austria, and France form an alliance to oppose Prussia and Russia. Talleyrand's clever move restored France to the family of nations. Now France was no longer the hated enemy but a necessary counterweight to Russia and Prussia. Threatened with war, Russia and Prussia moderated their demands and the crisis ended.

The Settlement

After months of discussion, quarrels, and threats, the delegates to the Congress of Vienna finished their work. Resisting Prussia's demands for a punitive peace, the allies did not punish France severely. They feared that a humiliated France would only prepare for a war of revenge. Moreover, Metternich continued to need France to balance the power of both Prussia and Russia. France had to pay a large indemnity over a five-year period and submit to allied occupation until the obligation was met.

Despite losing most of its conquests, France emerged with somewhat more land than it possessed before the Revolution. To guard against a resurgent France, both Prussia and Holland received territories on the French border. Holland obtained the southern Netherlands (Belgium); Prussia gained the Rhineland and part of Saxony, but not as much as the Prussians had desired. Nevertheless, Prussia emerged from the settlement significantly larger and stronger. Russia obtained Finland and a considerable part of the Polish territories, but not as much as the tsar had anticipated; the Congress prevented further Russian expansion into central Europe. The northern Italian province of Lombardy was restored to Austria, which also received adjacent Venetia. England obtained strategic naval bases: Helgoland in the North Sea, Malta and the Ionian Islands in the Mediterranean, the Cape Colony in South Africa, and Ceylon in the Indian Ocean. Germany was organized into a confederation of thirty-eight (later thirty-nine) states. Norway was given to Sweden. Legitimate rulers who had been displaced by the Revolution and Napoleon were restored to their thrones in France, Spain, Portugal, the Kingdom of the Two Sicilies, the Papal States, and many German states.

The conservative delegates at the Congress of Vienna have often been criticized for ignoring the liberal and nationalist aspirations of the different peoples and turning the clock back to the Old Regime. Critics have castigated the congress for dealing only with the rights of thrones and not the rights of peoples. But after the experience of two world wars in the twentieth century, some historians today are impressed with the peacemakers' success in restoring a balance of power that effectively stabilized international relations. No one country was strong enough to dominate the Continent; no Great Power was so unhappy that it resorted to war to undo the settlement. Not until the unification of Germany in 1870–71 was the balance of power upset; not until World War I in 1914 did Europe have another general war of the magnitude of the Napoleonic wars.

Revolutions, 1820–1829

Russia, Austria, Prussia, and Great Britain agreed to act together to preserve the territorial settlement of the Congress of Vienna and the balance of power. After paying its indemnity, France was admitted into this Quadruple Alliance, also known as the Concert of Europe. Metternich intended to use the Concert of Europe to maintain harmony between nations and internal stability within nations. Toward this end, conservatives in their respective countries censored books and newspapers, imprisoned liberal activists, and suppressed nationalist uprisings.

But repression could not contain the liberal and nationalist ideals unleashed by the French Revolution. The first revolution after restoration of the legitimate rulers occurred in Spain in 1820. Fearing that the uprising, with its quasi-liberal overtones, would inspire revolutions in other lands, the Concert of Europe empowered France to intervene. In 1823, a hundred thousand French troops crushed the revolution in Spain.

Revolutionary activity in Italy also frightened the Concert of Europe. In 1821, it authorized Austria to extinguish a liberal uprising in the Kingdom of the Two Sicilies. The Austrians also

Map 23.2 Europe, 1815 ▶
At the Congress of Vienna, Russia gained a considerable part of the Polish territories, Prussia acquired the Rhineland and part of Saxony, and Holland received Belgium. The northern Italian province of Lombardy was restored to the Hapsburg Empire, which also received adjacent Venetia.

0 200 400 Km.
0 200 400 Mi.
Kingdom of Prussia
Austrian Empire
Boundary of German Confederation
NORWAY (to Sweden)
SWEDEN
Stockholm
St. Petersburg
Riga
Moscow
North Sea
Baltic Sea
DENMARK
Copenhagen
RUSSIAN EMPIRE
GREAT BRITAIN
HELIGOLAND (Gr. Br.)
SCHLESWIG
HOLSTEIN
HANOVER
KINGDOM OF PRUSSIA
Berlin
Warsaw
POLAND
Kiev
UKRAINE
London
Amsterdam
KINGDOM OF THE NETHERLANDS
SAXONY
Prague
BOHEMIA
GALICIA
Frankfurt
LORRAINE
ALSACE
BADEN
WÜRTTEM-BERG
BAVARIA
Munich
AUSTRIAN EMPIRE
HUNGARY
BESSARABIA
MOLDAVIA
ATLANTIC OCEAN
Paris
FRANCE
SWITZERLAND
LOMBARDY
Milan
Venice
VENETIA
CROATIA
WALLACHIA
Black Sea
PIEDMONT
PARMA
MODENA
BOSNIA
SERBIA
BULGARIA
LUCCA
TUSCANY
PAPAL STATES
Elba
Corsica (France)
KINGDOM OF PIEDMONT-SARDINIA
Rome
Naples
NAPLES
OTTOMAN EMPIRE
Constantinople
PORTUGAL
Lisbon
Madrid
SPAIN
Sardinia
KINGDOM OF THE TWO SICILIES
ALBANIA
Ionian Is. (Gr. Br.)
GREECE
Mediterranean Sea
Sicily
GIBRALTAR (Gr. Br.)
Malta (Gr. Br.)

crushed an uprising in Piedmont, in northern Italy. Rulers in other Italian states jailed and executed liberal leaders, and several thousand Italians went into exile.

In both instances, Britain strongly opposed the actions of the alliance. It interpreted the alliance differently than Austria, Prussia, and Russia. The three eastern powers wanted the alliance to smother in the cradle all subversive movements that threatened the Old Order. To Metternich, the central problem of the age was suppressing revolutions, and he regarded the alliance as a means of preserving the status quo. Britain, however, viewed the alliance solely as a means of guarding against renewed French aggression. It did not consider intervention in the domestic affairs of other nations to be in its own interest.

A revolution also failed in Russia. During the Napoleonic wars and the occupation of France, Russian officers were introduced to French ideas. Contrasting French liberal ideas and ways with Russian autocracy, some officers resolved to change conditions in Russia. Like their Western counterparts, they organized secret societies and disseminated liberal ideas within Russia. When Alexander I died, these liberal officers struck. But representing only a fraction of the aristocracy and with no mass following among the soldiers, they had no chance of success. Their uprising in December 1825 was easily smashed by the new tsar, Nicholas I, and the leaders were severely punished. To prevent Western ideas from infiltrating his realm, Nicholas imposed rigid censorship and organized the Third Section, a secret police force, which spied on suspected subversives. The Decembrists had failed, but their courage would inspire future opponents of tsarist autocracy.

The revolutions in Spain, Italy, and Russia failed, but the Concert of Europe also suffered setbacks. Stimulated by the ideals of the French Revolution, the Greeks revolted against their Turkish rulers in 1821. Although the Turkish sultan was the legitimate ruler, Russia, France, and Britain aided the Greek revolutionaries, for they were Christians and the Turks were Muslims. Moreover, pro-Greek sentiments were very strong among educated western Europeans, who had studied the literature and history of ancient Greece and viewed the Greeks as struggling to regain their ancestral freedom. Not only the pressure of public opinion, but also the fear of Russian motives led Britain to join in the intervention. If Russia carried out its intention of aiding the Greeks on its own, no doubt the Russian bear would never release Greece from its hug. Britain could not permit this extension of Russian power in the eastern Mediterranean. Despite Metternich's objections, Britain, France, and Russia took joint action against the Turks.

In 1829, Greece gained its independence. The Metternich system, which aimed to preserve the territorial settlements made at Vienna and to protect traditional and legitimate rulers against liberal and nationalist revolutions, had been breached. The success of the Greeks heartened liberals in other lands.

Revolutions, 1830–1832

After Napoleon's defeat, a Bourbon king, Louis XVIII (1814–1824), ascended the throne of France. Recognizing that the French people would not accept a return to the Old Order, Louis pursued a moderate course. Although his pseudoconstitution, the Charter, declared that the king's power rested on divine right, it acknowledged that citizens possessed fundamental rights: freedom of thought and religion and equal treatment under the law. It also set up a two-house parliament. But peasants, urban workers, and most bourgeois could not meet the property requirements for voting. Louis XVIII was resisted by diehard aristocrats, or *ultras,* who wanted to erase the past twenty-five years of French history and restore the power and privileges of church and aristocracy. Their leader was the king's younger brother, the comte d'Artois, who, after Louis's death in 1824, ascended the throne as Charles X (1824–1830).

The new government aroused the hostility of the bourgeoisie by indemnifying the émigrés for the property they had lost during the Revolution, censoring the press, and giving the church greater control over education. In the election of 1830, the liberal opposition to Charles X won a decisive victory. Charles responded with the July Ordinances, which dissolved the newly elected Chamber of Deputies; the ordinances also deprived rich

LIBERTY LEADING THE PEOPLE, 1830, BY EUGENE DELACROIX (1799–1863). Early-nineteenth-century reformers found their rallying cry in liberty, a legacy of the French Revolution. In this painting, Delacroix, the leader of French romantic artists, glorifies liberty. (*Louvre/Réunion des Musées Nationaux.*)

bourgeois of the vote (less wealthy bourgeois did not have the vote) and severely curbed the press.

The bourgeoisie, students, and workers rebelled. They hoped to establish a republic, but the wealthy bourgeois who took control of the revolution feared republican radicalism. They offered the throne to the duc d'Orléans; Charles X abdicated and went into exile in Britain. The new king, Louis Philippe (1830–1848), never forgot that he owed his throne to the upper bourgeois. And the Parisian workers who had fought for a republic and economic reforms to alleviate poverty felt betrayed by the outcome, as did the still-disenfranchised petty bourgeois.

The Revolution of 1830 in France set off shock waves in Belgium, Poland, and Italy. The Congress of Vienna had assigned Catholic Belgium to Protestant Holland. From the outset, the Belgians had protested. Stirred by the events in Paris, Belgian patriots proclaimed their independence from Holland and established a liberal government. Inspired by the uprisings in France and Belgium, Polish students, intellectuals, and army officers took up arms against their Russian overlords. The revolutionaries wanted to restore Polish independence, a dream that poets, musicians, and intellectuals had kept alive. Polish courage, however, was no match for Russian might, and Warsaw fell in 1831. The tsar took savage revenge on the revolutionaries. In 1831–32, Austrian forces again extinguished a revolution in Italy. As in Poland, revolutionary leaders in Italy failed to stir the great peasant masses to the cause of Italian independence and unity.

THE RISE OF REFORM IN BRITAIN

Britain was the freest state in Europe in the early decades of the nineteenth century, but it was far from democratic. A constitutional monarchy, with many limits on the powers of king and state, Britain was nonetheless dominated by aristocrats. Landed aristocrats controlled both the House of Lords and the House of Commons—the Lords because they constituted its membership and the Commons because they patronized or sponsored men favorable to their interests. The vast majority of people, from the middle class as well as from the working class, could not vote. Many towns continued to be governed by corrupt groups. New industrial towns were not allowed to elect representatives to Parliament; often lacking a town organization, they could not even govern themselves effectively.

The social separation of noble and commoner was not as rigid in Britain as on the Continent. Younger sons of aristocrats did not inherit titles and were therefore obliged to make careers in law, business, the military, and the church. The upper and middle classes mingled much more freely than on the Continent, and the wealthiest merchants tended to buy lands, titles, and husbands for their daughters. Nonetheless, Parliament, the courts, local government, the established Anglican church, the monarch—all were part of a social and political system dominated by aristocratic interests and values. This domination had changed little despite the vast changes in social and economic structure that had taken place in the process of industrialization during the second half of the eighteenth century.

Some members of Parliament urged timely reforms. In 1828, Parliament repealed a seventeenth-century act that in effect barred Catholics and Nonconformists (non-Anglican Protestants) from government positions and from universities. In 1833, slavery was abolished within the British Empire. (The slave trade had been abolished earlier.) The Municipal Corporations Act (1835) granted towns and cities greater authority over their affairs; it created local governments that could begin to solve some problems of urbanization and industrialization. These municipal corporations could institute reforms such as sanitation, which Parliament encouraged by passing the first Public Health Act in 1848.

Increasingly, reform centered on extending suffrage and on enfranchising the new industrial towns. Middle-class men, and even workers, hoped to gain the right to vote. Because of population shifts, some sparsely populated regions, called *rotten boroughs,* sent representatives to the House of Commons, while many densely populated factory towns had little or no representation. Often a single important landowner controlled many seats in the Commons. Since voting was public, it made intimidation possible, and candidates frequently tried to influence voters with drinks, food, and even money.

Bitter feelings built up during the campaign for the Reform Bill of 1832. The House of Commons passed the bill to extend suffrage by some 200,000 men, almost double the number then entitled to vote. The House of Lords, however, refused to pass the bill. There were riots and strikes in many cities, and mass meetings, both of workers and of the middle class, took place all over the country. King William IV (1830–1837) became convinced, along with many politicians, that the situation was potentially revolutionary. To defuse it, he threatened to increase the number of the bill's supporters in the House of Lords by creating new peers. This threat brought reluctant peers into line, and the bill was passed. The Reform Act of 1832 extended the suffrage to the middle class and made the House of Commons more representative. The rotten boroughs lost their seats, which were granted to towns. Suffrage did not extend to workers, however, because there were high property qualifications.

During the 1830s and 1840s, reformers called Chartists agitated for democratic measures, such as universal manhood suffrage, the secret ballot, salaries and the abolition of property qualifications for members of Parliament, and annual elections of Parliament. The Chartists came from the ranks of both intellectual radicals and workers. Their platform remained the democratic reform program for the rest of the century, long after the death of Chartism itself at midcentury. All of the Chartists' demands, except annual elections for members of Parliament, were eventually realized.

The last political effort by the Chartists was led by Feargus O'Connor, a charismatic Irishman, who organized a mass demonstration to present a huge petition of six demands to Parlia-

CHARTIST CONVENTION. Chartists pressing for democratic reforms, April 1848. (*Illustrated London News, April 15, 1848.*)

ment in 1848. The cabinet ignored the great charter, which had signatures of at least two million names. The movement died out just as most of Europe burst into revolution. The working-class leadership of Chartism turned away from political programs almost exclusively to economic activity, such as trade unions, which could bring immediate benefits to workers.

Unlike the continental states, England avoided revolution. British politicians held that the reason was that they made timely reforms in the 1830s and 1840s and this lesson should guide the state in the future. British parliamentary govenment came to be the model of liberal, progressive, and stable politics, a symbol for all those who argued for reform rather than revolution. In the rest of Europe in 1848, however, such arguments were meeting with little success.

Revolutions of 1848: France

In 1848, often called *the year of revolution,* uprisings for political liberty and nationhood took place throughout Europe. The economic crisis of the previous two years had intensified unrest. Food riots broke out in many places. The decimation of the potato crop by disease and of the grain harvest by drought had caused terrible food shortages. Furthermore, a financial crisis precipitated by overspeculation had caused business failures, unemployment, and reduced wages. The common people blamed their governments for their misery and sought redress. Doubtless, economic hardship aggravated discontent with the existing regimes. But "it was the absence of liberty," concludes the historian Jacques Droz, "which . . . was most deeply resented by the peoples of Europe and led them to take up arms."[1]

The February Revolution

An uprising in Paris set in motion the revolutionary tidal wave that was to engulf much of Europe in 1848. The Revolution of 1830 had broken the back of the ultras in France. There would be no going back to the Old Regime. But King Louis Philippe and his ministers, moderates by temperament and philosophy, had no intention of going forward to democracy. A new law in 1831 broadened the franchise from fewer than 100,000 voters to 248,000 by 1846. Even so, only 3 percent of adult males qualified to vote.

The government of Louis Philippe was run by a small elite consisting of wealthy bourgeois bankers, merchants, and lawyers, as well as aristocrats who had abandoned the hope of restoring the Old Regime. This ruling elite championed the revolutionary ideas of equal treatment under the law and of careers open to talent, but fearing democracy, it blocked efforts to broaden the franchise. When the less wealthy bourgeoisie protested against the limited franchise, which still excluded professionals and small tradesmen, François Guizot, the leading minister, arrogantly proclaimed: "Get rich, then you can vote." The ruling elite had become a selfish, entrenched oligarchy, unresponsive to the aspirations of the rest of the nation. Intellectuals denounced the government for its narrow political base and voiced republican sentiments. To guard against republicanism and as a reaction to repeated attempts to assassinate the king, the government cracked down on radical societies and newspapers.

Radical republicans, or democrats, wanted to abolish monarchy and grant all men the vote. They had fought in the Revolution of 1830 but were disappointed with the results. Patriots and romantics, who looked back longingly on the glory days of Napoleon, also hated Louis Philippe's government. These French nationalists complained that the king, who dressed like a businessman and pursued a pacifist foreign policy, was not fit to lead a nation of patriots and warriors. Under Louis Philippe, they said, France could not realize its historic mission of liberating oppressed nationalities throughout Europe.

The strongest rumblings of discontent, barely heeded by the ruling elite, came from the laboring poor. Many French workers, still engaged mainly in pre–Industrial Revolution occupations, were literate and concerned with politics; they read the numerous books and newspapers that denounced social injustice and called for social change. Artisans and their families had participated in the great revolutionary outbreaks of 1789 and had defended the barricades in 1830. Favoring a democratic republic that would aid the common people, they felt betrayed by the regime of Louis Philippe, which had brought them neither political representation nor economic reform.

The few factory workers and the artisans in small workshops were becoming attracted to socialist thinkers who attacked capitalism and called for state programs to deal with poverty. Louis Blanc, a particularly popular socialist theorist, denounced capitalist competition and demanded that the government establish cooperative workshops. Owned by the workers themselves, these workshops would ensure employment for the jobless.

A poor harvest in 1846 and an international financial crisis in 1847, which drastically curtailed French factory production, aggravated the misery of the laboring poor. Prevented by law from striking, unable to meet the financial requirements for voting, and afflicted with unemployment, the urban workers wanted relief. Alexis de Tocqueville, in a speech before the Chamber of Deputies on January 29, 1848, captured the mood of the working class:

> *Do you not hear them repeating unceasingly that all that is above them is incapable and unworthy of governing them; that the present distribution of goods throughout the world is unjust; that property rests on a foundation which is not an equitable foundation? And do you not realize that when such opinions take root, when they spread in an almost universal manner, when they sink deeply into the masses, they are bound to bring with them*

> *sooner or later, I know not when nor how, a most formidable revolution?*
>
> *This, gentlemen, is my profound conviction: I believe that we are at this moment sleeping on a volcano. I am profoundly convinced of it.*[2]

The government, however, steadfastly refused to pass reforms. Its middle-class opponents sidestepped regulations against political assemblies and demonstrations by gathering at large banquets to protest. When the government foolishly tried to block future banquets, students and workers took to the streets in February 1848, denouncing Guizot and demanding reforms. Barricades went up. Attempting to defuse an explosive situation, Louis Philippe dismissed the unpopular Guizot. But the barricades, commanded by republicans, stayed, and the antigovernment demonstrations continued. When soldiers, confused by a shot that had perhaps gone off accidentally, fired directly into a crowd and killed fifty-two Parisians, the situation got out of hand. Unable to pacify the enraged Parisians, Louis Philippe abdicated. France became a republic, and the people of Paris were jubilant.

The June Days: Revolution of the Oppressed

Except for one workingman, the leadership of the provisional government established in February consisted of bourgeois. The new leaders were committed to political democracy, but only some, notably the socialist Louis Blanc, favored social reforms. Most of the ministers had little understanding of or sympathy for the plight of the laboring poor, and they viewed socialist ideas as a threat to private property. Although they considered it a sacred duty to fight for the rights of the individual, they did not include freedom from hunger and poverty among these rights. The middle class saw itself as separate from the laboring poor by reason of occupation and wealth. To the bourgeoisie, the workers were dangerous creatures, "the wild ones," "the vile mob."

Meanwhile, workers who could find jobs labored twelve and fourteen hours a day under brutalizing conditions. In some districts, one out of three children died before the age of five. Everywhere in France, beggars, paupers, prostitutes, and criminals were evidence of the struggle to survive.

The urban poor were desperate for jobs and bread. Socialist intellectuals, sympathetic to the plight of the workers, proposed that the state organize producer cooperatives run by workers. Some wanted the state to take over insurance companies, railroads, mines, and other key industries. To the property owners of all classes, such schemes smacked of madness.

The middle-class leaders of the new republic gave all adult males the vote and abolished censorship; however, their attempts to ease the distress of the urban poor were insincere and halfhearted. The government limited the workday to ten hours and legalized labor unions, but it failed to cope effectively with unemployment. The socialist Louis Blanc called for the creation of producer cooperatives in order to guarantee employment for the city poor. The republic responded by establishing national workshops, which provided some employment on public works projects. Most workers, however, received wages for doing nothing. Drawn by the promise of work, tens of thousands of laborers left the provinces for Paris, swelling the ranks of the unemployed. The national workshops provided work, food, and medical benefits for some of the unemployed. But to the workers, this was a feeble effort to deal with their monumental distress. To the property-owning peasantry and bourgeoisie, the national workshops were a waste of government funds. They viewed the workshops as nests of working-class radicalism, where plans were being hatched to change the economic system and seize their property.

For their participation in the February uprising against Louis Philippe, the workers had obtained meager benefits. When the government closed the workshops, working-class hostility and despair turned to open rebellion. Again, barricades went up in the streets of Paris.

The June Revolution in Paris was unlike previous uprisings in France. It was a revolt against poverty and a cry for the redistribution of property; as such, it foreshadowed the great social

THE BARRICADES. Parisian revolutionaries behind barricades clash with the army. (*Corbis-Bettmann.*)

revolutions of the twentieth century. The workers stood alone. To the rest of the nation, they were barbarians attacking civilized society. Aristocrats, bourgeois, and peasants feared that no one's property would be safe if the revolution succeeded. From hundreds of miles away, Frenchmen flocked to Paris to crush what they considered to be the madness within their midst.

Although they had no leaders, the workers showed remarkable courage. Women and children fought alongside men behind the barricades. After three days of vicious street fighting and atrocities on both sides, the army extinguished the revolt. Some 1,460 lives had been lost, including four generals. The June Days left deep scars on French society. For many years, workers would never forget that the rest of France had united against them; the rest of France would remain terrified of working-class radicalism.

In December 1848, the French people, in overwhelming numbers, elected Louis Napoleon—nephew of the great emperor—president of the Second Republic. They were attracted to the magic of Louis Napoleon's name, and they expected him to prevent future working-class disorders. The election, in which all adult males could vote, demonstrated that most Frenchmen were socially conservative; they were unsympathetic to working-class poverty and deeply suspicious of socialist programs.

REVOLUTIONS OF 1848: GERMANY, AUSTRIA, AND ITALY

Like an epidemic, the fever of revolution that broke out in Paris in February raced across the Continent. Liberals, excluded from participation in political life, fought for parliaments and constitutions; many liberals were also nationalists who wanted unity or independence for their nations. Some liberals had a utopian vision of a new Europe of independent and democratic states. In this vision, reactionary rulers would no longer stifle individual liberty; no longer would a people be denied the right of nationhood.

The German States: Liberalism Defeated

After the Congress of Vienna, Germany consisted of a loose confederation of thirty-nine independent states, of which Austria and Prussia were the most powerful. Jealous of their independence and determined to preserve their absolute authority, the ruling princes detested liberal and nationalist ideals. In the southern German states, which had been more strongly influenced by the French Revolution, princes did grant constitutions and establish parliaments to retain the loyalty of their subjects. But even in these states, the princes continued to hold the reins of authority.

The German nationalism that had emerged during the French occupation intensified during the restoration (the post-Napoleonic period), as intellectuals, inspired in part by the ideas of the Romantic Movement, insisted that Germans, who shared a common language and culture, should also be united politically. During the restoration, the struggle for German unity and liberal reforms continued to be waged primarily by students, professors, writers, lawyers, and other educated people. The great mass of people, knowing only loyalty to their local prince, remained unmoved by appeals for national unity.

The successful revolt against Louis Philippe, hostility against absolute princes, and an economic crisis combined to produce uprisings in the capital cities of the German states in March 1848. Everywhere, liberals clamored for constitutions, parliamentary government, freedom of thought, and an end to police intimidation. Some called for the creation of a unified Germany governed by a national parliament and headed by a constitutional monarch. The poor joined the struggle. The great depression of the 1840s had aggravated the misery of the German peasant and urban masses, and as the pressures of hunger and unemployment worsened, their discontent exploded into revolutionary fervor.

In the spring of 1848, downtrodden artisans, facing severe competition from the new factories, served as the revolution's shock troops. Unable to compete with the new machines, they saw their incomes fall and their work decrease. Skilled weavers working at home earned far less than factory hands, and some unemployed craftsmen were forced to take factory jobs, which they regarded as a terrible loss of status. These craftsmen wanted to restrict the growth of factories, curtail capitalist competition, and restore the power of the guilds, which had given them security and status.

Having lost hope that the absolute princes would aid them, craftsmen gave their support to bourgeois liberals, who, without this support, could not challenge the throne or wrest power from the aristocrats. In many German states, the actions of the embittered urban craftsmen determined the successful outcome of the insurrections. (Factory workers in the emerging industries showed no enthusiasm for revolution, despite the appeals of radical socialists.) Adding to the discomfort of the ruling princes was rioting in the countryside by peasants, goaded by crop failure, debt, and oppressive demands from the aristocracy.

Terrified that these disturbances would lead to anarchy, the princes made concessions to the liberals, whom they previously had censored, jailed, and exiled. During March and April 1848, the traditional rulers in Baden, Württemberg, Bavaria, Saxony, Hanover, and other states replaced reactionary ministers with liberals, eased censorship, established jury systems, framed constitutions, formed parliaments, and ended peasant obligations to lords.

In Prussia, tensions between the army and Berliners exploded into violence. Unable to subdue the insurgents, the army urged bombarding the city with artillery. Frederick William IV opposed the idea and ordered the troops to leave Berlin. The insurgents had won the first round. The Prussian king, like the other German princes, had to agree to the formation of a parliament and the admission of prominent liberals into the government.

But the triumph of the liberals in Prussia and the other German states was not secure. Although reforms liberalized the governments of the German states, the insurrections had not toppled the ruling dynasties. Moreover, the alliance between the bourgeois and the artisans was tenuous. The

Profile

Carl Schurz

Hulton Archive/Getty Images.

In 1848, Carl Schurz (1829–1906) was a student at the University of Bonn and felt destined for a career as a professor of history. To Schurz and his liberal-minded fellow students the news of the uprising in France seemed like the harbinger of an opportunity for reform in Germany as well. Under the guidance of one of his professors, Gottfried Kinkel, Schurz discovered his gifts for journalism and oratory and, at the age of nineteen, became a leader of revolutionary activities in Bonn. When the reactionary powers who at first granted concessions struck back at the revolutionaries, he took up arms in a futile effort to defend the short-lived democratic freedoms.

From a besieged city surrounded by Prussian forces, Schurz escaped through the sewers and eventually reached Switzerland. There he might have remained, but, on hearing that Professor Kinkel had been condemned to life imprisonment, he returned to Germany under an assumed name and plotted a daring rescue. The successful exploit, the flight through Germany, and a stormy sea voyage to Scotland made him a romantic hero throughout Germany.

artisans' violence frightened the property-owning middle class, which sought only moderate political reforms, preferably through peaceful means. In addition, the middle class saw restoration of the guild system, with its prohibitions on output and regulation of prices, as a reactionary economic measure.

Liberals took advantage of their successes in Prussia and other German states to form a national assembly charged with the task of creating a unified and liberal Germany. Representatives from all the German states attended the assembly, which met at Frankfurt. The delegates, including many articulate lawyers and professionals, came predominantly from the educated middle class; only a handful were drawn from the lower classes. After many long debates, the Frankfurt Assembly approved a federation of German states; it would have a parliament and would be headed by the Prussian king. Austria, with its many non-German nationalities, would be excluded from the federal union. Some radical democrats wanted to proclaim a German republic, but they were an ineffective minority. Most delegates were moderate liberals who feared that universal suffrage and the abolition of monarchy would lead to plebeian rule and the destruction of the social order. The deputies selected Frederick

England had become a haven for European revolutionaries, and Schurz lived there for a year and married. Despairing of ever returning to Germany, he emigrated to the United States in 1852. Speaking no English, his wife ill, his country and profession closed to him, he nearly gave way to depression. But he taught himself English and threw himself into the antislavery cause and Republican politics. His oratorical gifts had not deserted him, and in 1858 he campaigned for Abraham Lincoln in both English and German.

Lincoln became his friend and appointed Schurz as Minister to Spain in 1861. Within a year he returned to support emancipation and to fight in the Union army. After the Civil War he turned to journalism while remaining engaged in politics. In 1869 he was elected from Missouri to the U.S. Senate, and he joined the cabinet of President Rutherford B. Hayes as secretary of the interior in 1877. In this post he worked for the enlightened treatment of Indians and for civil service reform. After leaving the cabinet, he resumed his career as a journalist with a reputation as a veteran statesman, a political philosopher, and a distinguished German American.

William as emperor of the new Germany, but the Prussian king refused; he would never wear a crown given to him by common people during a period of revolutionary agitation.

While the delegates debated, the ruling princes recovered from the first shock of revolution and ordered their armies to crush the revolutionaries. The February Revolution in Paris had shown European liberals that authority could be challenged successfully; the June Days, however, had shown the authorities that revolutionaries could be beaten by professional soldiers. Moreover, the German middle class, frightened by lower-class agitation and unsympathetic to the artisans' demands to restrict capitalism and restore guilds, was losing its enthusiasm for revolution, and so, too, were the artisans. The disintegration of the alliance between middle-class liberals and urban artisans deprived the revolutionaries of mass support. A revival of the Old Order would not face much resistance.

In Prussia, a determined Frederick William ordered his troops to reoccupy Berlin. In March, the citizens of Berlin had fought against the king's troops, but in November, no barricades went up in Berlin. Prussian forces also assisted the other German states in crushing the new parliaments. The masses of workers and peasants did not fight to save the liberal governments, which fell one by one. A small minority of democrats resisted, particularly in Baden; many of these revolutionaries died in the fighting or were executed.

German liberalism had failed to unite Germany or to create a constitutional government dominated by the middle class. Liberalism, never securely rooted in Germany, was discredited. In the following decades, many Germans, identifying liberalism with failure, turned to authoritarian Prussia for leadership in the struggle for unification. The fact that authoritarians hostile to the spirit of parliamentary government eventually united Germany had deep implications for future German and European history.

Austria: Hapsburg Dominance

The Hapsburg Empire, the product of dynastic marriage and inheritance, had no common nationality or language; it was held together only by the reigning Hapsburg dynasty, its army, and its bureaucracy. The ethnic composition of the empire was enormously complex. Germans dominated; concentrated principally in Austria, they constituted about 25 percent of the empire's population. The Magyars predominated in the Hungarian lands of the empire. The great bulk of the population consisted of Slavs: Czechs, Poles, Slovaks, Slovenes, Croats, Serbs, and Ruthenians. There were also Italians in northern Italy and Romanians in Transylvania. The Hapsburg dynasty, aided by the army and the German-dominated civil service, prevented this multinational empire from collapsing into anarchy.

Metternich, it is often said, suffered from a "dissolution complex": he understood that the new forces of nationalism and liberalism could break up the Austrian Empire. Liberal ideas could lead Hapsburg subjects to challenge the authority of the emperor, and nationalist feelings could cause the different peoples of the empire to rebel against German domination and Hapsburg rule. To keep these ideas from infecting Austrian subjects, Metternich's police imposed strict censorship, spied on professors, and expelled from the universities students caught reading forbidden books. Despite Metternich's political police, the universities remained hotbeds of liberalism.

In 1848, revolutions spread throughout the Austrian Empire, starting in Vienna. Aroused by the abdication of Louis Philippe, Viennese liberals denounced Hapsburg absolutism and demanded a constitution, relaxation of censorship, and restrictions on the police. The government responded hesitantly and with limited force to the demonstrations of students and workers, and many parts of Vienna fell to the revolutionaries. The authorities used force that was strong enough to incense the insurrectionists and create martyrs but not strong enough to subdue them. Confused and intimidated by the revolutionaries, the government allowed freedom of the press, accepted Metternich's resignation, and promised a constitution. The Constitutional Assembly was convened and in August voted the abolition of serfdom. At the same time that the Viennese insurgents were tasting the heady wine of reform, revolts in other parts of the empire—Bohemia, Hungary, and northern Italy—added to the distress of the monarchy.

But the revolutionaries' victory was only temporary, and the defeat of the Old Order only illusory; the Hapsburg government soon began to recover its balance. The first government victory came with the crushing of the Czechs in Bohemia. In 1848, Czech nationalists wanted the Austrian Empire reconstructed along federal lines that would give Czechs equal standing with Germans. The Czechs called for a constitution for Bohemia and equal status for the Czech language in all official business. In June, students and destitute workers engaged in violent demonstrations, which frightened the middle and upper classes—both Czech and German. General Alfred zu Windischgrätz bombarded Prague, the capital of Bohemia, into submission and reestablished Hapsburg control.

In October 1848, Hapsburg authorities ordered the army to bombard Vienna. Against the regular army, the courageous but disorganized and divided students and workers had little hope. Imperial troops broke into the city, overcame resistance, and executed several of the revolutionary leaders. In March 1849, the Hapsburg leadership replaced the liberal constitution drafted by the popularly elected Constitutional Assembly with a more conservative one drawn up by its own ministers.

The most serious threat to the Hapsburg realm came from the Magyars in Hungary. Some twelve million people lived in Hungary, five million of whom were Magyars. The other nationalities comprised South Slavs (Croats and Serbs) and Romanians. The upper class consisted chiefly of Magyar landowners, who enjoyed tax exemptions and other feudal privileges. Drawn to liberal and modern ideas and fearful of peasant uprisings, some Hungarian nobles pressed for an end to serfdom and the tax exemptions of the nobility. Louis Kossuth (1802–1894), a member of the lower nobility, called for both social reform and a deepening of national consciousness. The great landowners, determined to retain their ancient privileges, resisted liberalization.

Led by Kossuth, the Magyars demanded local autonomy for Hungary. Hungary would remain within the Hapsburg Empire but would have its own constitution and national army and would control its own finances. The Hungarian leadership introduced liberal reforms: suffrage for all males who could speak Magyar and owned some property, freedom of religion, freedom of the press, the termination of serfdom, and the end of the privileges of nobles and church. Within a few weeks, the Hungarian parliament changed Hungary from a feudal to a modern liberal state.

But the Hungarian leaders' nationalist dreams towered above their liberal ideals. The Magyars intended to incorporate lands inhabited by Croats, Slovaks, and Romanians into their state (Magyars considered these lands an integral part of historic Hungary) and to transform these peoples into Hungarians. As the historian Hugh Seton-Watson has written,

> *Kossuth and his friends genuinely believed that they were doing the non-Hungarians a*

> *kindness by giving them a chance of becoming absorbed in the superior Hungarian culture. To refuse this kindness was nationalist fanaticism; to impose it by force was to promote progress. The suggestion that Romanians, Slovaks, or Serbs were nations, with a national culture of their own, was simply ridiculous nonsense.*[3]

In the spring of 1849, the Hungarians renounced their allegiance to the Hapsburgs and proclaimed Hungary an independent state, with Kossuth as president.

The Hapsburg rulers took advantage of the ethnic animosities inside and outside Hungary. They encouraged Romanians and Croats to resist the new Hungarian government. When Hapsburg forces moved against the Magyars, they were joined by an army of Croats, whose nationalist aspirations had been flouted by the Magyars. (The Slovaks fought alongside the Magyars.) Emperor Francis Joseph, who had recently ascended the Hapsburg throne, also appealed to Tsar Nicholas I for help. The tsar complied, fearing that a successful revolt by the Hungarians might lead the Poles to rise up against their Russian overlords. The Hungarians fought with extraordinary courage but were overcome by superior might. Kossuth and other rebel leaders went into exile; about one hundred rebel leaders were executed. Thus, through division and alliance, the Hapsburgs prevented the disintegration of the empire.

Italy: Continued Fragmentation

Italian nationalists, eager to end the humiliation of Hapsburg occupation and domination and to unite the disparate states into a unified and liberal nation, also rose in rebellion in 1848. Revolution broke out in Sicily six weeks before the February Revolution in Paris. Bowing to the revolutionaries' demands, King Ferdinand II of Naples granted a liberal constitution. The grand duke of Tuscany, King Charles Albert of Piedmont-Sardinia, and Pope Pius IX, ruler of the Papal States, also felt compelled to introduce liberal reforms.

Then the revolution spread to the Hapsburg lands in the north. The citizens of Milan, in Lombardy, built barricades and stood ready to fight the Austrian oppressor. When the Austrian soldiers attacked, they were fired on from nearby windows. From rooftops, Italians hurled stones and boiling water. After "Five Glorious Days" (March 18–22) of street fighting, the Austrians withdrew. The people of Milan had liberated their city. On March 22, the citizens of Venice declared their city free of Austria and set up a republic. King Charles Albert, who hoped to acquire Lombardy and Venetia, declared war on Austria. Intimidated by the insurrections, the ruling princes of the Italian states and Hapsburg Austria had lost the first round.

But soon everywhere in Italy the forces of reaction recovered and reasserted their authority. The Austrians defeated the Sardinians and reoccupied Milan, and Ferdinand II crushed the revolutionaries in the south. Revolutionary disorders in Rome had forced Pope Pius IX to flee in November 1848; in February 1849, the revolutionaries proclaimed Rome "a pure democracy with the glorious title of the Roman Republic." Heeding the pope's call for assistance, Louis Napoleon attacked Rome, destroyed the infant republic, and allowed Pope Pius to return. The last city to fall to the reactionaries was Venice, which the Austrians subjected to a merciless bombardment. After six weeks, the Venetians, weakened by starvation and cholera, surrendered. Reactionary princes still ruled in Italy; the Hapsburg occupation persisted in the north. Italy was still a fragmented nation.

Revolutions of 1848: An Assessment

The revolutions of 1848 in central Europe and Italy began with much promise but ended in defeat. The revolutionaries' initial success was due less to their strength than to the governments' hesitancy to use their superior force. The reactionary rulers overcame their paralysis, however, and moved decisively to smash the revolutions.

Boundaries after Congress of Vienna, 1815
Boundary of German Confederation
Centers of revolution, 1820s
Centers of revolution, 1830s
Centers of popular unrest in Britain, 1815–1848
Principal states affected by revolution, 1848
Centers of revolution, 1848
0 200 400 Km.
0 200 400 Mi.
SWEDEN AND NORWAY
St. Petersburg
Baltic Sea
North Sea
DENMARK
RUSSIAN EMPIRE
GREAT BRITAIN
IRELAND
Glasgow
Manchester
Birmingham
Bristol
London
KINGDOM OF THE NETHERLANDS
BEL.
Brussels
PRUSSIA
HANOVER
Posen
Berlin
Warsaw
POLAND
Dresden
Frankfurt
Prague
BOHEMIA
Brno
Cracow
Lemberg
ATLANTIC OCEAN
Paris
BAVARIA
Munich
Vienna
Salzburg
Pressburg
AUSTRIAN EMPIRE
Debrecen
Budapest
HUNGARY
Kolozsvar
Blaj
Jassy
FRANCE
SWITZ.
Lyons
La Coruña
Oviedo
Turin
Milan
Venice
Agram
Bucharest
Black Sea
Genoa
Modena
Pamplona
Florence
Macerata
PAPAL STATES
Saragossa
KINGDOM OF PIEDMONT SARDINIA
Madrid
Barcelona
Rome
Bari
Lisbon
PORTUGAL
SPAIN
Naples
Salerno
Valencia
OTTOMAN EMPIRE
KINGDOM OF THE TWO SICILIES
GREECE (Independence, 1829)
Cadiz
Mediterranean Sea
Palermo
Reggio
Sicily
Morea

The courage of the revolutionaries was no match for regular armies. Thousands were killed and imprisoned; many fled to America.

Class divisions weakened the revolutionaries in central Europe. The union between middle-class liberals and workers, which brought success in the opening stages of the revolutions, was only temporary. Bourgeois liberals favoring political reforms—constitution, parliament, and protection of basic rights—grew fearful of the laboring poor, who demanded social reforms—jobs and bread. To the bourgeois, the workers were radical Jacobins, a mob driven by dark instincts. When the workers engaged in revolutionary violence, a terrified middle class deserted the cause of revolution or joined the old elites in subduing the workers. These class divisions showed that the liberals' concern for political reforms—the extension of suffrage and parliamentary government—did not satisfy workers who were mired in poverty. The events of 1848 also showed that social issues—the demands of the working class for an alleviation of their misery—would become a prime consideration of European political life in the generations to come.

Intractable nationalist animosities helped to destroy all the revolutionary movements against absolutism in central Europe. In many cases, the different nationalities hated each other more than they hated the reactionary rulers. Hungarian revolutionaries dismissed the nationalist yearnings of the South Slavs and Romanians living in Hungary, who in turn helped the Hapsburg dynasty to extinguish the nascent Hungarian state. The Germans of Bohemia resisted Czech demands for self-government and the equality of the Czech language with German. When German liberals at the Frankfurt Assembly debated the boundary lines of a united Germany, the problem of Prussia's Polish territories emerged. In 1848, Polish patriots wanted to recreate the Polish nation, but German delegates at the convention, by an overwhelming majority, opposed returning the Polish lands seized by Prussia in the late eighteenth century. In addressing his fellow delegates, Wilhelm Jordan described the Poles as a people "which does not possess the same measure of human content as is given to the German kind" and denounced those Germans who would permit their kinsmen to live under Polish rule as traitors to their people. Then he justified Germany's claim to the Polish lands:

> *It is high time for us to wake up . . . to a healthy national egoism . . . which places the welfare and honor of the fatherland above everything else. . . . Frankly, the rules of theoretical justice never seem more pitiful to me than when they presume to fix the fate of nations. . . . No, I admit without blinking, our right is no other than the right of the stronger, the right of conquest.*[4]

Before 1848, democratic idealists envisioned the birth of a new Europe of free people and liberated nations. The revolutions in central Europe showed that nationalism and liberalism were not natural allies and that nationalists were often indifferent to the rights of other peoples. Disheartened by these nationalist antagonisms, John Stuart Mill, the English liberal statesman and philosopher, lamented that "the sentiment of nationality so far outweighs the love of liberty that the people are willing to abet their rulers in crushing the liberty and independence of any people not of their race or language."[5] In the revolutions of 1848, concludes the British historian Lewis Namier, "'nationality,' the passionate creed of the intellectuals, invades the politics of central and east-central Europe, and with 1848 starts the Great European War of every nation against its neighbors."[6]

Even though the liberal and nationalist aims of the revolutionaries were not realized, liberal gains were not insignificant. All Frenchmen obtained the right to vote; serfdom was abolished in Austria; and parliaments were established in Prussia and other German states.

Despite the establishment of parliaments, however, 1848 was a crucial defeat for German liberalism. Controlled by monarchs and aristocrats hostile to the democratic principles of 1848, the

◀ *Map 23.3* Europe's Age of Revolutions
In the decades after the Vienna settlement, Europe experienced a wave of revolution based chiefly on liberalism and nationalism.

postrevolutionary governments, using the methods of a police state, intimidated and persecuted liberals, large numbers of whom were forced to emigrate. The failure of the revolution and the reactionary policies of the postrevolutionary governments thwarted the growth of a democratic parliamentary system in Germany. Discredited by the failure of 1848, weakened by government intimidation and the loss of many liberals to emigration, and less committed to liberal ideals—which brought no gains in 1848—the German middle class in the period immediately after 1848 became apolitical or were willing to sacrifice liberal principles in order to achieve a united and powerful Germany. Nationalism would supersede liberalism as the principal concern of the German middle class. The failure of liberalism to take strong root in Germany would have dire consequences in the early twentieth century.

In later decades, liberal reforms, including legal guarantees of basic rights, would be introduced peacefully in several European countries—in Germany too, but there power still remained in the hands of preindustrial semifeudal elites, not with the middle class—for the failure of the revolutions of 1848 convinced many people, including liberals, that popular uprisings were ineffective ways of changing society. The Age of Revolution, initiated by the French Revolution of 1789, had ended.

Notes

1. Jacques Droz, *Europe Between Revolutions, 1815–1848* (New York: Harper Torchbooks, 1967), p. 248.
2. *The Recollections of Alexis de Tocqueville*, trans. Alexander Teixeira de Mattos (Cleveland, Ohio: Meridian Books, 1969), pp. 11–12.
3. Hugh Seton-Watson, *Nations and States* (Boulder, Colo.: Westview Press, 1977), p. 162.
4. Quoted in J. L. Talmon, *Political Messianism: The Romantic Phase* (New York: Praeger, 1960), p. 482.
5. Quoted in Hans Kohn, *Nationalism: Its Meaning and History* (Princeton, N.J.: Van Nostrand, 1965), pp. 51–52.
6. Lewis Namier, *1848: The Revolution of the Intellectuals* (Garden City, N.Y.: Doubleday, Anchor, 1964), p. 38.

Suggested Reading

Droz, Jacques, *Europe Between Revolutions* (1967). A fine survey of the period 1815–1848.

Duveau, Georges, *1848: The Making of a Revolution* (1967). France in 1848.

Fasel, George, *Europe in Upheaval: The Revolutions of 1848* (1970). A good introduction.

Fejtö, François, ed., *The Opening of an Era: 1848* (1973). Articles by eminent historians.

Langer, W. L., *Political and Social Upheaval, 1832–1852* (1969). A volume in *The Rise of Modern Europe* series; rich interpretation.

Robertson, Priscilla, *Revolutions of 1848* (1960). Vividly portrays events and personalities.

Sigmann, Jean, *1848: The Romantic and Democratic Revolutions in Europe* (1970). A useful survey.

Sperber, Jonathan, *The European Revolution, 1848–1851* (1994). A comprehensive overview.

Stearns, Peter N., *1848: The Revolutionary Tide in Europe* (1974). Strong on social factors.

Talmon, J. L., *Romanticism and Revolt* (1967). Forces shaping European history from 1815 to 1848.

Review Questions

1. What was Metternich's attitude toward the French Revolution? Toward Napoleon?
2. Assess the accomplishments and failures of the Congress of Vienna.
3. Between 1820 and 1832, where were revolu-

tions suppressed, and how? Where were revolutions successful, and why?

4. What reforms were introduced in Britain between 1815 and 1848?
5. What was the significance of the June Days?
6. Why did the revolutions of 1848 fail in the German states, the Austrian Empire, and Italy?
7. What were the liberal gains in 1848? Why were liberals and nationalists disappointed?

Part Five

An Age of Contradiction: Progress and Breakdown

1848–1914

1850

1860

1870

1880

1890

1900

Politics and Society	Thought and Culture
Second Empire in France (1852–1870) Commodore Perry opens Japan to trade (1853) Crimean War (1853–1856) Unification of Italy (1859–1870)	Stowe, *Uncle Tom's Cabin* (1851–52) Dickens, *Hard Times* (1854) Flaubert, *Madame Bovary* (1856) Darwin, *Origin of Species* (1859) Mill, *On Liberty* (1859)
Civil War in the United States (1861–1865) Bismarck in power in Germany (1862–1890) Unification of Germany (1866–1871) Settlement of 1867 splits Hapsburg territories into Austria and Hungary Reform Bill of 1867 in Great Britain Opening of Suez Canal (1869)	Hugo, *Les Misérables* (1862) Marx, *Capital* (1867) Dostoevski, *The Idiot* (1868–69) Tolstoy, *War and Peace* (1863–1869) Mill, *The Subjection of Women* (1869)
Franco-Prussian War (1870–71) Third Republic in France (1870–1940) Serbs gain independence from Ottoman Turks (1878)	Impressionism in art (1860–1886): Manet, Monet, Pissaro, Degas, Renoir Darwin, *The Descent of Man* (1871) Nietzsche, *The Birth of Tragedy* (1872) Ibsen, *A Doll's House* (1879)
French fight Chinese over Indochina (1883–85) Berlin Conference on Africa (1884) Reform Bill of 1884 in Great Britain	Postimpressionism in art (1880s–1890s): Cézanne, Gauguin, van Gogh, Munch, Matisse Zola, *The Experimental Novel* (1880) Spencer, *The Man Versus the State* (1884) Nietzsche, *The Anti-Christ* (1888)
Dreyfus affair in France (1894–1906) Sino-Japanese War (1894–95) Spanish-American War (1898) Battle of Omdurman in the Sudan (1898) Boer War in South Africa (1899–1902)	Le Bon, *The Crowd* (1895) Chamberlain, *The Foundations of the Nineteenth Century* (1899) Bernstein, *Evolutionary Socialism* (1899) Durkheim, *Suicide* (1897)
Boxer Rebellion in China (1900) Russo-Japanese War (1904–05) Anglo-French Entente Cordiale (1904) Anglo-Russian Entente (1907) Congo declared a Belgian colony (1908) Mexican Revolution (1911)	Freud, *The Interpretation of Dreams* (1900) Cubism in art: Picasso, Braque Abstract art: Mondrian, Kandinsky, Duchamp Planck: quantum theory (1900) Lenin, *What Is To Be Done?* (1902) Einstein: theory of relativity (1905) Weber, *The Protestant Ethic and the Spirit of Capitalism* (1904–05) Sorel, *Reflections on Violence* (1908)

Chapter 24

Thought and Culture in the Mid-Nineteenth Century: Realism and Social Criticism

The Stone Breakers (1849), by Gustave Courbet, illustrates the concern of realists for an accurate depiction of the details of everyday life. (Bildarchiv Foto Marburg/Art Resource, NY.)

- **Realism and Naturalism**
- **Positivism**
- **Darwinism**
  Natural Selection
  Darwinism and Christianity
  Social Darwinism
- **Religion in a Secular Age**
- **Marxism**
  A Science of History
  Class Conflict
  Destruction of Capitalism
  Marxism's Appeal and Influence
  Critics of Marx
- **Anarchism**
  Pierre Joseph Proudhon
  Mikhail Bakunin
- **Liberalism in Transition**
  John Stuart Mill
  Thomas Hill Green
  Herbert Spencer: Rejection of State Intervention
- **Feminism: Extending the Principle of Equality**

The second half of the nineteenth century was marked by great progress in science, a surge in industrialism, and a continuing secularization of life and thought. The principal intellectual currents of the century's middle decades reflected these trends. Realism, positivism, Darwinism, Marxism, and liberalism all reacted against romantic, religious, and metaphysical interpretations of nature and society and focused on the empirical world. In one way or another, each movement derived from and expanded the Enlightenment tradition. Adherents of these movements relied on careful observation and strove for scientific accuracy. This emphasis on objective reality helped stimulate a growing criticism of social ills; for despite unprecedented material progress, reality was often sordid, somber, and depressing. In the last part of the century, reformers, motivated by an expansive liberalism, a socially committed Christianity, or both, pressed for the alleviation of social injustice.

Realism and Naturalism

Realism, the dominant movement in art and literature in the mid 1800s, opposed the romantic veneration of the inner life and romantic sentimentality. The romantics exalted passion and intuition, let their imaginations transport them to a medieval past, which they deemed idyllic, and sought subjective solitude amid nature's wonders. Realists, in contrast, turned their attention to the external world and concentrated on social conditions, contemporary manners, and the familiar details of everyday life. With clinical detachment and meticulous care, they analyzed how people actually looked, worked, and behaved.

Like scientists, realist writers and artists carefully investigated the empirical world. For example, Gustave Courbet (1819–1877), who exemplified realism in painting, sought to practice what he called a "living art." He painted common people and commonplace scenes: laborers breaking stones, peasants tilling the soil or returning from a fair, a country burial, wrestlers, bathers, family groups. In a matter-of-fact style that sought to reproduce the environment just as it is, without any attempt at glorification or deviation, realist artists also depicted floor scrapers, rag pickers, prostitutes, and beggars. Gustave Flaubert (1821–1880) said of *Madame Bovary,* his masterpiece of realist literature: "Art ought . . . to rise above personal feelings and nervous susceptibilities! It is time to give it the precision of the physical sciences by means of a pitiless method."[1] Émile de Vogüé, a nineteenth-century French writer, described realism as follows:

> *They [realists] have brought about an art of observation rather than of imagination, one which boasts that it observes life as it is in its wholeness and complexity with the least possible prejudice on the part of the artist. It takes men under ordinary conditions, shows characters in the course of their everyday existence, average and changing. Jealous of the rigour of scientific procedure, the writer proposes to instruct us by a perpetual analysis of feelings and of acts rather than to divert us or move us by intrigue and exhibition of the passions. . . . The new art seeks to imitate nature.*[2]

Romantic writers had written lyrics, for lyric poetry is the language of feeling. The realists' literary genre was the novel because it lends itself admirably to depicting human behavior and social conditions. Realist novels were often serialized in the inexpensive newspapers and magazines, which the many newly literate common people could read. Thus, the commoners' interests helped shape the novels' content. Seeking to portray reality as it is, realist writers frequently dealt with social abuses and the sordid aspects of human behavior and social life.

In his large output of novels, Honoré de Balzac (1799–1850) described how social and economic forces affected people's behavior. Another Frenchman, Eugène Sue, gave harrowing accounts of slum life and crime in his serialized novel, *Les Mystères de Paris* (1842–43). George Sand (a woman writing under a male pen name) portrayed the married woman as a victim in *Indiana* (1832). A reviewer praised the book for presenting

> *a true, living world, which is our world . . . characters and manners just as we can observe them around us, natural conversations, scenes in familiar settings, violent, uncommon passions, but sincerely felt or observed and such as are still aroused in many hearts, under the apparent uniformity and monotonous frivolity of our lives.*[3]

Many regard Gustave Flaubert's *Madame Bovary* (1856) as the quintessential realistic novel. It tells the story of Emma Bovary, a self-centered wife living in a drab French provincial town who, interpreting the world from the prism of the romantic stories she reads, yearns for luxury, excitement, and romance. Disillusioned with her marriage to her devoted, hard-working, but dull husband, whom she detests, Emma commits adultery.

In this work, Flaubert strove to remain detached from his characters. Unlike romantics, he was concerned not with revealing his own emotions or opinions but with the accurate depiction of characters, situations, and dialogue. His goal, he said, was a book in which "the personality of the author is *completely* absent." Commenting on the realism of *Madame Bovary,* a contemporary novelist noted that it "represents an obsession with description. Details are counted one by one, all are given equal value, every street, every house, every room, every book, every blade of grass is described in full."[4] Also described fully and in great clinical detail is Emma's death from poisoning.

Russian writers were among the leading realists. In *A Sportsman's Sketches* (1852), the novelist, dramatist, and short-story writer Ivan Turgenev (1818–1883) provided a true-to-life picture of Russian rural conditions, particularly the brutal life of serfs. In an unpolemical style, Turgenev showed that serfdom debased not only the serfs but also their masters, the rural nobility, who regarded serfs as barely human. In *War and Peace* (1863–1869), Leo Tolstoy (1828–1910) vividly described the manners and outlook of the Russian nobility and the tragedies that attended Napoleon's invasion of Europe. In *Anna Karenina* (1873–1877), he probed class divisions and the complexities of marital relationships. Anton Chekhov (1860–1904) was a physician who turned to literature. His major dramas concentrate on the realities, often ugly, of provincial life

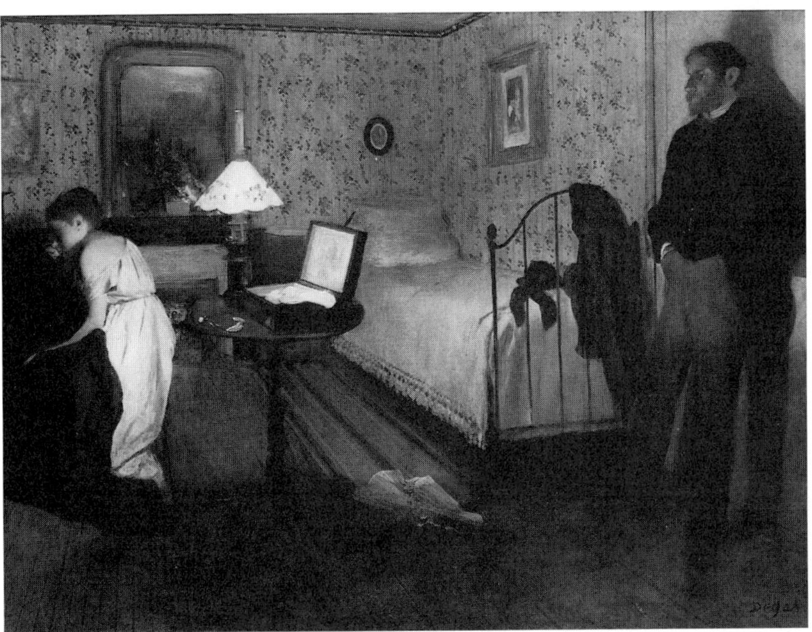

INTERIOR, **1868–69,** BY EDGAR DEGAS. Set in a world of poor shopkeepers and clerks, *Thérèse Raquin* (1867) was Émile Zola's first great success as a naturalist novelist. This Degas painting depicts the sexual tension and violent emotions that Zola sought to uncover in his work. (*Philadelphia Museum of Art, The Henry P. McIlhenny Collection in Memory of Francis P. McIlhenny.*)

among dissolute nobles who squander their money, drink excessively, and do nothing productive to better society. In essence Chekhov was describing a decadent social order in its last throes. Fydor Dostoevski (1821–1881), in his major novels, *Crime and Punishment* (1866), *The Idiot* (1868), *The Possessed* (1871), and *The Brothers Karamazov* (1880), showed a superb ability to create memorable characters, to probe minds, and to describe vividly and perceptively.

Among English writers, Elizabeth Gaskell, the wife of a Unitarian minister in Manchester, dealt compassionately with the plight of industrial workers in *Mary Barton* (1848) and *North and South* (1855). The novels of Charles Dickens—*Bleak House* (1853), *Hard Times* (1854), and several others—detailed the squalor of life, the hypocrisy of society, and the drudgery of labor in British industrial cities. Dickens skillfully created characters who, concerned only with safeguarding their privileged way of life, ignore the misery of the working class. These people run the schools, prisons law courts, and other government agencies that oppress the poor.

Literary realism evolved into naturalism when writers tried to demonstrate a causal relationship between human character and the social environment: that certain conditions of life produced predictable character traits in human beings. The belief that the law of cause and effect governed human behavior reflected the immense prestige attached to science in the closing decades of the nineteenth century.

The leading naturalist novelist, Émile Zola (1840–1902), had immense confidence in the scientific method and was convinced that it applied to literature. According to Zola, the novelist should proceed like a scientist performing an experiment. The "experimental novel," he wrote, shows "the

Profile

Charles Dickens

In his novels, Charles Dickens (1812–1870) criticized oppressive institutions and practices at home and abroad. In doing so, he helped to awaken the moral conscience of his day. In his early novels, Dickens deftly blends melodrama with playful humor and comedic characters, such as the Artful Dodger and Fagin, leaders of a den of pickpockets, prostitutes, and thieves in *Oliver Twist; or The Parish Boy's Progress* (1838). Dickens also demostrates how uncaring adults mistreat children, and he evokes sympathy for society's youthful victims—the orphan Oliver Twist and his friend, Nancy, who is brutally murdered by her boyfriend, Sikes, when she tries to help Oliver escape from Sikes's gang. In *The Life and Adventures of Nicholas Nickleby* (1839), Dickens exposes the abusive treatment of children. *In Bleak House* (1853), the factory worker Gridley disparages "the system" that prevents the workers from advancing or from bettering their working conditions. Dickens

The Granger Collection.

reciprocal effect of society on the individual and the individual on society." It shows "man living in social conditions produced by himself, which he modifies daily, and in the heart of which he himself experiences a continual transformation." This type of novel, Zola claimed,

> *is a consequence of the scientific evolution of the century; it continues and completes physiology, which itself leans for support on chemistry and medicine; it substitutes for the study of the abstract and the metaphysical man the study of the natural man, governed by physical and chemical laws, and modified by the influences of his surroundings; it is in one word the literature of our scientific age, as the classical and romantic literature corresponded to a scholastic and theological age.*[5]

In his own novels, Zola probed the slums, brothels, mining villages, and cabarets of France, examining how people were conditioned by the squalor of their environment. *Germinal* (1885), his greatest novel, graphically renders the terrible toil and drudgery endured by coal miners.

Realism was not restricted to the novel alone. The leading realist playwright, Henrik Ibsen (1828–1906), a Norwegian, examined with clinical precision the commercial and professional classes, their personal ambitions, business practices, and family relationships; his dramas drew attention to bourgeois pretensions, hypocrisy, and social conventions that thwart individual growth. Although Ibsen wrote about profound social issues, he viewed himself as a dramatist relating a piece of reality and not a social reformer agitating for reform.

blamed social institutions for the misery of the downtrodden.

Hard Times takes place in an industrial town called Coketown. Dickens's description of the town is a masterful example of realist writing.

> *It was a town of red brick, or of brick that would have been red if the smoke and ashes had allowed it; but, as matters stood it was a town of unnatural red and black like the painted face of a savage: It was a town of machinery and tall chimneys, out of which interminable serpents of smoke trailed themselves for ever and ever, and never got uncoiled. It had a black canal in it, and a river that ran purple with ill-smelling dye, and vast piles of buildings full of windows where there was a rattling and a trembling all day long, and where the piston of the steam-engine worked monotonously up and down, like the head of an elephant in a state of melancholy madness. It contained several large streets all very like one another, and many small streets still more like one another, inhabited by people equally like one another, who all went in and out at the same hours, with the same sound upon the same pavements, to do the same work, and to whom every day was the same as yesterday and tomorrow, and every year the counterpart of the last and the next.**

Dickens recognized that the monotony and stupefying conditions of industrial life crushed the spirit of the workers, curtailing both imagination and culture. Moreover, exploitation of the working class fostered class tensions, because the workers viewed government institutions as being impervious to their needs and intent only on protecting the privileged status of the entrepreneurs and industrial elites. Dickens used *A Tale of Two Cities* (1859) to issue a warning: if the political elites of England did not effectively address the need for social reform, England, like France, would become embroiled in revolutionary violence.

---

*Charles Dickens, *Hard Times* (New York: Penguin Books, 1985), p. 65.

In *Pillars of Society* (1877), Ibsen portrayed entrepreneurs who, aspiring for wealth and status, not only betray loved ones but also engage in unscrupulous business practices at the expense of their fellow citizens. The title is ironic, for the "pillars of society" are actually corrupt hypocrites.

In *A Doll's House* (1879), Ibsen took up a theme that shocked late-nineteenth-century bourgeois audiences: a woman leaving her husband and children in search of self-realization. Nora Helmer resents being a submissive and dutiful wife to a husband who does not take her seriously, who treats her like a child, a doll. Before walking out on Torvald, Nora tells him:

> *In all these eight years—longer than that—from the very beginning of our acquaintance, we have never exchanged a word on any serious subject. . . . When I was at home with papa, he told me his opinion about everything, and so I had the same opinions; and if I differed from him I concealed the fact, because he would not have liked it. He called me his doll-child, and he played with me just as I used to play with my dolls. And when I came to live with you . . . . I was simply transferred from papa's hands into yours. You arranged everything according to your own taste, and so I got the same tastes as you—or else I pretended to, I am really not sure which—I think sometimes the one and sometimes the other. . . . I have existed merely to perform tricks for you, Torvald. But you would have it so. You and papa have committed a great sin against me. It is your fault that I have made nothing of my life.*

By recognizing the truth about her life up to that point in time and then by resolving "to educate myself . . . to understand myself and everything about me," Nora now has the possibility of achieving individual freedom—of becoming a person in her own right.[6]

In striving for a true-to-life portrayal of human behavior and the social environment, realism and naturalism reflected attitudes shaped by science, industrialism, and secularism, which stressed the importance of the external world. The same outlook gave rise to positivism in philosophy.

Positivism

In the nineteenth century, science and technology continued to make astonishing strides. Combined with striking economic progress, these advances led many westerners to believe that a golden age was on the horizon. Viewing science as the highest achievement of the mind, intellectuals sought to apply the scientific method to other areas of thought. They regarded this method as a reliable way to approach all problems. Even history could be studied scientifically, they insisted, and society could be reorganized to conform with scientific laws of social development. Marxism was one attempt to fashion a science of society; another attempt was *positivism.*

According to the positivists, although people's knowledge of nature was vastly expanding, their understanding of society was deficient. This deficiency could be remedied by applying a strict empirical approach to the study of society. The philosopher must proceed like a scientist, carefully assembling and classifying data and formulating general rules that demonstrate regularities in the social experience. Such knowledge, based on concrete facts, would provide the social planner with useful insights. Positivists rejected metaphysics, which, in the tradition of Plato, tried to discover ultimate principles through reason alone, rather than through observation of the empirical world. For positivists, any effort to go beyond the realm of experience to a deeper reality would be a mistaken and fruitless endeavor. They restricted human knowledge only to what could be experienced and saw the method of science as the only valid approach to knowledge.

A leading figure in the emergence of positivism was Auguste Comte (1798–1857), an engineer with scientific training. Comte served as secretary to Saint-Simon until their association, punctuated by frequent quarrels, ended in 1824. But much of Saint-Simon's thought found its way into Comte's philosophy. Like Saint-Simon (and Marx), Comte called for a purely scientific approach to history and society: only by a proper understanding of the laws governing human affairs could society, which was in a state of intellectual anarchy, be rationally reorganized. He shared with Saint-Simon the view that the Enlightenment and the French Revolution had shattered the Old Regime but had not replaced it with new institutions and a new ideology; remedying this failure was the pressing need of the age.

Comte called his system positivism because he believed that it rested on sure knowledge derived from observed facts and was therefore empirically verifiable. Like others of his generation, he believed that scientific laws underlay human affairs and could be discovered through the methods of the geologist and the chemist: that is, through recording and systematizing observable data. "I shall bring factual proof," he said, "that there are just as definite laws for the development of the human race as there are for the fall of a stone."[7]

One of the laws that Comte believed he had discovered was the "law of the three stages." The human mind, he asserted, had progressed through three broad historical stages: theological, metaphysical, and scientific. In the theological stage, the most primitive of the three, the mind found a supernatural explanation for the origins and purpose of things, and society was ruled by priests. In the metaphysical stage, which included the Enlightenment, the mind tried to explain things through abstractions, such as "nature," "equality," "natural rights," or "popular sovereignty," which rested on hope and belief rather than on empirical investigation. The metaphysical stage was a transitional period between the infantile theological stage and the highest stage of society, the scientific, or positive, stage. In this culminating stage, the mind breaks with all illusions inherited from the past, formulates laws based on careful observation of the empirical world, and reconstructs society in accordance with these laws. People remove all mystery from nature and base their social legislation on laws of society similar to the laws of nature discovered by Newton.

Showing more insight than the philosophes, who tended to dismiss religion as a superstition and obsolete, Comte recognized that religion performs indispensable psychological and social functions. It is a powerful unifying force and a necessary outlet for human emotional needs. He therefore attempted to fashion a new religion for a new age: the Religion of Humanity, in which the veneration of the human race would supersede Christian teachings.

Because Comte advocated the scientific study of society, he is regarded as the principal founder of sociology; indeed, he coined the term. Comte's effort inspired many thinkers to collect and analyze critically all data pertaining to social phenomena. Émile Durkheim, a pioneer in the science of sociology, declared his indebtedness to Comte and, despite criticisms of Comte's work, recommended it as a superb introduction to the study of sociology. In trying to make the study of civilization an exact science, the English historian Henry T. Buckle (1821–1862), for example, looked at human culture as a product of climate, soil, and food; consequently, he thought that the achievements of western Europe were due to a favorable environment and the backwardness of Russia and Africa to an unfavorable one. Buckle believed that rigorous laws operated in the social world and that they could be best uncovered through statistical studies.

Although Comte attacked the philosophes for delving into abstractions instead of fashioning laws based on empirical knowledge, he was also influenced by the spirit of eighteenth-century philosophy. Like the philosophes, he valued science, criticized supernatural religion, and believed in progress. In this way, he accepted the Enlightenment's legacy, including the empirical and antitheological spirit of Diderot's *Encyclopedia* and Montesquieu's quest for historical laws governing society. Comte also acknowledged his debt to Condorcet, who saw intellectual and social progress as an inevitable condition of humanity.

A CARICATURE OF DARWIN. Darwin's theory of evolution created much controversy and aroused considerable bitterness. In this caricature, the apelike Darwin, holding a mirror, is explaining his theory of evolution to a fellow ape. (*Hulton/Corbis-Bettmann.*)

DARWINISM

Many contributed to the steady advance of science in the nineteenth century. In 1808, John Dalton, an English chemist, formulated the modern atomic theory. In 1831, an English chemist and physicist, Michael Faraday, discovered the principle of electromagnetic induction, on which the electric generator and electric motor are based. In 1847, Hermann von Helmholtz, a German physicist, formulated the law of conservation of energy, which states that the total amount of energy in the universe is always the same; energy that is used up is not lost but is converted into heat. In 1887, another German physicist, Heinrich Hertz, discovered electromagnetic waves—a discovery that later made possible the invention of radio, television, and radar. Almost two decades earlier, in 1869, Dmitri Mendeleev, a Russian chemist, constructed a periodic table for the elements, which helped to make chemistry more systematic and mathematical. In 1861, Louis Pasteur, a French scientist, initiated a revolution in medicine by proving that some diseases were caused by microbes, and he devised vaccines to prevent them.

Perhaps the most important scientific advance was the theory of evolution formulated by Charles Darwin (1809–1882). An English naturalist, Darwin did for biology what Newton had done for physics: he made it an objective science based on general principles. The Scientific Revolution of the seventeenth century had given people a new conception of space; Darwin radically altered our conception of time and biological life, including human origins.

Natural Selection

During the eighteenth century, almost all people had adhered to the biblical account of creation contained in Genesis. God had instantaneously created the universe and the various species of animal and plant life. He had given every river and mountain a finished and permanent form and made each species of animal and plant distinct from every other species. God had designed the bird's wings so that it could fly, the fish's eyes so that it could see under water, and human legs so that people could walk. All this, it was believed, had occurred some five or six thousand years ago.

Gradually, this view was questioned. In 1794, Erasmus Darwin, the grandfather of Charles Darwin, published *Zoonomia, or the Laws of Organic Life,* which offered evidence that the earth had existed for millions of years before the appearance of people and that animals experienced modifications, which they passed on to their offspring. Nearly forty years later, Sir Charles Lyell published his three-volume *Principles of Geology* (1830–1833), which showed that the planet had evolved slowly over many ages.

In December 1831, Charles Darwin sailed as a naturalist on the HMS *Beagle,* which surveyed the shores of South America and some Pacific islands. During the five-year expedition, Darwin collected and examined specimens of plant and animal life; he concluded that many animal species had perished, that new species had emerged, and that there were links between extinct and living species.

Influenced by Lyell's achievement, Darwin sought to interpret distant natural occurrences by means of observable processes that were still going on. He could not accept that a fixed number of distinct and separate species had been instantaneously created a mere five thousand years ago. In the *Origin of Species* (1859), and the *Descent of Man* (1871), Darwin used empirical evidence to show that the wide variety of animal species was due to a process of development over many millennia, and he supplied a convincing theory that explained how evolution operates.

Darwin adopted the Malthusian idea that the population reproduces faster than the food supply, causing a struggle for existence. Not all infant organisms grow to adulthood; not all adult organisms live to old age. The principle of *natural selection* determines which members of the species have a better chance of survival. The offspring of a lion, giraffe, or insect are not exact duplications of their parents. A baby lion might have the potential for being slightly faster or stronger than its parents; a baby giraffe might grow up to have a longer neck than its parents; an insect might have a slightly different color.

These small and random variations give the organism a crucial advantage in the struggle for food and against natural enemies. The organism favored by nature is more likely to reach maturity, to mate, and to pass on its superior qualities to its offspring, some of which will acquire the advantageous trait to an even greater degree than the parent. Over many generations, the favorable characteristic becomes more pronounced and more widespread within the species. Over millennia, natural selection causes the death of old species and the creation of new ones. Very few of the species that dwelt on earth ten million years ago still survive, and many new ones, including human beings, have emerged. People themselves are products of natural selection, evolving from earlier, lower, nonhuman forms of life.

Darwinism and Christianity

Like Newton's law of universal gravitation, Darwin's theory of evolution had revolutionary consequences in areas other than science. Evolution challenged traditional Christian belief. To some, it undermined the infallibility of Scripture and the conviction that the Bible was indeed the Word of God. Natural selection could explain the development of the organic world without reference to any divine design or ultimate purpose. Indeed, supernatural explanations of the origin of species now seemed superfluous and an obstacle to a scientific understanding of nature.

Darwin's theory touched off a great religious controversy between outraged fundamentalists, who defended a literal interpretation of Genesis, and advocates of the new biology. One theologian declared, "If the Darwinian theory is true, Genesis is a lie, the whole framework of the book of life falls to pieces, and the revelation of God to man, as we Christians know it, is a delusion and a snare."[8] A Methodist publication contended: "We regard this theory, which seeks to eliminate from the universe the immediate, ever-present, all pervasive action of a living and personal God, which excludes the possibility of the supernatural and the miraculous . . . as practically destructive of the authority of divine revelation, and subversive of the foundation of religion and morality."[9] In time, most religious thinkers tried to reconcile evolution with the Christian view that there was a Creation and that it had a purpose. These Christian thinkers held that God created and then directed the evolutionary process, that he steered evolution so that it would culminate in the human being.

Darwinism ultimately helped end the practice of relying on the Bible as an authority in questions of science, completing a trend initiated by Galileo. Darwinism thus contributed to the waning of religious belief and to a growing secular attitude that dismissed or paid scant attention to the Christian view of a universe designed by God and a soul that rises to heaven. For many, the conclusion was inescapable: nature contained no divine design or purpose, and the human species itself was a chance product of impersonal forces. The core idea of Christianity—that people were children of God participating in a drama of salvation—rested more than ever on faith rather than reason. Some even talked openly about the death of God. The notion that people are sheer accidents of nature was shocking. Copernicanism had deprived people of the comforting belief that the earth had been placed in the center of the universe just for them; Darwinism deprived them of the privilege of being God's special creation.

Social Darwinism

Darwin's theories were extended by others beyond the realm in which Darwin had worked. Social thinkers, who recklessly applied his conclusions to the social order, produced theories that had dangerous consequences. (Occasionally Darwin himself departed from his rigorous empiricism and drew murky conclusions about the mentally and physically handicapped and what he termed the "savage races.") Social Darwinists—those who transferred Darwin's scientific theories to social and economic issues—used the terms "struggle for existence" and "survival of the fittest" to buttress an often brutal economic individualism and political conservatism. Successful businessmen, they said, had demonstrated their fitness to succeed in the competitive world of business. Their success accorded with nature's laws and therefore was beneficial to society. Thus, American industrialist Andrew Carnegie (1835–1919) wrote in *The Gospel of Wealth* (1900):

> *We accept and welcome . . . the concentration of business, industrial and commercial, in the hands of a few and the law of competition . . . as being, not only beneficial, but essential to the future progress of the race. . . . We start, then, with a condition of affairs under which the best interests of the race are promoted, but which inevitably gives wealth to the few.*[10]

According to Social Darwinists, those who lost out in the socioeconomic struggle demonstrated their unfitness. Traditionally, failure had been ascribed to human wickedness or to God's plan. Now it was attributed to an inferior hereditary endowment.

Using Darwin's model of organisms evolving

and changing slowly over tens of thousands of years, conservatives insisted that society, too, should experience change at an unhurried pace. Instant reforms conflicted with nature's laws and wisdom and resulted in a deterioration of the social body.

The loose application of Darwin's biological concepts to the social world, where they did not apply, also buttressed imperialism, racism, nationalism, and militarism—doctrines that preached relentless conflict. Social Darwinists insisted that nations and races were engaged in a struggle for survival in which only the fittest survive and deserve to survive. In their view, war was nature's way of eliminating the unfit. Karl Pearson, a British professor of mathematics, stated in *National Life from the Standpoint of Science* (1900):

> *History shows me only one way, and one way only in which a higher state of civilization has been produced, namely the struggle of race with race, and the survival of the physically and mentally fitter race. . . . The path of progress is strewn with the wrecks of nations; traces are everywhere to be seen of the [sacrifice] of inferior races, and of victims who found not the narrow way to perfection. Yet these dead people are, in very truth, the stepping stones on which mankind has arisen to the higher intellectual and deeper emotional life of today.*[11]

"We are a conquering race," said the U.S. senator Albert J. Beveridge. "We must obey our blood and occupy new markets, and if necessary, new lands."[12] "War is a biological necessity of the first importance," claimed the Prussian general Friedrich von Bernhardi in *Germany and the Next War* (1911).[13]

Darwinian biology was used to promote the belief in Anglo-Saxon (British and American) and Teutonic (German) racial superiority. Social Darwinists attributed to racial qualities the growth of the British Empire, the expansion of the United States to the Pacific, and the extension of German power. The domination of other peoples—American Indians, Africans, Asians, Poles—was seen as the natural right of the superior race. British naturalist Alfred Russel Wallace, who arrived at the theory of evolution independently of Darwin, wrote in 1864:

> *The intellectual and moral, as well as the physical qualities of the European are superior; the same power and capacities which have made him rise in a few centuries from the condition of the wandering savage . . . to his present state of culture and advancement . . . enable him when in contact with savage man, to conquer in the struggle for existence and to increase at his expense.*[14]

Several writers and supporters of their countries' expansion described Native Americans, Africans, and Pacific Islanders as low forms of humanity whose subjection, even extinction, would be beneficial to the progress of civilization. For them the destruction of a "lower race" was justifiable, a biologically necessary and culturally worthy process. Thus in 1912, Paul Rohrbach, a German colonial official in Southwest Africa, wrote:

> *No false philanthropy or racial theory can convince sensible people that the preservation of a tribe of South Africa's kaffirs . . . is more important to the future of mankind than the spread of the great European nations and the white race in general.*
>
> *Not until the native learns to produce anything of value in the service of the higher race, i.e. in the service of its and his own progress, does he gain any moral right to exist.*[15]

Social Darwinism also affected racial attitudes in the United States. Too willingly, scholars, joining antiblack polemicists, attributed an inferior biological inheritance to blacks and some predicted their extinction, seeing them as losers in the Darwinian struggle for existence. Thus in 1905, William B. Smith, a Tulane University professor, wrote: "The vision . . . of a race vanishing before its superior is not at all dispiriting, but inspiring. . . . The doom that awaits the Negro has been prepared in like measures for all inferior races."[16]

The theory of evolution was a great achievement of the rational mind, but in the hands of the Social Darwinists it served to undermine the Enlightenment tradition. Whereas the philosophes emphasized human equality, Social Darwinists divided humanity into racial superiors and inferiors. The philosophes believed that states would increasingly submit to the rule of law to reduce violent conflicts; Social Darwinists, in contrast, regarded racial and national conflict as a biological necessity, a law of history, and a means of progress. In propagating a tooth-and-claw version of human and international relations, Social Darwinists dispensed with the humanitarian and cosmopolitan sentiments of the philosophes and distorted the image of progress. Their views promoted territorial aggrandizement and military buildup and led many to welcome World War I. The Social Darwinist notion of the struggle of races for survival became a core doctrine of the Nazi party after World War I and provided the "scientific" and "ethical" justification for genocide.

Religion in a Secular Age

In addition to Darwinism, other developments in the middle of the nineteenth century served to undermine traditional Christian belief. A growing secular attitude pushed religion to the periphery of human concerns for many people. New trends in biblical scholarship questioned the established opinion about the authenticity of the text of the Bible. Fortified by the discoveries of anthropologists and psychologists, "higher critics" examined the Old and New Testaments and the rise of Christianity in a historical and critical way. Generally, Protestant scholars, particularly Germans or those trained in Germany, took the lead in the new biblical scholarship.

In his *Life of Jesus* (1835), David Friedrich Strauss (1808–1874), a German theologian, examined the Gospels in a critical spirit, attempting to discern what was historically valid. He maintained that the New Testament was replete with myths, unconscious inventions by the Gospel writers, who embellished Jesus' life and words with their own messianic longings, and with inherited legends. The Gospels contain much mythical-religious content, Strauss said, but little history. Prior to the publication of Strauss's work, most students of religion had viewed the Gospels as a reliable historical source. But Strauss argued that the Jesus of faith is not the same as the Jesus of history. The belief that history, as presented in the Gospels, provided a firm basis for belief in Christian teachings was permanently undermined.

In *Essence of Christanity* (1841), Ludwig Feuerbach (1804–1872), a German philosopher and theologian, argued that the starting point of philosophy should be the human being and the material world, not God. "Religion is the dream of the human mind," he said, and God is a human creation, a product of human feelings and wishes. Human beings believe in the divine because they seek assistance from it in life and fear death.

Feuerbach treated religion as an expression of mythical thinking and God as an unconscious projection of human hopes, fears, and self-doubts. Christianity diminishes human beings in order to affirm God, said Feuerbach; Christians deny their own worth and goodness that they might ascribe all value to God. The human being, weak and self-hating,

> *sets God before him as the antithesis of himself. . . . God is the infinite, man the finite being; God is perfect, man imperfect; God eternal, man temporal; God almighty, man weak; God holy, man sinful. God and man are extremes: God is the absolutely positive, the sum of all realities; man the absolutely negative.*[17]

Religion, said Feuerbach, is a form of self-alienation, for human beings diminish their humanity when they invest their finest qualities in a nonexistent God and reserve their worst qualities for themselves. God represents the externalization of an idealized human being. When individuals measure themselves against this God-ideal, they see only miserable, contemptible, and worthless creatures. "To enrich God, man must become poor; that God may be all, man must become nothing. . . . [M]an is wicked, corrupt, incapable of good; but, on the other hand, God is the only good—the Good Being."[18] Humanity liberates itself, said Feuerbach, when it rejects God's existence and religions's claim to truth. He declared that it was his aim to change the friends of God into friends of human beings and the seekers of heaven into active, productive, and life-affirming individuals.

Confronted by this assault on orthodox belief, some Christians continued to believe that the Bible was true in all its parts, that it was the divinely inspired storehouse of knowledge about God and the world. These defenders of traditional Christianity rejected evolution and any other scientific discovery that appeared to be in conflict with their reading of Scripture. Danish philosopher Søren Kierkegaard (1813–1855) argued that true Christians commit themselves to beliefs that are seemingly unintelligible. For Kierkegaard, truth is subjective and personal, reached through passion and commitment. To find a truth that has an all-consuming meaning, to find an idea for which one can live and die—this should be the individual's highest aim. According to Kierkegaard, all philosophical systems fail because they are concerned with objective certainty and humanity in general and not with what truly matters—the individual standing alone and making choices based on passionately held beliefs. It is this experience that brings the individual face-to-face with God.

Because Christian truths surpass reason, Kierkegaard said that true Christians, strengthened by faith, plunge, with confidence, into the absurd. But it is this leap of faith that enables Christians to conquer the agonizing feeling that life, in its deepest sense, means nothing and to give meaning to their own existence. Such a faith, based on total commitment, is thus the true avenue of self-discovery.

Modernism, a movement of Catholic intellectuals, sought to liberalize the church, to make it more accepting of modern liberal political ideals and modern science, and to reexamine the Gospels and Catholic teaching in the light of modern biblical scholarship. In many of these instances, modernists took positions that directly challenged core Catholic principles. Thus, Alfred Firmin Loiry (1857–1940), a scholarly priest, questioned the historicity of the Virgin Birth and the bodily resurrection of Jesus, rejected the infalibility of papal and council pronouncements, and contended that Jesus did not impart God's permanent truths, that both he and the Gospels have to be interpreted within the context of their historical times.

Pope Pius X (1903–1914) strongly condemned modernism for undermining revelation and fostering agnosticism. The church also suppressed modernist journals, placed a number of modernist works on the *Index of Forbidden Books,* dismissed some modernist instructors, and excommunicated a number of the movement's staunchest supporters.

Marxism

The failure of the revolutions of 1848 and growing fear of working-class violence led liberals to abandon revolution and to press for reforms through the political process. In the last part of the nineteenth century, Marxists and anarchists became the chief proponents of revolution. Both liberalism and Marxism shared common principles derived from the Enlightenment. Their adherents believed in the essential goodness and perfectibility of human nature and claimed that their doctrines rested on rational foundations. They wanted to free individuals from accumulated superstition, ignorance, and prejudices of the past and to fashion a more harmonious and rational society. Both liberals and Marxists believed in social progress and valued the full realization of human talents.

Despite these similarities, the differences between liberalism and Marxism are profound. The goal of Marxism—the seizure of power by the working class and the destruction of capitalism—was inimical to bourgeois liberals; so, too, was the Marxist belief that violence and struggle were the essence of history, the instruments of progress, the vehicle to a higher stage of humanity. Liberals, who placed the highest value on the individual, held that through education and self-discipline people could overcome inequality and poverty. Marxists insisted that without a transformation of the economic system individual effort by the downtrodden would amount to very little.

Karl Marx (1818–1883) was born of German-Jewish parents (both descendants of prominent rabbis). To save his job as a lawyer, Marx's father converted to Protestantism. Enrolled at a university to study law, Marx switched to philosophy. In 1842, he was editing a newspaper, which was soon suppressed by the Prussian authorities for its outspoken ideas. Leaving his native Rhineland, Marx went to Paris, where he met another German, Friedrich Engels (1820–1895),

KARL MARX. Interpreting history in economic terms, Marx predicted that socialism would replace capitalism. He called for the proletariat to overthrow capitalism and to establish a classless society. (*Corbis-Bettmann.*)

who was the son of a prosperous textile manufacturer. Marx and Engels entered into a lifelong collaboration and became members of socialist groups. In February 1848, they published the *Communist Manifesto,* which called for a working-class revolution to overthrow the capitalist system. Forced to leave France in 1849 because of his political views, Marx moved to London, where he spent the rest of his life.

Although supported by Engels, Marx was continually short of funds, and at times he and his wife and daughters lived in dreadful poverty. In London, Marx spent years writing *Capital*—a study and critique of the modern capitalistic economic system, which, he predicted, would be destroyed by a socialist revolution.

A Science of History

As did other thinkers influenced by the Enlightenment, Marx believed that human history, like the operations of nature, was governed by scientific law. Marx was a strict materialist; rejecting all religious and metaphysical interpretations of both nature and history, he sought to fashion an empirical science of society. He viewed religion as a human creation—a product of people's imagination and feelings and a consolation for the oppressed. The happiness it brought he considered an illusion. Real happiness would come, said Marx, not by transcending the natural world but by improving it. Rather than deluding oneself by seeking refuge from life's misfortunes in an imaginary world, one must confront the ills of society and reform them. This last point is crucial. "The philosophers have only *interpreted* the world in different ways; the point is to *change it.*"[19]

The world could be rationally understood and changed, said Marx. People were free to make their own history, but to do so effectively, they must comprehend the inner meaning of history: the laws governing human affairs in the past and operating in the present. Marx adopted Hegel's view that history was not an assortment of unrelated and disconnected events, but a progressive development, which, like the growth of a plant, proceeded ineluctably according to its own inner laws. For both Hegel and Marx, the historical process was governed by objective and rational principles. Marx also adopted Hegel's view that history advanced dialectically: that the clash of opposing forces propelled history into higher stages.

However, Marx also broke with Hegel in crucial ways. For Hegel, it was the dialectical clash of opposing ideas that moved history into the next stage. For Marx, it was the clash of classes representing conflicting economic interests—what is called dialectical materialism—that accounted for historical change and progress. In Hegel's view, history was the unfolding of the Absolute Spirit, and a higher stage of development was produced by the synthesis of opposing ideas. According to Marx, Hegel's system failed because it was too metaphysical. It transcended the known world and downgraded reality to a mere attribute of Spirit. Marx saw Hegel's abstract philosophy as deflecting attention from the real world and its problems, which cried out for understanding and solution; it was a negation of life. For Marx, history was explainable solely in terms of natural processes—empirically verifiable developments.

As it is often said, Marx turned Hegel upside down. Hegel began with metaphysical consciousness—the Idea, Spirit, or God—which unfolded itself in human existence. Human beings and the human situation were attributes or emanations of the universal Idea, whose self-actualization gave essential meaning to the historical process. For Marx, the real relation of thought to human life was the exact reverse. The starting point and ultimate significance of history was to be found in the human social and economic environment, the natural conditions of life; thought was a product of these conditions. Marx valued Hegel's insight that history is a progressive and purposeful process, but he criticized Hegel for embedding this insight in metaphysical-theological fantasy. Hegel, said Marx, had made a mystical principle the real subject of history and thought. But, in truth, it is the "real man," the person who lives in and is conditioned by the objective world, the only true reality, who is the center of history. History is not Spirit aspiring to self-actualization but people becoming fully human, fulfilling their human potential. The moving forces in history, said Marx, were economic and technological factors: the ways in which goods were produced and wealth was distributed. They accounted for historical change and were the basis of all culture—politics, law, religion, morals, and philosophy. "The history of humanity," he concluded, "must therefore always be studied and treated in relation to the history of industry and exchange."[20]

According to Marx, material technology—the methods of cultivating land and the tools for manufacturing goods—determined society's social and political arrangements and its intellectual outlooks. For example, the hand mill, the loose yoke, and the wooden plow had given rise to feudal lords, whereas power-driven machines had spawned industrial capitalists. As material technology expanded, it came into conflict with established economic, social, and political forms, and the resulting tension produced change. Thus, feudal patterns could not endure when power machinery became the dominant mode of production. Consequently, medieval guilds, communal agriculture, and even the domestic production of goods gave way to free labor, private property, and the factory system of manufacturing. As Marx put it, the expansion of technology triggered a change from feudal social and economic relationships to capitalist ones. Ultimately, the change in economic-technological conditions would become the cause for great political changes.

This process was most clearly demonstrated by the French Revolution. Radical changes in the economic foundations of society had taken place since the Middle Ages without corresponding political changes. However, the forces of economic change could not be contained in outdated political forms. In France, this tension exploded into revolution. Whatever their conscious intentions, said Marx, the bourgeois leaders of the French Revolution had scattered feudal remnants to the wind; they had promoted free competition and commercial expansion and transferred power from the landed aristocracy to the leaders of finance and industry. Not every revolutionary change in history is explosive, according to Marx, but whenever major economic changes take place, political and social changes must follow.

Class Conflict

Throughout history, said Marx, there has been a class struggle between those who own the means of production and those whose labor has been exploited to provide wealth for this upper class. This dialectical, or opposing, tension between classes has pushed history forward into higher stages. In the ancient world, when wealth was based on land, the struggle was between master and slave, patrician and plebeian; during the Middle Ages, when land was still the predominant mode of production, the struggle was between lord and serf. In the modern industrial world, two sharply opposed classes were confronting each other: the capitalists owning the factories, mines, banks, and transportation systems, and the exploited wage earners (the proletariat).

The class with economic power also controlled the state, said Marx and Engels. That class used political power to protect and increase its property and to hold down the laboring class. "Thus the ancient State was above all the slaveowners' state for holding down the slaves," said Engels, "as a feudal State was the organ of the nobles for holding down the . . . serfs, and the modern representative State is the instrument of the exploitation of wage-labor by capital."[21]

According to Marx and Engels the class that controlled material production also controlled mental production: that is, the ideas held by the ruling class became the dominant ideas of society. These ideas, presented as laws of nature or moral and religious standards, were regarded as the truth by oppressor and oppressed alike. In reality, however, these ideas merely reflected the special economic interests of the ruling class. Thus, said Marx, bourgeois ideologists would insist that natural rights and laissez faire were laws of nature having universal validity. But these "laws" were born of the needs of the bourgeoisie in its struggle to wrest power from an obsolete feudal regime and to protect its property from the state. Similarly, nineteenth-century slaveholders convinced themselves that slavery was morally right: that it had God's approval and was good for the slave. Slave owners and capitalist employers alike may have defended their labor systems by citing universal principles that they thought were true, but in reality their systems rested on a simple economic consideration: slave labor was good for the pocketbook of the slave owner, and wage labor was good in the same way for the capitalist. They were unaware of the real forces motivating their thinking.

Destruction of Capitalism

Under capitalism, said Marx, workers knew only poverty. They worked long hours for low wages, suffered from periodic unemployment, and lived in squalid, overcrowded dwellings. Most monstrous of all, they were forced to send their young children into the factories. In *Capital,* Marx quotes a British official who declared in 1860:

> *Children of nine or ten years are dragged from their squalid beds at two, three, or four o'clock in the morning and compelled to work for a bare subsistence until ten, eleven, or twelve at night, their limbs wearing away, their frames dwindling, their faces whitening, and their humanity absolutely sinking into a stone-like torpor, utterly horrible to contemplate.*[22]

Capitalism also produced another kind of poverty, according to Marx: poverty of the human spirit. Under capitalism, the factory worker was reduced to a laboring beast, performing tedious and repetitive tasks in a dark, dreary, dirty cave—an altogether inhuman environment, which deprived people of their human sensibilities. Unlike the artisans in their own shops, factory workers found no pleasure and took no pride in their work; they did not have the satisfaction of creating a finished product that expressed their skills. Work, said Marx, should be a source of fulfillment for people. It should enable people to affirm their personalities and develop their potential. By treating people not as human beings but as cogs in the production process, capitalism alienated people from their work, from themselves, and from one another. Marx wrote:

> *[T]he worker . . . does not fulfil himself in his work but denies himself, has a feeling of misery rather than well-being, does not develop freely his mental and physical energies but is physically exhausted and mentally debased. . . . His work is not voluntary but imposed, forced labour. It is not the satisfaction of a need, but only a means for satisfying other needs. Its alien character is clearly shown by the fact that as soon as there is no physical or other compulsion it is avoided like the plague. . . .*
>
> *. . . [T]he more the worker expends himself in work, . . . the poorer he becomes in his inner life, and the less he belongs to himself. . . . The worker puts his life into the object, and his life then belongs no longer to himself but to the object.*[23]

Marx further asserted that capitalism dehumanized not only the workers but the capitalists as well. Consumed by greed and a ruthless competitiveness, they abused workers and each other and lost sight of life's true meaning: the fulfillment of the individual's creative potential. Marx's view of the individual owed much to the Western humanist tradition, which aspired to shape self-sufficient and productive human beings who strive to develop their intellectual, esthetic, and moral capacities and relate to others as subjects, not as objects. By reducing people to commodities and human relations to a cash nexus, said Marx, capitalism thwarted the realization of this humanist vision.

Marx believed that capitalist control of the economy and the government would not endure forever; capitalist society produced its own gravediggers—the working class. The capitalist system would perish just as the slave society of the ancient world and the feudal society of the Middle Ages had perished. For Marx, the destruction of capitalism was inevitable; it was necessitated by the law of historical materialism. From the ruins of a dead capitalist society, a new socioeconomic system, socialism, would emerge.

Marx predicted how capitalism would be destroyed. Periodic unemployment would increase the misery of the workers and intensify their hatred of capitalists. Small businesspeople and shopkeepers, unable to compete with the great capitalists, would sink into the ranks of the working class, greatly expanding its numbers. Society would become polarized into a small group of immensely wealthy capitalists and a vast proletariat, poor, embittered, and desperate. The monopoly of capital by the few would become a brake on the productive process. Growing increasingly conscious of their misery, the workers—aroused, educated, and organized by communist intellectuals—would revolt. "Revolution is necessary," said Marx, "not only because the *ruling* class cannot be overthrown in any other way, but also because only in a revolution *can the class which overthrows it* rid itself of the accumulated rubbish of the past and become capable of reconstructing society."[24] The working-class revolutionaries would smash the government that helped the capitalists maintain their dominance. Then they would confiscate the property of the capitalists, abolish private property, place the means of production in the workers' hands, and organize a new society. The *Communist Manifesto* ends with a ringing call for revolution:

> *The Communists . . . openly declare that their ends can be attained only by the forcible overthrow of all existing social conditions. Let the ruling classes tremble at a Communist revolution. The proletarians have nothing to lose but their chains. They have a world to win.*
>
> *Workingmen of all countries, unite!*[25]

Marx did not say a great deal about the new society that would be ushered in by the socialist revolution. With the destruction of capitalism, the distinction between capitalist and worker would cease and with it the class conflict. No longer would society be divided into haves and have-nots, oppressor and oppressed. Since this classless society would contain no exploiters, there would be no need for a state, which was merely an instrument for maintaining and protecting the power of the exploiting class. Thus, the state would eventually wither away. The production and distribution of goods would be carried out through community planning and communal sharing, replacing the capitalist system of competition. People would work at varied tasks, rather than being confined to one form of employment, just as Fourier had advocated.

A revolutionary change in the conditions of life, Marx predicted, would produce a radical transformation of the human being. No longer debased by the self-destructive pursuit of profit and property and no longer victims of capitalist exploitation, people would become finer human beings—altruistic, sensitive, cooperative, and creative. United with others in a classless society free of exploitation and no longer divided by divergent interests, individuals would become truly communal and truly free beings (surpassing the merely political freedom achieved in the bourgeois state)—that is, they would become truly human.

Marxism's Appeal and Influence

Marxism had immense appeal for both the downtrodden and intellectuals. It promised to end the injustices of industrial society; it offered explanations that claimed the certainty of science for all the crucial events of history; and it assured adherents that history guaranteed the triumph of their cause. Far from being a scientific system, however, Marxism had the features of a religious myth. It had adapted and secularized several Judeo-Christian themes: an apocalyptic struggle between good and evil brings history to an end; humanity's messianic hopes are realized when human beings, emancipated from the slavery of exploitation, undergo spiritual regeneration and fulfill the promise of their human nature; and militant proletarians serve as the agents of salvation. Ultimately faith, not science, assures the triumph of the proletariat and the redemption of humanity.

The writings of Marx (and later those of Lenin and Mao) became official dogma for the faithful. Those who deviated were branded as heretics and condemned for their sins. As Robert Tucker notes, it was this religious quality in Marxism that attracted many people to its cause:

> *Like medieval Christianity, Marx's system undertakes to provide an integrated all-inclusive view of reality, an organization of all significant knowledge in an interconnected whole, a frame of reference within which all possible questions of importance are answered. . . . This, of course, indicates a source of his system's appeal to some modern men in whom the hold of traditional religion has loosened but the craving for an all-inclusive world-view remains alive and strong.*[26]

Marx's influence grew during the second wave of industrialization in the closing decades of the nineteenth century, when class bitterness between the proletariat and the bourgeoisie seemed to worsen. Many workers thought that liberals and conservatives had no sympathy for their plight and that the only way to improve their lot was through socialist parties.

The emphasis Marx placed on economic forces has immeasurably broadened the perception of historians, who now explore the economic factors in historical developments. This approach has greatly expanded our understanding of Rome's decline, the outbreak of the French Revolution and the American Civil War, and other crucial developments. Marx's theory of class conflict has provided social scientists with a useful tool for analyzing social process. His theory of alienation has been adapted by sociologists and psychologists. Of particular value to social scientists is Marx's insight that the ideas people hold to be true and the values they consider valid often veil economic interests. On the political level, both the socialist parties of western Europe, which pressed for reform through parliamentary methods, and the communist regimes in Russia and China, which came to power through revolution, claimed to be heirs of Marx.

Critics of Marx

Critics point out serious weaknesses in Marxism. The rigid Marxist who tries to squeeze all historical events into an economic framework is at a disadvantage. Economic forces alone will not explain the triumph of Christianity in the Roman Empire, the fall of Rome, the Crusades, the French Revolution, modern imperialism, World War I, or the rise of Hitler. Economic explanations fall particularly flat in trying to account for the emergence of modern nationalism, whose appeal, resting on deeply ingrained emotional needs, crosses class lines. Most great struggles of the twentieth century have been not between classes but between nations.

Many of Marx's predictions or expectations have not materialized. Workers in Western lands did not become the oppressed and impoverished working class that Marx had described in the mid-nineteenth century. Because of increased productivity and the efforts of labor unions and reform-minded governments, Western workers improved their lives considerably, so that they now enjoy the highest standard of living in history. The tremendous growth of a middle class of professionals, civil service employees, and small-business people belies Marx's prediction that capitalist society would be polarized into a small group of very rich capitalists and a great mass of destitute workers. Marx believed that socialist revolutions would break out in the advanced industrialized lands. But the socialist revolutions of the twentieth century occurred in underdeveloped, predominantly agricultural states. The state in communist lands, far from withering away, grew more centralized, powerful, and oppressive. In no country where communist revolutionaries seized power have people achieved the liberty that Marx desired. Nor, indeed, have communists been able to sustain a viable economic system. The phenomenal collapse of communist regimes in the former Soviet Union and Eastern Europe in recent years testifies to Marxism's failure. All these failed predictions and expectations seem to contradict Marx's claim that his theories rested on an unassailable scientific foundation.

Anarchism

Anarchism was another radical movement that attacked capitalism. Like Marxists, anarchists denounced the exploitation of workers and the coercive authority of government and envisioned a stateless society. Only by abolishing the state, said anarchists, could the individual live a free and full life. To achieve these ends, a small number of anarchists advocated revolutionary terrorism; others, like the great Russian novelist Leo Tolstoy, rejected all violence. These anarchists sought to destroy the state by refusing to cooperate with it.

Pierre Joseph Proudhon

Anarchists drew inspiration from Pierre Joseph Proudhon (1809–1865), a self-educated French printer and typesetter. Proudhon criticized social theorists who devised elaborate systems that regimented daily life, conflicted with human nature, and deprived people of their personal liberty. He desired a new society that maximized individual freedom. He looked back longingly to preindustrial society, which he saw as free of exploitation and corruption and of great manufacturers and financiers. He respected the dignity of labor and wanted to liberate workers from the exploitation and false values of industrial capitalism. An awakened working class would construct a new moral and social order.

Proudhon believed that people would deal justly with one another, respect one another, and develop their full potential in a society of small peasants, shopkeepers, and artisans. Such a society would not require a government; government only fosters privilege and suppresses freedom:

> *To be governed is to be watched over, inspected, spied on, directed, legislated at, regulated, docketed, indoctrinated, preached at, controlled . . . censored, ordered about, by men who have neither the right nor the knowledge nor the virtue. To be governed means to be, at each operation, at each transaction, at each movement . . . registered, controlled, taxed . . . hampered, reformed, rebuked, arrested. It is to be, on the pretext of the general interest, taxed, drilled . . . exploited . . . repressed, fined, abused. . . . That's government, that's its justice, that's its morality.*[27]

Proudhon was less a theorist than a man who could express passionately the disillusionment and disgust with the new industrial society that was developing in Europe.

Mikhail Bakunin

Anarchism had a particular appeal in Russia, where there was no representative government and no way, other than petitions to the tsar, to legally redress injustice. A repressive regime, economic backwardness, a youth movement passionately committed to improving the lives of the masses, and a magnetic leader, Mikhail Bakunin (1814–1876), all contributed to shaping the Russian anarchist tradition. Bakunin was a man of action who organized and fought for revolution and set an example of revolutionary fervor. The son of a Russian noble, he left the tsar's army to study philosophy in the West, where he was attracted to the ideas of Proudhon and Marx. He was arrested for participating in the German revolution of 1848 and was turned over to tsarist officials. He served six years in prison and was then banished to Siberia, from which he escaped in 1861.

Bakunin devoted himself to organizing secret societies that would lead the oppressed in revolt. Whereas Marx held that revolution would occur in the industrial lands through the efforts of a class-conscious proletariat, Bakunin wanted all oppressed people to revolt, including the peasants (the vast majority of the population in central and eastern Europe). Toward this end, he favored secret societies and terrorism.

Marx and Bakunin disagreed on one crucial issue of strategy. Marx wanted to organize the workers into mass political parties; Bakunin held

Proudhon and His Daughters, by Gustave Courbet (1819–1877). Pierre Joseph Proudhon condemned the new industrial society, which he believed restricted workers and spread poverty. He sought a society that would maximize individual freedom. His call for freedom influenced many social thinkers and was adopted by nineteenth-century anarchists. (*Giraudon/Art Resource, NY.*)

that revolutions should be fought by secret societies of fanatic insurrectionists. Bakunin feared that after the Marxists overthrew the capitalist regime and seized power, they would become the new masters and exploiters, using the state to enhance their own power. They would, said Bakunin, become a "privileged minority . . . of *ex-workers,* who, once they become rulers or representatives of the people, cease to be workers and begin to look down upon the toiling people. From that time on they represent not the people but themselves and their claims to govern the people."[28] Therefore, said Bakunin, once the workers capture the state, they should destroy it forever. Bakunin's astute prediction that a socialist revolution would lead state power to intensify rather than disappear was borne out in the twentieth century.

Anarchists engaged in acts of political terrorism, including the assassination or attempted assassination of heads of state and key ministers, but they never waged a successful revolution. They failed to reverse the trend toward the concentration of power in industry and government, which would characterize the twentieth century.

Liberalism in Transition

In the early 1800s, European liberals were preoccupied with protecting the rights of the individual against the demands of the state. They championed laissez faire because they feared that state interference in the economy to redress social evils would threaten individual rights and the free market, which they thought were essential to personal liberty. They also favored property requirements for voting and officeholding because they were certain that the unpropertied and uneducated masses lacked the wisdom and experience to exercise political responsibility.

In the last part of the century, liberals began—not without reservation and qualification—to support extended suffrage and government action to remedy the abuses of unregulated industrialization. This growing concern for the welfare of the laboring poor coincided with and was influenced by an unprecedented proliferation of humanitarian movements on both sides of the Atlantic. Nurtured by the Enlightenment, as well as Christian teachings, reform movements called for the prohibition of child labor, schooling for the masses, humane treatment for prisoners and the mentally ill, equality for women, the abolition of slavery, and an end to war. By the beginning of the twentieth century, liberalism had evolved into liberal democracy, and laissez faire had been superseded by a reluctant acceptance of social legislation and government regulation. But from beginning to end, the central concern of liberals remained the protection of individual rights.

John Stuart Mill

The transition from laissez-faire liberalism to a more socially conscious and democratic liberalism is seen in the thought of John Stuart Mill (1806–1873), a British philosopher and statesman. Mill's *On Liberty* (1859) is the classic statement of individual freedom and minority rights: that the government and the majority may not interfere with the liberty of another human being whose actions do no injury to others.

Mill regarded freedom of thought and expression, the toleration of opposing and unpopular viewpoints, as a necessary precondition for the shaping of a rational, moral, and civilized citizen. Political or social coercion, said Mill, is also a barrier to the full development of individuality. Liberty is a supreme good that benefits both the individual and the community. When we silence an opinion, said Mill, we hurt present and future generations. If the opinion is correct, "we are deprived of the opportunity of exchanging error for truth." If the opinion is wrong—and of this we can never be entirely certain—we "lose the clearer perception and livelier impression of truth produced by its collision with error."[29] Therefore, government has no right to force an individual to hold a view

> *because it will be better for him to do so, because it will make him happier, or because in the opinions of others, to do so would be wise, or even right. These are good reasons for remonstrating with him, or reasoning with him, or persuading him, or entreating him, but not for compelling him or visiting him with any evil in case he do otherwise.*[30]

Mill would place limits on the power of government, for in an authoritarian state citizens cannot develop their moral and intellectual potential. Although he feared the state as a threat to individual liberty, Mill also recognized the necessity for state intervention to promote individual self-development: the expansion of individual moral, intellectual, and esthetic capacities. For example, he maintained that it was permissible for the state to require children to attend school against the wishes of their parents, to regulate hours of labor, to promote public health, and to provide workers' compensation and old-age insurance.

In *Considerations on Representative Government* (1861), Mill endorsed the active participation of all citizens, including the lower classes, in the political life of the state. However, he also proposed a system of plural voting in which education and character would determine the number of votes each person was entitled to cast. In this way, Mill, a cautious democrat, sought to protect the individual from the tyranny of a politically and intellectually unprepared majority.

Thomas Hill Green

The leading late-nineteenth-century figures in the shaping of a new liberal position in Britain were Thomas Hill Green (1836–1882), an Oxford University professor; D. G. Ritchie (1853–1903), who taught philosophy at Oxford and Saint Andrews; J. A. Hobson (1858–1940), a social theorist; and L. T. Hobhouse (1864–1929), an academic who also wrote for the *Manchester Guardian*. In general, these thinkers argued that laissez faire protected the interests of the economically powerful class and ignored the welfare of the nation. For example, Green valued private property but could not see how this principle helped the poor. "A man who possesses nothing but his powers of labor and who has to sell these to a capitalist for bare daily maintenance, might as well . . . be denied rights of property altogether."[31]

Green argued that the do-nothing state advocated by traditional laissez-faire liberalism condemned many citizens to destitution, ignorance, and despair. The state must preserve individual liberty and at the same time secure the common good by promoting conditions favorable for the self-development of the majority of the population. Liberalism, for Green, encompassed more than the protection of individual rights from an oppressive government. A truly liberal society, he said, gives people the opportunity to fulfill their moral potential and human capacities. And social reforms initiated by the state assisted in the realization of this broader conception of liberty. Green and other advocates of state intervention contended that the government has a moral obligation to create social conditions that permit individuals to make the best of themselves. Toward that end, the state should promote public health, ensure decent housing, and provide for education. The uneducated and destitute person cannot be morally self-sufficient or a good citizen, Green and other progressives argued.

Green and his colleagues remained advocates of capitalism but rejected strict laissez faire, which, they said, benefited only a particular class at the expense of the common good. Overcoming a traditional liberal mistrust of state power, they viewed the state as an ethical institution, assigned it a positive role in improving social conditions, and insisted that state actions need not threaten individual freedom.

In general, by the beginning of the twentieth century, liberals in Britain increasingly acknowledged the need for social legislation. The foundations for the British welfare state were being laid. On the Continent, too, social welfare laws were enacted. To be sure, the motives behind such legislation were quite diverse and often had little to do with liberal sentiments. Nevertheless, in several countries liberalism was expanding into political and social democracy, a trend that would continue in the twentieth century.

Herbert Spencer: Rejection of State Intervention

Many traditional liberals regarded state intervention—"creeping socialism," they called it—as a betrayal of the liberal principle of individual freedom. They held to the traditional liberal view that the plight of the downtrodden was not a legitimate concern of the state. The new liberalism, they argued, would make people dependent on the state, thereby stifling industriousness, self-reliance, and thrift. Paternalistic government would cripple the working class morally by turning them into "grown-up babies."

In *The Man Versus the State* (1884), the British philosopher Herbert Spencer rejected the idea "that evils of all kinds should be dealt with by the State." The outcome of state intervention, he said, is that "each member of the community as an individual would be a slave to the community as a whole . . . and the slavery will not be mild."[32] Committed to a philosophy of extreme individualism, Spencer never abandoned the view that the state was an evil and oppressive institution. He favored a society in which government would play the smallest role possible and individual freedom would be maximized, for when the power of the state is extended, however well-intentioned the motive, the freedom of the individual is restricted.

Spencer's extreme laissez faire and "rugged individualism" led him to oppose various forms of government intervention, including factory inspection, sanitary laws, pure food and drug requirements, a state postal system, compulsory public education, and public relief for the poor. "The function of Liberalism in the past was that of putting a limit to the powers of kings," he declared. "The function of true Liberalism in the future will be that of putting a limit to the powers of Parliament."[33]

A thoroughgoing individualist, Spencer saw the poor as incapable, weak, imprudent, and lazy—unfit to compete in the struggle for existence. For Spencer, state action was always misguided, for it tampered with nature's laws. "Instead of diminishing suffering, it eventually increases it. It favours the multiplication of those worst fitted for existence, and, by consequence, hinders the multiplication of those best fitted for existence—leaving, as it does, less room for them."[34] Government assistance creates an attitude of dependency among the poor; because they expect things to be done for them, they do not do things for themselves.

Feminism: Extending the Principle of Equality

Another example of the expansion of liberalism was the emergence of feminist movements in western Europe and the United States. Feminists insisted that the principles of liberty and equality expressed by the philosophes and embodied in the French Declaration of the Rights of Man and of the Citizen (1789) and the American Declaration of Independence be applied to women. Thus, Olympe de Gouges's *Declaration of the Rights of Woman* (1791), modeled after the Declaration of the Rights of Man and of the Citizen, the French Revolution's tribute to Enlightenment ideals, stated: "Woman is born free and remains equal to man in rights. . . . The aim of every political association is the preservation of the natural . . . rights of man and woman."[35] Mary Wollstonecraft's *Vindication of the Rights of Woman,* written under the influence of the French Revolution, protested against the prevailing subordination and submissiveness of women and the limited opportunities afforded them to cultivate their minds. She considered it an act of tyranny for women "to be excluded from a participation of the natural rights of mankind."[36] And in 1837, the English novelist and economist Harriet Martineau observed: "One of the fundamental principles announced in the Declaration of Independence is that governments derive their just power from the consent of the governed. How can the political condition of women be reconciled with this?"[37]

An American Feminist. Elizabeth Cady Stanton, who participated in the antislavery movement, was a principal founder of the American Woman's Suffragist Movement, which held its first convention in 1848 in Seneca Falls, New York. (*Bettmann/Corbis.*)

In the United States, in the 1830s, Angelina and Sarah Grimké spoke in public—something women rarely did—against slavery and for women's rights. In 1838, Sarah Grimké published *Letters on the Equality of the Sexes and the Condition of Women,* where she stated emphatically: "Men and women were Created Equal: they are both moral and accountable beings, and whatever is *right* for man to do is *right* for women. . . . How monstrous, how anti-Christian, is the doctrine that woman is to be dependent on man!"[38] The Woman's Suffrage Movement, holding its first convention in 1848 in Seneca Falls, New York, drew up a Declaration of Statements and Principles, which broadened the Declaration of Independence: "We hold these truths to be self-evident: that all men and women are created equal." The document protested "that woman has too long rested satisfied in the circumscribed limits which corrupt customs and a perverted application of the Scriptures have marked out for her" and called for the untiring effort of both men and women to secure for women "an equal participation with men in the various trades, professions, and commerce."[39]

In their struggle for equality, feminists had to overcome deeply ingrained premises about female inferiority and deficiencies. Even the philosophes, who often enjoyed the company of intelligent and sophisticated women in the famous salons, continued to view women as intellectually and morally inferior to men. Some philosophes, notably Condorcet, who wrote *Plea for the Citizenship of Women* (1791), argued for female emancipation, but they were the exception. Most philosophes concurred with Hume, who held that "nature has subjected" women to men and that their "inferiority and infirmities are absolutely incurable."[40] Rousseau, who believed that nature had granted men power over women, regarded traditional domesticity as a woman's proper role.

> *I would a thousand times rather have a homely girl, simply brought up, than a learned lady and a wit who would make a literary circle of my house and install herself as its president. A female wit is a scourge to her husband, her children, her friends, her servants, to everybody. From the lofty height of her genius, she scorns every womanly duty, and she is always trying to make a man of herself.*[41]

Nevertheless, by clearly articulating the ideals of liberty and equality, the philosophes made a women's movement possible. The growing popularity of these ideals could not escape women, who measured their own position by them. Moreover, by their very nature, these ideals were expansive. Denying them to women would ultimately be seen as an indefensible contradiction.

Opponents of women's rights argued that feminist demands would threaten society by undermining marriage and the family. An article in the *Saturday Review,* an English periodical, declared that "It is not the interest of States . . . to encourage the existence of women who are other than entirely dependent on man as well for subsistence as for protection and love. . . . Married life is a woman's profession."[42] And in 1870, a member of the House of Commons wondered "what would become, not merely of woman's influence, but of her duties at home, her care of the household, her supervision of all those duties and surroundings which make a happy home . . . if we are to see women coming forward and taking part in the government of the country."[43] This concern for the family combined with a traditional biased view of woman's nature, as one writer for the *Saturday Review* revealed:

> *The power of reasoning is so small in women that they need adventitious help, and if they have not the guidance and check of a religious conscience, it is useless to expect from them self-control on abstract principles. They do not calculate consequences, and they are reckless when they once give way, hence they are to be kept straight only through their affections, the religious sentiment and a well-educated moral sense.*[44]

No doubt, the following comment of Jules and Edmond Goncourt, two prominent French writers, reflected the mood of many other French intellectuals:

> *Men like ourselves need a woman of little breeding and education who is nothing but gaiety and natural wit, because a woman of that sort can charm and please us like an agreeable animal to which we may become quite attached. But if a mistress has acquired a veneer of breeding, art, or literature, and tries to talk to us on an equal footing about our thoughts and our feeling for beauty; if she wants to be a companion and partner in the cultivation of our tastes or the writing of our books, then she becomes for us as unbearable*

> *as a piano out of tune—and very soon an object of dislike.*[45]

In contrast to most of their contemporaries, some prominent men did support equal rights for women. "Can man be free if woman be slave?"[46] asked Shelley, who favored female suffrage. So too did Bentham and the political economist William Thompson, who wrote *Appeal of One Half of the Human Race* (1825). John Stuart Mill thought that differences between the sexes (and between the classes) were due far more to education than to inherited inequalities. Believing that all people—women as well as men—should be able to develop their talents and intellects as fully as possible, Mill was an early champion of female equality, including women's suffrage. In 1867, Mill, as a member of Parliament, proposed that the suffrage be extended to women (the proposal was rejected by a vote of 194 to 74).

In 1851, Mill had married Harriet Taylor, a long-time friend and a recent widow. An ardent feminist, Harriet Mill influenced her husband's thought. In *The Subjection of Women* (1869), Mill argued that male dominance of women constituted a flagrant abuse of power. He described female inequality as a single relic of an old outlook that had been exploded in everything else. It violated the principle of individual rights and hindered the progress of humanity:

> *. . . the principle which regulates the existing social relations between the two sexes—the legal subordination of one sex to the other—is wrong in itself, and now one of the chief hindrances to human improvement . . . it ought to be replaced by a principle of perfect equality, admitting no power or privilege on the one side, nor disability on the other.*[47]

Mill considered it only just that women be admitted to all the functions and occupations until then reserved for men. The struggle for female rights became a major issue in several lands at the end of the nineteenth century and the beginning of the twentieth.

❖ ❖ ❖

Notes

1. Quoted in George J. Becker, *Master European Realists of the Nineteenth Century* (New York: Ungar, 1982), pp. 30–31.
2. Cited in Damian Grant, *Realism* (London: Methuen, 1970), pp. 31–32.
3. Cited in F. W. J. Hemmings, ed., *The Age of Realism* (Atlantic Highlands, N.J.: Humanities Press, 1978), p. 152.
4. Quoted in Leonard J. Davis, "Gustave Flaubert," in *The Romantic Century,* ed. Jacques Barzun and George Stade, vol. 7 of *European Writers* (New York: Charles Scribner's Sons, 1985), p. 1382.
5. Émile Zola, *The Experimental Novel,* trans. Belle M. Sherman (New York: Haskell House, 1964), pp. 20–21, 23.
6. Henrik Ibsen, *A Doll's House,* in *Eleven Plays of Henrik Ibsen* (New York: Modern Library, n.d.), p. 85–87.
7. Quoted in Ernst Cassirer, *The Problem of Knowledge,* trans. William H. Woglom and Charles W. Hendel (New Haven, Conn.: Yale University Press, 1950), p. 244.
8. Quoted in Andrew D. White, *A History of the Warfare of Science with Theology in Christendom* (New York: Appleton, 1896), 1:71.
9. Excerpted in Richard Olson, ed., *Science as Metaphor* (Belmont, Calif.: Wadsworth, 1971), p. 124.
10. Andrew Carnegie, *The Gospel of Wealth* (New York: Century, 1900), pp. 4, 11.
11. Karl Pearson, *National Life from the Standpoint of Science* (London: Adam & Charles Black, 1905), pp. 21, 64.
12. Quoted in H. W. Koch, "Social Darwinism in the 'New Imperialism,'" in *The Origins of the*

First World War, ed. H. W. Koch (New York: Taplinger, 1972), p. 341.

13. Ibid., p. 345.
14. Quoted in John C. Greene, *The Death of Adam* (New York: Mentor Books, 1961), p. 313.
15. Quoted in Sven Lindqvist, *Exterminate the Brutes,* trans. Joan Tate (New York: New Press, 1996), pp. 150–151.
16. Quoted in George M. Fredrickson, *The Black Image in the White Mind* (New York: Harper Torchbooks, 1972), pp. 26–27.
17. Ludwig Feuerbach, *The Essence of Christianity,* trans. George Eliot (New York: Harper Torchbooks, 1957), p. 33.
18. Ibid., pp. 26–28.
19. Karl Marx, *Theses on Feuerbach,* excerpted in *Karl Marx: Selected Writings in Sociology and Social Philosophy,* ed. T. B. Bottomore and Maximilien Rubel (London: Watts, 1956), p. 69.
20. Karl Marx, *The German Ideology* (New York: International Publishers, 1939), p. 18.
21. Friedrich Engels, *The Origin of the Family, Private Property & the State,* in Emile Burns, *A Handbook of Marxism* (New York: Random House, 1935), p. 330.
22. Karl Marx, *Capital* (Chicago: Charles H. Kerr, 1912), 1:268.
23. Karl Marx, *Economic and Philosophical Manuscripts,* in *Karl Marx: Early Writings,* ed. T. B. Bottomore (New York: McGraw-Hill, 1963), pp. 122, 124–125.
24. Marx, *German Ideology,* p. 69.
25. Karl Marx, *Communist Manifesto,* trans. Samuel Moore (Chicago: Henry Regnery, 1954), pp. 81–82.
26. Robert Tucker, *Philosophy and Myth in Karl Marx* (Cambridge, England: Cambridge University Press, 1972), p. 22.
27. Quoted in James Joll, *The Anarchists* (New York: Grosset & Dunlap, 1964), pp. 78–79.
28. Excerpted in G. P. Maximoff, ed., *The Political Philosophy of Bakunin* (Glencoe, Ill.: The Free Press, 1953), p. 287.
29. John Stuart Mill, *On Liberty* (Boston: Ticknor & Fields, 1863), p. 36.
30. Ibid., p. 22.
31. Thomas Hill Green, *Lectures on the Principles of Political Obligation* (Ann Arbor: University of Michigan Press, 1967), p. 219.
32. Herbert Spencer, *The Man Versus the State* (London: Watts, 1940), pp. 34, 49–50.
33. Ibid., p. 152.
34. Quoted in Anthony Arblaster, *The Rise and Decline of Liberalism* (London: Basil Blackwell, 1984), p. 290.
35. Excerpted in Eleanor S. Riemer and John C. Fout, eds., *European Women: A Documentary History, 1789–1945* (New York: Schocken Books, 1980), pp. 63–64.
36. Mary Wollstonecraft, *Vindication of the Rights of Woman* (London: Dent, 1929), pp. 11–12.
37. Excerpted in Gayle Graham Yates, ed., *Harriet Martineau on Women* (New Brunswick, N.J.: Rutgers University Press, 1985), p. 134.
38. Excerpted in Miriam Schneir, ed., *Feminism: The Essential Historical Writings* (New York: Vintage Books, 1972), pp. 40–41.
39. Ibid., pp. 76, 82.
40. Quoted in Bonnie S. Anderson and Judith P. Zinsser, *A History of Their Own* (New York: Harper & Row, 1988), 2:113.
41. Jean Jacques Rousseau, *Emile*, trans. Barbara Foxley (London: Dent, Everyman's Library, 1974), p. 370.
42. Quoted in J. A. and Olive Banks, *Feminism and Family Planning in Victorian England* (Liverpool: Liverpool University Press, 1965), p. 43.
43. Ibid., p. 46.
44. Ibid., p. 47.
45. Robert Baldick, ed. and trans., *Pages from the Goncourt Journal* (New York: Penguin Books, 1984), p. 27.
46. Percy Bysshe Shelley, "The Revolt of Islam," canto 2, stanza 43, in *The Complete Poetical Works of Percy Bysshe Shelley,* ed. Thomas Hutchinson (London: Oxford University Press, 1929), p. 63.
47. John Stuart Mill, *The Subjection of Women,* in *On Liberty, Etc.* (London: Oxford University Press, 1924), p. 427.

Suggested Reading

Andreski, Stanislav, ed., *The Essential Comte* (1974). An excellent collection of excerpts from Comte's works.

Becker, George J., *Master European Realists of the Nineteenth Century* (1982). Discussions of Flaubert, Zola, Chekhov, and other realists.

Bullock, Alan, and Maurice Shock, eds., *The Liberal Tradition* (1956). Well-chosen selections from the writings of British liberals; the introduction is an excellent survey of liberal thought.

de Ruggiero, G., *The History of European Liberalism* (1927). A good starting point for a study of the subject.

Farrington, Benjamin, *What Darwin Really Said* (1966). A brief study of Darwin's work.

Grant, Damian, *Realism* (1970). A very good short survey.

Greene, J. C., *The Death of Adam* (1961). The impact of evolution on Western thought.

Hemmings, F. W. J., ed., *The Age of Realism* (1978). A series of essays exploring realism in various countries.

Hofstadter, Richard, *Social Darwinism in American Thought* (1955). A classic treatment of the impact of evolution on American conservatism, imperialism, and racism.

Joll, James, *The Anarchists* (1964). A fine treatment of anarchists, their lives and thought.

Manuel, Frank E., *The Prophets of Paris* (1965). Contains a valuable chapter on Comte.

Matthews, Betty, ed., *Marx: A Hundred Years On* (1983). Eleven essays by noted authorities.

McLellan, David, *Karl Marx: His Life and Thought* (1977). A highly regarded biography.

———, ed., *Karl Marx: Selected Writings* (1977). A balanced selection of Marx's writings.

Nochlin, Linda, *Realism* (1971). The nature of realism; realism in art.

Richter, Melvin, *The Politics of Conscience* (1964). A study of Thomas Hill Green and his age.

Tucker, Robert, *The Marxian Revolutionary Idea* (1969). Marxism as a radical social philosophy.

———, *Philosophy and Myth in Karl Marx* (1972). The relationship of Marxist thought to German philosophy. Good treatment of Marx's early writings.

———, ed., *The Marx-Engels Reader* (1972). Marx's essential writings.

Review Questions

1. How did realism differ from romanticism?
2. Realism and naturalism reflected attitudes of mind shaped by science, industrialism, and secularism. Discuss this statement.
3. What was the relationship between positivism and science?
4. What was Comte's "law of the three stages"?
5. The theory of evolution had revolutionary consequences in areas other than science. Discuss this statement.
6. Why were Social Darwinist theories so popular?
7. Compare and contrast the approaches to Christianity of Strauss, Feuerbach, and Kierkegaard.
8. What did Marx have in common with the philosophes of the Enlightenment?
9. What did Marx's philosophy of history owe to Hegel? How did it diverge from Hegel?
10. What relationship did Marx see between economics and politics?
11. What relationship did Marx see between economics and thought?
12. Why did Marxism attract followers?
13. Discuss Marx's historical importance.
14. What weaknesses in Marxism have critics pointed out?
15. Why was Marx convinced that capitalism was doomed? How would its destruction happen?
16. Why did Proudhon hate government?
17. In what ways did Bakunin and Marx differ?
18. Relate the theories of Mill, Green, and Spencer to the evolution of liberalism. Draw relevant comparisons and contrasts.
19. The feminist movement was an outgrowth of certain ideals that emerged during the course of Western history. Discuss this statement.
20. What arguments were used by opponents of equal rights for women?

Chapter 25

The Surge of Nationalism: From Liberal to Extreme Nationalism

Victor Emmanuel and Garibaldi at the Bridge of Teano (1860). The unification of Italy was the work of the romantic liberal Giuseppe Mazzini, the practical politician Count Cavour, and the seasoned revolutionary Giuseppe Garibaldi. Selflessly, Garibaldi turned over his conquests in the south to Victor Emmanuel in 1861. (Scala/Art Resource, NY.)

■ **The Unification of Italy**
Forces for and Against Unity
Failed Revolutions
Cavour and Victory over Austria
Garibaldi and Victory in the South
Italian Unification Completed

■ **The Unification of Germany**
Prussia, Agent of Unification
Bismarck and the Road to Unity

■ **Nationality Problems in the Hapsburg Empire**
Magyarization
German Versus Czech
South Slavs

■ **The Rise of Racial Nationalism**
Volkish Thought
Anti-Semitism: The Power and Danger of Mythical Thinking

The revolutions of 1848 ended in failure, but nationalist energies were too powerful to contain. In 1867, Hungary gained the autonomy it had sought in 1848, and by 1871, the unification of both Italy and Germany was complete.

The leading architects of Italian and German unification were not liberal idealists or romantic dreamers of the type who had fought in the revolutions of 1848; they were tough-minded practitioners of *Realpolitik,* "the politics of reality." Shrewd and calculating statesmen, they respected power and knew how to wield it; focusing on the actual world, they dismissed ideals as illusory, noble sentiments that impeded effective action. Realpolitik was the political counterpart of realism and positivism. All three outlooks shared the desire to view things coldly and objectively as they are, rather than as idealists would like them to be.

Nationalism, gaining in intensity in the last part of the nineteenth century, was to become the dominant spiritual force in European life. Once Germany was unified, Pan-Germans sought to incorporate Germans living outside the *Reich* (German empire) into the new Germany and to build a vast overseas empire. Russian Pan-Slavs dreamed of bringing the Slavs of eastern Europe under the control of "Mother Russia." Growing increasingly resentful of Magyar and German domination, the Slavic minorities of the Hapsburg Empire agitated for recognition of their national rights. In the late 1800s, nationalism became increasingly belligerent, intolerant, and irrational, threatening the peace of Europe and the liberal-humanist tradition of the Enlightenment.

The Unification of Italy

In 1848, liberals failed to drive the Austrians out of Italy and to unite the Italian nation. By 1870, however, Italian unification was achieved despite many obstacles.

Forces for and Against Unity

In 1815, Italy consisted of separate states. In the south, a Bourbon king ruled the Kingdom of the Two Sicilies; the pope governed the Papal States in central Italy; Hapsburg Austria ruled Lom-

Chronology 25.1 ❖ Unification of Italy

1821	Austria suppresses Carbonari rebellion
1831–32	Austria suppresses another Carbonari insurrection
1832	Mazzini forms Young Italy
March 1848	Austrians are forced to withdraw from Milan and Venice
November 1848	Liberal revolution forces pope to flee Rome
1848–49	Austria reasserts its authority in Milan and Venice; Louis Napoleon crushes revolutionaries in Rome
1858	Napoleon III agrees to help Piedmont-Sardinia against Austria
1859	War between Piedmont-Sardinia and Austria: Piedmont obtains Lombardy from Austria; Parma, Modena, Tuscany, and Romagna vote to join with Piedmont
1860	Garibaldi invades Kingdom of the Two Sicilies
March 17, 1861	Victor Emmanuel of Piedmont is proclaimed king of Italy
1866	Italy's alliance with Prussia against Austria results in annexation of Venetia by Italy
1870	Rome is incorporated into the Italian state and unity is achieved

bardy and Venetia in the north; and Hapsburg princes subservient to Austria ruled the duchies of Tuscany, Parma, and Modena. Piedmont in the northwest and the island of Sardinia were governed by an Italian dynasty, the House of Savoy. Besides these political divisions, Italy was divided economically and culturally. Throughout the peninsula, attachment to the local region was stronger than desire for national unity. Economic ties between north and south were weak; inhabitants of the northern Italian cities felt little closeness to Sicilian peasants. Except for the middle class, most Italians clung to the values of the Old Regime. Believing that society was ordered by God, they accepted without question rule by prince and pope and rejected the values associated with the French Revolution and the Enlightenment. To these traditionalists, national unity was also hateful. It would deprive the pope of his control over central Italy, introduce liberal ideas that would undermine clerical and aristocratic authority, and depose legitimate princes.

During the wars of the French Revolution, France had occupied Italy. The French eliminated many barriers to trade among the Italian states. They built roads, which improved links between the various regions, and they introduced a standard system of law over most of the land. The French also gave the Italian states constitutions, representative assemblies, and the concept of the state as a community of citizens.

The Italian middle class believed that expelling foreign rulers and forging national unity would continue the process of enlightened reform initiated by the French occupation and that this process would promote economic growth. Merchants and manufacturers wanted to abolish taxes on goods transported from one Italian state to another; they wanted roads and railways built to link the peninsula together; and they wanted to do away with the numerous systems of coinage and weights and measures, which complicated business transactions. Italians who had served Napoleon as local officials, clerks, and army officers resisted the restoration of clerical and feudal privileges, which denied them career opportunities.

Through works of history and literature, an intellectual elite awakened interest in Italy's glorious past. It insisted that a people who had built the Roman Empire and produced the Renaissance must not remain weak and divided, their land occupied by Austrians. These sentiments appealed particularly to university students and the middle class. But the rural masses, illiterate and preoccupied with the hardships of daily life, had little concern for this struggle for national revival.

Failed Revolutions

Secret societies kept alive the hopes for liberty and independence from foreign rule in the period after 1815. The most important of these societies was the Carbonari, which had clubs in every state in Italy. In 1820, the Carbonari, its members drawn largely from the middle class and the army, enjoyed a few months of triumph in the Kingdom of the Two Sicilies. Supported by the army and militia, they forced King Ferdinand I to grant a constitution and a parliamentary government. But Metternich feared that the germ of revolution would spread to other countries. Supported by Prussia and Russia, Austria suppressed the constitutional government in Naples and another revolution, which broke out in Piedmont. In both cases, Austria firmly fixed an absolute ruler on the throne. In 1831–32, the Austrians suppressed another insurrection by the Carbonari, in the Papal States. During these uprisings, the peasants had given little support; indeed, they seemed to side with the traditional rulers.

After the failure of the Carbonari, a new generation of leaders emerged in Italy. One of them, Giuseppe Mazzini (1805–1872), dedicated his life to the creation of a united and republican Italy—a goal he pursued with extraordinary moral intensity and determination. Mazzini was both a romantic and a liberal. As a liberal, he fought for republican and constitutional government and held that national unity would enhance individual liberty. As a romantic, he sought truth through heightened feeling and intuition and believed that an awakened Italy would lead to the regeneration of humanity. Mazzini believed that just as Rome had provided law and unity in the ancient world and the Roman pope had led Latin Christendom during the Middle Ages, so a third Rome, a newly united Italy, would usher in a new age of free nations, personal liberty, and equality. This era would represent great progress for humanity: peace, prosperity, and universal happiness would replace conflict, materialism, and self-interest. Given to religious mysticism, Mazzini saw a world of independent states founded on nationality, republicanism, and democracy as the fulfillment of God's plan.

After his release from prison for participating in the insurrection of 1831, Mazzini went into exile and founded a new organization, Young Italy. Consisting of dedicated revolutionaries, many of them students, Young Italy was intended to serve as the instrument for the awakening of Italy and the transformation of Europe into a brotherhood of free peoples. This sacred struggle, said Mazzini, demanded heroism and sacrifice.

Mazzini believed that a successful revolution must come from below—from the people, moved by a profound love for their nation. They must overthrow the Hapsburg princes and create a democratic republic. The Carbonari had failed, he said, because they had staged only local uprisings and had no overall plan for the liberation and unification of Italy. This could be achieved only by a revolution of the masses. Mazzini had great charisma, determination, courage, and eloquence; he was also a prolific writer. His idealism attracted the intelligentsia and youth and kept alive the spirit of national unity. He infused the *Risorgimento,* the movement for Italian unity, with spiritual intensity.

Mazzini's plans for a mass uprising against Austria and the princes failed. In 1834, a band of Mazzini's followers attempted to invade Savoy. But everything went wrong, and the invasion collapsed. Other setbacks occurred in 1837, 1841, and 1843–44. During the revolutions of 1848, however, Italian liberal-nationalists enjoyed initial successes. In Sicily, revolutionaries forced King Ferdinand to grant a liberal constitution. The rulers of Tuscany and Piedmont-Sardinia promised constitutions. After five days of fighting, revolutionaries drove the Austrians out of Milan in Lombardy. The Austrians were also forced to evacuate Venice, where a republic was proclaimed. The pope fled Rome, and Mazzini was elected to an executive office in a new Roman Republic. However, the forces of reaction, led by Hapsburg Austria, regained their courage and authority, and crushed the revolutionary movements one by one. French troops dissolved the infant Roman Republic and restored Pope Pius IX to power. Italy remained divided, and Austria still ruled the north.

Cavour and Victory over Austria

The failure of the revolutions of 1848 contained an obvious lesson: Mazzini's approach, an armed uprising by aroused masses, did not work because the masses were not committed to the nationalist cause and the revolutionaries were no match for the Austrian army. Italian nationalists now hoped that the Kingdom of Piedmont-Sardinia, ruled by an Italian dynasty, would expel the Austrians and lead the drive for unity. Count Camillo Benso di Cavour (1810–1861), the chief minister of Piedmont-Sardinia, became the architect of Italian unity.

Unlike Mazzini, Cavour was neither a dreamer nor a speechmaker but a cautious and practical statesman who realized that mass uprisings could not succeed against Austrian might. Moreover, mistrusting the common people, he did not approve of Mazzini's goal of a democratic republic. Cavour had no precise plan for unifying Italy. His immediate aim was to increase the territory of Piedmont by driving the Austrians from northern Italy and incorporating Lombardy and Venetia into Piedmont-Sardinia. But this expulsion could not be accomplished without allies, for Austria was a great power and Piedmont a small state. To improve Piedmont's image in foreign affairs, Cavour launched a reform program to strengthen the economy. He reorganized the currency, taxes, and the national debt; in addition, he had railways and steamships built, fostered improved agricultural methods, and encouraged new businesses. Within a few years, Piedmont became a progressive modern state.

In 1855, Piedmont joined England and France in the Crimean War against Russia. Cavour had no quarrel with Russia but sought the friendship of Britain and France and a chance to be heard in world affairs. At the peace conference, Cavour was granted an opportunity to denounce Austria for occupying Italian lands.

After the peace conference, Cavour continued to encourage anti-Austrian feeling among Italians and to search for foreign support. He found a supporter in Napoleon III (1852–1870), the French emperor, who hoped that a unified northern Italy would become an ally and client of France.

In 1858, Cavour and Napoleon III reached a secret agreement. If Austria attacked Piedmont, France would aid the Italian state. Piedmont would annex Lombardy and Venetia and parts of the Papal States. In return, France would obtain Nice and Savoy from Piedmont. With this agreement in his pocket, Cavour cleverly maneuvered Austria into declaring war (he did so by strengthening Piedmont's army and urging volunteers from Austrian-controlled Lombardy to join it), for it had to appear that Austria was the aggressor.

Supported by French forces and taking advantage of poor Austrian planning, Piedmont conquered Lombardy and occupied Milan. But Napoleon III quickly had second thoughts. If Piedmont took any of the pope's territory, French Catholics would blame their own leader. Even more serious was the fear that Prussia, suspicious of French aims, would aid Austria. For these reasons Napoleon III, without consulting Cavour, signed an armistice with Austria. Piedmont would acquire Lombardy, but no more. An outraged Cavour demanded that his state continue the war until all northern Italy was liberated, but King Victor Emmanuel of Piedmont accepted the Austrian peace terms.

The victory of Piedmont-Sardinia, however, proved greater than Cavour had anticipated. During the conflict, patriots in Parma, Modena, Tuscany, and Romagna (one of the Papal States) had seized power. These new revolutionary governments voted to join with Piedmont. Neither France nor Austria would risk military action to thwart Piedmont's expansion. In return for Napoleon III's acquiescence, Piedmont ceded Nice and Savoy to France.

Garibaldi and Victory in the South

Piedmont's success spurred revolutionary activity in the Kingdom of the Two Sicilies. In the spring of 1860, some one thousand red-shirted adventurers and patriots led by Giuseppe Garibaldi (1807–1882) landed in Sicily. They were determined to liberate the land from its Bourbon ruler, and they succeeded.

An early supporter of Mazzini, Garibaldi had been forced to flee Italy to avoid arrest for his revolutionary activities. He spent thirteen years in South America, where he took part in revolutionary movements. There he learned the skills of the revolutionary's trade and toughened his body and will for the struggle that lay ahead.

Garibaldi held progressive views. He supported the liberation of all subject nationalities, female equality, the right of workers to organize, racial equality, and the abolition of capital punishment. But the cause of Italian national unity was his true religion. Whereas Cavour set his sights primarily on extending Piedmont's control over northern Italy, Garibaldi dedicated himself to the creation of a unified Italy.

Garibaldi returned to Italy just in time to fight in the revolution of 1848. He was a brilliant leader who captivated the hearts of the people and won the poor and illiterate to the cause of Italian nationality. A young Italian who fought beside Garibaldi in 1849 said of his commander:

> *I shall never forget that day when I first saw him on his beautiful white horse. He reminded us of . . . our Savior . . . everyone said the same. I could not resist him. I went after him; thousands did likewise. He only had to show himself. We all worshipped him. We could not help it.*[1]

After the liberation of Sicily in 1860, Garibaldi invaded the mainland. He occupied Naples without a fight and prepared to advance on Rome. In this particular instance, Garibaldi's success confirmed Mazzini's belief that a popular leader could arouse the masses to heroic action.

Cavour feared that an assault on Rome by Garibaldi would lead to French intervention. Napoleon III had pledged to defend the pope's lands, and a French garrison had been stationed in Rome since 1849. Moreover, Cavour considered Garibaldi too impulsive and rash, too attracted to republican ideals, and too popular to lead the struggle for unification.

Cavour persuaded Napoleon III to approve an invasion of the Papal States by Piedmont to head off Garibaldi. A papal force offered only token opposition, and the Papal States of Umbria and the Marches soon voted for union with Piedmont, as did Naples and Sicily. Refusing to trade on his prestige with the masses to fulfill personal ambition, Garibaldi turned over his conquests to Piedmont's King Victor Emmanuel, who was declared king of Italy in 1861.

Italian Unification Completed

Two regions still remained outside the control of the new Italy: the city of Rome, ruled by the pope and protected by French troops; and Venetia, occupied by Austria. Cavour died in 1861, but the march toward unification continued. During the conflict between Prussia and Austria in 1866, Italy sided with the victorious Prussians and was rewarded with Venetia. During the Franco-Prussian War of 1870, France withdrew its garrisons from Rome; much to the anger of the pope, Italian troops marched in, and Rome was declared the capital of Italy.

The Unification of Germany

In 1848, German liberals and nationalists, believing in the strength of their ideals, naively underestimated the power of the conservative Old Order. After the failed revolution, some disenchanted revolutionaries retained only a halfhearted commitment to liberalism or embraced conservatism; others fled the country, weakening the liberal leadership. All liberals came to doubt the effectiveness of revolution as a way to transform Germany into a unified state; all gained new respect for the realities of power. Abandoning idealism for realism, liberals now thought that German unity would be achieved through Prussian arms, not liberal ideals.

Chronology 25.2 ❖ Unification of Germany

1815	German Confederation is formed
1834	Zollverein is established under Prussian leadership
1848	Liberals fail to unify Germany
1862	Bismarck becomes chancellor of Prussia
1864	Austria and Prussia defeat Denmark in a war over Schleswig-Holstein
1866	Seven Weeks' War between Austria and Prussia: Prussia emerges as the dominant power in Germany and organizes the North German Confederation
1870–71	Franco-Prussian War
January 18, 1871	William I becomes German kaiser

Prussia, Agent of Unification

During the late seventeenth and eighteenth centuries, Prussian kings had fashioned a rigorously trained and disciplined army. The state bureaucracy, often staffed by ex-soldiers, perpetuated the military mentality. As the chief organizations in the state, the army and the bureaucracy drilled into the Prussian people a respect for discipline and authority.

The Prussian throne was supported by the Junkers. These powerful aristocrats, who owned vast estates farmed by serfs, were exempt from most taxes and dominated local government in their territories. The Junkers' commanding position made them officers in the royal army, diplomats, and leading officials in the state bureaucracy. The Junkers knew that a weakening of the king's power would lead to the loss of their own aristocratic prerogatives.

In France in the late 1700s, a powerful and politically conscious middle class had challenged aristocratic privileges. The Prussian monarchy and the Junkers had faced no such challenge, for the Prussian middle class at that time was small and ineffectual. The idea of individual rights did not deeply penetrate Prussian consciousness, nor did it undermine the Prussian tradition of obedience to military and state authority.

Reforms from Above. The reform movement that began after Napoleon completely routed the Prussians at Jena (in 1806) arose from distress at the military collapse and at the apathy of the Prussian population. High bureaucrats and military men demanded reforms that would draw the people closer to their country and king. These leaders had learned the great lesson of the French Revolution: a devoted citizen army fights more effectively than oppressed serfs. To imbue all classes with civic pride, the reformers abolished hereditary serfdom, gave the urban middle class a greater voice in city government, laid the foundations for universal education, and granted full citizenship to Jews. To improve the army's morale, they eliminated severe punishments and based promotions on performance rather than birth.

But the reformers failed to give Prussia a constitution and parliamentary institutions. The middle class still had no voice in the central government. Monarchical power persisted, and the economic, political, and military power of the Junkers remained unbroken. Thus, liberalism had an unpromising beginning in Prussia. In France, the bourgeoisie had instituted reforms based on the principles of liberty and equality; in Prussia, the bureaucracy introduced reforms to strengthen the state, not to promote liberty. A precedent had been established: reform in Prussia would come from conservative rulers, not from the efforts of a middle class aroused by liberal ideals.

In 1834, under Prussian leadership, the German states, with the notable exception of Austria, had established the *Zollverein,* a customs union, which

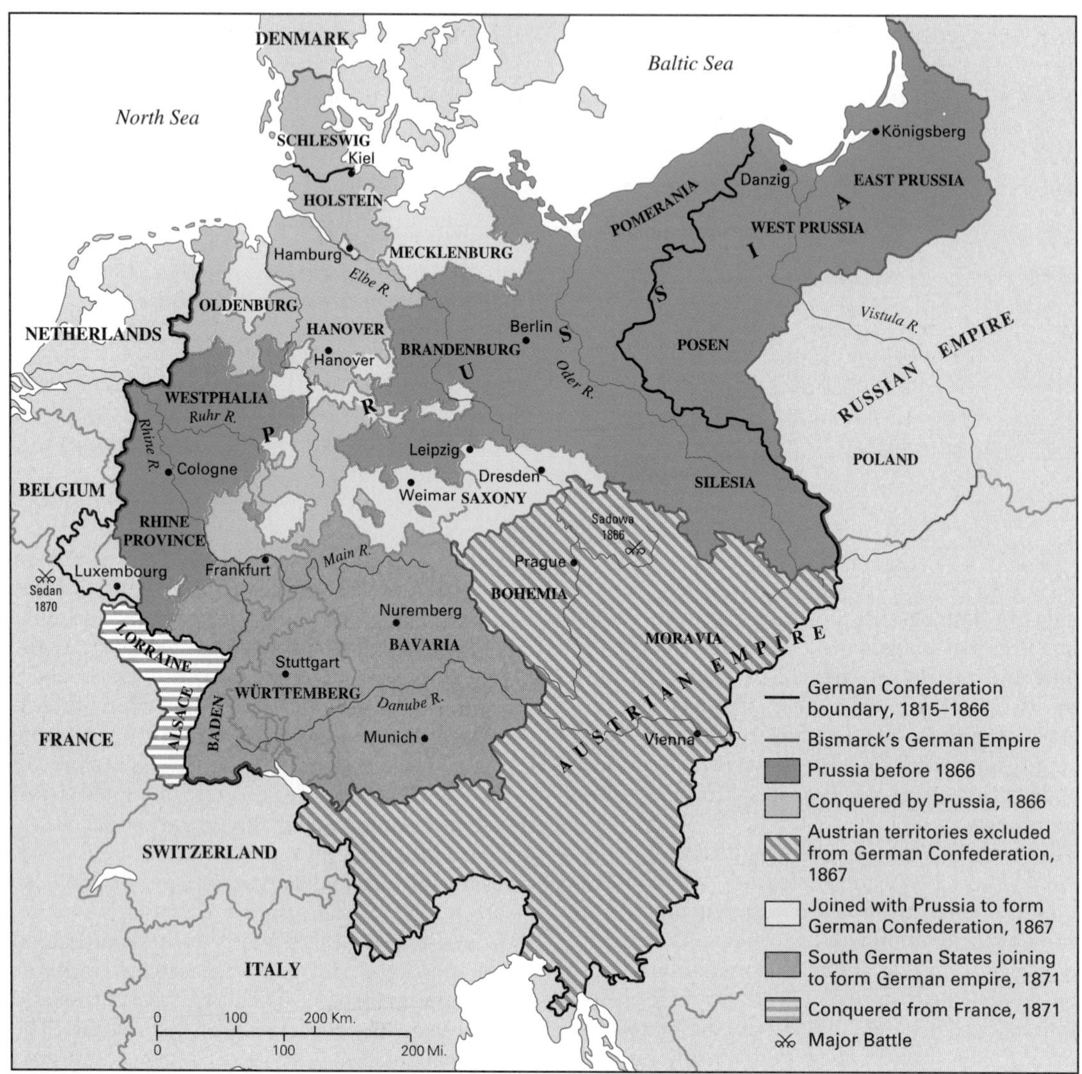

Map 25.1 Unification of Germany, 1866–1871 Between 1866 and 1871, Prussia fought wars against Denmark, Austria, and France, which resulted in the unification of Germany under Prussian leadership. Otto von Bismarck was the principal architect of German unification.

abolished tariffs between the states. The customs union stimulated economic activity and promoted a desire for greater unity. Businessmen, particularly, felt that having thirty-nine states in Germany was an obstacle to economic progress. The Zollverein provided the economic foundations for the political unification of Germany, and it led many Germans to view Prussia, not Austria, as the leader of the unification movement.

Liberals' Failure. Influenced by the legacy of the French Revolution, the ideas of legal equality, political liberty, and careers open to talent found favor with the Prussian bourgeoisie. Like the

French bourgeois of the Old Regime, Prussian bankers, manufacturers, and lawyers hated a system that denied them social recognition and political influence but rewarded idle sons of the nobility with the best positions. They also denounced government regulations and taxes, which hampered business, and they loathed the rigorous censorship, which stifled free thought. Peasants and artisans, concerned with economic survival, respectful of tradition, and suspicious of new ideas, did not identify with liberal principles.

During the revolution of 1848, liberals failed to wrest power from the monarchy and aristocracy and create a unified Germany. Frederick William IV (1840–1861) had refused the crown offered him by the Frankfurt Assembly. The Prussian monarch could not stomach German unity created by a revolution of commoners. But a German union fashioned and headed by a conservative Prussia was different and proved attractive to Frederick William. In 1849, Prussia initiated a diplomatic campaign toward this end. Austria resisted this maneuver because it was determined to retain its preeminence in German affairs. Faced with Hapsburg resistance, Prussia renounced its plans for a German union and agreed to the reestablishment of the German Confederation. This political humiliation taught Frederick William an obvious lesson: before Prussia could extend its hegemony over the other German states, Austrian influence in German affairs would have to be eliminated.

Bismarck and the Road to Unity

In 1858, Frederick William IV, by then mentally deranged, surrendered control of the government to his brother, who became William I (1861–1888), king of Prussia, when Frederick William died. William also regarded Austria as the chief barrier to the extension of Prussian power in Germany. This was one reason why he called for a drastic reorganization of the Prussian army. But the liberals in the lower chamber of the Prussian parliament blocked passage of the army reforms, for they feared that the reforms would greatly increase the power of the monarchy and the military establishment. Unable to secure passage, William withdrew the reform bill and asked the lower chamber for additional funds to cover government expenses. When Parliament granted these funds, he used the money to institute the army reforms. Learning from its mistake, the lower chamber would not approve the new budget in 1862 without an itemized breakdown.

A conflict had arisen between the liberal majority in the lower chamber and the crown. If the liberals won, they would, in effect, establish parliamentary control over the king and the army. At this critical hour, King William asked Otto von Bismarck (1815–1898) to lead the battle against Parliament.

Descended on his father's side from an old aristocratic family, Bismarck was a staunch supporter of the Prussian monarchy and the Junker class and a devout patriot. He yearned to increase the territory and prestige of his beloved Prussia and to protect the authority of the Prussian king, who, Bismarck believed, ruled by the grace of God. Liberals were outraged by Bismarck's domineering and authoritarian manner and his determination to preserve monarchical power and the aristocratic order. Set on continuing the reorganization of the army and determined not to bow to parliamentary pressure, Bismarck ordered the collection of taxes without Parliament's approval—an action that would have been unthinkable in Britain or the United States.

When the lower chamber continued to withhold funds, Bismarck dismissed the chamber, imposed strict censorship on the press, arrested outspoken liberals, and fired liberals from the civil service. The liberals protested against these arbitrary and unconstitutional moves, but they did not use force. Since the army fully supported the government and there was no significant popular support for challenging the government, an armed uprising would have failed. What led to a resolution of the conflict was Bismarck's extraordinary success in foreign affairs.

Wars with Denmark and Austria. To Bismarck, a war between Austria and Prussia seemed inevitable, for only by removing Austria from German affairs could Prussia extend its dominion over the other German states. Bismarck's first move, however, was not against Austria but

William I of Prussia. German emperor, in the Hall of Mirrors at Versailles (1871). (*The Mansell Collection.*)

against Denmark. The issue that led to the war in 1864 was enormously complex. Simplified, the issue was that Bismarck (and German nationalists) wanted to free the two duchies of Schleswig and Holstein from Danish control. Both territories, which contained a large number of Germans, had been administered by Denmark, but in 1863 Schleswig was incorporated into the Danish realm. Hoping to prevent Prussia from annexing the territories, Austria joined Prussia as an ally. After Denmark's defeat, Austria and Prussia tried to decide the disposition of the territories. Austria wanted a joint Austrian and Prussian occupation of the regions. But the negotiations broke down. Bismarck used the dispute to goad Austria into war. The Austrians, on their side, were convinced that Prussia must be defeated for Austria to retain its influence over German affairs.

In the Austro-Prussian war of 1866, Prussia, with astonishing speed, assembled its forces and overran Austrian territory. At the battle of Sadowa (or Königgrätz), Prussia decisively defeated the main Austrian forces and the Seven Weeks' War ended. Prussia took no territory from Austria, but the latter agreed to Prussia's annexation of Schleswig and Holstein and a number of small German states. Prussia, moreover, organized a confederation of North German states, from

OTTO VON BISMARCK. Bismarck (1815–1898), the Iron Chancellor, was instrumental in unifying Germany. A conservative, he resisted Parliament's efforts to weaken the monarch's power. Here he is portrayed in his youth, before becoming chancellor. (*Photo AKG London.*)

which Austria was excluded. In effect, Austria was removed from German affairs, and Prussia became the dominant power in Germany.

The Triumph of Nationalism and Conservatism over Liberalism. The Prussian victory had a profound impact on political life within Prussia. Bismarck was the man of the hour, the great hero who had extended Prussia's power. Most liberals forgave Bismarck for his authoritarian handling of Parliament. The liberal press, which had previously denounced Bismarck for running roughshod over the constitution, now lionized him. Prussians were urged to concentrate on the glorious tasks ahead and put aside the constitutional struggle, which, in contrast, appeared petty and insignificant.

Bismarck recognized the great appeal of nationalism and used it to expand Prussia's power over other German states and strengthen Prussia's voice in European affairs. By heralding his state as the champion of unification, Bismarck gained the support of nationalists throughout Germany. In the past, the nationalist cause had belonged to the liberals, but Bismarck appropriated it to promote Prussian expansion and conservative rule.

Prussia's victory over Austria, therefore, was a triumph for conservatism and nationalism and a defeat for liberalism. The liberal struggle for constitutional government in Prussia collapsed. The Prussian monarch retained the right to override parliamentary opposition and act on his own initiative. In 1848, Prussian might had suppressed a liberal revolution; in 1866, liberals, beguiled by Bismarck's military triumphs, gave up the struggle for responsible parliamentary government. They had traded political freedom for Prussian military glory and power.

The capitulation of Prussian liberals demonstrated the essential weakness of the German liberal tradition. German liberals displayed diminishing commitment to the principles of parliamentary government and growing fascination with power, military triumph, and territorial expansion. Bismarck's words, written in 1858, turned out to be prophetic: "Exalt his self-esteem toward foreigners and the Prussian forgets whatever bothers him about conditions at home."[2] The liberal dream of a united Germany had been preempted by conservatives. Enthralled by Bismarck's achievement, many liberals abandoned liberalism and threw their support behind the authoritarian Prussian state. And Germans of all classes acquired an adoration for Prussian militarism and for the power state, with its Machiavellian guideline that all means are justified if they result in the expansion of German power. In 1848, German liberals had called for "Unity and Freedom." What Bismarck gave them was unity and authoritarianism.

War with France. Prussia emerged from the war with Austria as the leading power in the North German Confederation; the Prussian king controlled the armies and foreign affairs of the states within the confederation. To complete the unification of Germany, Bismarck would have to draw the South German states into the new confederation. But the South German states, Catholic and hostile to Prussian authoritarianism, feared being absorbed by Prussia. Bismarck hoped that a war between Prussia and France would ignite the nationalist feelings of the South Germans, causing them to overlook the differences that separated them from Prussia.

Napoleon III, the emperor of France, was not averse to war either. The creation of a powerful North German Confederation had frightened the French, and the prospect that the South German states might one day add their strength to the new Germany was terrifying. Both France and Prussia had parties that advocated war.

A cause for war arose over the succession to the vacated Spanish throne. Under strong consideration was Prince Leopold of Hohenzollern-Sigmaringen, a distant relative of King William of Prussia. France vehemently opposed the candidacy of Leopold, for his accession might lead to Prussian influence being extended into Spain. William, seeking to preserve the peace, urged Prince Leopold to withdraw his name from consideration.

But William refused the French ambassador's demand that he give formal assurance that no Hohenzollern would ever again be a candidate for the Spanish crown. In a telegram sent from Ems to Berlin, he informed Bismarck of his conversation with the French ambassador. With the support of high military leaders, Bismarck edited the telegram. The revised version gave the impression that the Prussian king and the French ambassador had insulted each other. Bismarck wanted to inflame French feeling against Prussia and arouse German opinion against France. He succeeded. In both Paris and Berlin, crowds of people, gripped by war fever, demanded satisfaction. When France declared a general mobilization, Prussia followed suit; Bismarck had his war.

With the memory of the great Napoleon still strong, the French expected a quick victory. But the poorly prepared and incompetently led French army could not withstand the powerful Prussian military machine. The South German states, as Bismarck had anticipated, came to the aid of Prussia. Quickly and decisively routing the French forces and capturing Napoleon III, the Prussians went on to besiege Paris. Faced with starvation, Paris surrendered in January 1871. France was compelled to pay a large indemnity and to cede to Germany the border provinces of Alsace and Lorraine—a loss that French patriots could never accept.

The Franco-Prussian War completed the unification of Germany. On January 18, 1871, at Versailles, the German princes granted the title *kaiser* (emperor) to William I. A powerful nation had arisen in central Europe. Its people were educated, disciplined, and efficient; its industries and commerce were rapidly expanding; its army was the finest in Europe. Vigorous, confident, and intensely nationalistic, the new German Empire would be eager to play a greater role in world affairs. No nation in Europe was a match for the new Germany. Metternich's fears had been realized: a Germany dominated by Prussia had upset the balance of power. The unification of Germany created fears, tensions, and rivalries that would culminate in world war.

Nationality Problems in the Hapsburg Empire

In Italy and Germany, nationalism had led to the creation of unified states; in Austria, nationalism eventually caused the destruction of the centuries-old Hapsburg dynasty. A mosaic of different nationalities, each with its own history and traditions, the Austrian Empire could not survive in an age of intense nationalism. England and France had succeeded in unifying peoples of different ethnic backgrounds, but they did so during the Middle Ages, when ethnic consciousness was still rudimentary. The Austrian Empire, in contrast, had to weld together and reconcile antagonistic nationalities when nationalistic consciousness was high. The empire's collapse in the final stages of World War I was the culmination of years of antagonism between its different peoples.

In the first half of the nineteenth century, the Germans, constituting less than one-quarter of the population, were the dominant national group in the empire. But Magyars, Poles, Czechs, Slovaks, Croats, Romanians, Ruthenians, and Italians were experiencing national self-awareness. Poets and writers who had been educated in Latin, French, and German began to write in their mother tongues and extol their splendors. By searching their past for glorious ancestors and glorious deeds, writers kindled pride in their native histories and folklore and aroused anger against past and present injustices.

In 1848–49, the Hapsburg monarchy had extinguished the Magyar bid for independence, the Czech revolution in Prague, and the uprisings in the Italian provinces of Lombardy and Venetia. Greatly alarmed by these revolutions, the Austrian power structure resolved to resist pressures for political rights by strengthening autocracy and tightening the central bureaucracy. German and Germanized officials took over administrative and judicial duties formerly handled on a local level. An expanded secret police stifled liberal and nationalist expressions. The various nationalities, of course, resented these efforts at centralization and repression.

Magyarization

The defeats by France and Piedmont in 1859 and by Prussia in 1866 cost Austria its two Italian provinces. The defeat by Prussia also forced the Hapsburg monarchy to make concessions to the Magyars, the strongest of the non-German nationalities; for without a loyal Hungary, the Hapsburg monarchy could suffer other humiliations. The Settlement of 1867 split the Hapsburg territories into Austria and Hungary. The two countries retained a common ruler, Francis Joseph (1848–1916), who was emperor of Austria and king of Hungary. Hungary gained complete control over its internal affairs: the administration of justice and education. Foreign and military affairs, as well as common financial concerns, were dealt with by a ministry consisting of delegates from both lands.

With the Settlement of 1867, Magyars and Germans became the dominant nationalities in the empire. The other nationalities felt that the German-Magyar political, economic, and cultural domination blocked their own national aspirations. Nationality struggles in the half-century following the Settlement of 1867 consumed the energies of the Austrians and Hungarians. In both lands, however, the leaders failed to solve the problem of minorities, a failure that helped precipitate World War I and led to the dissolution of the empire during the last weeks of the war.

The nationality problems in Hungary differed substantially from those in Austria. Constituting slightly less than half the population of Hungary, the Magyars were determined to retain their hegemony over the other minorities: Romanians, Slovaks, Ruthenians, Serbs, Croats, and Jews. In the first phase of their national struggle, the Hungarians had sought to liberate their nation from German domination. In the second phase, after 1867, the landholding aristocracy, which ruled Hungary, tried to impose the Magyar language and traditions on the other nationalities. Non-Magyars who learned the Magyar language and considered themselves Hungarians could participate as equals in Hungarian society. Those who resisted were viewed as traitors and conspirators and faced severe penalties. Non-Magyars were largely excluded from voting and virtually barred from government jobs, which were reserved for Magyars or those who had adopted Magyar language and culture.

The government tightly controlled the non-Magyar peoples. It suppressed their cultural organizations and newspapers, and the great majority of public schools, even in predominantly non-Magyar regions, carried on instruction largely in Magyar. Protests by the nationalities against this forced Magyarization often led to jail sentences. The repressive measures strengthened the Slavs' and Romanians' hatred of the regime. At the same time, however, Magyarization brought economic and cultural opportunities. Jews in particular accepted the Magyar government and took advantage of what it offered.

But nationality movements within Hungary constituted less of a threat to the preservation of the Austro-Hungarian Empire than did Magyar nationalism itself. The Independence party, whose influence grew after 1900, began to demand a complete end to the link with Austria and the "cursed common institutions."

German Versus Czech

The Austrian population of the Dual Monarchy was made up of Germans (one-third) and Slavs (two-thirds). Hungary strove to forge a unified

The Young Czech Party Demonstrating in the Austrian Parliament (1900). The Hapsburg Empire was burdened by conflicts between its different nationalities. In Bohemia, Czechs and Germans often engaged in violent confrontations as Czechs pressed for recognition of their language and rights. (*Osterreichische Nationalbibliothek.*)

state by assimilating the non-Magyars; Austria, in contrast, made no deliberate effort to Germanize the Slavs. It did not try to make German the official language of the state or to dissociate non-Germans from their native traditions. In Austria, elementary school students were usually taught in their mother tongues. The state acknowledged the equal right of all the country's languages in the schools, in administration, and in public life. But the nationality problem was aggravated by the haughty attitude of the German Austrians, who considered themselves culturally superior to the Slavic peoples. Neither the Germans nor the Magyars would allow the Czechs and the South Slavs the same control over domestic affairs that had been granted the Magyars in the Settlement of 1867. The Germans believed that they had a historic mission to retain their dominance, an attitude that clashed with the Slavs' growing national consciousness.

The most serious conflict occurred in Bohemia between the Germans and the Czechs, the largest group of Slavs. The Czechs had the highest literacy rate in the Dual Monarchy, and Bohemia had become the industrial heartland of the empire. The emergence of a Czech university and Czech youth associations and the growth of Czech literature stimulated the development of national consciousness. Championed by a growing middle class, which had made considerable economic and cultural gains, nationalism among the Czechs of Bohemia intensified in the final decades of the nineteenth century. Between the Czechs and the Germans there was great animosity.

Concentrated primarily in the Sudetenland, the German Bohemians regarded themselves as culturally and morally superior to the Czechs and wanted to preserve their predominance in the government's administration. Considering the Czech language fit only for peasants and servants, the Sudeten Germans deemed it ridiculous that Czech be placed on an equal level with the

German tongue. The two groups argued over whether street signs and menus should be written in German or Czech. Czech nationalists wanted the same constitutional independence that had been granted to the Hungarians; Sudeten Germans demanded that Austria remain a centralized state governed by a German-dominated bureaucracy. Violent demonstrations, frenzied oratory, and strident editorials fanned the flames of hatred. Mounting resentment against the Czechs and growing admiration for Bismarck's new Germany led some Austrian Germans, particularly the Sudeten Germans, to seek union with Germany. Georg von Schönerer, the leader of the Austrian Pan-German movement, denounced both Slavs and Jews as racial inferiors and called for the creation of a Greater Germany.

The clash between Czechs and Germans turned uglier when in 1897 a new prime minister, Count Casimir Badeni, required government officials in Bohemia to know both the German and the Czech languages. This requirement was no hardship for Czech officials, since most of them already knew German. Few German officials, however, knew Czech or cared to learn it. Riots broke out in various cities, German and Czech deputies in Parliament engaged in fistfights, and the emperor was forced to dismiss Badeni. Eventually, the reform was dropped, but Czech-German hostilities remained intense.

South Slavs

The problem of the South Slavs in Austria—Serbs, Croats, and Slovenes—differed from that of the Czechs. No Czech state served as a magnet for the Czechs living within Austria, whereas in the Kingdom of Serbia (which gained full independence from the Ottoman Turks in 1878), the South Slavs had a foreign state to encourage their nationalist hopes. Serbian nationalists dreamed of extending their rule over their ethnic cousins, the South Slavs of Austria-Hungary. The Hapsburg monarchy viewed this vision of a Greater Serbia as a threat to its existence. This conflict was to trigger World War I.

The awakening of nationalism in the multiethnic Austro-Hungarian Empire raised the specter of dissolution. Could the forces of unity—the army, the bureaucracy, and loyalty to the Hapsburg dynasty—contain the centrifugal forces that threatened to shatter the empire into separate parts? A restructuring of the Dual Monarchy into a federated state that would give equality to the Slavs might have eased pressures within the empire, particularly since only extremists among the minorities were calling for independence. But the leading statesmen resisted the Slavs' demands. At the end of World War I, the empire was fractured into separate states based on nationality.

The Rise of Racial Nationalism

In the first half of the nineteenth century, nationalism and liberalism went hand in hand. Liberals sought both the rights of the individual and national independence and unification. Liberal nationalists believed that a unified state free of foreign subjugation was in harmony with the principle of natural rights, and they insisted that love of country led to love of humanity. "With all my ardent love of my nation," said Francis Palacky, a Czech patriot, "I always esteem more highly the good of mankind and of learning than the good of the nation."[3] Addressing the Slavs, Mazzini declared: "We who have ourselves arisen in the name of our national right, believe in your right, and offer to help you to win it. But the purpose of our mission is the permanent and peaceful organization of Europe."[4] Liberals expected that nationalism would unite a people in freedom and fellowship, foster a national cultural lowering, and promote idealism by leading people to set aside personal concerns for the good of the nation. They did not anticipate the emergence of an extreme nationalism that would subvert liberal values. The extreme nationalism of the late nineteenth and early twentieth centuries contributed to World War I and to the rise of fascism after the war. It was the seedbed of totalitarian nationalism.

Concerned exclusively with the greatness of the nation, extreme nationalists rejected the liberal emphasis on political liberty. Liberals regarded the state as a community of individuals voluntarily bonded by law and citizenship and entitled to the same rights. To extreme national-

CELEBRATION OF THE UNVEILING OF THE STATUE OF HERMANN (ARMINIUS) AT THE SITE OF TEUTOBERGER WALD. The Franco-Prussian War (1870–71) brought German unity and intensified nationalist feelings. German nationalists glorified the traditions and deeds of their ancient ancestors who overran the Roman Empire. Depicted here is the unveiling of the statue of Arminius, erected in 1875. Arminius was a tribal chieftain who defeated a Roman force in A.D. 9. German nationalism, which grew more extreme in succeeding decades, helped give rise to the world wars of the twentieth century. (*Bildarchiv Preussischer Kulturbesitz.*)

ists, however, the state was the highest development of a folkish-racial spirit inherited from their ancestors. In their eyes, profound and irreconcilable differences separated "their people" from those who did not share this ancestry. Even if they had dwelled in the land for centuries, such people were seen as dangerous aliens. Increasingly, they attacked parliamentary government as a barrier to national unity and greatness and maintained that authoritarian leadership was needed to meet national emergencies. The needs of the nation, they said, transcended the rights of the individual. Extreme nationalists also rejected the liberal ideal of equality. Placing the nation above everything, nationalists accused national minorities of corrupting the nation's spirit. In the name of national power and unity, they persecuted minorities at home and stirred up hatred against other nations. And they also glorified war as a symbol of the nations's resolve and will. At the founding of the Nationalist Association in Italy in 1910, one leader declared:

> *Just as socialism teaches the proletariat the value of class struggle, so we must teach Italy*

> *the value of international struggle. But international struggle is war? Well, then, let there be war! And nationalism will arouse the will for a victorious war, . . . the only way to national redemption.*[5]

Interpreting politics with the logic of emotions, extreme nationalists insisted that they had a sacred mission to regain lands once held in the Middle Ages, to unite with their kinfolk in other lands, or to rule over peoples considered inferior. They organized patriotic societies, denounced national minorities, particularly Jews, and created a cult of ancestors and a mystique of blood, soil, and a sacred national past. In these ancestral traditions and attachments, the nationalist found a higher reality akin to religious truth. Loyalty to the nation-state was elevated above all other allegiances. The ethnic state became an object of religious reverence; spiritual energies formerly dedicated to Christianity were now channeled into the worship of the nation-state, igniting primitive, dark, cruel feelings. In 1902, Friedrich Paulsen, a German philosopher, warned of the threat that nationalism posed to reason and morality:

> *A supersensitive nationalism has become a very serious danger for all the peoples of Europe; because of it, they are in danger of losing the feeling for human values. Nationalism, pushed to an extreme, just like sectarianism, destroys moral and even logical consciousness. Just and unjust, good and bad, true and false, lose their meaning; what men condemn as disgraceful and inhuman when done by others, they recommend in the same breath to their own people as something to be done to a foreign country.*[6]

By the beginning of the twentieth century, conservatives had become the staunchest advocates of nationalism, and the nationalism preached by conservative extremists was stripped of Mazzinian ideals of liberty, equality, and the fellowship of nations. Landholding aristocrats, generals, and clergy, often joined by big industrialists, saw nationalism as a convenient instrument for gaining a mass following in their struggle against democracy, social reform, and socialism. Championing popular nationalist myths and dreams and citing Social Darwinist doctrines, a newly radicalized right, dominated by the elite of German society, hoped to harness the instinctual energies of the masses, particularly the peasants and the lower middle class—shopkeepers, civil servants, and white-collar workers—to conservative causes. Peasants viewed liberalism and a godless Marxism as threats to traditional values, while the lower bourgeoisie feared the power of the organized proletariat. These people were receptive to the rhetoric of ultranationalists, who denounced democracy and Marxism as threats to national unity and Jews as aliens who endangered the nation. Nationalism was presented as a victory of idealism over materialism and as the subordination of class and personal interests to the general good of the nation.

Volkish Thought

Extreme nationalism was a general European phenomenon, but it was especially dangerous in Germany. Bismarck's triumphs lured Germans into a dream world. Many started to yearn for the extension of German power throughout the globe. The past, they said, belonged to France and Britain; the future, to Germany.

The most ominous expression of German nationalism (and a clear example of mythical thinking) was Volkish thought.[7] (*Volk* means "folk" or "people.") German Volkish thinkers sought to bind together the German people through a deep love of their language, traditions, and fatherland. These thinkers felt that Germans were animated by a higher spirit than that found in other peoples. To Volkish thinkers, the Enlightenment and parliamentary democracy were foreign ideas that corrupted the pure German spirit. With fanatical devotion, Volkish thinkers embraced all things German: the medieval past, the German landscape, the simple peasant, and the village. They denounced the liberal-humanist tradition of the West as alien to the German soul.

Among the shapers of the Volkish outlook was Wilhelm von Riehl (1823–1897), a professor at the University of Munich. He contrasted the artificiality of modern city life with the unspoiled existence in the German countryside. Berthold Auerbach (1812–1882) glorified the peasant as the ideal German. Paul de Lagarde (1827–1891), a professor of Oriental languages, called for a German faith, different from Christianity, that would unite the nation; he saw the Jews as enemies of Germany. Julius Langbehn (1851–1907) lauded a mystical and irrational life force as superior to reason and held that the Jews corrupted the German spirit.

Volkish thought attracted Germans frightened by all the complexities of the modern age: industrialization, urbanization, materialism, class conflicts, and alienation. Seeing their beloved Germany transformed by these forces of modernity, Volkish thinkers yearned to restore the sense of community, the spiritual unity, that they attributed to the preindustrial age. Only by identifying with their sacred soil and sacred traditions could modern Germans escape from the evils of industrial society. Only then could the different classes band together in an organic unity.

The Volkish movement had little support from the working class, which was concerned chiefly with improving its standard of living. It appealed mainly to farmers and villagers, who regarded the industrial city as a threat to native values and a catalyst for foreign ideas; to artisans and small shopkeepers, threatened by big business; and to scholars, writers, teachers, and students, who saw in Volkish nationalism a cause worthy of their idealism. The schools were leading agents for the dissemination of Volkish ideas.

Volkish thinkers looked back longingly to the Middle Ages, which they viewed as a period of social and spiritual harmony and reverence for national traditions. They also glorified the ancient Germanic tribes that overran the Roman Empire; they contrasted their courageous and vigorous German ancestors with the effete and degenerate Romans. A few tried to harmonize ancient Germanic religious traditions with Christianity.

Such attitudes led Germans to see themselves as a heroic people fundamentally different from and better than the English and French. It also led them to regard German culture as unique—innately superior to and, indeed, contravening the humanist outlook of the Enlightenment. Like their romantic predecessors, Volkish thinkers claimed that the German people and culture had a special destiny and a unique mission. They pitted the German soul against the Western intellect—feeling, intuition, spirit, and idealism against a drab rationalism. To be sure, the Western humanist tradition had many supporters in Germany, but the counterideology of Volkish thought was becoming increasingly widespread. This murky, irrational, radical nationalist, and antiliberal outlook shaped by these Volkish thinkers in the late nineteenth century would later undermine support for the democratic Weimar Republic established in Germany after World War I and provide Hitler with receptive listeners. Many of Hitler's supporters hoped that he would transform these Volkish longings into political realities.

Racist doctrines had a special appeal for Volkish thinkers. Racist ideologues saw race as the key to history. They maintained that not only physical features but also moral, esthetic, and intellectual qualities distinguished one race from another. In their view, a race demonstrated its vigor and achieved greatness when it preserved its purity; intermarriage between races was contamination that would result in genetic, cultural, and military decline. Unlike liberals, who held that anyone who accepted German law was a member of the German nation, racists argued that a person's nationality was a function of his or her "racial soul" or "blood."

Like their Nazi successors, Volkish thinkers claimed that the German race was purer than, and therefore superior to, all other races. Its superiority was revealed in such physical characteristics as blond hair, blue eyes, and fair skin: all signs of inner qualities lacking in other races. German racists claimed that Germans were the purest decendants of the ancient Aryans.* They held that the Aryans were a superior race and the creators of European civilization and that the Germans had inherited their superior racial qualities.

*The Aryans emerged some four thousand years ago, probably between the Caspian Sea and India. An Aryan tongue became the basis of most European languages. Intermingling with others, the Aryans lost their identity as a people.

Volkish thinkers embraced the ideas of Houston Stewart Chamberlain (1855–1927), an Englishman whose fascination with Germanism led him to adopt German citizenship. In *The Foundations of the Nineteenth Century* (1899), Chamberlain asserted in pseudoscientific fashion that races differed not only physically but also morally, spiritually, and intellectually, and that the struggle between races was the driving force of history. He attributed Rome's decline to the dilution of its racial qualities through the intermixing of races. The blond, blue-eyed, long-skulled Germans, possessing the strongest strain of Aryan blood and distinguished by an inner spiritual depth, were the true ennoblers of humanity—both physically superior and bearers of a higher culture. Chamberlain denied that Christ was a Jew, saying that he was of Aryan stock. As agents of a spiritually empty capitalism and divisive liberalism, the Jews, said Chamberlain, were undermining German society. Materialistic, cowardly, and devious, they were the very opposite of the idealistic, heroic, and faithful Germans. Chamberlain's book was enormously popular in Germany. Pan-German and other Volkish-nationalist organizations frequently cited it. Kaiser William II called *Foundations* a "Hymn to Germanism" and read it to his children.

Chamberlain's racist and anti-Semitic views make him a spiritual forerunner of Nazism, and he was praised as such by Alfred Rosenberg, the leading Nazi racial theorist in the early days of Hitler's movement. Joseph Goebbels, the Nazi propagandist, hailed Chamberlain as a "pathbreaker" and "pioneer" after meeting him in 1926. In 1923, Chamberlain, then sixty-eight years old, met Hitler, whose movement was still in its formative stage. Chamberlain subsequently praised Hitler as the savior of the Reich, and Hitler visited Chamberlain on his deathbed and attended his funeral.

German racial nationalists insisted that Germany had a unique mission; as a superior race, Germans had a right to dominate other peoples, particularly the "racially inferior" Slavs of eastern Europe. The Pan-German Association, whose membership included professors, schoolteachers, journalists, lawyers, and aristocrats, spread racial and nationalist theories and glorified war as an expression of national vitality. A statement from the association's journal sums up its philosophy:

THE PROTOCOLS OF THE ELDERS OF ZION. This infamous forgery, commissioned by the Russian secret police, became an international bestseller and contributed to outrages against Jews. Anti-Semitic organizations continue to publish and circulate it today. The picture is the actual cover of a French edition of the *Protocols,* c. 1934. (*The Wiener Library, London.*)

> *The racial-biological ideology tells us that there are races that lead and races that follow. Political history is nothing but the history of struggles among the leading races. Conquests, above all, are always the work of the leading races. Such men can conquer, may conquer, and shall conquer.*[8]

Anti-Semitism: The Power and Danger of Mythical Thinking

German racial nationalists singled out Jews as a wicked race and a deadly enemy of the German people. Anti-Semitism, widespread in late-nineteenth-century Europe, affords a striking example of the perennial appeal, power, and danger of mythical thinking—of elevating to the level of objective truth ideas that have no basis in fact but provide all-encompassing, emotionally satisfying explanations of life and history. By manufacturing the myth of the wicked Jew, the radical right confirmed the insight proffered by the political theorist Georges Sorel: people are moved and united by myths that offer simple, clear, and emotionally gratifying resolutions to the complexities of the modern world. Anti-Semitic organizations and political parties sought to deprive Jews of their civil rights, and anti-Semitic publications proliferated. The radical right saw Jew-hatred as a popular formula for mobilizing and uniting all social classes—a precondition for strengthening the nation and subverting liberal democracy.

In 1886, Edouard Drumont, a French journalist, published *Jewish France,* which argued that the Jews, racially inferior and believers in a primitive religion, had gained control of France. The book sold more than a million copies. Drumont blamed the Jews for introducing capitalism, materialism, and greed into France. Like medieval Christian anti-Semites, Drumont accused Jews of deicide and of using the blood of slaughtered Christian children for ritual purposes. (In rural France, the accusation of ritual murder, a deranged survival of the Middle Ages, still persisted, at times fomented by the clergy.) During the anti-Semitic outbursts accompanying the Dreyfus affair (see Chapter 26) when the French right was shouting "Death to the Jews," Drumont's newspaper (founded with Jesuit funds) tried to inflame public opinion with sensational polemics against the Jews. It blamed all the ills of France on the Jews, called for their expulsion from the country, and predicted that they would be massacred.

Romania barred most Jews from holding office and from voting, imposed various economic restrictions on them, and limited their admission into secondary schools and universities. The Romanian government even financed an international congress of anti-Semites, which met in Bucharest in 1886.

Russia placed a quota on the number of Jewish students admitted to secondary schools and higher educational institutions, confined Jews to certain regions of the country, and, "to purify the sacred historic capital," expelled around twenty thousand Jews from Moscow. Some government officials encouraged and even organized *pogroms* (mob violence) against Jews. Between 1903 and 1906, pogroms broke out in 690 towns and villages, most of them in the Ukraine, traditionally a hotbed of anti-Semitism. (Ukrainian folk songs and legends glorified centuries-old massacres of Jews.) The attackers looted, burned, raped, and murdered, generally with impunity. In Russia, and several other lands, Jews were put on trial for the old libel of ritual murder.

In Germany and Austria, hatred of the Jews developed into a systematic body of beliefs. As the historian Hans Kohn says, "Germany became the fatherland of modern anti-Semitism; there the systems were thought out and the slogans coined. German literature was the richest in anti-Jewish writing."[9] Like conservatives in other lands, German conservatives deliberately fanned the flames of anti-Semitism to win the masses over to conservative causes. The Christian Social Workers' party, founded in 1878 by Adolf Stöcker, a prominent Protestant preacher, engaged in anti-Semitic agitation in order to recruit the lower bourgeoisie to the cause of the Protestant church and the Prussian monarchy. In German-speaking Austria, Karl Lueger, a leader of the Christian Social party, founded by conservative German nationalists, exploited anti-Semitism to win elections in overwhelmingly Catholic Vienna. Georg von Schönerer, founder of the German National party in Austria, wanted to eliminate Jews from all areas of public life.

Anti-Semitism and the success of the Italians, Germans, Serbians, and others in achieving political independence stirred nationalist feelings among Jews. Jewish nationalism took the form of Zionism—a movement advocating the return of Jews to Palestine, their historic homeland. A key figure in the emergence of Zionism was Theodor Herzl (1860–1904), an Austrian journalist, who was horrified by the anti-Semitism he witnessed in Paris during the Dreyfus trial. In *The Jewish*

State (1896), he argued that the creation of a Jewish state was the best solution to the Jewish question. In 1897, in Switzerland, the first Zionist World Congress called for the establishment of a Jewish homeland in Palestine, which was then a province of the Ottoman Empire.

Anti-Semitism had a long and bloodstained history in Europe, stemming both from an irrational fear and hatred of outsiders with noticeably different ways and from the commonly accepted myth that the Jews as a people were collectively and eternally cursed for rejecting Christ. Christians saw Jews as the murderers of Christ—an image that provoked terrible anger and hatred.

During the Middle Ages, people believed and spread incredible tales about Jews. They accused Jews of torturing and crucifying Christian children in order to use their blood for religious ceremonies, poisoning wells to kill Christians, worshiping the Devil, and organizing a secret government that conspired to destroy Christianity. Jews were thought to be physically different from other people; they were said to have tails, horns, and a distinctive odor. Serving to propagate this myth was the decision of the Fourth Lateran Council (1215), which required Jews to wear a distinguishing mark on their clothing.

Although some medieval popes and bishops condemned these fables and sought to protect Jews from mob violence, the lower clergy and popular preachers spread the tales to the receptive masses. Periodically, mobs humiliated, tortured, and massacred Jews, and rulers expelled them from their kingdoms. Often barred from owning land and excluded from the craft guilds, medieval Jews concentrated in trade and moneylending—occupations that frequently earned them greater hostility. By the sixteenth century, Jews in a number of lands were forced by law to live in separate quarters of the town, called *ghettos.* Medieval Christian anti-Semitism, which depicted the Jew as vile and Judaism as repulsive, fertilized the soil for modern anti-Semitism.

In the nineteenth century, under the aegis of the liberal ideals of the Enlightenment and the French Revolution, Jews gained legal equality in most European lands. They could leave the ghetto, vote, hold offices, and participate in many activities that had been closed to them. Traditionally an urban people, the Jews, who were concentrated in the leading cities of Europe, took advantage of this new freedom and opportunity. Motivated by the fierce desire of outsiders to prove their worth and aided by deeply embedded traditions that valued education and family life, many Jews achieved striking success as entrepreneurs, bankers, lawyers, journalists, doctors, scientists, scholars, and performers. For example, in 1880, Jews, who constituted about 10 percent of the Viennese population, accounted for 38.6 percent of the medical students and 23.3 percent of the law students in Vienna. Viennese cultural life before World War I was to a large extent shaped by Jewish writers, artists, musicians, critics, and patrons. All but one of the major banking houses were Jewish. By the early 1930s, German Jews, who constituted less than 1 percent of the population, accounted for 10.9 percent of the doctors, 10.7 percent of the dentists, 5.1 percent of the editors and authors, and 16.3 percent of the lawyers. Thirty percent of the Nobel Prize winners in Germany were Jews.

But most European Jews—peasants, peddlers, and laborers—were quite poor. Perhaps five thousand to six thousand Jews of Galicia in Austria-Hungary died of starvation annually, and many Russian Jews fled to the United States to escape from desperate poverty. But the anti-Semites saw only "Jewish influence," "Jewish manipulation," and "Jewish domination." Aggravating anti-Semitism among Germans was the flight of thousands of Russian Jews into Austria and Germany. Poor, speaking Yiddish, a form of medieval German that sounded peculiar to nineteenth-century Germans, and having noticeably different customs, these Jews offended Germans and triggered primitive fears and hates.

Like other bourgeois, the Jews who were members of the commercial and professional classes gravitated toward liberalism. Moreover, as victims of persecution, they naturally favored societies that were committed to the liberal ideals of legal equality, toleration, the rule of law, and equality of opportunity. As strong supporters of parliamentary government and the entire system of values associated with the Enlightenment, the Jews became targets for those conservatives and Volkish thinkers, who repudiated the humanist and cosmopolitan outlook of liberalism and professed a militant nationalism. To Volkish thinkers, the West repre-

Profile

Theodor Herzl

Theodor Herzl (1860–1904), the founder of modern Zionism, was born in Budapest and received a law degree from the University of Vienna. Giving up law, he turned to writing stories and plays and working as a journalist. At the time of the Dreyfus trial—when an innocent Jewish army officer was railroaded and humiliated by the army and reviled by anti-Semites—Herzl was Paris correspondent for a prominent Viennese newspaper. Greatly distressed by French anti-Semites, who were shouting "Death to the Jews," Herzl became convinced that European Jews would never escape persecution. In *The Jewish State* (1896), he argued that security for Jews could be guaranteed only by a separate national state for Jews in their historic homeland:

Corbis-Bettmann.

sented an alien culture hostile to German racial-national identity, and the Jews, an alien race, symbolized the West. "Anti-Semitism was a manifestation of a rejection of the 'West' with which the Jews were identified," says the German historian Karl Dietrich Bracher, "because the Enlightenment and democracy were essential pre-conditions for their acceptance and progress."[10]

Anti-Semites invented a mythical evil to be blamed for all the social and economic ills caused by the rapid growth of industries and cities and for all the new ideas that were undermining the Old Order. Their anxieties and fears concentrated on the Jews, to whom they attributed everything they considered to be wrong with the modern age, all that threatened the German Volk.

The thought processes of Volkish anti-Semites demonstrate the mind's monumental capacity for self-delusion and irrational thinking. In the mythical world of Volkish thinkers, Jews were regarded as foreign intruders who could never be loyal to the fatherland; as a lower form of humanity that could infect and weaken the German race and debase its culture; and as international conspirators who were plotting to dominate Germany and the world. That last accusation was an updated version of the medieval myth that Jews were plotting to destroy Christendom. In an extraordinary display of irrationality, Volkish thinkers held that Jews throughout the world were gaining control over political parties, the press, and the economy in order to dominate the planet.

The myth of a Jewish world conspiracy found its culminating expression in a notorious forgery, the *Protocols of the Elders of Zion.* The *Protocols* was written in France in the 1890s by an unknown author in the service of the Russian secret police, which sought to justify the tsarist regime's

*We are a people—one people. We have honestly endeavored to merge ourselves in the social life of surrounding communities and to preserve only the faith of our fathers. We are not permitted to do so. In vain are we loyal patriots . . . ; in vain do we strive to increase the fame of our native land in science and art, or her wealth by trade and commerce. In countries where we have lived for centuries we are still cried down as strangers. . . . I think we shall not be left in peace. . . . [O]ld prejudices against us still lie deep in the hearts of people. . . . I say that we cannot hope for a change in the current . . . feeling. . . . The nations in whose midst Jews live are all either covertly or openly Anti-Semitic. . . . Palestine is our ever-memorable historic home. The very name of Palestine would attract our people with a force of marvellous potency.**

Herzl organized the first Zionist World Congress, which met in Basel, Switzerland, in 1897. He was elected president of the World Zionist Organization, a position he held until his death in 1904, at the age of forty-four. Herzl had little success in winning heads of state and Jewish bankers to the Zionist cause, but he did manage to make the Zionist movement into a recognized international organization. His drive and vision—"If you will it, it is no fairy tale"—inspired many Jews, particularly among the poor and persecuted Jewish masses of Russia and Poland, to struggle for the creation of a Jewish state in the land of Israel.

*Theodor Herzl, *The Jewish State* (New York: American Zionist Emergency Council, 1946), pp. 76–77, 85, 96.

anti-Semitic policies. The forger concocted a tale of an alleged meeting of Jewish elders in the Jewish cemetery of Prague. In these eerie surroundings, the elders plot to take over the world. First published in Russia in 1903, the *Protocols* was widely distributed after World War I and widely believed. Influenced by the *Protocols,* Russian anti-Semites interpreted the Russian Revolution of 1917 as an attempt by Jews to subjugate Christian Russia. German anti-Semites regarded the *Protocols* as convincing evidence that the Jews were responsible for starting World War I, for Germany's defeat, and for the revolution that toppled the monarchy. Nazi propagandists exploited the *Protocols* to justify their quest for power. Even after the *Protocols* was exposed as a blatant forgery, it continued to be translated and distributed. For anti-Semites, the myth of a Jewish world-conspiracy had become an integrating principle; it provided satisfying answers to the crucial questions of existence.

In the Middle Ages, Jews had been persecuted and humiliated primarily for religious reasons. In the nineteenth century, national-racial considerations augmented the traditional, biased Christian perception of Jews and Judaism. Christian anti-Semites believed that, through conversion, Jews could escape the curse of their religion. Racial anti-Semites, however, used the language of Social Darwinism. They said that Jews belonged to different species of the human race, that they were indelibly stained and eternally condemned by their biological makeup, and that their evilness and worthlessness derived from inherited racial characteristics, which could not be altered by conversion. As one anti-Semitic deputy stated in a speech before the German Reichstag (the lower chamber of the German parliament) in 1895,

> *If one designates the whole of Jewry, one does so in the knowledge that the racial qualities of this people are such that in the long run they cannot harmonize with the racial qualities of the Germanic peoples and that every Jew who at this moment has not done anything bad may nevertheless under the proper conditions do precisely that, because his racial qualities drive him to do it. . . . the Jews . . . operate like parasites . . . the Jews are cholera germs.*[11]

The Jewish population of Germany was quite small. In 1900, it was only about 497,000, or 0.95 percent of the total population of 50,626,000. Jews were proud of their many contributions to German economic and cultural life; they considered themselves patriotic Germans, relished German literature and music, and regarded Germany, a land of high civilization, as an altogether desirable place to live—a place of refuge in comparison with Russia, where Jews lived in terrible poverty and suffered violent attacks. German Jews, who felt that they already had a homeland, had little enthusiasm for Zionism.

German anti-Semitic organizations and political parties failed to get the state to pass anti-Semitic laws, and by the early 1900s, these groups had declined in political power and importance. But the mischief had been done. In the minds of many Germans, even in respectable circles, the image of the Jew as an evil and dangerous creature had been firmly planted. It was perpetuated by the schools, youth groups, the Pan-German Association, and an array of racist pamphlets and books. Late-nineteenth-century racial anti-Semites had constructed an ideological foundation on which Hitler would later build his movement. In words that foreshadowed Hitler, Paul de Lagarde said of the Jews: "One does not have dealings with pests and parasites; one does not rear them and cherish them; one destroys them as speedily and thoroughly as possible."[12]

It is, of course, absurd to believe that a nation of fifty million was threatened by a half-million citizens of Jewish birth, or that the eleven million Jews of the world (by 1900) had organized to rule the planet. The Jewish birthrate in Germany was low, the rate of intermarriage high, and the desire for complete assimilation into German life great. Within a few generations, the Jewish community in Germany might well have disappeared. Moreover, despite the paranoia of the anti-Semites, the German Jews and the Jews in the rest of Europe were quite powerless. There were scarcely any Jews in the ruling circles of governments, armies, civil services, or heavy industries. As events were to prove, the Jews, with no army or state and dwelling in lands where many despised them, were the weakest of peoples. But the race mystics, convinced that they were waging a war of self-defense against a satanic foe, were impervious to rational argument. Anti-Semites, said Theodor Mommsen, the great nineteenth-century German historian, would not listen to

> *logical and ethical arguments. . . . They listen only to their own envy and hatred, to the meanest instincts. Nothing else counts for them. They are deaf to reason, right, morals. One cannot influence them. . . . [Anti-Semitism] is a horrible epidemic, like cholera—one can neither explain nor cure it.*[13]

Racial nationalism, a major element in nineteenth-century intellectual life, attacked and undermined the Enlightenment tradition. Racial nationalists denied equality, scorned toleration, dismissed the idea of the oneness of humanity, and made myth and superstition vital forces in political life. They distorted reason and science to demonize and condemn an entire people and to justify humiliation and persecution. They presented a pathogenic racial ideology, fraught with unreason and hate, as something virtuous and idealistic. That many people, including the educated and the enlightened, accepted these racial doctrines was an ominous sign for Western civilization. It made plain the tenuousness of the rational tradition of the Enlightenment and showed how receptive the mind is to dangerous myths, and how easily human behavior can degenerate into inhumanity.

❖ ❖ ❖

Notes

1. Quoted in Christopher Hibbert, *Garibaldi and His Enemies* (Boston: Little, Brown, 1965), p. 45.
2. Quoted in Otto Pflanze, *Bismarck and the Development of Germany: The Period of Unification* (Princeton, N.J.: Princeton University Press, 1963), p. 232.
3. Quoted in Hans Kohn, *Pan-Slavism* (Notre Dame, Ind.: University of Notre Dame Press, 1953), pp. 66–67.
4. Quoted ibid., p. 44.
5. Cited in Edward R. Tannenbaum, *1900: The Generation Before the Great War* (Garden City, N.Y.: Doubleday, 1976), p. 337.
6. Quoted in Friedrich Meinecke, *The German Catastrophe* (Boston: Beacon Press, 1963), pp. 23–24.
7. This discussion is based largely on the works of George L. Mosse, particularly *The Crisis of German Ideology* (New York: Grosset & Dunlap Universal Library, 1964).
8. Cited in Horst von Maltitz, *The Evolution of Hitler's Germany* (New York: McGraw-Hill, 1973), p. 33.
9. Hans Kohn, *Nationalism: Its Meaning and History* (Princeton, N.J.: Van Nostrand, Anvil Books, 1955), p. 77.
10. Karl Dietrich Bracher, *The German Dictatorship,* trans. Jean Steinberg (New York: Praeger, 1970), p. 36.
11. Quoted in Raul Hilberg, *The Destruction of the European Jews* (Chicago: Quadrangle, 1967), pp. 10–11.
12. Quoted in Helmut Krausnick, Hans Buchheim, Martin Broszat, and Hans-Adolf Jacobsen, *Anatomy of the SS State,* trans. Richard Barry et al. (London: William Collins Sons, 1968), p. 9.
13. Quoted in Peter G. J. Pulzer, *The Rise of Political Anti-Semitism in Germany and Austria* (New York: Wiley, 1964), p. 299.

Suggested Reading

Beales, Derek, *The Risorgimento and the Unification of Italy* (1971). A comprehensive overview, followed by documents.

Fischer, Klaus P., *The History of an Obsession* (1998). A superb study of German-Jewish relations, particularly the delusionary character of anti-Jewish thinking.

Hamerow, T. S., *Restoration, Revolution, Reaction* (1958). An examination of Germany from 1815 to 1871, stressing the problems caused by the transition from agrarianism to industrialism.

———, ed., *Otto von Bismarck* (1962). A collection of readings from leading historians.

Hibbert, Christopher, *Garibaldi and His Enemies* (1965). A vivid portrait of the Italian hero.

Holborn, Hajo, *A History of Modern Germany, 1840–1945* (1969). A standard reference work.

Katz, Jacob, *From Prejudice to Destruction* (1980). A survey of modern anti-Semitism; views modern anti-Semitism as an outgrowth of traditional Christian anti-Semitism.

Kohn, Hans, *Nationalism: Its Meaning and History* (1955). A concise history of modern nationalism by a leading student of the subject.

Mosse, George L., *The Crisis of German Ideology* (1964). Explores the dark side of German nationalism.

———, *Toward the Final Solution* (1978). An analysis of European racism.

Pauley, B. F., *The Habsburg Legacy, 1867–1939* (1972). A good brief work on a complex subject.

Pflanze, Otto, *Bismarck and the Development of Germany* (1963). An excellent study of the political history of Germany from 1815 to 1871.

Pulzer, Peter G. J., *The Rise of Political Anti-Semitism in Germany and Austria* (1964). The relationship of anti-Semitism to changing socioeconomic conditions.

Rodes, John E., *The Quest for Unity: Modern Germany, 1848–1970* (1971). A good survey of German history.

Review Questions

1. What forces worked for and against Italian unity?
2. Mazzini was the soul, Cavour the brains, and Garibaldi the sword in the struggle for the unification of Italy. Discuss this statement.
3. Why is it significant that Prussia rather than the Frankfurt Assembly in 1848 served as the agent of German unification?

4. Prussia's victory over Austria was a triumph for conservatism and a defeat for liberalism. Discuss this statement.
5. What was the significance of the Franco-Prussian War for European history?
6. In the Hapsburg Empire, nationalism was a force for disunity. Discuss this statement.
7. What was the appeal of Volkish thought?
8. Why is racial nationalism a repudiation of the Enlightenment tradition and a regression to mythical thinking?
9. What is the relationship between medieval and modern anti-Semitism?
10. Anti-Semites attributed to Jews everything that they found repellent in the modern world. Discuss this statement.
11. Anti-Semitism demonstrates the immense power and danger of mythical thinking. Discuss this statement.

Chapter 26

The Industrial West: Responses to Modernization

The locomotive shown here is clearly a steam engine pulling carriages that are adaptations of horse-drawn carriages, much the same as the early automobiles were. (The Granger Collection.)

■ **The Advance of Industry**
Technological Takeoff
Accelerated Urbanization
Labor's Responses

■ **Great Britain: An Industrial Model**
Labor Unrest
The Irish Question
The Woman Question
Britain on the Eve of War

■ **France: Democratic or Authoritarian?**
Napoleon "le Petit"
After the Fall
Threats to the Republic
France on the Eve of War

■ **Germany: Forging an Empire**
Bismarck's "Struggle for Culture"
Germany on the Eve of War

■ **Italy: Unfulfilled Expectations**

■ **Russia: Tsarist Empire**

■ **The United States: Democratic Giant**

■ **A Golden Age?**

A "second industrial revolution" quickened the pace of industrialization, forcing much more rapid change in European society between 1870 and World War I. Mechanized industry, powered by new forms of energy, spread to all European states, though not to every region within them; it vastly increased the quantity of goods available to large segments of the population, and not just the wealthy. Indeed, new groups rose to authority and wealth. The generation before the First World War was truly the golden age of the middle classes, which gained wealth, power, and influence as social discrimination against them steadily diminished. Dazzled by the material benefits of a mass-producing society, many Europeans saw progress as inevitable. Those who were still left out of the consuming society struggled for their share.

The mechanization of basic goods industries had proceeded slowly and unevenly in the first half of the nineteenth century (see Chapter 21). Traditional economic production and social arrangements persisted alongside new technology and new methods of organizing labor. At midcentury, only Britain had become predominantly urban and an importer of food. Yet even Britain retained many aspects of an earlier rural, agrarian, privileged society alongside the new mercantile and manufacturing groups, which were gaining political and social power. In every country, traditional society ignored, resisted, and repressed the emerging forces and groups before reshaping basic institutions.

To deal with the major changes brought about by industrialization, governments expanded the role of the state, strengthening the central power over the diverse interests, regions, classes, and even nationalities. Civil wars, unification movements, and struggles for political representation usually ended with the central government becoming stronger. Sometimes the new balance of classes and regions meant the repression of dissent, regionalism, and tradition—the American Civil War, the Irish struggle for home rule, and the subjugation of minorities in newly unified Germany or tsarist Russia or Austria-Hungary are just some of the examples. In the half-century before the First World War, governments developed the machinery to control great numbers of citizens through military conscription, public ed-

Chronology 26.1 ❖ Europe in the Age of Industrialization

1845–47	Great famine in Ireland
1851	Louis Napoleon Bonaparte overthrows the Second Republic, becoming Emperor Napoleon III
1860s	Irish movement for republican form of government (the Fenians); Civil War in the United States; unification movements in German and Italian states; Dual Monarchy in Austria-Hungary
1861	Kingdom of Italy is formed; Tsar Alexander II emancipates the serfs and institutes reforms in Russia
1863	Emancipation of slaves in the United States
1864	Marx founds the First International Workingmen's Association
1867	Second Reform Bill passes, doubling the English electorate
1870–71	Franco-Prussian War; Paris Commune; creation of the German Empire
1873	Great Depression; the *Kulturkampf* in Germany
1875	German Social Democratic party founded
1880s	Parnell leads the Irish home rule movement
1881	Tsar Alexander II is assassinated
1884	Reform Bill grants suffrage to most English men
1889	Second International Workingmen's Association is founded
1891	Trans-Siberian Railroad constructed
1894–1906	The Dreyfus affair in France
1903–1905	Russo-Japanese War
1905	Revolution of 1905 in Russia
1909	Lloyd George introduces "people's budget"
1911	Power of House of Lords limited by act of Parliament

ucation, broad taxation, and, in some places, social legislation. Some governments encouraged nationalism, once thought dangerously democratic, as a way of absorbing masses of previously excluded people. Industrialization influenced the outcome of each of these struggles.

Industrialization affected international affairs as well. Population, area, and the size of the army were no longer adequate measures of national power. The amount of coal and iron production, the mileage and tonnage of railways and navies, the mechanization of industry, and the skill of the populace became important components. By 1914, production, trade, foreign markets, and political empires altered the balance of power, changing the positions of France, Russia, and Austria and tipping the scale toward the superior industrial might of Germany and the United States.

The Advance of Industry

Industry developed on the foundation of cheap labor and plentiful agricultural commodities, which were made easily and cheaply available by the development of a relatively inexpensive transportation and communication system. It took more than a century to lay that foundation, but by the 1850s, it was in place for almost all of Europe and parts of the Americas. On it was built a new economic world of growth and prosperity such as had not been seen before. *Revolution* accurately describes the radically new forms of business and labor organization, the massive accumulation of capital, the scientific and technological advance, and the new modes of marketing, distribution, and production. The apparently limitless change fostered a mentality of expendability: people could be replaced, raw materials replenished, nature rearranged, and even homelands exchanged.

Comparison with the midcentury quickly indicates the scope of the second industrial revolution. In 1850, most people were still farmers and much of industry produced tools and materials for farming. Even Britain had more domestic servants than factory hands and twice as many agricultural laborers as textile and clothing workers. Large factories were few; handicrafts still flourished. Electricity was too expensive to power lighting or drive machines; steel was too expensive to build with. Sailing ships still outnumbered steamships, and horses carried more freight than trains. On-the-job training was more common than schooling. Construction and machine making were a result of trial and error, not architectural and engineering knowledge.

This situation changed radically in two spurts: the first between 1850 and 1870; the second after the Great Depression of 1873, from the 1870s until World War I. During the first spurt, most of Europe and America consolidated earlier industrialization, extending it to previously untouched areas. The shift to machine production became permanent; steam power and other forms of energy were harnessed; and more sophisticated tools were introduced. The concentration of factory workers and production in industrial cities spurred many social changes. Labor organized unions primarily in the crafts. Social legislation was passed, especially laws for the protection of women and children. Governments, usually municipal rather than national, struggled to control water pollution, improve sanitation, and regulate housing conditions. In the more advanced industrial areas, the workplace changed; women and children were pushed out by unskilled male labor.

During the second spurt, beginning in the late 1870s but turning into a clear trend by the 1890s, in the major industrial countries of Germany and the United States, heavy industry became concentrated in large firms, capitalized by specialist banks. Cartels and monopolies—groups of companies that joined together in order to fix prices and giant firms able to dominate entire industries nationally and internationally—drastically altered the scale of development. Monopolies, run by boards of directors, some professional managers, and financiers, operated far-flung enterprises of enormous mechanized factories, manned by unskilled, low-paid, often seasonal workers. These industrial giants controlled the output, price, and distribution of commodities; they dominated smaller firms, financed and controlled research and development, utilized scientific advances, and expanded far beyond their national frontiers. Giant firms welded alliances with specialized banks all over Europe.

The "captains of industry"—the owners or managers of these large firms—possessed such extraordinary economic power that they often commanded political power as well. In much of Europe, such men were ennobled. Britain's railroad barons are early examples. In the United States, where bankers and entrepreneurs earned the epithet "robber barons," industrial titans could order politicians to represent their interests as "the oil senator" or "the railroad senator." These dynamic and powerful men, who could "cause" depressions or "own" cities, fascinated the public and obsessed their critics, obscuring the fact that the second industrial revolution was a broad movement, including thousands of small businesses, which were vulnerable to the booms and busts that the industrial giants tried to control.

The rapid growth and the powerful figures in great industries hid from contemporaries the fact that economic development was extremely uneven, even in advanced industrial states. The uneven development contributed to the political conflicts and social animosities, which, in turn, contributed to the uneven development. Industrialized Britain, for example, included rural, back-

Art of the Late Nineteenth and Twentieth Centuries

During the late nineteenth century, a number of art movements emerged that redefined both the objectives and the techniques of painters, sculptors, architects, and artisans. What set nineteenth-century art apart from works that came before was the realization among artists that they did not need to devote themselves to capturing reality as it was. They began to move away from representational art, pursuing instead a course that would bring them far along the road to abstraction—so far that by the early twentieth century, images bore almost no resemblance to the objects from which they were drawn.

As a point of departure, it is useful to consider the work of Jean François Millet (1814–1875), a French realist who brought scenes from everyday life to his canvas. Like the neoclassicists, Millet aspired to visual accuracy. Nonetheless, his work was innovative,

1. Jean François Millet. *The Gleaners,* 1857. *(Musée d'Orsay, Paris/Erich Lessing/Art Resource.)*

2. Paul Cézanne. *Madame Cézanne in the Conservatory*, c. 1880. *(Metropolitan Museum of Art, NY.)*

for he did not paint heroic, highly dramatic scenes but rather portrayed peasants and other common people at their usual tasks.

In *The Gleaners* (Figure 1) from 1857, Millet depicts, in a rhythmic composition, three heavy, slow-moving women harvesting a field of wheat. He uses color and light to convey their solid simplicity. In turning to everyday matters and bringing his canvas outside, Millet broke with tradition and set a precedent for the colorists of the later part of the century.

Art movements of the mid- and late nineteenth century include impressionism, a style that began in France and gained popularity both in Europe and in the newest emerging art center, the United States. A host of artists responded to the tenets of the impressionist movement, which heralded changes in color, line, and style. One hallmark of impressionists

3. Georges Seurat. *Sunday Afternoon on the Island of La Grande Jatte*, 1884–86. *(Art Institute of Chicago.)*

was their urge to paint *en plein air*, in nature—to take their easels out of the confining studio and set them down in fields, meadows, or anywhere else they could experience nature and put it on canvas, as Millet had done.

Art historians describe the impressionist movement as a revolution in color, in part because impressionist painters did not laboriously mix their paints on palettes but rather mixed colors on the canvas itself. But the impressionist movement, and the postimpressionists who followed, also heralded a revolution in line, in dimension, and in painting itself. What impressionists had in common was the desire to record realistically their immediate visual impression of a subject—for example, how a landscape appeared in a fleeting moment when light and atmosphere randomly coalesced.

The artists who followed are loosely called postimpressionists. Generally speaking, the term *postimpressionist* can be applied to almost any artist who worked after the 1880s. Usually, the artist had an impressionist phase and then experimented further not only with color but with form and space as well.

The paintings of Paul Cézanne (1839–1906) are some of the finest work of the postimpressionist era. He is best known for still lifes, but his portraits are also important reminders of the developments in the visual arts during the nineteenth century. The portrait of his wife, *Madame Cézanne in the Conservatory* (c. 1880) (Figure 2), illustrates many of the qualities of a postimpressionist work: overlapping brush strokes create depth and volume, and their rhythmic patterning adds texture to the flat canvas. Cézanne seems to be working at once in both a realistic and an impressionist genre. The face of the subject is rendered realis-

4. Vincent Van Gogh. *The Artist's Room in Arles*, 1889. *(Musée d'Orsay, Paris/Erich Lessing/Art Resource.)*

tically, as are the tree behind her and some other elements of the composition. But her hands, her dress, and most aspects of the background are impressionistic. This blending of styles and the experimentation with different vantage points and different elements that go into the overall composition demonstrate the approach tried by many artists of this period.

In his brief career, Georges Seurat (1859–1891) was able to take the lessons of the impressionists and give them a new twist. He, too, shared the impressionists' love of color and worked at using color in a wholly new way. Called pointillism, the technique used by Seurat required meticulous brush control and a deep understanding of the mechanics of color. Seurat's first pointillist work, *Sunday Afternoon on the Island of La Grande Jatte* (1884–86) (Figure 3) illustrates the care with which the artist rendered his images.

Typically, a painting by Seurat, which more often than not was preceded by a great many preliminary sketches and drawings, comprises literally millions of tiny individual dots and strokes of pure color, applied in such a way that the viewer's eye blends them into their final form. Thus, pointillism foreshadows the digitization used in electronic images today.

Seurat's contemporary, Vincent Van Gogh (1853–1890), is one of the best-known painters. The subject of biography, music, and endless fascination, Van Gogh could be classified as either a postimpressionist or an expressionist, although probably neither term would have found favor with the artist himself. Van Gogh's career spanned only ten years—even less time than that of Seurat—and some art historians call him the greatest Dutch artist since Vermeer and other painters of the seventeenth century.

Van Gogh's strengths lie in his use of color and his understanding of the medium of oil paint. His thickly applied brush strokes add light and shadow to his luminous canvases. One of his most famous paintings, *The Artist's Room in Arles* (1889) (Figure 4) suggests energy and motion even though it depicts a closed space. Van Gogh does not paint the

5. Paul Gauguin. *Ea Haereia oe (Where Are You Going?) (Hermitage, St. Petersburg, Russia/Scala/Art Resource, NY.)*

room realistically. Instead, he tries to capture feelings associated with the room, even if that means distorting the room's shape.

Among the other *-isms* that defined art in the late nineteenth century was primitivism, a movement "discovered" by progressive artists such as Pablo Picasso. Picasso looked to various sources for his inspiration, including Africa and the Far East. He also championed other artists who worked outside the mainstream.

In line with this tendency was the work of Paul Gauguin (1848–1903), who renounced not only impressionism but also the entire Western notion that a painter should reproduce the physical world as it actually appears. In 1891, attempting to escape what he viewed as a corrupt civilization, Gauguin abandoned France for the island of Tahiti, in the South Pacific. During his first two years in Tahiti, Gauguin painted sixty-six canvases, one of which was *Ea Haereia oe* (*Where Are You Going?*) Figure 5). In the two-dimensionality, intentional disproportion, rich coloration, and ambiguity of content of this painting, we see an

6. Pablo Picasso. *Les Demoiselles d'Avignon*, 1907. *(Musem of Modern Art, NY. Copyright ARS, NY.)*

attempt to revert to the pristine viewpoint of primitivism in which the artist's work is predominated more by imagination and feeling than by the restraints of sensory perception.

In the twentieth century, no single style predominated. It was a period of great experimentation and great changes. One of the most important movements of the early decades was abstraction, more easily defined visually than in words. Pablo Picasso (1881–1974) was one of the champions of the abstract movement. His *Les Demoiselles d'Avignon* (1907) (Figure 6) redefines the female form. This is not Boucher's *Venus*. Picasso's female forms are reductive—angular distortions of female bodies—and they hint at a number of cultural influences. While some may see suggestions of the classical in the forms of the three women to the left, there are also echoes of African sculpture; indeed, Picasso was influenced by both. But he was also inventive and sophisticated. His work reduces the visual to its most abstract elements. Changes in his style over his long and productive career indicate his receptiveness to influences from non-Western cultures as well as his own Western heritage.

The genre of abstraction that Picasso pioneered is called cubism. Among the host of cubist followers, many developed their own distinct cubist subcategories. Marc Chagall (1887–1985), a Russian painter whose works often strongly reflected his Jewish roots, worked in a cubist style that combined fantasy and reality. In *The Fiddler* (1911) (Figure 7), he blends elements of Russian and Jewish folktales with cubist renderings of scenes from everyday life.

By World War I, avant-garde artists had experimented with a multitude of abstract styles. At the Armory Show in New York City in 1913, many abstract painters made their debut on the North American continent. Generally favorably received by the art community (though not as welcomed by the average viewer), abstract painting began to gain a foothold outside Europe. Given the disfavor with which the National Socialists in Germany viewed nonrepresentational art, it was a good thing that America was willing to welcome avant-garde artists and their work.

In 1939, the Nazis—either by auction or destruction—got rid of many of the most famous abstract works in German museums. Some pieces were sold to museums or collectors in other European cities, only to fall victim once again to the strict anti-abstract sentiments of the Nazis as the war progressed; other works, and artists, were saved in the United States.

During and after World War II, art continued to be a compendium of various themes and movements. Not every artist worked in the abstract; some preferred to stick to realism. Still others painted in a style that came to be known as abstract expressionism.

The art of Piet Mondrian (1872–1944) may summarize the path taken by many abstract artists whose careers spanned both world wars. A Dutch painter, Mondrian started his career by working with representational images. Soon, however, he began to strip away all the elements of the representational, replacing reality with abstraction and reducing his canvases to simple, rhythmical, almost mathematically precise shapes and primary colors. He described his own work as neoplasticism; the paintings themselves suggest strict rules for balancing the horizontal and vertical, and color and space.

One of Mondrian's last works, *Broadway Boogie-Woogie* (1942–43) (Figure 8), amply illustrates the flatness and geometric precision of his neoplastic vision. The canvas shows only three colors and is divided only into horizontal and vertical space, yet it possesses a rhythmic

7. Marc Chagall. *The Fiddler,* 1911. *(Kunstsammlung Nordrhein-Westfalen, Duesseldorf, Germany/Erich Lessing/ Art Resource/©ARS, NY.)*

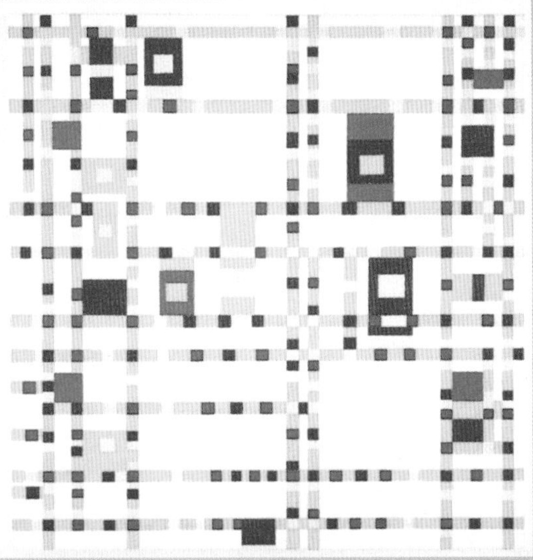

8. Piet Mondrian, *Broadway Boogie-Woogie,* 1942. *(Museum of Modern Art, NY.)*

9. Edward Hopper. *Nighthawks,* 1942. *(Art Institute of Chicago.)*

sense that reveals great skill and a fine grasp of how space and color can be used.

Not all art of the twentieth century was abstract. Some of the best representational art of any era belongs to this period. This is exemplified by the work of the American painter Edward Hopper (1882–1967). His haunting *Nighthawks* (1942) (Figure 9), painted the same year as Mondrian completed *Broadway Boogie-Woogie*, shows the reality of loneliness. It placed Hopper in the school of social realists, who painted true-to-life images of the world around them. Hopper depicted not cathedrals or temples but diners, barber shops, and movie theaters, using light and shadow as skillfully as Rembrandt.

ward Ireland, which furnished foodstuffs and laborers but shared in few benefits of industrialization. This economic deprivation, together with cultural and religious differences, fueled the Irish desire for autonomy. Until 1914, the central, southern, and eastern parts of Europe were also backwater areas, with some large-scale industries. In these regions economic oppression and repression of minorities went hand in hand. Often the lowest workers and the poorest peasants were ethnic and national minorities, who resented the power the dominant groups held over them. From the backwater areas hundreds of thousands of peasants and craftsmen, searching for a livelihood, immigrated to the Americas or British colonies. The movement from rural to urban areas was matched by an exodus on a scale unknown in history.

Britain alone developed industry according to free trade principles. Other governments built or subsidized "essential" industries (broadly defined to include transportation, communication, national banks, and above all, the production of war goods). The eastern empires remained economically and socially backward: overwhelmingly agricultural, with craftspeople manufact uring in consumer-oriented, small-scale operations of textiles and food processing. Even in industrially advanced Germany, megacartels such as the Krupp steelworks existed alongside handicraft labor.

Industrial work and wealth were unevenly and unequally distributed. The bourgeoisie included families rich enough to be elevated to the House of Lords or move in the German emperor's circle, as well as white-collar workers—the clerks in stores and government offices—and the poor but respected schoolteachers. In the second half of the century, middle-class values and interests provided standards of education, morality, and consumption for others to imitate. Traditional groups—artisans and peasantry—suffered considerable social dislocation as factory skills replaced craft skills and the use of agricultural machinery increased. Craftsmen and peasants became part of the industrial labor supply just when the introduction of heavy equipment reduced the total numbers of workers needed. Forced to move to cities, they competed for jobs. Men replaced women and children in rural and urban work. National and religious minorities replaced workers of the dominant groups.

Wages remained relatively stable after the 1870s, while the price of food and some other goods dropped. As a result, employed workers' purchasing power rose, and they spent more of their income on cheap consumer goods. Yet even the employed struggled, for they had lost family income when the state required their children to be trained in schools, something many workers resented. Their wives' income was lost, too, unless the women could find low-paying work as domestics, pieceworkers, seamstresses, or laundresses. Economic and social changes drastically altered the family and the role of each of its members. The cultural ideal of women in the home (the "cult of domesticity"), which appealed even to working-class wives in the prewar generation, depended on the ability of labor to support a family. To the degree that it could be achieved, it left the world of work a male domain.

The socioeconomic trends strongly affected political and social movements. As the middle class strove to inhibit and control labor, labor responded by broadening its organization to buttress its political and economic position. The rise in workers' standard of living and the improved working conditions did not narrow the gap between the workers and the owners. Indeed, the gap between the poor and the well-off, the powerless and the powerful, widened.

Technological Takeoff

Technology revolutionized production in undreamed-of ways, multiplying rather than merely adding to the goods and services. At midcentury, the trial-and-error tinkering of the artisan or the inventor began to be replaced by practical applications of scientific research to engineering, production, transportation, and communication. By 1900, German electrical, chemical, and mechanical industries routinely hired engineers and applied scientists to solve technical problems and produce new commodities, including artificial ones, of dyestuffs, fertilizers, and fuels. The Americans were not far behind. The Americans were early champions of scientific management—

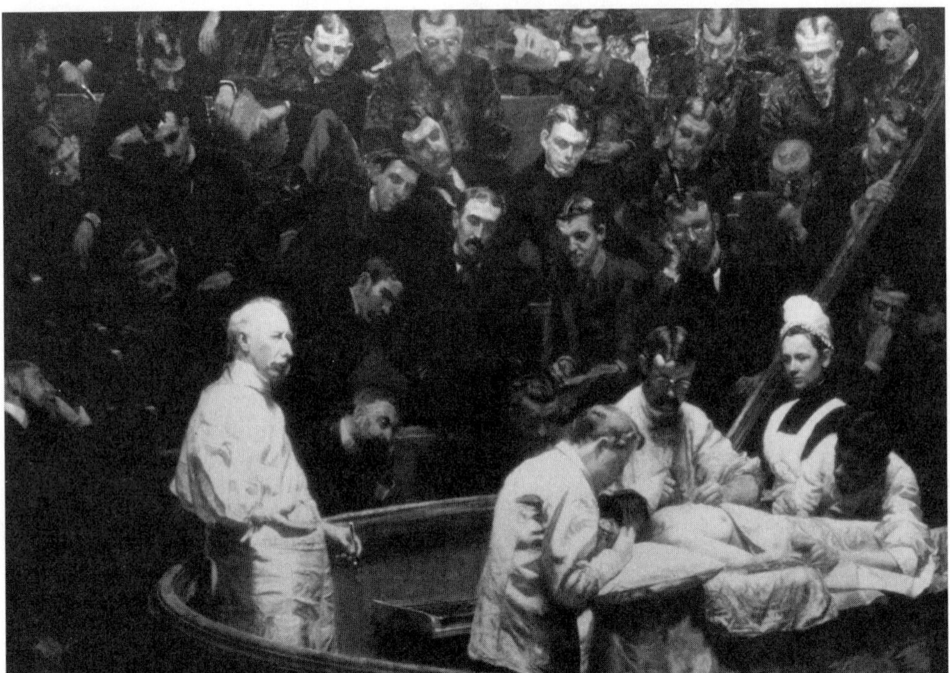

THE AGNEW CLINIC, BY THOMAS EAKINS. The great American painter has caught the atmosphere of medical school in the nineteenth century. Here, well-dressed and for the most part interested physicians observe a mastectomy operation. The combination of scientific study, expertise, and professional specialization lifted the practice of medicine from a trade to a science in the public's mind. (*University of Pennsylvania Art Collection, Philadelphia, Penn.*)

or "Taylorism," as it was called after Frederick Taylor, one of its leading proponents. Americans taught Taylorism in their new professional schools of business. Even European socialist critics of capitalism talked of "Taylorizing" production and management, taking the inefficiency out of capitalism.

The result was a "takeoff" of technology: each discovery opened a new runway down which industries could travel, and the new technologies were continually building feeder paths from one runway to another. This industrial takeoff, connecting industries to technological and scientific advances, can be illustrated by examining a few key industries: railroads, communications, and energy.

Railroads thrilled the public, along with investors and politicians, for railroads had the aura of progress that the cheaper, equally efficient, and labor-intensive (rather than capital-intensive) canals and roads did not. Railroads were the engine of industrial growth in Britain, stimulating the demand for coal and iron, steel, gravel, wood and tar, engineering training, and electronic signaling. With the development of Bessemer and Siemens processes, quality steel could be made cheaply and abundantly, causing a boom in the railroad and construction industries. Stronger steel machinery allowed a wider application of steam power in these industries, as well as others, including mining.

In the first period of consolidation, from 1850 to the 1870s, many railroad firms competed with each other. Further expansion required an unprecedented amount of capital accumulation, and the acquisition and use of funds was just as innovative as the invention of better engines and cars. The railroad moguls who could draw in the greatest amounts of capital soon swallowed up their rivals, acquiring immense personal and corporate fortunes. In countries that lacked moguls, government stepped in to amass the capital, build railroads, take over failing ones, and subsidize private builders by land or monopoly grants and contracts. It did so to foster commerce, maintain military power, and strengthen the central authority by bringing regions and groups into the national market. Railroads transformed North America and Eurasia, opening up vast unsettled areas. In the United States, there were more miles of railway (176,000) by 1870 than in all of Europe. It was the same in Canada. Railroads linked India's various regions. In Russia, in the 1890s, the Trans-Siberian Railroad, a fledgling line financed with reluctant French capital, carried millions of settlers eastward, to the desolate stretches of central Asia.

Shipping paralleled the epic expansion of railroads, bringing distant parts of the world together. The application of the steam-powered engine to ships was prohibitively expensive at first, just as it was for railroads and mining. In 1850, steam-powered ships constituted only 5 percent of the world's tonnage; by 1893, the figure had risen to half of all tonnage. In 1870, sailboats carried 4.5 million tons of goods, and steamships less than a million tons; by 1881, the tonnage was about equal, and by 1885, steam surpassed sail. By 1913, steam carried 11 million tons of goods, and sail only 800,000. The whole world was open to cheap, plentiful goods, products that often could swamp local crafts; simultaneously, Europe became the marketplace for much of the world.

Steam power fueled this massive increase in productivity from the middle of the century until its monopoly was broken at the turn of the century. Electricity became more competitive, powering whole industries and lighting great cities. Then two German engineers, Gottlieb Daimler and Karl Benz, perfected the internal combustion engine fueled by petroleum products, and applied it to a carriage. The automobile age was born. Ultimately, petroleum power democratized many aspects of the industrial process, fostering changes in production, organization, and consumption. Daimler developed a luxury automobile, the Mercedes; the American Henry Ford (1863–1947) produced his 1908 Model T for the "ordinary man." By 1914, his mass-production, conveyer-belt assembly-line techniques revolutionized industrial production. Another German's development of the diesel engine made the fuel for giant cargo ships, warships, and luxury liners much cheaper, more powerful, and more efficient. Steam, oil and gas, and electricity would power the twentieth century.

As they do today, communications pushed expansion, and industrial growth stretched communications. At the time, the rapid improvement of everyday postal services was much more important than spectacular inventions such as the telegraph, the telephone, and the radio. Development costs were so prohibitive for the telephone (invented by Alexander Graham Bell in 1876) and the wireless, or radio (invented by Guglielmo Marconi in 1895), that it took almost twenty-five years after invention for either device to be widely used even in industrial countries. Once costs were cut, however, communications grew exponentially, shrinking distances between markets and time between orders and delivery.

By the end of the nineteenth century, the Scientific and the Industrial Revolutions had joined forces. Scientific knowledge quickly became applied practice; inventions played a much greater role in industrial expansion than they had in the much slower, more cumulative earlier growth. More than half a century elapsed between Michael Faraday and James Maxwell's discovery of the fundamentals of electricity and the inventions of Thomas Edison, Bell, and Marconi. In a much shorter time, electricity provided power for lights, for urban and suburban trains, and for some factory engines. This same trend was evident in industrial chemistry. In 1850, almost all industrial materials were the ones people had been using for centuries: wood, stone, cotton, wool, flax, hemp, leather, plant dyes, and the base metals such as copper, iron, lead, and tin and their various alloys. From then onward, particularly in Germany, chemists discovered new elements and perfected formulas for alloys and other combinations. Dyes and coal-tar products

Painting of the Bowery by Louis Sontag (1895). This New York City street scene bursts with commercial energy and activity as the night is lighted by blazing electricity. The artist puts pushcarts, trolleys, horse-drawn cabs, and trains side by side, as he does the classic architecture of the theater and the four-story buildings housing shops and families on the Bowery. The city throbs with the energy of modern technology. (*Museum of the City of New York #32.275.2. Gift of William B. Miles.*)

(such as liquid fuel), aspirin and other drugs, saccharin, and disinfectants were developed. In medicine, too, the marriage of science and technology produced miraculous progeny. Anesthetics and antiseptics improved the chances of survival for hospitalized patients. The discovery and isolation of disease-causing bacteria by Louis Pasteur, a French chemist, made it possible to pinpoint the causes of some diseases, to quarantine the diseased, and to immunize or inoculate the healthy. By the end of the century, researchers had identified the causes of several killer diseases: typhoid, tuberculosis, cholera, tetanus, diphtheria, and leprosy.

Each new scientific breakthrough was quickly published for the general public in the popular scientific, medical, and technological press. Science exposed poor sanitation and squalor as the breeders of disease, and industrialized countries worked harder to ameliorate those conditions. Life expectancy increased, the death rate decreased, and the population in the more advanced

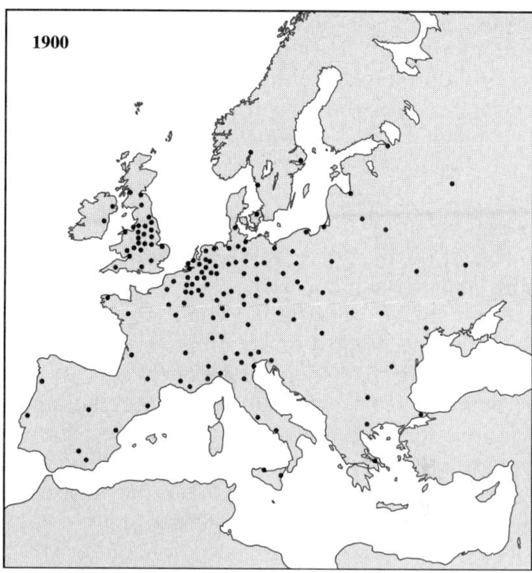

Map 26.1 European Cities of 100,000 or More, 1800–1900 Within a century, industrialization brought about the urbanization of northwestern Europe, particularly England, Belgium, western Germany, and northern France.

industrialized countries boomed despite the fact that couples practiced contraception as a way to maintain their standard of living.

In all, each advance—and we have discussed only a few key industries—brought social change, which forced changes in the political and social power of individuals, groups, and nations and pushed industrial and commercial development still further.

Accelerated Urbanization

Rapid industrial development urbanized northwestern Europe and the United States. More and larger cities, more densely populated, drew people from rural life and labor to mix with those who were city born and bred. Although the majority of England's population lived in cities of ten thousand as early as 1800, most other Europeans did not until the twentieth century, and most of the world waited in the countryside until after the Second World War. Although a commercial and not an industrial city, London had become a megalopolis of five million people by 1880; it was home to seven million by 1914. Between 1866 and the First World War, Berlin grew from half a million to two million. At unification, Germany had just three cities of more than a hundred thousand inhabitants; by 1903, it had fifteen. Paris increased in population from two million to three million between 1850 and World War I. By 1900, the United States was more heavily urbanized than Europe and had more cities of a million inhabitants than any other nation. These millions were immigrants, recently European peasants, or American farmers attacted to industrial labor.

Cities differed as did nations, but industrial ones seemed to grow more alike. Some of the worst ways in which they developed called for cooperative action by municipalities and government. By the end of the century, most of western Europe had taken some steps to provide sanitation, a public water supply, policing, and public transport. Streets were being laid and widened, housing was constructed, and some regulations were imposed on housing and commercial property. New professions of urban planner, transport and sanitation engineer, and social worker joined then replaced the well-meaning, civic-minded, urban-dwelling men and women volunteers who worked to alleviate the worst effects of urban industrial living.

The draw of the factory, the drama of the train, and the squalor and poverty of rural life brought village and rural people to the city, where they acclimated to the urban environment. Responding to the various pressures of education, the press, and patriotic campaigns, they became conscious of a national loyalty, which grew stronger as their regional, class, and religious allegiances waned. Maintaining traditional loyalties and minority identity became increasingly difficult in the process of industrialization and urbanization. There were exceptions: industrialization actually heightened minority identity among such industrially advanced peoples as the Czechs in Austria-Hungary and the Basques in Spain. Generally, however, if a minority culture managed to resist the pressures for integration, its success in doing so reflected the relative economic backwardness of the area. In Russia, the Austro-Hungarian Empire, the Iberian Peninsula, and southern Italy, discontented peasants rejected pressures for national integration. There, the peasants who held small pieces of land barely eked out a living, and landless peasants labored on great estates for landlords who paid them little despite the abundance they produced for export. As the landlord often spoke another language, the peasant's discontent stemmed from a mix of national or ethnic identity and economic woe.

Labor's Responses

Around the world, labor, too, was caught in the changing conditions of the second wave of industrialization. Giant enterprises required great armies of unskilled workers who toiled for low pay, usually by the day or by the job, if they were lucky enough (or shared enough of their wages with the foreman) to be chosen to work. When workers had low pay, irregular work, and minimal skills, the building of unions was almost impossible. Unskilled workers could not be fitted into craft unions. Technology increased the number of the unskilled, and it "deskilled" the craft workers, often pitting the two groups against each another. Skilled craftspeople watched as machines and unskilled workers—often foreigners or minorities or displaced peasants—took their places. Labor standards, the quality of goods, and wages all declined. Rising wages in any industry became an incentive to invent a machine to drive them back down.

Greater democracy helped labor. Where workers could vote, they pressed for government action against the social evils of industrialization and urbanization. In some countries, such as the United States, workers voted for the same political parties that other classes voted for. In other countries, such as Britain, workers did so at first but then organized their own party. In France, Germany, and Italy, workers joined socialist parties calling for the end of capitalism; in Italy, Spain, and parts of France, even more radical, anarchist parties gained worker support. Beginning in the 1860s and 1870s, workers demanded union recognition, minimum wages, maximum hours, and better working conditions even for nonunion workers. Laborers had to win over the general public, which was imbued with individualist, property-protecting values as well as class prejudices. Labor won public sympathy for the poorest of workers and for exploited women and children. In 1888, an English strike of women and girls who worked in match factories, where phosphorus endangered lives, drew public and press support, including sympathy strikes of other workers. The "match girls" made some gains. But the next year, when impoverished British dockworkers struck, there was little public sympathy for these rough-and-ready men. Australian and American dockworkers rescued them from sure defeat. They knew the horrible conditions of the job and realized how vulnerable a union of unskilled day laborers in any country actually was.

Between the "hungry forties" and the outbreak of World War I, the standard of living of many workers, both skilled craftspeople and factory hands, did improve, thanks to trade union organization, government intervention in the

"MATCH GIRLS." The "Match Girls" strike taught the public the human cost of cheap and dangerous products. Here the women pack phosphorus matches in a London factory. (*Hackney Archives Department, London.*)

economy, and the general increase in productivity. Nevertheless, most workers—and their families—lived in overcrowded, bleak, cold tenements, without ventilation or running water. They worked long hours—as many as fifty-five per week in trades where governments restricted the length of the workweek, and from seventy to seventy-five in unregulated trades. Their jobs were exhausting and monotonous. Women workers had a particularly hard life, spending the regulated number of hours in the factory and then doing piecework at home to make ends meet. In addition, they took care of the home and the children, of which there were usually five or more. Workers suffered from malnutrition, diseases (particularly tuberculosis), and lack of medical care for childbirth or accidents, even those that maimed and killed. Governments paid attention, taking the first steps to protect women and children and then extending reforms to male workers as laborers were drawn to socialist or labor parties, which believed that exploitation was built into the capitalist profit system. In the 1880s, Bismarck instituted reforms (see below), and by 1914, Britain, France, Austria, Italy, Denmark, and Switzerland provided some benefits for sick, injured, and elderly workers. These social welfare measures, however, offered only minimum assistance—much less than organized labor provided for itself from dues and welfare funds.

Socialist parties, which by the 1890s were often Marxist, grew phenomenally in Germany and rapidly in much of the rest of Europe. Even backward Russia had a Marxist socialist party. Socialists did not always agree on tactics; their views depended on their ideology and their country's political environment. Some socialists—men such as Wilhelm Liebknecht and August Bebel of Germany or Jules Guesde of France—insisted that reform would come only through a socialist-led revolution. Others—"revisionist" Marxists—argued that Marx's predictions needed to be adapted to new conditions, such as an improving standard of living and universal manhood suffrage. Two "revisionists"—in Germany, Eduard Bernstein, and in France, Jean Jaurès—urged socialists to build democracy, which, they believed, would then create socialism without revolution. Even in England, where Marxism was unimportant and democracy assumed, unionists organized the socialist Independent Labour party.

In the decade before 1914, a wave of strikes

swept through every industrial and industrializing country. Strikes were put down with violence: the dock strikes in London and Liverpool, the railroad workers' strike in France, and the miners' strikes in England and France, for example. There was no single united working class; there was no one program to solve workers' problems. The very ability of workers in England, France, and the United States to vote, speak, and organize to reform their conditions made it appear that those countries were on the verge of class warfare. Every year, the socialist parties and trade union congresses of the Second International (successor to Marx's First International Workingmen's Association) argued strategy and voted for the "hard line"—revolution to bring about socialism.

The revolutionary position was internationalist as well. Socialist congresses urged workers not to be tricked by the capitalists into fighting for their country should there be war. Worker solidarity was to reach across frontiers, and sometimes it did as in the dockworkers' strike. Although many middle- and upper-class Europeans feared that organized labor would follow socialist leadership, their fears were groundless; workers were deeply patriotic.

Great Britain: An Industrial Model

In 1850, foreigners and Englishmen alike believed England to be the most modern and progressive of states. It had made phenomenal industrial progress, and most of its people began to share a higher standard of living in the era of free trade after 1847. England was the model parliamentary government; it balanced an incomparable degree of political liberty with economic and social reforms, avoiding the extremes of revolution and reaction. Political parties competed to govern and in the process reformed evils and extended membership in the political community to previously excluded groups, such as labor or the Irish. That was the widely held view of Victorian England. The reality differed. "Country gentlemen" dominated British politics: titled aristocrats manned the cabinets and commanded the army and navy just as they did in central Europe. Great social mobility existed, but wealthy industrialists, merchants, and entrepreneurs who wanted a public life had to demonstrate a large measure of social conformity.

A century of industrial and commercial changes—and some good luck, like the discovery of gold in California and Alaska—brought prosperity and a sense of well-being, which shaped the politics of the time. Two men of quite different personalities and values were the central political figures whose competition stimulated reform: William E. Gladstone (1809–1898), a pious, sober man for whom politics was a struggle between the forces of liberal good and conservative evil; and the flamboyant Benjamin Disraeli (1804–1881), a novelist and a conservative, who loved the fascinating game of politics. They laid down the rules of the parliamentary game for others to admire and imitate. If the prime minister and his party failed to get a bill passed, the rules required a change in the governing party. He and his cabinet (men of his party drawn from the Parliament to run the government) had to resign or call a new election.

In 1867, when Gladstone failed to pass a bill to let some of the working class vote, Disraeli proposed suffrage for most city workers, not at all what anyone expected of the leader of the Conservatives. The measure carried, and suddenly the electorate was doubled. Both parties feared democracy, yet in the competition for power, democracy had become a reality. Overnight, compulsory elementary education became a necessity (other European states had state schools and compulsory education, but not England). In 1884, Gladstone's party extended the vote to most Englishmen. Women and many Irishmen still could not vote, but the belief grew that it was only a matter of time before liberal democracy would include even them.

The depression of 1873, however, undermined this conviction. English self-confidence was greatly diminished by industrial rivalry with Germany and the United States, imperial problems in South Africa and elsewhere, and the inability to resolve the Irish problem. Would "country gentlemen" admit women, the Irish, and labor into the political community? Could Britain be truly democratic? On the eve of the First World War, the demands for justice by each of these groups created a prolonged crisis for parliamentary government.

Labor Unrest

Lower-class militance seemed to subside for the half-century after 1848 despite the fact that none of the Chartists' democratic demands were realized. In the stable, prosperous middle decades of the century, British workers created the strongest labor movement in Europe. After the depression of 1873, in England, as in all the countries of Europe, technology altered conditions in whole industries, leading, in the 1880s, to a rise in militant industrial unions, termed "new unions." Unlike workers on the Continent, British workers were relatively untouched by Marxist ideas, managing to express their interests within the Liberal party. In the 1880s, however, widespread hardship caused by foreign competition and the general industrial downturn led some labor leaders to advocate English socialism. In 1893, J. Kier Hardie, a colorful nonconformist who represented a poor Welsh mining district in the House of Commons, formed the Independent Labour party. Sometimes in alliance with middle-class socialists, such as the Fabians, sometimes with Liberals, he and other union leaders hammered out a political and economic program.

The Labour party might never have gotten off the ground if it had not been for the Taff Vale decision (1901). The courts awarded damages to an employer picketed by a union. If workers could be fined for picketing or other actions "restraining trade," their unions would be broken and their treasuries depleted. This happened just as labor was mounting a campaign for protection against unemployment, accidents, sickness, and old age—benefits that German workers had obtained in the 1880s. Labor took to politics. By 1906, in a Liberal landslide, the new Labour party gained twenty-nine seats. The Liberals, led by David Lloyd George (1863–1945) and the then Liberal Winston Churchill (1874–1965), introduced a series of important social measures. They repealed the Taff Vale decision. Aided by the Labour party, they enacted a program of old-age pensions, labor exchanges to help the unemployed find work, minimum wages for certain industries, unemployment, and health insurance—in short, a program deeply influenced by Bismarck's social legislation. The House of Lords rejected the budget, forcing a constitutional crisis because the House of Commons is responsible for money bills. The Lords took this extreme action because "the people's budget" financed the social legislation by raising the income tax and levying inheritance taxes ("death duties") and "unearned" income taxes on rents, investments, and increases in the value of land. All these taxes were directed at the wealthy and the privileged.

The Liberals waged an all-out fight with the Lords, who saw their struggle as the defense of Britain and its empire against the Liberals' "socialist" campaign. Lloyd George sarcastically described the dukes as "five hundred men, ordinary men, chosen accidentally from among the unemployed." Class hatreds, unacknowledged for a couple of generations as part of the political balance that Britain had achieved, intensified and were bitterly and freely expressed. Miners, railway workers, and dockhands allied, calling a general strike. The people's budget ultimately passed.

Later, the Parliament Act of 1911 stipulated that the Lords could only delay the passage of a bill passed by the Commons, not prevent it. The machinery for democratic government in Britain was in place. Excluded groups had focused on democracy as the way to gain justice—not on social revolution. But a long coal strike in 1912 involved a million and a half workers, and only government intervention could stop it. Whether British liberal democracy would survive was uppermost in the minds of many on the eve of World War I.

The Irish Question

For members of Parliament, the Irish were a "question," and a troublesome one, for much of the nineteenth century. The great famine of 1845–47 brought unparalleled suffering to the Irish: a million of them died and another million emigrated.

Carson Reviewing Troops of Ulster Volunteers Before WWI. For almost a century the Irish demand for representation, then for home rule (or self-government), had met with political opposition in the British Parliament. With Parliament split, Irish nationalists and their opponents, Irish Protestants, armed for civil war. Here a leading member of Parliament supports the Irish Protestants who have volunteered for the civil war to keep Ireland in the British empire. The start of the first World War put this treasonous and revolutionary situation out of the public mind only for a couple years.(*Hulton Archive/Getty Images.*)

The sufferers saw England if not as the cause, then as callously indifferent to their plight. A revolutionary republican group, the Fenians, called for Irish independence, developing a variety of protests against British policy in Ireland. Fenian protests were remarkably successful; Gladstone said the Fenians provoked him to take up Irish reform. Like many English liberals, he thought that economic and religious reforms would end Irish discontent; therefore, he ended the tithe the Irish paid to the Anglican church and passed land legislation for Irish tenant farmers. Had these reforms been made in the 1840s and 1850s they might have appeased the Irish. By the 1880s, however, they were too little, too late; the issue had become home rule—that is, self-government within the British Empire. In the Commons, the Irish, led by the Protestant Charles Stewart Parnell, formed a separate bloc to force the Conservatives and the Liberals to reckon with the issue of home rule. Parnell's supporters used every known parliamentary tactic, and invented some new ones, to secure their goals. They denounced violence, but others urged violence. Terrorist acts aroused public passions; Parliament enacted extreme measures, suspending trial by jury and many other liberties in Ireland, which only intensified the hostilities. At the end of his life, Gladstone had split his party and failed, as would his Liberal successors, to achieve a reconciliation with the Irish. Parnell, whose political aura faded in a scandalous love affair, had also failed.

The continuing bitter struggle for home rule

made prewar British politics extremely volatile. The House of Lords, dominated by Tory imperialists (Conservatives), could not prevent the passage of home rule once the Parliament Act of 1911 became law. The Liberals pushed for the reform, but Tory imperialists thought the empire more important than elections and majority rule. Militant groups took the law into their own hands. The Irish Republican Brotherhood and the Gaelic League pressed for full independence; among the Protestant Irish, a private army, the Ulster Volunteers, was recruited, ready for war should home rule be enacted. Gangs smuggled guns (many from America), soldiers fired on demonstrators, and civil war seemed close. Some English Tory leaders threatened mutiny; one actually reviewed eighty thousand volunteer soldiers willing to fight against the English for the Protestant cause in Ireland.

In 1914, when Great Britain declared war on Germany, Ireland was uppermost in British minds. On the day the archduke of Austria was assassinated, the front pages of the British papers were filled with news of Irish protest, not with foreign affairs. With the onset of war, women and labor suspended their militant campaigns, pledging their loyalty to king and country. Many Irish fought for Britain in World War I, but the deferred promise of home rule angered many others. Some, like Sir Roger Casement, joined the Germans to fight for Ireland's independence. In 1916, on Easter Sunday, a group of Irish nationalists seized the Dublin post office in an insurrection; it was suppressed and the leaders executed.

After the war, Lloyd George negotiated a settlement. Ireland was divided, the south gaining self-government and the northern six counties of Ulster remaining part of the United Kingdom.

The Woman Question

The "woman question"—the issue of women's equality—was much older than the nineteenth-century struggle for the vote, which had begun in the antislavery and temperance campaigns in England and the United States. (The Anglo-American women reformers' network remained long after the end of slavery.) This question was more than a political concern in England, the English colonies, and the United States, where the suffrage movement was stronger than elsewhere in Europe. On the Continent, including Scandinavia, Germany, and even Russia, the "new woman" of the end of the century demanded sexual freedom, the right of divorce, child custody, and property ownership. Those demands would have been utopian dreams if the Industrial Revolution had not made it possible for women to work and to support themselves and their families. Nonetheless, husbands and fathers still had control of their children and the family property, education was unattainable for most, and employment was scarce and low paying. During the wave of industrial change on the eve of the First World War, the woman question came up again. Artists and intellectuals, such as Henrik Ibsen, George Bernard Shaw, and H. G. Wells, supported women's emancipation, and August Strindberg opposed it. Socialist feminists, such as the German Clara Zetkin, argued that only socialism could liberate women from responsibility for their children and from their lives of hard work in the home and in the economy. Socialist support was inconsistent on this issue. Conservatives, in contrast, were unified in their view that women's rights would destroy the family and undermine the nation. Ironically, radicals in France, Italy, and Spain, who ordinarily would have championed equality, opposed women's suffrage because they feared that priests and husbands would dominate the women. Finally, women themselves were torn between their role as wives and mothers and their desire for equality and some measure of protection.

Women had greater freedom in England than in most countries; there they could vote for and serve on school and local government boards. Without their volunteer work in schools and charity organizations, the educational and social support system of Britain would have floundered. But they could not vote for members of Parliament, their education was stunted, and they suffered from enormous social pressure to conform to traditional women's roles. The women's movement was far from united. Middle-class women and working-class women led very different lives. Many of the latter were much more concerned with economic security than with the right to vote. Although no longer limited to the most miserable and sometimes degrading labor, working-class women remained particularly vulnerable to the ups and downs of the economy. Many resented the middle-class women who gave them lessons in budgeting, housekeeping, and child-rearing when they desperately needed assistance. Even middle-class women were divided. Some feminists—Millicent Fawcett and Josephine Butler, for instance—thought that women should concentrate on self-improvement and legal efforts to raise their status in society. Others proposed radical and immediate action. Still others thought that the political road was the wrong one to take; if women wanted to be free, they needed to liberate themselves economically and socially from their dependence on men.

Despite the many aspects of women's rights, in England the "question" was posed as a suffrage issue. It was posed in particularly vivid ways—ways that threatened the accepted forms and norms of liberal politics. In the campaign for women's suffrage, suffragist tactics and government repression steadily escalated in violence. Many Liberals and some Labourites supported women's suffrage. Still, the leader of the Liberals advised women "to keep on pestering . . . but exercise the virtue of patience." A family of feminists called for an end to patience. Emmeline Pankhurst and her daughters Sylvia and Christabel urged demonstrations and disruptions of the House of Commons. When their petitions were ignored, they moved to more shocking actions: breaking windows, starting fires in mailboxes, etching with acid slogans in the golf greens, and chaining themselves to the gates of Parliament. In 1913, one militant killed herself in protest by jumping in front of the king's horse at the races. The suffragists' opponents argued that women were not rational enough to discuss politics. When law-breaking feminists were arrested, they staged hunger strikes. Ugly situations resulted. The police force-fed the demonstrators and subjected them to ridicule and rough treatment. Often the police would release half-starved suffragists to recover their health, then reimprison them ("cat and mouse" it was called). Ridiculed, humiliated, and punished—but, above all, legally ignored—feminists refused to accept the passive role that male-dominated society assigned them.

Women played a major part on the home front in World War I, and in 1918, women over thirty years of age were enfranchised in Britain. In some colonies (Australia, New Zealand), women had the right to vote. Finally, in 1928, British women gained the right to vote on the same terms as men, that is, they had to be twenty-one years old and to have six months' residency. After the war, women gained the right to vote in the United States, Germany, and the Soviet Union, but they would have to wait a long time for this right in France, Spain, Italy, and Switzerland.

Britain on the Eve of War

The bitter conflicts of prewar Britain showed the cracks in the country's self-image as a stable, liberal, constitutional regime. The elite learned that the tactics of the new politics—strikes, demonstrations, passive resistence, and terrorism—would destroy the liberal parliamentary institutions that many saw as the basis of Britain's greatness. Parliamentary government proved able to win a grueling world war, but issues of empire and economic depression would test the constitution once again as excluded groups fought for full democracy.

France: Democratic or Authoritarian?

The political fortunes of France in the nineteenth century differed greatly from Britain's. France's slow and uneven industrialization greatly affected its national and international affairs. Virtually each generation faced revolution and reaction, swinging from democratic revolution to authoritarian stability, from active participation of the people to rule by a single man or small group of men.

Napoleon "le Petit"

At midcentury, the personality and politics of Louis Napoleon Bonaparte (1808–1873), the nephew of the great Napoleon I, dominated

France. By an overwhelming majority, in an election in which all French males could vote, "the small" or "little" Bonaparte ("le Petit") was elected president of the Second French Republic, which a democratic social revolution had established in 1848. Within three years, he was dictator-emperor, the republic destroyed, and its destruction ratified by a plebiscite. This vote and subsequent elections were rigged. Bonaparte's imperialism, his willingness to support Catholics in Rome and in France, and his destruction of the republic outraged liberals and republicans, including Alexis de Tocqueville and Victor Hugo. The working class resented the dismantling of the republic. Most other French citizens, however, accepted the "little Napoleon."

Bonapartism was a mix of democratic, socialist, nationalist, and authoritarian ideas. It promised national glory, strong leadership, and social progress, which pleased many after the radical 1840s. Bonaparte combined the appearance of democracy—elections by universal manhood suffrage, plebiscites, a press, and intellectual debate—with economic expansion. At the same time, he suppressed opposition, censored the press, rarely convened the parliament, and manipulated both elections and debate. His close friends and his relatives were his advisers and administrators. Property owners, who liked stability at home, expansion abroad, railroad construction, and the rebuilding of Paris, liked him. He expressed concern for workers, whose suffering became acute as industrialization took hold. After a decade of authoritorian rule, he loosened the controls on the press and the legislature, legalized strikes, and granted workers a limited right to unionize. In 1869, when members of the opposition were elected, a new constitution with liberal safeguards for individual liberties was written. It turned Louis Napoleon Bonaparte into a constitutional parliamentary monarch like Queen Victoria in England. Was he a liberal nationalist who wanted to give France reforms once he had established his power? Or did he, like the great Napoleon, accept liberal change only when he feared an overthrow? Such questions became irrelevant the very next year, when France was defeated and occupied by Prussian troops.

After the Fall

As French armies collapsed, the people of Paris rose, refusing to accept defeat. The Paris Commune (1871) rejected both the corrupt Second Empire and the provisional government of Adolph Thiers. Thiers agreed to peace terms with Prussia and ended the wartime moratorium on the payment of rent and debts. The Communards (radical republicans) simply refused to obey the provisional government. The Communards included a wide range of opinion: the followers of Pierre Joseph Proudhon; groups of republican and socialist veterans of the Revolution of 1848 suddenly and unexpectedly liberated from prisons, hiding, and exile; and many ordinary republicans and patriots. For two months, the revolutionaries ruled Paris, inspired by the Jacobins of 1793 and the radicals of June 1848. Then the man who had accepted Bismarck's peace terms ordered French soldiers to attack Paris. The fighting was bitter and desperate, with many acts of terrorism and violence on both sides of this civil war. The defeated Communards were treated as traitors: twenty thousand men and women were executed without trial, and those who were tried received harsh sentences of death, life imprisonment, and transportation to prison colonies.

The Commune became legendary. It alarmed governing classes across Europe, who feared revolutionary socialism or anarchism. Many thought that the people should be ruled with an iron fist. International revolutionaries, too, thought that the Communards were the radicalized masses, forgetting that they had risen to save their country. Convinced that political leaders everywhere would be just as brutal in defending private property as Thiers had been, revolutionaries like Marx urged the masses to train themselves for violent insurrection. Other radicals, appalled by the bloodbath, argued that the revolutionary days of 1789, 1830, and 1848 were over because the modern state was too powerful. Workers would have to express their protests by votes and demonstrations.

The suppression of the Paris Commune marked a turning point in French political life. To French property owners, republican government meant radicalism, despite the fact that republicans had destroyed the Commune. A much wider

After the Fall: LaRoquette Prisoners Before the Firing Squad. The repression of the Paris Commune, which resisted the French provisional government when it tried to make peace with the Prussians, was a brutal bloodbath with atrocities on both sides. When it was over, almost eight thousand were sent into exile, five thousand imprisoned and fined, and many executed. Few could have predicted that the republic established then would survive to World War II. (*Corbis-Bettmann.*)

public supported a republican regime either by action or by apathy. Burdened by an indemnity and the loss of Alsace and part of Lorraine in the Franco-Prussian War and embittered by the experience of war and civil war, republican France slowly rebuilt national unity and regained its place in Europe.

Threats to the Republic

The government born from the next few years of political crisis would be the longest-lasting republic in the history of France (1870–1940). Its birth was accidental; with no king willing to rule, republicans did. The Third Republic had a powerful bicameral legislature—a senate and a chamber of deputies, which resembled the House of Commons—and a prime minister, who had to have its support. The president was a figurehead; republicans wanted no new Napoleon. Unlike Britain, France had many political parties, which expressed the deep differences—regional, political, religious, economic, and historical—among the French, but also exaggerated them.

Critics of the Third Republic gathered around a dashing republican general, Georges Boulanger (1837–1891), whose popularity reminded many of Napoleon III. Was France to swing back to authoritarianism again? The threat faded when

Boulanger dramatically committed suicide on the grave of his former mistress. Almost immediately, another scandal was exposed. Several republican deputies were involved in a giant stock swindle involving the financing of the Panama Canal. They tried to cover up the taking of bribes. The low level of public morality shocked the people. Many viewed all politics as immoral; others thought democracy was prone to corruption as in the United States and France. Prime ministers resigned in rapid succession; cabinets rose and fell frequently, giving the impression of a state without direction. Parliamentary life seemed to consist of wheeling and dealing; the Third Republic survived, but not without more trouble; in the process, politics took to the streets and the press.

The Dreyfus affair tore France apart for more than a decade. In 1894, Captain Alfred Dreyfus, an Alsatian-Jewish artillery officer, was wrongly accused of selling military secrets to the Germans. He was condemned to life imprisonment on Devil's Island, a deadly prison off the coast of French Guiana in South America. Anti-Semitic elements joined with all the Republic's opponents, including the army, the Catholic church, and monarchists, to block every attempt to clear Dreyfus. In the beginning, he had few friends; the vast majority felt that the honor off France and the army was at stake. Then a few radical republicans, including the writers Anatole France, Émile Zola, and the future war leader, Georges Clemenceau, came to Dreyfus's defense, mobilizing public opinion. University students demonstrated, insisting on a retrial and an overthrow of the verdict. After many humiliations, Dreyfus was finally cleared in 1906.

The radical republicans launched a fierce campaign to root out the antirepublicans and anti-Semitic elements. Anticlericalism had been strong in France for more than a century among certain groups; the Dreyfus affair seemed to justify all their fears. The radicals attacked the Catholic church, expelled religious orders, and confiscated their property. They tried to replace the influence of the parish priest with that of the district schoolmaster. Complete separation of church and state was ordered, making France a secular state. The Dreyfus case had exposed and exacerbated the divisions in French society.

France on the Eve of War

French economic development lagged. France had fewer and smaller industries than Britain or Germany, and more French people lived in rural areas or in small communities. In general, industry, trade unions, and socialist groups tended to be decentralized rather than national; artisans were much more influential than proletarians. For a generation after the suppression of the Paris Commune, labor was markedly antipolitical. Militants refused to cooperate with the Republic or any bourgeois government. In the 1880s, however, both trade unions and socialist political parties turned to democratic politics to gain social reform, such as pensions and regulations governing working conditions, wages, and hours. The ruling elite opposed such measures, which might have improved the lives of ordinary people. Socialists were ambivalent, thinking such reforms mere tokens to buy off workers. Many workers and intellectuals supported radical syndicalism (which advocated bringing industries and government under the control of workers) and even anarchism. Viewing a wave of strikes on the eve of the First World War as economic warfare, the government conscripted striking railway workers.

The Third Republic was not popular. The church, the army, socialism, and even memories of the monarchy and the empire inspired deeper passions than the Republic. The Republic survived because its enemies were divided. Few would have believed that France could fight and win the First World War.

Germany: Forging an Empire

The Prussian Bismarck created a German empire under his and Prussia's control. Prussia's king was emperor. All roads led to Berlin's Brandenburg Gate, where Bismarck decided the great issues, shaping the political environment for the next generation. For conservatives and liberals alike, the "Iron Chancellor" was the man of the hour.

Bismarck's constitution, like that of Napoleon III, was hardly liberal. Both men granted universal manhood suffrage and then manipulated the

Profile

Jean Jaurès

Jean Jaurès (1859–1914) was the most important socialist in the Third French Republic. A brilliant student, he advanced to the highest ranks of the university. He soon tired of teaching philosophy, however, and chose politics. He was the youngest member elected to the Chamber of Deputies. Deeply concerned about workers' problems, Jaurès believed that capitalism was creating a new feudalism in which the rich controlled the society. He led a socialist party convinced that only the working class struggled for justice and that their struggle could win over others.

Jaurès brought liberal republicans and socialists together for social reforms. He championed Alfred Dreyfus and argued that socialists had just as much at stake as liberals in questions of justice. Jaurès and French workers joined with intellectuals and students in demonstrating for and demanding a fair trial and freedom for the convicted Jewish officer. Many

Roger-Viollet.

votes and elections. The German government was federal, the twenty-four states had some powers, but foreign affairs and defense were in the hands of the emperor and his chancellor. The German kaiser, unlike Britain's monarch, had considerable control over lawmaking, foreign affairs, and the military. Aristocrats held the important positions in the military, the diplomatic corps, and the top echelon of the bureaucracy. The German Empire did not have Britain's two-party system, cabinet responsibility, or guarantees of civil liberties. Technically, the Reichstag could refuse to pass the budget, but politicians were usually unwilling to do that. Only the king-emperor could remove the chancellor or the cabinet members from office. Bismarck saw political parties as merely interest groups incapable of making policy for the country as a whole. He treated them as lobbyists. He cared little for liberal and democratic measures, maintaining an authoritarianism that would have significant consequences for Germany's future.

Bismarck's "Struggle for Culture"

To Bismarck, Catholics and socialists were internationalists who did not put Germany's interests first. Bismarck took advantage of the prejudice and misunderstanding by non-Catholics of the declaration of papal infallibility of 1871 to pass discriminatory laws against Catholics, restricting the Jesuits and requiring government supervision of the church and the education of priests in state socialists refused to take part in parliamentary politics; they thought Jaurès a bourgeois politician because he had been a university professor and never a worker. But those credentials brought a wide range of support as Jaurès campaigned vigorously for reforms that French workers still had not won. In 1905 the socialist parties of France joined together under his leadership during a time of strikes and repression. On the international scene, in the Second International, Jaurès was brilliant in his opposition to war, calling for all workers, not just French ones, to refuse to fight should their governments become belligerents.

In the last days before World War I, Jaurès was assassinated by a French nationalist fanatic who was afraid that the great speaker would convince his socialist followers to resist the war. The assassin was wrong. French workers—even socialists—defended their country in 1914 because they believed it to be the most democratic nation.

schools. All marriages had to be performed by state officials. Churchmen who rejected these laws were imprisoned or exiled. Almost 40 percent of Germany's people were Roman Catholic, and Bismarck's persecution actually strengthened the German Catholics' loyalty to their church and to the Catholic Center party. It weakened the liberals, who did not defend Catholic civil liberties. Prussian conservatives, though Protestant, resented Bismarck's anticlerical policy, which could be turned against Lutherans as well as Catholics. When Leo XIII became pope in 1878, Bismarck quietly opened negotiations to end the "struggle for culture" (*Kulturkampf*).

In the late 1870s, Bismarck attacked socialists—the other internationalists. Socialists were divided. One group, the German Workers' Association, was led by Ferdinand Lassalle (1825–1864), a charismatic lawyer-reformer who had the support of workers and trade unionists, as well as some influence with Bismarck himself. A nationalist, Lassalle concluded that if Germany enacted social reforms, workers would be just as patriotic as any other group. Marxists scoffed, opposing cooperation with the state, but there were more Lassalleans than Marxists. Consequently, they joined forces in 1875 to create a German Social Democratic party, the SPD. To crush the socialists, Bismarck sought to drive a wedge between workers and their leaders. He was sure that the liberals would respond as they had done when he had attacked the Catholics. When in 1878 two attempts were made on the emperor's life, Bismarck manipulated the public, blamed the socialists, and demanded that the party be outlawed and its leaders imprisoned. The few socialists were not a threat; their immediate practical program called for civil liberties and democracy in Germany. Only those with the narrowest of conservative views would have labeled the socialists as dangerous, but many in Germany, particularly the Prussian Junker class, held such a narrow view. Once again Bismarck was right about the liberals, who scarcely objected when special legislation outlawed subversive organizations and authorized the police to ban meetings and newspapers.

The Social Democratic party, like the Catholic Center party before, survived and strengthened its disciplined organization as the liberals grew weaker. Meanwhile, Bismarck wooed workers with social legislation. The effects of the rapid industrialization of the 1850s and 1860s disturbed Bismarck, as they did many conservatives. Germany was the first state to enact social legislation: insurance against sickness, disability, accidents, and old age. The employer, the state, and the worker each contributed small amounts to an insurance fund. Many people considered such measures socialist because the government taxed one group to support workers.

German socialists became the model for socialists elsewhere because they had greater numbers, as well as superior organization and leadership, and because Bismarck's social legislation had given German workers some protection. The Social Democratic party was not just a party but a way of life, offering members political activities, youth and women's divisions, athletic leagues, and cultural societies. Before World War I, union membership stood at roughly three million, and the Social Democratic party was the largest single party in Germany. The socialists talked revolution, but many members favored gradual reform, and most German workers were patriotic, even imperialistic.

Germany on the Eve of War

When Kaiser William II (1889–1918) ascended the throne, Germany possessed the most extensive sector of large-scale, concentrated industrial and corporate capitalism, as well as the largest and most powerful unions. Only the United States could rival the German giant capitalist in scale and concentration of industry. Germany's industrial growth was uneven, however. The heavy industries were quickly developing into giant monopolies or cartels, and mining and railroads were state owned and state operated, but the rapidity of expansion from craft to giant monopoly in some industries was more important than the percentage of the economy controlled by such industries. Many small firms were operating as well, and large-scale agricultural producers, particularly in the eastern regions, were still very powerful. Industrial unions had formed to deal with the monopolies, but workers in small firms were still organized by craft. While the population rose one-third in the single generation of 1882 to 1902, the industrial work force increased by 180 percent. Thirty-five percent of the active labor force of twenty-seven million people was in concentrated industries; many of these people moved directly from the farm to heavily concentrated industries in alien urban environments. Only peasants in Russia and peasant-immigrants in the United States experienced comparable dislocation.

In 1914, Germany was the most highly industrialized and powerful European nation, with the largest and most successful socialist party. Yet it was governed by a political regime that preserved aspects of an absolute monarchy. The constitution was a peculiar mixture of aristocratic Prussian power in the upper house and in the lower, democratic universal male suffrage manipulated to illiberal ends. The bureaucracy, the military, and the chancellor remained out of the reach of the voting populace. Bismarck's opportunistic maneuvers against Catholics, liberals, and socialists had undermined the development of a viable parliamentary government. The Social Democrats, ostensibly the party of revolution, were the only party that campaigned for chancellor responsibility, that is, for power of the Reichstag to reject the chancellor. In other countries such a measure would be advocated by liberals, but in Germany democratic and liberal measures were part of the campaign of socialists.

Italy: Unfulfilled Expectations

Italian nationalists expected greatness from the unification of their country, so long conquered, plundered, divided, and ruled by absolute princes. But the newly unified Italy faced serious problems. An overwhelmingly Roman Catholic country, like France, it was split by religious controversy. Liberals and republicans wanted a secular state, with civil marriage and public education, which was anathema to the church. Another divisive factor was Italy's long tradition of separate and rival states—an extreme version of the regional conflicts of other states. Many Italians doubted that the central government would deal justly with every region. Furthermore, few Italians could actually participate in the constitutional monarchy. Of the twenty-seven million citizens, only about two million could vote, even after the reforms of 1881, which tripled the electorate. Liberals could point out that almost every literate male could vote, but this achievement was small consolation to those who had fought for unification but were denied voting privileges when they failed a literacy test.

Among Italian workers, cynicism about the government was so deep that many turned to extreme radical movements, which advocated the rejection of authority and the tactics of terrorism, assassination, and general strikes. Disgust with parliamentary government led workers to believe that direct action would gain more than elections and parties. Advocates of direct action were much stronger in Italy than in France. Other alienated Italians included peasants from the poor rural south. Catholic, loyal to their landlord, and bitterly unhappy with their economic situation, they saw few signs of the new state aside from taxation and conscription.

The ruling elite brushed aside Italy's difficult social and economic problems. It concentrated instead on issues more easily expressed to an inexperienced political nation: nationalism, foreign policy, and military glory. The politicians trumpeted Italy's ambitions for Great Power status, justifying military expenditures beyond the means of such a poor state. They presented Italy's scramble for African and Mediterranean territories as the solution to its social ills. Exploiting others would pay for badly needed social reforms, and the raw materials gained would fuel industry. The failure of these promises to come true deepened the cynicism of a disillusioned people. On the eve of World War I, Italy was deeply divided politically. A wave of strikes and rural discontent gave sufficient warning to political leaders so that they declared neutrality, deciding, unlike Russia, not to risk the shaky regime by entering the war. But the appeals of expansionism were too great for them to maintain this policy.

Russia: Tsarist Empire

To the east, bordering on Germany, the vast Russian empire was considered part of Europe, although it differed fundamentally from western Europe. Stretching through the Eurasian landmass from Germany to China and Japan, covering one-sixth of the world's land surface, it suffered from incurable weaknesses. Unprotected by natural boundaries in its vast open spaces, it had been created by conquest. Its rulers lived in permanent dread of foreign invasion and internal breakup. Large distances, an adverse climate, and poor communications, as well as extensive ethnic, religious, and cultural diversity held together by force, made Russia a backward country. The great movements that had shaped the outlook of the modern West—the Renaissance, the Reformation, the Scientific Revolution, the Enlightenment, and the Industrial Revolution—had barely penetrated the lands to the east. Yet Russia's rulers, intermarrying with European royalty, always claimed, along with the western-educated elites, that their country was part of Europe. Their capital, Saint Petersburg, at the westernmost point of the Russian empire, was built to match the splendor of French royal architecture.

Russia's fortunes depended on its political order, which centered on the commands of the ruler. Peter the Great, in the early eighteenth century, had reorganized the tsarist government, centralizing the administration and forcing the nobility to serve the state; he also founded the Russian Academy of Sciences. At the end of the century, an exceptionally energetic ruler, Catherine the Great, inspired by French intellectuals such as Voltaire, strengthened the authority of the tsarist regime. Her successors, however, had reason to fear the liberal views of the Enlightenment. Russian officers, returning from western Europe after the defeat of Napoleon, asked why their country could not share in the civilized life they had just observed. They turned into revolutionaries and attempted a futile uprising in December 1825 at the accession of Nicholas I. Thereafter, fear of revolution always haunted the tsarist government.

To counter the subversive influence of western ideals and institutions, Nicholas I decreed an ideology of Russian superiority; called *official nationality*, it remained in force until 1917. The government's version of Russian nationalism taught the Russian people that the Orthodox church, the autocratic rule of the tsar, and Russia's Slavic culture made the Russian empire superior to the West. With the help of the secret police, the government tried to re-create the largely spontaneous unity of the leading western states by all-inclusive political controls, drawing a virtual iron curtain around the country to keep out dangerous foreign influences. The ideal was a monolithic regime, run like an army by a vigorous administration centered on the monarch; all Russians were to obey his wise and fatherly commands. But Nicholas's ambition to make Russia victorious in all comparisons with western Europe was thwarted in the Crimean War (1854–56), fought on Russian soil. English and French expeditionary forces defeated the Russian army and frustrated Russian efforts to gain political influence in the eastern Mediterranean area. Nicholas died before the war ended. A new regime began under Alexander II (1855–1881) in a mood of profound and widespread crisis. Alexander II was determined to preserve autocratic rule in Russia. However, he wanted Russia to achieve what had made western Europe strong: the energetic support and free enterprise of all its citizens. Whether stimulating popular initiative was possible without undermining autocracy was the key puzzle for him and for his successors to the end of the tsarist regime.

Alexander's boldest reforms included the emancipation of the serfs in 1861. They were liberated from bondage to the nobility and given land of their own, but not individual freedom. They remained tied to their villages and to their households, which owned the land collectively. Emancipation did not transform the peasants into enterprising and loyal citizens. For the nonpeasant minority, a package of other reforms brought new opportunities: limited self-government for selected rural areas and urban settlements, an independent judiciary, and the rule of law. Trial by jury was introduced, as well as a profession novel to Russians: the practice of law.

Meanwhile, Alexander reopened the borders, allowing closer ties with Europe. The rising class of businesspeople and professional experts looked west and conformed to western European middle-class standards. There was some relaxation in the repression of non-Russian minorities. The construction of railroads facilitated agricultural exports to the west and permitted the importing of goods and capital from the west. For some years, the economy boomed.

More significant in the long run was the flowering of Russian thought and literature among the intelligentsia. These were educated Russians who were shaped by Western schooling and travel yet still were prompted by the "Russian soul" and an intensity of inward feeling unknown in Western society. They quarreled with fierce sincerity about whether Russia should pursue superiority by imitating the West or by cultivating its own Slavic genius, possibly through a Pan-Slavic movement. Pan-Slavism, which glorified the solidarity of Russians with other Slavic peoples of eastern Europe, was a popular cause. Even more than the tsars, the intelligentsia hoped for a glorious Russia that would outshine the West.

The tsar, however, would not permit open discussion likely to provoke rebellion. Liberals advocating gradual change were thwarted by censorship and the police. The 1860s saw the rise of self-righteous fanatics ready to match the chicanery of the police and foment social revolution. By the late 1870s, they organized themselves into a secret terrorist organization, and in 1881, they assassinated Alexander II. The era of reforms ended, but the revolutionary underground continued, soon led by Marxist intellectuals.

The next tsar, Alexander III (1881–1894), a firm though unimaginative ruler, returned to the principles of Nicholas I. In defense against the revolutionaries, he perfected the police state, even enlisting anti-Semitism in its cause. He updated autocracy and stifled dissent, but he also promoted economic development. Russia had relied too heavily on foreign loans and goods; it had to build up its own resources. It also needed more railroads to bind its huge empire together. So in 1891 the tsar ordered the construction of the Trans-Siberian Railroad. Soon afterward, Minister of Finance Sergei Witte used the railroad expansion to boost heavy industry and industrialization generally.

In 1900, Witte addressed a farsighted memorandum to the young Nicholas II (1894–1917), who was hopelessly unprepared and out of tune with the times when he succeeded his father:

> *Russia more than any other country needs a proper economic foundation for its national policy and culture. . . . International competition does not wait. If we do not take energetic and decisive measures so that in the course of the next decade our industry will be able to satisfy the needs of Russia and of the Asiatic countries which are—or should be—under our influence, then the rapidly growing foreign industries will . . . establish themselves in our fatherland and the Asiatic countries mentioned above. . . . Our economic backwardness may lead to political and cultural backwardness as well.*[1]

Peasants in Russia. This photograph from the late nineteenth century shows Russian peasants in front of their home. (*Corbis-Bettmann.*)

Forced industrialization, however, also brought perils. It propelled the country into alien and often hated ways of life, created a discontented new class of workers, and impoverished agriculture. In addition, it promoted mobility, literacy, and contact with western Europe. Thus, it helped to increase political agitation among the professional classes, workers, peasants, and subject nationalities. Indispensable for national self-assertion and survival, industrialization strained the country's fragile unity.

The first jolt, the revolution of 1905, resulted from the Russo-Japanese War, in which Russia was defeated. Autocracy survived, although it was now saddled with a parliament, called the Imperial Duma, a concession to the revolution. The new regime, privately resisted by Nicholas II, started auspiciously. Russian art and literature flourished and the economy progressed. Agrarian reforms introduced the incentives of private property and individual enterprise in the villages. Nevertheless, popular resentment against government-sponsored modernization festered, waiting for opportunities to explode.

The four imperial rulers of Russia between 1825 and 1914 had labored under enormous difficulties in their efforts to match the power and prestige of the great states of Europe. Two of them met a violent end: Alexander II was assassinated, and Nicholas II was murdered. The other two died in weariness and failure. Although the awe that the tsars inspired among their subjects was real, their splendor was hollow. The tsars' high hopes for Russia's prominence in the world were frustrated by their failure to cope with the massive adversities confronting the country. Its hugeness and scarce means of communication, along with its ethnic, religious, and regional diversity, prevented the emergence of a collective national identity. The country also lacked an effective middle class. The members of the Russian intelligentsia and professional class were as ignorant as the tsars about their country's realities; some even dreamed of a Russia superior to the West. And the abysmally backward peasant masses, scattered over the largest country in the world, were poor material for building a modern state. Outwardly impressive, the Russian empire faced a grim future as the international competition for power escalated in World War I.

The United States: Democratic Giant

Within a generation of its bloody Civil War (1861–1865), the United States moved into the ranks of giant industrial powers, then to the status of a Great Power, and, by the end of World War I, to world leadership. In the mid-nineteenth century, however, the United States was essentially a nation of farmers, producing primary goods or raw materials. In the northeastern part of the country, craft industries supplied consumer goods for a domestic market, and advancing beyond basic craft goods was just as slow a process as it was in France and most of central Europe. Before the Civil War, the economy was primarily mercantile. Merchants were the commercial cement bonding the many small artisans, farmers, and exporters. Despite immigration from Europe and the use of slaves, there was a steady demand for cheap labor. Capital was even scarcer than labor. Americans were inventive, competitive, and socially democratic.

In many ways the early industrialization of the United States resembled that of Britain. Unskilled European immigrants and rural laborers furnished the manpower for New England textile mills, just as Irish and rural laborers had done for England. Both shared the blessings of a single government, able to provide a stable framework for commerce, and in the case of the United States, maintain tariffs against British competition. In both, government was noninterventionist—unwilling and unable to regulate private enterprise. Once a large internal market for cheap, standardized goods developed, entrepreneurs took the risks of investment and production on a large scale. Even more than the British, perhaps because of the much larger market for cheap goods, Americans took to machines that had standardized and interchangeable parts to produce such goods. (Eli Whitney, inventor of the cotton gin, began by producing interchangeable parts for handguns, for example.) Unlike Britain, however, the United States depended on an influx of capital (most of it English)—a dependence that continued even after the Civil War, when great sectors of the American economy moved from the work of artisans to modern concentrated industry. American industrialization gained momentum because of the sheer scale of industry—the westward extension of agriculture and transportation, and the exploitation of resources as private rather than public property. Other crucial factors were the cheap labor force and substantial foreign investment in large-scale corporations in heavy industries such as coal mining and iron and steel manufacture.

The role of government has often been underestimated in the United States. On both the regional and the national level, government encouraged free enterprise by allowing individuals and corporations to claim the nation's resources. It also fostered railroad building, tariff regulation, and free immigration—all of which contributed to the construction of an industrial giant. In terms of social problems, however, government took a laissez-faire stance. American politicians did much less than Europeans to support social legislation, including pensions and minimum wages; there was no Bismarck, Lloyd George, or Churchill to write social legislation. Yet until the end of the century, the United States had less labor strife than Europe and a relative absence of class conflict. Why? Did American workers share the dream of entrepreneurial success? Was the difficulty of forging class solidarity among varied ethnic groups of different cultures and languages decisive? Each new immigrant group (and later the rural blacks) did enter at the bottom, supplying cheap and competitive labor and experiencing violent reactions from their fellow workers from other ethnic and racial groups. By the end of the century, assimilated and politically active workers were able to prohibit Asian immigration. Congress did so after Chinese workers had built the transcontinental railroad. A Gentleman's Agreement excluded the Japanese.

Labor conflict between workers and employers

A New York Sweatshop, Photo by Jacob Riis (1849–1914). The latter half of the nineteenth century saw a proliferation of sweatshops. Adults and children alike, usually immigrants, labored long hours in appalling conditions for little pay. (*Corbis-Bettmann.*)

did flare up, however, in the decade before World War I. Generally, workers voted for one of the two major parties, but in the election of 1912, more than a million voted for the Socialist candidate. Not all of these voters were "foreigners" or recent immigrants, as contemporaries pretended. Many Americans were critical of the money power of giant cartels and monopolies, and both Theodore Roosevelt of the Republicans and Woodrow Wilson of the Democrats called for restrictions on monopolies, or trusts. Unrestricted competition, which gave cartels and trusts an unfair advantage, upset many Americans. Corporate ethics shocked them; business leaders as "robber barons" was not the American dream.

By 1914, the American market was the largest, most homogeneous, and most rapidly growing in the world. The United States was the largest industrial nation, producing more steel and coal than any other country. It was also the world's leader in automobiles, farming technology, electricity, and petroleum sectors. Its labor was the most productive and had the highest standard of living. The United States achieved this commanding position in a little more than a generation.

A Golden Age?

To thoughtful Europeans living in 1915, after a year of World War I, the nineteenth century must have seemed a golden era. They might have viewed it as a period of unparalleled peace and progress, full of the promise of all that well-meaning people considered modern: liberal institutions and democratic movements, autonomous nations, scientific and industrial progress, and individual human development. The century that had just ended seemed one of progress in the production of goods, the alleviation of want, the development of technology, and the application of science to industry and medicine. Part of that progress, in most minds, was the extension of constitutional and liberal government and the expression of humanitarian concern for others. Serfdom had been abolished in Europe; so had slavery in the United States and Brazil. Europeans spoke of self-government as a right. The importance of democracy had been acknowledged, and in most of Europe, universal manhood suffrage, if not universal suffrage, was in effect before the outbreak of the war.

The world had become smaller, more interdependent, and more cosmopolitan. Many westerners were more educated and probably better fed, housed, and clothed than their counterparts in preceding eras. Europe was at the height of its power in the nineteenth century. European productive capacities had reached out to most areas of the world, and European culture was brilliant—whether considered in the aggregate, or individually as German, French, English, or Italian culture.

Yet people looking back from the vantage point of 1915 must have realized, too, that something had gone wrong in the nineteenth century. Authoritarian governments persisted in central, eastern, and southern Europe. Traditional institutions and groups still exercised their privileges at the expense of others, often by brutally repressing opposition, especially regional and minority loyalties. Some had begun to have doubts when the revolutions of 1848 failed to reconcile national and class conflicts. Perhaps the bitter reaction to 1848, the harsh reality of the midcentury wars of unification, and the building of the centralized state had perverted the ideals of liberal government and individual freedom. Many doubted the wisdom of democratic government as they saw cynical leaders manipulate the passions of the masses. Perhaps the ideals of liberal government, individual freedom, national autonomy, and economic progress were not equally suited to every situation. In the last part of the nineteenth century and the first part of the twentieth, liberal-democratic ideals fell prey to authoritarianism, extreme nationalism, imperialism, class conflict, and racism. But despite a world war and mass destruction, liberal ideals would survive and spread.

❖ ❖ ❖

Note

1. Theodore Von Laue, *Sergei Witte and the Industrialization of Russia* (New York: Columbia University Press, 1963), p. 3.

Suggested Reading

Anderson, Bonnie, and Judith Zinsser, *A History of Their Own: Women in Europe from Prehistory to the Present,* vol. 2 (1988). A comprehensive survey of the movement for women's independence.

Blackbourn, David, and Geoff Eley, *The Peculiarities of German History* (1984). Critically examines traditional assumptions about Bismarck's Germany.

Davis, John, *Conflict and Control: Law and Order in Nineteenth Century Italy* (1988). A study of the north-south split in Italy and the various formal and informal ways conflict was controlled.

Ford, Colin, and Brian Harrison, *A Hundred Years Ago* (1983). An excellent social history of Britain, with fine photographs.

Foster, R. F., *Modern Ireland (1600–1972)* (1988). The best single-volume history.

Hobsbawm, Eric, *Nations and Nationalism Since*

1780 (1992). A good introduction to a complex subject.
———, *Nations and Nationalism Since 1780: Program, Myth, Reality* (1993). A sophisticated survey of developments in Europe.
Holborn, Hajo, *History of Modern Germany, 1840–1945,* vol. 3 (1969). A definitive work.
Johnson, D., *France and the Dreyfus Affair* (1967). The best of many books on this topic.
Joll, James, *Europe Since 1870* (1973). A valuable general survey, particularly good on socialism in the individual nations.
Kemp, Tom, *Industrialization in Nineteenth-Century Europe* (1985). A readable general survey incorporating recent scholarship.
Kropotkin, Peter, *Memoirs of a Revolutionist* (1967). A classic autobiography (written in 1889) of an aristocratic anarchist in tsarist Russia.
Mack Smith, Denis, *Italy: A Modern History,* rev. ed. (1969). An excellent survey, with emphasis on the failure of Italy to develop viable liberal institutions or economic solutions.
Mayer, Arno, *The Persistence of the Old Regime* (1981). The theme is the survival of traditional Europe until World War I.
Montgomery, David, *The Fall of the House of Labor: The Workplace, the State, and American Labor Activism, 1865–1925.* An important book for the changes of work life in the Industrial Revolution.
Nelson, Daniel, *Managers and Workers: Origins of the New Factory System in the United States, 1880–1920* (1975). An intelligent examination of the industrial growth that made the United States a Great Power.
Perkin, Harold, *The Third Revolution: Professional Elites in the Modern World* (1998). A comparative study of the rise of professional elites in the major powers.
Ragsdale, Hugh, *The Russian Tragedy: The Burden of History* (1996). A short history of Russia that sets the tsarist empire in historical perspective.
Seton-Watson, Christopher, *Italy from Liberalism to Fascism* (1981). An excellent survey of Italian history.
Sheehan, J. J., *German History (1770–1866)* (1989). The best on the subject.
Stedman Jones, Gareth, *Outcast London* (1971). An excellent study of British social problems and policy at the end of the century.
Weber, E., *Peasants into Frenchmen: Modernization of Rural France, 1870–1914* (1976). Describes the most important aspects of nation building.
Wehler, Hans, *The German Empire 1871–1918* (1986). A revisionist analysis in keeping with Blackbourn and Eley.
Wright, Gordon, *France in Modern Times,* 2nd ed. (1974). A good survey of the entire period.

Review Questions

1. Why was England seen by many as the model liberal nation in the middle decades of the nineteenth century?
2. How did the competition between political parties promote reform in Victorian England?
3. In what way did the Reform Bill of 1867 usher in a new era in British politics?
4. In England, the middle class and the workers often strove together for reform from 1860 to 1914. In France they rarely did so. Why?
5. Why did Louis Napoleon's policies lead some people to view him as a liberal, even a socialist, and others to see him as a conservative?
6. What was the general crisis of liberalism after 1870?
7. How did the conservatives attempt to win over the masses after 1870?
8. Historians disagree about the merits of the Bismarckian legacy to Germany. Discuss evidence for this disagreement.
9. For almost a generation after 1870, nationalism created a consensus supporting those who unified Germany and Italy. What economic, social, and political conflict seemed to undermine that consensus before World War I? Discuss this changed view of nationalism.
10. How did the ideology of official nationality undermine liberal reforms and inhibit industrialization in tsarist Russia?
11. How did industrial backwardness make it hard for tsarist Russia to achieve Great Power status?

12. What were the factors that raised the United States to a Great Power by 1914?
13. How were economic and social conditions connected to political crises in the Great Powers in the era before World War I?

Chapter 27

Western Imperialism: Global Dominance

Lithograph by Joseph Keppler, showing the Great Power of the West fighting over China. (Library of Congress.)

- **Emergence of the New Imperialism**
  - Conflicting Interpretations
  - A Global Economy
  - Control and Resistance
- **European Domination of Asia**
  - India
  - China
  - Japan
  - The Ottoman Empire
  - Southeast and Central Asia
- **The Scramble for Africa**
  - The Berlin Conference
  - Britain in Africa
  - Costs of Colonialism
- **Latin America**
- **The Legacy of Imperialism**

In the last two decades of the nineteenth century, European nations very rapidly laid claim to great portions of the world's surface. Russia and the United States pushed to the territorial limits of their continents and beyond. Westerners exploited the weakness of Japanese and Chinese dynasties forcing concessions to gain economic and political advantage in the Far East. They separated one by one the territories of the Ottoman Turkish ruler. The British deprived India of all semblance of independence, ruling it directly or indirectly through puppet princes. Europeans grabbed most of Africa, seizing goods, annexing territories, and carving out empires if local rulers were too weak or too self-interested to prevent it. Latin American development and prosperity became absolutely dependent on Europe and the United States.

From about 1880 to 1914, Europeans confronted each other, willing to fight over stretches of desert or rain forest that they could scarcely locate on the map. Asians and Africans who could not resolve conflicts among themselves found their lives controlled and their lands occupied by Europeans. Even those who were able to unite could not counter Western military and technological superiority.

European domination of most of the world continued until after World War II. The impact of imperialism—the domination by a country of the political, economic, or cultural life of another country, region, or people—contributed to both world wars and to the conflicting ideologies and crises of the cold war. It also played a part in the establishment of the interdependent global economy and culture that we have today.

Emergence of the New Imperialism

From the long perspective, European history has been one of expansion. It has also been a history of a struggle for domination of others—from the sixteenth-century explorations, conquests, and settlements of the Americas and the aggressive inroads in Southeast Asia and Africa for lucrative trade in spices, silks, luxury goods, and slaves to the eighteenth-century wars over trade and claims

Chronology 27.1 ❖ Expansion of Western Dominance

1830	The French move into Algeria
1839–1842	Opium War: the British defeat the Chinese, annexing treaty ports in China and opening them to Western trade
1853	U.S. naval forces open Japan to Western trade
1857–58	Sepoy Mutiny; Britain replaces the East India Company and governs India directly
1867	Mexicans led by Juárez execute Maximilian; Meiji Restoration in Japan
1869	Opening of Suez Canal
1876	Stanley sets up posts in the Congo for Leopold II of Belgium
1878	Congress of Berlin: Great Powers meet to prevent Russia from upsetting the balance of power in the Near East
1878–1881	British and Russian troops occupy Afghanistan
1881	The French take control of Tunisia
1882	Britain occupies Egypt
1883–85	The French fight the Chinese to claim Indochina
1884	Berlin Conference on Africa
1894–95	Sino-Japanese War: the British, Russians, and French intervene to take away Japan's gains
1896	Ethiopians defeat Italian invaders at Adowa
1898	Spanish-American War: the United States annexes the Philippines and Puerto Rico and occupies Cuba; the battle of Omdurman in the Sudan
1899–1902	Boer War between the British and the Afrikaners
1900	Boxers rebel against foreign presence in China
1904–1905	Russo-Japanese War: the Japanese defeat the Russians
1911	Mexican Revolution; Manchu dynasty is overthrown in China, a republic formed, and Sun Zhongshan (Sun Yat-sen) becomes its president; civil war breaks out in China
1919	Britain grants a legislative assembly in India; Gandhi's passive resistance movement broadens in response to the Amritsar Massacre; Kemal Atatürk emerges as the Turkish national leader; League of Nations mandate system established

to colonies. By the early 1800s, however, the old slaving stations in Africa had declined, as had the Caribbean sugar trade and the mines of Central and South America. Revolutionary wars had liberated the United States and Latin America and seemed to usher in a new era of trade and investment without political control. For most of the nineteenth century Europeans—at least those engaged in the growth of industry and the development of the nation—showed little interest in adding to the remnants of colonial empires. Advocates of free trade argued that commerce would go to whichever country could produce the best goods most cheaply. Efforts to add colonies would be better expended in improving industry, they said. They also hoped that Europeans had grown too civilized to fight over trade networks. European liberals, in particular, believed commerce was so interdependent that a major war would destroy the livelihoods of too many people and the power of states. Therefore, they believed war unlikely if not impossible.

Meanwhile, European influence over the rest of the world grew as European nations industrialized, expanding world trade and drawing previously untouched peoples into the network of supply and demand of raw materials, finished goods, and capital. The expansion of world trade and the spread of Western ideas and technology continued even without any extensions of political empires. Masses of European immigrants made new homes in North and South America, Australia, and New Zealand.

Suddenly, however, in the last decades of the century, Europeans switched abruptly from commercial penetration to active conquest, political control, and exploitation of previously unclaimed and, in many ways, untouched territories. Why did Europeans strive to claim and control the entire world?

Conflicting Interpretations

Some historians suggest that the new imperialism (to differentiate it from the *colonialism* of settlement and trade of the 1500s and 1600s) was a direct result of industrialization. With intensified economic activity and competition, Europeans struggled for raw materials, markets for their manufactured goods, and places to invest their capital for higher rates of return. In the late 1800s, many politicians and industrialists believed that annexing overseas territories was the only way for their nations to ensure the economic necessities for their people. Trusting the free market might mean triumph for competitor states. Captains of industry defended the search for new empires to their sometimes reluctant governments and compatriots, predicting dire economic consequences if their countries failed to get their share of the world markets.

Historians today, however, point out that most of the areas claimed by Europeans and Americans were not profitable sources of raw materials or wealthy enough to be good markets. For Europeans and Americans, the primary trading and investment venues were Europe and America rather than Asia or Africa. Some individual businesses made colonial profits, but most colonies proved unprofitable for the Western taxpayer. Between 1865 and 1914, for example, only 39 percent of British investment went to lands of the empire outside the British Isles, 28 percent of that amount going to the self-governing dominions. The average rate of return did not surpass that from home investments. In general, the colonies did not attract surplus European population that could contribute to the mother country's economy. The United States drew most of the European emigrants, who also streamed to Australia, Canada, New Zealand, and South America—lands already dominated by westerners. Two-thirds of British emigrants went outside the empire, mostly to the United States. Italians certainly did not migrate to Italy's African territories, and the French scarcely migrated at all.

The economic justifications of imperialism are inseparable from the intensely nationalistic ones. Policymakers hoped that possession of empires would solve economic problems, which were particularly pressing after the crash of 1873, and join together disparate social groups with pride in national power. The newly unified states, Germany and Italy, demanded colonies as recognition of their Great Power status; leaders in those two nations were convinced that Britain's standing depended on colonies and naval power. They were aware of the heavy tax burden on British subjects, the expenses of empire, and the greatly increased possibility of war with rival nations or resistant subjects. Nevertheless, these leaders chose an imperial course. Having lost ingloriously to Prussia in 1870, France also turned its attention overseas, hoping to recoup prestige and to add to its manpower and wealth for future European struggles. Many leaders hoped that imperialism would win them the loyalty of their own people. Some argued that the well-being of the workers depended on colonies. Others argued from strength: Americans, who built one of the world's great industrial powers after the Civil War, trumpeted their achievements by defeating the once-imperial Spain in Cuba and the Philippines. Still others urged imperialism from weakness. Economically backward Russia pushed east to the Pacific and south toward India for ports and resources to develop its commerce and industry. In the 1890s, Japan announced that it had joined the world's Great Powers by attacking China for control of Korea's raw materials and markets. Thus, both economically powerful states and struggling ones turned to imperialism.

On the eve of World War I, many socialists, including Vladimir Lenin, a revolutionary Marxist who would become one of the leaders of the Russian Revolution in 1917, argued that imperialism was inevitable in a highly advanced capitalist country. These socialists asserted that capitalist nations maintained their monopolistic economy and their political system by exploiting the less-developed world. Monopoly capitalism was condemned to periodic depressions due to lack of materials, markets, and capital, Lenin said. Unless the governments of capitalist countries could ensure high wages and profits for their own people by exploiting colonial peoples, working-class revolutions would break out. Powerful business interests also pushed their governments to the verge of war to safeguard their profits. At the same time, Lenin said, imperialism greatly accelerated both the development of capitalism and opposition to it among the victims of imperialism in Asia, Africa, and Latin America. He predicted that the struggle for empire would end in war between the Great Powers, which would draw the colonies into European affairs even faster than the operations of the market.

The nationalistic competition among the Europeans led them, for a time, to extend their power struggles to Africa and Asia. Far away from their European boundaries, leaders acquired territories for strategic reasons or to keep rivals out. For example, Britons worked to keep the Germans out of the Middle East because it might open the Indian Ocean—and the British-dominated Indian subcontinent—to them. They had to keep the Russians out of Afghanistan. Bismarck actually encouraged French expansion in Africa, hoping the inevitable conflict with the Italians and the British would distract them from Alsace and Lorraine, which Germany had taken in 1870. Overseas expansion could create yet another political rift to weaken the French government; at the least it would be expensive for France to maintain. But when Germany expanded its navy to strengthen its imperial position, Britain understood the move as hostile and moved quickly to ally with its rival France.

The British liked to think that they were merely defending their empire, particularly India. They defined enormous amounts of territory and water as essential. Other nations saw Britain as their primary rival for the spoils of imperialism—for "a place in the sun," as the Germans liked to phrase it. In Russia, a small clique of nobles and officers urged expansion, knowing that a move into Asia would bring conflict with Britain. Later, such a move meant conflict with Japan, driving the British and Japanese together. Since the conflicts between Europeans were played out in Asia and Africa, perhaps for a while they helped keep Europe itself relatively peaceful. In the long run, however, the tense atmosphere of imperialism—the militarism and the racism—contributed to a more devastating conflict in Europe, World War I, which engaged the empires as well.

The most extreme ideological expression of nationalism and imperialism was Social Darwinism. In the popular mind, the concepts of evolution justified the exploitation of "lesser breeds without the law" by superior races. This language of race and conflict, of superior and inferior people, had wide currency in the Western states. Social Darwinists vigorously advocated the acquisition of empires, saying that strong nations—by definition, those that were successful at expanding industry and empire—would survive and that others would not. To these elitists, all white men were more fit than nonwhites to prevail in the struggle for dominance; even among Europeans, some nations were deemed more fit than others for the competition. Usually, Social Darwinists thought their own nation the best, which sparked their competitive enthusiasm. But some feared that their people were incapable of endurance and sacrifice. Their fears

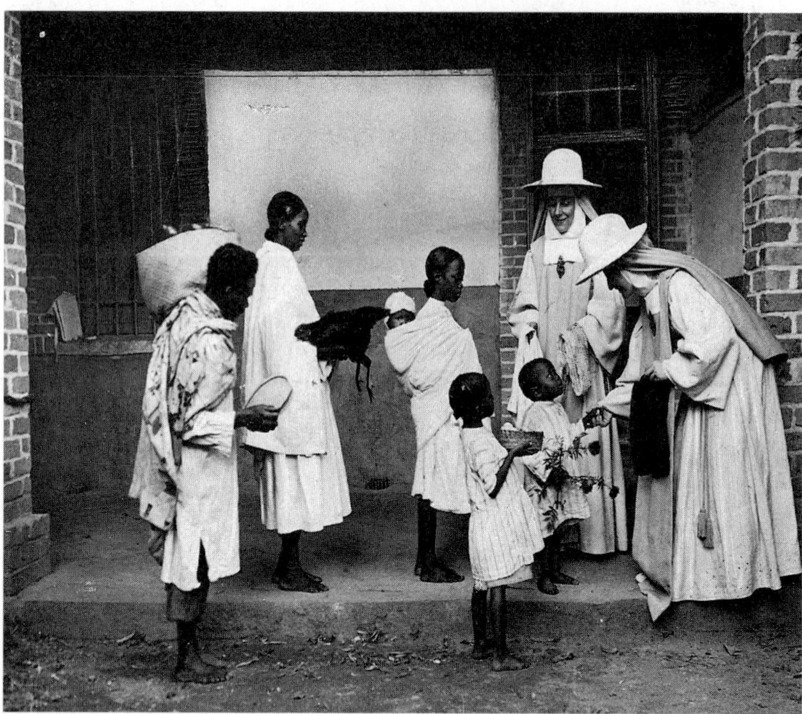

Roman Catholic Missionaries from France. Hats for protection against the tropical sun are a special adaptation of the traditional robes, or habits, worn by French nuns working on the island of Madagascar at the turn of the century. Catholics and Protestant denominations from every European nation strove for converts among African peoples. (*Roger-Viollet.*)

did not tame their imperialism, however. They thought colonies would train the people for the struggles ahead. Social Darwinists were blatantly racist; they even applied racial terms to their own lower class. Sometimes their Social Darwinism drove them to seek reforms. When working-class men proved physically unfit to serve in the Boer War, British imperialists urged health and education reforms to improve the British "race."

Not all advocates of empire were Social Darwinists. Some did not think of themselves as racists; but when they believed extending empire, law, order, and industry would raise "backward peoples" up the ladder of evolution to equality, they shared the assumptions of the Social Darwinists. In the nineteenth century, in contrast to the seventeenth and eighteenth centuries, Europeans, except for missionaries, rarely adopted the customs or learned the languages of local people. They had little sense that other cultures and other peoples had merit and deserved respect. Clearly, the European attitude toward other cultures had changed.

Many westerners believed that it was their duty as Christians to set an example and to educate others. Missionaries were the first to meet and learn about many peoples and the first to develop writing for those without a written language. Christian missionaries were ardently opposed to slavery, and throughout the century they went to unexplored African regions to preach against slavery, which was still carried on by Arab and African traders. But even missionaries thought preaching would not end the enslavement of those Africans who were vanquished in tribal wars. Some, like David Livingstone, hoped an expanding European economy would bring Africa to the world market and ultimately to freedom and progress.

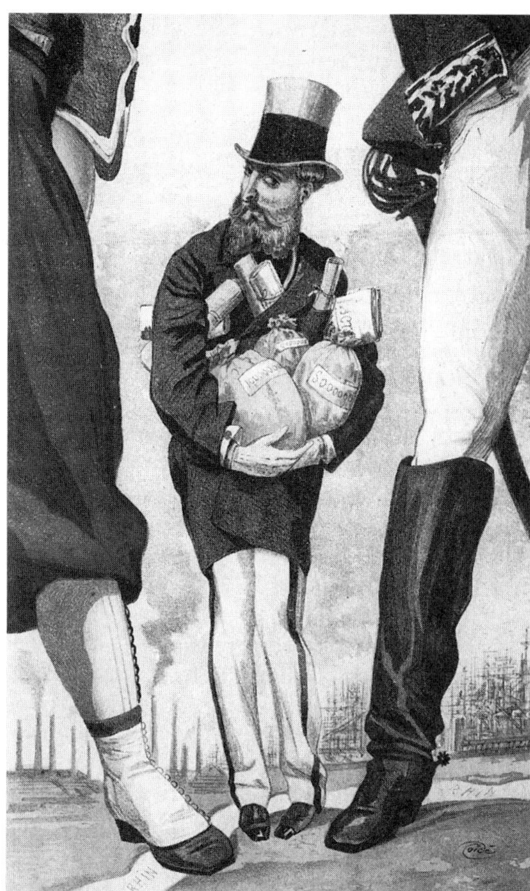

Leopold II of Belgium. The Belgian king had such extravagant tastes and habits that he operated as a private entrepreneur in the Congo, amassing a great fortune. His moneymaking created conditions that were so bad, akin to slavery, that Belgium's parliament took the territory away from him. His claim to the Congo, however, sparked the Great Powers into laying claim to much of Africa. (*Corbis-Bettmann.*)

Some of the passion for imperialism was sparked by interest in exotic places. At the end of the eighteenth century, the expeditions of Mungo Park, a Scottish explorer, on the Niger River in West Africa stimulated the romantic imagination. The explorations of Livingstone in the Congo Basin and of Richard Burton and John Speke (who raced with each other and with Livingstone to find the source of the Nile River) fascinated many Europeans during the second half of the nineteenth century. In the early 1800s, expeditions were a matter of adventure and scientific curiosity; they often included explorers from several countries. After the midcentury, national prestige became a goal in these forays. Sponsored by national geographic and exploratory societies and encouraged by their nation's military, explorers captured the public imagination in much the same way that astronauts do today. Explorers became public personalities; both the public and these celebrities saw exploration as an escape from a humdrum or stultifying existence at home.

Individuals and nations competed to find the highest mountain, the longest river, the highest waterfall, and the land never before seen by white men. Such challenges called men and women away from their ordinary lives, if not to experience then at least to dream of adventure. The mass press—the media of the day—spread stories of exotic peoples and customs, European bravery, and self-sacrificing heroes. The fiction of English authors Rudyard Kipling (1865–1936) and H. Rider Haggard (1856–1925) and their many inferior imitators stimulated the passion for faraway places and unknown peoples and helped shape the attitudes of the next generation. Kipling wrote: "Take up the White Man's Burden—/Send forth the best ye breed—/Go bind your sons to exile/To serve your captives' need." He also wrote of the Indian Gunga Din, whose brave death while serving his white masters won him their respect. Authors usually depicted heroism and glory and rarely described the exploitation, cruelty, and abuses of empire—until twentieth-century writers like Joseph Conrad, George Orwell, Olive Schreiner, and E. M. Forster began to probe imperialism's darker side.

A Global Economy

The Western economy became truly global by the end of the nineteenth century, thanks to new markets, new technology, and overseas trade and investment. As the Western powers industrialized, even small, backward European countries exploited raw materials and markets in the rest of the world. In many parts of Europe, even the working classes and the peasantry could buy goods from faraway places that had previously been available only to the very wealthy.

The underdeveloped areas of the world, in turn,

found markets for their crops and were able to buy European goods—at least the wealthy could. But being part of the world economy also made these areas subject to the smallest tremors on the European and American stock exchanges and to changing fashions of consumption. Participation in the world market brought wealth to a few people but meant hardship for many. It also meant the loss of traditional customs and social relationships.

Increasing crop production to satisfy European and American markets often created problems. Producing for the Western market meant turning land that had grown food for families over to export crops like coffee or indigo, thus reducing the local food supply. It often meant consolidation of small peasant holdings in the hands of richer peasants or landlords. Thus, market forces drove the poorer peasants off the land, into debt to the landlord or to the usurer, and into cities. For most of the nineteenth century, the peasants felt bonded to their traditional masters, but in the twentieth century, they came to see themselves as enslaved by foreigners who either controlled the government or the world market. The passionate desire to escape this bondage has fueled revolutionary and nationalist movements throughout the world.

Economic interdependence operated to the great advantage of Europeans and Americans, enriching the lives of consumers. Many Europeans and Americans dressed in Egyptian cotton, Australian wool, Chinese silk, and Argentinian leather and consumed Chinese tea or Colombian coffee; some had homes or offices furnished in hardwoods from Burma, Malaya, or Africa. Westerners could purchase all these goods, and many more, at prices so favorable that many luxury items became available to those who were not rich. Europeans and Americans could travel anywhere, using gold or easily available foreign currency, exchanged at a rate almost always favorable to them. They could invest their money in the raw materials or the government bonds of virtually any area of the world and expect a good return. They also expected their investments to be secure and their property and themselves to be protected. Non-Western political authorities unable to guarantee that security, for whatever reason, risked intervention, perhaps occupation, by European or American forces. In some non-Western areas, the governors had to grant *extraterritoriality,* or the right of Europeans to trial by their own laws in foreign countries. Europeans also often lived a segregated and privileged life in quarters, clubs, and whole sections of foreign lands or cities that were closed to native inhabitants.

Control and Resistance

Changing technology widened the gap between industrialized states and Asia and Africa. Europeans possessed the enormous power of industry and of military technology, and European nation-states could mobilize the support of all their citizens. These facts made it unlikely that a non-European country or people could successfully resist an industrialized European state intent on conquest. Yet Ethiopia was able to resist Italy's incursions, North Africans kept the French on the defensive in Algeria and Morocco, and the Japanese held off potential invaders.

Europeans established varying degrees of political control over much of the rest of the world. Control meant Europeans had to have the help of native elites, which perpetuated traditional powers or created a new class of leaders. Control could mean outright annexation and the governing of a territory as a colony. In this way, Germany controlled Tanganyika (East Africa) after 1886, France governed Algeria, and Britain ruled much of India. Control could also mean status as a protectorate, in which the local ruler continued to rule but was directed, or "protected," by a Great Power. In this way, the British controlled Egypt after 1882 and maintained authority over their dependent Indian princes, and France guarded Tunisia. There were also spheres of influence, where, without military or political control, a European nation had special trading and legal privileges that other Europeans did not have. At the turn of the century, the Russians and the British, each recognizing the other's sphere of influence, divided Persia (Iran). Some peoples were so completely dependent for trade and finance that they seemed politically independent only in the most technical sense. Cuba and the Philippines, for example, dared take no action that might upset their economic connections to the United States in the 1930s, not even action that might ease their debt crisis.

Nevertheless, many non-Europeans resisted

American and European economic penetration and political control. The very process of resistance shaped their history and their self-awareness. In many areas, such as the Ottoman Empire, China, and Japan, ruling governments found ways of limiting the political influence of Western trading interests. Some countries tried, as Egypt and Turkey did, to seek economic independence through modernization.

These forms of resistance were carried out by rulers who could command loyal subjects. Other resisters—individuals, groups, and regional communities—retained traditional ways, rejecting Western education and secularization, even renewing institutions, particularly religious ones, that were falling into disuse when the Europeans arrived. Such resistance became a statement of both national and individual identity. A few of the many instances of such resistance include the Sudanese Muslims' holy war led by the Mahdi Mohammed Ahmed. He and his followers attacked Egyptian fellow Muslims, whom he regarded as agents of the European nonbelievers, and the Europeans. The Boxer Rebellion in China and the Sepoy Mutiny in India are other examples of traditionalist resistance to outsiders. Still other resisters reacted with strongly nationalistic feelings and fought to strengthen the nationalism of their people, sometimes even going to Western universities, military schools, and factories to master the West's advanced technology. Mohandas Gandhi, Jawaharlal Nehru, Sun Yat-sen (Sun Zhongshan), Chiang Kai-shek (Jiang Jieshi), and Kemal Atatürk are national heros for resistance to the West.

In most cases, however, efforts at resistance brought non-European peoples more firmly under Western control. When their interests were threatened, Europeans generally responded by annexing the offending region or establishing a protectorate. Resistance continued, nonetheless. Whole peoples in Africa moved from place to place to escape European religion, taxes, and laws; and insurgent mountain people in Indochina and Algeria evaded French cultural influence or restricted it to the coastline for generations.

Europeans might dominate the ruler and perhaps the ruling elite, and they might make entire sectors of the economy dependent on their trade. They could also see the influence of their ideas and language on the youth and observe the decline of local traditions. But the level of European power differed in each area, and in many places Europeans were never fully in control. Each region has had a different history of European intervention. Nevertheless, Western domination seemed, to westerners and nonwesterners alike, a relentless force.

European Domination of Asia

India, China, and Japan were powerful kingdoms when the first European traders arrived in the age of exploration. For several hundred years, there were trading connections in which the European was the weaker party, dependent on the goodwill and interest of the Asians. In China and India, native craftspeople produced goods superior to European products, so Asians had little reason to trade with the West; Europeans had many incentives for commerce with the East. In the nineteenth century, when many more and much more powerful Europeans came to Asia, they encountered Chinese and Mogul empires that were weakened by internal problems. The situation gave Europeans an edge. The Asian kingdoms possessed a sense of cultural unity based on traditions and on the great religious and ethical systems of Hinduism, Buddhism, Islam, and Confucianism. Their loyalties were cultural and religious, not nationalism as Europeans knew it. Within a short time, the resentment of European domination developed into a national feeling, unifying diverse social and religious communities.

India

The history of the Indian subcontinent is a long one of a series of invasions, from Alexander the Great in the fourth century B.C. to the British in the eighteenth century. When Italian, Portuguese, and Spanish merchants came as traders, admirers, and imitators of the Mogul Empire, they found it ruled by a dynasty of highly advanced, wealthy, and religiously tolerant Muslim princes. When British traders arrived in the eighteenth century, the empire was disintegrating. The Muslim zealot Emperor Aurangzeb Alamgir (1658–1707) had launched a holy war that would tear apart Hindus and Muslims, as well as Sikhs, for half a cen-

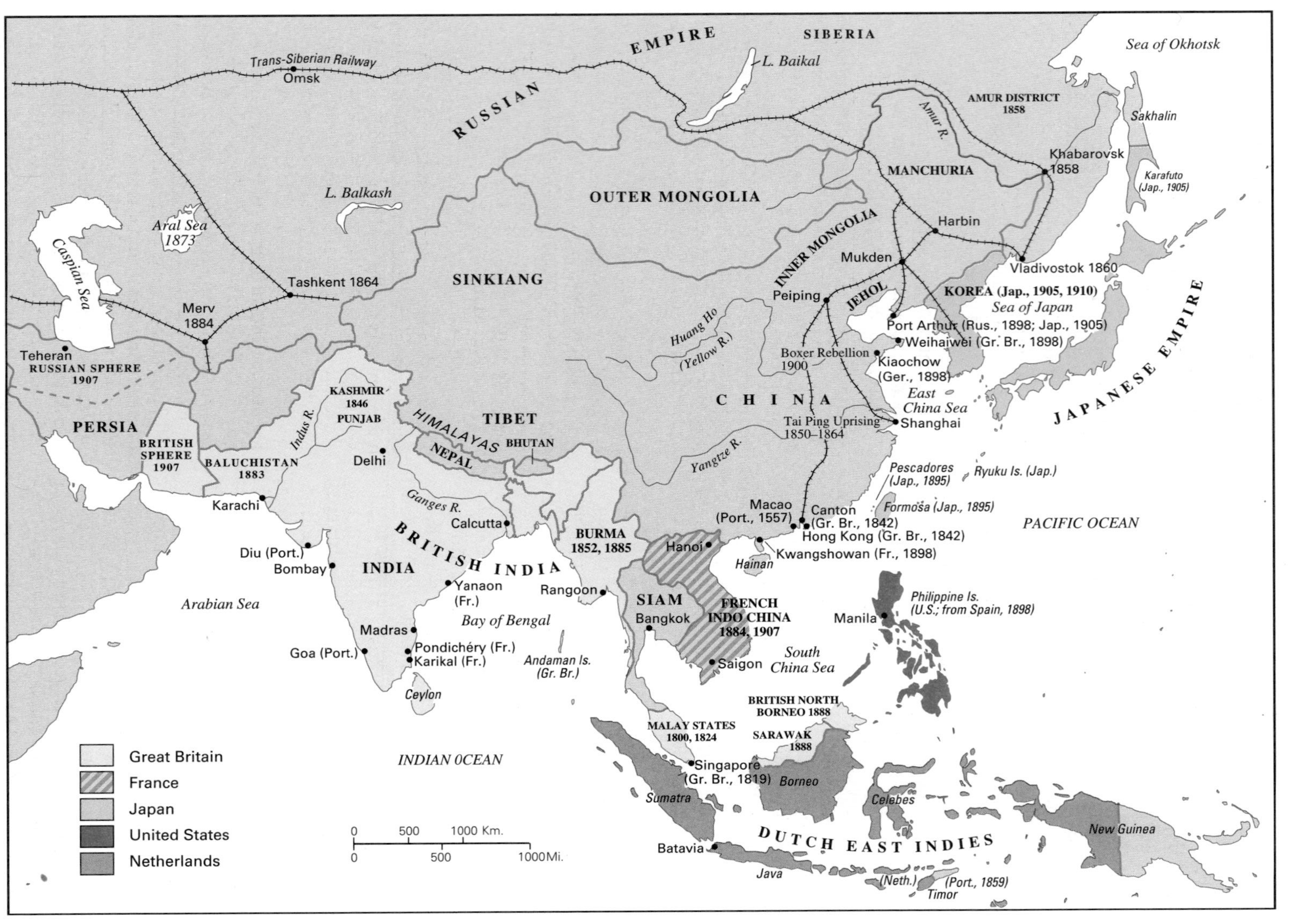
Trans-Siberian Railway
Omsk
RUSSIAN EMPIRE
SIBERIA
L. Baikal
Sea of Okhotsk
AMUR DISTRICT 1858
Amur R.
Sakhalin
Karafuto (Jap., 1905)
MANCHURIA
Khabarovsk 1858
L. Balkash
OUTER MONGOLIA
Aral Sea 1873
Caspian Sea
Harbin
INNER MONGOLIA
Mukden
Vladivostok 1860
SINKIANG
Tashkent 1864
Merv 1884
Peiping
JEHOL
KOREA (Jap., 1905, 1910)
Sea of Japan
Port Arthur (Rus., 1898; Jap., 1905)
Weihaiwei (Gr. Br., 1898)
JAPANESE EMPIRE
Huang Ho (Yellow R.)
Boxer Rebellion 1900
Kiaochow (Ger., 1898)
Teheran
RUSSIAN SPHERE 1907
KASHMIR 1846
PUNJAB
Indus R.
CHINA
East China Sea
PERSIA
BRITISH SPHERE 1907
HIMALAYAS
TIBET
NEPAL
BHUTAN
Tai Ping Uprising 1850–1864
Shanghai
BALUCHISTAN 1883
Delhi
Yangtze R.
Pescadores (Jap., 1895)
Ryuku Is. (Jap.)
Karachi
Ganges R.
Macao (Port., 1557)
Canton (Gr. Br., 1842)
Formosa (Jap., 1895)
PACIFIC OCEAN
Calcutta
BURMA 1852, 1885
Hong Kong (Gr. Br., 1842)
BRITISH INDIA
Diu (Port.)
Hanoi
Kwangshowan (Fr., 1898)
Bombay
INDIA
Hainan
Yanaon (Fr.)
Rangoon
Philippine Is. (U.S.; from Spain, 1898)
Arabian Sea
SIAM
FRENCH INDO CHINA 1884, 1907
Bangkok
Manila
Madras
Bay of Bengal
Goa (Port.)
Pondichéry (Fr.)
Karikal (Fr.)
Andaman Is. (Gr. Br.)
Saigon
South China Sea
Ceylon
BRITISH NORTH BORNEO 1888
MALAY STATES 1800, 1824
SARAWAK 1888
Great Britain
France
Japan
United States
Netherlands
INDIAN OCEAN
Singapore (Gr. Br., 1819)
Borneo
Sumatra
Celebes
0 500 1000 Km.
0 500 1000Mi.
DUTCH EAST INDIES
New Guinea
Batavia
Java
(Neth.)
(Port., 1859)
Timor

tury. The rivalries of powerful native princes, each of whom wished to succeed the emperor, worked to foreign advantage. India fell prey to the Europeans, and by the end of the century the British cleared out their rivals one by one. India became the jewel of the British Empire, the most completely governed Asian state.

British Rule. At first, British rule was indirect. Britain's East India Company was a regulated chartered monopoly enterprise under the control of Parliament, which exercised little control until the Sepoy Mutiny of 1857–58. (The Indians call this massive act of resistance the Great Rebellion.) This major popular uprising joined Muslim and Hindu soldiers with some native princes, who finally perceived that the British, rather than neighboring princes, posed the true threat to their authority. Peasants, who were victims of both their local landlords and the market, also participated. In a fierce war, the British, with the aid of faithful troops from the Punjab, repressed the uprising. The British ruled some states through dependent Indian princes, but after the Rebellion about two-thirds of the subcontinent was ruled directly by about a thousand British officials. Unlike the Chinese and the Japanese, the peoples of India lost all semblance of independence.

The men of the East India Company had mixed with the Indians, often marrying local women and adopting their customs and languages. But the British community felt so threatened by the uprising that it not only took all the authority it could into its hands but also maintained a social and legal separation from Indians. The civil service was British, trained in England and sent out to govern according to English law and customs. Later, an elite of Indians, educated in English and trained in law and administration, became part of the civil service. Along with soldiers drawn from the peoples with a military tradition, the Indian civil service (about four thousand Europeans and half a million Indians in 1900) ruled some three hundred million Indians of almost two hundred language groups, and several religions, races, and cultures. Today the territories that were British India are India, Pakistan, Bangladesh, and Myanmar (Burma). The British allowed friendly native princes to rule. Thus, the British created a powerful state with a single system of law, administration, and language. The subcontinent had some political unity, an English-educated elite, and a common resentment of British control. The British created the state; the many Indian communities created a nation.

India also acquired a modern railroad and communications system and an economy in which a segment was geared to meet the needs of the world market. The rest of the economy tried to supply local and regional demands. The railroad linked areas of food surplus with areas of need, reducing the incidence and impact of local famines, which had plagued India's history. Population increased as fewer people died of starvation and lives were saved with public projects of sanitation, hygiene, water and flood control, and Western medicine.

British rule also ended the century of war and disorder that accompanied the disintegration of the Mogul Empire; but it did not end the control that local landlords and usurers had over the lives of peasants. Many observers believe that the Indian masses benefited little from economic progress because landlords demanded payments that the poor could not afford. Moneylenders cheated the poor. In addition, the increase in population more than matched the increase in food. Even if they did not starve, most people suffered from malnutrition. What further aggravated the situation, these critics claim, was that the British flooded the Indian market with cheap, machine-produced English goods, thus driving native artisans out of business or even deeper into debt. Such detrimental consequences were not unique to India. They could be noted in many areas where the market economy and European rule disrupted traditional arrangements; their effect was most severe on the poorest and the weakest.

British racism excluded the Indian elite from clubs, hotels, and social gatherings and declared top government positions off-limits for Indians. Many of the traditional elite who profited from

◀ *Map 27.1* Asia, 1914 This map of Asia is deceptive. There are no markings or colors that can indicate the level of influence and control European and U.S. powers exercised over technically sovereign states of China, Siam (Thailand), and Persia (Iran).

MAHARAJA MADHAV RAO SCINDIA AND THE PRINCE OF WALES AFTER A HUNT IN INDIA (1905). The Prince of Wales (later George V) hunted with the maharaja on his visit to Gwalior. The maharaja is shown here as the quintessential English aristocrat after the hunt, surrounded by the kill. The British governed about one-fourth of India through the traditional princely rulers. A westernized Indian high society sent its sons to London to be educated and to learn the sports of British gentlemen. The British staged and took part in elaborate ceremonies honoring their princely allies. (*The Royal Commonwealth Society.*)

British connections resented the lack of respect for India's culture. In the 1880s, educated Indians demanded equality and self-government. They created the Indian National Congress, which, however, was neither national, because its members were upper-class Hindus, nor a congress, because it had no power to represent. At first, the Congress party sought home rule, or self-government within the empire. Eventually, it organized masses of Indians to gain independence.

The Anticolonial Campaign. Resistance to colonialism grew in militance throughout Asia when the Japanese defeated the Russians in 1904–1905 in the Russo-Japanese War. That victory inspired Indian nationalists. World War I brought greater solidarity among Indians, who, though opposed to British rule, had been far from united. Muslims had founded the Muslim League to speak for their minority community. (Many Hindus believed that the British favored the Muslims as part of a divide-and-conquer strategy.) The Indian elite found grounds for cooperation among the disparate communities, but the masses continued to be divided by differences of religion, class, and culture. These differences made Indian self-government seem distant even to Britons who wanted it.

In 1919, partly in response to agitation and partly as a reward for Indian loyalty during the war, the British granted India a legislative assembly. It would represent almost a million of the three hundred million people in the subcontinent. An elaborate scheme allotted representation by groups (that is, to Hindus, Muslims, Europeans, Anglo-Indians, and Sikhs) and by economic and social functions (that is, to rural, urban, university, landholding, and commercial classes). Although the British gave only some powers to this assembly, they appeared to acknowledge the principle of self-government.

At this very time, however, agitation and unrest

became most bitter. At Amritsar in the Punjab, a British officer commanded his Gurkha troops to fire into a peaceful demonstration until their ammunition was exhausted; 379 Indians died and 1,200 were wounded. Women and children were among the victims. The government punished the officer, but the British community in India gave him a fortune, honoring him for what he had done. The massacre and British behavior stung Indians to action—even those Indians who had advocated self-government within the British Empire.

Out of this feverish period emerged a gentle but determined revolutionary leader, Mohandas K. Gandhi (1869–1948). He had led resistance to the vicious system of racial discrimination in South Africa and, in the process, developed a doctrine of civil disobedience and nonviolent resistance. He believed that Indians' love of one another would overthrow British rule. His was a spiritually uplifting message, and a shrewd political tactic as well. Gandhi called on the Indian elite to give up their privileges, resign their positions, boycott British schools, and boycott all foreign goods. Freeing India required mass support as well as sacrifice. Gandhi rallied this support dramatically with "the march to the sea": a mass refusal to pay taxes on salt. Thrown in prison, Gandhi and his followers fasted for spiritual discipline. Their tactic also threatened the British with the possibility that the confined leaders would starve to death, setting off more civil disturbances. Gandhi promoted the boycott of foreign goods by spinning cotton and wearing simple native dress. To gain independence, he was even willing to sacrifice the higher standard of living that an industrial economy could bring to India. Most important, he was able to join traditional religious and cultural beliefs with political tactics to inspire Indians with nationalism.

Independence finally came after World War II exhausted Britain's resources, reduced its power, and stirred much of the world to struggle against racism and for liberty and democracy. There was no war between Britain and India—an accomplishment that many credit to the strength of Gandhi's moral leadership. But even his leadership could not prevent the partition of the country into Muslim Pakistan and predominantly Hindu India. Nor could it prevent bloody communal massacres and his own death at the hands of a Hindu nationalist assassin.

China

European intervention in China was very different. For centuries, Europeans had admired China for its wealth, art, and culture, and even for its imperial government, which ruled through mandarins (men who passed tests of Chinese learning). Unlike India, China excluded foreigners, whether they were missionaries, traders, or soldiers and sailors, in an effort to preserve traditional beliefs and shield them from Christianity, Western science, and secular ideologies.

When the British defeated the Chinese in the Opium War of 1839–1842, the Manchu dynasty was forced to open trade with the West. Before the war, such commerce had been controlled by native monopolists to whom the emperor had granted trading privileges. When the Chinese destroyed Indian opium being traded by the East India Company, the British aggressively asserted their right to free trade. In the subsequent war, Britain seized several trading cities along the coast, including Hong Kong. In the Treaty of Nanking (1842), the British insisted on determining Chinese tariffs. Furthermore, British subjects in China would be tried according to their own law (the right of extraterritoriality). These provisions undermined the emperor's ability to control the foreigners in his country.

Defeat forced the emperor to change. He revitalized the Manchu bureaucracy and cleaned up the official corruption, which weighed heavily on the poorest taxpayers. Nevertheless, widespread economic discontent led to the Taiping Rebellion of 1850–1864. This uprising seriously threatened the dynasty, which called on westerners to suppress the rebels. Britain and France extorted additional concessions. They forced the emperor to allow Chinese people to emigrate to become cheap, exploited laborers in South Africa and the United States.

For a time, the Europeans seemed content with trading rights in coastal towns and preferential treatment for their subjects. But Japan's easy victory in the Sino-Japanese War of 1894–95 encouraged Europeans to mutilate China. Britain, France, Russia, and Germany all scrambled for concessions, protectorates, and spheres of influence. China might have been carved up like Africa; however, each Western nation resisted any partition that might give an advantage to a

Profile

Gandhi

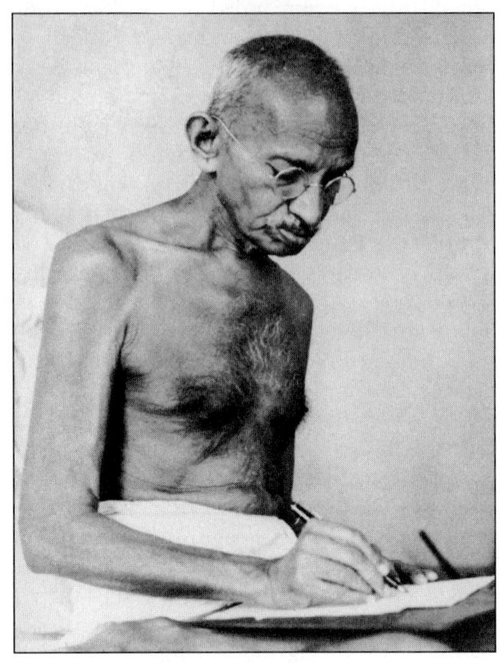

Hulton Archive/Getty Images.

Even before the First World War there was growing opposition to colonialism in Asia and Africa, but who would become the leaders of the national movements and what would be their demands? A most unlikely leader emerged in India. In a series of struggles a diminutive, gentle, pacifist, Mohandas Karamchand Gandhi (1869–1948), came to represent the most populous, most diverse, and largest colony in its stuggle for independence.

Gandhi began modestly within the framework of British government and law, asking that poor Indian immigrants in South Africa not be discriminated against. Returning to India he joined the Congress party, but he was not one of the elite who dominated that group. Eventually Gandhi transformed the Congress into a mass party that became a model and inspiration for other national movements. Victims of oppression throughout the world found his method of nonviolent resistance (*satyagraha*) the least bloody way to counter those who held all the weapons. Satyagraha called for a high degree of self-control and self-awareness, which Gandhi expressed in the language of the Indian religious and cultural tradition: Indians could free themselves once they thought of themselves

rival. To ensure American interests in China, the United States proclaimed the "Open Door" policy: that trade should be open to all and that the Great Powers should respect the territorial integrity of China. Whether the American action had any part in restraining the Western powers from partitioning China is unclear. The important treaty ports had already been apportioned and market capitalism, which Americans championed, was the most powerful threat to China's independence.

Chinese traditionalists organized secret societies to expel foreigners and punish those Chinese who accepted westernization. Usually, these societies opposed the Manchu dynasty itself, which had undermined traditional China. Sometimes, though, they allied with it. In 1900, encouraged by Empress Tzu-hsi, the Society of Righteous and Harmonious Fists (called the Boxers by Europeans) attacked foreigners throughout the north of China. An international army of Europeans, Japanese, and Americans suppressed the rebellion, seized Chinese treasures, and forced China to pay an indemnity. They also made China station foreign troops on its soil.

Chinese discontent with the dynasty deepened, and nationalistic opposition to the foreigners increased. When Japan defeated Russia in 1905, many Chinese urged their country to imitate the West, as the Japanese had done. Growing nationalism led to a boycott of American goods in 1905 to protest U.S. restrictions on Chinese immigrants. In 1911, nationalist revolutionaries, particularly strong among soldiers, workers, and students, as a nation and refused to carry out the commands of their rulers, but they must not lose control and respond to the savage acts of their rulers with savage acts of revenge. It was a difficult political message to accept for people who were not yet one nation and who had suffered repeated injustice and discrimination.

In 1919 at Amritsar in Punjab region, British governors brutally repressed a peaceful demonstration in which 1,500 Indians were killed or injured. Thereafter, Gandhi led thousands in a march to protest the British monopoly of salt; journalists and photographers from all over the world covered the protest. This simple man was turning the world of power and wealth upside down as Indians seemed willing to do without the benefits of industrialization and modern society to be free. Sophisticated Congress party leaders, such as Jawaharlal Nehru (1889–1964), supported Gandhi's strategy. In the 1930s the British jailed demonstrators repeatedly; Gandhi protested with hunger strikes. Rather than face his angry followers, British governors released him. Finally, in 1935 and 1937 Britain granted India provincial assemblies, but by then India's religious groups (Hindu and Muslim) were fragmented on every issue but independence, and radicals, including a communist party, regarded the aims of Gandhi and the Congress party as reactionary and bound to fail.

When World War II broke out the British declared war on behalf of India, arousing the nation. Although hundreds of thousands of Indian soldiers fought for the colonial rulers in the war, India refused to put its demands on hold. Gandhi spent months on a hunger strike for independence, and independence now became the country's slogan. At war's end, the British no longer had the power, the wealth, or the will to hold on to India. In 1947, the promise to partition India in two states, one Muslim and one Hindu, broke the subcontinent into violence, which all the efforts of the nonviolent movement could not prevent. Gandhi fasted once again—this time to calm his people and prevent civil war. Six months later an angry Hindu nationalist shot and killed Gandhi as he walked to morning prayers. The world mourned and India took another path.

overthrew the Manchu and declared a republic. Sun Zhongshan (Sun Yat-sen, 1866–1925) became president of the republic and head of the Nationalist party.

Espousing the Western ideas of democracy, nationalism, and social welfare (the three principles of the people, as Sun called them), the republic struggled to establish its authority over a China torn by civil war and ravaged by foreigners. Russia was claiming Mongolia; Britain, Tibet. Japan posed a danger as well. The northern warlords resisted any attempt to strengthen the republic's army because it might diminish their power. However, in the south, the republic more or less maintained control.

After Sun's death, the Guomindong (Kuomintang), under the authoritarian leadership of Jiang Jieshi (Chiang Kai-shek, 1887–1975), tried to modernize, using the military power of the state and introducing segments of a modern economic system. But faced with civil war, and attacked from both the right and the communist left under Mao Zedong (Mao Tse-tung, 1893–1976), and by the Japanese after 1931, the Guomindong made slow progress. A divided China continued to be at the mercy of outside interests until after World War II.

Japan

Like China, Japan was forced open by the West. By the 1850s, as in India and China, social dissension within Japan and foreign pressure combined to force the country to admit outside trade. In 1853,

Commodore Matthew C. Perry sailed into Tokyo Bay, making a show of American strength. The Japanese signed treaties that granted westerners extraterritoriality and control over tariffs.

A flood of violence ensued. The warrior nobility, the samurai, attacked foreigners and murdered members of their own government. They thought that trade would enhance the status of merchants, a social class they despised. In response to the samurai actions, U.S. and European ships destroyed important Japanese fortresses. Samurai seized the government, determined to preserve Japan's independence. This takeover—the Meiji Restoration of 1867—returned power to the emperor, or Meiji, from the feudal aristocracy, which had ruled in his name for almost seven hundred years.

The new government enacted a series of reforms, turning Japan into a powerful centralized state. Large landowners gave their estates to the emperor in exchange for compensation and high-level positions in the government. All classes were made equal before the law. As in France and Germany, universal military service was required, which diminished social privilege and helped to imbue Japanese of all classes with nationalism. The Japanese modeled their constitution on Bismarck's: there was a bicameral diet, or parliament, but the emperor kept authority.

The Meiji regime introduced modern industry and economic competition. The Japanese visited factories all over the West and hired westerners to teach industrial skills. The government, like central and eastern European governments, built defense industries, backed heavy industry and mining, and developed a modern communication system of railroads, roads, and telegraph. The government encouraged competitive consumer industries as well; it sold factories to wealthy family monopolies, the *zaibatsu,* which came to dominate the Japanese economy. Industry in Japan adopted traditional Japanese values and emphasized cooperation more than competition, paternalism rather than individualism, and deference rather than conflict. Westerners regarded the close cooperation of government and powerful families as something peculiar to the Japanese (neither capitalist nor socialist). Within little more than a generation of the Meiji Restoration, Japan moved from economic backwardness to a place among the top ten industrial nations. To underdeveloped countries, Japan became a model of a nation that borrowed from the West yet preserved its traditional values and social structure.

By 1900, Japan ended the humiliating treaties with the West and became an imperialist power in its own right. Japan won Taiwan and Korea in its war with China in 1894–95 despite Great Power intervention. The Great Powers grabbed greater spheres of influence from the helpless Chinese, infuriating the Japanese. In 1904, conflict over influence in Manchuria brought Japan and Russia to war, which Japan won. The victory of an Asian power over a Western power had a tremendous impact. Japan's victory in the Russo-Japanese War inspired anti-Western nationalist movements throughout Asia.

In World War I, Japan fought on the side of the Allies, emerging as the most powerful Asian state. It took over the former German holdings north of the equator, except for Germany's sphere of influence in China. (U.S. president Woodrow Wilson blocked that move at the Paris peace conference.) In the 1920s, the prosperous economy strengthened the middle class and increased the importance of the working class, reinforcing democratic institutions. But Japan's dependence on foreign trade meant that the nation was hard hit by the Great Depression of 1929, when the major states subjected its trade to tariffs. The depression weakened elements that contributed to peace, stability, and democracy in Japan and strengthened militarist and imperialist groups, which were set on control of Manchuria and China.

In the 1930s nationalists in Burma, India, Indochina, and Indonesia looked to Japan for support against Western imperialism. World War II, however, brought occupation and exploitation, not the independence and equality that these leaders hoped for.

The Ottoman Empire

Throughout the nineteenth century the Great Powers competed to inherit the estate of the "Sick Man of Europe" as Turkey was called then. Their competition ensured the sick man's demise. They claimed parts of the Balkans, central Asia, North Africa, and the Middle East. By the early twentieth century the traditional rivalry between Russia and Britain over central Asia was overshadowed by the German and British conflict in the Middle East.

COMMODORE PERRY AND THE U.S. SQUADRON MEETING JAPANESE IMPERIAL COMMISSIONERS AT YOKOHAMA (1854). Commodore Matthew Perry had opened Japan, against its will, to the West the preceding year. With the Meiji Restoration of 1867, a strong central government pushed Japan until it became one of the top ten industrial nations by 1900. Japan's imperialistic expansion brought it into conflict with China, Russia, and the Western imperialist powers. (*Culver Pictures.*)

The origins of the Anglo-German conflict seemed quite innocent and certainly not political. A group of German financiers proposed a railroad from central Turkey to Baghdad, on the Tigris River, with a connection down the Euphrates River to Basra and the Persian Gulf. Because the proposed new railroad would further open Turkey and its empire to the world market, the sultan was enthusiastic and offered to subsidize the project by guaranteeing the bonds and profits for the syndicate. The German backers of the railroad offered British and French investment groups a 25 percent share each, with 25 percent control to the Turks; the Germans kept the final quarter for themselves. The deal seemed fair; but the British government refused to allow British businessmen to invest.

Politics dominated economics; the British feared German ascendancy in an area so close to India and the Suez Canal. The repercussions of British action were far-reaching. A group of nationalistic Turkish officers denounced the sultan. They saw that one by one Europeans were taking the border territories of the Ottoman Empire. Reforms within the ruling elite alone seemed insufficient to the Young Turks, who demanded a stronger central government. Britain's action, together with German naval expansion, aggravated Anglo-German relations. The Germans came to see the British as their number one rival. In World War I, the Ottomans sided with the Germans, partly because of German influence over a generation of the Turkish elite and partly for fear of a Russian presence in the Caucasus, the Balkans, and the Black Sea areas.

Throughout World War I, the Allies secretly

negotiated the division of the Ottoman Empire. Hoping to weaken its contribution to the German war effort, Britain sponsored Arab independence movements in the Arabian peninsula and in the territories that are today Iraq, Syria, Lebanon, Jordan, and Israel. In the 1917 Balfour Declaration, Britain promised the Zionists a Jewish homeland in Palestine. The Allies also promised Greece and Italy that they would get Turkish land.

When the war was over, the Turks, led by Mustafa Kemal Atatürk, refused to accept the dismemberment of Turkish-speaking territory. They did accept the loss of Arab lands. The Turks drove the Allies out of Anatolia, declared a republic in 1923 under Atatürk's presidency, and moved the capital to Ankara, far away from the cosmopolitan city of Constantinople (Istanbul). Turkey, which became a secular state, was no longer the spiritual leader of millions of Muslims throughout the world. During Atatürk's presidency (1923–1938), the Turkish government banned traditional practices, such as veils for women, harems, and polygamy. European education and ideas flourished in the new republic. In Turkey the conflict between the modern and the traditional was resolved in favor of modern nationalism.

Among the Arabs, several forces fostered the desire for national self-determination, which grew during and after World War I. Britain schemed for a while to establish a puppet Muslim caliph but was rebuffed. The Arab chiefs welcomed British aid against the Turks but deeply resented intervention in their spiritual and local political affairs. They suspected that the Europeans were primarily interested in the area's oil. Arab nationalism, once encouraged against the Ottomans, could not be controlled when the Turks ceased to be a power. As nationalism developed, it often combined with religion to foment opposition, which plagued the imperialists between the world wars and afterward.

Southeast and Central Asia

The Great Power rush to claim territory was evident everywhere in Asia. As China, India, and the Ottoman Empire lost the ability to control border territories, European states tried to grab them. Indochina, Tibet, Korea, Burma, Afghanistan, and Persia were the objects of some power's design. The ensuing struggles between the Europeans for domination of southeast Asia, central Asia, and the Middle East were complicated further by conflict between the declining or disintegrating traditional empires and among the social forces of the region.

In southeast Asia, the French claimed Indochina (Vietnam, Laos, and Kampuchea today) and waged war with China (1883–85) to gain it. The French parliament threw out the government that gained the faraway and not obviously valuable territory, but France annexed the land nonetheless. Indochina was a prosperous agricultural region that traded with other Asians and hardly at all with France. Some of the French may have profited from the colony—merchants, civil servants, soldiers, priests, and scholars—but France as a whole was indifferent to its new acquisition.

From Indochina the French might have expanded into Siam (Thailand) as might the British from their base in Burma (Myanmar). Neither power was willing to let the other take Siam. Like Turkey in the Middle East, Siamese rulers were able to play the powers against each other to preserve some territorial integrity. By 1904 fear of Germany led Britain and France to put colonial differences aside.

Elsewhere throughout southeast Asia, Germany, the United States, Britain, and France competed for island naval stations and trading places. The Netherlands held on to a remnant of their seventeenth-century empire in the East Indies (Indonesia). Even colonies began to acquire colonies, as New Zealand and Australia pushed claims to Borneo and Tasmania. After World War I they claimed German colonies south of the equator. Some may have had economic motives, but national identity was equally important.

Just as the French and British competed in southeast Asia, and the Japanese and all the Great Powers competed in northern China and Korea, the Russians and the British confronted one another in central Asia. Russia's moves, south into Afghanistan and Persia (Iran), both of which bordered India, alarmed the British. They were sure that hostile forces on the borders would inspire rebellious Indian movements. In

Persia the British and Russians vied with one another to lend money to the shah to build a railroad to Teheran. At that moment Russians were borrowing money from the French for their own industrialization, but to create a claim they were willing to borrow more. At stake was control of the "top of the world," the passages to India. British and Russian troops fought each other in Afghanistan. When Britain was fighting the Boer War (see below) in South Africa, the Russians moved toward Persia, Tibet, and Afghanistan. These moves had little to do with economics and much to do with strategic control. The entire situation indicated the instability of relations between the Great Powers outside of Europe itself.

The rise of Germany made both Britain and Russia, longtime foes, willing to compromise. The Russians agreed to a British puppet ruler in Afghanistan. They divided Persia into three zones: one in the north for the Russians, one in the south for the British, and one in the middle for the Persians, to keep the two European powers separate.

This resolution of difficulties made British and Russian cooperation in Europe possible. An important piece in the system of alliances that led to World War I was in place. It had tremendous impact on Persia as well. Torn between Britain and Russia, Persia was neither independent nor stable. Its situation was further complicated after World War I, when its vast reserves of oil became valuable to the Great Powers. Reza Shah of the Pahlavi family gained control in 1925, abolishing foreigners' special privileges. In 1934, the shah granted the concession over the Bahrain Islands to an American firm, Standard Oil, thinking that foreigners whose interests seemed to be merely economic might be more easily controlled than foreigners with geopolitical designs. Yet as British power receded in the region during and after World War II, U.S. power took its place.

The response to European expansion and control throughout Asia before and after the First World War was nationalism. In a short time, in areas divided for centuries by ethnic and religious differences, states began organizing patriots into powerful movements to resist foreign domination. The strengthening of the nation would be the story of the period between the world wars; it would come to a dramatic climax in the aftermath of World War II.

The Scramble for Africa

The most rapid European expansion took place in Africa. As late as 1880, European nations ruled only a tenth of the continent. By 1914, Europeans claimed everything except Liberia (a small territory of freed slaves from the United States) and Abyssinia (Ethiopia). Only Russia, Austria-Hungary, and the United States did not scramble for African soil.

In the early nineteenth century, European powers laid some claims to Africa. The French moved into Algeria in 1830 only to spend a generation trying to pacify the populace. During the Napoleonic wars, Britain gained Capetown in South Africa, a useful provisioning place for ships bound for India and the East. The Boer cattlemen and farmers, who had migrated there from the Netherlands in the seventeenth century, were unwilling to accept British rule. To get away from the British, the Boers moved northward in a migration known as the Great Trek (1835–37), warring with native tribes along the way. By 1880, the Boers were firmly established in the interior of South Africa, in the Transvaal and the Orange Free State. In general, though, until the 1870s, interest in Africa seemed marginal and likely to decline.

Then the astounding activities of Leopold II, the king of Belgium, changed the picture. In 1876, as a private entrepreneur, he formed the International Association for the Exploration and Civilization of Central Africa. Leopold sent Henry Stanley (1841–1904) to the Congo River Basin to establish trading posts, sign treaties with the chiefs, and claim the territory for the association. Stanley, an adventurer and a newspaper reporter who had fought on both sides during the American Civil War, had earlier led an expedition to central Africa in search of David Livingstone, the popular missionary-explorer whom the public believed to be in danger. The human interest adventure story delighted thousands of readers. Imperialism became the fashion. For men like Stanley, Leopold's enterprise promised profit and adventure. For the Africans, it

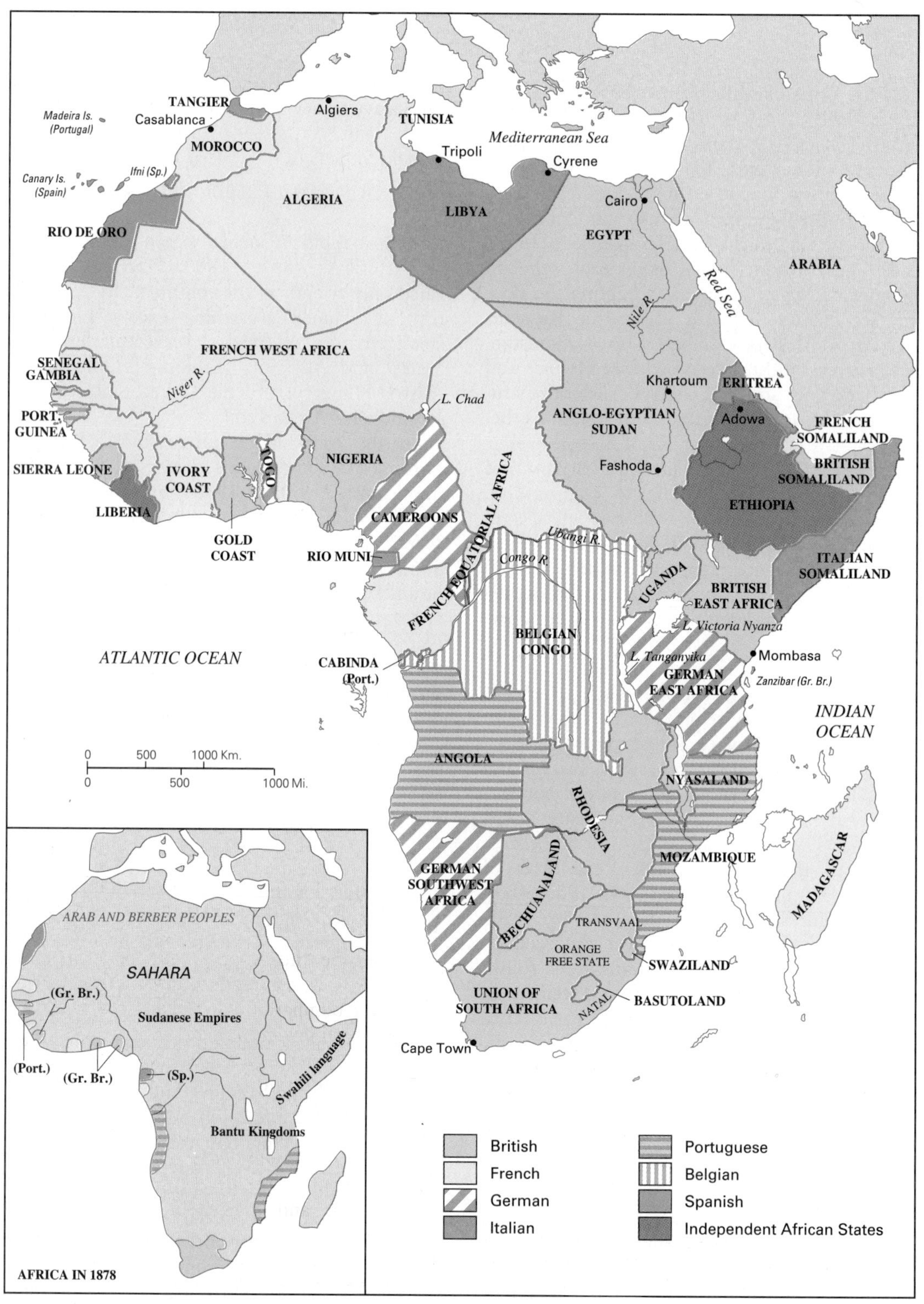

TANGIER
Madeira Is. (Portugal)
Casablanca
Algiers
TUNISIA
Mediterranean Sea
Tripoli
Cyrene
MOROCCO
Canary Is. (Spain)
Ifni (Sp.)
ALGERIA
LIBYA
Cairo
RIO DE ORO
EGYPT
ARABIA
Red Sea
Nile R.
FRENCH WEST AFRICA
SENEGAL
GAMBIA
Niger R.
Khartoum
ERITREA
L. Chad
PORT. GUINEA
ANGLO-EGYPTIAN SUDAN
Adowa
FRENCH SOMALILAND
NIGERIA
TOGO
SIERRA LEONE
IVORY COAST
Fashoda
BRITISH SOMALILAND
FRENCH EQUATORIAL AFRICA
LIBERIA
CAMEROONS
ETHIOPIA
GOLD COAST
Ubangi R.
RIO MUNI
Congo R.
ITALIAN SOMALILAND
UGANDA
BRITISH EAST AFRICA
BELGIAN CONGO
L. Victoria Nyanza
ATLANTIC OCEAN
CABINDA (Port.)
L. Tanganyika
Mombasa
GERMAN EAST AFRICA
Zanzibar (Gr. Br.)
INDIAN OCEAN
0 500 1000 Km.
0 500 1000 Mi.
ANGOLA
NYASALAND
RHODESIA
MOZAMBIQUE
GERMAN SOUTHWEST AFRICA
BECHUANALAND
MADAGASCAR
TRANSVAAL
ORANGE FREE STATE
SWAZILAND
UNION OF SOUTH AFRICA
BASUTOLAND
NATAL
Cape Town
ARAB AND BERBER PEOPLES
SAHARA
(Gr. Br.)
Sudanese Empires
(Port.)
(Gr. Br.)
(Sp.)
Swahili language
Bantu Kingdoms
AFRICA IN 1878
British
French
German
Italian
Portuguese
Belgian
Spanish
Independent African States

promised brutal exploitation. The French immediately established a protectorate on the north bank of the Congo.

The Berlin Conference

The scramble for African territory threatened European stability. Bismarck and Jules Ferry, the premier of France, called an international conference in Berlin in 1884 to lay some ground rules for the development of Africa south of the Sahara. Leopold (as businessman, rather than as the king of Belgium) was declared the personal ruler of the Congo Free State. The Congo Basin was made a free trade zone for merchants of every nation.

The nations at the conference agreed to stop slavery and the slave trade in Africa. Arabs and Africans still engaged in the slave trade. Before long, however, the Congo Association was trying to turn a profit with practices as vicious as those of the African slave traders. Edward D. Morel, an English humanitarian, and Roger Casement, a British civil servant who later became an Irish national hero, waged a vigorous campaign against Leopold for the Aborigines' Protection Society. They produced evidence that slavery, mutilation, brutality, and murder were commonly practiced to force blacks to work for rubber plantations in the Congo. In response to the outcry of world public opinion, the Belgian parliament declared the territory a Belgian colony in 1908, putting an end to Leopold's private enterprise.

Britain in Africa

Great Britain's activities in Africa exemplify the complicated motives, operations, and results of European imperialism. In the second half of the nineteenth century, Britain maintained only a few outposts along the coast of West Africa; even its hold on South Africa appeared to be loosening. From time to time, the British navy interfered with slave traders in Africa, but overall British interest there was minimal. In principle, Britain rejected empire. Its practice was another thing entirely.

◀ *Map 27.2* Africa, 1914 Africa's rapid dismemberment is pictured in these two maps. In 1878 there were few enclaves of Europeans along the coasts. By 1914 Africa had been carved up and all but Ethiopia and Liberia had been claimed.

Egypt. Local conditions in Egypt, including the construction of the Suez Canal (1859–1869), led to British occupation. For a generation (1805–1847), Mohammed Ali, governor of Egypt, had struggled for his independence from the sultan of the Ottoman Empire. Thereafter, strong *khedives* (Turkish governors), with British and French support, maintained Egypt's autonomy. Foreign investment and influence grew; successive khedives spent lavishly to modernize. Egypt fell deeply into debt to Europeans. The building of the Suez Canal, in which the khedive and British and French capitalists were the principal stockholders, brought the country to the verge of bankruptcy. In the long run, the existence of the canal promised Egypt trade and contact with the world economy, but its cost brought immediate disaster. When European creditors demanded cuts in the army as a way for Egypt to pay its debts, Egyptian soldiers rebelled. The combination of probable national bankruptcy and the khedive's apparent inability to keep law and order was a sufficient pretext to bring the British in as "protectors" in 1882.

The canal was the important waterway to India for the British. It was merely an investment to the French. The British invited France to join the occupation, but domestic politics prevented French participation. They deeply resented the British action; patriotic organizations vehemently protested the "insult" to French national honor. Meanwhile, British citizens hired ships to watch the naval bombardment of Egyptian ports as if war were a fireworks display.

Prime Minister William Gladstone, a "little Englander" (one who opposed empire), promised to withdraw British troops once the situation stabilized. Every day that the British remained, Egyptian discontent mounted against them, further threatening the stability of markets, investments, and even government. Egyptian opposition took two irreconcilable forms. Some Egyptians wanted a strong government and army so that they could throw the British out. Others hated all modernization, regarding it as a threat

The Secret of England's Greatness, by Thomas Jones Barker. In this painting, Queen Victoria presents a Bible in the audience chamber at Windsor. (*National Portrait Gallery, London.*)

to Islam. As the British became entrenched, vain attempts at resistance grew more violent.

The British did not withdraw from Egypt; in fact, they moved farther south into the Sudan, where devout Muslims were waging holy war against Egyptian authority. They resented foreign, non-Muslim influence over the khedive. The British, trying to strengthen the khedive's authority so that taxes would be collected, Egypt's budget balanced, and debts paid, were making the situation worse. An English general led ten thousand of the khedive's troops against the Sudanese Muslim followers of the Mahdi. The Egyptians were annihilated.

Costly occupation without stability angered British financiers. Gladstone's Liberal party argued against further action in the Sudan, but public opinion demanded action, so in 1885 Gladstone sent General Charles "Chinese" Gordon, famous for suppressing the Taiping Rebellion, as an observer to the Sudan. Gordon and the garrison were killed at Khartoum. Gordon's head was severed and placed on a pike. An enraged public accused Gladstone of having martyred the famous hero.

Gladstone refused to annex the Sudan. In 1898, when the Conservatives were in power, General Herbert Kitchener was sent to Africa, and his men, armed with machine guns, mowed down charging Muslims at Omdurman. The casualties were reported to be eleven thousand Muslims and twenty-eight Britons, which many Britons felt was appropriate revenge for Gordon's death.

The battle of Omdurman was an ugly victory; 1898 became a year of ugly confrontations and dubious victories for the British Empire. Immediately after the battle, British forces confronted a French exploratory mission under the command of Major Jean Baptiste Marchand at Fashoda in the Sudan. The French had marched from West Africa to the Sudan en route to Somaliland on the Red Sea in order to lay claim to territory from one side of Africa to the other. The British were moving south from Egypt and north from Kenya into the same territory. In the diplomatic crisis that followed, Britain and France were brought to the brink of war. Public passions were inflamed. Too divided by the Dreyfus affair at home (see Chapter 26) to risk a showdown with Britain, the French cabinet ordered Marchand to retreat. French public opinion was outraged. Behind the scenes, however, French diplomats began to negotiate with Britain to reconcile their two nations' ambitions. France could not challenge both Germany across the Rhine and Britain in Africa and Asia. The British, facing problems in Egypt and the Sudan, as well as mounting troubles in South Africa, also realized their limits. "Splendid isolation" was risky business if the whole world could be your battlefield and each of the Great Powers your enemy.

South Africa. Nothing underlined Britain's isolation more than the Boer War, which began in 1899. British relations with the Boers had been difficult since the Great Trek. They were aggravated when rich deposits of gold and diamonds were discovered in Boer territory.

The opposing leaders in these territories were strong and unyielding. Paul Kruger (1825–1904), the Boer president of the Transvaal, wanted independence, power, and access to the sea. He aimed to restrict the foreign prospectors, who were flooding into Boer territory by the thousands. The prime minister of Cape Colony, Cecil Rhodes (1853–1902), who had made a fortune in diamonds and gold in South Africa, acquired Rhodesia (Zimbabwe), a sizable and wealthy territory, for Britain. He dreamed of British red coloring the map of Africa from Cape Town to Cairo.

In 1895, Rhodes's close friend Leander Jameson led about six hundred armed men into the Transvaal to spark an uprising against Kruger, expecting British support. The raid failed, both men were disgraced, and Rhodes was censured by Parliament. Joseph Chamberlain, the imperialist colonial secretary in the British cabinet, was accused of complicity in the conspiracy but acquitted. Kaiser William II of Germany impetuously sent President Kruger a congratulatory telegram; the British took the diplomatic insult as symptomatic of their isolation. Accustomed to French opposition in every area of the globe, they now had to face the Germans.

Everything about the Boer War was unfortunate for the British. The Boers were formidable opponents—farmers by day and commandos by night, armed with the latest French and German rifles. Hatred for the British in the press of other European countries was almost universal. The war was exceptionally costly in both money and lives; it roused many Britons to a hysterical patriotism. Anti-imperialism gained strength, too. Humanitarians in London found some British tactics shameful. To deal with their stubborn foe, for example, the British herded, or "concentrated," whole settlements of Boers into compounds surrounded by barbed wire. The British won the major battles but had to contend with bitter guerrilla resistance.

The nasty war ended in 1902. Hoping to live together in peace with the Boers, the British made many concessions to them, including the right to use their own language, Afrikaans (English remained the official language). They also offered amnesty to any Boer who would swear allegiance to the British king. The settlement, which appeared generous to the belligerents, boded ill for the majority black population of South Africa. Boer autonomy meant that London would be able to do little to protect the rights of black Africans in the Boer territories. Few safeguards for blacks were written into the treaty or the constitution of the new Union of South Africa.

Costs of Colonialism

The cost of imperialism in Africa seemed high not only to the British and French but to other imperialists. Defeat at Adowa (1896) by Ethiopians belied Italian dreams of empire and national glory. Victory would not have alleviated Italy's economic problems, although it might have reduced political discontent. Germans could take little heart from their African acquisitions—Southwest Africa (Namibia), Southeast Africa (Tanzania, but not Zanzibar, which was British), the Cameroons, and Togo. The German colonies were the most efficiently governed (critics said the most ruthlessly controlled) but yielded few benefits, other than pride of ownership, because governing them was so costly. The Belgians obviously gained no prestige from the horrors perpetrated in the Congo. Serious thinkers contemplating the depths to which Europeans would sink in search of fortune and fame suggested the

Europeans were more barbarous than the Africans. Joseph Conrad, Roger Casement, and others pointed out Europeans' moral barbarity.

For the most part, honor was fleeting and profits illusory in African empires. Yet it appeared that Europeans might go to war with each other for African lands with few people and fewer resources. Such a war promised to be more deadly than the colonial conflicts between the technologically superior Europeans and the Africans and Asians. Only patient diplomacy and the growing threat of Germany kept England and France from coming to blows. Germany expressed its aggressive imperialism in a naval arms race with the British, which threatened the latter's power and national self-image. The "Teutonic cousins" eyed each other with deepening suspicion. This tension contributed to the alliances that the Great Powers made in the decade before World War I.

Latin America

The growing European influence in Latin America in the nineteenth century was yet another variety of imperialism. Although it involved neither direct rule, as in Africa and parts of Asia, nor a foreign threat, as in China and southeast Asia, it nonetheless gave Europeans and Americans control over much of Latin American life.

In the era of the American Revolution of 1776 and the French Revolution of 1789, Latin Americans colonists had rebelled against Spain. Britain and the United States encouraged them, in part to gain a free hand for trade that Spain had not allowed. They successfully forestalled attempts of the other Great Powers to restore Spain or to extend colonies after Napolean's fall. (The American president Monroe had warned against intervention and colonization there.)

For the entire nineteenth century, European trade and immigration penetrated South America. Argentina, Brazil, Chile, and other countries took in the Irish, Germans, Italians, eastern Europeans and Spaniards; like the United States, they became primarily immigrant nations. (A few countries—notably Mexico and Peru—attracted fewer Europeans, preserving an Amerindian or mestizo society.) Europeans also invested heavily. Britain and to a lesser degree France dominated the economy; they cooperated commercially with local merchants, loaned money, and negotiated favorable trade treaties for their citizens. By the end of the century, the United States was their competitor.

Both the Europeans and the local merchants and landowner elite exploited the lower classes. Brazil relied on African slave labor to produce for European markets; it was the last American nation to abolish slavery. Native Indians were pushed off their lands just as ruthlessly as they had been in North America.

Europe also dominated the Western Hemisphere culturally. In Latin America, a small, wealthy upper class imitated continental European culture. At Manaus in the Amazon region, using profits of rubber farms worked by enslaved Indians, rich South Americans built an ornate opera house resembling Milan's La Scala. Using the profits of cotton or coffee labor, wealthy North Americans lived like the British gentry. In Buenos Aires, Rio de Janeiro, and Santiago, merchants discussed the latest European intellectual fads. Both upper-class South and North Americans sent their children to Europe to attend school and to acquire "culture" before they entered business, agriculture, and government in their native lands. In these matters, the Latin American elite behaved much the same as westernizers among the elites of India, the Middle East, and southeast Asia. Some people in both Latin and North America, however, felt that New World countries must develop their own cultures, not imitate Britain or France. Significant local cultures did evolve.

The wealthy classes in Latin America depended on Europe for trade as well as culture. They became indebted to Europeans for funds to support their governments and build their railroads. For their part, the Europeans were content to gain the profits from commerce without direct colonization. If political dissension threatened to interfere with peaceful trade, Europeans had ways of letting the merchant class know the costs of that dissension. In general, dependent merchants maintained the conditions that Europeans thought were desirable for business. When the rules of free trade were violated, European vessels might blockade harbors or seize customhouses. But unlike the British in Egypt, Europeans in the Americas usually withdrew their troops or ships as soon as they had enforced their will.

Slaves Drying Coffee on a Plantation in Terreiros, Rio de Janeiro (c. 1882). Brazilian slaves toiled to produce one of Brazil's main exports to the world market. The world economy, which developed during the commercial revolution, emerged full force with the age of imperialism as more and more resources of the non-European world were produced, bought, and sold for overseas consumption. (*Photograph by Marc Ferrez; courtesy of Gilberto Ferrez.*)

An exception to this general policy of nonintervention was Napoleon III's attempt in 1867 to conquer Mexico and to install an Austrian archduke (Maximilian) on a bogus throne. The Mexicans, led by Benito Juárez (1806–1872), resisted the French invasion; the United States threatened. Napoleon thought better of his dreams of easy glory and abandoned the campaign, undertaken more to please members of his military than the French business community. The Mexicans executed Maximilian; the experience intensified Mexican nationalism.

Latin Americans were sheltered from direct European imperialism by the business interests of Britain and the United States, but they had little protection against the aggressions of the latter. As a formidable economic force, the United States entered the field of Great Powers. By the end of the century, the United States was able to energetically pursue its own interests, first in the Caribbean and Central America and then throughout Latin America. After the Spanish-American War (1898), the United States occupied Cuba and annexed Puerto Rico and the Philippines. It also restated the Monroe Doctrine. In the Roosevelt Corollary (1904), the United States announced that Europeans could not intervene in the Western Hemisphere even to protect their citizens or their business interests.

U.S. citizens, however, continued to interfere freely in Latin American affairs. They engineered the secession of Panama from Colombia in 1903 to obtain the rights to build the Panama Canal on favorable terms. The United States intervened repeatedly in the Caribbean, sending U.S. marines to occupy the Dominican Republic, Haiti, Nicaragua, and the port of Veracruz in Mexico. Seizing customs revenues for payment of debts and threatening Latin American governments, American "gunboat diplomacy" replaced English and French commercial power. Like Britain, the United States used force to maintain its interests while at the same time articulating a policy of free competition for trade and commerce—of open doors around the world, including Latin America.

In many ways, U.S. behavior resembled European imperialism. Like the European nations that acquired bases in China, the United States took Guantanamo Bay in Cuba, Fonseca in Nicaragua, and the Canal Zone in Panama, which was originally leased to the United States in perpetuity. Like European businesses, U.S. entrepreneurs invested so heavily in underdeveloped areas that they frequently controlled governments and ruling elites. In 1923, 43 percent of all U.S. foreign investment went to Latin America, 27 percent to Canada, only 22 percent to Europe (at a time when the United States was underwriting German recovery from World War I), and 8 percent to Asia and Africa. Foreign investment may have been a mere fraction of total American wealth, but it was significant to important segments of the national economy.

The United States practiced "dollar diplomacy" in Latin America. It used its economic power to influence politics just as Europeans had done in Morocco, Tunisia, Egypt, Persia, Turkey, and China. When corrupt members of dictatorial regimes borrowed money for national development or for their personal use and were unable to repay, the United States treated the governments like private companies or private individuals in default. The U.S. marines took customs, taxes, and treasuries until the debts were repaid. The customs revenues of Haiti (1915) and Santo Domingo (1904, 1916–1924) were collected for American bankers just as Britain and France had taken Egyptian revenues. Governments in Central America were U.S. puppets or clients, and the United States exercised just as much control over them as European countries had exercised in the Middle East or central Asia. The influence of the United States on Mexico under Porfirio Díaz (1876–1880, 1884–1911) resembled that of Germany and Britain on the Ottoman Empire.

The Latin American response to U.S. imperialism was like the response to European control in Asia and Africa: opposition and resistance. The strongest challenge to U.S. interests came with the Mexican Revolution of 1911. Mexican leaders—Emiliano Zapata, Victoriano Huerta, and Francisco "Pancho" Villa—had different motives for the overthrow of Díaz, but each saw the United States as part of the problem. Zapata wanted land reform, to break up the great estates and give land to the peasants; Huerta wanted to increase foreign investment in industry but keep Mexico, not the foreigners, in control. In 1916, Villa led a raid across the U.S. border. Woodrow Wilson ordered U.S. troops to chase him into Mexico. At that very moment, Wilson was preaching self-determination for European nations and expressing concern about the wrongs done to the weak by the strong in Europe; nonetheless, he violated Mexico's sovereignty when Mexico was torn by civil war.

After World War I, relations between the United States and Latin America remained troubled, particularly during the Great Depression, which had devastating effects on the countries that had begun to industrialize and build an export market. Only recently have U.S.–Latin American relations substantially improved.

The Legacy of Imperialism

World War I was a turning point in the history of imperialism, although neither mother countries nor colonies seemed aware of it at the time. Britain and France divided the German colonial spoils and replaced Turkish power in the Middle East. Both empires were at their territorial peak in 1919. Even more than before the war, leaders in both countries thought colonies essential to the well-being of their nations—for prestige, for manpower, and for trade. But the origins of decolonization also date from the postwar era. Wilson and Lloyd George, who championed national self-determination at Versailles, may have meant their slogans to apply to Europeans, not to the colonial world, but many intellectuals, both in the colonies and in Europe, argued that the principle of self-determination should apply to Asians and Africans. Liberal democrats in the West began to talk of training the colonies for eventual self-government or independence. In France, democrats talked of French citizens of all colors within the empire. In the colonies, forces for independence grew. Colonial intellectuals thought the democrats' timetable for equality or for self-government was too slow. Some found leadership in the anti-imperialist campaign of Lenin and the Bolsheviks.

Less than three decades later, World War II exhausted the European colonial powers. It depleted their soldiery, financial resources, and willingness to wage war against their rebellious colonies. During this war, the Allies relied on colonies for labor, soldiers, bases, and supplies. Colonies and British Commonwealth states like Australia made giant strides toward industrialization. At the very moment that colonies were most important to their mother countries, they were taking steps toward greater economic independence. Furthermore, the inability of the Europeans to avoid the war's slaughter and the racist destruction of the Jews undercut any moral authority westerners might have claimed. For British and French citizens, the postwar task was to realize peace, democracy, and social welfare at home. For many, this meant that the colonies, or at least some of them, would have to have self-determination, perhaps even independence. The question was not *if* there would be self-determination, but *when, where,* and *how* it would occur.

Today, almost a century after the rapid division of the world among the European and U.S. powers and decades after the decolonization of most of the world, the results of imperialism persist. Imperialism left a legacy of deep animosity in the countries of Asia, Africa, and Latin America. Although most nations have political independence, Western economic and cultural domination still exists and often influences the policies of autonomous governments. Much of the world is still poor and suffers from insufficient capital, unskilled leaders, and unstable governments. Many people in these poor areas believe that their countries' condition is the result of a century of Western exploitation.

Imperialism has been a source of great bitterness to former colonial peoples, not just because of economic exploitation but also because it was accompanied by racism and callous disregard for other cultures. Thus, many non-Westerners see little to admire in the values of the West. Their non-Western nationalism usually includes a strong anti-Western strain, some of which is expressed in religious and cultural conservatism or "fundamentalism." Politically, this anti-Western bent led some groups in some countries to procommunist or pro-Russian positions during the cold war or to the creation of their own versions of socialism, such as African socialism or Latin American revolutionary movements. In the aftermath of the cold war and decolonization, fundamentalism or traditionalism became a new political force opposing Western technological and economic competition. This political opposition is directed at the local elites as well. Local elites, even nationalist leader-heroes, are thought corrupted by the profits and values of globalism, which threatens to destroy traditional values, particularly religious ones, and livelihoods.

In today's economically interdependent world, the influence of Western ideas, institutions, technologies, and economic practices is apparent everywhere. English is an international language. The languages of computer technology are universal. African and Asian lands have adopted and adapted democracy, parliamentary and party government, military strategy and technology, socialism, and national boundaries left by Western powers. Intellectuals speak of a global village, so closely connected is the community of ideas shared by leading Africans, Asians, and Latin Americans with Europeans and North Americans. At the same time, many countries are acutely conscious of their hard-won nationhood and of their dependence on shifts in the world markets, which they cannot control.

❖ ❖ ❖

Suggested Reading

Baumgart, Winfried, *Imperialism* (1982). A critical examination of arguments and issues.

Brown, Judith, *Gandhi: Prisoner of Hope* (1990). An excellent biography illustrating the political wisdom of the saintly Gandhi.

Cain, P. A., and A. G. Hopkins, *British Imperialism: Innovation and Expansion, 1688–1914* (1993). This study emphasizes the importance of empire to Britain in the 1880–1914 era when banking, insurance, and service economy surpassed production.

Darby, Phillip, *Three Faces of Imperialism* (1987). British and American approaches to Asia and Africa.

Headrick, Daniel R., *The Tools of Empire: Technology and European Imperialism in the Nineteenth Century* (1981) and *Tentacles of Progress: Technological Transfer in the Age of Imperialism, 1850–1940* (1988). Interesting argument for the role of technology in imperialism.

Henderson, W. O., *Studies in German Colonial History* (1963). Several interesting essays on this topic, which is difficult to research in English sources.

Hobsbawm, Eric, *The Age of Empire* (1988). The third volume in his Marxist interpretation.

Hobson, J. A., *Imperialism: A Study* (1902). This book and those of Luxemburg and Lenin (see below) are the primary sources for the highly controversial theoretical analysis of capitalism as inherently imperialist.

Jeal, Tim, *Livingstone* (1974). A very readable biography of a fascinating life, with good background on Africa.

Langer, William, *European Alliances and Alignments, 1871–1890* and *Diplomacy of Imperialism, 1890–1902,* 2 vols. (1950). Indispensable sources for information about imperialism from the perspective of diplomatic history.

Lenin, V. I., *Imperialism: The Highest Stage in Capitalism* (1917).

Lieven, Dominic, *Empire: The Russian Empire and Its Rivals* (2000). A comparison of the British, Ottoman, Hapsburg, and Russian Empires.

Luxemburg, Rosa, *The Accumulation of Capital* (trans. 1963).

Mackenzie, John, *Propaganda and Empire* (1984). The best discussion of the importance of empire to Britain's self-definition.

May, Ernest, *Imperial Democracy* (1961). American expansionism discussed more thoroughly and less controversially than is usual.

Packenham, Thomas, *The Scramble for Africa* (1991). Colorful narrative history.

Phillips, Richard, *Mapping Men and Empire: A Geography of Adventure* (1997). Explores the role of science and adventure in imperialism.

Porter, Bernard, *The Lion's Share: A Short History of British Imperialism, 1850–1970* (1975). A good survey history.

Robinson, R. E., John Gallagher, and Alice Denny, *Africa and the Victorians: The Official Mind of Imperialism* (1961). An essential book for this fascinating subject; well written, controversial, emphasizing politics.

Schumpeter, Joseph, *Imperialism and Social Classes* (1951, 1989). A classic work by a great economist pointing to noneconomic causes of imperialism.

Thornton, A. P., *The Imperial Idea and Its Enemies: A Study in British Power,* 2nd ed. (1985). An interesting study of the ideas and policies of British imperialism.

Review Questions

1. How did industrialization change Europeans' relations with China, India, and Japan?
2. Why did imperialism grow after 1880? What rationalizations for European expansion were offered at the end of the nineteenth century?
3. What examples are there of successful resistance to Western imperialism?
4. How did imperialism fit in with the European alliance system? How did it cause it? How did imperialism undermine European stability under the alliance system?
5. What were the obstacles preventing Indian independence?
6. Why were Japan and China able to withstand imperialist expansion?
7. Why was Africa divided up in such a brief time?
8. How did imperialism threaten world peace in the early twentieth century?
9. How did competition for empire between England, France, and Russia make their friendship on the eve of World War I seem unlikely in 1900?
10. How was Turkey able to maintain itself in the nineteenth century against the encroachments of Europeans? How did Turkey respond to European threats in the twentieth century?
11. What problems in the Middle East and central Asia appear to have been resolved because Russia was defeated in World War I?

Chapter 28

Modern Consciousness: New Views of Nature, Human Nature, and the Arts

Evening on Karl Johan Street, by Edvard Munch. Munch's works often depicted anguish and horror. (Corbis-Bettmann.)

■ **Irrationalism**
Nietzsche
Dostoevski
Bergson
Sorel

■ **Freud: A New View of Human Nature**

■ **Social Thought: Confronting the Irrational and the Complexities of Modern Society**
Durkheim
Pareto
Le Bon
Weber

■ **The Modernist Movement**
Breaking with Conventional Modes of Esthetics
Modern Art

■ **Modern Physics**

■ **The Enlightenment Tradition in Disarray**

The modern mentality may be said to have passed through two broad phases: early modernity and late modernity. Formulated during the era of the Scientific Revolution and the Enlightenment, early modernity stressed confidence in reason, science, human goodness, and humanity's capacity to improve society for human betterment. Then in the late nineteenth and early twentieth centuries, a new outlook took shape. Late modern thinkers and scientists achieved revolutionary insights into human nature, the social world, and the physical universe; and writers and artists opened up hitherto unimagined possibilities for artistic expression.

These developments produced a shift in European consciousness. The mechanical model of the universe, which had dominated the Western outlook since Newton, was fundamentally altered. The Enlightenment view of human rationality and goodness was questioned, and the belief in natural rights and objective standards governing morality came under attack. Rules of esthetics that had governed the arts since the Renaissance were discarded. Shattering old beliefs, late modernity left Europeans without landmarks—without generally accepted cultural standards or agreed-on conceptions about human nature and life's meaning.

The late modern period was marked by extraordinary creativity in thought and the arts. Yet imaginative and fruitful as these changes were for Western intellectual and cultural life, they also helped create the disoriented, fragmented, and troubled era that characterized the twentieth century.

Irrationalism

While many intellectuals continued to adhere to the outlook identified with the Enlightenment, some thinkers in the late nineteenth century challenged the basic premises of the philosophes and their nineteenth-century heirs. In particular, they repudiated the Enlightenment conception of human rationality, stressing instead the irrational side of human nature. Regarding reason as sovereign, the philosophes had defined human beings by their capacity to think critically; now thinkers saw blind strivings and animal instincts as the primary fact of human existence. It seemed that reason exercised a very limited influence over human conduct, that impulses, drives, and instincts—all forces below the surface—determined behavior much more than did logical consciousness.

The problem of irrationalism is manifold. Some thinkers, while recognizing the weakness of reason, continued to value it and sought to preserve it as an essential ingredient of civilized life. Some studied manifestations of the irrational in myth, religion, the arts, and politics in a logical and systematic way in order to gain understanding of human nature and human behavior. Others, concentrating on the creative potential of the irrational, urged nourishing the feelings, which they considered vital to artistic creativity and a richer existence. Still others celebrated violence as a healthy expression of the irrational.

The new insights into the irrational side of human nature and the growing assault on reason had immense implications for political life. In succeeding decades, these currents of irrationalism would become ideologized and politicized by unscrupulous demagogues who sought to mobilize and manipulate the masses. The popularity of fascist movements, which openly denigrated reason and exalted race, blood, action, and will, demonstrated the naiveté of nineteenth-century liberals, who believed that reason had triumphed in human affairs.

Friedrich Nietzsche (1844–1900) with His Mother. Possessing the intuitive genius of a great poet, Nietzsche grasped the crucial problem afflicting the modern European soul: What path should the individual take in a world where God is dead? Nietzsche's answer to this question—the superman who creates his own values—lent itself to considerable misinterpretation and distortion and had little constructive social value. (*AKG, London.*)

Nietzsche

The principal figure in the dethronement of reason and the glorification of the irrational was the German philosopher Friedrich Nietzsche (1844–1900). Nietzsche's writings are not systematic treatises but rather collections of aphorisms, often containing internal contradictions. Consequently, his philosophy lends itself to misinterpretation and misapplication. Nazi theorists, for example, distorted Nietzsche to justify their notions of the German master race.

Nietzsche attacked the accepted views and convictions of his day as a hindrance to a fuller and richer existence. He denounced social reform, parliamentary government, and universal suffrage, ridiculed the vision of progress through science, condemned Christian morality, and mocked the liberal belief in man's essential goodness and rationality. According to Nietzsche, man must understand that life, which is replete with cruelty, injustice, uncertainty, and absurdity, is not governed by rational principles. There exist no absolute standards of good and evil whose truth can be demonstrated by reflective reason. Nothing is true; there is no higher purpose or sense to the universe or human existence. There is only the naked individual living in a godless and absurd world.

Modern bourgeois society, said Nietzsche, is decadent and enfeebled—a victim of the excessive development of the rational faculties at the expense of will and instinct. Against the liberal-rationalist stress on the intellect, he urged recognition of the dark, mysterious world of instinctual desires, the true forces of life. If the human will is smothered with excessive intellectualizing, the spontaneity that sparks cultural creativity and ignites a zest for living is destroyed. The critical and theoretical outlook destroys the creative instincts. For man's manifold potential to be realized, he must stop relying on the intellect and nurture again the instinctual roots of human existence.

Christianity, with all its prohibitions, restrictions, and demands to conform, also crushes the human impulse for life, said Nietzsche. Christian morality must be obliterated, for it is fit only for the weak, the slave. The triumph of Christianity in the ancient world, said Nietzsche, was a revolution of the lowest elements of society, the meek, the weak, and the ignoble, who sought to inherit the earth from their aristocratic superiors. It was nothing less than an attempt of resentful slaves and slavelike plebeians to prevent their aristocratic superiors from expressing their heroic natures and to strike back at the noble spirits whom they envied. They did so by condemning as evil the very traits that they themselves lacked—strength, power, assertiveness, and a zest for life—and by making their own base, wretched, and life-negating values the standard of all things. Then they saddled with guilt all those who deviated from the standard. This transvaluation of values engineered by Christianity, said Nietzsche, led to a deterioration of life and culture. In *The Anti-Christ* (1888), Nietzsche wrote:

> *Christianity has waged a war to the death against this* higher *type of man. . . . Christianity has taken the side of everything weak, base, ill-constituted, it has made an ideal out of opposition to the . . . instincts of strong life. . . . Christianity is a revolt of everything that crawls along the ground directed against that which is elevated.*[1]

The Christian virtues of love, compassion, and pity, Nietzsche added, are really only a facade hiding Christians' true feelings of envy, resentment, hatred, and revenge against their superiors, betters, and tormentors and desire for their own power.

Although the philosophes rejected Christian doctrines, they largely retained Christian ethics. Unlike the philosophes, Nietzsche did not attack Christianity because it was contrary to reason. He attacked it because, he said, it gave man a sick soul. It was life-denying. Blocking the free and spontaneous exercise of human instincts, it made humility, weakness, and self-abnegation virtues and pride a vice. In short, Christianity extinguished the spark of life. This spark of life, this inner yearning that is man's true essence, must again burn.

"God is dead," Nietzsche proclaimed. God is man's own creation. Christian morality is also dead. Dead also are all the inherited truths based on nature and reason. There are no higher worlds, no transcendental or metaphysical truths, no morality derived from God or nature, and no natural rights, scientific socialism, or inevitable progress. We are wandering through an eternal nothing in which all the old values and truths have lost their intelligibility. This *nihilism*—the belief that moral and social values have no validity—has caused a crisis in European life. But the death of God and of all transcendental truths can mean the liberation of man, insisted Nietzsche. Man can surmount nihilism by adopting a new orientation that gives primacy to the superior man, one who creates his own values and demonstrates self-mastery. He can overcome the deadening uniformity and mediocrity of modern civilization. He can undo democracy and socialism, which have made masters out of cattlelike masses, and surmount the shopkeeper's spirit, which has made man soft and degenerate. European society lacks heroic figures; everyone belongs to a vast herd, but there are no leaders.

According to Nietzsche, Europe could be saved only by the emergence of a higher type of man, the *superman* or *overman*, who would not be held back by the egalitarian rubbish preached by democrats and socialists. "A declaration of war on the masses by *higher* man is needed," said Nietzsche, to end "the dominion of *inferior* men." Europe requires "the annihilation of *suffrage universal*, i.e., the system through which the lowest natures prescribe themselves as laws for the higher."[2] Europe needs a new breed of rulers, a true aristocracy of masterful men. The superman is a new kind of man who breaks with accepted morality and sets his own standards. He does not repress his instincts but asserts them. He destroys old values and asserts his prerogative as master. Free of Christian guilt, he proudly affirms his own being; dispensing with Christian "thou shalt not," he instinctively says, "I will." He dares to be himself. Because he is not like other people, traditional definitions of good and evil have no meaning for him. He does not allow his individuality to be stifled. He makes his own values, those that flow from his very being.

The superman understands and exemplifies the ultimate fact of life: that "the most fearful and fundamental desire in man [is] his drive for power,"[3] that human beings crave and strive for power ceaselessly and uncompromisingly. It is perfectly natural for human beings to want to dominate nature and other human beings; inherent in human nature is the desire "to overpower, overthrow, . . . to become master, a thirst for enemies and antagonisms and triumphs."[4] This will to power is not a product of rational reflection but flows from the very essence of human existence. As the motivating force in human behavior, it governs everyday life and is the determining factor in political life. The enhancement of power brings supreme enjoyment: "The love of power is the demon of men. Let them have everything—health, food, a place to live, entertainment—they are and remain unhappy and low-spirited; for the demon waits and waits and will be satisfied. Take everything from them and satisfy this and they are almost happy—as happy as men and demons can be."[5] The masses, cowardly and envious, will condemn the superman as evil; this has always been their way. Thus, Nietzsche castigates democracy because it "represents the disbelief in great human beings and an elite society,"[6] and Christianity because it imposes an unnatural morality, one that affirms meekness, humility, and compassion.

The German philosopher Arthur Schopenhauer (1788–1860) had declared that beneath the conscious intellect is the will, a striving, demanding, and imperious force, which is the real determinant of human behavior. Schopenhauer held that the intellect is merely a tool of an alogical and irrational will. Life is an endless striving to fulfill ceaseless desires. Blind animal impulses, not the capacity for rational choice, are a human being's true essence. Schopenhauer sought to repress the will. He urged people to stifle desires and retreat into quietude to escape from life's agonies.

Nietzsche learned from Schopenhauer to appreciate the power of unconscious strivings that dominate human behavior, but he rejected Schopenhauer's condemnation and negation of the will, his flight from life. Instead, Nietzsche called for the heroic and joyful assertion of the will and the affirmation of life in order to redeem life from nothingness.

Supermen cast off all established values. Free of all restrictions, rules, and codes of behavior imposed by society, they create their own values. They burst on the world propelled by that something that urges people to want, take, strike, create, struggle, seek, dominate. They know that life is purposeless but live it laughingly, instinctively, fully. Supermen are people of restless energy who enjoy living dangerously, have contempt for meekness and humility, and dismiss humanitarian sentiments; they are noble warriors, hard and ruthless. Only a new elite, which distances itself from the masses and holds in contempt the Christian belief that all people are equal before God, can save European society from decadence.

The influence of Nietzsche's philosophy is still a matter of controversy and conjecture. Perhaps better than anyone else, Nietzsche grasped the crucial problem of modern society and culture: that with the "death of God" traditional moral values had lost their authority and binding power. In a world where nothing is true, all is permitted. Nietzsche foresaw that the future, an age without values, would be violent and sordid, and he urged individuals to face themselves and life free of illusion, pretense, and hypocrisy. Nietzsche is also part of a general nineteenth-century trend that sought to affirm the human being and earthly aspirations rather than God or salvation.

But no social policy could be derived from Nietzsche's heroic individualism, which taught that "there are higher and lower men and that a single individual can . . . justify the existence of whole millennia."[7] Nietzsche thought only of great individuals, humanity's noblest specimens, who overcome mediocrity and the artificiality of all inherited values. The social community and social injustice did not concern him. "The weak and ill-constituted shall perish: first principle of our philanthropy. And one shall help them to do so."[8] Surely, these words offer no constructive guidelines for dealing with the problems of modern industrial civilization.

Likewise, Nietzsche had no constructive proposals for dealing with the disintegration of rational and Christian certainties. Instead, his vitriolic attack on European institutions and values helped to erode the rational foundations of Western civilization. This assault appealed immensely to intellectuals in central Europe, who saw Nietzsche's philosophy as liberating an inner energy. Thus, many young people, attracted to Nietzsche, welcomed World War I; they viewed it as an esthetic experience and thought that it would clear a path to a new heroic age. They took Nietzsche's words literally: "A society that definitely and *instinctively* gives up war and conquest is in decline."[9]

Nazi theorists tried to make Nietzsche a forerunner of their movement. They sought philosophical sanction for their own thirst for power, contempt for the weak, ruthlessness, and glorification of action, as well as for their cult of the heroic and their Social Darwinistic revulsion for human equality. Recasting Nietzsche in their own image, the Nazis saw themselves as Nietzsche's supermen: members of a master race, who, by force of will, would conquer all obstacles and reshape the world according to their own values. Some German intellectuals were drawn to Nazism because it seemed a healthy affirmation of life, the life with a new purpose, for which Nietzsche called.

Nietzsche himself, detesting German nationalism and militarism, scoffed at the notion of German racial superiority, disdained (despite some unfortunate remarks) anti-Semitism, and denounced state worship. He would have abhorred Hitler and been dismayed at the twisting of his idea of the will to power into a prototype fascist principle. The men whom he admired were passionate but self-possessed individuals who, by mastering their own chaotic passions, would face life and death courageously, affirmatively, and creatively. Such men make great demands on themselves. Nevertheless, as Janko Lavrin points out, "Practically all the Fascist and Nazi theories can find some support in Nietzsche's texts, provided one gives them the required twist."[10] Nietzsche's extreme and violent denunciation of Western democratic principles, including equality, his praise of power, and his call for the liberation of the instincts, as well as his elitism, which denigrates and devalues all human life that is not strong and noble, and his spurning of humane values, provided a breeding ground for violent, antirational, antiliberal, and inhumane movements. His philosophy, which included loose talk about the virtues of pitiless warriors, the breeding of a master race, and the annihilation of the weak and the ill, is conducive to a politics of extremes that knows no moral limits.

Dostoevski

Like Nietzsche, the Russian novelist and essayist Fyodor Dostoevski (1821–1881) attacked the fundamental outlook of the Enlightenment, particularly as expressed by liberals and socialists. In contrast to their view that human beings are innately good, responsive to reason's promptings, and capable of constructing the good society through reason, Dostoevski perceived human beings as inherently depraved, irrational, and rebellious.

In *Notes from Underground* (1864), the narrator (the Underground Man) rebels against the efforts of rationalists, humanists, positivists, liberals, and socialists to define human nature according to universal principles and to reform society so as to promote greater happiness. He rebels against science and reason, against the entire liberal and socialist vision. He does so in the name of human subjectivity: the uncontainable, irrepressible, whimsical, and foolish human will. Human nature, says the Underground Man, is too volatile, too diversified to be schematized by the theoretical mind; it will struggle against reason's yoke.

For the Underground Man, there are no absolute and timeless truths that precede the individual and to which the individual should conform. There is only a terrifying world of naked wills vying with one another. In such a world, people do not necessarily seek happiness, prosperity, and peace—all that is good for them, according to "enlightened" thinkers. To the rationalist who aims to eliminate suffering and deprivation, Dostoevski replies that some people freely choose suffering and depravity because it gratifies them—for some, "even in a toothache there is enjoyment"—and they are repelled by wealth, peace, security, and happiness. They do not want to be robots in a rigorously planned and regulated social order, which creates a slot for everything, and they consider excessive intellectualizing—"over-acute consciousness"—a disease that keeps them from asserting their autonomy, their "independent choice."

> *[I]t seems that something that is dearer to almost every man than his greatest advantages must really exist . . . for which, if necessary, a man is ready to act in opposition to all laws, that is, in opposition to reason, honor, peace, prosperity. . . . One's own free unfettered choice, one's own fancy, however wild it may be, one's own fancy worked up at times to frenzy—why that is that very "most advantageous advantage" which we have overlooked, which comes under no classification and through which all systems and theories are continually being sent to the devil. . . . What man needs is simple independent choice, whatever that independence may cost and wherever it may lead.*[11]

It is this irrational will, Dostoevski tells us, that defines the individual's uniqueness and leads him to resist the blueprints drawn up by social theorists. For such crystal palaces—secular utopias designed to satisfy all human needs—do not satisfy what the individual needs most: the expression of one's own desires, no matter how foolish or capricious they might appear to the rational mind. So much for any theory that tries to reduce human nature, which is essentially peculiar, irrational, and incomprehensible, to a formula. If Dostoevski is right, if individuals do not act out of enlightened self-interest, if they are driven by instinctual cravings that resist reason's appeals, then what hope is there for social planners wishing to create the "good" society?

The Underground Man maintains that by following irrational impulses and engaging in irrational acts human beings assert their individuality; they prove that they are free. The Underground Man is totally free. He struggles to define his existence according to his own needs rather than the standards and values created by others. For him, freedom of choice is a human being's most priceless possession, and it derives not from the intellect but from impulses and feelings that account for our essential individuality. He considers the "rational faculty" as "simply one-twentieth of all my faculties of life"; life is more than reasoning, more than "simply extracting square roots."[12]

In rejecting external security and liberal and socialist concepts of progress—in aspiring to assert his own individuality even if this means acting against his own best interests—the Underground Man demonstrates that a powerful element of irrationality underlies human nature, an element that reason can neither understand nor satisfy.

Bergson

Another thinker who reflected the growing irrationalism of the age was Henri Bergson (1859–1941), a French philosopher of Jewish background. Originally attracted to positivism, Bergson turned away from the positivistic claim that science could explain everything and fulfill all human needs. Such an emphasis on the intellect, said Bergson, sacrifices spiritual impulses, imagination, and intuition and reduces reality and the soul to mere mechanisms. The methods of science cannot reveal ultimate reality, Bergson insisted. European civilization must recognize the limitations of scientific rationalism. Our capacity for intuition, whereby the mind achieves an immanent relationship with the object—becomes one with it—tells us more about reality than the method of analysis employed by science. The intuitive experience—something like the artist's instant comprehension of a natural scene—is a direct avenue to truth, which is closed to the calculations and measurements of science. Bergson's philosophy pointed away from science toward religious mysticism.

To his admirers, Bergson's philosophy liberated the person from the constraints of positivism, mechanism, and materialism. It also extolled the creative potential of intuition, the mystical experience, and the poetic imagination: those forces of life that resist categorization by the scientific mind. A protest against modern technology and bureaucracy—against all the features of mass society that seemed to stifle individual uniqueness and spontaneity—it sought to reaffirm the primacy of the individual in an increasingly mechanized and bureaucratic world. The popularity of Bergson's philosophy with its depreciation of reason, symptomized the unsuspected strength and appeal of the nonrational—another sign that people were searching for new alternatives to the Enlightenment world-view.

Sorel

Nietzsche and Dostoevski proclaimed that irrational forces constitute the essence of human nature; Bergson held that a nonrational intuition provides insights unattainable by the scientific mentality. The French social theorist Georges Sorel (1847–1922), who had given up engineering to follow intellectual pursuits, recognized the political potential of the nonrational. Like Nietzsche, Sorel was disillusioned with contemporary bourgeois society, which he considered decadent, unheroic, and life-denying. Like Nietzsche, he also denounced the liberal-democratic foundations of middle-class society. Whereas Nietzsche called for the superman to rescue society from decadence and mediocrity, Sorel placed his hopes in the workers, whose position made them courageous and virile. He saw them as bearers of higher values: as noble and determined producers struggling against exploiters and parasites.

Sorel wanted the proletariat to destroy the existing bourgeois-liberal-capitalist order and rejuvenate society by infusing it with dynamic and creative energy and a sense of moral purpose. The overthrow of decadent bourgeois society would be accomplished through a general strike: a universal work stoppage, which would bring down governments and give power to the workers. Sorel applauded violence, for it intensified the revolutionaries' dedication to the cause and spurred them to acts of heroism. It also accorded with his general conception that life is an unremitting battle and that history is a perpetual conflict between decay and vitality, between passivity and action. In his view, struggle purified, invigorated, and promoted creative change.

Sorel saw the general strike as having the appeal of a great mobilizing myth. What was important was not that the general strike actually take place, but that its image stir all the anticapitalist resentments of the workers and inspire them to carry out their revolutionary responsibilities. Sorel understood the extraordinary potency of myth: it structures and intensifies feelings, unifies people, and mobilizes and channels their energy into heroic action. Because they appeal to the imagination and the emotions, myths are an effective way of organizing the masses, buoying up their spirits, and moving them to revolt. By believing in the myth of the general strike, workers would soar above the moral decadence of bourgeois society and bear the immense sacrifices that their struggle called for.

Like Marx, Sorel believed that the goals of the worker could not be achieved through peaceful parliamentary means. He, too, wanted no reconciliation between bourgeois exploiters and oppressed workers. The only recourse for workers was direct action and violence. However, Marx considered violence simply as a means to a revolutionary end and would dispense with it once the end was achieved. Regarding violence as sublime—a means of restoring grandeur to a flabby world—Sorel valued it as an end in itself.

Sorel's condemnation of liberal democracy and his conviction that fabricated myths could serve as a powerful political weapon found concrete expression in the fascist movements after World War I. Sorel heralded the age of mass political movements committed to revolutionary violence and of myths manufactured by propaganda experts determined to destroy the liberal-rational tradition of the Enlightenment.

Freud: A New View of Human Nature

In many ways, Sigmund Freud (1856–1939), an Austrian-Jewish physician who spent most of his adult life in Vienna, was a child of the Enlightenment. Like the philosophes, he identified civilization with reason and regarded science as the avenue to knowledge. But in contrast to the philosophes, Freud focused on the massive power and influence of nonrational drives. Marx had argued that, although people believe that they think freely, in truth their beliefs and thoughts reflect the ideology of the ruling class. Freud, too, believed that our conscious thoughts are determined by hidden forces—namely, unconscious impulses.

Freud and His Daughter, Anna (1912). Sigmund Freud (1856–1939), the father of psychoanalysis, penetrated the world of the unconscious in a scientific way. He concluded that powerful drives govern human behavior more than reason does. His explorations of the unconscious produced an image of the human being that broke with the Enlightenment's view of the individual's essential goodness and rationality. (*Mary Evans Picture Library.*)

Whereas Nietzsche glorified the irrational and approached it with a poet's temperament, Freud recognized its potential danger. He sought to comprehend it scientifically and wanted to regulate it in the interests of civilization. Unlike Nietzsche, Freud did not belittle the rational but always sought to salvage respect for reason. In a letter to the Austrian novelist Stefan Zweig, Freud wrote that the essential task of psychoanalysis was "to struggle with the demon" of irrationality in a "sober way," to make it "a comprehensible object of science."[13] By "a sober way," he meant the scientific method, not Bergson's intuition or Nietzsche's inspired insights. Better than anyone, Freud recognized reason's limitations and the power of the nonrational, but he never wavered in his support of reason:

> *We may insist as often as we like, that man's intellect is powerless in comparison with his instinctual life, and we may be right in this. Nevertheless, there is something peculiar about his weakness. The voice of the intellect is a soft one, but it does not rest until it has gained a hearing. Finally, after a countless succession of rebuffs, it succeeds. This is one of the few points on which one may be optimistic about the future of mankind.*[14]

Freud's explorations of the world of the unconscious had a profoundly upsetting impact on our conception of the self. Freud himself viewed his theories as a great blow to human pride, to "man's craving for grandiosity":

> *Humanity has, in the course of time, had to endure from the hands of science two great outrages upon its naive self-love. The first was when it realized that our earth was not the center of the universe, but only a tiny speck in a world-system of a magnitude hardly conceivable; this is associated in our minds with the name of Copernicus. . . . The second was when biological research robbed man of his peculiar privilege of having been specially created, and relegated him to a descent from the animal world, implying an ineradicable animal nature in him: this transvaluation has been accomplished in our own time upon the investigations of Charles Darwin. . . . But man's craving for grandiosity is now suffering the third and most bitter blow from present-day psychological research which is endeavoring to show the "ego" of each of us that he is not even master in his own house, but that he must remain content with the veriest scrap of information about what is going on unconsciously in his own mind.*[15]

Freud held that people are not fundamentally rational and that human behavior is governed primarily by powerful inner forces, which are hidden from consciousness. Within the human mind, intense mental activity takes place that is independent of and unknown to consciousness. Primitive drives, strivings, and thoughts influence our behavior, often without our awareness, so that we may not know the real reasons for our actions. Freud considered not just the external acts of a person but also the inner psychic reality underlying human behavior.

Freud, of course, did not discover the unconscious. Romantic poets had sought the wellspring of creativity in a layer of mind below consciousness. The Greek tragedians, Shakespeare, Schopenhauer, Nietzsche, and Dostoevski, among others, had all penetrated the tangled world of the passions and marveled at its elemental power. Freud, who believed that artistic and literary creativity ultimately derives from primal instincts rooted in the unconscious, paid tribute to creative writers' intuition: "they are apt to know of a whole host of things between heaven and earth of which our philosophy has not yet let us dream. In their knowledge of the mind they are far in advance of us everyday people, for they draw upon sources which we have not yet opened up for science."[16] He described Nietzsche as a philosopher "whose guesses and intuitions often agree in the most astonishing way with the laborious findings of psychoanalysis."[17] Freud's great achievement was to explore the unconscious methodically and systematically with the tools and temperament of a scientist. He showed that the irrational contained a structure that could be empirically explained and rationally explored.

After graduating from medical school, Freud specialized in the treatment of nervous disorders. His investigations led him to conclude that childhood fears and experiences, often sexual in nature, accounted for neuroses: disorders in thinking, feeling, and behavior that interfere with everyday acts of personal and social life. Neuroses can take several forms, including hysteria, anxiety, depression, and obsessions. So painful and threatening were these childhood emotions and experiences that his patients banished them from conscious memory to the realm of the unconscious. To understand and treat neurotic behavior, Freud said, it is necessary to look behind overt symptoms and bring to the surface emotionally charged experiences and fears—childhood traumas—that lie buried in the unconscious, along with primitive impulses.

Freud probed the unconscious by urging his patients to say whatever came to their minds. This procedure, called free association, rests on the premise that spontaneous and uninhibited talk reveals a person's underlying preoccupations, his or her inner world, and the "demons" that are at the root of the person's emotional distress. A second avenue to the unconscious is the analysis of dreams. An individual's dreams, said Freud, reveal his or her secret wishes, often socially unacceptable desires, and frightening memories. Finding them too painful to bear, we lock up these wishes and memories in the deepest dungeons of the unconscious. But repressed emotions do not disappear; even in their cages, the demons remain active, continuing to haunt us and to generate conflicts. Our distress is real and even excruciating, but we do not know its source.

The *id*, the subconscious seat of the instincts, said Freud, is "a cauldron full of seething excitations" that constantly demand gratification. The id is primitive and irrational. It knows no values; it has no awareness of good and evil. Unable to endure tension, it demands sexual release, the termination of pain, or the cessation of hunger. When the id is denied an outlet for its instinctual energy, people become frustrated, angry, and unhappy. Gratifying the id is our highest pleasure. But the full gratification of instinctual demands is detrimental to civilized life. That is why the *ego*, which stands for reason, seeks to hold the id in check, to bring it in line with reality.

Freud postulated a harrowing conflict between the relentless strivings of our instinctual nature and the requirements of civilization. In Freud's view, civilization requires the renunciation of instinctual gratification and the mastery of animal instincts, a thesis he developed in *Civilization and Its Discontents* (1930). Although Freud's thoughts in this work were, no doubt, influenced by the great tragedy of World War I, the main theme could be traced back to his earlier writings. Human beings derive their highest pleasure from sexual fulfillment, said Freud, but unrestrained sexuality drains off psychic energy needed for creative artistic and intellectual life and directs human energies away from work needed to preserve communal life. Hence society, through the family, the priest, the teacher, and the police, imposes rules and restrictions on our animal nature.

But this is immensely painful. The human being is caught in a tragic bind. Society's demand to repress the instincts in the interest of civilization causes terrible frustration; equally distressing, the violation of society's rules under the pressure of instinctual needs evokes feelings of guilt. Either way, people suffer; civilized life simply entails too much pain for people. It seems that the price we pay for civilization is neurosis. Most people cannot endure the amount of instinctual renunciation that civilization requires. There are times when our elemental human nature rebels against all the restrictions and "thou shalt nots" demanded by society, against all the misery and torment imposed by civilization.

"Civilization imposes great sacrifices not only on man's sexuality, but also on his aggressivity,"[18] said Freud. People are not good by nature, as the philosophes had taught; on the contrary, they are "creatures among whose instinctual endowments is to be reckoned a powerful share of aggressiveness." Their first inclination is not to love their neighbor but to "satisfy their aggressiveness on him, to exploit his capacity for work without compensation, to use him sexually without his consent, to seize his possessions, to humiliate him, to cause him pain, to torture and to kill him."[19] Man is wolf to man, concluded Freud. "Who has the courage to dispute it in the face of all the evidence in his own life and in history?"[20] Civilization "has to use its utmost efforts in order to set limits to man's aggressive instincts," but "in spite of every effort these endeavors of civilization have not so far achieved very much."[21] People find it difficult to do without "the satisfac tion of this inclination to aggression."[22] When circumstances are favorable, this primitive aggressiveness breaks loose and "reveals man as a savage beast to whom consideration towards his own kind is something alien."[23] For Freud, "the inclination to aggression is an original self-subsisting disposition in man," and it "constitutes the greatest impediment to civilization." Civilization attempts "to combine single human individuals and after that families, then races, peoples and nations into one great unity. . . . But man's natural aggressive instinct, the hostility of each against all and of all against each, opposes this program of civilization."[24] Aggressive impulses drive people apart, threatening society with disintegration. For Freud, an unalterable core of human nature is ineluctably in opposition to civilized life. To this extent, everyone is potentially an enemy of civilization.

Freud's awareness of the irrational and his general pessimism regarding people's ability to regulate it in the interests of civilization did not lead him to break faith with the Enlightenment tradition, for Freud did not celebrate the irrational. He was too aware of its self-destructive nature for that. Civilization is indeed a burden, but people must bear it, for the alternative is far worse. In the tradition of the philosophes, Freud sought truth based on a scientific analysis of human nature and believed that reason was the best road to social improvement. Like the philosophes, he was critical of religion, regarding it as a pious illusion—a fairy tale in conflict with reason. Freud wanted people to throw away what he believed was the crutch of religion: to break away from childlike dependency and stand alone.

Also like the philosophes, Freud was a humanitarian who sought to relieve human misery by making people aware of their true nature, particularly their sexuality. He wanted society to soften its overly restrictive sexual standards because they were injurious to mental health. As a practicing psychiatrist, he tried to assist his patients in dealing with emotional problems. Freud wanted to raise to the level of consciousness hitherto unrecognized inner conflicts that caused emotional distress. One enduring consequence of the Freudian revolution is the recognition of the enormous importance played by childhood in the shaping of the adult's personality. The neurotic disorders that burden adults begin in early childhood. Freud urged that we show greater concern for the emotional needs of children.

Yet Freud also differed from the philosophes in crucial ways. Dismissing the Christian doctrine of original sin as myth, the philosophes had believed human nature to be essentially good. If people took reason for their guide, evil could be eliminated. Freud, however, asserted, in secular and scientific terms, a pessimistic view of human nature. He saw evil as rooted in human nature rather than as a product of a faulty environment. Education and better living conditions would not eliminate evil, as the philosophes had expected, nor would abolition of private property, as Marx had declared. The philosophes venerated reason; it had enabled Newton to unravel nature's mysteries and would permit people to achieve virtue and reform society. Freud, who wanted reason to prevail, understood that its soft voice had to compete with the thunderous roars of the id. Freud broke with the optimism of the philosophes. His awareness of the immense pressures that civilization places on our fragile egos led him to be generally pessimistic about the future.

Unlike Marx, Freud had no vision of utopia. He saw the crude, untameable, and destructive character of human nature as an ever present obstacle to harmonious social relations. That Freud was hounded out of Vienna by the Nazis and his four sisters were murdered by them simply for being Jewish is a telling footnote to his view of human nature, the power of the irrational, and the fragility of civilization.

Social Thought: Confronting the Irrational and the Complexities of Modern Society

The end of the nineteenth century and the beginning of the twentieth mark the great age of sociological thought. The leading sociological thinkers of the period all regarded science as the only valid model for correct thinking, and all claimed that their thought rested on a scientific foundation. They struggled with some of the crucial problems of modern society: How can society achieve coherence and stability when the customary associations and attachments that characterized village life are ruthlessly dissolved by the rapidly developing industrial-urban-capitalist order and when religion no longer unites people? What are the implications of the nonrational for political life? How can people preserve their individuality in a society that is becoming increasingly regimented? In many ways, twentieth-century dictatorships were responses to the dilemmas of modern society analyzed by these social theorists. And twentieth-century dictators would employ these social theorists' insights into group and mass psychology for the purpose of gaining and maintaining power.

Durkheim

Émile Durkheim (1858–1917), a French scholar of Jewish background and heir to Comte's positivism, was an important founder of modern sociology. Like Comte, he considered scientific thought to be the only valid model for modern society. A crucial element of Durkheim's thought was the effort to show that the essential ingredients of modern times—secularism, rationalism, and individualism—threaten society with disintegration. In traditional society, the social order was derived from God, and a person's place and function were assigned by God and determined by birth. Modern people, however, captivated by the principle of individualism, do not accept such restraints, said Durkheim. Instead, they seek to uplift themselves and demand that society allow them the opportunity. In the process, they reject or ignore the restraints that society must impose if it is to function. Their attitude leads to anarchy. Durkheim wanted to prevent modern society from disintegrating into a disconnected mass of self-seeking, antagonistic individuals. Like Rousseau, he held that the individual becomes fully human only as a member of a community.

The weakening of those traditional ties that bind the individual to society constituted, for Durkheim, the crisis of modern society. Without collective values and common beliefs, he felt, society was threatened with disintegration and the individual with disorientation. To a Western world intrigued by scientific progress, Durkheim emphasized the spiritual malaise of modern society. Modern people, said Durkheim, suffer from *anomie*—a collapse of values. They do not feel integrated into a collective community and find no purpose in life. In *Suicide* (1897), Durkheim maintained that "the exceptionally high number of voluntary deaths manifests the state of deep disturbances from which civilized societies are suffering and bears witness to its gravity."[25] The high level of boredom, anxiety, and pessimism also evidence the pathology of modern society. Modern people are driven to suicide by intense competition and the disappointment and frustration resulting from unfulfilled expectations and a lack of commitment to moral principles. People must limit their aspirations and exercise discipline over their desires and passions. They must stop wanting more. Religion once spurred people to view restraint and the renunciation of desires as virtues, but it can no longer do so.

Although Durkheim approved of modernity, he noted that modern ways have not brought happiness or satisfaction to the individual. Modern scientific and industrial society requires a new moral system, which would bind the various classes into a cohesive social order and help overcome the feelings of restlessness and dissatisfaction tormenting people. Like Saint-Simon, Durkheim called for a rational and secular system of morals to replace Christian dogma, which had lost its power to attract and to bind. If a rational and secular replacement for Christianity is not found, society would run the risk of dispensing with moral beliefs altogether, and it could not endure such a vacuum. Like the positivists, Durkheim insisted that the new moral beliefs must be discovered through the methods of science.

Durkheim hoped that occupational and professional organizations—updated medieval guilds—would integrate the individual into society and provide the moral force capable of restraining the selfish interests of both employer and worker. By curbing egoism, fostering self-discipline, and promoting altruism, these organizations could provide substitutes for religion.

Durkheim focused on a crucial dilemma of modernity. On the one hand, modern urban civilization has provided the individual with unparalleled opportunities for self-development and material improvement. On the other, the breakdown of traditional communal bonds caused by the spread of rationalism and individualism has produced a sense of isolation and alienation. In modern mass society, the individual feels like an outsider, a condition that has been exacerbated by the decline of Christianity. Twentieth-century totalitarian movements sought to integrate these uprooted and alienated souls into new collectivities: a proletarian state based on workers' solidarity or a racial state based on blood and soil.

Pareto

Like Comte, Vilfredo Pareto (1848–1923), an Italian economist and sociologist, aimed to construct a system of sociology on the model of the physical sciences. His studies led him to conclude that social behavior rests primarily not on reason but rather on nonrational instincts and sentiments. These deeply rooted and essentially changeless feelings are the fundamental elements in human behavior. Although society may change, human nature remains essentially the same. Whoever aims to lead and to influence people must appeal not to logic but to elemental feelings. Most human behavior is nonrational; nonlogical considerations also determine the beliefs that people hold. Like Marx and Freud, Pareto believed that we cannot accept a person's word at face value; we find the real cause of human behavior in human instincts and sentiments. People do not act according to carefully thought-out theories. They act first from nonlogical motivations and then construct a rationalization to justify their behavior. Much of Pareto's work was devoted to studying the nonrational elements of human conduct and the various beliefs invented to give the appearance of rationality to behavior that derives from feeling and instinct.

Pareto divided society into two strata: the elite and the masses. Elites have always existed, said Pareto, because human beings are unequal by nature and because the goods that all people seek cannot be shared equally. Because struggle is a general law of life, elites and masses will exist in all societies. The belief that a democracy constitutes rule by a people is a myth, said Pareto. In actuality, a small group of party leaders controls the political system. Pareto also rejected as naive Marx's vision of the end of the class struggle.

In the tradition of Machiavelli, Pareto held that a successful ruling elite must, with cunning, and if necessary with violence, exploit the feelings and impulses of the masses to its own advantage. Democratic states, he said, delude themselves in thinking that the masses are really influenced by rational argument. A staunch opponent of parliamentary democracy, Pareto predicted that new political leaders would emerge who would master the people through propaganda and force, appealing always to sentiment rather than to reason. To this extent, Pareto was an intellectual forerunner of fascism, which preached an authoritarian elitism. Mussolini praised Pareto and proudly claimed him as a source of inspiration. The extent to which Pareto, who died one year after Mussolini came to power, welcomed the fascist regime is a matter of conjecture. But the triumph of fascism did seem to confirm his convictions that democracy was ready to collapse and that a small minority of determined men, willing to use violence, could gain control of the state if the holders of power were reluctant to counter with force.

Le Bon

Gustave Le Bon (1841–1931), a French social psychologist, concentrated on mass psychology as demonstrated in crowd behavior, a phenomenon of considerable importance in an age of accelerating industrialization and democratization. "The substitution of the unconscious action of crowds for the conscious activity of individuals is one of the principal characteristics of the present age,"[26] Le Bon declared in the preface to *The Crowd* (1895). In the past, said Le Bon, rivalries between monarchs dominated Europe's political stage; "the opinion of the masses scarcely counted, and most frequently did not count at all."[27] But Europe has experienced a great transformation. In this new age, he said, the masses organized in socialist parties and unions are starting to determine the destinies of nations. Le Bon, who had contempt for democracy, intended his work to be a justification for rule by an authoritiarian elite.

Le Bon applied the term *crowd* to a large group of people in which individuality is submerged in the mass and the individual loses control over his or her ideas and emotions. A psychological crowd could be a street mob, a political party, or a labor union. An agglomeration of individuals "presents new characteristics very different from those of the individuals composing it. The sentiments and ideas of all the persons in the gathering take one and the same direction, and their conscious personality vanishes."[28] The crowd acquires a collective mind, in which critical thinking is swamped and "unconscious qualities obtain the upper hand."[29] Becoming increasingly intolerant and fanatical, the crowd member "descends several rungs in the ladder of civilization. Isolated, he may be a cultivated individual; in a crowd, he is a barbarian—that is, a creature acting by instinct."[30] Crowd behavior demonstrates convincingly that "the part played by the unconscious in all our acts is immense and that played by reason very small."[31] In a contest with sentiment, human reason is utterly powerless.

Le Bon also discussed the leaders of crowds and their means of persuasion. "A crowd is a servile flock that is incapable of ever doing without a master," he stressed. Leaders "are more frequently men of action than thinkers"; they are "morbidly nervous, excitable, . . . bordering on madness." Fanatically committed to their beliefs, they do not respond to logical argument. The masses, "always ready to listen to the strong-willed man,"[32] respond to the intensity of the leader's faith.

Both Mussolini and Hitler, who deliberately sought to seduce, manipulate, and dominate the masses, absorbed Le Bon's ideas, which had become commonplace in the early twentieth century. "I don't know how many times I have re-read *Psychologie des Foules* [*The Crowd*]," declared Mussolini. "It is an excellent work to which I frequently refer."[33] Hitler's analysis of the crowd—"sober reasoning determines their thoughts far less than emotion and feeling"—restates many of Le Bon's observations.

Weber

Probably the most prominent social thinker of the age, the German academic Max Weber (1864–1920) was a leading shaper of modern sociology. In Weber's view, Western civilization, unlike the other civilizations of the globe, had virtually eliminated myth, mystery, and magic from its conception of nature and society—the "disenchantment of the world," Weber called it. Most conspicuous in Western science, this process of rationalization, or "calculated action," was also evident in politics, law, and economics. Weber considered Western science to be an attempt to understand and master nature through reason, and Western capitalism an attempt to organize work and production in a rational manner. The Western state has a rational written constitution, rationally formulated law, and a bureaucracy of trained government officials who administer the affairs of state according to rational rules and regulations. Justice is not dispensed by wise elders but proceeds from codified law and established procedures.

The question of why the West, and not China or India, engaged in this process of rationalization intrigued Weber, and much of his scholarly effort went into answering it. Weber showed how various religious beliefs have influenced people's understanding of nature, shaped their values, social and political institutions, and economic behavior, and how they contributed to or blocked the development of rationalism. Weber's most famous thesis is that Protestantism, which saw work as a religious duty, a "calling," and hedonism as a sin, and which demanded a rational planning of one's life in accordance with God's will, produced an outlook compatible with the requirements of capitalism. Capitalism, said Weber, is not a thirst for money, a merely acquisitive desire that has been exhibited since the early days of civilization. The distinguishing feature of capitalism is the rational organization of all business activities, including the labor force, so that profits are continuous and calculable. The Protestant ethic gave religious approval to methodical and patient work and to saving and reinvesting, for it saw worldly success as a sign of God's approval.

Weber understood the terrible paradox of reason. Reason accounts for brilliant achievements in science and economic life, but it also despiritualizes life by ruthlessly eliminating centuries-old traditions, denouncing deeply felt religious beliefs as superstition, and regarding human feelings and passions as impediments to clear thinking. While giving people knowledge, the process of disenchantment has shattered the basis for belief in transcendental values; in a thoroughly disenchanted world, life is without ultimate purpose and the individual is soulless. This is the dilemma of modern individuals, said Weber. Secular rationality is shaping a world in which standards cannot claim ultimate sanction. A disenchanted world contains no inherited truths, no God-given answers to the human being's desperate need for meaning. We are now confronted with an immense and unprecedented burden: how to create for ourselves values that give meaning to life in a world deprived of certainty.

Secular rationality has produced still another awesome problem, said Weber. It has fostered self-liberation, for it enables human beings to overcome illusions and take control of the environment and of themselves, but it is also a means of self-enslavement, for it produces institutions, giant public and corporate bureaucracies, that in their relentless pursuit of efficiency encourage uniformity and depersonalization. Modern officials, said Weber, are emotionally detached. Concerned only with the efficient execution of tasks, they employ reason in a cold and calculating way; human feelings such as compassion and affection are ruled out as hindrances to effectiveness. In the name of efficiency, people are placed in "steel cages,"—that is, treating them impersonally as mere objects—depriving them of their individuality, personal liberty, and humanity. In the form of private and public bureaucratic hierarchies, reason has created the means for self-enslavement:

> *It is horrible to think that the world could one day be filled with nothing but those little cogs, little men clinging to little jobs and striving towards bigger ones. . . . This passion for bureaucracy . . . is enough to drive one to despair. . . . That the world should know no men but these: it is in such [a process] that we are already caught up, and the great question is, therefore, not how we can promote and hasten it, but what can we oppose to this machinery in order to keep a portion of mankind free from this parceling-out of the soul, from this supreme mastery of the bureaucratic way of life.*[34]

The prospect existed that people would refuse to endure this violation of their spiritual needs and would reverse the process of disenchantment by seeking redemption in the irrational. Weber himself, however, was committed to the ideals of the Enlightenment and to perpetuating the rational scientific tradition, which he felt was threatened by bureaucratic regimentation on the one hand and irrational human impulses on the other.

Like Freud, Weber was aware of the power of the nonrational in social life. One expression of the irrational that he analyzed in considerable depth was the charismatic leader who attracts people by force of personality. Charismatic leaders may be religious prophets, war heroes, or others who possess this extraordinary ability to attract and dominate others. People yearn for charismatic leadership, particularly during times of crisis. The leader claims a mission—a sacred duty—to lead the people during the crisis. The leader's authority rests on the people's belief in the mission and their faith in the leader's extraordinary abilities; a common allegiance to the charismatic leader unites the community. In an era that has seen its share of dictators and demogogues, the question of why people are drawn to the charismatic savior—why they succumb to his authority, and why they alter their lives in order to implement his vision—is of crucial concern to historians and social theorists.

The Modernist Movement

Breaking with Conventional Modes of Esthetics

At the same time as Freud and social thinkers were breaking with the Enlightenment view of human nature and society, artists and writers were rebelling against the traditional forms of artistic and literary expression that had shaped European cultural life since the Renaissance. Rejecting both classical and realist models, they subordinated form and objective reality to the inner life—to feelings, imagination, and the creative process. These avant-garde writers and artists found new and creative ways to express the explosive primitive forces within the human psyche that increasingly had become the subject of contemporary thinkers. Their experimentations produced a great cultural revolution, called *modernism*, which still profoundly influences the arts. In some ways, modernism was a continuation of the Romantic Movement, which had dominated European culture in the early nineteenth century. Both movements subjected to searching criticism cultural styles that had been formulated during the Renaissance and had roots in ancient Greece.

Even more than romanticism, modernism aspired to an intense introspection—a heightened awareness of self—and saw the intellect as a barrier to the free expression of elemental human emotions, the wellspring of creativity. Modernist artists and writers abandoned conventional literary and artistic models and experimented with new modes of expression. They liberated the imagination from the restrictions of conventional forms and enabled their audience, readers and viewers alike, to share in the process of creation, often unconcious, and to discover fresh insights into objects, people, and social conditions. They believed that there were further discoveries to be made in the arts, further possibilities of expression, that past masters had not realized. The consequence of their bold venture, wrote the literary critic and historian Irving Howe, was nothing less than the "breakup of the traditional unity and continuity of Western culture."[35]

Like Freud, modernist artists and writers probed beyond surface appearances for a more profound reality hidden in the human psyche. Writers such as Thomas Mann, Marcel Proust, James Joyce, August Strindberg, D. H. Lawrence, and Franz Kafka explored the inner life of the individual and the psychopathology of human relations in order to lay bare the self. They dealt with the predicament of men and women who rejected the values and customs of their day, and they depicted the anguish of people burdened by guilt, torn by internal conflicts, and driven by inner self-destructiveness. Besides showing the overwhelming might of the irrational and the seductive power of the primitive and the instinctual, they also broke the silence about sex that had prevailed in Victorian literature.

From the Renaissance through the Enlightenment and into the nineteenth century, Western esthetic standards had been shaped by the conviction that the universe embodied an inherent mathematical order. A corollary of this conception of the outer world as orderly and intelligible was the view that art should imitate reality. According to the sociologist Daniel Bell, from the Renaissance on, art was seen as "a mirror of nature, a representation of life. Knowledge was a reflection of what was 'out there' . . . a copy of what was seen."[36] Since the Renaissance, artists had deliberately made use of laws of perspective and proportion; musicians had used harmonic chords, which brought rhythm and melody into a unified whole; and writers had produced works according to a definite pattern, which included a beginning, middle, and end.

Modernist culture, however, acknowledged no objective reality of space, motion, and time that has the same meaning for all observers. Rather, reality can be grasped in a variety of ways; a multiplicity of frames of reference apply to nature and human experience. Consequently, reality is the way the viewer apprehends it to be through the prism of the imagination. "There is no outer reality," said the modernist German poet Gottfried Benn, but "only human consciousness, constantly building, modifying, rebuilding new worlds out of its own creativity."[37] Modernism is concerned less with the object itself than with how the artist transforms it, with the sensations that an object evokes in the artist's inner being, and with the meaning that the artist's imagination imposes on reality. "Conscientious and exact imitation of nature does not create a work of art," wrote Emil Nolde, a German expressionist painter. "A work becomes a work of art when one re-evaluates the values of nature and adds one's own spirituality."[38] Bell makes this point in reference to painting:

> *Modernism . . . denies the primacy of an outside reality, as given. It seeks either to rearrange that reality, or to retreat to the self's interior, to private experience as the source of its concerns and aesthetic preoccupations. . . . There is an emphasis on the self as the touchstone of understanding and on the activity of the knower rather than the character of the object as the source of knowledge. . . . Thus one discerns the intentions of modern painting . . . to break up ordered space . . . to bridge the distance between object and spectator, to "thrust" itself on the viewer and establish itself immediately by impact.*[39]

Dispensing with conventional forms of esthetics, which stressed structure and coherence, modernism propelled the arts onto uncharted seas. Modernists abandoned the efforts of realists and naturalists to produce a clinical and objective description of the external world; instead they probed subjective views and visions and the inner world of the unconscious. Recoiling from the middle-class, industrial civilization, which prized rationalism, organization, clarity, stability, and definite norms and values, modernist writers and artists were fascinated by the bizarre, the mysterious, the unpredictable, the primitive, the irrational, and the formless.

Writers experimented with new techniques to convey the intense struggle between the conscious and the unconscious and to connote the aberrations and complexities of human personality and the irrationality of human behavior. In particular, they devised a new way, the stream of consciousness, to reveal the mind's every level—both conscious reflection and unconscious strivings—and to capture how thought is punctuated by spontaneous outbursts, disconnected assertions, random memories, undifferentiated and freely associated words and sounds, hidden desires, and persistent fantasies. The stream of consciousness is not narrated memory but a flow of feelings and thoughts in which the boundary between consciousness and unconsciousness is blurred. It attempts to reveal the mystery and complexity of the inner person.

Modern artists deliberately plunged into the world of the unconscious in search of the instinctual, the fantastic, the primitive, and the mysterious, which they believed yielded a truth higher than that given by analytical thought. They embarked on a voyage into the mind's interior in the hopes of finding fantastic stimulants that would spark the creative imagination. Composers engaged in open revolt against the conventional rules and standards of musical composition. For example, the Austrian composer Arnold Schönberg (1874–1951) purposefully abandoned traditraditional scale and harmonic chords to produce atonal music that "seeks to express all that swells in us subconsciously like a dream."[40] The Russian composer Igor Stravinsky (1882–1971) experimented with both atonality and primitive rhythms. When Stravinsky's ballet *The Rite of Spring* was performed in Paris in 1913, the theater audience rioted to protest the composition's break with tonality, its use of primitive, jazzlike rhythms, and its theme of ritual sacrifice.

The modernist movement, which began near the end of the nineteenth century, was in full bloom before World War I and would continue to flower in the postwar world. Probably the

Profile

Joseph Conrad

The Granger Collection.

Behavior driven by the unconscious and the human being's capacity to act irrationally and cruelly—the dark side of human nature, which was the subject of Freud's investigations—intrigued many modernist writers, including the British novelist Joseph Conrad (1857–1924), born Jozel Teodor Konrad Korzenlowski. In 1862, when Conrad was not yet five years old, his father, who had participated in an insurrection to liberate Poland from Russian rule, was exiled to nothern Russia. In this harsh environment, his mother died of tuberculosis in 1865. His father, who translated the works of French and English authors in Polish, which the precocious young Conrad read voraciously, made the difficult decision to place his only child in the care of Joseph's maternal uncle in Poland, where he attended school. Joseph lost his father when he was twelve, and five years later, he left school to become an apprentice seaman on a French merchant ship. In 1878, speaking only a few words of English, he joined the British merchant navy.

During his twenty years at sea, Conrad visited exotic lands and experienced danger. These adventures found literary expression in Conrad's novels and short stories, including *An Outcast of the Islands* (1896), *Lord Jim* (1900), *Heart of Darkness* (1902), *Nostromo* (1904), and *The Secret Agent* (1907). But Conrad was far more than a masterful renderer of adventure

clearest expression of the modernist viewpoint is found in art.

Modern Art

In the late nineteenth century, artists began to turn away from the standards that had characterized art since the Renaissance. The history of modern painting begins with impressionism, a movement spanning the period 1860 to 1886. No longer committed to depicting how an object appears to the eye or to organizing space mathematically, artists searched for new forms of expression. They boldly strove to expand or break with the traditional formulas of composition (arrangement of visual elements) and the treatments of color and light. The impressionist movement was centered in Paris, and its leading stories. His reputation as one of England's finest novelists derives from both his compelling prose and his creative exploration of human depravity, a phenomenon to which he seemed irresistibly drawn. In 1891, after a four-month stay in the Congo Free State, a land notoriously exploited and brutalized by agents of the Belgian king Leopold II, Conrad suffered psychological trauma. His experiences in the heart of Africa led him to write his most compelling work, *Heart of Darkness.*

Kurtz, the principal character in *Heart of Darkness,* runs a very successful ivory trading post deep in the Congo. A poet, musician, and painter, Kurtz came to Africa imbued with humanitarian sentiments, intending to bring enlightenment to "savage" Africans. But in the primeval African jungle, his other self, long repressed by European values, comes to the fore. Kurtz becomes a depraved tyrant who decorates the fence poles around his house with human heads. The charismatic Kurtz has made disciples of the villagers, who view him as a godlike figure; they heed his every word and, at his command, launch murderous raids against nearby villages for more ivory. Kurtz engages in mysterious ceremonies—Conrad leaves the nature of these ceremonies to the reader's imagination, but it is likely that they are human sacrifices—that contribute to his uncanny power over the Africans.

Heart of Darkness expressed Conrad's revulsion for avaricious European imperialists, who, in their quest for riches, plundered and destroyed African villages and impressed the natives into forced labor. Their greeed, callousness, and brutality belied the altruism that they claimed was their motivation for coming to Africa. *Heart of Darkness* is also a tale of moral deterioration. The forbidding jungle environment, far from the restraints of European civilization, and the repulsive scramble for riches disfigure Kurtz, who is transformed into a sadist driven by dark urges no longer buried within his unconscious. The wilderness "whispered to him things about himself which he did not know, things of which he had no conception till he took counsel with this great solitude—and the whisper had proved irresistibly fascinating."*

When the dying Kurtz cries out "The horror! The horror!" in what Conrad says is "that supreme moment of complete knowledge,"† was he referring to his own moral collapse? Civilization, as Freud maintained, is very fragile; only a thin barrier separates it from barbarism. Given the right circumstances, all human beings are capable of the moral disfigurement experienced by Kurtz. Thus "darkness" refers not only to the jungle interior but also to the destructive tendencies that are at the core of human nature.

---

*Joseph Conrad, *Heart of Darkness* (New York: Barnes and Noble, 1994), p. 102.
†Ibid, p. 123.

figures were Edouard Manet, Claude Monet, Camille Pissaro, Edgar Degas, and Pierre Auguste Renoir. Taking Pissaro's advice—"Don't proceed according to rules and principles but paint what you observe and feel"—impressionists tried to give their own immediate and personal impression of an object or an event. They tried to capture how movement, color, and light appear to the eye at a fleeting instant.

Intrigued by the impact that light has on objects, impressionists left their studios for the countryside, where they painted nature under an open sky. They used bold colors and drew marked contrasts between light and dark to reflect how objects in intense sunlight seem to shimmer against their background.

Besides landscapes, the impressionists painted railways, bridges, and boulevards. They also painted people—in dance halls, cafés, theaters, and public gardens. Impressionistic painters wanted to portray life as it was commonly experienced in a rapidly industrializing and urbanizing world. And they always tried to convey their momentary impression of an event or figure.

In the late 1880s and the 1890s, several artists went beyond impressionism. Called postimpressionists, they further revolutionized the artist's sense of space and color. Even more than the impressionists, they sought to make art a vivid emotional experience and to produce a personal impression of reality rather than a photographic copy of objects.

One of the luminaries of this later movement, Paul Cézanne (1839–1906) came to Paris, the center of the Western art world, from the south of France. In 1882, he returned to the region of his birth, where he painted its natural scenery. By rigorously analyzing his own perception of objects, he made his way of seeing them the real subject of his paintings. When depicting objects in a group, Cézanne deliberately distorted perspective, subordinating the appearance of an individual object to the requirements of the total design. Cézanne tried to demonstrate that an object, when placed together with other objects, is seen differently than when it stands alone. His concern with form and design influenced the cubists (see below).

No longer bound by classical art forms, artists examined non-Western art, searching there for new forms of beauty and new ways of expression. The large number of artifacts and art objects from Asia, Africa, and the Pacific area coming into European capitals as souvenirs of imperialist ventures sparked interest in non-Western art, as did the finds of anthropologists and ethnographers. Paul Gauguin (1848–1903) saw beauty in carvings and fabrics made by such technologically primitive people as the Marquesans of Polynesia. He also discovered that art did not depend on skilled craftsmanship for its power. Very simple, even primitive, means of construction could produce works of great beauty.

A successful Parisian stockbroker, Gauguin abandoned the marketplace for art. He came to view bourgeois civilization as artificial and rotten. By severing human beings from the power of their own feelings, industrial civilization blunted the creative expression of the imagination and prevented people from attaining a true understanding of themselves. For these reasons, Gauguin fled to Tahiti. On this picturesque island, which was largely untouched by European ways, he hoped to discover humanity's original nature, without the distortion and corruption of modern civilization.

The postimpressionists produced a revolution not only of space but also of color, as exemplified by Vincent van Gogh (1853–1890). The son of a Dutch minister, van Gogh was a lonely, tortured, and impetuous soul. For a short period, he served as a lay preacher among desperately poor coal miners. When he moved to Paris in 1886, van Gogh came under the influence of the French impressionists. Desiring to use color in a novel way—his own way—van Gogh left Paris for the Mediterranean countryside, where he hoped to experience a new vision of sunlight, sky, and earth. Van Gogh used purer, brighter colors than artists had used before. He also recognized that color, like other formal qualities, could itself act as a language. He believed that the "real" color of an object does not necessarily express the artist's experience. Artists, according to van Gogh, should seek to paint things not as they are, but as the artists feel them. In *The Starry Night* he conveys his vision of a night sky not with tiny points of lights but with exploding and whirling stars in a vast universe, overwhelming the huddled dwellings built by human beings. The foreboding dark cypress intrudes into the sky's turbulence of intense yellow lights.

Practically unknown in his lifetime, van Gogh's art became extremely influential soon after his death. One of the first artists to be affected by his style was the Norwegian Edvard Munch (1863–1944), who discovered van Gogh's use of color while in Paris. In *The Dance of Life*, for example, Munch used strong, simple lines and intense color to explore unexpressed sexual stresses and conflicts. In *The Scream*, he deliberately distorted the human face and the sky, ground, and water to portray terror.

After the postimpressionists, art moved still farther away from reproducing exact likenesses of physical objects or human beings. Increasingly, artists sought to penetrate the deepest recesses of the unconscious, which they saw as the source of creativity and the abode of a higher truth. Paul Klee (1879–1940), a prominent twentieth-century

THE STARRY NIGHT (1889), BY VINCENT VAN GOGH. Van Gogh experienced wide mood swings—from extreme agitation to melancholy. His tumultuous temperament found expression in his paintings. *The Starry Night* conveys van Gogh's impression of a night sky. (*The Museum of Modern Art, New York. Acquired through the Lillie P. Bliss Bequest.*)

artist, described modern art as follows: "Each [artist] should follow where the pulse of his own heart leads. . . . Our pounding heart drives us down, deep down to the source of all. What springs from this source, whether it may be called dream, idea or phantasy—must be taken seriously."[41]

In Germany, the tendency to use color for its power to express psychological forces continued in the work of artists known as the German expressionists. In Ernst Ludwig Kirchner's (1880–1938) *Reclining Nude* of 1909, strong, acid yellows and greens evoke feelings of tension, stress, and isolation. Kirchner also used bold, rapid lines to define flat shapes, a technique borrowed from folk art and from non-Western native traditions.

In France, another group of avant-garde artists, the *fauves* (wild beasts), used lines, color, and form with great freedom to create new means of personal expression. Henri Matisse (1869–1954), the leading fauvist painter, freed color from every restriction. He painted broad areas with stunning pigment unrelated to the real colors of the subject. His novel use of color and design aroused a violent reaction. After examining the works of the fauves, a hostile French critic wrote: "What is presented here . . . has nothing to do with painting; some formless confusion of colors, blue, red, yellow, green, the barbaric and naive spirit of the child who plays with the box of colors he has just got as a Christmas present."[42] Rebelling against new currents in painting, critics failed to recognize the originality and genius of the fauves.

Between 1909 and 1914, a new style, called cubism, was developed by Pablo Picasso (1881–1973) and Georges Braque (1882–1963). They explored the interplay between the flat

Harmony in Red (1908), by Henri Matisse. In this early example of French fauvism, Matisse broke away from the representational renderings of his predecessors and set the tone for much of twentieth-century expressive painting. His use of line, color, and rhythmic motifs transforms the visual surface into brilliant designs and establishes a new pictorial language. (*The State Hermitage Museum, St. Petersburg.*)

world of the canvas and the three-dimensional world of visual perception. Like the postimpressionists, they sought to paint a reality deeper than what the eye sees at first glance. Cubist art presents objects from multiple viewpoints simultaneously. The numerous fragmentary images of cubist art make one aware of the complex experience of seeing. One art historian describes cubism as follows: "The cubist is not interested in usual representational standards. It is as if he were walking around the object he is analyzing, as one is free to walk around a piece of sculpture for successive views. But he must represent all these views at once."[43]

The colors used in early cubist art are deliberately banal, and the subjects represented are ordinary objects from everyday life. Picasso and Braque wanted to eliminate eye-catching color and intriguing subject matter so that the viewer would focus on the process of seeing itself.

In *Les Demoiselles d'Avignon*, Picasso painted five nudes. In each instance, the body is distorted in defiance of classical and Renaissance standards of beauty. The masklike faces show Picasso's debt to African art and, along with the angular shapes, deprive the subjects of individuality and personality. The head of the squatting figure combines a profile with a full face: Picasso's attempt to present multiple aspects of an object at the same time. The cubists' effort to depict something from multiple perspectives rather than from a single point in space and their need to deliberately deform objects in order to achieve this effect mark a radical break with artistic conventions.

Throughout the period 1890 to 1914, avant-garde artists were de-emphasizing subject matter

Les Demoiselles d'Avignon (1907), by Pablo Picasso. Picasso's painting exemplified new trends in art. Rather than conforming with classical and Renaissance conventions of representation, Picasso aimed to interpret visual reality in accord with his own sensibilities. (*Collection, The Museum of Modern Art, New York. Acquired through the Lillie P. Bliss Bequest.*)

and stressing the expressive power of such formal qualities as line, color, and space. It is not surprising that some artists finally began to create works that did not refer to anything seen in the real world. Piet Mondrian (1872–1944), a Dutch artist, came to Paris shortly before World War I. There he saw the cubist art of Picasso and Braque. By design, cubist paintings lacked visual depth; all the objects portrayed seemed to be contained within a space only a few inches deep. Cubists also reduced subject matter to insignificance. It seemed to Mondrian that the next step was to get rid of subject matter entirely. His painting *Broadway Boogie-Woogie*, for example, is devoid of representational content. Looking at Mondrian's paintings is a kinesthetic experience; the viewer senses the delicate interplay of balances and counterweights within the painting. By eliminating any reference to the visible world, Mondrian helped to inaugurate abstract art.

Another founder of abstract art was Wassily Kandinsky (1866–1944), a Russian residing in Germany. Kandinsky gradually removed all traces of the physical world from his paintings, creating a nonobjective art that bears no resemblance to the natural world. In declaring that he "painted . . . subconsciously in a state of strong inner tension,"[44] Kandinsky explicitly expressed a distinguishing quality of modern Western art: the artist's private inner experience of the world.

Black Weft, by Wassily Kandinsky. Kandinsky was a leader of a group of avant-garde painters in Munich, called *Der Blaue Reiter* (The Blue Rider), whose goal was to challenge the limits of artistic expression. In this painting, he has removed virtually all traces of the physical world, thereby creating a nonobjective artwork that bears little, or no, resemblance to the natural world. (*Musée des Beaux-Arts, Nantes, France/RMN/Art Resource, NY.*)

The revolution in art that took place near the turn of the twentieth century is reverberating still. These masters of modern art continue to inspire with their passion and vision. By breaking with the Renaissance view of the world as inherently orderly and rational and by stressing the power of the imagination, modern artists opened up new possibilities for artistic expression. They also exemplified the growing power and appeal of the nonrational in European life.

Modern Physics

Until the closing years of the nineteenth century, the view of the universe held by the Western mind was based mainly on the classical physics of Isaac Newton (1642–1727). This view included the following principles: (1) Time, space, and matter are objective realities, existing independently of the observer. (2) The universe is a giant machine whose parts obey strict laws of cause and effect. (3) The atom, indivisible and solid, is the basic unit of matter. (4) Heated bodies emit radiation in continuous waves. (5) Through further investigation, it will be possible to gain complete knowledge of the physical universe. Between the 1890s and the 1920s, this view of the universe was shattered by a second Scientific Revolution.

The discovery of x-rays by Wilhelm Konrad Roentgen in 1895, of radioactivity by Henri Bequerel in 1896, and of the electron by J. J. Thomson in 1897 led scientists to abandon the conception of the atom as a solid and indivisible particle. Rather than resembling a billiard ball, they said, the atom consists of a nucleus of tightly packed protons, separated from orbiting electrons by empty space.

In 1900, Max Planck, a German physicist, proposed the quantum theory, which holds that a heated body radiates energy not in a continuous unbroken stream, as had been believed, but in intermittent spurts, or jumps, called quanta. Planck's theory of discontinuity in energy radiation challenged a cardinal principle of classical physics: that action in nature was strictly continuous.

In 1905, Albert Einstein, a German-Swiss physicist of Jewish lineage, substantiated and elaborated Planck's theory by suggesting that all forms of radiant energy—light, heat, x-rays—move through space in discontinuous packets of energy. Then, in 1913, Niels Bohr, a Danish scientist, applied Planck's theory of energy quanta to the interior of the atom and discovered that the Newtonian laws of motion could not fully explain what happens to electrons orbiting an atomic nucleus.

As physicists explored the behavior of the atom further, it became apparent that its nature was fundamentally elusive and unpredictable. They soon observed that radioactive atoms throw off particles and transform themselves from atoms of one element into atoms of an entirely different element. But the transformation of a single atom in a mass of radioactive material could not be predicted according to inexorable laws of cause and effect. For example, it is known that over a period of 1,620 years half the atoms of the element radium decay and transform themselves into atoms of another element. It is impossible, however, to know when a particular atom in a lump of radium will undergo this transformation. Scientists can make accurate predictions only about the behavior of an aggregate of radium atoms. The transformation of any given radium atom is the result of random chance rather than of any known physical law. The fact that we cannot predict when a particular radioactive atom will decay calls into question the notion of classical physics that physical nature proceeds in an orderly fashion in accordance with strict laws of cause and effect.

Newtonian physics says that, given certain conditions, we can predict what will follow. For example, if an airplane is flying north at four hundred miles per hour, we can predict its exact position two hours from now, assuming that the plane does not alter its course or speed. Quantum mechanics teaches that in the subatomic realm we cannot predict with certainty what will take place; we can only say that, given certain conditions, it is probable that a certain event will follow. This principle of uncertainty was developed in 1927 by the German scientist Werner Heisenberg, who showed that it is impossible to determine at one and the same time both an electron's precise speed and its position. The science writer Alan E. Nourse explains:

> *[Heisenberg showed] that the very act of attempting to examine an electron any more closely in order to be more certain of where it was and what it was doing at a given instant* would itself alter where the electron was and what it was doing at the instant in question. *Heisenberg, in effect, was saying that in dealing with the behavior of electrons and other elementary particles the laws of cause and effect do not and cannot apply, that all we can do is make predictions about them on the basis of probability and not a very high degree of probability at that. . . . [T]he more certain we try to become about a given electron's* position *at a given instant, the wider the limits of probability we must accept with regard to what its* momentum *[speed] is at the same time, and vice versa. The more closely either one property of the electron or the other is examined, the more closely we approach certainty with regard to one property or the other, the more wildly uncertain the other property becomes. And since an electron can really only be fully described in terms of both its position and its momentum at any given instant,* it becomes utterly impossible to describe an electron at all *in terms of absolute certainties. We can describe it only in terms of uncertainties or probabilities.*[45]

In the small-scale world of the electron, we enter a universe of uncertainty, probability, and statistical relationships. No improvement in measurement techniques will dispel this element of chance

ALBERT EINSTEIN (1879–1955), A PRINCIPAL ARCHITECT OF MODERN PHYSICS. Forced to flee Nazi Germany, Einstein became a U.S. citizen. He was appointed to the Institute for Advanced Study at Princeton, New Jersey. (AP/Wide World.)

and provide us with complete knowledge of the universe.

Einstein himself could not accept a core principle of modern physics—that complete comprehension of reality was unattainable. Nevertheless, his theory of relativity was instrumental in shaping modern physics, for it altered classical conceptions of space and time. Newtonian physics had viewed space as a distinct physical reality, a stationary and motionless medium through which light traveled and matter moved. Time was deemed to be a fixed and rigid framework, the same for all observers and existing independently of human experience. For Einstein, however, neither space nor time had an independent existence, and neither could be divorced from human experience. When asked to explain briefly the essentials of relativity, Einstein replied: "It was formerly believed that if all material things disappeared out of the universe, time and space would be left. According to the relativity theory, however, time and space disappear together with the things."[46]

Contrary to all previous thinking, relativity theory holds that time differs for two observers traveling at different speeds. Imagine twin brothers involved in space exploration, one as an astronaut, the other as a rocket designer who never leaves earth. The astronaut takes off in the most advanced spaceship yet constructed, one that achieves a speed close to the maximum attainable in our universe—the speed of light. After traveling several trillion miles, the spaceship turns around and returns to earth. According to the experience of the ship's occupant, the whole trip took about two years. But when the astronaut lands on earth, he finds totally changed conditions. For one thing, his brother has long since died, for according to earth's calendars some two hundred years have elapsed since the rocket ship set out on its journey. Such an occurrence seemed to defy all commonsense experience, yet experiments supported Einstein's claims.

Motion, too, is relative. The only way we can describe the motion of one body is to compare it with another moving body. This means that there is no motionless, absolute, fixed frame of reference anywhere in the universe. The science writer Isaac Asimov illustrates Einstein's theory of the relativity of motion:

> *Suppose we on the earth were to observe a strange planet ("Planet X"), exactly like our own in size and mass, go whizzing past us at 163,000 miles per second relative to ourselves. If we could measure its dimensions as it shot past, we would find that it was foreshortened by 50 per cent in the direction of its motion. It would be an ellipsoid rather than a sphere and would, on further measurement, seem to have twice the mass of the earth.*
>
> *Yet to an inhabitant of Planet X, it would seem that he himself and his own planet were motionless. The earth would seem to be moving past him at 163,000 miles per second, and it would appear to have an ellipsoidal shape and twice the mass of* his *planet.*
>
> *One is tempted to ask which planet would really be foreshortened and doubled in mass, but the only possible answer is: that depends on the frame of reference.*[47]

In his famous equation, $E = mc^2$, Einstein showed that matter and energy are not separate categories but two different expressions of the same physical entity. The source of energy is matter, and the source of matter is energy. Tiny quantities of matter could be transformed into staggering amounts of energy. The atomic age was dawning.

The discoveries of modern physics transformed the world of classical physics. Whereas nature had been regarded as something outside the individual—an objective reality existing independently of ourselves—modern physics teaches that our position in space and time determines what we mean by reality and that our very presence affects reality itself. When we observe a particle with our measuring instruments, we are interfering with it, knocking it off its course; we are participating in reality. Nor is nature fully knowable, as the classical physics of Newton had presumed. Uncertainty, probability, and even mystery are inherent in the universe.

We have not yet felt the full impact of modern physics, but there is no doubt that it has been part of a revolution in human perceptions. As Jacob Bronowski, a student of science and culture, concludes,

> *One aim of the physical sciences has been to give an exact picture of the material world. One achievement of physics in the twentieth century has been to prove that that aim is unattainable. . . . There is no absolute knowledge. . . . All information is imperfect. We have to treat it with humility. That is the human condition; and that is what quantum physics says. . . . The Principle of Uncertainty . . . fixed once and for all the realization that all knowledge is limited.*[48]

That we cannot fully comprehend nature must inevitably make us less certain about our theories of human nature, government, history, and morality. That scientists must qualify and avoid absolutes has no doubt made us more cautious and tentative in framing conclusions about the individual and society. Like Darwin's theory of human origins, Freud's theory of human nature, and the transformation of classical space by modern artists, the modifications of the Newtonian picture by modern physicists contributed to the sense of uncertainty and disorientation that characterized the twentieth century.

The Enlightenment Tradition in Disarray

Most nineteenth-century thinkers carried forward the spirit of the Enlightenment, particularly in its emphasis on science and its concern for individual liberty and social reform. In the tradition of the philosophes, nineteenth-century thinkers regarded science as humanity's greatest achievement and believed that through reason society could be reformed. The spread of parliamentary government and the extension of education, along with the many advances in science and technology, seemed to confirm the belief of the philosophes in humanity's future progress.

But at the same time, the Enlightenment tradition was being undermined. In the early nineteenth century, the romantics revolted against the Enlightenment's rational-scientific spirit in favor of human will and feelings. Romantic nationalists valued the collective soul of the nation—ancient traditions rooted in a hoary and dateless past—over reason and individual freedom. Conservatives emphasized the limitations of reason and attacked the political agenda of the Enlightenment and the French Revolution.

In the closing decades of the nineteenth century, the Enlightenment tradition was challenged by Social Darwinists, who glorified violence and saw conflict between individuals and between nations as a law of nature and the avenue to progress. They considered the right of the powerful to predominate to be a right of nature beyond good and evil, and they castigated humanitarianism as weakness. Orthodox Marxists continued to teach that conflict between the proletariat and the industrial bourgeoisie was necessary for humanity's progress. Echoing Sorel, several thinkers trumpeted the use of force in social and political controversies. A number of thinkers, rejecting the Enlightenment view of people as fundamentally rational, held that subconscious drives and impulses govern human behavior more than reason does. If this is so, then the individual is not essentially autonomous, master of his or her own self. Several of these thinkers urged celebrating and extolling the irrational, which they regarded as the true essence of human beings and life. They glorified an irrational vitality, or Nietzsche's will to power, which transcended considerations of good and evil. "I have always considered myself a voice of what I believe to be a greater renaissance—the revolt of the soul against the intellect—now beginning in the world," wrote the Irish poet William Butler Yeats.[49] German advocates of "life philosophy" explicitly called the mind "the enemy of the soul."

Even theorists who studied the individual and society in a scientific way pointed out that below a surface of rationality lies a substratum of irrationality, which constitutes a deeper reality. The conviction was growing that reason was a puny instrument in comparison with the volcanic strength of nonrational impulses, that these impulses pushed people toward destructive behavior and made political life precarious, and that the nonrational did not bend very much to education. The Enlightenment's image of the autonomous individual who makes rational decisions after weighing the choices (a fundamental premise of liberalism and democracy) no longer seemed tenable. Often the individual was not the master of his or her own person; human freedom was limited by human nature.

Liberalism was also undermined by theorists who rejected the idea of natural rights. The view that all individuals are born with inalienable rights had provided the philosophical basis of classical liberalism. It was now argued, however, that natural rights were not a law of nature or a higher truth; rather, they were simply a human creation, a product of a specific set of circumstances at a particular stage in history, notably the emergence of the bourgeoisie. Could commitment to parliamentary government, the rule of law, and other liberal-democratic institutions and practices survive this assault on the core principle of liberalism?

Other theorists argued that ideas of right, truth, and justice do not have an independent value but are merely tools used by elites in their struggle to gain and maintain power. Opponents of liberalism and democracy utilized the theory of elites advanced by Pareto, as well as the new stress on human irrationality, as proof that the masses were incapable of self-government and that they had to be led by their betters. Many intellectuals of the right employed the new social theories to devalue the individualist and rational bases of liberal democracy bequeathed by the Enlightenment.

At the beginning of the twentieth century, the dominant mood remained that of confidence in Europe's future progress and in the values of European civilization. However, certain disquieting trends were already evident; they would grow to crisis proportions in succeeding decades. Although few people may have realized it, the Enlightenment tradition was in disarray.

The thinkers of the Enlightenment believed in an orderly, machinelike universe; the operation of natural law and natural rights in the social world; objective rules that gave form and structure to artistic productions; the essential rationality and goodness of the individual; and science and technology as instruments of progress. This coherent world-view, which had produced an attitude of certainty, security, and optimism, was in the process of dissolution by the early twentieth century. The commonsense Newtonian picture of the physical universe, with its inexorable laws of cause and effect, was fundamentally altered; the belief in natural rights and objective standards governing morality was undermined; and rules and modes of expression that were at the very heart of Western esthetics were abandoned. Confidence in human rationality and goodness weakened. Furthermore, science and technology were accused of forging a mechanical, bureaucratic, and materialistic world that stifled intuition and feelings, thereby diminishing the self. To redeem the self, some thinkers urged a heroic struggle, which was easily channeled into primitive nationalism and martial crusades. Thus, the radical attack on the moral and intellectual values of the Enlightenment, as well as on liberalism and democracy, included the denunciation of reason, the exaltation of force, a quest for the heroic, and a yearning for a new authority. It constitutes the intellectual background of the fascist movements that emerged after World War I. Holding the Enlightenment tradition in contempt and fascinated by power and violence, many people, including intellectuals, would exalt fascist ideas and lionize fascist leaders.

In the early twentieth century, then, the universe no longer seemed an orderly system, an intelligible whole; it seemed something fundamentally inexplicable. Human nature, too, seemed intrinsically unfathomable and problematic. To the question "Who is man?" Greek philosophers, medieval scholastics, Renaissance humanists, and eighteenth-century philosophes had provided a coherent and intelligible answer. By the early twentieth century, the old spiritual and intellectual certainties were rapidly eroding, Western intellectuals no longer possessed a clear idea of who the human being was. Individuals had become strangers to themselves, and life seemed devoid of an overriding purpose. Nietzsche sensed this:

> *Disintegration characterizes this time, and thus uncertainty: nothing stands firmly on its feet or on a hard faith in itself; one lives for tomorrow as the day after tomorrow is dubious. Everything on our way is slippery and dangerous, and the ice that still supports us has become thin: all of us feel the warm, uncanny breath of the thawing wind; where we still walk, soon no one will be able to walk.*[50]

This radical new disorientation led some intellectuals to feel alienated from Western civilization and even hostile toward it. At the beginning of the twentieth century, says the Dutch historian Jan Romein, "European man, who only half a century earlier had believed he was about to embrace an almost totally safe existence, and paradoxically enough did so in many ways, found himself before the dark gate of uncertainty."[51]

When the new century began, most Europeans were optimistic about the future, some even holding that European civilization was on the threshold of a golden age. Few suspected that European civilization would soon be gripped by a crisis that threatened its very survival. The powerful forces of irrationalism, which had been celebrated by Nietzsche, analyzed by Freud, and creatively expressed in modernist culture, would erupt with devastating fury in twentieth-century political life, particularly in the form of extreme nationalism and racism, which extolled violence. Disoriented and disillusioned people searching for new certainties and values would turn to political ideologies that openly rejected reason, lauded war, and scorned the inviolability of the human person. Dictators, utilizing the insights into the unconscious and the nonrational offered by Freud and social theorists, succeeded in manipulating the minds of people to an unprecedented degree.

These currents began to form at the end of the nineteenth century, but World War I brought them together in a tidal wave. World War I accentuated the questioning of established norms and the dissolution of Enlightenment certainties and caused many people to regard Western civilization as dying and beyond recovery. The war not only exacerbated the spiritual crisis of the preceding generation, but also shattered Europe's political and social order. It gave birth to totalitarian ideologies that nearly obliterated the legacy of the Enlightenment. The world wars of the twentieth century, with their millions of dead and mutilated, and the totalitarian experiments, which trampled on human dignity, bore out Nietzsche's warning that in a nihilistic world all is permitted.

❖ ❖ ❖

Notes

1. Friedrich Nietzsche, *Twilight of the Idols* and *The Anti-Christ,* trans. R. J. Hollingdale (New York: Penguin, 1972), pp. 117–118.
2. Friedrich Nietzsche, *The Will to Power,* trans. Walter Kaufmann and R. J. Hollingdale, ed. Walter Kaufmann (New York: Vintage Books, 1968), pp. 458–459.
3. Ibid., pp. 383–384.
4. Friedrich Nietzsche, *The Genealogy of Morals,* Essay I, sec. 13 (New York: Modern Library, 1954), p. 656.
5. Quoted in R. J. Hollingdale, *Nietzsche* (London: Routledge & Kegan Paul, 1973), p. 82.
6. Nietzsche, *Will to Power,* p. 397.
7. Ibid., p. 518.
8. Nietzsche, *Anti-Christ,* p. 116.
9. Nietzsche, *Will to Power,* p. 386.
10. Janko Lavrin, *Nietzsche* (New York: Charles Scribner's Sons, 1971), p. 113.

11. Fyodor Dostoevski, *Notes from Underground and The Grand Inquisitor,* trans. Ralph E. Matlaw (New York: Dutton, 1960), pp. 20, 23.
12. Ibid., p. 25.
13. Quoted in Peter Gay, *Freud: A Life for Our Time* (New York: Norton, 1988), p. xvii.
14. Sigmund Freud, *The Future of an Illusion,* trans. W. D. Robeson-Scott, rev. James Strachey (Garden City, N.Y.: Doubleday, 1964), p. 87.
15. Sigmund Freud, *A General Introduction to Psychoanalysis,* trans. Joan Riviere (Garden City, N.Y.: Garden City Publishing Co., 1943), p. 252.
16. Sigmund Freud, "Delusions and Dreams in Jensen's 'Gradiva,'" trans. James Strachey, in *The Standard Edition of the Complete Psychological Work of Sigmund Freud,* 2nd ed. (London: Hogarth Press, 1959), 9:8.
17. Sigmund Freud, "An Autobiographical Study," ibid., 20:60.
18. Sigmund Freud, *Civilization and Its Discontents* (New York: Norton, 1961), p. 62.
19. Ibid., p. 58.
20. Ibid.
21. Ibid., p. 59.
22. Ibid., p. 61.
23. Ibid., p. 59.
24. Ibid., p. 69.
25. Émile Durkheim, *Suicide: A Study in Sociology,* trans. John Spaulding and George Simpson (New York: Free Press, 1951), p. 391.
26. Gustave Le Bon, *The Crowd: A Study of the Popular Mind* (New York: Viking, 1960), p. 3.
27. Ibid., pp. 14–15.
28. Ibid., p. 23.
29. Ibid., p. 30.
30. Ibid., p. 32.
31. Ibid., p. 7.
32. Ibid., p. 118.
33. Quoted in Robert A. Nye, *The Origin of Crowd Psychology* (Beverly Hills, Calif.: Sage, 1975), p. 178.
34. Quoted in Robert Nisbet, *The Social Philosophers* (New York: Crowell, 1973), p. 441.
35. Irving Howe, ed., *The Idea of the Modern in Literature and the Arts* (New York: Horizon Press, 1967), p. 16.
36. Daniel Bell, *The Cultural Contradictions of Capitalism* (New York: Basic Books, 1976), p. 110.
37. Quoted in Howe, *Idea of the Modern,* p. 15.
38. Excerpted in Herschel B. Chipp, ed., *Theories of Modern Art* (Berkeley: University of California Press, 1968), p. 146.
39. Bell, *Cultural Contradictions,* pp. 110, 112.
40. Excerpted in Piero Weiss and Richard Taruskin, eds., *Music in the Western World: A History in Documents* (New York: Schirmer Books, 1984), p. 428.
41. Paul Klee, *On Modern Art,* trans. Paul Findlay (London: Faber & Faber, 1948), p. 51.
42. Quoted in Alfred H. Barr, Jr., ed., *Masters of Modern Art* (New York: Museum of Modern Art, 1954), p. 46.
43. John Canaday, *Mainstreams of Modern Art* (New York: Holt, 1961), p. 458.
44. Quoted in G. H. Hamilton, *Painting and Sculpture in Europe, 1880–1940* (Baltimore: Penguin Books, 1967), p. 133.
45. Alan E. Nourse, *Universe, Earth, and Atom* (New York: Harper & Row, 1969), pp. 554–555, 560.
46. Quoted in A. E. E. McKenzie, *The Major Achievements of Science* (New York: Cambridge University Press, 1960), 1:310.
47. Isaac Asimov, *Asimov's Guide to Science* (New York: Basic Books, 1972), pp. 354–355.
48. Jacob Bronowski, *The Ascent of Man* (Boston: Little, Brown, 1973), p. 353.
49. Quoted in Roland N. Stromberg, *Redemption by War* (Lawrence: Regents Press of Kansas, 1982), p. 65.
50. Nietzsche, *Will to Power,* p. 40.
51. Jan Romein, *The Watershed of Two Eras,* trans. Arnold J. Pomerans (Middletown, Conn.: Wesleyan University Press, 1978), p. 658.

Suggested Reading

Aschheim, Steven E., *The Nietzsche Legacy in Germany, 1890–1990* (1992). How Germans, including Nazis, interpreted Nietzsche.

Baumer, Franklin, *Modern European Thought* (1977). A well-informed study of modern thought.

Bradbury, Malcolm, and James McFarlane, eds., *Modernism, 1890–1930* (1974). Essays on various phases of modernism; valuable bibliography.

Gay, Peter, *Freud: A Life for Our Times* (1988). A highly recommended study.

Hamilton, G. H., *Painting and Sculpture in Europe, 1880–1940* (1967). An authoritative work.

Hollingdale, R. J., *Nietzsche* (1973). A lucid study.

Hughes, H. Stuart, *Consciousness and Society* (1958). Good on social thinkers.

Kaufmann, Walter, *Nietzsche* (1956). An excellent analysis of Nietzsche's thought.

Kolocotroni, Vassiliki, Jane Goldman, and Olga Taxidou, eds., *Modernism: An Anthology of Sources and Documents* (1998). Selections covering the breadth and variety of modernism.

Masur, Gerhard, *Prophets of Yesterday* (1961). Studies in European culture, 1890–1914.

Monaco, Paul, *Modern European Culture and Consciousness, 1870–1980* (1983). A useful survey.

Nelson, Benjamin, ed., *Freud and the Twentieth Century* (1957). A valuable collection of essays.

Roazen, Paul, *Freud's Political and Social Thought* (1968). The implications of Freudian psychology.

Rosenthal, Bernice, ed., *Nietzsche in Russia* (1986). Essays detailing Nietzsche's impact on Russian thought; good introduction by the editor.

Stromberg, Roland N., *An Intellectual History of Modern Europe* (1975). A fine text.

Zeitlin, I. M., *Ideology and the Development of Sociological Theory* (1968). Examines in detail the thought of major shapers of sociological theory.

Review Questions

1. What were Nietzsche's attitudes toward Christianity and democracy?
2. Why were the Nazis drawn to Nietzsche's thought?
3. What does Dostoevski's Underground Man mean when he says that life is more than "simply extracting square roots"?
4. How did Bergson reflect the growing irrationalism of the age?
5. How did Sorel show the political potential of the nonrational?
6. In what way was Freud a child of the Enlightenment? How did he differ from the philosophes?
7. For Durkheim, what constituted the crisis of modern society? How did he try to resolve it?
8. What do you think of Pareto's judgment that the masses in a democratic state are not really influenced by rational argument?
9. According to Le Bon, how are individuals transformed once they become part of a crowd? How does the leader sway the crowd?
10. For Weber, what was the terrible paradox of reason?
11. What were the standards of esthetics that had governed Western literature and art since the Renaissance? How did the modernist movement break with these standards?
12. Describe the view of the universe held by westerners around 1880. How was this view altered by modern physics?
13. In what ways was the Enlightenment tradition in disarray by the early twentieth century?

Part Six

World Wars and Totalitarianism: The West in Crisis

1914–1945

1910

1920

1930

1940

Politics and Society	Thought and Culture
World War I (1914–1918) United States declares war on Germany (1917) Bolshevik Revolution in Russia (1917) Wilson announces his Fourteen Points (1918) Treaty of Versailles (1919)	Bohr: Quantum theory of atomic stucture (1913) Stravinsky, *The Rite of Spring* (1913) Pareto, *Treatise on General Sociology* (1916) Spengler, *The Decline of the West* (1918, 1922) Dadaism in art (1915–1924) Barth, *The Epistle to the Romans* (1919)
Mussolini seizes power in Italy (1922) First Five-Year Plan starts rapid industrialization in the Soviet Union (1928) Forced collectivization of agriculture in the Soviet Union (1929) Start of the Great Depression (1929)	Wittgenstein, *Tractatus Logico-Philosophicus* (1921–22) Eliot, *The Waste Land* (1922) Cassirer, *The Philosophy of Symbolic Forms* (1923–1929) Mann, *The Magic Mountain* (1924) Surrealism in art (c. 1925) Hitler, *Mein Kampf* (1925–26) Hemingway, *The Sun Also Rises* (1926) Benda, *The Treason of the Intellectuals* (1927) Heidegger, *Being and Time* (1927) Lawrence, *Lady Chatterley's Lover* (1928) Remarque, *All Quiet on the Western Front* (1929)
Hitler becomes chancellor of Germany (1933) Hitler sends troops into the Rhineland (1936) Rome-Berlin Axis (1936) Stalin orders mass purges in the Soviet Union (1936–38) Spanish Civil War (1936–1939) Franco establishes a dictatorship in Spain (1939) Nazi-Soviet Non-Aggression Pact (1939) German troops invade Poland: World War II begins (1939)	Freud, *Civilization and Its Discontents* (1930) Ortega y Gasset, *The Revolt of the Masses* (1930) Jaspers, *Man in the Modern Age* (1930) Jung, *Modern Man in Search of a Soul* (1933) Toynbee, *A Study of History* (1934–1961) Keynes, *The General Theory of Employment, Interest, and Money* (1936) Steinbeck, *The Grapes of Wrath* (1939)
Germany invades Belgium, Holland, Luxembourg, and France (1940) Japan attacks Pearl Harbor: United States enters war against Japan and Germany (1941) War in Europe ends (1945) United States drops atomic bombs on Japan; Japan surrenders (1945)	Hemingway, *For Whom the Bell Tolls* (1940) Koestler, *Darkness at Noon* (1941) Fromm, *Escape from Freedom* (1941) Camus, *The Stranger* (1942) Sartre, *Being and Nothingness* (1943) Orwell, *Animal Farm* (1945)

Chapter 29

World War I: The West in Despair

Trench Warfare. Soldiers in the trenches had to endure earsplitting bombardments from heavy artillery and attacks from the enemy's trenches. They also had to deal with rats, lice, mud, the stench of rotting corpses, and the wails of the wounded unable to be rescued from no man's land. (The Art Archive.)

■ **Aggravated Nationalist Tensions in Austria-Hungary**

■ **The German System of Alliances**
The New German Empire
Bismarck's Goals

■ **The Triple Entente**
Fear of Germany
German Reactions

■ **Drifting Toward War**
The Bosnian Crisis
Balkan Wars
Assassination of Francis Ferdinand
Germany Abets Austria
The Question of Responsibility

■ **War as Celebration**

■ **Stalemate in the West**

■ **Other Fronts**

■ **Collapse of the Central Powers**
American Entry
Germany's Last Offensive

■ **The Peace Conference**
Wilson's Hope for a New World
Problems of Peacemaking
The Settlement
Assessment and Problems

■ **The Russian Revolution of 1917**
Problems of the Provisional Government
Lenin and the Rise of Bolshevism
Lenin's Opportunity
The Bolsheviks Survive

■ **The War and European Consciousness**

Prior to 1914, the dominant mood in Europe was one of pride in the accomplishments of Western civilization and confidence in its future progress. Advances in science and technology, the rising standard of living, the spread of democratic institutions, and Europe's position of power in the world all contributed to a sense of optimism, as did the expansion of social reform and the increase in literacy for the masses. Furthermore, since the defeat of Napoleon (1815), Europe had avoided a general war, and since the Franco-Prussian War (1870–71), the Great Powers had not fought one another. Reflecting on the world he knew before World War I, the historian Arnold Toynbee recalled that his generation had

> *expected that life throughout the World would become more rational, more humane, and more democratic and that, slowly, but surely, political democracy would produce greater social justice. We had also expected that the progress of science and technology would make mankind richer, and that this increasing wealth would gradually spread from a minority to a majority. We had expected that all this would happen peacefully. In fact we thought that mankind's course was set for an earthly paradise, and that our approach towards this goal was predestined for us by historical necessity.*[1]

Few people recognized that the West's outward achievements masked inner turbulence that was propelling Western civilization toward a cataclysm. The European state system was failing. By 1914, national states, fueled by explosive nationalism, were grouped into alliances that faced each other with ever mounting hostility. Nationalist passions, overheated by the popular press and expansionist societies, poisoned international relations. Nationalist thinkers propagated pseudoscientific racial and Social Darwinist doctrines, which glorified conflict and justified the subjugation of other peoples. Committed to enhancing national power, statesmen lost sight of Europe as a community of nations sharing a common civilization. Caution and restraint gave way to belligerency in foreign relations.

Chronology 29.1 ❖ World War I

June 28, 1914	Archduke Francis Ferdinand of Austria assassinated at Sarajevo
August 4, 1914	Germans invade Belgium
August 1914	Russians invade East Prussia and are defeated by Germans at the battle of Tannenberg
September 1914	The first battle of the Marne saves Paris
April 1915–January 1916	Gallipoli campaign: Allies withdraw after suffering 252,000 casualties
May 1915	Italy enters war on Allies' side
Spring 1915	Germany launches offensive that forces Russia to abandon Galicia and most of Poland
February 1916	General Pétain leads French forces at Verdun; Germans fail to capture the fortress town
June 1916	Russians suffer more than a million casualties in an offensive against Austrian lines
July–November 1916	Battle of the Somme: Allies suffer 600,000 casualties
January 1917	Germany launches unrestricted submarine warfare
March 1917	Tsarist regime is overthrown
April 6, 1917	United States declares war on Germany
May 1917	General Pétain restores French army's morale and discipline
July–November 1917	British defeat at Passchendaele
Fall 1917	Italian defeat at Caporetto
November 1917	Bolsheviks, led by Lenin, take command in Russia
January 1918	U.S. president Woodrow Wilson announces his Fourteen Points
1918–1920	Civil war and foreign intervention in Russia
March 1918	Russia signs Treaty of Brest-Litovsk, losing territory to Germany and withdrawing from the war
March 21, 1918	Germans launch a great offensive to end the war
June 3, 1918	Germans advance to within fifty-six miles of Paris
August 8, 1918	British victory at Amiens
October 1918	Turks are forced to withdraw from the war after several British successes
November 3, 1918	Austria-Hungary signs armistice with the Allies
November 11, 1918	Germany signs armistice with the Allies, ending World War I
January 1919	Paris Peace Conference
June 28, 1919	Germany signs Treaty of Versailles

The failure of the European state system was paralleled by a cultural crisis. Some European intellectuals attacked the rational tradition of the Enlightenment and celebrated the primitive, the instinctual, and the irrational. Increasingly, young people felt drawn to philosophies of action that ridiculed liberal bourgeois values and viewed war as a purifying and ennobling experience. Colonial wars, colorfully portrayed in the popular press, ignited the imagination of bored factory workers and daydreaming students and reinforced a sense of duty and an urge for gallantry among young men. These "splendid" little colonial wars helped fashion an attitude that made war acceptable, if not laudable. Yearning to break loose from their ordinary lives and to embrace heroic values, many Europeans regarded violent conflict as the highest expression of individual and national life.

"This peace is so rotten," complained a young German writer, George Heym, in 1912, longing for "a war, even an unjust one."[2] That same year, a survey of French students between the ages of eighteen and twenty-five showed that

> *the most cultivated elite among [them] find in warfare an aesthetic ideal. . . . These young men impute to it all the beauty with which they are in love and of which they have been deprived in ordinary life. Above all, [W]ar, in their eyes is the occasion for the most noble of virtues . . . energy, mastery, and sacrifice for a cause which transcends ourselves."*[3]

The popular historian Heinrich von Treitschke (1834–1896), whose lectures influenced many students who were to rise to positions of importance in the German army and administration, expressed the prevailing mood: "Those who preach the nonsense about everlasting peace do not understand the life of the [German] race. . . . [T]o banish war from history would be to banish all progress."[4] Friedrich von Bernhardi (1849–1930), a German general and influential military writer, considered war "a biological necessity of the first importance." In *Germany and the Next War* (1911), he wrote:

> *War is a biological necessity of the first importance, a regulative element in the life of mankind which cannot be dispensed with, since without it an unhealthy development will follow, which excludes every advancement of the race, and therefore all real civilization. . . .*
>
> *The struggle for existance is, in the life of Nature, the basis of all healthy development. . . . The law of the stronger holds good everywhere. . . .The weaker succumb. . . .*
>
> *The knowledge, therefore, that war depends on biological laws leads to the conclusion that every attempt to exclude it from international relations must be demonstrably untenable.*[5]

Although technology was making warfare more brutal and dangerous, Europe retained a romantic illusion about combat. "Even if we end in ruin it was beautiful," exclaimed General Erich von Falkenhayn, the future chief of the German general staff, at the outbreak of World War I.[6]

Although Europe was seemingly progressing in the art of civilization, the mythic power of nationalism and the primitive appeal of conflict were driving European civilization to the abyss. Few people recognized the potential crisis—certainly not the statesmen whose reckless blundering allowed the Continent to stumble into war.

Aggravated Nationalist Tensions in Austria-Hungary

On June 28, 1914, a young terrorist, with the support of the secret Serbian nationalist society called Union or Death (more popularly known as the Black Hand), murdered Archduke Francis Ferdinand, heir to the throne of Austria-Hungary. Six weeks later, the armies of Europe were on the march; an incident in the Balkans had sparked a world war. An analysis of why Austria-Hungary felt compelled to attack Serbia and why the other powers became enmeshed in the conflict shows how explosive Europe was in 1914. And nowhere were conditions more volatile than in Austria-Hungary, the scene of the assassination.

With its numerous nationalities, each with its own history and traditions and often conflicting aspirations, Austria-Hungary stood in opposition to nationalism, the most powerful spiritual force of the age. Perhaps the supranational Austro-Hungarian Empire was obsolete in a world of states based on the principle of nationality. Dominated by Germans and Hungarians, the empire remained unable either to satisfy the grievances or to contain the nationalist aims of its numerous minorities, particularly the Czechs and South Slavs (Croats, Slovenes, and Serbs).

The more moderate leaders of the ethnic minorities did not call for secession from the empire. Nevertheless, heightened agitation among several nationalities, which increased in the decade before 1914, greatly perturbed Austrian leaders. The fear that the empire would be torn apart by rebellion caused Austria to react strongly to any country that fanned the nationalist feelings of its Slavic minorities. This policy increased the tensions between Austria and small Serbia, which had gained its independence from the Ottoman Empire in 1878.

Captivated by Western ideas of nationalism, the Serbs sought to create a Greater Serbia by uniting with their racial kin, the seven million or so South Slavs living in the Hapsburg Empire. The shrill appeals by Serbian nationalists made Austrian leaders fear that the South Slavs might press for secession. Some of these leaders, notably Foreign Minister Count Leopold von Berchtold and Field Marshal Franz Conrad von Hötzendorf, urged the destruction of Serbia to eliminate the threat to Austria's existence.

Another irritant to Austria-Hungary was Russian Pan-Slavism, which called for the solidarity of Russians with their Slavic cousins in eastern Europe—Poles, Czechs, Slovaks, South Slavs, and Bulgarians. Pan-Slavism was based on a mystic conception of the superiority of Slavic civilization to Western civilization and of Russia's special historic mission to liberate its kin from Austrian and Turkish rule. Although Russian Pan-Slavs were few and did not dictate foreign policy, they constituted a significant pressure group. Moreover, their provocative and semireligious proclamations frightened Austria-Hungary, which did not draw a sharp line between Pan-Slavic aspirations and official Russian policy.

The tensions stemming from the multinational character of the Austro-Hungarian Empire in an age of heightened nationalist feeling set off the explosion in 1914. Unable to solve its minority problems and fearful of Pan-Slavism and Pan-Serbism, Austria-Hungary felt itself in a life-or-death situation. This sense of desperation led it to lash out at Serbia after the assassination of Archduke Francis Ferdinand.

The German System of Alliances

Perhaps the war might have been avoided, or at least limited to Austria and Serbia, if Europe in 1914 had not been split into two hostile alliance systems. Such a situation contains inherent dangers. Counting on the support of its allies, a country might pursue a more provocative and reckless course and be less conciliatory during a crisis. Furthermore, a conflict between two states might spark a chain reaction that draws in the other powers, transforming a limited war into a general war. That is what happened after the assassination. This dangerous alliance system originated with Bismarck.

The New German Empire

With its unification in 1870–71, Germany became an international power of the first rank, upsetting the balance of power in Europe. For the first time since the wars of the French Revolution, one nation was in a position to dominate the European continent. How a united and powerful Germany would fit into European life was the crucial problem in the decades following the Franco-Prussian War.

To German nationalists, unification both fulfilled a national dream and pointed to an even more ambitious goal: extending German power in Europe and the world. As the nineteenth century drew to a close, German nationalism became more extreme. Believing that Germany must either grow or die, nationalists pressed the government to build a powerful navy, acquire colonies, gain a much greater share of the world's markets, and expand German interests and influence in Europe. Sometimes these goals were expressed in the language of Social Darwinism: nations are engaged in an eternal struggle for survival and domination.

Militant nationalists preached the special destiny of the German race and advocated German expansion in Europe and overseas. Decisive victo-

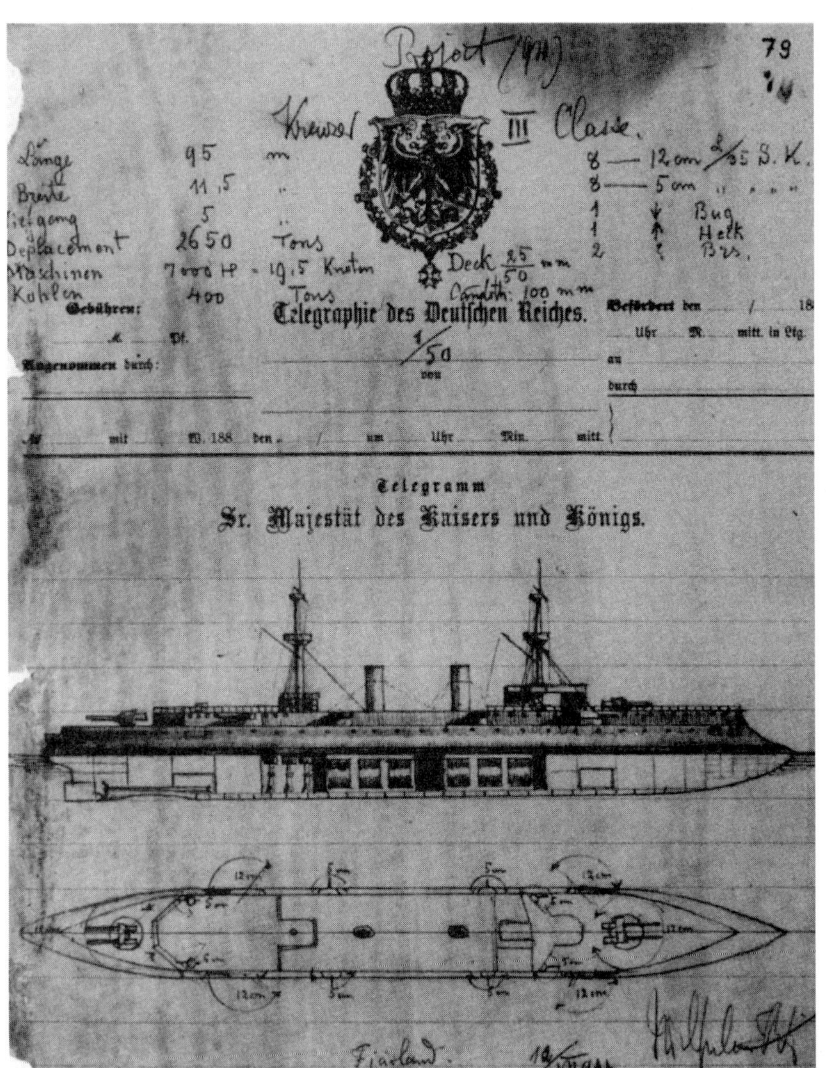

Blueprint for a Battle Cruiser. Emperor William II was determined to construct a great German navy that would challenge Britain's naval supremacy. This is his sketch for a battle cruiser. (*Bildarchiv Militärarchiv, Freiburg.*)

ries against Austria (1866) and France (1871), the formation of the German Reich, rapid industrialization, and the impressive achievements of German science and scholarship had molded a powerful and dynamic nation. Imbued with great expectations for the future, Germans became increasingly impatient to see the fatherland gain its "rightful" place in world affairs—an attitude that alarmed non-Germans.

Bismarck's Goals

Under Bismarck, who did not seek additional territory but wanted only to preserve the recently achieved unification, Germany pursued a moderate and cautious foreign policy. One of Bismarck's goals was to keep France isolated and friendless. Deeply humiliated by its defeat in the Franco-Prussian War and the loss of Alsace and Lorraine,

France found its nationalists yearning for a war of revenge against Germany. Victor Hugo expressed the "sacred anger" of the French: "France will have but one thought: to reconstitute her forces, gather her energy, . . . raise her young generation to form an army of the whole people. . . . Then one day she will be irresistible. Then she will take back Alsace-Lorraine."[7] Even though the French government, aware of Germany's strength, was unlikely to initiate a conflict, the issue of Alsace-Lorraine increased tensions between the two countries. Annexing the French provinces proved to be a serious blunder by Germany, for it made reconciliation impossible.

Bismarck also hoped to prevent a war between Russia and Austria-Hungary, since it could lead to German involvement, the breakup of Austria-Hungary, and Russian expansion in eastern Europe. To maintain peace and Germany's existing borders, Bismarck forged complex alliances. In the 1880s, he created the Triple Alliance, consisting of Germany, Austria-Hungary, and Italy, as well as an alliance with Russia.

A major weakness marred Germany's alliance system, however; Austria and Russia were potential enemies. Austria feared Russian ambitions in the Balkans and felt threatened by Russian Pan-Slavs. Bismarck knew that an alliance with Austria was essentially incompatible with Germany's treaty obligations to Russia. But he hoped that the arrangement would enable him to exercise a moderating influence over both eastern powers and prevent a war from erupting and upsetting the status quo. Besides, the treaty with Russia deprived France of a valuable ally.

Bismarck conducted foreign policy with restraint. He formed alliances not to conquer new lands, but to protect Germany from aggression by either France or Russia. His aim was to preserve order and stability in Europe, not to launch war. However, when the young Kaiser William II (1888–1918) ascended the throne, he clashed with the aging prime minister, and in 1890, Bismarck was forced to resign. Lacking Bismarck's diplomatic skills, his cool restraint, and his determination to keep peace in Europe, the new German leaders pursued a belligerent and imperialistic foreign policy in the ensuing years.

The first act of the new leadership was to let the treaty with Russia lapse, allowing Germany to give full support to Austria, which was deemed a more reliable ally. Whereas Bismarck had warned Austria to act with moderation and caution in the Balkans, his successors not only failed to hold Austria in check but actually encouraged Austrian aggression. This proved fatal to the peace of Europe.

The Triple Entente

Fear of Germany

When Germany broke with Russia in 1890, France was quick to take advantage of the situation. Worried by Germany's increasing military strength, expanding industries, growing population, and alliance with Austria and Italy, France eagerly courted Russia as an ally. It urged its bankers to invest in Russia, supplied weapons to the tsar, and arranged for the French and Russian fleets to exchange visits. In 1894, France and Russia entered into an alliance; the isolation forced on France by Bismarck ended.

Germany's growing military might also alarmed Great Britain. In addition, Germany had become a potent trade rival and strove to become a great colonial power as well—a goal demanded by German nationalists. But what troubled Britain most was Germany's decision to build a great navy. Germany was already the strongest land power on the Continent. Achieving naval parity with England would give Germany the potential to threaten Britain's overseas empire and to blockade the British Isles, depriving Britain of food and supplies. Germany's naval program was the overriding reason why Britain moved closer first to France and then to Russia. Germany's naval construction, designed to increase its stature as a Great Power but not really necessary for its security, was one indication that German leaders had abandoned Bismarck's policy of good sense. Eager to add the British as an ally and demonstrating superb diplomatic skill, France moved to end long-standing colonial disputes with Britain. The Entente Cordiale of 1904 accomplished this conciliation; England emerged from its self-imposed isolation.

Although the Franco-British understanding intensified German anxiety, Germany doubted that France and England, which had almost gone to war in 1898 in the Sudan, had overcome their deep animosities. Consequently, Chancellor Bernhard von Bülow (1849–1929) decided to test the

Entente Cordiale by provoking a crisis; he chose Morocco because earlier the British had resisted French imperialist designs there. He prodded a reluctant Kaiser William II to visit the Moroccan port of Tangier, a sign that Germany would support the Moroccan sultan against France. In January 1906, however, at the conference held in Algeciras, Spain, to resolve the crisis, Britain sided with France, which was given special rights in Morocco. Germany's efforts to disrupt the Anglo-French Entente Cordiale had failed.

Eager to counter Germany's Triple Alliance with a strong alliance of their own, French diplomats sought to ease tensions between their Russian ally and their new British friend. Two events convinced Russia to adopt a more conciliatory attitude toward Britain: a disastrous and unexpected defeat in the Russo-Japanese War of 1904–1905 and a working-class revolution in 1905. Shocked by defeat, its army bordering on disintegration, its workers restive, Russia was receptive to settling its imperial disputes with Britain over Persia, Tibet, and Afghanistan—a decision encouraged by France. In the Anglo-Russian Entente of 1907, as in the Anglo-French Entente Cordiale of 1904, the former rivals conducted themselves in a conciliatory, if not friendly, manner. In both instances, what engendered this spirit of cooperation was fear of Germany; both agreements represented a triumph for French diplomacy. The Triple Entente, however, was not a firm alliance, for there was no certainty that Britain, traditionally reluctant to send its troops to the Continent, would give more than diplomatic support to France and Russia in case of a showdown with Germany.

Europe was now broken into two hostile camps: the Triple Entente of France, Russia, and Britain and the Triple Alliance of Germany, Austria-Hungary, and Italy. The costly arms race and the maintenance of large standing armies by all the states except Britain served to increase fear and suspicion between the alliances.

German Reactions

Germany denounced the Triple Entente as a hostile anti-German coalition designed to encircle and crush Germany. To survive, Germany must break this ring. In the past, German arms had achieved unification; German military might would also end this threat to the fatherland. Considering Austria-Hungary its only reliable ally, Germany resolved to preserve the power and dignity of the Hapsburg Empire. If Austria-Hungary fell from the ranks of the Great Powers, Germany would have to stand alone against its enemies. At all costs, Austria-Hungary must not be weakened.

This assessment, however, suffered from dangerous miscalculations. First, Germany overstressed the hostile nature of the Triple Entente. In reality, France, Russia, and Britain drew closer together not to wage aggressive war against Germany but to protect themselves against burgeoning German military, industrial, and diplomatic power. Second, by linking German security to Austria, Germany greatly increased the chance of war. Growing more and more fearful of Pan-Serbism and Pan-Slavism, Austria might well decide that only a war could prevent its empire from disintegrating. Confident of German support, Austria would be more likely to resort to force; afraid of any diminution of Austrian power, Germany would be more likely to support Austria. In contrast to Bismarck, the new leadership thought not of restraining Austria but of strengthening it, by war if necessary.

Drifting Toward War

The Bosnian Crisis

After 1908, several crises tested the competing alliances. Particularly significant was the Bosnian affair, for it contained many of the ingredients that eventually ignited the war in 1914. The defeat by Japan in 1905 had diminished Russia's stature as a Great Power. The new Russian foreign minister, Alexander Izvolsky, hoped to gain a diplomatic triumph by compelling the Ottoman Turks to allow Russian warships to pass through the Dardanelles, fulfilling a centuries-old dream of extending Russian power into the Mediterranean. Izvolsky hoped that England and France, traditional opponents of Russia's Mediterranean ambitions but now Russia's allies, would not block the move. But certainly Austria would regard it as a hostile act.

Russia made a deal with Austria: if Austria would support Russia's move to open the Dardanelles, Russia would permit Austrian annexation of the provinces of Bosnia and Herzegovina. Officially part of the Ottoman Empire, these provinces had been administered by Austria-Hungary since 1878. The population consisted mainly of ethnic cousins of the Serbs. A formal annexation would certainly infuriate the Serbs, who hoped one day to make the region part of Greater Serbia. In 1908, Austria proceeded to annex the provinces, but Russia met stiff resistance from England and France when it presented its case for opening the strait to Russian warships. Austria had gained a diplomatic victory, while Russia suffered another humiliation. Even more enraged than Russia, Serbia threatened to invade Bosnia to liberate its cousins from Austrian oppression. The Serbian press proclaimed that Austria-Hungary must perish if the South Slavs were to achieve liberty and unity. A fiery attitude also prevailed in Vienna: Austria-Hungary could not survive unless Serbia was destroyed.

During this period of intense hostility between Austria-Hungary and Serbia, Germany supported its Austrian ally. To keep Austria strong, Germany would even agree to the dismemberment of Serbia and to its incorporation into the Hapsburg Empire. The crisis led Austria and Germany to coordinate battle plans in case a conflict between Austria and Serbia involved Russia and France. Unlike Bismarck, who tried to hold Austria in check, German leadership now coolly envisioned an Austrian attack on Serbia, and just as coolly offered German support if Russia intervened.

Map 29.1 The Balkans, 1914 Prior to 1914, the Balkans, with its different ethnic groups, was considered a powder keg. The most serious problem, which triggered World War I, was Austria-Hungary's fear of Serbian nationalists eager to create a Greater Serbia.

Balkan Wars

The Bosnian crisis pushed Germany and Austria closer together, brought relations between Austria and Serbia to the breaking point, and inflicted another humiliation on Russia. The first Balkan War (1912) continued these trends. The Balkan states of Montenegro, Serbia, Bulgaria, and Greece attacked a dying Ottoman Empire. In a brief campaign, the Balkan armies captured the Turkish Empire's European territory, with the exception of Constantinople. Because it was on the victorious side, landlocked Serbia gained the Albanian coast and thus a long-desired outlet to the sea. Austria, however, was determined to keep its enemy from reaping this reward, and Germany, as in the Bosnian crisis, supported its ally. Unable to secure Russian support, Serbia was forced to surrender the territory, which in 1913 became the state of Albania.

During a five-year period, Austria-Hungary had twice humiliated Serbia. Russia shared these humiliations, for it had twice failed to help its small Slavic friend and had been denied access to the Dardanelles at the time of the Bosnian crisis. Incensed Serbian nationalists accelerated their campaign of propaganda and terrorism against Austria. Believing that another humiliation would irreparably damage its prestige, Russia vowed to back Serbia in its next confrontation with Austria. And Austria, its patience exhausted and emboldened by German encouragement, wanted to end the Serbian threat once and for all. Thus, the ingredients for war between Austria and Serbia, a war that might easily draw in Russia and Germany, were present. Another incident might well start a war. It came on June 28, 1914.

The Assassination of Archduke Francis Ferdinand. Immediately after the assassination, Austrian authorities arrest one of the assassins. (*Bettmann/Corbis.*)

Assassination of Francis Ferdinand

Archduke Francis Ferdinand (1863–1914), heir to the throne of Austria, was sympathetic to the grievances of the South Slavs and favored a policy that would place the Slavs on an equal footing with Hungarians and Germans within the Hapsburg Empire. If such a policy succeeded, it could soothe the feelings of the Austrian Slavs and reduce the appeal of a Greater Serbia, the aim of the Black Hand.

On June 28, 1914, Francis Ferdinand was assassinated while making a state visit to Sarajevo, the capital of Bosnia. Young Gavrilo Princip, part of a team of Bosnian terrorists, fired two shots at close range into the archduke's car. Francis Ferdinand and his wife died within fifteen minutes. The conspiracy was organized by Dragutin Dimitrijevic, chief of intelligence of the Serbian army, who was linked to the Black Hand.* By killing the archduke, the terrorists hoped to bring to a boiling point tensions within the Hapsburg Empire and prepare the way for revolution.

Feeling that Austria's prestige as a Great Power and indeed its very survival as a supranational empire were at stake, key officials, led by the foreign minister, Count Leopold von Berchtold, decided to use the assassination as a pretext to crush Serbia. For years, Austrian leaders had yearned for war with Serbia in order to end agita-

*Serbia's prime minister, Nikola Pasic, learned of the plot and, through the Serbian envoy in Vienna, tried to get Austria to cancel Francis Ferdinand's visit. The Austrians, however, were not told of a specific assassination attempt, for Pasic did not want to admit that such an act of terrorism was being plotted on Serbian soil.

tion for the union of the South Slavs. Now, they reasoned, the hour had struck. But war with Serbia would require Germany's approval. Believing that Austria was Germany's only reliable ally and that a diminution of Austrian power and prestige threatened German security, German statesmen backed Austria, encouraging it to take up arms against Serbia. Both Germany and Austria wanted a quick strike to overwhelm Serbia before other countries were drawn in.

Germany Abets Austria

Confident of German backing, on July 23 Austria presented Serbia with an ultimatum and demanded a response within forty-eight hours. The terms of the ultimatum were so harsh that it was next to impossible for Serbia to accept them. This reaction was the one that Austria intended, as it sought a military solution to the crisis rather than a diplomatic one. But Russia feared that an Austrian conquest of Serbia was just the first step in an Austro-German plan to dominate the Balkans. Such an extension of German and Austrian power in a region close to Russia was unthinkable to the tsar's government. Moreover, after suffering repeated reverses in foreign affairs, Russia would not tolerate another humiliation. As Germany had resolved to back its Austrian ally, Russia determined not to abandon Serbia.

Serbia responded to Austria's ultimatum in a conciliatory manner, agreeing to virtually all Austrian demands. But it refused Austrian officials entry to investigate the assassination. Having already decided against a peaceful settlement, Austria insisted that rejecting one provision meant rejecting the entire ultimatum, and it ordered the mobilization of its army.

This was a crucial moment for Germany. Would it continue to support Austria, knowing that an Austrian attack on Serbia would most likely bring Russia into the conflict? Determined not to desert Austria and believing that a showdown with Russia was inevitable anyway, the German war party, with the military cajoling and persuading civilian authorities, continued to urge Austrian action against Serbia. They argued that it was better to fight Russia in 1914 than a few years later, when the tsar's empire, which already had a huge reserve of manpower and was rapidly building strategic railroads and expanding its Baltic fleet, would be stronger. The war party claimed that Germany's superior army could defeat both Russia and France, that Britain's army was too weak to make a difference, and that, in any case, Britain might remain neutral. Although Germany would have preferred a limited war, involving only Austria and Serbia, the idea of a general war did not dismay it. Indeed, the prospect of a war with Russia and France exhilarated some military leaders and statesmen. The permanent weakening of Russia and France would break the ring of encirclement, increase German territory, and establish Germany as the foremost power in the world.

On July 28, 1914, Austria declared war on Serbia. Russia, with the assurance of French support, proclaimed partial mobilization aimed at Austria alone. But the military warned that partial mobilization would throw the slow-moving Russian war machine into total confusion if the order had to be changed suddenly to full mobilization. Moreover, the only plans, particularly railway schedules, the Russian general staff had drawn up called for full mobilization, that is, for war against both Austria and Germany. Pressured by his generals, the tsar gave the order for full mobilization on July 30. Russian forces would be arrayed against Germany as well as Austria.

Because the country that struck first gained the advantage of fighting according to its own plans rather than having to improvise in response to the enemy's attack, generals tended to regard mobilization by the enemy as an act of war. Therefore, when Russia refused a German warning to halt mobilization, Germany, on August 1, ordered a general mobilization and declared war on Russia. Two days later, Germany also declared war on France, believing that France would most likely support its Russian ally. Besides, German battle plans were based on a war with both Russia and France; therefore, a war between Germany and Russia automatically meant a German attack on France.

When Belgium refused to allow German troops to march through Belgian territory into France, Germany invaded the small nation, which brought Britain, pledged since 1839 to guarantee Belgian neutrality, into the war. Britain could never tolerate German troops directly across the English Channel in any case, nor could it brook German mastery of western Europe. A century before, Britain had fought Napoleon to prevent France from becoming master of Europe; now it would fight Germany for the same reason. It was this fear that led Britain's naval and military commands to enter into joint planning with their French counterparts, which linked the two powers more closely. Should France be attacked, Britain would be unlikely to stay neutral.

The Question of Responsibility

The question of whether any one power was mainly responsible for the war has intrigued historians. In assessing blame, historians have focused on Germany's role. The German historian Fritz Fischer argues that Germany's ambition to dominate Europe was the underlying cause of the war. Germany encouraged Austria to strike at Serbia knowing that an attack on Serbia could mean war with Russia and its French ally. Believing that it had the military advantage, Germany was willing to risk such a war. Hence, "her leaders must bear a substantial share of the historical responsibility for the outbreak of general war in 1914."[8]

Attracted by Social Darwinist ideas that foresaw an inevitable racial struggle between Germans and Slavs, by militarist doctrines that glorified war, and by a nationalist drive for *Lebensraum*—more living space—continues Fischer, Germany sought to become the foremost economic and political power in Europe and to play a far greater role in world politics; to achieve this goal, it was willing to go to war. Fischer supports his position by pointing to Germany's war aims, drawn up immediately after the outbreak of war, which called for the annexation of neighboring territories and the creation of satellite states.

Fischer's critics, however, stress that Social Darwinism and militarism enthralled other European nations besides Germany. They argue further that Germany would have preferred a limited war between Austria and Serbia and before the war had no plans to dominate Europe. The plans for territorial acquisition, drawn up during the war, not before it, were not the reason why Germany went to war.

Historians also attribute blame to the other powers. Austria bears responsibility for its determination to crush Serbia and for its insistent avoidance of a negotiated settlement. Serbia's responsibility stems from pursuing an aggressive Pan-Serbian policy, which set Serbia on a collision course with Austria-Hungary. In 1913, the British ambassador to Vienna warned: "Serbia will some day set Europe by the ears, and bring about a universal war on the Continent. I cannot tell you how exasperated people are getting here at the continual worry which that little country causes to Austria."[9] Russia bears responsibility for instituting general mobilization, thereby turning a limited war between Austria-Hungary and Serbia into a European war; France, for failing to restrain Russia and indeed for encouraging its ally to mobilize; and England, for failing to make clear that it would support its allies. Had Germany seen plainly that Britain would intervene, it might have been more cautious.

Some historians, dismissing the question of responsibility, regard the war as an obvious sign that European civilization was in deep trouble. Viewed in the broad perspective of European history, the war marked a culmination of dangerous forces in European life: the glorification of power; fascination with violence and the nonrational; general dissatisfaction and disillusionment with bourgeois society; and, above all, explosive nationalism. It also underscored the diminishing confidence in the capacity of reason to solve the problems created by the Industrial Revolution and pointed to the flaws and perils of the alliance system.

War as Celebration

When war was certain, an extraordinary phenomenon occurred. Crowds gathered in capital cities, demonstrating allegiance to the various fatherlands and readiness to fight. Even socialists, who had pledged their loyalty to an international workers' movement, devoted themselves to their respective nations. War and its violence seemed to offer an escape from the dull routine of classroom, job, and home and from the emptiness, drabness, mediocrity, and pettiness of bourgeois society—from "a world grown old and cold and weary," as Rupert Brooke, a young British poet, put it.[10] To some, war was a "beautiful . . . sacred moment" that satisfied an "ethical yearning."[11] To many people, especially youth and intellectuals, war seemed a healthy and heroic antidote to what they regarded as an unbearably decadent and soul-destroying machine age and to bourgeois preoccupation with

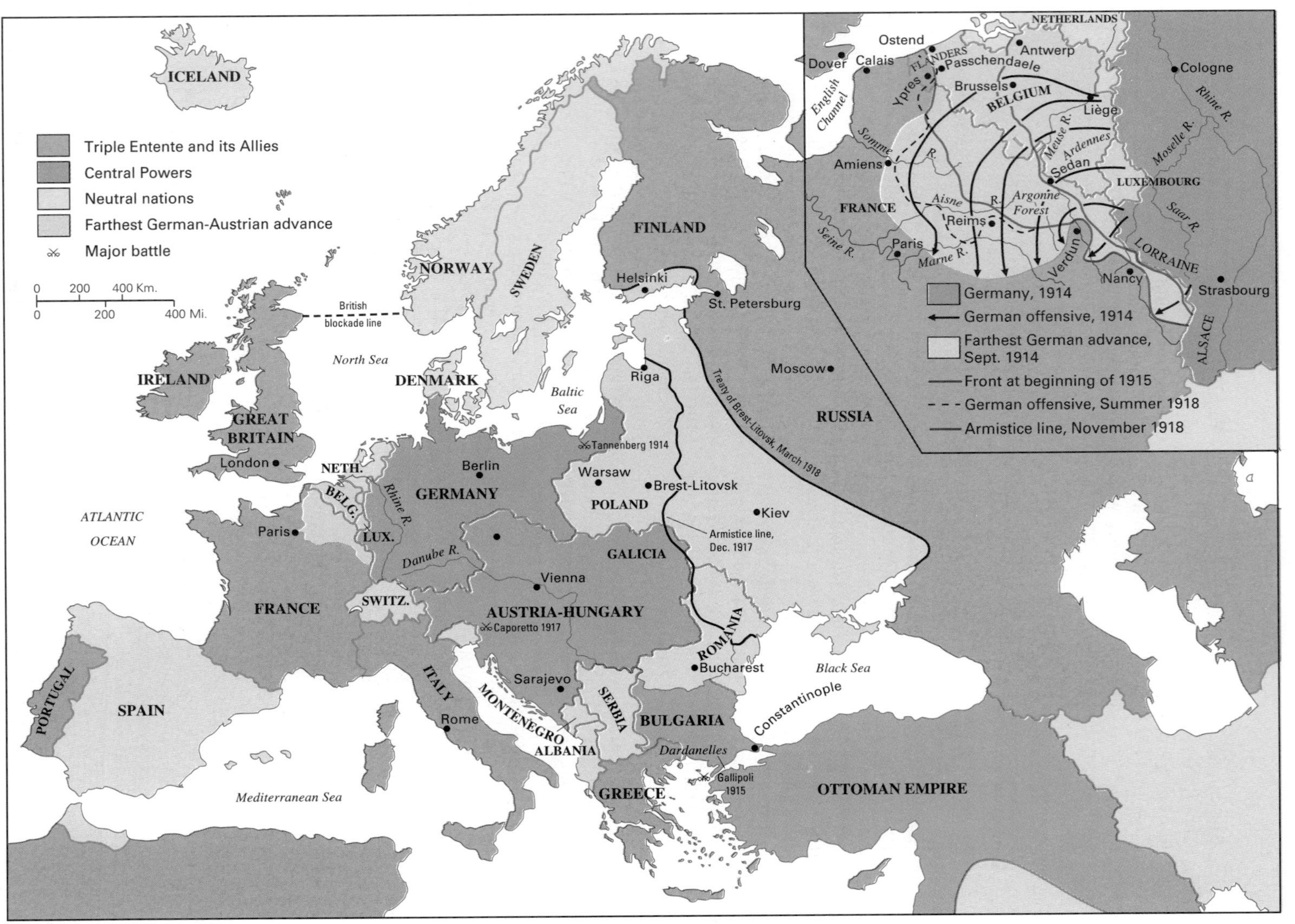
ICELAND
Triple Entente and its Allies
Central Powers
Neutral nations
Farthest German-Austrian advance
Major battle
0 200 400 Km.
0 200 400 Mi.
British blockade line
NORWAY
SWEDEN
FINLAND
Helsinki
St. Petersburg
IRELAND
GREAT BRITAIN
London
North Sea
DENMARK
Baltic Sea
Riga
Moscow
RUSSIA
Treaty of Brest-Litovsk, March 1918
Tannenberg 1914
NETH.
BELG.
LUX.
Rhine R.
Berlin
GERMANY
Warsaw
Brest-Litovsk
POLAND
Kiev
Armistice line, Dec. 1917
ATLANTIC OCEAN
Paris
Danube R.
GALICIA
Vienna
FRANCE
SWITZ.
AUSTRIA-HUNGARY
Caporetto 1917
ROMANIA
Bucharest
Black Sea
PORTUGAL
SPAIN
ITALY
Rome
Sarajevo
MONTENEGRO
ALBANIA
SERBIA
BULGARIA
Constantinople
Dardanelles
Gallipoli 1915
GREECE
OTTOMAN EMPIRE
Mediterranean Sea
NETHERLANDS
Ostend
Dover
Calais
FLANDERS
Passchendaele
Antwerp
Cologne
Ypres
Brussels
BELGIUM
Liège
English Channel
Rhine R.
Somme R.
Meuse R.
Ardennes
Moselle R.
Amiens
Sedan
LUXEMBOURG
FRANCE
Aisne R.
Argonne Forest
Saar R.
Reims
Seine R.
Paris
Marne R.
Verdun
LORRAINE
Nancy
Strasbourg
ALSACE
Germany, 1914
German offensive, 1914
Farthest German advance, Sept. 1914
Front at beginning of 1915
German offensive, Summer 1918
Armistice line, November 1918

work, profits, and possessions. More significantly, the outpouring of patriotic sentiments demonstrated the power that nationalism exerted over the European mind. Nationalism welded millions of people into a collectivity ready to commit body and soul to the nation, especially in its hour of need. For decades, state-directed education had indoctrinated youth with nationalist attitudes, beliefs, and myths designed to promote social cohesion. This training proved extraordinarily successful.

In Paris, men marched down the boulevards singing the stirring words of the French national anthem, the "Marseillaise," while women showered young soldiers with flowers. A participant recollected: "Young and old, civilians and military men burned with the same excitement. . . . thousands of men eager to fight would jostle one another outside recruiting offices, waiting to join up. . . . The word 'duty' had a meaning for them, and the word 'country' had regained its splendor."[12] These sentiments were echoed by another French soldier, Andre Fribourg, traveling to the front:

> *Our hearts beat with enthusiasm. A kind of intoxication takes possession of us. My muscles and arteries tingle with happy strength. The spirit is contagious. Along the track walkers wave to us. Women hold up their children. We are carried away by the greeting of the land, the mystery that the future holds, the thought of glorious adventure, and the pride of being chosen to share it.*[13]

Similarly, a German newspaper editorialized, "It is a joy to be alive. We wished so much for this hour. . . . The sword which has been forced into our hand will not be sheathed until our aims are won and our territory extended as far as necessity demands."[14] Writing about those momentous days, the British mathematician-philosopher Bertrand Russell (1872–1970) recalled his horror and "amazement that average men and women were delighted at the prospect of war. . . . [T]he anticipation of carnage was delightful to something like ninety per cent of the population. I had to revise my views on human nature."[15]

Soldiers bound for battle and wives and sweethearts seeing them off at train stations were in a holiday mood. "My dear ones, be proud that you live in such a time and in such a nation and that you . . . have the privilege of sending those you love into so glorious a battle," wrote a young German law student to his family.[16] The young warriors yearned to do something noble and altruistic, to win glory, and to experience life at its most intense.

The martial mood also captivated many of Europe's most distinguished intellectuals. They shared Rupert Brooke's sentiments: "Now God be thanked Who has matched us with His hour,/And caught our youth, and wakened us from sleeping."[17] In November 1914, Thomas Mann, the distinguished German writer, saw the war as "purification" and "liberation." "How could . . . the soldier in the artist," he asked, "not praise God for the collapse of a peaceful world with which he was fed up, so exceedingly fed up."[18] To the prominent German historian Friedrich Meinecke, August 1914 was "one of the great moments of my life which suddenly filled my soul with . . . the profoundest joy."[19]

Some intellectuals also welcomed the war because it unified the nation in a spirit of fraternity, which eliminated party squabbles and class differences and overcame individual isolation. Stefan Zweig (1881–1942), an Austrian writer, recalled how news of the war was greeted in Vienna:

> *As never before, thousands and hundreds of thousands felt what they should have felt in peace time, that they belonged together. . . . All differences of class, rank, and language were flooded over at that moment by the rushing feeling of fraternity. Strangers spoke to one another in the streets, people who had avoided each other for years shook hands, everywhere one saw excited faces. Each individual experienced an exaltation of his ego . . . he had been incorporated into the mass . . . and his person, his hitherto unnoticed person, had been given meaning.*[20]

War, in the view of some intellectuals, would spiritually regenerate the nation. It would resurrect glory, nobility, and heroism; it would

◀ *Map 29.2* World War I, 1914–1918
This map shows Europe divided into competing alliances and German advances into France and eastern Europe once war broke out.

awaken a spirit of self-sacrifice and dedication and give life an overriding purpose.

Thus, a generation of European youth marched off to war joyously, urged on by their teachers and cheered by their delirious compatriots. It must be emphasized, however, that both the soldiers who went off to war singing and the statesmen and generals who welcomed war or did not try hard enough to prevent it expected a short, decisive, and gallant conflict. Few envisioned what World War I turned out to be: four years of barbaric, senseless slaughter. The cheers of chauvinists, deluded idealists, and fools drowned out the words of those, principally socialists, labor leaders, pacifists, and left-leaning liberals, who realized that Europe was stumbling into darkness. "The lamps are going out all over Europe," said British Foreign Secretary Edward Grey. "We shall never see them lit again in our lifetime."

Stalemate in the West

On August 4, 1914, the German army invaded Belgium. German war plans, drawn up years earlier, chiefly by General Alfred von Schlieffen, called for the army to swing through Belgium to outflank French border defenses, envelop the French forces, and destroy the enemy by attacking its rear. With the French army smashed and Paris isolated, German railroads—an extensive system of tracks, carefully planned by the general staff, had been constructed in the previous decade—would rush the victorious troops to the eastern front to bolster the small force that had been assigned to hold off the Russians. The German military felt certain that the spirit and skill of the German army would ensure victory over the much larger Russian forces. But everything depended on speed. France must be taken before the Russians could mobilize sufficient numbers to invade Germany. The Germans were confident that they would defeat France in two months or less.

French strategy called for a headlong attack into Alsace and Lorraine. Inspired by Napoleon's stress on offensive warfare and convinced of French soldiers' unconquerable will and irresistible nerve, the French army prepared its soldiers only for offensive warfare. The field regulations proclaimed: "Battles are . . . struggles of morale. Defeat is inevitable as soon as the hope of conquering ceases to exist. Success comes . . . to him whose will is firmest and morale strongest."[21]

The French doctrine proved an instant failure. Although bayonet charges against machine-gun emplacements demonstrated the valor of French soldiers, they also revealed the incompetence of French generals. Making no effort at concealment or surprise and wearing striking red and blue uniforms, French soldiers were perfect targets. Marching into concentrated fire, they fell like pins. Everywhere the audacious attack was failing, but French generals, beguiled by the mystique of the offensive, would not change their tactics. In the first six weeks of the war, the French suffered an astounding 385,000 casualties, including 100,000 dead.

German success was not complete, however. Moving faster than anticipated, the Russians invaded East Prussia. In response, General Helmuth von Moltke transferred troops from the French front, hampering the German advance. By early September, the Germans had reached the Marne River, forty miles from Paris. With their capital at their backs, the regrouped French forces, aided by the British, fought with astounding courage. Meanwhile, the Germans were exhausted by long marches and had outrun their supplies. Moreover, in their rush toward Paris, they had unknowingly exposed their flank, which the French attacked. The British then penetrated a gap that opened up between the German armies, forcing the Germans to retreat. The first battle of the Marne had saved Paris. Now the war entered a new and unexpected phase: the deadlock of trench warfare.

For over four hundred miles across northern France, from the Alps to the North Sea, the opposing sides constructed a vast network of trenches. These trenches had underground dugouts, and barbed wire stretched for yards before the front trenches as a barrier to attack. Behind the front trenches were other lines, to which soldiers could retreat and from which support could be sent. Between the opposing armies lay "no man's land," a wasteland of mud, shattered trees, torn earth, and broken bodies. In the trenches soldiers were reduced to a primitive existence. Sometimes they stood knee-deep in freezing water or slimy mud; the stench from human waste, rotting corpses, and unwashed bodies overwhelmed the senses; rats, made more fecund by easy access to food, including decaying flesh, swarmed over the dead and scampered across the wounded and the sleeping;

WOMEN IN THE FACTORIES DURING WORLD WAR I. Women found employment in the war industry. Their patriotism and productive labor caused opposition to women's suffrage to dissipate. (*Corbis.*)

and ubiquitous lice caused intense discomfort and disease, which frequently required hospitalization for several weeks. After days of fearsome, earsplitting bombardments, even the most stouthearted were reduced to shivering, whimpering creatures. The agonizing cries and pleas of the wounded, left to die on the battlefield because it was too dangerous to attempt a rescue, shattered the nerves of the men in the trenches. Trench warfare was a futile battle of nerves, endurance, and courage, waged to the constant thunder of heavy artillery, which pulverized both ramparts and men.

But the most distinctive feature of trench warfare was butchery. As attacking troops climbed over their trenches and advanced bravely across no man's land, they were decimated by heavy artillery and chewed up by machine-gun fire. If they did penetrate the frontline trenches of the enemy, they were soon thrown back by a counterattack.

Despite a frightful loss of life, little land changed hands in this war of attrition. So much heroism, sacrifice, and death achieved nothing. The Allied generals in particular, unfeeling and totally lacking in imagination, ordered still greater attacks, hoping to wear down German manpower, which was inferior to their own. Once German reserves could not replenish losses, they reasoned, a breakthrough would be possible. But this strategy only increased the death toll, for the advantage was always with the defense, which possessed machine guns, magazine rifles, and barbed wire. Aided by radio and aerial reconnaissance, the defense could rush reinforcements to thwart an enemy attack. Tanks could redress the balance, but the generals, committed to old concepts, did not make effective use of them. And whereas the technology of the machine gun had been perfected, the motorized tanks often broke down. Gains and losses of land were measured in yards, but the lives of Europe's youth were squandered by the hundreds of thousands. In 1915, for example, France launched numerous attacks against German lines but never gained more than three miles in any one place. Yet these small gains cost France 1,430,000 casualties.

In 1915, neither side could break the deadlock. Hoping to bleed the French army dry and force its

Profile

Siegfried Sassoon

The Granger Collection.

At the outbreak of World War I, a number of British poets greeted the conflict as a glorious adventure, a God-given oportunity to experience life fully. After coming face to face with the horrors of trench warfare, several poets came to resent the effort to transform the indiscriminate slaughter of Europe's youth into an idealistic venture and used their talent to write antiwar poetry. Wilfred Owen (1893– 1918), Charles Hamilton Sorley (1895–1915), and Isaac Rosenberg (1890–1918) did not survive the war; Siegfried Sassoon (1886–1967) did, and his poetry remains a powerful protest againstwar.

Sassoon's father, Alfred Sassoon, came from a wealthy Jewish merchant family with roots in Baghdad and Bombay: the poet's grandfather had arrived in England in 1858, and the family quickly adjusted to Western ways. Alfred wed an Englishwoman, and Siegfried was reared as an Anglican. Leaving Cambridge University before completing a degree, Siegfried spent his time as a sportsman—hunting, racing horses, and playing cricket. Just before Britain declared war, he enlisted and achieved the rank of second lieutenant. After a younger brother and a close friend were killed in combat, Sassoon, determined to get revenge, displayed reckless bravery that earned him the nickname "Mad Jack." For his "conspicuous gallantry," Sassoon was awarded the Military Cross. But he was growing increasingly disillusioned with the slaughter, and his poetry depicted the war's futility.

surrender, the Germans in February 1916 attacked the town of Verdun, which was protected by a ring of forts. They chose Verdun because they knew the French could never permit a retreat from this ancient fortress. The Germans hoped that France, compelled to pour more and more troops into battle, would suffer such a loss of men that it would be unable to continue the war. However, the leadership of General Henri Philippe Pétain, the tenacity of the French infantry, and the well-constructed concrete and steel forts enabled the French to hold on. When the British opened a major offensive on July 1, the Germans had to channel their reserves to the new front, relieving the pressure on Verdun. Verdun was World War I's bloodiest battle. France and Germany together suffered perhaps a million casualties, including some 300,000 dead.

At the end of June 1916, the British, assisted by the French, attempted a breakthrough at the Somme River. On July 1, after seven days of in-

While recovering from a wound, Sassoon spoke with prominent pacifists, including the philosopher Bertrand Russell, and wrote a protest against the war in which he denounced Britain's leaders for not doing enough to end the slaughter. Fearing that Sassoon's vitriolic words would lead to a court-martial, his friend, the writer Robert Graves (1895–1985), convinced a medical board that Sassoon was suffering from shell shock, and he was sent to a convalescent hospital, where he continued to write antiwar poetry. Returning to the battlefront, Sassoon suffered a head wound in July 1918 and was sent back to England.

Sassoon's poetry expresses contempt for callous generals who, from a safe distance, order massive assaults against well-defended enemy lines that could cost the lives of tens of thousands of soldiers in just a few days. In "Base Details," he draws a sharp distinction between the "glum heroes" at the front and their "bald," "short of breath" "puffy" generals:

If I were fierce, and bald, and short of breath,
I'd live with scarlet Majors at the Base,
And speed glum heroes up the line to death.
You'd see me with my puffy petulant face,
Guzzling and gulping in the best hotel,
Reading the Roll of Honor. "Poor young chap,"
I'd say—"I used to know his father well;
Yes, we've lost heavily in this last scrap."
And when the war is done and youth stone dead,
I'd toddle safely home and die—in bed. *

After the war Sassoon wrote "Aftermath," in which he urges veterans to "swear by the slain of the War that you'll never forget":

Do you remember the rats; and the stench
Of corpses rotting in front of the front-line trench—
And dawn coming, dirty-white, and chill with a hopeless rain?
Do you ever stop and ask, 'Is it all going to happen again?'

Do you remember that hour of din before the attack—
And the anger, the blind compassion that seized and shook you then
As you peered at the doomed and haggard faces of your men?
Do you remember the stretcher-cases lurching back
With dying eyes and lolling heads—those ashen-grey
Masks of the lads who once were keen and kind and gay?

Have you forgotten yet? . . .
Look up, and swear by the green of the spring that you'll never forget.†

*Siegfried Sassoon, *Collected Poems* (New York: Viking Press, 1949), p. 75.
†Ibid., pp. 118–119.

tense bombardment intended to destroy German defenses, the British climbed out of their trenches and ventured into no man's land. But German positions had not been destroyed. Emerging from their deep dugouts, German machine gunners fired repeatedly at the British, who had been ordered to advance in rows. Marching into concentrated machine-gun fire, few British troops ever made it across no man's land. Out of 110,000 who attacked, 60,000 fell dead or wounded, "the heaviest loss ever suffered in a single day by a British army or by any army in the First World War," observes the British historian A. J. P. Taylor.[22] Some reached the German wire, only to become entangled in it. The Germans killed them with rifle fire and bayonets. For days the wounded lay in no man's land, their shrieks unheeded. The Germans suffered only 8,000 casualties, another powerful sign that in trench warfare advantage lay with the defense.

After this initial disaster, common sense and a concern for human life demanded that the attack be called off, but the generals, who rarely made an appearance at the front to observe the actual conditions of battle, continued to feed soldiers to the German guns. When the battle of the Somme ended in mid November, Britain and France had lost more than 600,000 men; yet the military situation remained essentially unchanged. In December 1916, the new commander in chief of the French forces, General Robert Nivelle, ordered another mass attack for April 1917. The Germans discovered the battle plans on the body of a French officer and withdrew to a shorter line on high ground, constructing the strongest defense network of the war. Although Nivelle knew that the French had lost the element of surprise, he went ahead with the offensive, which proved to be another bloodbath. Sometimes the fire was so intense that the French could not make it out of their own trenches. Although French soldiers fought with courage, the situation was hopeless. Still Nivelle persisted with the attack. After ten days, French casualties numbered 187,000.

The soldiers could endure no more. Spontaneous revolts, born of despair and military failure, broke out in rest areas as soldiers refused to return to the slaughter ground. In some instances, they shouted "Peace" and "To hell with the war." Mobs of soldiers seized trains to reach Paris and stir up the population against the war. Mutineers took control of barracks and threatened to fire on officers who interfered. The mutiny spread to the frontlines as soldiers told their officers that they would defend the trenches but not attack. The French army was disintegrating. "The slightest German attack would have sufficed to tumble down our house of cards and bring the enemy to Paris," recalled a French officer.[23]

General Pétain, the hero of Verdun, replaced the disgraced Nivelle. To restore morale, Pétain granted more leave, improved the quality of food, made the rest areas more comfortable, and ordered officers to show concern for their men. He visited the troops, listened to their complaints, and told them that France would engage in only limited offensives until the United States, which had just entered the war, reinforced the Allies in large numbers. These measures, combined with imprisonments and executions, restored discipline. The Germans, unaware of the full magnitude of the mutiny, had not put pressure on the front. By the time the Germans attacked, General Pétain had revitalized the army.

Other Fronts

While the western front hardened into a stalemate, events moved more decisively on the eastern front. In August 1914, according to plan, the bulk of the German army invaded France, hoping for a speedy victory, while a small force defended the eastern frontier against Russia. Responding to French requests to put pressure on Germany, the Russians, with insufficient preparation, invaded East Prussia. Defeated at the battle of Tannenberg (August 26–30, 1914), the Russians withdrew from German territory, which remained inviolate for the rest of the war.

Meanwhile, Germany's ally Austria was having no success against Serbia and Russia. Germany had to come to Austria's rescue. In the spring of 1915, the Germans made a breakthrough that forced the Russians to abandon Galicia and most of Poland. But Germany did not gain the decisive victory it had sought. Although badly battered, Russia remained in the war, forcing Germany to fight on two fronts.

In June 1916, the Russians launched an offensive, opening a wide breach in the Austrian lines. However, a German counteroffensive forced a retreat and cost the Russians more than a million casualties. Russia's military position deteriorated and its domestic unrest worsened.

In March 1917, food shortages and disgust with the great loss of life exploded into a spontaneous revolution. The tsar abdicated. Dominated by liberals, the new government opted to continue the war, despite the weariness of the Russian masses. In November 1917, a second revolution brought to power the Bolsheviks, or communists. In March 1918, the Bolsheviks ended Russia's role in the war by signing the punitive Treaty of Brest-Litovsk, in which Russia surrendered Poland, the Ukraine, Finland, and the Baltic provinces.

Some major battles involved belligerents who joined the conflict after August 1914—notably, the Ottoman Turks, who sided with the Germans, and the Italians, who joined the Allies. Intent on seizing the Dardanelles, the Allies met fierce Turkish resistance on the Gallipoli Peninsula. The Gallipoli cam-

BRITISH PROPAGANDA POSTER. The warring countries employed propaganda to strengthen the resolve of the soldiers and civilians on the "home front."(*Stock Montage.*)

paign (1915–16) cost the Allies 252,000 casualties, and they gained nothing. In 1917, the Italians were badly defeated by a combined German and Austrian force at Caporetto. Germany and Austria took some 275,000 prisoners.

Collapse of the Central Powers

American Entry

The year 1917 seemed disastrous for the Allies. The Nivelle offensive had failed, the French army had mutinied, a British attack at Passchendaele did not bring the expected breakthrough and added some three hundred thousand casualties to the list of butchery, and the Russians, torn by revolution and gripped by war weariness, were close to making a separate peace. But there was one encouraging development for the Allies. In April 1917, the United States declared war on Germany.

From the outset, America's sympathies lay with the Allies. To most Americans, Britain and France were democracies threatened by an autocratic and militaristic Germany. These sentiments were reinforced by British propaganda, which depicted the Germans as cruel "Huns." Since most war news came to the United States from Britain, anti-German feeling gained momentum. What precipitated America's entry was the German decision of January 1917 to launch a campaign of unrestricted submarine warfare. To deprive Britain of war supplies and to starve it into submission, the Germans resolved to torpedo both enemy and neutral ships in the war zone around the British Isles. Since the United States was Britain's principal supplier, American ships became a target of German submarines.

Angered by American loss of life and materiel, as well as by the violation of the doctrine of freedom of the seas, and fearful of a diminution of prestige if the United States took no action, President Woodrow Wilson (1856–1924) pressed for American entry. Also at stake was American security, which would be jeopardized by German domination of western Europe. As Secretary of State Robert Lansing wrote in a private memorandum just before the United States entered the war, "The Allies must not be beaten. It would mean the triumph of Autocracy over Democracy; the shattering of all our moral standards; and a real, though it may seem remote, peril to our independence and institutions."[24]

In initiating unrestricted submarine warfare, Germany gambled that the United States, even if it became a belligerent, could not intervene in sufficient numbers quickly enough to make a difference. The Germans lost their gamble. The United States broke diplomatic relations with Germany immediately on learning of the submarine campaign. Three weeks later, the British gave the Americans a message sent by German Foreign Secretary Arthur Zimmerman to the German ambassador in Mexico City and deciphered by British code experts. In the Zimmerman telegram, Germany proposed that in case of war between Germany and the United States, Mexico should join

Germany as an ally; in return, Mexico would receive Texas, New Mexico, and Arizona. This fantastic proposal further exacerbated anti-German feeling in the United States. As German submarines continued to attack neutral shipping, President Wilson, on April 2, 1917, urged Congress to declare war on Germany, which it did on April 6.

Although the United States may have entered the war to protect its own security, President Wilson told the American people and the world that the United States was fighting "to make the world safe for democracy." With America's entry, the war was transformed into a moral crusade: an ideological conflict between democracy and autocracy. In January 1918, Wilson enunciated American war aims in "Fourteen Points," which called for territorial changes based on nationality and the application of democratic principles to international relations. An association of nations would be established to preserve peace; it would conduct international relations with the same respect for law as was evidenced in democratic states. Thus, Wilson placed his hope for the future peace of the world in liberal nationalism and democracy, the two great legacies of the nineteenth century.

Germany's Last Offensive

With Russia out of the war, General Erich Ludendorff prepared for a decisive offensive before the Americans could land sufficient troops in France to help the Allies. A war of attrition now favored the Allies, who could count on American supplies and manpower. Without an immediate and decisive victory, Germany could not win the war. Ludendorff hoped to drive the British forces back to the sea, forcing them to withdraw from the Continent. Then he would turn his full might against the French. The great offensive began on March 21, 1918. The Germans breached the enemy lines, and the British retreated. Expanding their offensive, the Germans sought to split the British and French forces by capturing Amiens, the Allies' major communications center, and to drive the British back to the channel ports.

Suddenly, the deadlock had been broken; it was now a war of movement. Within two weeks, the Germans had taken some 1,250 square miles. But British resistance was astonishing, and the Germans, exhausted and short of ammunition and food, called off the drive. A second offensive against the British in April also had to be called off, as the British contested every foot of ground. Both campaigns depleted German manpower while the Americans were arriving in great numbers to strengthen Allied lines and uplift morale.

At the end of May, Ludendorff resumed his offensive against the French. Attacking unexpectedly, the Germans broke through and by June 3 advanced to within fifty-six miles of Paris. General John Pershing, head of the American forces, cabled Washington that "the possibility of losing Paris has become apparent."[25] But the offensive was already winding down as reserves braced the French lines. In the battle of Belleau Wood (June 6–25, 1918), the Americans checked the Germans. There would be no open road to Paris.

In mid July, the Germans tried again, crossing the Marne River in small boats. By August 3, the second battle of the Marne ended with the Germans being forced back over the river. Although they had thrown everything they had into their spring and summer offensives, it was not enough. The Allies had bent, but reinforced and encouraged by American arms, they did not break. Now they began to counterattack. On August 8, the British, assisted by the French and using tanks to great advantage, broke through east of Amiens. Ludendorff called August 8 "the black day of the German Army." The kaiser himself declared to his generals: "We have nearly reached the limit of our powers of resistance. The war must be ended."[26] The Allies, their confidence surging, continued to attack with great success in August and September.

Meanwhile, German allies, deprived of support from a hard-pressed Germany, were unable to cope. An Allied army of French, Britons, Serbs, and Italians compelled Bulgaria to sign an armistice on September 29. Shortly afterward, British successes in the Middle East forced the Turks to withdraw from the war. In the streets of Vienna, people were shouting "Long live peace! Down with the monarchy!" The Austro-Hungarian Empire was rapidly disintegrating into separate states based on nationality.

By early October, the last defensive position of the Germans crumbled. The army's spirit collapsed as well; war-weary soldiers sensing that the war was lost surrendered in large numbers and refused orders to return to the front. Fearing an Allied invasion of Germany, Ludendorff wanted an immediate armistice. But he needed to find a way to obtain favorable armistice terms from President Wilson and to shift the blame for the lost war from the military and the kaiser to the civilian leadership. Cynically, he urged the creation of a popular parliamentary government in Germany. But events in Germany went further than the general had anticipated. Whereas Ludendorff sought a limited monarchy, the shock of defeat and hunger sparked a revolution that forced the kaiser to abdicate.

On November 11, the new German Republic signed an armistice ending the hostilities. At 11 A.M., soldiers from both sides walked into no man's land and into a new day. A newspaper correspondent with the British army in France wrote: "Last night for the first time since August in the first year of the war, there was no light of gunfire in the sky, no sudden stabs of flame through darkness, no spreading glow above black trees where for four years of nights human beings were smashed to death. The Fires of Hell had been put out."[27]

The Peace Conference

Wilson's Hope for a New World

In January 1919, representatives of the Allied powers assembled in Paris to draw up peace terms; President Wilson was also there. The war-weary masses turned to Wilson as the prophet who would have the nations beat their swords into plowshares. In Paris, two million people lined the streets to cheer Wilson and throw bouquets; his carriage passed under a huge banner proclaiming "Honor to Wilson the Just." In Rome, hysterical crowds called him the god of peace; in Milan, wounded soldiers sought to kiss his clothes; in Poland, university students spoke his name when they shook hands with each other.

For Wilson, the war had been fought against autocracy. He hoped that a peace settlement based on liberal-democratic ideals would sweep away the foundations of war. Wilson proclaimed his message with a spiritual zeal that expressed his Presbyterian background and his faith in American democracy.

None of Wilson's principles seemed more just than the idea of self-determination: the right of a people to have its own state, free of foreign domination. In particular, this goal meant (or was interpreted to mean) the return of Alsace and Lorraine to France, the creation of an independent Poland, readjustment of the frontiers of Italy to incorporate Austrian lands inhabited by Italians, and an opportunity for Slavs of the Austro-Hungarian Empire to form their own states. Although Wilson did not demand the liberation of all colonies, the Fourteen Points did call for "a free, open-minded and absolutely impartial adjustment of all colonial claims" and a territorial settlement "made in the interest and for the benefit of the population concerned."

Aware that a harshly treated Germany might well seek revenge, engulfing the world in another cataclysm, Wilson insisted that there should be a "peace without victory." A just settlement would encourage a defeated Germany to work with the victorious Allies in building a new Europe. But on one point he was adamant: Prussian militarism, which he viewed as a principal cause of the war, must be eliminated. To create a better world, Wilson urged the formation of a League of Nations, an international parliament to settle disputes and discourage aggression. Wilson wanted a peace of justice to preserve Western civilization in its democratic and Christian form.

Problems of Peacemaking

How could such moralistic pronouncements translate into concrete peace provisions? "[N]o mortal man . . . could have hoped to bring about all the things that the world came to expect of Wilson," concludes the American historian Thomas A. Bailey. "Wilson's own people were bound to feel disillusioned; the peoples of the neutral and Allied countries were bound to feel deceived; and the peoples of the enemy countries were bound to feel betrayed."[28]

Wilson's negotiating position had also been undermined by the Republican party's victory in the congressional elections of November 1918. Wilson had appealed to the American people to elect Democrats as a vote of confidence in his diplomacy. But instead Americans sent twenty-five Republicans and fifteen Democrats to the Senate. Although the Republicans' success apparently stemmed from local and national, rather than international, issues, the outcome diminished Wilson's prestige at the conference table. In the view of his fellow negotiators, Wilson was trying to preach to Europe even though he lacked the support of his own country. Since the Senate had to ratify any American treaty, European diplomats worried that what

Wilson agreed to the Senate might reject, which is precisely what happened.

Attending the conference in person also weakened Wilson's negotiating position. As leader of the nation that had rescued the Allies and as initiator of a peace program that held the promise of a new world, Wilson occupied a position of honor, from which he could exert considerable influence and authority. But by haggling with the other representatives, he was knocked from his lofty pedestal and became all too human. "Messiahs tend to arouse less enthusiasm the more they show themselves," notes Bailey; "the role requires aloofness and the spell of mystery."[29]

A major obstacle to Wilson's peace program was France's demand for security and revenge. Nearly the entire war on the western front had been fought on French territory. France mourned the loss of half its young men. Many French industries and farms had been ruined. Particularly galling to the French was the flooding of mines and the general destruction of property carried out by the Germans in their retreat at the war's end. Viewing the Germans as savages and vandals, many in France were skeptical of Wilson's idealism. France's representative at the conference table, Georges Clemenceau (1841–1929), did not share Wilson's hope for a new world or his confidence in the future League of Nations. Instead, he demanded that Germany be severely punished and its capacity to wage war destroyed. He wanted guarantees that the wars of 1870–71 and 1914–18 would not be repeated. The latter war had shown that without the help of Britain and the United States, France would have been at the mercy of Germany. Because there was no certainty that these states would again aid France, Clemenceau wanted to use his country's present advantage to cripple Germany.

The intermingling of nationalities was another barrier to Wilson's program, for no one could create a Europe completely free of minority problems. Some nationalities would always feel that they had been treated shabbily, and the various nationalities were not willing to moderate their demands or lower their aspirations. "To most Europeans," states the German-American historian Hajo Holborn, "the satisfaction of their national dreams was an absolute end even when their realization violated the national determination of others."[30] For example, the Fourteen Points called for an independent Poland with secure access to the sea. But between Poland and the sea lay land populated by Germans. Giving this land to Poland would violate German self-determination; denying it to Poland would mean that the new country had little chance of developing a sound economy. No matter what the decision, one people would regard it as unjust. Similarly, to provide the new Czechoslovakia with defensible borders, it would be necessary to give it land inhabited principally by Germans. This, too, could be viewed as a denial of German self-determination, but not granting the area to Czechoslovakia would mean that the new state would not be able to defend itself against Germany.

Wilson and Clemenceau Arrive at Versailles, June 28, 1919. The idealism of President Wilson (center) clashed with Premier Clemenceau's (left) determination to enhance France's security. (*Hulton Deutsch Collection/Getty Images.*)

Secret treaties drawn up by the Allies during the war also interfered with Wilson's program. These agreements, dividing up German, Austrian, and Ottoman territory, did not square with the principle of self-determination. For example, to entice Italy into entering the war, the Allies had promised it Austrian lands that were inhabited predominantly by Germans and Slavs. Italy was not about to repudiate its prize because of Wilson's principles.

Finally, the war had aroused great bitterness, which persisted after the guns had been silenced. Both the masses and their leaders demanded retribution and held exaggerated hopes for territory and reparations. In such an atmosphere of postwar enmity, the spirit of compromise and moderation could not overcome the desire for spoils and punishment. A century earlier, when the monarchs had defeated Napoleon, they sought a peace of reconciliation with France. But setting aside their hatreds proved harder for democratic statesmen and nations than it had been for despotic monarchs and aristocratic diplomats.

The Settlement

After months of negotiations, often punctuated by acrimony, the peacemakers hammered out a settlement. Five treaties made up the Peace of Paris: one each with Germany, Austria, Hungary, Bulgaria, and Turkey. Of the five, the Treaty of Versailles, which Germany signed on June 28, 1919, was the most significant.

France regained Alsace and Lorraine, the territory lost to Germany in the Franco-Prussian War of 1870–71. The Treaty of Versailles also barred Germany from placing fortifications in the Rhineland. The French military had wanted to take the Rhineland from Germany and break it up into one or more republics under French suzerainty. Under this arrangement French control would extend to the Rhine River, which was a natural defensive border; French forces had only to destroy the bridges to prevent a German invasion of France. With Germany deprived of this springboard for invasion, French security would be immensely improved. Recognizing that the German people would never permanently submit to the amputation of the Rhineland, which was inhabited by more than five million Germans and contained key industries, Wilson and British Prime Minister David Lloyd George (1863–1945) resisted these French demands. They did not want to create an Alsace-Lorraine in reverse by awarding France a region that was overwhelmingly German. Nor could Wilson ever agree to such a glaring violation of the principle of self-determination.

Faced with the opposition of Wilson and Lloyd George, Clemenceau backed down and agreed instead to Allied occupation of the Rhineland for fifteen years, its demilitarization, and an Anglo-American promise of assistance if Germany attacked France in the future. This last point, considered vital by France, proved useless. The alliance went into effect only if both the United States and Britain ratified it. Since this so-called Security Treaty did not get past the U.S. Senate, Britain also refused to sign it. France had made a great concession on the Rhineland issue but received nothing in exchange. The French people felt that they had been duped and wronged.

A related issue concerned French demands for annexation of the coal-rich Saar Basin, which adjoined Lorraine. By obtaining this region, France would weaken Germany's military potential. France argued that this would be just compensation for the deliberate destruction of the French coal mines by the retreating German army at the end of the war. But here, too, France was disappointed. The final compromise called for a League of Nations commission to govern the Saar Basin for fifteen years, after which the inhabitants would decide whether their territory would be ceded to France or returned to Germany.

In eastern Germany, in certain districts of Silesia that had a large Polish population, a plebiscite determined the future of the region. As a result, part of Upper Silesia was ceded to Poland. The settlement also gave Poland a corridor cut through West Prussia and terminating in the Baltic port of Danzig, and Danzig itself was declared an international city to be administered by the League of Nations. The Germans would never resign themselves to this loss of territory that separated East Prussia from the rest of Germany.

The victorous nations were awarded control of German and Ottoman colonies. However, these nations held the colonies not outright but as mandates under the supervision of the League, which would protect the interests of the native peoples. Thus, the division of Ottoman and German colonies represented a compromise between traditional imperialism and Wilsonian idealism. The mandate system implied the ultimate end of colonialism, for it clearly opposed the exploitation of colonial peoples and asserted independence as the rightful goal for subject nations.

To strip Germany of any offensive capacity, the settlement abolished the German general staff and forbade military conscription in Germany. The German army was limited to a hundred thousand volunteers and deprived of heavy artillery, tanks, and warplanes. The German navy was limited to a token force, which did not include submarines.

The issue of war reparations caused great bitterness between Wilson and his French and British adversaries. The American delegation wanted the treaty to fix a reasonable sum that Germany would have to pay and specify the period of years allotted for payment. But, instead, the Treaty of Versailles left Germany with an open-ended bill, which would probably take generations to pay. Wilson had lost on the issue of reasonable reparations. Moreover, Article 231, which preceded the reparation clauses, placed sole responsibility for the war on Germany and its allies. The Germans responded to this accusation with contempt.

In separate treaties, the conference dealt with the dissolution of the Hapsburg Empire. In the closing weeks of the war, the Austro-Hungarian Empire had crumbled as the various nationalities proclaimed their independence from Hapsburg rule. In most cases, the peacemakers ratified with treaties what the nationalities had already accomplished in fact. Serbia joined with Austro-Hungarian lands inhabited by South Slavs to become Yugoslavia. Czechoslovakia arose from the predominantly Czech and Slovak regions of Austria. Hungary, which broke away from Austria to become a separate country, had to cede a considerable amount of land to Romania and Yugoslavia. Austria had to turn over to Italy the South Tyrol, which was inhabited by two hundred thousand Austrian Germans. This clear violation of the principle of self-determination greatly offended liberal opinion. Deprived of its vast territories and prohibited from union with Germany, the new Austria was a third-rate power.

Assessment and Problems

The Germans unanimously denounced the Treaty of Versailles, for in their minds the war had ended not in German defeat but in a stalemate. They regarded the armistice as the prelude to a negotiated settlement among equals, based on Wilson's call for a peace of justice. Instead, the Germans were barred from participating in the negotiations. And they viewed the terms of the treaty as humiliating and vindictive—designed to keep Germany militarily and economically weak. What standard of justice, they asked, allowed the Allies to take the German colonies, reduce the German military to a pitiful size without disarming themselves, ban Germany from the League of Nations, and saddle the country with impossible reparations? Why should Germany lose approximately one-eighth of its territory and one-tenth of its population? Why should the Allies blame the war on Germany; provide for the self-determination of Poles while precluding the union of German-speaking Austria with Germany; hand over to Italy some two hundred thousand Austrian Germans; place Germans under Polish rule; and declare the German port of Danzig a free city?

The Germans protested that, when the United States entered the war, Wilson had stated that the enemy was not the German people but their government. Surely, the Germans now argued, the new German democracy should not be punished for the sins of the monarchy and the military. To the Germans, the Treaty of Versailles was not the dawning of the new world that Wilson had promised but a vile crime.

Worn out by war, torn by revolutionary unrest, and desperately short of food, with its economy in disarray and with the Allies poised to invade, the new German republic had no choice but to sign the treaty. However, the sentiments of the German people were clearly and prophetically expressed by the Berlin *Vorwärts,* the influential Social Democratic newspaper: "We must never forget it is only a scrap of paper. Treaties based on violence can keep their validity only so long as force exists. Do not lose hope. The resurrection day comes."[31]

Critics in other lands also condemned the treaty as a punitive settlement, warning that it would only exacerbate old hatreds and enflame German nationalism. The treaty's defenders, however, insisted that had Germany won the war, it would have imposed a far harsher settlement on the Allies. They pointed to German war aims, which called for the annexation of parts of France and Poland, the reduction of Belgium and Romania to satellites, and German expansion in Africa. They pointed also to the Treaty of Brest-Litovsk, which Germany compelled Russia to sign in 1918, as an

Map 29.3 Post–World War I: Broken Empires and Changed Boundaries ▶

World War I led to the breakup of the Russian, Austro-Hungarian, and Ottoman Empires and the creation of several new countries, including Poland, Czechoslovakia, Yugoslavia, Lithuania, Latvia, and Estonia.

Boundaries of German, Russian, and Austro-Hungarian empires in 1914
Demilitarized Zone
Areas lost by Austro-Hungarian Empire
Areas lost by Russia
Areas lost by Germany
Areas lost by Bulgaria
Boundaries of 1926
0 200 400 Km.
0 200 400 Mi.
ATLANTIC OCEAN
North Sea
Baltic Sea
Mediterranean Sea
Black Sea
IRELAND
GREAT BRITAIN
NORWAY
SWEDEN
FINLAND
DENMARK
ESTONIA
LATVIA
LITHUANIA
EAST PRUSSIA
POLISH CORRIDOR
POLAND
SOVIET UNION
NETH.
BELG.
LUX.
RUHR
GERMANY
FRANCE
LORRAINE
ALSACE
SWITZ.
S. TYROL
AUSTRIA
CZECHOSLOVAKIA
GALICIA
HUNGARY
ROMANIA
BESSARABIA
CROATIA
YUGOSLAVIA
SERBIA
MONTENEGRO (To Yugoslavia, 1921)
ALBANIA
BULGARIA
GREECE
TURKEY
ITALY
SPAIN
PORTUGAL
Leningrad (St. Petersburg)
Stockholm
Kiel
Elbe R.
Danzig
Vistula R.
Amsterdam
Berlin
Warsaw
Kiev
Brussels
Cologne
Weimar
Frankfurt
Paris
Versailles
Prague
Rhine R.
Strasbourg
Vienna
Budapest
Dniester R.
Geneva
Milan
Venice
Trieste
Fiume
Zagreb
Belgrade
Bucharest
Sofia
Rome
Naples
Istanbul (Constantinople)
Athens
Crete

example of Germany's ruthlessness. An insatiable Germany deprived Russia of 34 percent of its population, 32 percent of its farmland, 54 percent of its industrial enterprises, and 89 percent of its coal mines. Furthermore, they noted that the peace settlement did reflect Wilson's principles: the new map of Europe was the closest approximation of the ethnic distribution of its peoples that Europe had ever known.

What is most significant about the Treaty of Versailles is that it did not solve the German problem. Germany was left weak but unbroken—its industrial and military power only temporarily contained, and its nationalist fervor not only undiminished but stoked by a peace treaty that all political parties viewed as unjust, dictated, and offensive to national pride. The real danger in Europe was German unwillingness to accept defeat or surrender the dream of expansion.

Would France, Britain, and the United States enforce the treaty against a resurgent Germany? The war had demonstrated that an Allied victory depended on American intervention. But in 1920, the U.S. Senate, angry that Wilson had not taken Republicans with him to Paris and fearing that membership in the League of Nations would involve America in future wars, refused to ratify the Treaty of Versailles. Britain, feeling guilty over the treatment of Germany, lacked the will for enforcement and even came to favor treaty revision. The responsibility for preserving the settlement therefore rested primarily with France, which was not encouraging. The Paris peace settlement left Germany resentful but potentially powerful—German industrial capacity was considerable, and only Russia had a larger population—and to the east lay small and weak states, some of them with sizable German minorities, that could not check a rearmed Germany.

The Russian Revolution of 1917

One consequence of the war that influenced the course of European and world history in momentous ways was the Russian Revolution of 1917 and the resultant triumph of the Bolsheviks. The people of Russia had initially responded to the war with a show of patriotic fervor. But the realities of war quickly dimmed this ardor. The ill-equipped and poorly led Russian armies suffered huge losses. In July 1915, the minister of war wrote this dismal report:

> *The soldiers are without doubt exhausted by the continued defeats and retreats. Their confidence in final victory and in their leaders is undermined. Ever more threatening signs of impending demoralization are evident. Cases of desertion and voluntary surrender to the enemy are becoming more frequent. It is difficult to expect enthusiasm and selflessness from men sent into battle unarmed and ordered to pick up the rifles of their dead comrades.*[32]

By 1916 the home front began to fall apart. Shops were empty, money had no value, and hunger and cold stalked the working quarters of cities and towns. Factory workers, many of them women replacements for husbands, brothers, and sons who were at the front, toiled long hours for wages that could not keep up with the accelerating inflation. When they protested, the goverment resorted to heavy-handed repression. By January 1917, nearly all Russians, soldiers and civilians alike, had lost trust in their autocratic government. But Tsar Nicholas II, determined to preserve autocracy, resisted any suggestion that he liberalize the regime for the sake of the war effort.

Autocracy was ready to collapse at the slightest blow. In early March (February 23 by the calendar* then in use), a strike, riots in the food lines, and street demonstrations in Petrograd (formerly Saint Petersburg) flared into sudden, unpremeditated revolution. The soldiers, who in 1905 had stood by the tsar, rushed to support the striking workers. The Romanov dynasty, after three hundred years of rule (1613–1917), came to an end. A Provisional Government was set up—provisional until a representative Constituent Assembly, to be elected as soon as possible, could establish a permanent regime.

*Until March 1918, events in Russia were dated by the Julian calendar, thirteen days behind the Gregorian calendar used in the West. By the Julian calendar the first revolution occurred in February, the second in October.

Problems of the Provisional Government

The collapse of autocracy was followed by what supporters in Russia and the West hoped would be a liberal democratic regime pledged to give Russia a constitution. In reality, however, the course of events from March to November 1917 resembled a free-for-all—a no-holds-barred fight for the succession to autocracy, with only the fittest surviving. Events demonstrated the desperate state of the Russian Empire. Its vast size promoted internal disunity; increasing hardships raised the fury of the accumulated resentments to raw brutality among the masses. National minorities took advantage of the anarchy to dismember the country.

Among the potential successors to the tsars, liberals of various shades seemed at first to enjoy the best chances. They represented the educated and forward-looking elements in Russian society that had arisen after the reforms of the 1860s: lawyers, doctors, professional people of all kinds, intellectuals, businesspeople and industrialists, many landowners, and even some bureaucrats. Liberals had opposed autocracy and earned a reputation for leadership.

Liberals had joined the March revolution reluctantly, for they were afraid of the masses and the violence of the streets. They dreaded social revolution that could result in the seizure of factories, dispossession of landowners, and tampering with property rights. Although most leaders of the Provisional Government had only modest means, they were "capitalists," believing in private enterprise as the best way of promoting economic progress. Their ideal was a constitutional monarchy, its leadership entrusted to the educated and propertied elite familiar with the essentials of statecraft.

Unfortunately, the liberals misunderstood the mood of the people. Looking to the Western democracies—including, after April 1917, the United States—for political and financial support, the liberals decided to continue the war on the side of the Allies. The decision antagonized the war-weary masses, along with the Russian soldiers, almost two million of whom had deserted. The liberals also antagonized the Russian peasants by not confiscating and redistributing the landlords' lands free of charge. As Russian nationalists who wanted their country to remain undivided, the liberals opposed national minorities—Finns, Ukrainians, Georgians, and others—who sought self-determination; hence, they lost the minorities' support.

The peasants began to divide the landlords' land among themselves, and more soldiers deserted in order to claim a share. The breakdown of the railways stopped factory production; enraged workers ousted factory managers and owners. Consumer goods grew scarce and prices soared, and the peasants could see no reason to sell their crops if they could buy nothing in return. Thus, the specter of famine in the cities arose. Hardships and anger mounted. Adding to the disorder were the demands of the non-Russian nationalities for self-determination and even secession.

Freedom in Russia was leading to dissolution and chaos. The largely illiterate peasant masses had no experience with or understanding of the institutions, habits, and attitudes of a free society. Without their cooperation, Russian liberalism collapsed. This outcome demonstrated the difficulty of establishing Western liberal democratic forms of government in countries lacking a sense of unity, a strong middle class, and a tradition of responsible participation in public affairs.

By July 1917, when Aleksandr Kerensky (1881–1970), a radical lawyer of great eloquence, took over the leadership of the Provisional Government, it had become clear that law and order could be upheld only by brute force. In late August and early September, a conspiracy led by an energetic young general, Lavr Kornilov, sought to establish a military dictatorship. Kornilov had the support not only of the officer corps and the tsarist officials but also of many liberals fed up with anarchy. What stopped the general was not Kerensky's government (which had no troops) but the workers of Petrograd. Their agitators demoralized Kornilov's soldiers, proving that a dictatorship of the right had no mass support. The workers also repudiated Kerensky and the Provisional Government, as well as their own moderate leaders; henceforth, they supported the Bolsheviks.

Lenin and the Rise of Bolshevism

Revolutionary movements had a long history in Russia, going back to the early nineteenth century, when educated Russians began to compare their country unfavorably with western Europe. They,

THE TSAR IN EXILE. Nicholas II and his children, living in reduced circumstances, take the sun on a roof in Tobolsk, Siberia. The imperial family was later transferred to Ekaterinburg and then murdered in 1918. (*Hulton Deutsch Collection/Getty Images.*)

too, wanted constitutional liberty and free speech in order to make their country modern. Prohibited from speaking out in public, they went underground, giving up their liberalism as ineffective. They saw revolutionary socialism, with its idealistic vision and compassion for the multitude, as a better ideology in the harsh struggle with the tsar's police. By the 1870s, many socialists had evolved into austere and self-denying professional revolutionaries who, in the service of the cause, had no moral scruples, just as the police had no scruples in the defense of the tsars. Bank robbery, murder, assassination, treachery, and terror were not seen as immoral if they served the revolutionary cause.

In the 1880s and 1890s, revolutionaries learned industrial economics and sociology from Marx; from Marxism they also acquired a vision of a universal and inevitable progression toward socialism and communism, which satisfied their semireligious craving for salvation in this world, not the next. Marxism also allied them with socialist movements in other lands, giving them an internationalist outlook. History, they believed, was on their side, as it was for all the proletarians and oppressed peoples in the world.

By 1900, a number of able young Russians had rallied to revolutionary Marxism; almost all of them were educated or came from privileged families. The most promising was Vladimir Ilyich Ulyanov, known as Lenin (1870–1924), the son of a teacher and school administrator who had attained the rank of a nobleman. Lenin had studied law but practiced revolution instead. His first contribution lay in adapting Marxism to Russian conditions; to do so, he took considerable liberties with Marx's teaching. His second contribution followed from the first: outlining the organization of an underground party capable of surviving against the tsarist police. It was to be a tightly knit conspiratorial elite of professional revolutionaries. Its headquarters would be safely located abroad, and it would have close ties to the masses, that is, to the workers and other potentially revolutionary elements.

Women Demonstrate in Petrograd in 1917. The collapse of the tsarist regime was followed by a period of political fermentation, meetings, and concern about food shortages. Women demonstrated for increased bread supplies. The poster reads, "Comrades, workers, and soldiers, support our demands!" (*Sovfoto.*)

Two other prominent Marxists were Leon Trotsky (1879–1940) and Joseph Stalin (1879–1953). Trotsky, whose original name was Lev Bronstein, was the son of a prosperous Jewish farmer from southern Russia and was soon known for his brilliant pen. Less prominent until after the Revolution, Stalin (the man of steel) was originally named Iosif Dzhugashvili; he was from Georgia, beyond the Caucasus Mountains. Bright enough to be sent to the best school in the area, he dropped out for a revolutionary career. While they were still young, Lenin, Trotsky, and Stalin were all hardened by arrest, imprisonments, and exile to Siberia. Lenin and Trotsky later lived abroad, while Stalin, following a harsher course, stayed in Russia; for four years before 1917, he was banished to bleakest northern Siberia and conditioned to ruthlessness for life.

In 1903, the Russian Marxists split into two factions, the moderate Mensheviks, so named after finding themselves in a minority (*menshinstvo*) at a rather unrepresentative vote at the Second Party Congress, and the extremist Bolsheviks, who at that moment were in the majority (*bolshinstvo*). They might more accurately have been called the "softs" and the "hards." The "softs" (Mensheviks) preserved basic moral scruples; they would not stoop to crime or undemocratic methods for the sake of political success. For that the "hards" (Bolsheviks) ridiculed them, noting that a dead, imprisoned, or unsuccessful revolutionary was of little use.

Meanwhile, Lenin perfected Bolshevik revolutionary theory. He violated Marxist tradition by paying close attention to the revolutionary potential of peasants (thereby anticipating Mao Zedong). Lenin also looked closely at the numerous peoples in Asia who had recently fallen under Western imperialist domination. These people, he sensed, constituted a potential revolutionary force. In alliance with the Western—and Russian—proletariat, they might overthrow the

V. I. LENIN. Red Army soldiers leaving for battle in the civil war are addressed by Lenin in Moscow in May 1920. (*Sovfoto.*)

worldwide capitalist order. The Bolsheviks, the most militant of all revolutionary socialists, were ready to assist in that gigantic struggle.

Lenin was a Russian nationalist, as well as a socialist internationalist; he had a vision of a modern and powerful Russian state destined to be a model in world affairs. Russian communism was thus nationalist communism. The Bolsheviks saw the abolition of income-producing property by the dictatorship of the proletariat as the most effective way of mobilizing the country's resources. Yet the Bolshevik mission was also internationalist. The Russian Revolution was intended to set off a world revolution, liberating all oppressed classes and peoples around the world and achieving a higher stage of civilization.

Lenin's Opportunity

On April 16, 1917, Lenin, with German help, arrived in Petrograd from exile in Switzerland. (The Germans provided Lenin with a secret train to take him to Petrograd; they hoped that the Bolshevik leader, who wanted Russia to withdraw from the "capitalist" war, would initiate a revolution and gain power.) The Provisional Government, he said, could not possibly preserve Russia from disintegration. Most of the soldiers, workers, and peasants would repudiate the Provisional Government's cautious liberalism in favor of a regime expressing their demand for peace and land. Nothing would stop them from avenging themselves for centuries of oppression. Lenin also felt that only complete state control of the economy could rescue the country from disaster. The sole way out, he insisted, was the dictatorship of the proletariat backed by *soviets* (councils) of soldiers, workers, and peasants, particularly the poorer peasants.

Lenin prepared his party for the second stage of the Revolution of 1917: the seizure of power by the Bolsheviks. His slogan, "Peace, Land, and Bread," held a magnetic attraction for the desperate Russian masses. The Bolsheviks' determined effort to win over the disheartened soldiers proved particularly effective. Many of the people who supported the Bolsheviks interpreted Lenin's other powerful slogan—"All Power to the Soviets"—to mean that the Bolsheviks aimed to create a democratic socialist state that would institute needed social reforms. They did not anticipate the creation of Bolshevik dictatorship.

Conditions favored the Bolsheviks, as Lenin had predicted. The Bolsheviks obtained majorities in the soviets. The peasants were in active revolt, seizing the land themselves. The Provisional Government lost all control over the course of events; three years of warfare had caused the disintegration of Russian society. On November 6 (October 24 by the old calendar), Lenin urged immediate action: "The government is tottering. It must be *given the death blow* at all costs." On the following day, the Bolsheviks, meeting little resistance, seized power. Lenin permitted elections for the Constituent Assembly that had been scheduled by the Provisional Government. In a free election, the Bolsheviks received only 24 percent of the vote. After meeting once in January 1918, however, the Constituent Assembly was disbanded by the Bolsheviks.

The Bolsheviks Survive

Lenin contended that he was guiding the Russian proletariat and all humanity toward a higher social order, symbolizing—in Russia and much of the world—the rebellion of the disadvantaged against Western (or "capitalist") dominance. That is why, in 1918, he changed the name of his party from Bolshevik to Communist, which implied a concern for the human community. For Lenin, as for Marx, a world without exploitation was humanity's noblest ideal.

But staggering adversity confronted Lenin after his seizure of power. In the prevailing anarchy, Russia lay open to the German armies. Under the Treaty of Brest-Litovsk, signed in March 1918—the lowest point in Russian history for over two hundred years—Russia lost Finland, Poland, and the Baltic provinces, all regions inhabited largely by non-Russians. It also lost the rebellious Ukraine, its chief industrial base and breadbasket. Yet Lenin, with the country in shambles, had no choice but to accept the humiliating terms.

The War and European Consciousness

"There will be wars as never before on earth," predicted Nietzsche. World War I bore him out. Modern technology enabled the combatants to kill with unprecedented efficiency; modern nationalism infused both civilians and soldiers with the determination to fight until the enemy was totally beaten. Exercising wide control over its citizens, the modern state mobilized its human, material, and spiritual resources to wage total war. As the war hardened into a savage stalemate, statesmen did not press for a compromise peace but rather demanded ever more mobilization, ever more escalation, and ever more sacrifices.

The Great War profoundly altered the course of Western civilization, deepening the spiritual crisis that had produced it. How could one speak of the inviolability of the individual when Europe had become a slaughterhouse, or of the primacy of reason when nations permitted the slaughter to go unabated for four years? How could the mind cope with this spectacle of a civilization turning against itself, destroying itself in an orgy of organized violence? How could it explain students leaving their schoolbooks to become, as one participant said, "nocturnal beasts of prey hunting each other in packs"[33]? A young French soldier, shortly before he was killed at Verdun, expressed the disillusionment that gripped the soldiers in the trenches: "Humanity is mad! It must be mad to do what it is doing. What a massacre! What scenes of horror and carnage, I cannot find words to translate my impressions. Hell cannot be so terrible. Men are mad!"[34] The war, said British poet Robert Graves, provoked an "inward scream" that still reverberates. The agony caused by the astronomical casualty figures—some 9.4 million dead and twenty-one million wounded, many of them pathetically mutilated and disfigured—touched millions of homes. Now only the naive could believe in continuous progress. Western civilization had entered an age of violence, anxiety, and doubt.

World War I was a great turning point in the history of the West. The war left many with the gnawing feeling that Western civilization had lost its vitality and was caught in a rhythm of breakdown. It seemed that Western civilization was fragile and perishable, that Western people, despite their extraordinary accomplishments, were never more than a step or two away from barbarism. Surely, any civilization that could allow such senseless slaughter to last four years had entered its decline and could look forward to only the darkest of futures.

European intellectuals were demoralized and disillusioned. The orderly, peaceful, rational world of their youth had been destroyed. The Enlightenment world-view, weakened in the nineteenth century by the assault of romantics, Social Darwinists, extreme nationalists, race mystics, and glorifiers of the irrational, was now disintegrating. The enormity of the war had shattered faith in the capacity of reason to deal with crucial social and political questions. It appeared that civilization was fighting an unending and seemingly hopeless battle against the irrational elements in human nature and that war would be a continuous phenomenon in the twentieth century.

Scientific research had produced more efficient weapons to kill and maim Europe's youth. The achievements of Western science and technology, which had been viewed as a boon for humanity

KÄTHE KOLLWITZ: THE SURVIVORS (1922). With an estimated ten million dead and twenty-one million wounded, World War I shattered the hope that western Europe had been making continuous progress toward a rational and enlightened civilization. (*National Gallery of Art, Washington, D.C., Rosenwald Collection © Estates of Käthe Kollwitz, ARS, New York 1991.*)

and the clearest testament to the superiority of European civilization, were called into question. Confidence in the future gave way to doubt. The old beliefs in the perfectibility of humanity, the blessings of science, and ongoing progress now seemed an expression of naive optimism, if not post-Christian myths that the war had exposed as fraudulent. As A. J. P. Taylor concludes,

> *The First World War was difficult to fit into the picture of a rational civilization advancing by ordered stages. The civilized men of the twentieth century had outdone in savagery the barbarians of all preceding ages, and their civilized virtues—organization, mechanical skill, self-sacrifice—had made war's savagery all the more terrible. Modern man had developed powers which he was not fit to use. European civilization had been weighed in the balance and found wanting.*[35]

Western civilization had lost its spiritual center. The French writer Paul Valéry summed up the mood of a troubled generation, for whom the sun seemed to be setting on the Enlightenment:

> *The storm has died away, and still we are restless, uneasy as if the storm were about to break. Almost all the affairs of men remain in a terrible uncertainty. We think of what has disappeared, and we are almost destroyed by what has been destroyed; we do not know*

> *what will be born, and we fear the future, not without reason. We hope vaguely, we dread precisely; our fears are infinitely more precise than our hopes; we confess that the charm of life is behind us. There is no thinking man . . . who can hope to dominate this anxiety, to escape from this impression of darkness. . . . But among all these injured things is the Mind. The Mind has indeed been cruelly wounded; its complaint is heard in the hearts of intellectual men; it passes a mournful judgment on itself. It doubts itself profoundly.*[36]

Having lost confidence in the power of reason to solve the problems of the human community, in liberal doctrines of individual freedom, and in the institutions of parliamentary democracy, many people turned to fascism as a simple saving faith. Far from making the world safe for democracy, as Wilson and other liberals had hoped, World War I gave rise to totalitarian movements, which would nearly destroy democracy.

The war produced a generation of young people who had reached their maturity in combat. Violence had become a way of life for millions of soldiers hardened by battle and for millions of civilians aroused by four years of propaganda. The relentless massacre of Europe's young men had a brutalizing effect. Violence, cruelty, suffering, and even wholesale death seemed to be natural and acceptable components of human existence. The sanctity of the individual seemed to be liberal and Christian claptrap.

The fascination with violence and contempt for life persisted in the postwar world. Many returned veterans yearned for the excitement of battle and the fellowship of the trenches—what one French soldier called "the most tender human experience." After the war, a young English officer reminisced: "There was an exaltation, in those days of comradeship and dedication, that would have come in few other ways."[37] A fraternal bond united the men of the trenches. Many veterans also shared a primitive attraction to war's fury. A Belgian veteran expressed it this way:

> *The plain truth is that if I were to obey my native animal instincts—and there was little hope for anything else while I was in the trenches—I should enlist again in any future war, or take part in any sort of fighting, merely to experience again that voluptuous thrill of the human brute who realizes his power to take away life from other human beings who try to do the same to him. What was first accepted as a moral duty became a habit and the habit . . . had become a need.*[38]

And no doubt Julian Grenfell spoke for many other combat soldiers when he declared in November 1914: "I *adore* war. I have never been so well or so happy. . . . The fighting excitement vitalizes everything, every sight and word and action."[39] The brutalizing effect of the war is evident in this statement by a German soldier, for whom the war never ended:

> *People told us that the War was over. That made us laugh. We ourselves are the War. Its flame burns strongly in us. It envelops our whole being and fascinates us with the enticing urge to destroy. We . . . marched onto the battlefields of the postwar world just as we had gone into battle on the Western Front: singing, reckless, and filled with the joy of adventure as we marched to the attack; silent, deadly, remorseless in battle.*[40]

The British novelist D. H. Lawrence (1885–1930) understood that the brutality and hate unleashed by the war had ruined old Europe and would give rise to even greater evils. On the day the armistice was signed, he warned prophetically:

> *I suppose you think the war is over and that we shall go back to the kind of world you lived in before it. But the war isn't over. The hate and evil is greater now than ever. Very soon war will break out again and overwhelm you. . . .The crowd outside thinks that Germany is crushed forever. But the Germans will soon rise again. Europe is done for. . . . The war isn't over. Even if the fighting should stop, the evil will be worse because the hate will be dammed up in men's hearts and will show itself in all sorts of ways.*[41]

The veterans who aspired to recapture the exhilaration experienced in combat made ideal recruits for extremist political movements that glorified action and promised to rescue society from a decadent liberalism. Hitler and Mussolini, both ex-soldiers imbued with the ferocity of the front, knew how to appeal to them. The lovers of violence and the harbingers of hate who took control of fascist parties would come within a hairsbreadth of destroying Western civilization. The intensified nationalist hatreds following World War I also helped fuel the fires of World War II. The Germans vowed to regain lands lost to the Poles. Some Germans, like the embittered Hitler, were consumed by anguish over a defeat that they believed never should have happened and over the humiliating Treaty of Versailles; a desire for revenge festered in their souls. Italy, too, felt aggrieved because it had not received more territory from the dismembered Austro-Hungarian Empire. Mussolini would cleverly exploit these feelings in his bid for power.

Yet, while some veterans clung to an aggressive militarism, others aspired to build a more humane world. Such veterans embraced democratic and socialist ideals and resolved that the bloodbath would never be repeated. Tortured by memories of war, European intellectuals wrote pacifist plays and novels and signed pacifist declarations. Indeed, in the 1930s, an attitude of "peace at any price" discouraged resistance to Nazi Germany in its bid to dominate Europe.

During World War I, new weapons were introduced, particularly the tank and the fighter plane, which revolutionized the future of warfare. Just prior to World War II, imaginative military planners recognized that planes and tanks, properly deployed, could penetrate and smash the enemy's defenses, circumventing the stalemate of trench warfare. Planes also meant terror from the skies, for bombs could pulverize a city, killing and maiming tens of thousands of civilians.

World War I was total war; it encompassed the entire nation and had no limits. States demanded total victory and total commitment from their citizens. They regulated industrial production, developed sophisticated propaganda techniques to strengthen morale, and exercised ever greater control over the lives of their people, organizing and disciplining them like soldiers. This total mobilization of nations' human and material resources provided a model for future dictators. With ever greater effectiveness and ruthlessness, dictators would centralize power and manipulate thinking. The ruthless dictatorships that emerged in Russia, Germany, and Italy were products of the war. The war gave Communists the opportunity to seize power in Russia, and the mentality of the front helped to mold the fascist movements that emerged in Italy and Germany. The barbarism of the trenches would be eclipsed in the postwar era by the horrors inflicted on people by totalitarian regimes.

❖ ❖ ❖

Notes

1. Arnold Toynbee, *Surviving the Future* (New York: Oxford University Press, 1971), pp. 106–107.
2. Quoted in Roland N. Stromberg, *Redemption by War* (Lawrence: Regents Press of Kansas, 1982), p. 24.
3. Excerpted in John W. Boyer and Jan Goldstein, eds., *Twentieth Century Europe,* vol. 9 of *University of Chicago Readings in Western Civilization*, ed. John W. Boyer and Julius Kirshner (Chicago: University of Chicago Press, 1987), p. 26.
4. Heinrich von Treitschke, *Politics*, excerpted in *Germany's War Mania* (New York: Dodd, Mead, 1915), pp. 222–223.
5. Friedrich von Bernhardi, *Germany and the Next War,* trans. Allan H. Fowles (New York: Longmans, Green, and Company, 1914), pp. 18, 24.
6. Quoted in James Joll, "The Unspoken Assumptions," in *The Origins of the First World War*, ed. H. W. Koch (New York: Taplinger, 1972), p. 325.
7. Quoted in Barbara Tuchman, *The Guns of August* (New York: Macmillan, 1962), pp. 46–47.
8. Fritz Fischer, *Germany's Aims in the First World War* (New York: Norton, 1967), p. 88.
9. Quoted in Joachim Remak, *The Origins of World War I* (New York: Holt, 1967), p. 135.
10. Rupert Brooke, "Peace," in *Collected Poems of Rupert Brooke* (New York: Dodd, Mead, 1941), p. 111.
11. Quoted in Joachim C. Fest, *Hitler* (New York: Harcourt Brace Jovanovich, 1973), p. 66.

12. Roland Dorgelàs, "After Fifty Years," in *Promise of Greatness*, ed. George A. Panichas (New York: John Day, 1968), pp. 14–15.
13. Excerpted in Joe H. Kirchberger, ed., *The First World War: An Eyewitness to History* (New York: Facts on File, 1992), p. 45.
14. Quoted in Tuchman, *The Guns of August*, p. 145.
15. Bertrand Russell, *The Autobiography of Bertrand Russell, 1914–1944* (Boston: Little, Brown, 1968), pp. 4, 6.
16. Quoted in Robert G. L. Waite, *Vanguard of Nazism* (New York: Norton, 1969), p. 22.
17. Brooke, "Peace," p. 111.
18. Quoted in Peter Gay, *Freud: A Life for Our Time* (New York: Norton), p. 348.
19. Quoted in Koch, *Origins of the First World War*, p. 318.
20. Stefan Zweig, *The World of Yesterday* (New York: Viking, 1970), p. 223.
21. Quoted in Tuchman, *Guns of August*, p. 51.
22. A. J. P. Taylor, *A History of the First World War* (New York: Berkeley, 1966), p. 84.
23. Quoted in Richard M. Watt, *Dare Call It Treason* (New York: Simon & Schuster, 1963), p. 215.
24. Quoted in Daniel M. Smith, *The Great Departure* (New York: Wiley, 1965), p. 20.
25. Quoted in S. L. A. Marshall, *The American Heritage History of World War I* (New York: Dell, 1966), p. 334.
26. Quoted in John Terraine, *To Win a War: 1918, the Year of Victory* (Garden City, N.Y.: Doubleday, 1981), p. 102.
27. Excerpted in Louis L. Snyder, ed., *Historic Documents of World War I* (Princeton, N.J.: Van Nostrand, 1958), p. 183.
28. Thomas A. Bailey, *Woodrow Wilson and the Lost Peace* (Chicago: Quadrangle Books, 1963), p. 29.
29. Ibid., p. 209.
30. Hajo Holborn, *The Political Collapse of Europe* (New York: Knopf, 1966), p. 102.
31. Quoted in Bailey, *Woodrow Wilson,* p. 303.
32. Excerpted in Ronald Kowalski, *The Russian Revolution, 1917–1921* (New York: Routledge, 1997), p. 20.
33. Quoted in Michael Adas, *Machines as the Measure of Man* (Ithaca, N.Y.: Cornell University Press, 1989), p. 376.
34. Quoted in Alistair Horne, *The Price of Glory* (New York: Harper, 1967), p. 240.
35. A. J. P. Taylor, *From Sarajevo to Potsdam* (New York: Harcourt, Brace & World, 1966), pp. 55–56.
36. Paul Valéry, *Variety* (New York: Harcourt, Brace, 1927), pp. 27–28.
37. Quoted in Modris Eksteins, *Rites of Spring: The Great War and the Birth of the Modern Age* (New York: Doubleday Anchor Books, 1989), p. 232.
38. Quoted in Eric J. Leed, *No Man's Land: Combat and Identity in World War I* (New York: Cambridge University Press, 1979), p. 201.
39. Quoted in Reginald Pound, *The Lost Generation of 1914* (New York: Coward-McCann, 1964), p. 80.
40. Quoted in Robert G. L. Waite, *Vanguard of Nazism* (New York: Norton, 1969), p. 42.
41. Quoted in Samuel Hynes, *A War Imagined* (New York: Atheneum, 1991), p. 266.

Suggested Reading

Albrecht-Carrie, René, *The Meaning of the First World War* (1965). How the war upset Europe's delicate equilibrium.

Bailey, Thomas, *Woodrow Wilson and the Lost Peace* (1963). A critical interpretation of the role of the United States at the peace conference.

Berghahn, V. R., *Germany and the Approach of War in 1914* (1975). Relates German foreign policy to domestic problems.

Essame, H., *The Battle for Europe, 1918* (1972). The last campaign.

Falls, Cyril, *The Great War* (1961). A good narrative of the war.

Figues, Orlando, *A People's Tragedy* (1996). A thorough, detailed, anecdotal, and comprehensive study of the Russian Revolution.

Fischer, Fritz, *Germany's Aims in the First World War* (1967). A controversial work stressing Germany's responsibility for the war.

Fussell, Paul, *The Great War and Modern Memory*

(1977). The influence of the Great War on British writers.

Geiss, Imanuel, ed., *July 1914* (1967). Selected documents.

Gilbert, Martin, *The First World War* (1994). Contains illuminating anecdotal material.

Horne, Alistair, *The Price of Glory* (1967). Brilliantly recaptures the battle of Verdun.

Joll, James, *The Origins of the First World War* (1984). Excellent work of synthesis.

Koch, H. W., ed., *The Origins of the First World War* (1972). Useful essays, particularly those dealing with the glorification of war before 1914.

Kowalski, Ronald, ed., *The Russian Revolution, 1917–1921* (1997). A useful collection of original sources.

Lafore, Laurence, *The Long Fuse* (1971). A beautifully written study of the causes of the conflict.

Leed, Eric J., *No Man's Land*: *Combat and Identity in World War I* (1979). The impact of the war on the men who participated in it.

Marshall, S. L. A., *The American Heritage History of World War I* (1966). Probably the best account available.

Panichas, George A., ed., *Promise of Greatness* (1968). Recollections of the war by people of prominence.

Remak, Joachim, *The Origins of World War I* (1967). A fine introduction.

Remarque, Erich Maria, *All Quiet on the Western Front* (1969). First published in 1929, this novel has become a classic.

Schmitt, Bernadotte, E., *The World in the Crucible, 1914–1919* (1984). The war and its aftermath. A volume in the distinguished *Rise of Modern Europe* series.

Service, Robert, *The Russian Revolution, 1900–1927* (1990). A brief overview.

Strachan, Hew, ed., *The Oxford Illustrated History of the First World War* (1998). Essays by an international team of specialists on many phases of the war.

Stromberg, Roland N., *Redemption by War: The Intellectuals and 1914* (1982). Analysis of the reasons why so many intellectuals welcomed the war.

Terraine, John, *To Win a War: 1918, the Year of Victory* (1981). The final campaign; contains numerous passages from primary sources.

Thomson, G. M., *The Twelve Days* (1964). Just prior to the hostilities.

Tuchman, Barbara, *The Guns of August* (1962). A beautifully written account of the opening weeks of World War I.

Watt, Richard M., *Dare Call It Treason* (1963). A brilliant study of the French army mutinies of 1917.

Williams, John, *The Other Battleground* (1972). A comparison of the home fronts in Britain, France, and Germany.

Winter, J. M., *The Experience of World War I* (1995). Excellent illustrations and eyewitness accounts are intgrated into a gripping narrative.

Review Questions

1. How did the nationality problems in Austria-Hungary contribute to the outbreak of World War I?
2. What were the principal purposes of Bismarck's system of alliances?
3. What condition led to the formation of the Triple Entente? How did Germany respond to it?
4. After the assassination of Archduke Francis Ferdinand, what policies were pursued by Austria-Hungary, Germany, Russia?
5. Was World War I inevitable?
6. In assessing responsibility for the war, what arguments have been advanced by historians for each of the major countries involved?
7. Why did many Europeans welcome the war?
8. What battle plans did Germany and France implement in 1914? What prevented Germany from reaching Paris in 1914?
9. Identify and explain the historical significance of the battles of Verdun and the Somme.
10. Why did the United States enter the war?
11. What was Wilson's peace program? What obstacles did he face?
12. What happened to Austria-Hungary as a result of the war and the peace settlement?
13. Why did the tsarist regime collapse in March 1917?
14. Why did the Provisional Government and liberal democracy fail in 1917?
15. How did World War I transform the consciousness of Europeans?

Chapter 30

An Era of Totalitarianism

The Nazi Mass Rally. The most effective means of uniting the masses, said Hitler, was the mass rally. Bombarded by the cheers of thousands of voices, by marching units, by a forest of banners, and by explosive oratory, the individual becomes convinced of the truth of the party's message. (AP/Wide World Photos.)

- **The Nature of Totalitarianism**
- **Communist Russia**
  War Communism and the New Economic Policy
  One-Party Dictatorship
  The Stalin Revolution
- **The Nature of Fascism**
- **The Rise of Fascism in Italy**
  Postwar Unrest
  Mussolini's Seizure of Power
- **The Fascist State in Italy**
  Consolidation of Power
  Control of the Masses
  Economic Policies
  The Church and the Fascist Regime
- **The New German Republic**
  Threats from Left and Right
  Economic Crisis
  Fundamental Weaknesses of the Weimar Republic
- **The Rise of Hitler**
  The Early Years
  The Nazi Party
  Hitler's World-View
  Hitler Gains Power
- **Nazi Germany**
  The Leader-State
  Economic Life
  Nazism and the Churches
  Shaping the "New Man"
  Anti-Semitic Legislation
  Mass Support
- **Liberalism and Authoritarianism in Other Lands**
  The Spread of Authoritarianism
  The Western Democracies

In the 1930s, the term *totalitarianism* was used to describe the Fascist regime in Italy, the National Socialist regime in Germany, and the Communist regime in the Soviet Union. To a degree that far exceeds the ancient tyrannies and early modern autocratic states, these dictatorships aspired to and, with varying degrees of success, attained control over the individual's consciousness and behavior and all phases of political, social, and cultural life. To many people it seemed that a crises-riddled democracy was dying and that the future belonged to these dynamic totalitarian movements.

Totalitarianism is a twentieth-century phenomenon, for such all-embracing control over the individual and society could be achieved only in an age of modern ideology, technology, and bureaucracy. The totalitarian state was more completely established in Germany and the Soviet Union than in Italy, where cultural and historic conditions impeded the realization of the totalitarian goal of monolithic unity and total control.

In *Totalitarian Dictatorship and Autocracy* (1956), Carl J. Friedrich and Zbigniew K. Brzezinski viewed fascist and communist dictatorships as "historically unique and *sui generis*"[1]—different in nature from ancient Oriental despotisms, the Roman Empire, the tyrannies of the Renaissance city-states, or the absolute monarchies of modern Europe. "Broadly speaking, totalitarian dictatorship is a new development; there has never been anything quite like it before." They contended further that "fascist and communist totalitarian dictatorships are basically alike."[2] The ideological aims and social and economic policies of Hitler and Stalin differed fundamentally. However, both Soviet Russia and Nazi Germany shared the totalitarian goal of total domination of the individual and institutions and employed similar methods to achieve it. Mussolini's Italy is more accurately called authoritarian, for the party-state either did not intend to control all phases of life or lacked the means to do so. Moreover, Mussolini hesitated to use the ruthless methods that Hitler and Stalin employed so readily.

The Nature of Totalitarianism

Striving for total unity, control, and obedience, the totalitarian dictatorship is the antithesis of liberal democracy. It abolishes all competing political parties, suppresses individual liberty, eliminates or regulates private institutions, and utilizes the modern state's bureaucracy and technology to impose its ideology and enforce its commands. The party-state determines what people should believe—what values they should hold. There is no room for individual thinking, private moral judgment, or individual conscience. The individual possesses no natural rights that the state must respect. The state regards individuals merely as building blocks, human material to be hammered and hewed into a new social order. It seeks to create an efficiently organized and stable society—one whose members do not raise troublesome questions or hold unorthodox opinions.

Nevertheless, the totalitarian dictatorship is also an unintended consequence of liberal democracy. It emerged in an age in which, because of the French and Industrial Revolutions, the masses had become a force in political life. The totalitarian leader seeks to gain and preserve power by harnessing mass support. Hitler, in particular, built a party within the existing constitutional system and exploited the electoral process in order to overthrow the democratic government.

Unlike previous dictatorial regimes, the dictatorships of both the left and the right sought to legitimatize their rule by gaining the masses' approval. They claimed that their governments were higher and truer expressions of the people's will. The Soviet and Nazi dictatorships established their rule in the name of the people—the German Volk or the Soviet proletariat.

A distinctive feature of totalitarianism is the overriding importance of the leader, who is seen as infallible and invincible. The masses' slavish adulation of the leader and their uncritical acceptance of the dogma that the leader or the party is always right promote loyalty, dedication, and obedience and distort rational thinking.

Totalitarian leaders want more than power for its own sake; in the last analysis, they seek to transform the world according to an all-embracing ideology, a set of convictions and beliefs that, says Hannah Arendt, "pretend[s] to know the mysteries of the whole historical process—the secrets of the past, the intricacies of the present, the uncertainties of the future."[3] The ideology constitutes a higher and infallible truth based on a law of history or social development that, says Karl Dietrich Bracher, "reduce[s] the past and the future to a single historical principle of struggle, no matter whether by state, nation, people, race, or class."[4] The ideology contains a dazzling vision of the future—a secular New Jerusalem—that strengthens the will of the faithful and attracts converts. "This utopian and chiliastic outlook of totalitarian ideologies," declare Friedrich and Brzezinski, "gives them a pseudoreligious quality. In fact, they often elicit in the less critical followers a depth of conviction and a fervor of devotion usually found only among persons inspired by a transcendent faith."[5] Like a religion, the totalitarian ideology provides its adherents with beliefs that make society and history intelligible, that explain all of existence in an emotionally gratifying way. A distinguishing feature of both communist and Nazi ideologies was the dogmatic belief that conflict—between classes for Marxists and between nations and races for Nazis—was the driving force in history.

The ideology—a "grand transcendent fiction [or] *metamyth*" in Brzezinski's apt phrase—promises to transform the social order in accordance with an ultimate and exclusive truth propagated by the party, thereby satisfying a human yearning for complete certitude.[6] Like a religion, it creates true believers, who feel that they are participating in a great cause—a heroic fight against evil—that gives meaning to their lives. During World War II, a German soldier fighting on the eastern front wrote to his brother that the battle "is for a new ideology, a new belief, a new life! I am glad that I can participate. . . . in this war of light and darkness."[7]

Also like a religion, the totalitarian party gives isolated and alienated individuals a sense of belonging, a feeling of camaraderie; it enables a person to lose himself or herself in the comforting and exhilarating embrace of a mass movement. The radical Russian anarchist Bakunin had sensed the seductive power of the community when he stated: "I do not want to be I, I want to be We."[8]

Not only did the totalitarian religion-ideology supply followers with a cause that claimed absolute goodness; it also provided a Devil. For the Soviets, the source of evil and the cause of all the

Chronology 30.1 ❖ Totalitarianism

November 1917	Bolsheviks, led by Lenin, take command in Russia
1918–20	Civil war and foreign intervention in Russia
March 1918	Treaty of Brest-Litovsk
July 1918	Nicholas II of Russia and his family are murdered
March 1919	Communist International is formed
1921–28	New Economic Policy
1922	Stalin becomes general secretary of the Communist party
1922	Mussolini rises to power
1923	Hitler's failed Beer Hall Putsch and subsequent imprisonment
January 1924	Lenin dies
1924	Constitution of the Union of Soviet Socialist Republics takes effect
1928	First Five-Year Plan starts rapid industrialization in Russia
October 1929	The Great Depression begins
1929	Stalin in sole command in Russia; collectivization of agriculture begins
1933	Hitler elected chancellor of Germany
1936	Stalin constitution: socialism achieved
1936–38	Stalin's terror purges
1936–39	Spanish Civil War
November 1938	Nazi pogrom—*Kristallnacht*
1939	Hitler invades Poland; World War II breaks out
June 1941	Hitler invades the Soviet Union

people's hardships were the degenerate capitalists, reactionary peasants who resisted collectivization, the traitorous Trotskyites, or the saboteurs and foreign agents, who impeded the realization of the socialist society. For the Nazis, the Devil was the conspirator Jew. These "evil" ones must be eliminated in order to realize the totalitarian movement's vision of the future. Thus, totalitarian regimes liquidate large segments of the population designated as "enemies of the people." Historical necessity or a higher purpose demands and justifies their liquidation. The appeal to historical necessity has all the power of a great myth. Presented as a world-historical struggle between the forces of good and the forces of evil, the myth incites fanaticism and numbs the conscience. Traditional rules of morality have no meaning; seemingly decent people engage in terrible acts of brutality with no remorse, convinced that they are waging a righteous war.

Totalitarians are utopians inspired by idealism; they seek the salvation of their nation, their race, or humanity. They believe that the victory of their cause will usher in the millennium, a state of harmony and bliss. Such a vision is attractive to people burdened by economic insecurity or spiritual disorientation. The history of the twentieth century demonstrates how easily utopian beliefs can be twisted into paranoid fantasies, idealistic sentiments transformed into murderous fanaticism, and destructive components of human nature mobilized and directed by demagogues.

Unlike earlier autocratic regimes, the totalitarian dictatorship is not satisfied with its subjects' outward obedience; it demands the masses' unconditional loyalty and enthusiastic support. It strives to control the inner person: to shape thoughts, feelings, and attitudes in accordance with the party ideology, which becomes an official creed. It does not rule by brute force alone but seeks to create a "new man," one who dedicates himself body and soul to the party and its ideology. Such unquestioning, faithful subjects can be manipulated by the party. The disinterested search for truth, justice, and goodness—the exploration of those fundamental moral, political, and religious questions that have characterized the Western intellectual tradition for centuries—is abandoned. Truth, justice, and goodness are what the party deems them to be, and ideological deviation is forbidden.

The totalitarian dictatorship deliberately politicizes all areas of human activity. Ideology pervades works of literature, history, philosophy, art, and even science. It dominates the school curriculum and influences everyday speech and social relations. The state is concerned with everything its citizens do: there is no distinction between public and private life, and every institution comes under the party-state's authority. If voluntary support for the regime cannot be generated by indoctrination, then the state unhesitatingly resorts to terror and violence to compel obedience. People live under a constant strain. Fear of the secret police is ever present; it produces a permanent state of insecurity, which induces people to do everything that the regime asks of them and to watch what they say and do.

Communist Russia

In 1918, Lenin's infant Communist government was threatened with civil war. Tsarist officers had gathered troops in the south; other anticommunist centers rose in Siberia, and still others in the extreme north and along the Baltic coast. The political orientation of these anticommunist groups, generally called Whites in contrast to the communist Reds, combined all shades of opinion, from moderate socialist to reactionary, the latter usually predominating. The Whites received support from foreign governments, which freely intervened. Until their own revolution in November 1918, the Germans occupied much of southern Russia. England, France, and the United States sent troops to points in northern and southern European Russia; England, Japan, and the United States also sent troops to Siberia. At first they wanted to offset German expansion, but later they hoped to overthrow the Communist regime. In May and June 1918, Czech prisoners of war, about to be evacuated, precipitated anticommunist uprisings along the Trans-Siberian Railroad, bringing the civil war to fever pitch.

In July 1918, Communists murdered Nicholas II and his entire family. In August, a noncommunist socialist nearly assassinated Lenin, while White forces in the south moved to cut off central Russia from its food supply. In response, the Communists speeded the buildup of their own Red Army. Recruited from the remnants of the tsarist army and its officer corps, the Red Army was reinforced by compulsory military service and strict discipline; Trotsky reintroduced the death penalty, which had been outlawed by the Provisional Government. Threatened with death if they refused, many tsarist officers served in the Red Army. They were closely watched by Trotsky's ruthless political commissars, who were also responsible for the political reliability and morale of the troops. Trotsky ordered the formation of "blocking units" to machine-gun retreating soldiers. The civil war was brutal; both sides butchered civilians and their own comrades.

In November 1918, thanks to the Allied victory and the American contribution to it, the German menace ended. Yet foreign intervention stepped up in response to the formation of the Communist International (Comintern), an organization founded by Lenin to guide the international revolutionary movement that he expected to issue from the world war. Lenin sought revolutionary support from abroad for strengthening his hand at home; his enemies reached into Russia to defeat at its source the revolution that they feared in their own countries. At the same time, the civil war rose to its climax.

Hard-pressed as Lenin's party was, by the autumn of 1920 it had prevailed over its enemies. The Whites were divided among themselves and discredited by their association with the tsarist regime; the Communists had greater popular support, the advantage of interior communications, and superior political skills. The war-weary foreign interventionists called off their efforts to overthrow the Communist regime by force.

The communist victory in the civil war exacted a staggering price. Reds and Whites alike carried the tsarist tradition of political violence to a new pitch of horror (some of it later described in novels by Boris Pasternak and Mikhail Sholokhov). The entire population, including the Communist party and its leaders, suffered in the war. Some 1.2 million combatants on both sides perished. In addition, the Communists killed some 250,000 peasants who resisted grain requisitions and executed tens of thousands of political opponents. Adding to the death toll were some 100,000 Jews, victims of pogroms perpetrated largely by the Whites. Compounding the nation's anguish was the famine of 1921–22, which claimed some five million victims.

War Communism and the New Economic Policy

Besides the extreme misery brought on by the world war and civil war, the Russian people had to endure the rigors of the policy known as "war communism." It was introduced in 1918 to deal with the plummeting agricultural and economic production, rampant inflation, and desperate hunger in the cities. Under war communism, the state took over the means of production and greatly limited private ownership; it conscripted labor and, in effect, confiscated grain from the peasants. War communism devastated the economy even further and alienated workers and peasants. The state-run factories were mismanaged, workers stayed away from their jobs or performed poorly, and peasants resisted the food requisition detachments that the government sent to seize their grain.

There was even open rebellion. In March 1921, sailors at the Kronstadt naval base and workers in nearby Petrograd—people who in 1917 had been ready to give their lives for the Revolution—rose against the repression that had been introduced during the civil war; they called for the establishment of socialist democracy. Trotsky ruthlessly suppressed that uprising, but the lesson was clear: the Communist regime had to retreat from war communism and to restore a measure of stability to the country.

In 1921, the Communist party adopted the New Economic Policy (NEP), which lasted until 1928. Under a system that Lenin characterized as "state socialism," the government retained control of finance, industry, and transportation—"the commanding heights" of the economy—but allowed the rest of the economy to return to private enterprise. Peasants, after giving part of their crops to the government, were free to sell the rest in the open market; traders could buy and sell as they pleased. With the resumption of small-scale capitalism, an air of normal life returned.

One-Party Dictatorship

While the Communists were waging a fierce struggle against the Whites, they instituted a militant dictatorship run by their party. Numbering about five hundred thousand members in 1921, the Communist party was controlled by a small, intimate group, the politburo (political bureau), which assumed a dictatorial role. The key leaders—Lenin, Trotsky, Stalin, and a few others—determined policy, assigned tasks, and appointed important officials. The party dominated all public agencies; its leaders held the chief positions in government. No other political parties were tolerated, and trade unions became agents of the regime. Never before had the people of Russia been forced into such compulsory unity and abject dependence on their government.

Impatient with the endless disputes among righteous and strong-willed old revolutionaries, Lenin, in agreement with other top leaders, demanded unconditional submission to his decisions. He even ordered that dissidents be disciplined and political enemies be terrorized. No price was too high to achieve monolithic party unity. Believing that they were creating a new and better society that would serve as a model for the rest of humanity, the Communists felt no moral objection to the use of force or even terror, including executions and forced-labor camps. The dreaded Cheka, a ruthless secret police organization, executed some two hundred thousand people from 1919 to 1925. The means Lenin employed for ruling his backward country denied the human values that Marx had taken from the Enlightenment and put into his vision of a socialist society. Lenin was perfectly willing to use state terror to promote the class struggle.

The Communists abolished the power of the

FORGING SOCIALISM. Men and women work equally in this socialist realist propaganda poster from 1921. (*From* Art of the October Revolution, *Mikail Guerman. Aurora Publishers, Leningrad. Reproduced by permission of V/O Vneshtorgizdat.*)

Orthodox church, which was the traditional ally of tsarism and the enemy of innovation. They were militant atheists, believing with Marx that religion was the "opium of the people"; God had no place in their vision of a better society. Above all, they wiped out—by expropriation, discrimination, expulsion, and execution—the educated upper class of bureaucrats, landowners, professional people, and industrialists.

The Communist party promised "to liberate woman from all the burdens of antiquated methods of housekeeping, by replacing them by house-communes, public kitchens, central laundries, nurseries, etc."[9] But traditional values, particularly in the Asian parts of the Soviet Union, hardly favored equality between the sexes, especially in political work. The practical necessity of combining work with family responsibility, moreover, tended to keep women out of managerial positions in the party and the organizations of the state, but the ideal remained alive.

The Communists never ceased to stress that they worked strenuously for the welfare of the vast majority of the population. They received much acclaim for their emphasis on providing housing, food, and clothing and making education, theater, and other cultural activities, previously reserved for the elite, available to the masses. Although the Communists were not opposed to some private ownership of property, they outlawed income-producing property that enabled capitalists to employ (or exploit, as the Communists said) others for their own profit.

For Lenin, socialism meant reeducating the unruly masses to higher standards of individual conduct and economic productivity that would be superior to capitalism. In the spring of 1918, he complained that Russian workers had not yet matched capitalist performance: "The Russian worker is a bad worker compared with the workers of the advanced, i.e., western countries." To overcome this deficiency, Lenin urged competition—socialist competition—and hammered home the need for "iron discipline at work" and "unquestioning obedience" to a single will, that of the Communist party. There was no alternative: "Large-scale machinery calls for absolute and strict unity of will, which directs the joint labors of hundreds and thousands and tens of thousands of people. A thousand wills are subordinated to one will."[10]

In those words lay the essence of subsequent Soviet industrialization. The economy was to be monolithic, rationally planned, and focused on pursuing a single goal: overcoming the weaknesses of Russia so disastrously demonstrated in the war. Allowing workers to make their own decisions, Lenin held, would perpetuate Russian backwardness. Instead, he called for a new "consciousness," a hard-driving work ethic expressed in the Russian Marxist revolutionary vocabulary.

In attempting to transform their Soviet Russia into a modern industrialized state that would serve as a model for the world, the Communists imposed a new autocracy even more authoritarian than the old. In order to survive, Russia would be rebuilt against the people's will, if necessary. In the view of the party leaders, the masses always needed firm guidance. The minds of the people, therefore, came under unprecedented government control. In education, from kindergarten through university, in the press, on radio, and in literature and the arts, the Communist party tried to fashion people's thoughts to create the proper "consciousness."

The party made Marxism-Leninism the sole source of truth, eliminating as best it could all rival creeds, whether religious, political, or philosophical. Thinking was to be as reliably uniform as machine processes and totally committed to the party. Moreover, thoughts were to be protected against subversive capitalist influences. Soviet Russia, the party boasted, had risen to a superior plane of social existence and would attract other revolutionary states to its federal union, until eventually it covered the entire world. Lest Soviet citizens doubt their new superiority, the party prohibited all uncontrolled comparison with other countries.

Lenin molded Soviet Russia into an international revolutionary force, the champion of anticapitalism and of the liberation of colonial peoples. The Russian Revolution inspired nationalistic ambitions for political self-determination and cultural self-assertion among a growing number of peoples around the world, especially in Asia. It appealed particularly to intellectuals educated in the West (or in westernized schools) yet identifying themselves with their downtrodden compatriots.

To have a political tool for world revolution, Lenin created the Communist—or Third—International (Comintern). The most radical successor to earlier socialist international associations, it helped organize small Communist parties in western Europe, which in time became dependable, though rather powerless, agents of Soviet Russia. In Asia, where no proletariat existed, Lenin tried to work closely with incipient nationalist movements. Lenin and the Bolshevik Revolution gained the admiration and instinctive loyalty of colonial and semicolonial people in what would come to be called the Third World.

In 1923, a new constitution laid down federal guidlines for Soviet Russia, henceforth officially known as the Union of Soviet Socialist Republics (U.S.S.R.) or the Soviet Union. Having captured the attention of the world, the Soviet Union now stood out as the communist alternative to the capitalist West.

The Stalin Revolution

Lenin died in 1924, and the task of achieving the goal that he had set was taken up by Stalin. The "man of steel" was crude and vulgar, toughened by the revolutionary underground and tsarist prisons and by the roughest aspects of Russian life. Relentlessly energetic but relatively inconspicuous among key Bolsheviks, Stalin had been given, in 1922, the unwanted and seemingly routine task of general secretary of the party. He used this position to his own advantage, building up a reliable party cadre—apparatus men, or *apparatchiki*, as they came to be called—and dominating the party as not even Lenin had done. When he was challenged, particularly by Trotsky and his associates, in the protracted struggles for the succession to Lenin, it was too late to unseat him. None of Stalin's rivals could rally the necessary majorities at the party congresses; none could match Stalin's skill in party infighting or in making rough and anarchic people into docile members of the Communist party apparatus.

Industrialization. To Stalin, Russia's most pressing need was not world revolution but the fastest possible buildup of Soviet power through industrialization. The country could not afford to risk near-annihilation again, as it had done in the world war and then in the civil war. Communist pride dictated that the country be made as strong as possible. Stalin set forth the stark reckoning of Russian history in a speech delivered in 1931, three years after launching a program of massive industrialization:

> *Those who fall behind get beaten, But we do not want to be beaten. No, we refuse to be beaten. One feature of the history of old Russia was the continual beatings she suffered for falling behind, for her backwardness. All beat her—for her backwardness, for military backwardness, cultural backwardness, political backwardness, for industrial backwardness, for agricultural backwardness. She was beaten because to do so was profitable and could be done with impunity. . . . You are backward, you are weak—therefore you are wrong, hence you can be beaten and enslaved. You are mighty, therefore you are right, hence we*

FORCED LABOR IN THE GULAG. All those accused of disloyalty to the party and not killed outright ended up in one of the gulags, or forced-labor camps. Forced labor was designed as a punishment and also as a means of obtaining raw materials from inhospitable regions in the far north. In this photo, deported peasants and political prisoners using primitive technology are engaged in constructing the canal linking Leningrad with the White Sea. Millions perished in the gulags. (*David King Collection, London, England.*)

> *must be wary of you. Such is the law of the exploiters. . . . That is why we must no longer lag behind.*[11]

Stalin decided on all-out industrialization at the expense of the toiling masses. Peasants and workers, already poor, would be required to make tremendous sacrifices of body and spirit to overcome the nation's weaknesses.

Abandoning the NEP, Stalin decreed a series of Five-Year Plans, the first and most experimental one commencing in 1928. The industrialization drive was heralded as a vast economic and social revolution, undertaken by the state according to a rational plan. The emphasis lay on heavy industry: the construction of railroads, power plants, steel mills, and military hardware, such as tanks and warplanes. Production of consumer goods was cut to the minimum, and all small-scale private trading, revived under the NEP, came to an end—with disastrous results for the standard of living. Having just come within sight of their pre-1914 standard of living, Russians now found their expectations dashed.

A new grim age of drastic material hardships and profound anguish began. Harsh punishments, including denial of food cards and imprisonment, were meted out for lateness, slowness, or incompetence. Many people, however, particularly the young, were fired to heroic exertions. They were proud to sacrifice themselves for the building of a superior society. And many common factory workers had the opportunity to attend school and become engineers and administrators, tying them to the regime. When the Great Depression in the capitalist countries put millions out of work, no Soviet citizen suffered from unemployment; in the 1930s, gloom pervaded the West, but confidence and hope, artificially fostered by the party, buoyed up many people in Soviet Russia. The first two Five-Year Plans dramatically and rapidly increased Russia's industrial infrastructure as factories, mines, dams, and railroads were feverishly constructed. At no time, though, did the planning produce Western-style efficiency, and workers, who labored in a herculean way, actually suffered a decline in real wages. The regime concentrated on heavy industry, not consumer goods or improving the standard of living.

Collectivization. Meanwhile, a different and far more brutal revolution overtook Soviet agriculture: peasants were forcibly integrated into the planned economy through collectivization. Agriculture—peasants, their animals, and their fields—was subjected to the same rational control as industry. Collectivization meant the pooling of farmland, animals, and equipment to achieve efficient, large-scale production. The Communist solution for the backwardness of Russian agriculture had long been for the peasants to become like workers. But knowing the peasants' distaste for the factory, their attachment to their own land, and their stubbornness, the party had hesitated to carry out its ambitious scheme. In 1929, however, Stalin believed that, for the sake of industrialization, he had no choice. If the Five-Year Plan was to succeed, the government had to receive planned crops of planned size and quality at planned times. This could be accomplished, Stalin thought, only by destroying the independent peasantry and creating huge agricultural factories. With collectivization, the ascendancy of the party over the people of Russia became almost complete.

The peasants paid a ghastly price. Stalin declared war on the Russian countryside. He ordered that the *kulaks*, the most enterprising and well-to-do peasants, be "liquidated as a class." Many were killed outright, and millions were deported to forced-labor camps in the far north, where most ultimately perished from hunger or abuse. Their poorer and less efficient neighbors were herded onto collective farms at the point of a bayonet.

The peasants struck back, sometimes in pitched battles. The horror of forced collectivization broke the spirit even of hardened officials. "I am an old Bolshevik," sobbed a secret police colonel to a fellow passenger on a train; "I worked in the underground against the Tsar and then I fought in the civil war. Did I do all that in order that I should now surround villages with machine guns and order my men to fire indiscriminately into crowds of peasants? Oh, no, no!"[12] Typically, however, the local officials and activists who stripped the peasants of their possessions and searched for hidden grain viewed themselves as idealists building a new society that was in the best interests of a suffering humanity; they infused their own ruthlessness into the official orders. Their dedication to the triumph of communism overcame all doubts caused by the sight of starving people and the sounds of wailing women and children.

Defeated but unwilling to surrender their livestock, the peasants slaughtered their animals, gorging themselves in drunken orgies against the days of inevitable famine. The country's cattle herds declined by one-half, inflicting irreparable secondary losses as well. The number of horses, crucial for rural transport and farm work, fell by one-third. Crops were not planted or not harvested, the Five-Year Plan was disrupted, and from 1931 to 1933 millions starved to death.

The suffering was most cruel in the Ukraine, where famine killed approximately seven million people, many after extreme abuse and persecution. In order to buy industrial equipment abroad so that industrialization could proceed on target, the Soviet Union had to export food, as much of it as possible and for prices disastrously lowered by the Great Depression. Let the peasants in the Ukrainian breadbasket perish so that the country could grow strong! Moreover, Stalin relished the opportunity to punish the Ukrainians for their disloyalty during the civil war and their resistance to collectivization.

By 1935, practically all farming in Russia was collectivized. The kulaks had been wiped out as a class, and the peasants, ever rebellious under the tsars, had been cowed into permanent submission. In theory, the collective farms were run democratically, under an elected chairman; in practice, they followed as best they could the directives handed down from the nearest party office. People grumbled about the rise of a new serfdom. Agricultural development had been stifled.

Total Control. To quash resistance and mold a new type of suitably motivated and disciplined citizen, Stalin unleashed a third revolution, the revolution of totalitarianism. Only communist regimentation, he believed, could liberate Russia from its historic inferiority. Moreover, the totalitarian state accorded with his desire to exercise total control over the party and the nation. Stalin's totalitarianism aimed at a complete reconstruction of state and society, down to the in-

Map 30.1 The Union Republics of the Union of Soviet Socialist Republics (U.S.S.R.) The Soviet Union consisted of many different nationalities whose nationalist aspirations were held in check by the repressive regime.

nermost recesses of human consciousness. It called for "a new man," suited to the needs of Soviet industrialism.

The revolution of totalitarianism encompassed all cultural activity. All media of communication—literature, the arts, music, the stage—were forced into subservience to the Five-Year Plan and Soviet ideology. In literature, as in all art, an official style was promulgated. Called *socialist realism*, it was expected to describe the world as the party saw it or hoped to shape it. Novels in the social realist manner told how the romances of tractor drivers and milkmaids or of lathe operators and office secretaries led to new victories of production under the Five-Year Plan. Composers found their music examined for remnants of bourgeois spirit; they were to write simple tunes suitable for heroic times. Everywhere huge, high-color posters showed men and women hard at work with radiant faces, calling others to join them; often Stalin, the wise father and leader, was shown among them. In this way, artistic creativity was locked into a dull, utilitarian straitjacket of official cheerfulness; creativity was allowed only to boost industrial productivity. Behind the scenes, all artists were disciplined to conform to the will of the party or be crushed.

Education, from nursery school to university, was likewise harnessed to train dutiful and loyal citizens, and Soviet propaganda made a cult of Stalin that bordered on deification. Thus, a writer declared in 1935:

> *Centuries will pass and the generations still to come will regard us as the happiest of mortals, as the most fortunate of men, because we . . . were privileged to see Stalin, our inspired leader. Yes, and we regard ourselves as the*

> *happiest of mortals because we are the contemporaries of a man who never had an equal in world history. The men of all ages will call on thy name, which is strong, beautiful, wise, and marvellous. Thy name is engraven on every factory, every machine, every place on the earth, and in the hearts of all men.*[13]

But still the Russian masses resisted the enforced change to the large-scale, rigid regimentation of modern industrialism. Against that dogged resistance, Stalin unleashed raw terror to break stubborn wills and compel conformity. Terror had been used as a tool of government ever since the Bolsheviks seized power. Lenin, who had provided theoretical justification for terror in the struggle against tsarism, employed it after the Revolution (and the tsars had also used it, moderately and intermittently). After the start of the first Five-Year Plan, show trials were staged in which engineers who disagreed with Stalin's production timetable were denounced as saboteurs. The terror used to herd the peasants onto collective farms was even greater. Stalin also used terror to crush opposition and to instill abject fear in the ranks of the party and in Russian society at large.

Purges had long been used to rid the party of weaklings. After 1934, however, they became an instrument of Stalin's drive for unchallenged personal power. In 1936, his vindictive terror broke into the open. The first batch of victims, including many founders of the Communist party, were accused of conspiring with the exiled Trotsky to set up a "terrorist center" and of scheming to terrorize the party. After being sentenced to death, they were immediately executed. In 1937, the next group, including prominent Communists of Lenin's day, were charged with cooperating with foreign intelligence agencies and wrecking "socialist reconstruction," the term for Stalin's revolution; they too were executed. Shortly afterward, a secret purge decimated the military high command—almost half the country's seventy thousand officers were either shot or sent to the camps—for which the country paid a heavy price when Germany attacked in 1941.

In 1938, the last and biggest show trial advanced the most bizarre accusation of all: sabotage, espionage, and attempting to dismember the Soviet Union and kill all its leaders (including Lenin in 1918). In the public hearings, some defendants refuted the public prosecutor, but in the end all confessed, usually after torture and threats to their family, before being executed. Western observers were aghast at the cynical charges and at the physical and mental tortures used to obtain the confessions.

The great trials, however, involved only a small minority of Stalin's victims; many more perished in silence without benefit of legal proceedings. The terror first hit members of the party, especially the Old Bolsheviks, who had joined before the Revolution; they were the most independent-minded members and therefore the most dangerous to Stalin. But Stalin also decimated the cultural elite that had survived the Lenin revolution. Thousands of engineers, scientists, industrial managers, scholars, and artists disappeared; they were shot or sent to forced-labor camps, where most of them perished. Their relatives also suffered, often fired from their jobs, evicted from their apartments, exiled to remote regions, and even sentenced to labor camps. No one was safe. To frighten the common people in all walks of life, men, women, and even children were dragged into the net of Stalin's secret police, leaving the survivors with a soul-killing reminder: submit or else.

Stalin may have orchestrated the terror, but large numbers of party members believed that terror, which was decimating their own ranks, was necessary. The memory of the vicious civil war, when domestic and foreign enemies sought to overthrow the new Bolshevik regime, and the resistance of the kulaks to collectivization created a siege mentality among the Communist leadership. Everywhere they saw anti-Soviets plotting against the party; they defined these enemies as Trotskyites, former kulaks, Whites who had fought in the civil war, members of outlawed anti-Soviet political parties, foreign agents, and criminals—cattle and horse thieves, contraband smugglers, bandits, and so on. Party officials saw terror as a legitimate way both of protecting the party to which they were ideologically committed and from which they derived prestige, power, and material benefits, and of protecting the Soviet experiment, which they viewed as humanity's best hope.

The toll of the purges is reckoned in many millions; it included Trotsky, who in 1940 was murdered in Mexico. The bloodletting was ghastly, as Stalin's purge officials themselves followed each other into death and ignominy. Stalin, however, was untroubled by the waste of life. By showing party officials and the Russian masses how vulnerable they were, how dependent they were on his will, he frightened them into servility. No doubt, the terror was also an expression of his craving for personal power and his vengeful and suspicious, some say clinically paranoid, nature. He saw enemies everywhere, took pleasure in selecting victims, and reveled in his omnipotence. For good reason, Stalin has been called a twentieth-century Ivan the Terrible. Like the sixteenth-century tsar, for whom he expressed admiration, Stalin stopped at no brutality in order to establish personal autocracy.

But more than a craving for personal power motivated Stalin. He regarded himself as Lenin's heir, responsible for securing and expanding the Revolution and defending it against foreign and domestic enemies. The only way to do this was to create a powerful Soviet Union through rapid modernization. Stalin, who had passed through the hands of the tsarist police and participated in the carnage of the civil war, believed that without the total obedience of the Russian peoples the Soviet state and society could not be effectively modernized and that terror was necessary to compel compliance. Stalin, as much a Russian patriot as a Marxist, did not forget the threat to Russia's survival after World War I. He was keenly aware of the political ambitions of Mussolini, of Japanese expansionism in the Far East, and eventually of German rearmament under Hitler. As he had said in 1931, if the Soviet Union did not make the utmost effort to strengthen itself within ten years, it could not withstand another attack; its peoples would perish under foreign domination. In Stalin's mind, totalitarianism was necessary to save Russia from foreign enemies that would devour it. Ten years after Stalin's warning of 1931, Hitler's armies invaded the Soviet Union, ready to exploit, enslave, and annihilate its citizens and seize its territory. The expansion of industrial capacity under Stalin was a key reason why Russia ultimately defeated the Nazi invaders.

The Nature of Fascism

Liberals viewed the Great War as a conflict between freedom and autocracy and expected an Allied victory to accelerate the spread of democracy throughout Europe. Right after the war, it seemed that liberalism would continue to advance as it had in the nineteenth century. The collapse of the autocratic German and Austrian Empires had led to the formation of parliamentary governments throughout eastern and central Europe. Yet within two decades, in an extraordinary turn of events, democracy seemed in its death throes. In Spain, Portugal, Italy, and Germany, and in all the newly created states of central and eastern Europe except Czechoslovakia, democracy collapsed, and various forms of authoritarian government emerged. The defeat of democracy and the surge of authoritarianism was best exemplified by the triumph of totalitarian fascist movements in Italy and Germany; with brutal frankness, their leaders proclaimed that individual freedom, a relic of a dying liberal age and a barrier to national greatness, would be dispensed with.

The emergence of fascist movements in more than twenty European lands after World War I was a sign that liberal society was in a state of disorientation and dissolution. The cultural pessimism, disdain for reason, elitism, romantic glorification of action and heroism, and contempt for liberal values voiced by many intellectuals and nationalists before the war found expression after the war in the antidemocratic and irrational fascist ideologies, which altered European political life. Fascism marked the culmination of the counter-Enlightenment mentality inherent in the extreme nationalism and radical conservatism of the late nineteenth century and in the repudiation of modern Western civilization by disenchanted intellectuals.

As a Europe-wide phenomenon, fascism was a response to a postwar society afflicted with spiritual disintegration, economic dislocation, political instability, and thwarted nationalist hopes. A general breakdown of meaning and values led people to search for new beliefs and new political arrangements. Fascism was an expression of fear that the Bolshevik Revolution would spread westward. It was also an expression of hostility to democratic values and a reaction to the failure of liberal institutions to solve the problems of modern industrial society. Disillusioned with liberal government that failed to cope with massive social and economic problems, particularly during the Depression, many Europeans were tempted by authoritarian alternatives that would dispense with parliamentary government and the protection of individual rights. Anything seemed better than the ineffectual parliaments that appeared helpless in the face of mounting misery.

Fascist movements were marked by a determination to eradicate liberalism and Marxism—to undo the legacy of the French Revolution of 1789 and the Bolshevik Revolution of 1917. Fascists believed that theirs was a spiritual revolution, that they were initiating a new era in history and building a new civilization on the ruins of liberal democracy. "We stand for a new principle in the world," said Mussolini. "We stand for the sheer, categorical, definitive antithesis to the world of democracy . . . to the world which still abides by the fundamental principles laid down in 1789."[14] The chief principle of Nazism, said Hitler, "is to abolish the liberal concept of the individual and the Marxist concept of humanity, and to substitute for them the Volk community, rooted in the soil and united by the bond of its common blood."[15] The fascists' uniforms, songs, flags, parades, mass rallies, and cult of physical strength and violence all symbolized this call for a reawakened and reunited people.

Fascists accused liberal society of despiritualizing human beings and transforming them into materialistic creatures whose highest ideal was moneymaking. Regarding liberalism as bankrupt and parliamentary government as futile, many people yearned for a military dictatorship. To fascists and their sympathizers, democracy seemed an ineffective and enfeebled Old Order ready to be overthrown. Idealistic youth and intellectuals rejoiced in fascist activism. They saw fascism as a revolt against the mediocrity of the liberal state and modern mass society and a reaffirmation of the noblest human qualities: heroism and dedication to one's people. Fascists saw themselves as participants in a dynamic mass movement that would rectify the weaknesses and irresolution of parliamentary government and rid the nation of corrosive foreign influences. For them, the triumph of fascism would mark a new beginning for their nation and a new era in world history.

The fascist vision of a regenerated nation—a New Order led by a determined and heroic elite—arising from the ruins of a decadent Old Order had the appeal of great myth; it evoked belief, commitment, and loyalty. The myth of rebirth—a nation cured of evil and building a new and vigorous society—had a profound impact on people dissatisfied with liberal society and searching for new beliefs. The myth of the nation reborn answered a metaphysical yearning to give meaning to life and history. It provided an emotionally gratifying world-view at a time when many people had lost confidence in liberal-democratic ideals and institutions.

Fascists regarded Marxism as another enemy, for class conflict divided and weakened the state. To fascists, the Marxist call for workers of the world to unite meant the death of the national community. Fascism, in contrast, would reintegrate the proletariat into the nation and end class hostilities by making people at all levels feel that they were a needed part of the nation. Fascism thus offered a solution to the problem of insecurity and isolation in modern industrial society.

Attacking the rational tradition of the Enlightenment, fascism exalted will, blood, feeling, and instinct. Intellectual discussion and critical analysis, said fascists, cause national divisiveness; reason promotes doubt, enfeebles the will, and hinders instinctive, aggressive action. Fascism made a continual appeal to the emotions as a means of integrating the national community. This flow of emotion fueled irrational and dangerous desires, beliefs, and expectations, which blocked critical judgment and responsible action. Glorifying action for its own sake, fascists aroused and manipulated brutal and primitive impulses and carried into politics the combative spirit of the trenches. They formed private armies, which attracted veterans—many of them rootless, brutal, and maladjusted men who sought to preserve the loyalty, camaraderie, and violence of the front.

Fascist ideology exalted the leader, who, it was believed, intuitively grasped what was best for the nation. It also called for rule by an elite of dedicated party members. The leader and the party would relieve the individual of the need to make decisions. Convinced that the liberal stress on individual freedom promoted national divisiveness, fascists pressed for monolithic unity: one leader, one party, one ideology, and one national will.

Fascism drew its mass support from the lower middle class: small merchants, artisans, white-collar workers, civil servants, and peasants of moderate means, all of whom were frightened both by big capitalism and by Marxism. They hoped that fascism would protect them from the competition of big business and prevent the hated working class from establishing a Marxist state, which would threaten their property. The lower middle class saw in fascism a noncommunist way of overcoming economic crises and restoring traditional respect for family, native soil, and nation. Furthermore, many of these people saw fascism as a way of attacking the existing social order, which denied them opportunities for economic advancement and social prestige.

Although a radicalized middle class gave fascist movements their mass support, the fascists could not have captured the state without the aid of existing ruling elites: landed aristocrats, industrialists, and army leaders. In Russia, the Bolsheviks had to fight their way to power; in Italy and Germany, the old ruling order virtually handed power to the fascists. In both countries, fascist leaders succeeded in reassuring the conservative elite that they would not institute widespread social reforms or interfere with private property and would protect the nation from communism. Even though the old elite often abhorred fascist violence and demagoguery, it entered into an alliance with the fascists to protect its interests. In Germany, the elite could not have installed Hitler into power had he not had the electoral backing of a significant number of Germans.

In their struggle to bring down the liberal state, fascist leaders aroused primitive impulses and tribal loyalties; they made use of myths and rituals to mobilize and manipulate the masses. Organizing their propaganda campaigns with the rigor of a military operation, fascists stirred and dominated the masses and confused and undermined their democratic opposition, breaking its will to resist. Fascists were most successful in countries with weak democratic traditions. When parliamentary government faltered, it had few staunch defenders, and many people were drawn to charismatic demagogues who promised direct action.

The proliferation of fascist movements demonstrated that the habits of democracy are not quickly learned, easily retained, or even desired. Particularly during times of crisis, people lose patience with parliamentary discussion and constitutional procedures, sink into nonrational modes of thought and behavior, and are easily manipulated by unscrupulous politicians. For the sake of economic or emotional security and national grandeur, they will often willingly sacrifice political freedom. Fascism starkly manifested the immense power of the irrational; it humbled liberals, making them permanently aware of the limitations of reason and the fragility of freedom.

The fascist goal of maximum centralization of power was furthered by developments during World War I: the expansion of bureaucracy, the concentration of industry into giant monopolies, and the close cooperation between industry and the state. The instruments of modern technology—radio, motion pictures, public address systems, telephone, and teletype—made it possible for the state to indoctrinate, manipulate, and dominate its subjects.

The Rise of Fascism in Italy

Postwar Unrest

Although Italy was on the winning side in World War I, it resembled a defeated nation. Food shortages, rising prices, massive unemployment, violent strikes, workers occupying factories, and peasants squatting on the uncultivated periphery of large estates created a climate of crisis. These dismal conditions contrasted sharply with the vision of a postwar world painted by politicians during the war. Italy required effective leadership and a reform program, but party disputes paralyzed the liberal government. With several competing parties, the liberals could not organize a solid majority that could cope with the domestic crisis.

The middle class was severely stressed. To meet accelerating expenses, the government increased taxes, but the burden fell unevenly on small landowners, small business owners, civil service workers, and professionals. Moreover, the value of war bonds, purchased primarily by the middle class, declined considerably because of inflation. Instead of being able to retrieve the good old days and their former status once the war ended, these solid citizens found that their economic position continued to deteriorate.

Large landowners and industrialists feared that their nation was on the verge of a Bolshevik-style revolution. They took seriously the proclamations of the socialists: "The proletariat must be incited to the violent seizure of political and economic power and this must be handed over entirely and exclusively to the Workers' and Peasants' Councils."[16] In truth, Italian socialists had no master plan to seize power. Peasant squatters and urban strikers were responding to the distress in their own regions and did not significantly coordinate their efforts with those in other localities. Besides, when workers realized that they could not keep factories operating, their revolutionary zeal waned and they started to abandon the plants. The workers' and peasants' poorly led and futile struggles did not portend a Red revolution. Nevertheless, the industrialists and landlords, with the Bolshevik Revolution still vivid in their minds, were taking no chances.

Adding to the unrest was the national outrage at the terms of the peace settlement. Italians felt that despite their sacrifices—five hundred thousand dead and one million wounded—they had been robbed of the fruits of their victory. Although Italy had received the Brenner Pass and Trieste, it had been denied the Dalmatian coast, the Adriatic port of Fiume, and territory in Africa and the Middle East. Nationalists blamed the liberal government for what they called a "mutilated victory." In 1919, a force of war veterans, led by the poet and adventurer Gabriele D'Annunzio (1863–1938), seized Fiume, to the delirious joy of Italian nationalists and the embarrassment of the government. D'Annunzio's occupation of the port lasted more than a year, adding fuel to the flames of Italian nationalism and demonstrating the weakness of the liberal regime in imposing its authority on rightist opponents.

MUSSOLINI WITH HIS TROOPS. The Italian dictator deliberately tried to sustain an image of a virile warrior. Although Mussolini established a one-party state, he was less successful than Hitler or Stalin in creating a totalitarian regime. (*AP/Wide World.*)

Mussolini's Seizure of Power

Benito Mussolini (1883–1945) was born in a small village in east-central Italy. Proud, quarrelsome, violent, and resentful of the humiliation he suffered for being poor, the young Mussolini was a troublemaker and was often brought before school authorities. But he was also intelligent, ranking first on final examinations in four subjects. After graduation, Mussolini taught in an elementary school, but this work did not suit his passionate temperament. From 1902 to 1904, he lived in Switzerland, where he broadened his reading, lectured, and wrote. He also came under the influence of anarchists and socialist revolutionaries.

Returning to Italy, Mussolini was labeled a dangerous revolutionary by the police. As a reward for his zeal and political agitation, which led to five months in prison for inciting riots, in 1912 he was made editor of *Avanti*, the principal socialist newspaper. During the early days of World War I, he was expelled from the Socialist party for advocating Italian intervention in the war. After Italy entered the war, Mussolini served at the front and, during firing practice, suffered a serious wound, for which he was hospitalized.

In 1919, Mussolini organized the Fascist party to realize his immense will to power. The quest for power, the yearning for action and a release of dynamic energy, more than a set of coherent doctrines, characterized the young movement. A supreme opportunist rather than an ideologist, Mussolini exploited the unrest in postwar Italy in order to capture control of the state. He attracted converts from among the discontented, the disillusioned, and the uprooted. Many Italians, particularly the educated bourgeois who had been inspired by the unification movement of the nineteenth century, viewed Mussolini as the leader who would gain Fiume, Dalmatia, and colonies and win Italy's rightful place of honor in international affairs.

Hardened war veterans, who had been told that they would be rewarded for their sacrfices at the front but instead confronted unemployment and landlessness, were drawn to fascism's dynamism. So too were veterans eager to escape the boredom and idleness of civilian life, which seemed so squalid in comparison with the high drama of battle. These demobilized soldiers welcomed an opportunity to wear the uniforms of the Fascist militia (Black Shirts), parade in the streets, and fight socialist and labor union opponents. Squads of Fascist Black Shirts (*squadristi*) raided socialist and trade union offices, destroying property and beating the occupants. As socialist Red Shirts responded in kind, it soon appeared that Italy was drifting toward civil war.

Hoping that Mussolini would rescue Italy from Bolshevism, industrialists and landowners contributed large sums to the Fascist party. The lower middle class, fearful that the growing power of labor unions and the Socialist party threatened their property and social prestige, viewed Mussolini as a protector. Middle-class university students, searching for adventure and an ideal, and army officers, dreaming of an Italian empire and hostile to parliamentary government, were also attracted to Mussolini's party. Intellectuals disenchanted with liberal politics and parliamentary democracy were intrigued by his philosophy of action. Mussolini's nationalism, activism, and anticommunism gradually seduced elements of the power structure: capitalists, aristocrats, army officers, the royal family, and the church.

In 1922, Mussolini made his bid for power. Speaking at a giant rally of his followers in late October, he declared: "Either they will give us the government or we shall take it by descending on Rome. It is now a matter of days, perhaps hours." A few days later, thousands of Fascists began the March on Rome. Some members of Parliament demanded that the army defend the government against a Fascist coup. It would have been a relatively simple matter to crush the twenty thousand Fascist marchers, armed with little more than pistols and rifles, but King Victor Emmanuel III (1869–1947) refused to act. The king's advisers, some of them sympathetic to Mussolini, exaggerated the strength of the Fascists. Believing that he was rescuing Italy from terrible violence, the king appointed Mussolini prime minister.

Mussolini had bluffed his way to power. Fascism had triumphed not because of its own strength—the Fascists had only 35 of the 535 seats in Parliament—but because the liberal government, irresolute and indecisive, did not counter force with force. In the past, the liberal state had not challenged Fascist acts of terror; now it feebly surrendered to Fascist blustering and threats. No doubt, liberals hoped that, once in power, the Fascists would forsake terror, pursue moderate aims, and act within the constitution. But the liberals were wrong; they had completely misjudged the antidemocratic character of fascism.

The Fascist State in Italy

Consolidation of Power

In October 1922, when Italy's liberal government capitulated, the Fascists by no means held total power. Anti-Fascists still sat in Parliament, and only four of the fourteen ministers in Mussolini's cabinet were Fascists. Cautious and shrewd, Mussolini resisted the extremists in his party, who demanded a second revolution: the immediate and preferably violent destruction of the Old Order. In this early stage of Fascist rule, when his position was still tenuous, Mussolini sought to maintain an image of respectability and moderation. He tried to convince the power structure that he intended to operate within the constitution, and he did not seek dictatorial power. At the same time, he gradually secured his position and turned Italy into a one-party state. In 1923, the Acerbo electoral law, approved by both chambers of the parliament, decreed that the party with the most votes in a national election (provided that the figure was not less than 25 percent of the total votes cast) would be granted two-thirds of the seats in the Chamber of Deputies. In the elections of 1924, which were marred by Fascist terrorism, Mussolini's supporters received 65 percent of the vote. Even without the implementation of the new electoral law, the opponents of fascism had been enfeebled. Mussolini had consolidated his power.

When socialist leader Giacomo Matteotti protested Fascist terror tactics, Fascist thugs killed him (in 1924). Although Mussolini had not ordered Matteotti's murder, his vicious attacks against his socialist opponent inspired the assassins. Repelled by the murder, some sincere democrats withdrew from the Chamber of Deputies in protest and some influential Italians called for Mussolini's dismissal. But the majority of liberals, including the leadership, continued to support Mussolini. And the king, the papacy, the army, large landowners, and industrialists, still regarding Mussolini as the best defense against internal disorder and Marxism, failed to back an anti-Fascist movement.

Pressed by the radicals within the Fascist party, Mussolini moved to establish a dictatorship. In 1925–26, he eliminated non-Fascists from his cabinet and dissolved opposition parties. He also smashed the independent trade unions, suppressed opposition newspapers, replaced local mayors with Fascist officials, and organized a secret police to round up troublemakers. Many anti-Fascists fled the country or were deported.

Mussolini then turned on the extremist Fascists, the local chieftains (*ras*) who had led squadristi in the early days of the movement. Lauding violence, daring deeds, and the dangerous life, the ras were indispensable during the party's formative stage. But Mussolini feared that their radical adventurism posed a threat to his personal rule. And their desire to replace the traditional power structure with people drawn from their own ranks could block his efforts to cooperate with the established elite: industrialists, aristocratic landowners, and army leaders. Consequently, Mussolini expelled some squadristi leaders from the party and gave others positions in the bureaucracy to tame them.

Mussolini was less successful than Hitler and Stalin in fashioning a totalitarian state. The industrialists, the large landowners, the church, and to some extent even the army never fell under the complete domination of the party. Nor did the regime possess the mind of its subjects with the same thoroughness as the Nazis did in Germany. Life in Italy was less regimented and the individual less fearful than in Nazi Germany or Communist Russia. The Italian people might cheer Mussolini, but few were willing to die for him.

Control of the Masses

Like Communist Russia and Nazi Germany, Fascist Italy used mass organizations and mass media to control minds and regulate behavior. As in the Soviet Union and the Third Reich*, the Fascist regime created a cult of the leader. "Mussolini goes forward with confidence, in a halo of myth, almost chosen by God, indefatigable and infallible, the instrument employed by Providence for the creation of a new civilization," wrote the philosopher Giovanni Gentile.[17] To convey the image of a virile leader, Mussolini had himself photographed barechested or in a uniform with a steel helmet. Other photographs showed him riding horses, driving fast cars, flying planes, and playing with lion cubs. Mussolini frequently addressed huge throngs of admirers from his balcony. His tenor voice, grandiloquent phrases, and posturing—jaw thrust out, hands on hips, rolling eyes—captivated audiences. Idolatry from the masses, in turn, intensified Mussolini's feelings of grandeur. Elementary school textbooks depicted Mussolini as the savior of the nation, a modern-day Julius Caesar.

Fascist propaganda urged that the grandeur of the Roman Empire be restored through conquest. It also inculcated habits of discipline and obedience: "Mussolini is always right." "Believe! Obey! Fight!" Propaganda also glorified war: "A minute on the battlefield is worth a lifetime of peace." It enticed Italians with a utopian vision—a proud, powerful, and vigorous nation imbued with the martial spirit of their Roman ancestors. The press, radio, and cinema idealized life under fascism, implying that fascism had eradicated crime, poverty, and social tensions. Schoolteachers and university professors were compelled to swear allegiance to the Fascist government and to propagate Fascist ideals, while students were urged to criticize instructors who harbored liberal attitudes. Millions of youths belonged to Fascist organizations, in which they participated in patriotic ceremonies and social functions, sang Fascist hymns, and wore Fascist uniforms. They submerged their own identities in the group.

*Third Reich was the official Nazi designation for the Hitler regime as the presumed successor of the Holy Roman Empire, 800–1806 (the First Reich), and the German Empire, 1871–1918 (the Second Reich). The Nazis boasted that the Third Reich would last a thousand years.

Economic Policies

Fascists denounced economic liberalism for promoting individual self-interest, and socialism for instigating conflicts between workers and capitalists, which divided and weakened the nation. The Fascist way of resolving tensions between workers and employers was to abolish independent labor unions, prohibit strikes, and establish associations or corporations, which included both workers and employers from a given industry. In theory, representatives of labor and capital would cooperatively solve labor problems in a particular industry. In practice, the representatives of labor turned out to be Fascists who protected the interests of the industrialists. Although the Fascists lauded the corporative system as a creative approach to modern economic problems, in reality it played a minor role in Italian economic life. Big business continued to make its own decisions, paying scant attention to the corporations.

Nor did the Fascist government solve Italy's long-standing economic problems. To curtail the export of capital and reduce the nation's dependence on imports in case of war, Mussolini sought to make Italy self-sufficient. To win the "battle of grain," the Fascist regime brought marginal lands under cultivation and urged farmers to concentrate on wheat rather than other crops. Although wheat production thus increased substantially, total agricultural output declined because wheat was planted on land better suited to animal husbandry and fruit cultivation. To make Italy industrially self-sufficient, the regime limited imports of foreign goods, with the result that Italian consumers paid higher prices for Italian-manufactured goods. Mussolini posed as the protector of the little people, but under his regime the power and profits of big business grew and the standard of living of small farmers and urban workers declined. Government attempts to grapple with the depression were halfhearted. Aside from providing family allowances—an increase in income with the birth of each child—the Fascist regime did little in the way of social welfare.

The Church and the Fascist Regime

Although anticlerical since his youth, Mussolini practiced expediency. He recognized that coming to terms with the church would improve his image with Catholic public opinion. The Vatican regarded Mussolini's regime as a barrier against communism and as less hostile to church interests and more amenable to church direction than a liberal government. Pope Pius XI (1922–1939) was an ultraconservative whose hatred of liberalism and secularism led him to believe that the Fascists would increase the influence of the church in the nation.

In 1929, the Lateran Accords recognized the independence of Vatican City, repealed many of the anticlerical laws passed under the liberal government, and made religious instruction compulsory in all secondary schools. The papal state, Vatican City, became a small enclave within Rome over which the Italian government had no authority. Relations between the Vatican and the Fascist government remained fairly good throughout the 1930s. One crisis arose in 1931 when Mussolini, pushed by militant anticlericals within his party, dissolved certain Catholic youth groups as rivals to Fascist youth associations; but a compromise that permitted the Catholic organizations to function within certain limits eased tensions. When Mussolini invaded Ethiopia and intervened in the Spanish Civil War, the church supported him. Although the papacy criticized Mussolini for drawing closer to Hitler and introducing anti-Jewish legislation, it never broke with the Fascist regime.

The New German Republic

In the last days of World War I, a revolution brought down the German government, a semi-authoritarian monarchy, and led to the creation of a democratic republic. In October 1918, the German admirals ordered the German navy to engage the British in the English Channel, but the sailors, anticipating peace and resentful of their officers (who commonly resorted to cruel discipline), refused to obey. Joined by sympathetic soldiers, the mutineers raised the red flag of revolution. The revolt soon spread as military men and workers demonstrated for peace and reform and in some regions seized authority. Reluctant to fire on their comrades and also fed up with the war, German troops did not move to crush the revolutionaries.

On November 9, 1918, the leaders of the government announced the end of the monarchy, and

Rosa Luxemburg Speaking in Stuttgart. A prominent member of the Social Democrats, Luxemburg rejected the argument of revisionists that capitalism could be reformed and revolution avoided. She was sentenced to prison for opposing Germany's entry into the war. Immediately after the war she emerged as one of the leaders of the newly established German Communist party, or Spartacists. The attempted uprising of the Spartacists in 1919 was crushed, and Luxemburg was murdered by the Free Corps. (© *Topham, The Image Works.*)

Kaiser William II fled to Holland. Two days later, the new German republic, headed by Friedrich Ebert (1871–1925), a Social Democrat, signed an armistice agreement ending the war. Many Germans blamed the new democratic republic for the defeat—a baseless accusation, for the German generals, knowing that the war was lost, had sought an armistice. This legend that traitors, principally Jews and Social Democrats, cheated Germany of victory was created and propagated by the conservative right—generals, high-ranking bureaucrats, university professors, and nationalists, who wanted to preserve the army's reputation and bring down the new and hated democratic Weimar Republic.

In February 1919, the recently elected National Assembly met at Weimar and proceeded to draw up a constitution for the new state. The Weimar Republic—born in revolution, which most Germans detested, and military defeat, which many attributed to the new government—faced an uncertain future.

Threats from Left and Right

Dominated by moderate socialists, the infant republic faced internal threats from both the radical left and the radical right. In January 1919, the newly established German Communist party, or Spartacists, disregarding the advice of their leaders, Rosa Luxemburg and Karl Liebknecht, took to the streets of Berlin and declared Ebert's government deposed. To crush the revolution, Ebert turned to the Free Corps: volunteer brigades of ex-soldiers and adventurers, led by officers loyal to the emperor, who had been fighting to protect the eastern borders from encroachments by the new states of Poland, Estonia, and Latvia. The men of the Free Corps relished action and de-

THE GERMAN INFLATION, 1923. As the value of the mark plummeted, many Germans lost their entire savings, which had taken a lifetime to accumulate. Here children play with now worthless banknotes. (*Hulton-Deutsch Collection/Corbis.*)

spised Bolshevism. They suppressed the revolution and murdered Luxemburg and Liebknecht on January 15. In May 1919, the Free Corps also marched into Munich to overthrow the soviet republic set up there by communists a few weeks earlier.

The Spartacist revolt and the short-lived soviet republic in Munich (and others in Baden and Brunswick) had a profound effect on the German psyche. The communists had been easily subdued, but fear of a communist insurrection remained deeply embedded in the middle and upper classes—a fear that drove many into the ranks of the Weimar Republic's right-wing opponents.

In March 1920, the republic was threatened by the radical right. Refusing to disband as the government ordered, detachments of the right-wing Free Corps marched into Berlin and declared a new government, headed by Wolfgang Kapp, a staunch German nationalist. President Ebert and most members of the cabinet and National Assembly fled to Stuttgart. Insisting that it could not fire on fellow soldiers, the German army, the Reichswehr, made no move to defend the republic. A general strike called by the labor unions and the socialist parties prevented Kapp from governing, and the coup collapsed. However, the Kapp Putsch demonstrated that the loyalty of the army to the republic was doubtful and that important segments of German society supported the overthrow, by violence, if necessary, of the Weimar Republic and its replacement by an authoritarian government driven by a nationlist credo.

Economic Crisis

In addition to uprisings by the left and right, the republic was burdened by an economic crisis. During the war, Germany had financed its military expenditures not by increasing taxation but through short-term loans, accumulating a huge debt that now had to be paid. A trade deficit and enormous reparation payments worsened the nation's economic plight. Unable to meet the deficit in the national budget, the government simply printed more money, causing the value of the German mark to decline precipitously. In 1914, the mark stood at 4.2 to the dollar; in 1919, at 8.9 to the dollar; and in early 1923, at 18,000 to the dollar. In August 1923, a dollar could be exchanged for 4.6 million marks and in November, for 4 billion marks. Bank savings, war bonds, and pensions, representing years of toil and thrift, became worthless. Blaming the government for this disaster, the ruined middle class became more receptive to ultrarightist movements that aimed to bring down the republic.

With the economy in a shambles, the republic defaulted on reparation payments. Premier Raymond Poincaré (1860–1934) of France took a hard line. In January 1923, he ordered French troops into the Ruhr, the nerve center of German industry. Responding to the republic's call for passive resistance, factory workers, miners, and railroad workers in the Ruhr refused to work for the French. To provide strike benefits for the

Ruhr workers, the government printed yet more money, making inflation even worse.

In August 1923, Gustav Stresemann became chancellor. The new government lasted only until November 1923, but during those one hundred days, Stresemann skillfully placed the republic on the path to recovery. Warned by German industrialists that the economy was at the breaking point, Stresemann abandoned the policy of passive resistance in the Ruhr and declared Germany's willingness to make reparation payments. Stresemann issued a new currency backed by a mortgage on German real estate. To reduce public expenditures, which contributed to inflation, the government fired some civil service workers and lowered salaries; to get additional funds, it raised taxes; to protect the value of the new currency, it did not print another issue. Inflation receded, and confidence was restored.

A new arrangement regarding reparations also contributed to the economic recovery. Recognizing that in its present economic straits Germany could not meet its obligations to the Allies or secure the investment of foreign capitalists, Britain and the United States pressured France to allow a reparation commission to make new proposals. In 1924, the parties accepted the Dawes Plan, which reduced reparations and based them on Germany's economic capacity. During the negotiations, France agreed to withdraw its troops from the Ruhr—another step toward easing tensions for the republic.

From 1924 to 1929, economic conditions improved. Foreign capitalists, particularly Americans, were attracted by high interest rates and the low cost of labor. Their investments in German businesses stimulated the economy. By 1929, iron, steel, coal, and chemical production exceeded prewar levels. The value of German exports also surpassed that of 1913. This spectacular boom was partly due to more effective methods of production and management and the concentration of related industries in giant trusts. Real wages were higher than before the war, and improved unemployment benefits made life better for the workers. It appeared that Germany had also achieved political stability, as threats from the extremist parties of the left and the right subsided. Given time and economic stability, democracy might have taken firmer root in Germany. But then came the Great Depression. The global economic crisis that began in October 1929 revealed how weak the Weimar Republic was.

Fundamental Weaknesses of the Weimar Republic

German political experience provided poor soil for transplanting an Anglo-Saxon democratic parliamentary system. Before World War I, Germany had been a semi-autocratic state ruled by an emperor who commanded the armed forces, controlled foreign policy, appointed the chancellor, and called and dismissed Parliament. This authoritarian system blocked the German people from acquiring democratic habits and attitudes. Still accustomed to rule from above, still adoring the power state, many Germans sought the destruction of the Weimar Republic.

Traditional conservatives—the upper echelons of the civil service, judges, industrialists, large landowners, and army leaders—were contemptuous of democracy and were avowed enemies of the republic. They wanted to restore a pre-1914 authoritarian government, which would fight liberal ideals and protect the fatherland from Bolshevism. These traditional conservatives regarded the revolution against the monarchy in the last weeks of the war as a treacherous act and the establishment of a democratic republic as a violation of Germany's revered tradition of hierarchical leadership. Nor did the middle class feel a commitment to the liberal-democratic principles on which the republic rested. The traditionally nationalistic middle class identified the republic with defeat in war and the humiliation of the Versailles treaty. Rabidly antisocialist, this class saw the leaders of the republic as Marxists who would impose a working-class state on Germany.

Right-wing intellectuals often attacked democracy as a barrier to the true unity of the German nation. In the tradition of nineteenth-century Volkish thinkers, they scorned reason and political freedom and glorified instincts, race, and action. In doing so, they turned many Germans against the republic, eroding the popular support on which democracy depends. As the German historian Kurt Sontheimer puts it,

> *The submission of a large part of German intellectual society to the National Socialist*

> *Weltanschauung [world-view] . . . would have been inconceivable without the anti-democratic intellectual movement that preceded it and that, in its contempt for everything liberal, had blunted people's sensibilities to the inviolable rights of the individual and the preservation of human dignity. . . . Nothing is more dangerous in political life than the abandonment of reason. . . . The intellect must remain the controlling, regulating force in human affairs. The anti-democratic intellectuals of the Weimar period . . . despised reason and found more truth in myth or in the blood surging in their veins. . . . Had they a little more reason and enlightenment, these intellectuals might have seen better where their zeal was leading them and their country.*[18]

The Weimar Republic also showed the weaknesses of the multiparty system. With the vote spread over a number of parties, no one party held a majority of seats in the parliament (Reichstag), and so the republic was governed by a coalition of several parties. But because of ideological differences, the coalition was always unstable and in danger of failing to function. This is precisely what happened during the Great Depression. When effective leadership was imperative, the government could not act. Political deadlock caused Germans to lose what little confidence they had in the democratic system. Support for the parties that wanted to preserve democracy dwindled, and extremist parties that aimed to topple the republic gained strength.

Supporting the republic were Social Democrats, Catholic Centrists, and German Democrats; a coalition of these parties governed the republic during the 1920s.* Seeking to bring down the republic were the Communists, on the left, and two rightist parties, the Nationalists and the National Socialist German Workers' party, led by Adolf Hitler.

*The Social Democrats hoped one day to transform Germany into a Marxist society, but they had abandoned revolutionary means and pursued a policy of moderate social reform. The largest party until the closing months of the Weimar Republic, the Social Democrats were committed to democratic principles and parliamentary government. The Catholic Center party opposed socialism and protected Catholic interests but, like the Social Democrats, supported the republic. The German Democratic party consisted of middle-class liberals who also opposed socialism and supported the republic. Although the right-wing German People's party was more monarchist than republican, on occasion it joined the coalition of parties that sought to preserve the republic.

The Rise of Hitler

The Early Years

Adolf Hitler (1889–1945) was born in the town of Braunau am Inn, Austria, on April 20, 1889, the fourth child of a minor civil servant. Much of his youth was spent in Linz, a major city in Upper Austria. A poor student at secondary school, although by no means unintelligent, Hitler left high school and lived idly for more than two years. In 1907, the Vienna Academy of Arts rejected his application for admission. After the death of his mother in December 1907 (his father had died in 1903), Hitler drifted around Vienna, viewing himself as an art student. Contrary to his later description of these years, Hitler did not suffer great poverty, for he received an orphan's allowance from the state and an inheritance from his mother and an aunt. When the Vienna Academy again refused to admit him in 1908, he did not seek to learn a trade or to work steadily but earned some money by painting picture postcards.

Hitler was a loner, often given to brooding and self-pity. He found some solace by regularly attending Wagnerian operas (much admired by German nationalists for their glorification of German folk traditions), by fantasizing about great architectural projects that he would someday initiate, and by reading. He read a lot, especially in art, history, and military affairs. He also read the racial, nationalist, anti-Semitic, and Pan-German literature that abounded in multinational Vienna. This literature introduced Hitler to a bizarre racial mythology: a heroic race of blond, blue-eyed Aryans battling for survival against inferior races. The racist treatises preached the danger posed by mixing races, called for the liquidation of racial inferiors, and marked the Jew as the embodiment of evil and the source of all misfortune.

In Vienna, Hitler came into contact with Georg von Schönerer's Pan-German movement. For Schönerer, the Jews were evil not because of their religion, not because they rejected Christ, but because they possessed evil racial qualities.

Schönerer's followers wore watch chains with pictures of hanged Jews attached. Hitler was particularly impressed with Karl Lueger, the mayor of Vienna, a clever demagogue who skillfully manipulated the anti-Semitic feelings of the Viennese for his own political advantage. In Vienna, Hitler also acquired a hatred for Marxism and democracy and the conviction that the struggle for existence and the survival of the fittest are the essential facts of the social world. His years in Vienna emptied Hitler of all compassion and scruples and filled him with a fierce resentment of the social order, which, he felt, had ignored him, cheated him, and condemned him to a wretched existence.

When World War I began, Hitler was in Munich. He welcomed the war as a relief from his daily life, which lacked purpose and excitement. Volunteering for the German army, Hitler found battle exhilarating, and he fought bravely, twice receiving the Iron Cross.

The experience of battle taught Hitler to prize discipline, regimentation, leadership, authority, struggle, and ruthlessness. The shock of Germany's defeat and of revolution intensified his commitment to racial nationalism. To lead Germany to total victory over its racial enemies became his obsession. Like many returning soldiers, he required vindicating explanations for lost victories. His own explanation was simple and demagogic: Germany's shame was due to the creators of the republic, the "November criminals"; and behind them was a Jewish-Bolshevik world conspiracy.

The Nazi Party

In 1919, Hitler joined the German Workers' Party, a small right-wing group and one of the more than seventy extremist military-political-Volkish organizations that sprang up in postwar Germany. Displaying fantastic energy and extraordinary ability as a demagogic orator, propagandist, and organizer, Hitler quickly became the leader of the party, whose name was changed to National Socialist German Workers' party (commonly called Nazi). As leader, Hitler insisted on absolute authority and total allegiance—a demand that coincided with the postwar longing for a strong leader who would set right a shattered nation. Without Hitler, the National Socialist German Workers' party would have remained an insignificant group of discontents and outcasts. Demonstrating a Machiavellian cunning in politics, Hitler tightened the party organization and perfected the techniques of mass propaganda.

Like Mussolini, Hitler incorporated military attitudes and techniques into politics. Uniforms, salutes, emblems, flags, and other symbols imbued party members with a sense of solidarity and camaraderie. At mass meetings, Hitler was a spellbinder who gave stunning performances. His pounding fists, throbbing body, wild gesticulations, hypnotic eyes, rage-swollen face, and repeated, frenzied denunciations of the Versailles treaty, Marxism, the republic, and Jews inflamed and mesmerized the audience. Many listeners—and his speeches generally attracted people already hostile to the Weimar Republic—were swayed by Hitler's earnestness, conviction, and self-confidence. They believed that Hitler and his movement could restore Germany's strength and pride. Hitler instinctively grasped the innermost feelings of his audience: its resentments and its longings. "The intense will of the man, the passion of his sincerity seemed to flow from him into me. I experienced an exaltation that could be likened only to religious conversion," said one early admirer.[19]

In November 1923, Hitler attempted to seize power in Munich, in the state of Bavaria, as a prelude to toppling the republic. The attempt, which came to be known as the Beer Hall Putsch, failed, and the Nazis made a poor showing; they quickly scattered when the Bavarian police opened fire. Ironically, however, Hitler's prestige increased, for when he was put on trial, he used it as an opportunity to denounce the republic and the Versailles treaty and to proclaim his philosophy of racial nationalism. His impassioned speeches, publicized by the press, earned Hitler a nationwide reputation and a light sentence: five years' imprisonment, with the promise of quick parole. While in prison, Hitler dictated *Mein Kampf*, a rambling and turgid work, which contained the essence of his worldview.

The unsuccessful Munich putsch taught Hitler a valuable lesson: armed insurrection against superior might fails. He would gain power not by force but by exploiting the instruments of democracy: elections and party politics. He would use apparently legal means to destroy the Weimar Republic and impose a dictatorship. As Nazi propaganda expert Joseph Goebbels would later express it, "We have openly declared that we use

ADOLF HITLER. In this painting by a German artist, Hitler is idolized as a heroic medieval knight. (*U.S. Army.*)

democratic methods only to gain power and that once we had it we would ruthlessly deny our opponents all those chances we had been granted when we were in the opposition."[20]

Hitler's World-View

Some historians see Hitler as an unprincipled opportunist and a brilliant tactician who believed in nothing but cleverly manufactured and manipulated ideas that were politically useful in his drive for power. To be sure, Hitler was concerned not with the objective truth of an idea but with its potential political usefulness. He was not a systematic thinker like Marx. Whereas communism claimed the certainty of science and held that it would reform the world in accordance with rational principles, Hitler proclaimed the higher validity of blood, instinct, and will and regarded the intellect as an enemy of the soul. Hitler, nevertheless, possessed a remarkably consistent ideology. As Hajo Holborn explains,

> *Hitler was a great opportunist and tactician, but it would be quite wrong to think that ideology was for him a mere instrumentality for gaining power. On the contrary, Hitler was a doctrinaire of the first order. Throughout his political career he was guided by an ideology . . . which from 1926 onward [did] not show any change whatsoever.*[21]

Hitler's thought comprised a patchwork of nineteenth-century anti-Semitic, Volkish, Social Darwinist, antidemocratic, and anti-Marxist ideas. From these ideas, many of which enjoyed wide popularity, Hitler constructed a world-view rooted in myth and ritual. Given to excessive daydreaming and never managing to "overcome his youth with its dreams, injuries, and resentments,"[22] Hitler sought to make the world accord with his fantasies—struggles to the death between races, a vast empire ruled by a master race, and a thousand-year Reich.

German thought, particularly after Nietzsche, was permeated by the idea of crisis: that Germany and Europe were experiencing a unique historical upheaval. The unexpected loss in World War I intensified the feeling among Germans that the nation required a radical transformation, a new beginning. Hitler conceived himself as a man of destiny leading a movement of world-historical significance; he had a mission to rescue the nation by imbuing Germans with a rejuvenating ideology, one that was inherent in their primordial past.

Racial Nationalism. Nazism rejected both Judeo-Christian and Enlightenment traditions and sought to found a new world order based on racial nationalism. For Hitler, race was the key to understanding world history. He believed that Western civilization was at a critical juncture. Liberalism was dying, and Marxism, that "Jewish invention," as he called it, would inherit the future unless it was opposed by an even more powerful world-view. "With the conception of race National Socialism will carry its revolution and recast the world," said Hitler.[23] As the German barbarians had overwhelmed a disintegrating Roman Empire, a reawakened, racially united Germany, led by men of iron will, would undo the humiliation of the Versailles treaty, carve out a vast European empire, and deal a decadent liberal civilization its deathblow. It would conquer Russia, eradicate communism, and reduce to serfdom the subhuman Slavs, "a mass of born slaves who feel the need of a master."[24]

In the tradition of crude Volkish nationalists and Social Darwinists, Hitler divided the world into superior and inferior races and pitted them against each other in a struggle for survival. For him, this fight for life, that is, for territory and resources, was a law of nature and of history. The Germans, descendants of ancient Aryans, possessed superior racial characteristics; a nation degenerates and perishes if it allows its blood to be contaminated by intermingling with lower races. Conflict between races was desirable, for it strengthened and hardened racial superiors. It made them ruthless—a necessary quality in this Darwinian world. As a higher race, the Germans were entitled to conquer and subjugate other races. Germany must acquire *Lebensraum* (living space) by expanding eastward at the expense of the racially inferior Slavs.

The Jew as Devil. An obsessive and virulent hatred of Jews dominated Hitler's mental outlook. In waging war against the Jews, Hitler believed that he was defending Germany from its worst enemy, a sinister force that stood in total opposition to the new world he envisioned. In Hitler's mythical interpretation of the world, the Aryan was the originator and carrier of civilization. As descendants of the Aryans, the German race embodied creativity, bravery, and loyalty. As a counterpart, Jews, who belonged to a separate biological race, personified the vilest qualities. "Two worlds face one another," said Hitler in a statement that clearly reveals the mythical character of his thought, "the men of God and the men of Satan! The Jew is the anti-man, the creature of another god. He must have come from another root of the human race. I set the Aryan and the Jew over and against each other."[25] Everything Hitler despised—liberalism, intellectualism, pacifism, parliamentarianism, internationalism, communism, modern art, and individualism—he attributed to Jews.

For Hitler, the Jew was the mortal enemy of racial nationalism. The moral outlook of the ancient Hebrew prophets, which affirmed individual worth and made individuals morally responsible for their actions, was totally at odds with Hitler's morality, which subordinated the individual to the national community. Hitler once called conscience a Jewish invention. The prophetic vision of the unity of humanity under God and the belief in equality, justice, and peace were also contrary to Hitler's creed that all history is a pitiless struggle between races and that only the strongest and most ruthless deserve to survive.

Hitler's anti-Semitism served a functional purpose as well. By concentrating all evil in one enemy, "the conspirator and demonic" Jew, Hitler provided true believers with a simple, all-embracing, and emotionally satisfying explanation for their misery. By defining themselves as the racial and spiritual opposites of Jews, true believers of all classes felt joined together in a Volkish union. By seeing themselves engaged in a heroic battle for self-preservation and racial survival against a demonic enemy that embodied evil, they strengthened their will. Even failures and misfits gained self-respect. Anti-Semitism provided insecure and hostile people with powerless but recognizable targets on whom to focus their antisocial feelings.

The surrender to myth served to disorient the intellect and unify the nation. When the mind accepts an image such as Hitler's image of Jews as vermin, germs, and satanic conspirators, it has lost all sense of balance and objectivity. Such a disoriented mind is ready to believe and to obey, to be manipulated and to be led, to brutalize and to tolerate brutality; it is ready to be absorbed into the collective will of the community. That many people, including intellectuals and members of the elite, accepted these racial ideas shows the enduring power of mythical thinking and the vulnerability of reason. In 1933, the year Hitler took power, Felix Goldmann, a German-Jewish writer, commented astutely on the irrational character of Nazi anti-Semitism: "The present-day politicized racial anti-Semitism is the embodiment of myth, . . . nothing is discussed . . . only felt, . . . nothing is pondered critically, logically or reasonably, . . . only inwardly perceived, surmised. . . . We are apparently the last [heirs] of the Enlightenment."[26]

The Importance of Propaganda. Hitler understood that in an age of political parties, universal suffrage, and a popular press—the legacies of the French and Industrial Revolutions—the successful leader must win the support of the masses. To do so, Hitler consciously applied and perfected elements of circus showmanship, church pageantry, American advertising, and the techniques of propaganda that the Allies had used to stir their civilian populations during the war. To be effective, said Hitler, propaganda must be aimed principally at the emotions. The masses are not moved by scientific ideas or by objective and abstract knowledge, but by primitive feelings, terror, force, and discipline. Propaganda must reduce everything to simple slogans incessantly repeated and must concentrate on one enemy. The masses are aroused by the spoken, not the written, word—by a storm of hot passion erupting from the speaker, "which like hammer blows can open the gates to the heart of the people."[27]

The most effective means of stirring the masses and strengthening them for the struggle ahead, Hitler had written in *Mein Kampf*, is the mass meeting. Surrounded by tens of thousands of people, individuals lose their sense of individuality and no longer see themselves as isolated. They become members of a community bound together by an esprit de corps reminiscent of the trenches during the Great War. Bombarded by the cheers of thousands of voices, by marching units, by banners, by explosive oratory, individuals become convinced of the truth of the party's message and the irresistibility of the movement. Their intellects overwhelmed, their resistance lowered, they lose their previous beliefs and are carried along on a wave of enthusiasm. Their despair over the condition of their nation turns to hope, and they derive a sense of belonging and mission. They feel that they are participants in a mighty movement that is destined to regenerate the German nation and initiate a new historical age. "The man who enters such a meeting doubting and wavering leaves it inwardly reinforced; he has become a link to the community."[28]

Hitler Gains Power

When Hitler left prison in December 1924, after serving nine months, he proceeded to tighten his hold on the Nazi party. He relentlessly used his genius for propaganda and organization to strengthen the loyalty of his cadres and to instill in them a sense of mission. In 1925, the Nazi party counted about 27,000 members; in 1929, it had grown to 178,000, with units throughout Germany. But its prospects seemed dim, for since 1925, economic conditions had greatly improved—Germany's exports had even surpassed those of Britain—and the republic seemed politically stable. In 1928, the National Socialists (NSDAP) received only 2.6 percent of the vote. Nevertheless, Hitler never lost faith in his own capacities or his destiny. He continued to build his party and waited for a crisis that would rock the republic and make his movement a force in national politics.

The Great Depression, which began in the United States at the end of 1929, provided that crisis. Desperate and demoralized people lined up in front of government unemployment offices. Street peddlers, beggars, and youth gangs proliferated; suicides increased, particularly among middle-class people shamed by their descent into poverty, idleness, and uselessness. As Germany's economic plight worsened, the German people became more amenable to Hitler's radicalism. The Nazis tirelessly expanded their efforts. Everywhere, they staged mass rallies, plastered walls with posters, distributed leaflets, and engaged in street battles with their opponents of the left. Hitler promised all things to all groups, avoided debates, provided simple explanations for Germany's misfortunes, and insisted that only the Nazis could rescue Germany. Nazi propaganda attacked the communists, the "November criminals," the democratic system, the Versailles treaty, reparations, and the Jews. It depicted Hitler as a savior. Hitler would rescue Germany from chaos; he understood the real needs of the Volk; he was sent by destiny to lead Germany in its hour of greatest need. These propaganda techniques worked. The Nazi party went from 810,000 votes in 1928 to 6.4 million in 1930, and its representation in the Reichstag soared from 12 to 107.

The Social Democrats (SPD), the principal defenders of democracy, could draw support only from the working class; to the middle class, they were hated Marxists. Moreover, in the eyes of many Germans, the SPD was identified with the status quo, that is, with economic misery and national humiliation. Swallowing right-wing propaganda, they held the founders and leaders of the Weimar Republic responsible for the defeat in World War I and the diminution of Germany's power in world affairs. The SPD simply had no program that could attract the middle class or give it hope for a better future.

To the lower middle class, the Nazis promised effective leadership and a solution to the economic crisis. For this segment of society, the Great Depression was the last straw, the final evidence that the republic had failed and should be supplanted by a different kind of regime. Germans of the lower middle class craved order, authority, and leadership and abhorred the endless debates and factional quarrels of the political parties. To them parliamentary government was fatally flawed. They wanted Hitler to protect Germany from the communists and from organized labor and to revive the economy. The traumatic experience of the Great Depression caused many bourgeois—until then apathetic about voting—to cast ballots. The depression was also severe in England and the United States, but the liberal foundations of these countries were strong. In Germany they were not, because the middle class had not committed itself to democracy, nor indeed did it have any liking for it. Democracy endured in Britain and the United States; in Germany, it collapsed.

But Nazism was more than a class movement. It appealed to the discontented and disillusioned from all segments of the population: embittered veterans, romantic nationalists, idealistic intellectuals, industrialists and large landowners frightened by communism and social democracy, rootless and resentful people who felt that they had no place in the existing society, the unemployed, lovers of violence, and newly enfranchised youth yearning for a cause. The Social Democrats spoke the rational language of European democracy. The Communists addressed themselves to only a part of the nation, the proletariat, and were linked to a foreign country, the Soviet Union. The Nazis reached a wider spectrum of the population, and their promise to unite the German people in a racial brotherhood dedicated to restoring German honor and power touched deeper feelings.

And always there was the immense attraction of Hitler, who tirelessly worked his oratorical magic on increasingly enthusiastic crowds, confidently promising leadership and national rebirth. Many Germans were won over by his fanatical sincerity, his iron will, and his conviction that he was chosen by fate to rescue Germany. What a new party member wrote after hearing Hitler speak expressed the mood of many Germans: "There was only one thing for me, either to win with Adolf Hitler or to die for him. The personality of the Fuehrer had me totally in its spell."[29] Many others, no doubt, voted for Hitler not because they approved of him or his ideas, but because he was a strong opponent of the Weimer Republic, which they viewed as weak and contemptible. What these people wanted, above all, was the end of the republic they hated.

Meanwhile, the parliamentary regime failed to function effectively. According to Article 48 of the constitution, during times of emergency the president was empowered to govern by decree, that is, without Parliament. When President Paul von Hindenburg (1847–1934), the aging field marshal, exercised this emergency power, the responsibility for governing Germany was in effect transferred from the political parties and Parliament to the president and chancellor. Rule by the president, instead of by Parliament, meant, for one thing, that Germany had already taken a giant step away from parliamentary government in the direction of authoritarianism.

In the election of July 31, 1932, the Nazis received 37.3 percent of the vote and won 230 seats, far more than any other party but still not a majority. Determined to become chancellor, Hitler refused to take a subordinate position in a coalition government. Franz von Papen, who had resigned from the chancellorship, persuaded Hindenburg, whose judgment was distorted by old age, to appoint Hitler chancellor. In this decision, Papen had the support of German industrialists, aristocratic landowners, and the Nationalist party.

As in Italy, the members of the ruling elite were frightened by internal violence, unrest, and the specter of communism. They had abhorred the creation of the Weimar Republic, and the government's ineffectiveness in coping with crises only confirmed their disdain for parliamentary democracy. They thought Hitler a vulgar man, a lowly corporal, and they detested his demagogic incitement of the masses. But they regarded him as a useful instrument to fight communism, block social reform, break the back of organized labor, and rebuild the armament industry. They expected him to break the shackles of the hated Versailles treaty, which the Weimar Republic had passively accepted, restore the strength of the military, and in international affairs pursue a more assertive policy reminiscent of the days of the emperor. They also hoped that the charismatic Hitler would revive the nation's spirit and pride, which had eroded under the republic. And, traditionally anti-Semitic, they welcomed an opportunity to restrict the role of

Jews in Germany's political, economic, and cultural life.

Hitler had cleverly reassured these traditional conservatives that the Nazis would protect private property and business and go slow with social reform. They would have preferred a dictatorship under Hindenburg, a respected general who shared their views and upbringing, but a dictatorship under Hitler still seemed to them better than the Weimar Republic, which they had hated since its inception.

Like the Italian upper class, which had assisted Mussolini in his rise to power, the old conservative ruling elite intrigued to put Hitler in power. Ironically, this decision was made when Nazi strength at the polls was beginning to ebb. Expecting to control Hitler, conservatives calculated badly, for Hitler could not be tamed. They had underestimated his political skills, his ruthlessness, and his obsession with racial nationalism. Hitler had sought power not to restore the Old Order but to fashion a new one. The new leadership would be drawn not from the traditional ruling segments but from the most dedicated Nazis, regardless of their social background.

Never intending to rule within the spirit of the constitution, Hitler, who took office on January 30, 1933, quickly moved to assume dictatorial powers. In February 1933, a Dutch drifter with communist leanings set a fire in the Reichstag. Hitler persuaded Hindenburg to sign an emergency decree suspending civil rights on the pretext that the state was threatened by internal subversion. The chancellor then used these emergency powers to arrest, without due process, Communist and Social Democratic deputies.

In the elections of March 1933, Nazi thugs broke up Communist party meetings, and Hitler called for a Nazi victory at the polls to save Europe from Bolshevism. Intimidated by street violence and captivated by Nazi mass demonstrations and relentless propaganda, the German people elected 288 Nazi deputies in a Reichstag of 647 seats. With the support of 52 deputies of the Nationalist party and in the absence of Communist deputies, who were under arrest, the Nazis now had a secure majority. Hitler then bullied the Reichstag into passing the Enabling Act (in March 1933), which permitted the chancellor to enact legislation independently of the Reichstag. With astonishing passivity, the political parties had allowed the Nazis to dismantle the government and make Hitler a dictator with unlimited power. Hitler had used the instruments of democracy to destroy the republic and create a dictatorship. And he did it far more thoroughly and quickly than Mussolini.

Nazi Germany

Mussolini's fascism exhibited much bluster and bragging, but Fascist Italy did not have the industrial and military strength or the total commitment of the people necessary to threaten the peace of Europe. Nazism, in contrast, demonstrated a demonic quality, which nearly destroyed Western civilization.

Hitler's sinister, fanatical, and obsessive personality had a far greater impact on the German movement than Mussolini's character had on Italian fascism. Also contributing to the demonic radicalism of Nazism were certain deeply rooted German traditions, which were absent in Italy: Prussian militarism, adoration of the power state, and belief in the special destiny of the German Volk. These traditions made the German people's attachment to Hitler and Nazi ideology much stronger than the Italian people's devotion to Mussolini and his party.

The Leader-State

The Nazis moved to subjugate all political and economic institutions and all culture to the will of the party. There could be no separation between private life and politics: ideology must pervade every phase of daily life and all organizations must come under party control. There could be no rights of the individual that the state must respect. The party became the state, and its teachings the soul of the German nation. Joseph Goebbels (see below) summed up this totalitarian goal: "It is not enough to reconcile people more or less to our regime, to move them towards a position of neutrality towards us, we want rather to work on people until they are addicted to us."[30] An anonymous Nazi poet expressed the totalitarian credo in these words:

> *We have captured all the positions*
> *And on the heights we have planted*

> *The banners of our revolution.*
> *You had imagined that that was all that we wanted*
> *We want more*
> *We want all*
> *Your hearts are our goal,*
> *It is your souls we want.*[31]

The Third Reich was organized as a leader-state, in which Hitler, the *fuehrer* (leader), embodied and expressed the real will of the German people, commanded the supreme loyalty of the nation, and held omnipotent power. As a Nazi political theorist stated, "The authority of the Fuehrer is total and all-embracing . . . it embraces all members of the German community. . . . The Fuehrer's authority is subject to no checks or controls; it is circumscribed by no . . . individual rights; it is . . . overriding and unfettered."[32] Virtually all crucial decisions in foreign affairs were made by Hitler. Yet, at the same time, the Nazi state comprised organizations and individuals competing with one another for influence, power, and plunder.

To strengthen the power of the central government and coordinate the nation under Nazism, the regime abolished legislatures in the various German states and appointed governors who would make certain that Nazi directives were carried out throughout the country. The Nazis took over the civil service and used its machinery to enforce Nazi decrees. In this process of *Gleichschaltung* (coordination), the Nazis encountered little opposition. The political parties and the trade unions collapsed without a struggle.

In June 1933, the Social Democratic party was outlawed, and within a few weeks, the other political parties simply disbanded on their own. In May, the Nazis had seized the property of the trade unions, arrested the leaders, and ended collective bargaining and strikes. The newly established German Labor Front, an instrument of the party, became the official organization of the working class. Although there is evidence that the working class in 1933 would have resisted the Nazis, the leadership never mobilized proletarian organizations. With surprising ease, the Nazis imposed their will on the nation.

Hitler made strategic but temporary concessions to the traditional ruling elite. On June 30, 1934, Nazi executioners swiftly murdered the leaders of the SA (Nazi storm troopers who had battled political opponents) to eliminate any potential opposition to Hitler from within the party. With this move, Hitler also relieved the anxieties of industrialists and landowners, who feared that Ernst Röhm, the head of the SA, would persuade Hitler to remove them from positions of power and to implement a program of radical social reform, threatening their property.

The execution of the SA leaders (including Röhm) was also approved by the generals, for they regarded the SA as a rival to the army. In August, all German soldiers swore an oath of unconditional allegiance to the fuehrer, cementing the alliance between the army and National Socialism. The army tied itself to the Nazi regime because it approved of the resurgence of militaristic values and applauded the death of the Weimar Republic. As the German historian Karl Dietrich Bracher concludes, "Without the assistance of the Army, at first through its toleration and later through its active cooperation, the country's rapid and final restructuring into the total leader state could not have come about."[33]

Economic Life

Hitler had sought power not to improve the living standards of the masses but to convert Germany into a powerful war machine. Economic problems held little interest for this dreamer, in whose mind danced images of a vast German empire. For him, the "socialism" in National Socialism meant not a comprehensive program of social welfare but the elimination of the class antagonisms that divided and weakened the fatherland. Radicals within the party wanted to deprive the industrialists and landowners of power and social prestige and to expropriate their property. The more pragmatic Hitler wanted only to deprive them of freedom of action; they were to serve, not control, the state. Germany remained capitalist, but the state had unlimited power to intervene in the economy. Unlike the Bolsheviks, the Nazis did not destroy the upper classes of the Old Regime. Hitler made no war against the industrialists. He wanted from them loyalty, obedience, and a war machine. German businessmen prospered but exercised no influence on political decisions. The profits of industry rose, and workers lauded the regime for ending the unemployment crisis.

Nazism and the Churches

Nazism conflicted with the core values of Christianity. "The heaviest blow that ever struck humanity was the coming of Christianity," said Hitler to intimates during World War II.[34] Had Germany won the war, the Nazis would no doubt have tried to root Christianity out of German life. In 1937, the bishop of Berlin defined the essential conflict between Christianity and Nazism:

> *The question at stake is whether there is an authority that stands above all earthly power, the authority of God, Whose commandments are valid independent of space and time, country and race. The question at stake is whether individual man possesses personal rights that no community and no state may take from him; whether the free exercise of his conscience may be prevented and forbidden by the state.*[35]

Nazism could tolerate no other faith alongside itself. Recognizing that Christianity was a rival claimant for the German soul, the Nazis moved to repress the Protestant and Catholic churches. In the public schools, religious instruction was cut back and the syllabus changed to omit the Jewish origins of Christianity. Christ was depicted not as a Jew, heir to the prophetic tradition of Hebrew monotheism, but as an Aryan hero. The Gestapo (secret state police) censored church newspapers, scrutinized sermons and church activities, forbade some clergymen to preach, dismissed the opponents of Nazism from theological schools, and arrested some clerical critics of the regime.

The clergy were well represented among the Germans who resisted Nazism; some were sent to concentration camps or executed. But these courageous clergy were not representatives of the German churches, which, as organized institutions, capitulated to and cooperated with the Nazi regime. Both the German Evangelical and German Catholic churches demanded that their faithful give Hitler their loyalty; both turned a blind eye to Nazi persecution of Jews. Even before World War II and the implementation of genocide, many Evangelical churches banned baptized Jews from entering their temples and dismissed pastors with Jewish ancestry. During the war both Catholic and Evangelical churches condemned resistance and found much to admire in the Third Reich; and both supported Hitler's war. When Germany attacked Poland, starting World War II, the Catholic bishops declared: "In this decisive hour we encourage and admonish our Catholic soldiers, in obedience to the Fuehrer, to do their duty and to be ready to sacrifice their whole existence."[36] Both churches urged their faithful to fight for fatherland and fuehrer, pressured conscientious objectors to serve, and celebrated Nazi victories.

The German churches, which preached Christ's message of humanity, failed to take a stand against Nazi inhumanity for a variety of reasons. Many German church leaders feared that resistance would lead to even more severe measures against their churches. Traditionally, the German churches had bowed to state authority and detested revolution. Church leaders also found some Nazi ideas appealing. Intensely nationalistic, antiliberal, antirepublican, anticommunist, and anti-Semitic, many members of the clergy were filled with hope when Hitler came to power. They anticipated that Hitler would restore respect for traditional Christian morality, which, they believed, had been undermined by the secularism, materialism, and vice rampant in the republic. And he would declaw the Communists, who had declared war on Christianity. The prominent Lutheran theologian who "welcomed that change that came to Germany in 1933 as a divine gift and miracle"[37] voiced the sentiments of many members of the clergy. Such feelings encouraged prolonged moral nearsightedness, not a revolt of Christian conscience. When the war ended, the German Evangelical church leaders lamented:

> *[W]e know ourselves to be one with our people in a great company of suffering and in a great solidarity of guilt. With great pain do we say: "Through us endless suffering has been brought to many people and countries. . . . We accuse ourselves for not witnessing more courageously, for not praying more faithfully, for not loving more ardently."*[38]

Shaping the "New Man"

Propaganda had helped the Nazis come to power. Now it would be used to consolidate their hold on the German nation and shape a "new man," committed to Hitler, race, and Volk. Hitler was a radical revolutionary who desired not only the outward form of power but also control over the inner person, over the individual's thoughts and feelings. The purpose of Nazi propaganda was to condition the mind to revere the fuehrer and to obey the new regime. Its intent was to deprive individuals of their capacity for independent thought. By concentrating on myths of the race and the infallibility of the fuehrer, Nazi propaganda sought to disorient the rational mind and give the individual new standards to believe in and obey. Propaganda aimed to mold the entire nation to think and respond as the leader-state directed. Even science had to conform to Nazi racial ideology. Thus, Johannes Stark, a Nobel Prize winner, declared that scientific thought is a function of race:

> *[N]atural science is overwhelmingly a creation of the Nordic-Germanic blood component of the Aryan peoples. . . . The Jewish spirit is wholly different in its orientation. . . . True, Heinrich Hertz made the great discovery of electromagnetic waves, but he was not a full-blooded Jew. He had a German mother, from whose side his spiritual endowment may well have been conditioned.*[39]

The Ministry of Popular Enlightenment, headed by Joseph Goebbels (1897–1945), controlled the press, book publishing, the radio, the theater, and the cinema. A holder of a doctoral degree in the humanities, Goebbels was intelligent and a master in the art of propaganda. Viewing Hitler as a Nietzschean superman, a man of destiny who was inculcating Germans with a saving faith, Goebbels was completely devoted to the fuehrer. He was also vain, cynical, and contemptuous of the very masses he manipulated. But the German people were not merely passive victims of clever and ruthless leaders. "The effective spread of propaganda and the rapid regimentation of cultural life," says Bracher, "would not have been possible without the invaluable help eagerly tendered by writers and artists, professors and churchmen." And the manipulation of the minds of the German people "would not have been effective had it not been for profound historically conditioned relations based . . . on a pseudo-religious exaggerated nationalism and on the idea of the German mission."[40] Although some intellectuals showed their abhorrence of the Nazi regime by emigrating, the great majority gave their support, often with overt enthusiasm. Some individuals rejected Nazi propaganda, but the masses of German people came to regard Nazism as the fulfillment of their nationalist longings.

The Nazis tried to keep the emotions in a state of permanent mobilization, for Hitler understood that the emotionally aroused are most amenable to manipulation. Goose-stepping SA and SS (elite military and police) battalions paraded in the streets; martial music quickened the pulse; Nazi flags decorated public buildings; loudspeakers installed in offices and factories blared the Nazi message, and all work stopped for important broadcasts. Citizens were ordered to greet each other with "Heil Hitler," a potent sign of reverence and submission.

The regime made a special effort to reach young people. All youths between the ages of ten and eighteen were urged and then required to join the Hitler Youth, and all other youth organizations were dissolved. At camps and rallies, young people paraded, sang, saluted, and chanted: "We were slaves; we were outsiders in our own country. So were we before Hitler united us. Now we would fight against Hell itself for our leader."[41]

Nazification of Education. The schools, long breeding grounds of nationalism, militarism, antiliberalism, and anti-Semitism, now indoctrinated the young in Nazi ideology. The Nazis instructed teachers in how certain subjects were to be taught; and to ensure obedience, members of the Hitler Youth were asked to report suspicious teachers. Portraits of Hitler, along with Nazi banners, were displayed in classrooms. War stories, adventures of the Hitler Youth, and ancient Nordic legends replaced fairy tales and animal stories in reading material for the young. The curriculum upgraded physical training and sports, curtailed religious instruction, and introduced many courses in "racial science." Decidedly anti-intellectual, the Nazis stressed character building over book learning. They intended to train young people to serve the leader and the racial community—to imbue them with a sense of fellowship for their Volkish kin, that sense of camaraderie found on the battlefield. Expressions of individualism and independence were suppressed.

The universities quickly abandoned freedom of the mind, scientific objectivity, and humanist values. "We repudiate international science, we repudiate the international community of scholars, we repudiate research for the sake of research. Sieg Heil!" declared one historian.[42] Even before the Nazi takeover, many university students and professors had embraced Volkish nationalism and right-wing radicalism. Two years before Hitler came to power, for example, 60 percent of all undergraduates supported the Nazi student organization, and anti-Semitic riots broke out at several universities. Horst von Maltitz observes:

> *For seventy years or more, the professors had preached aggressive nationalism, the German destiny of power, hero worship, irrational political Romanticism, and so forth, and had increasingly deemphasized, if not eliminated, the teachings of ethical and humanist principles. . . . Essentially neither [professors nor students] wanted to have anything to do with democracy. In the Weimar Republic . . . both groups, on the whole, seemed equally determined to tear down that Republic. The professors did their part by fiery lectures, speeches, and writings; the students did theirs in noisy demonstrations, torch-light parades, vandalism, and physical violence. . . . When Hitler came to power, both professors and students fell all over themselves to demonstrate their allegiance.*[43]

In May 1933, professors and students proudly burned books considered a threat to Nazi ideology. Many academics praised Hitler and the new regime. Some 10 percent of the university faculty, principally Jews, Social Democrats, and liberals, were dismissed, and their colleagues often approved. "From now on it will not be your job to determine whether something is true but whether it is in the spirit of the National Socialist revolution," the new minister of culture told university professors.[44] Numerous courses on Nazi ideology were introduced into the curriculum.

Giant Rallies. Symbolic of the Nazi regime were the monster rallies staged at Nuremberg. Scores of thousands roared, marched, and worshiped at their leader's feet. These true believers, the end product of Nazi indoctrination, celebrated Hitler's achievements and demonstrated their loyalty to their savior. Everything was brilliantly orchestrated to impress Germans and the world with the irresistible power, determination, and unity of the Nazi movement and the greatness of the fuehrer. Armies of youths waving flags, storm troopers bearing weapons, and workers shouldering long-handled spades paraded past Hitler, who stood at attention, his arm extended in the Nazi salute. The endless columns of marchers, the stirring martial music played by huge bands, the forest of flags, the chanting and cheering of spectators, and the burning torches and beaming spotlights united the participants into a racial community. "Wherever Hitler leads we follow," thundered thousands of Germans in a giant chorus. The Nuremberg rallies were among the greatest theatrical performances of the twentieth century.

Terror. Another means of ensuring compliance and obedience was terror. Its instrument, the SS, had been organized in 1925 to protect Hitler and other party leaders and to stand guard at party meetings. Under the leadership of Heinrich Himmler (1900–1945), a fanatical believer in Hitler's racial theories, the SS was molded into an elite force of disciplined, dedicated, and utterly ruthless men. Myopic, narrow-chested, and sexually prudish, Himmler contrived a cult of manliness. He envisioned the SS, who were specially selected for their racial purity and physical fitness, as a new breed of knights: Nietzschean supermen who would lead the new Germany.

The SS staffed the concentration camps established to deal with political prisoners. Through systematic terror and torture, the SS sought to deprive the inmates of their human dignity and to harden themselves for the struggles that lay ahead. The knowledge that these camps existed and that some prisoners were never heard from again was a strong inducement for Germans to remain obedient.

Anti-Semitic Legislation

The Nazis deprived Jews of their German citizenship and instituted many anti-Jewish measures designed to make them outcasts. Thousands of Jewish doctors, lawyers, musicians, artists, and professors were barred from practicing their pro-

Young Nazis Burning Books in Salzburg, Austria, in 1938. Heinrich Heine, the great nineteenth-century German-Jewish poet, once said that people who burn books end up burning people. (© *Topham/The Image Works.*)

fessions, and Jewish members of the civil service were dismissed. A series of laws tightened the screws of humiliation and persecution. Marriage or sexual encounters between Germans and Jews were forbidden. Universities, schools, restaurants, pharmacies, hospitals, theaters, museums, and athletic fields were gradually closed to Jews. As a rule, German academic and clerical elites did not protest; many agreed with the National Socialists' edicts. The Jews were simply abandoned.

In November 1938, using as a pretext the assassination of a German official in Paris by a seventeen-year-old Jewish youth, whose family the Nazis had mistreated, the Nazis organized an extensive pogrom. Nazi gangs murdered scores of Jews, destroyed 267 synagogues, and burned and vandalized 7,500 Jewish-owned businesses all over Germany—an event that became known as Night of the Broken Glass (*Kristallnacht*). Twenty thousand Jews were thrown into concentration camps. The Reich then imposed on the Jewish community a fine of one billion marks. These measures were a mere prelude, however. During World War II, genocidal murder of European Jewry became a cardinal Nazi objective.

Mass Support

The Nazi regime became a police state, symbolized by mass arrests, the persecution of Jews, and concentration camps that institutionalized terror. Yet fewer heads rolled than people expected, and in many ways life seemed normal. The Nazis established the totalitarian state without upsetting the daily life of the majority of the population. Moreover, Hitler, like Mussolini, was careful to maintain the appearance of legality. By not abolishing Parliament or repealing the constitution, he could claim that his was a legitimate government.

To people concerned with little but family, job, and friends—and this includes most people in any country—life in the first few years of the Third Reich seemed quite satisfying. Most Germans believed that the new government was trying to solve Germany's problems in a vigorous and sensible manner, in contrast to the ineffective

Weimar leadership. By 1936, the reinvigoration of the economy, stimulated in part by rearmament, had virtually eliminated unemployment, which had stood at 6 million jobless when Hitler took power. An equally astounding achievement in German eyes was Hitler's bold termination of the humiliating Versailles treaty, the rebuilding of the war machine, and the restoration of power in international affairs. It seemed to most Germans that Hitler had awakened a sense of self-sacrifice and national dedication among a people dispirited by defeat and depression. He had united a country torn by class antagonisms and social distinctions and given people a sense of national pride. Workers had jobs, businessmen profits, and generals troops, and the bonds of community had been greatly strengthened—what could be wrong?

Many intellectuals, viewing Hitlerism as the victory of idealism over materialism and of community over selfish individualism, lent their talents to the regime and endorsed the burning of books and the suppression of freedom. To them, Hitler was a visionary, an agent for the rebirth and regeneration of the fatherland, who had shown Germany and the world a new way of life—a new creed.

Thus, having regained confidence in themselves and their nation, many Germans rejoiced in Hitler's leadership, did not regret the loss of political freedom, and remained indifferent to the plight of the persecuted, particularly Jews. Moreover, Hitler's popularity and mass support rested on something far stronger than propaganda and terror, for he had won the hearts of a sizable proportion of the German people. To many Germans, Hitler was exactly as Nazi mythology depicted him, a man of destiny and a savior of the nation who "stands like a statue grown beyond the measure of earthly man."[45]

There was some opposition and resistance to the Hitler regime. Social Democrats and Communists organized small cells. Some conservatives, who considered Hitler to be a threat to traditional German values, and some clergy, who saw Nazism as a pagan religion in conflict with Christian morality, also formed small opposition groups. But only resistance from the army could have toppled Hitler. Some generals, even before World War II, urged such resistance. The overwhelming majority of German officers, however, preferred the new regime, which had restored Germany's military might and pride and had given them the opportunity for professional advancement, or they considered it dishonorable to break their oath of loyalty to Hitler. And most of these officers would remain loyal until the bitter end. Very few Germans realized that they were ruled by evil men driven by an evil ideology, that their country, an advanced industrial society with an impressive tradition of high culture, was passing through a long night of barbarism. Still fewer considered resistance.

Liberalism and Authoritarianism in Other Lands

The Spread of Authoritarianism

After World War I, in country after country, parliamentary democracy collapsed and authoritarian leaders came to power. In most of these countries, liberal ideals had not penetrated deeply; liberalism met resistance from conservative elites.

Spain and Portugal. In both Spain and Portugal, parliamentary regimes faced strong opposition from the church, the army, and large landowners. In 1926, army officers overthrew the Portuguese republic that had been created in 1910, and gradually, Antonio de Oliveira Salazar (1889–1970), a professor of economics, emerged as dictator. In Spain, after antimonarchist forces won the election of 1931, King Alfonso XIII (1902–1931) left the country, and Spain was proclaimed a republic. But the new government, led by socialists and liberals, faced the determined opposition of the ruling elite. The reforms introduced by the republic—expropriation of large estates, reduction of the number of army officers, dissolution of the Jesuit order, and closing of church schools—only intensified the Old Order's hatred.

The difficulties of the new Spanish republic mounted: workers, near starvation, rioted and engaged in violent strikes; the military attempted a coup; and Catalonia, with its long tradition of separatism, tried to establish its autonomy. Imitating the example of France (described later in this chapter), the parties of the left, including the Communists, united in the Popular Front, which came to power in February 1936. In July 1936,

Profile

Charles Maurras

Roger-Viollet.

Some historians view Action Française, an ultranationalist, antidemocratic, and anti-Semitic, organization founded in 1898–99 by Charles Maurras (1868–1952), as a forerunner of the fascist movements that emerged in the aftermath of World War I. In the tradition of early-nineteenth-century French conservatives, Maurras held that the collective takes precedence over the individual: "The primary reality, more real than the individual and more real also than the world," he declared, "is *la patrie,* the Country."* He regarded the religious individualism of the Reformation, the political individualism of the French Revolution, and the cultural individualism of romanticism as forces of national division and discord. The principle of equality, he said, permitted rule by the mediocre and the incompetent.

To save France from class war, political factions, capitalist exploitation, and spiritual disintegration—all consequences of unbridled individualism in his eyes—Maurras championed integral nationalism. It sought the integration of the nation around Catholicism, France's ancestral religion; monarchy, a deeply rooted French tradition; and hierarchy, leadership based on birth and talent. Maurras valued France of the Old Regime, for it was monarchical, hierarchical, and community minded. Hostile and foreign elements—he meant specifically Masons, Protestants, Jews, alien residents, and recently naturalized citizens—must be deprived of political

General Francisco Franco (1892–1975), stationed in Spanish Morocco, led a revolt against the republic. He was supported by army leaders, the church, monarchists, landlords, industrialists, and the Falange, a newly formed fascist party. Spain was torn by a bloody civil war. Aided by Fascist Italy and Nazi Germany, Franco won in 1939 and established a dictatorship.

Eastern and Central Europe. Parliamentary government in eastern Europe rested on weak foundations. Predominantly rural, these countries lacked the sizable professional and commercial classes that had promoted liberalism in western Europe. Only Czechoslovakia had a substantial native middle class with a strong liberal tradition. The rural masses of eastern Europe, traditionally subjected to monarchical and aristocratic authority, were not used to political thinking or civic responsibility. Students and intellectuals, often gripped by a romantic nationalism, were drawn to antidemocratic movements.

rights and influence. Such people, he argued, had no deep roots in the French nation; they could never be truly French. Maurras hoped that army leaders, inspired by the Action Française philosophy, would overthrow the Third Republic and reestablish monarchical rule.

Maurras was strongly anti-Semitic, holding that "Jewish capitalism" and "Jewish democracy" were corrupting the French soul. He attributed a destructive individualism to Judaism, for it had conceived the idea of one God who had endowed everyone with a conscience: "it is in the Law and the Prophets . . . that are to be found the first expressions in antiquity of the individualism, egalitarianism, humanitarianism, and social and political idealism that were to mark 1789."[†] He saw the Jews as agents of revolution and as alien conspirators. Action Française waged a fierce campaign against a pardon for Dreyfus, the Jewish army officer who was falsely convicted of treason. At times, it engaged in organized vandalism and violence against his supporters. For decades Maurras's paper fomented anti-Semitism with vicious editorials such as the following: *"Down with the Jews!*Those whom we make the mistake of treating as if they were our equals display a ridiculous ambition to dominate us. They shall be put in their place and it will be our pleasure to do so."

Student members of the Action Française joined with young royalists to form the Camelots du Roi (hawkers of the king), which sold the Action Française newspaper in the streets, acted as guards at the organization's meetings, and participated in anti-Republic and nationalist demonstrations. The organized violence of Camelots du Roi presaged the fascist terror tactics after World War I. In this sense, the Camelots could be viewed as the first storm troopers.

Support for Action Française came principally from the army, the nobility, the clergy, and middle-class professionals. Between 1910 and 1926, Action membership ranged from thirty thousand to forty thousand. The group posed no threat to the state, but its cult of la patrie, condemnation of democracy, celebration of war, virulent anti-Semitism, employment of organized violence, and call for a leader to resurrect the nation anticipated and coincided with fascism.

After France's defeat in World War II, Maurras supported the authoritarian Vichy regime and denounced the resistance movement. He applauded Vichy's laws that made Jews second-class citizens, and his paper published the hiding places of Jews so that they could be rounded up and sent to German concentration camps. After the liberation of France, Maurras was sentenced to life imprisonment but was released in 1951 for medical reasons.

---

*Quoted in Michael Sutton, *Nationalism, Positivism and Catholicism: The Politics of Charles Maurras and French Catholics, 1890–1914* (Cambridge: Cambridge University Press, 1982), p. 26.

[†]Ibid., p. 8.

Right-wing leaders also played on the fear of communism. When parliamentary government failed to solve internal problems, the opponents of the liberal state seized the helm. Fascist movements, however, had little success in eastern Europe. Rather, authoritarian regimes headed by traditional ruling elites—army leaders or kings—extinguished democracy there.

With the dissolution of the Hapsburg Empire at the end of World War I, Austria became a democratic republic. From the start, it suffered from severe economic problems. The Hapsburg Empire had been a huge free-trade area. Food and raw materials had been permitted to circulate unimpeded throughout the empire. The new Austria lacked sufficient food to feed the population of Vienna and needed raw materials for its industries. Worsening its plight was the erection of tariff barriers by each of the states formerly part of the Hapsburg Empire. Between 1922 and 1926, the League of Nations had to rescue Austria from bankruptcy. The Great Depression aggravated

Austria's economic position. Many Austrians believed that only *Anschluss* (union) with Germany could solve Austria's problems.

Austria was also burdened by a conflict between the industrial region, including Vienna, and the agricultural provinces. Factory workers were generally socialist and anticlerical; the peasants were strongly Catholic and antisocialist. The Social Democrats controlled Vienna, but the rural population gave its support to the Christian Social party. Each party had its own private army: the workers had the *Schutzbund*, and the provincials the *Heimwehr*.

In the early 1920s, under the guidance of its Social Democratic mayor, Vienna introduced a number of social reforms—including free kindergartens, hospitals, and burials, and subsidized housing projects—that significantly improved conditions for the working class. The middle class, which bore the brunt of the tax burden needed to pay for these reforms designed specifically for the working class, saw the Social Democrats, who dominated Vienna, as implacable enemies. During the Great Depression, Chancellor Engelbert Dollfuss (1892–1934) sought to turn the country into a one-party state. In February 1934, police and Heimwehr contingents raided Social Democratic headquarters. When the Social Democrats called a general strike, Dollfuss bombarded worker's strongholds, including huge municipal housing projects, killing 193 civilians. After the workers were subdued, the Dollfuss government tried and imprisoned more than one thousand socialists, outlawed leftist trade unions, and disbanded the Social Democratic party. Austria had joined the ranks of authoritarian states.

When Hitler came to power in Germany, Austrian Nazis pressed for Anschluss. In July 1934, a band of them assassinated Dollfuss, but a Nazi plot to capture the government failed. Four years later, however, Hitler would march into Austria, bringing about the Anschluss desired by many Austrians.

The new Hungary that emerged at the end of World War I faced an uprising by communists inspired by the success of the Bolsheviks in Russia. Béla Kun (1885–1937), supported by Russian money, established a soviet regime in Budapest in March 1919. But Kun could not win the support of the peasants and was opposed by the Allies, who helped crush the revolutionary government. In 1920, power passed to Admiral Miklós Horthy (1868–1957), who instituted a brief white terror, which exceeded the red terror of the Kun regime. During the Great Depression, the Horthy government, which favored the large landholders, was challenged by the radical right, which preached extreme nationalism, anti-Semitism, and anticapitalism and tried to win mass support through land reform. Its leader, Gyula Gömbös (1886–1936), who served as prime minister from 1932 to 1936, sought to align Hungary with Nazi Germany. Wishing to regain territories lost as a result of World War I and aware of Hitler's growing might, Hungary drew closer to Germany in the late 1930s.

Poland, Greece, Bulgaria, and Romania became either royal or military dictatorships. In September 1940, a year after World War II started, the fascist Iron Guard seized power in Romania and engaged in the mass murder of Jews. In January 1941, the Iron Guard was crushed by the military. The new state of Czechoslovakia, guided by President Tomáš Masaryk (1850–1937) and Foreign Minister Eduard Beneš (1884–1948), who were both committed to the liberal-humanist tradition of the West, preserved parliamentary democracy. Its most serious problem came from the 3.25 million Germans living within its borders, primarily in the Sudetenland. The German minority founded the Sudetenland German party, which modeled itself after Hitler's Nazi party. Hitler later exploited the issue of the Sudetenland Germans to dismember Czechoslovakia.

The Western Democracies

While liberal governments were failing in much of Europe, the great Western democracies—the United States, Britain, and France—continued to preserve democratic institutions. In Britain and the United States, fascist movements were merely a nuisance. In France, fascism was more of a threat because it exploited deeply ingrained hostility in some quarters to the liberal ideals of the French Revolution.

The United States. The central problem faced by the Western democracies was the Great Depression, which started in the United States. In the 1920s, hundreds of thousands of Americans had bought stock on credit; this buying spree sent stock prices soaring well beyond what the stocks were actually worth. In late October 1929, the stock market was hit by a wave of panic selling; prices plummeted. Within a few weeks, the value of stocks listed on the New York Stock Exchange fell by some $26 billion. A terrible chain reaction followed over the next few years. Businesses cut production and unemployment soared; farmers unable to meet mortgage payments lost their land; banks that had made poor investments closed down. American investors withdrew the capital they had invested in Europe, causing European banks and businesses to fail. Throughout the world, trade declined and unemployment rose.

When President Franklin Delano Roosevelt (1882–1945) took office in 1933, more than thirteen million Americans—one-quarter of the labor force—were out of work. Hunger and despair showed on the faces of the American people. Moving away from laissez faire, Roosevelt instituted a comprehensive program of national planning, economic experimentation, and reform, known as the New Deal. Although the U.S. political and economic system faced a severe test, few Americans turned to fascism or communism. The government engaged in national planning but did not break with democratic values and procedures.

Britain. Even before the Great Depression, Britain faced severe economic problems. Loss of markets to foreign competitors hurt British manufacturing, mining, and shipbuilding; rapid development of water and oil power reduced the demand for British coal, and outdated mining equipment put Britain in a poor competitive position. To decrease costs, mine owners in 1926 called for salary cuts; the coal miners countered with a strike and were joined by workers in other industries. To many Britons, the workers were leftist radicals trying to overthrow the government. Many wanted the state to break the strike. After nine days, industrial workers called off their strike, but the miners held out for another six months, only to return to work with longer hours and lower pay. Although the general strike failed, it did improve relations between the classes, for the workers had not called for revolution and they had refrained from violence. The fear that British workers would follow the Bolshevik path abated.

The Great Depression cast a pall over Britain. The Conservative party leadership tried to stimulate exports by devaluing the British pound and to encourage industry by providing loans at lower interest rates, but in the main, it left the task of recovery to industry itself. Not until Britain began to rearm did unemployment decline significantly. Despite the economic slump of the 1920s and the Great Depression, Britain remained politically stable, a testament to the strength of its parliamentary tradition. Neither the communists nor the newly formed British Fascist party gained mass support.

France. In the early 1920s, France was concerned with postwar rebuilding. From 1926 to 1929, France was relatively prosperous. Industrial and agricultural production expanded, tourism increased, and the currency was stable. Although France did not feel the Great Depression as painfully as did the United States and Germany, the nation was hurt by the decline in trade and production and the rise in unemployment.

The political instability that had beset the Third Republic almost since its inception continued, and hostility to the Republic mounted. The rift between liberals and conservatives, which had divided the country since the Revolution and grown worse with the Dreyfus affair, continued to plague France during the depression. The French right, particularly the radicals, whose numbers had been increasing since the 1880s, had traditionally rejected the ideals of liberty, equality, individual rights, and parliamentary government associated with the Enlightenment and the French Revolution, and was violently anti-Marxist. Negating liberal ideals and democractic government, the right endorsed an authoritarian and hierarchical system, which would oppose social reform and protect right-wing interests, and extreme nationalism, which would integrate all classes and restore France's greatness. As the leading parties failed to solve the nation's problems, a number of fascistic groups gained strength. On February 6, 1934, right-wing gangs threatened to invade the Chamber of Deputies. What brought on the crisis was the exposure of the shady dealings of Alexander Stavisky, a financial manipulator with high government connections, including parliamentary deputies and a cabinet minister. Antirepublican forces on the right, with their paramilitary units, saw the scandal as an opportunity to replace the Third Republic with an authoritarian regime. The resulting violence left hundreds wounded and several dead. The whole affair was too poorly organized to constitute a serious threat to the government. But to the parties of the left—socialists, communists, and radicals—the events of February 6–7 constituted a rightist attempt to establish a fascist regime.

Fear of growing fascist strength at home and in Italy and Germany led the parties of the left to form the Popular Front. In 1936, Léon Blum (1872–1950), a socialist, heir of Enlightenment humanism, and a Jew, became premier. Blum's Popular Front government instituted more reforms than any other ministry in the history of the Third Republic. At the time he took office, French workers in many industries were not unionized, worked ten or more hours a day six days a week without vacations, and were poorly compensated. To end a wave of strikes that tied up production, Blum gave workers a forty-hour workweek and holidays with pay and guaranteed them the right to collective bargaining. He took steps to nationalize the armaments and aircraft industries. To reduce the influence of the wealthiest families, he put the Bank of France under government control. By raising prices and buying wheat, he aided farmers. Conservatives and fascists denounced Blum as a Jewish socialist who was converting the fatherland into a communist state. "Better Hitler than Blum," grumbled French rightists.

Despite significant reforms, the Popular Front could not revitalize the economy. In 1937, the Blum ministry was overthrown and the Popular Front, always a tenuous alliance, fell apart. Through democratic means the Blum government had tried to give France its own New Deal, but the social reforms passed by the Popular Front only intensified hatred between the working classes and the rest of the nation. France had preserved democracy against the onslaught of domestic fascists, but it was a demoralized and divided nation that confronted a united and dynamic Nazi Germany.

❖ ❖ ❖

Notes

1. Carl J. Friedrich and Zbigniew K. Brzezinski, *Totalitarian Dictatorship and Autocracy* (New York: Praeger, 1961), p. 5.
2. Ibid., p. 7.
3. Hannah Arendt, *The Origins of Totalitarianism* (New York: World, Meridian Books, 1958), p. 469.
4. Karl Dietrich Bracher, *The Age of Ideologies,* trans. Erwald Osers (New York: St. Martin's Press, 1984), p. 83.
5. Friedrich and Brzezinski, *Totalitarian Dictatorship and Autocracy,* p. 13.
6. Zbigniew Brzezinski, *Out of Control* (New York: Charles Scribner's Sons, 1993), p. 19.
7. Quoted in Omer Bartov, *Hitler's Army: Soldiers, Nazis, and War in the Third Reich* (New York: Oxford University Press, 1992), p. 166.
8. Quoted in Arendt, *Origins of Totalitarianism,* p. 330.
9. "All-Russian Communist Party (Bolsheviks), 1919," in *Soviet Communism: Programs and Rules. Official Texts of 1919, 1952, 1956, 1961,* ed. Jan F. Triska (San Francisco: Chandler, 1962), p. 23.
10. V. I. Lenin, "The Immediate Tasks of the Soviet Government," in *The Lenin Anthology,* ed. Robert C. Tucker (New York: Norton, 1975) pp. 448 ff.
11. J. V. Stalin, "Speech to Business Executives" (1931), in *A Documentary History of Communism from Lenin to Mao,* ed. Robert V. Daniels (New York: Random House, 1960), 2:22.
12. Quoted in Isaac Deutscher, *Stalin: A Political Biography* (New York: Oxford University Press, 1966), p. 325.
13. Excerpted in T. H. Rigby, ed., *Stalin* (Englewood Cliffs, N.J.: Prentice-Hall, 1966), p. 111.
14. Quoted in Zeev Sternhill, "Fascist Ideology," in *Fascism: A Reader's Guide,* ed. Walter Laqueur (Berkeley: University of California Press, 1976), p. 338.
15. Quoted in John Weiss, *The Fascist Tradition* (New York: Harper & Row, 1967), p. 9.
16. Quoted in F. L. Carsten, *The Rise of Fascism* (Berkeley: University of California Press, 1969), p. 53.

17. Quoted in Max Gallo, *Mussolini's Italy* (New York: Macmillan, 1973), p. 218.
18. Kurt Sontheimer, "Anti-Democratic Thought in the Weimar Republic," in *The Path to Dictatorship, 1918–1933,* trans. John Conway, intro. Fritz Stern (Garden City, N.Y.: Doubleday Anchor Books, 1966), pp. 47–49.
19. Quoted in Joachim C. Fest, *Hitler,* trans. Richard and Clara Winston (New York: Harcourt Brace Jovanovich, 1974), p. 162.
20. Quoted in Karl J. Newman, *European Democracy between the Wars* (Notre Dame, Ind.: University of Notre Dame Press, 1971), p. 276.
21. Hajo Holborn, *Germany and Europe* (Garden City, N.Y.: Doubleday Anchor Books, 1971), p. 215.
22. Fest, *Hitler,* p. 548.
23. Quoted in Alan Bullock, *Hitler: A Study in Tyranny* (New York: Harper Torchbooks, 1964), p. 400.
24. *Hitler's Secret Conversations, 1941–1944,* with an introductory essay by H. R. Trevor Roper (New York: Farrar, Straus & Young, 1953), p. 28.
25. Quoted in Lucy S. Dawidowicz, *The War Against the Jews, 1933–1945* (New York: Holt, Rinehart & Winston, 1975), p. 21.
26. Quoted in Uri Tal, "Consecration of Politics in the Nazi Era," in *Judaism and Christianity Under the Impact of National Socialism,* ed. Otto Dov Kulka and Paul R. Mendes Flohr (Jerusalem: Historical Society of Israel, 1987), p. 70.
27. Adolf Hitler, *Mein Kampf,* trans. Ralph Mannheim (Boston: Houghton Mifflin, 1962), p. 107.
28. Ibid., p. 479.
29. Cited in Ian Kershaw, "Hitler and the Germans," in *Life in the Third Reich,* ed. Richard Bessel (New York: Oxford University Press, 1987), pp. 43–44.
30. Quoted in David Welch, ed., *Nazi Propaganda* (Totowa, N.J.: Barnes & Noble, 1983), p. 5.
31. Quoted in J. S. Conway, *The Nazi Persecution of the Churches* (New York: Basic Books, 1968), p. 202.
32. Quoted in Helmut Krausnick, Hans Buchheim, Martin Broszart, and Hans-Adolf Jacobsen, *Anatomy of the SS State* (London: Collins, 1968), p. 128.
33. Karl Dietrich Bracher, *The German Dictatorship,* trans. Jean Steinberg (New York: Praeger, 1970), p. 243.
34. *Hitler's Secret Conversations,* p. 6.
35. Quoted in Hans Rothfels, "Resistance Begins," in *Path to Dictatorship,* pp. 160–161.
36. Quoted in Guenter Lewy, *The Catholic Church and Nazi Germany* (New York: McGraw-Hill, 1965), p. 226.
37. Quoted in Hermann Graml et al., *The German Resistance to Hitler* (Berkeley: University of California Press, 1970), p. 206.
38. Quoted in Conway, *Nazi Persecution,* p. 332.
39. Excerpted in George L. Mosse, ed., *Nazi Culture* (New York: Grosset & Dunlap, 1966), pp. 206–207.
40. Bracher, *German Dictatorship,* pp. 248, 251.
41. Quoted in T. L. Jarman, *The Rise and Fall of Nazi Germany* (New York: New York University Press, 1956), p. 182.
42. Quoted in Horst von Maltitz, *The Evolution of Hitler's Germany* (New York: McGraw-Hill, 1973), pp. 433–434.
43. Ibid., pp. 438–439.
44. Quoted in Bracher, *German Dictatorship,* p. 268.
45. Quoted in Fest, *Hitler,* p. 532.

Suggested Reading

Communist Russia

Cohen, Stephen, *Bukharin and the Bolshevik Revolution* (1980). Argues that there existed more moderate alternatives to Stalin's policies.

Conquest, Robert, *The Harvest of Sorrow: Soviet Collectivization and the Terror-Famine* (1986). The human consequences of collectivization.

Deutscher, Isaac, *Trotsky: 1879–1940,* 3 vols., *The Prophet Armed* (1954), *The Prophet Unarmed* (1959), *The Prophet Outcast* (1963). The classic work on Trotsky.

Ginzburg, Eugenia, *Journey into the Whirlwind* (1967). A woman's experiences under the terror.

Laqueur, Walter, *Stalin: The Glasnost Revelations* (1990). Effects of the truth about Stalin on the Soviet people.

Mandelstam, Nadezhda, *Hope Against Hope: A Memoir* (1976). A searing account of life during Stalin's purges by the widow of one of the victims.

Medvedev, Roy, *Let History Judge: The Origins and Consequences of Stalinism,* rev. ed. (1990). Includes newly available material on Stalin's crimes of the 1930s.

Pasternak, Boris, *Doctor Zhivago* (1958). A Nobel Prize–winning novel about the tragedies of Russian life from Nicholas II to Stalin.

Razgon, Lev, *True Stories* (1997). A survivor's account of Stalin's camps.

Scott, John, *Behind the Urals: An American Worker in Russia's City of Steel* (1942, repr. 1973). A firsthand account of life under the first Five-Year Plan.

Sholokhov, Mikhail, *And Quiet Flows the Don; The Don Flows Home to the Sea,* 2 vols. (1934, 1940). A Nobel Prize–winning novel about the brutalizing effects of war, revolution, and civil war.

Solzhenitsyn, Aleksandr I., *The Gulag Archipelago,* 3 vols. (1973–1975). The classic account of Stalin's terror.

Tucker, Robert C., *Stalin as a Revolutionary* (1973). A psychological study of the young Stalin.

———, *Stalin in Power: The Revolution from Above, 1928–1941* (1990).

———, ed., *The Lenin Anthology* (1975). For those who want a taste of Lenin's writings.

———, ed., *Stalinism: Essays in Historical Interpretation* (1977). Essays on Stalin by prominent scholars.

Volkogonov, Dmitri, *Stalin: Triumph and Tragedy* (1991). The first Soviet biography based on hitherto unavailable archive material.

Von Laue, Theodore H., *Why Lenin? Why Stalin? Why Gorbachev?* 3rd ed. (1993). A brief survey of the rise and fall of the Soviet Union.

Fascism and Nazism

Allen, William Sheridan, *The Nazi Seizure of Power* (1965). An illuminating study of how the people of a small German town reacted to Nazism during the years 1930–1935.

Bissel, Richard, ed., *Life in the Third Reich* (1987). Essays dealing with various aspects of life in Hitler's Germany; good overviews.

Bracher, Karl Dietrich, *The German Dictatorship* (1970). A highly regarded analysis of all phases of the Nazi state.

Broszat, Martin, *The Hitler State* (1981). A detailed anatomy of the internal structure of the Third Reich.

Bucheim, Heim, *Totalitarian Rule* (1968). The nature and characteristics of totalitarianism, by a German scholar.

Bullock, Alan, *Hitler: A Study in Tyranny* (1964). An excellent biography.

Burleigh, Michael, and Wolfgang Wippermann, *The Racial State: Germany 1933–1945* (1991). Persecution of Jews, Gypsies, mentally handicapped, and homosexuals; analysis of racially motivated social policies of the Nazi regime.

Cassels, Alan, *Fascist Italy* (1968). A clearly written introduction.

Conway, J. S., *The Nazi Persecution of the Churches* (1968). Nazi persecution of the churches and the capitulation of the clergy.

Fest, Joachim C., *Hitler* (1974). An excellent biography.

Fischer, Klaus, *Nazi Germany: A New History* (1995). Probably the best one-volume treatment of Nazi Germany available.

Fritzsche, Peter, *Germans into Nazis* (1998). Tries to explain why Germans were attracted to the Nazi movement.

Haffner, Sebastian, *The Meaning of Hitler* (1979). A German journalist's inquiry into Hitler's successes and failures.

Jackel, Eberhard, *Hitler's Weltanschauung* (1972). An analysis of Hitler's world-view.

Kirkpatrick, Ivone, *Mussolini: A Study in Power* (1964). A solid biography.

Laqueur, Walter, ed., *Fascism: A Reader's Guide* (1976). A superb collection of essays.

Mack Smith, Denis, *Mussolini* (1982). By a leading historian of modern Italy.

Maltitz, Horst von, *The Evolution of Hitler's Germany* (1973). In trying to explain how it was possible, the author discusses the German roots of Nazism.

Mayer, Milton, *They Thought They Were Free* (1955). The lives of ordinary citizens who became Nazis.

Mosse, George L., *Nazi Culture* (1966). A representative collection of Nazi writings with a fine introduction.

Noakes, J., and G. Pridham, eds., *Nazism 1919–1945* (1983). A useful collection of primary sources in two volumes.

Paxton, Robert O., *Europe in the Twentieth Century* (1975). A first-rate text with an excellent bibliography.

Peukert, Detlev J. K., *Inside Nazi Germany* (1982). How ordinary citizens responded to Nazi rule.

Rees, Laurence, *The Nazis: A Warning from History* (1997). A companion volume to the BBC documentary, its principal virtue lies in the testimonies of former Nazis.

Reuth, Ralf Georg, *Goebbels* (1993). A highly acclaimed biography newly translated into English.

Rogger, Hans, and Eugen Weber, eds., *The European Right* (1966). A valuable collection of essays on right-wing movements in various European countries.

Rosenbaum, Ron, *Explaining Hitler* (1998). Interviews with leading historians about Hitler's life and career. The author knows how to ask questions and to interpret answers.

Spielvogel, Jackson J., *Hitler and Nazi Germany* (1988). Clearly written, up-to-date survey.

Turner, Henry A., ed., *Reappraisals of Fascism* (1975). A collection of useful essays.

Review Questions

1. How did the Soviet leaders view the position of Russia in the world? What were their aims and ambitions? How did their goals compare with those of other states?
2. How do you explain the fact that the Communist regime was far more ruthless in its methods of government than the tsarist regime? Which regime made Russia more powerful?
3. What do you think of the Leninist view that what was accomplished by voluntary cooperation in the West had to be achieved by compulsion in Russia? How do you account for the high degree of voluntary cooperation in American society? Why was it lacking in Russia?
4. What motivated Stalin to make terror a government policy? What motivated Communist bureaucrats to participate in Stalin's inhumanities?
5. How would you describe the differences between the conditions shaping American history and the conditions shaping Russian history in the years covered by this chapter? To what extent can American ways of thinking be applied to the conditions prevailing in Russia in the years treated in this chapter—or in general?
6. How did fascist principles, as Mussolini said, "stand for the sheer, categorical, definitive antithesis to the world of democracy . . . to the world which still abides by the fundamental principles laid down in 1789"?
7. Why did some Italians support Mussolini? In what ways was Mussolini less effective than Hitler in establishing a totalitarian state?
8. How was Hitler's outlook shaped by his experiences in Vienna?
9. What was the significance of the Munich putsch of 1923?
10. What were Hitler's attitudes toward democracy, the masses, war, the Jews, and propaganda?
11. What made Hitler's views attractive to Germans?
12. How was Hitler able to gain power? How did the Nazis extend their control over Germany?
13. In what ways did Nazism conflict with the core values of Christianity? What was the general policy of the Nazis toward the churches? Why did the German churches generally fail to take a stand against the Nazi regime?
14. What was the purpose of the giant rallies?
15. By 1939, most Germans were enthusiastic about the Nazi regime. Explain this statement.
16. What lessons might democratic societies draw from the experience of fascist totalitarianism?
17. After World War I, in country after country, parliamentary democracy collapsed and authoritarian leaders came to power. Explain.
18. How did the United States, Britain, and France try to cope with the Great Depression?

Chapter 31

Thought and Culture in an Era of World Wars and Totalitarianism

Guernica, by Pablo Picasso, a passionate protest against fascism and the horrors of war. (Giraudon/Art Resource, Copyright 1991 ARS, N.Y./SPADEM.)

■ **Intellectual and Artists in Troubled Times**
Postwar Pessimism
Literature and Art: Innovation, Disillusionment, and Social Commentary
Communism: "The God That Failed"
Reaffirming the Christian World-View
Reaffirming the Ideals of Reason and Freedom

■ **Existentialism**
Intellectual Background
Basic Principles
Nineteenth-Century Forerunners
Twentieth-Century Existentialists

■ **The Modern Predicament**

The presuppositions of the Enlightenment, already eroding in the decades before World War I, seemed near collapse after 1918—another casualty of trench warfare. Economic distress, particularly during the depression, also profoundly disoriented the European mind. Westerners no longer possessed a frame of reference, a common outlook for understanding themselves, their times, or the past. The core values of Western civilization—the self-sufficiency of reason and the inviolability of the individual—no longer seemed inspiring or binding.

The crisis of consciousness evoked a variety of responses. Having lost faith in the purpose of Western civilization, some intellectuals turned their backs on it or found escape in their art. Others sought a new hope in the Soviet experiment or in fascism; still others reaffirmed the rational-humanist tradition of the Enlightenment. Christian thinkers, repelled by the secularism, materialism, and rootlessness of the modern age, urged westerners to find renewed meaning and purpose in their ancestral religion. A philosophical movement called existentialism, which rose to prominence after World War II, aspired to make life authentic in a world stripped of universal values.

Intellectuals and Artists in Troubled Times

Postwar Pessimism

After World War I, Europeans looked at them selves and their civilization differently. It seemed that in science and technology they had unleashed powers that they could not control, and belief in the stability and security of European civilization appeared to be an illusion. Also illusory was the expectation that reason would banish surviving signs of darkness, ignorance, and injustice and usher in an age of continual progress. European intellectuals felt that they were living in a "broken world." In a time of heightened brutality and mobilized irrationality, the values of old Europe seemed beyond recovery. "All the great words," wrote D. H. Lawrence, "were cancelled out for that generation."[1] The fissures discernible in European civilization before 1914 had grown wider and deeper. To be sure, Europe also had its optimists—those who found reason for hope in the League of Nations and in the easing of international tensions and improved economic conditions in the mid 1920s. However, the Great Depression and the triumph of totalitarianism intensified feelings of doubt and disillusionment.

The somber mood that gripped intellectuals in the immediate postwar period had been anticipated by Freud in a series of papers published in 1915 under the title "Thoughts for the Times on War and Death." The war, said Freud, stripped westerners of those cultural restraints that had served to contain a murderous primeval aggressiveness, and it threatened to inflict irreparable damage on European civilization:

> *We cannot but feel that no event has ever destroyed so much that is precious in the common possessions of humanity, confused so many of the clearest intelligences or so thoroughly debased what is highest. . . . [T]he war in which we had refused to believe broke out, and it brought—disillusionment. . . . It tramples in blind fury on all that comes in its way, as though there were to be no future and no peace among men after it is over. It cuts all the common bonds between the contending peoples, and threatens to leave a legacy of embitterment that will make any renewal of these bonds impossible for a long time to come.*[2]

A pessimistic outlook also pervaded Freud's *Civilization and Its Discontents* (1930), in which he held that civilized life was forever threatened by the antisocial and irrational elements of human nature.

Other expressions of pessimism abounded. In 1919, Paul Valéry stated: "We modern civilizations have learned to recognize that we are mortal like the others. We feel that a civilization is as fragile as life."[3] "We are living today under the sign of the collapse of civilization,"[4] declared the humanitarian Albert Schweitzer in 1923. In the midst of the depression, Arnold Toynbee wrote: "The year 1931 was distinguished from previous years . . . by one outstanding feature. In 1931 men and women all over the world were seriously contemplating and frankly discussing the possibility that the Western system of Society might break down and cease to work."[5] The German philosopher Karl Jaspers noted in 1932 that "there is a growing awareness of imminent ruin tantamount to a dread of the approaching end of all that makes life worthwhile."[6]

Disillusionment and gloom also permeated works of fiction and poetry. The novels of Aldous Huxley rejected belief in progress and expressed a disenchantment with the modern world. Ernest Hemingway's *The Sun Also Rises* (1926) described a lost postwar generation. In *All Quiet on the Western Front* (1929), Erich Maria Remarque dealt with the horrors of the war and their impact. A German soldier in the novel ponders the war's effect on youth:

> *I am twenty years old; yet I know nothing of life but despair, death, fear, and fatuous superficiality cast over an abyss of sorrow. I see how peoples are set against one another, and in silence, unknowingly, foolishly, obediently, innocently slay one another. I see that the keenest brains of the world invent weapons and words to make it yet more refined and enduring. . . . all my generation is experiencing these things with me. . . . What do they expect of us if a time ever comes when the war is over? Through the years our business has been killing. . . . Our knowledge of life is limited to death. What will happen afterwards?*[7]

In the poem "The Second Coming" (1919), William Butler Yeats conveys his sense of the dark times:

> *Mere anarchy is loosed upon the world,*
> *The blood-dimmed tide is loosed, and everywhere*
> *The ceremony of innocence is drowned;*
> *The best lack all conviction, while the worst*
> *Are full of passionate intensity.*
> *Surely some revelation is at hand*
> *Surely the Second Coming is at hand.*[8]

T. S. Eliot's "The Waste Land" (1922) also expresses a feeling of foreboding. In his image of a collapsing European civilization, Eliot creates a macabre scenario. Hooded hordes, modern-day barbarians, swarm over plains and lay waste cities. Jerusalem, Athens, Alexandria, Vienna, and London—each once a great spiritual or cultural center—are now collapsing.[9]

Other writers and thinkers also focused on the crises facing the Western world. Carl Gustav Jung, a Swiss psychologist who broke with Freud, stated in *Modern Man in Search of a Soul* (1933):

> *I believe I am not exaggerating when I say that modern man has suffered an almost fatal shock, psychologically speaking, and as a result has fallen into profound uncertainty. . . . The revolution in our conscious outlook, brought about by the catastrophic results of the World War, shows itself in our inner life by the shattering of our faith in ourselves and our own worth. . . . I realize only too well that I am losing my faith in the possibility of a rational organization of the world, the old dream of the millennium, in which peace and harmony should rule, has grown pale.*[10]

In 1936, the Dutch historian Johan Huizinga wrote in a chapter entitled "Apprehension of Doom":

> *We are living in a demented world. And we know it. . . . Everywhere there are doubts as to the solidity of our social structure, vague fears of the imminent future, a feeling that our civilization is on the way to ruin. . . . almost all things which once seemed sacred and immutable have now become unsettled, truth and humanity, justice and reason. . . . The sense of living in the midst of a violent crisis of civilization, threatening complete collapse, has spread far and wide.*[11]

In 1939, as the war clouds darkened, E. M. Forster, the distinguished British novelist, lamented:

> *During the present decade thousands and thousands of innocent people have been killed, robbed, mutilated, insulted, imprisoned. We, the fortunate exceptions, learn of this from the newspapers and from refugees, we realize that it may be our turn next, and we know that all these private miseries may be the prelude to an incalculable catastrophe, in which the whole of western civilization . . . may go down. Perhaps history will point to these years as the moment when man's inventiveness finally outbalanced his moral growth, and toppled him downhill.*[12]

The most influential expression of pessimism was Oswald Spengler's *The Decline of the West.* The first volume was published in July 1918, as the war was drawing to a close, and the second volume in 1922. The work achieved instant notoriety, particularly in Spengler's native Germany, which was shattered by defeat. Spengler viewed history as an assemblage of many different cultures that, like living organisms, experience birth, youth, maturity, and death. What contemporaries pondered most was Spengler's insistence that Western civilization had entered its final stage and that its death could not be averted.

Spengler defined a culture as a spiritual orientation that pervades a people's literature, art, religion, philosophy, politics, and economics; each culture has a distinctive style, which distinguishes it from other cultures. The ancient Greeks, wrote Spengler, viewed themselves as living in a clearly defined and finite world. Hence, classical sculpture was characterized by the life-size nude statue; architecture, by the temple with small columns; and political life, by the small city-state rather than by a kingdom or an empire. Modern westerners have a different cultural orientation, said Spengler; they exhibit a Faustian urge to expand, to reach out. Thus, Europeans developed perspectival art, which permits distance to be depicted on a canvas; they sailed the oceans and conquered vast regions of the globe; and they invented the telephone and telegraph, making possible quick communication over great distances.

According to Spengler, cultures had to pass through three necessary stages: a heroic youth, a creative maturity, and a decadent old age. In its youth, during the Renaissance, said Spengler, Western culture experienced the triumphs of Michelangelo, Shakespeare, and Galileo; in its maturity, during the eighteenth century, Western culture reached its creative height in the music of Mozart, the poetry of Goethe, and the philosophy of Kant. But now, Faustian culture, entering old age, was showing signs of decay: a growing materialism and skepticism; a disenchanted proletariat; rampant warfare and competition for empire; and decadent art forms. "Of great painting or great music there can no longer be, for Western people, any question," Spengler concluded.[13]

To an already troubled Western world, Spengler offered no solace. The West, like other cultures and like any living organism, was destined to die. Its decline was irreversible and its death inevitable; the symptoms of its degeneration were already evident. Spengler's gloomy prognostication buttressed the fascists, who claimed that they were creating a new civilization on the ruins of the dying European civilization.

Literature and Art: Innovation, Disillusionment, and Social Commentary

Postwar pessimism did not prevent writers and artists from continuing the cultural innovations begun before the war. In the works of D. H. Lawrence, Marcel Proust, André Gide, James Joyce, Franz Kafka, T. S. Eliot, and Thomas Mann, the modernist movement achieved a brilliant flowering. Often these writers gave expression to the troubles and uncertainties of the postwar period.

Franz Kafka (1883–1924), whose major novels, *The Trial* and *The Castle*, were published after his death, did not receive recognition until after World War II. Yet perhaps better than any other novelist of his generation, Kafka grasped the dilemma of the modern age. There is no apparent order or stability in Kafka's world. Human beings strive to make sense out of life, but everywhere ordinary occurrences thwart them. They are caught in a bureaucratic web, which they cannot control; they live in a nightmare society dominated by oppressive, cruel, and corrupt officials and amoral torturers. In Kafka's world, cruelty and injustice are accepted facts of existence, power is exercised without limits, and victims cooperate in their own destruction. Traditional values and ordinary logic do not operate. Our world, thought to be secure, stable, and purposeful, easily falls apart. Like Kierkegaard, Kafka understood the intense anxiety that torments modern people.

Franz Kafka (1883–1924). The troubled Czech-Jewish writer expressed the feelings of alienation and aloneness that burden people in the modern age. (*Corbis-Bettmann.*)

In *The Trial*, for example, Josef K., an ordinary man who has no consciousness of wrongdoing, is arrested. "K. lived in a country with a legal constitution, there was universal peace, all the laws were in force; who dared seize him in his own dwelling?"[14] Josef K. is never told the reason for his arrest, and he is eventually executed, a victim of institutional evil that breaks and destroys him "like a dog." In these observations, Kafka anticipated the emerging totalitarian state. (Kafka's three sisters perished in the Holocaust.)

A German-speaking Jew in the alien Slav environment of Czechoslovakia, Kafka died of tuberculosis at an early age. In voicing his own deep anxieties, Kafka expressed the feelings of alienation and isolation that characterize the modern individual. He explored life's dreads and absurdities, offering no solutions or consolation. In Kafka's works, people are defeated and unable to comprehend the irrational forces that contribute to their destruction. Although the mind yearns for coherence, Kafka tells us that uncertainty, if not chaos, governs human relationships. We can be sure neither of our own identities nor of the world we encounter, for human beings are the playthings of unfathomable forces, too irrational to master.

A brooding pessimism about the human condition pervades Kafka's work. One reason for the intensified interest in Kafka after World War II, observes Angel Flores, "is that the European world of the late 30's and 40's with its betrayals and concentration camps, its resulting cruelties and indignities, bore a remarkable resemblance to the world depicted by Kafka in the opening decades of the century. History seems to have imitated the nightmarish background evoked by the dreamer of Prague."[15]

Before World War I, the German writer Thomas Mann (1875–1955) had earned a reputation for his short stories and novels, particularly *Buddenbrooks* (1901), which portrayed the decline of a prosperous bourgeois family. At the outbreak of the war, Mann was a staunch conservative who disliked democracy. After the war, he drew closer to liberalism, supporting the Weimar Republic and attacking the Nazi cult of irrationalism.

In *Mario and the Magician* (1930), Mann explicitly attacked Italian fascism and implied that it would require armed resistance. In 1931, two years before Hitler took power, Mann, in an article entitled "An Appeal to Reason," described National Socialism and the extreme nationalism it espoused as a rejection of the Western rational tradition and a regression to primitive and barbaric modes of behavior. Nazism, he said, "is distinguished by . . . its absolute unrestraint, its orgiastic, radically anti-humane, frenziedly dynamic character. . . . Everything is possible, everything is permitted as a weapon against human decency. . . . Fanaticism turns into a means of salvation . . . politics becomes an opiate for the masses . . . and reason veils her face."[16]

After Hitler's seizure of power, Mann went to Switzerland and eventually to the United States, where he remained a resolute foe of totalitarianism. In 1938, he described the crisis of reason that afflicted his generation: "The twentieth century has in its first third taken up a position of reaction against classic rationalism and intellectualism. It has surrendered to admiration of the unconscious, to a glorification of instinct. And the bad instincts have accordingly been enjoying a heyday."[17]

In *The Magic Mountain*, begun in 1912 and completed in 1924, Mann had reflected on the decomposition of bourgeois European civilization. The novel is set in a Swiss sanitarium, just prior to World War I. The patients, drawn from several European lands, suffer from tuberculosis and are diseased in spirit, as well as body. The sanitarium symbolizes Europe. It is the European psyche that is sick and rushing headlong into a catastrophe.

One patient, the Italian Ludovico Settembrini, stands for the humanist ideals of the Enlightenment: reason, individual liberty, and progress. While Mann is sympathetic to these ideals, he also indicts Settembrini for his naive faith in progress, his shallow view of human nature, which gives little significance to the will, and his lofty rhetoric. Overestimating the power of the rational, Settembrini foolishly believes that people will mend their ways once they are enlightened by reason. Thus, he even claims that he cured a sick person merely by looking at him "rationally." Settembrini represents a decaying liberalism.

Pitted against Settembrini is Leo Naphta, a Spanish-trained Jesuit of Jewish-Polish descent, who represents the revolt against reason in Mann's generation. Naphta completely rejects the Italian's liberal-humanist values. An authoritarian, he insists that people do not need freedom but need only authority and discipline imposed by state or church. He is a fanatic, accepting torture and terror as a way to impose authority. Convinced that the dictatorship of the proletariat is the means of salvation demanded by the age, Naphta embraces Marxism. Borrowing from medieval mysticism, Nietzschean irrationalism, and Marxist militancy, he attacks every facet of the existing liberal order.

Another character, a wealthy Dutch planter from Java named Mynheer Peeperkorn, is nonintellectual, illogical, and inarticulate, but he radiates pure vitality and emotional intensity. This charismatic personality dwarfs the humanist Settembrini and the authoritarian Naphta and dominates the patients, who find him irresistible.

The Magic Mountain, which ends with the advent of World War I, raised, but did not resolve, crucial questions. Was the epoch of rational-humanist culture drawing to a close? Did bourgeois Europe welcome its spiritual degeneration in the same way that some of the patients in the sanitarium had a will to illness? How could Europe rescue itself from decadence?

D. H. Lawrence (1885–1930), the son of an illiterate British coal miner, was saddened and angered by the consequences of industrial society: the deterioration of nature, tedious work divorced from personal satisfaction, and a life-denying quest for wealth and possessions. He looked back longingly on preindustrial England and wanted people to reorient their thinking away from moneymaking and suppression of the instincts. In his works he dealt with the clash between industrial civilization, which regiments human beings in the name of efficiency, and the needs of human nature. Thus in *Women in Love* (1920), the new owner of the family coal mine, determined to utilize modern management techniques in order to extract greater wealth from the business, dismisses the human needs of the workers:

> *Suddenly he had conceived the pure instrumentality of mankind. There had been so much humanitarianism, so much talk of sufferings and feelings. It was ridiculous. The sufferings and feelings of individuals did not matter in the least.... What mattered was the pure instrumentality of the individual. As a man as of a knife: does it cut well? Nothing else mattered.*
>
> *Everything in the world has its function, and is good or not good in so far as it fulfills this function.... Was a miner a good miner? Then he was complete.*[18]

In *Lady Chatterly's Lover* (1928), a highly erotic novel, Lawrence affirmed sexual passion as both necessary and beneficial for human well-being and criticized cultural norms that disfigured it with distaste, shame, and guilt.

Like nineteenth-century romantics, Lawrence found a higher truth in deep-seated passion than in reason; this led him to rail against Christianity for stifling human sexuality. Like Nietzsche, he believed that excessive intellectualizing destroyed the life-affirming, instinctual part of human nature. In 1913, he wrote:

> *My great religion is a belief in the blood, the flesh, as being wiser than the intellect. We can go wrong in our minds. But what our blood feels and believes and says is always true. The intellect is only a bit and a bridle. What do I care about knowledge. All I want is to answer to my blood without fribbling intervention of mind, or moral, or what not. . . . We have got so ridiculously mindful, that we never know that we ourselves are anything.*[19]

Shattered by World War I, disgusted by fascism's growing strength, and moved by the suffering of the depression, many writers became committed to social and political causes. Remarque's *All Quiet on the Western Front* was one of many antiwar novels. In *The Grapes of Wrath* (1939), John Steinbeck captured the suffering of American farmers losing their land when it became the Dust Bowl or driven from it by foreclosure during the depression. George Orwell's *The Road to Wigan Pier* (1937) recorded the bleak lives of English coal miners. Few issues stirred the conscience of intellectuals as did the Spanish Civil War, and many of them volunteered to fight with the Spanish republicans against the fascists. Ernest Hemingway's *For Whom the Bell Tolls* (1940) expressed the sentiments of these thinkers.

The new directions taken in art before World War I—abstractionism and expressionism—continued in the postwar decades. Picasso, Mondrian, Kandinsky, Matisse, Rouault, Braque, Modigliani, and other masters continued to refine their styles. In addition, new art trends emerged, mirroring the trauma of a generation that had experienced the war and lost its faith in Europe's moral and intellectual values.

In 1915 in Zurich, artists and writers founded a movement, called Dada, to express their revulsion against the war and the civilization that spawned it. From neutral Switzerland, the movement spread to Germany and Paris. Dadaists viewed artistic and literary standards with contempt, rejected God, and glorified unreason. They celebrated nihilism for its own sake. "Through reason man becomes a tragic and ugly figure,"

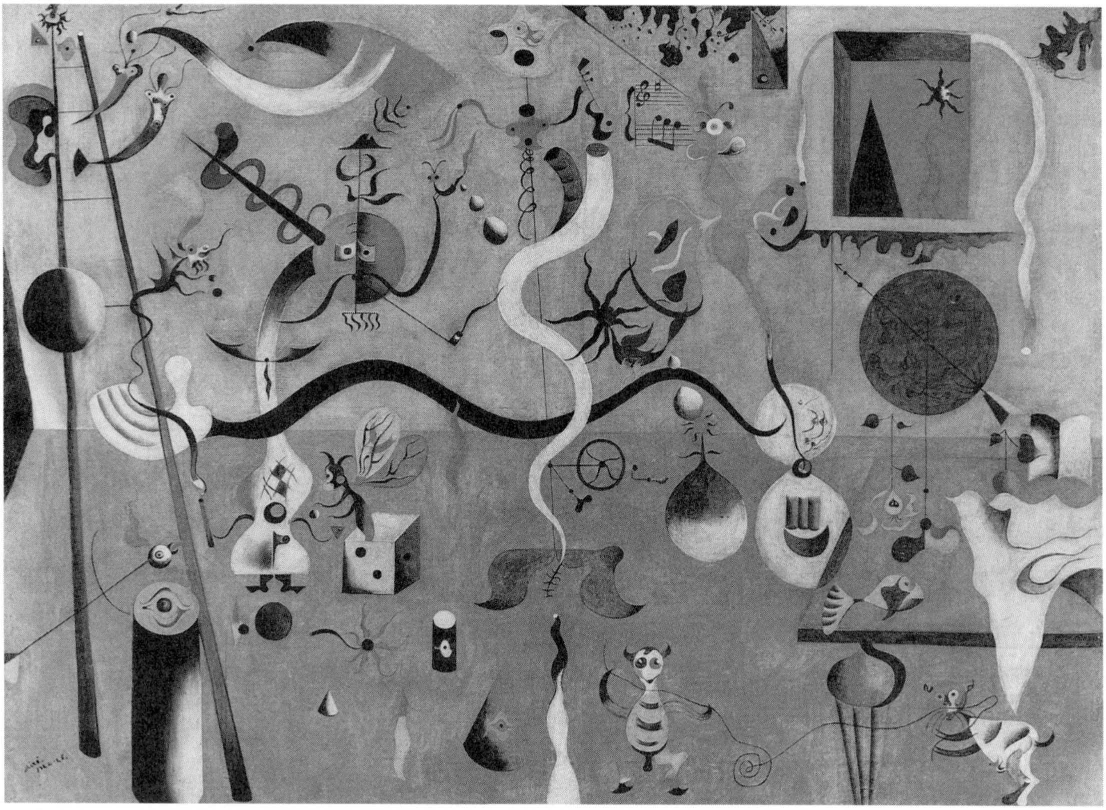

Harlequin's Carnival (1924), by Joan Miró (1893–1983). In one of the first surrealist paintings, Miró makes visible an inner world of fantasy and humor populated by an array of imaginary creatures. (*Albright-Knox Art Gallery, Buffalo, New York, Room of Contemporary Art Fund, 1940. Copyright 1991 ARS, N.Y., ADAGP.*)

said one Dadaist; "beauty is dead," said another. Dada shared in the postwar mood of disorientation and despair. Dadaists regarded life as essentially absurd (*Dada* is a nonsense term) and cultivated indifference. "The acts of life have no beginning or end. Everything happens in a completely idiotic way," declared the poet Tristan Tzara, one of Dada's founders. Tzara elevated spontaneity above reason:

> *What good did the theories of the philosophers do us? Did they help us to take a single step forward or backward? . . . We have had enough of the intelligent movements that have stretched beyond measure our credulity in the benefits of science. What we want now is spontaneity because everything that issues freely from ourselves, without the intervention of speculative ideas . . . represents us.*[20]

For Dadaists, the world was nonsensical, and reality disordered; hence, they offered no solutions to anything. "Like everything in life, Dada is useless," said Tzara.[21]

Dadaists showed their contempt for art (one art historian calls Dada "the first anti-art movement on record"[22]) by producing works that were deliberately senseless, purposeless, and chaotic,

Angel of Hearth and Home, by Max Ernst (1891–1976). Ernst formed part of the transition from Dada to surrealism. His paintings expressed a profound anxiety. André Breton called him "the most magnificently haunted mind in Europe." (*© 1995 Artists Rights Society (ARS), New York/SPADEM/ADAGP, Paris.*)

and apparently devoid of artistic value. Marcel Duchamp's *Bicycle Wheel* is an example, as is his *Mona Lisa* with a mustache. Despite the Dadaists' nihilistic aims and "calculated irrationality," says the art historian H. W. Janson, "there was also liberation, a voyage into unknown provinces of the creative mind." Thus, Duchamp's painting with the nonsense title *Tu m'* was "dazzlingly inventive [and] far ahead of its time."[23]

Dada ended as a formal movement in 1924 and was succeeded by surrealism. Surrealists inherited from Dada a contempt for reason. They stressed fantasy and made use of Freudian insights and symbols in their art to reproduce the raw state of the unconscious and to arrive at truths beyond reason's grasp. To penetrate the interior of the mind, said André Breton, a French surrealist poet, the writer should "write quickly without any previously chosen subject, quickly enough not to dwell on and not to be tempted to read over what you have written."[24] Writing should not be dictated by the intellect but should flow automatically from the unconscious. Surrealists tried to portray the world of fantasy and hallucination, the marvelous and the spontaneous. Breton urged artists to live their dreams, even if it meant seeing "a horse galloping on a tomato." In the effort to break through the constraints of rationality so that they might reach a higher reality—that is, a "surreality"—leading surrealists such as Max Ernst (1891–1976), Salvador Dali (1904–1989), and Joan Miró (1893–1983) produced works of undeniable artistic merit.

Artists, like writers, expressed a social conscience. George Grosz combined a Dadaist sense of life's meaninglessness with a new realism to depict the moral degeneration of middle-class

German society. In *After the Questioning* (1935), Grosz, then living in the United States, dramatized Nazi brutality; in *The End of the World* (1936), he expressed his fear of another impending world war. Käthe Kollwitz, also a German artist, showed a deep compassion for the sufferer: the unemployed, the hungry, the ill, and the politically oppressed.

In a series of paintings, *The Passion of Sacco and Vanzetti* (1931–32), American artist Ben Shahn showed his outrage at the execution of two radicals. William Gropper's *Migration* (1932) dramatized the suffering of the same dispossessed farmers described in Steinbeck's novel *The Grapes of Wrath*. Philip Evergood, in *Don't Cry Mother* (1938–1944), portrayed the apathy of starving children and their mother's terrible helplessness.

In his etchings of maimed, dying, and dead soldiers, German artist Otto Dix produced a powerful visual indictment of the Great War's cruelty and suffering. Service in the German army during World War I made Max Beckmann acutely aware of violence and brutality, which he expressed in *The Night* (1918–19) and other paintings. Designated a "degenerate artist" by the Nazis, Beckmann went into exile. In *Guernica* (1937), Picasso memorialized the Spanish village decimated by Nazi saturation bombing during the Spanish Civil War. *White Crucifixion* (1938) by Marc Chagall, a Russian-born Jew who had settled in Paris, depicted the terror and flight of Jews in Nazi Germany.

Communism: "The God That Failed"

The economic misery of the depression and the rise of fascist barbarism led many intellectuals to find a new hope, even a secular faith, in communism. They praised the Soviet Union for supplanting capitalist greed with socialist cooperation; replacing a haphazard economic system marred by repeated depressions with one based on planned production; and providing employment for everyone when joblessness was endemic in capitalist lands. Equating socialism with humanitarianism and capitalism with injustice, they believed that the Soviets were reorganizing society for the benefit of humanity. The American literary critic Edmund Wilson said that in the Soviet Union one felt at the "moral top of the world where the light never really goes out."[25] The British political theorists Sidney and Beatrice Webb declared that there was no other country "in which there is actually so much widespread public criticism and such incessant reevaluation of its shortcomings as in the USSR."[26] To these intellectuals, it seemed that in the Soviet Union a vigorous and healthy civilization was emerging and that only communism could stem the tide of fascism. Many of these deluded people, ignoring or refusing to recognize the reality of Stalin's terror, continued to embrace the Soviet system. For others, however, the attraction was short-lived. Sickened by Stalin's purges and terror, the denial of individual freedom, and the suppression of truth, they came to view the Soviet Union as another totalitarian state and communism as another "god that failed."

One such intellectual was Arthur Koestler. Born in Budapest of Jewish ancestry and educated in Vienna, Koestler worked as a correspondent for a leading Berlin newspaper chain. He joined the Communist party at the very end of 1931 because he "lived in a disintegrating society thirsting for faith," was moved by the suffering caused by the depression, and saw communism as the "only force capable of resisting the onrush of the primitive [Nazi] horde."[27] Koestler visited the Soviet Union in 1933, experiencing firsthand both the starvation brought on by forced collectivization and the propaganda that grotesquely misrepresented life in Western lands. Although his faith was shaken, he did not break with the party until 1938, in response to Stalin's liquidations.

In *Darkness at Noon* (1941), Koestler explored the attitudes of the Old Bolsheviks who were imprisoned, tortured, and executed by Stalin. These dedicated Communists had served the party faithfully, but Stalin, fearful of opposition, hating intellectuals, and driven by megalomania, denounced them as enemies of the people. The leading character in *Darkness at Noon,* the imprisoned Rubashov, is a composite of the Old Bolsheviks. Although he is innocent, Rubashov, without being physically tortured, publicly confesses to political crimes that he never committed.

Rubashov is aware of the suffering that the party has brought to the Russian people:

Profile

Charlie Chaplin

Culver Pictures.

Charles Spencer (Charlie) Chaplin was born in London in 1889 to music hall entertainers. His mother, Hannah Chaplin, taught young Charles the art of pantomine. Touring the United States with an English company, he was hired by Mack Sennett to act in the popular Keystone Comedies. Insightful, intelligent, musical, and artistic, Chaplin transformed silent film comedy, which was largely slapstick, into an art form.

In *The Tramp* (1915), Chaplin played a gentleman tramp, the character with which he would always be identified. The "little tramp" wore baggy pants, a derby, fingerless gloves, and a shabby dress coat, handled a bamboo cane with great dexterity, and shuffled as he

> *[I]n the interests of a just distribution of land we deliberately let die of starvation about five million farmers and their families in one year. . . . [to liberate] human beings from the shackles of industrial exploitation . . . we sent about ten million people to do forced labour in the Arctic regions and the jungles of the East, under conditions similar to those of antique galley slaves. . . . to settle a difference of opinion, we know only one argument: death. . . . Our poets settle discussions on questions of style by denunciations to the Secret Police. . . . The people's standard of life is lower than it was before the Revolution, the labour conditions are harder, the discipline is more inhuman. . . . Our Press and our schools cultivate Chauvinism, militarism, dogmatism, conformism and ignorance. The arbitrary power of the Government is unlimited, and unexampled in history. Freedom of the Press, of opinion and of movement are as thoroughly exterminated as though the proclamation of the Rights of Man had never been. We have built up the most gigantic police apparatus, with informers made a national institution, and with the most refined scientific system of physical and mental torture. We whip the groaning masses of the country towards a theoretical future happiness, which only we can see.*[28]

Pained by his own complicity in the party's crimes, including the betrayal of friends, Rubashov questions the party's philosophy that the individual should be subordinated and, if necessary, sacrificed to the regime. Nevertheless, Rubashov remains the party's faithful servant. True believers do not easily break with their walked. Critics applauded Chaplin's skill as both actor and director in *The Kid* (1921), which also starred the six-year-old Jackie Coogan. The interaction between the little tramp and the young boy, who had been abandoned, brought tears and smiles to audiences. It also revealed Chaplin's social conscience. Abandoned by his alcoholic father, he knew poverty as a youth.

Chaplin's skill as a social commentator was demonstrated in two classic works: *Modern Times* (1936) and *The Great Dictator* (1940). In *Modern Times,* Chaplin satirized labor in the modern mechanized factory. In one memorable scene, Charlie is tightening nuts on a conveyer belt when the boss orders a speedup. Desperately trying to increase his pace, Charlie moves hyperactively and spasmodically. His mind is also affected. When he sees a secretary wearing a dress with ornaments resembling the nuts that he has been turning, Charlie chases her, determined to apply his wrench to the nutlike ornaments. In the *Great Dictator,* Chaplin mocked Mussolini and Hitler and expressed outrage at German anti-Semitism. He made the film, he said, for "the return of decency and kindness."

After World War II, Chaplin continued to act and direct, but his later works—*Monsieur Verdoux* (1947), *Limelight* (1952), and *A King in New York* (1957)—were not well received. Identified with leftist causes, Chaplin was refused reentry into the United States in 1952. Twenty years later, he returned to the United States and received on honorary Academy Award. In 1975, he was knighted by Queen Elizabeth II. He died at the end of 1977.

faith. By confessing to treason, Rubashov performs his last service for the Revolution. For the true believer, everything—truth, justice, and the sanctity of the individual—is properly sacrificed to the party.

Reaffirming the Christian World-View

By calling into question core liberal beliefs—the essential goodness of human nature, the primacy of reason, the efficacy of science, and the inevitability of progress—World War I led thinkers to find in Christianity an alternative view of the human experience and the crisis of the twentieth century. Christian thinkers, including Karl Barth, Paul Tillich, Reinhold Niebuhr, Christopher Dawson, Jacques Maritain, and T. S. Eliot, asserted the reality of evil in human nature. They assailed liberals and Marxists for holding too optimistic a view of human nature and human reason; postulating a purely rational and secular philosophy of history; and anticipating an ideal society within the realm of historical time. Reinhold Niebuhr (1892–1971), a leading American Protestant theologian, declared in 1941: "The utopian illusions and sentimental observations of modern liberal culture are really all derived from the basic error of negating the fact of original sin."[29] For these thinkers, the Christian conception of history as a clash between human will and God's commands provided an intelligible explanation of the tragedies of the twentieth century. Karl Barth (1886–1968), the Swiss-German Protestant theologian, called for a reaffirmation of the Christ who inspires faith, the uniqueness of Christianity, and the spiritual power of divine revelation. The true meaning of history, he said,

The Night (1918–19), by Max Beckmann (1884–1950). Max Beckmann's paintings gave expression to the disillusionment and spiritual unease that afflicted postwar Germany. When the Nazis included his works in the Degenerate Art Exhibition (1937), he left the country. In *The Night,* Beckmann, himself a veteran of the front, depicts brutal men engaging in terrible violence. (*Kunstsammlung Nordrhein-Westfalen, Dusseldorf, © Estate of Max Beckmann/ARS, New York, 1991.*)

is not to be found in the liberals' view of the progress of reason and freedom or in the Marxist conception of economic determinism. Rather, it derives from the fact that history is the arena in which the individual's faith is tested.

Jacques Maritain (1882–1973), a leading Catholic thinker, denounced core elements of the modern outlook: the autonomy of the individual, the autonomy of the mind, and a nonreligious humanism. He urged that the Christian philosophy of Thomas Aquinas be revived, for he believed that it successfully harmonized faith and reason. Maritain argued that "anthropomorphic humanism," which held that human beings by themselves alone can define life's purpose and create their own values, has utterly failed. Without guidance from a transcendental source, reason is powerless to control irrational drives, which threaten to degrade human existence. Without commitment to God's values, we find substitute faiths in fanatic and belligerent ideologies and unscrupulous leaders.

A strong advocate of political freedom, Maritain stressed the link between modern democracy and the Christian Gospels, which proclaimed "the natural equality of all men, children of the same God and redeemed by the same Christ . . . [and] the inalienable dignity of every soul fashioned in the image of God." He insisted that "the democratic state of mind and . . . the democratic philosophy of life requires the energies of the Gospel to penetrate secular existence, taming the irrational to reason."[30] These energies would control the human propensity for self-centeredness, wickedness, and hatred of others. To survive, secular democracy must be infused with Christian love and compassion.

The English Catholic thinker Christopher Dawson (1889–1970) stressed the historic ties between Christianity and Western civilization. He wrote in 1933: "If our civilization is to recover its vitality, or even to survive, it must . . . realize that religion is . . . the very heart of social life and the root of every living culture."[31]

In 1934, the British historian Arnold Toynbee (1889–1975) published the first three volumes of his monumental work, *A Study of History*, in which he tried to account for the rise, growth, breakdown, and disintegration of civilization. Underlying Toynbee's philosophy of history was a religious orientation, for he saw religious prophets as humanity's greatest figures and the world's major religions as humanity's greatest achievement. Toynbee attributed the problems of Western civilization to its breaking away from Christianity and embracing "false idols," particularly the national state, which, he said, had become the object of westerners' highest reverence.

Toynbee regarded nationalism as a primitive religion, inducing people to revere the national community rather than God. This deification of the parochial—tribal or local—community intensified the brutal side of human nature and provoked wars among people sharing a common civilization. To Toynbee, Nazism was the culmination of the worst elements in modern European nationalism, "the consummation . . . of a politico-religious movement, the pagan deification and worship of parochial human communities which had been gradually gaining ground for more than four centuries in the Western world at large."[32] The moral catastrophe of Nazism, he said, demonstrates the inadequacy of liberal humanism, for the Enlightenment tradition proved a feeble barrier to the rise and spread of Nazism. The secular values of the Enlightenment, divorced from Christianity, cannot restrain human nature's basest impulses. For the West to save itself, said Toynbee, it must abide by the spiritual values of its religious prophets.

Reaffirming the Ideals of Reason and Freedom

Several thinkers tried to reaffirm the ideals of rationality and freedom that totalitarian movements had trampled. In *The Treason of the Intellectuals* (1927), Julien Benda (1867–1956), a French cultural critic of Jewish background, castigated intellectuals for intensifying hatred between nations and classes. "Our age is indeed the age of the intellectual organization of political hatreds," he wrote. Intellectuals who stir up hatred between nations, said Benda, do not pursue justice or truth but proclaim that "even if our country is wrong, we must think of it in the right." They scorn outsiders, extol harshness and action, and proclaim the superiority of instinct and will to intelligence; or they "assert that the intelligence to be venerated is that which limits its activities within the bounds of national interest." The logical end of this xenophobia, said Benda, "is the organized slaughter of nations and classes."[33]

José Ortega y Gasset (1883–1955), descendant of a Spanish noble family, gained international recognition with the publication of *The Revolt of the Masses* (1930). According to Ortega, European civilization, the product of a creative elite, was degenerating into barbarism because of the growing power of the masses, for the masses lacked the mental discipline and the commitment to reason needed to preserve Europe's intellectual and cultural traditions. Ortega did not equate the masses with the working class and the elite with the nobility; an attitude of mind, not a class affiliation, distinguished the "mass-man" from the elite.

The mass-man, said Ortega, has a commonplace mind and does not set high standards for himself. He is inert until driven by an external compulsion. He does not enter into rational dialogue with others, defend his opinions logically, or accept objective standards. Faced with a problem, he "is satisfied with thinking the first thing he finds in his head" and "crushes . . . everything that is different, everything that is excellent, individual, qualified, and select. Anybody who is not like everybody, who does not think like everybody, runs the risk of being eliminated."[34] Such intellectually vulgar people, declared Ortega, cannot understand or preserve the processes of civilization. The fascists exemplify this revolt of the masses, for "under fascism there appears for the first time in Europe a type of man who . . . simply shows himself resolved to impose his opinions. This is the new thing: the right not to be reasonable, the 'reason of unreason.'" The danger lay in "the masses . . . having decided to rule society without the capacity for doing so."[35] Rejecting reason, the mass-man glorifies violence: the ultimate expression of barbarism. If European civilization is to be rescued from fascism and communism, said Ortega, the elite must sustain civilized values and provide leadership.

A staunch defender of the Enlightenment tradition, Ernst Cassirer (1874–1945), a German philosopher of Jewish lineage, emigrated after Hitler came to power, eventually settling in the United States. Just prior to Hitler's triumph, Cassirer wrote of the need to uphold and reenergize that tradition: "The age which venerated reason and science as man's highest faculty cannot and must not be lost even for us. We must find a way not only to see that age in its own shape but to release again those original forces which brought forth and molded this shape."[36]

In his posthumous work, *The Myth of the State* (1946), Cassirer described Nazism as the triumph of mythical thinking over reason. The Nazis, said Cassirer, cleverly manufactured myths—of the race, the leader, the party, the state—that disoriented the intellect. Germans who embraced these myths surrendered their capacity for independent judgment, leaving themselves vulnerable to manipulation by the Nazi leadership. Cassirer warned:

> *In politics we are always living on volcanic soil. We must be prepared for convulsions and eruptions. In all critical moments of man's social life, the rational forces that resist the rise of old mythical conceptions are no longer sure of themselves. In these moments the time of myth has come again. For myth has not been really vanquished and subjugated. It is always there, lurking in the dark and waiting for its hour and opportunity. This hour comes as soon as the other binding forces of man's social life . . . lose their strength and are no longer able to combat the demonic mythical powers.*[37]

To contain the destructive powers of political myths, Cassirer urged strengthening the rational-humanist tradition and called for the critical study of political myths, for "in order to fight an enemy you must know him. . . . We should carefully study the origin, the structure, the methods, and the technique of the political myths. We should see the adversary face to face in order to know how to combat him."[38]

Like Cassirer and many other German-Jewish intellectuals, Erich Fromm (1900–1980), a social theorist and psychoanalyst, settled in the United States after the Nazis took power. In *Escape from Freedom* (1941), Fromm explained the triumph of Nazism within the wider context of European history. When the Middle Ages ended, he said, the individual grew increasingly independent of external authority and experienced new possibilities for personal development. The individual's role in the social order was no longer rigorously determined by birth. Increasingly, the world was explained in natural terms, freeing people from magic, mystery, and authority; and the possibility for the full development of human potential here on earth was proclaimed. In the political sphere, this new orientation culminated in the democratic state. However, as westerners grew more "independent, self-reliant, and critical," they became "more isolated, alone, and afraid."[39]

During the Middle Ages, said Fromm, the individual derived a sense of security from a structured social system, which clearly defined the role of clergy, lords, and serfs, and from a Christian world-view, which made life and death purposeful. Modern westerners have lost this sense of security. Dwelling in impersonal cities, threatened by economic crises, no longer comforted by the medieval conception of life's purpose, they are often tormented by doubts and overwhelmed by feelings of aloneness and insignificance. People try to overcome this "burden of freedom" by surrendering themselves to a person or power that they view "as being overwhelmingly strong"; they trade freedom for security by entering into "a symbiotic relationship that overcomes . . . aloneness."[40] Because modern industrial society has made the individual feel powerless and insignificant, concluded Fromm, fascism is a constant threat. Fromm would meet the challenge of fascism by creating social conditions that lead the individual to be free yet not alone, to be critical yet not filled with doubts, to be independent yet feel an integral part of humankind.

George Orwell (1903–1950), a British novelist and political journalist, wrote two powerful indictments of totalitarianism: *Animal Farm* (1945) and *1984* (1949). In *Animal Farm,* based in part on his experiences with communists during the Spanish Civil War, Orwell satirized the totalitarian regime built by Lenin and Stalin in Russia. In *1984,* Orwell, who was deeply committed to human dignity and freedom, warned that these great principles are now permanently menaced by the concentration and abuse of political power. "If you want a picture of the future, imagine a boot stamping on a human face forever," says a member of the ruling elite as he tortures a victim in the dungeons of the Thought Police.[41]

The society of *1984* is ruled by the Inner Party, which constitutes some 2 percent of the population. Heading the Party is Big Brother—most likely a mythical figure created by the ruling elite to satisfy people's yearning for a leader. The Party indoctrinates people to love Big Brother, whose picture is everywhere. Party members are conditioned to accept unquestioningly the Party's orthodoxy, with all its contradictions and reversals. Doublethink, the prescribed way of thinking, brainwashes people into holding two contradictory beliefs simultaneously. The Party's political philosophy is revealed in three slogans: "WAR IS PEACE," "FREEDOM IS SLAVERY," "IGNORANCE IS STRENGTH." The Ministry of Truth resorts to thought control to dominate and manipulate the masses and to keep Party members loyal and subservient. Independent thinking is destroyed. Objective truth no longer exists. Truth is whatever the Party decrees at the moment. If the Party were to proclaim that two plus two equals five, it would have to be believed.

Anyone thinking prohibited thoughts is designated a thought-criminal, a crime punishable by death. The Thought Police's agents are ubiquitous. Using hidden microphones and telescreens, they check on Party members for any signs of deviance from Party rules and ideology. Posters displaying Big Brother's picture carry the words "BIG BROTHER IS WATCHING YOU." Convinced that "who controls the past controls the future," the Ministry of Truth alters old newspapers to make the past accord with the Party's current doctrine. In this totalitarian society of the future, all human rights are abolished, people are arrested merely for their thoughts, and children spy on their parents. The society is brutalized by processions of chained prisoners of war, by public mass executions, and by the Two Minutes Hate ritual, which rouses participants to a frenzy against Party enemies. A steady supply of cheap gin and pornography keeps the masses (proles) dull-witted and out of political mischief.

Orwell's anti-utopian novel focuses on Winston Smith, who works for the Ministry of Truth and is arrested by the Thought Police for harboring anti-Party sentiments. Smith rebels against the Party in order to reclaim his individuality—to think and feel in his own way rather than in accordance with the Party's dictates. Tortured, humiliated, and brainwashed, Smith confesses to crimes that both he and the Party know he did not commit.

The Inner Party seeks to capture the inner mind, to transform people into mindless robots. O'Brien of the Thought Police tells Smith: "You will be hollow. We shall squeeze you empty, and then we shall fill you with ourselves." Thus, the Party does not kill Smith but "reshapes" him, by breaking his will and transforming him into a true believer in Big Brother. Smith comes to believe that "the struggle was finished. He had won the victory over himself. He loved Big Brother."[42]

Existentialism

Intellectual Background

The philosophical movement that best exemplified the anxiety and uncertainty of Europe in an era of world wars was existentialism. Like writers and artists, existentialist philosophers were responding to a European civilization that seemed to be in the throes of dissolution. Although existentialism was most popular after World War II, expressing the anxiety and despair of many intellectuals who had lost confidence in reason and progress, several of its key works were written prior to or during the war.

What route should people take in a world where old values and certainties had dissolved, where universal truth was rejected and God's existence denied? How could people cope in a society where they were menaced by technology, manipulated by impersonal bureaucracies, and overwhelmed by feelings of anxiety? If the universe is devoid of any overarching meaning, what meaning could one give to one's own life? These questions were at the crux of existentialist philosophy.

Basic Principles

Existentialism does not lend itself to a single definition, for its principal theorists did not adhere to a common body of doctrines. For example, some existentialists were atheists, like Jean Paul Sartre, or omitted God from their thought, like Martin Heidegger; others, like Karl Jaspers, believed in God but not in Christian doctrines; still others, like Gabriel Marcel and Nikolai Berdyaev, were Christians; and Martin Buber was a believing Jew. Perhaps the essence of existentialism appears in the following principles, although not all existentialists would subscribe to each point or agree with the way it is expressed.

1. Reality defies ultimate comprehension; there are no timeless truths that exist independently of and prior to the individual human being. Existence—our presence in the here-and-now—precedes and takes precedence over any presumed absolute values. The moral and spiritual values that society tries to impose cannot define the individual person's existence. Our traditional morality rests on no foundation whose certainty can either be demonstrated by reason or guaranteed by God. There are simply no transcendent absolutes; to think otherwise is to surrender to illusion.
2. Reason alone is an inadequate guide to living, for people are more than thinking subjects who approach the world through critical analysis. They are also feeling and willing beings, who must participate fully in life and experience existence directly, actively, and passionately. Only in this way does one live wholly and authentically.
3. Thought must not merely be abstract speculation but must have a bearing on life; it must be translated into deeds.
4. Human nature is problematic and paradoxical, not fixed or constant; each person is like no other. Self-realization comes when one affirms one's own uniqueness. One becomes less than human when one permits one's life to be determined by a mental outlook—a set of rules and values—imposed by others.
5. We are alone. The universe is indifferent to our expectations and needs, and death is ever stalking us. Awareness of this elementary fact of existence evokes a sense of overwhelming anxiety and depression.
6. Existence is essentially absurd. There is no purpose to our presence in the universe. We simply find ourselves here; we do not know and will never find out why. Compared with the eternity of time that preceded our birth and will follow our death, the short duration of our existence seems trivial and inexplicable. And death, which irrevocably terminates our existence, testifies to the ultimate absurdity of life.
7. We are free. We must face squarely the fact that existence is purposeless and absurd. In doing so, we can give our life meaning. It is in the act of choosing freely from among different possibilities that the individual shapes an authentic existence. There is a dynamic quality to human existence; the individual has the potential to become more than he or she is.

Nineteenth-Century Forerunners

Three nineteenth-century thinkers—Søren Kierkegaard, Fyodor Dostoevski, and Friedrich Nietzsche—were the principal forerunners of existentialism. Their views of reason, will, truth, and existence greatly influenced twentieth-century existentialists.

Kierkegaard. A Danish religious philosopher and Lutheran pastor, Kierkegaard held that self-realization as a human being comes when the individual takes full responsibility for his or her life. The individual does so by choosing one way of life over another. In making choices, said Kierkegaard, the individual overcomes the agonizing feeling that life in its deepest sense is nothingness.

For Kierkegaard, the highest truth is that human beings are God's creatures. However, God's existence cannot be demonstrated by reason; the crucial questions of human existence can never be resolved in a logical and systematic way. In Kierkegaard's view, the individual knows God through a leap of faith, not through systematic reasoning. In contrast to the Christian apologists who sought to demonstrate that Christian teachings did not conflict with reason, Kierkegaard denied that Christian doctrines were objectively valid. For him, Christian beliefs were absurd and irrational and could not be harmonized with reason. True Christians, said Kierkegaard, confidently embrace beliefs that are incomprehensible, if not absurd.

Twentieth-century existentialists took from Kierkegaard the idea that an all-consuming dread is the price of existence. "I stick my finger into existence," said Kierkegaard,"—it smells of nothing. Where am I? What is this thing called the world? Who is it who has lured me into the thing, and now leaves me here? Who am I? How did I come into the world? Why was I not consulted?"[43] The sense that we live in a meaningless world drives us to the edge of the abyss. This overwhelming dread can cause us to flee from life and to find comfort in delusions. But it can also spark courage, since it is an opportunity to make a commitment. For both Kierkegaard and twentieth-century existentialists, the true philosophical quest is a subjective experience: the isolated individual, alone and without help, choosing a way of life, to which he or she is deeply committed. Only in this way does the individual become a whole person. Kierkegaard's dictum that "it is impossible to exist without passion"—that our actions matter to us—is at the heart of existentialism.

Dostoevski. Although existentialist themes pervade several of Dostoevski's works, it is in *Notes from Underground* (1864) that he treats explicitly the individual's quest for personal freedom, identity, and meaning and the individual's revolt against established norms—themes that are crucial to the outlook of twentieth-century existentialists.

Nietzsche. Friedrich Nietzsche was an important forerunner of existentialism for several reasons. He stated that philosophical systems are merely expressions of an individual's own being and do not constitute an objective representation of reality; there is no realm of being that is the source of values. Nor does religion provide truth, for God is dead. And, asked Nietzsche, is not this godless world absurd? Nietzsche held that modern westerners had lost all their traditional supports. To overcome nothingness, said Nietzsche, individuals must define life for themselves and celebrate it fully, instinctively, and heroically. Nietzsche's insistence that individuals confront existence squarely, without hypocrisy, and give it meaning—their own meaning—was vital to the shaping of existentialism.

Twentieth-Century Existentialists

Heidegger. The German philosopher Martin Heidegger (1889–1976), generally regarded as the central figure in the development of existentialist thought, presents a problem to students of philosophy. First, Heidegger rejected being classified as an existentialist. Second, he wrote in a nearly incomprehensible style, which obscured his intent. Third, in 1933, Heidegger, recently elected rector of the University of Freiburg, joined the National Socialist party and publicly praised Hitler and the Nazi regime. The following year, he resigned as rector and gave no further support to the Third Reich, although he did continue to sympathize with some Nazi ideals. Heidegger's dalliance with Nazism caused some thinkers either to dismiss him or to minimize his importance as a valid philosopher.

In his pathbreaking book, *Being and Time* (1927), Heidegger asked: what does it mean *to be*, to say *I am*? Most people shun this question, said Heidegger; consequently, they live inauthentically, merely accepting a way of life set by others. Such people, he said, have "fallen from being"; they do not reflect on their existence or recognize the various possibilities and choices that life offers. Rather, they flee from their own selves and accept society's values without reflection. Neither their actions nor their goals are their own; they have forfeited a human being's most distinctive qualities: freedom and creativity.

To live authentically, declared Heidegger, the individual has to face explicitly the problem of Being; that is, one has to determine one's own existence, create one's own possibilities, and make choices and commitments. Choosing, said Heidegger, is not just a matter of disengaged thought, for the human creature is more than a conscious knower. The authentic life encompasses the feelings, as well as the intellect; it is a genuine expression of a person's whole being.

Coming to grips with death, said Heidegger, provides us with the opportunity for an authentic life. The trauma of our mortality and finiteness, the image of the endless void in which Being passes into non-Being, overwhelms us with dread; we come face to face with the insignificance of human existence, with directionless lives. To escape this dread, said Heidegger, some people immerse themselves in life's petty details or adopt others' prescribed values. But dread of death is also an opportunity. It can put us in touch with our uniqueness, our own Being, letting us take hold of our own existence to make life truly our own.

The authentic life requires, said Heidegger, that we see ourselves within the context of historical time, for we cannot escape the fact that our lives are bound by conditions and outlooks inherited from the past. Human beings are thrown into a world that is not of their own making. They dwell in a particular society, which carries with it the weight of the past and the tensions and conflicts of the present. Without knowledge of these conditions, Heidegger declared, events and things will always impose themselves on us, and we will not have the courage to reject conventions that we had no part in shaping. Although our future is related to the past, it is not determined by it.

Jaspers. Karl Jaspers (1883–1969), a German psychiatrist turned philosopher, was a leading figure in the existentialist movement. Jaspers fell into disfavor with the Nazi regime (he advocated liberal-humanist values, and his wife was Jewish) and lost his position as professor of philosophy at Heidelberg University. Like Kierkegaard, Jaspers held that philosophy and science cannot provide certainty. Also like Kierkegaard, he sought to discover the genuine self through an encounter with life. Like Heidegger, he held that while death makes us aware of our finitude, thereby promoting anxiety, it also goads us to focus on what is truly important and to do so immediately. Jaspers insisted that the individual has the power to choose. To be aware of this freedom and to use it is the essence of being human:

> *Man is always something more than what he knows of himself. He is not what he is simply once for all, but is a process; he is . . . endowed with possibilities through the freedom he possesses to make of himself what he will by the activities on which he decides.*[44]

Feelings of guilt and anxiety inevitably accompany free will, said Jaspers. Nevertheless, we must have the courage to make a choice, for it is in the act of choosing that the individual shapes his or her true self.

Although Jaspers rejected revealed religion, dogma, and the authority of churches, he did postulate what he called "philosophical faith." He thought of human existence as an encounter with Transcendence: "the eternal, indestructible, the immutable, the source [that] . . . can be neither visualized nor grasped in thought."[45] Jaspers did not equate Transcendence with God in the conventional sense, but the concept is laden with theistic qualities. Although not a traditional Christian, Jaspers was no atheist.

Sartre. The outlook of several French existentialists—Jean Paul Sartre (1905–1980), Maurice Merleau-Ponty (1908–1961), Albert Camus (1913–1960), and Simone de Beauvoir (1908–1987)—was shaped by their involvement in the resistance to Nazi occupation during World War II. Sartre, the leading French existentialist, said that their confrontation with terror and torture

Jean Paul Sartre and Simone de Beauvoir. Sartre and de Beauvoir were two of the principal exponents of existentialism. (*G. Pierre/Corbis-Sygma.*)

taught them "to take evil seriously." Evil is not the effect of ignorance that might be remedied by knowledge or of passions that might be controlled, said Sartre; rather, it is a central fact of human existence and is unredeemable. Facing capture and death, the members of the French resistance understood what it is to be a solitary individual in a hostile universe. Living on the cutting edge of life, they rediscovered the essence of human freedom: they could make authentic choices. By saying no to the Nazis and resisting them, they confronted existence squarely. They faced the central problem that concerned Sartre: what does it mean to be a human being?

Sartre served in the French army at the outbreak of World War II and was captured by the Germans. Released after the French surrender, he taught philosophy while serving in the resistance. His principal philosophical work was *Being and Nothingness* (1943). In addition to his philosophical writings, Sartre, after World War II, gained international acclaim for his novels and plays, many of them, particularly *Nausea* (1938) and *No Exit* (1944), written from an existentialist point of view.

In contrast to Kierkegaard and Jaspers, Sartre defined himself as an atheist and saw existentialism as a means of facing the consequences of a godless universe. Atheistic existentialism, he said, begins with the person and not with God, a preestablished ethic, or a uniform conception of human nature.

For Sartre, existence precedes essence: that is, there are no values that precede the individual metaphysically or chronologically to which he or she must conform. There exists no higher realm of Being and no immutable truths that serve as ultimate standards of virtue. It is unauthentic to submit passively to established values, which one did not participate in making. The individual has nothing to cling to; he or she is thrown into the world "with no support and no aid."[46]

It is the first principle of existentialism, said Sartre, that we must each choose our own ethics, define ourselves, and give our own meaning to our life. Through our actions, we decide how we shall create ourselves. According to Sartre, we are what we do; each individual is "nothing else than the ensemble of his acts, nothing else than his life. . . . man's destiny is within himself." As free conscious beings, we are totally responsible for defining our lives and for giving them meaning and value. "Not only is man what he conceives himself to be, but he is also what he wills himself to be," Sartre said, and "existentialism's first move is to make every man aware of what he is and to make full responsibility of his existence rest on him."[47]

In Sartre's view, a true philosophy does not engage in barren discourses on abstract themes; it makes commitments and incurs risks. We are not objectified instruments, determined and shaped by material forces, as Marxism teaches. Nor do unconscious drives determine our actions, as Freud contended. For Sartre, we are not helpless prisoners of our genes, of the environment, of historical forces, or of culture. Rather, we alone are responsible for who we are and for the feelings that torment, trap, and immobilize us. True, the conditions in which we find ourselves impinge on our existence, but it is up to us to decide what to do about them. Thus, said Sartre, a French man or woman had to choose between being a patriot or a traitor during the German occupation. Similarly, an alcoholic made poor choices and continues to make them.

We have the capacity to plunge decisively, audaciously into life and constantly to recreate ourselves. We have no control over the fact that we exist; existence is simply given to us. But each individual does decide his or her own peculiar essence. We do so by the particular way we choose to live. The realization that we have the freedom to decide for ourselves what kind of person we are going to be, and what meaning we give to our lives, can be liberating and exhilarating. But it can also fill us with a dread that immobilizes or that leads us to seek refuge in a role selected for us by others. When we abdicate the responsibility of choosing a meaning for our lives, said Sartre, we live in "bad faith."

Camus. Reared and educated in French-ruled Algeria, Albert Camus gained an instant reputation in 1942 with the publication of *The Stranger*, a short novel, and *The Myth of Sisyphus*, a philosophical essay. During World War II, he served in the French resistance. His most important books in the decade after the war were two works of fiction, *The Plague* (1947) and *The Fall* (1956), as well as *The Rebel* (1951), a collection of interpretive essays on historical, philosophical, and esthetic topics.

Camus dealt with the existential theme of the individual struck by the awareness of God's nonexistence and of an impending rendezvous with an eternity of nothingness. Does this mean that my life is without meaning? That my actions do not matter? Camus rejected both suicide and nihilism as responses to this absurdity of existence. Even though existence has no higher meaning and the universe is indifferent to us, we must still accept "the desperate encounter between human inquiry and the silence of the universe."[48] Life may be absurd, but this absurdity is no justification for resignation.

Camus expressed a distaste for abstractions and ideologies because they led their adherents to torture and murder. These beliefs, claiming certainty, cause people to lose sight of their fellows as flesh-and-blood individuals and provide justification for barbarous criminal acts. In 1946, he wrote: "We have seen lying, degradation, killing, deportation, and torture and, each time, it was not possible to persuade those who did it not to do it, because they were sure of themselves and because one does not persuade an abstraction, that is, the representative of an ideology."[49] Ultimately, Camus saw a moralistic humanism that promoted human fraternity and human dignity as a worthwhile response to the absurdity of the human condition. Human beings should aspire to serve "those few values without which a world . . . isn't worth living in, without which a man . . . is not worthy of respect."[50]

In *The Stranger*, Meursault, an insignificant French shipping clerk, kills an Algerian Arab for no particular reason. It was as if shooting him or not shooting him came to the same thing. Convicted and sentenced to death, Meursault examines his own life, which he has lived without awareness, imagination, passion, or commitment, as revealed in the novel's opening lines: "Maman died today. Or yesterday, maybe, I don't know."[51] Meursault displays a shocking indifference to his mother's death, not because of any hate for her but simply because that is the way he lives. Neither her death nor his own life is very important to him. Committed to nothing, moved by nothing, indifferent to marriage and career, the essential values of modern society, and not given to introspection or reflection, he merely lives passively from day to day, a stranger to himself and to life. It is just such an attitude that human beings must strive to overcome, suggests Camus. Facing death, Meursault grasps an existential truth: even in a meaningless universe that is indifferent to his fate, he must strive to give meaning to his life.

For Camus, neither religion nor philosophy provides a basis for human values or can tell us with certainty what is right or wrong. No final authority can be found in a transcendental heaven or in reason's dictates. Thus, when a priest tries to make Meursault aware of his guilt and his spiritual needs, the condemned man responds: "He seemed so certain about everything, didn't he. And yet none of his certainties was worth one hair of a woman's head."[52] Values may not be absolute or eternal, maintained Camus, but he did urge living by values that advance human dignity and warm human relations; we must find a life-enhancing alternative to the nihilistic conclusion that life is valueless and meaningless. Reason and experience will never enable us to ascribe a transcendent or ultimate significance to life. Nevertheless, they are effective and helpful guides to escape the nihilistic abyss and to make life worth living.

Religious Existentialism. Several thinkers are classified as religious existentialists, among them Nikolai Berdyaev (1874–1948), an exile from Communist Russia; Martin Buber (1878–1965), a Jew who fled Nazi Germany; and Gabriel Marcel (1889–1973), a French Catholic. During World War I, Marcel served with the French Red Cross, accounting for soldiers missing in battle. This shattering experience brought the sensitive thinker face to face with the tragedy of human existence. A growing concern with the spiritual life led him to convert to Catholicism in 1929.

The modern individual, said Marcel in 1933, "tends to appear to himself and to others as an agglomeration of functions." A person is viewed as an entrepreneur, a laborer, a consumer, a citizen. The hospital serves as a repair shop, and death "becomes, objectively and functionally, the scrapping of what has ceased to be of use and must be written off as a total loss."[53] In such a functional world, maintained Marcel, people are valued for what they produce and possess. If they do not succeed as merchants, bookkeepers, or ticket-takers, people judge them and they judge themselves as personal failures. Such an outlook suffocates spirituality and deprives the individual of the joy of existence. It produces an "intolerable unease" in the individual, "who is reduced to living as though he were in fact submerged by his function. . . . Life in a world centered on function is liable to despair because in reality this world is empty, it rings hollow."[54]

Marcel wanted people to surpass a functional and mechanical view of life and explore the mystery of existence—to penetrate to a higher level of reality. Marcel held that one penetrates ultimate reality when one overcomes egocentricity and exists for others, when one loves and is loved by others. When we exist through and for others, when we treat another person not as an object performing a function but as a "thou" who matters to us, we soar to a higher level of existence. When we are actively engaged with others in concrete human situations, we fulfill ourselves as human beings; when we actively express love and fidelity toward others, life attains a higher meaning. Such involvement with others, said Marcel, provides us with a glimpse of a transcendent reality and is a testimony to God's existence. Marcel maintained that faith in God overcomes the anxiety and despair that characterize the modern predicament. It also improves the quality of human relationships, for if we believe that all people matter to God, they are more likely to matter to us.

The Modern Predicament

The process of fragmentation that had begun in European thought and the arts at the end of the nineteenth century accelerated after World

War I. Increasingly, philosophers, writers, and artists expressed disillusionment with the rational-humanist tradition of the Enlightenment. They no longer shared the Enlightenment confidence in reason's capabilities or in human goodness, and they viewed perpetual progress as an illusion.

For some thinkers, the crucial problem was the great change in the European understanding of truth. Since the rise of philosophy in ancient Greece, Western thinkers had believed in the existence of objective, universal truths: truths that were inherent in nature and applied to all peoples at all times. (Christianity, of course, also taught the reality of truth as revealed by God.) It was held that such truths—the natural rights of the individual, for example—could be apprehended by the intellect and could serve as a standard for individual aspirations and social life. The recognition of these universal principles, it was believed, compelled people to measure the world of the here-and-now in the light of rational and universal norms and to institute appropriate reforms. Philosophy had the task of reconciling human existence with the objective order.

During the nineteenth century, the existence of universal truth came into doubt. A growing historical consciousness led some thinkers to maintain that what people considered truth was merely a reflection of their culture at a given stage in history—their perception of things at a specific point in the evolution of human consciousness. These thinkers, called historicists, held that universal truths were not woven into the fabric of nature. There are no natural rights of life, liberty, and property that constitute the individual's birthright; there are no standards of justice or equality that are inherent in nature and ascertainable by reason. It was people, said historicists, who elevated the beliefs and values of an age to the status of objective truth. The normative principles—the self-evident truths proclaimed by Jefferson—that for the philosophes constituted a standard for political and social reform and a guarantee of human rights were no longer linked to the natural order, to an objective reality that could be confirmed by reason. As Hannah Arendt noted, "We certainly no longer believe, as the men of the French Revolution did, in a universal cosmos of which man was a part and whose natural laws he had to imitate and conform to."[55]

This radical break with the traditional attitude toward truth contributed substantially to the crisis of European consciousness that marked the first half of the twentieth century. Traditional values and beliefs, either those inherited from the Enlightenment or those taught by Christianity, no longer gave Europeans a sense of certainty and security. People were left without a normative order to serve as a guide to living—and without such a guide might be open to nihilism. For if nothing is fundamentally true—if there are no principles of morality and justice that emanate from God or can be derived from reason—then it can be concluded, as Nietzsche understood, that everything is permitted. Some scholars interpreted Nazism as the culminating expression of a nihilistic attitude grown ever more brutal.

By the early twentieth century, the attitude of westerners toward reason had also undergone a radical transformation. Some thinkers, who had placed their hopes in the rational tradition of the Enlightenment, were distressed by reason's inability to resolve the tensions and conflicts of modern industrial society. Moreover, the growing recognition of the nonrational—of human actions determined by hidden impulses—led to doubts that reason plays the dominant role in human behavior. The intellect did not seem autonomous and self-regulating but instead seemed subject to the rebellious demands of unconscious drives and impulses. Men's and women's propensity for goodness, their capacity to improve society, and their potential for happiness seemed severely limited by an inherent irrationality. Indeed, civilization itself seemed threatened by people's instinctual needs, as Freud had proclaimed.

Other thinkers viewed the problem of reason differently. They attacked reason for fashioning a technological and bureaucratic society that devalued and crushed human emotions and stifled individuality; these thinkers insisted that human beings cannot fulfill their potential, cannot live wholly, if their feelings are denied. They agreed with D. H. Lawrence's critique of rationalism: "The attribution of rationality to human nature, instead of enriching it, now seems to me to have impoverished it. It ignored certain powerful and valuable springs of feeling. Some of the spontaneous, irrational outbursts of human nature can have a sort of value from which our schematism was cut off."[56]

These thinkers pointed out that reason was a double-edged sword: it could demean, as well as ennoble and liberate, the individual. They attacked all theories that subordinated the individual to a rigid system. They denounced positivism for reducing human personality to psychological laws, and Marxism for making social class a higher reality than the individual. Rebelling against political collectivization, which regulated individual existence according to the needs of the corporate state, they assailed modern bureaucracy and technology. These creations of the rational mind, they claimed, had fashioned a social order that devalued and depersonalized the individual, denying people an opportunity for independent growth and a richer existence. According to these thinkers, modern industrial society, in its drive for efficiency and uniformity, deprived people of their uniqueness and reduced human beings to cogs in a mechanical system.

Responding to the critics of reason, other philosophers maintained that it was necessary to reaffirm respect for the rational tradition, first proclaimed by the ancient Greeks and given its modern expression by the Enlightenment philosophes. Reason, said these thinkers, was indispensable to civilization. What they advocated was broadening the scope of reason to accommodate the insights into human nature offered by the romantics, Nietzsche, Freud, modernist writers and artists, and others who explored the world of feelings, will, and the subconscious. They also stressed the need to humanize reason so that it could never threaten to reduce a human being to a thing.

In the decades shaped by world wars and totalitarianism, intellectuals raised questions that went to the heart of the dilemma of modern life. How can civilized life be safeguarded against human irrationality, particularly when it is channeled into political ideologies that idolize the state, the leader, the party, or the race? How can individual human personality be rescued from a relentless rationalism that reduces human nature and society to mechanical systems and seeks to regulate and organize the individual as it would any material object? Do we, as human beings, have the moral and spiritual resolve to use properly the technological and scientific creations of modern civilization, or will they devour us? Do the values associated with the Enlightenment provide a sound basis on which to integrate society? Can the individual find meaning in what many came to regard as a meaningless universe? World War II gave these questions a special poignancy.

❖ ❖ ❖

Notes

1. Quoted in Barbara Tuchman, *The Guns of August* (New York: Macmillan, 1962), p. 440.
2. Sigmund Freud, "Thoughts for the Times on War and Death," in the *Standard Edition of the Complete Psychological Works of Freud,* vol. 14, ed. James Strachey (London: Hogarth Press, 1957), pp. 275, 278.
3. Quoted in Hans Kohn, "The Crisis in European Thought and Culture," in *World War I: A Turning Point in Modern History*, ed. Jack J. Roth (New York: Knopf, 1967), p. 28.
4. Quoted in Franklin L. Baumer, "Twentieth-Century Version of the Apocalypse," *Cahiers d'Histoire Mondiale* (Journal of World History), 1 (January 1954):624.
5. Quoted in William McNeill, *Arnold J. Toynbee: A Life* (New York: Oxford University Press, 1989), p. 152.
6. Baumer, "Apocalypse," p. 624.
7. Erich Maria Remarque, *All Quiet on the Western Front*, trans. A. W. Wheen (Boston: Little, Brown, 1929), p. 224.
8. W. B. Yeats, "The Second Coming," in *Col-*

lected Poems of W. B. Yeats (New York: Macmillan, 1956), pp. 184–185.

9. T. S. Eliot, "The Waste Land," in *Collected Poems, 1909–1962* (New York: Harcourt, Brace, 1970), p. 67.
10. Carl Gustav Jung, *Modern Man in Search of a Soul*, trans. W. S. Dell and Cary F. Baynes (New York: Harcourt, Brace, 1933), pp. 231, 234–235.
11. Johan Huizinga, *In the Shadow of Tomorrow* (London: Heinemann, 1936), pp. 1–3.
12. E. M. Forster, "Post-Munich," in *Two Cheers for Democracy* (New York: Harcourt, Brace & World, 1951), p. 21.
13. Oswald Spengler, *The Decline of the West*, trans. Charles F. Atkinson (London: Allen & Unwin, 1926), p. 40.
14. Franz Kafka, *The Trial,* trans. Willa and Edwin Muir (New York: Knopf, 1957), p. 7.
15. Angel Flores, ed., *The Kafka Problem* (New York: Gordian Press, 1975), p. xxi.
16. Thomas Mann, "An Appeal to Reason," excerpted in *Sources of the Western Tradition,* ed. Marvin Perry et al., vol. 2, 5th ed. (Boston: Houghton Mifflin, 1991), p. 366.
17. Thomas Mann, "Schopenhauer," in *Essays of Three Decades,* trans. H. T. Lowe-Porter (New York: Knopf, 1968), p. 409.
18. D. H. Lawrence, *Women in Love* (New York: Penguin Books, 1979), p. 215.
19. Harry T. Moore, ed., *The Collected Letters of D. H. Lawrence* (New York: Viking, 1962), 1:180.
20. Tristan Tzara, "Lecture on Dada (1922)," trans. Ralph Mannheim, in *The Dada Painters and Poets*, ed. Robert Motherwell (New York: Witterborn, Schultz, 1951), pp. 250, 248.
21. Ibid., p. 251.
22. Edward Lucie-Smith, in Donald Carrol and Edward Lucie-Smith, *Movements in Modern Art* (New York: Horizon Press, 1973), p. 49.
23. H. W. Janson, *History of Art*, 2nd ed. (Englewood Cliffs, N.J.: Prentice-Hall, 1977), p. 661.
24. André Breton, *What Is Surrealism*? trans. David Gascoyne (London: Faber & Faber, 1936), p. 62.
25. Quoted in David Caute, *The Fellow Travellers* (New York: Macmillan, 1973), p. 64.
26. Ibid., p. 92.
27. Richard Crossman, ed., *The God That Failed* (New York: Bantam Books, 1951), pp. 15, 21.
28. Arthur Koestler, *Darkness at Noon* (New York: Macmillan, 1941), pp. 158–159.
29. Reinhold Niebuhr, *The Nature and Destiny of Man* (New York: Charles Scribner's Sons, 1941), I:273.
30. Jacques Maritain, *Christianity and Democracy* (New York: Charles Scribner's Sons, 1944), pp. 44, 62.
31. Quoted in C. T. McIntire, ed., *God, History, and Historians* (New York: Oxford University Press, 1977), p. 9.
32. Arnold J. Toynbee, *Survey of International Affairs, 1933* (London: Oxford University Press, 1934), p. 111.
33. Julien Benda, *The Betrayal of the Intellectuals*, trans. Richard Aldington (Boston: Beacon Press, 1955), pp. 21, 38, 122, 162.
34. José Ortega y Gasset, *The Revolt of the Masses* (New York: Norton, 1957), pp. 63, 18.
35. Ibid., p. 73.
36. Ernst Cassirer, *The Philosophy of the Enlightenment*, trans. Fritz C. A. Koelln and James P. Pettegrove (Boston: Beacon Press, 1955), pp. xi–xii.
37. Ernst Cassirer, *The Myth of the State* (New Haven, Conn.: Yale University Press, 1946), p. 280.
38. Ibid., p. 296.
39. Erich Fromm, *Escape from Freedom* (New York: Avon Books, 1965), p. 124.
40. Ibid., pp. 173, 246.
41. George Orwell, *1984* (New York: Harcourt, Brace, 1949; paperback, New American Library, 1961), p. 220.
42. Ibid., pp. 211, 245.
43. Quoted in T. Z. Lavine, *From Socrates to Sartre: The Philosophic Quest* (New York: Bantam Books, 1984), p. 322.
44. Karl Jaspers, *Man in the Modern Age*, trans.

Eden and Cedar Paul (Garden City, N.Y.: Doubleday Anchor Books, 1951), p. 159.

45. Quoted in John Macquarrie, *Existentialism* (Baltimore: Penguin Books, 1973), p. 246.

46. Jean Paul Sartre, *Existentialism,* trans. Bernard Frechtman (New York: Philosophical Library, 1947), p. 28.

47. Ibid., pp. 38, 42, 18–19.

48. Albert Camus, *The Rebel*, trans. Anthony Bower (New York: Knopf, 1956), p. 6.

49. Quoted in Roy Pierce, *Contemporary French Political Thought* (New York: Oxford University Press, 1966), p. 125.

50. Quoted in Germaine Brée, *Camus* (New Brunswick, N.J.: Rutgers University Press, 1961), p. 9.

51. Albert Camus, *The Stranger*, trans. Matthew Ward (New York: Vintage Books, 1988), p. 3.

52. Ibid., p. 120.

53. Gabriel Marcel, "On the Ontological Mystery," in *The Philosophy of Existentialism*, trans. Manya Harari (Secaucus, N.J.: Citadel Press, 1980), p. 10.

54. Ibid., p. 12.

55. Cited in Harry S. Kariel, *In Search of Authority* (Glencoe, Ill.: Free Press, 1964), p. 246.

56. Cited in Anthony Arblaster, *The Rise and Decline of Western Liberalism* (Oxford: Basil Blackwell, 1984), p. 81.

Suggested Reading

See also books suggested for reading at the end of Chapter 28.

Barrett, William, *Irrational Man* (1958). Especially good on the cultural roots of existentialism.

Blackham, H. J., *Six Existentialist Thinkers* (1952). Useful analyses of Kierkegaard, Nietzsche, Jaspers, Marcel, Heidegger, and Sartre.

———, ed., *Reality, Man and Existence* (1965). Essential works of existentialism.

Cruickshank, John, ed., *Aspects of the Modern European Mind* (1969). A useful collection of sources in modern intellectual history.

Kaufmann, Walter, ed., *Existentialism from Dostoevsky to Sartre* (1956). The basic writings of existentialist thinkers.

Macquarrie, John, *Existentialism* (1972). A lucid discussion of existentialism.

McIntire, C. T., ed., *God, History, and Historians* (1977). Selections from Christian thinkers; many deal with the crises of the twentieth century.

McIntire, C. T., and Marvin Perry, eds., *Toynbee Reappraisals* (1989). Essays on Toynbee's life and thoughts.

Pawel, Ernst, *The Nightmare of Reason* (1984). A biography of Kafka.

Wagar, W. Warren, ed., *European Thought Since 1914* (1968). A valuable collection of sources.

Review Questions

1. What factors contributed to a mood of pessimism in the period after World War I?
2. What signs of decay did Spengler see in Western civilization?
3. In what ways did Kafka grasp the dilemma of the modern age? Do his insights still apply today?
4. In *The Magic Mountain*, Mann reflected on the decomposition of bourgeois European civilization. Discuss this statement.
5. What was D. H. Lawrence's attitude toward industrial society? Do you agree with him?
6. In what ways were both Dada and surrealism an expression of the times?
7. How did art and literature express a social conscience during the 1920s and 1930s?
8. Why were many intellectuals attracted to communism in the 1930s?
9. What is the theme of *Darkness at Noon*?
10. How did Toynbee interpret nationalism and Nazism?
11. What did Ortega mean by the "mass-man"? What dangers were presented by the mass-man?
12. Why did Benda entitle his book *The Treason of the Intellectuals*?
13. What was Cassirer's attitude toward the Enlightenment? How did he interpret Nazism?

14. How did Fromm explain the rise of Nazism?
15. What were some of the conditions that gave rise to existentialism? What are the basic principles of existentialism?
16. In what ways do the works of these thinkers express existentialist themes: Heidegger, Jaspers, Sartre, Camus, and Marcel?
17. What do you like or dislike about existentialism?

Chapter 32

World War II: Western Civilization in the Balance

D-Day. The invasion of Normandy was a decisive turning point in World War II. The landing at Omaha Beach almost ended in a disaster for the Americans, many of whom drowned in the rough waters or were killed by heavy German fire before they could reach the beach. (A.E. French/Getty Images.)

- **The Aftermath of World War I**
- **The Road to War**
  Hitler's Foreign Policy Aims
  Breakdown of Peace
  Czechoslovakia: The Apex of Appeasement
  Poland: The Final Crisis
- **The Nazi Blitzkrieg**
  The Fall of France
  The Battle of Britain
  Invasion of Russia
- **The New Order**
  Exploitation and Terror
  Extermination
  Resistance
- **Turn of the Tide**
  The Japanese Offensive
  Defeat of the Axis Powers
- **The Legacy of World War II**

From the early days of his political career, Hitler dreamed of forging in central and eastern Europe a vast German empire that would bring the millions of Germans living there under the rule of the Third Reich. He believed that only by waging a war of conquest against Russia could the German nation gain the living space and security it required and, as a superior race, deserved. War was an essential component of National Socialist ideology; it also accorded with Hitler's temperament. For the former corporal from the trenches, the Great War had never ended. Hitler aspired to political power because he wanted to mobilize the material and human resources of the German nation for war and conquest. Whereas historians may debate the question of responsibility for World War I, few would deny that World War II was Hitler's war.

> *It appears to be an almost incontrovertible fact that the Second World War was brought on by the actions of the Hitler government, that these actions were the expression of a policy laid down well in advance in* Mein Kampf, *and that this war could have been averted up until the last moment if the German government had so wished.*[1]

Western statesmen had sufficient warning that Hitler was a threat to peace and the essential values of Western civilization, but they failed to rally their people and take a stand until Germany had greatly increased its capacity to wage aggressive war.

The Aftermath of World War I

World War I showed that Germany was the strongest power on the European continent. In the east, the German army triumphed over Russia. In the west, Britain and France could have hoped for no more than a deadlock without the aid of the United States. The Treaty of Versailles weakened Germany but did not permanently cripple it.

In the decade after the war, responsibility for preserving the peace settlement rested essentially with France. The United States had rejected the

Chronology 32.1 ❖ Road to World War II

1931	Japan invades Manchuria
March 1935	Hitler announces German rearmament
October 1935	Italy invades Ethiopia
1936–1939	Spanish Civil War
March 7, 1936	Germany remilitarizes the Rhineland
October 1936	Berlin-Rome Axis is formed
November 1936	German-Japanese anticommunist pact
July 1937	Japan invades China
March 13, 1938	Anschluss with Austria, which becomes a German province
September 1938	Munich Agreement: Britain and France approve Germany's annexation of Sudetenland
1939	Franco establishes a dictatorship in Spain
March 1939	Germany invades Czechoslovakia
April 1939	Italy invades Albania
May 22, 1939	Pact of Steel between Hitler and Mussolini
August 23, 1939	Nonaggression pact between Germany and Russia
September 1, 1939	Germany invades Poland
September 3, 1939	Britain and France declare war on Germany

treaty and withdrawn from European affairs; Soviet Russia was consolidating its Revolution; and Britain, burdened with severe economic problems, disarmed, and traditionally hostile to Continental alliances, did not want to join with France in holding Germany down. France sought to contain Germany by forging alliances with the new states of eastern Europe, which the French hoped would serve as a substitute for alliance with a now untrustworthy Communist Russia. Thus, in the 1920s, France entered into alliances with Poland, Czechoslovakia, Romania, and Yugoslavia. But no combination of small eastern European states could replace Russia as a counterweight to Germany. Against Hitler's Germany, the French alliance system would prove useless.

In the area of international relations, a feeling of hope prevailed during the 1920s. The newly created League of Nations provided a supranational authority to which nations could submit their quarrels. At the Washington Naval Conference (1921–22), the leading naval powers—the United States, Britain, France, Italy, and Japan—agreed not to construct new battleships or heavy cruisers for a ten-year period and established a ratio for these large ships between them. It was hoped that avoiding a naval arms race would promote international peace.

In the Locarno Pact (1925), Germany, France, and Belgium agreed not to change their existing borders, which meant, in effect, that Germany had accepted both the return of Alsace and Lorraine to France and the demilitarization of the Rhineland—two provisions of the Versailles treaty. The Locarno Pact held the promise of a détente between France and Germany. But it was only an illusion of peace, for Germany gave no such assurances for its eastern border with Czechoslovakia and Poland, France's allies.

Other gestures that promoted reconciliation followed. In 1926, Germany was admitted to the League of Nations, and in 1928, the Kellogg-

Briand Pact renouncing war was signed by most nations. The signatories condemned war as a solution for international disputes and agreed to settle quarrels through peaceful means. Ordinary people welcomed the Kellogg-Briand Pact as the dawning of a new era of peace, but because the pact contained no clauses for its enforcement, this agreement, too, fostered only the illusion of peace.

Nevertheless, between 1925 and 1930, hopes for reconciliation and peace were high. Recovery from the war and increased prosperity coincided with the easing of international tensions. As evidence of the new spirit of conciliation, France and Britain withdrew their forces from the Rhineland in 1930, four years ahead of the time prescribed by the Versailles treaty.

The Road to War

Hitler's Foreign Policy Aims

After consolidating his power and mobilizing the nation's will, Hitler moved to implement his foreign policy objectives: the destruction of the Versailles treaty, the conquest and colonization of eastern Europe, and the domination and exploitation of racial inferiors. In some respects, Hitler's foreign policy aims accorded with the goals of Germany's traditional rulers. Like them, Hitler sought to make Germany the preeminent power in Europe. During World War I, German statesmen and generals had sought to conquer extensive regions of eastern Europe, and in the Treaty of Brest-Litovsk, Germany took Poland, the Ukraine, and the Baltic states from Russia. But Hitler's racial nationalism—the subjugation and annihilation of inferior races by a master German race—marked a break with the outlook of the old governing class. Germany's traditional conservative leaders had not revoked the civil rights of German Jews and had sought to Germanize, not enslave, the Poles living under the German flag.

In foreign affairs, Hitler demonstrated the same blend of opportunism and singleness of purpose that had brought him to power. He behaved like a man possessed, driven by a fanatical belief that his personal destiny was tied to Germany's future. Here, too, he displayed an uncanny understanding of his opponents' weaknesses; and here, too, his opponents underestimated his skills and intent. As in his climb to power, he made use of propaganda to undermine his opponents' will to resist. The Nazi propaganda machine, which had won the minds of the German people, became an instrument of foreign policy. Nazi propaganda tried to win the support of the twenty-seven million Germans living in Europe and the Americas, outside the borders of the Reich proper. To promote social and political disorientation in other lands, the Nazis propagated anti-Semitism on a worldwide basis and tried to draw international support for Hitler as Europe's best defense against the Soviet Union and Bolshevism. The Nazi anticommunist campaign "convinced many Europeans that Hitler's dictatorship was more acceptable than Stalin's and that Germany—'the bulwark against Bolshevism'—should be allowed to grow from strength to strength."[2]

As Hitler had anticipated, the British and the French backed down when faced with his violations of the Versailles treaty and threats of war. Haunted by the memory of World War I, Britain and France went to great lengths to avoid another catastrophe—a policy that had the overwhelming support of public opinion. Moreover, Britain suffered from a bad conscience regarding the Versailles treaty. Woefully unprepared for war from 1933 to 1938 and believing that Germany had been treated too severely, Britain was amenable to making concessions to Hitler. Although France had the strongest army on the Continent, it was prepared to fight only a defensive war—the reverse of its World War I strategy. France built immense fortifications, called the Maginot Line, to protect its borders from a German invasion, but it lacked a mobile striking force that could punish an aggressive Germany. The United States, concerned with the problems of the Great Depression and standing aloof from Europe's troubles, did nothing to strengthen the resolve of France and Britain. Since both France and Britain feared and mistrusted the Soviet Union, the grand alliance of World War I was not renewed. There was an added factor: suffering from a failure of leadership and political and economic unrest that eroded national unity, France was experiencing a decline in morale and a loss of nerve. It consistently turned to Britain for direction.

British statesmen championed a policy of appeasement: giving in to Germany in the hope that a satisfied Hitler would not drag Europe through another world war. British policy rested on the

APPEASEMENT. Haunted by the memory of World War I, many French and British officials and ordinary citizens would go to great lengths to appease Germany in order to avoid a second world war. Soon after Hitler's remilitarization of the Rhineland, cartoonist David Lowe called the leaders of England and France spineless. (*London Evening/Solo Standard.*)

disastrous illusion that Hitler, like his Weimar predecessors, sought peaceful revision of the Versailles treaty and that he could be contained through concessions. This perception was as misguided as the expectation of Weimar conservatives that the responsibility of power would compel Hitler to abandon his National Socialist radicalism. Some British appeasers, accepting the view that Nazi propaganda cleverly propagated and exploited, also regarded Hitler as a defender of European civilization and the capitalist economic order against Soviet communism.

In *Mein Kampf*, Hitler had explicitly laid out his philosophy of racial nationalism and *Lebensraum* (living space). As dictator, he had established a one-party state, confined political opponents to concentration camps, and persecuted Jews. But the proponents of appeasement did not properly assess these signs. They still believed that Hitler could be reasoned with. Appeasement, which in the end was capitulation to blackmail, failed. Germany grew stronger and the German people more devoted to the fuehrer. Hitler did not moderate his ambitions, and the appeasers did not avert war.

Breakdown of Peace

To realize his foreign policy aims, Hitler required a formidable military machine. Germany had to rearm. The Treaty of Versailles limited the size of the German army to a hundred thousand volunteers, restricted the navy's size, forbade the production of military aircraft, heavy artillery, and tanks, and disbanded the general staff. Throughout the 1920s, Germany evaded these provisions, even entering into a secret arrangement with the

ICELAND
Germany and Italy
Italian possessions in Africa before 1935
German aggressions, 1935–1939
Italian aggressions, 1935–1939
0 200 400 Km.
0 200 400 Mi.
NORWAY
SWEDEN
FINLAND
ESTONIA
Baltic Sea
LATVIA
Moscow
North Sea
DENMARK
IRELAND
Memel
LITHUANIA
GREAT BRITAIN
NETHERLANDS
Danzig
EAST PRUSSIA
SOVIET UNION
London
Berlin
POLISH CORRIDOR
ATLANTIC OCEAN
Brussels
BELGIUM
GERMANY
SUDENTENLAND 1938
Warsaw
RHINELAND 1936
Weimar
POLAND
Paris
Prague
LUXEMBOURG
Nuremberg
CZECHOSLOVAKIA 1939
Munich
Vienna
FRANCE
SWITZERLAND
AUSTRIA 1938
HUNGARY
ROMANIA
SPAIN (Civil War, 1936–1939)
PORTUGAL
Madrid
Barcelona
ITALY
YUGOSLAVIA
Black Sea
BULGARIA
Rome
ALBANIA 1939
GREECE
TURKEY
Mediterranean Sea
LIBYA
ERITREA
AFRICA
ETHIOPIA 1935–1936
IT. SOMALILAND
A F R I C A

Soviet Union to establish training schools for German pilots and tank corpsmen on Russian soil.

In March 1935, Hitler declared that Germany was no longer bound by the Versailles treaty. Germany would restore conscription, build an air force (which it had been doing secretly), and strengthen its navy. The German people were ecstatic over Hitler's boldness. France protested but offered no resistance. Britain negotiated a naval agreement with Germany, thus tacitly accepting Hitler's rearmament.

A decisive event in the breakdown of peace was Italy's invasion of Ethiopia in October 1935. Mussolini sought colonial expansion and revenge for the defeat that the African kingdom had inflicted on Italian troops in 1896. The League of Nations called for economic sanctions against Italy, and most League members restricted trade with the aggressor. But Italy continued to receive oil, particularly from American suppliers. Believing that the conquest of Ethiopia did not affect their vital interests and hoping to keep the Italians friendly in the event of a clash with Germany, neither Britain nor France sought to restrain Italy, despite its act of aggression against another member of the League of Nations. The Fascists claimed they were civilizing a backward African nation. In the process, tens of thousands of Ethiopians perished, victims of saturation bombing, poison gas, and mistreatment in concentration camps into which they had been herded.

Mussolini's subjugation of Ethiopia discredited the League of Nations, already weakened by its failure to deal effectively with Japan's invasion of the mineral-rich Chinese province of Manchuria in 1931. At that time, the League formed a commission of inquiry and urged nonrecognition of the puppet state of Manchukuo created by the Japanese, but the member states did not restrain Japan. The invasion of Ethiopia, like the invasion of Manchuria, showed the League's reluctance to use force to resist aggression.

On March 7, 1936, Hitler marched troops into the Rhineland, violating both the Versailles treaty and the Locarno Pact. German generals had cautioned Hitler that such a move would provoke a French invasion of Germany and reoccupation of the Rhineland, which the German army, still in the first stages of rearmament, could not repulse. But Hitler gambled that France and Britain, lacking the will to fight, would take no action.

Hitler had assessed the Anglo-French mood correctly. Britain was not greatly alarmed by the remilitarization of the Rhineland. After all, Hitler was not expanding the borders of Germany but only sending soldiers to Germany's frontier. Such a move, reasoned British officials, did not warrant risking a war. France viewed the remilitarization of the Rhineland as a grave threat. It deprived France of the one tangible advantage that it had obtained from the Treaty of Versailles: a buffer area. Now German forces could concentrate in strength on the French frontier, either to invade France or to discourage a French assault if Germany attacked Czechoslovakia or Poland, France's eastern allies. France lost the advantage of being able to retaliate by invading a demilitarized zone.

Three factors explain why France did not try to expel the twenty-two thousand German troops that occupied the zone. First, France would not act alone, and Britain could not be persuaded to use force. Second, the French general staff overestimated German military strength and thought only of defending French soil from a German attack, not of initiating a strike against Germany. Third, French public opinion showed no enthusiasm for a confrontation with Hitler.

The Spanish Civil War of 1936–1939 was another victory for fascism. Nazi Germany and Fascist Italy aided Franco; the Soviet Union supplied the Spanish republic. The republic appealed to France for help, but the French government feared that the civil war would expand into a European war. With Britain's approval, France proposed the Nonintervention Agreement. Italy, Germany, and the Soviet Union signed the agreement but continued to supply the warring parties. By October 1937, some sixty thousand Italian "volunteers" were fighting in Spain. Hitler sent between five and six thousand men and hundreds of planes, which proved decisive. By comparison, the Soviet Union's aid was meager. Viewing the conflict as a struggle between democracy and fascism, thousands of Eu-

◄ *Map 32.1* German and Italian Aggressions, 1935–1939 German aggression from 1936 to 1939 included the militarization of Rhineland (1936), Anchluss with Austria (1938), and the dismemberment of Czechoslovakia (1938–1939).

ropeans and Americans volunteered to fight for the republic.

Without considerable help from France, the Spanish republic was doomed, but Prime Minister Léon Blum continued to support nonintervention. He feared that French intervention would cause Germany and Italy to escalate their involvement, bringing Europe to the edge of a general war. Moreover, supplying the republic would have dangerous consequences at home because French rightists were sympathetic to Franco's conservative-clerical authoritarianism. In 1939, the republic fell, and Franco established a dictatorship, imprisoning or banishing to labor camps more than one million Spaniards and executing another two hundred thousand.

The Spanish Civil War provided Germany with an opportunity to test weapons and pilots. It also demonstrated that France and Britain lacked the determination to fight fascism. In addition, the war widened the breach between Italy and Britain and France that had opened when Italy invaded Ethiopia, and it drew Mussolini and Hitler closer together. In October 1936, Mussolini sent his foreign minister to meet with Hitler in Berlin. The discussions bore fruit, and on November 1, Mussolini proclaimed that a Rome-Berlin "Axis" had been created.

One of Hitler's aims was the incorporation of Austria into the Third Reich. The Treaty of Versailles expressly prohibited the union of the two countries, but in *Mein Kampf*, Hitler insisted that an Anschluss was necessary for German Lebensraum. In February 1938, under intense pressure from Hitler, Austrian chancellor Kurt von Schuschnigg promised to accept Austrian Nazis in his cabinet and agreed to closer relations with Germany. Austrian independence was slipping away, and increasingly, Austrian Nazis undermined Schuschnigg's authority. Seeking to gain his people's support, Schuschnigg made plans for a plebiscite on the issue of preserving Austrian independence. An enraged Hitler ordered his generals to draw up plans for an invasion of Austria. Hitler then demanded Schuschnigg's resignation and the formation of a new government headed by Arthur Seyss-Inquart, an Austrian Nazi.

Believing that Austria was not worth a war, Britain and France informed the embattled chancellor that they would not help in the event of a German invasion. Schuschnigg then resigned, and Austrian Nazis began to take control of the government. Under the pretext of preventing violence, Hitler ordered his troops to cross into Austria, and on March 13, 1938, Austrian leaders declared that Austria was a province of the German Reich.

Many Austrians welcomed the Anchluss. The idea of a Greater Germany appealed to their Pan-German sentiments, and they hoped that Hitler's magic would produce economic recovery. Moreover, depriving Jews of their rights, property, and occupations had widespread appeal among traditionally anti-Semitic Austrians. The Viennese celebrated by ringing church bells, waving swastika banners, and spontaneously beating, robbing, and humiliating Jews, including tearing Torah scrolls, shearing the beards of rabbis, and forcing whole families to scrub sidewalks. The Austrians' euphoria over the Anchluss and their sadistic treatment of helpless of Jews astonished many observers, including the German occupiers.

Czechoslovakia: The Apex of Appeasement

Hitler obtained Austria merely by threatening to use force. Another threat would give him the Sudetenland of Czechoslovakia. Ethnic Germans, numbering some 3.25 million, predominated in the Sudetenland. The region contained key industries and strong fortifications; since it bordered Germany, it was also vital to Czech security. Deprived of the Sudetenland, Czechoslovakia could not defend itself against a German attack. Encouraged and instructed by Germany, the Sudeten Germans, led by Konrad Henlein, shrilly denounced the Czech government for "persecuting" its German minority and depriving Sudeten Germans of their right to self-determination. The Sudeten Germans agitated for local autonomy and the right to profess the National Socialist ideology. Behind this demand was the goal of German annexation of the Sudetenland and the destruction of Czechoslovakia.

While negotiations between the Sudeten Germans and the Czech government proceeded, Hitler's propaganda machine accused the Czechs of hideous crimes against the German minority and warned of retribution. Hitler also ordered his generals to prepare for an invasion of Czechoslovakia and to complete the fortifications along the French border. Fighting between Czechs and Sudeten Germans heightened the tensions. Seeking to preserve peace, Prime Minister Neville Chamberlain (1869–1940) of Britain offered to confer with Hitler, who then extended an invitation.

Britain and France held somewhat different positions toward Czechoslovakia, the only democracy in eastern Europe. In 1924, France and Czechoslovakia had concluded an agreement of mutual assistance in the event that either was attacked by Germany. Czechoslovakia had a similar agreement with Russia, but with the provision that Russian assistance depended on France's first fulfilling the terms of its agreement. Britain had no commitment to Czechoslovakia. Some British officials, swallowing Hitler's propaganda, believed that the Sudeten Germans were indeed a suppressed minority entitled to self-determination. They also thought that the Sudetenland, like Austria, was not worth a war that could destroy Western civilization. Hitler, they said, only wanted to incorporate Germans living outside of Germany; he was only carrying the principle of self-determination to its logical conclusion. Once these Germans lived under the German flag, Hitler would be satisfied. In any case, Britain's failure to rearm adequately between 1933 and 1938 weakened its position. The British chiefs of staff believed that the nation was not prepared to fight and that it was necessary to sacrifice Czechoslovakia to buy time.

Czechoslovakia's fate was decided at the Munich Conference (September 1938), attended by Chamberlain, Hitler, Mussolini, and Prime Minister Édouard Daladier (1884–1970) of France. The Munich Agreement called for the immediate evacuation of Czech troops from the Sudetenland and its occupation by German forces. Britain and France then promised to guarantee the territorial integrity of the truncated Czechoslovakia. Both Chamberlain and Daladier were praised by adoring crowds in their respective countries for keeping the peace.

Critics of Chamberlain have insisted that the Munich Agreement was a tragic blunder. Chamberlain, they say, was a fool to believe that Hitler could be bought off with the Sudetenland. Hitler regarded concessions by Britain and France as signs of weakness; they only increased his appetite for more territory. Second, argue the critics, it would have been better to fight Hitler in 1938 than a year later, when war actually did break out. In the year following the Munich Agreement, Britain increased its military arsenal, but so did Germany, which strengthened western border defenses, built submarines, heavy tanks, and planes, and trained more pilots.

Had Britain and France resisted Hitler at Munich, it is likely that the fuehrer would have attacked Czechoslovakia. But the Czech border defenses, built on the model of the French Maginot Line, were formidable. The Czechs had a sizable number of good tanks, and the Czech people were willing to fight to preserve their nation's territorial integrity. By itself, the Czech army could not have defeated Germany. But while the main elements of the German army were battling the Czechs, the French, who could mobilize a hundred divisions, could have broken through the German West Wall, which was defended by only five regular and four reserve divisions; then they could have invaded the Rhineland and devastated German industrial centers in the Ruhr. (Such a scenario, of course, depended on the French overcoming their psychological reluctance to take the offensive.) And there was the possibility, although probably a slim one, that the Soviet Union would have fulfilled its agreement and come to Czechoslovakia's aid.

After the annexation of the Sudetenland, Hitler plotted to extinguish Czechoslovakia's existence. He encouraged the Slovak minority in Czechoslovakia, led by a fascist priest, Josef Tiso, to demand complete separation. On the pretext of protecting the Slovak people's right of self-determination, Hitler ordered his troops to enter Prague. In March 1939, Czech independence came to an end.

The destruction of Czechoslovakia was of a different character from the remilitarization of the Rhineland, the Anschluss with Austria, and the annexation of the Sudetenland. In all these previous cases, Hitler could claim the right of German self-determination, Woodrow Wilson's grand principle. The occupation of Prague and the end of Czech independence, though, showed that Hitler really sought European hegemony. Outraged statesmen demanded that the fuehrer be deterred from further aggression.

Poland: The Final Crisis

After Czechoslovakia, Hitler turned to Poland, demanding that the free city of Danzig be returned to Germany and that railways and roads, over which

Chronology 32.2 ❖ World War II

September 27, 1939	Poland surrenders
November 1939	Russia invades Finland
April 1940	Germany attacks Denmark and Norway
May 10, 1940	Germany invades Belgium, Holland, and Luxembourg
May 27–June 4, 1940	British and French troops are evacuated from Dunkirk
June 22, 1940	France surrenders
August–September 1940	Battle of Britain
September 1940	Japan begins conquest of Southeast Asia
October 1940	Italian troops cross into Greece
April 6, 1941	Germany attacks Greece and Yugoslavia
June 22, 1941	Germany launches offensive against Russia
December 7, 1941	Japan attacks Pearl Harbor: United States enters the war against Japan and Germany
1942	Tide of battle turns in the Allies' favor: Midway (Pacific Ocean), Stalingrad (Soviet Union), and El Alamein (North Africa)
April–May 1943	Uprising of Jews in Warsaw ghetto
September 1943	Italy surrenders to Allies, following invasion
June 6, 1944	D-day—Allies land in Normandy
August 1944	Paris is liberated; Poles rise up against German occupiers
January 1945	Soviet troops invade Germany
March–April 1945	Allies penetrate Germany
May 7, 1945	Germany surrenders unconditionally
August 1945	United States drops atomic bombs on Hiroshima and Nagasaki; Soviet Union invades Manchuria; Japan surrenders

Germans would enjoy extraterritorial rights, be built across the Polish Corridor, linking East Prussia with the rest of Germany. Poland refused to restore the port of Danzig, which was vital to its economy. The Poles would allow a German highway through the Polish Corridor but would not permit German extraterritorial rights. France informed the German government that it would fulfill its treaty obligations to aid Poland. Chamberlain also warned that Britain would assist Poland.

On May 22, 1939, Hitler and Mussolini entered into the Pact of Steel, promising mutual aid in the event of war. The following day, Hitler told his officers that Germany's real goal was the destruction of Poland. "Danzig is not the objective. It is a matter of expanding our living space in the east, of making our food supplies secure. . . . There is therefore no question of sparing Poland, and the decision remains to attack Poland at the first suitable opportunity."[3] In the middle of June, the army presented Hitler with battle plans for an invasion of Poland.

Britain, France, and the Soviet Union had been engaged in negotiations since April. The Soviet Union wanted a mutual-assistance pact, including joint military planning, and demanded bases in Poland and Romania in preparation for a German attack. Britain was reluctant to endorse these demands, fearing that a mutual-assistance pact with Russia might cause Hitler to embark on a mad adventure that would drag Britain into war. Moreover, Poland would not allow Russian troops on its soil, fearing Russian expansion.

At the same time, Russia was conducting secret talks with Nazi Germany. Unlike the Allies, Hitler could tempt Stalin with territory that would serve as a buffer between Germany and Russia. Moreover, a treaty with Germany would give Russia time to strengthen its armed forces. On August 23, 1939, the two totalitarian states signed a nonaggression pact, which stunned the world. A secret section of the pact called for the partition of Poland between the two parties and Russian control over Latvia and Estonia (later the agreement was amended to include Lithuania). By signing such an agreement with his enemy, Hitler had pulled off an extraordinary diplomatic coup: he blocked the Soviet Union, Britain, and France from duplicating their World War I alliance against Germany. The Nazi-Soviet Pact was the green light for an invasion of Poland, and at dawn on September 1, 1939, German troops crossed the frontier. Two days later, when Germany did not respond to their demand for a halt to the invasion, Britain and France declared war on Germany.

The Nazi Blitzkrieg

Germany struck at Poland with speed and power, implementing tactical concepts of a mobile armored offensive worked out by German military planners between the wars. The German air force, the Luftwaffe, destroyed Polish planes on the ground, attacked tanks, pounded defense networks, and bombed Warsaw, terrorizing the population. Tanks opened breaches in the Polish defenses, and mechanized columns overran the foot-marching Polish army, trapping large numbers of soldiers. The Polish high command could not cope with the incredible speed and coordination of German air and ground attacks. By September 8, the Germans, moving rapidly across Poland's flat terrain, advanced to the outskirts of Warsaw. On September 17, Soviet troops invaded Poland from the east. On September 27, Poland surrendered. In less than a month, the Nazi *blitzkrieg* (lightning war) had vanquished Poland.

The Fall of France

For Hitler, the conquest of Poland was only the prelude to a German empire stretching from the Atlantic to the Urals. When weather conditions were right, he would unleash a great offensive in the west. Meanwhile, the six-month period following the defeat of Poland was nicknamed the "phony war," for the fighting on land consisted only of a few skirmishes on the French-German border. Then, in early April 1940, the Germans struck at Denmark and Norway. Hitler wanted to establish naval bases on the Norwegian coast from which to wage submarine warfare against Britain, and to ensure delivery of Swedish iron ore to Germany through Norwegian territorial waters.

Denmark surrendered within hours. A British-French force tried to assist the Norwegians, but the landings, badly coordinated and lacking in air support, failed. The Germans won the battle of Norway. But the Norwegian campaign produced two positive results for the Allies: Norwegian merchant ships escaped to Britain to be put into service; and Winston Churchill (1874–1965), who had opposed appeasement, replaced Chamberlain as British prime minister. (The German victory in Norway eroded Chamberlain's support in the House of Commons, and he was forced to give up the helm.) Dynamic, courageous, and eloquent, Churchill had the capacity to stir and lead his people in the struggle against Nazism.

On May 10, 1940, Hitler launched his offensive in the west with an invasion of neutral Belgium, Holland, and Luxembourg. While armored forces penetrated Dutch frontier defenses, airborne units seized strategic airfields and bridges. On May 14, after the Luftwaffe had bombed Rotterdam, destroying the center of the city and killing many people, the Dutch surrendered.

A daring attack by glider-borne troops gave Germany possession of two crucial Belgian bridges, opening the plains of Belgium to German panzer (tank) divisions. Believing that this was the

Hitler's Greater Germany
Allied with Germany
Occupied by Germany and its allies
Advances by Allied forces
Major battle
NORTHERN IRELAND
IRELAND
GREAT BRITAIN
Battle of Britain (Fall 1940)
London
Dunkirk
English Channel
Invasion of Normandy (June 6, 1944)
NORMANDY
NETHERLANDS
Rotterdam
Antwerp
BELGIUM
Bastogne
Battle of the Bulge (Dec. 1944)
Sedan
Paris
Western Front, Feb. 1945
ATLANTIC OCEAN
North Sea
NORWAY
Oslo
SWEDEN
Stockholm
Baltic Sea
DENMARK
Copenhagen
FINLAND
Helsinki
L. Ladoga
Leningrad
Riga
Moscow
SOVIET UNION
Smolensk
Tula
Russian Front, Dec. 1941
Russian Front, Spring 1944
Russian Front, Feb. 1945
Elbe R.
Berlin
Posen
Warsaw
GERMANY
POLAND
Pinsk
Kiev
Stalingrad
Volga R.
Don R.
Caspian Sea
UKRAINE
Krakow
CZECHOSLOVAKIA
SLOVAKIA
Rhine R.
Vienna
AUSTRIA
HUNGARY
Budapest
Russian Front, Nov. 1942
FRANCE
SWITZERLAND
Vichy
VICHY FRANCE (Occupied Nov. 1942)
Yalta
ROMANIA
Bucharest
Black Sea
Bologna
Italian Front, Feb. 1945
YUGOSLAVIA
Sofia
ITALY
Monte Cassino (May 1944)
BULGARIA
Madrid
Lisbon
PORTUGAL
SPAIN
Rome
Anzio
ALBANIA
Ankara
TURKEY
Salerno (Sept. 1943)
GREECE
Gibraltar (Gr. Br.)
Sicily (July 1943)
Athens
SYRIA
SP. MOROCCO
Algiers
Tunis
Crete
Cyprus
Casablanca (Nov. 1942)
Malta (Gr. Br.)
LEBANON
Rommel defeated in Tunisia (May 1943)
FRENCH MOROCCO
ALGERIA (Vichy France)
Mediterranean Sea
PALESTINE (Br. Mandate)
Alexandria
El Alamein (Summer 1942)
TUNISIA
TRANS-JORDAN (Br. Mandate)
0 200 400 Km.
0 200 400 Mi.
Suez Canal
LIBYA
Nile R.
Cairo
EGYPT

main German attack, French troops rushed to Belgium to prevent a German breakthrough, but the greater menace lay to the south, on the French frontier. Meeting almost no resistance, German panzer divisions had moved through the narrow mountain passes of Luxembourg and the dense Forest of Ardennes in southern Belgium. On May 12, German units were on French soil near Sedan. Thinking that the Forest of Ardennes could not be penetrated by a major German force, the French had only lightly fortified the western extension of the Maginot Line. The failure to counterattack swiftly was a second mistake. The best elements of the Anglo-French forces were in Belgium, but the Germans were racing across northern France to the sea, which they reached on May 20, cutting the Anglo-French forces in two.

The Germans now sought to surround and annihilate the Allied forces converging on the French seaport of Dunkirk, the last port of escape. But probably fearing that German tanks would lose mobility in the rivers and canals around Dunkirk, Hitler called them off just as the troops prepared to take the port. Instead, he ordered the Luftwaffe to finish off the Allied troops, but fog and rain prevented German planes from operating at full strength, and British pilots inflicted heavy losses on the attackers. The Allies took advantage of this breathing space to tighten their defenses and prepare for a massive evacuation. While the Luftwaffe bombed the beaches, some 338,000 British and French troops were ferried across the English Channel by destroyers, merchant ships, motorboats, fishing boats, tugboats, and private yachts. Abandoning their equipment on the beaches, the British saved their armies to fight another day. Hitler's decision to hold back his tanks made the miracle of Dunkirk possible.

Meanwhile, the battle for France was turning into an even worse disaster for the French. Whole divisions were cut off or in retreat, and millions of refugees in cars and carts and on motorcycles and bicycles fled south to escape the advancing Germans. On June 10, Mussolini also declared war on France. With authority breaking down and resistance dying, the French cabinet appealed for an armistice, which was signed on June 22 in the same railway car in which Germany had agreed to the armistice ending World War I.

◀ *Map 32.2* World War II: The European Theater By 1942 Germany ruled virtually all of Europe from the Atlantic to deep into Russia. Germany's defeat in Stalingrad in Russia and El Alamein in North Africa were decisive turning points.

How can the collapse of France be explained? Neither French military leaders, who experienced the debacle, nor historians are in agreement as to the relative strength of the French and German air forces. It is likely that the Germans and the French (including the British planes based in France) had some three thousand planes each. But many French planes—in what still remains a mystery—stayed on the airfields. The planes were available, but the high command either did not use them or did not deploy them properly. Unlike the Germans, the French did not comprehend or appreciate the use of aviation in modern warfare. As for tanks, the French had as many as the Germans, and some were superior. Nor was German manpower overwhelming. France met disaster largely because its military leaders, unlike the Germans, had not mastered the psychology and technology of motorized warfare. "The French commanders, trained in the slow-motion methods of 1918, were mentally unfitted to cope with Panzer pace, and it produced a spreading paralysis among them," says the British military expert Sir Basil Liddell Hart.[4] Put succinctly, the French were badly outgeneraled. One also senses a loss of will among the French people: a consequence of internal political disputes dividing the nation, poor leadership, the years of appeasement and lost opportunities, and German propaganda, which depicted Nazism as irresistible and the fuehrer as a man of destiny. It was France's darkest hour.

According to the terms of the armistice, Germany occupied northern France and the coast. The French military was demobilized, and the French government, now located at Vichy, in the south, and headed by Marshal Henri Philippe Pétain, the hero of World War I, would collaborate with the German authorities in occupied France, even to the point of passing racial laws and deporting Jews, including two thousand orphans under the age of six, to Nazi murder factories. The leaders of Vichy and their supporters, many of them prominent intellectuals and anti-Dreyfusards in their youth, shared in the antidemocratic, anti-Marxist, and anti-Semitic tradition of the radical right that had arrayed itself against the Third French Republic since the late nineteenth century. Refusing to recognize defeat, General Charles de Gaulle (1890–1970) escaped to London and organized the Free French forces. The Germans gloried in their revenge, and the French wept in their humiliation. The British gathered their courage, for they now stood alone.

The Battle of Britain

Hitler expected that, after his stunning victories in the west, Britain would make peace. The British, however, continued to reject Hitler's peace overtures, for they envisioned only a bleak future if Hitler dominated the Continent. "The Battle of Britain is about to begin," Churchill told his people. "Upon this battle depends the survival of Christian civilization. . . . if we fail, then . . . all we have known and cared for will sink into the abyss of a new Dark Age."[5]

With Britain unwilling to come to terms, Hitler proceeded in earnest with invasion plans. A successful crossing of the English Channel and the establishment of beachheads on the English coast depended on control of the skies. Marshal Hermann Goering assured Hitler that his Luftwaffe could destroy the British Royal Air Force (RAF), and in early August 1940, the Luftwaffe began massive attacks on British air and naval installations. Virtually every day during the "Battle of Britain," weather permitting, hundreds of planes fought in the sky above Britain. "Never in the field of human conflict was so much owed by so many to so few," said Churchill of the British pilots, who rose to the challenge. On September 15, the RAF shot down sixty aircraft, convincing Hitler that Goering could not fulfill his promise to destroy British air defenses, and on September 17 the fuehrer postponed the invasion of Britain "until further notice." The development of radar by British scientists, the skill and courage of British fighter pilots, and the unwillingness of Germany to absorb more losses in planes and trained pilots saved Britain in its struggle for survival.

With the invasion of Britain called off, the Luftwaffe concentrated on bombing English cities, industrial centers, and ports, in the hopes of eroding Britain's military potential and undermining civilian morale. Every night for months, the inhabitants of London sought shelter in subways and cellars to escape German bombs, while British planes rose time after time to make the Luftwaffe pay the price. British morale never broke during the "Blitz."

Britain, by itself, had no hope of defeating the Third Reich. What ultimately changed the course of the war were Germany's invasion of the Soviet Union in June 1941 and Japan's attack on the United States in December 1941. With the entry of these two powers, a coalition was created that had the human and material resources to reverse the tide of battle.

Invasion of Russia

The obliteration of Bolshevism and the conquest, exploitation, and colonization of Russia were cardinal elements of Hitler's ideology: in Russia, the Nazi empire would take control of wheat, oil, manganese, and other raw materials, and the fertile Russian plains would be settled by the master race. German expansion in the east could not wait for the final defeat of Britain. In July 1940, Hitler instructed his generals to formulate plans for an invasion of Russia. On December 18, Hitler set May 15, 1941, for the beginning of Operation Barbarossa, the code name assigned for the blitzkrieg against the Soviet Union. Events in the Balkans, however, forced Hitler to postpone the date to the latter part of June.

Seeking to make Italy a Mediterranean power and to win glory for himself, Mussolini had ordered an invasion of Greece. In late October 1940, Italian troops stationed in Albania—which Italy had occupied in 1939—crossed into Greece. The poorly planned operation was an instant failure; within a week, the counterattacking Greeks advanced into Albania. Hitler feared that Britain, which was encouraging and aiding the Greeks, would use Greece to attack the oil fields of Romania, which were vital to the German war effort, and to interfere with the forthcoming invasion of Russia. Another problem emerged when a military coup overthrew the government of Prince Paul in Yugoslavia, which two days earlier had signed a pact with Germany and Italy. Hitler feared that the new Yugoslav government might gravitate toward Britain. To prevent any interference with Operation Barbarossa, the Balkan flank had to be secured. On April 6, 1941, the Germans struck at

Stalingrad, February 1943. In the photograph, the Russians are rescuing the bombed-out city of Stalingrad from the Nazi invaders. (*Sovfoto.*)

both Greece and Yugoslavia. Yugoslavia was quickly overrun, and Greece, although aided by fifty thousand British, New Zealand, and Australian troops, fell at the end of April.

For the war against Russia, Hitler assembled a massive force: some four million men, thirty-three hundred tanks, and two thousand planes. Evidence of the German buildup abounded, but a stubborn Stalin ignored these warnings. Desperate to avoid war with Nazi Germany, Stalin would take no action that he feared might provoke Hitler. Consequently, the Red Army was vulnerable to the German blitzkrieg. In the early hours of June 22, 1941, the Germans launched their offensive over a wide front. Raiding Russian airfields, the Luftwaffe destroyed twelve hundred aircraft on the first day, most of them on the ground, a clear example of Stalin's failure to heed warnings of an impending German attack. The Germans drove deeply into Russia, cutting up and surrounding the disorganized and unprepared Russian forces. Contributing to the rout was the poor quality of Russian commanders, a consequence of Stalin's purge of Red Army officers, many of them trained and competent professionals, a few years earlier.

The Russians suffered terrible losses. In a little more than three months, two and a half million Russian soldiers were killed, wounded, or captured, and fourteen thousand tanks destroyed. Describing the war as a crusade to save Europe from "Jewish-Bolshevik subhumans," German propaganda claimed that victory was assured.

But there were also disquieting signs for the Nazi invaders. The Russians, who had a proven capacity to endure hardships, fought doggedly and courageously for the motherland, and the government would not consider capitulation. At first many Russians, particularly in Ukraine, welcomed the German invaders, who they hoped would liberate them from Stalin's tyranny. But German ruthlessness against the local population, whom Nazi ideology marked for exploitation and servitude, strengthened the resolve of the Russian people. Russian reserve strength was far greater than the Germans had estimated. Increasing the Red Army's strength was the drafting of hundreds of thousands of prisoners from labor camps and the recruitment of hundreds of thousands of women, who saw action as artillery and anti-aircraft gunners, fighter pilots, tank personnel, and snipers. The Wehrmacht (German army), far from its supply lines, ran short of fuel, vehicles, and spare parts and had to contend with primitive roads that turned into seas of mud when the autumn rains came. One German general described the ordeal: "The infantryman slithers in the mud, while many teams of horses are needed to drag each gun forward. All wheeled vehicles sink up to their axles in the slime. Even tractors can only move with great difficulty. A large portion of our heavy artillery was soon stuck fast. . . . The strain that all this caused our already exhausted troops can perhaps be imagined."[6] Conditions no longer favored the blitzkrieg.

Early and bitter subzero weather hampered the German attempt to capture Moscow. Without warm uniforms, tens of thousands of Germans suffered from frostbite; without antifreeze, guns did not fire. The Germans advanced to within twenty miles of Moscow, but on December 6, a Red Army counterattack forced them to postpone the assault on the Russian capital. The Germans were also denied Leningrad, which since September had been almost completely surrounded and under constant bombardment. During this epic siege, which lasted for two and a half years, the citizens of Leningrad displayed extraordinary courage in the face of famine, disease, and shelling that cost nearly one million lives, more than the combined losses of Britain and the United States for the entire war.

By the end of 1941, Germany had conquered vast regions of Russia but had failed to bring the country to its knees. There would be no repetition of the collapse of France. Moreover, by moving machinery and workers east far beyond the German reach, the Soviets were able to replenish their military hardware, which was almost totally destroyed during the first six months of the war. Driven by patriotic fervor—and by fear of the omnipresent NKVD agents searching for malingerers—Russian factory workers, many of them the wives and daughters of soldiers, toiled relentlessly, heroically. Soon they were producing more planes and tanks than Germany. The Russian campaign demonstrated that the Russian people would make incredible sacrifices for their land and that the Nazis were not invincible.

The New Order

By 1942, Germany ruled virtually all of Europe, from the Atlantic to deep into Russia. Some conquered territory was annexed outright; other lands were administered by German officials; in still other countries, the Germans ruled through local officials sympathetic to Nazism or willing to collaborate with the Germans. On this vast empire, Hitler and his henchmen imposed a New Order.

Exploitation and Terror

"The real profiteers of this war are ourselves, and out of it we shall come bursting with fat," said Hitler. "We will give back nothing and will take everything we can make use of."[7] The Germans systematically looted the countries they conquered, taking gold, art treasures, machinery, and food supplies back to Germany and exploiting the industrial and agricultural potential of non-German lands to aid the German war economy. Some foreign businesses and factories were confiscated by the German Reich; others produced what the Germans demanded. Germany also requisitioned food from the conquered regions, significantly reducing the quantity available for local civilian consumption. German soldiers were fed with food harvested in occupied France and Russia; they fought with weapons produced in Czech factories. German tanks ran on oil delivered by Romania, Germany's satellite. The Nazis also made slave laborers of conquered peoples. Some seven million people from all over Europe were wrested from their homes and transported to Germany. These forced laborers, particularly the Russians and Poles, whom Nazi ideology classified as a lower form of humanity, lived in wretched, unheated barracks and were poorly fed and overworked; many died of disease, hunger, and exhaustion.

The Nazis ruled by force and terror. The prison cell, the torture chamber, the firing squad, and the concentration camp symbolized the New Order. In the Polish province annexed to Germany, the Nazis jailed and executed intellectuals and priests, closed all schools and most churches, and forbade Poles from holding professional positions. In the region of Poland administered by German officials, most schools above the fourth grade were shut down. Himmler insisted that it was sufficient for Polish children to learn "simple arithmetic up to five hundred at the most; writing of one's name; a doctrine that it is a divine law to obey the Germans and to be honest, industrious, and good."[8] The

Germans were particularly ruthless toward the Russians. Soviet political officials were immediately executed; many prisoners of war were herded into camps and deliberately starved to death. In all, the Germans took prisoner some 5.5 million Russians, of whom more than 3.5 million perished, primarily from starvation. These prisoners of war were supervised not by the notorious SS, who ran the extermination camps, but by the regular army, the Wehrmacht, whose officers made deliberate decisions to starve Russian prisoners.

German soldiers routinely abused innocents: they stripped Russian peasants of their winter clothing and boots before driving them into the freezing outdoors to die of cold and starvation, slaughtered large numbers of hostages, burned whole villages to the ground in reprisal for partisan attacks, and deported massive numbers of people for slave labor. To the German invaders the Russians were "Asiatic bestial hordes" led by sinister "subhuman" Jews who aimed to destroy Germany. Recent studies, largely by German historians, demonstrate how committed the Wehrmacht command was to Nazi ideological aims, how willing it was to propagate Nazi ideology among the troops—letters and diaries reveal how ideologically devoted average soldiers were to Nazism—and how implicated both the high command and common soldiers were in war crimes, including the extermination of the Jews.

Extermination

Against the Jews of Europe, the Germans waged a war of extermination. The task of imposing the "Final Solution of the Jewish Problem" was given to Himmler's SS, and they fulfilled these grisly duties with fanaticism and bureaucratic efficiency. In exterminating the Jewish people, the Nazis believed they were righteous and courageous and serving a higher good—the defense of the sacred Volk. In striking at the Jews, they were also destroying essential values of the Western tradition—reason, freedom, equality, toleration, respect for human dignity, and individualism—which they despised and with which the Jews, because of their unique historical experience, were identified.

Regarding themselves as idealists who were writing a glorious chapter in the history of Germany, the SS tortured and murdered with immense dedication. The minds of the SS were dominated by the mythical world-view of Nazism, as the following tract issued by SS headquarters reveals:

> *Just as night rises up against the day, just as light and darkness are eternal enemies, so the greatest enemy of world-dominating man is man himself. The sub-man—that creature which looks as though biologically it were of absolutely the same kind, endowed by Nature with hands, feet and a sort of brain, with eyes and mouth—is nevertheless a totally different, a fearful creature, is only an attempt at a human being, with a quasi-human face, yet in mind and spirit lower than any animal. Inside this being a cruel chaos of wild, unchecked passions: a nameless will to destruction, the most primitive lusts, the most undisguised vileness. A sub-man—nothing else! . . . Never has the sub-man granted peace, never has he permitted rest. . . . To preserve himself he needed mud, he needed hell, but not the sun. And this underworld of sub-men found its leader: the eternal Jew!*[9]

Special squads of SS—the *Einsatzgruppen*, trained for mass murder—followed on the heels of the German army into Russia. Entering captured villages and cities, they rounded up Jewish men, women, and children, herded them to execution grounds, and slaughtered them with machine-gun and rifle fire at the edge of open trenches, which sometimes were piled high with thousands of victims, including severely wounded people, who would suffocate to death when the pit was filled with earth. Aided by Ukrainian, Lithuanian, and Latvian auxiliaries, along with contingents from the Romanian army, the Einsatzgruppen massacred some 1.3 million Jews. Units of the Wehrmacht actively participated in the rounding up of Jews and sometimes in the shootings. Despite the denials of staff officers after the war, evidence from their own files reveals that they knew fully well that the extermination of the Jews was state policy that units of the Wehrmacht were helping to implement.

In Poland, where some 3.3 million Jews lived, the Germans established ghettos in the larger cities. Jews from all over the country were crammed into these ghettos, which were sealed off from the rest of the population. The German administration de-

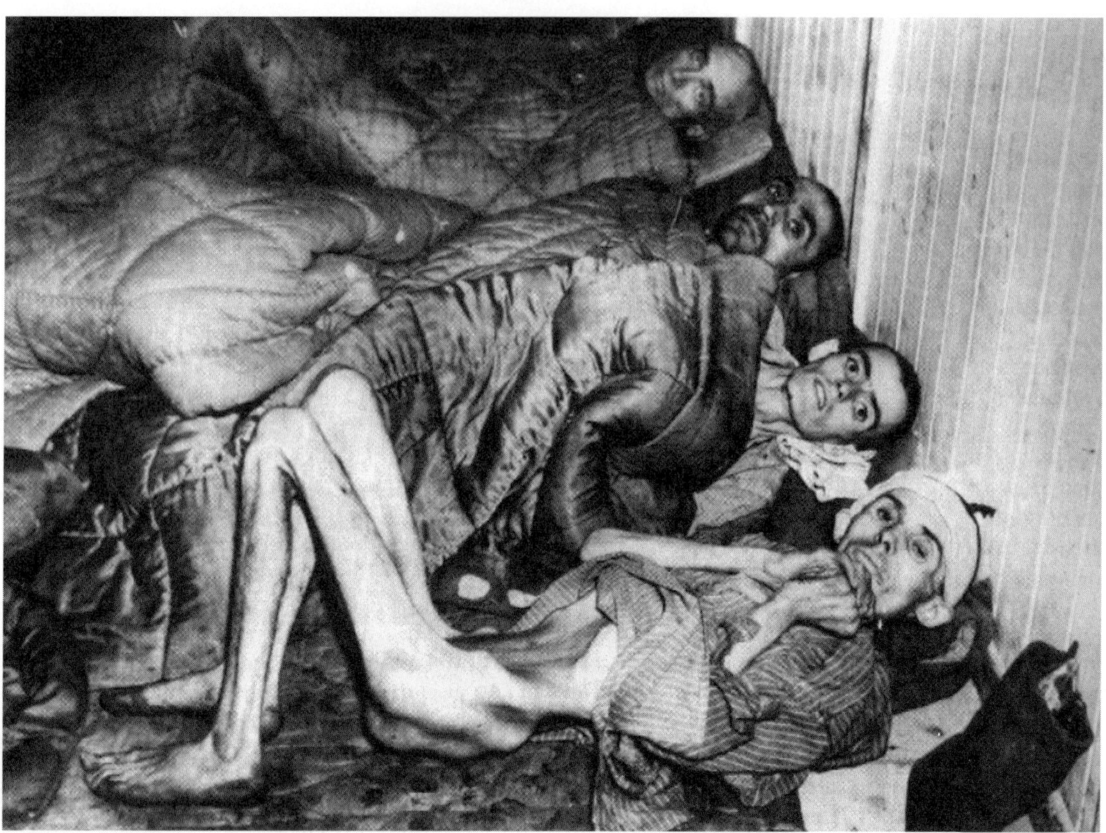

CONCENTRATION CAMP SURVIVORS. Thousands of emaciated and diseased inmates of German concentration camps died in the weeks after liberation by the Allies. These camps will forever remain a monument to the capacity of human beings for inhumanity. (© *Topham/The Image Works.*)

liberately curtailed the food supply, and many Jews died of malnutrition, disease, and beatings. In the ghettos, the Polish Jews struggled to maintain community life and to preserve their spirit. They established schools (forbidden by the German authorities), prayed together (also forbidden), organized social services, and kept hidden archives so that future ages would have a historical record of their ordeal.

The mass killings, however, posed problems for the Germans. These murders were too public, whereas the Germans wanted to keep the Final Solution as secret as possible. Furthermore, the face-to-face killing of civilians, including women and children, could be too hard on the psyche of the personnel charged with carrying out such orders. To overcome these problems, the Germans transformed concentration camps, originally established for political prisoners, into killing centers, and they also built new ones for this purpose.* Jews from all over Europe were rounded up—for "resettlement," they were told. The victims dismissed rumors that the Germans were engaged in genocide. They simply could not believe that any nation in the twentieth century was capable of such evil. "Why did we not fight back?"† a survivor

*Some 2.5 million to 3 million Jews were gassed in Nazi death factories built in Poland—Chelmno, Treblinka, Sobibur, Belzec, Lublin, Majdanek, and Auschwitz-Birkenau, the largest.

†Jewish resistance is discussed in the next section of this chapter.

asks, and answers: "I know why. Because we had faith in humanity. Because we did not really think that human beings were capable of committing such crimes."[10]

Jammed into sealed cattle cars, eighty or ninety to a car, the victims traveled sometimes for days, without food or water, choking from the stench of vomit and excrement and shattered by the crying of children. Disgorged at the concentration camps, they entered another planet:

> *Corpses were strewn all over the road; bodies were hanging from the barbed-wire fence; the sound of shots rang in the air continuously. Blazing flames shot into the sky; a giant smoke cloud ascended about them. Starving, emaciated human skeletons stumbled forward toward us, uttering incoherent sounds. They fell down right in front of our eyes gasping out their last breath.*
>
> *Here and there a hand tried to reach up, but when this happened an SS man came right away and stepped on it. Those who were merely exhausted were simply thrown on the dead pile. . . . Every night a truck came by, and all of them, dead or not, were thrown on it and taken to the crematory.*[11]

SS doctors quickly inspected the new arrivals, "the freight," as they referred to them. Rudolf Hoess, the commandant of Auschwitz—the most notorious of the murder factories—described the procedure:

> *The "final solution" of the Jewish question meant the complete extermination of all Jews in Europe. I was ordered to establish extermination facilities at Auschwitz in June, 1941. . . . It took from three to fifteen minutes to kill people in the death chamber, depending upon climatic conditions. We knew when the people were dead because their screaming stopped. We usually waited about one-half hour before we opened the doors and removed the bodies. After the bodies were removed our special commandos took off the rings and extracted the gold from the teeth of the corpses. . . .*
>
> *The way we selected our victims was as follows. . . . Those who were fit to work were sent into the camp. Others were sent immediately to the extermination plants. Children of tender years were invariably exterminated since by reason of their youth they were unable to work. . . . We endeavored to fool the victims into thinking that they were to go through a delousing process. Of course, frequently they realized our true intentions, and we sometimes had riots and difficulties due to that fact. Very frequently women would hide their children under clothes, but of course when we found them we would send the children in to be exterminated.*[12]

The naked bodies, covered with blood and excrement and intertwined with each other, were piled high to the ceiling. To make way for the next group, a squad of Jewish prisoners emptied the gas chambers of the corpses and removed gold teeth, which, along with the victims' hair, eyeglasses, and clothing, were carefully collected and catalogued for the war effort. Later, the bodies were burned in crematoriums specially constructed by I. A. Topf and Sons of Erfurt. The chimneys vomited black smoke, and the stench of burning flesh permeated the entire region. Jewish leaders in the United States and Britain, who got word of the killings, pleaded with the Allies to bomb the rail lines to Auschwitz and the gas chambers, but the Allies did nothing. The killing process went on relentlessly. Between 1.1 million and 1.5 million people died in Auschwitz—90 percent of them Jews. Non-Jewish victims included political prisoners and Soviet prisoners of war.

Auschwitz was more than a murder factory. It also provided the German industrial giant, I. G. Farben, which operated a factory adjoining the camp, with slave laborers, both Jews and non-Jews. The working pace at the factory and the ill treatment by guards were so brutal, reported a physician and inmate, that "while working many prisoners suddenly stretched out flat, turned blue, gasped for breath, and died like beasts."[13]

Auschwitz also allowed the SS, the elite of the master race, to shape and harden themselves according to the National Socialist creed. A survivor recalls seeing SS men and women amuse themselves with pregnant inmates. The unfortunate women were "beaten with clubs and whips, torn by dogs, dragged by the hair, and kicked in the stomach with heavy

Profile

Hans and Sophie Scholl

In February 1943, Hans Scholl, age twenty-five, a medical student, and his twenty-two-year-old sister, Sophie Scholl, who was studying biology and philosophy, were executed by the Nazis for high treason. The Scholls belonged to the White Rose, a small group of idealistic students at the University of Munich who urged passive resistance to the National Socialist regime. The White Rose hoped that if more Germans were aware of the Nazi regime's inhumane character they would withdraw their loyalty.

The Scholls had once been enthusiastic members of the Hitler Youth, but over the years they grew increasingly disillusioned with Nazism. Their outlook was shaped by their anti-Nazi father, by a commitment to the German humanist tradition best represented by Schiller and Goethe, and by Kurt Huber, a professor of philosophy and psychology at their university, who spoke to trusted students of a duty "to enlighten those Germans who are still unaware of

AKG, London.

German boots. Then, when they collapsed, they were thrown into the crematory—alive."[14] By systematically overworking, starving, beating, terrorizing, and degrading the inmates, by making them live in filth and sleep sprawled all over each other in tiny cubicles, the SS deliberately sought to strip prisoners of all human dignity, to make them appear and behave as "subhuman," and even make them believe that they were "subhuman," as the National Socialist ideology asserted. The SS relished their absolute power over the inmates.

Many concentration camp inmates went mad or committed suicide; some struggled desperately, defiantly, and heroically to maintain their humanity. When prisoners, exhausted, starved, diseased, and beaten, became unfit for work, which generally happened within a few months, they were sent to the gas chambers. Perhaps the vilest assault on human dignity ever conceived, Nazi extermination camps were the true legacy of National Socialism, and the SS, the true end product of National Socialist indoctrination and idealism.

The SS were often ideologues committed to racist doctrines, which, they believed, were supported by the laws of biology. They were true believers driven by a utopian vision of a new world order founded on a Social Darwinist fantasy of racial hierarchy. To realize this mythic vision of ultimate good, the Jews, whom Nazi ideology designated as less than human and the source of all evil, had to be destroyed; the defense of the fatherland required the elimination of the Jews. Other SS, and their army of collaborators, were simply ordinary people doing their duty as they had been trained, following orders the best way they knew how. They were morally indifferent bureaucrats, concerned with techniques and effectiveness, and careerists and functionaries seeking to impress superiors with their ability to get the job done. These people quickly adjusted to the routine of mass murder.

the evil intentions of our government." Hans was also swayed by the persecution of Jews he had witnessed when he was in transport through Poland to the Russian front.

On walls in Munich, the Scholls painted signs: "Down with Hitler," and "Freedom." Stowing their anti-Nazi leaflets in luggage, the students traveled by railroad to several German cities to drop them off. The following excerpts come from three of White Rose's four leaflets:

> *Who among us has any conception of the dimensions of shame that will befall us and our children when one day the . . . most horrible of crimes—crimes that infinitely outdistance every human measure—reach the light of day? (First leaflet)*

> *Our present "state" is the dictatorship of evil. . . . it is your right—or rather, your moral duty—to eliminate this system. (Third leaflet)*

> *We are trying to achieve a renewal from within of the severely wounded German spirit. This rebirth must be preceded, however, by the clear recognition of all the guilt with which the German people have burdened themselves, and by an uncompromising battle against Hitler. (Fourth leaflet)**

On February 18, 1943, Hans and Sophie were spotted dropping leaflets in the university by the building superintendent, who reported them to the Gestapo. On February 23, Hans, Sophie, and Christoph Probst, also a medical student, were executed. Several days before she died, Sophie stated: "What does my death matter if through us thousands of people will be stirred to action and awakened?" Hans's last words, "Long live freedom," echoed through the prison. Kurt Huber and other members of the group were executed on July 13, 1943.

*Inge Scholl, *Students Against Tyranny,* trans. Arthur R. Schultz (Middletown, Conn.: Wesleyan University Press, 1970), pp. 36, 73, 81–82, 56.

Thus, as Konnilyn G. Feig observes, the thousands of German railway workers "treated the Jewish cattle-car transports as a special business problem that they took pride in solving so well."[15] The German physicians who selected Jews for the gas chambers were concerned only with the technical problems and efficiency, and those doctors and scientists who performed unspeakable medical experiments on Jews viewed their subjects as laboratory animals, as the following correspondence between an I. G. Farben plant and the commandant of Auschwitz testifies: "In contemplation of experiments of a new soporific drug we would appreciate your procuring for us a number of women. . . . We propose to pay not more than 170 marks a head. If agreeable, we will take possession of the women. We need approximately 150. . . . Received the order of 150 women. Despite their emaciated condition, they were found satisfactory. . . . The tests were made. All subjects died. We shall contact you on the subject of a new load."[16]

The German industrialists who worked Jewish slave laborers to death considered only cost-effectiveness in their operations. So, too, did the firms that built the gas chambers and the furnaces, whose durability and performance they guaranteed. An eyewitness reports that engineers from Topf and Sons experimented with different combinations of corpses, deciding that "the most economical and fuel-saving procedure would be to burn the bodies of a well-nourished man and an emaciated woman or vice versa together with that of a child, because, as the experiments had established, in this combination, once they had caught fire, the dead would continue to burn without any further coke being required."[17] Hoess, the commandant of Auschwitz, who exemplified the bureaucratic mentality, noted that his gas chambers were more efficient than those used at Treblinka because they could accommodate far more people. The Germans were so concerned with efficiency and cost that—to conserve ammunition or gas and not slow down the pace from the time victims were ordered to undress until they were hurried into the chambers—toddlers were taken from their mothers and thrown live into burning pits or mass graves.

When the war ended, the SS murderers and those who had assisted them returned to families and jobs, resuming a normal life, free of remorse and untroubled by guilt. "The human ability to normalize the abnormal is frightening indeed," observes the sociologist Rainer C. Baum.[18] Mass murderers need not be psychopaths. It is a "disturbing psychological truth," notes Robert Jay Lifton, that "ordinary people can commit demonic acts."[19]

There have been many massacres during the course of world history. And the Nazis murdered many non-Jews in concentration camps and in reprisal for acts of resistance. What is unique about the Holocaust—the extermination of European Jewry—was the Nazis' determination to murder without exception every single Jew who came within their grasp, and the fanaticism, ingenuity, cruelty and systematic way with which they pursued this goal. Despite the protests of the army, the SS murdered Jews whose labor was needed for the war effort, and when Germany's military position was desperate, the SS still diverted military personnel and railway cars to deport Jews to the death camps.

The Holocaust was the fulfillment of Nazi racial theories. Believing that they were cleansing Europe of worthless life and a dangerous race that threatened Germany, Nazi executioners performed their evil work with dedication, assembly-line precision, and moral indifference—a gruesome testament to human irrationality and wickedness. Using the technology and bureaucracy of a modern state, the Germans killed approximately 6 million Jews: *two-thirds* of the Jewish population of Europe. Some 1.5 million of the murdered were children; almost 90 percent of Jewish children in German-occupied lands perished. Tens of thousands of entire families were wiped out without a trace. Centuries-old Jewish community life vanished, never to be restored. Burned into the soul of the Jewish people was a wound that could never entirely heal. Written into the history of Western civilization was an episode that would forever cast doubt on the Enlightenment conception of human goodness, rationality, and the progress of civilization.

Resistance

Each occupied country had its collaborators, including many right-wing intellectuals, who welcomed the demise of democracy, saw Hitler as Europe's best defense against communism, approved of Nazi measures against Jews, and profited from the confiscation of Jewish property and the sale of war material. In nearly every country occupied by or allied to Nazi Germany, local government officials and the police willingly assisted the Germans in rounding up, hunting down, and deporting Jews to the extermination camps. In Lithuania the local population was responsible for murdering more than half of the country's 140,000 Jewish victims (95 percent of Lithuania's Jewish population perished).

Each occupied country also produced a resistance movement that grew stronger as Nazi barbarism became more visible and prospects of a German defeat more likely. The Nazis retaliated by torturing and executing captured resistance fighters and killing hostages—generally, fifty for every German killed.

In western Europe, the resistance rescued downed Allied airmen, radioed military intelligence to Britain, and sabotaged German installations. Norwegians blew up the German stock of heavy water needed for atomic research. The Danish underground sabotaged railways and smuggled into neutral Sweden almost all of Denmark's eight thousand Jews just before they were to be deported to the death camps. The Greek resistance blew up a vital viaduct, interrupting the movement of supplies to German troops in North Africa. After the Allies landed on the coast of France in June 1944, the French resistance delayed the movement of German reinforcements and liberated sections of the country. Belgian resistance fighters captured the vital port of Antwerp.

The Polish resistance, numbering some three hundred thousand at its height, reported on German troop movements and interfered with supplies destined for the eastern front. In August 1944, with Soviet forces approaching Warsaw, the Poles staged a full-scale revolt against the German occupiers. The Poles appealed to the Soviets, camped ten miles away, for help. Thinking about a future Russian-dominated Poland, the Soviets did not move. After sixty-three days of street fighting, remnants of the Polish underground surrendered, and the Germans destroyed what was left of Warsaw.

Russian partisans numbered several hundred thousand men and women. Operating behind the German lines, they sabotaged railways, destroyed trucks, and killed scores of thousands of German soldiers in hit-and-run attacks.

The mountains and forests of Yugoslavia provided excellent terrain for guerrilla warfare. The leading Yugoslav resistance army was headed by Josip Broz (1892–1980), better known as Tito. Moscow-trained, intelligent, and courageous, Tito organized the partisans into a disciplined fighting force, which tied down a huge German army and ultimately liberated the country from German rule.

Jews participated in the resistance movements in all countries and were particularly prominent in the French resistance. Specifically Jewish resistance organizations emerged in eastern Europe, but they suffered from shattering hardships. They had virtually no access to weapons. Poles, Ukrainians, Lithuanians, and other peoples of eastern Europe with a long history of anti-Semitism gave little or no support to Jewish resisters—at times, even denounced them to the Nazis or killed them. For centuries, European Jews had dealt with persecution by complying with their oppressors, and they had unlearned the habit of armed resistance that their ancestors had demonstrated against the Romans. The Germans responded to acts of resistance with savage reprisals against other Jews, creating a moral dilemma for any Jew who considered taking up arms. Nevertheless, revolts did take place in the ghettos and concentration camps. In the spring of 1943, the surviving Jews of the Warsaw ghetto, armed only with a few guns and homemade bombs, fought the Germans for several weeks.

Italy and Germany also had resistance movements. After the Allies landed in Italy in 1943, bands of Italian partisans helped to liberate Italy from fascism and the German occupation. In Germany, army officers plotted to assassinate the fuehrer. On July 20, 1944, Colonel Claus von Stauffenberg planted a bomb at a staff conference attended by Hitler, but the fuehrer escaped serious injury. In retaliation, some five thousand suspected anti-Nazis were tortured and executed in exceptionally barbarous fashion. Suspended by piano wire from meat hooks, they slowly strangled in front of cameras so that Hitler could observe their excruciating death at his leisure.

Turn of the Tide

The Japanese Offensive

While Germany was subduing Europe, its ally, Japan, was extending its dominion over areas of Asia. Seeking raw materials and secure markets for Japanese goods and driven by a xenophobic nationalism, Japan in 1931 had attacked Manchuria in northern China. Quickly overrunning the province, the Japanese established the puppet state of Manchukuo in 1932. After a period of truce, the war against China was renewed in July 1937. Japan captured leading cities, including China's principal seaports, and inflicted heavy casualties on the poorly organized Chinese forces, obliging the government of Jiang Jieshi (Chiang Kai-shek) to withdraw to Chungking in the interior.

In 1940, after the defeat of France and with Britain standing alone against Nazi Germany, Japan eyed Southeast Asia—French Indochina, British Burma and Malaya, and the Dutch East Indies. From these lands, Japan planned to obtain the oil, rubber, and tin vitally needed by Japanese industry and enough rice to feed the nation. Japan hoped that a quick strike against the American fleet in the Pacific would give it time to enlarge and consolidate its empire. On December 7, 1941, the Japanese struck with carrier-based planes at Pearl Harbor in Hawaii. Taken by surprise—despite warning signs—the Americans suffered a total defeat: the attackers sank 17 ships, including 7 of 8 battleships; destroyed 188 airplanes and damaged 159 others; and killed 2,403 men. The Japanese lost only 29 planes. After the attack on Pearl Harbor, Germany declared war on the United States. Now the immense American industrial capacity could be put to work against the Axis powers—Germany, Italy, and Japan. American factories produced planes, tanks, and ships at a pace and scale that astonished both friend and foe. The American arsenal supplied Britain and the Soviet Union with badly needed equipment.

Defeat of the Axis Powers

By the spring of 1942, the Axis powers held the upper hand. The Japanese Empire included the coast of China, Indochina, Thailand, Burma, Malaya, the Dutch East Indies, the Philippines,

Japanese Empire, 1931
Japanese Empire, 1942
Extent of Japanese expansion
Allied advances
SOVIET UNION
ASIA
MONGOLIA
MANCHURIA
Peiping
(Peking)
KOREA
JAPAN
Tokyo
Hiroshima
Nagasaki
CHINA
Shanghai
Taiwan
BURMA
Hong
Kong
THAILAND
FRENCH
INDOCHINA
Okinawa
1945
Iwo Jima
1945
Mariana Is.
Saipan
Guam
1944
Manila
Philippine Is.
Leyte 1944
MALAYA
Singapore
Borneo
Sumatra
Dutch East Indies
Java
New
Guinea
Caroline Is.
Marshall
Is.
Wake
Tawara
1943
Gilbert Is.
Solomon Is.
Guadalcanal
1942
Attu
Kiska
1943
Aleutian Is.
PACIFIC OCEAN
Midway 1942
Hawaiian Is.
Pearl Harbor
INDIAN OCEAN
AUSTRALIA
Brisbane
0 500 1000 Km.
0 500 1000 Mi.

and other islands in the Pacific. Germany controlled Europe almost to Moscow. When the year ended, however, the Allies seemed assured of victory. Three decisive battles—Midway, Stalingrad, and El Alamein—reversed the tide of war.

At Pearl Harbor, the Japanese had destroyed much of the American fleet. Assembling a mighty flotilla (eight aircraft carriers, eleven battleships, twenty-two cruisers, and sixty-five destroyers), Japan now sought to annihilate the rest of the United States' Pacific fleet. In June 1942, the main body of the Japanese fleet headed for Midway, eleven hundred miles northwest of Pearl Harbor; another section sailed toward the Aleutian Islands, in an attempt to divide the American fleet. But the Americans had broken the Japanese naval code and were aware of the Japanese plan.

On June 4, 1942, the two navies fought a strange naval battle; it was waged entirely by carrier-based planes, for the two fleets were too far from each other to use their big guns. Demonstrating marked superiority over their opponents and extraordinary courage, American pilots destroyed 4 aircraft carriers and downed 322 Japanese planes. The battle of Midway cost Japan the initiative. With American industrial production accelerating, the opportunity for a Japanese victory had passed.

After being stymied at the outskirts of Moscow in December 1941, the Germans renewed their offensive in the spring and summer of 1942. Hitler's goal was Stalingrad, the great industrial center located on the Volga River; control of Stalingrad would give Germany command of vital rail transportation and access to the oil fields of the Caucasus. The battle of Stalingrad was an epic struggle in which Russian soldiers and civilians contested for every building and street of the city. In this urban battlefield, scarred by mile after mile of destroyed buildings and mountains of rubble, the combatants were separated by mere yards, snipers lurked in the maze of ruins, and tough Russian soldiers stealthily and ceaselessly attacked at night with bayonets and daggers; here the blitzkrieg, which had brought the Germans immense success in their earlier offensives, did not apply. Ironically, massive German bombing raids, which had left almost every structure in ruins, provided the Russian fighters with perfect cover from which to harass the enemy. Superior German technical skills and generalship were of no value in close-quarter combat in basements and sewers and amid the rubble and skeletons of buildings. So brutal was the fighting that at night half-crazed dogs sought to escape the city by swimming across the river. One German soldier wrote in his diary at the end of December: "The horses have already been eaten. . . . The soldiers look like corpses or lunatics looking for something to put in their mouths. They no longer take cover from Russian shells; they haven't the strength to walk, run away and hide."[20]

A Russian counterattack in November, planned by General (later Marshal) Georgi Zhukov, caught the Germans in a trap. Not believing that the Russians had sufficient reserve armies and tanks or the competence to launch a massive counteroffensive, German commanders were taken by surprise. With his soldiers exhausted and desperately short of food, medical supplies, weapons, and ammunition, Friedrich Paulus, commander of the Sixth Army, urged Hitler to order a withdrawal before the Russians closed the ring. The fuehrer refused, persuaded, in part, by the pompous Herman Goering's assurance that his Luftwaffe would be able to supply the beleaguered army by air. It was an empty promise; the lack of available transport planes and terrible winter weather, which limited the number of flights and hampered maintenance crews, who had to work outdoors on primitive Russian airfields, doomed the airlift. After suffering tens of thousands of additional casualties, their position hopeless, the remnants of the Sixth Army surrendered on February 2, 1943. Some 260,000 German soldiers had perished in the battle of Stalingrad, and another 110,000 were taken prisoner. Russian morale soared.

The Soviet high command, which had performed terribly in the early days of the German offensive, distinguished itself at Stalingrad. At the battle of Kursk in July 1943, Russian military leaders again demonstrated an increasing ability

◀ *Map 32.3* World War II: The Pacific Theater The battle of Midway was a major turning point in the Pacific Theater. The map also shows the island hopping of the Americans that brought them closer to Japan. The battles of Iwo Jima and Okinawa were particularly brutal.

to master the technique of modern warfare. Analyzing correctly that the Germans would attack the Kursk salients, Zhukhov turned the area into a fortress. Immense numbers of heavy artillery, mines, antitank ditches, tanks, and planes, including dive-bombers equipped with cannon capable of destroying tanks, were set in place. A huge reserve force was positioned to repair breaches opened by panzer attacks. In an epic encounter, over three hundred German tanks were destroyed in one day. "Soviet success at Kursk . . . was the most important single victory of the war," concludes one military historian. "It was the point at which the initiative passed to the Soviet side. . . . The German front in the east was forced . . . to fall back along its entire length. . . . There was a long way to go to take the fight into Europe and to reach Berlin, but Kursk had unhinged the German front irreversibly."[21]

In January 1941, the British were routing the Italians in northern Africa. Hitler assigned General Erwin Rommel (1891–1944) to halt the British advance. Rommel drove the British out of Libya and, with strong reinforcements, might have taken Egypt and the Suez Canal. But Hitler's concern was with seizing Yugoslavia and Greece and preparing for the invasion of Russia. At the beginning of 1942, Rommel resumed his advance, intending to conquer Egypt. The British Eighth Army, commanded by General Bernard L. Montgomery, stopped him at the battle of El Alamein in October 1942. The victory of El Alamein was followed by an Anglo-American invasion of northwestern Africa in November 1942. By May 1943, the Germans and Italians were defeated in North Africa.

After securing North Africa, the Allies, seeking complete control of the Mediterranean, invaded Sicily in July 1943 and quickly conquered the island. Mussolini's fellow Fascist leaders turned against him, and the king dismissed him as prime minister. In September, the new government surrendered to the Allies, and in the following month, Italy declared war on Germany.

Italian partisans, whose number would grow to three hundred thousand, resisted the Germans, who were determined to hold on to central and northern Italy. At the same time, the Allies fought their way up the peninsula. The fighting in Italy, vicious and costly, would last until the very end of the war. Captured by partisans, Mussolini was executed (April 28, 1945) and his dead body, hanging upside down, was publicly displayed.

On June 6, 1944, D-day, the Allies landed on the beaches of Normandy in France. They had assembled a massive force for the liberation of Europe: two million men and five thousand vessels, the greatest armada in history. Although they suspected an imminent landing, the Germans did not think that it would occur in Normandy, and they dismissed June 6 as a possible date because weather conditions were unfavorable. The success of D-day depended on securing the beaches and marching inland. On some beaches the soldiers struggled ashore in the face of intense enemy fire. At Omaha Beach, the Americans almost did not make it. Weighed down by heavy equipment, men drowned as they were tossed by high waves; others were killed or wounded by machine-gun fire before reaching the beach. Much of the heavy armor was lost. Those who stumbled ashore hugged the embankment and sheltered themselves behind whatever barrier they could find to escape the German guns firing from the cliffs. Traumatized by the devastation and death surrounding them, and often leaderless, the soldiers, many of them facing combat for the first time, seemed paralyzed. But amid the chaos, says the official army account,

> *At half-a-dozen or more points on the long stretch, they found the necessary drive to leave their cover and move out over the open beach flat toward the bluffs. . . . [T]he decisive factor was leadership. Wherever an advance was made, it depended on the presence of some few individuals, officers and noncommissioned officers, who inspired, encouraged, or bullied their men forward by making the first forward moves. . . . Colonel [George A. Taylor] summed up the situation in a terse phrase: "Two kinds of people are staying on this beach, the dead and those who are going to die—now let's get the hell out of here."*[22]

Having established beachheads, the Allies rushed more men and supplies into battle. Still believing that Normandy was only a feint, that the main attack would be directed at Pas de Calais, the Germans continued, in what was a fatal blunder, to hold back their crack reserves. Adding to the Germans' woes was the destruction of the French transportation system by Allied planes just prior

HIROSHIMA AFTER THE ATOMIC BOMB. The mass destruction of Hiroshima ushered in a new age. Nuclear weapons gave humanity the capacity to destroy civilization. (*Corbis-Bettmann.*)

to the invasion. German troops sent to fortify the defenses at Normandy met delay after delay. Aided by control of the air, the Allies overwhelmed the German defenders. By the end of July, they had built up their strength in France to a million and a half. In the middle of August, Paris rose up against the German occupiers and was soon liberated.

As winter approached, the situation looked hopeless for Germany. Brussels and Antwerp fell to the Allies; Allied bombers were striking German factories and mass-bombing German cities in terror raids that took a horrendous toll of life. The air war eroded Germany's industrial potential, devastated the transportation system, preventing supplies from reaching the fronts, and caused morale to plummet. Desperate, Hitler made one last gamble. In mid December 1944, he launched an offensive to split the Allied forces and regain the vital port of Antwerp. The Allies were taken by surprise in the battle of the Bulge, but a heroic defense by the Americans at Bastogne helped stop the German offensive.

While their allies were advancing in the west, the Russians were continuing their drive in the east, advancing into the Baltic states, Poland, and Hungary. By February 1945, they stood within one hundred miles of Berlin.

Also in February, the Allies in the west were battling the Germans in the Rhineland, and on March 7, 1945, American soldiers, seizing a bridge at Remagen that the Germans had failed to destroy, crossed the Rhine into the interior of Germany. By April 1945, British, American, and Russian troops were penetrating into Germany from east and west. From his underground bunker near the chancellery in Berlin, a physically exhausted and emotionally unhinged Hitler engaged in wild fantasies about new German victories. On April 30, 1945, with the Russians only blocks away, the fuehrer took his own life. In his last will and testament, Hitler again resorted to the vile lie: "It is not true that I or anybody else in Germany wanted war in 1939. It was wanted and provoked exclusively by those international statesmen who either were of Jewish origin or worked for Jewish interests."[23] On May 7, 1945, a demoralized and devastated Germany surrendered unconditionally.

After the victory at Midway in June 1942, American forces attacked strategic islands held by Japan. American troops had to battle their way up beaches and through jungles tenaciously defended by Japanese soldiers, who believed that death was preferable to the disgrace of surrender. In March 1945, twenty-one thousand Japanese perished on Iwo Jima; another hundred thousand died on Okinawa in April 1945 as they contested for every inch of the island. On August 6, 1945, the United States dropped an atomic bomb on Hiroshima, killing more than seventy-eight thousand people and demolishing 60 percent of the city. President Harry S Truman said that he ordered the atomic attack to avoid an American invasion of the Japanese homeland, which would have caused hundreds of thousands of casualties.

Truman's decision has aroused considerable debate. Some analysts say that dropping the bomb was unnecessary, that Japan, deprived of oil, rice, and other essentials by an American naval blockade and defenseless against unrelenting aerial bombardments, was close to surrender and had indicated as much. It has been suggested that with the Soviet Union about to enter the conflict against Japan, Truman wanted to end the war immediately, thus depriving the U.S.S.R. of an opportunity to extend its influence in East Asia. On August 8, Russia did enter the war against Japan, invading Manchuria. After a second atomic bomb was dropped on Nagasaki on August 9, the Japanese asked for peace.

The Legacy of World War II

World War II was the most destructive war in history. The total war waged by the combatants also enveloped civilians, who were victims of reprisals, genocide, slave labor, and aerial bombardment of cities. Estimates of the number of dead range as high as fifty million, including twenty-five million Russians, who sacrificed more than the other participants in both population and material resources. The war produced a vast migration of peoples unparalleled in modern European history. In accordance with an agreement made with Russia at a conference at Yalta in February 1945, Britain and America compelled some two million Russian prisoners of war, slave laborers, and those who had been recruited into the German army to return to the Soviet Union, many against their will. Ten percent of these deportees were executed and 70 percent sent to labor camps. The Soviet Union annexed the Baltic lands of Latvia, Lithuania, and Estonia, forcibly deporting many of the native inhabitants into central Russia. The bulk of East Prussia was taken over by Poland, and Russia annexed the northeastern portion. Millions of Germans fled the invading Russians, who, bent on revenge for the misery the Nazis had inflicted on their kin and country, committed numerous atrocities, including indiscriminate killing and mass rape, before Soviet authorities ended the mayhem. Millions more Germans were driven out of Poland, Czechoslovakia, Yugoslavia, Romania, and Hungary, places where their ancestors had lived for centuries, by vengeful eastern Europeans. Moreover, leaders in these countries, driven by nationalist aspirations, welcomed an opportunity to rid their nations of an ethnic minority, particularly since so many of these Germans had aided the Nazi occupiers. In 1945–46, some twelve million to thirteen million Germans were driven westward. Expelled from their homes, often with only a few minutes' warning, they had to leave almost everything behind. Herded into internment camps, they were brutalized by Polish and Czech guards who relished the opportunity to torment Germans. Tens of thousands died from malnutrition, disease, exposure, and mistreatment; thousands more committed suicide.

Material costs were staggering. Everywhere cities were in rubble; bridges, railway systems, waterways, and harbors destroyed; farmland laid waste; livestock killed; coal mines wrecked. Homeless and hungry people wandered the streets and roads. Europe faced the gigantic task of rebuilding. Yet Europe did recover from this material blight, and with astonishing speed.

The war produced a shift in power arrangements. The United States and the Soviet Union emerged as the two most powerful states in the world. The traditional Great Powers—Britain, France, and Germany—were now dwarfed by these superpowers. The United States had the atomic bomb and immense industrial might—its economy, previously suffering from the Great Depression, boomed during the war; the Soviet Union had the largest army in the world and was extending its dominion over eastern Europe. With Germany defeated, the principal incentive for Soviet-American cooperation evaporated.

After World War I, nationalist passions intensified. After World War II, western Europeans progressed toward unity. The Hitler years convinced many Europeans of the dangers inherent in extreme nationalism, and fear of the Soviet Union prodded them toward greater cooperation.

World War II accelerated the disintegration of Europe's overseas empires. The European states could hardly justify ruling over Africans and Asians after they had fought to liberate European lands from German imperialism. Nor could they ask their people, exhausted by the Hitler years and concentrating all their energies on reconstruction, to fight new wars against Africans and Asians pressing for independence. In the years just after the war, Great Britain surrendered India, France lost Lebanon and Syria, and the Dutch departed from Indonesia. In the 1950s and 1960s, virtually every colonial territory gained independence. In those instances where the colonial power resisted independence for the colony, the price was bloodshed.

The consciousness of Europe, already profoundly damaged by World War I, was again grievously wounded. Nazi racial theories showed that even in an age of sophisticated science the mind remains attracted to irrational beliefs and mythical imagery. Nazi atrocities proved that people will torture and kill with religious zeal and machinelike indifference. This regression to mythical thinking and savagery bears out Walter Lippmann's contention that "men have been barbarians much longer than they have been civilized. They are only precariously civilized, and within us there is the propensity, persistent as the force of gravity, to revert under stress and strain, or under temptation, to our first natures."[24] And the behavior of German intellectuals also contained a painful lesson, says German historian Karl Dietrich Bracher: "The intellectuals who supported the Nazis in one way or another all document that the mind can be temporarily seduced, that people can be bribed with careers and fame, that thinking people, especially, are tempted by an irrational cult of action and are peculiarly susceptible to 'one-dimensional' answers and promises of salvation."[25]

The Nazi assault on reason and freedom demonstrated anew the precariousness of Western civilization. This assault would forever cast doubt on the Enlightenment conception of human goodness, secular rationality, and the progress of civilization through advances in science and technology.

The Holocaust was heightened irrationality and organized evil on an unprecedented scale. Auschwitz, Treblinka, Sobibor, and the other death factories represent the triumph of human irrationality over reason—the surrender of the mind to a bizarre racial mythology that provided a metaphysical and pseudoscientific justification for mass murder. They also represent the ultimate perversion of reason. A calculating reason manufactured and organized lies and demented beliefs into a structured system with its own inner logic, and employed sophisticated technology and administrative techniques to destroy human beings spiritually and physically. Science and technology, venerated as the great achievement of the Western mind, had made mass extermination possible. The philosophes had not forseen the destructive power inherent in reason.

Both the Christian and the Enlightenment traditions had failed the West. Some intellectuals, shocked by the irrationality and horrors of the Hitler era, drifted into despair. To these thinkers, life was absurd, without meaning; human beings could neither comprehend nor control it. In 1945, only the naive could have faith in continuous progress or believe in the essential goodness of the individual. The future envisioned by the philosophes seemed more distant than ever. Nevertheless, this profound disillusionment was tempered by hope. Democracy had, in fact, prevailed over Nazi totalitarianism and terror. Moreover, fewer intellectuals were now attracted to antidemocratic thought. The Nazi dictatorship convinced many of them, even some who had wavered in previous decades, that freedom and human dignity were precious ideals and that liberal constitutional government, despite its imperfections, was the best means of preserving these ideals. Perhaps, then, democratic institutions and values would spread throughout the globe, and the newly established United Nations would promote world peace.

Notes

1. Pierre Renouvin, *World War II and Its Origins* (New York: Harper & Row, 1969), p. 167.
2. Z. A. B. Zeman, *Nazi Propaganda* (New York: Oxford University Press, 1973), p. 109.
3. *Documents on German Foreign Policy, 1918–1945,* vol. 6 (London: Her Majesty's Stationery Office, 1956), series D, no. 433.
4. Basil H. Liddell Hart, *History of the Second World War* (New York: Putnam, 1970), pp. 73–74.
5. Winston S. Churchill, *The Second World War: Their Finest Hour* (Boston: Houghton Mifflin, 1949), 2:225–226.
6. Quoted in William L. Shirer, *The Rise and Fall of the Third Reich* (New York: Simon & Schuster, 1960), p. 860.
7. *Hitler's Secret Conversations, 1941–1944,* with an introductory essay by H. R. Trevor Roper (New York: Farrar, Straus & Young, 1953), p. 508.
8. Quoted in Gordon Wright, *The Ordeal of Total War* (New York: Harper Torchbooks, 1968), p. 124.
9. Quoted in Norman Cohn, *Warrant for Genocide* (New York: Harper Torchbooks, 1967), p. 188.
10. Gerda Weissman Klein, *All but My Life* (New York: Hill & Wang, 1957), p. 89.
11. Judith Sternberg Newman, *In the Hell of Auschwitz* (New York: Exposition, 1964), p. 18.
12. *Nazi Conspiracy and Aggression* (Washington, D.C.: U.S. Government Printing Office, 1946), 6:787–789.
13. Quoted in Joseph Borkin, *The Crime and Punishment of I. G. Farben* (New York: Free Press, 1978), p. 143.
14. Gisella Perl, *I Was a Doctor in Auschwitz* (New York: International Universities Press, 1948), p. 80.
15. Konnilyn G. Feig, *Hitler's Death Camps* (New York: Holmes & Meier, 1979), p. 37.
16. Quoted in Erich Kahler, *The Tower and the Abyss* (New York: George Braziller, 1957), pp. 74–75.
17. Quoted in Steven T. Katz, "Technology and Genocide: Technology as a 'Form of Life,'" in *Echoes from the Holocaust,* ed. Alan Rosenberg and Gerald E. Meyers (Philadelphia: Temple University Press, 1988), p. 281.
18. Rainer C. Baum, "Holocaust: Moral Indifference as the Form of Modern Evil," in *Echoes from the Holocaust,* p. 83.
19. Robert Jay Lifton, *The Nazi Doctors* (New York: Basic Books, 1968), p. 5.
20. Richard Overy, *Why the Allies Won* (New York: Norton, 1995), p. 82.
21. Ibid., p. 96.
22. *Omaha Beachhead,* prepared by the War Department Historical Division (Washington, D.C., 1945), pp. 58, 71.
23. Excerpted in George H. Stein, ed., *Hitler* (Englewood Cliffs, N.J.: Prentice-Hall, 1968), p. 84.
24. Walter Lippmann, *The Public Philosophy* (Boston: Little, Brown, 1955), p. 86.
25. Karl Dietrich Bracher, *Turning Points in Modern Times,* trans. Thomas Dunlap (Cambridge, Mass.: Harvard University Press, 1995), p. 198.

Suggested Reading

Adams, R. J. Q., *British Politics and Foreign Policy in the Age of Appeasement, 1935–1939* (1993). The nature, purpose, and meaning of appeasement.

Ambrose, Stephen E., *D-Day* (1994). Based on oral histories from people who were there.

Bartow, Omer, *Hitler's Army* (1992). Excellent material on the indoctrination of the German soldier.

Bauer, Yehuda, *A History of the Holocaust* (1982). An authoritative study.

Baumont, Maurice, *The Origins of the Second*

World War (1978). A brief work by a distinguished French scholar.

Bell, P. M. H., *The Origins of the Second World War in Europe* (1986). An intelligent survey.

Browning, Christopher R., *The Path to Genocide* (1992). Essays on launching the Final Solution; particularly good insights into the attitudes of lower- and middle-echelon bureaucrats who participated in mass murder.

Calvocoressi, Peter, and Guy Wint, *Total War* (1972). A good account of World War II.

Campbell, John, ed., *The Experience of War* (1989). A team of specialists provides a topical approach to the war.

Cohn, Norman, *Warrant for Genocide* (1967). An astute analysis of the mythical components of modern anti-Semitism.

Dear, I. C. B., *The Oxford Companion to World War II* (1995). A superb reference work.

Des Pres, Terrence, *The Survivors* (1976). A sensitive analysis of life in the death camp.

Eubank, Keith, *The Origins of World War II* (1969). A brief introduction; a good bibliographical essay.

Gilbert, Martin, and Martin Gott, *The Appeasers* (1963). A study of British weakness in the face of Hitler's threats.

Hilberg, Raul, *The Destruction of the European Jews* (1967). A monumental study of the Holocaust.

Hildebrand, Klaus, *The Foreign Policy of the Third Reich* (1973). An assessment of Nazi foreign policy.

Klee, Ernst, Willi Dressen, and Volker Riess, eds., *The Good Old Days* (1988). Documents show perpetrators and bystanders not only as indifferent to the suffering of Jews but also as deriving pleasure from it.

Marks, Sally, *The Illusion of Peace* (1976). The failure to establish peace in the period 1918–1933.

Marrus, Michael R., *The Holocaust in History* (1987). An excellent summary of key issues and problems.

Michel, Henri, *The Shadow War* (1972). An analysis of the European resistance movement, 1939–1945.

———, *The Second World War,* 2 vols. (1975). Translation of an important study by a prominent French historian.

Overy, Richard, *Why the Allies Won* (1995). A brilliant analysis.

Remak, Joachim, *The Origins of the Second World War* (1976). A useful essay, followed by documents.

Weinberg, Gerhard L., *A World at Arms* (1994). A recent study based on extraordinary knowledge of the sources.

Wiesel, Elie, *Night* (1960). A moving personal record of the Holocaust.

Ziemke, Earl F., *Stalingrad to Berlin: The German Defeat in the East* (1968). Old but still useful.

Review Questions

1. What efforts promoted international reconciliation during the 1920s? How did these efforts foster only an illusion of peace?
2. What were Hitler's foreign policy aims?
3. Why did Britain and France practice a policy of appeasement?
4. Discuss the significance of each of the following: Italy's invasion of Ethiopia (1935), Germany's remilitarization of the Rhineland (1936), the Spanish Civil War (1936–1939), Germany's union with Austria (1938), the occupation of Prague (1939), and the Nazi-Soviet Pact (1939).
5. What factors made possible the quick fall of France?
6. What problems did the German army face in Russia?
7. Describe the New Order that the Nazis established in Europe.
8. In your opinion, what is the meaning of the Holocaust for Western civilization? For Jews? For Christians? For Germans?
9. Discuss the significance of each of the following battles: Midway (1942), Stalingrad (1942–43), El Alamein (1942), and D-day (1944).
10. What is the legacy of World War II?

Part Seven

The Contemporary World: The Global Age

Since 1945

1940

1950

1960

1970

1980

1990

2000

Politics and Society	Thought and Culture
Yalta agreement (1945) United Nations established (1945) Marshall Plan for recovery of Europe (1947) State of Israel established (1948) North Atlantic Treaty Organization (NATO) established (1949) Division of Germany (1949) Triumph of communism in China (1949)	Wiener, *Cybernetics* (1948) Orwell, *1984* (1949) de Beauvoir, *The Second Sex* (1949)
Korean War (1950–1953) European Economic Community (EEC) established (1957) Sputnik launched; space age begins (1957)	Camus, *The Rebel* (1951) Discovery of DNA by Crick and Watson (1951–53) Djilas, *The New Class* (1957) Chomsky, *Syntactic Structures* (1957) Snow, *The Two Cultures and the Scientific Revolution* (1959)
Berlin Wall built (1961) Cuban missile crisis (1962) Vietnam War (1963–1973)	Carson, *Silent Spring,* (1962) Pope John XXIII, *Pacem in Terris* (1963) McLuhan, *Understanding Media* (1964) Levi-Strauss, *The Savage Mind* (1966)
Détente in East-West relations (1970s)	Solzhenitsyn, *The Gulag Archipelago* (1974–1978) Wilson, *Sociobiology* (1975)
Gorbachev becomes leader of Soviet Union (1985) Explosion at Chernobyl nuclear power plant (1986) Peaceful overthrow of Communist governments in Eastern Europe (1989) Berlin Wall demolished (1989)	Creation of the Internet (1983) Gorbachev, *Perestroika* (1987)
Reunification of Germany (1990) Charter of Paris for a New Europe (1990) Official end of cold war (1990) Persian Gulf War (1991) Yeltsin elected Russian president (1991) Yugoslav federation breaks up and war begins (1991) Collapse of the Soviet Union (1991) Czechoslovakia splits into Czech Republic and Slovakia (1993) European Union ratifies the Maastricht Treaty (1993) Elections for new Russian constitution and parliament (1993) War breaks out between Russia and Chechnya (1994) Dayton Agreement ends civil war in former Yugoslavia (1995)	Huntington, *The Clash of Civilization and the Remaking of World Order* (1996) Vatican Commission for Religious Relations with the Jews, "We Remember: A Reflection of the 'Shoah' [the Hebrew name for Holocaust]" (1998)
Terrorist attacks on World Trade Center and the Pentagon (September 11, 2001)	Human genome sequence completed (2001) Discovery of skull of earliest known hominid ancestor that lived in central Africa between six and seven million years ago (2002)

Chapter 33

Europe After World War II: Recovery and Realignment, 1945–1989

The Berlin Wall, swiftly erected by the East German Communist regime in 1961, divided the city of Berlin for twenty-eight years. (Corbis-Bettmann.)

■ **The Cold War**
Origins
Cold War Mobilization
Arms Race and Space Race
The Vietnam War

■ **Building a New Europe**

■ **The Soviet Bloc**
Stalin's Last Years
After Stalin: Thaw, Détente, Perestroika, and Glasnost

■ **Decolonization**

At the end of World War II, Winston Churchill lamented: "What is Europe now? A rubble heap, a charnel house, a breeding ground for pestilence and hate."[1] Everywhere the survivors counted their dead. War casualties were relatively light in western Europe. Britain and the Commonwealth suffered 460,000 casualties; France, 570,000; and Italy, 450,000. War casualties were heavier in the east: 5 million people in Germany, 6 million in Poland (including 3 million Jews), 1 million in Yugoslavia, and more than 25 million in the Soviet Union. The material destruction had been unprecedentedly heavy in the battle zones, particularly in the east, where Hitler's and Stalin's armies had fought without mercy to people, animals, or the environment. Industry, transportation, and communication had come to a virtual standstill. Now members of families searched for each other; prisoners of war made their way home; Jews from extermination camps or from hiding places returned to open life; and displaced persons by the millions sought refuge.

Europe was politically cut in half; Soviet troops had overrun eastern Europe and penetrated into the heart of Germany. The Yalta agreement of February 1945, signed by Roosevelt, Churchill, and Stalin, turned the prevailing military balance of power into a political settlement. The Soviet Union imposed its grim dictatorship on the Western-oriented countries in eastern and southeastern Europe.

Yet there was hope. In the spring of 1945, the United States rallied the victorious Allies, including the Soviet Union, to a farsighted political initiative, establishing the United Nations. In its charter, reflecting basic aspects of Western thinking, the new organization pledged

> *To save succeeding generations from the scourge of war, which twice in our lifetime has brought untold sorrow to mankind, and to reaffirm faith in fundamental human rights, in the dignity and worth of the human person, in the equal rights of men and women and of nations large and small . . . to promote social progress and better standards of life in larger freedom.*[2]

Chronology 33.1 ❖ Europe, 1945–1989

1945	United Nations founded; eastern Europe occupied by Red Army
1947	Cold war starts; Truman Doctrine; Marshall Plan inaugurated
1948	Stalinization of eastern Europe
1949	NATO formed; first Soviet atomic bomb exploded
1953	Stalin dies
1956	Khrushchev's secret speech on Stalin's crimes; Polish October; Hungarian uprising is crushed
1957	European Economic Community established; sputnik launched—the space age begins
1961	Berlin Wall built, dividing the city of Berlin
1962	Cuban missile crisis
1963–1973	Vietnam War
1964	Khrushchev ousted; a new team of leaders, lead by Brezhnev, succeeds him
1968	Student uprising in France; Czechoslovakia's "socialism with a human face"
1969	American landing on the moon
1979	Soviet Union invades Afghanistan
1982	Brezhnev dies
1985	Gorbachev becomes U.S.S.R. leader
1988	Communist dictatorship in Poland ends; civilian government takes office
1989	Overthrow of Communist regimes in Eastern Europe

Three years later, the members of the United Nations underscored the charter's purpose in the Universal Declaration of Human Rights. The declaration announced that the "recognition of the inherent dignity and of the equal and inalienable rights of all members of the human family is the foundation of freedom, justice and peace in the world."[3] These ringing phrases, often restated in subsequent U.N. documents, extended to all humanity the ideals by which in recent times Western societies had professed to guide their political practice.

By promoting a global organization based on these ideals, the United States stepped forward as the heir and guardian of the Western tradition. A superpower, it was striving to shape the new world order of the global age that was emerging from the defeat of Germany and Japan. The material wealth of the United States, its industrial efficiency, and the ideals of democratic freedom embedded in its institutions helped rebuild democratic government and generate prosperity in western Europe. The United States also impressed people around the world, inspiring imitation even in hostile countries.

Thus, American influence speeded up the westernization of the world. Japan and Pacific Rim countries were drawn into the mainstream of Western business and culture. Decolonization created a multitude of new states in Asia and Africa, patterned, however painfully, after the Western model of statehood. For better or for worse, all the world's peoples were becoming linked in rapidly increasing political and economic interdependence, a process that was accelerated by immigrants from poor countries streaming toward the rich.

These changes took place over the next decades under the shadow of the cold war, the worldwide conflict between the two victors in World War II, the United States and the Soviet Union. Each offered its form of government and guiding ideals as a model for the entire world. While proudly presenting the communist vision as the guide to the future, Stalin remained afraid of Western—especially American—superiority. Trying to help his vast country catch up to Western achievements, he also gave high priority, after his country's losses in two world wars, to external security, expanding his control over the Soviet Union's neighboring states in eastern Europe.

The Cold War

Origins

The cold war (the American financier Bernard Baruch coined the phrase in 1947) stemmed from the divergent historical experiences and the incompatible political ambitions of the United States and the Soviet Union. As the European continent lay in a shambles, the proud outsiders to the west and east dominated the global scene. The challenge that started the cold war came before the end of World War II. As the Red Army moved through eastern Europe, the fate of the peoples of that region hung in the balance. Would Stalin treat them as a conquered people, knowing that left to their own devices they would return to their traditional anti-Russian orientation?

As the Red Army occupied Poland, Stalin installed a pro-Soviet regime. Other countries in eastern Europe suffered the same fate. Ever worried about the security of his country's western boundaries, Stalin incorporated most eastern European countries into a buffer zone for protection against Western attack. The local populations and their sympathizers in western Europe and the United States viewed the Soviet occupation of eastern Europe as a dire calamity. But short of starting another war, Western countries were powerless to intervene. For the next forty-five years, the two parts of the Continent would be known as Eastern Europe and Western Europe: two camps of opposing ideologies. To quote Churchill's famous words, "From Stettin in the Baltic to Trieste in the Adriatic, an iron curtain has descended across the Continent."[4] Now the Western democracies had to close ranks against the communist menace. American leaders were profoundly concerned: they had the responsibility of rallying Western Europe, and possibly the world, against universal communism.

Cold War Mobilization

Alarmed Americans viewed the Soviet occupation of eastern Europe as part of a communist expansion that threatened to extend to the rest of the world. In March 1947, fearing Soviet penetration in the eastern Mediterranean, President Truman proclaimed the Truman Doctrine: "It must be the policy of the United States to support free peoples who are resisting attempted subjugation by armed minorities or by outside pressures."[5] The Truman Doctrine was the centerpiece of the new policy of *containment,* of holding Soviet power within its then current boundaries. U.S. military and economic support soon went to Greece and Turkey. Thus, a sharp reversal took place in American foreign policy; prewar American isolation gave way to worldwide vigilance against any Soviet effort at expansion.

Later that year, the United States took a major step toward strengthening the West. In June 1947, Secretary of State George C. Marshall announced an impressive program of economic aid, formally called the European Recovery Program but widely known as the Marshall Plan. By 1952, when the plan terminated, it had supplied Europe with a total of $13.15 billion in aid—a modest pump-priming for the subsequent record upswing in U.S., Western European, and even global prosperity. Western Europe recovered, and the United States gained economically strong allies and trading partners.

In 1948 Stalin, seeking greater control in East Germany, cut off access to West Berlin. In response, the United States and Britain organized a massive airlift of supplies to the city, preserving the western outpost in East Germany.

The United States in 1950, with United Nations support, went to war for two years to defend South Korea against an invasion by Communist North Korea and its powerful Chinese ally. For a time thereafter, hysterical fear of communist infiltration into the U.S. government and among intellectuals gripped the American public. Apprehensions about national security were accompanied by a massive ideological mobilization of American opinion against the communist threat.

The United States strove to contain Soviet power by establishing in 1949 the North Atlantic Treaty Organization. NATO linked the armed forces of the United States, Canada, Portugal, Norway, Iceland, Denmark, Italy, Britain, France, and the Benelux countries (an acronym for Belgium, the Netherlands, and Luxembourg). Greece and Turkey soon joined; West Germany was included in 1956, and Spain in 1982. The American influence also provided the foundations for political stability under democratic constitutions, as well as for material prosperity based on free enterprise in a market economy. In response to NATO, the Soviet Union formed the Warsaw Pact, consisting of the armed forces of the Soviet Union and its European satellites.

THE SPACE PROGRAM. The first American astronauts from Project Mercury in 1961 were ready to venture into space. Front left to right: Walter M. Schirra, Donald K. Slayton, John H. Glenn (later elected a U.S. senator), and Malcolm S. Carpenter. Back left to right: Alan B. Shepard, Virgil T. Grissom, and Leroy G. Cooper. (*Corbis-Bettmann.*)

Arms Race and Space Race

Military alliances and forces were backed up by ever more powerful armaments. Sooner than expected, in 1949, the Soviet Union exploded its own atomic device. Thereafter, the arms race escalated to hydrogen bombs and intercontinental ballistic missiles (ICBMs). Threatened by Soviet ICBMs, the United States lost its territorial invulnerability, which its geography had implied until then. The arms race proved a source of profound intellectual and moral alarm. Said Albert Einstein, "The unleashed power of the atom has changed everything save our modes of thinking, and thus we drift toward unparalleled catastrophes."[6] Catastrophe was barely avoided in 1962. When the Soviet Union, under Nikita Khrushchev, prepared to place nuclear missiles in the newly established Communist regime in Cuba, trying to offset U.S. missiles in Turkey, President John F. Kennedy demanded their removal. For a terrifying moment, as the world held its breath, the cold war threatened to turn into a hot nuclear exchange. Fortunately, diplomacy prevailed. A secret deal was struck: Soviet missiles were taken out of Cuba in exchange for the removal of obsolete American missiles from Turkey; in addition the United States promised not to attack Cuba. The Cuban missile crisis ended peacefully.

The U.S.-Soviet rivalry extended into outer space. In 1957, the Soviet government sent the first *sputnik* (satellite) into orbit around the earth, shocking complacent Americans into a keen awareness of their vulnerability. For some years, the Soviet Union remained ahead in the

Map 33.1 **Western Europe After 1945** To counter the communist threat from the Soviet Union, Western European countries, formerly enemies, cooperated for their mutal protection. The majority of countries joined NATO for security against communist attack, and six countries with Europe formed the Common Market (the forerunner of the European Union) to facilitate trade and economic integration.

prestigious field of space exploration, sending the first astronaut, Yuri Gagarin, into orbit in 1961. The United States caught up in 1969 by landing a man on the moon.

All along, science and technology contributed to the escalation of the ominous arms race. Determined to gain the advantage in order to discourage an enemy attack, each side developed ever more sophisticated weapons and long-range delivery systems that, if used, could have destroyed

BOGGED DOWN IN VIETNAM. Americans defended South Vietnam against a threatened takeover by Communist North Vietnam. Between 1964 and 1973, U.S. involvement in the unsuccessful Vietnam War cost tens of thousands of Vietnamese and American lives, ruined South Vietnam, and polarized U.S. public opinion over the morality of the war. (*AP/Wide World Photos.*)

all civilized life. In addition, other countries were acquiring nuclear arms: England, France, China, Israel, India, and Pakistan. The increasing fear of nuclear war, however, prompted efforts to scale down the arms race.

In 1968, one hundred members of the United Nations signed the Nuclear Non-Proliferation Treaty, promising to abstain from developing nuclear arms; other U.N. members soon joined them. In 1969, the superpowers began the Strategic Arms Limitations Talks (SALT), agreeing in 1972 to a temporary limit on offensive strategic weapons.

The Vietnam War

From the start, the cold war led humanity along the brink of nuclear apocalypse. The conflict remained, however, a *cold* war, because the superpowers abstained from armed confrontation. The United States, however, did get drawn into a protracted hot war with Communist North Vietnam, which, under the leadership of Ho Chi Minh, waged a guerrilla war to take over South Vietnam. If the communists prevailed, apprehensive Americans argued, all the other countries in East and Southeast Asia would fall like dominoes to communist rule. Under President Lyndon B. Johnson, U.S. support of South Vietnam escalated into the undeclared and increasingly unpopular Vietnam War.

The U.S. government shipped to Vietnam nearly half a million soldiers, equipped with chemical weapons and advanced electronic gear. Yet victory eluded the American forces despite the fact that more explosives were dropped on tiny Vietnam than the Allies had dropped during World War II.

Opposition to the war among the American public increased, especially after North Vietnam launched a new wave of attacks early in 1968. Peace talks between the United States and North Vietnam started in April of that year. Despite con-

Map 33.2 Southeast Asia and the Vietnam War In order to prevent the spread of communism to South Vietnam, the United States supported the South Vietnamese government in its war against the communist north. The Ho Chi Minh Trail was the supply route used by North Vietnamese Communist guerrilla fighters infiltrating South Vietnam. When the supply route was bombed, the war spilled over into Cambodia and Laos.

tinuing negotiations, President Richard M. Nixon, elected in late 1968, extended the war by secretly bombing communist bases and supply routes in neighboring Cambodia and Laos. Protests in America mounted until, at last, in 1973, by agreement with North Vietnam, the United States withdrew its forces from the area. In 1975, the North Vietnamese swept aside the inept South Vietnamese army and unified the country under a communist dictatorship. Ho Chi Minh had triumphed against the mightiest nation in the world.

Yet defeat in Vietnam undermined neither America's domestic unity nor its position in the world. American patriotism peaked during the presidency of Ronald Reagan. Despite racial tensions and unresolved problems stemming from generational poverty, the United States continued to stand out as a model of democracy, industrial productivity, and the good life, much admired around the globe.

Building a New Europe

U.S. military and economic preeminence after the war prepared the way for the spread of American culture and lifestyle abroad. The languages of Western Europe became permeated with American words and phrases. Young people, especially, favored American popular music, American fashions, and the casual American way of life. Most importantly, however, the United States set a model for economic and political cooperation. As Winston Churchill declared in 1946, "We must build a kind of United States of Europe."[7] After two ruinous world wars, people at last began to feel that the price of violent conflict had become excessive; war no longer served any national interest. Furthermore, the extension of Soviet power made some form of Western European unity desirable, although procommunist sympathy lingered among workers and intellectuals.

Since the countries of Western Europe were not prepared to submerge their separate national traditions under a common government, they started with economic cooperation. Even that began rather modestly, with the creation of the European Coal and Steel Community (ECSC) in 1951. It drew together the chief Continental consumers and producers of coal and steel, the two materials essential for rebuilding Western Europe. The ECSC comprised France, West Germany, the three Benelux countries, and Italy.

Emboldened by the ECSC's success, the six countries in 1957 established the European Economic Community (EEC). Also known as the Common Market, it created a free market among the member states and sought to improve living conditions within them. In 1973, Great Britain, Ireland, and Denmark joined the original members in what now became the European Community (EC); in 1981, Greece, and in 1986, Spain and Portugal became members. The EC constituted the largest single trading bloc, conducting more than one-fifth of the world's commerce. In this framework of growing cooperation, the

Profile

Margaret Thatcher

Margaret Thatcher (b. 1925), a lower-middle-class grocer's daughter, was an anomaly in the upper-class, male-dominated Conservative party, of which she became the leader in 1975. For four years, while the Conservatives were out of office, she honed the convictions that made her famous. Socialism, she argued, was responsible for Britain's decline; only adhering to free-market principles, dismantling the welfare state, and weakening the trade unions, whose frequent strikes caused widespread misery, would restore prosperity. The Conservative victory in the 1979 election made Thatcher the first woman prime minister in British history. She put her principles into practice.

At first, financial and service industries did well, but unemployment doubled as the government stopped subsidizing inefficient indus-

Jacob Sutton/Getty Images.

major countries of Western Europe experienced a political and economic revival, which contributed to Western superiority in the cold war.

Impoverished by the war and vulnerable in its dependence on imported food and raw material, Great Britain lost its leading role in world politics after 1945; it peacefully dismantled its colonial possessions. The postwar Labour government, allied with powerful trade unions, provided Britons with a measure of economic security through social programs and extensive government control over important branches of the economy. Such controls, however, placed Britain at a disadvantage vis-à-vis its European competitors, prolonging the wartime austerity.

Under Winston Churchill, the Conservative prime minister elected in 1951, the British people started their postwar years of moderate prosperity; in 1959 Churchill's successor, Harold Macmillan, told his countrymen: "You never had it so good." Yet the voters were not so sure. For the next fifteen years they shifted twice from the Conservatives to the Labour party before electing Margaret Thatcher in 1978, the first woman prime minister. She dominated English politics for the next decade.

The "Iron Lady" fought inflation and rigorously encouraged individual initiative and private enterprise. During the Thatcher years, the British economy improved, and London regained its former luster as a financial center. But Britain was not without severe civic tensions—terrorism by the Irish Republican Army seeking to drive Britain from Northern Ireland, and resentment at the influx of Indians, Pakistanis, West Indians, and other people from former colonies. In addition, despite their EC membership, the English clung to their traditional insular detachment from their neighbors on the Continent.

Across the English Channel, France, liberated from German occupation, was reorganized democratically under the Fourth Republic and soon achieved respectable economic growth, despite frequent changes of government (twenty-six in tries and factories closed. During three years of "Thatcherism," support for her Conservative government eroded. Then came the Argentinian attack on the Falkland Islands, which stirred British patriotism. Military victory under Thatcher's leadership led to her reelection in 1983.

The prime minister aroused strong feelings. She was admired by some and detested by others. Her personal strength was widely recognized; she was known as the "Iron Lady." During her second term in office, she fought successfully for tough laws to limit trade union power; she also dismantled state-owned enterprises and sold off publicly owned housing. Under her leadership, the country's defense was modernized and health care and education were privatized. She also provided vigorous leadership in foreign affairs and forged a particularly close relationship with President Reagan. Although her inflexibility and self-righteousness made her enemies, the opposition Labour party, lacking strong leadership, could not prevail against her. Her third election victory, in 1987, made her the longest-serving British prime minister in the twentieth century.

Thatcher's opposition to closer integration of Britain in the European Community and a domestic furor over the attempt to replace real estate taxes with an outrageously high local tax led to outright rebellion within her government. In 1990, her leadership was challenged, and she resigned as prime minister in order to preserve party unity.

She remains active in politics, and her membership in the House of Lords as Baroness Thatcher still gives her public prominence.

twelve years). The short-lived governments assisted in the organization of Western European defense that laid the groundwork for the European Economic Community, and they promoted political reconciliation with Germany.

A major problem that France faced in these years was decolonization. In Indochina, the colonial liberation movement inflicted a resounding defeat on the French army in 1954. In Algeria, French settlers and soldiers were determined to thwart independence. The long and bloody Algerian conflict had serious repercussions.

In 1958, the agitation to keep Algeria under French control, supported by certain army circles, reached a dangerous point. To prevent a right-wing coup aided by the army, General Charles de Gaulle stepped forward. He had been the leader of the Free French forces in World War II and president for a brief period after the war. He now restored order and established the Fifth Republic, with a strong executive authority. Aspiring to give France its rightful place in the world, he extended the economic modernization of the early 1950s achieved under the Fourth Republic. He also encouraged the development of science and technology and cemented ties with the new African states that were formerly under French rule. To strengthen patriotic devotion to the nation, he insisted that France have its own nuclear force, and he pulled his country out of NATO. To rescue France from a protracted and divisive conflict, he consented to Algerian independence in 1962 over the protest of the army.

In 1968, domestic opposition erupted dramatically when students and workers, supported by the Communist party, staged demonstrations in Paris, demanding educational reform and social justice. Attempts by the police to break up the demonstrations provoked violent street fights. Alarmed, de Gaulle quickly called a general election, in which a frightened electorate gave him a landslide victory. Unable to revise the constitution in his favor, however, he resigned in 1969.

France produced no leader equal in stature to

de Gaulle; his successors could not rally the French people as he had done. The Fifth Republic continued with a government based on a centrist coalition subject to endless friction and attacked by extremists—Communists on the left promoted cooperation with Moscow, while nationalists on the right stirred up hatred toward North African immigrants. In 1981, however, a sudden shift occurred on the left of the political spectrum. The Communists joined forces with the Socialist party and helped to elect its leader, François Mitterrand as president. Now French politics turned socialist; industries and banks were nationalized and government jobs increased. But the socialist remedies applied by Mitterrand failed, forcing the government into a period of austerity by the mid 1980s.

Despite the economic and political uncertainties of the times, Mitterrand maintained the Gaullist tradition. His country was the third largest nuclear power and the fourth largest economy in the world. All along, France was a leading architect of European unity without surrendering its own character.

Italy, half the size of France yet larger in population by a few million, became a democratic republic in 1946. Its government, however, was weak and unstable. The average life span of an Italian cabinet was less than a year. The country offered a sharp contrast between north and south. The north was efficient and prosperous; the south was backward and infiltrated by the Mafia. Centered in Sicily, the Mafia was a source of political corruption and even occasional terror against the government.

The Italian economy proved to be a surprising success despite the fact that the government was perennially in debt and unemployment ran high, especially in the south. Even more than France, Italy was flooded by legal and illegal immigrants from Asia and Africa, straining the country's resources.

In 1945, its cities in ruins, Germany had been defeated, occupied, and branded as a moral outcast. Divided among the four occupying powers—the United States, Britain, France, and the Soviet Union—the German nation was politically extinct. Extensive eastern lands were lost to Poland and the Soviet Union; some territory was returned to France. By 1949, two new and chastened Germanys had emerged. West Germany (the Federal Republic of Germany), formed from the three western zones of occupation, faced hostile, Soviet-dominated East Germany (the German Democratic Republic). The former capital city of Berlin, inside East Germany, was similarly divided into western and eastern zones of occupation. The partition of Germany signified the destruction of Germany's traditional identity and ambition. The national trauma reached a climax in August 1961, when the East German government suddenly threw up a wall between East and West Berlin and tightly sealed off East from West Germany. West Germany thus became the crucial frontier of the cold war, radiating Western superiority into the Soviet bloc.

The cold war proved a boon to the West Germans; it contributed to their integration into the emerging new Europe and to the reduction of old hatreds. Located next door to the Red Army, the West Germans, along with the Western armed forces stationed on their soil, were in a strategic position for defending Western Europe. Moreover, German industrial expertise was indispensable for rebuilding the Western European economy. On this basis, West Germany (far larger than its Communist counterpart to the east and the most populous of all Western European countries) began to build a new political identity.

The architect of the new West Germany was Konrad Adenauer, its chancellor from 1949 to 1963. He sought to restore respect for Germany in cooperation with the leading states of Western Europe and the United States. As a patriot, he reestablished a cautious continuity with the German past; he also shouldered responsibility for the crimes of the Nazi regime and assumed the payment of indemnifications and pensions to the Jewish victims and survivors of the Nazi era, as well as the payment of reparations to the state of Israel, which had been established in 1948. Under Adenauer's guidance, the West Germans also threw themselves into rebuilding their economy; the whole world soon admired the German "economic miracle." As a result, democracy put down roots among the West German people, strengthening their solidarity with their former European enemies. West Germany was admitted to NATO in 1957 and, together with East Germany, to the United Nations in 1972; it joined France in promoting the European Community.

After the Adenauer era, German voters shifted

from center-right to center-left. Chancellor Willy Brandt (1969–1974) took the initiative for an "opening toward the East," contributing to a temporary relaxation of tensions between the superpowers. During these years, West Germany's booming economy and a generous admission policy attracted ambitious "guest workers," many from Turkey. Political extremists did not endanger political stability, except for one party, the Greens, which called attention to the destruction of the environment, industrial pollution, and the dangers of nuclear power. Loosely organized, the Greens expressed a romantic alienation from contemporary society and politics. In 1982, the voters turned conservative, electing the leader of the Christian Democratic Union, Helmut Kohl, chancellor. Kohl continued Adenauer's policy of integrating West Germany, now the most prominent country in Western Europe, into the cold war alliance against Soviet communism.

The Soviet Bloc

For Soviet Russia, World War II was another cruel landmark in the succession of wars, revolutions, and crises afflicting the country since 1914. Nothing basically changed after its end. The vast country's weaknesses persisted, even though it had extended its boundaries far to the west. The liberation from terror and dictatorship, which many soldiers had hoped for as a reward for their heroism, never occurred. The epic struggle against the Nazi invaders had further hardened Stalin. Sixty-six years old in 1945, he displayed in his last years an unrelenting ruthlessness and a suspiciousness that turned into paranoia.

Stalin found no reason to relax control. Wherever he looked, he saw cause for concern. The government, the party, communist ideology, the economy—all were in disarray. Thus, the Soviet Union slid from war into the uneasy peace of the cold war, staggering through the hardships and hunger of the war's aftermath, mourning its dead soldiers, and desperately short of men. A shrill, dogmatic superpatriotism became mandatory for all Soviet citizens. It extolled Russia's achievements, past and present, over those of the West. Even scientists had to submit, sometimes at a fearful cost to research.

Stalin's Last Years

In his last years, Stalin withdrew into virtual isolation, surrounded by a few fawning and fearful subordinates. When on March 5, 1953, the failing dictator died of a stroke, his assistants sighed with relief. Many other people wept. To them, Stalin was the godlike leader and savior of the nation. The human costs of his regime were immense, but of his achievements in raising Soviet power there can be no doubt. By 1949, Soviet Russia possessed the atomic bomb. By 1953, at the same time as the United States, it had the hydrogen bomb as well.

Stalin also bequeathed to his successors a population tamed and even cowed, yet more literate and adapted to urban-industrial life. But one traditional source of insecurity remained: the humiliating comparison with the superior West. Stalin's successors faced a hard task. How could they preserve the Soviet Union's superpower status while reducing the inhumanity of Stalinism?

In addition they had to cope with the consequences of Soviet domination of Eastern Europe. By the end of 1948 virtually all the countries in eastern and southeastern Europe, as well as eastern Germany, had emerged as "people's democracies." The Soviet Union claimed the right to intervene at will in the internal affairs of its satellites. Thus, the pall of Stalinism hung over war-torn and impoverished Eastern Europe. The puppet regimes leveled the formerly privileged classes, curtailing or abolishing private enterprise. The economy was socialized and rigid, and hasty plans were implemented for industrialization and the collectivization of agriculture. Religion and the churches were repressed, and political liberty and free speech stamped out. Even the "proletarian masses" derived few benefits from the artificial revolution engineered from Moscow because Stalin drained the countries under his control of their resources for the sake of rebuilding the Soviet Union. Contact with Western Europe or the United States was banned. Each satellite country existed in isolation, surrounded by borders fortified with barbed wire and watchtowers set along mined corridors. Fear reached deep into every house and into individual souls as little Stalins copied their mentor's style in East Berlin, Warsaw, Prague, Budapest, and Sofia.

The one exception was Yugoslavia, where Marshal Tito set up his anti-Stalinist communist regime with commercial ties to Western Europe.

Communist parties elsewhere were guided by Moscow; Soviet troops remained strategically stationed in the area. The Warsaw Treaty Organization (the Warsaw Pact), which was a military instrument for preserving the ideological and political unity of the bloc and for counterbalancing NATO, coordinated the armies of the satellite countries with the Red Army.

After Stalin: Thaw, Détente, Perestroika, and Glasnost

After Stalin's death, a team headed by Nikita Khrushchev (1954–1964) assumed leadership. Khrushchev was the driving force behind the "thaw" that emptied the forced-labor camps and allowed most of the nationalities forcibly resettled during the war to return to their native regions. Privileged Russians were allowed to catch a glimpse of the West. Khrushchev himself visited the United States, observing that "We must study the capitalist economy attentively . . . study the best that the capitalist countries' science and technology have to offer . . . in the interests of socialism."[8] In a secret speech (soon known around the world) at the Twentieth Party Congress in February 1956, Khrushchev even dared to attack Stalin himself. His audience gasped with horror as he recited the facts: "Of the 139 members and candidates of the party's Central Committee who were elected at the 17th Congress (1934), 98 persons, i.e., 70%, were arrested and shot."[9] Without criticizing the Soviet system, Khrushchev acknowledged and rejected the excesses of Stalinism.

Khrushchev's revelations created a profound stir and prompted defection from Communist ranks everywhere. Among the Soviet satellite countries, the first rumbles of protest were heard in June 1956, in Poland. The crisis came to a head in October: would Poland revolt, inviting invasion by the Red Army, or would Khrushchev ease Soviet control? The Soviet boss yielded in return for a Polish pledge of continued loyalty to the Soviet Union. Thereafter, Poland breathed more freely, clinging to its Catholic faith as a cornerstone of its national identity.

Although the "Polish October" ended peacefully, events moved to a brutal showdown in Hungary. On October 20, 1956, an uprising in Budapest led to an anti-Soviet outburst, forcing Soviet troops to withdraw from the country. Next, a moderate Communist government, eager to capture popular sentiment, called for Western-style political democracy and Hungary's withdrawal from the Warsaw Pact. Thoroughly alarmed, and with the backing of Mao and even Tito, the Soviet leaders struck back. On November 4, 1956, Soviet troops reentered Hungary and brutally crushed all opposition.

Reaffirming Soviet superiority in 1959, Khrushchev boasted to alarmed Americans: "We will bury you." In 1962, he claimed that "Soviet society has become the most highly educated society in the world," predicting that by 1970 the Soviet Union would "surpass the strongest and richest capitalist country, the USA, in per capita production."[10] His extravagant promises, however, antagonized wide sections of state and party administration. In October 1964, while he was on vacation, his comrades in the politburo unceremoniously ousted him for "ill health" or, as they later added, his "hare-brained schemes." He was retired and allowed to live out his years in peace.

Khrushchev was succeeded by a group of leaders acting in common. Among these men, Leonid Brezhnev (1964–1982) gradually rose to the fore. Under his leadership, the government of the U.S.S.R. turned from a personal dictatorship into an oligarchy: the collective rule of a privileged minority. Brezhnev's style stressed reasoned agreement rather than command. Soviet officials breathed more easily, and Soviet society in turn grew less authoritarian.

The post-Stalin permissiveness was never without risks, as was shown in Czechoslovakia in 1968. A new group of Communists, led by Alexander Dubček, sought to liberalize their regime. Their goal was a "humanist democratic socialism," or "socialism with a human face"—a Communist party supported by public goodwill rather than by the secret police.

On August 21, East German, Polish, Hungarian, and Soviet troops, under the provisions of the Warsaw Pact, carried out a swift and well-prepared occupation of Czechoslovakia but failed to break the rebellious will of its Communists. While Soviet tanks rumbled through Prague, an extraordinary Czechoslovak party congress se-

SOVIET TANKS IN AFGHANISTAN. The inability of Soviet forces to build popular support or to subdue Afghan tribesmen, who waged relentless guerrilla warfare, forced the Soviet Union to withdraw in 1989. Afghanistan became a cold war battleground as the United States provided arms to Afghan freedom fighters. (*Corbis.*)

cretly met in choked fury. Never had the Soviet leaders encountered such resistance by party members. Nonetheless, the revolt ended in failure. The party was purged; all reforms were canceled; and the country was reduced to abject hopelessness. But the Soviet Union paid a high price. A cry of moral outrage resounded around the world; protests were heard even in Moscow.

In the 1970s, international relations entered a limited phase of peaceful cooperation, called *détente*. The Soviet Union had achieved a rough parity in nuclear weapons with the United States; henceforth it was protected by deterrence just like the United States. For a brief period, the country enjoyed some civic contentment; it inspired Brezhnev's boast that "capitalism is a society without a future."[11] His confidence led in 1979 to the Soviet invasion of Afghanistan, in support of a faltering pro-Soviet regime installed in Kabul, the Afghan capital, following a 1978 coup. Muslim tribal communities, however, opposed Marxist policies, and a countrywide revolt gathered strength. The government's survival became increasingly dependent on Soviet military equipment and advisers.

The massive Soviet invasion failed to establish control outside the major cities. The Soviet army was under constant guerrilla attack by Afghan freedom fighters, the *mujahidin,* drawn from independent tribes normally at war with each other; hatred of the Soviet invaders temporarily united them. The inability of the Soviet forces to build upon popular support, or to train the Afghan army into an effective defense against rebel forces, led to eight years of costly and inconclusive warfare. Afghanistan became a cold war battleground as the mujahidin received arms and assistance from the United States, Saudi Ara-

German territory to Poland
Acquired by Soviet Union, 1939–1945
Soviet satellites
Communist, nonsatellite nation
"Iron Curtain" after 1950
0 200 400 Km.
0 200 400 Mi.
ATLANTIC OCEAN
North Sea
Baltic Sea
Black Sea
Caspian Sea
Adriatic Sea
Mediterranean Sea
G. of Finland
ICELAND
IRELAND
Dublin
GREAT BRITAIN
London
NORWAY
Oslo
SWEDEN
Stockholm
FINLAND
Helsinki
Leningrad
ESTONIA
LATVIA
LITHUANIA
BELORUSSIA
UKRAINE
Kiev
Dnieper R.
SOVIET UNION
Moscow
Volga R.
CRIMEA
BESSARABIA
DENMARK
Copenhagen
NETHERLANDS
Amsterdam
BELGIUM
Brussels
LUX.
FRANCE
Paris
Seine R.
Rhône R.
WEST GERMANY
Bonn
Hamburg
Elbe R.
Rhine R.
Munich
EAST GERMANY
Berlin
POLAND
Warsaw
Gdansk (Danzig)
Vistula R.
CZECHOSLOVAKIA
Prague
AUSTRIA
Vienna
SWITZERLAND
HUNGARY
Budapest
ROMANIA
Bucharest
Danube R.
BULGARIA
Sofia
YUGOSLAVIA
Belgrade
ALBANIA
Tirane
GREECE
Athens
TURKEY
Ankara
Istanbul
SYRIA
IRAQ
IRAN
ITALY
Rome
Po R.
Corsica
Sardinia
Sicily
SPAIN
Madrid
Ebro R.
PORTUGAL
Lisbon

bia, Pakistan, and other countries, and maintained a strong resistance movement against Soviet forces. Finally a U.N.-brokered agreement resulted in the withdrawal of Soviet forces by 1989.

The domestic backlash in the Soviet Union against the unpopular war, in which fifteen thousand Soviet soldiers died (about one million Afghans perished), was considerable. In addition, the Reagan administration in the United States had used the war as a pretext to begin a massive arms buildup; and especially after the poor showing of Soviet troops in Afghanistan, the Soviets felt obliged to match the huge U.S. defense expenditures. The attempt to do so strained the declining Soviet economy to the breaking point and was one of the factors leading up to the collapse of the Soviet Union.

The Brezhnev years permitted a relaxation of the authoritarian discipline. The country could be opened, cautiously, to the outside world. Young people, for instance, were allowed access to Western styles of music and dress. More issues of state policy were opened to public debate, and more latitude was granted to artistic expression. Interest in religion revived. Prominent dissidents were punished, but less brutally than in the past. Andrei Sakharov, the distinguished scientist who had helped develop the Soviet hydrogen bomb and subsequently became a vigorous advocate of human rights, was exiled from Moscow and placed under house arrest. Other outspoken critics, including the writer Alexandr Solzhenitsyn, were expelled from the country or allowed to emigrate. Less prominent dissidents were confined to mental hospitals, following a practice begun under the tsars.

The brief era of public satisfaction induced widespread complacency and corruption. Comparisons with the West also caused a loss of patriotic dedication. Voices were heard on the street protesting that Marxism-Leninism "tastes like stale bread." Not surprisingly, economic productivity declined, and opposition stirred among the Soviet satellite states. The Communist claim to superiority faded; the Soviet Union was falling behind in the cold war. One by one, the satellite governments in Eastern Europe resumed ties with capitalist states. How could the Soviet government retain control over its satellites while allowing them greater independence?

Brezhnev's successors were old men who survived in office for only a short time. In 1985, at last a younger, energetic Communist, Mikhail Sergeyevich Gorbachev, assumed control, admitting privately that "everything is rotten through and through."

It was the fate of Mikhail Gorbachev to preside over his country's collapse. Self-confident and articulate, he strove to integrate his country into the main currents of modern life through a dramatic retreat from communist theory and practice.

Gorbachev's domestic reforms proceeded under the barrage of two slogans: *perestroika* (restructuring) and *glasnost* (openness). The reforms aimed at "a genuine revolutionary transformation" of Soviet life and institutions.[12] The goals that Lenin and Stalin had tried to reach through totalitarian controls were now to be achieved by voluntary civic cooperation. Perestroika promised to reorganize the state and society and to revive individual creativity. Liberated at last, Soviet citizens were to take the initiative in government at the grassroots level and participate in national affairs. Thus, with the help of the most advanced technology, they could satisfy their yearning for a higher standard of living. Glasnost, in turn, was to take the Stalinist lid off public opinion and permit at long last an uninhibited discussion of the country's problems. It would rid public thinking of the official propoganda lies and promote open debate. As Gorbachev observed in 1986, "Communists always need the truth."[13] Both perestroika and glasnost sought to transform the Soviet system into a true democracy under the Communist party. Meanwhile, contacts with the outside world increased. Western ideals, culture, and respect for human rights penetrated Soviet minds as never before. Summed up by Gorbachev as "the most thoroughgoing upheaval in our country's history,"[14] these changes entailed unforseen perils: the breakup of

◀ *Map 33.3* Eastern Europe After 1945 During and after World War II the Soviet Union extended its rule halfway across Europe. Repressive communist governments in Eastern Europe were controlled by Moscow. Yugoslavia, under President Tito, defied Moscow and became a communist state with links to Western Europe and the United States.

the Soviet bloc in Eastern Europe and the collapse of the Soviet Union.

Decolonization

World War II, in which many colonial soldiers loyally fought for their masters, stirred up demands among non-Western peoples for an end to Western colonial rule and for political independence. After all, freedom and self-determination were prominent Allied war slogans. Exhausted by the war, European colonial powers had little strength left for colonial rule, and the mighty groundswell for decolonization, supported by the superpowers and the ideals of the United Nations, eventually abolished all overseas empires and propelled their former subjects into independent statehood.

Decolonization quickly became a major issue in the cold war as the two superpowers competed with each other for control over the emerging states of Africa and Asia. Both sides, in their ignorance of local cultures, found themselves entangled in the intricacies of local power struggles, especially in tropical Africa, which was frequently involved in protracted civil wars bordering on anarchy.

The decolonization of Asia began in 1946 when the United States granted independence to the Philippines. In 1947, India and Pakistan attained sovereign statehood; in 1948, independent Burma and Ceylon (later renamed Sri Lanka) emerged. In 1949, Holland was forced to grant independence to Indonesia. More ominously in that year, China turned communist, encouraging anticolonialism in Asia and Africa. After granting independence to Laos in 1954, the French were driven from Cambodia and Vietnam the same year, leaving the Americans to defend South Vietnam against the communist revolutionaries of North Vietnam until 1973.

After the mid 1950s, the European rulers started the process of decolonizing the highly diverse continent of Africa. In 1956, British troops were withdrawn from the Suez Canal, and in the following year the British Gold Coast, renamed Ghana, achieved independence—the first sub-Saharan country to do so. Its leader, Kwame Nkrumah (1909–1972), had already indicated his guiding policy, which also inspired other African leaders: "Capitalism is too complicated a system for a newly independent nation. Hence the need for a socialistic society" and possibly for "emergency measures of a totalitarian kind."[15] In 1961, Nkrumah toured the Soviet bloc; he was ousted in 1964. Meanwhile France, responding to an up-

Jomo Kenyatta (c. 1894–1978) Wearing a leopard skin over his Western-style suit, Kenyatta brandishes a fly whisk, a symbol of authority. Imprisoned by the British for his opposition to colonial rule, he became the leader of independent Kenya in 1963. Under his slogan, *Harambee* (pulling together), he built a strong, stable government and a capitalist-oriented economy. (*Anthony Howard/Camera Press/ Retna.*)

Map 33.4 Former European Colonies ▶
Agitation for independence started after World War I. It gained momentum after World War II, and reached a crescendo in the 1960s, resulting in the birth of dozens of new countries. The colonial powers failed to groom their successors for governmental responsibilities, and in some countries independence led to protracted conflicts, extending to the present day.

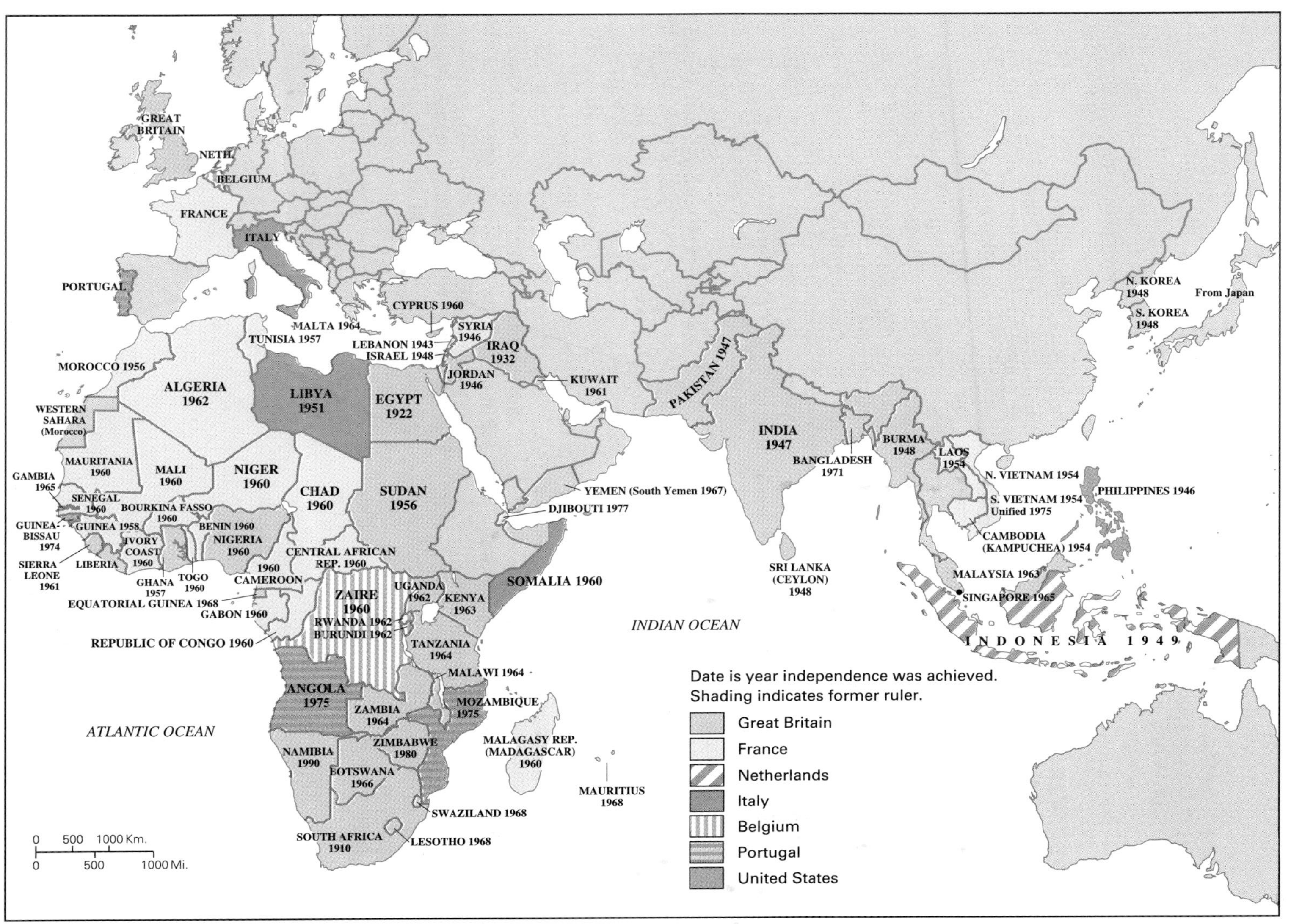

GREAT BRITAIN
NETH.
BELGIUM
FRANCE
ITALY
PORTUGAL
CYPRUS 1960
MALTA 1964
TUNISIA 1957
SYRIA 1946
LEBANON 1943
ISRAEL 1948
IRAQ 1932
JORDAN 1946
KUWAIT 1961
MOROCCO 1956
ALGERIA 1962
LIBYA 1951
EGYPT 1922
WESTERN SAHARA (Morocco)
MAURITANIA 1960
MALI 1960
NIGER 1960
CHAD 1960
SUDAN 1956
GAMBIA 1965
SENEGAL 1960
BOURKINA FASSO 1960
GUINEA-BISSAU 1974
GUINEA 1958
BENIN 1960
IVORY COAST 1960
NIGERIA 1960
CENTRAL AFRICAN REP. 1960
SIERRA LEONE 1961
LIBERIA
GHANA 1957
TOGO 1960
1960 CAMEROON
EQUATORIAL GUINEA 1968
GABON 1960
REPUBLIC OF CONGO 1960
ZAIRE 1960
UGANDA 1962
KENYA 1963
RWANDA 1962
BURUNDI 1962
SOMALIA 1960
TANZANIA 1964
MALAWI 1964
ANGOLA 1975
ZAMBIA 1964
MOZAMBIQUE 1975
ZIMBABWE 1980
NAMIBIA 1990
BOTSWANA 1966
MALAGASY REP. (MADAGASCAR) 1960
MAURITIUS 1968
SWAZILAND 1968
SOUTH AFRICA 1910
LESOTHO 1968
ATLANTIC OCEAN
YEMEN (South Yemen 1967)
DJIBOUTI 1977
PAKISTAN 1947
INDIA 1947
BANGLADESH 1971
SRI LANKA (CEYLON) 1948
INDIAN OCEAN
BURMA 1948
LAOS 1954
N. VIETNAM 1954
S. VIETNAM 1954
Unified 1975
CAMBODIA (KAMPUCHEA) 1954
PHILIPPINES 1946
MALAYSIA 1963
SINGAPORE 1965
INDONESIA 1949
N. KOREA 1948
S. KOREA 1948
From Japan
Date is year independence was achieved.
Shading indicates former ruler.
Great Britain
France
Netherlands
Italy
Belgium
Portugal
United States
0 500 1000 Km.
0 500 1000 Mi.

swelling of nationalist fervor, had freed all its colonies by 1960, except for Algeria, which did not gain independence until 1962, after a cruel war, and Djibouti, which opted for continued union with France and did not become independent until 1977.

Pushed by the trend of the times, the Belgians in 1960 pulled out of the Congo, leaving behind some thirty Congolese university graduates to fill four thousand administrative posts and precipitating a civil war in the unprepared country. The Congo's first leader, Patrice Lumumba, was assassinated, and after a period of continuing turmoil the army seized power in 1965 under General Joseph Mobutu (1930–1997). As President Mobutu Sese Seko, he renamed his country Zaire and stayed in power for thirty-two years, treating the country with its immense mineral wealth as his private fiefdom. He amassed one of the world's largest fortunes and purchased luxurious mansions abroad while poverty raged among his people. During the cold war, he proved to be a firm ally of Western powers, combating procommunist regimes in Africa. In return, he received foreign aid from Western countries, which closed their eyes to the human rights abuses and corruption in his regime.

Decolonization swept through African lands ruled by Britain. The former colonial peoples had not been prepared by education or by administrative experience to take over responsibility. In 1951, the British foreign secretary, Herbert Morison, had characterized independence for African countries as "giving a child of ten a latch-key, a bank account and a shotgun."[16] In 1961, Tanganyika became independent, joining with Zanzibar to form Tanzania in 1964 under the leadership of Julius Nyerere (1921–1999). He presided until the 1980s over a socialist development program, assisted by Communist China. In 1962, Uganda was decolonized; it was led by Milton Obote as a socialist one-party state, until he was overthrown in 1971 by Idi Amin, a barbarous dictator who lasted in power until 1980. Nigeria, an ethnically divided state, attained independence in 1960 but was soon caught in a civil war costing a million lives. In that war, Britain, Italy, and the Soviet Union, in an unusual alignment, competitively assisted the Nigerian government, while France aided the separatists. In 1964, having gained independence the previous year, Kenya turned into a republic under Jomo Kenyatta, who ruled as an authoritarian president in a one-party state leaning toward the West. The following year, a white supremacist party defied Britain by declaring unilateral independence in the British colony of Rhodesia. It finally yielded to African rule in 1980, and Rhodesia became the new state of Zimbabwe.

Portugal, the last European state to decolonize, held on to its African colonies as long as possible. Finally, in 1975, it abandoned Angola in the midst of a bloody civil war between the American-supported government and a liberation movement supported by the Soviet Union with Cuban assistance. Only the Republic of South Africa, independent since 1910, remained under repressive white minority rule until 1994.

Decolonization often sparked protracted and brutal struggles of building modern states among peoples who were utterly unprepared for this effort and who were also divided by their past animosities, as well as by the competition between the superpowers. Nor did peoples with different traditions adjust to the institutions and procedures of Western democracy. Even today in many parts of Africa, one-party dictatorships remain in power, often dressed up as democracies.

❖ ❖ ❖

Notes

1. Quoted in Walter Laqueur, *Europe Since Hitler* (Baltimore: Penguin Books, 1970), p. 118.
2. "The Charter of the United Nations," *Yearbook of the United Nations* (Dordrecht, Netherlands: Martin Nijhoff, 1989), 39:1378.
3. "Universal Declaration of Human Rights," *Yearbook of the United Nations, 1948–49* (New York: Columbia University Press, 1950), p. 535.

4. Winston S. Churchill, "Sinews of Peace; Address, March 5, 1946," *Vital Speeches of the Day*, March 15, 1946, p. 3.
5. "The Truman Doctrine," in *Major Problems in American Foreign Policy: Documents and Essays,* ed. Thomas G. Paterson (Lexington, Mass.: Heath, 1978), 2:290.
6. Ralph E. Lapp, "The Einstein Letter That Started It All," *New York Times Magazine*, August 2, 1964, p. 64.
7. Quoted in Roger Morgan, *West European Politics Since 1945* (London: Batsford, 1972), p. 91.
8. *Current Soviet Policies II. The Documentary Record of the 20th Party Congress and Its Aftermath* (New York: Praeger, 1957), p. 141.
9. Nikita S. Khrushchev in *The Crimes of the Stalin Era: Special Report to the 20th Congress of the Communist Party of the Soviet Union,* annotated by Boris I. Nicolaevsky (New York: The New Leader, 1956), p. 20.
10. *Current Soviet Policies IV. The Documentary Record of the 22nd Congress of the Communist Party of the Soviet Union* (New York: Columbia University Press, 1962), pp. 64, 15.
11. Leonid Brezhnev, *Following Lenin's Course* (Moscow: Progress Publishers, 1976), 5:480.
12. Mikhail Gorbachev, "Political Report to the 27th Party Congress," *Current Digest of the Soviet Press,* March 26, 1986, p. 12.
13. Ibid., p. 26.
14. Mikhail Gorbachev, "On the Path to a Market Economy; Speech . . . [to] the USSR Supreme Soviet," *Current Digest of the Soviet Press,* October 24, 1990, p. 3.
15. Kwame Nkrumah, *The Autobiography of Kwame Nkrumah* (Edinburgh: Thomas Nelson, 1957), p. x.
16. Quoted in David Reynolds, *One World Divisible: A Global History Since 1945* (New York: Norton, 2000), p. 88.

Suggested Reading

Craig, Gordon, *The Germans* (1982). Key aspects of post–World War II Germany.

Fursenko, Aleksandr, and Timothy Naftali, *"One Hell of a Gamble": Khrushchev, Castro, and Kennedy, 1958–1964* (1997). An excellent account of the Cuban Missile Crisis.

Kennedy, Paul, *The Rise and Fall of the Great Powers: Economic Change and Military Conflict from 1500 to 2000* (1987). An economic analysis of five hundred years of Western civilization and a projection into the future.

Mahoney, Daniel J., *De Gaulle: Statesmanship, Grandeur and Modern Democracy* (1996). A perceptive, short biography.

McNamara, Robert S., *In Retrospect: The Tragedy and Lessons of Vietnam* (1995). A candid apology for Vietnam by the secretary of defense who waged the war.

Medvedev, Roy, *Khrushchev: The Years in Power* (1976). A sympathetic biography by a prominent former dissident.

Riddell, Peter, *The Thatcher Decade: Britain in the 1980s* (1989). A *Financial Times* editor analyzes the Iron Lady's policies and leadership style.

Solzhenitsyn, Alexandr, *Cancer Ward* (1968). A novel using a cancer ward in a hospital as a metaphor for Stalin's Soviet Union. Based on the author's experiences.

Review Questions

1. What were the origins of the cold war? Could it have been avoided?
2. Some people called the cold war "the third world war." Would you agree?
3. What do you consider the biggest changes that occurred in Western Europe after 1945?
4. What was the postwar role of the United States in Western Europe? How did it contribute to the present strength of those European countries?
5. How do you assess Stalin's accomplishments in rebuilding the Soviet Union after World War II?
6. How did Khrushchev and Brezhnev change the Stalinist heritage? What effect did their policies have on the Soviet people?
7. How firm was the hold of the Soviet Union on its Eastern European satellites?
8. What benefits were expected from decolonization? What were the actual consequences?

Chapter 34

The Troubled Present

The destruction of the World Trade Center's twin towers by members of Al Qaeda, a terrorist organization headed by Osama bin Laden, mobilized the United States to take the offensive against international terrorism. (AP/World Wide Photos.)

■ **The Demise of Communism**
1989: Year of Liberation
The Collapse of the Soviet Union
The Death of an Ideal

■ **The Post–Cold War World**
Post-Communist Russia and the Former Soviet Republics
Central and Eastern Europe After 1989
Western Europe

■ **Our Global Age: Tensions and Concerns**

Since 1989, momentous events have utterly changed the world. The superpower polarization of world politics ended, and a new, multicentered, unstable world order has emerged. Western civilization and its ideals have been transformed into a transcultural worldwide modernity. At the same time, however, traditional cultural diversity still simmers. The end of the cold war introduced a new uncertainty into human affairs. On the one hand, global interdependence promotes peaceful cooperation; on the other, it causes a clash of cultural traditions, giving rise to contagious violence and extremism.

The Demise of Communism

1989: Year of Liberation

The collapse of the Soviet Union, the communist superpower, was one of the most striking events in recent history. The Soviet leaders after Stalin could not reduce the gap in living standards and the quality of life between the Soviet system and Western capitalism. By comparison, the West was making impressive progress. This fact, increasingly recognized throughout the Soviet bloc, undermined its carefully enforced communist conformity. Disloyalty grew throughout the multinational and multiethnic Soviet empire. By the 1980s, it was common knowledge, admitted in the highest ranks of the Communist party, that the Soviet system had stifled rather than advanced creativity and efficiency.

Perestroika and glasnost spread among the peoples of Eastern Europe, resentful of Soviet domination and worried by widespread economic hardships. During 1989 and 1990, Eastern Europeans showed their distaste for Communist leadership and demanded freedom and self-determination. Poland took the lead.

Traditionally anti-Russian, the Poles had long resented their country's economic decline. The slightest relaxation of Soviet control encouraged Polish nationalism, which always found expression in the Roman Catholic church. When a Polish cardinal became Pope John Paul II in 1978, patriotism surged. In 1980, workers led by an electrician, Lech Walesa, succeeded, with the blessing of the church, in forming an independent labor union, called Solidarity. Pressured by relentless strikes, the

Chronology 34.1 ❖ From Cold War to Globalism

1989	Year of liberation in Eastern Europe; Berlin Wall demolished
1990	Soviet republics call for independence; Soviet economy in crisis; reunification of Germany; Charter of Paris for a New Europe; official end of cold war
1991	Persian Gulf War; Yeltsin elected Russian president; collapse of Soviet Union; Yugoslav federation breaks up and war begins
1993	Czechoslovakia splits into Czech Republic and Slovakia; elections for new Russian constitution and parliament; European Union ratifies Maastricht Treaty
1994	South Africa elects multiracial government; war breaks out between Russia and Chechnya
1995	Dayton Agreement ends civil war in Bosnia
1996	Yeltsin reelected president of Russia
1998	Russian currency collapses
1999	Poland, Hungary, and the Czech Republic join NATO; Yeltsin resigns; Chechen war reopens; ethnic cleansing of Kosovo; Serbia bombed
2000	Putin elected president of Russia
2001	Terrorist attack on World Trade Center; war on terrorism in Afghanistan

Polish government briefly recognized the union, despite threats of Soviet intervention. In December 1981, however, a military dictatorship, under General Wojciech Jaruzelski, imposed martial law.

Solidarity persisted underground until 1988, when public pressure forced Jaruzelski to end his dictatorship and appoint a civilian government. Solidarity was legalized in January 1989; in April the Communist party gave up its monopoly of political power in Poland. In the first free election, Solidarity triumphed, leading to the formation of a noncommunist government. After ten years of struggle, Poland, the largest country in Eastern Europe, achieved political independence by essentially peaceful means. In December 1990, Lech Walesa was elected president. Encouraged by events in Poland and a resurgence of patriotic feeling, Hungary abolished its Communist bureaucracy in May 1989 and embraced the ideals of democracy and free enterprise.

A more dramatic upheaval occurred in East Germany. On November 6, 1989, when almost a million antigovernment demonstrators crammed the streets of East Berlin, the Communist government resigned. On November 9, in an explosion of patriotic fervor, the Berlin Wall was breached. Young people danced on top of the wall and tens of thousands of East Germans flocked into West Berlin, welcomed with flowers, champagne, and money for buying West German goods. East Germany was ready to be united with West Germany, with Gorbachev's approval.

The exhilaration over breaching the Berlin Wall reverberated in the countries still under Communist rule. By mid December 1989, a multiparty system was installed in Bulgaria, which

Map 34.1 Post-Cold War Europe and the ▶ Former Soviet Union Instead of the stark postwar division of Europe into three blocs—Western Europe, Eastern Europe, and the Soviet Union—the continent is now a patchwork of independent countries, some with new names. Russia remains the largest country, but the former Soviet Republics have claimed their territory on Russia's eastern and southern borders. Within Europe, East and West Germany have reunited, while Yugoslavia has split up.

ICELAND
0 200 400 Km.
0 200 400 Mi.
ATLANTIC OCEAN
RUSSIA
FINLAND
NORWAY
Helsinki
Oslo
SWEDEN
St. Petersburg
Stockholm
Tallinn
ESTONIA
North Sea
Riga
LATVIA
Moscow
IRELAND
DENMARK
Baltic Sea
Dublin
GREAT BRITAIN
LITHUANIA
Vilnius
Volga R.
Copenhagen
Gdańsk (Danzig)
Minsk
Hamburg
London
Amsterdam
Elbe R.
BELARUS
KAZAKHSTAN
NETHERLANDS
Berlin
Warsaw
Vistula R.
Don R.
Brussels
GERMANY
BELGIUM
POLAND
Kiev
Dnieper R.
Paris
Luxembourg
Prague
CZECH REPUBLIC
Seine R.
UKRAINE
LUX.
Rhine R.
Danube R.
SLOVAKIA
FRANCE
Vienna
Bratislava
MOLDOVA
Caspian Sea
Bern
SWITZERLAND
AUSTRIA
Budapest
Chisinau
Rhône R.
HUNGARY
Ljubljana
SLOVENIA
Po R.
Zagreb
ROMANIA
CRIMEA
CROATIA
Belgrade
Bucharest
GEORGIA
PORTUGAL
Ebro R.
BOSNIA AND HERZEGOVINA
SERBIA
Danube R.
Black Sea
Tbilisi
Baku
Lisbon
Madrid
Adriatic Sea
Sarajevo
SPAIN
ITALY
BULGARIA
Yerevan
Corsica
Rome
Sofia
ARMENIA
MONTENEGRO
Skopje
Istanbul
AZERBAIJAN
Tirana
MACEDONIA
Sardinia
Ankara
IRAN
ALBANIA
TURKEY
Mediterranean Sea
GREECE
IRAQ
Athens
Sicily
SYRIA

Profile

Václav Havel

The Czech playwright and president, Václav Havel, was born in 1936 to prosperous parents in Prague. After military service, he joined a theater group in Prague as a stagehand and discovered his vocation. His plays, written in the 1960s and 1970s, were satires and parables of life under totalitarianism. They were banned by the Communist government from performance or publication in Czechoslovakia but were produced abroad to wide acclaim.

In 1977, Havel was among the founders of the dissident human rights movement, Charter 77, and became its spokesman. His activities exposed him to constant police harassment, and he was imprisoned for five years.

His career as a political leader began in 1989, when communism crumbled in Eastern

Wide World Photos.

had joined the quest for democratic government and private enterprise.

The end of the year produced the final victories in the revolution of 1989. Romania's Nicolae Ceausescu, persisting in his own ruthless dictatorship, had paid no attention to the drift of the times. But on December 21, students disrupted a mass demonstration organized on his behalf in the capital city of Bucharest. The crowd followed the students' lead, and even the army turned against Ceausescu. On December 25, he and his wife were tried and executed. The most repulsive representative of Communist rule, defying to the last the trend toward democratic freedom, had ignominiously fallen.

On the same day, Czechoslovakia joined the triumphant finale of the crusade against communism with the election of Václav Havel as president. The most daring and articulate dissident in his country, Havel had led a swift "velvet revolution" against the Czech Communist government. The election of this previously imprisoned dissident playwright, a profound thinker deeply committed to the Western humanist tradition, was a joyous landmark in a momentous year of liberation.

The message spread quickly into Yugoslavia, a fragile federation of six ethnically conscious member republics, among whom Serbia was dominant. Less rigidly controlled than other Eastern European countries, Yugoslavia enjoyed close relations with Western Europe. Yet in 1989, the government could not prevent public protest, encouraged by the news of the Communist downfall in other lands. On December 26, its Communist party caved in and suggested the formation of a multiparty system, which was duly adopted in January 1990. The new freedom soon undermined the unity of the Yugoslav federation—a bitter war would follow in Bosnia.

By the end of 1989, except for Albania, where

Europe. In the absence of democratic politicians, intellectuals in Prague established the Civic Forum to guide the country toward democracy. Havel, with his talent for promoting unity, became the chief negotiator. His skillful leadership contributed to Czechoslovakia's astonishingly swift and smooth transition to democracy. Immensely popular, he was elected president in December 1989.

Although the era of intellectuals in politics was brief, Havel remained in office. He resigned in 1992, protesting the division of Czechoslovakia, but returned as president of the Czech Republic. Despite a bout with lung cancer, he has continued to use his moral authority in the service of government and his literary gifts in political writings, explaining the policies, problems, and achievable hopes of his country to Czechs and to readers worldwide.

MIKHAIL GORBACHEV. Soviet leader Gorbachev and his wife visit Vilnius, the capital of Lithuania, following the declaration of independence by the Lithuanian Communist party. Gorbachev warned demonstrators: "If we should separate, it is the end of perestroika." (*Alain Nogues/Sygma.*)

the Communist party held on until free elections in February 1991, all of Eastern Europe had liberated itself from Soviet domination—a breathtaking change, accomplished unexpectedly within a single year and dealing a deadly blow to the Soviet Union itself.

The Collapse of the Soviet Union

The repudiation of communism in Eastern Europe intensified the disintegration of Soviet rule at the center. Gorbachev's glasnost released the bitterness accumulated under Stalinist repression, revealed the widespread environmental damage caused by promoting industrial progress at any price, and activated the immense diversity of attitudes and values among the various nationalities that comprised the Soviet Union. As a result, the cohesion of the Soviet Union weakened. Clamoring for independence, the Lithuanians, Latvians, and Estonians set off similar demands among Ukrainians, Byelorussians, Georgians, Armenians, and the peoples of central Asia. Ethnic violence escalated disastrously. The biggest blow to Soviet unity came in 1990, when the Russian republic, the largest member of the Soviet Union, declared its limited independence under the leadership of Boris Yeltsin.

As political fragmentation increased, the Soviet economy, battered by decades of inefficient production and distribution of food and consumer goods, collapsed. The breakdown of effective government led to crime, corruption, and violence—evils always simmering under the surface of Soviet life. In late 1990, a Moscow newspaper described the public mood in grim terms:

> *Our society is in many ways inexorably drifting toward the danger point of ungovernability and decline. Economic collapse, paralysis of political authority, outbreaks of ethnic unrest, the illusory nature of social safeguards, rampant crime, and the visible impoverishment of a starving, tired people, which has spawned a general spiritual emptiness, apathy, bitterness and confusion—these are but a few signs . . . of mounting and potentially explosive public discontent. . . . As the store shelves grow emptier, narrow-minded, rudimentary sentiments have become increasingly prevalent: why the hell do we need this restructuring, all this openness, with pluralism to boot? We'd rather have sausage and order.*[1]

Obviously, the spiritual rebirth and the revolution in people's minds that Gorbachev had hoped for had not occurred. In October 1990, he himself conceded in the face of failure that "unfortunately, our society is not ready for the procedures of a law-based state. We don't have that level of political culture, those traditions. All that will come in the future."[2]

The future, however, deepened the country's disunity. On August 19, 1991, hard-line Communists, hostile to Gorbachev's reforms, staged a coup, imprisoning him in his Crimean vacation home and deposing him as president of the Soviet Union, in preparation for a new Communist dictatorship. Yet the conspirators, all of them high officials appointed by Gorbachev, grossly misjudged popular attitudes. Revulsion against the Communist party was even stronger than the yearning for sausage and order. The KGB's vanguard forces defected to Yeltsin, who led a fervent street protest at risk to his life. The emotional outburst in favor of freedom and democracy quickly spread from Moscow to Leningrad (recently renamed Saint Petersburg, as under the tsars) and other cities. The coup collapsed in less than three days. When Gorbachev returned to Moscow, he faced, as he said, "a different country." The Communist party, now repudiated by Gorbachev himself, was swept aside by public disdain, and the Soviet Union broke apart.

Within two weeks, twelve of the fifteen union republics—the Baltic republics of Latvia, Lithuania, and Estonia foremost among them—declared their independence. The remaining republics soon followed suit. On December 24, 1991, the Soviet Union was officially dissolved, and Gorbachev was dismissed from office. The only trace left of the former unity was the ill-defined Commonwealth of Independent States (CIS). Holding out a vague hope for future cooperation among the diverse peoples of the former Soviet Union, it was eventually joined by all the former Soviet republics apart from the Baltic states.

The huge empire that for centuries had cast its shadow over Europe and the world perished. Even more significantly, the Soviet system, which had challenged Western ascendancy since the end of World War I, collapsed, together with its ideological presumption of worldwide communist happiness. Freedom, democracy, and private enterprise—the ideals of the American superpower—won the cold war.

The Death of an Ideal

The sudden and unexpected collapse of communism in Eastern Europe in 1989 seemed to discredit Marxism irrevocably. Reformers in Eastern European lands liberated from Communist oppression expressed revulsion for the socialist past and a desire to regenerate their countries with an infusion of Western liberal ideals and institutions. Havel, the newly elected president of a free Czechoslovakia, expressed this disillusionment with the past and hope for a new democratic future:

> *The worst of it is that we live in a spoiled moral environment. We have become morally ill because we are used to saying one thing and thinking another. We have learned not to believe in anything, not to care about each other, to worry only about ourselves. . . . The previous regime, armed with a proud and intolerant ideology, reduced people into the means of production. . . . Many of our citizens died in prison in the 1950's. Many were executed. Thousands of human lives were destroyed.*

The Wall Came Tumbling Down. The Berlin Wall, symbol of the division of Germany, was breached in November 1989. Young people excitedly clambered onto the partially demolished wall, while East and West Berliners thronged the streets. (*Regis Bossu/Sygma.*)

> *Perhaps you are asking what kind of republic I am dreaming about. I will answer you: a republic that is independent, free democratic, a republic with economic prosperity and also social justice.*[3]

Marxism is a failed ideology propped up only by force in the few surviving Communist regimes. "Scientific socialism," which claimed to have deciphered the essential meaning and direction of history, is neither scientific nor relevant to current needs. It is merely another idea that was given too much credence and is now ready to be swept into the dustbin of history. The political theorist Francis Fukuyama suggests that the decline of communism and the end of the cold war reveal a larger process at work, "the ultimate triumph of Western liberal democracy":

> *The twentieth century saw the developed world descend into a paroxysm of ideological violence, as liberalism contended first with the remnants of absolutism, then bolshevism and Fascism, and finally an updated Marxism that threatened to lead to the ultimate apocalypse of nuclear war. But the century that began full of self-confidence in the ultimate triumph of Western liberal democracy seems at its close to be returning full circle to where it started . . . to an unabashed victory of economic and political liberalism. The triumph of the West, of the Western idea, is evident first of all in the total exhaustion of viable systematic alternatives to Western liberalism. . . . What we may be witnessing . . . is the end point of mankind's ideological evolution and the universalization of Western liberal democracy as the final form of government.*[4]

The Post–Cold War World

Post-Communist Russia and the Former Soviet Republics

Throughout the 1990s and into the new century, the Russian Federal Republic has been struggling to bring its political and economic systems into conformity with the Western model while coping with its loss of territory and superpower status. The collapse of the Soviet Union revealed Russia to be a weak, poorly developed society, beset by profound problems.

Yeltsin's "Shock Therapy." Marred by mismanagement, waste, and lack of incentives, the Soviet economic system had failed miserably in comparison with Western capitalism. In order to reform the economy and improve the standard of living of the Russian people, which lagged far behind living standards in Western lands, President Yeltsin, emerging in 1990 as the leader of the new Russia, made a sudden switch in 1992 from a state-run economy to private ownership and a capitalist market system. This precipitous transfer of state firms to private ownership—"shock therapy"—in many ways proved a disaster. The chief beneficiaries of privatization were often the same inefficient managers who had controlled the economy during the Soviet era and amassed wealth by unscrupulous means. As a result of industrial decline and the withdrawal of government subsidies, ruinous inflation reduced millions of people dependent on pensions to hand-to-mouth subsistence. Many working Russians also sank into poverty as real wages plummeted some 40 percent from 1992 to 1998. Workers often had to wait two to six months for their paychecks, and unemployment soared. In sum, the achievement of economic security, no less than the attainment of participatory democracy, was likely to be a long and painful process. The Russian economist Georgi Arbatov describes the negative consequences of the attempt to inject capitalism directly into the Russian economy:

> *The poorly conceived transition program resulted in an unprecedented decline of the national economy. By 1998 Russian GDP was only about one-half its 1990 level, with the crisis spread to virtually all areas of production. Russian industry found itself unable to compete even in its own domestic markets. All of this was accompanied by a sharp reduction in investment and a disintegration of scientific and technological potential. We are now witnessing processes of pauperization and de-intellectualization, accompanied by criminalization, as Russia increasingly takes on the appearance of a Third World republic.*
>
> *The standard of living of most Russians has decreased dramatically. . . . Life has become especially hard for the millions of people who are dependent on pensions, many of whom now live in impoverished conditions. Their savings were practically eliminated by inflation, and the level of pensions is below the minimum necessary, even by the official calculations, for bare survival. Their situation is aggravated by the tremendous increase in the prices of medicines and the lower quality and reduced availability of subsidized health care.*
>
> *. . . Education has deteriorated drastically. Higher education is not free anymore and is unaffordable for many. Even more serious are the problems of unemployment and the financial difficulty that a young family has in getting a house and raising children.*[5]

With popular unrest mounting and facing op-

Contemporary Art

After World War II, myriad styles emerged or continued to develop. The best known of them was abstract expressionism. Art historians cite the realities of the post–World War II era—the aftermath of the atom bomb, the cold war—as the impetus for a number of movements or subgroups of abstract expressionism. The artists shared an outlook that championed individuality and espoused the freedom to express themselves purely through the use of color and abstract, nonrepresentational forms. As the century progressed, each artist felt even more freedom of expression, leading to a proliferation of styles. Artists were also subject to an ever more critical audience. Viewers felt freer in their ability to criticize art and in their efforts to understand the artists and the work they had created.

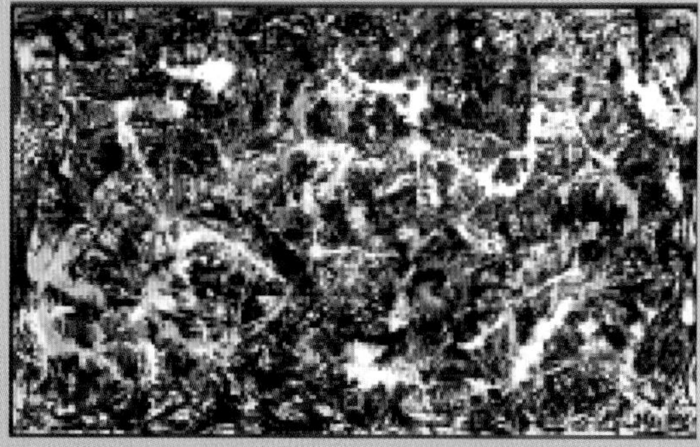

1. Jackson Pollock. *Convergence,* 1952. *(Albright Knox Art Gallery, Buffalo.)*

The most famous abstract expressionist, whose style is known as action painting, was Jackson Pollock (1912–1956). He completed his first action painting in 1950. Pollock poured and splattered his colors on the canvas, instead of applying them with a brush or palette knife. He used a liquid paint that he dripped onto huge unstretched canvases spread on the floor. By positioning the canvas on the floor below him, Pollock felt closer to it—he became part of the painting. Able to walk around the canvas, Pollock worked on it from all sides. As he painted, there emerged a harmony, an easy rhythmic give and take between artist and painting, from which the painting acquired a life of its own. His *Convergence* (1952) (Figure 1) may at first seem to be merely an accident, a canvas used as a drop cloth. But each application of color was made in a controlled and studied manner. The artist knew exactly what he was doing every time he dripped, sprayed, or splattered his canvas. One might say that his paintings have a tactile, kinesthetic quality that is evident in the linear, agitated shapes on the canvas, virtually reflecting the motion of Pollock's body as he worked on the canvas below him.

The work of Helen Frankenthaler (1928–) carried further the abstract expressionism initiated by Pollock. It may be characterized as color-field or minimalist painting. In the 1950s, she was impressed with Pollock's work and adapted his technique to her own purposes. She, too, spilled paint on canvas, spreading, rubbing, and brushing colors into expansive shapes. A switch from oil paint to acrylic paints in the sixties enabled her to produce abstract and ethereal effects unlike the energetic

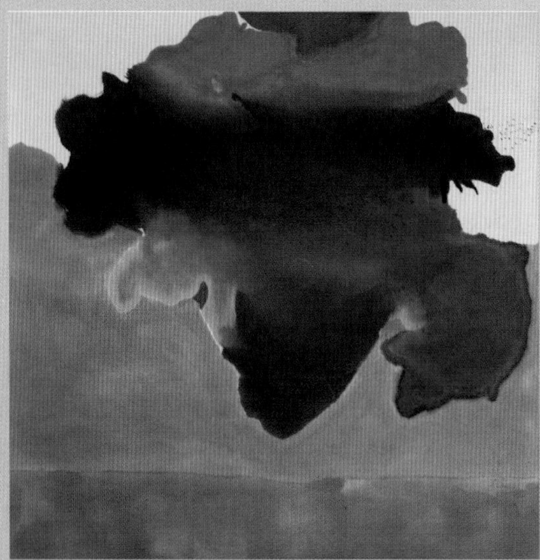

2. Helen Frankenthaler. *The Bay*, 1963. *(Founders Society Purchase with funds from Dr. and Mrs. Hilbert H. DeLawter. Photograph © 1991 The Detroit Institute of Arts.)*

3. Jasper Johns. *Three Flags*, 1958. Encaustic on canvas, 308 7/8 × 45 × 5 in. (784 × 115.6 × 12.7 cm.) *(Fiftieth Anniversary Gift of the Gilman Foundation, Inc., The Lauder Foundation, A. Alfred Taubman, an anonymous donor, and Purchase 80.32 ©Jasper Johns/Licensed by VAGA/New York.)*

linear motion present in Pollock's paintings. In *The Bay* (1963) (Figure 2), Frankenthaler creates a sense of volume, spatial unity, and emotional feeling through the tranquil juxtaposition of translucent colors on a flat, two-dimensional surface.

Abstract expressionism spawned its own antagonists. Pop art was a reaction against nonrepresentational abstract art, which pop artists thought was pretentious and overly serious. Pop artists were influenced by earlier movements that ridiculed the notion of "art for art's sake," scoffed at the idea of the unique art object, and presented ready-made objects such as bicycle wheels and urinals as works of art. The phrase *pop art* was first used in England in the late 1950s to signify paintings that exalted postwar consumerism and celebrated popular culture.

Foremost among the early painters in the pop art movement in the United States was Jasper Johns (1930–). Largely self-taught as an artist, in 1954 he began to paint common objects such as targets, maps, and especially, flags. Four years later he executed one of his most famous paintings: *Three Flags* (Figure 3) is literally three canvases superimposed on each other, creating a reverse perspective, in which the smallest flag moves into the space of the viewer. *Three Flags* is simultaneously a painting and a relief sculpture. The ambiguous meaning of the painting was hotly debated at the time. Was it a realistic representation of the American flag, was it subtle satirical derision of it, or was some esoteric meaning implicit in its seemingly naive obviousness?

The work of sculptors during the second half of the twentieth century reveals both continuity with the sculpture of the pre–World War II period and radical change. Sculptors began to experiment. The major movement from the 1970s was minimalism—simple, symmetrical sculpture made of modern materials that engaged the viewer and, by implication, spurned depicting the human body.

One of the most important minimalist sculptors was David Smith (1906–1965), who flourished during the abstract expressionist era.

4. David Smith. *Cubi XIX. (The Tate Gallery, London/Art Resource, NY.)*

Smith began to sculpt in metal in 1933. During the 1950s and early 1960s, he produced several series of sculptures, including his Cubi series, inspired by cubism. *Cubi XIX* (Figure 4), of 1964, is representative of the series. All the cubis are constructed of monumental cubes, cubic rectangles, and cylinders, which Smith himself constructed out of polished and brushed stainless steel. The carefully balanced cubis are meant to be displayed outdoors where they capture and reflect every change in the natural light.

The most famous architect of the early twenty-first century is Frank O. Gehry (1929–). His work is found not only in the United States but also in Japan and several European countries. Gehry's view of architecture has evolved out of his profound interest in painting and sculpture and his friendships with contemporary artists. His theory of architecture embodies the conviction that architecture is an art form among art forms, like painting and sculpture, expressive of human feeling. Known for his innovative use of materials, Gehry is famous for the way he twists, turns, and bends metal into shapes that affect the emotions. One of his most recent ventures, the Guggenheim Museum at Bilbao, Spain (Figure 5), was opened in 1997.

Gehry's Guggenheim Museum is a perfect illustration of his ability to elevate architecture to the rank of an expressive artistic form not bound by the stultifying rules that consigned previous architectural works to the status of mechanically produced redundant, box-like forms. The Bilbao Guggenheim itself is a work of art, a form of sculptural architecture. The building consists of organically interrelated contrasting shapes composed of a multiplicity of materials, ranging from limestone and glass to titanium. It houses nineteen galleries with thirty-six thousand square feet of exhibition space. It not only attracts numerous visitors—1,300,000 in its inaugural year—but provides the city of Bilbao with a dramatic architectural centerpiece that has had the intended effect of reinvigorating the Basque region's recession-plagued economy and revitalizing its cultural life.

5. Guggenheim Musuem in Bilbao, Spain *(Superstock.)*

YELTSIN'S LAST CAMPAIGN. Boris Yeltsin, dressed for ethnic appeal in the city of Kazan, campaigned for reelection as president of Russia in 1996. News of his subsequent heart attack in the middle of the campaign was hushed up, and he won reelection. His health continues to be precarious. (*Sichov/Sipa Press.*)

position from Communist hardliners, Yeltsin was forced to slow his liberalization of the economy; the social costs—public confusion over bewildering changes, a sharp decline in the standard of living, and the loss of productivity leading to shortages—were too high. "No more experiments," advised slogans spray-painted on walls.

Adding to the intractable problems of the new Russia were soaring crime and corruption. Yeltsin consolidated his power by making alliances with a small group of businessmen, the "oligarchs," who had grown wealthy by acquiring former state-owned enterprises at extremely low prices. They plundered the firms for assets, concentrating Russia's wealth in their own hands, and they gained control of banks "that operate in a pathological fashion." As law enforcement deteriorated, organized crime became a major force in Russian life, as described by three Russian economists:

> *The Russian economy has been transformed into a highly corrupt and criminalized economic system. Rampant crime and corruption have degraded everyday life, obstructed legitimate business activity, and impaired the functioning of government. . . . Though the proclivity for corruption and illegality predates the economic transition, primary blame resides with the reform strategy. . . .*
>
> *Taking advantage of weak law enforcement, Mafia influences have become prominent in all facets of Russian life. An estimated 200,000 active criminal groups existed in Russia by the mid-1990s, including 5,500 large organizations. In addition to extortion, their activities included burglary, embezzlement, and criminal misappropriation of both public and business funds.*[6]

The oligarchs financed Yeltsin's bid for reelection as president, which he won with an astonishing 65 percent of the vote in 1996 despite suffering a heart attack during the election campaign. At age sixty-six and in frail health, Yeltsin could no longer provide effective leadership for his vast fragmented country, and in 1997 he frankly acknowledged the difficulties that he and his country faced: "After creating a new political system, we failed to outfit it with new tools of government, and we ourselves did not learn to govern in a new way."[7]

Nevertheless, by winning reelection with the support of the oligarchs, Yeltsin vanquished the Communists in the Duma, the new legislature. In addition, by permitting the oligarchs to buy up the major state enterprises, he smashed Soviet central planning. It would be impossible in these circumstances to reinstate communism in Russia. But the situation was dangerous because many key enterprises, including banks and the media, were now controlled by unscrupulous oligarchs. In return for their support of Yeltsin, they became an inner political circle in the Kremlin, controlling the country's policies. No wonder Russians began to feel that the government itself had been "privatized."

In August 1998 everything changed. The dysfunctional banking system precipitated a second currency collapse, wiping out Russians' savings and livelihoods. Among the casualties were the majority of the oligarchs. Some were ruined by the collapse of their banks, others went abroad, and the remainder backed out of public life. Suddenly their political influence, which had been paramount since 1995, diminished dramatically, and a new generation of businessmen began to emerge.

Yeltsin resigned on New Year's Eve 1999. His grasp of events had become increasingly uncertain, and he was obviously incapable of ruling. He thus became the first Russian leader to give up power voluntarily. In his demoralized, bankrupt, and corrupt post-Communist country, Yeltsin contended with problems beyond the capacity of the most astute politician. He made appalling mistakes, but he was determined to go down in history as the man who made the restoration of communism in Russia impossible. It was no mean achievement.

Putin: Clamping Down and Reaching Out. Yeltsin's chosen successor, Vladimir Putin, determined to make his mark as a strongman during his short term as Yeltsin's prime minister by reopening the war in Chechnya, a small Islamic enclave in the Caucasus, at war for centuries with the conquering Russians. After two years of ruthless fighting, at great political damage to Yeltsin, the defeated Russian armies withdrew in 1996, leaving the burden of the final settlement of Chechnya's independence to the future. The war resumed in 1999 when Chechen rebels invaded neighboring Dagestan in an effort to establish a united Islamic state in the Caucasus. At the same time a terrorist attack on apartment blocks in Russian cities killed more than three hundred people and maimed many more. Putin put the blame for the attack on Chechens and stormed into the Caucasus to force the invaders out of Dagestan. The Chechen capital, Grozny, was razed; the main victims were elderly Russian residents, the rebels having already escaped to the mountains. Russian troops took control of the war-devastated Caucasus region, but the Chechen leaders remained at large and continued guerrilla attacks on Russian soldiers.

Putin became president of Russia at a time when modest economic stability was beginning to emerge. His objective has been to establish a strong centralized state under the rule of law. He destroyed the remaining political influence of the oligarchs in order to reassert executive power. More alarmingly, he has increased goverment control of the media (previously owned by two of the oligarchs) and curbed the freedom of the press if it is used "for anti-state purposes" (in his words), a move that has alienated Russian liberals. Nevertheless, exhausted by years of turmoil, the Russians have supported Putin; they have welcomed the imposed order along with emerging financial stability and slight economic growth.

The oligarchs have been succeeded by eight large business groups who have created monopolies by systematically buying up entire sectors of Russian industry. Private companies in the coal, steel, automobile, aluminum, and timber industries have been aggressively taken over by business tycoons. The new tycoons, four of whom are under forty, differ from the oligarchs in that they are beginning to modernize the industries that they control; they invest in their companies, pay taxes, and forge connections with Western industry. A growing body of new business law circumscribes their tactics to a limited extent.

Unlike the oligarchs the new tycoons wield no direct political clout, but the size of their holdings alone makes them influential in the governments's economic decisions. They also exercise more control over provincial goverments far from Moscow. The chief danger is to small businesses, which had been recently increasing in number; they are traditionally the engine of growth in new economies, but now face takeover threats from the big groups.

By 2002, cautious optimism was visible. Russia's oil and gas are in demand abroad, and a nascent middle class is emerging. Profits are still leaving the country, but at a slower rate, and more money is being reinvested in the economy. Foreign investment, which dried up during the corrupt and chaotic Yeltsin years, is returning.

Russia's international role shrank during the first two years of Putin's administration, when internal affairs were the prime focus of the government. However, Russia still has a nuclear arsenal, and this gives it a formidable position in the world. Despite misgivings about Western intentions toward Russia, and sensitivity about their loss of superpower status, Russians are adopting more positive feelings toward the West. The emergence of this new attitude had coincided with Putin's policies, which clearly indicate his conviction that Russia's future lies westward.

In the spring of 2002 Putin set a course of strategic integration with the United States and Europe. With President George W. Bush he signed a bilateral arms control treaty to reduce nuclear arsenals, and at the same time Russia was made a junior member of NATO. Because NATO's historical mission had been a military alliance against the Soviet Union, Russia had hitherto regarded NATO as a threat. But Putin evidently regards the prestige of membership in NATO as an opportunity for integration with the West, and as a means of maintaining Russia's image as a great power.

The gap between Russia and the West remains enormous. Russia is still a huge poor country riddled with crime and corruption; it is burdened with a crumbling infrastructure, high inflation, and desperate rural poverty. Its health and social services are in disarray, and drug addiction, AIDS, drug-resistant tuberculosis, and alcoholism run rampant. Life expectancy has declined over the past decade, and deaths outnumber births. Real incomes of Russians are only now starting to approach the levels reached in 1990.

Unrealistic optimism at the time of the Soviet collapse that Russia would emerge as a free, democratic, and market-oriented state changed to pessimism during the 1990s. Building a democratic civic society took centuries in the West; Russia in its weakened state cannot achieve that in one generation. But there are positive signs, and it is in the interests of the West to assist Russia; for if Russia unravels, the whole Eurasian continent will be destabilized.

The Former Soviet Republics. Deep uncertainty prevails in the states that succeeded the former Soviet republics: Belarus, Ukraine, Moldova, Georgia, and the Muslim states of central Asia, which include Azerbaijan, Kazakhstan, Turkmenistan, and Uzbekistan. Reorganized through dubious elections, the majority of the states are still dominated by the Communist legacy of overregulated, centrally planned economies. The precipitous breakdown of trading patterns after the Soviet collapse resulted in economic turmoil. The privatization of major industries has proceeded slowly, if at all, and government corruption and regulation have hampered foreign investment, leading to continued impoverishment of the populations of the states.

The Muslim countries are governed by repressive one-party governments, and the growth of Islamic extremism has destabilized the region. The Muslim states clustered around the Caspian Sea have extensive oil and gas reserves. Cooperative ventures with western European and American oil companies have given these states access to potential wealth.

Central Asia, located at the intersection of Europe, Asia, and the Middle East, provides porous borders for traffic in weapons, terrorists, and narcotics. After centuries of compulsory unity imposed by tsars and commissars, the diverse and divided inhabitants in the huge area between Europe and East Asia have to learn how to manage by themselves. This is no small task for people untrained in the techniques of civic cooperation required for effective modern states.

Central and Eastern Europe After 1989

After a century of war, occupation, and dictatorship, hopes ran high in the former Soviet satellite countries of central and eastern Europe. Western ideals of freedom and democracy had penetrated deep into the eastern lands and had heightened popular expectations. By 1990, however, the euphoria of the previous year began to vanish. How could democratic government and market economies be adapted to the tension-ridden traditions of that troubled area, now suspended between the remnants of Communist rule and the glittering promise of Western life?

Funeral in Bosnia. A funeral of one of the tens of thousands of Muslim victims of the civil war in the former Yugoslavia, which raged from 1992 to 1995. The principal aggressor was Serbia, intent on seizing territory in Bosnia and Croatia in order to create a "greater Serbia." (*Anthony Suau/Liaison.*)

The countries that were closest to western Europe geographically—Poland, Hungary, and the Czech Republic—were also closest to Western political and economic systems and eager to move toward full democracy and market economies. Poland achieved a quick but painful transition to a free-market economy; Czechoslovakia followed a similar course. Hungary, the most enterprising of the Communist countries, loosened its economy further. Yet people were unprepared for an open market economy and suspicious of capitalism.

As a result of economic and social insecurities, the pace of privatization of business slowed, most prominently in Poland, where in 1993 a majority voted in favor of leadership under an ex-Communist. A similar trend surfaced in Hungary a year later, when the former Communist party, renamed the Hungarian Socialist Workers party, took office after a massive election victory. The Czechs, bound by tradition to western European culture, fared somewhat better; after January 1993, they were relieved of their association with less advanced Slovakia. The Communist party was outlawed, but political disunity among a multiplicity of noncommunist parties prevented effective privatization. Everywhere inflation, unemployment, outdated industrial enterprises, and ignorance of market conditions held down economic development.

Yet after 1995, the economic prospects began to improve, with the help of Western aid. Poland, Hungary, and the Czech Republic shifted their economic emphasis from east to west, increasing trade and economic integration with western Europe. They expect political stability and security as a result of their integration into NATO in 1999.

In the 1990s, the former Yugoslavia became the most troubled region of Europe. Cobbled together after World War I as an artificial state composed of sharply different ethnic groups dominated by Serbia, Yugoslavia was torn apart by the nationalist ambitions set off by the collapse of the Soviet Union. In July 1991, Slovenia seceded; Croatia and Bosnia attempted to follow in 1992, ending Serbian domination. Because there were large Serbian populations in both Croatia and Bosnia, Yugoslav president Slobodan Milosevic, a Serb nationalist, refused to give up control and unleased the Serb army, augmented by Bosnian Serbs, on the two countries. Ethnic hatred exploded, centered on Bosnia, a splintered mountainous region. Its major ethnic groups—43 percent Muslim, 17 percent Catholic Croat, and 31 percent Orthodox Serb—were scattered in multiethnic communities; there were few ethnically consolidated areas.

Muslims, Croats, and Serbs ruthlessly fought each other. The Bosnian Serbs, hoping to join with Serbia in a Greater Serbia, conquered 70 percent of Bosnia, conducting a brutal "ethnic cleansing" of Muslims while submitting Sarajevo, Bosnia's capital, to bloody bombardment. All sides, but most of all the Serbs, committed heinous atrocities, provoking moral outrage. A U.N. force of sixty thousand men vainly tried to halt ethnic cleansing by Serbs.

In August 1995, Croatia went on the offensive to drive Serbs out of its territory, and NATO used its air force for the first time in its fifty-year history, against the Bosnian Serbs. In November 1995, the United States stepped forward, in negotiations held in Dayton, Ohio, to promote peace. The Dayton Agreement proposed a Bosnian government equally shared by Muslims, Croats, and Serbs. As the fighting died down, the U.N. forces were replaced by smaller NATO units, including American troops and even some Russian soldiers. A measure of normality returned to Sarajevo. But the outrageous inhumanities of the Bosnian civil war posed troubling questions. Why were western European countries so reluctant to intervene? Why did the United States enter so late? Can a foreign military presence soften deeply entrenched local hatreds?

Europeans and Americans were forced to reconsider these questions when violence erupted between Serbs and ethnic Albanians in the Yugoslav province of Kosovo. This is a sacred place for Serbs, the site of Orthodox shrines and of the battle of Kosovo in 1389, in which the Ottoman Turks defeated the Serbs, ruling Kosovo until 1912. The Serbs regard the battle as the birth of the Serb nation. Ethnic antagonism has persisted between Serbs and the predominantly Muslim Albanians who form 90 percent of the population of two million. In 1998, President Milosevic, seeking to shore up his power by manipulating Serbian nationalist feelings, sent Serbian forces to crush Albanian separatists fighting for an independent Kosovo.

Repelled by the forced expulsions and massacres of innocent villagers, NATO felt compelled to intervene. Despite a threat of NATO air strikes, Milosevic, a dictator whose hands already were stained with the blood of thousands of victims in Bosnia, refused to allow a NATO peacekeeping force into Kosovo. NATO launched air strikes on Serbia in March 1999. At the same time special Serbian forces, determined to drive Albanians out of Kosovo, stormed into the region. Carrying the practice of ethnic cleansing to a new level of brutality, they terrorized and murdered Albanians, systematically burned villages, confiscated valuables, and compelled their victims to flee the province. Hundreds of thousands of Albanian refugees streamed out of the country into neighboring lands, creating a massive humanitarian crisis.

The unrelenting NATO bombardment of Yugoslavia, expected to be brief and decisive, continued for eleven weeks—so too did the ethnic cleansing of Kosovo—until Milosevic capitulated. Eventually the Kosovo Albanians were allowed to return to their ravaged country. A force of forty thousand NATO and U.N. troops remained in Kosovo to assist with relief efforts, prevent revenge attacks on the remaining Serb population, and enable an administration to be put in place to guarantee Kosovo's autonomy. As a first step, elections were held in November 2001 for a provincial assembly.

The U.N. International Criminal Tribunal for the Former Yugoslavia indicted President Milosevic and Bosnian Serb and Croatian leaders and military commanders on charges of genocide and crimes against humanity. President Milosevic ran for reelection in a fraudulent campaign in September 2000. This brazen act sparked massive protests in Belgrade and forced him from office. Facing the threat of a cutoff of Western aid for rebuilding the shattered country, Serbia eventually arrested him and transferred him to the custody of the U.N. Tribunal to face charges. His trial began in 2002.

The new low-key president of Yugoslavia, Vojislav Kostunica, has said that Yugoslavs "want to live in an ordinary, average state in which everything is more or less average—the economy, standard of living, industrial growth, banks, welfare, health care, the media."[8] Yugoslavia, however, is a shattered country, mired in poverty, dependent on foreign aid, and shrunken to a dysfunctional federation consisting of Serbia, Montenegro, and Kosovo. Montenegro is demanding independence, and Kosovo is currently a U.N. protectorate, secured by a NATO-led peacekeeping force and bent upon eventual independence. Even President Kostunica's modest vision is unlikely to be achieved in the near future.

Western Europe

Since the end of World War II, the Western European states have engaged in a slow process of economic, political, and cultural integration. The collapse of the Soviet power supplied a sudden jolt for accelerating this trend. In 1991, in the Dutch city of Maastricht, the members of what was then called the European Community transformed themselves into the European Union (EU). This organization is shaping Europe into a unified political and economic force, with the help of a common monetary unit, the euro, which competes with the U.S. dollar as a currency for worldwide use. Tied to the global economy with an impact second only to the United States, this new Europe is emerging as a powerful presence in world affairs. EU countries are also members of NATO, which in 2002 admitted its former adversary, Russia, as a junior partner.

Implementing the EU's objectives has proved no easy task. Many Europeans have unanswered questions about the future of their countries. Are they surrendering their identity, along with their sovereignty, to the EU? Are Europeanization and globalization (the latter frequently defined as "American imperialism") going to change irrevocably their national status? The problem is that Europeans do not identify with the EU, personified by remote Eurocrats headquartered in Brussels, Belgium. An unelected European Commission makes the decisions, and the elected European Parliament is a weak institution. The Eurocrats argue that making policies more accountable to public opinion would slow the pace of European integration. As the EU moves into new areas—a common economic policy based on a common currency (the euro) and a projected common foreign policy—decisions will become ever more remote from the ground-floor influence of public opinion in member countries. Another question is linked to the worries about identity and change: will immigration transform homogeneous societies into multiethnic, multinational ones? The reluctance of governing political parties to open the immigration question has given far-right-wing parties another reason to attack the EU.

Center-left governments in EU countries are being challenged by the resurgent right wing. In Austria, Jorg Haider's ultra-right-wing Freedom party is a member of the governing coalition. In France, with alarming success, Jean Marie Le Pen augmented his anti-immigration platform with an appeal to the "little people ruined by Euro-Globalization." Denmark, Holland, and Portugal all have growing right-wing parties. Many Europeans feel that immigration is a legitimate cause for alarm, for every year thousands of illegal immigrants enter the EU area from all over the world. Some are genuinely fleeing oppression and danger in their own countries; others are in search of jobs; most are unskilled. Unlike the United States, European nations have very limited immigration, so people entering countries illegally have to apply for asylum—that is, they have to prove that they would be in danger if forced to return to their countries of origin. Asylum can be granted on humanitarian grounds, but in most countries it does not extend to would-be immigrants looking for jobs.

The treatment of asylum seekers who enter a country illegally varies from country to country. Both Germany and England, which have the greatest number, forbid them to work but give

GROWING ETHNIC DIVERSITY IN EUROPE. In recent decades, Western Europe has become the home for an increasing number of people from outside the Continent. Turkish guest workers have settled in Germany; millions of people from former colonial possessions in North Africa and sub-Saharan Africa now reside in France; immigrants from India, Pakistan, and the Caribbean, regions once part of the British Empire, now live in Britain. Cultural clashes, competition for employment, criminality, and pressure on welfare services have, at times, led to a xenophobic reaction against immigrants. (*AP/World Wide Photos.*)

them housing and welfare checks while they wait for their applications to be considered; this wait can take up to two years. Asylum seekers are bitterly resented by citizens who perceive them to be living idly on the generosity of the welfare state. Although European countries are comparatively prosperous, unemployment is high, and when jobs are few, immigration is seen as a threat. The EU is trying to draw up a code harmonizing the way EU countries deal with this problem, but right-wing rhetoric is complicating any attempt to liberalize the myriad asylum laws.

Throughout Europe, right-wing parties exploit the immigration issue by charging that immigrants cause crime. By playing on fears for personal safety, these parties hope to win people to their cause. This is a clever ploy, for explicit appeals to racial hatred are considered unacceptable reminders of the Nazi past.

The biggest challenge to the EU derives from its eastward expansion reaching as far as Turkey. This will be a long-term process, given the economic and political instability of the states applying to join, the majority of them burdened by their communist past. Because the EU is integrating politically as well as economically, any country applying for membership has not only to demonstrate economic progress toward a market economy but also to conform to acceptable standards of democracy and human rights. By 2000, applications for admission had been received from twelve countries: Bulgaria, Cyprus, the Czech Republic, Estonia, Hungary, Latvia, Lithuania, Malta, Poland, Romania, Slovakia, and Slovenia.

If all are admitted, the population of the EU will approach five hundred million. A major concern is that most of these candidates have weak economies and would be in need of financial assistance at enormous expense to the EU. Hitherto, countries accepted into membership were fully democratic with mature market economies. Can the EU choose to neglect countries that fall short of this ideal, or should it help them to achieve it? In past years, membership in the EU has allowed Greece, Spain, Portugal, and Ireland, all with per capita incomes below the EU average, to escape economic and industrial backwardness.

The European Union is a conglomerate of diverse countries large and small, all linked by their common European history. It includes two nuclear powers, France and the United Kingdom. Reunited Germany is the most populous and most influential country.

In the United Kingdom, Prime Minister Margaret Thatcher resigned in 1990 in the face of conservative criticism. Her successor, John Major, maintained an uncertain majority in Parliament, increasingly troubled by political scandals and the rising popularity of the Labour party. In the election of 1997, that party, revitalized by Tony Blair, its young and lively leader in close touch with the people, scored an impressive victory. Under his leadership, the Labour party has moved to the political center. It endorsed a pro-business, pro-enterprise policy, limiting benefits for the poor, and jettisoned the old working-class/state-ownership image. This policy has given the country an unusually strong economy, and London is a vibrant worldwide financial center. Socially, however, the picture is less bright; educational standards in schools have fallen, the health service is in crisis, and crime (in a formerly law-abiding country) has increased. The industrial north of England has been neglected and is currently the largest ricipient of EU structural funds, which makes this region one of the most deprived in Europe. Looking across the Channel to Europe, the English wonder why their public services are so inferior to those in other EU countries.

In Northern Ireland, where Protestants and Catholics had long been at war with each other, Blair helped to end the conflict and create an elected assembly. After three difficult years, the peace process was finally on track. It was a huge gamble that terrorists and bigots, who have spent decades trying to destroy each other, could act rationally in a democratic assembly. The potential for violence in Northern Ireland still remains high.

Britain continues to play an important role in international affairs. It aided the United States, its close ally, in the Gulf War of 1991, when an international coalition led by the United States prevented Saddam Hussein from annexing Kuwait to Iraq. Britain also participated in NATO actions to counter Serbian aggression in the Balkans, and in the war against the Taliban in Afghanistan following the tragic events of September 11, 2001.

France, including the Mediterranean island of Corsica, has a population of fifty-eight million and is the largest territorial state in western Europe. Proud of their historical tradition, the French cherish their past and are uneasy about the intrusion of alien ways, especially from the United States. Following de Gaulle, the French goverment still wants to play its part in world affairs, for instance, in opposing American policies in the Mideast. At the same time, however, it works closely with NATO to reduce violence in the Balkans. Its chief concern is cooperation with Germany in creating an effective European Union that balances French and German aspirations. France also wants to preserve its influence in Africa, generously donating financial aid to economic development.

At home, French politics are in reasonably stable order. The socialist François Mitterrand, president until 1995, named Jacques Chirac, a moderate conservative, as his prime minister in 1986. Succeeding Mitterrand as president, Chirac was forced to name a socialist, Lionel Jospin, to head the goverment. The two men were each suited to their jobs, but personal rivalry made for a difficult relationship, especially when Jospin challenged Chirac for the presidency in 2002. A fragmented vote resulted in an upset when Jean Marie Le Pen, the far-right leader of the National Front party, qualified for a runoff election against Chirac. The result sent shock waves through France, where demonstrations against Le Pen gathered force and Chirac campaigned vigorously, claiming that international respect for France would be wrecked if Le Pen—an anti-immigration, anti-EU, antiglobalization, antisemitic, racist candidate—won a large proportion of the vote. He received only 18 percent of the vote, but the affair revealed a troubling undercurrent in French society.

With its eighty-three million people, Germany has the largest population in Europe and is proud of the peaceful reunification of its western and eastern parts in 1990. Helmut Kohl, as chancellor of West Germany, was the architect of the reunited Germany; he poured huge amounts of West German money into what had been the Communist German Democratic Republic, hoping for quick integration. However, attitudes and habits developed under communism have persisted; the seventeen million former East Germans, with no experience of democracy, still feel themselves to be second-class citizens. More than a decade after reunification, a sour mood of disillusionment persists. Unemployment is at 20 percent because communist-era factories have closed and no new industries have been established. East Germans feel sidelined by reunification. The rise in right-wing violence since reunification is particularly severe in the old East Germany, where neo-Nazis and skinheads, usually under-employed and alienated youth, have been responsible for outbreaks of lawlessness and brutality against "outsiders"—immigrants and Jews—whom they regard as parasites draining away the country's resources and diluting its national character.

A hopeful symbol of reunification was the relocation of the German capital from Bonn to Berlin, the traditional German capital city, which for more than forty years had been surrounded by territory under communist control. Greatly expanded, Berlin is fast becoming a major European center, exploring close ties with central and eastern Europe and even Russia.

Kohl had taken a leading role in promoting European economic and political unity, with due regard for French national pride. As the European community expands, Germany will certainly benefit; it already runs the third largest economy in the world and a stable federal regime.

Kohl's conservative chancellorship ended after sixteen eventful years. In 1998, Germans elected Gerhard Schröder, leader of the Social Democrats, as his successor. Schröder's party formed a coalition with the Greens, who scaled down their environmental and pacifist radicalism. Like England and France, Germany is now ruled by a moderate left-wing government. And like his French colleague, Schröder has to balance the customary high level of social benefits against the pressures of global economic competition, while unemployment remains high.

Our Global Age: Tensions and Concerns

In the twenty-first century, globalization continues relentlessly; the world is being knit ever closer together by the spread of Western ideals, popular culture (particularly American), free-market capitalism, and technology. Government officials and business and professional people all over the world dress in Western clothes. Women follow Western fashions in dress and makeup. People line up to eat at McDonald's, see a Hollywood movie, or attend a rock concert. Everywhere people are eager to adopt the latest technology that originated in the West but is now also manufactured in other, particularly Asian, lands. Advanced technology intensifies the means of communication, not only through television and radio but also with faxes, e-mail, cellular phones, or the Internet—all means of instantaneous individual communication that have become commonplace in the past decade.

These developments promote shared interests among individuals and businesses, some of them multinational corporations, throughout the globe, reducing the importance of national frontiers. All these factors combined are reshaping non-Western societies in a relentless adjustment that causes both deep hardships and possibilities for a better life.

The ideals of freedom and democracy, historical accomplishments of Western civilization, exert a powerful influence worldwide; they are also part of the process of westernization. Unlike technology, they cannot be easily put into practice outside the countries of their origin. However, they inspire human ambitions everywhere. They have even become part of the rhetoric of dictatorships.

At the same time, strong cultural traditions still divide the world. Traditional ways of life, often at odds with the demands of modernization, remain deeply ingrained in many lands. Among people deeply committed to their own cultural traditions or feeling left behind by modernization, the process of globalization has provoked a powerful backlash, nowhere more so than in the Muslim world. The hatred of radical Muslim fundamentalists for the West, which they see as a threat to traditional Islam, is a striking example of the clash of cultures in a world being increasingly connected.

On September 11, 2001, nineteen Muslim Arabs, most of them from Saudi Arabia, hijacked four planes: two of them they crashed into the World Trade Center in New York, bringing down both towers; a third plane rammed into the Pentagon in Washington, D.C., causing severe damage; the fourth plane, apparently headed for the White House, crashed in a field in Pennsylvania when passengers attacked the hijackers. In all, more than three thousand people perished in the worst terrorist attack in history. The meticulously planned operation was the work of Al Qaeda, an international terrorist network of militant Muslims, or Islamists as they call themselves. In 1998, it was responsible for the deadly bombings of the American embassies in Kenya and Tanzania, which killed hundreds, and in 2000, it detonated a bomb next to the U.S. destroyer Cole in the harbor of Aden, costing the lives of seventeen American sailors.

The leader of Al Qaeda, Osama bin Laden, scion of an immensely wealthy Saudi family, operated from Afghanistan with the protection of the radical fundamentalist Taliban, who ruled the country, transforming it into a repressive regime based on a rigid interpretation of Islamic law. In particular, the Taliban imposed oppressive rules for women, permitting beatings by male relatives, prohibiting females from working, barring them from schools, and demanding that they wear a garment—the burka—that covered them from head to foot. Violators could be severely beaten, imprisoned, or executed.

When Taliban leaders refused to turn bin Laden over to the United States, President George W. Bush, supported by an international coalition, launched a military campaign whose ultimate goal was the destruction of international terrorism. The United States showed a fierce resolve unexpected by bin Laden who thought that the Americans would not risk sending troops to fight in the forbidding Afghan terrain and against people who had defeated the Soviet Union. Local Afghan forces opposed to the Taliban, assisted by American airpower, which proved decisive, defeated the Taliban in a few weeks. The new leaders of Afghanistan would no longer permit their country to serve as a haven and training center for radical Islamic terrorists.

On numerous occasions President Bush and his chief advisers declared that the attack on Afghanistan was directed against "evil doers" and not against Muslims in general or their faith. However, bin Laden and his followers view their struggle against the United States as a holy war against the infidel. Bin Laden and other Arabs from Morocco to Yemen devoted to a militant Islam had fought in Afghanistan to drive out the Soviets. During that conflict, bin Laden and his cohorts drew up plans for the creation of an Islamic world-state governed by Islamic law, a revival of the medieval caliphate. In 1998, bin Laden told his followers that the stationing of American troops in Saudi Arabia, "the land of the two holy Mosques," demonstrated that America "had spearheaded the crusade against the Islamic nation." A religious fanatic and absolutist who cannot tolerate pluralism, bin Laden wants to drive westerners and Western values out of Islamic lands; he is also a theocrat, who would use the state's power to impose a narrow, intolerant version of Islam on the Muslim world. He and his followers are zealots who are convinced that they are doing God's will. Recruits for suicide missions are equally convinced that they are waging holy war against the enemies of God and their centers of evil, for which they will be richly rewarded in Paradise.

To be sure, the actions of bin Laden and his followers violate core Islamic teachings against killing civilians. At the same time, however, terrorists find religious justification for their actions in Islamic tradition. The early followers of Muhammad, says Bernard Lewis, divided the world

> *into two houses: the House of Islam, in which a Muslim government ruled and Muslim law prevailed, and the House of War, the rest of the world . . . ruled by infidels. Between the two, there was to be a perpetual state of war until the entire world either embraced Islam or submitted to the rule of the Muslim state. . . . For Osama bin Laden, 2001 marks the resumption of the war for the religious dominance of the world that began in the seventh*

Afghanistan After the Taliban. After the defeat of the Taliban, which had harbored and encouraged Al Qaeda terrorists, Hamid Karzai became president of an interim government in Afghanistan with the support of the United States. President Karzai struggled to deal with his nation's immense problems: local warlords who resisted the Kabul government, pockets of surviving Taliban fighters, the return of hundreds of thousands of refugees after the ouster of the Taliban, and the destruction, caused by years of warfare and drought, of great stretches of once fertile land. (*Reuters NewMedia Inc./Corbis.*)

> *century. For him and his followers, this is the moment of opportunity. Today America exemplifies the civilization that embodies the leadership of the House of War, and it . . . has become degenerate and demoralized, ready to be overthrown.*[9]

The hatred of radical Muslims for the West shows that in an age of globalism the world is still divided by strong cultural traditions. It also reveals how the problems confronting the Middle East—authoritarian governments, the suppression of human rights, rampant corruption, mushrooming populations, high unemployment, and the ongoing Arab-Israeli conflict—have a global impact. All of these factors have led many disillusioned young people to place their hopes for a better life not in democratic reforms but in a radical Islam that promises to restore a glorious past and guarantee entrance to Paradise. Fostering this outlook are the numerous religious schools financed by Saudi Arabia that have been established in many parts of the Muslim world. In these schools youngsters are given no secular education and from an early age are indoctrinated in the tenets of radical Islamism: hatred of the

West, holy war against the infidel, the Jew as Devil, and the virtue of martyrdom for the faith.

Before September 11, Al Qaeda operated in Muslim lands from Indonesia to Morocco with little fear of government interference and received huge sums from wealthy Arabs in the Persian Gulf and from worldwide Muslim organizations purporting to be raising funds only for charitable purposes. Al Qaeda members also found a haven in western European lands where they coordinated their operations generally unrestrained by the authorities. The successful engagement in Afghanistan, American pressure on other lands that had harbored terrorists, and rigorous international efforts to destabilize Al Qaeda's vast financial network greatly weakened the terrorist organization. But thousands of Al Qaeda fighters crossed from Afghanistan into Pakistan, and the seething discontent in the Muslim world, particularly among Arabs, provides Al Qaeda with recruits, including zealots willing to inflict maximum casualites on civilians, even if doing so means blowing themselves up in the process. After September 11, several Al Qaeda operations were thwarted, including attempts to explode airplanes. But in 2002, an Al Qaeda affiliate rammed a fuel truck into a historic Tunisian synagogue, killing nineteen people, most of them German tourists. And it is believed that in the same year the Al Qaeda network was responsible for a bus attack in Karachi that killed eleven French engineers, a bombing of the U.S. consulate in Karachi that took the lives of twelve Pakistanis, the kidnapping and beheading of the American journalist Daniel Pearl, the blowing up of a French oil tanker off Yemen, the killing of an American marine in Kuwait, and the bombing of a nightclub in Bali, Indonesia, that killed more than 180 people, most of them westerners on holiday. With Al Qaeda cells located in scores of countries—and many freelancers, inspired by bin Laden's ideology, eager to attack Western interests—and bin Laden unaccounted for, international terrorism remains a threat to world stability. Making the situation more ominous is the uncovering of evidence that Al Qaeda has sought to obtain weapons of mass destruction.

The events of September 11 may have signaled a new type of warfare for a new century. Free and open societies like the United States are vulnerable to attack, less from states that are deterred by America's might—as in the cold war—than by stateless conspiratorial groups employing modern computers, communications, and banking systems to organize and finance terrorism. Such groups are not deterred by America's arsenal. And there is the fearful prospect that a rogue state will supply these groups with biological, chemical, and eventually nuclear weapons to wage war by proxy.

International terrorism is a major source of concern in today's interconnected world. There are others. Western science, medicine, humanitarianism, and economic progress have produced an unprecedented population explosion in Asia, Africa, the Middle East, and Latin America. For countless millennia the world's population remained almost stationary, slowly beginning to grow in the eighteenth century. At the height of Western imperialism, in 1900, the world's population reached 1.6 billion. Fifty years later, it reached 2.5 billion, and by the year 2000 it skyrocketed to 6.1 billion. Despite immense losses of life in two world wars, totalitarian terror, local famines, and other calamities, the world's population nearly quadrupled within a century.

The economic disparity between the rich and the poor, which sharply separates the industrialized from the developing countries, is further cause for concern. By all accounts, the trend will get worse. As a U.N. report of 1996 concluded, the gap between rich and poor "will move from inequitable to inhuman."[10]

The growth of the urban population is equally alarming. Megacities of 10 million and more people have multiplied in developing countries, the biggest being Mexico City, with 16.6 million inhabitants. Within a quarter of a century, 61 percent of the world's population is expected to live in cities. One billion urban households are too poor to feed their crowded people; Guangzhou, the biggest city in southern China, averages 5.7 people per room. These cities often contain vast, squalid slums, lack sewage facilities, clean water, and clean air, and are infected with mosquitoes that spread malaria. Crime, violence, and corruption add to the misery of the world's slum dwellers.

Violence is escalating throughout the world. In the first half of the 1990s, at least 3.2 million

TYRANT OF IRAQ. In 2002 President George W. Bush threatened to go to war in order to remove Saddam Hussein, the ruthless dictator of Iraq. In the past, Saddam attacked Iran and Kuwait and used poison gas against the rebellious Kurdish minority. And he continued to stockpile dangerous chemical and biological weapons, and his scientists were forging ahead with atomic weapons. (*AP/World Wide Photos.*)

people were killed in local political conflicts, most of them civilians, not counting the untold number of victims of daily crime. Most frightening for the future is the development of weapons of mass destruction by states that do not share Western democratic values. North Korea, a ruthless Communist dictatorship, possesses nuclear weapons. Saddam Hussein, the brutal head of Iraq—he used poison gas against his own people, routinely murders army leaders and government officials in order to contain opposition, and invaded neighboring Kuwait, precipitating the Gulf War—is feverishly building an arsenal of biological and chemical weapons and may be close to having a nuclear capability. Iran, headed by Islamic fundamentalists who support terrorism against the infidel, is also moving ahead with weapons of mass destruction.

How can peaceful global interdependence be advanced, given the persistent cultural and political differences that divide the world, promoting hatred and inciting violence? How can tiny individuals on our crowded planet gain a sense of control over their personal circumstances, as well as over the ever more complex institutions under which they live? How is it possible to gain the world-mindedness that would enable us to be cooperative citizens of our earthly habitat even under grave adversity? Can the present generation of Western peoples, above all, Americans, help shape the development of the global community in accordance with the highest ideals of Western civilization: reason, freedom, and respect for human dignity?

❖ ❖ ❖

NOTES

1. "Drifting Toward the Danger Point" [from *Izvestia*], *Current Digest of the Soviet Press,* November 21, 1990, p. 26.
2. Quoted in Anthony Lewis, "Et Tu Eduard," *New York Times,* December 21, 1990, sec. A, p. 39.
3. From "Havel's Vision—Excerpts from Speech by the Czech President," *New York Times,* January 2, 1990, p. A13.
4. Francis Fukuyama, "The End of History," *The National Interest,* Summer 1989, pp. 3, 4.
5. Georgi Arbatov, "Origins and Consequences of 'Shock Therapy,'" in *The New Russia: Transition Gone Awry,* ed. Lawrence R. Klein and

Marshall Pomer (Stanford, Calif.: Stanford University Press, 2001), pp. 173–174.

6. Svetlana P. Glinkina, Andrei Grigoriev, and Vakhtang Yakobidze, "Crime and Corruption," ibid., pp. 233, 237.
7. Boris Yeltsin, "Yeltsin Addresses Parliament on the State of the Nation," *Current Digest of the Post-Soviet Press,* April 9, 1997, p. 1.
8. Quoted in Tim Judah, "Goodbye to Yugoslavia?" *New York Review of Books,* February 8, 2001, p. 44.
9. Bernard Lewis, "Revolt of Islam," *The New Yorker,* November 19, 2001, pp. 52, 62.
10. United Nations Development Programme, *Human Development Report, 1996* (New York: Oxford University Press, 1996), p. iii.

Suggested Reading

Aron, Leon, *Yeltsin: A Revolutionary Life* (2000). A political biography of the larger-than-life but flawed figure.

Cohen, Leonard J., *Serpent in the Bosom: The Rise and Fall of Slobodan Milosevic* (2000). Violence and genocide in pursuit of an ethnic vision.

Freeland, Chrystia, *Sale of the Century: Russia's Wild Ride from Communism to Capitalism* (2000). A colorful account of the takeover of state-owned firms by Russian oligarchs.

Friedman, Thomas L., *The Lexus and the Olive Tree: Understanding Globalization* (1999). The rules and logic of the new international system.

Garron-Ash, Timothy, *The Magic Lantern: The Revolution of '89 Witnessed in Warsaw, Budapest, Berlin and Prague* (1990). A lively account of the death of communism in eastern Europe, conveying the exhilaration of the time.

Geddes, Andrew P., *Immigration and European Integration: Toward Fortress Europe* (2000). Migration into and within the European Union countries.

Gorbachev, Mikhail S., *Memoirs* (1996). The tumultuous years of reform in the Soviet Union.

Gordon, Philip, and Sophie Meunier, *The French Challenge: Adapting to Globalization* (2001). The problems of French hostility to globalization.

Havel, Václav, *Summer Meditations* (1992). An excellent selection of essays by the president of the Czech Republic.

Hodge, James F., and Gideon Rose, eds., *How Did This Happen: Terrorism and the New War* (2001). Wide-ranging essays on the attack of September 11, 2001.

Judah, Tim, *Kosovo: War and Revenge* (2000). An even-handed history of Kosovo throughout the twentieth century.

Pond, Elizabeth, *Beyond the Wall: Germany's Road to Unification* (1993). An account of the new Germany by a veteran journalist with an optimistic view of the future of Europe.

Putin, Vladimir, *First Person: An Astonishingly Frank Self-Portrait by Russia's President* (2000). Interviews with the enigmatic president and commentary from family and friends.

Rashid, Ahmed, *Jihad: The Rise of Militant Islam in Central Asia* (2002). Analysis of Islamic movements in a volatile area.

Remnick, David, *Lenin's Tomb* (1993). A superb, Pulitzer Prize–winning account of the last years of the Soviet Union.

Rieff, David, *Slaughterhouse: Bosnia and the Failure of the West* (1995). The responsibility of the Western nations for the Bosnian genocide.

Sachs, Jeffrey, *Poland's Jump to the Market Economy* (1993). An account of the dramatic economic restructuring in Poland since 1989. (The author has been an economic adviser in Poland and Russia.)

Soros, George, *On Globalization* (2002). On the need for social awareness by global institutions.

Review Questions

1. Why was the "revolution" of 1989 in eastern Europe a relatively peaceful one?
2. What effects did the end of the cold war have on global politics?
3. How, in the light of Russian history, the conditions of the country, and the attitude of its peoples, do you react to a Russian patriot's opinion, expressed after the election of December 1993: "Universal suffrage, dumped on Russia like the other fruits of European liberties, does not work in Russia"?
4. What are the main problems facing the European Union in the next five years?
5. Terrorism has been frequently called "the dark side of globalization." What does this phrase mean?

Epilogue

Reaffirming the Core Values of the Western Tradition

In recent years, modern Western civilization has come under severe attack from several quarters, including religious thinkers, intellectuals loosely called postmodernists, advocates of the poor and oppressed, and militant Muslims. Some religious thinkers deplore the modern age for its espousal of secular rationality, the central legacy of the Enlightenment. These thinkers argue that reason without God degenerates into an overriding concern for technical efficiency—an attitude of mind that produces Auschwitz, Stalin's labor camps, weapons of mass destruction, and the plundering and polluting of the environment. The self without God degenerates into selfish competition, domination, exploitation, and unrestrained hedonism. Human dignity conceived purely in secular terms does not permit us to recognize the *thou* of another human being, to see our neighbor as someone who has been dignified by God; and removing God from life ends in spiritual emptiness and gnawing emotional distress. These critics of the Enlightenment tradition urge the reorientation of thinking around God and transcendent moral absolutes. Without such a reorientation, they argue, liberal democracy cannot resist the totalitarian temptation or overcome human wickedness.

Postmodernists argue that modernity founded on the Enlightenment legacy, which once was viewed as a progressive force emancipating the individual from unreasonable dogmas, traditions, and authority, has itself become a source of repression through its own creations: technology, bureaucracy, consumerism, materialism, the nation-state, ideologies, and a host of other institutions, procedures, and norms. Aversion to a technoscientific culture and to its methodology leads postmodernists to devalue the principle of objectivity in the social sciences and to give greater weight to the subjective, to feelings, intuition, fantasy, to the poetry of life. Postmodernists contend that the evaluation of data and reasoned arguments, no matter how logical they seem, reveal only personal preferences and biases. In their view, science has no greater claim to truth than does religion, myth, or witchcraft. In a world marked by cultural diversity and individual idiosyncrasies, there are no correct answers, no rules that apply everywhere and to everyone. Moreover, like those who point out the dangers of reason not directed by spiritual values, postmodernists argue that reason fosters oppressive governments, military complexes, and stifling bureaucracies. Nor has it solved our problems.

Expressing disdain for Western humanism, which ascribes an inherent dignity to human beings, urges the full development of the individual's potential, and regards the rational, self-determining human being as the center of existence, postmodernists claim that humanism has failed. The humanist vision of socialist society ended in Stalinism, and liberal humanism proved no more effective a barrier to Nazism than did Christianity. In our own day, they ask, has the rational humanist tradition been able to solve the problems of overpopulation, worldwide pollution, world hunger, poverty and war that ravage our planet? Closer to home, has reason coped successfully with urban blight, homelessness, violence, racial tensions, or drug addiction? Moreover, postmodernists contend that the Western tradition, which has been valued as a great and creative human achievement, is fraught with gender, class, and racial bias. In their view, it is merely a male, white, Eurocentric interpretation of things, and the West's vaunted ideals are really a cloak of hypocrisy intended to conceal, rationalize, and legitimate the power, privileges, and preferences of white, European, male elites.

People who identify with victims of exploitation, discrimination, and persecution throughout the globe also attack the Western tradition. They point to the modern West's historic abuses: slavery, imperialism, racism, ethnocentrism, sexism, class exploitation, and the ravaging of the environment. They accuse westerners of marginalizing the poor, women, and people of color by viewing them as the "other." Furthermore, they condemn the West for arrogantly exalting Western values and achievements and belittling, or even destroying, indigenous peoples and cultures. Finding Western civilization intrinsically flawed, some critics seek a higher wisdom in non-Western traditions—African, Asian, or Native American.

Radical Muslims, who were responsible for or identify with the events of September 11, view Western civilization as a threat to traditional Islam. Their vision of an Islamic society based on a strict interpretation of the Koran clashes head on with core principles of Western democracy—separation of church and state, religious toleration, protection of basic rights, and female equality.

Defenders of the Enlightenment heritage argue that this heritage, despite its flaws, still has a powerful message for us. They caution against devaluing and undermining the modern West's unique achievements: the tradition of *rationality,* which makes possible a scientific understanding of the physical universe and human nature, the utilization of nature for human betterment, and the identification and reformation of irrational and abusive institutions and beliefs; the tradition of *political freedom,* which is the foundation of democratic institutions; the tradition of *inner freedom,* which asserts the individual's capacity for ethical autonomy, the ability and duty to make moral choices; the tradition of *humanism,* which regards individuals as active subjects, with both the right and the capacity to realize their full human potential; the tradition of *equality,* which demands equal treatment under the law; and the tradition of *human dignity,* which affirms the inviolable integrity and worth of the human personality and is the driving force behind what is now a global quest for social justice and human rights.

The modern struggle for human rights—initiated during the Enlightenment, advanced by the French Revolution, and embodied in liberalism—continues in the contemporary age. Two crucial developments in this struggle are the civil rights movement in the United States and the feminist movement. Spokespersons for these movements have used ideas formulated by Western thinkers in earlier struggles for liberty and equality. Thus, one reason for the success of Martin Luther King's policy of direct action was that he both inspired and shamed white America to live up to its Judeo-Christian and democratic principles. Although written more than twenty-five years ago, the insights of French social theorist Jacques Ellul still apply:

> *[T]he essential, central, undeniable fact is that the West was the first civilization in history to focus attention on the individual and on freedom. . . . The West, and the West alone, is responsible for the movement that has led to the desire for freedom. . . . Today men point the finger of outrage at slavery and torture. Where did that kind of indignation originate? What civilization or culture cried out that slavery was unacceptable and torture scandalous? Not Islam, or Buddhism, or Confucius, or Zen, or the religions and moral codes of Africa and India! The West alone has defended the inalienable rights of the human person, the dignity of the individual. . . . The West attempted to apply in a conscious, methodical way the implications of freedom. . . . [T]he West discovered what no one else had discovered: freedom and the individual. . . . I see no other satisfactory model that can replace what the West has produced.**

The roots of these ideals are ultimately found in the West's Greek and Judeo-Christian heritage, but it was the philosophes of the Enlightenment who clearly articulated them for the modern age. To be sure, these ideals are a goal, not a finished achievement, and nothing should make westerners more appreciative of the preciousness of these ideals and more alert to their precariousness than examining the ways they have been violated and distorted over the course of centuries. It is equally true that every age has to rethink and revitalize this tradition in order to adapt it to the needs of its own time.

Therefore, it is crucial in this age of globalism, with its heightened sense of ethnic and cultural diversity, that westerners become sensitized to the histories and traditions of all cultures. But it is equally crucial in an era of global interdependence and tension that westerners continuously affirm and reaffirm the core values of their heritage and not permit this priceless legacy to be dismissed or negated. As the history of our century demonstrates, when we lose confidence in this heritage, we risk losing our humanity, and civilized life is threatened by organized barbarism.

*Jacques Ellul, *The Betrayal of the West,* trans. J. O'Connell (New York: Seabury, 1978), pp. 17–19, 29.

Index

Abbasid caliphs, 207, 209, 210
Abbesses, 224
Abbey of Fulda, 218
Abelard, Peter, 265–267
Aborigines' Protection Society, 687
Abraham, 34
Absolute Spirit, 538, 539, 540
Absolutism, 378, 380, 390, 392, 398–399, 405, 427, 437, 468, 475–476, 484
Abstract art, 717–718
Abu Bakr, 206
Abyssinia, 685
Accounting procedures, 364
Achilles, 55–56, 105
Acre, 249
Acropolis of Athens, 50(illus.)
Action Française, 800, 801
Actium, battle of, 138, 142
Address to the Christian Nobility of the German Nation (Luther), 332
Adenauer, Konrad, 878
Adrianople, battle of, 165
Advancement of Learning (Bacon), 420
Aegean Basin, 63(illus.)
Aegean civilizations, 52–54. *See also* Ancient Greece
Aegean islands, 54
Aeneid (Virgil), 154
Aeschylus, 93
Afghanistan: British and Russian interests in, 684, 685, 735; European interests in, 684; Soviet invasion of, 880; Taliban in, 904, 906; post-Taliban, 907(illus.)
Africa: prehistoric civilization in, 5; trade with, 352, 353, 509; European expansion in, 685–690; map of, 686; decolonization of, 884–885. *See also* North Africa; West Africa; *specific countries*
Afrikaans, 689
Agamemnon, 55–56
Age of Pericles, 66, 69, 70
Age of Reason. *See* Enlightenment
Agincourt, battle of, 284
Agriculture: in early Near Eastern, 8–10; Sumerian, 11; in Israelite Kingdom, 36; in Roman Republic, 133–134; manorialism and, 222, 224, 225, 234; in Middle Ages, 225, 229–231(illus.), 280–281, 362(illus.), 509; plantation, 358, 359, 360(illus.); on manors, 361; enclosure, 361–362, 511; convertible husbandry and, 362–363; in Eastern Europe, 363; in France, 468, 511; capitalist, 509, 510; revolution in, 509–512; in global economy, 674; in Soviet Union, 774
Ahmed, Mahdi Mohammed, 675
Ahura Mazda, 28
Aisha (wife of Muhammad), 207
Akhetaten, Pharaoh, 21, 22
Akkad, 12
Alans, 165
Alaric, 165
Albania, 848, 892, 901
Albert the Great (Albertus Magnus), 270–271
Alchemy, 412
Alcuin of York, 218–219
Alexander I, tsar of Russia, 502, 562, 566
Alexander II, tsar of Russia, 660, 661
Alexander III, tsar of Russia, 660
Alexander the Great, Macedonian king, 57, 71, 86, 88, 89, 103, 104, 105–106, 111, 117
Alexandria, Egypt, 108, 109, 111, 156, 410
Alexius, Byzantine emperor, 246, 249
Alfonso XIII, king of Spain, 799
Alfred the Great, 237
Algeria, 674, 685, 877–878, 886
Ali, Mohammed, 687
Allah, 204, 206
All Quiet on the Western Front (Remarque), 810, 814
Almagest (Ptolemy), 156, 410–411
Al Qaeda, 888(illus.), 904, 906, 907, 908
Alsace, 733–734, 742, 749, 751, 837
Ambrose, Saint, 188–189
Amenhotep IV, Pharaoh, 21
American colonies, 358, 359
American Revolution, 454–456, 468–470, 544
Amerindians, 358–359
Amin, Idi, 886
Amorite dynasty, 24
Amos, 44, 45
Amsterdam, 384, 399
Anabaptists, 342–343
Anarchism, 602–603
Anatolia, 246, 684
Anatomy, 419
Anaximander, 76
Ancient Egypt: overview, 17, 99; Old Kingdom to Middle Kingdom, 17–18; religion in, 18–19; myths in, 18–20, 29, 56; divine kingship in, 19–20; science and mathematics in, 20–21; New Kingdom and decline of, 21–23, 35; achievements of, 30; influence of, 34, 106; fall to Rome, 103; Alexander the Great and, 105. *See also* Egypt
Ancient Greece: literature in, 30, 54–56, 259; philosophy in, 30, 40, 75–89, 112, 182–184, 259; overview, 51–52; chronology of, 52; early Aegean civilizations and, 52–54; Sparta, 54, 58–59, 62, 66–69; rise of Hellenic civilization in, 54–57; maps of, 55, 63; religion in, 56–57, 79; evolution of city-state in, 57–58; politics in, 57–58, 69–72, 84; Athens, 59–62; Delian League, 62–63; Persian Wars, 62–63, 79; democracy in, 63–68, 84–85; slavery in, 64–66; Age of Pericles, 66–67; Peloponnesian War, 66–69, 71–72, 79, 82, 84, 97–98; Fourth Century, 69; philosophy in, 75–89, 182–184, 208; art in, 89; poetry in, 89–91; homosexuality in, 90; drama in, 90–96; view of history in, 96–98; achievements of, 98–99, 811; influence of, 106, 124, 127, 153, 157, 207, 208, 209, 301. *See also* Greece; Hellenistic Age
Andalusia, 381
Angles, 237
Anglican church, 340, 393, 397, 418
Anglo-French Entente Cordiale of 1904, 735
Anglo-Russian Entente of 1907, 735
Anglo-Saxons, 214, 237, 238
Angola, 886

Animal Farm (Orwell), 823
Anna Karenina (Tolstoy), 586
Annals (Tacitus), 155
Anselm, Saint, 265
Anthony, Mark, 136–138, 142, 143
Antichrist, 327–328
The Anti-Christ (Nietzsche), 698
Antigonids, 106
Antioch, 249
Antiochus III, Seleucid king, 106
Antiochus IV, Seleucid king, 109
Anti-Semitism: in early Christians, 187–188; in Middle Ages, 212, 232, 254–256, 631; in Germany, 555, 627–634, 787–790, 792–793, 795, 797–798, 851–856; Volkish thought and, 627–632; rise of late-nineteenth century, 630–634; Dreyfus trial and, 655; Church and, 795; Action Française and, 800, 801; World War II and, 838, 839, 847–848, 851–856; in Austria, 842. *See also* Jews; Judaism
Antoninus Pius, 149
Antwerp, 384, 399
Apollonius of Rhodes, 110
Apostles, 176, 184–185
Appeal of One Half of the Human Race (Thompson), 608
Aqueduct at Pont du Gard, 150
Aquinas, Saint Thomas, 268–270, 273, 277, 289, 411, 820
Arab-Israeli conflict, 907
Arabs: in Byzantine Empire, 202, 204; conversion to Islam, 204–206; Mongol invasions and Ottoman dominance, 209–210; in Frankish Gaul, 217; galleys, 353; radical Islam and, 908. *See also* Islam; Islamic civilization; Muslims
Aragon, 241, 381
Aramaeans, 25, 28
Aramaic, 28, 109
Arbatov, Georgi, 896
Archimedes of Syracuse, 112
Architecture: Persian, 27(illus.), 28; Minoan, 53; Greek, 80(illus.), 144; Hellenistic, 107, 109; Etruscan, 120; Roman, 144(illus.), 147, 157; medieval, 275, 276(illus.), 277; Renaissance, 315. *See also* Art
Arch of Titus, 33(illus.)
Arendt, Hannah, 767, 830
Areopagus Council, 61–62
Argentina, 690
Arianism, 186
Aristarchus, 111
Aristides, Aelius, 153
Aristophanes, 95–96, 110
Aristotle: background, 86; critique of Plato, 86–87; ethical thought of, 87–88; political thought of, 88–89, 103; Alexander the Great and, 105, 111; influence of, 111, 419; commentaries on, 208, 209, 212, 213; Latin translations of, 212; medieval rediscovery of, 263–264, 267–270, 272, 423; concept of natural slaves, 358; cosmology of, 411–414, 416
Arius, 186
Arkwright, Richard, 513
Armenia, 148, 149, 892
Arminius, 626(illus.)
Arms race, 872–874, 879
Arndt, Ernst Moritz, 554
Arouet, François Marie. *See* Voltaire
Art: prehistoric, 7–8, 7(illus.); ancient Near Eastern, 28, 30; Early Christian, 30, 171(illus.), 193(illus.); Aegean, 53; Greek, 65(illus.), 67(illus.), 78(illus.), 89; Roman, 102(illus.), 123(illus.), 131, 153, 157; Hellenistic, 105(illus.), 108(illus.), 111; Etruscan, 122(illus.); medieval, 261(illus.), 263(illus.), 266(illus.), 282(illus.), 285(illus.), 286(illus.), 288(illus.), 294(illus.), 312, 362(illus.); Renaissance, 300(illus.), 304(illus.), 307, 311–316; Gothic, 312; Dutch, 400; of Romantic period, 531, 533; realism in, 585–586; impressionist, 712–714; modern, 712–718, 814–817; postimpressionist, 714; expressionist, 715, 814; cubist, 715–717; abstract, 717–718, 814; Dadaist, 814–816; surrealist, 816, 817. *See also* Architecture
Artisans, 521
The Art of Love (Ovid), 154–155
Aryans, 787, 790
Ashurbanipal, king of Assyria, 26
Asia: railroads in, 643; European domination of, 675–685; map of, 676; European imperialism in southeast and central, 684–685; decolonization of, 884–885. *See also specific countries*
Asia Minor, 54, 105, 106, 111, 135, 203, 209, 249
Asimov, Isaac, 720
Assembly, Greek, 62, 63, 64
Assyria, 26, 35, 36
Assyrians, 23, 25–26, 36
Astrology, 412
Astronomy: Mesopotamian, 16; Egyptian, 18; Babylonian, 30, 108; Hellenistic, 108, 111; Ptolemaic, 156—157, 413–414; Muslim golden age, 208; ancient Greek, 410, 413; Copernicus, 412–414, 416; Tycho and Kepler, 414–415; Galileo, 415–416; Newton, 416–418. *See also* Science
Asylum seekers, 902–903
Atatürk, Kemal, 675, 684
Atheists, 433, 436, 827
Athens: growth and development of, 57, 58, 59; democracy in, 59–62; Delian League, 62–63, 67; Persian Wars, 62–63, 79; democracy in, 63–66, 84–85; Pericles and, 66–67; Peloponnesian War, 67–69, 70, 98; politics in, 70–72; Sophists, 79; Hellenistic, 111. *See also* Ancient Greece
Atomism, 114
Atonism, 22–23
Attica, 60, 62, 67
Auden, W. H., 99
Auerbach, Berthold, 628
August Decrees, 474, 475
Augustine, Saint, 189–192, 191(illus.), 265
Augustus (Octavian), Roman Emperor, 120, 137, 138, 139, 141(illus.), 142–146, 152, 153, 154
Aurangzeb Alamgir, Emperor, 675, 677
Auschwitz, 853, 855, 863
Australia: imperialist interests of, 684; industrialization in, 693; World War II and, 849
Austria: Thirty Years' War, 385; emergence of 402; map, 404; during Enlightenment, 449, 450, 453; war with France, 476–478; Napoleon and, 498, 503; Congress of Vienna

and, 564; Concert of Europe and, 566; revolutions in 1848, 576, 577, 614, 615; abolishment of serfdom in, 579; Italian unification and, 615; conflict with Prussia, 616, 619–621; nationalism in, 622–625; anti-Semitism in, 630, 631; Jewish population in, 631; hostility with Serbia, 736–739; aftermath of World War I and, 751, 752, 801; authoritarianism in, 802; antecedents of World War II and, 842; right-wing government in, 902
Austro-Hungarian Empire: industrialization in, 509, 646; nationalist tensions in, 731–732; antecedents of World War I, 733–739; Russia and, 734; Germany and, 735; Serbia and, 736–739; World War I and, 739, 748, 749; end of, 752, 762
Austro-Prussian War of 1866, 620–621
Authoritarianism: in post-World War I Europe, 777–778; spread of, 799–802. *See also* Communism; Fascism
Automotive industry, 643
Avars, 201
Averroës (Ibn-Rushd), 208–209, 270
Avicenna (Ibn-Sina), 208, 271
Avignon popes, 287–288
Azerbaijan, 899
Azores, 353
Aztecs, 355, 374, 382

Babeuf, Gracchus, 482(illus.)–483
Babylon, 36, 37, 105
Babylonia, 26, 27, 35
Babylonian Captivity, 36–37, 287
Babylonians, 15, 16, 46
Bacon, Francis, 309, 420–421, 422
Bacon, Roger, 271, 293
Bactria, 105. *See also* Afghanistan
Badian, E., 130
Baghdad, 207, 209, 210
Bailey, Thomas A., 749
Bakunin, Mikhail, 602–603, 767
Balboa, Vasco Nuñez de, 355
Balfour Declaration, 684
Balkans: Middle Ages, 201, 202, 249; pre-World War I, 731, 734, 738; World War II and, 848; Serbia's aggression in, 904
Balkan Wars, 736
Ball, John, 283–284
Baltic states, 746, 759, 838, 861. *See also* Estonia; Latvia; Lithuania
Balts, 246, 351
Balzac, Honoré de, 586
Bangladesh, 677
Banking: innovations in, 364; industrialization and, 515–517; in Russian Federal Republic, 897, 898
Bank of France, 497
Barbarossa, Frederick, 246, 249
Baring family, 516
Barker, Thomas Jones, 688
Barth, Karl, 819–820
Baruch, Bernard, 871
Basil, Saint, 185
Basques, 646
Bassi, Laura, 440
Bastille, 462(illus.), 473
Battle of Britain, 848
Battle of Hastings, 237
Battle of Issus (Syria), 102(illus.), 105
Battle of the Nile, 490
Battle of Trafalgar, 500
Baum, Rainer C., 856
Bavaria, 217, 218, 453
Bayle, Pierre, 432, 433, 447
Bebel, August, 647
Beccaria, Cesare, 441–442
Beckmann, Max, 817
Bede, Venerable, 215
Bedouins, 206
Beer Hall Putsch, 788
Beethoven, Ludwig, 531, 533
Being and Nothingness (Sartre), 827
Being and Time (Heidegger), 825–826
Belarus, 899
Belgium, 449, 478; French annexation of, 498; Napoleon and, 504; transportation industry in, 516; Congress of Vienna and, 567; Congo and, 689, 884–885; World War I and, 738, 742; World War II and, 845, 847, 856, 861; NATO and, 872
Belisarius, 215
Bell, Alexander Graham, 643
Bell, Daniel, 710
Bellini, Giovanni, 315
Benda, Julien, 821
Benedict, Saint, 185
Benedictine monks of Cluny, 242
Benedict XI, Pope, 287
Beneš, Eduard, 802
Ben Matthias, Joseph. *See* Josephus, Flavius
Benn, Gottfried, 711
Bentham, Jeremy, 550, 608
Benz, Karl, 643
Bequerel, Henri, 718
Berbers, 217
Berchtold, Leopold von, 594, 732, 737
Berckheyde, G. A., 349
Berdyaev, Nikolai, 824, 829
Bergson, Henri, 701–702
Berlin Wall, 868(illus.), 890, 895(illus.)
Bernhardi, Friedrich von, 594, 731
Bernstein, Eduard, 647
Bessemer, Henry, 515
Beveridge, Albert J., 594
Bible, 34, 38–39. *See also* Hebrew Scriptures; New Testament
Bill of Rights, 456
bin Laden, Osama, 888, 906–907, 908
Biology, 418–419. *See also* Science; Scientific Revolution
Biró, Mathias Devái, 341
The Birth of Venus (Botticelli), 314
Bishop of Rome, 184–185
Bishops, 184, 186
Bismarck, Otto von, 619, 620, 621(illus.), 622, 627, 647, 649, 687, 732, 733, 734
Black Death. *See* Bubonic plague
Black Hand, 731, 737
Black Shirts, 781

Blair, Tony, 904
Blake, William, 532, 533
Blanc, Louis, 571
Blandina, 180–181
Bleak House (Dickens), 520, 587, 588, 589
Blitzkrieg, 498
Blood libel, 255–256
Blum, Léon, 804, 842
Boccaccio, 308
Boerhaave, Herman, 419
Boer War, 672, 685, 689
Boethius, 212–213, 237
Bohemia, 341, 401, 450, 576, 579, 624
Bohemian church, 325
Bohr, Niels, 719
Boleyn, Anne, 340, 394
Bologna, 303
Bolsheviks/Bolshevism, 746, 755–759, 770, 772, 774, 776, 777, 778, 779, 781, 786, 802, 817, 838
Bonaparte, Louis Napoleon (Napoleon III), 615, 616, 622, 652–653, 655, 691
Bonaparte, Napoleon: Alexander the Great and, 105; painting of, 488(illus.); rise to power, 489–491; chronology of career of, 490; character of, 491–492; France and, 492–497; Europe and, 497–498, 500; fall of, 500–504, 530; legend of, 504
Bonapartism, 653
Boniface, Saint, 217, 218(illus.)–219
Boniface VIII, Pope, 285, 286, 287
Book burnings, 343, 798
Bookkeeping, double-entry, 364
Books of Instruction (Ancient Egypt), 18
The Book of the Courtier (Castiglione), 310, 312
Bora, Katharina von, 332–334
Borneo, 684
Bosnia, 735–737, 892, 900(illus.), 901
Boston Tea Party, 455(illus.)
Botticelli, Sandro, 314
Boulanger, Georges, 654
Bourbon dynasty, 388–392, 493, 503
Bourgeoisie. *See* Middle class
Bowra, C. M., 56
Boxer Rebellion, 675, 680
Boyle, Robert, 309, 409, 419–420, 422
Bracher, Karl Dietrich, 532, 767, 794, 863
Braidwood, Robert J., 10
Brandenburg Gate, 655
Brandt, Willy, 879
Braque, Georges, 715–716
Brazil, 358, 360(illus.), 385, 690, 691(illus.)
Brethren of the Common Life, 316, 317, 326–327
Breton, André, 816
Brezhnev, Leonid, 880–881, 883
Bright, John, 39
British Parliament, 238, 291, 340, 380, 386, 393, 396, 397, 454, 549, 568, 648
Bronstein, Lev. *See* Trotsky, Leon
Brooke, Rupert, 739, 741
The Brothers Karamazov (Dostoevski), 587
Broz, Josip (Tito), 857
Bruges, 281, 284
Brunelleschi, Filippo, 313
Bruno, Giordano, 344
Brunswick, duke of, 477
Brutus, Marcus Junius, 138, 152
Brzezinski, Zbigniew K., 766, 767
Buber, Martin, 824, 829
Bubonic plague, 167, 255, 273(illus.), 281–282, 304. *See also* Plague
Buckle, Henry T., 591
Buddenbrooks (Mann), 813
Buddhism, 675
Bulgaria, 736, 748, 751, 802, 890
Bulgars, 201, 204
Bülow, Bernhard von, 734–735
Burckhardt, Jacob, 301–302
Burghers, 235
Burgundians, 211, 242
Buridan, Jean, 272
Burke, Edmund, 541, 542, 549
Burma, 677, 682, 684, 857, 884
Burrows, Millar, 44
Burton, Richard, 673
Bush, George W., 899, 906, 909
Business. *See* Commerce and trade
Butler, Josephine, 652
Butterfield, Herbert, 485
Byelorussia, 892
Byzantine civilization: overview, 199–200; conflict with Roman Church, 200; imperial growth and decline of, 200–204, 215; map of, 201; impact of, 204; Greek influence on, 208; translation of works from, 261, 270

Caesar, Julius, 105, 129, 130, 137–138(illus.), 152
Calculus, 410
Caligula, 147
Callimachus, 110
Calvin, John, 318, 331, 336, 337, 338, 342
Calvinism, 336–338, 341, 396, 397, 399, 400, 427
Cambodia, 875, 884
Cambyses, 28
Camelots du Roi, 801
Cameroons, 689
Camus, Albert, 826, 828–829
Canaan, 34, 35
Canaanites, 25
Canada, NATO and, 872
Canaries, 353
Candide (Voltaire), 435, 442–443
Cannae, battle of, 127, 134, 165
Canon of Medicine (Avicenna), 271
Canossa, 244
The Canterbury Tales (Chaucer), 262
Cape of Good Hope, 354
Capet, Hugh, 386
Capetian dynasty, 284
Capitalism: domestic system, 364; explanation of, 368; mercantile, 368–370; during Enlightenment, 443–444; Marx and, 599–600; monopoly, 671; Weber and, 709
Capital (Marx), 597, 599
Carbonari, 614

Cardinals, 243
Carneades of Cyrene, 116
Carnegie, Andrew, 593
Carnivals, 370, 371, 372
Carolingian dynasty, 217, 239
Carolingian Renaissance, 218–220
Carpenter, Malcolm S., 872(illus.)
Carthage, 124, 125, 126, 127, 133, 139
Carthaginians, 125, 130
Cartwright, Edmund, 513
Cartwright, John, 463
Casement, Roger, 687, 690
Cassiodorus, 213
Cassirer, Ernst, 291, 535, 822
Castellany, 221
Castiglione, Baldesar, 310, 312–313
Castile, 241, 254, 272, 353, 381
Castlereagh, Robert Stewart, Viscount, 562, 563
Çatal Hüyük (Turkey), 9
Catalonia, 241, 381, 799
Catharism, 252, 253, 254
Cathedral of Saint Sernin, 276(illus.)
Cathedral School of Notre Dame, 262, 265
Cathedral schools, 261–262
Catherine of Aragon, 340
Catherine the Great, Russian empress, 405, 452(illus.), 453, 659
Catholic Center party, 657
Catholic Centrists (Germany), 787
Catholic Church. *See* Roman Catholic Church
Catholicism. *See* Christianity; Roman Catholic Church
Catholic Reformation, 343–345
Cato the Elder, 131, 133
Catullus, 90, 131–132
Cave painting, 7(illus.)–8
Cavour, Count Camillo Benso di, 615, 616
Ceausescu, Nicolae, 890
Censorship: by Catholic Church, 317, 344, 390, 445, 447; prevalence of, 427; in Russia, 452–453
Central Europe: authoritarian governments in, 800–802; post-communist, 899–902. *See also specific countries*
Centuriate Assembly, 121–122
Cervantes Saavedra, Miguel de, 319
Ceylon, 564, 884
Cézanne, Paul, 714
Chagall, Marc, 817
Chaldeans, 26–28, 36
Chamberlain, Houston Stewart, 629
Chamberlain, Joseph, 689
Chamberlain, Neville, 843, 845
Chambers, Ephraim, 447
Chansons de geste, 273
Chaplin, Charlie, 818(illus.)–819
Chaplin, Hannah, 818
Chapuy, Jean-Baptiste, 484(illus.)
Chariot races, 158
Charivari, 371
Charlemagne, 217–220, 237, 400
Charles Albert, king of Piedmont-Sardinia, 577
Charles I, king of England, 387, 396, 397
Charles II, king of England, 397–398
Charles IV, king of France, 284
Charles IX, king of France, 387
Charles the Bald, 221
Charles V, Holy Roman Emperor, 331, 332, 334, 335–336, 340, 383, 385, 399, 401
Charles VI, Austrian emperor, 450
Charles VIII, king of France, 306, 386
Charles X, king of France, 566
Charter of Nobility, 452
Chartists, 468–469, 649
Chaucer, Geoffrey, 262
Chechnya, 898
Chekhov, Anton, 586–587
Cheka, 770
Chemistry, 419–420
Chénier, André, 463
Chiang Kai-shek (Jiang Jieshi), 675, 681, 857
Children's Crusade, 249
Chile, 690
China: rise of nationalism in, 680–681; trade with, 232, 352, 353; gunpowder and, 352; resistance to influence of West in, 675, 680; European intervention in, 679–680, 692; communist takeover of, 884; Tanzania and, 885
Chirac, Jacques, 904
Chivalry, 223
Chlotilde, 216
Chopin, Frederic, 531
Christ. *See* Jesus Christ
Christianity: origins of, 40, 48, 142, 169, 172–179; spread of, 104, 113, 117, 183(illus.), 199; cult of Mithras and, 160; chronology of, 173; Judaism in first century B.C. and, 173–174; Jesus and, 175–177; Saint Paul and, 177–179; universalism and, 179, 181; appeal of, 179–181; Roman Empire and, 181–182; Greek philosophy and, 182–184, 193, 259, 261, 263–264, 267–270; Hellenization of, 183–184; bishop of Rome and, 184–185; monasticism and, 185; scriptural tradition and doctrinal disputes and, 185–186; society and, 186–187, 551; Jews and, 187–188, 254–256, 631, 633; world-view of, 188–192, 819–821; Augustinian, 189–192, 191(illus.); classical humanism and, 191–194; Byzantine Empire, 199, 200, 202–204, 203, 204; crusades and, 203; influence of, 204; Latin Christiandom, 211, 212, 213, 220, 236, 242; medieval civilization and culture, 213–216; Frankish empire and, 216–220; education of clergy, 218–219; in feudal society, 223, 224; Crusades and, 246–250; dissenters and reformers and, 250–253; medieval world-view based on, 262–264; Aquinas and, 268–270, 273, 277, 289; as bridge to modern world, 290–291; humanism and, 308, 309, 316, 317, 318, 319, 321; medieval church in crisis and, 325–328; mysticism and, 326–327, 562; Indian conversions, 357, 358; witchcraft and, 372; cosmology and, 411; Scientific Revolution and, 423–424; Enlightenment and, 432–435, 457; romantics' view of, 534; conservatism and, 543; Saint-Simon and, 552; Darwinism and, 593–596; Nietzsche and, 698–700; Nazism and, 795. *See also* Eastern Orthodox Church; Papacy; Protestantism; Reformation; Roman Catholic Church; *specific denominations*
Christianity Not Mysterious (Toland), 433

Christians: relationship between Jews and, 187–188, 212, 232, 254–256, 631, 633; in Islamic lands, 207
Christian Social Workers' party, 630
Christine de Pisan, 292–293
Chrysostom, John, Saint, 188
Churchill, Winston, 649, 845, 869, 871, 875, 876
Church of San Lorenzo, 313
Church of the Holy Wisdom (Hagia Sophia), Constantinople, 203(illus.)
Cicero, 123, 132, 138, 212, 308, 309
Ciompi revolt, 303
Cisalpine Gaul, 131
City-states: Sparta, 54, 58–59, 62, 66–69; Athens, 57, 58, 59–62; evolution of, 57–58; Delian League, 62; decline of, 69–70, 103, 120, 133–134, 179; theoretical reason in, 79–80; Seleucids, 107; Roman Republic, 124, 139; Roman Empire, 153; northern Italy, 302–306; monarchies in, 378. *See also* Polis
The City of God (Saint Augustine), 189, 190
The City of Ladies (Christine de Pisan), 292–293
Civil disobedience, 679
Civil humanism, 310
Civilization and Its Discontents (Freud), 704, 810
Civilizations: rise of, 5–9; first, 9–10; Mesopotamian, 11–17; Egyptian, 17–23; Hittite, 24–25; Assyrian, 25–26; Neo-Babylonian, 26–27; Persian, 27–28
The Civilization of the Renaissance in Italy (Burckhardt), 301
Civil law, Roman, 157, 201
Civil War (United States), 662, 685
Clairvaux, Bernard, 266
Class conflict, 598–599
Classical humanism, 191–194
Claudius, 152
Cleisthenes, 61–62, 64, 66
Clemenceau, Georges, 655, 750(illus.), 751
Clement of Alexandria, 183
Clement V, Pope, 287
Clement VII, Pope, 288
Cleon, 95
Cleopatra, 136(illus.)–138, 142
Clericis Laicos, 286
Clodia, 131
The Clouds (Aristophanes), 95–96
Clovis, 210(illus.), 216–217
Cluniac monks, 242, 246
Cluny, 242
Coal, 514
Cobbert, William, 549
Code Napoléon, 494–495, 500
Code of Hammurabi, 15–16
Colbert, Jean Baptiste, 389
Cold War, 693; chronology of, 870; origins of, 871; mobilization during, 871–872; arms race and space race during, 872–874; Vietnam war and, 874–875; decolonization and, 884–885
Coleridge, Samuel Taylor, 534
Collectivization, 774
Collingwood, R. G., 96
Colloquies (Erasmus), 317
Colonialism, 670, 678–679, 689–690. *See also* Imperialism
Colonies. *See* American colonies
Colosseum of Rome, 147, 158
Columbus, Christopher, 355, 382
Commentaries (Caesar), 136
Commerce and trade: Egypt and, 16, 20; Mesopotamians and, 16; Mycenaeans and, 53–54; Greeks and, 54; Hellenistic period and, 108; Roman Empire and, 151; Middle Ages and, 212, 232, 233(illus.), 236, 303; northern Italian city-states and, 303; European expansion and, 351–357, 363–370, 368; roles between Old and New World and, 456. *See also* Economy
Committee of Public Safety, 478, 479, 480
Commodus, 150, 167
Common law, 201, 237, 393
Commonwealth of Independent States (CIS), 894
Communards, 653
Communication, 515
Communism: in Soviet Union, 767–777, 869, 871–883; in Russia, 769–772; war, 770; in Germany, 784–785, 793, 838; in Spain, 799; fear of, 801, 872; in Hungary, 802; disillusionment with, 817–819, 889; Cold War and, 871; in France, 878; in China, 884; demise of, 889–896; in Russian Federal Republic, 898; in North Korea, 909. *See also* Fascism; Marxism; Totalitarianism
Communist International (Comintern), 769, 772
Communist Manifesto (Marx & Engels), 597, 600
Communitarians, 551
Complutensian Polyglot Bible, 318, 319
Comte, Auguste, 590, 706
Concentration camps, 852(illus.)–857
Concert of Europe, 564, 566
Conciliar Movement, 288
Concordat of 1801, 494
Concordat of Bologna, 387
Concordat of Worms, 244, 246
Condorcet, Marquis de, 465, 607
Condottieri, 306, 311, 320
Confederation of Rhine, 498
Confessions (Saint Augustine), 189
The Confessions (Rousseau), 531
Confucianism, 675
Congo, 689, 886
Congo Free State, 687
Congress of Vienna: Metternich and, 560–563; crisis over Saxony and Poland, 563–564; settlement of, 564, 567
Conrad, Joseph, 673, 690, 712, 712(illus.)–713
Conrad III, German emperor, 249
Conservatism: explanation of, 530; overview of, 541; French Revolution and, 541–543; social stability and, 543; Prussia and, 621
Considerations on Representative Government (Mill), 604
The Consolation of Philosophy (Boethius), 213, 237
Constable, John, 531
Constantine, Roman emperor, 164, 166, 168, 182, 203(illus.)
Constantinople, 199–200, 202–203, 232, 247, 249
Constitution: Roman, 121–124; of United States, 455–456
Constitutional states, 378
Consumerism, 370
Containment, 871
Continental System (Napoleon), 500–501
Convention of Public Safety (French Revolution), 478
Convertible husbandry, 363

Cooper, Leroy G., 872(illus.)
Cooper, Thomas, 442
Copernicus, Nicolaus, 411–414, 416, 424
Copyhold, 361
Corpus Juris Civilis, 201, 272
Corsica, 126, 904
Cort, Henry, 514
Cortés, Hernando, 352, 355, 382
Cosmologists, 76–78, 80, 81, 410–411, 412, 413, 414
Cosmopolitanism, 104, 106–109
Cottage industry, 364
Cotton gin, 513
Cotton industry, 513, 514(illus.)
Council of Basel, 325
Council of Chalcedon, 186
Council of Clermont, 246
Council of Constance, 325
Council of Five Hundred, 64
Council of Four Hundred, 60, 64
Council of Nicaea, 186
Council of Pisa, 288
Council of Ten, 306
Council of the Areopagus, 61–62
Council of Trent, 344–345
Counter Reformation, 343–345, 371, 402, 424
Courbet, Gustave, 584(illus.), 585, 603
Covenant (Hebrew), 41–43, 47
Crassus, 136, 137
Crates, 109
The Creation of Adam (Michaelangelo), 315
Crécy, battle of, 284, 286(illus.)
Crete, 53
Crime and Punishment (Dostoevski), 587
Crimean War, 615, 659–660
Criminal justice, 440–442
Critias, 69, 79
Critique of Pure Reason (Kant), 537
Croatia, 901
Croats, 577, 625, 732
Crompton, Samuel, 513
Cromwell, Oliver, 397, 399(illus.)
Cromwell, Thomas, 340
Crusades: origin of, 203; overview of, 246; papacy and, 246–247, 249; motivation for, 247; map of, 248; impact of, 250, 351, 353
Cuba, 691, 692, 872
Cuban Missile Crisis, 872
Cubism, 715–717
Culture: language development and, 6–7; Greek, 75–99; Hellenistic, 107–117; during Roman Republic, 130–132; during Roman Empire, 153–160; during Byzantine period, 204; waning of classical, 212–213; monasteries and, 213, 214, 215; during Middle Ages, 259–277; during Renaissance, 307–308, 311–316, 320–321; traditional popular, 370–371; reform of popular, 371–372; globalization and, 905–907
Cuneiform writing, 11, 16, 25
Cuthbert of Canterbury, Archbishop, 219
Cynicism, 116–117
Cyprus, 106
Cyrillic, 204
Cyrus the Great, 28, 37
Czechoslovakia: World War I peace settlement and, 750, 752; democracy and, 777, 800, 802; aftermath of World War I and, 837; alliance with France, 837; World War II and, 842–843, 862; 1968 invasion of, 880–882; end of communism in, 892
Czech Republic, 453–454, 900–901
Czechs: during Byzantine Empire, 204; nationalism of, 576, 579, 623, 624, 625; industrialization and, 646; in Austro-Hungarian Empire, 732

Dacia, 148
Dadaist, 814–816
Dagestan, 898
Daimler, Gottlieb, 643
Daladier, Édouard, 843
D'Alembert, Jean, 448, 457
Dali, Salvador, 816
Dalton, John, 591
Damascus, Pope, 188
Danes, 237
D'Annunzio, Gabriele, 780
Dante Alighieri, 274–275
Danton, Jacques, 480
Darby, Abraham, 516
Darby, Abraham, II, 516
Darby, Abraham, III, 517
Darby family, 514, 516–517
Dardanelles, 735, 746
Darius I, king of Persia, 62
Darius III, king of Persia, 105
Dark Age, 54, 56–57
Darkness at Noon (Koestler), 817–819
d'Artois, comte, 473
Darwin, Charles, 591(illus.), 592–594
Darwin, Erasmus, 592
Darwinism: overview of, 591–592; natural selection and, 592; Christianity and, 593–596; Social, 593–596, 627, 633, 671–672, 721, 729, 732, 739, 790, 854
David, 35
David, Jacques Louis, 472, 488
David (Michaelangelo), 315
Dawes Plan, 786
Dawson, Christopher, 819, 821
Dayton Agreement, 901
D-Day, 860
Dead Sea, 173
Dead Sea Scrolls, 38(illus.), 173–174
de Beauvoir, Simone, 826, 827(illus.)
de Bonald, Louis, 541
Deborah, 43
Decembrists, 566
Decius, Roman emperor, 181
Declamation Concerning the False Decretals of Constantine (Valla), 309–310
Declaration of Independence, 454, 469, 606, 607
Declaration of Statements and Principles, 607
Declaration of the Rights of Man and of the Citizen, 474–475, 476, 479, 483–484, 606
Declaration of the Rights of Women (de Gouges), 606
The Decline of the West (Spengler), 811

Decolonization, 884–885
The Defender of the Peace (Marsiglio of Padua), 287
Degas, Edgar, 587(illus.), 713
de Gaulle, Charles, 848, 877, 904
de Gouges, Olympe de, 606
Deists, 433, 434
Delacroix, Eugene, 555(illus.)
de las Casas, Bartolomé, 358–359
Delian League, 62–63, 67, 68
de Maistre, Joseph, 541
Democracy: primitive, 15; Greek, 59–68, 84–85; liberalism and, 546–549; radicalism and, 549–550; labor and, 646; in post-World War I Europe, 777; United States as model of, 875
Democracy in America (Tocqueville), 547
Democritus, 77, 114
Demosthenes, 69, 70(illus.), 71
Denmark: under Grand Empire, 498; Bismarck and, 620; World War II and, 845, 856; NATO and, 872; European Community membership, 876; right-wing parties in, 902
Depression of 1873, 640, 648. *See also* Great Depression
Descartes, René, 421(illus.), 422, 434
Descent of Man (Darwin), 592
Despotism: in northern Italian city-states, 303, 304, 306; enlightened, 402, 449–450, 452–453, 497
Détente, 881
d'Holbach, 442, 465
Dialectics, 81–82, 92
Dias, Bartholomeu, 354
Diaspora, 177
Díaz, Porfirio, 692
Dickens, Charles, 520, 587, 588, 589
Diderot, Denis, 442, 443, 447(illus.), 448, 449, 453, 591
Dimitrijevic, Dragutin, 737
Diocletian, Roman emperor, 164, 166, 168, 181–182
Diogenes, 117
Dionysus, 91, 92
Dionysus cult, 57
Directory (French Revolution), 482, 491
Disease: during early civilizations, 10; among New World natives, 355, 357, 359; advances in prevention and treatment of, 644. *See also* Bubonic plague; Plague
Disraeli, Benjamin, 648
Diu, 353
The Divine Comedy (Dante), 264, 275(illus.), 277, 532(illus.)
Dix, Otto, 817
Dollfuss, Engelbert, 802
A Doll's House (Ibsen), 589–590
Domesday Book, 237
Domestic system of cottage industry, 364
Dominic, Saint, 253
Dominican Republic, 691
Dominicans, 253, 373
Domitian, 147, 152
Donatello, 314
Donation of Constantine, 310
Don Quixote (Cervantes), 319
Dorians, 54, 58
Dostoevski, Fydor, 587, 700–701, 704, 825
Double-entry bookkeeping, 364
Doyle, William, 380
Draco, 60
Draconian, 60
Drama: Greek, 90–96; Roman, 131; Shakespearean, 319–320; realism in, 586–587, 588–590. *See also* Literature
Dreyfus, Alfred, 655, 656, 801
Dreyfus affair, 630, 632, 655, 689, 801, 803
Droz, Jacques, 569–570
Drumont, Edouard, 630
Dual Monarchy, 623, 624, 625
Dubček, Alexander, 880
Duchamp, Marcel, 816
du Châtelet, Madame, 424, 435, 440
du Cobenzl, Comte, 450
Dumont, J., 392
Dura-Europos synagogue, 42(illus.), 44(illus.)
Durkheim, Émile, 706–707
Dutch East Indies, 857
Dutch Republic, 427, 429, 432, 436, 449. *See also* Netherlands
The Dying Slave (Michaelangelo), 315
Dzhugashvili, Iosif. *See* Stalin, Joseph

Eakins, Thomas, 642(illus.)
Early Renaissance Art, 312–314
East Africa, 5
Eastern Europe: agricultural change, 363; during Enlightenment, 453–454; industrialization in, 509; authoritarian governments in, 800–802; Soviet domination of, 879–881, 883; demise of communism in, 880, 889–890, 892, 894–896; map of, 883; post-communist, 899–902. *See also specific countries*
Eastern Orthodox Church: language of, 200; origin of, 200; Crusades and, 247, 254; power of, 659
East Germany (German Democratic Republic): Stalin and, 871–872, 878; reunification of, 890, 895(illus.), 905
East India Company, 454, 677
East Indies, 352, 366
Ebert, Friedrich, 784
Ecclesiastical History of the English People (Bede), 215
Economic thought: during Enlightenment, 443–445; liberal, 545–546
Economy: in Roman Empire, 167–169; in Latin Christiandom, 212, 232; feudal, 222; in Middle Ages, 229–235, 280–282; during European expansion, 350–370; in Portuguese empire, 353–355; in Spanish empire, 355, 357; slavery and slave trade and, 357–359; price revolution and, 359–361; agricultural expansion and, 361–363; trade and industrial expansion, 363–368; growth of capitalism and, 368–370; in Napoleon's France, 496–497; beginning of global, 673–674; in Weimar Republic, 785–786; in Nazi Germany, 794–795; in Russian Federal Republic, 896–898; in central and eastern Europe, 899–902. *See also* Commerce and trade
Edessa, 249
Edict of Milan, 182
Edict of Nantes, 338, 390
Education: Sumerians and, 16; Sophists and, 78–79; in Middle Ages, 259–262; in Enlightenment, 440, 453; for females, 440, 496; in Napoleon's France, 495–496; in Great

Britain, 525; in Soviet Union, 772, 775–776; in Nazi Germany, 796–797; teaching radical Islamism, 907–908
Edward III, king of England, 284, 286
Edward VI, king of England, 340, 394, 395
Edwin Smith Surgical Papyrus, 21
Egypt: Hellenistic, 106, 107, 127; Ptolemaic, 106; during Roman Empire, 159; in early Christian period, 185; during Byzantine Empire, 201–202; Ottomans and, 210; Napoleon in, 490; Great Britain and, 674, 687–689, 692; modernization in, 675; World War II and, 860. *See also* Ancient Egypt
Einsatzgruppen, 851
Einstein, Albert, 719, 720(illus.), 721–722
Elba, 503, 504
Eleanor of Aquitaine, 240
Electricity, 643
Eleusinian cult, 57
Eliot, T. S., 810–812, 819
Elite culture, 370, 371
Elizabethan age, 394–395
Elizabeth I, queen of England, 316, 340, 394(illus.)–395
Ellul, Jacques, 912
Émile (Rousseau), 440
Emperor worship, 146
Empire building. *See* Imperialism
Empyrean Heaven, 263
Enclosure, 361–362, 511
Encomenderos, 357
Encomiendas, 357
Encyclopedia (Diderot), 443, 447–448, 591
Engels, Friedrich, 551, 596–599
England: monasteries in, 214; trade in, 232, 365–366, 369–370; rise of, 237–238; Magna Carta and, 238, 291, 393; Parliament and, 238, 291, 340, 380, 386, 393, 396, 397, 454, 549, 568; expulsion of Jews from, 255; wage regulations and, 282; peasant revolt in, 284; Hundred Years' War and, 284–285, 386; during Renaissance, 316; during Reformation, 335, 338, 340, 344, 393; slave trade and, 358; agriculture in, 363; textile industry in, 364, 513; consumerism in, 370; distribution of political power in, 381; Spanish invasion of, 384–385, 394, 395; growth of power in, 386; Louis XIV and, 390; limited monarchy in, 392–399; constitution of, 393; Protestantism and, 393, 395, 396, 397, 398; Tudors in, 393–396; Revolutions in, 396–399; during Enlightenment, 427, 429, 433, 443–444, 448–449, 453; flight of French Protestants to, 429; interest in New World, 448–449; Seven Years' War and, 449, 453, 454; American Revolution and, 454–456; Napoleon and, 500–501; industrialization in, 508, 509, 511–521, 524–525, 641, 648–652. *See also* Great Britain
English Factory Acts, 524–525
English humanism, 319–320
English Revolutions: 1640–1660, 397, 435, 470; 1688–1689, 398, 399, 433, 470
Enlightened despotism, 402, 449–450, 452–453, 497
Enlightenment: Scientific Revolution and, 410; Spinoza and, 422; overview of, 427–429, 533; chronology of, 428; formation of public and secular culture during, 429–432; salons during, 430; Freemasons and, 430–431; scientific academies during, 432; alternatives to orthodoxy and, 432–435; Voltaire and, 434–435; political thought during, 435–438; Locke and, 436–437; Montesquieu and, 437; Rousseau and, 437–438; epistemology and education during, 438–440; social thought during, 438–443; humanitarianism during, 440–443, 504; economic thought during, 443–445; High Enlightenment, 445, 447–448; European expansion, 446(illus.); French Revolution and, 448, 469–470, 484, 485; warfare and, 448–449; enlightened despotism and, 449–450, 452–453; eastern Europe during, 453–454; American Revolution and, 454, 456; modern world and, 456–457, 531, 809, 830, 912; conservatism and, 543; Jews and, 631; Modernism vs., 710, 721–723
Enquiry Concerning Human Understanding (Hume), 536
Entente Cordiale of 1904, 734–735
Entertainment: Roman, 158; pantomine, 818–819. *See also* Drama
Epic of Gilgamesh, 15
Epictetus, 155
Epicureanism, 113–116, 132
Epicurus, 113–115(illus.), 115(illus.), 132, 152
Epidaurus theater (Greece), 74(illus.)
Epidemics, 10, 167, 255, 273(illus.), 281–282, 304
Epistemology, 434, 438–440
Epistles (Saint Paul), 185
Equites, 129
Erasmian humanism, 317–318
Erasmus, Desiderius, 317(illus.)–318, 327, 344
Eratosthenes, 111–112
Ernst, Max, 816
Esarhaddon, king of Assyria, 26
Escape from Freedom (Fromm), 822
Essay Concerning Human Understanding (Locke), 438
Essay on the Principle of Population (Malthus), 545
Essays (Montaigne), 318
Essence of Christianity (Feuerbach), 595
Essenes, 173, 174, 175
Estancias, 357
Estates General, 240, 386, 400, 469, 470, 471, 472, 473, 474
Estonia, 784, 862, 892, 894
Ethics: Egyptian, 18; Aristotle and, 87–88; Mosaic Law and, 175
Ethics (Aristotle), 88
Ethiopia, 674, 689, 783, 841, 842
Etruscans: origin of, 120; culture of, 120–121; art of, 122(illus.); Roman expansion and, 124
Etymologiae (Isidore of Seville), 213
Eucharist, 242, 254, 342, 432
Euclid, 111, 213, 262
Eugène, Prince, viceroy of Italy, 500
Eugene of Savoy, Prince, 402
Eugenius II, Pope, 249
Euphrates River, 10, 11, 27
Euripides, 79, 94–95
Europe: rise of, 199, 200(illus.), 210–213; political and economic transformation of, 210–212; Latin Christendom, 210–213, 232, 242; waning of classical culture in, 212–213; Charlemagne and, 219–220; invasions and, 220(illus.)–221, 229; revival of trade and, 232, 233(illus.); rebirth of towns in, 234–235; rise of states in, 236–241; bubonic plague in, 282; population growth in,

Europe: (*cont.*)
335, 352, 360–361, 363, 509–510; economic transformation in, 350–370; commercial revolution chronology of, 351; expansion of, 351–359; Portuguese empire and, 353–355, 356; Spanish empire and, 355, 356, 357; maps of, 356, 367, 391, 446, 451, 499, 564, 578, 645, 740, 753, 840, 846, 858, 873, 883, 886; slavery and slave trade and, 357–359; price revolution in, 359–361; agricultural expansion in, 361–363; trade and industrial expansion in, 363–366, 368; growth of capitalism in, 368–370; popular culture in, 370–372; witchcraft and witch craze in, 372–374; Napoleon and, 497–504 (*See also* Bonaparte, Napoleon); post-World War II, 875–879; right-wing parties in, 902, 903; immigration trends in, 902–903. *See also specific countries and areas*
European Coal and Steel Community (ECSC), 875
European Community (EC), 875
European Economic Community (EEC), 875
European Recovery Program, 871
European Union (EU), 902, 903, 904
Eusebius, 180
Evangelical churches, 795
Evans, Arthur, 53
Everett, Robert A., 188
Evergood, Philip, 817
The Exchequer, 237
Excommunication, 251
Existentialism: explanation of, 809; background of, 823–824; basic principles of, 824; nineteenth-century forerunners of, 824–825; twentieth-century, 825–829; religious, 829
Exodus (Hebrew), 39, 43, 48
Extraterritoriality, 674
Ezra, 37

Fabians, 649
Factory workers, 521, 522–525
Falange, 800
Falkenhayn, Erich von, 731
Falkland Islands, 877
Al-Farabi, 208
Faraday, Michael, 591, 643
Farel, William, 337
Farming. *See* Agriculture
Farrington, Benjamin, 111
Fascism: nature of, 777–779; Marxism and, 778; in Italy, 779–783, 793; in Spain, 799–800, 841–842; Action Française and, 800, 801; fear of, 804. *See also* Totalitarianism
Fauvism, 716, 717(illus.)
Fawcett, Millicent, 652
Feast of Fools, 371
February Revolution, 570–571, 575
Federal Republic of Germany. *See* West Germany (Federal Republic of Germany)
Feig, Konnilyn G., 855
Feminist movements, 606–608, 912
Fenians, 650
Ferdinand II, king of Naples, 577, 614
Ferdinand II, king of Spain, 352, 381–383, 401
Ferrara, 303
Feudal society: characteristics of, 221–222, 236; vassalage and, 222–223, 238, 240; law in, 223; warriors in, 223–224; noblewomen in, 224; agrarian life in, 224–225; towns in, 235; effect of Crusades on, 250; post-medieval, 290; liberty and, 291; rejection of, 294; in northern Italy, 303; in Portugal, 353; monarchies and, 378. *See also* Serfdom
Feuerbach, Ludwig, 595
Fief, 222
Fifth Republic, 878
Finland: Congress of Vienna and, 564; World War I and, 746, 759
First Crusade, 249
First Estate (France), 464
First Intermediate Period (Ancient Egypt), 17
First Punic War, 125–126
Fischer, Fritz, 739
Five Good Emperors, 150
Five-Year Plans, 773, 774, 775, 776
Flanders, 232, 283, 284, 399
Flaubert, Gustave, 586
Flavian dynasty, 147
Florence, Italy, 234, 284, 303, 306, 310, 313, 315, 364
Flores, Angel, 813
Fonte, Bartolommeo della, 309
Food gathering. *See* Hunting-gathering societies
Ford, Henry, 643
Forster, E. M., 673, 811
For Whom the Bell Tolls (Hemingway), 814
The Foundations of the Nineteenth Century (Chamberlain), 629
Four Hundred (Ancient Greece), 68–69
Fourier, Charles, 552
Fourth Crusade, 203, 249, 254
Fourth Lateran Council, 256, 631
Fourth Republic, 878
France: cave painting in, 7(illus.); Greco-Roman civilization in, 136, 150(illus.); origin of, 221; trade and, 232, 365, 366; rise of, 238–240; map of, 239; government of, 241; Jews in, 255, 847–848; peasant revolts in, 283, 284; Hundred Years' War and, 284–285, 386; papal power in, 285–287; during Renaissance, 316; during Reformation, 331, 336, 337, 338, 387; slave trade and, 358, 442, 494–495; agriculture in, 363, 511; industrialization in, 364, 508, 509; textile industry in, 364; witchcraft in, 373; Thirty Years' War and, 385, 388; medieval kings in, 386; growth of power in, 386–392; Roman Catholic Church and, 387, 388, 445, 447, 655; Protestants in, 387–388, 429, 432, 464, 494; religion in, 387–388; Louis XIV and, 388–390, 392, 429; Grand Empire and, 400, 498; during Enlightenment, 427, 429, 432, 434, 435, 444, 448–449; lodges and clubs in, 430, 431; scientific academics in, 432; interest in New World, 448–449; Seven Years' War and, 449, 453, 454; American Revolution and, 454–455, 468; Second Estate in, 465; bourgeoisie in, 465–466; Third Estate in, 465–468; First Estate in, 466; peasantry in, 466–468, 473, 474, 478; administration and financial disorder in, 468–469; war with Austria and Prussia, 476–478; Jacobins in, 478–479; Napoleon and, 489–500; government of Directory in, 491; government

during Napoleon, 493; religion during Napoleon, 493–496; Code of Napoléon in, 495; education during Napoleon, 495–496; economy during Napoleon, 496–497; Napoleonic warfare and, 497–498; failure to conquer England, 500–501; fall of Napoleon in, 500–504; Peninsular War and, 501; domination of Germany, 501–502; invasion of Russia, 502–503; European coalition against, 503–504; Napoleon's legacy in, 504; international investment and, 516; urbanization in, 519, 520; Congress of Vienna and, 562, 564, 565; Concert of Europe and, 564; actions against Turks, 566; revolution of 1830, 566, 567, 570; revolutions of 1848, 569–572, 575; Crimean War and, 615; Franco-Prussia War, 621–622; anti-Semitism in, 630; urbanization of, 645; socialism in, 647; labor strikes in, 648; Louis Napoleon Bonaparte and, 653–654; Third Republic and, 654–654–655; imperialist interests of, 671; interest in China, 679; southeast Asian interests of, 684; interests in Africa, 685, 687, 688, 689, 690; German policy toward, 733–734; alliance with Russia, 734, 735; World War I and, 741–744, 742, 746–748; aftermath of World War I and, 750–752, 754, 836–837; rebuilding of post-World War I, 803–804, 838; fear of fascism in, 804; antecedents of World War II and, 838–842; World War II and, 845, 847–848, 856, 857, 863; NATO and, 872; decolonization by, 877–878, 884, 885; right-wing challenges in, 902, 904–905; as European Union member, 904; state of contemporary, 904. *See also* French Revolution

France, Anatole, 655

Franciscans, 253

Francis Ferdinand, Austrian archduke, 731, 737

Francis I, king of France, 316, 331, 336, 387, 394

Francis of Assisi, Saint, 253

Francken, Frans, 384(illus.)

Franco, Francisco, 382, 800, 842

Franco-Dutch War, 390, 403

Franco-Prussian War, 616, 621–622, 626(illus.), 654, 729, 733, 751

Frankfort, Henri, 18

Franklin, Benjamin, 427, 430, 442, 454

Franks: establishment of kingdom of, 211, 216–217; Charlemagne and, 217–218; Carolingian renaissance and, 218–220; breakup of Charlemagne's empire and, 220–221; Saladin and, 250, 251

Frederick I, king of Prussia, 403

Frederick I (Barbarossa), Holy Roman Emperor, 246, 249

Frederick II, king of Sicily, 254

Frederick of Saxony, 331

Frederick the Great, king of Prussia, 403, 430–453, 435, 440, 449, 452

Frederick William I, king of Prussia, 403–404

Frederick William II, Prussian elector, 403

Frederick William III, king of Prussian, 502

Frederick William IV, king of Prussia, 575, 619

Free Corps, 784–785

The Freedom of the Christian Man (Luther), 332

Free enterprise, 368. *See also* Capitalism

Free French forces, 848, 878

Freemasons, 429–431(illus.), 450

French Revolution: events leading to, 392; clubs and lodges and, 430, 431; scientific academies and, 430, 431; Enlightenment and, 448, 469–470, 484, 485; impact of, 453, 530, 544; storming the Bastille, 462(illus.), 473; overview, 463; Old Regime and, 463–471; chronology of, 464; map and, 467; American Revolution and, 469–470; clash between nobility and Third Estate during, 471; moderate stage of, 471–476, 553; National Assembly, 471–476, 472(illus.); great fear and, 473–474; October Days and, 474; san-culottes and, 476; foreign invasion and, 476–478; radical stage of, 476–483, 549, 553; Jacobins and, 478–479; nationalism and, 479, 485, 486, 498, 504, 530, 553, 564; nation in arms and, 479; Republic of Virtue and Reign of Terror and, 479–481; fall of Robespierre, 481–483; meaning of, 483–486; industrialization and, 508, 511; conservatism and hostility to, 541–543; liberalism and, 546–547; German people's view of, 554; occupation of Italy during, 613

Frescoes, 313

Freud, Anna, 703(illus.)

Freud, Sigmund, 94n, 533, 702–706, 723, 810, 830

Fribourg, Andre, 741

Friedrich, Carl J., 766, 767

Friedrich, Caspar David, 533

Frisia, 218

Fromm, Erich, 822–823

Fronde, 388

Fukuyama, Francis, 895–896

Fulbert, Canon, 265, 266, 267

Gadol, Joan, 277

Gaelic League, 651

Gagarin,Yuri, 873

Galen, 156, 157, 262, 271, 418, 419

Galicia, 631, 746

Galileo Galilei, 272, 345, 408, 409, 415(illus.)–416, 416, 418, 422, 424, 593, 811, (illus.)

Galleys, 353

Gallican church, 387

Gallipoli campaign, 746–747

Gallus, Roman emperor, 181

Gama, Vasco da, 354

Gamaliel, Rabban, 177

Gandhi, Mohandas K., 675, 679, 680(illus.)–681

Gargantua and Pantagruel (Rabelais), 318

Garibaldi, Giuseppe, 616

Gaskell, Elizabeth, 587

Gauguin, Paul, 714

Gaul, 130, 136, 151, 159, 185, 211, 215, 216

Geneva, 344

Genghis Khan, 209

Genoa, 246, 303, 351

Gentile, Giovanni, 782

Gentiles, 177, 178

Geocentric theory, 263

Geoffrin, Madame, 430

Geography, 111–112, 114(illus.)

Geometry, 111

George, David Lloyd, 649, 751

George V, king of England, 678

Georgia, 892, 899

German Democratic party, 787
German Democratic Republic. *See* East Germany (German Democratic Republic)
German expressionism, 715
German humanism, 318
Germania (Tacitus), 155
Germanic language, 24
Germanic law, 211, 223, 272
Germanic tribes: during Roman Empire, 150, 151, 155, 162, 164, 165, 166, 168, 199, 214; during Middle Ages, 201, 204, 211–212, 214, 215
German Labor Front, 794
German National party, 630
German Social Democratic party, 657–658
German Workers' Association, 657
German Workers' party, 788
Germany: Franks and, 211; origin of, 221; trade and, 232; rise of, 240–241; Jews in, 255, 627–634.634, 631; during Renaissance, 316; during Reformation, 331, 332, 333, 334, 335, 336, 343, 344, 401; expansion of, 351; scientific academics in, 432; nineteenth-century unification of, 501–502, 508, 555, 564, 574, 575, 612, 616–622, 732; industrialization in, 508, 509, 657–658; limited liability in, 517; urbanization in, 519; Hegel and, 540; nationalism in, 554–555, 573, 580, 627–629; anti-Semitism in, 555, 627–634, 787–790, 792–793, 795, 797–798; Congress of Vienna and, 564; revolution of 1848, 573–575; establishment of parliament in, 579–580; map of, 618; Bismarck and, 619, 620, 621(illus.), 622, 627, 647, 649, 655–658; Volkish thought in, 627–632; Weimar Republic, 628, 784–787, 792, 813; technological advances in, 641, 643; urbanization of, 645; socialist parties in, 647; women's movement in, 651; socialism in, 657–658; on eve of World War I, 658; imperialist interests of, 670, 674, 689, 692; interest in China, 679; Ottoman Empire and, 682–684; antecedents of World War I, 731–739; naval power of, 733(illus.), 734; Triple Alliance, 734, 735; World War I and, 739, 742–749; settlement of World War I and, 749–752, 754, 762, 839, 841; Treaty of Versailles and, 751, 752, 754, 839, 841; fascism in, 779; end of monarchy in, 783–785; economic crisis in, 785–786; rise of Hitler in, 787–788; Nazi party in, 788–789; Hitler's world-view and, 789–791; Hitler's gain in power in, 790–793; characteristics of Nazism, 793–799; aftermath of World War I and, 836, 837; road to World War II, 838–839, 841–845; in World War II, 845, 847–862; resistance movement in, 857; defeat of, 857–862; legacy of World War II and, 862–864; partition of, 878; immigration and asylum seekers in, 902–903; state of contemporary, 905; Nazism's New Order and, 850-857. *See also* East Germany (German Democratic Republic); West Germany (Federal Republic of Germany)
Germany and the Next War (Bernhardi), 594, 731
Germinal (Zola), 588
Ghana, 884
Ghent, 234, 284
Ghettos, 631, 851–852, 857
Gide, André, 812
Giles of Rome, 287
Giorgione, 315–316
Giotto, 312–313
Girondins, 477, 478, 480
Giza pyramids, 4(illus.)
Gladiators, 158, 187
Gladstone, William E., 648, 650, 687, 688
Glasnost, 883, 889, 892
Glenn, John H., 872(illus.)
Globalization: effects of, 902; conflict and, 905–907
Glorious Revolution, 397, 544
Gnosticism, 252
Goa, 354
Godwin, Mary, 536–537
Goebbels, Joseph, 629, 788–789, 793, 796
Goering, Hermann, 848, 859
Goethe, Johann, 532, 811, 854
Golden Rule, 175, 552
Goldmann, Felix, 790
Gold trade, 354, 355
Gömbös, Gyula, 802
Gombrich, E. H., 316
Goncourt, Edmond, 607–608
Goncourt, Jules, 607–608
Gorbachev, Mikhail Sergeyevich, 883–884, 890, 892(illus.), 893, 894
Gordon, Charles "Chinese," 688
Gospels, 185, 187, 215, 255
The Gospel of Wealth (Carnegie), 593
Gothic architecture, 275, 276(illus.), 277
Gothic art, 312
Goths, 165
Government by consent, 291
Goya, Francisco, 501(illus.)
Gracchan revolution, 134–135
Gracchus, Cornelia, 152
Gracchus, Gaius, 134–135, 152
Gracchus, Tiberius, 134–135, 152
Granada, 357, 381
Grand Armée de la Russie, 502, 503(illus.)
Grand Duchy of Warsaw, 498
Grand Empire, 498–500, 499(illus.)
Grand Lodge (Freemasons), 430, 431
Grand National Consolidated Trades Union, 524
The Grapes of Wrath (Steinbeck), 814, 817
Graves, Robert, 759
Gravity, 417, 418
Great Britain: Parliament and, 238, 291, 340, 380, 386, 393, 396, 397, 454, 549, 568, 648; economic thought in, 443–445; Napoleon and, 500–501; industrialization in, 508, 509, 511–521, 524–525, 641, 648–652; coal production in, 515; transportation in, 515; finance in, 516, 517; urbanization in, 518, 519, 520; labor unions, 524, 646, 648; efforts to reduce poverty in, 524–525; radicalism and, 549; Congress of Vienna and, 562, 564; actions against Turks, 566; Concert of Europe and, 566; rise of reform in, 567–569; abolishment of slavery, 568; Crimean War and, 615; labor strikes in, 646, 647(illus.), 648; Irish independence and, 650–651; women's movement in, 651–652; imperialist interests of, 671, 674, 692; in Egypt, 674, 687–689; rule of India by, 677–678,

680–681; interest in China, 679; interest in Tibet, 681; Ottoman Empire and, 682–684; interests in southeast Asia, 684; interests in central Asia, 684–685; interests in Africa, 685, 687, 688, 689, 690; Boer War and, 689; antecedents to World War I and, 734–735, 739; World War I and, 739, 744–748; aftermath of World War I and, 752, 754, 836, 838–839; Great Depression in, 803; antecedents of World War II and, 838–842; World War II and, 845, 847–848, 860, 862, 863, 869; NATO and, 872; European Community membership, 876; Thatcher and, 876–877; conflict in North Ireland, 877, 904; decolonization by, 884–885; Nigeria and, 885; immigration and asylum seekers in, 902–903; as European Union member, 904; state of contemporary, 904. *See also* England
Great Council, 238
Great Depression: Japan and, 682; Latin America and, 692; Soviet Union and, 773, 774; Germany and, 791–792; Austria and, 802; United States and, 802–803, 838; Great Britain and, 803; social effects of, 810
Great Exhibition of 1851, 526
Great Fear (French Revolution), 474, 477
Great Rebellion (India), 677
Great Schism, 288, 325
Great Trek, 685, 689
Greco-Roman civilization: characteristics of, 103, 104, 156, 199; France and, 136; spread of, 151; limitations and decline of, 158, 159, 160, 163, 166, 172, 179, 189, 210. *See also* Roman Empire
Greece: during Hellenestic Age, 106, 107, 108, 117; during Middle Ages, 212; independence of, 566; revolt against Turks, 566; Balkan Wars and, 736; authoritarianism in, 802; World War II and, 848, 849, 856; U.S. economic and military support for, 871; NATO and, 872; European Community membership, 876; as European Union member, 904. *See also* Ancient Greece
Greek fire, 202
Greek language, 24, 109, 200, 212
Greek Orthodox Church. *See* Eastern Orthodox Church
Greek War of Independence, 555
Green, Thomas Hill, 605
Greenland, 221
Green party (Germany), 879, 905
Gregorian calendar, 754n
Gregorian reform, 242–244, 246
Gregory I, the Great, Pope, 215–216, 237
Gregory IX, Pope, 251
Gregory VII, Pope, 243, 244, 247, 253
Gregory XI, Pope, 288
Grenfell, Julian, 761
Grey, Edward, 742
Grimké, Angelina, 606
Grimké, Sarah, 606
Grissom, Virgil T., 872(illus.)
Gropper, William, 817
Grosseteste, Robert, 271
Grosz, George, 816–817
Guangzhou, China, 908
Gudea, King (Mesopotamian ruler), 14(illus.)
Guernica (Picasso), 808(illus.), 817
Guesde, Jules, 647
Guilds, 234, 500
Guise family, 338
Guizot, François, 570, 571
Gulags, 773(illus.)
Gulf War of 1991, 904, 909
Guomindong (Kuomintang), 681
Gutenberg, Johann, 316
Gymnasia, 107

Hadith, 207
Hadrian, 148–149, 152, 157
Haggard, H. Rider, 673
Hagia Sophia, Constantinople, 203(illus.)
Haider, Jorg, 902
Haiti, 691, 692
Halley, Edmund, 416
Hamlet (Shakespeare), 319–320
Hammond, Mason, 57
Hammurabi, 15, 24
Hannibal, 126–127, 129, 133, 134, 165
Hanukkah, 109
Hapsburgs: during Reformation, 341; Ferdinand and Isabella, 381–383; in Spain, 382–386; Charles V, 383; Philip II, 383–385; in Netherlands, 399; Holy Roman Empire in reigns of, 401, 402; Austrian, 402, 450, 453, 561, 562, 563, 575–577, 615, 622–625, 737, 752, 801
Hardenberg, Prince Karl von, 563
Hardie, J. Kier, 649
Hard Times (Dickens), 587, 589
Hargreaves, James, 513
Hart, Sir Basil Liddell, 847
Harvey, William, 409, 418, 419
Hastings, battle of, 237
Hatchepsut, Queen, 22(illust.), 23
Havel, Václav, 892, 893(illus.), 894–895
Hazor, 36(illus.)
Heart of Darkness (Conrad), 712, 713
Hebrew language, 109
Hebrews: religion of, 22–24, 38–41, 51; origin of, 25, 34–35; influences on, 34; chronology of, 35; Israelite kingdom and, 35–36; conquest, captivity and restoration of, 36–37; map and, 37; individual and moral autonomy and, 40–41; law of, 42–43, 47, 109, 173, 175; historical time and, 43–44, 96; prophets of, 44–45; social justice and, 45; universalism and, 46–47; individualism and, 47–48; legacy of, 48, 51; during Roman Empire, 147–149; Christianity and, 178–179, 182, 187–188, 193. *See also* Anti-Semitism; Jews; Judaism
Hebrew Scriptures, 34, 38–39, 40, 41, 42, 48, 109, 110, 173, 177, 185–186, 187, 206, 256, 595
Hector, 56
Hedonism, 114
Hegel, G.W.F., 538–541, 597–598
Hegira, 206
Heidegger, Martin, 824, 825, 826
Heine, Heinrich, 798
Heinlein, Konrad, 842
Helgoland, 564
Hellenic Age, 54–57, 103, 104, 107. *See also* Ancient Greece

Hellenism: stages of, 103; spread of, 107–109, 117, 130, 131; Jews and, 109–110; influence of, 142, 163; decline of, 172
Hellenistic Age: overview of, 103–104, 117; philosophy of, 103–104, 109, 112–117, 120; Alexander the Great and, 105–106; art of, 105(illus.), 108(illus.), 111, 157; competing dynasties during, 106; cosmopolitanism and, 106–109; maps of, 107, 114; Jews in, 109–110; literature of, 110; view of history and, 110–111; science during, 111–112, 114; Rome and, 127, 153; rationalism and, 160; religion during, 160, 161. *See also* Ancient Greece
Hellenization, of Christianity, 183–184
Hellespont, 62
Helmholtz, Hermann von, 591
Héloise, 265–267
Hemingway, Ernest, 810, 814
Henlein, Konrad, 842
Henrican Revolution, 393, 395, 396
Henry I, king of England, 237
Henry II, king of England, 237, 240
Henry II, king of France, 338, 387
Henry III, king of France, 387
Henry IV, Holy Roman Emperor, 243, 244
Henry IV, king of France, 388
Henry of Navarre, 338
Henry the Navigator, prince of Portugal, 352, 353
Henry V, king of England, 284
Henry VI, Holy Roman Emperor, 246
Henry VII, king of England, 393
Henry VIII, king of England, 319, 331, 338, 340, 393, 394, 396(illus.)
Heraclius, Byzantine emperor, 203
Herculaneum, 147
Herder, Johann Gottfried, 554
Heresy, 289, 332, 373, 383
Heresy trials, 251
Herlihy, David, 307
Hermes Trismegistus, 412
Herodotus, 17, 62, 96–97, 98
Hertz, Heinrich, 591–592
Herzegovina, World War I and, 735–736
Herzl, Theodor, 630–633, 632(illus.)
Hesiod, 90–91
Heym, George, 731
Hidalgos, 355, 357, 383
Hieroglyphics, Egyptian, 18–19
High Enlightenment, 447–448. *See also* Enlightenment
Hildebrand, 243
Hill, Christopher, 366
Himmler, Heinrich, 797, 850, 851
Hindenburg, Paul von, 792
Hinduism, 675
Hindus, in India, 678
Hippocrates, 78, 262, 271, 418
Hiroshima, Japan, 861(illus.), 862
Hispania, 381
Historical and Critical Dictionary (Bayle), 432–433, 447
Histories (Herodotus), 97
Histories (Polybius), 112
Histories (Tacitus), 155
History: Hebrew view of, 43–44, 96; Greek view of, 96–98; Hellenistic view of, 110–111; Roman Empire view of, 154–155; Christian view of, 192–193; Marxist view of, 597–598
History of Rome (Livy), 154
History of the Goths (Cassiodorus), 213
Hitler, Adolf, 761–762, 767, 778, 787–799, 789(illus.), 836, 838–839, 841–845, 847–850, 856, 860, 861, 869
Hittin, 250
Hittites, 24–25, 35
Hobbes, Thomas, 435–436, 444
Hobhouse, L. T., 605
Hobsbawm, E. J., 556
Hobson, J. A., 605
Ho Chi Minh, 874, 875
Hoess, Rudolf, 853, 855
Hohenzollern dynasty, 403, 450, 452
Holborn, Hajo, 750, 789
Holland. *See* Netherlands
Hollingdale, R. J., 554
Holocaust, 851–856, 863
Holstein, 620
Holy Roman Empire: papacy and German rulers during, 243, 244, 246; map of, 245(illus.); separation of Sicily during, 254; conflict with Italy during, 303; Reformation and, 331, 338, 382; monarchies and, 380, 385; failure to unify Germany and, 400–402; Prussia and, 403
Holy Synod, 405
Homer, 52, 54–56, 57
Homeric epics, 54–56, 105
Horace, 90, 133, 152, 154
Horemheb, Pharaoh, 22
Horthy, Miklós, 802
Hosea, 44
Hötzendorf, Franz Conrad von, 732
House of Commons (Great Britain), 238, 568, 649, 650, 652, 654, 845. *See also* British Parliament
House of Lords (Great Britain), 238, 568, 649, 651. *See also* British Parliament
House of Orange, 399, 400, 449
House of Savoy, 613
Howard, John, 441
Howe, Irving, 710
Hroswitha of Gandersheim, 224
Huber, Kurt, 854, 855
Huerta, Victoriano, 692
Hugh Capet, 239
Hugo, Victor, 531, 533, 653, 734
Hugo the Iron, 249
Huguenots, 338, 387, 388
Huizinga, Johan, 811
Humanism: Greek, 82, 99, 131, 212; Hellenistic, 104, 112; Roman, 131, 142, 160, 161, 212; Christianity and, 191–194, 308, 309, 316, 317, 318, 319, 371; medieval, 212; during Renaissance, 308–311, 316–321, 324; civil, 310; Erasmian, 317–318; French, 318; Spanish, 318–319; English, 319–320; mysticism and, 326–327; during Reformation, 341; rejection of Western, 911

Humanitarianism: Greek, 65; Stoic, 155; crime and punishment and, 440–442; during Enlightenment, 440–443; slavery and, 442–443; social equality and, 443
Human rights: in Greek city-states, 65; origin of concept of, 443
Hume, David, 433–434, 536, 537
Humors, 418
Hundred Years' War, 284–285
Hungarian Socialist Workers party, 900
Hungary: Turkish conquest of, 210; Magyars and, 221; Reformation and, 341; Austrian Hapsburgs in, 402; during Enlightenment, 449, 450, 453–454; nationalism in, 453, 623; revolution in 1848, 576, 579; independence of, 577, 612, 623–624; aftermath of World War I and, 751, 752; Communism in, 802; World War II and, 861, 862; uprising in, 880; end of communism in, 890; economic and social status of, 900–901
Huns, 164–165, 199
Hunting-gathering societies, 6–8
Hurrians, 24
Hus, Jan, 289, 325, 326, 327
Husbandry, 363
Hussein, Saddam, 904, 909
Hussites, 325
Huxley, Aldous, 810
Hydra, 65
Hydrostatics, 112
Hyksos, 18, 21

Iberian Peninsula, 352, 381
Ibsen, Henrik, 588–590, 651
Iceland, 221; NATO and, 872
Idealism: explanation of, 535; Hume's empiricism and, 535–537; Kant and, 537–538; Hegel and, 538–541; totalitarians and, 768
The Idiot (Dostoevski), 587
Illiad (Homer), 54, 55, 56, 154
Imams, 207
Immaculate Conception, 224
Imperial Duma, 661
Imperialism: in ancient Near East, 23–28; in Athens, 62–63, 71; in Rome, 127; chronology of nineteenth- and twentieth-century, 669; conflicting interpretations of, 670–673; emergence of, 675, 676(illus.); in Asia, 675–685; in Africa, 685–690; in Latin America, 690–692; United States, 691–692; legacy of, 692–693
Impressionism, 712–714
Incas, 355, 359
Index of Prohibited Books, 317, 344
India: mathematics in, 208; trade in, 232, 352, 354; British interests in, 671; imperialist interests in, 675, 677; British rule of, 677–678, 680–681, 863; anticolonial campaign in, 678–679; independence of, 679, 863, 884
Indiana (Sand), 586
Individual, Hebrew concept of, 40–41, 47–48
Individualism, in Renaissance Italy, 308
Indochina, 682, 684, 857, 877
Indo-Europeans, 18, 23–24, 26, 28
Indonesia, 682, 863, 884, 904, 908
Indulgences, selling of, 329, 330(illus.)
Industrialization: in Roman Empire, 168; agriculture and, 363, 509–511; in France, 364, 508, 509, 652–655; in Germany, 508, 509, 657–658; in Italy, 508–509, 658–659; overview of, 508–509; in Russia, 509, 659–662; in United States, 509, 662–663; in Great Britain, 511–521, 524–525, 641, 648–652; urbanization and, 518–520, 645–646; between 1870 and World War I, 638–639; chronology of, 639; overview of, 639–641; technology and, 641–645; scientific advances and, 643–645; labor movement and, 646–648; in Japan, 682; in Soviet Union, 772–774
Industrial Revolution: events leading to, 370; Scientific Revolution and, 422; events leading to, 444; in Great Britain, 508, 509, 511–521, 524–525; overview, 508–509; origins of, 509–510; agriculture and, 510–511; technological advances and, 513–515; financial aspects of, 515–517; societal transformation and, 517–518; urbanization and, 518–520; social structure and, 520–522; working class and, 522–524; poverty and, 524–525; impact of, 526–527
Industrial socialism, 553
Industrial workers, 522–524
Industry: expansion of, 363–365; centers of, 367(illus.); "captains of," 640
Ingeborg of Denmark, 253
Innocent III, Pope, 249, 252, 253, 254
Inquisition, 341, 344, 373, 382, 399, 400, 441(illus.)
Institutes of the Christian Religion (Calvin), 338
Intercontinental ballistic missiles (ICBMs), 872
International Association for the Exploration and Civilization of Central Africa, 685
International Criminal Tribunal for the Former Yugoslavia (United Nations), 901–902
International Style, 312, 314
Investiture Controversy, 243, 244
Ionian Islands, 564
Ionians, 54, 62, 75–77
Iran, 909
Iraq: creation of, 684; attempt to annex Kuwait, 904; U.S. threat of attack on, 909
Ireland: conversion to Christianity, 214; monasteries in, 214, 215; during Reformation, 344, 345; famine of 1845–1847, 546, 649–650; voting rights in, 648–649; independence of, 649–651; European Community membership, 876; conflict in North Ireland, 877, 904; as European Union member, 904
Irish Republican Army, 876
Irish Republican Brotherhood, 651
Irnerius, 272
Iron curtain, 871. *See also* Cold War
Iron industry, 514–517
Irrationalism: explanation of, 696–697; Nietzsche and, 697–700; Dostoevski and, 700–701; Bergson and, 701–702; Sorel and, 702; Freud and, 705. *See also* Rationalism
Isaac, 34
Isabella, queen of Castile, 352, 381–383
Isaiah, 45
Isidore of Seville, 213
Islam: during Byzantine Empire, 202, 203, 204; principles of, 204–206; Hegira, 206; Jews and, 206, 207; expansion

Islam: *(cont.)*
of, 209(illus.); cultural unity and, 675; modernization as threat to, 687–688, 906–908; radical, 906–908. *See also* Muslims
Islamic civilization: founding of new religion, 204–206; society in, 206–207; golden age of, 207–209; Mongol invasions and Ottoman dominance in, 209–210; translation of works from, 261, 270
Islamists, 906
Isocrates, 105
Isonomy, 64
Israel, German reparations to, 879
Israelites. *See* Hebrews
Italian Confederation, 125
Italy: during Roman conquest, 124–125, 130, 135; Augustus and, 146; during Roman Empire, 150; during Byzantine Empire, 203, 215; Ostrogoths and, 211; papacy and, 215; trade in, 232; German interests in, 240–241; as birthplace of Renaissance, 302–308; city-states in northern, 303–306; map of, 305; Renaissance society in, 306–308; during Reformation, 340–341; French invasion of, 386, 613; Napoleon and, 489, 497, 498; industrialization in, 508–509, 658–659; urbanization in, 519; unification of, 555, 611(illus.), 612–616, 658–659; Concert of Europe and, 564; revolutions in, 567, 577, 614–615; imperialist interests of, 670, 689; World War I and, 746, 748, 749, 750; aftermath of World War I in, 762, 779, 780; postwar unrest in, 779–780; rise of fascism in, 779–781; Mussolini and, 780–782, 793; fascist state in, 781–783, 841; control of masses in fascist, 782; church in fascist, 783; economics in fascist, 783; invasion of Ethiopia, 841, 842; World War II and, 857, 860; NATO and, 872; as democratic republic, 878; Nigeria and, 885
Ivan IV, the Terrible, 405

Jacob, 34
Jacobins, 440, 443, 478, 553, 653, 479, 480, 481, 482, 485, 489, 495, 497, 541, 547, 554
Jacquerie uprising, 283, 284
Jaeger, Werner, 56
Jaffa, 249
James I, king of England, 396
James II, king of England, 398
Jameson, Leander, 689
Janson, H. W., 816
Japan: western imperialism and, 671, 674, 681–682, 683(illus.); resistance to influence of West in, 675; in Russo-Japanese War, 678, 680; industrialization and economic development in, 682; invasion of Manchuria, 841; World War II and, 857, 859, 861(illus.), 862; post-World War II, 870
Jarmö (Iraq), 9
Jaruzelski, Wojciech, 890
Jaspers, Karl, 810, 824, 826, 827
Jaurès, Jean, 647, 656–657
Jefferson, Thomas, 428, 830, l454
Jeremiah, 44, 46(illus.), 47
Jericho, 9
Jerome, Saint, 166, 188
Jerusalem, 35–36, 109, 147, 148, 149, 246, 247, 249, 250
Jesuits, 343, 344, 421, 440, 453, 656
Jesus Christ, 172, 173, 174, 175, 176, 177, 178, 179, 180, 182, 184, 185, 186, 187, 188, 190, 192, 204, 242
Jewish France (Drumont), 630
The Jewish State (Herzl), 630–633
The Jewish Wars (Josephus), 148, 149
Jews: religion of, 22–24, 38–41, 51; origin of, 25, 34–35, 37; individual and moral autonomy of, 40–41; law, 41–43, 47, 109, 173, 175; prophets of, 44–45; social justice and, 45; universalism and, 46–47; individualism and, 47–48; Hellenism and, 109–110; during Roman Empire, 147–149; Jesus and, 172–173; during first century B.C., 173–174; of Diaspora, 177–178; anti-Semitism and, 187–188, 212, 232, 254–256, 627–634; Muhammad and, 206; in Islamic lands, 207; during Middle Ages, 212, 232, 254–256, 631, 633; Crusades and, 249, 250, 254; as medieval translators, 270; Spain and, 357, 380, 382, 383; under Napoleon, 494, 500; German anti-Semitism and, 555, 627–634, 768, 787–790, 792–793, 795, 797–798, 838, 839; Pogroms against, 630; Zionism and, 630–631; Enlightenment and, 631; profile of nineteenth-century, 631; Mussolini and, 783; Hitler and, 788–790, 839; Church and persecution of, 795; World War II and, 838, 839, 847–848, 851–856; extermination of, 851–856, 869; in resistance movements, 857; German reparations to, 879. *See also* Hebrews; Judaism
Jihad, 249
Jiménez de Cisneros, Francisco, 318–319
Joan of Arc, 284
John, king of England, 237–238, 240, 253–254
John, Prester, 352
John, Saint, 185
John of Paris, 287
John of Salisbury, 293
John Paul II, Pope, 889
Johnson, Lyndon B., 874
John the Baptist, 175
Jones, A.H.M., 65
Jordan, 684
Joseph, king of Spain, 501
Joseph II, Holy Roman Emperor, 402, 403(illus.), 450, 452
Josephus, Flavius, 148–149
Jospin, Lionel, 904
Joyce, James, 710, 812
Juárez, Benito, 691
Judah, 36, 37, 47
Judah Maccabeus, 109
Judaism: law and, 42–43, 47, 109, 173, 175, 179; during first century B.C., 173–175; Jesus and, 175–177; Christianity and, 178–179, 182, 187–188, 193; influence of, 204. *See also* Anti-Semitism; Hebrews; Jews
Judea, 109, 147, 148, 159, 175
Judith, 43
Julian calendar, 754n
Julio-Claudian dynasty, 147
Julius Caesar (Shakespeare), 319
Julius II, Pope, 315
June Days, 571–572, 575
Jung, Carl Gustav, 811
Junkers, 403, 404, 452, 617
Junks, 353
Jus civile, 157

Jus gentium, 157–158
Justinian, Byzantine emperor, 200, 201, 204, 212, 215, 272
Juvenal, 155

Kafka, Franz, 710, 812(illus.)–813
Kampuchea, 684
Kandinsky, Wassily, 717, 718(illus.)
Kant, Immanuel, 427, 428, 430, 443, 457, 537–538, 811
Kapp, Wolfgang, 785
Karzai, Hamid, 907(illus.)
Kassites, 24
Kay, John, 513
Kazakhstan, 899
Keats, John, 533, 537
Kellogg-Briand Pact, 837–838
Kennedy, John F., 872
Kenya, 886
Kenyatta, Jomo, 884(illus.), 886
Kepler, Johannes, 412, 414–415, 416, 418, 422
Keppler, Joseph, 667(illus.)
Kerensky, Aleksandr, 755
Khrushchev, Nikita, 872, 880
Khufu, pyramid of, 20
Kierkegaard, Søren, 596, 812, 824–825, 826, 827
King, Martin Luther, 912
King Arthur and his Round Table, 273
Kingdom of Piedmont-Sardinia, 614, 615
Kingdom of Serbia, 625
Kingdom of the Two Sicilies, 564, 612, 614, 616
King Lear (Shakespeare), 319
King Lidd's men, 521
Kipling, Rudyard, 673
Kirchner, Ernst Ludwig, 715
Kis, Stephen, 341
Kitchener, Herbert, 688
Kitto, H.D.F., 56, 57
Klee, Paul, 714–715
Knights, 222, 223, 246, 247, 249, 274, 351
Koestler, Arthur, 817
Kohl, Helmut, 879, 905
Kohn, Hans, 630
Koine dialect, 181
Kollwitz, Kathe, 760(illus.)
Königgrätz, 620
Koran, 204, 205, 206, 207, 208, 209, 357
Korea, 682, 684, 872, 909
Korean War, 872
Kornilov, Lavr, 755
Kosovo, 901, 902
Kossuth, Louis, 576, 577
Kostunica, Vojislav, 902
Kristallnacht, 798
Kruger, Paul, 689
Kun, Béla, 802
Küng, Hans, 172–173
Kuwait, 904, 908, 909

Labor strikes, 646, 647(illus.), 648, 649
Labor unions: development of, 524, 646–647; in Great Britain, 524, 646, 648; Owen and, 553; in France, 655
Lady Chatterley's Lover (Lawrence), 814
Lagarde, Paul de, 628, 634
La Gioconda (Leonardo), 315
Laissez-faire doctrine, 444–445
Langbehn, 628
Language: during Paleolithic Age, 6–7; Sumerian, 11, 12; Indo-European, 24. *See also* Literature
Lansing, Robert, 747
Laos, 684, 875, 884
Lascaux, France, 7(illus.)
Lassalle, Ferdinand, 657
The Last Supper (Leonardo), 315
Lateran Accords, 783
Late Renaissance Art, 314–316
Latifundia, 168
Latin America, European influence in, 690–692
Latin Christendom, 210–213, 220, 232, 236, 242, 250. *See also* Middle Ages
Latin language, 24, 121, 210, 211, 212, 214, 259, 273
Latvia, 784, 851, 862, 892, 894
Lavoisier, Marie Anne, 422
Lavrin, Janko, 700
Law: Mesopotamian, 15–16; Hebrew, 42–43, 47, 109, 173, 175; Roman, 59, 127, 129, 157–158, 201, 204, 211, 272; Sophists, 79; common, 201, 237, 393; Koranic, 207; Germanic, 211, 223, 272; feudal, 223; English, 237
Law of nations, 157–158
Law of the maximum, 479
Lawrence, D. H., 710, 761, 809, 812, 814, 830–831
League of Nations: Wilson and, 749, 750; creation of, 751; Germany and, 752, 837–838; Austria and, 801; hope for success of, 810; function of, 837; Italy's invasion of Ethiopia and, 841
Leakey, Richard E., 5
Lebanon, 684, 863
Le Bon, Gustave, 708
Lefebvre, Georges, 476, 491
Legislative Assembly (French Revolution), 477
Legnano, battle of, 246
Lemercier, Népomucène, 533
Lenin, Vladimir, 671, 756–759, 758(illus.), 769, 770, 771, 772, 776, 777, 823, 884
Lent, 370
Leo III, Pope, 217
León, 241, 253
Leonardo da Vinci, 314, 315(illus.)
Leopold I, Austrian emperor, 402
Leopold II, king of Belgium, 673(illus.), 685, 687
Leo X, Pope, 387
Leo XIII, Pope, 657
Le Pen, Jean Marie, 902, 904–905
Lepidus, 138
Les Mystères de Paris (Sue), 586
Letters Concerning the English Nation (Voltaire), 435
Letters on the Equality of the Sexes and the Condition of Women (Grimké), 606–607
Levi, Mario Attilio, 66
Leviathan (Hobbes), 435–436
Lewis, Bernard, 906–907

Liberalism: French Revolution and, 484, 530; overview of, 543–544; sources of, 544; economic theory and, 545–546; democracy and, 546–549; nationalism and, 555–556; German, 579–580; Marxism vs., 596; in transition, 604–606; nationalism and, 625–626; Jews and, 631; modernism and, 722; post-World War I period and, 777, 783, 912; economic, 783
Liberia, 685
Liberty: Greek concept of, 66; feudalism and, 291; individual, 544–545
Libya, 860
Libyans, 23
Liebknecht, Karl, 784, 785
Liebknecht, Wilhelm, 647
Liege homage, 222
Life of Jesus (Strauss), 595
The Life and Adventures of Nicholas Nickleby (Dickens), 588
Lifton, Robert Jay, 856
Liga, 416
Lilburne, John, 397
Limited liability, 517
Lincoln, Abraham, 575
Lioba, 219
Lippmann, Walter, 863
Lis, Stephen, 341
Literacy, 199, 218, 219, 261
Literature: Mesopotamian, 15; Egyptian, 18–19; Greek, 30, 54–56, 259; Hebrew, 30; Hellenistic, 110; Roman, 131, 154; medieval, 273–275; about industrial cities, 520; Romantic period, 531; realism in, 586–587; naturalism in, 587–590; modernist, 710, 711, 712–713; of socialist realism, 775; Pan-German, 787; postwar pessimism in, 810–814. *See also* Drama; Language; Poetry
Lithuania: during Reformation, 341, 342; extermination of Jews and, 851; World War II and, 851, 856, 862; independence of, 892(illus.), 894
Little Brothers, 253
Livia, 147, 151(illus.), 152
Livingston, David, 672, 673, 685
Livy, 127, 154, 311
Locarno Pact, 837, 841
Locke, John, 410, 434, 435, 436(illus.)–437, 440, 442, 444, 448, 454, 457, 537, 544
Lodges, 430–431
Logos, 115, 116, 184, 185
Loiry, Alfred Firmin, 596
Lollards, 289, 325
Lombards, 201, 215, 216, 217
Lombardy, 564, 577, 612–615, 623
Longbows, 284
Lorraine, 733–734, 742, 749, 751, 837
Lothair, 221
Louis Philippe, king of France, 567, 570, 571, 573, 576
Louis the Pious, 220–221
Louis VI, king of France, 239
Louis VII, king of France, 240, 249
Louis XIII, king of France, 388
Louis IX, king of France, 240
Louis XIV, king of France, 373, 377, 388–390, 392, 402, 427, 429, 432, 466, 470
Louis XVI, king of France, 473, 476–477, 541
Louis XVIII, king of France, 503, 504, 566
Loyola, Ignatius, 343
Lucian, 116
Lucretius, 132
Ludendorff, Erich, 748–749
Lueger, Karl, 630, 788
Luke, Saint, 185
Lumumba, Patrice, 886
Luther, Hans, 328
Luther, Martin, 323(illus.), 324, 328–337, 341, 342
Lutheranism, 331–332, 333, 334, 335, 336, 340–341, 345, 401
Luxembourg, 845, 847, 872
Luxemburg, Rosa, 784, 785
Lyceum, 86, 111
Lyell, Sir Charles, 592
The Lyrical Ballads (Wordsworth), 533
Lysistrata (Aristophanes), 95

Macedonia, 105, 112, 127, 133
Macedonians, 69, 70, 71, 106, 107, 110, 125
Machiavelli, Niccolò, 310–311, 317, 320, 386, 435
Macmillan, Harold, 876
Madame Bovary (Flaubert), 586
Madeira, 353
Madhav Rao Scindia, Maharaja, 678
Magellan, Ferdinand, 355
Magic: sympathetic, 8; Mesopotamian, 16–17; Egyptian, 19; Near Eastern, 30; in Roman Empire, 160; mystery cults, 179; witchcraft, 373; Scientific Revolution and, 412, 419, 420
The Magic Mountain (Mann), 813
Maginot Line, 838, 843
Magna Carta, 238, 291, 393
Magnus, Albertus, 270–271
Magyars, 212, 221, 224, 229, 261, 575, 576, 612, 623
Mahdi, 207, 688
Maimonides (Moses ben Maimon), 256
Major, John, 904
Malacca, 354
Malaya, 857
Malleus Maleficarum, The Hammer of Witches, 373
Malta, 564
Malthus, Thomas R., 545, 546, 592
Maltitz, Horst von, 797
Manchu dynasty, 679, 680, 681
Manchukuo, 841
Manchuria, 682, 841, 857, 862
Manet, Edouard, 713
Manichaeism, 189, 252
Mann, Thomas, 710, 812, 813
Manorialism, 222, 224, 225, 234
Manors, 361
The Man Versus the State (Spencer), 605
Mantua, 303
Mao Zedong, 681, 880
Marat, Jean-Paul, 448
Marathon, 62
Marcel, Gabriel, 824, 829
Marchand, Jean Baptiste, 688
Marches, 616
Marconi, Guglielmo, 643

Marcus Aurelius, 149–150, 153, 155–156, 162, 180
Maria Theresa, Austrian queen, 402, 403(illus.), 449, 450
Marie Antoinette, Queen of France, 473
Mario and the Magician (Mann), 813–814
Maritain, Jacques, 819, 820, 821
Maritime insurance, 364–365
Marius, 135
Mark, Saint, 185
Market towns, 365(illus.)
Marriage: in Roman society, 152; in feudal society, 224; in Renaissance Italy, 307; women's rights and, 607
Marshall, George C., 871
Marshall Plan, 871
Marsiglio of Padua, 287
Martel, Charles, 217
Martin, Émile, 515
Martin, Pierre, 515
Martineau, Harriet, 606
Martin of Tours, Saint, 185
Marx, Karl, 96, 346, 541, 551, 590, 596–603, 597(illus.), 702, 705–706, 771
Marxism: background of, 596–598; class conflict and, 598–599; destruction of capitalism and, 599–600; appeal and influence of, 600–601, 831; criticisms of, 601–602; Russia and, 756, 757; fascism and, 778; as failed ideology, 894–895. *See also* Communism
Marxist socialist parties, 647
Mary, Virgin (mother of Jesus), 224
Mary Barton (Gaskell), 587
Mary I, queen of England, 340, 394, 395
Mary, queen of Scotland, 395
Masada, 147
Masaryk, Tomáš, 802
Masonic lodges, 429–431, 447
Massys, Quentin, 317
Match girls, 646, 647(illus.)
Mathematical Composition (Ptolemy), 156
Mathematics: Mesopotamians and, 16; Egyptian, 20; Greek, 77, 78; Babylonian, 78; Hellenistic, 111; during Muslim golden age, 207, 208; during Scientific Revolution, 410, 424
Mathilda of Tuscany, 244
Matisse, Henri, 715, 716(illus.)
Mattathias, 109
Matteotti, Giacomo, 782
Matthew, Saint, 185
Maurras, Charles, 800(illus.)–801
Maximilian I, Holy Roman Emperor, 331, 401
Maxwell, James, 643
Mazarin, Cardinal, 388
Mazzini, Guiseppe, 614, 615, 616, 625
Mecca, 204, 206
Medea (Euripides), 94–95
Medes, 26
Medicis, Catherine de, 338, 387
Medicis, Cosimo de, 306
Medicis, Lorenzo de (the Magnificent), 306
Medicis family, 306, 310
Medicine: Mesopotamian, 16–17; Egyptian, 20–21, 30; Greek, 78; Hellenistic, 111; during Muslim golden age, 208; during Scientific Revolution, 418–419; diagnostic, 419; during Enlightenment, 440; scientific breakthroughs in, 644. *See also* Science
Medina, 206
Meditations (Marcus Aurelius), 149, 155
Meiji Restoration of 1867, 682
Meinecke, Friedrich, 741
Mein Kampf (Hitler), 788, 791, 839, 842
Melians, 72
Melos, 72
Menander, 110, 131
Mendeleev, Dmitri, 592
Menes, 17
Mensheviks, 757
Mercantile capitalism, 364, 368–370
Mercantilism, 369–370
Merleau-Ponty, Maurice, 826
Merovech, 217
Merovingians, 217
Mesopotamia: map of, 11; overview of, 11–12, 99; religion of, 12–15; myths of, 13, 29, 56; government and law in, 15–16; business and trade in, 16; writing, mathematics, astronomy and medicine in, 16–17, 30, 96; influence of, 34, 106; Alexander the Great and, 105
Messana, 125
Messenians, 58
Messiah, 174, 176, 178
Metalwork, 9
Metaphysics, 77
Metternich, Prince Klemens von, 560–561, 563, 564, 566, 575–576, 614, 622
Mexican Revolution of 1911, 692
Mexico: Spanish conquest of, 355, 382–383; Napoleon III and, 691; World War I and, 747–748
Mexico City, 908
Michaelangelo Buonarroti, 314, 315, 811
Micromegas (Voltaire), 435
Middle Ages: chronology of, 196–197, 200, 230, 281; origin of, 199; Byzantine Empire during, 199–204; Islamic civilization during, 204–210; Latin Christendom, 210–213, 220, 232, 242; anti-Semitism in, 212, 232, 254–256, 631; relationship between Christians and Jews in, 212, 232, 254–256, 631, 633; Church as shaper of civilization in, 213–216; kingdom of Franks during, 216–221; feudal society in, 221–225; agriculture in, 225, 229–231(illus.), 280–281, 362(illus.), 509; economic expansion in, 229–241; rise of states in, 236–241; papal power in, 241–254; anti-Semitism in, 254–256, 631; revival of learning in, 259–262; world-view during, 262–264, 291; philosophy and theology in, 264–270; science in, 270–272; revival of Roman law in, 272; literature in, 273–275; architecture in, 275–277; economic problems in, 280–281; Black Death in, 281–283; rebellions during, 282–284; Hundred Years' War and, 284–285, 386; decline of papacy in, 285–289; breakup of Thomistic synthesis in, 289–290; as link to modern world, 290–295, 301; elite vs. popular culture in, 370; monarchy in, 386; cosmology in, 410–411; romantics' view of, 534; liberalism and, 544
Middle class: Greek, 54; Roman, 159, 167; medieval, 235; in France, 465–466, 470–471, 497; industry and commerce and, 520–521; in Russia, 661–662

Middle Kingdom (Ancient Egypt), 17–18
Milan, Italy, 234, 303, 306, 577, 614, 615
Military, Roman, 124–125, 135, 146, 162–163, 167
Mill, John Stuart, 545, 579, 604, 608
Millenarianism, 327, 328, 343
Milosevic, Slobodan, 901–902
Minoan civilization, 52, 53
Miró, Joan, 815, 816
Missionaries: in New World, 358–359; imperialism and, 672; in Africa, 672(illus.)
Mithraism, 160, 161(illus.), 180, 181
Mithridates, 135
Mitterrand, François, 878, 904
Mobutu, Joseph, 886
Moderna, 613, 615
Modernism: explanation of, 596; Enlightenment vs., 710, 721–723; break with conventional esthetics and, 710–712; art and, 712–718, 814–817; physics and, 718–721
Modernity: early, 696; late, 696
Modern Man in Search of a Soul (Jung), 811
Modern world: Christianity and, 290–291; Middle Ages and, 290–295, 301; Renaissance and, 320–321; Reformation and, 345–346; Enlightenment and, 456–457; Industrial Revolution and, 526–527; irrationalism and, 696–705; globalization and, 890, 902, 905–907, 912; rejection of, 911–912
Mogul Empire, 677
Moldova, 899
Moltke, Helmuth von, 742
Mommsen, Theodor, 634
Mona Lisa (Leonardo), 315, 316
Monarchy: Mesopotamian, 15; Egyptian, 19–20, 107; Assyrian, 25–26; Persian, 28; Greek, 59; Hellenistic, 106, 107; Etruscan, 121; Roman emperors, 142–144, 146; Byzantine, 200–201; Germanic, 211; in England, 237–238, 392–399; in France, 239–240, 386–392; in Germany, 240–241; effect of Crusades on, 250; authority of, 291; during Reformation, 345; state building by, 378, 380–381; in Hapsburg Spain, 381–386; medieval, 386; in Netherlands, 399–400; in Holy Roman Empire, 400–402; in Austria, 402; enlightened despotism, 402, 449–450, 452–453, 497; in Prussia, 403–404; in Russia, 404–405. *See also specific countries or areas*
Monasteries: origin of, 185; during Middle Ages, 213, 214, 215, 242, 261
Monasticism: rise of, 185; during Middle Ages, 214, 215, 218
Mondrian, Piet, 717
Monet, Claude, 713
Mongolia, 281, 681
Mongols, 166, 209–210
Monks, 185, 214–215
Monopoly capitalism, 671
Monotheism: Atonism vs., 22–23; Hebrews and, 35, 39–40, 48; founding of Islam, 204. *See also* Christianity; Islam; Judaism
Monroe Doctrine, 691
Montaigne, Michel de, 318, 373
Monte Cassino, Italy, 185
Montenegro, 736, 902
Montesquieu, Baron de la Brède et de, 435, 437, 442, 457, 465, 544
Montgomery, Bernard L., 860
More, Thomas, 319
Morel, Edward D., 687
Morison, Herbert, 886
Morocco, 674, 692, 735
Mosaic Law, 109, 173, 175, 179. *See also* Judaism
Moses, 22, 35, 37, 44
Moses (Michaelangelo), 315
Mosque of Mohammed Ali, Cairo, 205(illus.)
Mosques, 205
Mozart, Wolfgang Amadeus, 430, 431(illus.), 811
Muhammad, 204–207
Mujahidin, 881
Mumford, Lewis, 10
Mun, Thomas, 369, 370
Munch, Edvard, 695(illus.), 714
Munich Conference, 843
Municipal Corporations Act, 568
Mursilis I, Hittite king, 24
Music, 711, 775
Muslim League, 678
Muslims: in Byzantine Empire, 202–204; Jews and, 206, 207; state and society of, 206–207; in Spain, 209, 239, 246, 250, 261, 270, 380, 381, 382, 383; invasions in Europe, 212, 221, 224, 239, 261; Crusades and, 246–250; during conquest and expansion, 352, 353; slave trade and, 357; in India, 678; fundamentalist, 687–688, 906–908; in Albania, 901; in former Yugoslavia, 901; globalization and, 906–907. *See also* Arabs; Islam; Islamic civilization
Mussolini, Benito, 761–762, 766, 777, 778, 780(illus.)–783, 788, 793, 841, 842, 843, 848
Mutual aid societies, 524
Myanmar, 677
Mycenae, 53
Mycenaean civilization, 52, 53, 54, 55
Mystery cults, 160–161
Mysticism: in Roman Empire, 160; Christian, 326–327, 562; humanism and, 326–327; during Scientific Revolution, 412
Myth: during Paleolithic Age, 7–8; Mesopotamian, 13, 29, 56, 76; Egyptian, 18–20, 29, 56, 76; ancient Near Eastern, 29–30; Greek, 52, 75; in Hitler's world-view, 789
The Myth of the State (Cassirer), 822

Namibia, 689
Namier, Lewis, 579
Naples, 306, 616
Napoleon Bonaparte. *See* Bonaparte, Napoleon
Napoleon III. *See* Bonaparte, Louis Napoleon (Napoleon III)
Narmer, 17
National Assembly (France), 472(illus.)–473, 474, 475, 476, 477
National Convention (French Revolution), 477, 478
Nationalism: French Revolution and, 479, 485, 486, 498, 504, 530, 553; rise of European, 504, 530, 553–555; liberalism and, 555–556, 625–626; late-nineteenth century, 612; racial, 625–634, 729, 788–790, 838, 839; Russian, 659; Arab, 684; in Asia, 685; World War I and, 729, 731–733, 741

Nationalist Association (Italy), 626
National Socialist German Workers' party, 787, 788, 791. *See also* Nazi party
Naturalism, 587–590
Natural Life from the Standpoint of Science (Pearson), 594
Natural selection, 592
Nature: Hebrew view of, 40; medieval view of, 193, 291, 409; modern view of, 291–292; scientific view of, 411–416, 420, 423; magical power of, 412; Renaissance view of, 412; romantics' view of, 533–534
Nausea (Sartre), 827
Navigation Act, 366
Nazi party, 788–789, 791–792
Nazism: Social Darwinism and, 595; Chamberlain and, 629; Nietzsche and, 697, 700; ideology and, 768, 863; fascist Italy and, 782; anti-Semitism and, 788–790, 797–798, 851–856; rise of, 788–793; propaganda and, 790–791, 796, 838, 839, 849; leader state and, 793–794; Germany and, 793–799; economics and, 794–795; churches and, 795; education and, 796–797; support for, 798–799; Austria and, 802; later viewpoints regarding, 821, 822, 826; foreign policy and, 838–839; Wehrmacht's commitment to, 851; Holocaust and, 851–856, 863; legacy of World War II and, 863–864. *See also* World War II
Near East, ancient: Paleolithic Age and, 5–8; chronology of, 6; religion in, 7, 9–10, 28–29, 39, 40, 57; Neolithic Age and, 8–9; first civilizations in, 9–10; Mesopotamia and, 11–17; Egypt and, 17–23; empire builders and, 23–28; myths of, 29–30; achievements of civilizations in, 30
Nebuchadnezzar, King, 26–27, 46–47
Necker, Jacques, 473
Necker, Madame, 430
Nefertiti, Queen, 21(illus.)
Nehemiah, 37
Nehru, Jawaharlal, 675
Nelson, Horatio, 490, 500
Neo-Babylonians, 26–27
Neolithic Age, 8–9
Neo-Platonism, 162, 212, 411–412, 416
Nero, Roman emperor, 147, 155
Nerva, 147–148, 150, 151
Netherlands: trade in, 232, 365, 366; government in, 241; during Reformation, 335, 338; slave trade and, 357–358; agriculture in, 362–363; textile industry in, 364; government in, 380, 399–400; political power distribution in, 381; Hapsburgs and, 385; Louis XIV and, 390; Calvinism and, 399, 400, 427; Spain and, 399, 400; during Enlightenment, 427, 447, 450, 453; flight of French Protestants to, 429, 432; education of females in, 440; industrialization in, 511, 512; urbanization in, 518; Congress of Vienna and, 564, 567; interests in East Indies, 684; World War II and, 845; NATO and, 872; independence of Indonesia, 884; right-wing parties in, 902
New Comedy (Menander), 131
New Deal, 803
New Economic Policy (NEP), 770, 773
New Harmony, Indiana, 553
New Kingdom (Ancient Egypt), 18, 21–23
New Lanark cotton mills, 553
New Model Army, 397
New Poor Law, 525
New Stone Age. *See* Neolithic Age
New Testament: origin of, 174, 175; explanation of, 185–186, 188; influence of, 186–187; German translation of, 332
Newton, Isaac, 272, 309, 409, 410, 412, 416–418, 417, 422, 424, 434, 443, 448, 706, 718, 719
New World: Portuguese in, 353, 354; Spanish in, 355, 356; slave trade, 357, 358, 359; Anglo-French rivalry over control of, 448–449; trade with, 509
New Zealand, 684, 849
Nibelungenlied, 273
Nicaragua, 691, 692
Nice, 478, 615
Nicene Creed, 186
Nicholas I, tsar of Russia, 566, 659, 660
Nicholas II, Pope, 243
Nicholas II, tsar of Russia, 660–661, 754, 756(illus.), 769
Nicomachean Ethics (Aristotle), 87
Niebuhr, Reinhold, 819
Nietzsche, Friedrich, 697(illus.)–700, 704, 721, 723, 759, 814, 825, 830
Nigeria, 886
Nihilism, 698
Nile River, 10, 17, 20
Nimes, France, 150
Ninety-five Theses (Luther), 329–330
Nineveh, 202
Nivelle, Robert, 746
Nixon, Richard M., 875
Nkrumah, Kwame, 884
Noblewomen, 224, 274
No Exit (Sartre), 827
Nonintervention Agreement, 841
Nonviolent resistance, 679
Normans, 203, 237, 246, 270, 392–393
North Africa: during Byzantine Empire, 201, 202, 211; Ottomans and, 210; Crusades and, 249; French interest in, 674; World War II and, 860. *See also specific countries*
North and South (Gaskell), 587
North Atlantic Treaty Organization (NATO), 872, 878, 879, 899, 901, 902, 904
North German Confederation, 621–622
North Ireland, 877, 904
North Korea, 872, 909
Northmen. *See* Vikings
Norway: Congress of Vienna and, 564; World War II and, 845, 856; NATO and, 872
Notes from Underground (Dostoevski), 700–701, 825
Notre Dame Cathedral, 276(illus.)
Nourse, Alan E., 719
Nouveau riches, 307, 350
Nubia, 18, 20
Nubians, 18, 23
Numidia, 135
Nuns, 214, 215, 219, 224
Nyerere, Julius, 886

Obote, Milton, 886
Ockham, William of, 290
O'Connor, Feargus, 568–569
Octavian. *See* Augustus (Octavian), Roman Emperor

Odyssey (Homer), 54, 154
Oedipus Rex (Sophocles), 94
Of Crime and Punishment (Beccaria), 441
Official nationality, 659
Oil, 685, 899
Old Kingdom (Ancient Egypt), 17–18
Old Stone Age. *See* Paleolithic Age
Old Testament. *See* Hebrew Scriptures
Oligarchy: Greek-city states and, 59, 61, 68, 69; Roman, 123
Oliver, Roland, 358
Oliver Twist (Dickens), 588
Olympian religion, 57
Olympus, Mount, 57
Omdurman, battle of, 688
On Ecclesiastical Power (Giles of Rome), 287
On Kingly and Papal Power (John of Paris), 287
On Liberty (Mill), 604
On the Nature of Things (Lucretius), 132
On the Revolutions of the Heavenly Spheres (Copernicus), 413
Open Door policy, 680
Open-field system, 361
Operation Barbarossa, 848–849
Opium War, 679
Opticks (Newton), 417, 418
Optics, 208, 271
Oration on the Dignity of Man (della Mirandola), 309
Origen, 188
Origin of the Species (Darwin), 592
Orléans, 284
Orphic cult, 57
Ortega y Gasset, José, 821–822
Orwell, George, 673, 814, 823
Ostracism, 61
Ostrogoths, 165, 201, 211, 213, 215
Ottoman Empire, 204, 210, 325, 402, 449, 453, 631, 675, 682–684, 736
Otto the Great, 240, 400
Ovid, 90, 154–155
Owen, Robert, 553
Owen, Wilfred, 744
Oxford University, 262, 427
Ozment, Steven, 269–270

Pachomius, Saint, 185
Pacific Rim countries, 870
Pact of Steel, 844
Padua, 303
Paine, Thomas, 439, 549–550
Painting. *See* Art
Pakistan: independence of, 677, 679, 884; support for Soviet-occupied Afghanistan, 883; Muslim fundamentalists in, 908
Palacky, Francis, 625
Paleolithic Age, 5–8
Palestine: ancient, 26, 34; Hellenistic, 106; during Roman Empire, 149, 176; Jesus and, 172, 176; during Byzantine Empire, 201–202; Seljurk Turks and, 209; Mongols and, 210; Crusades and, 249; Jewish homeland in, 631, 684
Panama, 691, 692
Panama Canal, 516, 552, 655, 691
Pan-German Association, 629, 634
Pankhurst, Christabel, 652
Pankhurst, Emmeline, 652
Pankhurst, Sylvia, 652
Pan-Serbism, 732, 739
Pan-Slavism, 732, 734
Pantheon, 144(illus.)
Papacy: bishops of Rome, 184–185; during Byzantine era, 200; during Middle Ages, 215–216; relationship with Franks, 217; Germany and, 240–241; power of, 241–254; sacraments and, 242; Gregorian reform and, 242–244, 246; Crusades and, 246–250; dissenters and reformers and, 250–253; Innocent III and, 253–254; decline of, 285–290, 303–304; Great Schism and, 288; heresies and, 289; monarchies and, 378. *See also* Roman Catholic Church
Papal States, 217, 287, 306, 577, 612, 614, 615, 616
Papen, Franz von, 792
Paracelsus, 419
Pareto, Vilfredo, 707–708, 722
Paris, France, 234, 284, 429, 430, 645
Paris Commune, 653–655, 654(illus.)
Park, Mungo, 673
Parlement of Paris, 386
Parliament Act of 1911, 649, 651
Parliaments: British, 238, 291, 340, 380, 386, 393, 396, 397, 454, 549, 568, 648; origin of, 241, 393
Parma, 613, 615
Parmenides, 77, 83
Parnell, Charles Stewart, 650
Parochialism: Hebrews and, 46; city-states and, 106, 120
Parthenon, 80(illus.)
Parthia, 148, 149
Parthians, 137, 148, 149, 151
Pasic, Nikola, 737n
Pasternak, Boris, 770
Pasteur, Louis, 592, 644
Patriarchs (Hebrew), 34
Patrick, Saint, 214
Patroclus, 56
Patron-client relationship (Roman), 122–123
Paul, prince of Yugoslavia, 848
Paul, Saint, 177–179, 185, 187
Paulsen. Friedrich, 627
Paulus, Friedrich, 859
Pax Romana: explanation of, 144, 146–147; map of, 145; successors of Augustus and, 147–150; constructive rule during, 151–152; social conditions during, 152; orderly world community and, 152–153; culture during, 153–158; literature during, 154; view of history during, 154–155; philosophy during, 155–156; science during, 156–157; art and architecture during, 157; law during, 157–158; entertainment during, 158; unrest during, 159; collapse of, 162; military during, 167
Peace of Augsburg, 335
Peace of God, 223–224
Peace of Lodi, 306
Peace of Paris, 751
Peace of Westphalia, 385
Pearl, Daniel, 908

Pearl Harbor, 857, 859
Pearson, Karl, 594
Peasantry: in Roman Empire, 159; farming methods of, 215; feudal society and, 222, 224–225; revolts of, 282–283; Hundred Years' War and, 285; in France, 466–468, 473, 474, 478, 485, 511–512; in Russia, 661(illus.)
Peasants' Revolt, 283, 325, 335
Peloponnesian League, 59, 67
Peloponnesian peninsula, 54, 58
Peloponnesian War, 66–69, 71–72, 79, 82, 84, 95, 97–98, 113
Peloponnesus, 53
Peninsular War, 501
Pentagon terrorist attack, 888(illus.), 904, 906
Pentateuch, 38
Pepin II of Heristal, 217
Pepin the Short, 217
Perestroika, 883, 889
Pergamum, 106, 127
Pericles, 66–68, 71, 115
Perry, Matthew C., 682, 683(illus.)
Pershing, John, 748
Persia: Egypt and, 23; as unifier of Near East, 27–28; conflict between Greece and, 96–97; Alexander the Great and, 105–106; influence of, 106; during Roman Empire, 164; Byzantines and, 201–202; Greek influence on, 208; Seljurk Turks and, 209; Mongols and, 210; early twentieth-century, 674; European interests in, 684, 692; Russian interests in, 684–685, 735; Pahlavi rule in, 685
Persian language, 24
The Persians (Aeschylus), 93
Persian Wars, 62–63, 79, 96–97, 105
Peru, 355
Pessimism: postwar, 809–812; in literature, 812–814; in art, 814–817
Pétain, Henri Philippe, 744, 746, 847
Peter, Saint, 184, 242, 243
Peter the Great, Russian tsar, 405, 452, 659
Peter the Hermit, 247
Petrarch, 308–309, 310
Peyre, Henri, 469
Phalansteries, 552
Pharaohs, 17–23
Pharisees, 173, 174, 177
Philip Augustus of France, 239–240, 249, 253
Philip II, king of Spain, 355, 359, 383–385, 395, 399, 401
Philip II of Macedonia, 69, 70, 71, 86, 105
Philip IV, king of France, 240, 284, 285, 286, 287
Philip VI, king of France, 284
Philip of Hesse, 343
Philippics, 70
Philippines, 691, 857, 859, 884
Philistines, 35, 42(illus.)
Philo of Alexandria, 109–110, 177
Philosophes, 427–445, 457, 491, 531, 535, 541, 542, 544, 594, 595. *See also* Enlightenment
Philosophical Dictionary (Voltaire), 442
Philosophical relativists, 79
Philosophy: Greek, 30, 40, 75–89, 112, 182–184, 259, 261; Ionian, 75–76; cosmologists and, 76–78; Sophists, 78–79; Socrates, 79–82; Plato, 82–87; Aristotle, 86–89, 103, 105, 111, 208, 209, 212, 213, 263–264, 267–270; Hellenistic, 103–104, 109, 112–117, 120; Epicureanism, 113–115; stoicism, 115–116; skepticism, 116; cynicism, 116–117; Roman, 132, 155–156, 161–162; spiritualization of, 161–162; Christianity and, 182–184, 193, 264–270, 410; during Muslim golden age, 207, 208, 209; medieval, 264–270, 409; Aquinas, 268–270, 273, 277, 289; Descartes, 421, 422; Spinoza, 421–422. *See also specific philosophers*
Phoenicia, 106
Phoenicians, 24, 25, 35, 125
Physics, 718–721
Picasso, Pablo, 715–716, 717(illus.), 808(illus.), 817
Pico della Mirandola, Giovanni, 309
Piedmont, 613, 614, 616, 623
Piedmont-Sardinia, 614, 615
Pilate, Pontius, 147
Pillars of Society (Ibsen), 589
Pindar, 90
Pisa, 246
Pisistratus, 61
Pissaro, Camille, 713
Pius II, Pope, 288
Pius IX, Pope, 577
Pius X, Pope, 596
Pius XI, Pope, 783
Pizarro, Francisco, 355
Plague: in ancient Greece, 67; bubonic, 167, 255, 281–282, 304; during Late Roman Empire, 167. *See also* Disease
Plank, Max, 719
Plantagenet, Henry, 240
Plantation agriculture, 358, 359, 360(illus.), 691(illus.)
Plataea, 62
Plato: influences on, 77, 83; background of, 82–83; theory of ideas, 83–84, 110; theory of just state, 84–86, 190; Aristotle's critique of, 86–87; view of God, 109–110, 184; Renaissance revival of, 411–412
Platonic Academy (Athens), 212
Plautus, 131
Plea for the Citizenship of Women (Condorcet), 607
Plebeian Assembly, 122
Plebeians, 121–122, 124, 125
Plotinus, 162
Plutarch, 70, 137
Poetry: Greek, 89–91; Roman, 154; medieval, 273–274, 292; Romantic era, 531, 532, 533, 536, 537; World War I and, 764–765; postwar pessimism in, 810–811; surrealist, 816. *See also* Literature
Pogroms, 630, 770
Poincaré, Raymond, 785
Poitiers, battle of, 284
Poland: during Reformation, 341–342; during Enlightenment, 453; Congress of Vienna and, 563; Russia's interest in, 563, 567, 746; Germany's claim to, 579, 939; aftermath of World War I and, 749, 750, 751, 759, 784, 837; authoritarianism in, 802; alliance with France, 837; World War II and, 843–845, 850–852, 856, 861, 862, 869; Red Army occupation of, 871; end of communism in, 880, 889–890; economic and social status of, 900–901
Polis, 57–58, 72, 88, 103, 106, 112, 117, 120, 162. *See also* City-states

Polish Diet, 342
Political thought: Aristotle and, 88–89, 103; during Renaissance, 310–311; during Enlightenment, 435–438; liberalism and, 543–544
Politics: of ancient Greece, 57–58, 69–72, 84; of Roman Republic, 134–135; of Latin Christiandom, 210–212; of northern Italian city-states, 303–304, 306; development of state and, 405–406; labor movement and, 646
Politics (Aristotle), 88
Polybius, 111, 112–113, 125, 154
Polytheism, 18
Pompeii, 147
Pompey, 136, 137
Pontius Pilate, 147, 176
Poor Law, 525
Pope Leo X with Two Cardinals (Raphael), 315
Popular culture: traditional, 370–371; reform of, 371–372; witchcraft and, 372–374
Popular Front, 799, 804
Population growth: in Roman Empire, 167–168; in Middle Ages, 232; in Europe, 335, 352, 360–361, 363, 509–510, 644–645; of German Jews, 634; twentieth-century, 908
Porphyry, 212
Portugal: expansion of, 352, 353, 354, 355, 356(illus.); slave trade and, 357; independence from Spain, 385; trade with England, 501; authoritarian rule in, 799; NATO and, 872; European Community membership, 876; decolonization by, 886; right-wing parties in, 902; as European Union member, 904
Porus, Indian king, 105
Positivism, 590–591, 701, 706
The Possessed (Dostoevski), 587
Postimpressionism, 714
Postmodernism, 911
Postwar pessimism: overview of, 809–812; in literature, 812–814; in art, 814–817
Pottery, 8, 9
Poverty: industrialization and, 524–525; gap between wealth and, 908
Praise of Folly (Erasmus), 317, 327
Predestination, 331, 343
Price, Richard, 439
Price revolution: impact of, 359–361; agriculture and, 361–363; trade and industry expansion and, 363, 364, 365, 368
Priestley, Joseph, 439
Primitive democracy, 15
Primogeniture, 362, 365–366, 369
The Prince (Machiavelli), 310, 317
Princip, Gavilo, 737
Principate, 143
Principia Mathematica (Newton), 410, 416–417, 422, 427, 435
Principles of Geology (Lyell), 592
Principles of Political Economy (Ricardo), 546
Printing press, 316, 317, 422. *See also* Publishing
Prisons, 440–442
Private enterprise, 368. *See also* Capitalism
Privy Council, 393, 395
Probst, Christoph, 855
Propaganda: World War I, 747(illus.); Soviet, 775–776; Nazi, 790–791, 796, 838, 839, 849
Prophets, Hebrew, 44–48, 204
Protagoras, 79
Protestant ethic, 345–346
Protestantism: origin of, 288, 324; censorship and, 317; Lutheranism, 331–332, 333, 334, 335, 336; Calvinism, 336–338; Counter Reformation, 343–345; impact of, 345–346, 385; monarchies and, 380; Saint Bartholomew's Day Massacre and, 387; in France, 387–388, 429, 432, 464, 494; in England, 393, 395, 396, 397, 398; Scientific Revolution and, 419
Protestant Reformation. *See* Reformation
Protocols of the Elders of Zion, 629(illus.)
Protocols of the Elders of Zion, 632–633
Proudhon, Pierre Joseph, 602, 603(illus.), 653
Proust, Marcel, 710, 812
Prussia: emergence of, 403–404; map of, 404; education in, 440; during Enlightenment, 440, 449, 450, 451; war with France, 476–478; Napoleon and, 498, 501–504, 503; Congress of Vienna and, 562, 564; Saxony and, 563; Concert of Europe and, 566; reform in, 573–575; establishment of parliament in, 579; conflict with Austria, 616, 619–621; German unification and, 617–622
Prussians, 246, 351
Ptolemaic system, 156–157
Ptolemies, 106, 125, 136, 137
Ptolemy, 156, 208, 262, 263, 410–411
Public Health Act of 1848, 568
Publishing: invention of printing press, 316; during Renaissance, 316–317; literacy and popular culture and, 371; in Netherlands, 400; during Enlightenment, 427, 433, 447
Puerto Rico, 691
Puritans, 396, 397, 454
Putin, Vladimir, 898, 899
Pynda, battle of, 112
Pyramids, Egyptian, 4(illus.), 17, 18, 20
Pythagoras, 77
Pythagoreans, 77, 412

Qaeda. *See* Al Qaeda
Quadruple Alliance, 564. *See also* Concert of Europe
Quakers, 397, 442
Quantum mechanics, 719

Rabelais, François, 318
Racial nationalism, 625–634, 633, 729, 788, 789, 790, 838, 839. *See also* Anti-Semitism
Racial superiority, Social Darwinism and, 594, 595
Racism, of British in India, 677–678
Radical Reformation, 342–343
Radio, 643
Railroad industry, 515, 516, 642–643, 660, 677
Ramsay, chevalier, 447
Randall, J. H., Jr., 295
Raphael Santi, 314, 315
Rationalism: in ancient Near East, 30; Greek, 40, 58, 72, 75–86, 98–99, 160, 182–184; Sophist, 79; Socratic, 80–82; Platonism, 82–86, 190; Hebrew, 109; Roman, 162; Augustinian, 191; classical humanism, 191, 192, 193; medieval, 264–265, 291; Aquinas, 268–269, 289,

290; Ockham and, 290; Napoleon and, 491–492; reaffirming ideals of, 821–823, 911, 912. *See also* Enlightenment; Irrationalism
Ravenna, 201, 217
Reagan, Ronald, 875, 877, 883
Realism, 585–590
Realpolitik, 612
Reconquest, 352
Red Army, 769, 849, 871, 880
Reflections on the Revolution in France (Burke), 541, 549
Reflections on the State of France (de Maistre), 541
Reformation: events leading to, 288, 289, 324; impact of, 317, 318, 371; medieval church in crisis, 325–328; chronology of, 326; mysticism and humanism during, 326–327; end of world and, 327–328; as break with Catholicism, 328–331; Luther and, 328–335; in France, 331, 336–338, 387; in Germany, 331, 332, 333, 334, 335, 336, 343, 344, 401; salvation and, 331; spread of, 331–332, 335–336; in England, 335, 338, 340, 344, 394; Calvin and Calvinism and, 336–338; map, 339; in Spain, 340, 341, 382, 383; in southern and eastern Europe, 340–342; radical, 342–343, 373; Catholic response to, 343–345; modern age and, 345–346; in Austria, 402
Reform Bill of 1832, 568
Reichstag, 656
Reign of Terror, 480(illus.)–481, 541
Relativism, 79, 81
Religion: ancient Near Eastern, 7, 9–10, 28–29, 39, 40, 57; Mesopotamian, 12–15; Egyptian, 18–19; Hebrew, 22–23, 38–48, 51; monotheism, 22–23, 35, 39–40, 48, 182; Hittite, 25; Persian, 28; Greek, 56–57, 79; Roman, 121, 123–124, 160–162, 178; Hellenistic, 160; Mithraism, 160, 161(illus.); dissenters and reformers, 250–253; as integrating feature of Middle Ages, 291; dogmatism and, 318; during Reformation, 324–326; European expansion and, 352; in French state, 387–388; deism, 433–434; in Napoleonic France, 493–494; positivism and, 591; Darwinism and, 593–596; Asian, 675; communism and, 771. *See also specific religions*
Religion of Humanity, 591
Religious existentialists, 829
Remarque, Erich Maria, 810, 814
Rembrandt van Rijn, 400
Renaissance: art in, 300(illus.), 311–316; overview of, 301–302; chronology of, 302; in Italy, 302–308; map, 305; humanism and, 308–310, 317–321; political thought in, 310–311; spread of, 316–320; birth of modern age during, 320–321; Platonists and, 411–412
Renoir, Pierre Auguste, 713
Republicanism, 303–304, 306
Republican states, 378
Republic of Virtue, 479, 480
The Republic (Plato), 84, 85, 86, 88, 190, 319
Respublica Christiana, 236
Revivals, religious, 523
The Revolt of the Masses (Ortega), 821–822
Revolutions: English Revolution of 1640–1660, 397, 435, 470; English Revolution of 1688–1689, 398, 399, 433, 470; Dutch, 449; Brussels, 450; American, 454–456, 469–470; French, 463–486; chronology of, 561; of 1820–1829, 564, 566; of 1830–1832, 566–567; of 1848 in France, 569–572; of 1848 in Germany, 573–575; of 1848 in Austria, 575–577; assessment of 1848, 577, 579–580; of 1848 in Italy, 577. *See also specific revolutions*
Reza Shah, 685
Rhazes (al-Razi), 208
Rhineland, 316, 449, 478, 564, 751, 838, 841, 843, 861
Rhodes, Cecil, 689
Rhodesia, 689, 886
Richard, I, the Lion-Hearted of England, 240, 249
Ricardo, David, 546
Richelieu, Cardinal, 388, 390
Riehl, Wilhelm von, 627–628
Ritchie, D. G., 605
The Road to Wigan Pier (Orwell), 814
Robespierre, Maximilien, 448, 479–482, 485
Roentgen, Wilhelm Konrad, 718
Rohan Book of Hours, 288(illus.)
Röhm, Ernst, 794
Rohrbach, Paul, 594
Roland, Paladin, 352
Romagna, 615
Roman Catholic Church: language of, 200; split with Eastern Orthodox, 200; as unifier, 213–214; as shaper of medieval civilization, 213–216; monks and papacy and, 214–216; Franks and, 217; Immaculate Conception and, 224; sacraments and, 242; Gregorian reform and, 242–244, 246; Crusades and, 246–250; dissenters and reformers, 250–253; Innocent III and, 253–254; anti-Semitism and, 254–256; church law and, 272; conflict with France, 285–287; Great Schism and, 287–288; papal power and, 287–289; heresies and, 289; censorship by, 317, 344, 390; medieval church in crisis, 325–328; Reformation and, 328–331, 340, 343–345, 345, 346; Luther and, 332–333; in Spain, 381, 383; in France, 387, 388, 445, 447, 464, 655; in England, 394, 395, 396; scientific ideas and, 424; in Poland, 453, 889; Napoleon and, 494; Jews and, 631, 795; in Germany, 656–657; fascism and, 783. *See also* Christianity; Papacy
Roman Empire: overview of, 142; Augustus and foundations of, 142–144, 146; chronology of, 143; map of, 145; Pax Romana and, 146–158; Jews in, 147–149; successors of Augustus, 147–150; time of happiness, 150–153, 158; culture of, 153–160; literature of, 154; poetry of, 154; view of history, 154–155; philosophy in, 155–156, 161–162; science in, 156–157; art and architecture in, 157; law in, 157–158, 211; decline and fall of, 158, 166–169, 212; entertainment in, 158; internal unrest in, 158–159; social and economic weaknesses of, 159; stagnation and transformation in, 159–160; religion of, 160–162; third-century crisis in, 162–163; Constantine and, 164; Diocletian and, 164; tribal migrations and invasions in, 164–166; legacy of, 169; Christianity and, 181–182, 213–214
Romanesque architecture, 275, 276(illus.)
Roman Forum, 119(illus.)
Romania: during Roman Empire, 165; anti-Semitism in, 630; authoritarianism in, 802; alliance with France, 837; World War II and, 848, 850, 862; end of communism in, 890, 892

Roman law, 127, 129, 157–158, 201, 204, 211, 259
Romanov, Michael, Russian tsar, 405
Romanov dynasty, 754
Romanovs, 405
Roman Republic: limitations of, 104; Hellenistic kingdoms and, 106, 113; Polybius on, 112–113; Etruscans and, 121; overview of, 120; constitution of, 120–124; chronology of, 121; Greek influence in, 124, 127, 153, 157; uniting Italy, 124–125; conquest of Mediterranean world and, 125–127; consequences of expansion and, 127–130; map of, 128; culture of, 130–132; collapse of, 132–139, 143; agriculture in, 133–134; Gracchan revolution and, 134–135; rival generals in, 135–136; Julius Caesar and, 136–138; last years of, 138–139
Romanticism: overview of, 530–531; characteristics of, 531–533; nature, God, and history and, 533–535; impact of, 535; nationalism and, 554
Rome: as spiritual capital of Christianity, 210, 215; eleventh and twelfth century, 304; unification of Italy and, 616. *See also* Roman Empire; Roman Republic
Rommel, Erwin, 860
Roosevelt, Franklin D., 803, 869
Roosevelt, Theodore, 663
Roosevelt Corollary, 691
Rosenberg, Isaac, 744
Rostovtzeff, Michael, 160
Rothschild family, 516
Rotterdam, 399
Rotton boroughs, 568
Rousseau, Jean Jacques, 437–438(illus.), 442, 448, 457, 531, 549, 607
Royal Society of London, 422, 429
Rudolf, king of Germany, 244
Rule of law, 291
Rule of Saint Benedict, 185
Rus, Jacob, 663(illus.)
Ibn-Rushd (Averroës), 208–209, 270
Russell, Bertrand, 741
Russia: Huns and, 164–165; Byzantine Empire and, 204; Mongols and, 209; bubonic plague in, 281; emergence of, 404–405; during Enlightenment, 452; Napoleon and, 498, 502–503, 503; industrialization in, 509; Congress of Vienna and, 562, 564; interest in Poland, 563, 567; actions against Turks, 566; Concert of Europe and, 566; tsarist autocracy in, 566; Crimean War and, 615; anti-Semitism in, 630, 632–633; plight of Jews in, 631, 634; socialist parties in, 647; women's movement in, 651; imperial rulers prior to World War I, 659–662; in Russo-Japanese War, 678, 680; interest in China, 679; interest in Mongolia, 681; interest in central Asia, 684–685; Austria-Hungary, 731, 733–739; antecedents of World War I, 732, 734–736, 738–739; Pan-Slavism in, 732, 734; alliance with France, 734, 735; Austria-Hungary and, 734–736; interest in Afghanistan, 735; World War I and, 742, 746, 747, 752; aftermath of World War I and, 754, 759, 762, 837; provisional government in, 755; Lenin and rise of Bolshevism and, 755–759; Marxism and, 756; communist, 769–772; war communism and new economic policy in, 770; one-party dictatorship in, 770–772; in World War II, 848–851, 857, 859–862, 869. *See also* Russian Federal Republic; Soviet Union
Russian Academy of Sciences, 659
Russian Federal Republic: establishment of, 896–898; economic conditions in, 898–899; Putin and, 898–899; NATO and, 899, 902; social conditions in, 899. *See also* Russia; Soviet Union
Russian Orthodox church, 405
Russian Revolution of 1917, 671; events prior to, 754; provisional government and, 755; Lenin and rise of Bolshevism and, 755–759; events following, 769
Russo-Japanese War, 661, 678, 682, 735, 772

Saar Basin, 751
Sacraments, 242, 328–329
Sadducees, 173, 174
Sadok, 173
Sadowa, 620
Saint Bartholomew's Day Massacre, 338, 387
Saint-Just, Louis-Antoine de, 485
Saint Peter's Basilica, 329
Saint-Simon, Comte de, 551–552, 590
Sakharov, Andrei, 883
Saladin, 249, 250(illus.)–252
Salamis, 62
Salazar, Antonio de Oliveira, 799
Sallust, 133, 152
Salons, 429, 430, 448
Salvation, 329–331, 345, 432
Salvianus of Marseilles, 167
Sand, George, 520, 586
San Domingo, 494
Sans-culottes, 476, 480–482, 484
Sanskrit, 24
Santo Domingo, 692
Sappho, 89–90
Sarajevo, 901
Sardinia, 126, 215, 246, 613, 614
Sargon the Great (Mesopotamian ruler), 12
Sartre, Jean-Paul, 824, 826–827(illus.), 828
Sasson, Siegfried, 744–745
Satan, 187
Saudi Arabia, 883, 906, 907
Saul, 35, 177. *See also* Paul, Saint
Savonarola, Girolamo, 372
Savoy, 478, 613, 614, 615
Saxons, 217, 237
Saxony, 563, 564
Scandinavia: trade in, 232; during Reformation, 335, 336; women's movement in, 651
Schliemann, Heinrich, 52–53
Schiller, Friedrich von, 531, 854
Schirra, Walter M., 872(illus.)
Schlegel, A. W., 531
Schlegel, Friedrich, 531, 533
Schleswig, 620
Schlieffen, Alfred von, 742
Scholasticism, 259, 265, 291, 308, 411, 419, 422
Scholl, Hans, 854–855
Scholl, Sophie, 854–855
Schönberg, Arnold, 711
Schönerer, Georg von, 630, 787

Schopenhauer, Arthur, 699, 704
Schreiner, Olive, 673
Schröder, Gerhard, 905
Schubert, Franz, 531
Schurz, Carl, 574(illus.)–575
Schuschnigg, Kurt von, 842
Schweitzer, Albert, 810
Science: in Mesopotamia, 16; in Egypt, 20–21; mythology and, 29–30; Hellenistic, 111–112, 114; in Roman Empire, 156–157; in Muslim golden age, 207, 208; in Middle Ages, 270–272, 291; in Enlightenment, 440, 535–537; idealism and, 535–538; Darwinism and, 591–596; industrialization and, 643–645; warfare and, 759–760. *See also* Astronomy; Biology; Chemistry; Medicine
Scientific academies, 432
Scientific management, 641–642
Scientific method, 410
Scientific Revolution, 309; overview of, 409–410; medieval cosmology and, 410–411; Renaissance neo-Platonism and, 411–412; magic and mystical thought and, 412; Copernicus and, 412–413; laws of planetary motion and, 414–415; Galileo and, 415–416; Newton and, 416–418; biology, medicine, and chemistry and, 418–420; Bacon and, 420–421; Descartes and, 421–422; social implications of, 422; impact of, 423–424, 427, 592; Enlightenment and, 456
Scientific socialism, 895
Scipio Africanus, 127
Scotland: Reformation in, 335, 338, 344; education in, 440; during Enlightenment, 440, 444; urbanization in, 519
Scotus, Duns, 289
Second Crusade, 240, 249
Second Empire, 653
Second Estate (France), 465
Second Intermediate Period (Ancient Egypt), 18
Second Punic War, 126–127, 129, 130
Secularism: trends toward, 291; in Renaissance Italy, 307–308; in Enlightenment, 429–432; in Industrial Revolution, 527
Seimens, William, 515
Seleucia, 127, 148
Seleucids, 106, 107, 125
Seljuk Empire, 203, 246
Seljuk Turks, 203, 209, 246, 249
Semites, 18
Sempronia, 152
Senate, Roman, 143
Seneca, Lucius Annaeus, 155
Sennett, Mack, 818
Sepoy Mutiny, 677
September Massacres, 477
September 11 terrorist attacks, 888(illus.), 904, 906, 908
Serbia: Austria-Hungary attack on, 731, 732; Balkan Wars and, 736; Austrian hostility with, 737–739; World War I and, 746, 748, 752; as independent country, 892, 901, 902, 904
Serbs, 204, 732, 736
Serfdom: explanation of, 222, 225; decline of, 231, 664; in towns, 235; in Eastern Europe, 363, 452; in Ukraine, 452; in France, 466–467, 500; in Prussia, 502; in Russia, 660. *See also* Feudal society
Sermon on the Mount, 174, 187
Servants, 521–522
Servetus, Michael, 344
Seton-Watson, Hugh, 576–577
Settlement of 1867, 623
Seven Weeks' War, 620
Seven Years' War, 449, 453, 454, 468
Severn bridge, 517
Seyss-Inquart, Arthur, 842
Shahn, Ben, 817
Shakespeare, William, 319–320, 704, 811
Shaw, Bernard, 651
Shelley, Percy Bysshe, 536–537, 608
Shepard, Alan B., 872(illus.)
Shi'a, 207
Shiel, James, 51
Shi'ites, 206, 207
Shipping industry, 364–366, 643
Sholokhov, Mikhail, 770
Siam, 684
Siberia, 769
Sic et Non (Abelard), 266
Sicily, 67, 68, 98, 125, 126, 130, 209, 215, 246, 250, 254, 261, 270, 281, 306, 577, 616
Sieyès, Abbé, 471
Sigismund, Holy Roman Emperor, 403
Silesia, 449, 453, 751
Silver trade, 361
Simon, 109, 184
Ibn-Sina (Avicenna), 208, 271
Sino-Japanese War, 679
Sistine Chapel (Vatican), 315
Skepticism, 116, 318, 433, 434
Slavery/slave trade: Egypt and, 21, 34–35; Hebrews and, 34–35, 43; Greek city-states and, 64–66; Carthaginian, 127; in Roman Republic, 130, 133–134, 152; in Roman Empire, 152; early Christian view of, 187; Portuguese, 353–354; in European expansion period, 357–359; impact of, 374; during Enlightenment, 442–443; Toussaint L'Ouverture and, 495; in Great Britain, 568
Slavic language, 24
Slavs, 201, 204, 246, 351, 732, 737, 739, 749
Slayton, Donald K., 872(illus.)
Slovakia, 900
Slovaks, 204
Slovenes, 625, 732
Slovenia, 901
Smith, Adam, 444, 445, 552
Smith, Edwin, 21
Smith, William B., 594
Snake goddess (Crete), 53(illus.)
Sobibor, 863
Soboul, Albert, 470
Social Darwinism, 593–596, 627, 633, 671–672, 721, 729, 732, 739, 790, 854
Social Democrats (Germany), 658, 784, 787, 791, 794, 799, 802
Social equality, 443

Socialism: explanation of, 442; emergence of, 530, 550–551; technocratic, 551–552; psychological, 552; industrial, 553; women's movement and, 651; in France, 656–657; in Germany, 657–658; in United States, 663; in Russia, 771; in Germany, 794
Socialist parties, 646, 647
Socialist realism, 775
Social justice, 45
The Social Contract (Rousseau), 435, 437, 448, 549
Social thought: epistemology and education, 438–440; during Enlightenment, 438–443; humanitarianism and, 440–443
Social War (Roman Republic), 135
Social welfare, 647
Society of Jesus, 343
Society of Righteous and Harmonious Fists, 680
Socrates: background of, 80–81; dialectics of, 81–82, 92; execution of, 82; teachings of, 83, 84, 85, 131, 191, 213, 540; Aristophanes and, 96, 116
Solidarity (Poland), 889–890
Solomon, 35, 36
Solon of Athens, 60–62, 64, 76, 93, 124
Solzhenitsyn, Alexandr, 883
The Song of Roland, 273
Sontag, Louis, 644(illus.)
Sontheimer, Kurt, 786–787
Sophists, 78–79, 80, 81, 97–98
Sophocles, 92–94, 212
Sophrosyne, 79
Sorel, Georges, 630, 702, 721
Sorley, Charles Hamilton, 744
South Africa, 564, 679, 680, 685, 689, 885
South Korea, 872
South Slavs, 625, 732, 737
South Tyrol, 752
Sovereignty: rise of, 378–406; chronology of, 379; concept of, 405. *See also* Monarchy
Soviet Union: ideology and, 767–768, 817; one-party dictatorship and, 770–772; establishment of, 772; industrialization in, 772–774; Stalin revolution and, 772–777; collectivization in, 774; total control in, 774–777; map of, 775; in World War II, 848–851, 857, 859–860, 861, 862, 863, 869; post-World War II, 862–863, 871, 879; Cold War and, 869, 871–883; U.S. arms race and space race with, 872–874; domination of Eastern Europe by, 879–881, 883, 889–892; in Afghanistan, 883; collapse of, 884, 892–894; Nigeria and, 885. *See also* Russia; Russian Federal Republic; *specific countries*
Space race, 872–874
Spain: Carthaginian expansion in, 126–127; Romans in, 129(illus.), 130; Byzantine civilization in, 201; Muslims in, 209, 239, 246, 250, 261, 270, 380, 381, 384.382; Visigoths and, 211; trade in, 232, 365, 366, 368, 369; during Renaissance, 316; during Reformation, 340, 341, 382, 383; expansion and, 352, 355, 356(illus.), 357; Jews and, 357, 380, 382, 383; Hapsburgs in, 381–386; invasion of England, 384–385, 394, 395; Thirty Years' War and, 385; Louis XIV and, 390; Netherlands and, 399, 400; Napoleon and, 501, 503; industrialization in, 646; Mussolini and, 783; fascism and, 799–800, 841–842; NATO and, 872; European Community membership, 876; as European Union member, 904
Spanish-American War, 691
Spanish Armada, 385, 394, 395
Spanish Civil War of 1936–1939, 841
Spanish humanism, 318–319
Spanish March, 217
Sparta: founding of, 54; growth and development of, 58–59; Persian Wars and, 62; Peloponnesian War and, 66, 67, 68, 98; in fourth century, 69. *See also* Ancient Greece
Spartacists, 784, 785
Spartacus, 130
Speke, John, 673
Spencer, Herbert, 605–606
Spengler, Oswald, 811–812
Spice trade, 352, 354–355, 363, 366
Spinning jenny, 513, 514
Spinoza, Benedict de, 421–422
The Spirit of the Laws (Montesquieu), 435, 437
A Sportsman's Sketches (Turgenev), 586
Sputnik, 872
Sri Lanka, 884
St. John (Leonardo), 315
Stalin, Joseph, 757, 770, 772–871, 773, 774, 775, 776, 777, 817, 823, 849, 869, 871, 879–880, 884
Stamp Act, 454
Standard Oil, 685
Stanley, Henry, 685
Stanton, Elizabeth Cady, 606(illus.)
Stark, Johannes, 796
The Starry Messenger (Galileo), 415
States: rise of, 236–241; monarchs as builders of, 378, 380–381; modern political development and, 405–406
Stavisky, Alexander, 803
Steam power, 513–514, 515, 643
Steamship lines, 516
Steen, Jan, 400
Steinbeck, John, 814
Stephen II, Pope, 217
Stephen of Cloyes, 249
Stöcker, Adolf, 630
Stoicism, 115–116, 124, 132, 142, 155, 162, 184, 185, 213
The Story of My Misfortunes (Abelard), 266, 267
Straits of Bosporus, 199
The Stranger (Camus), 828–829
Strato, 111
Strauss, David Friedrich, 595
Stravinsky, Igor, 711
Stresemann, Gustav, 786
Strindberg, August, 651, 710
The Structure of the Human Body (Vesalius), 419
Struggle of the Orders (Rome), 121, 157
Stuart kings, 396–397, 436
Stubbe, Phillip, 372
A Study of History (Toynbee), 821
The Subjection of Women (Mill), 608
Sudan, 675, 688, 734
Sudetenland, 624–625, 802, 842–843
Sue, Eugène, 586
Suebi, 165

Suez Canal, 516, 552, 683, 687, 860
Sugar industry, 360, 363
Suicide (Durkheim), 706
Sulla, 135–136
Sumer, 9, 10, 15
Sumerian harp, 12(illus.)
Sumerians, 9, 11–13, 16, 24, 30. *See also* Mesopotamia
Summa Theologica (Aquinas), 268, 277
Sunnis, 207
The Sun Also Rises (Hemingway), 810
Sun Yat-sen (Sun Zhongshan), 675, 681
Surrealism, 816, 817
Sweden: Napoleon and, 498, 503; Congress of Vienna and, 564; World War II and, 856
Switzerland, during Reformation, 335, 337, 338
Sympathetic magic, 8
Syracuse, 67, 98
Syria: ancient, 26, 28; Hellenistic, 106, 109; early Christianity in, 185; during Byzantine Empire, 201–202; Seljuk Turks and, 209; Mongols and, 210; Ottomans and, 210; during Middle Ages, 212; Crusades and, 247(illus.), 249; creation of, 684; France and, 863
Syria Palestine, 149

Tacitus, 143, 155
Taft Vale decision, 649
Taiping Rebellion, 688
Taiwan, 682
A Tale of Two Cities (Dickens), 589
Taliban, 904, 906
Talleyrand-Périgord, Charles Maurice de, 563
Talmud, 256
Tamerlane, 210
Tanak. *See* Hebrew Scriptures
Tanganyika, 674, 886
Tanzania, 689, 886
Tarentum, 58
Tarsus, 177
Tasmania, 684
Tauberbischofsheim, 219
Taxes: in Roman Empire, 129, 164, 166; Byzantine, 204; in Islamic lands, 207; in feudal society, 225; parliamentary consent for, 241; during Hundred Years' War, 284; in France, 468, 475
Taylor, A.J.P., 745, 760
Taylor, Frederick, 642
Taylor, Harriet, 608
Technocratic socialism, 551–552
Technological advances: during Middle Ages, 290; drive for expansion and, 352–353; industrialization and, 513–515, 641–645; warfare and, 759–760; arms and space races and, 872–874
Telegraph, 515, 643
Telephone, 643
Temperance, 523
The Tempest (Giorgione), 316
Templars, 287
Ten Commandments, 42, 43
Ten Hours Act, 525
Ten lost tribes, 36
Terence, 131, 152, 224
Terrorism: in Russian Federal Republic, 898; by fundamentalist Muslim groups, 904, 906, 908, 909
Terrorist attacks of September 11, 888(illus.), 904, 906, 908
Tertullian, 182, 184
Tetzel, 329
Textile industry, 364, 553
Textiles, 232
Thailand, 857
Thales of Miletus, 76
Thatcher, Margaret, 876(illus.)–877, 904
Theater at Epidaurus (Greece), 74(illus.)
Themistocles, 62
Theocracy: Roman, 121; Muslim, 207; Calvinist, 337
Theocritus, 110
Theodora, Byzantine empress, 200–201
Theodorakopoulos, John N., 76
Theodoric I, 212
Theodoric the Great, 211
Theodosius I, Roman emperor, 182
Theogony (Hesiod), 90, 91
Theophrastus, 111
Thermidorean Convention, 489
Thermidoreans, 482
Thermopylae, 62
Thespis, 91
Thiers, Adolph, 653
Third Crusade, 249
Third Estate (France), 465–468, 471, 472, 473
Third Reich, 782, 794–799, 842, 848
Third Republic, 654–656, 803, 804
Third Section, 566
Thirty Tyrants (Ancient Greece), 69
Thirty Years' War, 385, 388, 401, 402, 403
Thompson, William, 608
Thomson, J. J., 718–719
Thrace, 130
Three-field system, 230
Thucydides, 66, 68, 70, 71, 72, 97–98, 113, 154
Thuringia, 218
Thutmose II, Pharaoh, 22
Tiberius, 172
Tibet, 681, 684, 685, 735
Tigrus River, 10, 11, 25
Tillich, Paul, 819
Timaeus (Plato), 109–110
Time of happiness (Roman Empire), 150–153, 158
Tiso, Josef, 843
Tito, Marshal (Josip Broz), 857, 879
Titus, 147
Tocqueville, Alexis de, 547(illus.)–548, 570–571, 653
Togo, 689
Toland, John, 418, 433
Tolstoy, Leo, 586, 602
Toolmaking, 6, 8
Torah. *See* Judaism; Mosaic Law
Totalitarianism: explanation of, 766; nature of, 767–769; chronology of, 768; communist Russia and, 769–777; nature of fascism and, 777–779; fascism in Italy and, 779–783; new German republic and, 783–787; rise of Hitler and, 787–793; Nazi Germany and, 793–799; au-

Totalitarianism: *(cont.)*
thoritarianism and, 799–802; social effects of, 810. *See also* Communism; Fascism; Nazism
Tours, battle of, 217
Toussaint L'Ouverture, François Dominique, 494 (illus.)–495
Toynbee, Arnold, 729, 810, 821
Trade. *See* Commerce and trade
Trajan, Emperor, 126(illus.), 148
Transportation, innovations in, 515
Trans-Siberian Railroad, 660
Transubstantiation, 335
Transvaal, 689
The Treason of the Intellectuals (Benda), 821
Treatise of Human Nature (Hume), 536
Treatise on the Unity and Trinity of God (Abelard), 267
The Treatise on the Three Imposters, 433
Treaty of Augsburg, 401
Treaty of Brest-Litovsk, 746, 752, 754, 759, 838
Treaty of Karlowitz, 402
Treaty of Verdun, 221
Treaty of Versailles, 751, 752, 754, 762, 836, 838, 839, 841
Treblinka, 855, 863
Treitschke, Heinrich von, 731
Trench warfare, 742–743, 762
Trial by jury, 237
The Trial (Kafka), 812
Tribal Assembly, 122, 135
Tribune of the People, 482, 483
Triple Alliance, 734, 735
Triple Entente, 735
The Trojan Women (Euripides), 95
Trojan War, 55
Trotsky, Leon, 757, 769, 770, 776
Trotskyites, 768
Troubadours, 273, 274(illus.)
Troy, 55–56
Truce of God, 223–224
Truman, Harry S., 862, 871
Truman Doctrine, 871
Tucker, Robert, 601
Tudor dynasty, 340, 393–396
Tunis, 246
Tunisia, 674, 692, 908
Turgenev, Ivan, 586
Turkey: modernization in, 675; European imperialism and, 682–684, 692; modern nationalism in, 684; aftermath of World War I and, 751; U.S. economic and military support for, 871, 872; NATO and, 872
Turkmenistan, 899
Turks: Seljuk, 203, 209, 246, 249; Ottoman, 204, 210, 325, 449, 746, 748, 901; crusades against, 246; Spanish war against, 355, 383; control of Hungary, 402; Greek revolt against, 566
Tuscany, 613, 614, 615
Tutankhamen, Pharaoh, 21–22
Twelfth-Century Awakening, 219, 261, 302
Twelve Disciples, 176, 181, 184, 187
Twelver Shi'ites, 207
Twelve Tables, 122, 157
Two-field system, 230
Two Treatises of Government (Locke), 435, 436, 437, 438
Tycho Brahe, 414
Tyldesley, Joyce, 23
Tyre, 35, 105
Tzara, Tristan, 815
Tzu-hsi, Empress, 680

Uganda, 886
Ukraine: during Roman Empire, 165; serfdom in, 452; pogroms against Jews in, 630; World War I and, 746, 838; World War II and, 849; independence of, 892, 899
Ukrainians: during Byzantine Empire, 204; extermination of Jews, 851
Ulster Volunteers, 651
Ulyanov, Vladimir Ilyich. *See* Lenin, Vladimir
Umbria, 616
Unam Sanctam, 285, 286
Unconscious, 702–704
Union of Soviet Socialist Republics (U.S.S.R). *See* Soviet Union
Union of Utrecht, 399
Union or Death society, 731
United East India Company, 366
United Nations: establishment of, 869–870; decolonization and, 884; International Criminal Tribunal for the Former Yugoslavia, 901–902
United Provinces. *See* Netherlands
United States: American Revolution, 454–456, 469–470; industrialization in, 509, 662–663; transportation in, 515; limited liability in, 517; urbanization in, 519, 645; technological advances in, 641–643; women's suffrage in, 651; Latin American interests of, 691–692; World War I and, 747–752, 754; aftermath of World War I and, 749–752, 754; Great Depression in, 802–803; World War II and, 857, 859, 860, 861, 862–863; emergence as superpower, 862–863, 870; Cold War and, 871–874; NATO and, 872; Vietnam and, 875; support for Soviet-occupied Afghanistan, 883; decolonization by, 885; radical Muslims' hatred for, 906–907
Universal Declaration of Human Rights (United Nations), 870
Universal gravitation, 417
Universalism: Persian empire and, 28; Hebrews and, 47; Hellenistic, 104, 179; Christianity and, 179, 181
Universities, medieval, 259, 260(illus.), 261–262
University at Bologna, 262, 302
University at Padua, 302
University of Alcalá, 318
University of France, 496
University of Paris, 262, 270, 272
Urban II, Pope, 246, 247, 254
Urbanization: in early Near East, 9, 10; in Middle Ages, 234–235; industrialization and, 518–520, 645–646; map of, 645; trends toward, 908
Urban labor, 468
Urban VI, Pope, 288(illus.)
Utilitarianism, 550
Utopia (More), 319
Uzbekistan, 899

Valencia, 241
Valens, Roman emperor, 165

Valerian, Roman emperor, 181
Valéry, Paul, 760–761, 810
Valla, Lorenzo, 309, 310
Vandals, 165, 201, 211, 215
Van Eyck, Jan, 314(illus.)
van Gogh, Vincent, 714, 715(illus.)
van Swieten, Gerard, 450
Vassalage, 222–223, 238, 240
Vatican City, 783
Velde, Jan van del, 400
Venetia, 564, 577, 613, 615, 616, 623
Venice, Italy, 234, 249, 303, 306, 351, 577
Vermeer, Jan, 400
Versailles, 389(illus.)
Vesalius, Andreas, 419, 420(illus.)
Vespasian, 147, 152
Vesuvius, Mount, 147
Victor Emmanuel, king of Piedmont, 615, 616
Victor Emmanuel III, king of Italy, 781
Vienna, 210
Vietnam, 684, 884
Vietnam War, 874(illus.)–875(illus.)
Vikings, 212, 221, 224, 229, 237, 239, 261
Villa, Francisco "Pancho," 692
The Vindication of the Rights of Women (Wollstonecraft), 439, 606
Vindiciae contra Tyrannos, 387
Virgil, 154
Visigoths, 165, 190, 201, 211
Vogüé, Émile de, 586
Volkish thought, 627–632, 786, 788, 789, 790
Volksgeist, 554
Voltaire, 427, 430, 432, 434–435, 442, 443, 448, 450, 457, 541, 659
Voting rights, 651, 652
Vryonis, Speros, 204

Wady Qumran Manuscripts. See Dead Sea Scrolls
Wagner, Richard, 531, 787
Waldensians, 252
Waldo, Peter, 252, 253, 341
Walesa, Lech, 889, 890
Wallace, Alfred Russel, 594
War and Peace (Tolstoy), 586
War communism, 770
Warfare: in early civilizations, 10; Sumerians and, 12; in Roman Republic, 124–125; feudal system and, 223–224, 281; in Enlightenment, 448–449, 448–450; Napoleonic, 497–498, 500; lightning, 498; trench, 742–743, 762; World War I and, 742–743, 762; glorification of, 761–762; by terrorist groups, 908
War of the Austrian Succession, 468
War of the Roses, 393
War of the Spanish Succession, 390
Warsaw ghetto, 857
Warsaw Treaty Organization (Warsaw Pact), 880, 881
Washington, George, 454
Washington Navel Conference, 837
Watt, James, 422, 423(illus.), 513
Watt, W. Montgomery, 208
The Wealth of Nations (Smith), 444, 445
Webb, Beatrice, 817
Weber, Max, 346, 708–710
Weimar Republic, 628, 784–787, 788, 792, 813
Wellesley, Sir Arthur, 501
Wellington, duke of, 504
Wells, H. G., 651
Wessex, 237
West Africa: trade with, 352–354; slave trade and, 357–359, 374; exploration of, 673. *See also specific countries*
West Germany (Federal Republic of Germany): NATO and, 872, 879; establishment of, 878; Cold War and, 878–879; reunification of, 890, 895(illus.), 905
West Indies, 355, 358
Westphalia, 402
White Rose, 854, 855
Whites, 769, 770
Whitney, Eli, 513, 662
Whore of Babylon, 327–328
Wilkinson, John, 517
William I, kaiser of Germany, 619, 620(illus.), 622
William II, kaiser of Germany, 629, 658, 689, 734, 735, 784
William III, king of England, 398
William IV, king of England, 568
William of Ockham, 290
William the Conqueror, 237, 238, 240, 392
William the Pig, 249
William the Silent, Prince of Orange, 399
Wilson, John A., 22, 34
Wilson, Lyn Hatherly, 90
Wilson, Woodrow, 663, 682, 692, 747, 748, 749, 750(illus.), 751, 752, 754, 843
Windischgrätz, Alfred zu, 576
Winstanley, Gerrard, 397
Witches/witchcraft, 342, 372–374
Witte, Sergei, 660
Wolff, Betje, 443
Wollstonecraft, Mary, 428, 439(illus.), 606
Wolsey, Cardinal, 319
Woman's Suffrage Movement, 607
Women: Hebrew, 43; Greek, 65, 88, 152; in Roman Empire, 152; in Roman Republic, 152; early Christian view of, 180, 187; in medieval society, 224, 234–235, 238(illus.), 273–274; in Renaissance Italy, 307; as medieval mystics, 326; as witches, 373; political power of, 381; as scientists and mathematicians, 424, 429; salons for, 430; lodges for, 431; education for, 440, 496; during Enlightenment, 443; equality of, 552; feminist movements, 606–608; conditions for working, 646, 647; voting rights for, 648–649; World War I and, 652, 743(illus.); communism and, 771
Women in Love (Lawrence), 814
Women's rights: Wollstonecraft and, 439; movement for, 651–652
Wood, Charles, 546
Wordsworth, William, 533
Working class, 522–524
Works and Days (Hesiod), 90, 91
World Trade Center attack, 888(illus.), 904, 906
World War I: events leading to, 625; role of women in, 652; Germany prior to, 658; Italy prior to, 659; United States

World War I: *(cont.)*
prior to, 662–663; imperialism and, 671, 692; Japan in, 682; Ottomans in, 683–684; alliances and, 685, 732–734; modernism and, 723; state of Europe prior to, 729, 731; chronology of, 730; tensions in Austria-Hungary and, 731–732; Triple Entente and, 734–735; Bosnian crisis and, 735–736; Balkan wars and, 736; Assassination of Francis Ferdinand and, 737–738; Germany abets Austria and, 738–739; public view of, 739, 741–742; responsibility for, 739; stalemate in West and, 742–746; eastern front and, 746–747; Gallipoli campaign and, 746–747; U.S. entry in, 747–748; Germany's last offensive in, 748–749; peacemaking following, 749–752; aftermath of, 750–754, 762, 779, 780, 784, 836–838; Treaty of Versailles and, 751, 752, 754, 762, 836, 838, 839, 841; assessment and problems following, 752, 754; Russian Revolution of 1917 and, 754–759; effects of, 759–762; Hitler and, 788; pessimism following, 809–812
World War II: impact of, 692–693; events leading to, 762; ideology and, 767; events leading to, 837; antecedents of, 838–839, 841–842; aggression and, 842–843; Poland and, 843–845; chronology of, 844; fall of France during, 845, 847–848; Nazi blitzkrieg during, 845, 847–850; Battle of Britain during, 848; invasion of Russia during, 848–850; exploitation and terror during, 850–851; Hitler's New Order in, 850–857; extermination during, 851–856; resistance during, 856–857; defeat of Axis powers and, 857, 859–862; Japanese offensive and, 857; legacy of, 862–864, 869–871
Writing: Sumerian, 11, 16, 30; Egyptian, 18–19; Phoenician, 25
Wycliffe, John, 289, 325, 326, 327, 340
Wyfrid, 218. *See also* Boniface, Saint

Xerxes, 62, 93, 97, 105

Yahweh, 35, 37, 39, 46
Yalta agreement, 869
Yeats, William Butler, 722, 810
Yeltsin, Boris, 893, 894, 896–898, 897(illus.)
Yemen, 908
Yeomanry, 362
Yiddish, 631
Young Hegelians, 540–541
Yugoslavia: Treaty of Versailles and, 752; alliance with France, 837; World War II and, 848–849, 857, 862, 869; Tito and, 879; end of communism in, 892; violence in former, 901–902

Zacharias, Pope, 218
Zaire, 886
Zalaszowska, Catherine, 342
Zama, battle of, 127, 129
Zanzibar, 689, 886
Zapata, Emiliano, 692
Zarathustra, 28
Zealots, 173, 174, 176
Zedekiah, King, 46, 47
Zeno, 115
Zetkin, Clara, 651
Zeus, 57, 60, 90, 109
Zhukov, Georgi, 859, 860
Ziggurats, 13
Zimbabwe, 689, 885
Zimmerman, Arthur, 747
Zionism, 630–631, 632, 633
Zionist World Congress, 631
Zola, Émile, 520, 587–588, 655
Zollverein, 617–618
Zoonomia (Erasmus Darwin), 592
Zoroastrianism, 28
Zosimus, 164
Zweig, Stefan, 703, 741
Zwingli, Ulrich, 335